October 15–18, 2017
Amsterdam, The Netherlands

Association for Computing Machinery

Advancing Computing as a Science & Profession

CHI PLAY'17

Proceedings of the Annual Symposium on Computer-Human Interaction in Play

Sponsored by:

ACM SIGCHI

Supported by:

Dutch Game Garden, EA, EPIC, University of Applied Sciences, Hogeschool van Amsterdam, IJSfontein, Mediamatic, Persuasive Gaming in Context, SONY, and Technische Universiteit Eindhoven

Association for Computing Machinery

Advancing Computing as a Science & Profession

The Association for Computing Machinery
2 Penn Plaza, Suite 701
New York, New York 10121-0701

Notice to Past Authors of ACM-Published Articles
ACM intends to create a complete electronic archive of all articles and/or other material previously published by ACM. If you have written a work that has been previously published by ACM in any journal or conference proceedings prior to 1978, or any SIG Newsletter at any time, and you do NOT want this work to appear in the ACM Digital Library, please inform permissions@acm.org, stating the title of the work, the author(s), and where and when published.

ISBN: 978-1-4503-4898-0 (Digital)

ISBN: 978-1-4503-5675-6 (Print)

Additional copies may be ordered prepaid from:

ACM Order Department
PO Box 30777
New York, NY 10087-0777, USA

Phone: 1-800-342-6626 (USA and Canada)
+1-212-626-0500 (Global)
Fax: +1-212-944-1318
E-mail: acmhelp@acm.org
Hours of Operation: 8:30 am – 4:30 pm ET

CHI PLAY 2017 Welcome

It is our great pleasure to welcome you to the fourth *ACM SIGCHI Annual Symposium on Computer-Human Interaction in Play - CHI PLAY '17. See more at:* http://chiplay.org.

From the General Chairs & Program Chairs

CHI PLAY is an international and interdisciplinary conference series for researchers and professionals across all areas of play, games, and human-computer interaction (HCI), we call it: "player-computer interaction." CHI PLAY highlights and fosters discussion of current high-quality research in games, and HCI. It forms the foundations for the future of digital play. This year is the fourth year of the symposium, which is already proving to be a premier forum for presentation of research results and experience reports on leading-edge issues of novel games and playful interaction, player experience evaluations, tangible play, serious games, gamification, exertion games, games user research, player psychology, social game and play systems, play & game developer applications and theory. The mission of the symposium is to share insights into game and play interaction design and analysis that fulfil the needs of developers, researchers, and designers and identify new directions for future research and development in HCI and games. CHI PLAY gives researchers and practitioners a unique opportunity to share their perspectives with others interested in the various aspects of HCI in games and play. The symposium provides a meeting place for practitioners and academics where participants present and discuss peer-reviewed academic papers and the latest breaking results and approaches from industry.

This year we feature two new tracks. As CHI PLAY 2017 brings together research and industry, we tried something fresh, a new track called 'Spotlight Papers', which will highlight significant work from both industry and research from innovative implementations to thought-provoking case studies. Authors were asked to bring a demonstration, video or prototype next to a max 10-page paper submission.

We also feature a state of the art exhibition where over 20 state games and other products of playful interaction of industry as well individual developers are showcased. Both the exhibition, which is open to the public, and the conference take place in beautiful and unconventional venues on the water front of Amsterdam as well as in its newly formed innovation hub in the centre of the city.

The call for papers attracted submissions from across the continents. We selected a program committee of experts in human-computer interaction and game research to lead the scientific review process. All full papers were blind reviewed by peer reviewers as well as a committee member. Accepted papers are published in the ACM Digital Library. The program committee reviewed and accepted the following:

Venue/Track	*Reviewed*	*Accepted*	*Proportion*
Full Technical Papers	178	46	26%
Works-in-Progress	83	51	61%
Spotlights	31	11	35.5%
Play Exhibition	76	25	33%

Putting together CHI PLAY '17 was a team effort. We are very grateful to the contributors of this conference: our staff at the conference, our partners, our volunteers, the authors who submitted their high-quality work and thus provided the content of the program, the program committee, who managed the reviews on a short timeline, our reviewers who ensured a top-quality conference, and our local organizing committee.

We hope that you will find this program interesting and thought-provoking and that the event will provide you with a valuable opportunity to share ideas with other researchers and practitioners from institutions around the world.

Ben Schouten
CHI PLAY 17 General co-chair
Eindhoven University of Technology, Amsterdam & University of Applied Sciences, the Netherlands

Zach Toups
CHI PLAY 17 General co-chair
New Mexico State University, USA

Panos Markopoulos
CHI PLAY 17 General co-chair
Eindhoven University of Technology, The Netherlands

Paul Cairns
CHI PLAY 17 Technical program co-chair
University of York , UK

Tilde Bekker
CHI PLAY 17 Technical program co-chair
Eindhoven University of Technology, the Netherlands

From the Paper Chairs

CHI PLAY has become one of the leading conferences on player-computer interaction. This year's CHI PLAY 2017 saw again a steep increase in high-quality and diverse submissions, testifying to the ever-growing importance of research on games and play, and the recognition of the conference.

To ensure a high-quality review process, we received the help of 40 program committee members - 31 associate chairs and 9 ninja reviewers from Finland, USA, Austria, Ireland, Denmark, Australia, UK, Switzerland, Germany, the Netherlands, Canada, Spain, Sweden and Belgium. Each associate chair supervised in turn 3 or more reviewers, hence ensuring that every paper received at least three high-quality reviews. Borderline scoring papers or papers with diverging scores received an additional reviewer and/or were discussed at a virtual program chair meeting. In this manner, we strived to accept only high-quality research papers while still encouraging a diversity of research approaches and contributions, as befits this domain that spans arts, design, engineering, computer science, and human sciences.

We want to thank all authors who submitted to CHI PLAY 2017. We also want to thank our 341 external reviewers for their time. Finally, we are profoundly grateful to our associate chairs and ninja reviewers. It is their scientific expertise and dedication that renders it possible to make CHI PLAY successful.

Perttu Hämäläinen
CHI PLAY 17 Papers co-chair
Aalto University, Finland

Vero Vanden Abeele
CHI PLAY 17 Papers co-chair
KU Leuven, Belgium

From the Work in Progress, Spotlights and Exhibition Chairs

Work-in-Progress contributions, or WIPs for short, provide a unique opportunity for late-breaking results to be presented as a poster at the conference. WIPs should open up new research questions, evoke discussion and debate, and outline a future research agenda. WIPs were reviewed on several criteria such as relevance to the CHI PLAY community, clarity of writing and presentation, and their "in-progress" nature. So, this track is not a venue for summative pieces of work, but an opportunity to share ideas from ongoing projects. We received 83 submissions, and each submission was peer-reviewed by at least two reviewers from a pool of 102. We accepted 51 submissions, leading to an acceptance rate of 61%.

The *Spotlight track* is a new venue for CHI PLAY that aims to highlight significant work from industry and research – from innovative implementations to thought-provoking case studies. The track is particularly suitable for individuals, studios, and companies who want to showcase their work and share lessons learned from success and failure. Submissions were reviewed by a committee of 7 jury members recruited from academia and industry. Each submission received two reviews and a meta-review from one of the track chairs. An online jury meeting took place, where borderline submissions were discussed before a final list of accepted papers was collated. We received 31 submissions; we accepted 11, giving an acceptance rate of 35.5%. Furthermore, an additional 3 submissions were fast-tracked by the Papers chairs to be included as a Spotlight. We want to thank all authors who submitted to this new track and to express our gratitude to our fantastic jury members who helped select an exciting set of submissions for the conference.

We are also proud to announce that the 2017 edition of the conference hosts an *Play Exhibition* of games and playable artifacts, showcasing some highlights of game design from the industry as well as independent developers in the Netherlands. CHI PLAY is at the crossroads of research, design, and experimentation, so we called it "Dutch Courage": an homage to the risk-taking, daring attitude that many developers demonstrate as they innovate the field. From an initial list of more than seventy games, twenty-five were finally selected for "Dutch Courage," taking into account new types of gameplay and interaction with players.

The exhibition co-chairs assembled an extensive list of Dutch games, soliciting contributions from researchers and practitioners, and examining the nominees of recent editions of the Dutch Game Awards. The exhibition represents a broad variety in technological perspectives, that range from PC-based games, to touchscreen interfaces, tangible interfaces such as breath-taking and mixed-reality installations. Moreover, the games and other playful artifacts are authentic and uncompromising designed to engage, in both serious settings as healthcare and education as well as entertainment and arts. "Dutch Courage" is open to the public during the days of the conference. We are grateful to MediaMatic, a space dedicated to new media arts since 1983, for hosting the exhibition, as well as to the Dutch Game Garden for the networking and support. We would like to thank all the exhibitors, organizers and volunteers who made it happen.

Luc Geurts
CHI PLAY 17 Work in Progress co-Chair
KU Leuven, Belgium

Hartmut Koenitz
CHI PLAY 17 Work in Progress co-Chair
HKU University of the Arts, the Netherlands

Jo Iacovides
CHI PLAY 17 Spotlight Papers co-chair
Open University, UK

Max Birk
CHI PLAY 17 Spotlight Papers co-chair
University of Saskatchewan, Canada

Gabriele Ferri
CHI PLAY 17 Exhibition co-chair
Amsterdam University of Applied Sciences, the Netherlands

Menno Deen
CHI PLAY 17 Exhibition co-chair
Dutch Game Garden, the Netherlands

Table of Contents

Session 3: Player and Parent Preferences

Session Chair: Gabriele Ferri *(Amsterdam University of Applied Sciences)*

Session 4: Taking Serious Games Seriously

Session Chair: Vero Vanden Abeele *(KU Leuven)*

Session 5: Tools to Analyse Games

Session Chair: Luc Geurts *(KU Leuven)*

Session 8: Beyond the Typical Player Experience

Session Chair: Panos Markopoulos *(Eindhoven University of Technology)*

Session 9: VR and Other Novel IO Technology

Session Chair: Perttu Hämäläinen *(Aalto University)*

CHI PLAY 2017 Conference Organizers

General Chairs: Ben Schouten (Eindhoven University of Technology and Amsterdam University of Applied Sciences, the Netherlands)
Panos Markopoulos (Eindhoven University of Technology, the Netherlands)
Zachary Toups (New Mexico State University, USA)

Technical Program and Proceedings: Paul Cairns (University of York, UK)
Tilde Bekker (Eindhoven University of Technology, the Netherlands)

Papers: Vero Vanden Abeele (KU Leuven, Belgium)
Perttu Hämäläinen (Aalto University, Finland)

Spotlight Papers: Jo Iacovides (Open University, UK)
Max Birk (University of Saskatchewan, Canada)

Work-in Progress: Luc Geurts (KU Leuven, Belgium)
Hartmut Koenitz (HKU University of the Arts, the Netherlands)

Student Game Competition: Joshua Tannenbaum (University of California Irvine, USA)
Erik van der Spek (Eindhoven University of Technology, the Netherlands)
Martijn Kors (Eindhoven University of Technology, the Netherlands)

Workshops and Courses: Kathrin Gerling (Lincoln University, UK)
Rafael Bidarra (Delft University of Technology, the Netherlands)

Doctoral Consortium: Peta Wyeth (Queensland University of Technology, Australia)
Sebastian Deterding (University of York, UK)

Publicity and Social Media: Josh Andres (RMIT University, Australia)
Marierose van Dooren (Delft University of Technology, the Netherlands)

Student Volunteers: Erik Harpstead (Carnegie Mellon University, USA)
Frank Nack (University of Amsterdam, the Netherlands)

Local Arrangements: Monique van Reijen (Amsterdam University of Applied Sciences, the Netherlands)
Wouter Sluis-Thiescheffer (Fontys University of Applied Sciences, the Netherlands)

Play Exhibition: Gabriele Ferri, (Amsterdam University of Applied Sciences, the Netherlands)
Menno Deen (Dutch Game Garden, the Netherlands)

Industry and Sponsors: Jan Willem Huisman (IJsfontein Playful Learning, the Netherlands)
Wieke Schrakamp (IJsfontein Playful Learning, the Netherlands)
Veronica Zammitto (Electronic Arts, Vancouver, Canada)

Special Liaisons: Joost Raessens (Utrecht University, the Netherlands)

Ninja Reviewers: Katherine Isbister (University of California, US)
Rilla Khaled (Concordia University, Canada)
Peta Wyeth (Queensland University of Technology, Australia)
Anna Cox (University College Londen, UK)
Annika Waern (University of Uppsala, Sweden)
Jerry Fails (Montclair State University)
Mark Hancock (University of Waterloo, Canada)
José Zagal (University of Utah, USA)
Jan Van Looy (Imec & Universiteit Gent, Belgium)

Jury members Spotlight Papers: Rilla Khaled (Concordia University, Canada)
Kristina Rothe (Turn 10 Studios, USA)
Zhenyu "Cole" Zhu (Tencent, China)
Alena Denisova (Swansea University, Wales)
Ben Kirman (University of York, England)
Ian Livingston (Electronic Arts, Canada)
Hanna Wirman (The Hong Kong Polytechnic University, Hong Kong)

Jury members Play Exhibition: Menno Deen (Dutch Game Garden, the Netherlands)
Gabriele Ferri (Amsterdam University of Applied Sciences, the Netherlands)
Ben Schouten (Eindhoven University of Technology, the Netherland
Sabina Dirks (Dutch Game Association, the Netherlands)

CHI PLAY 2017 Sponsor & Supporters

Sponsor: SIGCHI

Supporters in alphabetical order:

Dutch Game Garden

EA

EPIC GAMES

Fontys University of Applied Sciences

Hogeschool van Amsterdam

ijsfontein

Mediamatic

PERSUASIVE GAMING IN CONTEXT
FROM THEORY-BASED DESIGN TO VALIDATION AND BACK

SONY

TU/e Technische Universiteit Eindhoven University of Technology

How to Play

Ian Bogost
Georgia Institute of Technology
ibogost@gatech.edu

ABSTRACT

It's the same as ever: Games are popular but still mysterious. More and more people play them, but deep understanding of what they are and how they work remains out of reach. A dark shadow of unseemliness still shrouds them.

Meanwhile, ordinary people really want to know about and get involved in game design, but they don't know what it is. This is true of parents curious or concerned about the medium, of young people interested in careers in it, sometimes from ordinary folks wondering why they're so drawn to *Candy Crush*.

And yet, still nobody has a good answer. There are business books that talk about leveraging games for commercial and organizational ends. There are books about how gamers are resilient, and there are books about what the heck games even are and where they came from. There are textbooks, too, but they either lean heavy on theory, or devolve into how-to programming guides for the latest software platform.

Those approaches don't really answer what a game is and what elements comprise one. In the way that it's possible to answer for a novel, or a film, or a painting, or a software program, or a building. (Furthermore, decades of efforts to ontologize and categorize games don't seem to have helped.)

And yet, people are interested in that knowledge—whether to understand their *Candy Crush* kick, or to design informal activities for themselves or their families, or to pursue a career in or around game design. Sometimes people mistake games for computer games, and think that they have to understand programming to grasp them, or to make them. But just as plot, character, setting, narration, and other elements make the novel what it is, so there are similar concepts for games. Even if game designers don't always agree on what those might be, and even if definitions and ontology have become theoretically unpopular, it is useful to lay them out for ourselves—and for the general public.

CHI PLAY 2017, October 15–18, 2017, Amsterdam, The Netherlands.
ACM ISBN 978-1-4503-4898-0/17/10.
DOI: https://doi.org/10.1145/3116595.3116641

ACM Classification Keywords

H.5.2. User Interfaces, Theory and Methods; K.8 Personal Computing, Games.

Author Keywords

Play, games research, ontology, education, aesthetics

BIOGRAPHY

Ian Bogost is an author and an award-winning game designer. He is the Ivan Allen College Distinguished Chair in Media Studies and Professor of Interactive Computing at the Georgia Institute of Technology, where he also holds an appointment in the Scheller College of Business. Bogost is a Founding Partner at Persuasive Games LLC, an independent game studio, and a Contributing Editor at *The Atlantic*, where he writes regularly about technology and popular culture.

Connecting through Play by Design

Katherine Isbister
University of California, Santa Cruz
katherine.isbister@ucsc.edu

ABSTRACT
Game designers and developers have long been at the vanguard of creating technology-enhanced experiences to evoke and encourage connection among people. Consider for example the creation of home game consoles in the 1970s—a rich shared-screen engaging multi-person experience offered far earlier than business applications for computer-supported cooperative work that emerged in the 1980s [1]. Yet this aspect of the games field is under-appreciated by technologists as well as the general public.

In this keynote I will highlight examples of the tradition within game development of design to support connection. I will present examples of design techniques innovated by the game community that encourage connection. And I will present research from my lab that sketches directions for the future of technology interfaces for games and play as well as everyday interaction. I'll conclude with a call to action for the CHI-Play community to bridge their knowledge to those in the technology field who are shaping the fabric of how we engage one another in everyday life.

ACM Classification Keywords
H.5.2. User Interfaces

Author Keywords
Emotion and games; social connection; wearables; virtual reality; embodied play.

BIOGRAPHY
Katherine Isbister is Professor of Computational Media at the University of California, Santa Cruz, where she Directs the Center for Games and Playable Media, and the Social Emotional Technology Lab. Isbister was founding Director of the Game Innovation Lab at New York University. She is a Distinguished Scientist of the ACM, as well as a Founding Fellow of the Higher Education Video Game Alliance. Isbister has received honors including MIT Technology Review's Young Innovator award, a Humboldt Experienced Researcher fellowship, and a Lenore Annenberg and Wallis Annenberg Fellowship in Communication at Stanford University's Center for Advanced Study in the Behavioral Sciences 2014-2015.

Isbister's research bridges Human Computer Interaction and Game Design—her team builds and researches playful computer-supported experiences that push the boundaries of moment-to-moment engagement with technology. Isbister is the author of several books on game design and development [2-4]. Her latest, *How Games Move Us: Emotion by Design*, addresses how games can be designed to evoke empathy and connection for players.

REFERENCES
1. Grudin, J. 1994. Computer-Supported Cooperative Work: History and Focus. *Computer 27*(5): 19-26.
2. Isbister, K. 2016. *How Games Move Us: Emotion by Design*. MIT Press.
3. Isbister, K. and Schaffer, N. 2008. *Game Usability: Advice from the Experts for Advancing the Player Experience.* Morgan Kaufmann.
4. Isbister, K. 2006. *Better Game Characters by Design: A Psychological Approach*. Morgan Kaufmann

CHI PLAY 2017, October 15–18, 2017, Amsterdam, The Netherlands.
ACM ISBN 978-1-4503-4898-0/17/10.
DOI: https://doi.org/10.1145/3116595.3116642

Gamification through the Application of Motivational Affordances for Physical Activity Technology

Dennis L. Kappen
Humber College and University of Ontario Institute of Technology, Ontario, Canada
dennis.kappen@humber.ca

Pejman Mirza-Babaei
University of Ontario Institute of Technology
Oshawa, Ontario, Canada
pejman.m@acm.org

Lennart E. Nacke
University of Waterloo
Waterloo, Ontario, Canada
Lennart.Nacke@acm.org

ABSTRACT
Motivational affordances are attributes of interactive technologies or game elements that promote participation in physical activity (PA) routines. Although these affordances have been previously integrated into technologies in non-tailored approaches, the motivations of adults for PA are specific (e.g., to improve one's health, wellness, or fitness). There are no previous comparisons of either the motivation to participate in PA or motivational affordances that facilitate PA in different age groups. Therefore, we conducted an online survey with 150 participants using the Exercise Motivations Inventory-2 scale (EMI-2) together with long-form questions to explore motivational affordances and PA technology preferences in four age groups. Our results suggest health-related pressures are significant motivations for PA in different age groups. Additionally, a content analysis of preferences allowed us to distinguish between gamified motivational affordances and feedback elements. These results provide age-group-specific gamification design guidelines for incorporating motivational elements in PA technology.

Author Keywords
Motivational affordances; gamification; physical activity; motivation; user experience design

ACM Classification Keywords
H.1.2. User/Machine Systems: Human Factors; K.8.0 Personal Computing: Games.

INTRODUCTION
Successful commercial fitness games, such as Nintendo's Wii Fit games or Majesco's Zumba Fitness games, are designed with the general population in mind and are not tailored to appeal to specific age groups. While fitness-tracking technologies like Fitbit [71], Nike+ FuelBand [70], and Google Fit [72] have enabled people to become motivated and track their physical activity (PA), it is not clear how people in different age groups use these technologies. There are major differences in the motivation to keep fit between younger adults [57] and older adults [48]. As the population ages, older adults are trying to lead healthier lifestyles while maintaining their physical and mental wellness [1,8]. Not all older adults pursue fitness in the same way, and they often face more substantial cognitive and physical challenges compared to younger populations [63]. Thus, it is important to compare the motivations and preferences of adults within different age groups.

Motivational affordances [23,38] for the facilitation of PA are elements that help facilitate intrinsic or extrinsic motives to participate in PA. This idea follows from gamification, which is the application of strategies from game design (e.g., actions, challenges, and achievements) to daily activities to help make people's actions more engaging [14]. Research has shown that gamified fitness applications have the potential to engage people in regular PA [38].

Habits of playing and reasons for not playing exergames (combining PA and gaming technology) studied in age groups (<24, 25-34, 35-44 and >45) revealed preferences in exergame technology, resource and temporal issues [30]. However, the motivations of adults in different age groups including seniors (65+) to become more physically active (PA motivations) have not been studied in detail. Adult preferences for motivational elements that facilitate participation in PA (PA facilitation) have also not been explored before. Thus, we conducted a survey study that combined open-ended answers and self-report scales, including the Exercise Motivations Inventory (EMI-2) [40], to compare the PA motivations of adults in different age groups (18-29, 30-49, 50-64, and >65 years old) and to elucidate their preferences for motivational elements that facilitate PA.

There were significant differences in the motives to participate in PA in the *health pressures* and *ill health avoidance* EMI-2 dimensions among the four age groups. Additionally, we identified differences in the motivational affordances preferred by the different age groups, and used these to develop age-group-specific design guidelines.

We make four strong contributions to the CHI PLAY community: (1) We provide empirical evidence of significant

CHI PLAY '17, October 15-18, 2017, Amsterdam, Netherlands

ACM ISBN 978-1-4503-4898-0/17/10...$15.00
https://doi.org/10.1145/3116595.3116604

differences in motives for becoming physically active among different age groups. (2) We specify age-group-specific motivational affordances, because our results suggest people in different age groups have different preferences regarding motivational affordances. (3) We classify motivational elements into gamified motivational affordances and feedback elements facilitated by a content analysis. (4) Finally, we deliver age-specific design guidelines for incorporating motivational elements into technologies used to facilitate PA. A better understanding of how interactive technologies can meet the needs of adults in different age groups should enable us to create meaningful fitness and PA technologies.

RELATED WORK

Many commercial systems have combined gamification with PA [38] as a behaviour-change strategy to help individuals achieve health and fitness goals. For example, fitness trackers have been shown to motivate workout activities by providing feedback [52]. Initially, we will review the literature on the motivation to participate in PA, the relevance of gamification, and fitness and motivational affordances in a PA context.

Comparison of Motivation to Participate in PA

A systematic review of PA and exercise motivation grounded in Self-Determination Theory (SDT) emphasized the importance of autonomous (identified and intrinsic) over extrinsic regulation in promoting PA [65]. Participation in exercises depended on habit formation that needed a minimum of four bouts of exercise over a six-week period [32]. Technology apps like *Lift* (now: *coach.me*[1]) have been shown to support habit formation for tracking diet, exercise, spirituality, personal hygiene, education and personal growth, but they require continual usage [56]. However, this previous study did not address PA or motivational affordances. Additionally, while intrinsic rewards have been shown to promote exercise in the initial phase, habit formation helped to maintain participation in exercises over time [18,54]. Furthermore, while motives for participating in PA differ across type of activity, age, and gender in adults [47], this previous study did not identify any motivational affordances of technology-assisted PA. To explain why it is important to compare the motivation to participate in PA in different age groups, we will first discuss younger adults and older adults in the context of PA and the use of motivational affordances in gamified technology.

Younger adults and PA

Self-determined situational motivation (the reason why someone does something in a particular situation) drives self–determined contextual motivation (the understanding of why someone is doing something), and social factors have been shown to positively predict the motivation of younger adults to participate in exercise and PA [35]. Studies involving younger populations participating in Tae Kwan Do and aerobics have revealed exercise adherence improved when motives were enjoyment, competence, and social interaction, as opposed to motives focused on fitness or appearance [61]. Motivational affordances provided by a wrist-worn activity monitor were shown to have only a short-term positive effect on PA and sedentary activity (SED) in young men [24]. Monitoring of physical activity metrics and tracking was shown to be motivating because of the increased awareness of one's own behaviour [46]. While college students reported that enjoyment and challenge were intrinsic motives for participation in PA, extrinsic motives included appearance, weight, and stress management [39]. Motivational affordances are made possible through persuasive technologies and gamification, and foster social collaboration and PA [66]. Goal-setting in the form of a daily step count has been shown to facilitate increased PA [6]. In the game ***Fish' n' Steps***, participants were encouraged to overcome a sedentary lifestyle by having their daily step count determine the growth and actions of an animated fish [36]. However, the preferences for motivational affordances by younger adults in technology-facilitated PA have not been investigated.

Older Adults and PA

Previous studies [5] have examined the benefits of gaming activities and how older adults use game technology [3]. This research has focused predominantly on the relevance of gaming and its applicability in rehabilitation, physical and cognitive training, leisure and entertainment, and adult learning. While older adults often participate in aerobic activity classes, dancing, yard work or gardening, swimming and water aerobics [17], or even Tai Chi [55], cognitive changes and increasing physical challenges associated with aging reduce the opportunities of older adults to play digital games or exercise using video games [37]. Playful applications, such as motion-based video games, hold the promise of encouraging accessible PA in older adults [19]. Prior research has demonstrated that these game applications may have beneficial effects on the physical and emotional wellbeing of an aging population [27,63]. Motivational characteristics, such as purposeful interactions, customization of activities, fostering of independence, building relationships, sharing and accommodating preferences [28], are commonly seen with older adults, and these relate to their lifestyle attitudes. PA motivation for older adults with persuasive technologies depended on social, physical and intrinsic triggers [58]. Additionally, as a result of improved wellness and decreased sedentary time [1], prescriptive interventions with casual video games have been suggested to prevent and treat stress [59], and thus to improve the mood of participants.

Behaviour-Change and Motivational Affordances

While gamification relies on intrinsic and extrinsic motivations provided by a gamified application, Larsen found a user's external motivation could increase their internal motivation over time [34]. The fact that human behavior can

[1] https://www.coach.me

be influenced using game design principles in decision-making applications and services [29] suggests that it may be possible to identify behaviour-change elements to foster intrinsic motivation. Customization of these gamification elements based on demographics or age groups may contribute to the personalization of playful technologies. This customization of playful technologies necessitates the understanding of specific preferences of triggers that motivate gameful PA [31]. The association of different skill atoms with different age groups—based on preferences, needs, and wants—is critical for the design of technology artifacts. The exploration of physical activities through gamification [20] could help provide access to activities that would otherwise be precluded by age-related challenges. Therefore, the investigation of motivational affordances based on demographic characteristics such as age groups should promote our understanding of how to implement game design elements in technological artifacts. Although a few research projects have studied behaviour change in fitness and health apps (see below), there has not been a detailed comparison of motivational affordances facilitating PA technology based on age groups.

While Lister et al. reported how gamification can change health behaviours by using game elements in fitness and health apps [38], their study did not compare age group-specific preferences. King et al. reported strategies to influence health behaviours, which led to the collective aim to develop digital 'games with a purpose' [33]. However, they did not address any demographic-specific strategies. Other researchers have applied motivational affordances to help maintain adherence to mundane and boring activities such as exercise and daily physical activities [22], but that study focused on a demographic comprised of younger adults. Commercial devices and websites (such as Fitbit [71], Nike+ FuelBand [70], Fitocracy [73] and FitOrbit [74]) have leveraged the quantification of achievements to motivate users. However, little research has been done on the motives for using these technologies among adults in different age groups.

A study of exercise habits in younger participants (mean age = 21) revealed that adherence (continued participation in PA or exercise routines) was associated with motives focused on enjoyment, competence, and social interaction rather than personal fitness or appearance [61]. Health benefits resulting from the observation of fitness routines [50] are linked to the motivation of older adults (mean age = 78) to initiate and maintain fitness activities [53]. Research on intrinsic and extrinsic motivations in older adults (mean age = 63.8 years) [11] explored their activity levels (inactives, actives, sustained maintainers) against dimensions of health and fitness, weight management, appearance, stress management, enjoyment, emotion, and sociality. For younger adults (mean age = 18.6 years) who were actively involved in PA, studies have shown that intrinsic motivation has a greater effect than extrinsic motivation [7]. None of the studies mentioned above compared age groups and they all specifically focused on either a young population or an older population. In contrast, our study offers a comparison of different age groups, preferences for motivational affordances in PA technology and PA.

Toward a Survey Study of Motivational Affordances

Survey studies have been used in investigations of personality-targeted gamification [25], the social influence on gamification [22] and persona development [44]. We specifically examined recent CHI papers on survey studies to obtain methods and procedures for reporting survey results [4,25].

While research has shown gamification can be used to add motivational affordances to mundane activities such as exercise routines and physical activity [38], it is important that we investigate the *relevance* of these affordances in different age groups. Additionally, physical activity is important in all life stages, and while health technologies and gamified fitness strategies have been widely adopted by the younger population, little research has been done on the motivational affordances facilitated by technology among different groups. Previous studies [11,42] have examined the intrinsic and extrinsic motivations of older adults and younger adults to engage in physical activity [49,57]. PA could include daily activities like work, yard and garden activities, walking for leisure and/or routine exercises. However, to the best of our knowledge, no previous study has compared motivational affordances preferred by adults in different age groups using gamified fitness applications to influence PA participation. Here, we describe a survey study that sought to identify the similarities and differences in motives to participate in PA and the influence of motivational affordances as a technology facilitator for PA.

THEORETICAL DEVELOPMENT

Self-Determination Theory (SDT) posits the self-regulation of uninteresting activities is an inherently motivational construct that occurs through the process of internalization. The facilitation of internalization [12] serves as a catalyst to engage with a gamified application. However, the expectation of extrinsic rewards can marginalize intrinsic motivation [13,60]. Intrinsic motivation is facilitated when autonomy, competence, and relatedness—the three psychological needs of human motivation—are satisfied [62]. From the perspective of the intersection of SDT and PA, integrated regulation was an important predictor of exercise behaviour [16]. In middle-aged adults (mean age = 31.8 years) using PA technology social comparison provided greater motives to participate in PA [69]—while the effects of extrinsic motivational affordances (e.g., virtual rewards) were inconclusive.

To select a scale for our study, we reviewed different measures used by researchers to study motivation and PA: (1) The Intrinsic Motivations Inventory (IMI) [43] addressed the need for the accurate assessment of psychological constructs in a competitive sport setting. According to a study that used the IMI, apparent intrinsic motivation may be extrinsic—fueled by rewards such as weight loss, improvements in physical appearance, and social recognition [41]. (2) The Self-Motivation Inventory [15] aimed to identify variations in adherence to physical activity and dropouts [21] within female and male participants. (3) The Exercise Motivations Inventory (EMI) [40] and Exercise Motivations Inventory-2 (EMI-2) [41] proposed a collection of exercise participation motives in adults that could be applied to both exercisers and non-exercisers. (4) The Psychological Need Satisfaction in Exercise scale (PNSE)[67] validated high levels of need satisfaction in exercise contexts. We decided to use the EMI-2, because the focus of our study was to compare *motives* to participate in PA between age groups.

Based on the focus towards investigating PA motives and preferences towards motivational affordances, the theoretical development in this study consisted of the triangulation of three domains: (1) Motivation to participate in PA, (2) Motivational Affordances, and (3) PA.

Research Questions

Participation in daily PAs, exercises, or fitness routines is critical to overcome a sedentary lifestyle and helps to maintain and improve health and wellbeing in adults of all ages. Motivation to participate in PA can be achieved through gamified behaviour-change strategies [2,28,51]. However, there has been little research on the differences in the motives to participate in PA among age groups. Using devices and apps to monitor physical activities and exercise routines makes it possible to also monitor progression or regression over time [38]. Many of these apps situate motivational affordances to help foster intrinsic and/or extrinsic PA motivation [64]. Additionally, the understanding of age-group-specific preferences for these motivational affordances is critical if we hope to integrate them into the design of PA technologies. While a non-tailored, generalised approach is being used in current fitness-tracking and gamified PA technology, more research is needed to understand the preferences for these motivational affordances in adults in different age groups. Thus, we asked the following research questions:

RQ1: Are there differences in the motivation to participate in PA between adults from different age groups?

RQ2: Does the choice of motivational affordances differ between age groups?

STUDY DESIGN AND METHODS

We conducted a survey study using a questionnaire in both online and printed formats. A recruitment drive for participants was carried out through email and blog posts, by posting the survey link through social media channels such as Twitter, LinkedIn, and Facebook, and through recruitment at community centres and fitness centres.

Survey Design

We included a "by hand" option for participation because we were also targeting older adults (65+). This questionnaire was a compilation of EMI-2 [41]—a revised Exercise Motivations scale—demographic questionnaires, and questions on preferences for motivational affordances to participate in PA. The EMI-2 is a multidimensional, 51-item scale designed to assess an individual's motives to participate in exercise. These 51 items are categorised into 14 dimensions (Stress Management, Revitalization, Enjoyment, Challenge, Social Recognition, Affiliation, Competition, Health Pressures, Ill Health Avoidance, Positive Health, Weight Management, Appearance, Strength & Endurance, and Nimbleness). We extended the applicability of this scale by replacing the term 'exercise' with 'physical activity', so that it included a wide range of activities defined as light, moderate, or strenuous PA, which is relevant for older adults [10].

Participants

Data were collected over a four-month period (April 2016-July 2016). Participants were offered the option of a chance to win one of three Amazon.ca gift cards, each valued at $30 CDN. In total, 192 participants took part in the survey: 22 respondents filled the survey by hand and responses were then transferred to the survey database, and 170 responses were completed in an online questionnaire format. Forty-two of the total survey responses had to be purged because of incomplete data, resulting in 150 complete responses.

DATA ANALYSIS AND RESULTS

Participant Demographics

Most PA guidelines are defined for age groups: adults (18-64) and older adults (65+) groups [9,68]. However, to compare the needs and preferences of adults in different age groups, we used age cohorts from a study on adults and gaming [26]. Based on this research study, we binned the data into four age groups: 18-29 years old (G1), 30-49 years old (G2), 50-64 years old (G3), and 65+ years old (G4). These groups were coded 1-4 for data analysis. Gender was equally distributed (F=75, M=75) in the total sample population and gender distribution within each group is shown in Table 1.

We collected demographic information from participants (as a percentage of the overall sample population) regarding

	Total Participants	(N=150)
Age (years)	(1) 18-29 (17, 11.3%) (GF=11, GM=6)	M=25.7, SD=2.5
	(2) 30-49 (58, 38.7%) (GF=28, GM=30)	M=39, SD=5.85
	(3) 50-64 (43, 28.7%) (GF=25, GM=18)	M=56.9.SD=3.9
	(4) 65+ (32, 21.3%) (GF=11, GM=21)	M=71.9, SD=4.9
Devices used to play digital games	Smartphones	35.0%
	Cell-Phones	11.7%
	Tablets	22.3%
	Desktop PC	9.7%
	Laptop computers	9.7%
	Game Consoles	7.8%
	Online	1.9%
	All on the list	1.9%

Table 1: Demographics; GF= Gender Female, GM= Gender Male, N = Total, M =Mean, SD = Standard Deviation.

their age, gender, hours spent sitting per day, hours spent sleeping per day, inclination to play digital games, devices used to play games, time spent in physical activity per day, apps used to monitor physical activities and devices used to monitor physical activities. Detailed information not shown in Table 1 is shown in our supplementary materials.

From the total sample (N=150), more than half of the respondents (60.1%) spent more than five hours sitting per day, and slept for 7-8.5 hours per day (54.4%). While a high percentage of the respondents did not play any digital games (52%), among those who did, smart phones (35%), tablets (22.3%) and cell-phones (11.7%) were the most desirable media for playing digital games. Additionally, while a high percentage of the respondents spent less than an hour per day participating in PA (28%) and did not use any apps (71.3%) or devices to monitor their PA (60.7%), Fitbit (19.1%) and pedometers (17%) were most often used by the remaining respondents. Our data indicate that, of the respondents who played digital games, mobile devices were preferred for digital games and wearable tracking devices were preferred technology choices.

Data Analyses

We used a mixed-method approach to analyse the data. Survey responses from the EMI-2 questionnaire were analysed quantitatively. Content analysis was carried out on the long-form text responses buy identifying frequencies of motivational affordances and grouping them into the question categories.

Reliability and Normality

All 14 dimensions of the EMI-2 scale [41] had high reliabilities, Cronbach's α =.90. The scale reliability with dimensions deleted is shown in the supplementary materials. Data from the 51-item, 14-dimension EMI-2 scale were non-normal (Kolmogorov-Smirnov test).

Motivational differences between age groups

Non–normal data from the four groups binned according to age groups were tested using the Kruskal-Wallis test for differences. Only two dimensions, 'health pressures', $H(3) = 7.96$, $p < .05$, and 'ill health avoidance', $H(3) = 8.90$, $p < .05$, differed significantly between the age groups. This indicated that among the age groups, 'health pressures' and 'ill health avoidance' facilitated participation in PA.

DV (control)	Age Category	Statistic
HP	30-49 years old	U=358, r = -.20
	50-64 years old	U=224, r = -.30
	65+ years old	U=165, r = -.32
IHA	30-49 years old	U=284, r = -.30
	50-64 years old	U=206, r = -.34
	65+ years old	U=146, r = -.38

Table 2: Mann-Whitney U statistic. EMI-2 scale dimensions: HP = health pressures; IHA = ill health avoidance.

Pairwise comparisons using the Mann-Whitney test were performed to follow up the above finding and to investigate further differences between age groups within the two dimensions identified above. We used G1 (18-29 years old) as a control group and compared the results with those in the other three age groups. Health pressures (HP) and ill health avoidance (IHA) and dependent variables (DV) were significant with G2 (30-49 years old), G3 (50-64 years old) and G4 (65+), as shown in Table 2 (all $p < .05$). Additionally, to investigate the trends in dimensions between age groups we used the Jonckheere-Terpstra statistic to test for ordered patterns of the averages of the 14 EMI dimensions of the four age groups. Jonckheere's test revealed a significant trend in health pressures ($J = 4795$, $z = 2.78$, $r = .22$), ill health avoidance ($J = 4579$, $z = 2.02$, $r = .16$), and nimbleness ($J = 4716$, $z = 2.495$, $r = .20$) (all $p < .05$).

Motivational Affordances for PA

The respondents answered the following questions:

1. What *types of feedback* do you look for in an app to help you with PA?
2. Can you suggest attributes in the app that could *motivate* you to participate in PA?
3. Can you suggest attributes in the app that *do not motivate (negative attributes)* you to participate in PA?
4. Can you suggest attributes in the app which could *help facilitate goals* for PA?
5. Can you suggest any attributes which could help you *continue to participate in physical activity* sessions over a longer period of time?

A content analysis of the answers to long-form text questions in the survey was performed using Excel (Microsoft, Inc.). Long-form text data were categorised based on the motivational affordances for PA [23,38]. The frequencies of the attributes were determined as a percentage of the total number of attributes (n_{att}) listed by the respondents per age group. While the content analysis revealed many attributes for each question, we report excerpts of the percentages of the attributes for each of the question categories. The remaining percentages for the attributes are shown in the supplementary materials.

Feedback types: The comparison of the *feedback types* looked for by each group showed respondents in each group sought different feedback types. Table 3 shows the excerpts of the percentages feedback attributes in each group.

Representative responses from G1: for **calories**: *'I would look for calories'; 'calories burnt'; 'calorie counter';* for **heart rate**: *'[...]it would be good to see heart rate';* for **step-counters:** *'noting steps is like hitting a mark'.*

G2: for **calories**: *'[...]used for calorie count/ calories burned'*; for **distance travelled** and **step counters**: *'step counter to see the distance between places and sometimes how much calories need to be burn(ed) if I eat a certain type of food'; 'the number of calorie / weight / progression / number of steps'.*

G3: for **time**: *'want to do this often'; 'the more I do it, the faster I go; 'check time taken to do this'*; *'performance improvement over time';* for **points**: *'like to see my points'*; for **feedback**: *'step counters and calorie counters'*; *'[...]with Fitbit: Step and miles counter'*; *'immediate feedback on number of steps taken'*.

Age Cat	Types of Feedback
18-29 (n_{att}=51)	Calories (15.7%), heart rate (13.7%) step counters (9.8%)
30-49 (n_{att}=110)	Calories (18.2%), distance travelled (15.5%), step counters (16.4%)
50-64 (n_{att}=88)	Time (19.3%), points (17%), feedback (11.4%)
65+ (n_{att}=117)	Step-counters (17.9%), distance travelled (14.5%), calories (14.5%)

Table 3: Feedback types

G4: for **step-counters** and **distance travelled**: *'feedback on steps'*; *'steps, I walk a lot';' If an iPhone app could detect walking'*; and **calories**: *'calories monitoring device'*; *'calories burnt'*.

Motivation to participate in PA: Excerpts of percentages of three preferences of attributes that could *motivate to participate* in PA in each of the four age groups are shown in Table 4.

Age Cat	Affordances
18-29 (n_{att}=44)	Badges (11.4%), progression (11.4%), goals (9.1%)
30-49* (n_{att}=96)	Calories (10.4%), step-counters (8.3%), progression (6.3%),
50-64** (n_{att}=57)	Calories (12.3%), distance travelled (12.3%), weight loss (8.8%)
65+ (n_{att}=94)	Step-counters (10.6%), distance travelled (10.6%), progression (6.4%)
	* no monitoring (12.5%)
	** no monitoring (21.1%)

Table 4: Affordances to help participate in PA

Representative responses from G1: for **badges**: *'[...]I like receiving badges'*; *'[...]anonymous competition between friends resulting in like Fitbit badges'*; for **progression**: *'[...]seeing how far behind I am compared to friends'*; *'progress indicator towards goals'*; *'comparison of past few results towards a goal'*.

G2: for **calories**: *'[...]need to know calories and general trend'; calories burned';* for **progression**: *'the Nike running app has motivated me to run more based on the tracking my progression and setting up challenges'*; *'along with daily stats it also provides tips which is specific to you'*; *'daily progress chart'*; *'logging of activities'*.

G3: for **calories**: '[...]*good to know how much I burned'*; for **distance travelled**: *'I love the stats on the Fitbit [...] weekly totals of (km) walked'*.

G4: for **distance travelled**: *'I like walking, so distance is important'*; *'distance monitoring device';* for **progression**: *'comparisons to previous similar exercise / i.e. cycling routes same climbs and compare times'*; *'show progress or improvement'*.

Negative attributes: Table 5 shows excerpts of percentages of *negative attributes* that affect participation in PA.

Age Cat	Negative Attributes
18-29 (n_{att}=9)	Step counters (44.4%), social sharing (33.3%), points (22.2%),
30-49 (n_{att}=53)	Challenges (17%), step counters (13.2%), badges, dist. travelled (7.5%),
50-64 (n_{att}=27)	Challenges (18.5%), step counters (18.5%), calories (14.8%)
65+ (n_{att}=81)	Time (17%), challenges (10%), progression (8.9%)

Table 5: Negative attributes

Representative responses from G1: *'[...]***step-counters-** *I've never used one and don't care to try[...]seems unnecessary'*; *'[...]too much pressure with counting and maintaining steps[...]'.* for **social affordances**: *'[...]social aspects don't interest me'; '[...]I do not like the pressure of sharing'.*

G2: for **challenges**: *'[...]the competition side of the physical activities'*; for **step counters**: *'[...]too much time it takes to learn something, too much fiddling'*; for **social affordances**: *'[...]too much social stuff, I don't need to share every time I take a deep breath[...]'*; *'[...]other people don't motivate me, I prefer to work out alone[...]'; '[...]Notifications from the app which tell you that your friend is doing better than you, really annoying I feel like that's childish[...]'.*

G3: for **challenges**: *'I do not like competition[...]'*; *'[...]days with little activity are motivating as well, because you don't want to have them very often'*.

G4: for **time**: *'watching the clock is a stress'*; for **challenges**: *'[...]do not like challenges that are tough'; 'fear of falling'; 'complex steps'; 'complex routines'; 'easy to remember (difficulty)'; 'fear of exertion'; 'Intensity of physical activity'*; for **progression***: '[...]as the day progresses I am less likely to be active or want to start anything'.*

Affordances that facilitate goals for PA: Table 6 shows the excerpts of percentages of attributes that *help in facilitating PA*.

Age Cat	Affordances
18-29 (n_{att}=34)	Goals (14.7%), challenges (11.8%), step counters (11.8%)
30-49 (n_{att}=78)	Challenges (14.5%), goals (12.0%), progression (9.6%)
50-64 (n_{att}=65)	Choice (14.1%), goals (9.4%), step-counters (7.8%)
65+ (n_{att}=112)	Goals (8.9%), badges (8%), challenges (7.1%)

Table 6: Affordances that facilitate goals for PA

Representative responses from G1: for **goals**: *'I'd need to have goals for what I want to accomplish in mind'*; *'[...]calculating goals for me based on diet[...]'*.

G2: for **goals** and **challenges**: *'[...]the goals that I have for my life help decide my activity goals'*; *'[...]I've used a running app in the past which trains you to reach a specific running goal (5km runs)'*; *'[...]cumulative milestones like run 500 km in a year or other milestones like fastest 10km run'*.

G3: for **goals**: *'[...]prefer to achieve goals'*; *'[...]burn off calories'*; *'[...]benchmark in terms of physical activity expected for age - to compare myself against the benchmark'*.

G4: for **goals**: *'[...]simple routines'*; *'[...]easy to remember and recall steps'*; *'[...]I do the same activities over and over again'*; *'[...]age related goal suggestions'*; *'[...]incremental goals'*; *'[...]simple steps and routines'*.

Continuance of PA: Table 7 shows excerpts of the attributes that could facilitate *continuance of PA over a longer time* frame.

Age Cat	Affordances
18-29 (n_{att}=37)	Badges (16.2%), goals (16.2%), progression (13.5%)
30-49 (n_{att}=56)	Progression (10.7%), step counters (10.7%), time (10.7%),
50-64 (n_{att}=55)	Goals (12.7%), step counters (10.9%), feedback (9.1%)
65+ (n_{att}=86)	Feedback (15.1%), progression (14%), goals (12.8%)

Table 7: Continuance in PA over a longer time

Representative responses from G1: for **badges**: *'[...]I think virtual badges are neat'*; *'[...] some kind of game/badge element with goals for completing a given exercise'*; *'incentives'*; *'stars'*; *'badges'*.

G2: for **progression**: *'[...]a graphical completion chart'*; *'progression history'*; *'[...]tracking progress of how you are improving'*; *'[...] tracking over time to show progress'*.

G3: for ***goals***: *'[...]like training targets'*; *'[...]do nature stuff'*; *'[...]good heath'*; *'[...]speed to complete 6 km of walking per night'*; *'[...]willingness to have a healthy body'*.

G4: for **feedback**: *'Involuntary updates (perhaps weekly) delivered to me with graphic information indicating progress'*; *'I prefer improvements on daily and weekly basis'*; *'[...]more interaction and feedback on an app like using my Fitbit'*; *'[...]need feedback on improvements[...]'*; *'[...]advice of family physician'*; *'[...]praise'*.

While **social affordance** generally had a lower percentage for facilitating the continuance of PA, a few comments regarding this affordance were: *'[...]someone to compete with directly and share[...]'*; *'[...]social linking to track progress easily and participate remotely in shared exercise with friends'* (G2); *'[...]prefer a consistent social group' (G3)*; *'I need a social environment for higher motivation to initiate and stick to physical activity' (G4)*. The content analysis provided insights into the preferences of respondents from the four age groups for motivational affordances that facilitate PA or serve as triggers to help foster motivation in PA.

DISCUSSION

In this study, we surveyed motives to participate in PA and compared preferences for motivational affordances for technology-facilitated PA among four age groups. Health tracking and the gamification of physical exercise are becoming part of our daily routines. However, a range of affordances that are used in these wearable and online applications are generalized towards a generic population, and are not tailored towards the exercise motivations of specific demographic populations. The presumption that the design of these applications can involve the universal adaptation of these systems to different age groups may be flawed. Our survey study helps to shed more light on this issue by providing insights into age-specific motivations for PA. Our survey study analysed positive and negative attributes that could help facilitate or hinder technology-facilitated PA.

Comparison of Motivational Differences of Age Groups

In our study, we reduced the 51 scale items into 14 dimensions as suggested by the EMI-2 literature [41]. The 14 dimensions for motives to participate in PA had high reliability. Non-parametric tests revealed significant results only for the health pressures and ill health avoidance dimensions. Based on the EMI-2, this result indicated that advice from doctors, the desire to prevent illness prevalent in the family and the need to recover from an illness took precedence over scale items from other dimensions. Similarly, avoidance of heart disease, prevention of health problems, avoidance of ill health and the desire to stay healthy were significant motivations in the ill health dimension. Furthermore, a pairwise comparison between two groups (using G1 as a control group) revealed significant results for the three other age groups in the health pressures and ill health avoidance dimensions. These two dimensions are important motives for participating in PA for all age groups.

We observed a statistically significant trend of higher median scores (Jonckheere-Terpstra statistic) within the health pressures, ill health avoidance, and nimbleness dimensions. These findings help to answer our RQ1 regarding differences in motivation to participate in PA between adults from different age groups.

Motivational Affordances for Different Age Groups

Feedback Types

A content analysis of long-form survey responses showed the following. Firstly, the most popular *feedback type* that age groups 1 and 2 refer to was feedback on *calories*. *Time* taken to complete a task was a popular feedback preferred by group 3, whereas *step counters* was popular with the older demographic. We could argue that possibly keeping track of calories matters more during our active years in life, while later in life we want more specific feedback like scheduling our exercise around our (often family) life and even later we want to ensure we are staying active and remain mobile at all. Often a little walk can do wonders to an otherwise sedentary retirement lifestyle. It is possible the participants in group 4 walked more than those in the other groups, which made *distance travelled* the second-most favourite type of feedback preferred by this group. We would like to assume that this likely refers to feedback that incentivizes walks and promotes mobility for older adults. For the design of gamified health applications to facilitate PA in these age groups, this means that these types of feedback elements can be given greater focus.

The least-favoured types of feedback were achievement, choice, cost (G1); weight loss (G2); achievement, cost, distance travelled and sound (G3) and achievement, cost, sharing and weight loss (G4). This is interesting because in the following discussion we outline that badges are important to the younger age group (G1) and that they do not have negative feelings about challenge. It is arguable that the form of achievement feedback matters for this age group more than for other age groups. Another disparity is seen for G2, who clearly liked feedback on their calorie consumption but would not prefer to see actual weight loss indicated. This could be because weight loss at that age might be challenging (simply because we are generally entering our working life and it is hard to find time for losing weight when we are starting families and securing our advancement on the job market). To avoid frustration, it is easier to show progress and monitoring of calories than to indicate (possibly slower) weight loss for this age group.

Motivational Affordances Facilitating PA

In terms of *motivational affordances* to facilitate PA, the most popular affordances were *badges* and *progression* for G1, *calories* for G2 and G3, and *step counters* for G4. This suggests that extrinsic motivational affordances are more popular with the younger age group and tracking metrics (and setting goals to track intrinsic motivation) are more favoured by older age groups G2, G3 and G4. We should note that many of the respondents in G1 were part of the millennial generation. This generation grew up surrounded by video games and it is possible that they more generally understand extrinsic rewards like badges. This generation also likes challenge as part of their health-tracking routines and possibly finds it more attractive to mask caloric progress in badge systems (that can possibly be shared in their social circles as well).

The least popular motivational affordances were trailing feedback (G1), competition, comparison with friends and negative feedback (G2), competition and comparison with friends (G3), and levels (G4). This implies that participants in G2 and G3 were reluctant to share their performance and metrics with others, as were those in the older age group for complex or difficult PA. This might highlight a shift from the older generations towards the millennial generation (G1) in terms of how they share their personal information related to their wellbeing and fitness.

Regarding *negative attributes*, *step counters* (G1), *challenges* (G2 and G3), and *time* were the least favourite of the motivational attributes. This is consistent with the finding that the least favourable *motivational affordance* for both G2 and G3 was *competition*. *Time* was the least favorable negative attribute for G4, which also implies that the time taken for PA was a negative pressure in this group.

Regarding *attributes that aid/facilitate goals for PA*, the survey responses were coherent. *Goals* (G1), *challenges* (G2), *choice* (G3) and *goals* (G4) were the most popular of the attributes. Interestingly, *challenges* were also a *negative attribute* for respondents in G2. Further investigation of the responses indicated that respondents were averse to *challenge pressure* (negative attribute) as opposed to challenges as an attribute. We could interpret these findings as G1 wanting to be rewarded for their progression, G2 and G3 wanting to know that they are progressing toward targets, and G4 wanting to know if they are improving or progressing towards maintaining their health at all.

The least favoured attributes were *achievement* (G1), *sound* and *device* (G2), *narrative* (G3) and *sound* and *calories* (G4). One respondent (G3) was quite interested in narratives, but indicated that the relevance of the narrative was important to the context of the app design. Again, we can see how calorie tracking is of little importance for older adults (G4) and how, controversially, the millennial generation (G1) does not like achievement yet finds badges highly valuable.

Favourite Attributes of PA Technology

Regarding physical activity or exercise adherence (continuance of PA over time), *badges* (G1), *progression* (G2), *goals* (G3) and *feedback* (G4) were key favourites within each category of technology attributes. In G4, feedback as a generic term meant to get feedback on improvements, form-checking and gait. Again, older adults are more interested in remaining active than in achieving physical targets or fitness goals. In contrast to this, the results from the other age groups were more fitness-related.

Form-checking and speed (G1), cost (G2), speed and quests (G3), and health data (G4), as in the privacy of personal information, were the least favourable attributes that could hinder participation in PA. G1's preference for badges but no regard to form-checking could imply an interest in quick fixes and apps that provide rewarding feedback instead of critical feedback aimed at improvement of form (or speed). It is interesting that G3 seems to be averse to quests, because many people of that generation might be baby boomers and are less interested in game mechanics as part of their fitness-tracking applications.

Age-group-specific Design Guidelines

Our survey study focused on comparing the motivation to participate in PA between four age groups and investigating preferences for motivational affordances in PA facilitated by technology. While the motivation to participate in PA differed significantly in the health pressures and ill health dimensions of the EMI-2, a content analysis of long-form survey questions provided design guidelines for tailoring motivational affordances by age group.

Age Cat	Design Guidelines for PA Technology
18-29	**Motivation for PA:** While fostering intrinsic motivation through affordances like goals and progression, it is also critical to integrate extrinsic motivational affordances like badges and rewards. **Facilitating goals for PA:** Incorporate accomplishment affordances while fostering challenge within the context of PA **Continuance of PA:** Provide the opportunity to earn badges and rewards while working towards goals
30-49	**Motivation for PA:** Incorporate feedback elements like calories and distance travelled while providing daily progression and comparisons with a social circle. **Facilitating goals for PA:** While integrating a combination of short-term goals/long-term goals, and challenges, provide progression affordance in the form of reaching milestones **Continuance of PA:** Integrate progression in the form of visual graphs to show progress over time and achievement of goals
50-64	**Motivation for PA:** While integrating feedback elements like calories and distance travelled to facilitate walking, incorporate weekly progression elements to foster intrinsic motivation. **Facilitating goals for PA:** Provide the opportunity to achieve goals with provisions for comparison with benchmarked PA markers **Continuance of PA:** Provide the opportunity to set up goals with feedback on progression
65+	**Motivation for PA:** Provide monitoring of activities to encourage walking using feedback elements like step-counters and distance metrics while indicating progress or improvement as affordances from a feel-good perspective. **Facilitating goals for PA:** Integrate simple routines and challenges while providing opportunities to earn badges **Continuance of PA:** Integrate feedback elements to provide involuntary feedback, praise and improvement

Table 8: Design guidelines to integrate motivational affordances for PA technology

We categorised these age-group-specific design guidelines based on our long-form survey responses into three types: (1) motivation to participate in PA, (2) facilitating goals for PA, and (3) continuance of PA. Our suggested design guidelines are shown in Table 8. These guidelines are important for designers because it helps to customize and personalize motivational affordances for the design of age-centric PA technology. As an example, based on these guidelines, fitness applications like Fitbit or Nike Fuelband could deliver goals and progressive challenges with a mix of rewards and badges while fostering challenges and promoting the feeling of accomplishment among potential customers in G1. In contrast, customers in G4 could be provided with simple routines intermingled with praise for the completion of simple tasks to enable a feeling of validation for their efforts.

Motivational Affordances and Feedback/Tracking Metrics

	Motivational Elements
Gamified motivational affordances (**Intrinsic elements**)	Goals Challenges Progression Achievements Choice/options Quests Social sharing
Gamified motivational affordances (**Extrinsic elements**)	Badges Rewards Points Incentives Leaderboards
Feedback elements	Calorie tracker Step-counters Distance travelled Daily notifications Time spent Heart rate Breathing rate Sleep cycle Sound inputs Weight loss indicator Physical form-checker Gait/posture-checker

Table 9: Differentiating gamified motivational affordances and feedback elements

From a technology-facilitated PA solution perspective, it is important to distinguish between gamification elements and feedback/tracking metrics (Table 9). Our content analysis findings indicate gamification elements are important as motivational affordances. A few of these intrinsic elements that could play a role in fostering motivational participation in PA are goals, challenges, progression, achievements, choice quests, and social sharing leading to a feel-good context. Extrinsic elements such as badges, rewards, incentives, points, and leaderboards were also key findings in this survey study. As indicated in related literature, many of these extrinsic elements may also support intrinsic motivation to different degrees of intensity [11,22,45]. Many levels of feedback elements or tracking metrics of PA activities can also serve as motivational affordances in technology-facilitated PA, including calorie tracking, step counters, distance travelled, daily notifications, time spent, heart rate, breathing rate, speed, sleep cycle, sound inputs and weight loss indicators. Additional attributes such as physical form-checking, posture correction and gait-checking were also desirable attributes. However, it is important to consider the target demographic when designing PA technology. As our study showed, strong differences in preferences for feedback types and key motivators exist between the millennial generation and older generations. To ensure that PA technology is adopted within the target demographic group, different design decisions must be made early on in the technology design process. We hope that our design guidelines provide a helpful starting point for the development of successful PA technology for different demographics.

Motivations for Physical Activity

Prior studies have shown motivation for PA has intrinsic and extrinsic components [11,15,41]. However, our survey study revealed that the driving force for fostering participation in PA is the desire to maintain good health. The definition of good health can shift over time as people age, where younger people have a stronger tendency to get quick feedback on the things they track, and middle-aged people prefer the ability to set their own goals and follow individual health and fitness targets. Older adults generally use PA technology to ensure their mobility and to maintain physical health.

Thus, our findings help identify and differentiate motivational affordances in adults in different age groups. Our findings also help to differentiate (1) feedback/tracking metrics from (2) gamification elements, thereby helping to minimize the confusion in their application. While both elements serve as motivational affordances for participation in PA, they are distinctly different in function and usage, as explained in the subsection above. As we clearly showed in Table 9, all of the elements are available for the design of motivational PA technology and the emphasis on which ones to use should come from designers, who are informed about their target demographic. In user experience design in general, contextual inquiry (i.e., field studies where designers observe user interactions with similar products as the planned product) is recommended as a first step towards designing a successful interactive product. For building successful PA technology, we would recommend augmenting any findings coming from contextual inquiries with information about demographic tendencies presented here.

Applications that serve as technology-facilitators for PA will need to apply this distinction between feedback metrics and gamification elements diligently. While feedback is a generic term and a gamification element is not, our content analysis indicates that it is important to distinguish feedback elements in the form of tracking PA from feedback within a gamification context. We hope that this differentiation will help designers establish gamification elements and feedback/tracking elements for PA facilitated by technology.

Limitations and Future Research Directions

While the survey study had many participants, G1 included only 17 participants. The small sample size of this age group could be a limitation to this study. While surveys may have their own limitations (e.g. the number of questions presented), this survey study allows us to understand the overall preferences of respondents within these binned age groups. An interview-based qualitative study over a longer period of time would be a possible next step to understand the detailed motivational affordances (intrinsic and extrinsic) that facilitate PA. This would also make it possible to understand the changes in motivational affordances over time. We plan to use these findings to investigate specific motivational affordances and tracking metrics for select age groups to enable the identification and evaluation of gamification elements, tracking elements or feedback metrics. Additionally, the influence of these motivational affordances (intrinsic and extrinsic) can lead to a better understanding of their applicability and influence on intrinsic and extrinsic motivations to participate in PA.

CONCLUSION

While health technologies and gamified fitness strategies have been widely adopted, there has been little research to support the differentiation of motivational affordances for PA in specific age groups to maintain PA routines. This paper contributes to our understanding of the design of gamified PA technology.

Firstly, we provide evidence that health pressures and ill health avoidance significantly influence participation in PA. Furthermore, to the best of our knowledge, this work provides new insights into the differentiation of motivational affordances to be tailored for different age groups, with the goal of helping researchers and designers better understand design challenges when creating PA applications for different age groups. This is an important step in the development of meaningful health technology applications for both young and old adults. This would allow individuals to apply technology for the initiation, maintenance and adherence of PA to promote physical and mental wellbeing. Finally, this research identified a difference between gamified motivational elements and feedback elements, and we provide age-group-specific design guidelines that could be critical for the development of customisable and tailored technology for PA. These are valuable contributions to the growing body of work in human-computer interaction and games.

ACKNOWLEDGMENTS

We thank Dr. Elisa Mekler for providing helpful comments on previous versions of this document. We would like to thank SSHRC (895-2011-1014), NSERC (RGPIN- 418622-

2012), CFI (35819) and Mitacs (IT07255) for funding this work. All aspects of this study complied with the research ethics guidelines provided at UOIT.

REFERENCES

1. Faisal A Barwais, Thomas F Cuddihy, and L Michaud Tomson. 2013. Physical activity, sedentary behavior and total wellness changes among sedentary adults: a 4-week randomized controlled trial. *Health and quality of life outcomes* 11, 1: 183. https://doi.org/10.1186/1477-7525-11-183
2. Shlomo Berkovsky, Mac Coombe, Jill Freyne, Dipak Bhandari, and Nilufar Baghaei. 2010. Physical Activity Motivating Games: Virtual Rewards for Real Activity. In *Proc. of the 28th international conference on Human factors in computing systems - CHI '10*: 243. Retrieved from http://portal.acm.org/citation.cfm?doid=1753326.1753362
3. Marie-Louise Bird, Brodie Clark, Johanna Millar, Sue Whetton, and Stuart Smith. 2015. Exposure to "Exergames" Increases Older Adults' Perception of the Usefulness of Technology for Improving Health and Physical Activity: A Pilot Study. *JMIR Serious Games* 3, 2: 1–8. https://doi.org/10.2196/games.4275
4. Julia Ayumi Bopp, Elisa D. Mekler, and Klaus Opwis. 2016. Negative Emotion, Positive Experience? In *Proc. of the 2016 CHI Conference on Human Factors in Computing Systems - CHI '16*: 2996–3006. https://doi.org/10.1145/2858036.2858227
5. Philipp Brauner, André Calero Valdez, Ulrik Schroeder, and Martina Ziefle. 2013. Increase Physical Fitness and Create Health Awareness through Exergames and Gamification. The Role of Individual Factors , Motivation and Acceptance Increase Physical Fitness and Create Health Awareness through Exergames and Gamification. *In Proc of SouthCHI 2013*, 349–362.
6. Dena M. Bravata, Crystal Smith-Spangler, Vandana Sundaram, Allison L Gienger, Nancy Lin, Robyn Lewis, Christopher D Stave, Ingram Olkin, and John R. Sirard. 2007. Using Pedometers to Increase Physical Activity A Systematic Review. *JAMA* 298, 19: 2296–2304.
7. Janet Buckworth, Rebecca E. Lee, Gail Regan, Lori K. Schneider, and Carlo C. DiClemente. 2007. Decomposing intrinsic and extrinsic motivation for exercise: Application to stages of motivational readiness. *Psychology of Sport and Exercise* 8, 4: 441–461. https://doi.org/10.1016/j.psychsport.2006.06.007
8. Laurien M. Buffart, Tessa Westendorp, Rita J. Van Den Berg-Emons, Henk J. Stam, and Marij E. Roebroeck. 2009. Perceived barriers to and facilitators of physical activity in young adults with childhood-onset physical disabilities. *Journal of Rehabilitation Medicine* 41, 11: 881–885. https://doi.org/10.2340/16501977-0420
9. Canadian Society of Exercise Physiology. 2012. Canadian Physical Activity and Sedentary Behaviour Guidelines. https://doi.org/978-1-896900-30-8
10. Lilian Cheung. 2015. Examples of Moderate and Vigorous Physical Activity. Harvard T.H. Chan School of Public Health: *Obesity Prevention Source*. Retrieved August 10, 2016 from https://www.hsph.harvard.edu/obesity-prevention-source/moderate-and-vigorous-physical-activity/
11. Marie Dacey, Amy Baltzell, and Len Zaichkowsky. 2008. Older adults' intrinsic and extrinsic motivation toward physical activity. *American Journal of Health Behavior* 32, 6: 570–582. https://doi.org/10.5555/ajhb.2008.32.6.570
12. Edward L. Deci, Haleh Eghrari, Brian C. Patrick, and Dean R. Leone. 1994. Facilitating Internalization: The Self Determination Theory Perspective. *Journal of Personality* 62, 2: 119–42.
13. Edward L. Deci, Richard Koestner, and Richard M Ryan. 1999. A meta-analytic review of experiments examining the effects of extrinsic rewards on intrinsic motivation. *Psychological Bulletin*, 627–668.
14. Sebastian Deterding, Dan Dixon, Rilla Khaled, and Lennart E. Nacke. 2011. From Game Design Elements to Gamefulness : Defining " Gamification ." *MindTrek'11, September 28-30, 2011, Tampere, Finland.*, 9–15.
15. R K Dishman and W Ickes. 1981. Self-motivation and adherence to therapeutic exercise. *Journal of Behavioral Medicine* 4, 4: 421–38. Retrieved from http://www.ncbi.nlm.nih.gov/pubmed/16019873
16. Lindsay R Duncan, Craig R Hall, Philip M Wilson, and O Jenny. 2010. Exercise motivation: a cross-sectional analysis examining its relationships with frequency, intensity, and duration of exercise. *The International Journal of Behavioral Nutrition and Physical Activity* 7: 7. https://doi.org/10.1186/1479-5868-7-7
17. Bassem Elsawy and Kim E Higgins. 2010. Physical Activity Guidelines for Older Adults. *American Family Physician* 81, 1: 55–59. Retrieved from http://www.ncbi.nlm.nih.gov/pubmed/20052963
18. Benjamin Gardner and Phillippa Lally. 2013. Does intrinsic motivation strengthen physical activity habit? Modeling relationships between self-determination, past behaviour, and habit strength. *Journal of Behavioral Medicine* 36, 5: 488–497. https://doi.org/10.1007/s10865-012-9442-0
19. Kathrin Gerling, Ian Livingston, Lennart E. Nacke, and Regan Mandryk. 2012. Full-body motion-based game interaction for older adults. In *Proc. of CHI '12*, 1873–1882. https://doi.org/10.1145/2207676.2208324
20. Kathrin M Gerling. 2011. Exploring the Potential of Gamification Among Frail Elderly Persons. In *Ext Abs CHI 2011*, 1–4.

21. Hinda Goldberg. 1983. Involment in Physical Activity as a Function of Attitude Toward Physical Activity and Self-Motivation. York University, Toronto, Ontario.
22. Juho Hamari and Jonna Koivisto. 2015. "Working out for likes": An empirical study on social influence in exercise gamification. *Computers in Human Behavior* 50: 333–347. https://doi.org/10.1016/j.chb.2015.04.018
23. Juho Hamari, Jonna Koivisto, and Harri Sarsa. 2014. Does gamification work? - A literature review of empirical studies on gamification. *Proceedings of the Annual Hawaii International Conference on System Sciences*: 3025–3034. https://doi.org/10.1109/HICSS.2014.377
24. Anna Maiju Jauho, Riitta Pyky, Riikka Ahola, Maarit Kangas, Paula Virtanen, Raija Korpelainen, and Timo Jämsä. 2015. Effect of wrist-worn activity monitor feedback on physical activity behavior: A randomized controlled trial in Finnish young men. *Preventive Medicine Reports* 2: 628–634. https://doi.org/10.1016/j.pmedr.2015.07.005
25. Yuan Jia, Bin Xu, Yamini Karanam, and Stephen Voida. 2016. Personality-targeted Gamification. *Proceedings of the 2016 CHI Conference on Human Factors in Computing Systems - CHI '16*: 2001–2013. https://doi.org/10.1145/2858036.2858515
26. Sydney Jones and Susannah Fox. 2009. Pew Internet Project Data: Adults and video games. *Online*, September: 1–9. https://doi.org/10.1080/00150190490429231
27. Younbo Jung, Koay Jing Li, Ng Sihui Janissa, Wong Li Chieh Gladys, and Kwan Min Lee. 2009. Games for a better life: Effects of Playing Wii Games on the Well-Being of Seniors in a Long-Term Care Facility. *Proceedings of the Sixth Australasian Conference on Interactive Entertainment - IE '09*: 1–6. Retrieved from http://portal.acm.org/citation.cfm?doid=1746050.1746055
28. Dennis L. Kappen, Lennart E. Nacke, Kathrin M. Gerling, and Lia E. Tsotsos. 2016. Design Strategies for Gamified Physical Activity Applications for Older Adults. In *Proceedings of the Annual Hawaii International Conference on System Sciences-49*, 1309–18.
29. Dennis L Kappen and Lennart E Nacke. 2013. The Kaleidoscope of Effective Gamification: Deconstructing Gamification in Business Applications. In *Proceedings of the First International Conference on Gameful Design, Research, and Applications - Gamification '13*, 119–122.
30. Tuomas Kari, M Makkonen, P Moilanen, and L Frank. 2012. The Habits of Playing and the Reasons for not Playing Exergames: Age Differences in Finland. In *In Proc. of the IADIS International Conferences Interfaces and Human Computer Interaction 2012 and Game and Entertainment Technologies 2012, Section II*, 29–38. Retrieved from https:/proceedings.nsf/0/e554d83474d02f5bc1257a2a0032a7d4/$FILE/P37_Kari_33. pdf
31. Tuomas Kari, Jenni Piippo, Lauri Frank, Markus Makkonen, and Panu Moilanen. 2016. To Gamify or Not to Gamify? Gamification in Exercise Applications and Its Role in Impacting Exercise Motivation. *29th Bled eConference*, July: 393–405. Retrieved from https://www.researchgate.net/publication/304899543_To_Gamify_or_Not_to_Gamify_Gamification_in_Exercise_Applications_and_Its_Role_in_Impacting_Exercise_Motivation
32. Navin Kaushal and Ryan E. Rhodes. 2015. Exercise habit formation in new gym members: a longitudinal study. *Journal of Behavioral Medicine* 38, 4: 652–663. https://doi.org/10.1007/s10865-015-9640-7
33. Dominic King, Felix Greaves, Christopher Exeter, and Ara Darzi. 2013. "Gamification": Influencing Health Behaviours with Games. *Journal of the Royal Society of Medicine* 106, 3: 76–8. https://doi.org/10.1177/0141076813480996
34. Richard Stålnacke Larsson. 2013. Motivations in Sports and Fitness Gamification. Umea University.
35. Genevie L. Lavigne, Nicolas Hauw, Robert L. Vallerand, Philippe Brunel, Celine Blanchard, Isabelle Cadorette, and Christophe Angot. 2009. On the Dynamic Relationships between Contextual (or General) and Situational (or State) Motivation toward Exercise and Physical A ctivity : A Longitudinal Test of the Top -Down and Bottom -Up Hypotheses. *International Journal of Sport and Exercise Psychology*, 7: 147–168.
36. James J Lin, Lena Mamykina, Silvia Lindtner, Gregory Delajoux, and Henry B Strub. 2006. Fish ' n ' Steps : Encouraging Physical Activity with an Interactive Computer Game. *Proceedings of the 8th International Conference on Ubiquitous Computing (UbiComp'06)*, 261–278.
37. James J Lin, Lena Mamykina, Silvia Lindtner, Gregory Delajoux, and Henry B Strub. 2006. Fish ' n ' Steps : Encouraging Physical Activity with an Interactive Computer Game. In *UbiComp 2006, LNCS 4206*, 261–278.
38. Cameron Lister, Joshua H West, Ben Cannon, Tyler Sax, and David Brodegard. 2014. Just a Fad? Gamification in Health and Fitness Apps. *JMIR Serious Games* 2, 2: 1–12. https://doi.org/10.2196/games.3413

39. Kilpatrick Marcus, Edward Hebert, and John Bartholomew. 2005. College Students' motivation for physical activity: Differentiating Men's and Women's Motives for Sport Participation and exercise. *Journal of American College Health 54*, 87–94.
40. David Markland. 1999. The Exercise Motivations Inventory. *www.FitnessLogistics.com*. Retrieved August 20, 2016 from www.FitnessLogistics.com
41. David Markland and David K Ingledew. 1997. The measurement of exercise motives: Factorial validity and invariance across gender of a revised Exercise Motivations Inventory. *British Journal of Health Psychology* 2: 361–376.
42. Hannah R. Marston. 2013. Digital Gaming Perspectives of Older Adults: Content vs. Interaction. *Educational Gerontology* 39, 3: 194–208. https://doi.org/10.1080/03601277.2012.700817
43. Edward McAuley, Terry Duncan, and Vance V. Tammen. 1989. Psychometric Properties of the Intrinsic Motivation Inventory in a Competitive Sport Setting: A Confirmatory Factor Analysis. *Research Quarterly* 60, 1: 45–58.
44. Jennifer (Jen) McGinn and Nalini Kotamraju. 2008. Data-driven persona development. *Proceeding of the twenty-sixth annual CHI conference on Human factors in computing systems - CHI '08*: 1521–1524. https://doi.org/10.1145/1357054.1357292
45. Elisa D Mekler, Florian Br, Klaus Opwis, and Alexandre N Tuch. 2013. Do Points , Levels and Leaderboards Harm Intrinsic Motivation ? An Empirical Analysis of Common Gamification Elements. In *Gamification 2013*, 66–73.
46. Jochen Meyer, Jutta Fortmann, Merlin Wasmann, and Wilko Heuten. 2015. Making Lifelogging Usable: Design Guidelines for Activity Trackers. *Multimedia Modeling* 8936, Lecture Notes in Computer Science: 323–334. https://doi.org/10.1007/978-3-319-14442-9_39
47. Keyvan Molanorouzi, Selina Khoo, and Tony Morris. 2015. Motives for adult participation in physical activity: type of activity, age, and gender. *BMC public health* 15, 1: 66. https://doi.org/10.1186/s12889-015-1429-7
48. Seyedeh Ameneh Motalebi, Jamileh Amirzadeh Iranagh, Abbas Abdollahi, and Kong Lim. 2014. Applying of theory of planned behavior to promote physical activity and exercise behavior among older adults. *Journal of Physical Education and Sport* 14, 4: 562–568.
49. Lorraine Murray. 2006. Sport, Exercise and Physical Activity: Public Participation, Barriers and Attitudes. *Executive, Scottish.*
50. Robert J Nied and Barry Franklin. 2002. Promoting and prescribing exercise for the elderly. *American family physician* 65, 3: 419–26. Retrieved from http://www.ncbi.nlm.nih.gov/pubmed/11858624
51. Hannah E Payne, Victor Ba Moxley, and Elizabeth MacDonald. 2015. Health Behavior Theory in Physical Activity Game Apps: A Content Analysis. *JMIR serious games* 3, 2: e4. https://doi.org/10.2196/games.4187
52. Pedro Pereira, Emília Duarte, Francisco Rebelo, and Paulo Noriega. 2014. A review of gamification for health-related contexts Theoretical aspects on gamification. In *Proceedings of the Third International Conference on Design, User Experience, and Usability. User Experience Design for Diverse Interaction Platforms and Environments - Volume 8518*, 742–753.
53. Edward M. Phillips, Jeffrey C. Schneider, and Greg R. Mercer. 2004. Motivating Elders to Initiate and Maintain Exercise. *Archives of Physical Medicine and Rehabilitation* 85, July: 52–57. https://doi.org/10.1016/j.apmr.2004.03.012
54. L Alison Phillips, Pier-éric Chamberland, Eric B Hekler, Jessica Abrams, Miriam H Eisenberg, L Alison Phillips, Eric B Hekler, Jessica Abrams, and Miriam H Eisenberg. 2016. Intrinsic Rewards Predict Exercise via Behavioral Intentions for Initiators but via Habit Strength for Maintainers. *Sport, Exercise, and Performance Psychology*, November. https://doi.org/http://dx.doi.org/10.1037/spy0000071
55. Tony Pigford. 2010. Feasibility and Benefit of Using the Nintendo Wii Fit for Balance Rehabilitation in an Elderly Patient Experiencing Recurrent Falls. *Journal of Student Physical Therapy Research* 2, 1: 12–19.
56. Ian Renfree, Daniel Harrison, Paul Marshall, Katarzyna Stawarz, and Anna L. Cox. 2016. Don't Kick the Habit: The Role of Dependency in Habit Formation Apps. *Proceedings of the 2016 CHI Conference Extended Abstracts on Human Factors in Computing Systems - CHI EA '16*: 2932–2939. https://doi.org/10.1093/ajae/aaq155
57. Mark Rice, Wah Pheow Tan, Jeremy Ong, Lih Jie Yau, Marcus Wan, and Jamie Ng. 2013. The dynamics of younger and older adult's paired behavior when playing an interactive silhouette game. *Proceedings of the SIGCHI Conference on Human Factors in Computing Systems - CHI '13*: 1081–1091. https://doi.org/10.1145/2470654.2466138
58. Natalia Romero, Janienke Sturm, Tilde Bekker, Linda de Valk, and Sander Kruitwagen. 2010. Playful persuasion to support older adults' social and physical activities. *Interacting with Computers* 22, 6: 485–495. https://doi.org/10.1016/j.intcom.2010.08.006

59. Carmen V Russoniello, Kevin O'Brien, and Jennifer M Parks. 2009. The effectiveness of casual video games in improving mood and decreasing stress *Journal of CyberTherapy and Rehabilitation* 2, 1.

60. Richard M. Ryan and Edward L. Deci. 2000. Intrinsic and Extrinsic Motivations: Classic Definitions and New Directions. *Contemporary Educational Psychology* 25, 1: 54–67. https://doi.org/10.1006/ceps.1999.1020

61. Richard M. Ryan, Christina M. Frederick, Deborah Lepes, Noel Rubio, and Kennon M. Sheldon. 1997. Intrinsic Motivation and Exercise Adherence. *International Journal of Sport Psychology* 28, 4: 335–354.

62. Richard M. Ryan, C. Scott Rigby, and Andrew Przybylski. 2006. The Motivational Pull of Video Games: A Self-Determination Theory Approach. *Motivation and Emotion* 30, 4: 344–360. https://doi.org/10.1007/s11031-006-9051-8

63. Karen A Schutzer and B Sue Graves. 2004. Barriers and motivations to exercise in older adults. *Preventive Medicine* 39, 5: 1056–61. https://doi.org/10.1016/j.ypmed.2004.04.003

64. Grace Shin and Mohammad H Jarrahi. 2014. Studying the Role of Wearable Health-Tracking Devices in Raising Users ' Self-Awareness and Motivating Physical Activities. In *WISH 2014 - Workshop on Interactive Systems in Healthcare*, 1–5.

65. Pedro J Teixeira, Eliana V Carraça, David Markland, Marlene N Silva, and Richard M Ryan. 2012. Exercise, physical activity, and self-determination theory: a systematic review. *The international journal of behavioral nutrition and physical activity* 9, 1: 78. https://doi.org/10.1186/1479-5868-9-78

66. X Tong, Diane Gromala, Chris D Shaw, and Carman Neustaedter. 2016. Examining the Efficiency of Gamification Incentives for Encouraging Physical Activity – Social Collaborations or Interactive Mobile Games ? In *PervasiveHealth2016*, 1–10.

67. Philip M Wilson, W Todd Rogers, Wendy M Rodgers, and T Cameron Wild. 2006. The Psychological Need Satisfaction in Exercise Scale. *Journal of Sport and Exersise Psychology*, 28: 231–251.

68. World Health Organization. 2010. Global Recommendations on Physical Activity for Health. *Geneva: World Health Organization*: 60. https://doi.org/10.1080/11026480410034349

69. Oren Zuckerman and Ayelet Gal-Oz. 2014. Deconstructing gamification: evaluating the effectiveness of continuous measurement, virtual rewards, and social comparison for promoting physical activity. *Personal and Ubiquitous Computing*: 1705–1719. https://doi.org/10.1007/s00779-014-0783-2

70. 2014. Nike+ FuelBand. Retrieved November 5, 2015 from http://www.nike.com/ca/en_gb/c/running/nikeplus/gps-app

71. 2015. FitBit. Retrieved November 5, 2015 from www.fitbit.com

72. 2015. Google Fit. Retrieved October 10, 2015 from https://fit.google.com/

73. 2015. Fitocracy. Retrieved November 10, 2015 from www.fitocracy.com

74. 2015. FitOrbit. Retrieved October 12, 2015 from www.fitorbit.com

Life Tree: Understanding the Design of Breathing Exercise Games

Rakesh Patibanda, Florian 'Floyd' Mueller
Exertion Games Lab
RMIT University
Melbourne, Australia
{rakesh, floyd}@exertiongameslab.org

Matevz Leskovsek
Breathinglabs.com
University of Ljubljana
Slovenia
mat@breathinglabs.com

Jonathan Duckworth
CiART Lab
RMIT University
Melbourne, Australia
jonathan.duckworth@rmit.edu.au

ABSTRACT
Regular breathing exercises can be a beneficial part of leading a healthy life. Digital games may have the potential to help people practice breathing exercises in an engaging way, however designing breathing exercise games is not well understood. To contribute to such an understanding, we created *Life Tree* as the culmination of three prototypal breathing games. *Life Tree* is a virtual reality (VR) game in which a player controls the growth of a tree by practicing pursed-lip breathing. We selected VR head-mounted display technology because it allows players to focus and limit external distractions, which is beneficial for breathing exercises. 32 participants played *Life Tree* and analysis of the collected data identified four key themes: 1) Designing Breathing Feedback; 2) Increasing Self-Awareness of Breathing and Body; 3) Facilitating Focused Immersion; and, 4) Engagement with Breathing Hardware. We used these themes to articulate a set of breathing exercise game design strategies that future game designers may consider to develop engaging breathing exercise games.

Author Keywords
Breathing exercises; game design; virtual reality; wellbeing; mindfulness.

ACM Classification Keywords
H.5.m. Information interfaces and presentation (e.g., HCI): Miscellaneous.

INTRODUCTION
Breathing is a core activity of our everyday life and yet we are mostly unaware of it [26]. Breathing is one of the only conscious physical activities that directly affects our heart, therefore, we can successfully treat illnesses such as hypertension and arrhythmia by controlling our breathing [21]. Practicing breathing exercises is considered one of the most fundamental ways for the development of both physical and mental well-being. It can reduce stress and promote feelings of relaxation [14, 32, 37, 50]. The way we do our breathing affects our whole body [61]. In particular, practicing breathing exercises may help reduce breathing related disorders such as Attention Deficit Hyperactivity Disorder (ADHD), Chronic Obstructive Pulmonary Disease (COPD) and Asthma [14, 27, 28] while improving our quality of life [14]. Several researchers suggest that digital games can support the practice of breathing exercises to improve wellbeing of players [19, 26, 39, 53, 60]. Furthermore, Moraveji [3] says that, *"breathing is one of the only conscious things we have control of, and digital feedback could help understand our breathing pattern and alter it, if necessary."* These perceptions of breathing informed our core motivation to use the interactive nature of digital games [52] to help players practice breathing exercises such as pursed-lip breathing, in an engaging way.

The design of digital games using the breath of players as a control mechanism has emerged in recent years with works such as *Breath controlled amusement park rides*, *Breathalising games* and *Breathtaking Journey* [35, 41, 57]. These games seem to entertain players, however, they do not appear to help practice breathing exercises, which can also support the wellbeing of players. Also, while some preliminary game research exists (such as with *AirFlow*, *ChillFish* and *DEEP* [49, 55, 58]), in which researchers have developed games to support the practice of breathing exercises, this research does not specifically present strategies on how to design engaging breathing exercise games. Recent developments in mobile and ubiquitous computing hardware technology, such as with Breathing+ [38], Zephyr [24] and sensors in smartphones like the microphone [42] have made it possible for game designers to sense players' breathing. Accordingly, we see this as an opportunity to use breathing as a control mechanism.

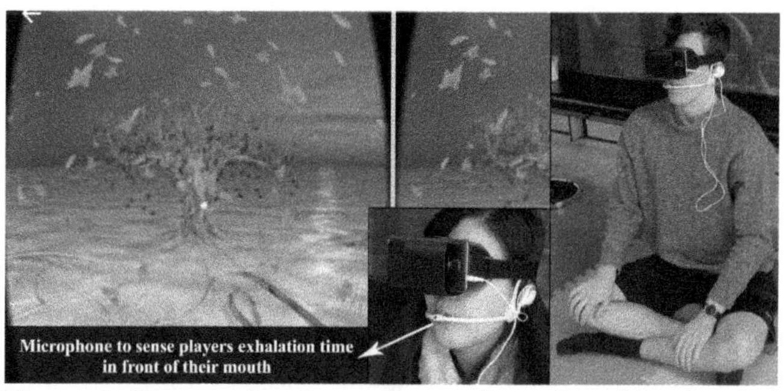

Figure 1. Players play the game wearing a breathing headset and a virtual reality head-mounted display.

CHI PLAY 2017, October 15–18, 2017, Amsterdam, The Netherlands.

ACM ISBN 9978-1-4503-4898-0/17/10...$15.00
https://doi.org/10.1145/3116595.3116621

Our intention with this paper is to better understand the opportunities and challenges in designing games that help players practice breathing exercises and answer our research question: *How do we design engaging breathing exercise games?* In order to answer this question, we first discuss the relationship between breathing and body posture. We also discuss technologies available to measure breathing, and list previous research on breathing in various forms of interactive media. We then discuss the design of our three initial prototype games that led to the design of our final game, *Life Tree* (figure. 1), a VR game that helps players practice pursed-lip breathing. Further, we describe a user study carried out to understand subjective experiences of participants' playing *Life Tree* before presenting a thematic analysis of the data captured. This data informs four overarching themes that we use to articulate of set of design strategies that may act as a stepping stone for future designers interested in designing breathing exercise games.

BACKGROUND

In order to design engaging breathing exercise games, designers may want to make use of the following considerations from existing literature as per our knowledge on breathing and, interactive media that uses breathing as a control mechanism.

Breathing and Body Posture

Body posture has been shown to significantly affect the way we breathe [6, 40]. Hewitt [26] suggests that breathing exercises can be practiced using different body-postures. He suggests that sitting down cross-legged with the hands resting on our thighs gives us greater stability and has been used for thousands of years by Yogis [54] (a historic term for Yoga practitioners). As such, considering the right body posture may play an important role for the design of breathing exercise games.

Pursed-Lip Breathing

Pursed-Lip Breathing (PLB) [12] is performed by exhaling through tightly pressed lips (pursed lips) and inhaling through the nose with a closed mouth. Physicians, physical therapists, occupational therapists, and respiratory therapists teach this breathing technique to their patients to ease shortness of breath and to promote deep breathing [26]. In a study conducted to design personalised relaxation techniques involving breathing exercises for oncology patients, researchers asked patients to practice PLB and observed a significant decrease in their stress levels [43]. We have therefore chosen PLB as the breathing exercise technique players can practice while playing *Life Tree*.

Breathing and Interactive Media

Breathing as a control mechanism has been put to creative uses: for navigating an immersive virtual world through the metaphor of diving [36]; and for enabling two-way communication [57]. Devices for measuring breathing have also entered the market, for example, the Sensawaft Breath Controlled Mouse [45], Breathing+ headset [38] and Spire [33]. Breathing as a control mechanism has been used in some game interfaces from simply blowing out candles on a digital screen, to the sensory deprivation game, *Deep Sea* [5]. *Deep Sea* is an audio only breathing first-person shooter game [5]. This game serves as an example of how breathing can be used as a novel control mechanism. *The Journey to Wild Divine* [7] is a study that investigates a biofeedback management tool to teach breathing techniques to children with Attention Deficit Hyperactivity Disorder (ADHD). Children played the game by manipulating their heart rate using breathing techniques taught in the game. This game indicated that a breathing game has the potential to produce positive developments for children with ADHD [2]. *ChillFish* [55] is another breathing game for children with ADHD to help them retain attention on practicing breathing exercises. The gameplay is based on an underwater 2D world, where the player's character collects as many starfishes as possible. This research suggests that doctors treating breathing disorders such as ADHD might want to use creative solutions such as games.

The incorporation of music in breathing is a widespread practice [22]. Researchers have used music as the central entity being controlled by breathing: *Sonic Cradle* [59] is a non-visual interactive system that promotes mindfulness using breathing to control the ambient music. This study suggests that meditative processes such as practicing breathing exercises could be enhanced by using certain kinds of music. *Breathing Light* and *Soma Carpet* are two applications by Somaesthetic designers [29]. Somaesthetics allows the design of interactions that subtly support directing users' attention inwards, towards their own body [29, 30]. *Breathing Light* consists of an enclosure made of fabric and string curtains that one crawls under, creating a room within a room, effectively shutting out the external world. Inside this enclosure, a breathing sensor controls an ambient light that will dim in cadence with the participant's breathing. *Soma Carpet* is a system that has the ability to direct the participant's attention by providing heat feedback to different parts of one's body while one follows the instructions of a pre-recorded breathing exercise lesson. Here, *Soma Carpet* draws attention to the importance of self-awareness of one's own body while breathing. Their research suggests that game designers may want to consider using subtle feedback: that is, feedback that does not disturb the breathing experience for users, such as the dimming of lights in *Breathing Light*. External stimuli such as heat in *Soma Carpet* might also help direct the users' attention towards their own body while practicing breathing exercises.

Marshall et al. [41] explored the potential of breathing as a control mechanism for *Bronco Ride*, an amusement park ride. They use breathing as a control mechanism in amusement park rides to: 1) encourage the rider to hold their breath; and, 2) use rapid breathing to power up the ride. Tennent et al. [57] explored the potential for breathing as a control mechanism in gaming. They developed five games using breathing as an exclusive, secondary and ambient control mechanism. In order to sense the breathing of players they developed a custom gas mask and used it with gaming interfaces such as keyboard and mouse to control parts of the game. Using their research, we are better able to understand the challenges and opportunities in designing breathing exercise games.

Breathing and virtual reality

Davies [19] was one of the first to use breathing as a control mechanism with her project, *Osmose* [19]. *Osmose* is an immersive interactive virtual reality installation with a head-mounted display and real-time motion tracking based on breathing and balance. Players gently float in order to navigate through the different worlds within *Osmose*. Davies filled the virtual world of *Osmose* with simple particle systems. These particle systems were used as ambiguous representations of objects in the world of *Osmose* such as a water stream or birds. Importantly, Davies used this technique to help players feel centered to their physical bodies during immersion, in a way that is similar to the effect of practicing meditation.

DEEP is another VR game that has been developed to support children with anxiety disorders [58]. *DEEP's* main aim is to provide an immersive and relaxing experience with no explicit tasks or goals. The player's diaphragm expansions are recorded (using a variable resistor/stretch sensor) and used as feedback. A study of *DEEP* showed reduced levels of stress and anxiety in children. These findings confirm the potential of using VR technology in the design of breathing exercise games. *Breathtaking Journey* [35] is a Mixed-Reality (MR) game providing a first-person perspective of a refugee's journey. It has been developed to research the influence of multi-sensory experiences on presence, empathy and ultimately on attitude change. The aim of the game is to avoid detection by stopping your breath while the enemies are on the prowl. Players wear a custom-built mask having the ability to measure breathing in order to play the game.

In summary, breathing as a control mechanism has been used for entertainment in games, however, it has rarely been explored in the context of helping players practice breathing exercises. While we were inspired by the philosophical literature on breathing exercises [26], we also drew design tactics from existing work [41, 57] and used them in the design of *Life Tree*.

Hardware to Measure Breathing and Software

Digital games discussed in the previous sections such as *DEEP* and the *breath controlled amusement park ride* [41] have used custom-built strap devices to measure breathing. Devices like Zephyr [24] are readily available on the market to calculate aspects of breathing such as breathing rate, tidal volume, etc. These aspects can be easily sensed and considered by game designers as input. Exhalation is important for PLB [12] and Breathing+ is a headset specifically designed [38] to measure the exhalation time of players while practicing PLB. Breathing+ can be connected to the 3.5 mm headset jack of either your smart phone or desktop computer. The microphone in front of the player's mouth (fig. 1) helps calculate exhalation time. While this device can only calculate exhalation time, it is light and one of the most portable devices available. This is one reason why we chose this device to sense breathing in our games. In addition, research suggests that strapped measuring devices such as Zephyr were judged uncomfortable by participants [20]. We used Unity 3D (version 5.4.4) to develop our games and Maya (version 2016) to design and animate 3D objects in our games.

In the next section, we describe the design of our three initial VR prototypes and present our learnings through a Formal Analysis of Gameplay (FAOG). FAOG is a method that provides an understanding of a game system by deriving design primitives, which are a combination of 1) Components, 2) Actions and, 3) Goals [9]. FAOG allows us to determine these design primitives by repeatedly playing our own games and writing in detail about them. We used this method to play test our prototype games repeatedly with five fellow researchers and heuristically evaluate the prototypes while noting the design primitives that worked well with breathing exercises. These learnings then informed the design of our final game, *Life Tree*.

DESIGNING INITIAL BREATHING EXERCISE GAMES

Our idea before developing *Life Tree* was to experiment with different ways to design engaging breathing feedback to support the practice of breathing exercises. We designed different kinds of breathing feedback in these three initial VR prototypes: 1) *Space Gaze*; 2) *Focus Tree;* and, 3) *Outlandish Whisper*. We refined these prototypes by playing them repeatedly with fellow researchers (fig. 3) who have expertise in game design and also with researchers conducting research on breathing applications (non-game ones). This informed the final design of *Life Tree*. Breathing exercises are best practiced in short intervals [26], therefore, all our games were designed to be played for 2-3 minutes.

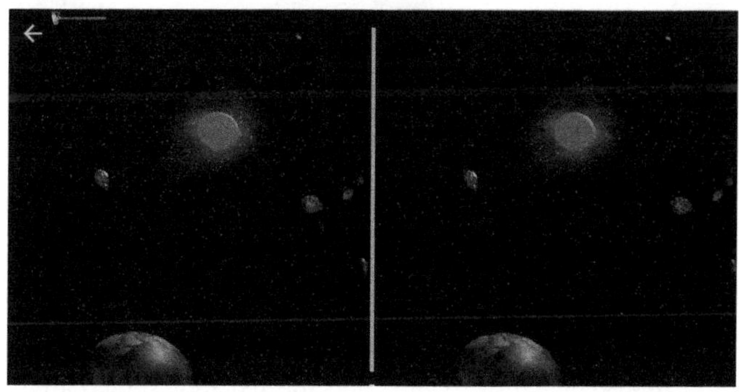

Figure 2. Blue oxygen that players collect to survive.

Prototype 1: Space Gaze

In *Space Gaze*, players practice PLB to move gently inside the virtual environment and collect oxygen (fig.2) in order to maintain the oxygen level in the atmosphere and survive in the game. To provide breathing feedback, we explored the slow movement of the player's viewpoint and, as the end goal we experimented with the survival mechanic [51]. Players see a blue shimmering light, i.e., the oxygen while wearing the HMD. The player's viewpoint moves upward in space on exhalation and moves down during inhalation to help players collect the oxygen. By conducting a FAOG, we concluded that the slow motion of the player's viewpoint in the virtual environment could help them focus on their breathing. However, it also appeared that the survival mechanism in the game could distract players from focusing on their breathing, making them anxious.

Prototype 2: Focus Tree

In Focus Tree, the viewpoint of players slowly revolves around an island while they practice PLB. On inhaling, clouds cover the island to block the view of players; and on exhaling, clouds get blown away allowing players to view the island (fig.3). Trees start growing on the island when the players exhale. The aim of the game is to grow as many trees as possible within the time limit. Rhythmic breathing leads to the growth of more trees on the island and non-rhythmic breathing leads to lesser growth. Conducting a FAOG suggested that participants liked the naturalistic game environment in the form of a green island, flowing water, trees growing and playing with the colours of the tree as a result of their breathing exercise. We observed that players enjoyed how the feedback with the growth of trees as a result of rhythmic breathing was embedded into the environment of the game. However, we found that showing the remaining game time caused stress to the players.

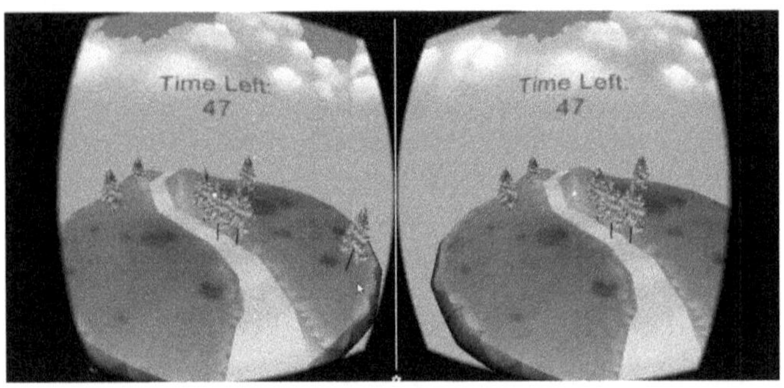

Figure 3. The clouds dissipate with every exhalation.

Prototype 3: Outlandish Whisper

In *Outlandish Whisper*, players dive into a world filled with ambiguous particles to practice PLB. We wanted to explore breathing feedback by allowing players to feel as if they are exhaling something out of their body and inhaling something into their body. When players inhale, they see that they are inhaling gold particles and when they exhale, they exhale red particles. The rationale for selecting these colours was that gold represents fresh oxygen and the red represents carbon dioxide. Further, blue particles were generated whenever the game detects that the players are breathing in rhythm. When participants were breathing non-rhythmically, a pre-recorded voice instructed participants to gently focus on their breathing again. We noted that players liked the responsiveness of the breathing feedback. It seemed that players liked the subtleness of rhythmic breathing feedback embedded into the environment. We noticed that players liked the pre-recorded voice instructions before the game started, as they believed this helped them understand the goal of the game. Players did not like the pre-recorded voice instructions being played during the game as it seemed to distract them from focusing on their breathing.

LIFE TREE: DESIGN AND DEVELOPMENT

Our aim with the design of *Life Tree* was to create an immersive and engaging way to practice PLB. We made the following design decisions using findings from our initial three prototypes and based on the literature on breathing. *Life Tree* is a VR game that helps players practice PLB. The environment of the game consists of a tree submerged in the middle of the water. The game lasts approximately two and a half minutes. Players wear the HMD along with the Breathing+ headset as shown in fig. 1.

Overview of *Life Tree's* Gameplay

As the game begins, players see a colorless tree standing in the middle of a body of water. If players exhale at this point in time, they can see leaves being blown towards the tree. A pre-recorded voice instruction informs players to sit down cross-legged. As the players sit down, an animation of the tree getting submerged into the water is triggered in order to replicate their bodily action. This is achieved by using the input acceleration in the y-direction (if input.acceleration.y <= -1.1f). Once the players sit down, the game menu pops up. To start the game, players have to target (using head orientation) the reticle (VR pointer) on the start button and exhale continuously for three seconds. As a way to introduce visual breathing feedback before the game starts, players can see leaves being blown towards the menu button on exhalation while navigating the game. This action performed by the players starts the game which, in turn, triggers a sound of rhythmic breathing in the background that lasts for 30 seconds. Players can follow the rhythm by inhaling and exhaling for at least three seconds. In order to give them visual feedback, the trunk of the tree expands on inhalation and contracts on exhalation. The animation of the tree contracting is played until the maximum frame number is reached. If the players' exhalation time is lesser than the maximum frame number then it is played only until that particular time frame (if frame is "f", f <= f (max)). Similarly, when players inhale, the animation of the tree expanding is played till the minimum frame (f (min) <= f).

In order to visualise the exhalation of players, we use particle effects of leaves being blown towards the tree. The colour of the leaves changes to a bluish-green shade if the players breathe rhythmically, otherwise, it changes to a greenish-brown shade. If the time difference between two consecutive exhalations is less than two seconds and the current exhale time is longer than one second, it is considered as rhythmic breathing. Further, if the difference between two consecutive exhalations is more than three seconds then it is considered as non-rhythmic breathing. If the breathing of players is non-rhythmic then the system starts to blur the view of players in the game (It starts from value "0" and is increased by a value of 0.03f for every update, i.e., 0 <= Blur Value <= 3.

Similarly, on rhythmic breathing, the *Blur Value* is decreased by 0.03f). This is effective only 20 seconds after the game starts. The goal of the game is for players to make the tree as colourful as possible by breathing rhythmically and keeping the game in focus for as long as they can. In order to design *Life Tree,* we considered the following concepts: 1) Designing Focus; 2) Encouraging Players to Sit in a Cross-Legged Posture; 3) Designing for Self-Reflection and Awareness of Breathing; and, 4) Designing Audio.

Figure 4. The game encouraging a player into the right body posture to play the game.

Designing to Nurture Player's Focus on Breathing
Practitioners of breathing exercises benefit from being able to focus on their breathing [26]. We wanted to embed breathing feedback in the game environment in a similar way to that which had worked well with *Focus Tree* and *Outlandish Whisper*. Players liked the use of naturalistic visuals in *Focus Tree*, with the trees and leaves. We applied our learning from *Focus Tree* and designed naturalistic visuals for Life Tree. A tree is the only visual element in the game. We chose an illustration of a tree from the works of Apostolescu [4].

Designing to Encourage Right Body Posture
To encourage players to move into the right body posture to play *Life Tree*, we used a soothing pre-recorded female voice asking them to sit down in a cross-legged posture placing their hands on their thighs (fig.4). These are initial instructions to get players into the right position before the start of the actual gameplay. We used this as players liked the initial voice instructions in *Outlandish Whisper.*

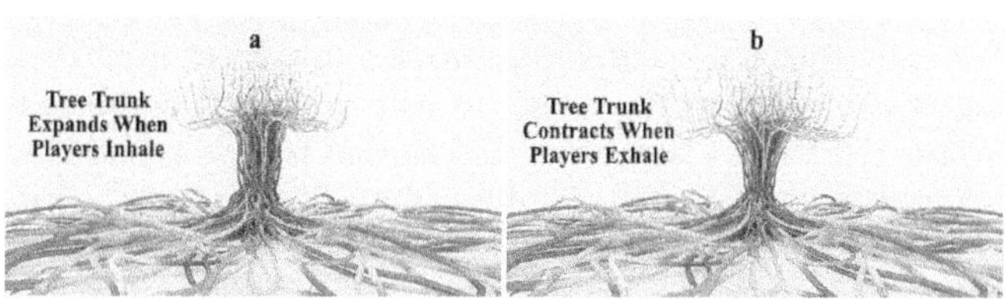

Figure 5a shows the tree expanding when players inhale and 5b shows the tree contracting when players exhale.

Designing to Increase Awareness of Breathing and Body
Focusing on one's breathing leads to awareness of both breathing pattern, and body movement while practicing breathing exercises [26, 61]. We learned from *Outlandish Whisper* that players did not like the pre-recorded voice instructions during the game. As an approach to design breathing feedback for *Life Tree* we imagined the trunk of the tree in our game to be the lungs of the player's body. When a player inhales, the trunk of the tree expands and when the player exhales, the trunk of the tree contracts (fig 5. a & b).

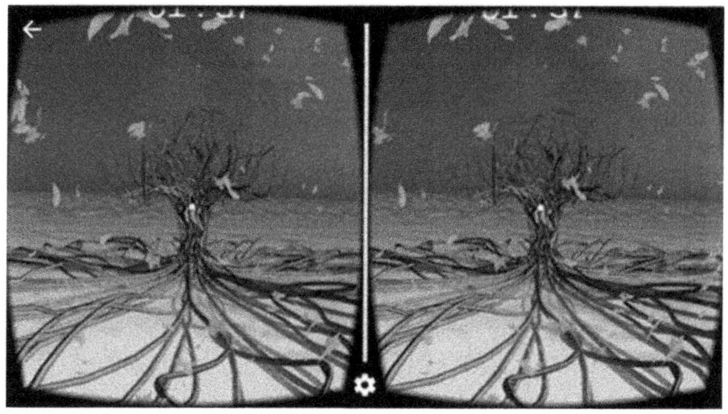

Figure 6. Lifeless tree when the game begins along with feedback of leaves on exhalation.

Furthermore, we used the tree's texture as breathing feedback. The tree looks lifeless and gray in colour at the beginning of the game. The tree is filled with colour exponentially as players practice PLB (fig.7). The saturation value of the tree increases slowly from 0 (black) to 1 (actual colour of the tree). The players add colour to the tree based on their breathing rhythm. We used leaves (fig. 6 & 7) as a way to help players visualise and understand that their exhale is recognised by the Breathing+ headset. Breathing is widely considered as a subconscious activity [44]. Therefore, in order to not distract them from focusing on their breathing, we slowly blurred the game's view as a subtle way to give feedback to players that they were not breathing in rhythm.

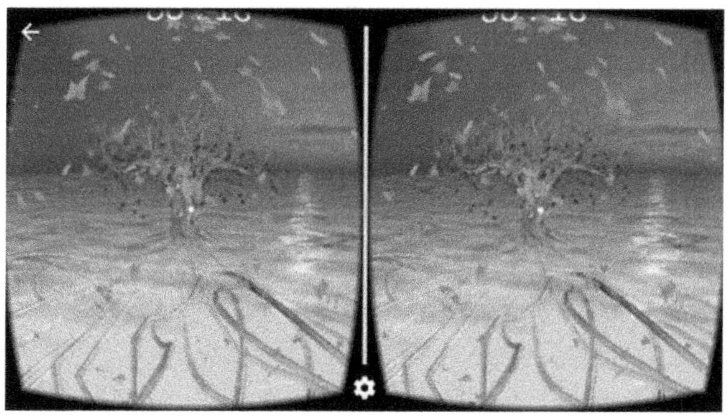

Figure 7. The full of life tree at the end of the game.

Designing Audio to Enhance the Cognitive Experience of Practicing Breathing Exercises
Based on player feedback from *Focus Tree* and *Outlandish Whisper*, we avoided pre-recorded voice instructions in the background. In *Life Tree*, players listen to a rhythmic inhalation and exhalation sound at the start of the game to understand how to perform the breathing exercise. The sound lasts for 30 seconds before fading out. We believe the ambiguous breathing sound might help players understand the kind of breathing exercise they have to perform in the

game without disturbing the focus on their breathing. Furthermore, we used instrumental music of an Indian instrument called "Veena" as the background score for the game. A study by Clayton [16] suggests the Veena's music has been used to enhance the effect of practicing Yoga, which involves the practice of breathing exercises in various body postures.

USER STUDY AND DATA ANALYSIS

Ethical approval was obtained to conduct our research with 32 participants. Prior to the start of the game session, we briefed participants about PLB and *Life Tree*. Participants were free to play the game multiple times. Post the game session, all 32 participants (16 males and 16 female) answered questions in the Game Experience Questionnaire (GEQ) [31, 47] and were subsequently interviewed. The GEQ questions were measured on a 7-point Likert Scale with answers ranging from "Strongly Agree" to "Strongly Disagree". The average age of the participants was 25, with a standard deviation of three years. In the interviews, participants answered questions regarding their experience playing *Life Tree*, their feeling after the game session, PLB, situations in which they would like to play the game and follow-up questions based on their answers. Participants were video and audio recorded while playing the game and while they were being interviewed.

Interviews were transcribed. A question and its answer by a participant were put together and considered as one unit of data. In total, there were 642 units of data included in the analysis. An inductive thematic analysis was then conducted on the data [11]. This method was deemed appropriate, as the design of breathing exercise games is an emerging and crudely understood topic, for which limited relevant theory currently exists. Two researchers independently read all units of the data three times, and each researcher initially identified every data unit with a category code. These independent codes given by the two researchers were discussed and refined separately until agreement was reached on a total of 25 codes. The coding categories were then examined and cross-referenced with the data and further analysed for overarching themes that affected player experience, which were again reviewed by both researchers.

THEMES DESCRIBING PLAYER EXPERIENCE

Overall, participants liked playing *Life Tree*. They reported that *"the game was very fascinating and de-cluttering"*. They also thought of it as a novel experience. P17, a female participant said, *"It is really good. I feel surprised about that game because I have not experienced such a kind of game before. It really felt special for me"*.

We now unpack the player experience further by articulating four overarching themes: 1) Designing Breathing Feedback; 2) Increasing Self-Awareness of Breathing and Body; 3) Facilitating Focused Immersion; and, 4) Engagement with Breathing Hardware.

Theme 1: Designing Breathing Feedback

This theme describes participants' discussion of the breathing feedback design in *Life Tree*. 174 of the total 642 units of data were described by this theme, which consists of two category codes: 1) *Non-interruptive breathing feedback during gameplay* (mentioned in 106 units); and, 2) *Initial breathing guidance after starting the game* (mentioned in 68 units).

Non-interruptive breathing feedback during gameplay

Participants discussed the non-interruptive nature of the breathing feedback, i.e., the way in which feedback kept them informed about their breathing while ensuring they did not lose attention on their breathing rhythm. This seems to resonate with the high score of 5.78 (SD = 0.89) for the parameter *Flow* measured using the GEQ. *Flow* refers to the mental state of operation in which players performing actions in a game are fully immersed in a feeling of energised focus, full involvement, and enjoying the actions they are performing in the game [15, 17]. All the 32 participants liked the feedback with green leaves that they saw on exhalation. P3 said, *"I liked the visual representation of the breathing in the form of leaves. It showed me how I was exhaling, how hard I was exhaling and whether I was exhaling or not"*. Participant P1, when asked about the one thing she would like to keep in the game, said, *"Just that sense of reassurance you get with the feedback using leaves; that you are doing it right and not in your face about it."*

Ten participants said that they did not see the game getting blurred as they were breathing in the desired rhythm throughout the game. Seventeen out of the remaining 22 participants liked how the game informed and nudged them in a subtle way when they went out of rhythm, by blurring the view of the game. Participant P17 said, when asked about the one thing he wanted to keep in the game, *"The blurry part of the game. It helps me understand if I am breathing rhythmically or not in a way that does not distract me from my breathing"*. We noted that participants enjoyed seeing the tree become colourful over the course of the game. Participant P4 said, *"It felt like I was giving life to the tree because I saw colours creeping into it and it also helped me understand that I was breathing rhythmically"*.

We embedded the breathing feedback into the tree trunk, i.e., the environment of the game, to help players become self-aware of their own breathing. This design feature appeared to help achieve self-awareness of breathing. P27 said, *"The tree changes its form based on my exhale and inhale. This helped me become aware of my own breathing"*. While participants became self-aware of their own breathing with the help of this feature, 10 participants also perceived this as imitation of their own breathing and enjoyed the tree imitating their breathing pattern. These participants also suggested that this imitation encouraged them to breathe rhythmically. Participant P32 said, *"The breathing of the tree was imitating my breathing pattern. I felt that there was someone else breathing along with the tree. It was kind of prompting me to breathe rhythmically".* We observed that 22 participants liked our design choice with embedding classical Indian music as the background. These participants felt the music helped them calm their nerves and relax. P3 said, *"The kind of music that was playing along with the game was very fascinating as it made me feel relaxed and calmed my nerves".*

While 22 participants felt imaginative while playing the game, only eight participants could describe this imaginative feeling caused while playing *Life Tree*. Participant P12 said, *"It was interesting as I was enjoying the seasons in the game. I felt like I was in spring season then later I felt I was in autumn because what I was seeing made me feel very creative and imaginative."* We use the word, 'imaginative' as the colours changing in the tree due to their rhythmic breathing were never meant to be perceived as change in seasons. However, it looked like the combination of the features helped users become imaginative and creative with their thoughts. We believe this is the reason why *Sensory and Imaginative Immersion* got a relatively high score, i.e., 4.85 (SD = 1.09) on the Likert Scale.

Initial breathing guidance after starting the game

Twenty-five participants liked the sound of rhythmic breathing at the beginning of the game. Twenty participants had prior experience of using breathing exercise applications like the Headspace app [25, 48] and indicated that the initial sound of rhythmic breathing was enough to understand that they had to breathe rhythmically to play the game. We designed a breathing poster to recruit our participants who were interesting in breathing exercises. This is the reason why we had a large number of participants with prior experience with breathing exercises. Participant P7 said, *"I like the sound of the breathing that comes initially. It helped me understand that I had to breathe like the rhythmic sound being played or at least breathe rhythmically.* Seven participants liked the idea of the ambiguous breathing sound at the beginning, however, they had difficulty understanding its purpose. This is reflected by the average score of 3.88 (SD = 1.3) for the parameter *Competence* measured with the help of the GEQ. Competence is the ability to perform a particular task in a game [52] and, in this case, it is the practice of pursed-lip rhythmic breathing . Participant P26 said, *"The bit that I disliked was the breathing sound at the beginning as I did not know if I was supposed to follow that pattern or not".* Seven of these 10 participants suggested adding a tutorial mode at the beginning of the game. Participants P3 and P11 said, *"It was a little hard to understand the game at the beginning. A little bit more instructions, maybe a guided tutorial mode would be really good to go with".*

Theme 2: Increasing Self-Awareness of Breathing and Body

This theme describes how *Life Tree* helped participants become aware of their breathing and body. Ninety-three of the total 642 units of data were described by this theme, which consists of three category codes: 1) *Awareness of body movement* (19 units); 2) *Mindful practice of breathing exercises* (44 units); and, 3) *Feeling after the game session* (28 units).

Awareness of body movement

29 participants commented on how *Life Tree* made them more aware of their breathing and body movement while playing. Participant P9 said, *"I was able to feel my own breathing. I was also able to experience my whole body move and I could hear my heart beat as well".* When participants were asked about what facilitated this self-awareness, they said that the synchronisation between their breathing pattern and breathing feedback in the game pushed them to concentrate and continue breathing rhythmically. P7 said, *"It made my body feel good while I exerted pressure on my diaphragm and lungs. It was also nice to see the game's response towards my breathing".*

Mindful practice of breathing exercises

Eighteen participants discussed how the blurring of the game's view on breathing non-rhythmically nudged them to become mindful about their breathing and pushed them to breathe rhythmically. P23 said, *"I felt that I was not doing it right and that is why the tree was not in focus. To get back into rhythm I had to become more aware of my abdomen expanding and contracting to get it into a rhythm".* As described by Bergomi et al. [8] the process of becoming self-aware of one's own feelings and inner sensations is referred to as *awareness towards inner experiences*, one of the factors that helps an individual become mindful. Eight participants even compared the experience of playing *Life Tree* to applications they use in general to practice mindfulness, which involves the practice of breathing exercises such as the Headspace app [25]. These participants suggested that the breathing feedback in *Life Tree* helped them become aware, and in turn, more mindful of, their breathing. P9 said, *"I felt more aware of my breathing while playing Life Tree than while using the application I generally use, i.e., Headspace [25]. I guess it is because of the more interactive nature of this game where you visualise your breathing."*

Feeling after the game session

Twenty-six participants discussed how they felt good after playing the game. Eight participants spoke about how they felt exhausted in a good way. For example, P10 said, *"I feel a little exhausted after playing the game but I feel that this is good exhaustion".* This reflects on the relatively high score of 3.93 (SD = 1.07) for the parameter *Tiredness* measured using the GEQ. Twenty-one participants spoke about becoming calmer and feeling good about themselves after the game session. P29 said, *"After I finished playing the game I feel quite good and happier than I was before playing the game".* We thought that this good post-game feeling was a result of the virtual environment that helped players concentrate on their own breathing and the soothing music. P16 said, *"I feel very peaceful and relaxed after playing the game because of the immersive environment and music".* P3 mentioned how the music made him calmer and said, *"The kind of music that was playing along with the game was very fascinating as it made me feel relaxed and calmed my nerves".* This discussion reflects the high score of 4.86 (SD = 1.4) for the parameter *Positive Experience* measured using the GEQ.

Theme 3: Facilitating Focused Immersion

This theme describes how *Life Tree* helped participants experience focused immersion. Focused immersion is referred to as a state of mind experienced by players while doing an activity in which they feel that the time flies [1]. One hundred and fifty-seven units of the total 642 units of data were characterised by this theme, consisting of two category codes: 1) *Immersiveness leading to flow* (99 units); and, 2) *Breathing as the focal point* (58 units).

Immersiveness leading to flow

Participants suggested that the repetitive nature of the task, i.e., breathing rhythmically, was one reason why they felt it to be an immersive experience. Participant P4 said, *"It was an easy repetitive thing to do and once I got the hang of it, I did not really need to consciously think about it as I was totally immersed while enjoying the responsiveness of the feedback I got with my breathing".* This suggests that the rhythmic breathing activity in the game, synchronised with the responsiveness of the breathing feedback, might create an immersive experience for participants. While 30 participants thought of rhythmic breathing as an easy repetitive action, 16 participants found it to be challenging, as they still had to focus on their breathing to ensure it was rhythmic. P8 said, *"It was quite fun to see the leaves being blown towards the tree and then challenging myself to focus more on my breath to breathe rhythmically".* These descriptions by the participants reflect nicely the score of 3.91 (SD = 0.72) for the parameter of *Challenge* measured using the GEQ.

Breathing as the focal point

Twenty-four participants said that they were able to focus on their breathing while playing *Life Tree*. Participant P17 said, *"I tried to practice breathing exercises with my partner but it is difficult to not let my mind wander. So, one thing I particularly liked about it was it gave me something to focus on. I can usually wait for a while and listen to my breathing, but I over think a lot anyway and this was cool about the game, because at least for the time I was playing the game, I was looking at the tree and focusing on it and the environment and did not think a lot about other things".* This strengthens our belief that a simplistic visual design allows participants to focus on their breathing while giving them enough breathing feedback to understand and alter their breathing pattern, if necessary. Further, the use of a HMD also appeared to help participants feel focused while playing the game, as 20 participants spoke about how immersive an experience *Life Tree* was for them. For example, participant P26 said, *"I was really engrossed in the game and I was not really thinking of anything else".* As participants started to get the hang of what they had to do in the game, they appeared to experience being in a state of flow, which is an altered sense of time [15, 18, 56]. P32 said, *"Two and a half minutes playing the game; I did not even realise. It felt like 20 seconds or something. I felt the time fly by when I was playing the game".*

Theme 4: Engagement with Breathing Hardware

This theme describes the participants' engagement with technology used to sense breathing in *Life Tree*. Eighty-three of the total 642 units were characterised by this theme, consisting of two category codes: 1) *Awareness of breathing with hardware* (66 units); and, 2) *Ease of using the breathing hardware* (17 units).

Awareness of breathing with hardware

Twelve participants mentioned that apart from the breathing feedback, the headset also helped them become more aware of their breathing as they were able to hear their own breathing sound reverberating through the microphone in front of them. P2 said, *"I could also feel the sound of my breath through the mouthpiece as well. I could hear the air through the hole in front of mouth. This helped me understand if I was breathing correctly into the headset or not".* This tells us that the physical design of the sensor could additionally help players receive breathing feedback, at least on exhalation.

Ease of using the breathing hardware

Participants adjusted their headset to ensure that the microphone was close enough to their mouth. However, participants could not adjust the width of the headset (i.e., loosen the headset to fit the size of their face) and seven of them discussed how uncomfortable wearing the headset felt. P24 said, *"I was really not comfortable wearing the headset as my head is a little too wide".* Furthermore, the microphone only had a small hole in front of their mouth and they had to aim and blow into the hole to register their exhalation. P8 said, *"I sometimes had to exhale quite hard and sometimes had to aim into the microphone for it to register my breathing".* Participants also suggested that due to this uncomfortable feeling, they had to adjust their headset a few times while playing the game and in consequence lost their focus on breathing. P14 said, *"I was enjoying the visuals and the breathing feedback but then suddenly I had to adjust my breathing headset over my ear and this disturbed by rhythm and focus".*

STRATEGIES TO DESIGN BREATHING EXERCISE GAMES

In addition to the four themes discussed above, which might be particularly useful as descriptive tools for researchers, we now present a set of prescriptive strategies to serve as guiding tools for game designers interested in creating engaging breathing exercise games. These strategies are based on the reported experience of our participants as well as our craft knowledge that comes from designing three prototype games and *Life Tree*. We reference this discussion back to each of the themes in order to showcase how these strategies could help future designers design engaging breathing exercise game experiences.

1. Consider Using Subtle Onboarding to Help Players Engage with the Breathing Exercises

Our results with *Initial breathing guidance after starting the game* under "Theme 1: Designing Breathing Feedback" suggest that participants enjoyed and understood how to play *Life Tree.* Results suggest that experienced players understood and liked the subtle use of the sound of rhythmic breathing in the background and recognised that it helped them understand the breathing pattern they had to follow to play the game. However, inexperienced players valued pre-recorded voice instructions to help understand the breathing pattern they had to follow in the game. On the whole, participants liked the subtleness of feedback and they also suggested that it helped them understand the actions in the game without disturbing their focus on breathing. Consequently, we suggest designers to consider what we call "subtle onboarding", as previously suggested by Zichermann [62], by which we mean informing players regarding the breathing pattern they have to perform in the game. Based on our results, we extend the notion of "subtle onboarding" to the design of breathing exercise games and recommend designers consider the use of subtle audio feedback that allows players to understand the breathing pattern they have to perform in the game while sustaining their focus on breathing.

2. Consider Using Non-Interruptive Breathing Feedback to Support Self-Awareness of Breathing During Gameplay

Our results with *Non-interruptive breathing feedback during gameplay* under "Theme 1: Designing Breathing Feedback" indicate that players can profit when designers develop an immersive and non-interruptive environment for breathing exercise games. Participants suggested that the synchronous breathing feedback with the tree, together with the leaves getting blown onto the tree, helped with the overall experience of *Life Tree's* immersive nature. They also suggested that the non-interruptive nature of the breathing feedback helped them become self-aware of their breathing and become immersed in the practice of breathing exercises. As previously suggested by Chen [15], an immersive environment can be created by designing feedback that does not distract players from the task that they are doing. Further, Bouvier et al. [10] suggest that an immersive environment can heighten the self-awareness of players while playing games. Based on our results, we recommend that designers consider creating what we call *Non-interruptive breathing feedback during gameplay*, which means designing breathing feedback that does not distract players from their breathing during gameplay to create an immersive game environment while nourishing and amplifying the player's self-awareness of their breathing pattern. In order to achieve this, designers might want to consider using visuals effects such as particles that sync with the theme of the game; for example, the use of leaves to provide breathing feedback in *Life Tree.*

3. Consider Using the Objects in the Game Environment to Provide Imitative Breathing Feedback

Results with *Initial breathing guidance after starting the game* under "Theme 1: Designing Breathing Feedback" suggest that players might like it more when the objects in the game environment are used to provide breathing feedback. For example, participants liked how the tree was giving them feedback about their breathing pattern by expanding and contracting its trunk on inhalation and exhalation. They also suggested that this helped them enhance their feeling of immersion while practicing breathing exercises; at least for the time they were playing the game. Therefore, we extend the notion of breathing feedback to the design of breathing exercise games and propose to designers that they use the objects in the environment of the game to provide what we call "imitative breathing feedback", i.e., breathing feedback designed in a way which allows players to feel as if the objects in the game are imitating their breathing pattern in a playful way.

4. Consider Using a Minimalist Approach to Designing Naturalistic Visuals to Help Players Focus on their Breathing

Players need to focus on their breathing while practicing breathing exercises [26]. Further, breathing exercises should help players to relax and calm their minds [2, 3]. Our results from "Theme 2: Self-Awareness of Breathing and Body" and "Theme 3: Facilitating Focused Immersion", suggest that players enjoyed the simplistic visuals in *Life Tree.* We noted that this simplistic visual design in the game helped them focus better on their breathing pattern as it created less focal points. Players also suggested that they liked how naturalistic the visuals were in *Life Tree* and how this helped foster relaxation and calm their minds. "naturalistic" here refers to natural objects such as the tree, leaves and water in the game. As previously suggested by Carroll et al. [13], following "The Minimalist Approach", defined as, *"designing for focus by showing things that matter the most for effective learning and performance,* helps foster focus in the minds of the players. Based on our results, we extend this notion of "The Minimalist Approach" to breathing exercise games and recommend designers consider the following approaches to help players focus on their breathing:

- Designers may consider designing minimal focal points in the game to help nurture focus in the minds of players while playing breathing exercise games.
- Designers may consider designing minimal naturalistic visuals in their game environment to help players relax and be calm while playing breathing exercise games.

5. Consider the Intimate Placement of Breathing Hardware and how it can Affect Breathing Performance

Players being comfortable with the technology worn when playing games is an important factor to consider [23]. Our results with "Theme 4: Engagement with Breathing Hardware", suggest that hardware used to sense breathing in the game needs to be comfortable and consider that everyone's body is different. Our results suggest that participants lost their attention on their breathing briefly a few times due to irritation caused by the obstructive nature of the hardware design. Furthermore, participants suggested that the breathing hardware was unable to capture their breathing a few times while playing *Life Tree*. Therefore, these factors might have resulted in their loss of focus on their breathing. Gemperle et al. [23] define wearability as *"the interaction between the human body and the wearable object"*. They suggest 13 guidelines for wearability such as considering unobtrusive placement, considering size variation, considering comfortable attachments, considering the sensory interaction and more. We extend this notion of wearability to consider the following approaches to designing breathing hardware that support the design of breathing exercise games:

- Design for adjustability; for example, by using lightweight straps that can be extended to fit either on the waist or around the head, and provide easy adjustment of the breathing hardware
- Breathing hardware should have high fidelity to ensure that every breath is sensed accurately. We suggest breathing hardware designers consider using sensors that cover a larger area of the mouth and nose to increase sensing accuracy, which will, in turn increase focus of players on their breathing.
- Since breathing is a bodily activity, a full body clothing system could also be designed in order to measure parameters of breathing such as breathing rate, tidal volume etc. This form of hardware design to measure breathing could increase the factor of wearability by making use of the standardised sizing systems set by the clothing industry.

6. Consider Designing Breathing Hardware that Helps Players Hear their Own Breathing

This strategy suggests how self-awareness of breathing can be increased with the choice of sensors used in the design of hardware. Our results with "Theme 4: Engagement with Breathing Hardware", suggest that participants liked to hear their own breathing sounds and that hardware used to measure breathing in the game can increase self-awareness of the player's breathing. As indicated by Gemperle et al. [23], sensory interaction includes both active and passive interaction and this is a valuable feature for any wearable device. *Active* refers to the primary function of the wearable and *passive* refers to the additional function perceived by the users. According to these researchers, it is important to be sensitive of how players interact with a wearable, especially something that is placed on the human body. We acknowledge this and extend this notion to the design of hardware that detects breathing by recommending hardware designers use sensors that capture the sounds of the player's breathing and replay the amplified sound back to the players in real-time. This can assist a player become aware of his or her own breathing pattern while playing the game.

LIMITATIONS AND FUTURE WORK

Our research contributes both to the theory and practice of game design by evaluating player experience using four themes and the six breathing exercise game design strategies. However, we have not tested the strategies with other designers. It is also unclear if participants would like to use *Life Tree* repeatedly or if the breathing technique led to their improved well-being. We also acknowledge that the current work cannot claim to show that a breathing game is superior to regular breathing exercises with respect to the user motivation or potential health benefits. However, it would be interesting for longitudinal studies to explore such questions. On a similar note, the design guidelines are largely based on qualitative data. Thus, it would be relevant for future work to empirically validate the proposed guidelines.

CONCLUSION

Our research may provide useful insights for designers who are interested in designing breathing exercise games that are engaging and enjoyable to play. Furthermore, in the future, we hope our research will help pulmonologists look at creative ways to treat breathing related problems such as Attention Deficit Hyperactivity Disorder (ADHD), Chronic Obstructive Pulmonary Disease (COPD) and, the 235 million children who suffer from Asthma [34]. Our research could also be used by meditation practitioners to support the practice of mindfulness.

In conclusion, game designers can explore the design of breathing exercise games to help people learn proper breathing techniques in an engaging way. Breathing related disorders such as COPD could rise to become the third most common illness in the world by 2020 [46]. Game designers could help improve the lives of millions of such individuals and nudge them towards leading a healthy life by designing engaging breathing exercise games.

ACKNOWLEDGEMENTS

We would like to thank all the volunteers who participated in the study and would especially like to thank Dr. Matevz Leskovsek from Breathing Labs.

REFERENCES

1. Ritu Agarwal and Elena Karahanna. 2000. Time flies when you're having fun: Cognitive absorption and beliefs about information technology usage. *MIS quarterly*, 665-694. http://dx.doi.org/10.2307/3250951.
2. Krestina L. Amon and Andrew Campbell. 2008. Can Children with AD/HD Learn Relaxation and Breathing Techniques through Biofeedback Video Games? *Australian Journal of Educational & Developmental Psychology 8*, 72-84.
3. Lawrence Ampofo. 2015. Podcast #22 Neema Moraveji: The Benefits of Calming Technology - Digital Mindfulness. Digital Mindfulness, Retrieved on January 05, 2017 from http://digitalmindfulness.net/podcast-22-neema-moraveji-the-benefits-of-calming-technology/.

4. Matei Apostolescu. 2016. The workz of Matei Apostolescu. Retrieved on January 05, 2017 from http://www.013a.com/html/tree_zero_three.htm.

5. Robin Arnott. 2015. Deep Sea. Retrieved on January 05, 2017 from http://wraughk.com/deepsea/.

6. Ahmet Baydur, Rodney H. Adkins, and Joseph Milic-Emili. 2001. Lung mechanics in individuals with spinal cord injury: effects of injury level and posture. *Journal of Applied Physiology 90*, 2, 405-411. http://jap.physiology.org/content/jap/90/2/405.full.pdf.

7. Corwin Bell. 2003. The journey to wild divine. *The Wild Divine Project: Las Vegas, NV, USA*.

8. Claudia Bergomi, Wolfgang Tschacher, and Zeno Kupper. 2013. Measuring mindfulness: first steps towards the development of a comprehensive mindfulness scale. *Mindfulness 4*, 1, 18-32. http://dx.doi.org/10.1007/s12671-012-0102-9.

9. Staffan Bjork and Jussi Holopainen. 2004. *Patterns in Game Design (Game Development Series)*. Charles River Media.

10. Patrice Bouvier, François De Sorbier, Pascal Chaudeyrac, and Venceslas Biri. 2008. Cross-benefits between virtual reality and games. In *International Conference and Industry Symposium on Computer Games, Animation, Multimedia, IPTV, Edutainment and Security (CGAT'08)*, France, 10pp., https://hal-upec-upem.archives-ouvertes.fr/hal-00622350.

11. Virginia Braun and Victoria Clarke. 2006. Using thematic analysis in psychology. *Qualitative research in psychology 3*, 2, 77-101.

12. E. H. Breslin. 1992. The pattern of respiratory muscle recruitment during pursed-lip breathing. *CHEST Journal 101*, 1, 75-78. http://dx.doi.org/10.1378/chest.101.1.75.

13. John M. Carroll and Hans Van Der Meij. 1998. Ten misconceptions about minimalism. *Minimalism beyond the Nurnberg funnel*, 55-90. http://dx.doi.org/10.1109/47.503271.

14. Kavita D. Chandwani, Bob Thornton, George H. Perkins, Banu Arun, N. V. Raghuram, H. R. Nagendra, Qi Wei, and Lorenzo Cohen. 2010. Yoga improves quality of life and benefit finding in women undergoing radiotherapy for breast cancer. *Journal of the Society for Integrative Oncology 8*, 2.

15. Jenova Chen. 2007. Flow in games (and everything else). *Communications of the ACM 50*, 4, 31-34. http://dx.doi.org/10.1145/1232743.1232769.

16. Martin Clayton. 2005. Communication in Indian raga performance. *Musical communication*, 361-381.

17. Ben Cowley, Darryl Charles, Michaela Black, and Ray Hickey. 2008. Toward an Understanding of Flow in Video Games. *Comput. Entertain. 6*, 2 (2008/07//), 20:21-20:27. http://dx.doi.org/10.1145/1371216.1371223.

18. Mihaly Csikszentmihalyi. 1996. Flow and the psychology of discovery and invention. *New Yprk: Harper Collins*. http://www.bioenterprise.ca/docs/creativity-by-mihaly-csikszentmihalyi.pdf.

19. Char Davies and John Harrison. 1996. Osmose: towards broadening the aesthetics of virtual reality. http://papers.cumincad.org/data/works/att/b81d.content.pdf.

20. Hilko Ehmen, Marten Haesner, Ines Steinke, Mario Dorn, Mehmet Gövercin, and Elisabeth Steinhagen-Thiessen. 2012. Comparison of four different mobile devices for measuring heart rate and ECG with respect to aspects of usability and acceptance by older people. *Applied Ergonomics 43*, 3, 582-587. http://dx.doi.org/10.1016/j.apergo.2011.09.003.

21. William J. Elliott and Joseph L. Izzo Jr. 2006. Device-guided breathing to lower blood pressure: case report and clinical overview. *Medscape General Medicine 8*, 3, 23.

22. Robert Fried. 1990. Integrating music in breathing training and relaxation: I. Background, rationale, and relevant elements. *Biofeedback and Self-Regulation 15*, 2, 161-169. http://dx.doi.org/10.1007/BF00999146.

23. Francine Gemperle, Chris Kasabach, John Stivoric, Malcolm Bauer, and Richard Martin. 1998. Design for wearability. In *Wearable Computers, 1998. Digest of Papers. Second International Symposium on* IEEE, 116-122. http://dx.doi.org/10.1109/ISWC.1998.729537.

24. Jono Hailstone and Andrew E. Kilding. 2011. Reliability and validity of the Zephyr™ BioHarness™ to measure respiratory responses to exercise. *Measurement in Physical Education and Exercise Science 15*, 4, 293-300. http://dx.doi.org/10.1080/1091367X.2011.615671.

25. Inc Headspace. 2010. Headspace - meditation - Android Apps on Google Play. Retrieved on January 05, 2017 from https://play.google.com/store/apps/details?id=com.getsomeheadspace.android&hl.

26. James Hewitt. 2012. *The Complete Yoga Book: The Yoga of Breathing, Posture and Meditation*. Random House.

27. Anne E. Holland, Catherine J. Hill, Alice Y. Jones, and Christine F. Mcdonald. 2012. Breathing exercises for chronic obstructive pulmonary disease. *Cochrane*

Database Syst Rev 10. http://dx.doi.org/10.1002/14651858.CD008250.

28. E. Holloway and F. S. Ram. 2004. Breathing exercises for asthma. *Cochrane Database Syst Rev 1*. http://dx.doi.org/10.1136/thorax.58.8.649.

29. Kristina Höök, Martin Jonsson, Anna Ståhl, and Johanna Mercurio. 2016. Somaesthetic Appreciation Design. In *Proceedings of the SIGCHI Conference on Human Factors in Computing Systems (CHI'16), San Jose, CA, USA*. http://dx.doi.org/10.1145/2858036.2858583.

30. Kristina Höök, Anna Ståhl, Martin Jonsson, Johanna Mercurio, Anna Karlsson, and Eva-Carin Banka Johnson. 2015. Cover story somaesthetic design. *interactions 22*, 4, 26-33.

31. Wijnand Ijsselsteijn, Karolien Poels, and Yvonne Aw De Kort. 2008. The Game Experience Questionnaire: Development of a self-report measure to assess player experiences of digital games. *TU Eindhoven, Eindhoven, The Netherlands*.

32. Inhand. In Hand Mobile App helps bring balance to our daily stresses and anxieties. Retrieved on January 05, 2017 from https://play.google.com/store/apps/details?id=uk.inhand.

33. Amelia Keller. 2015. Investigating Calm User Experiences of Meditation Applications.

34. Marko Kokic. 2015. World Health Organization | Chronic respiratory diseases (CRDs). World Health Organization, Retrieved on January 05, 2017 from http://www.who.int/respiratory/en/.

35. Martijn Jl Kors, Gabriele Ferri, Erik D Van Der Spek, Cas Ketel, and Ben Am Schouten. 2016. A Breathtaking Journey.: On the Design of an Empathy-Arousing Mixed-Reality Game. In *Proceedings of the 2016 Annual Symposium on Computer-Human Interaction in Play* ACM, 91-104. http://dx.doi.org/10.1145/2967934.2968110.

36. Ben Kuchera. 2015. Deep is a virtual reality 'game' that wants to teach you how to breathe. polygon, Retrieved on January 05, 2017 from http://www.polygon.com/2015/3/2/8133675/deep-vr-meditation.

37. Pyoung Sook Lee. 1999. Theoretical bases and technical application of breathing therapy in stress management. *Journal of Korean Academy of Nursing 29*, 6, 1304-1313. http://dx.doi.org/10.4040/jkan.1999.29.6.1304

38. Matevz Leskovsek. 2015. Breathing Labs - Breathing Package. Retrieved on January 05, 2017 from http://www.breathinglabs.com/breathing-package/.

39. Ann M. Maclarnon and Gwen P. Hewitt. 1999. The evolution of human speech: The role of enhanced breathing control. *American Journal of Physical Anthropology 109*, 3, 341-363. http://dx.doi.org/10.1002/(SICI)1096-8644(199907)109:3<341::AID-AJPA5>3.0.CO;2-2.

40. M. Makhsous, James Bankard, and L. Fang. 2004. Lung capacity and airflow change due to different sitting posture. *Med Rehabil 84*, 332-337.

41. Joe Marshall, Duncan Rowland, Stefan Rennick Egglestone, Steve Benford, Brendan Walker, and Derek Mcauley. 2011. Breath control of amusement rides. In *Proceedings of the SIGCHI Conference on Human Factors in Computing Systems* ACM, 73-82. http://dx.doi.org/10.1145/1978942.1978955.

42. Pere Marti-Puig, Gerard Masferrer, and Moises Serra. 2014. Low-complex Real-Time Breathing Monitoring System for Smartphones. In *CCIA*, 257-260.

43. Deborah Mast, Judy Meyers, and Ann Urbanski. 1987. Relaxation techniques: A self-learning module for nurses: Unit II. *Cancer Nursing 10*, 4, 217-225. http://journals.lww.com/cancernursingonline/Fulltext/1987/08000/Relaxation_techniques__A_self_learning_module_for.8.aspx.

44. Patrick Mckeown. 2008. *Asthma-free Naturally: Everything You Need to Know to Take Control of Your Asthma*. Conari Press.

45. Paul Miller. 2010. Zyxio's 'sensawaft' tech lets you control a cursor with your breath, you lazy jerk. Engadget, Retrieved on January 05, 2017 from https://www.engadget.com/2010/01/08/zyxios-sensawaft-tech-lets-you-control-a-cursor-with-your-bre/.

46. Christopher J. L. Murray and Alan D. Lopez. 1997. Alternative projections of mortality and disability by cause 1990–2020: Global Burden of Disease Study. *The Lancet 349*, 9064, 1498-1504. http://dx.doi.org/10.1016/S0140-6736(96)07492-2.

47. Kent L. Norman. 2013. Geq (game engagement/experience questionnaire): a review of two papers. *Interacting with computers 25*, 4, 278-283. http://dx.doi.org/10.1093/iwc/iwt009.

48. Inmaculada Plaza, Marcelo Marcos Piva Demarzo, Paola Herrera-Mercadal, and Javier García-Campayo. 2013. Mindfulness-based mobile applications: Literature review and analysis of current features. *JMIR mHealth and uHealth 1*, 2. http://dx.doi.org/10.2196/mhealth.2733.

49. Yongqiang Qin, Chris J. Vincent, Nadia Bianchi-Berthouze, and Yuanchun Shi. 2014. AirFlow: designing immersive breathing training games for

COPD. In *CHI'14 Extended Abstracts on Human Factors in Computing Systems* ACM, 2419-2424. http://dx.doi.org/10.1145/2559206.2581309.

50. Kelley Raab. 2014. Mindfulness, self-compassion, and empathy among health care professionals: a review of the literature. *Journal of Health Care Chaplaincy 20*, 3, 95-108. http://dx.doi.org/10.1080/08854726.2014.913876.

51. Vanessa Rementilla. 2016. Invisible Teacher: How Might Digital Leisure Games Foster Critical Thinking and Grit? http://openresearch.ocadu.ca/id/eprint/1366.

52. Katie Salen and Eric Zimmerman. 2004. *Rules of play: Game design fundamentals*. MIT press.

53. Martin E. P. Seligman. 2012. *Flourish: A Visionary New Understanding of Happiness and Well-being*. Atria Books, New York, NY.

54. Sanchari Sinha, Som Nath Singh, Y. P. Monga, and Uday Sankar Ray. 2007. Improvement of glutathione and total antioxidant status with yoga. *The Journal of Alternative and Complementary Medicine 13*, 10, 1085-1090. http://dx.doi.org/10.1089/acm.2007.0567.

55. Tobias Sonne and Mads Møller Jensen. 2016. Evaluating the ChillFish Biofeedback Game with Children with ADHD. In *Proceedings of the The 15th International Conference on Interaction Design and Children* ACM, 529-534. http://dx.doi.org/10.1145/2930674.2935981.

56. Penelope Sweetser and Peta Wyeth. 2005. GameFlow: a model for evaluating player enjoyment in games. *Computers in Entertainment (CIE) 3*, 3, 3-3. http://dx.doi.org/10.1145/1077246.1077253.

57. Paul Tennent, Duncan Rowland, Joe Marshall, Stefan Rennick Egglestone, Alexander Harrison, Zachary Jaime, Brendan Walker, and Steve Benford. 2011. Breathalising games: understanding the potential of breath control in game interfaces. In *Proceedings of the 8th International Conference on Advances in Computer Entertainment Technology* ACM, 58. http://dx.doi.org/10.1145/2071423.2071496.

58. Marieke Van Rooij, Adam Lobel, Owen Harris, Niki Smit, and Isabela Granic. 2016. DEEP: A Biofeedback Virtual Reality Game for Children At-risk for Anxiety. In *Proceedings of the 2016 CHI Conference Extended Abstracts on Human Factors in Computing Systems* ACM, 1989-1997. http://dx.doi.org/10.1145/2851581.2892452.

59. Jay Vidyarthi, Bernhard E. Riecke, and Diane Gromala. 2012. Sonic Cradle: designing for an immersive experience of meditation by connecting respiration to music. In *Proceedings of the designing interactive systems conference* ACM, 408-417. http://dx.doi.org/10.1145/2317956.2318017.

60. Daphna Vilozni, Ephraim Bar-Yishay, Ilan Gur, Yehuda Shapira, Shirley Meyer, and Simon Godfrey. 1994. Computerized respiratory muscle training in children with Duchenne muscular dystrophy. *Neuromuscular Disorders 4*, 3, 249-255. http://dx.doi.org/10.1016/0960-8966(94)90026-4.

61. Damon Young. 2015. *How to Think About Exercise*. Picador.

62. Gabe Zichermann and Christopher Cunningham. 2011. *Gamification by design: Implementing game mechanics in web and mobile apps*. O'Reilly Media, Inc.

AutoGym: An Exertion Game for Autonomous Driving

Sven Krome
RMIT University
Melbourne, Australia
sven.krome@rmit.edu.au

Jussi Holopainen
University of Lincoln
Lincoln, UK
jholopainen@lincoln.ac.uk

Stefan Greuter
RMIT University
Melbourne, Australia
stefan.greuter@rmit.edu.au

ABSTRACT
In-car exercises are a promising way to keep the inactive driver of future autonomous cars in good shape and alert of the situation around them. To explore how to implement exercises into the car context, we designed AutoGym, an in-car fitness program that translates frustrating traffic into a fun exertion game. To progress in the game, the players must anticipate changes to the traffic situation they are exposed to in the car and work-out against their prediction. In this paper, we present the conceptual design of AutoGym and report what we have learnt from an explorative user study with 28 participants. Furthermore, from the design process and the evaluation, we derived three strategies for implementing exertion games. We found that these strategies helped to conceptualize exertion games as a playful embodiment of the dynamics of driving and as such, can positively influence the experience of control, orientation and situational awareness i.e. experiential factors that can be crucial for facilitating future autonomous driving in a pleasurable and safe way.

Author Keywords
Exertion Games; Autonomous Driving; Games.

ACM Classification Keywords
H.5.m. Information interfaces and presentation (e.g., HCI): Miscellaneous.

INTRODUCTION
Driving a car is arguably not the healthiest form of transportation. The suboptimal sitting posture, combined with a very restricted space for movement, often results in physical fatigue and an uncomfortable transportation experience. Especially professional drivers and long-distance commuters, spending several hours in vehicles, are at risk of physical and mental suffering [15]. Autonomous driving technology relieves the driver from the driving task, enabling a much wider range of interactions and movements within the driving context. In order to explore the possibilities of in-car exercise games, we designed AutoGym, an in-car exertion game that motivates exercise through an integration of the driving context as a game element. Physical exercise as health, wellness and stress management method is widely accepted [4]. Exertion games are one gameful strategy to motivate physical exercise [9]. The general concept of exertion games is to package physical exercise into a gameful experience and thereby facilitate and motivate exercise in a more pleasurable and fun way.

Even though autonomous driving is expected to allow the inactive driver a bigger range of movements, the spatial dimensions of a standard passenger car will naturally restrain the player's movements and their body position. But even in this restricted space, a large variety of physical exercises are possible. For example, several self-help books provide a repertoire of instructions for in-car exercise and promise to increase wellbeing during transportation [1,11,18]. However, a gameful, fun and motivating approach to in-car exercise, which seamlessly integrates exertion within the car context, has not been available. To explore a new way of motivating in-car exertion we studied a proof-of-concept implementation of AutoGym with 28 participants in a lab-based simulator.

RELATED WORK
The car as a space for activities and entertainment beyond the driving task is almost as old as the automobile itself. However, for a long time, music and other forms of auditory content were the only feasible entertainment alternatives for the active driver. For passengers, however, researchers have explored a wide range of entertainment opportunities, from immersive media consumption to a large variety of games and even physical interactions.

Car Passenger Games
Substantial research on interactive passenger entertainment has been conducted by Oscar Juhlin. Investigating the road as a medium for social encounters, Juhlin suggested several in-car prototypes to establish a social connection between the player/user, co-passengers, road users and the transportation environment. For instance, the *Backseat Gaming Project* [6] investigated how an interactive story can unfold through defined points-of-interest along the travel route. Like most research on passenger games, the aim was to entertain children to avoid boredom. However, besides simply entertaining the kids in the rear of the car, the researchers have also suggested games for various other purposes.

CHI PLAY '17, October 15–18, 2017, Amsterdam, Netherlands

ACM ISBN 978-1-4503-4898-0/17/10...$15.00
https://doi.org/10.1145/3116595.3116626

Sundström et al. [14] suggested three games that aim to encourage children to sit safely in the car. The authors used driving features, such as g-force and the alternation of light/shadow, as basis for designing core-experiences into their games. All of the three games aim to have the kids sit in a safe position as a side effect of the game play. For example, in the game *emo-car* the player has to mimic the "feeling" of the car with facial expressions. Since the facial expressions of the player are only properly registered if the player sits in an upright position in front of the camera, the player only performs well when sitting safely. In other words, to progress in the game, the child must perform the desired behavior i.e. sit upright.

Wilfinger et al. [17] conceptualized *RiddleRide* an educational in-car multiplayer quiz game that was aimed to connect adults and children with points-of-interest while on a car trip. Each player plays the game on their individual mobile device. To make the quiz suitable for all age groups, the answer modality provided adapted difficulty levels suited for adults and children. Similarly, Broy et al. [3] suggested *nICE* an in-car multiplayer game that facilitates collaborative and communicative experiences among passengers and the driver based on an image puzzle that needs to be uncovered by playing several mini-games. Additionally, Zuckerman et al. [19] developed *Mileys* a digital in-car game with the purpose to connect children with their families and their environment.

Research on in-car games indicate that the integration of contextual data such as location, e.g. [3,19], or the dynamics of driving, e.g. [14], is a promising approach for an engaging gameplay while driving. Even though all the above mentioned games are targeted at children, we believe that an appropriate implementation of the driving context would also motivate adult drivers to engage in games and even in exercises.

Interactive driver entertainment and gamification

Although researchers have suggested an integration of the driver and interactive in-car entertainment, such as [3], driver-focused approaches have been insufficient due to safety considerations. Solitary driver applications have to be secondary activities that are *augmenting* the driving tasks such as safe-driving and/or eco-driving gamification approaches [5]. In contrast to passenger entertainment most of these approaches focused on the design of visual feedback such as points, leaderboards and virtual rewards based on a target activity such as fuel efficient driving.

With autonomously driven cars, the driving task becomes a secondary activity, and the implementation of gamification needs to be adapted accordingly. Depending on the level of automation, gamification of supervisory tasks and situational awareness become a central focus but also wellbeing and dynamic sitting will likely become gamification challenges of the future. For example, Terken et al. [16] suggested an interactive in-car environment for stress reduction in commuting scenarios. The system projects immersive virtual environments into the interior of the car that can be explored by a tangible interface. This system is intended for higher-level driving automation that does not require an ongoing supervisory control. This enables the system to be independent from the driving situation and does not require situational-awareness of the driver. Investigating creative activities in stop-and-go traffic, Krome et al. [7] suggested AutoJam, an in-car music game that is played on a stationary steering wheel within an autonomously driven car. In AutoJam we concluded, that an integration of traffic into the music game can facilitate a consistent feeling of progression even when the car was not moving and as such positively influence the traffic experience.

In-car exertion tools and occupational health

Besides the aforementioned self-help books for in-car exercises that mostly focus on stretching and strengthening exercises [1,11,18], a large variety of mobile foot-rockers and mini-exercise bikes are available for travel and office use. Figure 1 shows an example of a commercially available foot stepper of the company *Gamercize*. These devices aim to integrate exercise and video game activities.

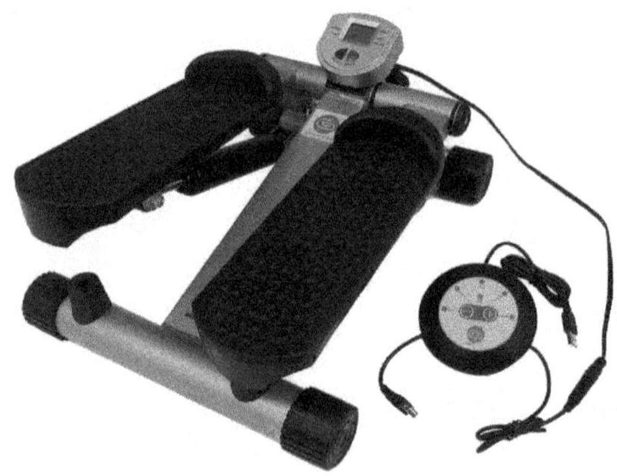

Figure 1: Commercially available Power Stepper *(c) Richard Coshott, BY-SA 2.0*

Similarly, some airlines suggest that passengers on long distance flights engage in onboard exercise programs and the car tuner *Becker Automotive Design* [12] offers to build a full body exercise machine into a Cadillac Escalade to enable exercise on-the-go. Research has confirmed that exercise is beneficial to the wellbeing of office workers [10]. Despite the benefits of exercises and the advancements of autonomously driven cars, neither motivational aspects of in-car exercises nor the importance of maintaining a situational awareness being driven by an autonomous car have been investigated by research or industry. In approaching this research context, we aim to explore how a gameful interaction system can motivate in-car exercises by using the driving context as a playable input in the system.

PROTOTYPE CONCEPT

AutoGym is an exertion game for future driving experiences in autonomous cars. Based on a commuter pilot study [8], we selected a rush hour driving scenario within Melbourne's city traffic. Within the context of an autonomously driven car, we envisaged that the inactive driver could engage in other non-driving activities while maintaining awareness of the traffic situation.

The AutoGym prototype consisted of a mini-exercise bike positioned on the driver's lap that was manually operated by hand. The resistance of the mini-exercise bike was linked to the car's speed, i.e. the faster the car drives, the higher the resistance of the exercise bike. When the car stopped completely, the resistance was at its minimum, allowing the player to turn the wheel without much effort. The resistance increased to the maximum at a speed of 60 km/h. Maximum resistance made it almost impossible to spin the wheel. A touchscreen tablet pc, displayed the game interface and the interactions via the exercise bike. Figure 2 shows the implementation of AutoGym on the passenger side of a test vehicle that was driven by another driver to simulate the experience of being in an autonomously driven vehicle.

Figure 2: In-car setup of AutoGym with manually operated exercise bike. The resistance of the bike was linked to the car's speed. The game was displayed on a touch screen PC in front of the driver on the dashboard.

GAME AND INTERFACE DESIGN

The objective of AutoGym is to complete a whole exercise program (represented as the ring seen in Figure 3) consisting of segments that the player needed to complete though workout on the exercise bike. The length of a segment represented the amount of time in which the player had to finish the segment through a work-out via the exercise bike. The longer the segment, the longer the player has to turn the spinning wheel on the exercise bike to complete it.

As soon as a segment was selected, a countdown is initiated visualized by an increasing status bar on the inside of the segment. Each turn on the exercise bike was rewarded with audio feedback and a progress visualization. Figure 4 illustrates the game loop.

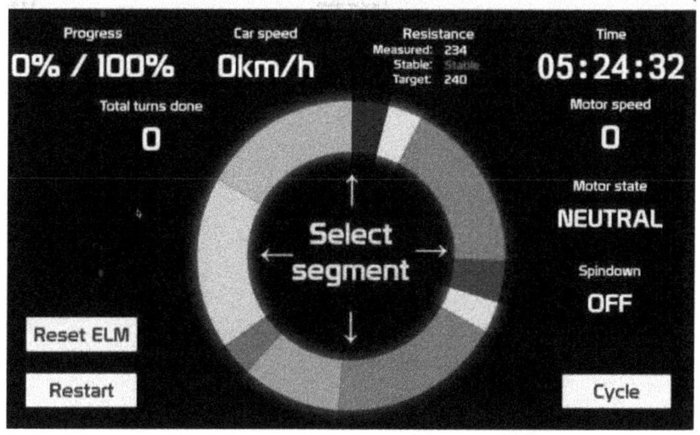

Figure 3: AutoGym Graphical User Interface.

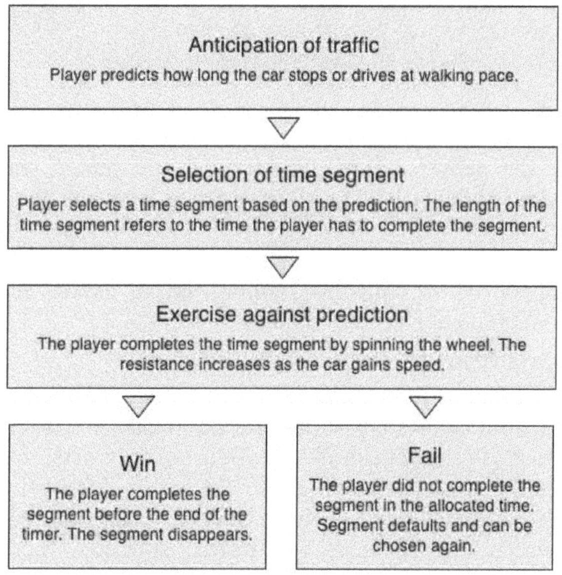

Figure 4: *AutoGym* Interaction Loop.

The decisions required from the player to successfully complete the game consist of three complementary steps: (1) The anticipation and prediction of the traffic situation, (2) The translation of the prediction into a time segment and (3) the completion of the time segment by turning the exercise bike often and fast enough before the countdown of the time segment expires.

The game is finished as soon as the player successfully completed all segments of the ring. Upon completion, the player is presented with performance statistics showing the overall turns, the time and the failed attempts.

TECHNICAL IMPLEMENTATION

For the AutoGym prototype we modified an off-the-shelf mini-exercise bike with adjustable resistance. We exchanged the manual adjustment system with a high-torque electrical motor that was controlled by an Arduino microcontroller with H-Bridge Shield to enable the motor to turn in both directions. We attached two additional sensors to the exercise wheel: a magnetic sensor to register the turns and a slider sensor to measure and adjust the resistance by the motor.

Figure 5: AutoGym Technical Setup.

Figure 5 shows the technical implementation of the AutoGym exertion interface consisting of the mini-exercise bike, the sensors, a high torque electric motor and an *Arduino* with H-Bridge Shield to change the motor's direction of rotation. The hardware was connected to the output device via the serial port. The game interface was developed with Unity3D running on a laptop in the simulator and a tablet pc in the car.

EVALUATION

To investigate the impact of AutoGym, we conducted a lab-based simulator study with 28 participants. The study assessed (1) the impact of AutoGym on the users' feeling and satisfaction of playing, (2) the users' motivation of traffic-based contextual exercises and (3) the users' perception of the car and traffic situation. For the assessment, we chose a mixed qualitative and quantitative study design with the goal to explore the user experiences and compare them with the results from the standardized questionnaires.

STUDY PROCEDURE

After receiving formal consent, the participants were briefed on the purpose and scenario of the study: A regular rush-hour commute in a fully autonomous car. The study consisted of four components as shown in Figure 6.

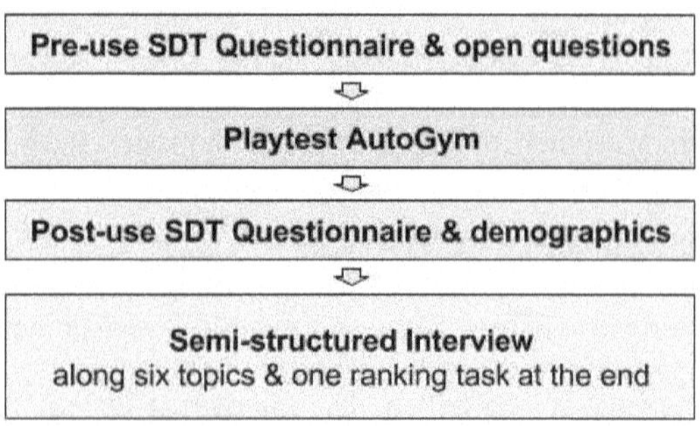

Figure 6: AutoGym Study Procedure. Before and after the playtest, the participants completed a questionnaire and a semi-structured interview at the end.

The pre- and post-questionnaire consisted of five scales from Sheldon's self-determination questionnaire [13]: autonomy-scale, competency-scale, stimulation-scale (two items from physical thriving and one item from the pleasure-scale), security-scale, and self-esteem scale. The test procedure was concluded by a semi-structured interview of 10-30 minutes. The interview was guided by 10 topics regarding the user experience, the difficulties, the experience of traffic and the game as well as a final ranking task on the most prominent feelings.

SIMULATOR SETUP

We tested AutoGym in an improved simulator setup based on a traffic clip recorded on an evening commute during rush-hour traffic in Melbourne. The video footage of the commute was played on a 46" TV screen to maximize immersion. When the video was recorded, we also recorded the car speed based on an OBD-II application. The simulator was playing the video in sync with the speed data that was controlling the exercise bikes resistance. Figure 7 shows the simulator setup.

Figure 7: AutoGym Simulator Setup.

PARTICIPANTS

For the user study, 28 volunteers were recruited through snowball sampling via word-of-mouth and social media channels. Participation was completely voluntary and not rewarded. Table 1 shows an overview of the participants grouped by occupation.

Table 1: Overview of participants grouped by occupation.

Occupation	Sex (f/m)	Avg. age
Post graduate students	5 / 6	26.00
Researchers / academic staff	4 / 5	33.33
Creative industry	0 / 4	29.50
Technician / IT	1 / 2	33.00
Maternity leave	1 / 0	30.00

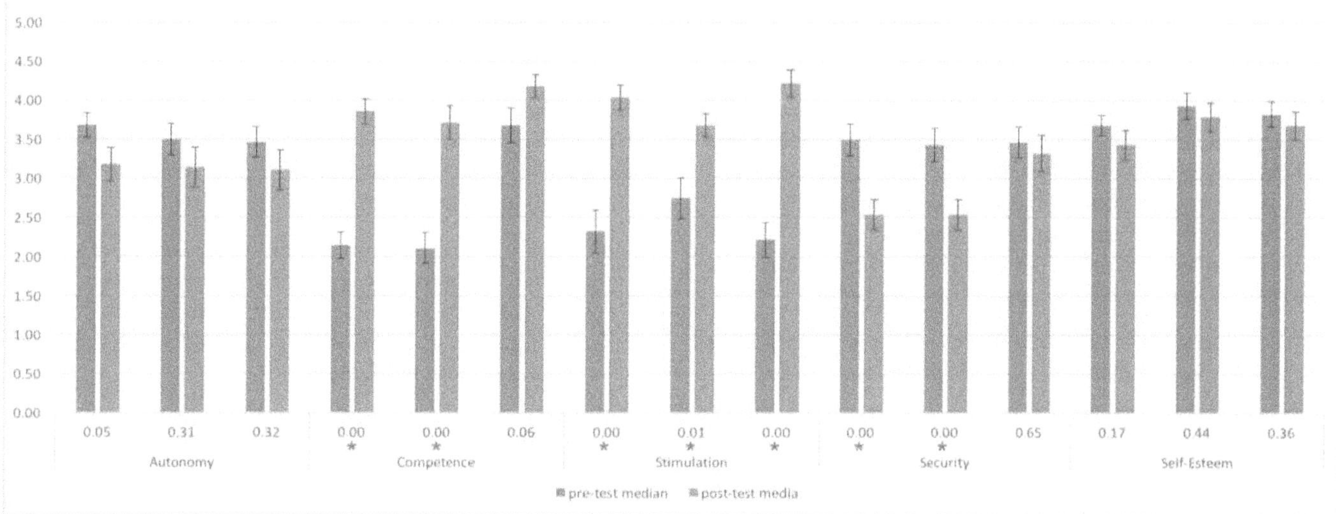

Figure 8: Questionnaire results. Means of each item of the five scales with p-Value for each pair of items below. Pre (blue) and post (orange) questionnaire.

FINDINGS

Pre / Post Questionnaires

The data of the pre- and post-questionnaires was imported into SPSS for analysis. Figure 8 shows the results of each item of the pre-and post-questionnaires. To analyze the data, we performed a paired t-test for each pair of pre-and post-questionnaire items. The comparison of pre-and post-values shows that the items from the autonomy and self-esteem scale do not have any significant differences, even though a slight tendency can be recognized.

The most significant difference can be found on the stimulation scale ($p<.001$ for all three items). After playing *AutoGym*, the users valued the *AutoGym* experience as significantly more stimulating than the experience during their usual commute. Similarly, the first two items of the competency scale show a significant difference ($p<.001$) much more than the third item. These items inquired about the "successful completion of a difficult task" and "mastering a hard challenge". From these results, we imply that *AutoGym* was experienced by the players as a gameful and challenging activity that lead to a significant feeling of competence and mastery, at least in comparison to the participants' last commute.

Interestingly, the two first security items show a very significant decrease between pre- and post- questionnaire. Of interest is the first security item because it inquires if the user felt "structured and predictable" while using *AutoGym*. In comparison to a usual commute, participants valued the *AutoGym* experience as less predictable and structured. This can be an indication for a novelty effect. However, it can also be interpreted that the exposure to traffic i.e. making the traffic the topic of the game had an impact on the players' perception of the situation.

Besides the SDT scales, the pre-test questionnaire also contained several questions about the participants' demographic as well as their driving history, such as car ownership.

The pre-test questionnaire also contained two open questions that asked about previous commuting experiences. For example, one of the questions was "Describe your last commuting trip in one word". As expected, the last commute was described as a negative experience, most common words used being stress, boredom, or frustration.

On one hand, we can conclude from the questionnaires that the participants have a negative evaluation of their last commute. On the other hand, the results from the SDT items were mostly as expected, except for the decreasing security items that requires further investigations.

Semi-Structured Interviews

The interviews were between 10 to 30 minutes long and pre-structured by ten topics. All interviews were audio recorded and conducted immediately after the post-test questionnaire. The recordings were transcribed and analyzed with NVivo software using a thematic analysis approach [2]. After an initial open coding session in which the participants' transcripts were coded based on the contextual meaning, we compared the identified nodes and clustered them into 13 categories with several sub-categories. In the following we report on the six categories that, we assume, are particularly descriptive for designing exertion games in the context of autonomous driving.

A. General evaluation and difficulties

All 28 participants were able to finish the *AutoGym* game: five participants completed without failure, 17 participants repeated one segment, five participants two and only one participant repeated three segments before completing the game. In the interviews, most participants described the *AutoGym* as easy and not very physically challenging. All participants reported they would like to play it again, particularly in different traffic conditions.

The general attitude was very positive, participants described the AutoGym experience as fun, interesting and satisfying. However, the participants were unsure about the nature of *AutoGym* experience, undecided if they should consider AutoGym a game, an exercise tool or a substitute for driving. For example, one participant proposes:

> *Games like this would definitely be a substitute for driving. It translates the driving to another high-level task* (male, 26).

The build-up of expectation also influenced the interpretation:

> *I was expecting more an arcade game. Right now it's more an exercise. I could see that after a few times the novelty wears off* (female, 31).

Contrary to this, the idea of embedding exertion into games was questioned because it blurred the exercise part.

> *If that'd be in an autonomous car, it's a good way to kill down time. However, I don't know what the purpose of gamifying the exercise [was]. If it's for the exercise, I'd work out effectively* (male, 28).

Interestingly, the differences in determining the character of AutoGym, was expressed in most of the participants' answers. The perception was changing depending on topic or question. We believe that this interpretive openness resulted from linear mapping of the speed and the bike's resistance, which would allow participants' to evaluate the game depending on their effort and physical strength.

B. Perceived Control: self, car, traffic

One implicit design assumption of AutoGym was that the physical connection between the player and driving (facilitated by the exertion challenge) would increase the player's feeling of control over the situation. Participants reported that AutoGym would establish a feeling of control, however, the locus and impact differed depending on the interpretation. For example, one interpretation was that it is a physical challenge. By winning, despite the resistance, the player imposes control over the situation:

> *I felt good but I felt that I didn't predict the traffic very well. My instinct was saying let's do this despite the traffic. It was also that I was able to do it because it was quite easy. [...] So like a trick to exert more control over the situation* (male, 32).

In accordance with our assumption, many participants reported that they gained control and orientation because it allowed them to feel the car behavior:

> *When the resistance was going harder I felt good because I was going again. Especially during [the] workout I was primarily looking at the application and the resistance signaled me to look up again* (female, 21).

Most interestingly, not only the physical experience of driving facilitated that feeling but also the prediction challenge i.e. the anticipation of traffic, seems to increase sovereignty by allowing the player to act on it.

> *If you are stuck in traffic, you feel out of control, but the game influenced that perception. With it [AutoGym] you can train yourself to read the traffic, and by reading and understanding traffic, it is less scary* (female, 34).

C. Sources of Pleasure: self-efficacy, relatedness to the car, mastery of traffic

We designed AutoGym to enable a faster progression in the exercise program, the slower the car drives. The most rewarding moment should be when the car comes to a halt with almost zero resistance on the spinning bike. Since the participants had different physical strength, they interpreted the reward structure differently. For example, some players felt more rewarded if they were able to complete a section despite higher resistance:

> *I understood the idea that you are rewarded by good predictions with less resistance but I'm quite the opposite. You could reward me with more resistance. For me, it's empty energy going away. [...] In the end it was me who chose the prediction, so I have to fight my own prediction and seeing that the prediction was right or not was quite satisfying* (male, 26).

On the other hand, the physical experience of driving was not only reported as orientation but also as a pleasurable experience in itself:

> *I felt the resistance changes were very comfortable to experience. I'd like to play this with closed eyes and guess based on the resistance how fast the car is driving. It could even be more fun* (female, 34).

Mastery was not only related to physical exertion, predicting the traffic was reported as a skill that could be trained and improved:

> *I felt very good. Like winning. A feeling of mastery. I was able to predict the stops quite good. My predictions were improving over time* (female, 23).

D. Experiencing the car: competition, collaborator, companion

Even though the playtests took place in a lab-based simulator, the participants reported that they could imagine how they would perceive the car during playing AutoGym. On the one hand, the car was interpreted as the one to compete with: *I was busy beating the car* (male, 26). On the contrary, the interpretation was based on an exchange or sharing of work with the car, by taking over the work from the car. We interpreted this as a collaboration.

> *It's interesting to feel what the car feels. If the car works, you can rest and enjoy. [...] You get communicated how the car feels and translate it in an activity [...] when it stops, you take over the physical movement* (male, 25).

However, the alignment of car speed and resistance was also reported as counter-intuitive, especially when the players associated themselves with the car:

> *My mind assumes that when the car rests, I would be resting. I want to be more aligned with the car. It was a big effort to start being busy and physical when my car rests. I felt a little disconnected to the car* (female, 46).

E. Traffic Perception: Context, Opponent, Playground

As expected, time and traffic was experienced as much faster while playing AutoGym. All participants reported that they did not experience a feeling of waiting:

> *Usually I feel bored but with this game I wanted the traffic to stop so I can work out* (female, 22)

However, for the players able to turn the exercise bike even in higher speeds, the traffic situation transformed into a physical challenge for work out.

> *I was experiencing the traffic through the changes in resistance and the more resistance the faster the car and the more I was challenged* (male, 25)

Whereas a few participants reported that the traffic was impossible to predict, others reported that the prediction task connected them with the traffic. Traffic becomes a playground for informed decisions.

> *Yeah. I'm someone who likes to play with the traffic anyway. You will start to learn patterns. If I take a gamble and lose I'll be 2 minutes later so I take the risk* (male, 31).

F. Motivation of Exertion: abreaction, sympathy, progression

One central topic of the interview was the motivation to perform exercises while in traffic. The participants answered this question from several perspectives. Most prominently, participants reported how they would use AutoGym for integrating sport into their daily life. In particular, exercise seemed to be a good activity to deal with frustrating traffic situations.

> *When I stuck in the traffic it makes sense to deal with frustration. It's a good abreaction. I'd play that in difficult traffic* (male, 28).

Moreover, the stimuli of the traffic situation had a natural effect to start interacting. As manual drivers, we are already conditioned to acting when in traffic. It seems a natural interaction that you start getting active when you see a change in traffic; in the sense of piggy-backing exertion onto traffic:

> *The traffic light, the cars in front of us. Especially the break light in front of me. If they turned on 20m in front, our impulse is to break and then you felt the decrease of resistance* (male, 23).

Lastly, a participant reported that sympathizing with the car can also result in exertion as a way of facilitating the driving task:

> *Somehow you can contribute [to driving]. I can show sympathy with the car. The car works hard; I work hard too* (male, 28).

DESIGNING EXERTION-GAMES FOR AUTONOMOUS DRIVING

The results clearly demonstrated that the connection between AutoGym and the driving context through the prediction and resistance mechanics of the game affected both the experience of the exertion task, as well as the driving situation. The exertion task, mediated by the experience of the car speed, had an impact on the perception of the car and the driving context. It appears as if the physical investment of exertion was facilitating the player's concept of who is in control of the situation, who sets the challenge and the motivation to continue. Table 2 summarizes the findings of the interviews by aligning them into three possible configurations. These three suggested configurations are an attempt to understand implementations of in-car exertion, based on the connection of the three core aspects of the experience: perception of traffic, perceived locus of control, and the motivation for exertion. The interviews indicated that the participants interpreted the AutoGym experience based on their physical

Table 2: Three Implementation Strategies with selected criteria from the findings.

Implementation of Exertion	Role of car as	Traffic perception	Exertion motivation	Perceived control	Sources of Pleasure
(1) Driving substitute	Competitor	Context	Fitness and abreaction	self / overcome the car	Self-efficacy / mastery
(2) Identification	Companion	Opponent	Sympathy with car	aligned with the car	Relatedness / feeling for car
(3) Contribution	Collaborator	Playground	Progression	over traffic	Mastery / understanding traffic

ability to control the game by exercising even when the car drove relatively fast. This motivation to exercise had a particularly strong effect on the interpretation of the perceived loci of control. Hence, each of the following implementation strategies can be seen as a possible configuration for designing traffic-based exertion games that are based on prediction and resistance mechanics.

Implementation Strategy 1: Exertion as a Driving Substitute

AutoGym substitutes the driving task by providing a new challenge for mastering the traffic: physical exertion. From a design perspective, exertion as a substitute was implemented by a linear and continuous mapping of car speed and resistance. This allows the players, depending on their physical strength, to dominate the car's driving behavior. Hence, the challenge was to beat the car. The car was perceived as a competitor that must be overcome to win the game. In other words, the rewarding moment was to impose their own power on top of the car's power. The higher the speed, the more challenging the game. In contrast to the original concept, the stop phases became time for recovery.

The traffic situation was relevant mostly as the source of the driving behavior but not as the focus of the activity. By overcoming the car as a competitor, the player experienced control as self-efficacy. The player was in control of the driving task by mastering the power and speed of the car through physical exercise. This implies that exercise and fitness motives were of similar importance to the pleasure of exertion in an unusual context.

The focus of implementing exertion as a driving substitute might be on making the car and driving dynamics a physical experience. The game component, such as the prediction mechanics of AutoGym, should be designed to support the experience of imposing their own power. Ultimately, this implementation leads to an in-car exercise program and would not necessarily be embedded in a game context. The traffic was a challenging moment of harder and easier intervals, similar to popular interval workouts. In future autonomous cars, it might be possible to represent the player's performance data through the driving style of the car which open new perspectives of external motivations.

Implementation Strategy 2: Exertion through Car Identification

This strategy was also based on a physical experience of the car's power. However, exertion was less strongly motivated by competition but by sympathy and progress. The car was perceived as a companion with whom the player shares the workload, in order to progress in traffic. Exertion was not the core-experience of the interaction system. Exertion was rather a medium to build a physical connection to the car thus making the traffic progression more tangible. The core experience was a consistent progression through an exercise program and traffic.

Traffic was not a motivation for exercising, such as in implementation strategy 1 nor the motivation for the gameplay as in strategy 3. The general assumption was that neither traffic nor physical exercise are fun. However, it was pleasurable to feel the progression through the power and the dynamics of the driving. Furthermore, the players gained orientation and control by feeling what the car was doing. The player was in a physically mediated dialogue with the car's driving dynamics having only one goal: progression, mediated by an understanding of the situation through the exertion tasks.

Interaction needs to be aligned with the dynamics of driving. An indirect implementation of speed could enforce that. Subsequently, this concept could also be implemented by an inverted mapping of speed and resistance as one participant suggested: *When the car works, I want to work as well.*

Implementation Strategy 3: Exertion for Driving Contribution

In contrast to the two former strategies, this configuration relied on the prediction mechanic as the core experience of the game. Exercise and the feeling for the car (the core-experiences of the other two implementations) were only an additional motivational affordance of a correct prediction. Avoiding or minimizing exertion by a precise prediction of traffic was the goal and challenge of the setup.

In this implementation, traffic was the playground and object of investigation i.e. it needed to be understood in order to progress in the game. The gameplay resembled a dialogue between the car and the inactive driver, which led to an interpretation of the car as a collaborator for progressing in the game (and the traffic respectively). Similar to strategy 2, the workload was shared between car and player. In other words, the player contributed to the driving activity by reading and communicating the traffic situation correctly.

This change the location of perceived control. Control was established through understanding the traffic and the driving situation. A correct prediction instilled a feeling of success and control over the traffic. It reframed traffic as something that can be understood and overcome. In that way, traffic lost its subjective characteristics of being uncontrollable, and potentially disastrous, and turned it into a playable environment.

This interpretation facilitated the exchange between the work of the car and the exertion activity. When the car stopped, the workload was transferred to the player. In particular, the exercise bike was associated with the concept of charging the car, such as a metaphor for an electric car. This could potentially add another layer of motivation for exertion. In any case, since this implementation relied on precise decisions, it would require a strict enforcement of the game rules. Wrong predictions should have severe consequences for the exercise routine. A linear connection between speed and resistance would not be required because the core experience was reading the traffic situation.

LIMITATION

The presented implementation strategies attempt to describe three possible configurations of aligning exertion games with the autonomous driving context. In this paper we posed this alignment as implications resulting mainly from the interviews, as well as from experiences and reflections of the design process. The 28 semi-structured interviews provided a comprehensive repository of user experiences, although only a subset of these experiences directly informed the three presented implications. In contrast to this, the questionnaires provided only few unexpected insights and the small number of cases does not allow a generalization of the results.

Furthermore, to increase the sample size, we tested AutoGym in a lab-based simulator setup. We assume that this setup had a major influence on the players' perception of the car, and of course, the experience of safety and a feeling of control. On the contrary, this setup allowed the participant to focus completely on the game without the distraction of a real driving situation. Because of these reasons, we believe that the implications provide an idealized concept of exertion implementation strategies.

In the design process and the lab-based study of AutoGym we explicitly excluded the safety constraints of current autonomous driving such as handover times and the physical dimensions of the interface. A legal implementation of AutoGym would require a level of automation technologies not yet available. Nevertheless, by designing and testing the concept AutoGym we investigated the traffic and driving situation as a playable input for a secondary activity. The impact on the situational awareness and as such an improved safety of autonomous driving has only been investigated indirectly and subjectively via the interviews. In future studies, it will be crucial to investigate the safety context of such an exertion-game, in terms of quantifiable situational awareness, emergency behavior and hand-over situations.

The AutoGym prototype has a limited scope of resistance. Over the length of the study, the strength of the resistance decreased which required us to readjust the resistance several times. Participants who followed right after the adjustment, had a slightly higher base-resistance then others. This might have influenced their experience. However, since everyone successfully completed the game, we believe that this effect can be marginalized.

Ultimately, the participants differed in their individual physical strength. Since we could not align the resistance with the personal strength, the physical effort required from the participant was not equal. We believe that these differences facilitated the individual interpretations which resulted in a rich variety of experiential aspects.

CONLUSION

This paper presented AutoGym, an in-car exertion game that integrates stop-and-go traffic as a playable input and thus forces the player to maintain situational awareness during autonomous driving. We reported the results from a lab-based simulator study with AutoGym that offer insight on the player experience and the impact on the motivation to engage in contextualized exertion.

We articulated three implementations that are based on generic configurations of the identified experience factors. The broader context of this work is the exploration of non-driving activities for autonomous driving that aims to compensate for this loss of operational control through a meaningful in-car integration.

AutoGym enabled a direct translation of driving dynamics into an interactive exertion experience. This made it suitable for exploring the fertile experiential tensions of the autonomous driving context. The suggested implementation strategies provide a blueprint for future explorations of in-car exertion games. Ultimately, AutoGym shows that even frustrating stop-and-go traffic can be a fun and healthy experience. In that way, we hope to inspire designers to continue exploring exertion as a healthy way to make up for the experiential caveats of autonomous driving.

REFERENCES

1. Melissa Addey. 2016. *Happy Commuter: Over 100 ways to improve and enjoy your commute*. Letterpress Publishing.
2. Virginia Braun and Victoria Clarke. 2006. Using thematic analysis in psychology. *Qualitative research in psychology* 3, 2, 77–101.
3. Nora Broy, Sebastian Goebl, Matheus Hauder, et al. 2011. A cooperative in-car game for heterogeneous players. *Proceedings of the 3rd International Conference on Automotive User Interfaces and Interactive Vehicular Applications - AutomotiveUI '11*, ACM Press, 167. http://doi.org/10.1145/2381416.2381443
4. Martha Davis, Elizabeth Robbins Eshelman, and Matthew McKay. 2008. *The Relaxation and Stress Reduction Workbook*. New Harbinger Publications.
5. Stefan Diewald, Andreas Möller, Luis Roalter, Tobias Stockinger, and Matthias Kranz. 2013. Gameful Design in the Automotive Domain: Review, Outlook and Challenges. *Proceedings of the 5th International Conference on Automotive User Interfaces and Interactive Vehicular Applications*, ACM, 262–265. http://doi.org/10.1145/2516540.2516575
6. Oskar Juhlin. 2010. *Social media on the road: The future of car based computing*. Springer London, London. http://doi.org/10.1007/978-1-84996-332-9

7. Sven Krome, Joshua Batty, Stefan Greuter, and Jussi Holopainen. 2017. Autojam: Exploring interactive music experiences in stop-and-go traffic. *Proceedings of the 2017 Conference on Designing Interactive Systems*, ACM, 441–450.

8. Sven Krome, Steffen P Walz, and Stefan Greuter. 2016. Contextual Inquiry of Future Commuting in Autonomous Cars. *Proceedings of the 2016 CHI Conference Extended Abstracts on Human Factors in Computing Systems*, ACM, 3122–3128.

9. FF Mueller and Stefan Agamanolis. 2009. A framework for exertion interactions over a distance. *Proceedings of the 2009 ACM SIGGRAPH Symposium on Video Games* 1, 212, 143–150.

10. Karin I Proper, Marjan Koning, Allard J Van der Beek, Vincent H Hildebrandt, Ruud J Bosscher, and Willem van Mechelen. 2003. The effectiveness of worksite physical activity programs on physical activity, physical fitness, and health. *Clinical journal of sport medicine* 13, 2, 106–117.

11. Ricarda Rasch and Günther Krusemark. 2006. *Fit im Auto: Übungen im Auto und auf dem Rastplatz; Entspannung, Konzentration, Stressabbau*. AirPlay-Entertainment.

12. Christian Seabaugh. 2012. The Ultimate Hybrid? Custom Cadillac Escalade Comes with Exercise Bike. Retrieved from http://www.automobilemag.com/news/the-ultimate-hybrid-custom-cadillac-escalade-comes-with-exercise-bike-159265/

13. Kennon M Sheldon, Andrew J Elliot, Youngmee Kim, and Tim Kasser. 2001. What Is Satisfying About Satisfying Events ? Testing 10 Candidate Psychological Needs. 80, 2, 325–339. http://doi.org/10.1037//O022-3514.80.2.325

14. Petra Sundström, Axel Baumgartner, Elke Beck, et al. 2014. Gaming to Sit Safe: The Restricted Body as an Integral Part of Gameplay. *Proceedings of the 2014 conference on Designing interactive systems*, ACM, 715–724.

15. Adrian H AH Taylor and Lisa Dorn. 2006. Stress, fatigue, health, and risk of road traffic accidents among professional drivers: the contribution of physical inactivity. *Annual review of public health* 27, 16, 371–91. http://doi.org/10.1146/annurev.publhealth.27.021405.102117

16. Zoë Terken, Roy Haex, Luuk Beursgens, et al. 2013. Unwinding After Work: An In-car Mood Induction System for Semi-autonomous Driving. *Proceedings of the 5th International Conference on Automotive User Interfaces and Interactive Vehicular Applications*, ACM, 246–249. http://doi.org/10.1145/2516540.2516571

17. David Wilfinger, Alexander Meschtscherjakov, Martin Murer, Sebastian Osswald, and Manfred Tscheligi. 2011. Are we there yet? a probing study to inform design for the rear seat of family cars. *Lecture Notes in Computer Science (including subseries Lecture Notes in Artificial Intelligence and Lecture Notes in Bioinformatics)* 6947 LNCS, 657–674. http://doi.org/10.1007/978-3-642-23771-3_48

18. D Yarnell. 2009. *Autometrics: A Complete Manual on How to Workout in Your Car*. CreateSpace Independent Publishing Platform.

19. Oren Zuckerman, Guy Hoffman, and Ayelet Gal-Oz. 2015. In-car game design for children: Promoting interactions inside and outside the car. *International Journal of Child-Computer Interaction.* http://doi.org/10.1016/j.ijcci.2015.03.001

13 Game Lenses for Designing Diverse Interactive Jogging Systems

Florian 'Floyd' Mueller[1], Chek Tien Tan[1,2], Rich Byrne[1], Matt Jones[3]
[1]Exertion Games Lab, RMIT University, Melbourne, Australia
[2] Singapore Institute of Technology, Singapore
[3]Swansea University, Swansea, UK
{floyd, chek, rich}@exertiongameslab.org, always@acm.org

ABSTRACT
HCI is increasingly interested in designing technology for being physically active, and in many cases focuses on jogging. We find that many current approaches seem to view jogging only through a lens of athletic performance. However, jogging is multifaceted, yet there is so far no collated list of alternative lenses through which jogging could be viewed at by designers. In this paper, we draw on game design thinking to articulate 13 lenses through which designers can examine jogging. These 13 lenses are derived from related work and our combined experience of having designed and studied three different jogging systems. The lenses enable a structured articulation of key opportunities that interactive technology offers for jogging designers. With our work, we aim to support designers who want to create diverse interactive jogging systems so that more people can profit from the many benefits of jogging.

Author Keywords
Jogging; running; whole-body interaction; sport; exertion.

ACM Classification Keywords
H5.2. Information Interfaces and presentation (e.g., HCI): User Interfaces.

INTRODUCTION
Jogging – a prevalent sporting activity – has sparked a wide variety of interactive jogging support systems including many mobile apps (e.g. RunKeeper [6], Nike+ [7] and MapMyRun [38]) and also an array of different wearables (e.g. sports watches [64], sensing sport socks [2] and sports smartglasses [30]). Interaction design research also has its fair share of systems exploring how interactive technology can support the jogging experience (e.g. [11, 18, 20, 32, 40, 43, 51, 54, 56, 60, 61, 79, 80, 81]).

Experiential lenses:	
1. The jogger's challenge	How to facilitate a jogging flow?
2. The jogger's play	How to support movement as play?
3. The premise of the jog	How to support the setting of the jog?
4. The jogger's character	Who is the jogger?
5. The story of the jog	How to support the jog as a narrative?
Instrumental lenses:	
6. The social jogger	Who is involved in the jog?
7. The jogger's objective	What is the jogger striving for?
8. The procedure of the jog	What actions are required?
9. The rules of the jog	What actions are allowed?
10. The jogger's resources	What assets can the jogger use?
11. The jogger's conflict	What is in the jogger's way?
12. The boundaries of the jog	Where does the jogging start and end?
13. The outcome of the jog	What is the result of the jog?

Fig. 1. 13 lenses when designing for jogging

We, the authors, have also designed several novel jogging systems and studied them over the years as well as engaged in jogging ourselves (three of us went from no jogging to completing marathons). We decided to come together to collate our experiences and discuss where the field is heading, which was where we found that it appears that many current approaches seem to view jogging only from the perspective of improving athletic performance, i.e. helping joggers to run further and faster. We acknowledge that striving for athletic performance improvement can be a key driver for many joggers, however, jogging is multifaceted [32], and we believe there are many more design lenses through which designers can examine jogging. However, to our knowledge, so far, there does not exist a structured articulation of what these design lenses could be. We believe that such an articulation could enable the beginning of a systematic inventory of the opportunities that interactive technology can offer to joggers, and with our work, we hope to begin such an inventory.

In order to structure such perspectives through which to view jogging, we believe we can learn from game design thinking, as jogging, like most sports, can be regarded as a

CHI PLAY '17, October 15–18, 2017, Amsterdam, Netherlands

ACM ISBN 978-1-4503-4898-0/17/10…$15.00
https://doi.org/10.1145/3116595.3116607

form of play. Inspired by this parallel, we have drawn significantly from game design literature, being especially inspired by its language (such as the labeling of our lenses with game design terminologies like "rules", "challenge", or "objective"), which we appropriate in the articulation of our design lenses. Furthermore, the choice of using lenses was also inspired by game designer Shell [71] who has previously used lenses to articulate how interactive and playful experiences can be viewed from multiple perspectives, which in turn has been used to support designers of these experiences. We therefore believe the jogging community can learn from the CHI PLAY community (and vice versa) when it comes to supporting the playfully active human.

Our aim is to inspire and guide designers to create diverse interactive jogging systems. To achieve this, we present a set of 13 experiential and instrumental lenses through which jogging can be viewed, and place a particular focus on identifying technology opportunities (we present 26 opportunities in total, 2 for each lens). With our lenses, which we created to be readily accessible and actionable for practitioners, we want to help designers think differently about jogging, departing from the prevalent approach that sees exertion only as a mechanical activity for improving physiological functioning; instead, expanding the focus to also consider a set of instrumental and experiential aspects.

Designers can use our lenses as guidance when it comes to creating novel jogging systems to check whether they have considered different aspects of the multifaceted experience that jogging embodies. However, we do not think a system can cover all perspectives, but believe that having a set of perspectives can structure an initial ideation process. Furthermore, we believe our 13 lenses do not represent a complete set that covers every possible jogging support system nor will they accommodate all joggers (for example joggers who do not like using technology), but rather, we see them as a starting point towards future investigations. In particular, we compile knowledge from three future-oriented systems to inform the future of the jogging-technology phenomenon. We believe the 13 lenses could not have been deduced by simply observing a single case study.

Furthermore, we build on our personal jogging experiences from engaging with jogging for over 15 years as well as intimate knowledge of having conducted over half a dozen jogging studies over the years. This includes findings not previously reported in our papers, such as what we learned from pilot studies, early prototypes and failed technology attempts. We also acknowledge that our own jogging experiences might taint our findings with particular jogging preferences. In fact, they offer an intimate account across a range of 4 researchers from 3 countries, all being both joggers and HCI designers. As such, our work echoes HCI trends in autobiographical design [55], designing for movement through moving oneself [27, 39] and autoethnography [63], all of which highlight that bodily experiences are best understood when experienced by oneself, while allowing no information to be lost in communication or interpretation between participant and researcher. Furthermore, autoethnography allows for rapid design iterations that capitalizes on the designer's tacit knowledge which is a key benefit of reflective practice [63].

Our lens development was aided by the authors' prior work with sports scientists, physiologists and related literature. However, we provide a designer's perspective that especially draws from insights gained from the collated design practice. This designer's perspective is grounded in practice-based design research, promoting the diversity of enquiry methods in HCI, and in particular answers calls for more design-led enquiry [25]. Our primary contribution therefore sits in the design research tradition [28] taking the form of 13 guiding lenses and 26 opportunities for the design of future jogging support systems. The paper also introduces previously unpublished jogging work "PaceTunes", thus also offering a system and study contribution.

We believe our findings are timely as there is an increased attention, both commercially and academically, on advances in technology to support jogging. We believe our work can aid the design of a range of technologies to support jogging and other endurance activities, possibly even extending to sports in general [58, 82, 84, 85, 86]. As such, we present knowledge in the design research tradition [28] in the form of 13 experiential and instrumental lenses when designing for jogging. These lenses are derived from an examination of the literature and from practical experiences of having designed and studied three jogging systems.

A note on "jogging"

A distinction can be made between walking, jogging/running and sprinting in terms of biomechanics [37], however differentiating between jogging and running is not so easy. Sometimes jogging is considered a lower speed version of running [26], however, based on our experiences across 3 different cultures (Australia, UK and Germany), it seems that the use is culturally influenced [75]. For the purpose of this paper, we use the word jogging to encapsulate running at a slow pace for a longer period, within an amateur setting (therefore excluding professionals but include enthusiasts who participate in amateur races).

RELATED WORK

Jogging has been examined through particular lenses previously. For example, sports psychology examined jogging through a motivational lens [15, 54]. Prior work has also examined jogging through the experience of *going* jogging [73], taken up in our set of experiential lenses. Designing for jogging can also learn from perspectives of being physically active. For example, several movement-focused research projects [23, 34, 36, 45, 72, 83] highlight the expressive power of bodily movement and its potential

Fig. 2. a) Jogging over a Distance, b) Joggobot & c) PaceTunes

in a public context. These works led us to lenses that consider the larger public space, such as jogging in a park.

Tholander et al. presented an ethnographic study of joggers' use of sports gear and found that joggers embrace the opportunity to engage with technology [76]. Interaction design researchers have therefore developed their own jogging systems; we can differentiate between the following key approaches: instructional technology, gamification and social facilitation. Instructional technology aims to improve a jogger's technique, for example by giving gait feedback through sound [57] (considered under our *procedure* lens). Other research has aimed to gamify jogging, offering virtual worlds to transport joggers into alternative realities [62] (considered under *premise*). Design research has also aimed to support the social aspect of jogging, for example by sharing heart rate data with fellow joggers [41] and audience members [18, 20] (considered under *social*). Unfortunately these distinct lenses rarely cross over, for example, instructional technology systems do not usually consider social support and vice versa. Furthermore, some facets of jogging mentioned in the ethnographic literature (such as the need for replenishing water) have not yet been fully explored by design research (for a starting point see Khot et al. [31]). We see an opportunity to bring the field forward by presenting a collated design-focused articulation of a set of lenses researchers can look through when designing for jogging.

THREE JOGGING SYSTEMS

The three novel jogging systems (the first two have been described previously [47, 49, 52]) all highlighted a different technology, accommodated different jogging contexts with a focus on different social experiences (Fig. 2 a, b, c).

Jogging over a Distance

Jogging over a Distance (JoD) connects two joggers in different geographical locations and with different athletic abilities through the use of heart rate data (Fig. 1a) [46-49]. An initial 18-person study with mono-audio connections [59] and a subsequent 32-person study using stereo audio [47] showed how the system was able to support "social joggers" i.e. people who use exercise to socialize and socialize through the exercise [59]. With JoD, two joggers plan to run at the same time, each equipped with a mobile phone, headphones, microphone and heart rate monitor. Each jogger can hear live audio of their jogging partner while they run. Relative to their target heart rate (which the joggers enter beforehand), the jogger's heart rate affects the audio location in a 2D plane (oriented horizontally around the jogger's head). If the other jogger is "in front", the sound appears to come from the front, and the further "in front", the softer the audio volume. If both joggers perform at their preferred heart rate (or have both slowed at the same percentage from their baseline), they hear the audio right beside them, as if running side-by-side. This way, the jogger is able to detect whether the partner is putting in more, the same, or less "effort" based on relative heart rate.

Joggobot

Joggobot (JBot) is a flying quadcopter that serves as an embodied jogging companion for solo joggers (Fig. 1b). It uses assisted GPS to fly along a fixed path at a speed the user determines beforehand. A study with 13 joggers revealed that participants found jogging with a quadcopter exciting, as Joggobot not only served as pacemaker, but also as an entertaining companion (sensor inaccuracies combined with wind made the quadcopter sometimes appear to have "a mind of its own" [52, 53]). Furthermore, they described the quadcopter as a fellow partner that also invested physical effort since it also made noise and showed signs of exertion, facilitating a sense of connectedness between the jogger and quadcopter.

PaceTunes

PaceTunes (PT) is designed to support joggers who set themselves objectives for their run (e.g. distance runners). In order to achieve such objectives, controlling one's pace is often crucial. PaceTunes aims to support joggers keeping their desired pace by combining the joy of listening to music with the objective of controlling pace (Fig. 1c). The jogger's pace is calculated via GPS and compared to a baseline the jogger can set him/herself. The jogger listens to music which is spatialized similar to the microphone-captured voices in JoD: the music appears to be in front of the jogger if jogging too slow, behind if jogging too fast, or surrounding the jogger when the pace is as desired.

A study with six joggers revealed that all participants could easily detect the music "distance" and were able to use it to pace their jog. Overall, they described the system as useful and intuitive [12]. In particular, the study highlighted how the music was used as a platform for the unfolding story of the jogging experience as participants became fatigued. The study also highlighted that music is not for everyone, for example, it was noted that some joggers preferred "listening" to their own body, e.g. breathing.

Method used in developing the lenses

Based on related work, our own jogging experiences and our collated experiences designing and studying these three systems, we formulated a set of lenses that can be used for designing future jogging systems, which we complemented with easy-to-remember questions designers can ask (Fig. 1).

Our process began by articulating what we have learned and what we thought were missed opportunities. Then we compared our experiences with findings from related work and results from our studies. Subsequently, three of the authors came together into the same location and discussed over the course of two months commonalities and differences of their experiences, which often resulted in heated discussions, as jogging can be a very personal and affective experience (for example, the authors each have very different opinions about which jogging apps they prefer). We then further refined our findings by thinking-through-writing. We discussed our written results and tried to find logical groupings. These groupings formed the basis for our lenses, which we supplemented with opportunities derived from further discussions, iterative articulations, assemblages of our past jogging experiences, design explorations and related work, with a particular focus on what the future may hold for interactive jogging systems.

We believe that jogging designers can learn from game design thinking, hence we also drew from our 15 years of combined experience in teaching game and play design. In particular, as our discussion evolved, we began to notice strong parallels between our central findings and how well they relate to Fullerton et al.'s work, which we used both when naming our lenses and to highlight the instrumental and experiential aspects of play and leisure [24]. Our lenses include a set of questions because we were inspired by the work on designing for movement, where practitioners appreciated an easy-to-remember format that also appeals to industry [50]. We selected lenses that we believe are underexplored and felt that 13 lenses allowed us to reach a natural saturation that is in line with prior work [24] and a suitable number to both capture the necessary principles and remain manageable for implementation within design practice. We suggest to designers to read through all the lenses, but also acknowledge that not all lenses can (or should be) be implemented in a single system.

THE JOGGING LENSES

We present 5 experiential (1-5) and 8 instrumental (6-13) lenses. The experiential lenses are concerned with the visceral aspects that unfold throughout the jogging experience, whereas the instrumental lenses are aimed to provide an underlying structure to support the jog. The experience-focused view on jogging aligns with current popular jogging culture accounts [44] that recommend shifting our perspective of seeing jogging as a task to be accomplished (such as when doctors prescribe physical activity) to seeing jogging as an opportunity to facilitate personal growth [3, 83]. By considering the instrumental lenses, designers can support the "mechanics" of jogging. Therefore the instrumental lenses can be thought of as the "usability" tools in the designer's toolkit, while the experiential lenses are the "experiential" tools.

In each lens below, as well as posing a design inspiring question, we articulate two exemplar key opportunities (labeled "O1" and "O2") interactive technology offers to designers. We complement each lens with an "additional insight" section in order to provide designers with practical suggestions from our work in the field. Where applicable, we also describe next to each heading which of our 3 system's research stage (or combination thereof) the lens relates to most pertinently: the design process (D), the evaluation (E) or post-reflection that included moments such as "we wish we would have considered more of this (lens)" (R).

EXPERIENTIAL LENSES

1. The jogger's challenge — JoD JBot PT
How to facilitate a jogging flow? — D DE E

The jogger's challenge can be thought of as the difficulty of the jog. Most often this challenge is not constant, but rather dynamic, i.e. a jog usually gets increasingly challenging over time. Csikszentmihalyi describes an appropriate level of challenge as one that is "just enough" to require an amount of effort that creates a sense of both accomplishment and enjoyment [17]. Designers have an opportunity to craft the circumstances that lead to the right amount of challenge over the course of the jog in order to facilitate "being in the zone" or "flow" [17, 32].

O1: Managing challenge through sensing bodily responses
The jog gets more challenging as a person's resources diminish; we find that managing this challenge can benefit from tracking these resources. JoD is an example of the opportunity of technology to sense bodily responses (such as heart rate) to facilitate the right amount of challenge: JoD utilized the relative (instead of absolute) heart rate to balance joggers' abilities, which was welcomed by study participants. Faster joggers could run with slower joggers allowing both of them to experience an optimal challenge, facilitating the emergence of flow.

O2: Facilitating challenge by drawing from a history of jogs
When studying PaceTunes, we asked joggers about their past jogs in order to identify a challenging pace that could promote the emergence of flow. Similarly, most mobile jogging apps show how a jogger's pace changes over multiple jogs in order to allow the setting of new goals. Technology supports this facilitation of an optimal challenge through the ability to record and analyze a history of jogs. A current limitation, however, is that there are insufficient analysis models to suggest appropriate future challenges (for example, there is no good algorithm to automatically set a route or pace based on previous jogs, the weather, or how the jogger "feels" before the run).

Additional insight
Our interviews suggest that joggers actively seek the appropriate challenge that puts them into a state of flow, however, getting into this state is not easy. In particular, the beginning of the jog can often be dis-engaging. In response, we point out that challenge changes over time as the jogger experiences fatigue, and designers should therefore consider and take advantage of this inherent dynamic.

2. The jogger's play JoD JBot PT
How to support movement as play? DE E DR
The jogger's play can be thought of as the freedom to act within the structured rules of jogging (see lens 9). This self-regulation [44] presents an opportunity for playful engagement, through highlighting the joy of movement and supporting self-expression through movement.

O1: Highlighting the joy of movement
Our Joggobot study and subsequent experience of exhibiting the device at various venues taught us that technology has the potential to remind people of the "joy of movement" [72]. When people experienced Joggobot for the first time, they often tried a wide range of "feel-good" movements in order to interact with the device. An analogy that highlights this joy of movement is the recent barefoot jogging trend. Although jogging barefoot may appear to be physically risky and hence seen as detrimental to enjoyment, the freedom to move one's toes and feel the terrain is believed to facilitate a richer experience than running with shoes. We agree with Segura et al. that highlighting the joy of movement can be key to supporting being physically active [72].

O2: Supporting self-expression through movement
Jogging can also be supported via the idea of self-expression, where technology can help joggers express themselves through their jogs. For example, we find it intriguing that some joggers use the GPS tracking functionality of their jogging apps to create low-fidelity etch-a-sketch-like drawings using their jogging route, which they then share on social media [21]. Opportunities lie in designing technologies that facilitate the creation of these art forms instead of currently being "user hacks".

Additional insight
One of our JoD participants appropriated the technology to give her remote jogging partner a (verbal) guided tour through the park she was jogging in. This included spotting some horses, to which she enthusiastically ran to in order to describe them over the headphones. It appeared that moving through the park was a form of play for her that she enjoyed sharing with her jogging partner. However, this conflicted with her partner who wanted to treat the jog more "seriously", as she was training for a 10k run. This anecdote exemplifies that designers can engage technology to support the joy of movement, however, they also need to manage any conflict arising from existing objectives joggers (or their partners) might have.

3. The premise of the jog JoD JBot PT
How to support the setting of the jog? ER E R
For most joggers the setting is a park, an urban footpath or a running track. We identify two key ways for how technology can support the setting of the jog: transforming the existing premise or introducing a new premise.

O1: Transforming the existing premise
The introduction of objects that distort the perception of a setting can often transform a premise. Designers can exploit this to offer novel and interesting experiences [69]. For example, the use of a quadcopter transformed the existing premise of a jog in a park into a futuristic scenario: participants told us they felt like they were in a sci-fi movie, promoting the emergence of a jogging fantasy world that they said assisted in motivating them.

O2: Introducing a new premise
Digital games are typical examples of how technology can introduce a new premise, often putting the player in alternate universes via visuals and sounds. Similar opportunities exist for jogging designers. Park et al. [61] and Campbell et al. [13] both demonstrated how joggers can be introduced a new alternate premise through virtual worlds. Consolvo et al. [16] introduced a virtual flower garden to nurture by means of physical activity, while Lin et al. [35] provided virtual fish as a way to introduce an aquarium as a new premise. Commercially, Pokémon Go introduced a world full of Pokémon to catch.

Additional insight
We see great potential for technology to engage with premise when designing for jogging. However, we also note that the original premise (the setting of the actual jog)

should remain part of the experience, even if only for the purpose of safety: for example, a VR headset might introduce a highly immersive new premise, however, could be outright dangerous for urban joggers.

4. The jogger's character — Who is the jogger?

JoD JBot PT
DR ER R

The jogger's character refers to the embodied being within the technology-supported jogging experience. Technology can support the development of existing characters, allowing participants to take on various roles as seen in role-playing games [24], but also introduce new characters.

O1: Developing the existing character

In the GoodGym project [5] the existing character is quite cunningly developed: joggers are paired with isolated elderly people, where the jogger commits to jog by regularly delivering small items such as milk. The GoodGym website uses character development quite cleverly: it addresses the jogger as "the athlete" and the elderly as "the coach" (rather than simply as "the delivery person" and "the elderly") to engage both users tightly into the GoodGym experience.

O2: Introducing a new character

Joggobot is one example of how technology can introduce a new character. It presented a quadcopter as an embodied jogging companion, sometimes resulting in the joggers affectionately naming their quadcopter and assigning it a gender ("*She* made me work hard today"). This is in stark contrast with interactions joggers usually have with most other jogging systems, such as jogging apps.

Additional insight

By addressing the participant as "the jogger" (rather than "the user"), jogging systems can contribute positively to character development that follows a trajectory from "going jogging" to "becoming a jogger". However, challenges can arise when developing a fictitious character as there is potential that participants might transfer fantasy abilities to their own abilities and overestimate them, leading to over-exertion and injury. Designers should therefore develop the character (and associated fictitious abilities) in conjunction with joggers' existing and improving abilities.

5. The story of the jog — How to support the jog as a narrative?

JoD JBot PT
DE ER D

By supporting the jog as a narrative, designers are reminded that a key characteristic of the jog is that the jogger can ask "what happens next if I ...?" [70]. As such, the jogging experience can be articulated as a story that is filled with uncertainty, and as a consequence, it motivates people to participate in order to address this uncertainty [33].

O1: Introducing a new interactive story

We believe the idea of a story offers opportunities to use technology to transform an "ordinary" jog into a "dramatic" experience. One of the few examples that uses this is "Run, Zombies!" [4], which audibly depicts an apocalyptic world infested by zombies. Slowly unfolding the audio story allows a jogger to become engrossed in that alternate universe. In the "I Seek the Nerves Under Your Skin" project the system plays a poem to its end only if participants keep running [40]. Similarly, PaceTunes introduced a new "story" in the form of an MP3 song, where the participants needed to keep running in order to hear the entire song. We can envision future systems where the run and the story are even more tightly linked, for example where changes in jogging direction affect how the story unfolds, similar to the "Choose Your Own Adventure" novels from the 1980s.

O2: Highlighting the existing story of the jog to support storytelling

Jogging systems such as those by Garmin highlight the existing story of the jog: they make GPS and heart rate data available online after the jog, allowing for storytelling around the jog. Many joggers share this data with jogging community websites and articulate their associated experience in a story-like format, for example the following "jogging story" is supplemented with location, pace, elevation and heart rate data: "This was by far my toughest run in a long time. The run was going swell into [sic] I turned the corner to head west, straight into 30-40mph wind gusts. The eighth mile was probably the slowest and most excruciating 7:42 I've ever ran..." [1].

Additional insight

We found "Zombies, Run!" helped us turn our monotone jogs into interval training by making us repeatedly intersperse short sprints in order to escape the zombies. As such, the system reframed the jogging activity through the means of the narrative.

INSTRUMENTAL LENSES

We now articulate the 8 instrumental lenses.

6. The social jogger — Who is involved in the jog?

JoD JBot PT
DE DER DER

Jogging is often a solo activity, but it is also undertaken with friends, in a jogging group or with complete strangers (e.g. during a race). Furthermore, joggers share their paths with others (often non-joggers). Joggers also often plan their jogs with others both on- and offline regarding where and when to jog. In this sense jogging is a social activity even when a jogger jogs alone. Considering this social aspect can be key in motivating exercise [42]. We therefore suggest that designers ask: "Who is involved in the jog?"

O1: Supporting jogger-jogger and jogger-spectator relationships across distance and time during the jog

JoD demonstrated that technology can enhance the jogging experience by connecting joggers in geographically distant locations (jogger-jogger), while the Nike+ system [7] connects joggers across time by enabling comparisons asynchronously. As such, technology offers an opportunity to support the social jogger across both distance and time. Furthermore, Joggobot participants noted how their jog was affected when by-standers commented on the quadcopter (jogger-spectator). We therefore highlight the opportunity to use technology to incorporate spectators (as with most interactive experiences [65]); for inspiration see the work that relays a jogger's heart rate to remote audience members [19]. Most current jogging apps support jogger-jogger and jogger-spectator relationships, focusing on relationships *after* the jog. In contrast, we highlight an opportunity to also support the jogger *during* the run.

O2: Balancing different jogging abilities
One key hindrance for people to join their jogging friends can be their different fitness levels [47, 59]. Technology can offer an opportunity to balance joggers of different abilities by a) either connecting them while jogging at different speeds (like in JoD) or b) altering the effort required for one of the joggers (for example by using an exoskeleton that gives a jogger a physical "boost").

Additional insight
We have found that in general joggers welcome technology that enables them to embrace jogging as a social experience (i.e. JoD and Joggobot). In particular, we found that joggers appreciate technology that allows them to be in control of the extent to which they engage socially, rather than prescribe the social interaction [49], especially as social interaction becomes more difficult with increasing fatigue.

7. The jogger's objective — What is the jogger striving for?

JoD JBot PT D ER DR

This lens highlights what the jogger is striving for. Sports science has previously identified health and fitness, well-being, athletic challenge and social reasons as common objectives [15] with more recent research [32] highlighting that joggers often have more than one objective. Therefore it can be necessary to consider multiple objectives, including in-the-moment objectives concerned with the immediate jog as well as across multiple jogs.

O1: Introducing new objectives
Technology can facilitate the introduction of new objective(s). For example, both JoD and PaceTunes introduced the new objective of regulating heart rate and pace to maintain virtual audio locations. Participants indicated that these new objectives offered opportunities for engagement, thus reducing the monotony that can sometimes occur when jogging.

O2: Divide and conquer
It has been previously argued that dividing larger objectives into smaller ones can help users achieve their objectives [66], including in exertion activities [9]. Technology can help joggers achieve their larger objective by dividing it as well, as in PaceTunes, where the system allowed joggers to increase the target pace between runs in small increments in order to achieve their overall target pace.

Additional insight
JoD showed that joggers can welcome the introduction of new objectives, such as maintaining a partner's relative pace [46]. However, our study also highlighted that participants' personal jogging objective (such as jogging for a specific duration) could clash with a newly introduced objective, such as when the jogging partner did not want to jog for the same duration. This conflict could have been managed by matching up participants with similar goals. Similar to guideline 3 in the work by Knaving et al. [32], we make designers aware that they should consider any existing objectives before introducing new ones while managing any conflict that may arise.

8. The procedure of the jog — What actions are required to achieve the objective?

JoD JBot PT DR ER DR

The procedure of the jog consists of the sequence of actions required by the jogger to achieve his/her objective(s). Designers should ask how they could support the jogger in achieving his/her objective through specific actions, in particular the "ongoing action" and the "special action".

O1: Ongoing action
We refer to the action of putting one foot in front of the other as the predominant ongoing action and highlight the opportunity of technology to support this, for example by providing guidance on running technique through sonification [10, 57]. In order to support this ongoing action most systems require a "starting" and "resolving" action such as a button-press that turns the system on and off respectively. For example, PaceTunes participants had to take the device out of their pocket and press the start button when they began their jog. They also had to press a button when the jog was complete. As designers we need to be aware that "in the wild" [67] a jogger's ongoing action is not necessarily always clearly encapsulated by an obvious start and finish. With PaceTunes issues arose when participants had to pause at a traffic light: the joggers did not know if they should pause the system and how this would affect their target pace. The Strava app addresses this by automatically pausing after a few seconds of inactivity. Therefore we highlight the opportunity to utilize starting and resolving actions to support the ongoing action.

O2: Special action
With the introduction of technology, "special actions" become important. A "special action" refers to any action external to the core mechanic of jogging. One example is raising the wrist to check one's heart rate on a sports watch. Another example is from an early version of JoD where the balancing functionality that triggered the audio spatialization had to be manually activated. This special action disturbed the core jogging mechanic, and hence in the subsequent version, activation was made automatic.

Additional insight
Designers can use special actions to create new jogging experiences, for example Park et al.'s work required joggers to flail their arms during their jogs to control virtual characters [62]. Knaving et al. [32] recommended that designers minimize the use of special actions that could interfere with the ongoing jogging action, otherwise joggers

might perceive the activity as "not jogging anymore" and rather see it as a new activity (e.g. an upper arm workout).

9. The rules of the jog
What actions are allowed?

JoD JBot PT
D ER E

The rules of the jog define allowable actions for the jogger. A typical rule for many joggers is to not stop running, even when it gets very challenging to do so. The jogger voluntarily adheres to the rules [74], as this can facilitate a strive for competence [66]. We identify two key technology opportunities when it comes to rules: technology can a) help enforce existing rules and b) enable new rules.

O1: Enforcing rules

In professional running competitions judges enforce the rules, however, casual joggers are often their own enforcers. Technology can help here: for example, the Runkeeper app has a virtual trainer that enforces the rules, i.e. the distance is non-editable. It also has a mode where the jogger can specify his/her own rules, i.e. set a target time, and the tracking system enforces these user-set rules.

O2: Enabling new rules

With technology, designers can consider enabling new rules. For example, PaceTunes prescribed that participants had to jog outdoors due to the system's dependence on GPS. Participants willingly adhered to this new rule as the system awarded them with a novel jogging experience, however, designers need to be aware that new rules might be perceived as restricting, contrasting the rather "open" nature of jogging (compared to most other sports activities that have plenty of rules, e.g. basketball).

Additional insight

With PaceTunes, we found that the new rule of having to jog outdoors led to an emergence of play around the GPS's limitations: participants tried to jog under trees to explore the limitations of the system, and how the music would be affected. This phenomenon of exploring sensing "seams" (i.e. the borderline between where sensing works and where it does not) and its positive effects on user experiences has been previously articulated [14], and we highlight the opportunity to facilitate this by enabling new "seams".

10. The jogger's resources
What assets can the jogger use to accomplish the objective?

JoD JBot PT
DE R DER

The jogger's resources are assets that the jogger can use towards accomplishing his/her objective(s). The main internal resource is the finite amount of stamina that the jogger has in order to complete the run. External resources include a sports drink or a downhill section of the running course. Technology offers unique opportunities to manage internal resources and to introduce new external resources.

O1: Managing internal resources

Although humans have a good sense of what tiredness feels like, joggers often want more precision on the limit of their internal resources. Systems can measure them (e.g. biofeedback) while allowing joggers to compare them with others' and their own prior data. For example the JoD heart rate data gave joggers an indication of internal resources.

O2: Introducing new external resources

Prior jogging support systems have shown that technology offers the opportunity to introduce new external resources, for example GPS jogging watches provide navigational information [43] for joggers to regulate their jogging routes. Another example is the "power-song" resource by the Nike+ app where the jogger can press a button to play a motivational song to gain a psychological boost.

Additional insight

We highlight that resources should have real utility, i.e. they need to be useful for the jogger to achieve the objective. For example, we find virtual resources, such as the health packs in "Zombies, Run!" [78], can fall short when it comes to utility as they often focus on providing utility in a virtual world which may or may not match up with any jogging objective in the physical world.

11. The jogger's conflict
What is in the jogger's way?

JoD JBot PT
DER E DER

Conflicts are obstacles that prevent the jogger from accomplishing his/her objective(s). Research on motivation has previously examined obstacles that prevent people from engaging in jogging [42]. These obstacles are mostly seen from a health intervention perspective and are therefore considered negative, however, flow theory reminds us that obstacles are not necessarily always negative, and can in fact contribute to a sense of challenge that is key to attaining a positive flow experience [17]. These obstacles can be categorized as both internal and external.

O1: Internal obstacles

In our studies, the participants sometimes experienced a form of obstacle internal to their bodies, such as stitches, mental fatigue or cramps. Technology offers an opportunity to highlight the range of possible internal obstacles that might occur and thereby help participants cope with them. For example, we can envision sensing systems enhanced with machine learning algorithms that could predict cramps. We noticed during testing JoD that the technology amplified breathing difficulties. Participants said they used the amplified breathing noise of their partner (the microphone was close to their mouths) to assess when their partner was exhausted and as a consequence slowed down.

O2: External obstacles

This concerns obstacles which are external to the jogger's body. An example is the physical jogging environment that could include cars (on the road) or bicycles (on jogging paths), causing the jogger to slow. This external obstacle became particularly pertinent in PaceTunes, where pausing due to traffic was conflicting with the system asking for a consistent pace. Technology can highlight these external obstacles, or implement ways around them. For example, we can envision a future version of PaceTunes that suggests alternative jogging paths with fewer cars, using a combination of GPS and traffic data. Alternatively, the jogger could be encouraged to slow down, such as in Monster and Gold [11], by introducing virtual monsters as external obstacles the jogger is encouraged to avoid.

Additional insight

One of our JoD participants almost could not participate on the day of our study due to an injury that restricted him from jogging. However, since he was able to use a bicycle we were able to test the design on the bicycle instead. We did not consider this in our initial design, but in hindsight, could have exploited the opportunity to support multiple sports activities thanks to the use of heart rate as the input mechanism, hence reframing the obstacle.

12. The boundaries of the jog Where and when does the jogging start and end?

JoD JBot PT
ER ER DE

The boundaries of the jog are what separate the jogging activity from "everything else", both pragmatically and conceptually. This highlights boundary aspects such as whether a jogging system should also include any stretching exercises, or whether running to catch a bus could be sensed as part of the training regime. Conceptually, the start and end of a jog can be seen as play boundaries that demarcate the "magic circle" [70]. Designers can utilize technology to either highlight or blur these boundaries.

O1: Highlighting boundaries

In PaceTunes, the music demarcated when the jog "was happening", essentially highlighting via audio the magic circle. Similarly the raising and lowering of the Joggobot suggested when the jogging activity was about to begin and end, communicating it clearly not only to the jogger, but also to bystanders.

O2: Blurring boundaries

Joggobot interviews suggested that technology could also blur these boundaries. Participants expressed that they would like to take Joggobot home after the jog, so that the quadcopter would hover near their door when identifying opportune times for jogging. Some commercial systems similarly blur the boundary of the jog: they not only analyze the jogging activity but also the jogger's sleep patterns, suggesting that a good jogging session begins with a good night's sleep.

Additional insight

We found that for many joggers, jogging is a way of life that extends beyond the jogging track. To support this, joggers can now use a range of devices to monitor other aspects of their life to identify opportunities that will support their jogging activities (what food to eat, how long to sleep, etc.). We find that incorporating such devices to encompass wider boundaries is an interesting way forward, especially how to make sense of the devices' data in a way that is meaningful to the jogger.

13. The outcome of the jog What is the result of the jog?

JoD JBot PT
DE E DER

A typical outcome of a jog is the successful completion of a route, but it can also be an enhanced mood. We believe technology can support the outcome of a jog in two key ways: by articulating outcomes and by quantifying them.

O1: Articulating outcomes

Joggobot interviews revealed that participants appreciated when the battery of the quadcopter went dead, as it communicated to them that the quadcopter was "tired", and that it was therefore just as acceptable for them to also be tired. We can see this as an example of the quadcopter as a human training analogue, where the trainer explicitly gives their permission for the jogger to rest. On the other hand, joggers may perceive the robot as a "buddy" and feel that when the quadcopter is tired, they too are free to admit they are also tired, and thus exhaustion becomes an acceptable outcome of a jog.

O2: Quantifying outcomes

Many mobile jogging apps and wearables (e.g. MapMyRun, Fitbit devices [22]) allow joggers to log quantified outcomes like distance and step count, therefore facilitating awareness of quantified physical activity outcomes [68]. Interviews with JoD participants revealed that the joggers wanted to know what their heart rate was during the run. While the system did not reveal this data, in a future version of the system we could make this data available.

Additional insight

Our findings suggest that it is important to contextualize outcomes, for example, jogging apps can connect to digital scales, articulating the outcome of the jog in weight loss. However, since jogging and weight loss have a complex relationship, it is important to inform joggers what the newly articulated and quantified outcomes can mean.

TEMPORAL ASPECTS

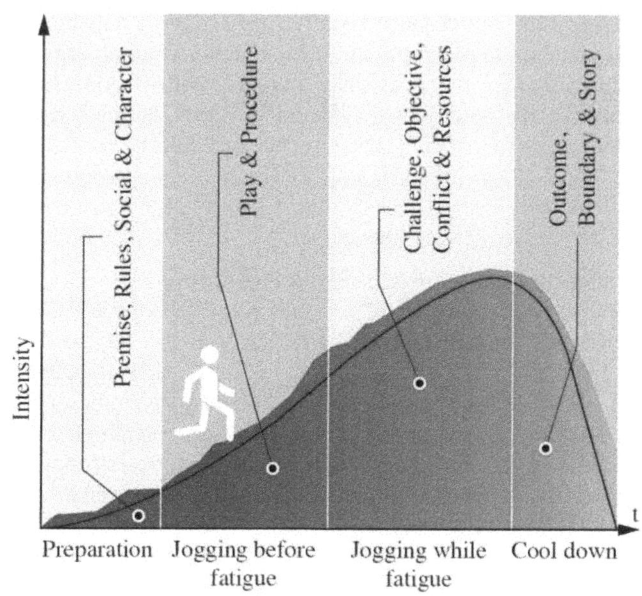

Fig. 3. The lenses across time

The jogging experience often changes significantly over time: in the beginning of a session, jogging is mostly easy, but at the end, it can be very difficult. In response, we now extend our 13 lenses across a time-based structure, inspired by previous work around time-based structures for embodied interactions [8][29].

We focus on the following key stages of the jog: preparation, jogging before fatigue, jogging while fatigue, and cool down. We acknowledge that these stages could be further categorized (such as distinguishing between different heart rate zones), however, leave this for future work. Furthermore, we confine our discussion so that each lens is covered just once in the entire jog (Fig. 3).

Premise, Rules, Social & Character

The lenses "premise", "rules", "social" and "character" can be applied particularly in the preparation stage, the period right before the actual jogging activity. Establishing how to support the setting of the jog (*premise*) can contribute towards the jogger's initial motivation. For example, an app could make the jogger aware of a more scenic route in a nearby park rather than using the road. The app could also stress what actions are allowed (*rules*), such as staying within a certain heart rate zone. Furthermore, the system could involve other *social* actors, such as avatars of professional athletes that demonstrate stretching exercises, fostering the development of the jogger seeing him/herself as a "world-class athlete" *character* in response to the question "Who is the jogger?"

Play & Procedure

The lenses "play" and "procedure" can be applied particularly in the stage before fatigue kicks in. Joggers have a big opportunity to experience movement as *play* while they are not yet exhausted. Technology can highlight opportunities for play, for example by allowing joggers to "create" music through mapping running actions to sounds. Asking what actions are required (*procedure*) can inspire designers to think about how to support a good jogging technique e.g. by providing joggers with feedback to minimize their vertical displacement. Such motor-sensory feedback systems [77] seem to be particularly useful for this stage, as the jogger is not yet at a high exhaustion level and can therefore process cognitive information more easily when compared to the next stage.

Challenge, Objective, Conflict & Resources

The lenses "challenge", "objective", "conflict" and "resources" can be applied particularly in the stage where fatigue kicks in. Entering the "flow zone" is likely during this stage, so designers should consider how technology can ensure joggers are neither over- or under-*challenged*; for example, by measuring fatigue indicators, or introducing additional *objectives* that the jogger can strive for. Technology could predict through advanced sensors what is in the jogger's way (*conflict*) in the form of potential injury, warning the jogger. Lastly, designers might want to ask what assets the jogger can use (*resources*), for example to make the jogger aware of any water fountains nearby.

Outcome, Boundary & Story

The lenses "outcome", "boundary" and "story" can be applied particularly in the "cool down" stage after completing the jogging action. Designers could think about how the result of the jog is presented (*outcome*), for example, an outcome could be the average pace. By looking at where the jogging starts and ends (*boundaries*), designers can identify opportunities to incorporate benefits of the jog into other, everyday activities. For example, a system could identify the geographical location where the jog concluded to suggest activities after the run such as a recovery treatment nearby. By considering the jog as a narrative (*story*), designers could think about how they conclude the experience and transition it to the next jog.

LIMITATIONS

We acknowledge that our work only tangentially considers specific forms of running such as long-distance and cross-country. Nevertheless, as we see our work as a starting point towards further investigations into other sports, we believe our lenses still have strong utility. Furthermore, as this work focuses on the jogging activity itself, we only indirectly address any activities in-between jogging (e.g. strength training, injury rehabilitation, or negotiations with family members about how much time is available for jogging). Opportunities for exploration in regards to this have been highlighted elsewhere [32, 76], nevertheless we hope our lenses could be extended to incorporate such aspects in future work. Lastly, although some of our joggers jogged multiple times [47], many of our personal insights are based on single exposures of our systems; we acknowledge that additional and longer term engagements could reveal further insights.

CONCLUSIONS

In sum, our work contributes to the emerging area of designing for technology-supported jogging as made popular by recent mobile and wearable technology trends. Based on related work, our own jogging experiences and having designed, built and studied three jogging systems, we present a set of 13 lenses designers could examine jogging through when designing technology to support it. The strength of our work lies in its practical design focus, articulating the first structured understanding of 26 opportunities for jogging designers. With this work we aim to aid designers in creating novel and diverse systems that support joggers. In consequence, we hope jogging participation increases, and ultimately, more people profit from the many benefits of jogging.

ACKNOWLEDGEMENTS

We thank everyone who has helped with this work in one form or another, especially everyone who jogged with us. Thanks also to Stefan Agamanolis, Martin Gibbs, Frank Vetere and Jennifer Sheridan. Florian 'Floyd' Mueller thanks the Australian Research Council (DP110101304).

REFERENCES

1. Dailymile. Retrieved January 10, 2017 from http://www.dailymile.com/people/Jzelm9/entries/13139370.
2. Sensoria Fitness. Retrieved January 10, 2017 from http://www.sensoriafitness.com/.
3. Florian Mueller and Sarah Jane Pell. 2016. Technology Meets Adventure: Learnings from an Earthquake-Interrupted Mt. Everest Expedition. In *Proceedings of the Joint Conference on Pervasive and Ubiquitous Computing*. ACM, 2971683, 817-828. http://dx.doi.org/10.1145/2971648.2971683
4. Zombies, Run! Retrieved January 10, 2017 from http://www.zombiesrungame.com.
5. Goodgym. Retrieved January 10, 2017 from http://www.goodgym.org/.
6. Runkeeper. Retrieved January 10, 2017 from http://runkeeper.com.
7. Apple. Apple - Nike + Ipod. Retrieved January 10, 2010 from http://www.apple.com/ipod/nike.
8. Steve Benford, Gabriella Giannachi, Boriana Koleva and Tom Rodden. 2009. From Interaction to Trajectories: Designing Coherent Journeys through User Experiences. In *Proceedings of the Conference on Human factors in computing systems*. ACM, 1709-718. http://doi.acm.org/10.1145/1518701.1518812
9. Ian Bogost. 2005. The Rhetoric of Exergaming. In *Proceedings of Digital Arts and Cultures (DAC) Conference*.
10. Jordi Bolíbar and Roberto Bresin. Sound Feedback for the Optimization of Performance in Running. *SMC Sweden 2012 Sound and Music Computing, Understanding and Practicing in Sweden* (2012), 39.
11. Fabio Buttussi and Luca Chittaro. Smarter Phones for Healthier Lifestyles: An Adaptive Fitness Game. *IEEE Pervasive Computing* 9, 4 (2010), 51–57. http://dx.doi.org/doi:10.1109/MPRV.2010.52
12. Richard Byrne. Adapting Running Pace with Music. Unpublished thesis, 2008.
13. Taj Campbell, Brian Ngo and James Fogarty. 2008. Game Design Principles in Everyday Fitness Applications. In *Proceedings of the Conference on Computer supported cooperative work*. ACM, 249-252.
14. Matthew Chalmers, Marek Bell, Barry Brown, Malcolm Hall, Scott Sherwood and Paul Tennent. 2005. Gaming on the Edge: Using Seams in Ubicomp Games. In *Proceedings of the Conference on Advances in computer entertainment technology*. ACM, 306-309. http://dx.doi.org/10.1145/1178477.1178533
15. Peter J Clough, John Shepherd and Ronald Maughan. Motives for Participation in Recreational Running. *Journal of Leisure Research* (1989).
16. Sunny Consolvo, David W. McDonald, Tammy Toscos, Mike Y. Chen, Jon Froehlich, Beverly Harrison, Predrag Klasnja, Anthony LaMarca, Louis LeGrand, Ryan Libby, Ian Smith and James A. Landay. 2008. Activity Sensing in the Wild: A Field Trial of Ubifit Garden. In *Proceedings of the SIGCHI Conference on Human Factors in Computing Systems*. ACM, 1357335, 1797-1806. http://dx.doi.org/10.1145/1357054.1357335
17. Mihaly Csikszentmihalyi. *Flow: The Psychology of Optimal Performance*. New York: Harper and Row, 1990.
18. Franco Curmi, Maria Angela Ferrario, Jen Southern and Jon Whittle. 2013. Heartlink: Open Broadcast of Live Biometric Data to Social Networks. In *Proceedings of the SIGCHI conference on Human Factors in computing systems*. ACM, 1749-1758. http://dx.doi.org/10.1145/2470654.2466231
19. Franco Curmi, Maria Angela Ferrario and Jon Whittle. 2014. Bioshare: A Research Tool for Analyzing Social Networks Effects When Sharing Biometric Data. In *Proceedings of the 2014 companion publication on Designing interactive systems*. ACM, 101-104. http://dx.doi.org/10.1145/2598784.2602793
20. Franco Curmi, Maria Angela Ferrario, Jon Whittle and Florian Mueller. 2015. Crowdsourcing Synchronous Spectator Support: (Go on, Go on, You're the Best)^{N-1}. In *Proceedings of the Conference on Human Factors in Computing Systems*. ACM, 757-766. http://dx.doi.org/10.1145/2702123.2702338
21. EJ Dickson. 2014. Woman Uses Nike+ App to Draw Penises All over San Francisco. Retrieved January 10, 2017 from http://www.dailydot.com/lol/nike-plus-penis-drawing/.
22. Fitbit. 2012. Retrieved January 10, 2017 from Fitbit. http://fitbit.com.
23. Maiken Hillerup Fogtmann, Jonas Fritsch and Karen Johanne Kortbek. 2008. Kinesthetic Interaction - Revealing the Bodily Potential in Interaction Design. In *Proceedings of OZCHI '08: Conference of the computer-human interaction special interest group (CHISIG) of Australia on Computer-Human Interaction*. ACM.
24. Tracy Fullerton, Christopher Swain and Steven Hoffman. *Game Design Workshop*. Morgan Kaufmann, 2004.

25. William Gaver. 2012. What Should We Expect from Research through Design? In *Proceedings of the SIGCHI Conference on Human Factors in Computing Systems*. ACM, 937-946. http://dx.doi.org/10.1145/2207676.2208538

26. Marnix GJ Gazendam and At L Hof. Averaged Emg Profiles in Jogging and Running at Different Speeds. *Gait & posture* 25, 4 (2007), 604-614.

27. Kristina Höök, Martin Jonsson, Anna Ståhl and Johanna Mercurio. 2016. Somaesthetic Appreciation Design. In *Proceedings of the Conference on Human Factors in Computing Systems (CHI'16), San Jose, CA, USA*.

28. Kristina Höök and Jonas Löwgren. Strong Concepts: Intermediate-Level Knowledge in Interaction Design Research. *ACM Trans. Comput.-Hum. Interact.* 19, 3 (2012), 1-18. http://dx.doi.org/10.1145/2362364.2362371

29. Amy Huggard, Anushka De Mel, Jayden Garner, Cagdas Chad Toprak, Alan D Chatham and Florian Mueller. 2013. Understanding a Socially Awkward Digital Play Journey. In *Proceedings of DiGRA 2013*. ACM.

30. Recon Instruments. 2015. Recon. Retrieved January 10, 2015 from reconinstruments.com.

31. Rohit Khot, Jeewon Lee, Larissa Hjort, Deepti Aggarwal and Florian Mueller. 2015. Tastybeats: Designing Palatable Representations of Physical Activity. In *Proceedings of the Conference on Human Factors in computing systems*. ACM. 2933-2942. http://dx.doi.org/10.1145/2702123.2702197

32. Kristina Knaving, Pawel Wozniak, Morten Fjeld and Staffan Bjork. 2015. Flow Is Not Enough: Understanding the Needs of Advanced Amateur Runners to Design Motivation Technology. In *Proceedings of the Conference on Human Factors in Computing Systems*. ACM, 2013-2022. http://dx.doi.org/10.1145/2702123.2702542

33. R. Scott Kretchmar. *Practical Philosophy of Sport and Physical Activity*. Human Kinetics Publishers (Champaign, IL, USA), 2005.

34. Astrid Larssen, Lian Loke, Tony Robertson, Jenny Edwards. 2004. Understanding Movement as Input for Interaction–a Study of Two Eyetoy Games. In *Proceedings of OzCHI '04*.

35. James Lin, Lena Mamykina, Silvia Lindtner, Gregory Delajoux and Henry Strub. 2006. Fish'n'steps: Encouraging Physical Activity with an Interactive Computer Game. In *Proceedings of UbiComp 2006: Ubiquitous Computing*. 261-278.

36. Lian Loke, Astrid Larssen, Toni Robertson and Jenny Edwards. Understanding Movement for Interaction Design: Frameworks and Approaches. *Personal and Ubiquitous Computing* 11, 8 Special Issue Movement-Based Interaction (2007), 691-701.

37. Roger A Mann and John Hagy. Biomechanics of Walking, Running, and Sprinting. *The American Journal of Sports Medicine* 8, 5 (1980), 345-350.

38. mapmyrun.com. 2010. Mapmyrun. Retrieved January 10, 2017 from http://www.mapmyrun.com/.

39. Elena Márquez Segura, Laia Turmo Vidal, Asreen Rostami and Annika Waern. Year. Embodied Sketching. In *Proceedings of the 2016 CHI Conference on Human Factors in Computing Systems*. ACM, 6014-6027.

40. Joe Marshall and Steve Benford. 2011. Using Fast Interaction to Create Intense Experiences. In *Proceedings of the Conference on Human factors in computing systems*. ACM, 1255-1264. http://dx.doi.org/10.1145/1978942.1979129

41. Matthew Mauriello, Michael Gubbels and Jon E Froehlich. 2014. Social Fabric Fitness: The Design and Evaluation of Wearable E-Textile Displays to Support Group Running. In *Proceedings of the Conference on Human Factors in Computing Systems*. ACM, 2833-2842.

42. Mary McElroy. *Resistance to Exercise: A Social Analysis of Inactivity*. Human Kinetics Publishers (Champaign, IL, USA), 2002.

43. David K McGookin and Stephen A Brewster. 2013. Investigating and Supporting Undirected Navigation for Runners. In *Proceedings of CHI'13 Extended Abstracts on Human Factors in Computing Systems*. ACM, 1395-1400.

44. Stu Mittleman and Katherine Callan. *Slow Burn: Burn Fat Faster by Exercising Slower*. HarperCollins, 2001.

45. Jin Moen. Kinaesthetic Movement Interaction: Designing for the Pleasure of Motion. Unpublished PhD thesis, Stockholm: KTH, 2006.

46. Florian Mueller, Shannon O'Brien and Alex Thorogood. 2007. Jogging over a Distance: Supporting a "Jogging Together" Experience Although Being Apart. In *Proceedings of CHI '07: Conference on Human Factors in Computing Systems*. ACM, 2579 - 2584.

47. Florian Mueller, Frank Vetere, Martin Gibbs, Darren Edge, Stefan Agamanolis, Jeniffer Sheridan and Jeffrey Heer. 2012. Balancing Exertion Experiences. In *Proceedings of SIGCHI Conference on Human Factors in Computing Systems*. ACM, 1853-1862.

48. Florian Mueller, Frank Vetere, Martin Gibbs, Stefan Agamanolis and Jennifer Sheridan. 2010. Jogging over a Distance: The Influence of Design in Parallel Exertion Games. In *Proceedings of Sandbox '10: the 5th ACM SIGGRAPH Symposium on Video Games*. ACM, 63-68.

49. Florian Mueller, Frank Vetere, Martin Gibbs, Darren Edge, Stefan Agamanolis and Jennifer Sheridan. 2010. Jogging over a Distance between Europe and Australia. In *Proceedings of the symposium on User interface software and technology*. ACM, 189-198. http://dx.doi.org/10.1145/1866029.1866062

50. Florian Mueller and Katherine Isbister. 2014. Movement-Based Game Guidelines. In *Proceedings of the SIGCHI Conference on Human Factors in Computing Systems*. ACM, 2191-2200. http://dx.doi.org/10.1145/2556288.2557163

51. Florian Mueller, Joe Marshall, Rohit Ashok Khot, Stina Nylander and Jakob Tholander. 2014. Jogging with Technology: Interaction Design Supporting Sport Activities. In *Proceedings of the extended abstracts of the ACM conference on Human factors in computing systems*. ACM, 1131-1134. http://dx.doi.org/10.1145/2559206.2559209

52. Florian Mueller and Matthew Muirhead. 2015. Jogging with a Quadcopter. In *Proceedings of the 33rd Annual ACM Conference on Human Factors in Computing Systems*. ACM, 2023-2032. http://dx.doi.org/10.1145/2702123.2702472

53. Florian Mueller and Matthew Muirhead. 2014. Understanding the Design of a Flying Jogging Companion. In *Proceedings of the adjunct publication of the 27th annual ACM symposium on User interface software and technology*. ACM, 2658786, 81-82. http://dx.doi.org/10.1145/2658779.2658786.

54. Lama Nachman, Amit Baxi, Sangeeta Bhattacharya, Vivek Darera, Piyush Deshpande, Nagaraju Kodalapura, Vincent Mageshkumar, Satish Rath, Junaith Shahabdeen and Raviraja Acharya. 2010. Jog Falls: A Pervasive Healthcare Platform for Diabetes Management. In *Proceedings of Pervasive Computing*. Springer, 94-111.

55. Carman Neustaedter and Phoebe Sengers. Autobiographical Design: What You Can Learn from Designing for Yourself. *interactions* 19, 6 (2012), 28-33.

56. Shahriar Nirjon, Robert F Dickerson, Qiang Li, Philip Asare, John A Stankovic, Dezhi Hong, Ben Zhang, Xiaofan Jiang, Guobin Shen and Feng Zhao. 2012. Musicalheart: A Hearty Way of Listening to Music. In *Proceedings of the 10th ACM Conference on Embedded Network Sensor Systems*. ACM, 43-56.

57. Stina Nylander, Mattias Jacobsson and Jakob Tholander. 2014. Runright: Real-Time Visual and Audio Feedback on Running. In *Proceedings of CHI '14 Extended Abstracts on Human Factors in Computing Systems*. ACM, 583-586. http://dx.doi.org/10.1145/2559206.2574806

58. Stina Nylander, Jakob Tholander, Florian Mueller and Joe Marshall. 2014. Hci and Sports. In *Proceedings of CHI '14 Extended Abstracts on Human Factors in Computing Systems*. ACM, 2559223, 115-118. http://dx.doi.org/10.1145/2559206.2559223

59. Shannon O'Brien and Florian Mueller. 2007. Jogging the Distance. In *Proceedings of the SIGCHI conference on Human Factors in computing systems*. ACM, 523-526.

60. Nuria Oliver and Fernando Flores-Mangas. 2006. Mptrain: A Mobile, Music and Physiology-Based Personal Trainer. In *Proceedings of the 8th conference on Human-computer interaction with mobile devices and services*. ACM, 21-28. http://dx.doi.org/10.1145/1152215.1152221

61. Taiwoo Park, Uichin Lee, Bupjae Lee, Haechan Lee, Sanghun Son, Seokyoung Song and Junehwa Song. 2013. Exersync: Facilitating Interpersonal Synchrony in Social Exergames. In *Proceedings of the 2013 conference on Computer supported cooperative work*. ACM, 409-422.

62. Taiwoo Park, Chungkuk Yoo, Sungwon Peter Choe, Byunglim Park and Junehwa Song. 2012. Transforming Solitary Exercises into Social Exergames. In *Proceedings of the ACM 2012 conference on Computer Supported Cooperative Work*. ACM, 863-866. http://dx.doi.org/10.1145/2145204.2145332

63. Sebastiaan Pijnappel and Florian Mueller. Year. 4 Design Themes for Skateboarding. In *Proceedings of the SIGCHI conference on Human Factors in computing systems*. ACM, 1271-1274.

64. Polar. 2015. Polar. Retrieved January 10, 2015 from polar.com.

65. Stuart Reeves, Steve Benford, Claire O'Malley and Mike Fraser. 2005. Designing the Spectator Experience. In *Proceedings of the SIGCHI Conference on Human Factors in Computing Systems*. ACM, 1055074, 741-750. http://dx.doi.org/10.1145/1054972.1055074.

66. Scott Rigby and Richard Ryan. *Glued to Games: How Video Games Draw Us in and Hold Us Spellbound*. Praeger, 2011.

67. Yvonne Rogers. Interaction Design Gone Wild: Striving for Wild Theory. *interactions* 18, 4 (2011), 58-62. http://dx.doi.org/10.1145/1978822.1978834

68. Brenda Rooney, Kathy Smalley, Jennifer Larson and Sarah Havens. Is Knowing Enough? Increasing Physical Activity by Wearing a Pedometer. *WMJ-MADISON-* 102, 4 (2003), 31-36.

69. Daniela K. Rosner, Hidekazu Saegusa, Jeremy Friedland and Allison Chambliss. 2015. Walking by Drawing. In *Proceedings of the 33rd Annual ACM Conference on Human Factors in Computing Systems*. ACM, 2702467, 397-406. http://dx.doi.org/10.1145/2702123.2702467

70. Katie Salen and Eric Zimmerman. *Rules of Play: Game Design Fundamentals*. The MIT Press (Boston, MA, USA), 2003.

71. Jesse Schell. *The Art of Game Design: A Book of Lenses*. Morgan Kaufmann, 2008.

72. Elena Marquez Segura, Annika Waern, Jin Moen and Carolina Johansson. 2013. The Design Space of Body Games: Technological, Physical, and Social Design. In *Proceedings of the SIGCHI conference on Human Factors in computing systems*. ACM, 3365-3374. http://dx.doi.org/10.1145/2470654.2466461

73. Richard Shipway and Immy Holloway. Running Free: Embracing a Healthy Lifestyle through Distance Running. *Perspectives in public health* 130, 6 (2010), 270-276.

74. Bernard Suits. *The Grasshopper: Games, Life and Utopia*. Broadview Press, 2005.

75. Jonh R. Taylor. On Running and Jogging. *Cognitive Linguistics (includes Cognitive Linguistic Bibliography)* 7, 1 (1996), 21. http://dx.doi.org/10.1515/cogl.1996.7.1.21

76. Jakob Tholander and Stina Nylander. 2015. Snot, Sweat, Pain, Mud, and Snow: Performance and Experience in the Use of Sports Watches. In *Proceedings of the 33rd Annual ACM Conference on Human Factors in Computing Systems*. ACM, 2913-2922.

77. Jelle van Dijk, Remko van der Lugt and Caroline Hummels. 2014. Beyond Distributed Representation: Embodied Cognition Design Supporting Socio-Sensorimotor Couplings. In *Proceedings of the 8th International Conference on Tangible, Embedded and Embodied Interaction*. ACM, 181-188.

78. Emma Witkowski. 2013. Running from Zombies. In *Proceedings of The 9th Australasian Conference on Interactive Entertainment: Matters of Life and Death*. ACM.

79. Pawel Wozniak, Kristina Knaving, Staffan Bjork and Morten Fjeld. 2015. Rufus: Remote Supporter Feedback for Long-Distance Runners. In *Proceedings of the Conference on Human-Computer Interaction with Mobile Devices and Services*. ACM, 115-124. http://dx.doi.org/10.1145/2785830.2785893

80. Mahmoud Hassan, Florian Daiber, Frederik Wiehr, Felix Kosmalla, Antonio Krueger. Footstriker: An Ems-Based Foot Strike Assistant for Running. *Proc. ACM Interact. Mob. Wearable Ubiquitous Technol.* 1, 1 (2017), 1-18. http://dx.doi.org/10.1145/3053332

81. Chek Tien Tan, Richard Byrne, Simon Lui, Weilong Liu and Florian Mueller. 2015. Joggar: A Mixed-Modality Ar Approach for Technology-Augmented Jogging. In *Proceedings of SIGGRAPH Asia 2015 Mobile Graphics and Interactive Applications*. ACM, 2818434, 1-1. http://dx.doi.org/10.1145/2818427.2818434

82. Florian Mueller, Darren Edge, Frank Vetere, Martin Gibbs, Stefan. Agamanolis, Bert Bongers and Jennifer Sheridan. 2011. Designing Sports: A Framework for Exertion Games. In *Proceedings of the Conference on Human Factors in Computing Systems*. ACM, 2651-2660.

83. Florian Mueller and Damon Young. 2017. Five Lenses for Designing Exertion Experiences. In *Proceedings of the 2017 CHI Conference on Human Factors in Computing Systems*. ACM, 3025746, 2473-2487. http://dx.doi.org/10.1145/3025453.3025746

84. Florian Mueller, Joe Marshall, Rohit Ashok Khot, Stina Nylander and Jakob Tholander. 2015. Understanding Sports-HCI by Going Jogging at Chi. In *Proceedings of the 33rd Annual ACM Conference Extended Abstracts on Human Factors in Computing Systems*. ACM, 2727688, 869-872. http://dx.doi.org/10.1145/2702613.2727688

85. Florian Mueller, Joe Marshall, Rohit Ashok Khot, Stina Nylander and Jakob Tholander. 2016. Jogging at CHI. In *Proceedings of the 2016 CHI Conference Extended Abstracts on Human Factors in Computing Systems*. ACM, 1119-1122.

86. Florian Mueller. Digital Sport: Merging Gaming with Sports to Enhance Physical Activities Such as Jogging. In *Digital Sport for Performance Enhancement and Competitive Evolution: Intelligent Gaming Technologies*, 2009, 150-166.

Lessons From Designing a Game to Support Playfulness in Multisensory Stimulation Environments

Nuno Castelhano
Department of Informatics Engineering,
University of Coimbra, Portugal
nscc@dei.uc.pt

Licínio Roque
Department of Informatics Engineering,
University of Coimbra, Portugal
lir@dei.uc.pt

ABSTRACT

We report on the design research process of a game as experimental model to support a ludic context between an occupational therapist and a child with intellectual disability. Having a multisensory stimulation environment as context for integration, the prototype was tested with eleven children playing it for the first time. Test results were coded as time-based events taking place during the play sessions, from which the ability of the participants to use and control the game became evident. The content analysis of the video recordings accounts for gameplay instances that show the adequacy of the designed solution in mobilizing playfulness, and describes a ludic context marked by abundant child-therapist verbal and non-verbal interactions. Authors draw lessons from this process to the design of games to support playfulness in such contexts: provide a context for player-therapist interaction, empower body as interface, enable flexibility of performance, coordinate multisensory stimulus, provide ludic cues, enable personalization of presence.

Author Keywords

Multisensory Stimulation Environments; Videogame design; Playfulness; Intellectual disability.

ACM Classification Keywords

C.3 SPECIAL-PURPOSE AND APPLICATION-BASED SYSTEMS - Real-time and embedded systems; K.4.2 Social Issues - Assistive technologies for persons with disabilities; K.8.0 General Games

INTRODUCTION

This work presents the test results of the "Malha" videogame, designed for integration in multisensory stimulation environments, as mediator for therapy, delivered as educational support, with children with intellectual disability.

CHI PLAY '17, October 15–18, 2017, Amsterdam, Netherlands

ACM ISBN 978-1-4503-4898-0/17/10…$15.00
https://doi.org/10.1145/3116595.3116599

Multisensory stimulation environments, also known as Snoezelen rooms, are now a common resource in organizations delivering services to persons with disability. Originally created to allow moments of relaxation and stimulation to persons with severe disabilities through contact and control of the sensory environment [21], they are now used and tested with diverse populations and with different objectives, *e.g.* people with dementia [12,25,40,47], in palliative day care [4] or for chronic pain management [36], alongside with interventions in the area of disability [20,30], that focus not only in health, but also in educational purposes, supporting personal development [8,37].

These rooms are characterized as spaces in which sensory stimulation can be controlled and fit to the needs of the users. This is accomplished through numerous devices that allow visual, auditory, tactile or olfactory experiences.

The idea to design a videogame for this context, having children with intellectual disability as target population, stems not only in its compatible properties for sensory stimulation, as artefact, but mainly to use it as a mediator agent of playfulness. By mobilizing playfulness skills, other therapy purposes might be followed on that base, having the multisensory environment as an operational context, alternative from commonly used spaces.

This opportunity is particularly relevant to the domain of Occupational Therapy in which child play is recognized as a twofold area for intervention, whether to act upon those competences, whether as means to achieve other objectives [23,38]. In any case, the adequate interaction between therapist and the child is a key element to succeed, considering that the expectancy to deal with client engagement in this relation falls directly into the competences of the therapist [10].

In this article we start by briefly reviewing our research approach and the design guidelines that inspired and oriented the prototype development. The following sections describe the conditions in which the prototype play tests were prepared and conducted. The results presented are time-logged events emerging from the test sessions, further analyzed and discussed to argue about the competence of the designed solution, in creating and maintaining a rich ludic context between child and therapist.

OUR RESEARCH APPROACH

Context and motivation

The domain and process of occupational therapy encompasses the very large spectrum of human activity, from which the areas of occupation, client factors, performance skills, performance patterns, context and environment, and activity demands, are considered to support engagement in participation and health [1].

Children with intellectual disability are considered as a target population for the intervention of occupational therapy, mostly because of expected limitations in their opportunities for participation, due to reduced cognitive and social skills [22]. Intellectual disability is a term commonly associated with a health and development condition that results in a human performance below the average, causing a disturbed functionality in two or more areas of adaptive behaviour, like self-care, learning, communication and others [43]. As diverse and particular as they may be, the needs of children with intellectual disability and the expectations of their parents or representatives, concern the domain and process of occupational therapy.

Play is highlighted as one area in which participation is a recognized limitation for the personal development of a child with intellectual disability, in the matters of social interaction, of opportunities for play and exploration, and of personal mobility [16,32]. In this line of thought, the skills related with play may be the priority for the intervention delivered by the occupational therapist. His/her role in the success of the therapeutic relation is, obviously, determinant, and several authors refer the importance of a full commitment, allied with personal development and reflective practice [10,13,15,34]. In fact, with regards to the intervention with children with intellectual disability, providing for challenge and purposeful context, to foster motivation and participation, is paramount for the therapist.

This is where the search for appropriate resources gains relevance. We have been following a socio-cultural approach and qualitative methods to understand the use and potential of multisensory stimulation environments, concerning the integration of the computer-mediated ludic activity as a facilitator for occupational therapy intervention. In our research we have found that multisensory stimulation rooms are considered as play-friendly contexts, and from that perspective, powerful intervention allies for occupational therapists [9].

Multisensory stimulation environments, and Snoezelen rooms in particular, originated in the late 70's, in the Netherlands, to serve as a value activity context to persons with severe disabilities. In our days they can be found mostly in organizations delivering services to persons with disability, in hospitals, schools, or even in residential homes. In all cases, they might be used for leisure, therapy or educational purposes - a popularity exceedingly supported by an idea of innovation and of positive impacts for everyone using it [46]. Of course, the indisputable success of multisensory stimulation rooms contrasts with what is actually safe to say about their use, in regards to scientific knowledge. The efficacy of the original Snoezelen intervention as therapy is still to be sufficiently supported by evidence [3,19,26,27].

The field of Human Computer Interaction is inspiring the development of multisensory stimulation environments. Several projects and experiences are expanding their usefulness for disability, for example, engaging social interaction of children with autism spectrum disorder [4], enhancing sensory experience of children with profound developmental disabilities [7], or exploring new interaction possibilities with smart objects [14,48].

If we go back to the original idea, however, we find that the room is merely meant to be explored and enjoyed, with no focus on therapy [21]; therefore, there is a relevant difference in using the room as intervention therapy, from using it as support for a therapeutic relation. From our point of view, these rooms should be considered, for their special characteristics, as desirable places to deliver play intervention, and not as a treatment, or an intervention *per se*.

A Model for Playfulness

From the scientific area of occupational therapy emerged a model conceptualizing child playfulness, considering it as an observable and measurable behaviour. As proposed by Bundy [5], playfulness is bounded to a mutual act of interpretation of ludic cues between actors; a contextual frame in which verbal and non-verbal cues intend to communicate how one wants to be treated and to proceed in the play interaction. This interaction of ludic cues enclosures the presence (or absence) of actions related to three constructive dimensions: perception of control, source of motivation and freedom to suspend reality. As tentatively presented in Figure 1, playfulness is more likely present in a ludic interaction, as much as evidences of internal control, intrinsic motivation and freedom to suspend reality are perceived in that context of child activity.

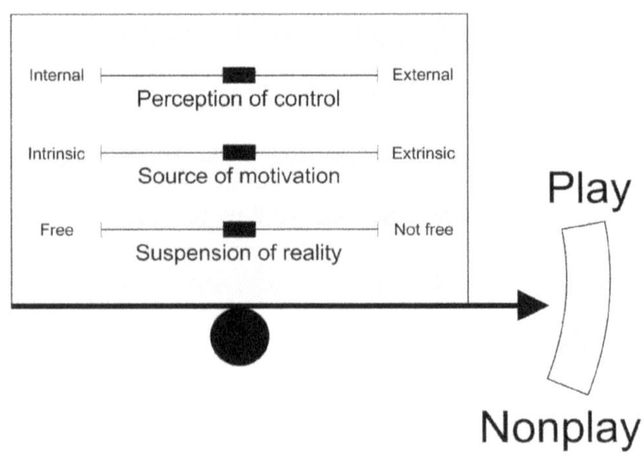

Figure 1: Bundy's model of playfulness [5].

Bundy also developed an evaluation protocol, called the Test of Playfulness, to be used as an assessment tool of child play. This test has been studied for psychometric properties [6,17], revealing its reliability and validity, and used to study how engaging in virtual play impacts children's playfulness [41].

A DESIGN RESEARCH EXERCISE

Awareness of Problem

Exploring multisensory environments as contexts for play can have a valuable contribution to play therapy, *e.g,* in dealing with developmental cases. Considering the multisensory room as a resource and also that it allows the child for an alternative context of exploration and play, here we aim to study how a videogame designed with specific characteristics might act as mediator for playfulness. In addition, we intend to find out which aspects would make it more supportive of playfulness in children with disability, which could inform the design guidelines.

To pursue this agenda, we envisioned a Design Research exercise that involves the following steps:

a) Recognizing a problem here formulated as designing a game to be used in multisensory stimulation environments, that could foster playfulness as a basis for developmental intervention with intellectually challenged children;

b) Elaborating a design proposal that takes into account guidelines for aspects of an activity that can contribute to a playful attitude in children;

c) Developing a proof of concept prototype for such a game design proposal;

d) Evaluate the emergent gameplay in a manner that enables identification of when and how playfulness was effectively being supported, through coding and content analysis of video registers of gameplay;

All things considered, this project was thought to be an empirical contribution to add knowledge about the use of multisensory stimulation environments by occupational therapists, with children with intellectual disability, privileging a videogame as mediator. To that end we reflected on its functionality and main characteristics.

Design Proposal and Rationale

Literature is copious about accessibility in videogame design, presenting useful knowledge, for example, in the shape of design guidelines [2,31] or as design patterns [11].

The following design guidelines were proposed as comprehensive orienting features to shape a game that would respond to the brief of supporting playfulness in the context of the multisensory environments while ensuring adaptation to the target audience.

- *Empower body as interface*

Our first concern was about aligning skill in manipulation of devices, usually necessary to play videogames, with the expected difficulties of the players with reduced fine motor control. This was addressed by anticipating that all actions necessary to play the game would result entirely from mapping body movement through sensor technology.

- *Enable flexibility of performance*

In regards to assist player performance, we recognized the importance of including some degree of flexibility in body movement recognition, to tolerate for involuntary movements, and assist internal perception of control.

- *Coordination of multisensory stimuli*

Another concern was how sensory stimulation could be achieved, especially how visual and auditory elements in the game could act upon fun and playfulness. Internal perception of control and intrinsic motivation could be enhanced by offering continuous gratification of body movement and encouragement during the play experience.

- *Offer Ludic Cues*

Besides the playful opportunity offered through responsive representations, the design includes some stimulus features reserved for the key moments in the gameplay (scoring, winning) to act as reinforcements of experimentation, and would also to allow the exploration of *ludic cues* as invitations or provocations for the playful interaction.

- *Personalization of presence*

Another important feature considered was allowing for meaningful player choice. The design would cater to the importance of empowering the child, and to grant opportunity for the personalization of presence in the game.

We found these guidelines closely connected to Hernandez *et al* [18] broad recommendations to address the potential limitations of our target audience. Although referring to the design of action videogames for children with cerebral palsy, their general advice is to keep things as simple as possible, for example by reducing the need of timed actions and the consequences of errors, by limiting available actions and compensating for differences in motor skills.

Inspiration for the design

A popular Portuguese traditional game, called "Malha" provided the inspiration for the prototype. This game has very simple rules. It is played in teams of two players that, in turns, will try to hit a small object located at a throwing distance. This object is a wooden or metal obelisk-shaped solid figure, called the "pino". The players use a set of hand-sized flattened iron or stone discs (the "malha") as throwing objects, weighing between 200gr and 500gr each. Every throw aiming for the target will hit or miss, but also marks a position status of proximity towards the target. Each team will score points by overturning the target or by placing the closest "malha" to the target, after each round. Victory is achieved by accumulating points in respect to a predetermined goal.

Most of the characteristics of the original game were transposed to our digital design; however, to expand on playfulness, we added fantasy elements, via representational and behavioural aspects on the virtual "malhas" and "pinos". The designed "Malha" videogame is a duel of skilfulness between two players that, in turns, will throw the "malha" (the rounded object), to try and hit the obelisk shape object (the "pino").

In our prototype, each player can embody his own "malha" after the throw and during flight, by exercising a limited degree of control of flight direction. While one player controls the "malha", the other player takes over the "pino", exercising lateral position control in defensive movements, escaping the "malha" direction. These movements are accompanied by booing and cheering sound expressions; a final "dance of victory", accompanied with graphic fireworks was also included.

Developing the Game as Proof of Concept Prototype

As previously said, our prototype is an elaboration over the traditional "Malha" game. The game was developed in Unity 3D to use a combination of short throw projector and Microsoft Kinect 2 sensor as part of its interface. Two players can play it side by side, facing a wall-size projected image. All game controls are enabled through interpreting player body movement.

Throws are recognized by the sensor as forward movements of one arm, facing the projection. This is considered an adequate gesture to reproduce an object throw in Kinect based games [44]. Tilt movements of the upper-body are monitored in both players for orientation of the "malha" flight and the "pino" defensive movements. All navigation is made through tilt movements, for browsing, and with the forward movement of the right arm for selections.

As depicted in Figure 2, navigation allows a quick play, with randomly selected elements, or the choice menu in which players can select representational features for the "malhas", or power-ups that condition their behaviour (like light/heavier "malhas", for faster or slower flights). Two scenario themes are also available for staging the duel: winter or spring scenarios.

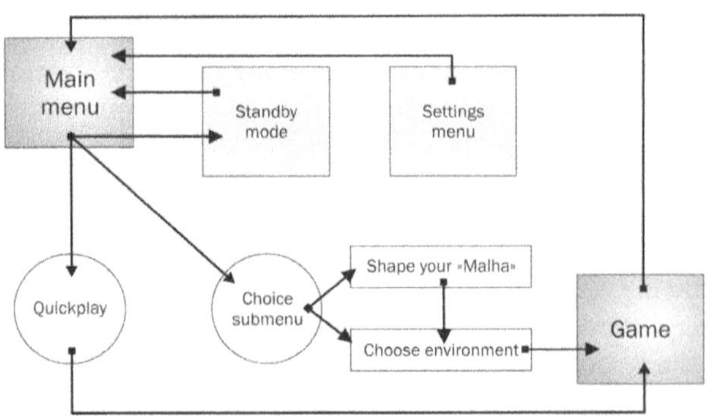

Figure 2: Navigation options across the game interface

After the initial tests of game interface sensitivity, we noticed it was quite hard to use Kinect to drive game components, therefore we decided to include some tolerance of body movements and adjust target detection range to make targets reasonably easier to hit. These assistive features were included in the programming code.

Figure 3: Video screenshots from recordings of the "Malha" game

Figure 4: Video screenshot of the "malha" before hitting the "pino"

Figures 3 and 4 present two video screenshots of the game environment. In the upper left and right corners are the scores for each player. In the centre, a right arm holding a "malha" ready to throw, towards the "pino", the small object in the centre. The player silhouettes are also visible in the lower corners. Choice of left/right was not yet fitted at this time, but would be a requirement for a larger audience. Figure 4 presents a moment when the "malha" hits the "pino".

PLAY TESTING SESSIONS AND EVALUATION

Testing Scenario and Population

Three organizations delivering occupational therapy support to children with intellectual disability were involved. They were asked to allow the use of their multisensory stimulation environments, with the participation of their therapists. A group of six interested therapists was gathered from these contacts, five occupational therapists (presented in Table 1 as OT) and one speech therapist (presented in Table 1 as ST).

The convenience criteria used for the selection of the participant group of children were the following: age between 5 and 11 years old, baseline communication skills and personal movement control, and the circumstance of receiving any sort of therapeutic support, complementary to school curricula, by any of the participant therapists.

The legal representatives of the suggested children were contacted to obtain an informed consent term, explaining how the test sessions were to happen, and how the wellbeing of the child would be preserved. A group of eleven children participated, with a profile as described in Table 1.

Child #	Age	Sex	Diagnosis	Therapist
1	10	F	CP	OT 1
2	10	F	CP	OT 1
3	7	M	CP	OT 1
4	10	F	ID	OT 2
5	10	M	ADHD	OT 3
6	8	M	ASD	OT 2
7	5	M	ASD	OT 4
8	9	F	ASD	ST
9	9	F	ASD	ST
10	10	M	US	OT 4
11	9	F	ID	OT 5

Table 1: Characterization of the participant children

Four children in this group had a diagnosis of Autism Spectrum Disorder (#6-9). Three of Cerebral Palsy (#1-3), all with difficulties with balance and one that depended on product support for daily mobility. Two of the children had a diagnosis of intellectual disability (#4, #11), one of attention deficit hyperactivity disorder (#5). One had an undiagnosed syndrome, causing a moderate delay in intellectual and motor development (#10). All children were receiving individually planned occupational therapy support, mostly aiming for the improvement of social competences and for intellectual stimulation, as complement to school curricular activities.

Data collection procedures

Two multisensory stimulation environments were used; both typical Snoezelen rooms. All sessions were recorded in video by two cameras simultaneously, one focusing on the players interactions and the other, the videogame projection on the wall.

The video footage of each session was fully edited into a single movie, synchronizing both cameras on screen, to allow a structured observation of events. Prior to the test sessions, therapists were instructed about the game functionality, in particular about the necessary movements to control the game. They proposed the play activity to the children, and respected their eventual refusal in playing the game. Session data was captured after some initial quick play for players to get comfortable with the technology.

Data analysis method

The method used for data analysis was based on the detailed observation and coding of the video recordings with two main purposes: a) to gather information about how the players played the game, in regards to ability and control over actions; b) to look into the resulting ludic context for understanding the operative agency of this particular videogame, as mediator for playfulness.

We followed separately content analysis and thematic analysis procedures in this matter, as suggested in the literature [42], which resulted in a timesheet log for each test session. The time position for the events was registered for session number, minute and second when each event is visible in the footage.

A first chronological map was started with task and time performance, as adequately suggested for usability tests in HCI [29], by gathering events directly related to how the players played the game. This major content set was called "Gameplay Instances". A base log was previously created with the following categories of events, registered as described:

- Start: the moment when the game starts.
- Throw: when one of the players executes a throwing movement.
- Drive: when one of the players controls the correspondent in game avatar (*i.e.* the "malha's" flight, or the "pino's" dodging).
- Golden Goal: when the "malha" hits the "pino".
- Control Lost: when sensor failed to recognize the player.
- Final: the moment when the game ends.

In a second observation of the same data, the throwing movements and avatar drives were coded according to perceived intentionality, *i.e.* the cases when players intentionally tried to control avatars as instructed, as opposed to erratic movements.

A separate set of time-event data was coded through thematic analysis, for the verbal and non-verbal communication of the players. This set of data was organized in subjective categories, by open coding method, according to the apparent intention of the player, or the suggested meaning of the message to the researchers.

Observer agreement [33] was globally performed between authors as a reliability method, both for the validation of the coding scheme used in the content analysis, related to gameplay instances, and for the thematic analysis of verbal communication. In this process, a preliminary event log produced by the first author was presented to the second. Consensus was achieved on conflicting or unclear logged events into the final events log for each test session.

A complementary session analysis was also conducted, in which we aimed for a third-party evaluation of the play sessions, resorting to a translated version of the "Test of Playfulness". For this matter we asked four of the participant therapists to score the children's playfulness through the footage observation. This task was prepared in a way that the available therapists would not evaluate their own sessions.

RESULTS AND ANALYSYS

Regarding to the technical performance of the hardware and software, the game worked as expected in both environments. Some issues with navigation and choice in character configuration were registered in the test sessions in room 2. We found that initial character and environment choice were not intentional, but accidental, in the majority of cases. This caused some difficulties in the initial identification of the correct character by the players, but did not influence the rest of the game once resolved.

Control was momentarily lost in three occasions in sessions 1 and 10, when sensor failed to recognize the player. This was caused by the seated position of the child while playing the game. The game was repeated in sessions 1, 2 and 5, as requested by the child, therefore the quantity of registered instances is superior for these cases. The average length of the play sessions was measured in 4':01" (s.d. of 00':43").

Gameplay instances

Figure 5 presents the timelines for logged events in each session related to child control of the game. The following categories of data are presented left to right: moments when control was lost; moments when the "malha" is pitched; moments directly related to control of game avatars (*i.e.* the "malha" flight and the "pino" dodging movements), and finally, moments when golden goal is achieved.

Concerning the classification of the "malha" throws, two types were observed: intentional and accidental. In the first case, the player intentionally moved as required to perform the "malha" throw. The second case logged moments when unintentional movements were recognized by the hardware, therefore resulting in unexpected throws.

Regarding to the avatar control instances, three types were observed: a deliberate and intentional drive, when the child actually performs the movement towards avatar control, as opposing to a erratic and tentative driving movements (both about the "Malha" flight and the "Pino" dodge movements); a total absence of control effort was also logged in sessions 10, 7 and 2 (presented as No drive).

A first analysis of Figure 5 shows the greater amount of instances reflecting the ability of the child to interact and play the game (Intentional Throw and Consequent drive), as opposed to the antagonist events (Accidental throw, Erratic drive and No drive). In sessions 3, 4 and 5 the game was played almost without any control problems. The total percentage of adequate movements was calculated in 77% for throws and in 71% for avatar control. The golden goal was achieved by the child in 8 of the 11 sessions.

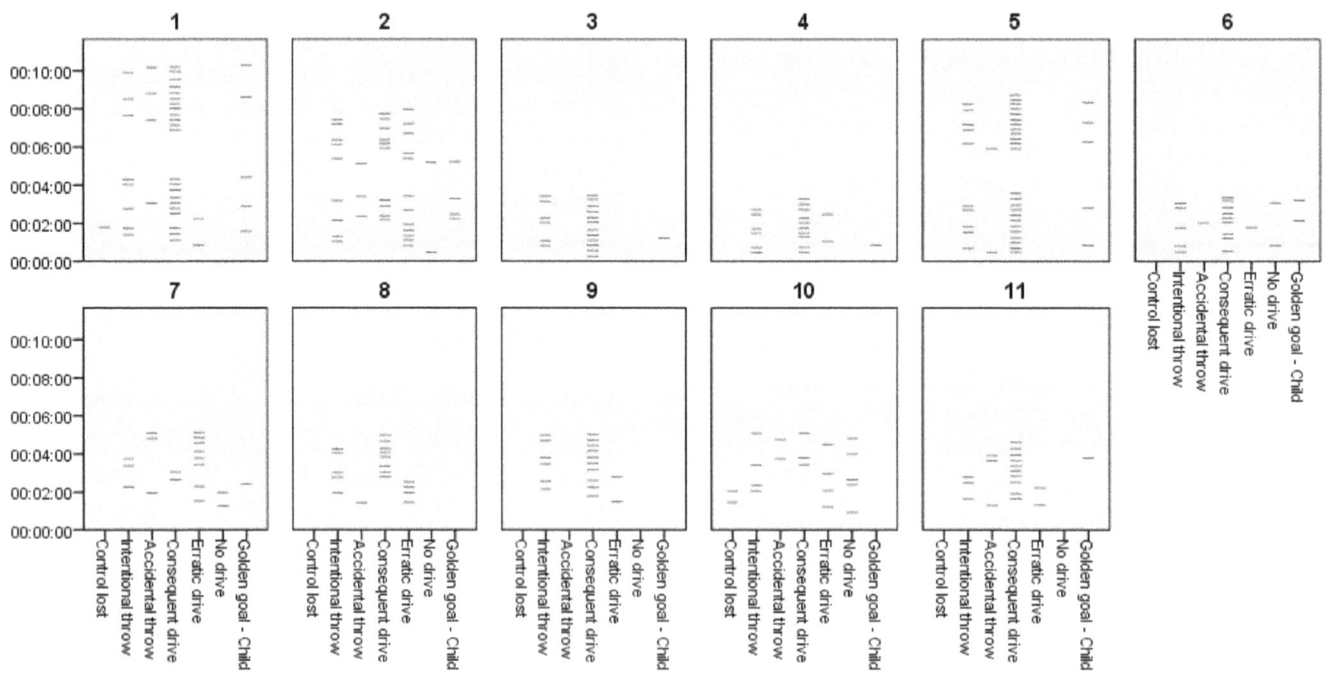

Figure 5: Session timelines of gameplay instances related to child control

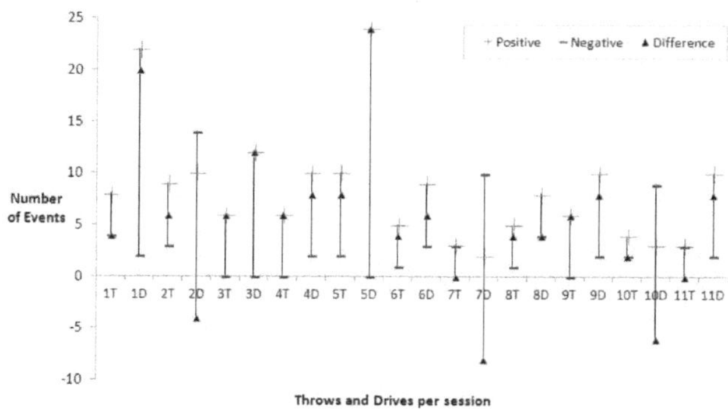

Figure 6: Balance between adequate and inadequate movements

Figure 6 presents a frequency difference between throws (T) and drives (D) considered adequate (+) and inadequate movements (-), as a presumed indicator for game control. This graphic allows a comparative view of how the game was controlled by the participant children; to some extent, apart from child 7 and 10, all were able to exercise a fair amount of control of actions, both in throws and drives.

Gameplay interactions

A second set of data was gathered from logging verbal and non-verbal interactions between child and therapist within sessions, considered as representations of participation in a ludic context for its enclosed descriptive potential.

Child interaction events

The registered child interactions were organized in various categories. In general this set of data supports the idea that they were interested in the activity, and that their participation is marked by moments of joy, fun and curiosity. Table 2 shows eight categories of content divided in verbal (V) and non-verbal (NV) events.

In the most representative category are logged moments in which the child clearly manifested fun, as depicted in the following examples: *"(NV) screams of excitement, after launch, while the malha flies to the pino."* (S2, 00'32"); *"(V) You are the red one! You are the red one!"* (S4, 00'32"); *"(NV) Reacts as if he took the hit, retreating unsteadily"* (S5, 08'54").

From this category we separated moments of evident satisfaction for being able to control the game characters, which happened in the majority of the test sessions (except for sessions 3 and 10): *"(NV) Arms up and jump to fall on his knees in sign of victory. (V) This is cool..."* (S5, 5'19"); *"(V) I did it! (NV) Tcham, tcham! (Success dodging)" (S2, 1'45"); (NV) Claps and vertically swings arms in sign of victory*" (S1, 8'38").

Along with these two categories, the events classified as signs of adherence and acceptance of the ludic context, are also found relevant. The following examples account for moments when the child shows the will to persist in the proposed activity: *"(NV) Claps hands in content."* (S3, 1'15"); *"(NV) Looks at OT and smiles back."* (S4, 3'26"); *"(NV) Dances to the music, always checking the projection."* (S7, 05'36").

Moments of frustration and disappointment where also present in the majority of sessions (except for session 4 and with greater frequency in session 2). The logged events in this category gather the negative reactions resulting of gameplay, for example when failing to hit the "pino", as depicted in the following events: *"(NV) Lets body slide down the chair. Laughs slightly, because he was close to hit the pino."* (S3, 00'55"); *"(NV) Throws himself on the mattress after fail."* (S5, 7'02"); *"(V) Move! (to the malha in projection)"* (S7, 3'26").

C.#	T.#	Joy		Acceptance		Disappoint		Gloat/Mock		Fun		Expectancy		Curiosity		Observation		Σ
		v	nv	v	nv	v	nv	v	Nv	v	nv	v	nv	v	nv	v	nv	
1		1	3	1	2	1	1	1		1	5		5					21
2	OT1	6	3	3	4	3	10		5	2	3		1					40
3					3		1				3		1		1			9
4	OT2	1	1		2					1	3		1		1			10
5	OT3	1	6	2	2		1	5		3	8	1		2	1	2		34
6	OT2	2	1			2			1	1	2		2	1	1			13
7	OT4	1		4	1	5				2				3				16
8	ST	1		2			1				1		1					6
9		1		2		5	1		1			1						11
10	OT4			5	1	1				1	6		1	1		2		18
11	OT5		2	3		2			1	1		1				1		11
Total		14	16	22	15	19	15	6	8	12	31	3	12	7	4	5		189

Table 2: Frequency instances of gameplay interactions by the participant children, organized by category themes

Mocking about the adversary performance was also registered as a category of relevant events (with major frequency in sessions 2 and 5). This is exemplified in the following quotes: *"(NV) Hand booing to projection. Moves randomly in the chair while screaming."* (S2, 6'39"); *"(V) What?! Was it a point? (NV) Falls on his knees."* (S5, 3'23"). In some cases, these events appear associated with the sounds in the game: *"(NV) child responds with another mocking sound."* (S6, 03'28"); *"(NV) Screams in reaction to a gloating sound in the game."* (S2, 6'32").

Expectation feelings, along with attention and impatience about the game events were also perceived in almost all sessions (except for session 7): *"(NV) Oh, oh... (Claps hands with expectation)"* (S10, 2'42"); *"(NV) Jumps repeatedly at the mattress"* (S4, 00'5"); *(V) Yes! Yes! (NV) Looks at the projection area with expectation."* (S9, 00'28").

The moments of environment observation, most of the times related to the game, resulted as curiosity logged events: "*(NV) Smiles and reacts to gloating sound in the game."* (S3, 00'23"); *"(V) I have hit one of those!"* (S7, 6'12"); *"(V) What do we do now?"* (S10, 4'42"). This category is clearly connected to the contextual interpretation of the child.

Therapist interaction events

The communication interactions of the therapists were also diverse, as presented in Table 3. In the majority of cases they addressed the child to support their game play, for example, how to interact with avatars or about the game functionality: *"(V) You've got me! Now it's my turn, you must dodge... Move! Move!"* (S6, 03'18"), or *"(V) Ok! That's it! Try to get me! There you go! Oh... no! You are going to get me! Ah! Almost! Now It's my turn to throw"* (S9 3'50").

These examples account for simple verbal instructions, however, more illustrative events were also logged: *"(V) Now it's my turn. Now you must dodge. Just keep your feet on the ground. I'm going to throw! (NV) After throw OT touches child's shoulder to orient movement"* (S6, 1'03"); *"(V) It looks like a giant coin and over there, at the end, is the pino that we try to hit. Sometimes I am the malha, and you are the pino. Then, we change roles. The malha will try to hit the pino and the pino must run away. Ok?"* (S11, 00'14").

Another relevant category constructed over the gameplay interactions gathers moments when the therapist intends to involve the child in the ludic context, inviting for participation, and frequently allowing focus on the game activity: *"(V) Get ready! I'm going to throw again..."* (S5, 3'28"), or *"(V) Go on, say Ah, Ah, Ah! (imitates sound in the game)"* (S10, 01'08"). Complementing and cheering the child performance were also frequently logged events. This happened both for success or failure moments: *(V) You've already scored three points! Oh! You've got me! I can't believe it!"* (S11, 03'45"), *"(V) Ok! Try to get me! Ok... almost there! Almost, you almost did it!* (S9, 04'42").

The gloating and mocking interventions where also observed in the collected data, as shown in the following cases: *"(V) Oh, I'm going to get you! (gloating sound in game) Oh! And it makes fun of me! Ok..."* (S11, 04'20"), or *"(NV) Looks at child and imitates the gloating sound in the game Tó-Tó"* (S4, 3'26"). The last category of events gathers interactions in which the therapist is searching for meaning in the game events: *"(V) Was that me?" (S2, 5'19"), or "(V) Who's to play now? I think it's me now!" (S7, 4'00").*

Playfulness evaluation

The four participant raters received basic training in a translated version of the original Test of Playfulness. This preliminary instrument consists in 21 items that reflect a one-dimensional concept of playfulness, through the combined presence of intrinsic motivation, internal control, freedom to suspend reality, and framing (interpretation of ludic cues). Items are scored in a Likert Scale with respect to three dimensions: Extent (0- rarely or never, 1- some of the time, 2- much of the time, 3- almost always), Intensity (0- not, 1- mildly, 2- moderately, 3- highly), and Skilfulness (0- unskilled, 1- slightly skilled, 2- moderately skilled, 3- highly skilled). Unseen items are scored as not applicable (NA).

C.#	T.#	Game cues		Explain		Cheer		Invite		Gloat/mock		Question		Σ
		v	nv	v	nv	v	nv	v	nv	v	nv	v	nv	
1		9		7		8		9		1				34
2	OT1	6		6		2	1	8	1	1	1	1		27
3		3		1		2		4						10
4	OT2	5		5		4		4		1	1			20
5	OT2	10		2		7	1	14		4				38
6	OT3	9		2		7		3		1				22
7	OT4	9		7		3		11				2		32
8	ST	13		4				5		1				23
9		2	3	3		7		6		3				24
10	OT4	5		2		3		15		1		2		28
11	OT5	2		10		4		4		6				26
Total		73	3	49	0	47	2	83	1	19	2	5	0	284

Table 3: Frequency instances of gameplay interactions by the participant therapists, organized by category themes.

ToP Item subscale	S1	S2	S3	S4	S5	S6	S7	S8	S9	S10	S11	ITEM MAX
Motivation	16	17	14	15	16	13	11	14	12	13	18	18
Freedom to suspend reality	10	23	5	16	17	10	11	2	3	12	20	30
Control	8	10	9	9	9	9	5	8	4	7	9	12
Shared items	23	24	14	20	24	16	15	9	11	21	20	27
Framing	11	12	8	11	11	10	9	6	8	11	12	12
Not Applicable	6	2	7	4	4	6	4	9	9	4	3	-
Raw total score	68	86	50	71	77	58	51	39	38	64	79	99

Table 4: Item subscale scores in ToP, as evaluated by therapists

Considering that each of ToP items relates with one or more of the represented constructs of playfulness in Bundy's model [45], we accounted for the item subscale scores of the ToP, to characterize playfulness as evaluated by therapists. Those values are presented in Table 4. Playfulness was evaluated with lower values in sessions 8 and 9. For the remaining sessions, scores are above the middle point of a maximum possible score (99). The most surprising data, however, is the high scores registered in "Motivation" and "Framing" items, across all sessions, in which values are close to a maximum obtainable. These values seem to contrast with items related to "Freedom to Suspend Reality", scarcely recognized.

DISCUSSION

The test sessions allowed the observation of the "Malha" videogame as mediator of a ludic context, in two multisensory stimulation environments, between a group of selected children and their therapist. The content analysis of the video recordings resulted in structured data, not only about how the intentions of design were fulfilled, but also about the created ludic context.

In regards to the intentions of design, considered as the previously defined set of orienting guidelines, the technological solution functionality is considered adequate, although not novel; in fact, our proposal is similar to other projects that emphasize graphics, animation and auditory design as key elements for user engagement [28]. The wall projection of the game, the recognition of player movement and the sensor calibration, allowed control of the necessary game actions, even among children that demonstrated lower skill levels.

Concerning the general ability to play the game, our results illustrate that all children were able to perform the intentional throws and exercise control of the avatars, with more or less difficulty. It is important to stress out that all children played the game for the first time, regardless of their personal disadvantages. In addition, the tests suggested the need to improve the choice and avatar configuration menus. Despite the fact that this moment captured the interest of players, it resulted frequently in difficulties about the correct identification of the avatar they were controlling.

The resulting observation data supports the idea that the "Malha" game was able to create and mediate a rich and diverse ludic context that mobilized the child playfulness. We found this particular ludic context marked by abundant interactions between the therapist and the child, mainly motivated by the search of control of the game avatars. This is perceptible in the variety of the latent emotions, elicited in our content analysis. The challenge offered by the "Malha" game, being characterized by feelings of joy and frustration, and occasionally marked by adversary mocking, is a close experience to the physical game, hereby expanded by its fantasy elements. To some extent, the "Malha" game favoured the presence of this referential layer of communicative interaction between the therapist and the child. This meta-discourse composed of interpretation, reflective remarks, verbal incentives, *etc.*, emerging from the ludic context, can act as a supporting layer to improve the therapeutic relation. On hindsight, we can recognize that there was an underlying intrinsic rationale in the proposed design that could also be distilled as a design guideline:

- *Provide a context for player-therapist interaction*

In summary, body as interface, flexible avatar control and the coordination of sensory stimuli into ludic cues, seemed to work as supportive aspects of the proposed design for child playfulness in our experience, which add value to the spectrum of videogame design guidelines in the area of disability. In spite of starting from a basic challenge, we think our design focus on playfulness also pulls away from the challenge dimension, by lowering the perception of formal game elements in favour of a more experientially rewarding activity. The resulting play context is prone to act as a basis for a more exploratory engagement, enabling diverse forms of participation [39].

Data also supports the presence of the theoretical dimensions of Bundy's playfulness model, namely internal control, intrinsic motivation, and the framing of ludic cues. Of course, the results concerning the administration of the ToP should be interpreted with caution; they merely represent the interpretation of the participant therapists. Nevertheless, the ToP provided a complementary structured observation of the test sessions regarding playfulness.

These results fall under the main scope of Occupational Therapy as an example of how a videogame can contribute to a therapeutic relationship by mobilizing playfulness and interaction. Furthermore, this therapeutic relationship must be considered in its call for the occupational therapists full personal involvement and the building of mutual confidence, especially in determining child interest and motivation [24].

CONCLUSION

The contribution of this work to the HCI field of knowledge is both empirical and constructive [35]; empirical, in the sense of testing and describing the agency effect of a designed videogame in supporting a therapeutic relation in the context of multisensory stimulation environments, between a child with intellectual disability and its therapist. It is constructive, in the sense that it adds information and method exploration into understanding the use of videogames in multisensory environments. To the best of our knowledge, few exploratory studies rely on content analysis to describe and understand a ludic relationship between an occupational therapist and children with intellectual disability having a videogame as mediator.

The multisensory stimulation environments are already being promisingly explored and expanded by the area of HCI, with the socio-cultural issues of disability in the agenda. However, understanding their contribution for child playfulness, particularly in the complexities of intellectual disability, is still a challenge ahead.

In summary, the described ludic context is clearly the main result of the use of the "Malha" game in multisensory stimulation environments. From this point of view, we conclude that this work provides an input to understand player experience, and the awareness of how playfulness can be mobilized and supported in a short ludic session. To that end we can contribute a set of guidelines that were instrumental in our design: Provide a context for player-therapist interaction, empower body as interface, enable flexibility of performance, coordinate multisensory stimulus, provide ludic cues, enable personalization of presence.

ACKNOWLEDGEMENTS

Author thanks to Titan Forged Games Team for their involvement in this design project.

REFERENCES

1. American Occupational Therapy Association. 2008. Occupational Therapy Practice Framework: Domain & Process. *American Journal of Occupational Therapy* 62, 6: 625–683.
2. Barrie Ellis, Gareth Ford-Williams, Lynsey Graham, Dimitris Grammenos, Ian Hamilton, Ed Lee, Jake Manion, and Thomas Westin. 2017. Game Accessibility Guidelines. *gameaccessibilityguidelines.com*. Retrieved from http://gameaccessibilityguidelines.com
3. Betsy H. Botts, Patti A. Hershfeldt, and Robyn J. Christensen-Sandfort. 2008. Snoezelen® - Empirical Review of Product Representation. *Focus on Autism and Other Developmental Disabilities* 23, 3: 138–147.
4. Scott Brown and Jeffrey Tzu Kwan Valino Koh. 2014. Responsive Multisensory Environments As a Tool to Facilitate Social Engagement in Children with an Autism Spectrum Disorder. In *SIGGRAPH Asia 2014 Designing Tools For Crafting Interactive Artifacts* (SA '14), 1:1–1:4. https://doi.org/10.1145/2668947.2668949
5. Anita C. Bundy. 1997. Play and Playfulness: what to look for. In *Play in Occupational Therapy for Children* (1st ed.), Diane Parham and Linda Fazio (eds.). Mosby, St. Louis, MO, 52–66.
6. Anita C. Bundy, Lori Nelson, Margaret Metzger, and Kathleen Bingaman. 2001. Validity and Reliability of a Test of Playfulness. *OTJR: Occupation, Participation and Health* 21, 4: 276–292. https://doi.org/10.1177/153944920102100405
7. Héctor A. Caltenco and Henrik Svarrer Larsen. 2014. Designing for Engagement: Tangible Interaction in Multisensory Environments. In *Proceedings of the 8th Nordic Conference on Human-Computer Interaction: Fun, Fast, Foundational* (NordiCHI '14), 1055–1058. https://doi.org/10.1145/2639189.2670274
8. Mark Carter and Jennifer Stephenson. 2012. The Use of Multi-Sensory Environments in Schools Servicing Children with Severe Disabilities. *Journal of Developmental and Physical Disabilities* 24, 1: 95–109. https://doi.org/10.1007/s10882-011-9257-x
9. Nuno Castelhano, Fabiana Silva, Márcia Rezende, Licínio Roque, and Lívia Magalhães. 2013. Ludic Content in Multisensory Stimulation Environments: An Exploratory Study about Practice in Portugal. *Occupational Therapy International* 20, 3: 134–143. https://doi.org/10.1002/oti.1347
10. Rosemary Caulton and Rayna Dickson. 2007. Finding an explanation for what we do. In *Contemporary Issues in Occupational Therapy: Reasoning and Reflection*, J. Creek and A. Lawson-Porter (eds.). John

Wiley & Sons Ltd, Chichester, 87–114. Retrieved from https://books.google.pt/books?id=f1HxBr_N3YwC

11. Jinghui Cheng, Cynthia Putnam, and Doris C. Rusch. 2015. Towards Efficacy-Centered Game Design Patterns For Brain Injury Rehabilitation: A Data-Driven Approach. In *Proceedings of the 17th International ACM SIGACCESS Conference on Computers & Accessibility* (ASSETS '15), 291–299. https://doi.org/10.1145/2700648.2809856
12. JCC Chung and CKY Lai. 2002. Snoezelen for dementia. *Cochrane Database of Systematic Reviews*, 4.
13. Ellen S. Cohn, Barbara A. Boyt Schell, and Elizabeth Blesedell Crepaeu. 2010. Occupational Therapy as a Reflective Practice. In *Handbook of Reflection and Reflective Inquiry: Mapping a Way of Knowing for Professional Reflective Inquiry*, N. Lyons (ed.). Springer US, 131–158. Retrieved from https://books.google.pt/books?id=2nOpVDNKMBYC
14. Franca Garzotto, Mirko Gelsomini, Alessandro Pappalardo, Claudio Sanna, Erica Stella, and Michele Zanella. 2016. Using Brain Signals in Adaptive Smart Spaces for Disabled Children. In *Proceedings of the 2016 CHI Conference Extended Abstracts on Human Factors in Computing Systems* (CHI EA '16), 1684–1690. https://doi.org/10.1145/2851581.2892533
15. Alison J. Gerlach, Gail Teachman, Debbie Laliberte-Rudman, Rebecca M. Aldrich, and Suzanne Huot. 2017. Expanding beyond individualism: Engaging critical perspectives on occupation. *Scandinavian Journal of Occupational Therapy*: 1–9. https://doi.org/10.1080/11038128.2017.1327616
16. Ellen M. Hamm. 2006. Playfulness and the Environmental Support of Play in Children With and Without Developmental Disabilities. *OTJR-Occupation, Participation and Health* 26, 3: 88–96.
17. Lynne Harkness and Anita C. Bundy. 2001. The Test of Playfulness and Children with Physical Disabilities. *OTJR: Occupation, Participation and Health* 21, 2: 73–89. https://doi.org/10.1177/153944920102100203
18. Hamilton A. Hernandez, Zi Ye, T.C. Nicholas Graham, Darcy Fehlings, and Lauren Switzer. 2013. Designing Action-based Exergames for Children with Cerebral Palsy. In *Proceedings of the SIGCHI Conference on Human Factors in Computing Systems* (CHI '13), 1261–1270. https://doi.org/10.1145/2470654.2466164
19. James Hogg, Judith Cavet, Loretto Lambe, and Mary Smeddle. 2001. The use of "Snoezelen" as multisensory stimulation with people with intellectual disabilities: a review of the research. *Research in Developmental Disabilities* 22: 353–372.
20. Guillian A. Hotz, Andrea Castelblanco, Isabel M. Lara, Alyssa D. Weiss, Robert Duncan, and John Kuluz. 2006. Snoezelen: A controlled multi-sensory therapy for children recovering from severe brain injury. *Brain Injury* 20, 8: 879–888.
21. Jan Hulsegge and Ad Verheul. 1988. *Snoezelen - Another World*. ROMPA, UK.
22. Matthew King, Nora Shields, Christine Imms, Monique Black, and Clare Ardern. 2013. Participation of children with intellectual disability compared with typically developing children. *Research in developmental disabilities* 34, 5: 1854–1862. https://doi.org/10.1016/j.ridd.2013.02.029
23. Heather Miller Kuhaneck, Kari J. Tanta, Allison Kristine Coombs, and Heather Pannone. 2013. A Survey of Pediatric Occupational Therapists' Use of Play. *Journal of Occupational Therapy, Schools, & Early Intervention* 6, 3: 213–227. https://doi.org/10.1080/19411243.2013.850940
24. H.M. Kuhaneck, S.L. Spitzer, and E. Miller. 2010. *Activity Analysis, Creativity and Playfulness in Pediatric Occupational Therapy: Making Play Just Right*. Jones & Bartlett Learning.
25. J. Minezes L. Letts, J. Berenyi M. Edwards, and C. O'Neill and C. O'Toole K. Moros. 2011. Effectiveness of Interventions Designed to Modify and Maintain Perceptual Abilities in People With Alzheimer's Disease and Related Dementias. *American Journal of Occupational Therapy* 65, 5: 505–513.
26. C. Yuen-yi Lai. 2003. The use of multisensory environments on children with disabilities: a literature review. *British Journal of Therapy and Rehabilitation* 10, 8: 358–363. https://doi.org/10.12968/bjtr.2003.10.8.13513
27. G.E. Lancioni, A.J. Cuvo, and M.F. O'Reilly. 2002. Snoezelen: an overview of research with people with developmental disabilities and dementia. *Disability and Rehabilitiation* 24, 4: 175–184.
28. Cecilia Sik Lanyi and David Joseph Brown. 2010. Design of Serious Games for Students with Intellectual Disability. In *Proceedings of the 2010 International Conference on Interaction Design & International Development* (IHCI'10), 44–54. Retrieved from http://dl.acm.org/citation.cfm?id=2227347.2227353
29. Jonathan Lazar, Jinjuan Heidi Feng, and Harry Hochheiser. 2009. *Research Methods in Human-Computer Interaction*. John Wiley & Sons, Glasgow.
30. Meir Lotan and Michele Shapiro. 2005. Management of young children with Rett disorder in the controlled multi-sensory (Snoezelen) environment. *Brain & Development* 27: S88–S94.

31. Mark C. Barlet and Steve D. Spohn. 2012. *Includification: a practical guide to game acessibility*. The AbleGamers Foundation. Retrieved from https://www.includification.com/AbleGamers_Includification.pdf

32. H. McConachie, A.F. Colver, R.J. Forsyth, S.N. Jarvis, and K.N. Parkinson. 2006. Participation of disabled children: how should it be characterised and measured? *Disability and Rehabilitiation* 28, 18: 1157–1164.

33. K.A. Neuendorf. 2002. *The Content Analysis Guidebook*. SAGE Publications, London.

34. Janet Njelesani, Gail Teachman, Evelyne Durocher, Yani Hamdani, and Shanon K. Phelan. 2015. Thinking critically about client-centred practice and occupational possibilities across the life-span. *Scandinavian Journal of Occupational Therapy* 22, 4: 252–259. https://doi.org/10.3109/11038128.2015.1049550

35. Antti Oulasvirta and Kasper Hornbæk. 2016. HCI Research As Problem-Solving. In *Proceedings of the 2016 CHI Conference on Human Factors in Computing Systems* (CHI '16), 4956–4967. https://doi.org/10.1145/2858036.2858283

36. P. Schofield. 2002. Evaluating Snoezelen for relaxation within chronic pain management. *British Journal of Nursing* 11, 12: 812, 814–21.

37. Paul Pagliano. 2012. *The Multisensory Handbook: A guide for children and adults with sensory learning disabilities*. David Fulton (Routledge), London.

38. L.D. Parham and L.S. Fazio. 2008. *Play in Occupational Therapy for Children*. Mosby Elsevier.

39. Luis Lucas Pereira and Licínio Roque. 2012. Towards a Game Experience Design Model Centered on Participation. In *CHI '12 Extended Abstracts on Human Factors in Computing Systems* (CHI EA '12), 2327–2332. https://doi.org/10.1145/2212776.2223797

40. R. Padilla. 2011. Effectiveness of environment-based interventions for people with Alzheimer's disease and related dementias. *American Journal of Occupational Therapy* 65, 5: 514–22.

41. Denise Reid. 2011. Doing play in a virtual environment. In *Advanced Computational Intelligence Paradigms in Healthcare*, Sheryll Brahnam and C. Jain Lakhmy (eds.). Springer, Berlin, 253–268.

42. J. Saldana. 2009. *The Coding Manual for Qualitative Researchers*. SAGE Publications. Retrieved from https://books.google.pt/books?id=msuOE0UfXpUC

43. Nora Shields, Matthew King, Monique Corbett, and Christine Imms. 2014. Is participation among children with intellectual disabilities in outside school activities similar to their typically developing peers? A systematic review. *Developmental neurorehabilitation* 17, 1. https://doi.org/10.3109/17518423.2013.836256

44. Chaklam Silpasuwanchai and Xiangshi Ren. 2015. Designing Concurrent Full-body Gestures for Intense Gameplay. *Int. J. Hum.-Comput. Stud.* 80, C: 1–13. https://doi.org/10.1016/j.ijhcs.2015.02.010

45. Geva Skard and Anita C. Bundy. 2008. Test of Playfulness. In *Play in Occupational Therapy for Children* (2nd ed.), Diane Parham and Linda S. Fazio (eds.). Mosby, St. Louis, MO, 71–93.

46. Jennifer Stephenson. 2002. Characterization of Multisensory Environments: Why Do Teachers Use Them? *Journal of Applied Research in Intellectual Disabilities* 15: 73–90.

47. E.-Y. Yoo S.-Y. Kim and S.-H. Park and J.-H. Park M.-Y. Jung. 2012. A systematic review of the effects of occupational therapy for persons with dementia: A meta-analysis of randomized controlled trials. *NeuroRehabilitation* 31, 2: 107–115.

48. Emmanouil Zidianakis, Ioanna Zidianaki, Danae Ioannidi, Nikolaos Partarakis, Margherita Antona, George Paparoulis, and Constantine Stephanidis. 2015. Employing Ambient Intelligence Technologies to Adapt Games to Children's Playing Maturity. In *Universal Access in Human-Computer Interaction. Access to Learning, Health and Well-Being: 9th International Conference, UAHCI 2015, Held as Part of HCI International 2015, Los Angeles, CA, USA, August 2-7, 2015, Proceedings, Part III*, Margherita Antona and Constantine Stephanidis (eds.). Springer International Publishing, Cham, 577–589. https://doi.org/10.1007/978-3-319-20684-4_56

GlowPhones: Designing for Proxemics Play with Low-Resolution Displays in Location-based Games

Timothy Merritt[1],Christine Linding Nielsen[2], Frederik Lund Jakobsen[2], Jens Emil Grønbæk[2]
[1]Department of Computer Science, Aalborg University, Aalborg, Denmark
[2]Department of Computer Science, Aarhus University, Aarhus, Denmark
merritt@cs.aau.dk,christinelinding@gmail.com,frederik_lund@hotmail.com,jensemil@cs.au.dk

Figure 1: *Left:* Players navigate to stage locations in the dark forest using light cast from the mobile phone. *Center:* Game stages involve social challenges supported by novel use of smartphone sensors and actuators. Here the player 'mixes' a color by carefully rotating and orienting the screen. *Right:* players complete the final game stage by lighting up sensor panels simultaneously.

ABSTRACT
Location-based mobile games often utilize built-in sensors for supporting game experiences tied to the physical world, yet the visual user interface remains constrained to the small high-resolution screen. GlowPhones is a location-based mobile social game using low-resolution displays to augment the physical space and move the attention away from the mobile screen. Players explore the physical world and collaborate to overcome challenges relying on the screen glow intensity emitted from the phone's screen and light flash frequency of the camera flash for navigation. Three game stages explore proxemics play using low-resolution light displays designed to require social competition, physical cooperation and bodily contact challenging cultural norms. A user study was conducted in a public forest during the night. Spatial analysis of proxemics and F-formations in conjunction with a Game Experience Questionnaire provide insights about the experiential and socio-spatial qualities of low-resolution displays. Qualitative examples offer new strategies for proxemics play.

Author Keywords
Games; proxemics; play; whole-body interaction; mobile social interaction

CHI PLAY '17, October 15-18, 2017, Amsterdam, Netherlands

ACM ISBN 978-1-4503-4898-0/17/10...$ 15.00
DOI: https://doi.org/10.1145/3116595.3116598

ACM Classification Keywords
H5.2 Information interfaces and presentation: User Interfaces.

INTRODUCTION
Location-based games provide experiences orchestrated to respond to the player location as well as actions or situational context [3]. The players are often encouraged to explore and interact with the physical world, yet with intense focus on the small screen of the mobile phone, there are challenges to the richness of social interactions for collocated players and a diminished capacity to attend to stimuli in the physical environment.

We introduce GlowPhones, a mobile social game platform that aims to bring player focus, social interaction and game events out into the physical world using sensors and actuators already in the smartphone. Low-resolution displays are used as a design resource in a mobile social gaming experience to draw attention of the players toward the environment and their co-players. The interactions embedded in the physical world allow for exploring different strategies for proxemics play. In the GlowPhones game, the user navigates to key locations aided by the visual cues provided by changes in the reflected light from the phone into the surroundings. Two low-resolution navigation modes were explored: *screen glow intensity* and *light flash frequency*. In screen glow intensity mode, players must orient the screen toward the ground to activate a navigation mode that uses intensity of glow from the smartphone screen with higher brightness indicating approach to the target geofence. In light flash frequency mode, players orient the camera toward the ground so that cast light illuminates the surroundings and the frequency of camera flash events increases indicating approach to the target geofence. Game stages were designed to explore social play between two people through three different challenges of competitive play, collaborative physical play, and forced collaboration. In the remaining sections we describe the system design, the study conducted "in the wild" of a city forest park at night, and finally we review gathered data from logged game events and feedback from players to provide insights into the player experience. Characteristics of GlowPhones that encourage collaboration and playful proxemic behavior are identified to inspire future development of low-resolution displays for mobile social games. Our discussion of design implications for low-resolution displays suggest new strategies for supporting social interaction as well as involving proxemics play in mobile social games.

RELATED WORK

Low-Resolution and Rich Communication

Previous work on limited and minimal communication tools suggest that 'richness' in communication media should not entirely focus on bandwidth and accuracy of interpretation [41] but rather should focus on the social interactions of people and 'suggestive' communication, embracing ambiguity [9], and aesthetics of the bodily experience [38]. Low bandwidth communication, even down to one-bit communication channels can be used for rich human communication [19]. Pousman and Stasko provided an analysis of the design space for ambient information systems that provides a language for discussing the formal qualities of displays [39]. They present four design dimensions including information capacity, notification level, representational fidelity, and aesthetic emphasis to describe and discuss existing systems and implications for future design opportunities. 'Information capacity was described as the number of data elements that are represented, with high information capacity possible with full resolution screens, while low information capacity systems convey fewer data elements as in the Ambient Orb [7] which uses simple glow levels and subtle color change events to encode information. Display technologies with low information capacity have been explored for use in various contexts including auditory mediation [5], low-resolution visual displays [42] [1], and even low resolution haptic cues to provide navigation and directional guidance [46]. We use the term, "low-resolution displays" as a general term which recognizes the low information capacity of a media yet is independent of the representational fidelity.

Robinson et al. argue for thinking beyond the high-resolution screen of the small mobile device in the design of rich user experiences [44]. They discuss examples of designing ambient media to shift focus into the physical world as in the "Babbage Cabbage technique" of engineering plants to change color as a means of embedding digitally controlled information into the environment [8]. Various other forms of ambient living media have been proposed [4] including glowing bacteria in peripheral display system that provides a low bandwidth of information regarding social media and interpersonal relationships. In that work, the authors recognize that high bandwidth displays of the mobile and personal computer may not be the most effective way to make an impression on the user. Harrison et al. explore the expressive capabilities of 'point lights' or single pixel light sources which are often found on electronic devices and appliances drawing attention to the richness of single pixel displays [13].

There are also examples of physical and social games using low resolution screens to bring the visible game elements into the physical space [22]. Low resolution does not diminish the usefulness of a display - on the contrary, when less information is provided, attention can be more focused on a task. Research on low resolution wearable displays for traffic safety demonstrated that low resolution can yield highly visible indicators for interactions in public [40]. While many mobile experiences are designed for daytime use, when the sun has set, we experience light and changes in the environment more clearly [28]. Interaction in the dark reduces the overall visual feedback and leads people to be more aware of their body and the surrounding space [51]. We noticed that the light given off by the mobile phone screen and the camera flash can be extremely bright, especially in a dark environment.

Social Interaction and Spatial Behavior

The interplay between bodies and space and its effects on social experiences have been widely explored within the research field of interaction design for the medical context [47], social play and mobile games [14, 15]. In this endeavor, research from social psychology has shown to be instrumental. The study of proxemics [12] accounts for how people use features in the environment as ways of structuring their social relationships. It further suggests that personal expectations and cultural attitudes impact the behavior in social encounters as much as the built environment. These ideas have been extended to interaction design in understanding the spatial relationships between people and technology [11, 30, 36, 24, 29]. Krogh et al. argue that a literacy in proxemics (i.e., a socio-spatial literacy) can be used as a design resource for actively designing spatial interventions that have impact on the experienced social space [24]. Furthermore, the F-formation system [20] has been proposed for categorizing people's facing formations with a set of spatial patterns. The o-space of an F-formation describes the shared physical space in front of the people facing each other, whereas the transactional segment denotes the immediate visual space in front a single person [20]. This language for spatial behavior has been adopted in HCI to provide implications for interaction design [30, 36, 29, 48]. New F-formations have been identified from a study of people cooking together, e.g. *spooning* as an intimate enactment of social cooking [36].

Physical, Social, and Location-Based Games

Within games research, the *magic circle* [45] is commonly described as a metaphorical circle within the game experience where special rules apply [18]. We recognize that in designing a game experience, users can be willing to have fun engaging in activities and following rules, while suspending disbelief and engaging in the narrative of the game world.

[1]Jim Campbell portfolio `http://www.jimcampbell.tv/portfolio/low_resolution_works/`

Using physical space as game elements in social games has been explored to enhance social engagement, e.g., through Mueller et al.'s concept of Proxemics Play [32]. The concept extends the traditional proxemic zones using wireless technologies to challenge cultural norms and facilitate exploration of proxemic zones through play. The use of proximity sensors in social play has further been used to encourage social interaction between people in public streets [35] and as a means for supporting exploratory educational experiences [23] and mixed reality entertainment for the family [21].

Location-based or locative media explores tagging and mapping of the real world, assigning content and interactions to spaces, places, people or things [49]. Tagging is either done with virtual tagging of the world or by tracing the action of subjects in the world. It is concerned with lived place and historical surface creating a geospatial experience and can make us reflect on our spatial and social selves [6]. When designing location-based games, the creation and orchestration of game content and activities is key to a successful game experience. Geocaching is a commonly utilized game mechanic embedding goals within the game into real-world physical caches pursued and found by the players [34, 48]. Pokémon Go [1] provides an Augmented Reality realization of fictional characters placed at specific locations in the physical world however, social interaction is minimal. Current mobile phones have powerful built-in sensors that can support unique gaming experiences that bring the focus beyond the small individual screen and back to the physical and social interactions [17, 27, 43, 16].

RESEARCH PROBLEM

We are intrigued by low bandwidth, low-resolution displays as a design resource in a mobile social gaming experience, specifically in the capacity to draw attention of the players toward the environment and their co-players. *How can we design enjoyable mobile social game experiences that shift focus away from the high resolution screen of the smartphone and into the physical and social environment?*

GLOWPHONES GAME

GlowPhones is a location-based mobile game that serves as a research platform to explore proxemics play and low-resolution displays. The game play is inspired by orienteering and requires players to navigate to target locations in the real world where they face challenges related to a narrative. Navigation with GlowPhones is provided through the available light sources on a typical smartphone illuminating the area around the player through the brightness of the screen or the frequency of camera flash events. Two players can advance the story by completing three game stages, which present players with social challenges that explore playful proxemic arrangements of players and technology. Built-in smartphone sensors are used to create new spatial experiences for co-players, encouraging them to be creative with their bodies and mobile devices in the surrounding space. The central point of each stage was marked with a physical lantern that would light up and play a sound when completed. We developed the game narrative to fit within the physical environment and incorporates physical features and unique spatial experiences available in the Riis Skov (Riis forest) [50] city park including a monumental building, a bridge over a stream, and a lookout point overlooking the city of Aarhus, Denmark (see Figure 1). The motivation in terms of proxemics is to change the experienced social space in mobile games from players being in private spheres with their individual devices to a shared interactive space using the surroundings for display and interaction. The study investigates how these aspects of interaction fostered intimate and social zones between players, as well as engaging players with the site. The design rationale behind using shared low-resolution light display with limited information and sensors for physical interaction is to make the game an aesthetic and social experience with less emphasis on efficient use, but more on the inherent social qualities of exploration and play [38].

Game Play

The game play of GlowPhones involves three stages. Each stage involves different physical interactions of social play as depicted in Figure 2 between the navigation and challenge stages, which are explained as part of an unfolding narrative. In short, the narrative is a story about a spacecraft that has to be rebuilt in order to launch it. It is presented at various times to the user through screen cards displayed on the mobile screen and based around a fictitious rocket that has crashed in the forest. The players are asked to help fix and relaunch the rocket in order to complete the game (see Figure 2).

Figure 2: The game consists of three stages. A: The players mix chemicals by rotating phone to find color. B: Players jump together to charge the spacecraft battery. C: The players cooperate to light up the panels placed around a tree to launch the space craft. Before each stage there is an initial navigation stage.

Stage 1: Color Match – Competition

The players compete against each other to find specific colors (chemicals) on the screen by rotating the device physically in any direction. When the phone is in motion, the onscreen color is continually modified through palette rotations influenced by the internal orientation sensor (see Figure 2(A)). Fine motor skills are required in order to position the device in precise angles to find the right colors. The first player to find the three colors has successfully mixed the chemicals to build the battery. The stage completion is also signalled by the activation of a lantern hung in a nearby tree (at the center of the geofence).

Stage 2: Jump Together – Physical Collaboration

The target location of the second stage *Jump Together* was on top of a bridge spanning over a creek, approximately 7 meters above the water (see Figure 2(B)). Players are prompted by a screen message to “charge the spacecraft battery” by holding hands and jumping up and down.The phone’s accelerometer detects the motion and an onscreen animation of the battery charge level visualizes their progress. Once the battery is fully charged, a lantern attached to the railing of the bridge is activated signalling stage completion.

Stage 3: Light Up Panels – Forced Cooperation

In the final stage, the players have to physically locate and activate two light sensitive panels, one located on either side of a tree (see Figure 2(C)). In order to stand out among the objects in the forest, four 1cm diameter retroreflective stickers were affixed to the sensor housing. Once the players enter the 25m radius of the geofence, the camera light activates and players are instructed to ignite the rocket by activating the sensors. When the players have located the panels, they have to simultaneously shine light on each of the two panels. When the task is solved, a lantern on the ground next to the tree plays music and activates a play of lights through internally mounted LED strips to indicate that the spacecraft launches and the players have completed the game.

Challenging Proxemics in the Game Stages

From the perspective of proxemics, players relate to each other and their personal zone [12] including their phone. The game challenges proxemic zones in different ways by playing with proxemic barriers. The *"Jump Together"* stage deliberately crosses the barrier between players’ personal zones. The *"Light Up Panels"* stage separates players’ zones with a visual barrier, but players still depend on each other in how they have separate roles for solving the same task (inspired by Goddard et al. [10]). On the other hand, the *"Color Match"* stage is competitive and players are in close proximity allowing for awareness of their co-player’s game state through peeking at the screen.

Navigation Methods

The navigation to the stations was provided with two strategies for light-based navigation including *light flash frequency* (see Figure 3), similar to Harrison et al. ‘blink decreasing’ and ‘blink increasing’ light behaviors [13] an *screen glow intensity* (see Figure 4), similar to what Harrison et al. called ‘staircase continuous’ light behavior [13]. The methods display the straight-line distance to the stations through modulating the light emitted from the mobile. To supplement the light-based navigation and avoid wild detours in the forest, the narrative supplies initial cues to help guide the players toward the stations making reference to environmental details such as ‘...the station is found toward the water.’

Light flash frequency utilizes the camera flash bulb but does not take a photo. It serves to light up the surroundings for a brief moment and through the strobe frequency it is used to provide proximity feedback. This navigation method is implemented with ten levels comparing the distance and setting the strobe light intensity from 1 flash per 10 seconds at a distance greater than 400m increasing up to 5 flashes per second at the geofence. *Screen glow intensity* is controlled by varying the size of white circle on a black screen that expands when the user approaches the geofence. The circle size is inversely mapped to the distance to the geofence, making the circle grow in small steps upon approaching the geofence thus emitting more light and providing a noticeable increase in glow level. We mapped the area surrounding the circle to blink red if the newest GPS registered location is further away or green if the player is getting closer. We utilized the orientation sensor in the mobile phone to enforce a rule that the player must orient the screen toward the ground so that they can only see the back of the phone when looking down on it carried in their hand. If the phone is turned over in the hopes of peeking at the screen, the screen turns off until the player returns the phone to the screen-down position. This design consideration is among the more significant choices in GlowPhones. It imposes an unconventional way of holding a mobile device, however, it resonates with the proxemics motivation of turning the surroundings, rather than the device screen, into an interactive space.

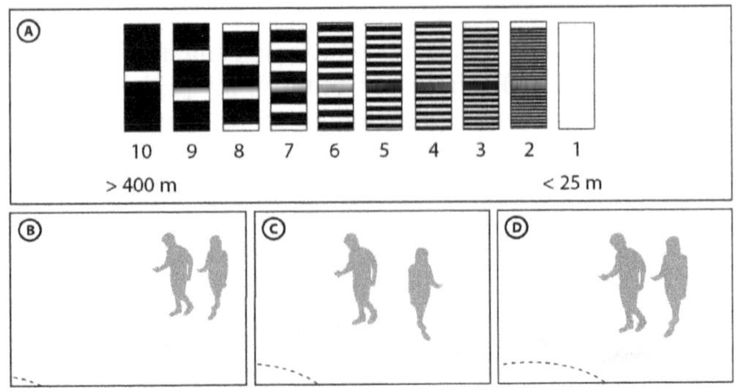

Figure 3: **Light flash frequency navigation.** A: Flashing frequency varies from 1 flash per 10 seconds at a distance greater than 400m increasing to 5 flashes per second at the geofence. B-D: Flash frequency increases as the player approaches the geofence (marked with a dashed line). C: The player closest to the geofence has more frequent light flashes than the player on the right.

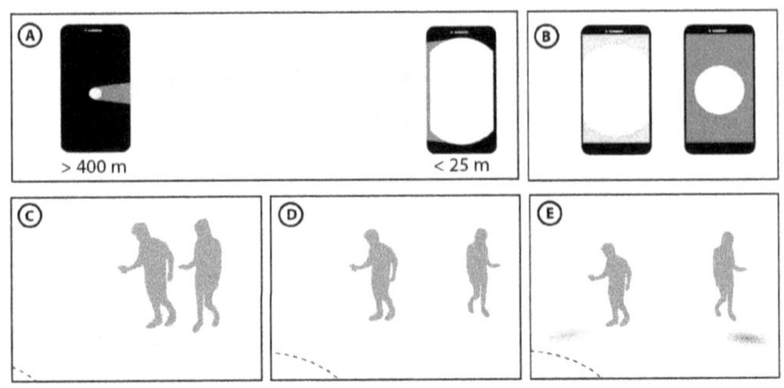

Figure 4: **Screen glow intensity navigation.** A: The white circle grows in size linearly as the player approaches the geofence. B+E: A green border indicates ‘approaching geofence’, red indicates ‘retreating from geofence’. C-D: The glowing circle is biggest thus casting more light for the person closest to the geofence.

TECHNICAL IMPLEMENTATION

The central part of the system is the application that runs on Android devices utilizing built-in sensors for game challenges and navigation. The navigation and challenges run on the devices, but are connected to physical stations in the forest in different ways. Either by sending information of the winner, when the challenge is completed, or receiving information when the station has been activated by a connecting player in the forest. At each station, a lantern is placed, which carries a Particle Photon [37] that offers a connection as a wireless access point to the devices within range and additional components including Neopixel RGB LEDs, an 8 ohm speaker and battery. The challenges are activated when the user's GPS coordinate reaches a geofence (see Figure 5).

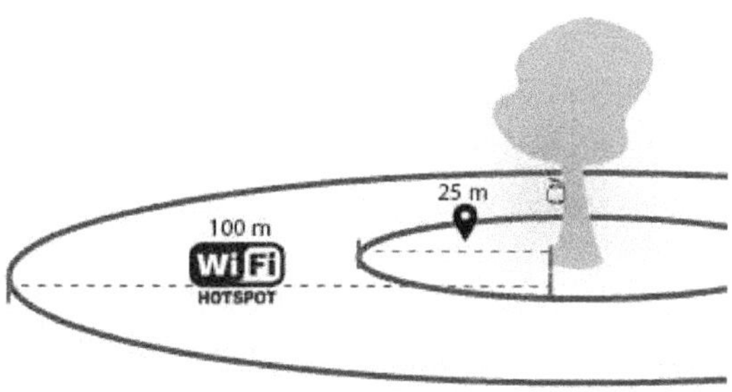

Figure 5: Geofence at game stations. The outer perimeter shows the WiFi range which reaches up to 100m. The inner perimeter is the fixed geofence with bounds at 25m radius around the physical lantern placed on a tree. Placing the geofence well within the WiFi range ensured that phones would join up to the access point well before reaching the target.

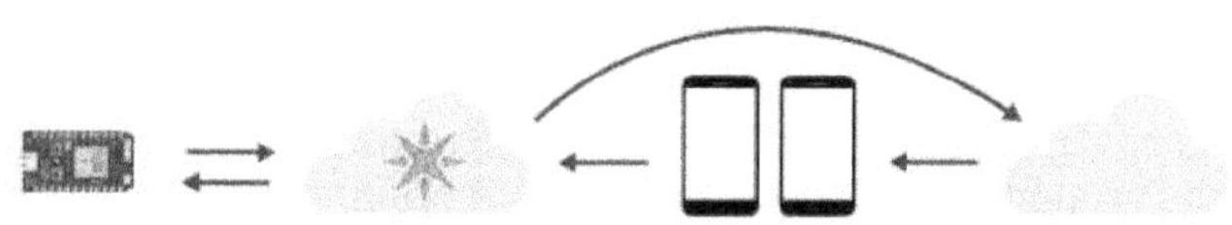

Figure 6: The connections between the phones and the Photons. Stage 1&2 only send data to the Photon, but stage 3 also receives information from cloud through an external website.

The technical implementation of GlowPhones is illustrated in Figure 6. The mobile phones send messages to the Photons through the Particle Cloud. The code on the Photon then reads the messages and runs the appropriate code. The Particle Cloud supports subscribing to events using webhooks. When Photon code has been executed, an event is sent to an external website, and the phones look for updated information about the last time the code has been executed. Exchanged data allows the connected devices to notify the Particle to light up the lantern when a game has been completed, and react when a physical task is completed.

Evaluation

We utilized the GlowPhones system as an experimental platform to explore low resolution mobile gaming. We conducted a study in the wild and gathered data using the mobile phones and self-reported data using the GEQ (Game Experience Questionnaire) and interviews to explore the game experience relating to game features, navigation modes, and suggestions for improvements. Seven dyads took part in the study, fourteen participants in total with 11 male and 3 females ranging from 22 to 31 years and average of 24.6 years of age and all participants claim to have experience in playing mobile games. The evaluation was conducted over three consecutive days in the darkness of the evening hours ensuring that the public forest park would be dark enough to allow the players to navigate using the light cast from the mobile phones. Before each session, the two participants were shortly briefed with an open-ended interview [25] to establish their general experience with mobile phones. The participants were then introduced to a basic overview of the 2 navigation modes and an indication that the game would involve 3 stages. The two participants were given mobile phones with the GlowPhones game installed. We asked some participants to wear an action camera that would document their play, and study facilitators followed the participants to be available for answering questions during the game play and to observe player behavior. Each session lasted one hour, with approximately 30 minutes for completing the game stages and 30 minutes for answering the questionnaire and interviews. Proxemics [12] and F-formations [20] served as an analytical lens, through which we observed participants. We did not, however, tell participants that we were observing spatial behavior. Based on observations from four facilitators, interesting qualitative examples from the evaluation were observed and analysed in terms of their proxemic configurations of people, technology and physical space. F-formations were used to analyse the social play experience from a spatial perspective, highlighting how players organized themselves during competitive and collaborative play ranging from social to more intimate configurations. In the first stage, the participants navigated using the light flash frequency mode. The facilitators followed the players just within hearing and visual range, in order to observe proxemics, F-formations and communication between the players. In the second stage, the players navigate using the intensity of screen glow. In the third stage, the players were asked to choose the navigation method they would prefer for finding the target location in the final stage "Light Up Panels". At the completion of the final stage, participants were guided to the vehicle at the starting location and were asked to complete the GEQ. When the questionnaires were completed, contextual interviews were conducted with both players together.

RESULTS

An encouraging result from this study is that all participants understood and utilized the light-based navigation and enjoyed the game experience. We examine the feedback from contextual interviews and GEQ to provide further insights into how the players reacted to the 2 modes of navigation and the 3 game stages. Taken as a whole, the results suggest rich potential in developing mobile social games using low-resolution displays and physical bodily interaction.

Logged Location Data

The route between the stages covered approximately 1 km in a forest area of roughly 0.8 km^2. Collected position data from the mobile phones has been visualized on a heatmap (see Figure 7). The heatmap gives a visual overview of the field and stages. The map shows that the participants tended to stay on the paths, however, some groups took a different route for a short time, but eventually found the way back to the trail with the stage location. Some participants noted that it was part of the enjoyment of the game to temporarily 'get lost' and explore different areas of the forest.

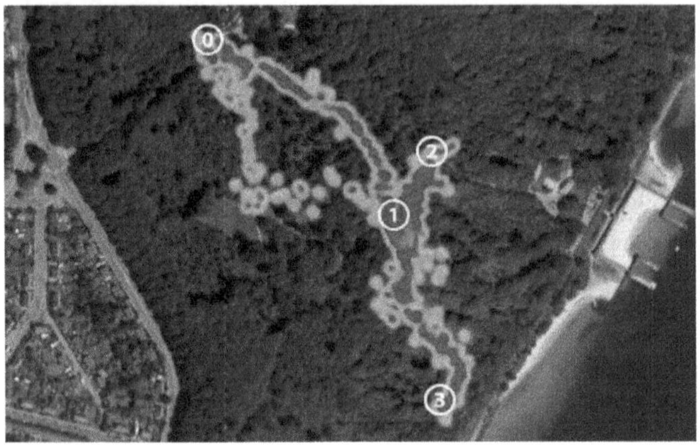

Figure 7: Heatmap of player movements during the game in Riis Skov [50] city park in Aarhus, Denmark. 0) Game starting location, 1) Stage 1, the chemical factory, 2) Stage 2, the power plant 3) Final stage, spacecraft launchpad.

Game Experience Questionnaire

The results of the game experience questionnaire (GEQ) suggest that players had overall a very positive game experience. This is reflected in the high score for positive affect (M = 2.89, SD = 0.74) and the relatively low scores for negative affect (M = 0.75, SD = 0.73) and very low scores for the tension dimension (M = 0.55, SD = 0.68). The high average score for competence (M = 2.27, SD = 1.04) suggests players felt capable of playing the game and comparable to prior studies noted in [33]. Flow (M = 1.74, SD = 0.95) and immersion scores (M = 1.94, SD = 0.33) suggest that players were involved in the game experience to a moderate level. The game was not rated as highly challenging and was an easy game to play (M = 1.11, SD = 0.80) which ensured that all participants could complete the stages and experience each challenge, but future iterations could explore more difficult challenges. Figure 8 shows average gameplay experience scores.

General Responses to Light-based Navigation

The navigation methods had distinct ways of displaying proximity information as seen in figure 3 and 4. Contextual interviews provide additional insights into the player experience with each and overall, the feedback suggests the navigation modes yielded much emphasis on the forest and the surroundings.

> "In relation to the use of the screen to navigate (screen glow), it made me more aware of the forest, because I was forced to look where I walked. The light tells you where to go, that was actually fun" - Participant 14

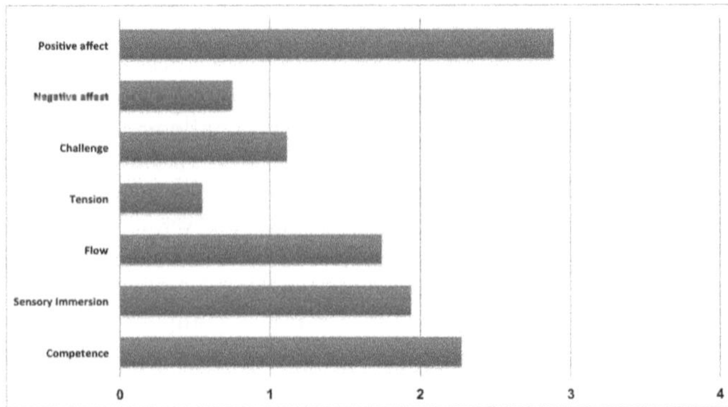

Figure 8: Average gameplay component scores recorded from playing GlowPhones game.

Participants overall preferred navigating with the light flashes over screen glow. Of the 14 participants, 9 preferred the light flashes, whereas 5 preferred the glowing screen. The participants that preferred the glowing screen valued the color change events and understood the glow level and color as a navigation method. One of the advantages of screen glow intensity navigation is the larger bandwidth of information it communicates including the proximity to the geofence and color change events for alerting the player if moving away from the target direction. Additionally, the glowing screen exhibited some unexpected use, which will be elaborated on in the following.

Light Flash Frequency Navigation Method

Generally, the light flashes allowed for a natural upright posture (see Figure 3(B-D)) where players could point the light at the ground right next to each other or pointing outward toward the forest and pathways. Figure 9(A-B) illustrates how the light flash mode allowed for an awareness of the co-player's display. The wide V-shaped formation [36] allows the players to have a peripheral awareness of each other, while primarily facing towards the same reflection on e.g. a tree. This formation was seen used when players were within the geofence (causing their lights to stop flashing and remain on) looking for physical clues of the next task station (see figure 10(right)). Generally, participants found the light flash navigation entertaining but also challenging.

> "I also think the flash was fun because you had to really keep an eye on when it flashed more and there was an extra challenge that you could only see the path ahead in flashes." - Participant 6

Some participants tried to find patterns by counting the seconds between the flashes, and often stopped to look around if the rate changed [Session 1]. Some considered splitting so they could cover a larger area [Session 1, 5]. When participants were walking in a side-by-side formation [20] (see Figure 9(B)), it was apparent that the light flashes were perceived to have a higher frequency because the blinking among devices was not synchronized, yet the cast light overlapped resulting in a perceived increased frequency while the flashes were out of phase [Session 1, 2]. This highlighted a socio-spatial consequence of light reflections, i.e., that a social awareness was enabled by the display being projected out into the players' shared visual space of overlapping transactional segments [20]. Participants also engaged in playful teasing against each other e.g. when players faced each other to use the flashlight for temporarily blinding their co-player [Session 3] (see Figure 9(C)). This shows how simple interfaces can lead to playful social behaviors with players inventing meaning and utilizing the technology for other purposes not intended or specified by the designers as also seen in [19].

Only a few participants chose to use the two navigation modes at the same time, however, in those dyads which did, they seemed to fall into roles. The player using the light flashes walked in front, because of the stronger light source. The participants collaborated and discussed the feedback from the different phones [Session 1].

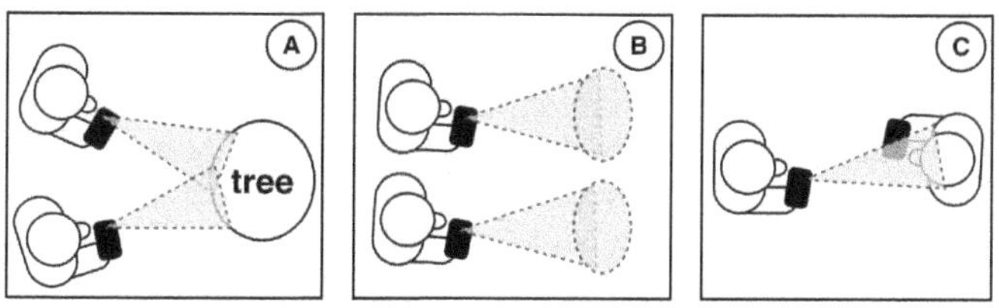

Figure 9: F-formations of players interacting with light in flash frequency mode. A: *Wide V-shaped* - using surroundings to combine reflections. B: *Side-by-side* - interpreting blinking patterns. C: *Face-to-face* - using flash to tease each other in the dark.

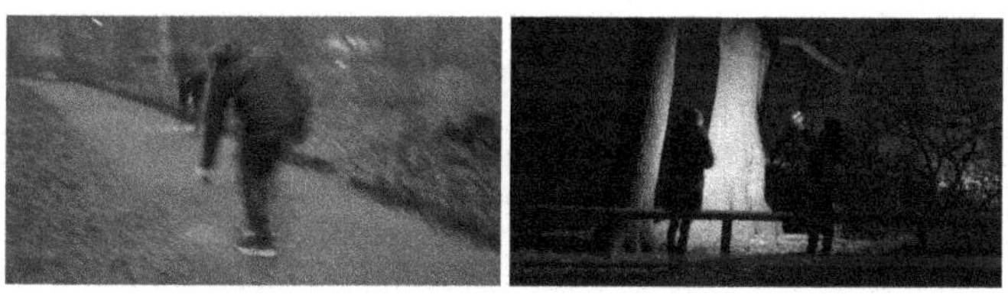

Figure 10: Players' use of surroundings. *Left:* Participants seen crouching down to better see the light emitted from the glowing circle. *Right:* The light reflection as a shared display: The participants often combined the light sources to cooperate locating the light panels placed within the environment.

Screen Glow Intensity Navigation Method

The players understood and could navigate with the light cast on the ground from the screen glow when standing upright with the screen oriented toward the ground. In two sessions, players turned the phone to look at the screen, which causes the screen to turn black and they asked the facilitators why that happens [Session 3, 4]. In some sessions, players appropriated the screen glow in various ways to increase visibility by adjusting their body position, as illustrated in Figure 11. Two players crouched down to move the phone closer to the ground surface as seen in Figure 10, surprisingly few tried to

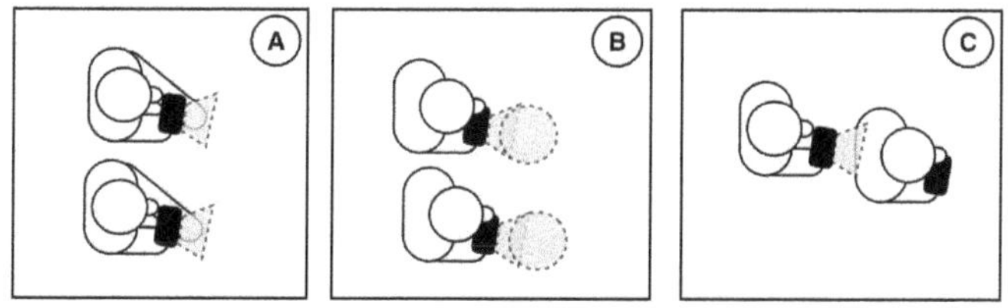

Figure 11: F-formations of players interacting with light in screen glow mode, using tactics to get nearer a reflecting surface. A: *Cupping* with hands, B: *Crouching* closer to the ground, C: *Spooning* by using the back of a participant.

bypass it by holding the phone overhead to peek at the display from underneath [Session 1]. Others were not so satisfied with this method. Due to the short distance to the second location, they were not able to make it work. The changes in glow intensity depends on the distance between the last locations, however some participants walked very slowly and were attending to the color cues. Interestingly, the more intense focus and slow movement actually reduced the usefulness of the cues [Session 1]. One participant felt that the feedback came at random times, and would like to be able to activate it themselves [Session 5]. The feedback colors were sometimes wrong, causing a dyad to count three samples: two red and one green, and then concluded it was the wrong direction because there was more red blinks than green [Session 6].

Because of the unusual angle of the phone, the participants adapted various unexpected spatial configurations for better interpreting the low-resolution output. These examples reveal particular social behavior in how they mimic each others' spatial behavior. Two players held their hand a few centimeters below the glowing screen, shortening the distance to the reflection claiming in the interview that this helped them see the color.

Similarly, two players crouched down to hover the phone over the ground surface (see Figure 11(B) and Figure 10(left)). [Session 1]. In one session, players complemented each other, when one player used the other player's back to better discern the changes in the information given from the screen glow (see Figure 11(C)) [Session 5]. These examples illustrate how nontraditional interaction with the mobile display can cause creative social use of technology.

Social Interactions During Game Tasks

The tasks in the three game stages were designed to explore different social interactions: the *Color Match* game was a competitive task, *Jump Together* involved physical collaboration, and *Light Up Panels* enforced verbal collaboration in a collective task. During the tasks at the three stages, the limited information and vague cues from the narrative served the purpose of encouraging collaborative sense making. Especially in stage 3, as players were locating light sensors, they discussed what the cues meant while simultaneously exploring the physical surroundings near the tree in stage 3. Furthermore, dialogue between the two players suggest that the complexity of the task and the mapping between digital and physical information made them pay extra attention to the surroundings during this task.

Players found the *Jump Together* task quite funny and did not hesitate to engage in the challenge. This suggests that even simple prompts by the game can invite and lead players to cross cultural barriers for bodily contact. While not so surprising for the players who were a romantic couple to hold hands, we discussed this topic further with all participants revealing additional details that contributed to the willingness for hand holding. As noted by Participant 2,

> "The jumping game was fun, because it took me by surprise, also with the fact that the screen was filled out [battery metaphor] was quite different so it made it fun."

Some players reflected in the contextual interview that it would be easy to hack the system by merely shaking the phone, yet when they were asked why they went along with holding hands, it became apparent that hacking the system didn't come to mind until after the game [Session 3, 6].

Physical Lanterns and Disturbed Night Vision

The lanterns were intended as a simple reward to indicate progression in the game – sharp chirping sounds came from the lantern to raise the awareness. However, few participants paid attention to the lanterns. Before *Color Match*, most participants discovered the lantern from the subtle default light emitted, but only very few noticed the lantern light up upon stage completion. The feedback from the interviews suggests that it was not easily noticed among the brightness of the mobile phones; this night blindness can be a challenge as noted in other work [26]. During *Jump Together* none of the participants were aware of the lantern light up. However, at the *Light Up Panels* task all participants discovered the lantern light upon stage completion. The retro-reflective dots on the light panels captured the attention of most players when their camera flashlights illuminated it from a distance.

CHALLENGING THE PERSONAL MOBILE DISPLAY

The main design goal of GlowPhones was to move user attention away from the mobile display by utilizing low-resolution output that would encourage users to attend more to the environment and surroundings. The following discusses design qualities and challenges of designing 'away from the mobile display'.

From Personal to Shared Navigation

A few design decisions in the navigation design took part in nudging the user to attend to the physical surroundings by intervening with traditional use of smartphones. 1) The game is location-based, and the game is designed for a night-time experience re-purposing the phone as a "smart torch" with location awareness information. 2) Site-specific cues in the narrative that built on the players' common knowledge of the site. 3) Light from the phone projecting onto the real world is used for navigation and is visible to both players and spectators. When using the screen glow intensity for navigation, players were forced to orient their phone's screen downward and away from their eyes in order to activate the navigational guidance. Making the simple intervention of nudging users to point their display to the environment and relying on the information reflected from the surfaces around them (e.g., the ground or the trees) changes the mobile display from a private to a shared peripheral display as seen in Figure 10. This could be seen in how they had shared access to the patterns of light being reflected in the environment from each phone, or how they used each other in the interaction, as described with Figures 9 and 11. These examples can be contrasted to the proxemic behavior usually unfolding when two people have the device information facing towards themselves, such as the screen-focused interaction in Pokémon Go. Thus, a shared experience can be designed for by intentionally intervening with the traditional spatial configurations of technology and users.

Transitioning between Mobile and Spatial Display

It is especially challenging to design transitions between interaction with the mobile screen and the lanterns in the physical surrounding space. If a sound or light event emanates from the mobile, the player will likely look at it. Comparing how the participants reacted to the different stages reveals how some design aspects make participants more attentive to the environment than others. In stage 3, most players clearly understood that they finished their task just from the ambient information and the glowing lantern in the tree. While this worked well in stage 3, the design of stages 1 and 2 seemed to compete more with the attention required towards the phone. Especially in stage 1, when players try to find a color by rotating the screen, the mobile screen captured the participants' attention more and only one group discovered the lantern in the nearby tree. They either did not notice it or were blinded by the light emitted from their phones. During the user studies, the brightness of the screens were adjusted to a minimum, however, the participants still reported being blinded by the screen light when consecutively having to refocus on the environment. This points towards a more general challenge for using light-based communication in a night game in the forest. 8 ohm speakers were embedded in the lanterns, however, in stage 1 and 2 the sound events did not seem to be loud enough to compete with the attention toward the screens or the task. In future iterations of the game, sound could be further explored as a low-resolution modality in combination with light flashing away from the user's eye to make information in the surroundings more discoverable in low-light conditions.

AESTHETICS OF LIMITED INFORMATION

The playful interactions in GlowPhones highlights the potential of aesthetic interaction [38] and further the value of the body in the physical world in combination with virtual elements to drive a social game experience [10, 23]. The following discusses social and aesthetic qualities of limited information.

Designing Aesthetic Navigation

One of the inherent qualities of using low-resolution displays is that it provides users with ambiguous or incomplete information, affording users to interpret, try to make sense of it, or encouraging the player to look for other pieces of contextual information to supplement. While this might seem like an odd choice in a navigation system given that it would be less efficient than e.g. Google Maps, it provides guidance through more aesthetic and playful qualities [52] that can be desirable in a gaming experience. The two navigation methods used in GlowPhones do not aim at increasing the efficiency for using navigation, but rather to encourage social interaction and persuade users to look elsewhere for cues to their navigation. This can be compared to being a "puzzle" that the players need to overcome. The navigation methods used in GlowPhones give ambiguous and complex information to the players, who need to interpret the cues to determine where to move in order to approach the target location.

Limited Information Allows for Human Communication

The GlowPhones navigation design allows for the user to have a higher awareness of the surrounding forest. This quality has some similarities to the puzzle solving used in Geocaching games [34]. It potentially gives the players a higher engagement with the game play, other players, and the surroundings. The users were able to find the selected locations through triangulation of the data provided from the game. Throughout the game, the players engaged with informational prompts and onscreen content including the narrative, stage challenges, and ambient light-based navigation methods. Furthermore, the paths in the physical environment were, for most players, as important as the digital information. If there was a path in the direction that seemed to increase intensity in the light, players assumed it was an indication that they were on the right track. While it is challenging to design transitions in user attention between the phone screen and the physical surroundings, mixing digital and physical elements can create complexity. Our study shows that seeking contextual information beyond the low-resolution display is encouraged by its limited information. Furthermore, the relationship between information encourages interpretation, and this has shown to encourage engagement with the system and other users [9, 10]. Gaver et al. thus suggest to deliberately use ambiguity to give rise to uncertainty and encourage discussion. The imprecision of the navigation methods in GlowPhones seemed to encourage much verbal communication between the two players about how to interpret the signals. Kaye et al.'s minimal intimate object [19] reveals how low-resolution displays can offer new means for remote intimate communication. In cooperative gameplay for separated players, small movements and actions can lead to interpretation and mentalizing of co-players to understand intentions [31]. Since GlowPhones is a collocated interactive experience with similar low-resolution elements, it offers an example of what material aspects of low resolution mean for proxemics and collocated collaboration. Our observations indicate that the complexity of the navigation task combined with limited information encouraged verbal communication about where to go or how to interpret the flashes from the phones. This suggests that moving the complexity away from the mobile screens encourages collaboration. And it further illustrates how the limited information allows for the communication to extend into the interpersonal communication between players during interaction and game play.

PROXEMICS PLAY WITH LOW-RESOLUTION DISPLAYS

This section discusses the experiential qualities of low-resolution displays in social games from the perspective of proxemics. The low-resolution design of GlowPhones provides a good case for illustrating how design features of technology have the potential in persuading certain spatial behavior of users and hence influence the social experience in a collocated social game. The following identifies key spatial features in low-resolution displays that suggest new strategic elements in designing for proxemics play.

Dimmed Light Causes Creative F-formations

Experimenting with different light sources from the mobile phone led to important findings regarding properties of low-resolution displays. Harrison et al. suggests that expanding light displays with varying color, size, directionality, diffuseness, and shape would enhance the expressive capability of light displays, however, increasing the complexity. [13]. Our study further explores these physical phenomena and their socio-spatial significance and meaning in a gaming experience. A key design decision was to detect the *directionality* of the device (screen glow navigation) to force the screen to face downwards. Through experiments it became clear that people's traditional use of mobile phones is competing with this interaction concept. Traditional use in mobile games is to face the screen of the phone towards the player where they need to focus.

The short range of light with screen glow navigation exhibited surprising playful bodily configurations of players and technology. Analysing players' spatial behavior, some of the F-formations were reminiscent of those in related work. In Figure 11(A-B) both participants cupped the light or crouched, whereas in Figure 11(C), one player used the back of the other to be able to see higher intensity light from the reflection of screen light. The latter is reminiscent of the *spooning* pattern – identified in Paay et al.'s study of people cooking together [36] – which exhibits a particular intimate enactment between the participants. What is to be noted here is that spatial properties of the actuation (e.g., light) takes part in shaping the social experience, suggesting a new area to explore for proxemics play. While the Kaye et al.'s minimal intimate objects [19] offered new means for remote intimate communication using low resolution, our study illustrates how low-resolution displays serve as collocated intimate communication objects through their spatial consequences, e.g. the glowing screen's short distance resulted in dyads using a spooning formation.

Playing with Proxemic Barriers

An important argument from our study is that it provides an example of how simple design strategies can play with proxemic zones of players in the game. Related work on proxemics play provide strategies for how wireless technologies can make people cross cultural barriers. In the examples of Musical Embrace and Jelly-Stomp [32], players are enticed to lower the distance between each other by exploiting physical properties of sensors (e.g. sensing pressure/touch or breaking Bluetooth reception), potentially causing physical contact between strangers. Observations of the *Jump Together* game complements [32] in suggesting that proxemics play can be

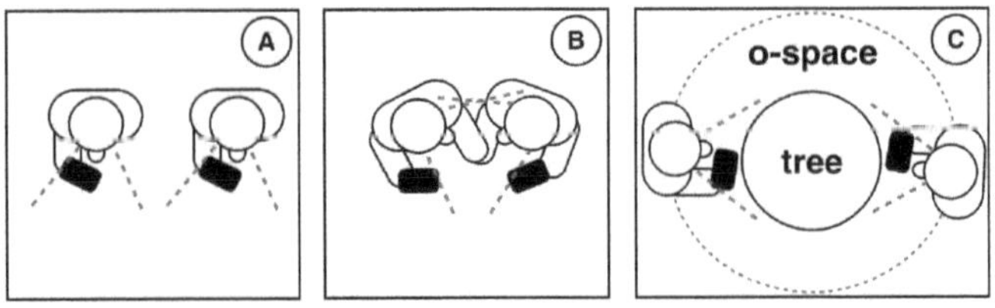

Figure 12: Transactional segments of players in the three game stages creating proxemic zones. A: *Cocoon* - Players' segments were constrained by the attention from bright screens. B: *Hand holding* - Players crossed personal zones to solve task. C: *Separation* - Players' o-space is separated by a tree.

designed for in very simple game modifications. In our case, the distance between players is deliberately lowered by encouraging touch through the narrative. A particular design goal in the *Jump Together* stage was to design for proxemics play by crossing cultural barriers. Deliberate use of hand holding for completing a task (see Figure 12(B)) encouraged the participants to engage on a social level that would otherwise be uncommon in everyday life. Surprisingly every pair of participants engaged in this activity without trying to cheat the system, even though it was occasionally followed by a comment that the hand holding could not be detected by the system (i.e., no sensor enforces hand holding). This suggests, as articulated in [10] that the "magic circle" of the game world extends beyond the sensors and actuators of the mobile device and into the social behaviors and reactions when the game calls for engaging people in activities that challenge cultural norms and expectations.

Furthermore, we extend this idea of playing with proxemic barriers by deliberately creating barriers between players. Goddard et al. use the example of the mobile game Spaceteam [2] in how it necessitates collaboration through verbal communication between players by the asymmetry in the design [10]. The players have, as reported in that work, complementary roles in that their individual interfaces contain different information that the others might be dependent on. As opposed to screen sharing, players are forced to constantly keep an eye on their individual screens, while verbally communicating crucial information to one's collaborators. Similarly in GlowPhones, the designed spatial configuration in the *Light Up Panels* task consisted of light sensors strategically placed on opposite sides of the tree to create an intentional visual barrier between the participants. In the F-formation depicted in Figure 12(C), the tree acts as a barrier between the participants' transactional segments right in their o-space [20], forcing them out of a traditional social space (i.e., [12]) with face-to-face contact, into a spatial configuration where they were physically separated. The task to solve the puzzle of the stage involved a tightly-coupled collaboration between the two participants, where they had to synchronously light up the panels. This encouraged them to verbalize their actions in order to succeed. Hence, inspired by Spaceteam, the design of *Light Up Panels* illustrates how restricting visual access to shared resources (i.e., deviating from traditional physical means of communication) through an unconventional F-formation with a physical barrier can increase verbal communication. Furthermore, both examples of playing with proxemic barriers in interaction design illustrate very simple strategies and game modifications for engaging proxemics in play. We hope this encourages designers to look into even simpler design strategies than those proposed by Mueller at al. [32].

Light as Awareness of Zones

Mueller et al. discuss the potential of interaction design in making people discover wireless and proxemics zones [32]. GlowPhones extends this strategy with an analytical focus on light as a medium for creating zones. The *Color Match* task provides an illustration for comparison with the other two tasks in relation to proxemic zones. *Color Match* requires no collaboration between the participants, and thus in comparison, the proxemic zones are separated, given that the participants neither interact through the task, nor through physical closeness. Being collocated they had a peripheral awareness of the other's screen, however, users were often observed to be concentrated on their private displays, indicated by the fact that no one noticed the lantern lighting up when one completed the task. As mentioned in statements from participants, they were aware how the blinding from a bright screen limited their ability to attend to the surroundings. In this way, the light source highlights where the attention is during *Color Match* and creates a 'cocoon' zone around each individual player with a screen (see Figure 12(A)) that constrains their awareness to the surroundings. Similar to this argument, the light flashes and lanterns act as indicators of zones, making the zones more visible. The blurry and invisible zone of the Wifi range around the task stations were made visible when the lanterns lit up from interactions on the phone. Furthermore, the geofence was made tangible with the light flashes that changed from a blinking pattern to constant light. Along those lines, the observed F-formations around the navigation interactions (see Figure 9 and 11) illustrate how they would actively engage with each others' personal zones using the cones projecting from the light sources. The results from this study indicate a potential in using light as an ambient interface for awareness of wireless and proxemic zones [32].

CONCLUSION

We presented GlowPhones, a location-based mobile game that brings play into the physical world utilizing low-resolution light-based navigation and site-specific challenges. In this work, we demonstrate how low-resolution displays can turn mobile devices from private into shared displays that encourage users to look away from their devices and engage with the surrounding site. Limited information encourages users to collaborate and look for information in the physical world. Low-resolution displays have limited bandwidth, yet 'richness' in the medium as shown with GlowPhones comes from aesthetic qualities in how it triggers emotions in the players including piqued curiosity and stimulation of playful proxemic behaviors. We hope this work encourages additional research exploring new areas of proxemics play with low-resolution displays.

REFERENCES

1. Pokémon Go. `http://www.pokemongo.com`. Accessed: 2016-11-04.
2. Spaceteam. `http://spaceteam.ca/`. Accessed: 2016-06-04.
3. BENFORD, S., ANASTASI, R., FLINTHAM, M., DROZD, A., CRABTREE, A., GREENHALGH, C., TANDAVANITJ, N., ADAMS, M., AND FARR, J. R. Coping with uncertainty in a Location-Based game. *IEEE Pervasive Computing 2*, 3 (July 2003), 34–41.
4. CHEOK, A. D., KOK, R. T., TAN, C., FERNANDO, O. N. N., MERRITT, T., AND SEN, J. Y. P. Empathetic living media. In *DIS '08: Proceedings of the 7th ACM conference on Designing interactive systems* (New York, NY, USA, 2008), ACM, pp. 465–473.
5. CHUMKAMON, S., TUVAPHANTHAPHIPHAT, P., AND KEERATIWINTAKORN, P. A blind navigation system using RFID for indoor environments. In *2008 5th International Conference on Electrical Engineering/Electronics, Computer, Telecommunications and Information Technology* (May 2008), vol. 2, IEEE, pp. 765–768.
6. DE LANGE, M. *Moving circles: Mobile media and playful identities*. 2010.
7. DEVICES, A. Ambient orb, 2005.
8. FERNANDO, O. N., CHEOK, A. D., MERRITT, T., PEIRIS, R. L., FERNANDO, C. L., RANASINGHE, N., WICKRAMA, I., AND KARUNANAYAKA, K. Babbage cabbage: Biological empathetic media. In *VRIC Laval Virtual Proceedings* (Apr. 2009), pp. 363–366.
9. GAVER, W. W., BEAVER, J., AND BENFORD, S. Ambiguity as a resource for design. In *Proceedings of the SIGCHI Conference on Human Factors in Computing Systems* (New York, NY, USA, 2003), CHI '03, ACM, pp. 233–240.
10. GODDARD, W., GARNER, J., AND JENSEN, M. M. Designing for social play in co-located mobile games. In *Proceedings of the Australasian Computer Science Week Multiconference* (New York, NY, USA, 2016), ACSW '16, ACM, pp. 68:1–68:10.
11. GREENBERG, S., MARQUARDT, N., BALLENDAT, T., DIAZ-MARINO, R., AND WANG, M. Proxemic interactions: the new ubicomp? *interactions 18*, 1 (2011), 42–50.
12. HALL, E. T. *The Hidden Dimension*. 1966.
13. HARRISON, C., HORSTMAN, J., HSIEH, G., AND HUDSON, S. Unlocking the expressivity of point lights. In *Proceedings of the SIGCHI Conference on Human Factors in Computing Systems* (New York, NY, USA, 2012), CHI '12, ACM, pp. 1683–1692.
14. ISBISTER, K. Connecting through play. *interactions 23*, 4 (June 2016), 26–33.
15. ISBISTER, K., ABE, K., AND KARLESKY, M. Interdependent wearables (for play): A strong concept for design. In *Proceedings of the 2017 CHI Conference on Human Factors in Computing Systems* (New York, NY, USA, 2017), CHI '17, ACM, pp. 465–471.
16. ISBISTER, K., MÁRQUEZ SEGURA, E., KIRKPATRICK, S., CHEN, X., SALAHUDDIN, S., CAO, G., AND TANG, R. Yamove! a movement synchrony game that choreographs social interaction. *Human Technology 12* (2016), 74–102.
17. JOSELLI, M., AND CLUA, E. gRmobile: A framework for touch and accelerometer gesture recognition for mobile games. In *2009 VIII Brazilian Symposium on Games and Digital Entertainment* (2009), IEEE, pp. 141–150.
18. JUUL, J. The magic circle and the puzzle piece. In *Conference proceedings of the philosophy of computer games* (2008), vol. 56.
19. KAYE, J. ., LEVITT, M. K., NEVINS, J., GOLDEN, J., AND SCHMIDT, V. Communicating intimacy one bit at a time. In *CHI '05: CHI '05 extended abstracts on Human factors in computing systems* (New York, NY, USA, 2005), ACM, pp. 1529–1532.
20. KENDON, A. Spatial organization in social encounters: The f-formation system. *Conducting interaction: Patterns of behavior in focused encounters* (1990), 209–238.
21. KHOO, E., MERRITT, T., AND CHEOK, A. Designing a mixed reality intergenerational entertainment system. In *The Engineering of Mixed Reality Systems*, E. Dubois, P. Gray, and L. Nigay, Eds., Human-Computer Interaction Series. Springer London, London, 2010, ch. 7, pp. 121–141.
22. KHOO, E. T., MERRITT, T., AND CHEOK, A. D. Designing physical and social intergenerational family entertainment. *Interacting with Computers 21*, 1-2 (Jan. 2009), 76–87.
23. KHOO, E. T., MERRITT, T., FEI, V. L., LIU, W., RAHAMAN, H., PRASAD, J., AND MARSH, T. Body music: physical exploration of music theory. In *Sandbox '08: Proceedings of the 2008 ACM SIGGRAPH symposium on Video games* (New York, NY, USA, 2008), ACM, pp. 35–42.
24. KROGH, P. G., PETERSEN, M. G., O'HARA, K., GRØNBÆK, J. E., AND RASMUSSEN, M. K. Sensitizing concepts for socio-spatial literacy in hci. *Proceedings of Chi'17* (2017).
25. KVALE, S. *Doing interviews*. Sage, 2008.
26. LÖCHTEFELD, M., LAUTEMANN, N., GEHRING, S., AND KRÜGER, A. ambiPad: Enriching mobile digital media with ambient feedback. In *Proceedings of the 16th International Conference on Human-computer Interaction with Mobile Devices & Services* (New York, NY, USA, 2014), MobileHCI '14, ACM, pp. 295–298.

27. LUCERO, A., HOLOPAINEN, J., AND JOKELA, T. Mobicomics: Collaborative use of mobile phones and large displays for public expression. In *Proceedings of the 14th International Conference on Human-computer Interaction with Mobile Devices and Services* (New York, NY, USA, 2012), MobileHCI '12, ACM, pp. 383–392.

28. MARCH, W., NAFUS, D., SWAN, L., AND TAYLOR, A. S. Night and darkness: interaction after dark. In *CHI'08 Extended Abstracts on Human Factors in Computing Systems* (2008), ACM, pp. 3985–3988.

29. MARSHALL, P., ROGERS, Y., AND PANTIDI, N. Using f-formations to analyse spatial patterns of interaction in physical environments. In *Proceedings of the ACM 2011 Conference on Computer Supported Cooperative Work* (New York, NY, USA, 2011), CSCW '11, ACM, pp. 445–454.

30. MENTIS, H. M., O'HARA, K., SELLEN, A., AND TRIVEDI, R. Interaction proxemics and image use in neurosurgery. In *Proceedings of the 2012 ACM annual conference on Human Factors in Computing Systems - CHI '12* (New York, New York, USA, 2012), ACM Press, p. 927.

31. MERRITT, T., AND MCGEE, K. Protecting artificial team-mates: More seems like less. In *Proceedings of the SIGCHI Conference on Human Factors in Computing Systems* (New York, NY, USA, 2012), CHI '12, ACM, pp. 2793–2802.

32. MUELLER, F., STELLMACH, S., GREENBERG, S., DIPPON, A., BOLL, S., GARNER, J., KHOT, R., NASEEM, A., AND ALTIMIRA, D. Proxemics play: Understanding proxemics for designing digital play experiences. In *Proceedings of the 2014 Conference on Designing Interactive Systems* (New York, NY, USA, 2014), DIS '14, ACM, pp. 533–542.

33. NACKE, L. E., STELLMACH, S., SASSE, D., AND LINDLEY, C. A. Gameplay experience in a gaze interaction game, Apr. 2010.

34. NEUSTAEDTER, C., TANG, A., AND JUDGE, T. Creating scalable location-based games: lessons from geocaching. *Personal Ubiquitous Comput. 17*, 2 (Feb. 2013), 335–349.

35. PAASOVAARA, S., AND OLSSON, T. Proximity-based automatic exchange of data in mobile gaming: Studying the experiences of streetpass users. In *Proceedings of the 9th Nordic Conference on Human-Computer Interaction* (New York, NY, USA, 2016), NordiCHI '16, ACM, pp. 26:1–26:10.

36. PAAY, J., KJELDSKOV, J., SKOV, M. B., AND O'HARA, K. F-formations in cooking together: A digital ethnography using youtube. In *IFIP Conference on Human-Computer Interaction* (2013), Springer, pp. 37–54.

37. PARTICLE INDUSTRIES INC. Particle photon. `https://store.particle.io/`. Accessed: 2017-07-24.

38. PETERSEN, M. G., IVERSEN, O. S., KROGH, P. G., AND LUDVIGSEN, M. Aesthetic interaction: a pragmatist's aesthetics of interactive systems. In *Proceedings of the 5th conference on Designing interactive systems: processes, practices, methods, and techniques* (2004), ACM, pp. 269–276.

39. POUSMAN, Z., AND STASKO, J. A taxonomy of ambient information systems: Four patterns of design. In *Proceedings of the Working Conference on Advanced Visual Interfaces* (New York, NY, USA, 2006), AVI '06, ACM, pp. 67–74.

40. PUPPENDAHL, T. G., BECHTOLD, O., STRASSEL, L., JAKOB, D., BRAUN, A., AND KUIJPER, A. Enhancing traffic safety with wearable low-resolution displays. In *Proceedings of the 2nd International Workshop on Sensor-based Activity Recognition and Interaction* (New York, NY, USA, 2015), WOAR '15, ACM.

41. RASMUSSEN, M. K., LEHOUX, N., OCNARESCU, I., AND KROGH, P. G. I'Ll knock you when I'M ready...: Reflecting on media richness beyond bandwidth and imitation. In *Proceedings of the Designing Interactive Systems Conference* (New York, NY, USA, 2012), DIS '12, ACM, pp. 106–115.

42. RICHARD GRUSIN, JOHN G. HANHARDT, R. S. J. C. *Jim Campbell: Material Light*. Hatje Cantz, 2010.

43. ROBBINS, H., AND ISBISTER, K. Pixel motion: A surveillance camera-enabled public digital game. In *FDG* (2014).

44. ROBINSON, S., MARSDEN, G., AND JONES, M. *There's Not an App for That: Mobile User Experience Design for Life*, 1 ed. Morgan Kaufmann, Dec. 2014.

45. SALEN, K., AND ZIMMERMAN, E. *Rules of play: Game design fundamentals*. MIT press, 2004.

46. SCHMIDT, A., KLEEMANN, M., MERRITT, T., AND SELKER, T. Tactile communication in extreme contexts: Exploring the design space through kiteboarding. In *Human-Computer Interaction – INTERACT 2015*, J. Abascal, S. Barbosa, M. Fetter, T. Gross, P. Palanque, and M. Winckler, Eds., vol. 9299 of *Lecture Notes in Computer Science*. Springer International Publishing, 2015, pp. 37–54.

47. SONNE, T., MERRITT, T., MARSHALL, P., LOMHOLT, J. J., MÜLLER, J., AND GRØNBÆK, K. Calming children when drawing blood using breath-based biofeedback. In *Proceedings of the 2017 Conference on Designing Interactive Systems* (New York, NY, USA, 2017), DIS '17, ACM, pp. 725–737.

48. TONG, L., SERNA, A., PAGEAUD, S., GEORGE, S., AND TABARD, A. It's not how you stand, it's how you move: F-formations and collaboration dynamics in a mobile learning game. In *Proceedings of the 18th International Conference on Human-Computer Interaction with Mobile Devices and Services* (New York, NY, USA, 2016), MobileHCI '16, ACM, pp. 318–329.

49. TUTERS, M., AND VARNELIS, K. Beyond locative media: Giving shape to the internet of things. *Leonardo 39*, 4 (2006), 357–363.

50. VISITAARHUS. Riis forest. `http://www.visitaarhus.com/ln-int/riis-forest-gdk653297`. Accessed: 2017-07-24.

51. VONGSATHORN, L., O'HARA, K., AND MENTIS, H. M. Bodily interaction in the dark. In *Proceedings of the SIGCHI Conference on Human Factors in Computing Systems* (2013), ACM, pp. 1275–1278.

52. ZWINDERMAN, M., ZAVIALOVA, T., TETTEROO, D., AND LEHOUCK, P. Oh music, where art thou? In *Proceedings of the 13th International Conference on Human Computer Interaction with Mobile Devices and Services* (New York, NY, USA, 2011), MobileHCI '11, ACM, pp. 533–538.

A Framework Supporting Selecting Space to Make Place in Spatial Mixed Reality Play

Hitesh Nidhi Sharma[1] **Sultan A. Alharthi**[1] **Igor Dolgov**[2] **Zachary O. Toups**[1]
[1]Play & Interactive Experiences for Learning Lab, Dept. Computer Science
[2]Perception, Action, & Cognition in Mediated Artificial & Natural Environments Lab, Dept. Psychology
New Mexico State University, Las Cruces, New Mexico, USA
hitesharmaa@gmail.com, salharth@nmsu.edu, id@nmsu.edu, z@cs.nmsu.edu

ABSTRACT
Studies of mixed reality systems, especially games and play, have proliferated in the human-computer interaction literature, yet little research has directly addressed how designers *select* physical *spaces* to *make places*. A space is a physical area, while a place is a space infused with meaning. Mixed reality games that make use of physical space *make and/or alter places*. Selection of a space as a setting for a mixed reality play raises questions around immersion, safety, and user experience design. The present research analyzes the mixed reality literature through grounded theory to derive guidelines for selecting space and making place in mixed reality play. We consider 71 papers and 17 games after filtering over 240 papers for how they address space. We contribute a framing for mixed reality spaces on two axes: one that reflects space continuity and one that reflects space specificity requirements. From the framework, we provide design implications for space selection.

Author Keywords
Mixed reality; augmented reality; games; play; space; outdoor; framework; grounded theory.

ACM Classification Keywords
H.5.1 Information Interfaces and Presentation (e.g. HCI): Multimedia Information Systems

INTRODUCTION
The proliferation of lightweight computing devices and wireless networking, coupled with the ability to track users outdoors, has led to the advent of outdoor *mixed reality play*. Mixed reality play combine virtual reality information with physical reality experience. The present research is concerned with what we call *spatial mixed realities*, those in which information is linked to physical locations (i.e., *location-aware games*, *location-based games*, *location-based activities* [P10]). Applications of spatial mixed reality have included tourism [19], education [6, 20, 37, 46, 54, 57], and, especially, games [P7, P53].

CHI PLAY '17, October 15–18, 2017, Amsterdam, Netherlands

ISBN 978-1-4503-4898-0/17/10... $15.00
DOI: https://doi.org/10.1145/3116595.3116612

Spatial mixed realities take place in physical environments that afford and constrain action through a combination of layout, size, climate, history, purpose, and/or social contracts. All of these must be considered by designers while developing the virtual reality component of their work. The present research supports designers and researchers when selecting space. Thus, this paper aims to answer:

1. *What are the salient variables that mixed reality play designers need to consider when selecting space?*
2. *How might these variables impact the experience?*

The answers to these questions provide implications for those designing mixed reality play with regards to physical location and layout.

To address the research questions, we look to prior designers' considerations in outdoor spaces and analyze these with grounded theory. We target the research literature as a primary data source because, until recently, most mixed reality systems appear as research projects and art installations. To begin, we identified all research published in *Proceedings of the ACM Conference on Human Factors in Computing Systems* (CHI) and the *Proceedings of the International Symposium on Mixed and Augmented Reality* (ISMAR) from October 1999 through June 2015. We used open coding to identify research domains related to mixed reality systems development. We then engaged in open, axial, and selective coding on specific research domains to identify and classify articles that provide insight on the selection of outdoor space. As a point of constant comparison, we then incorporate published mobile games and an additional corpus of papers.

In response to our research questions, we develop a descriptive framework from our axial codes for space selection in mixed reality. The resulting space-selection framework provides designers and researchers insight into how to select outdoor spaces and places for mixed reality play. The framework has two axes: space continuity and specificity requirements. We bring together best practices, identify problems faced by researchers, and make recommendations based on the literature.

Reporting Conventions

In the present research, we use papers and games as data sources for grounded theory analysis. We include an Extended Bibliography that, like the References section, reports on papers we collected as data, but may also cite directly for their insights. Papers from the Extended Bibliography are cited prefixed with a "P" (e.g., [P44]). Likewise, we include a Ludography of mixed reality games that are not reported upon in the literature, but that we include as part of our analysis. Games from the Ludography are prefixed with a "G" (e.g., [G8]).

Paper Outline

We start by discussing background topics related to mixed reality, then deeply develop the concepts of space and place. We cover prior frameworks for mixed reality systems, which influenced our grounded theory analysis of research samples. We describe our methodology for acquiring, filtering, and evaluating the prior research through grounded theory. As results, we present our axial coding scheme that develops a space-selection framework, as well as general observations on the dataset. We then discuss specific design implications for the design of mixed reality play, addressing the research questions.

MIXED REALITY GAMES

Broadly, all games that connect virtual and physical[1] reality [41] in some meaningful way through sensors, networks, computers, and databases are *mixed realities* [4, 8, P7]. These range from *augmented reality*, in which conformal 3D imagery is integrated with a perspective on the physical world, as with most aircraft head-up displays and *Pokèmon GO* [G8], to *augmented virtuality*, in which physical-world artifacts and spaces are integrated into a virtual world.

Many games fall in between the extremes of augmented reality and augmented virtuality. Spatial mixed realities connect virtual information to physical-world locations [2] (e.g., [22, 30]) by tracking users' locations with sensors, like the Global Positioning System (GPS) [9, 30, 60]. In many games, a player's physical-world location is mapped to a virtual-world location isomorphically, yet, in others, this connection is more abstract.

Although related, mixed reality games should not be confused with *alternate reality games*, a form of play involves narrative interaction and puzzle solving [16], which "take the substance of everyday life and weave it into narratives that layer additional meaning, depth, and interaction upon the real world" [P46, p37].

Pervasive games are form of mixed reality, which are "a ludic form of mixed reality entertainment with goals, rules, competition, and attacks, based on the utilization of Mobile Computing and/or Pervasive Computing technologies" [P29, p12].

[1] Throughout, we distinguish the physical world from virtual worlds. We avoid the term "real world", because the connected mixed reality experience of physical and virtual realities compose a player's real world experience.

Affordance Theory

Norman's [45] theory of *affordances* explains how potential interaction is mapped to available action in the physical environment through form and/or design. Norman's theory, which draws upon but also diverges from J.J. Gibson's original conceptualization of affordances [24], accounts for how people use *mental models* [23, 34] to understand the interactive potential afforded by their environments. Affordances, especially those that are otherwise not perceivable, may be augmented by *signifiers* that indicate where and how one may interact with an object or environment. *Constraints* limit interaction through physical characteristics or cultural conventions. Constraints, when considered as a component of design, prevent incorrect interactions.

Affordances, signifiers, and constraints impact how a physical-world space may be used for the purposes of spatial mixed reality. For example, while open layout affords walking, running, and jumping, it also prevents hiding.

Games and Play

Many spatial mixed reality systems are games or playful systems. Salen and Zimmerman [48], through a review of the prior literature and with a nod to Huizinga [33] and Caillois [10], arrive at play as a superset of games, as well as a component of them. Games are systems of *rules*, which limit action, and *play*, which is the freedom to make choices in the context of the rules. *Games* result in a quantifiable outcome, while *play* does not. In the context of spatial mixed reality, the affordances and constraints of the physical world function as rules.

UNDERSTANDING SPACE AND PLACE

To have a clear understanding of the role of the physical world in mixed realities, we develop a discussion of the prior framings of *space* and *place*. We connect these to the concepts of *aura* and *magic circle*.

Space

Space refers to a physical setting [1, 29, 55]; the value of a space depends on the perspective and tasks of the people within it. According to Tuan [55], one of the foremost philosophers on space and place, we perceive space through senses, experiencing it through having room to move around. Humans primarily perceive space through vision, which provides a reference for distance, size, and relationships among entities in one's surroundings. While vision is primary, other senses support experience of space: smell might provide a sense of mass and distance; sound provides information about size and distance; and touch provides information about size, mass, and texture [55].

Spaces provide affordances and constraints to users of mixed reality systems [P69]. Physical-world setting, space, is a critical component of any mixed reality system, as mixed reality systems connect virtual realities to physical space. Many mixed reality systems use vision and sound to give users a sense of the surrounding virtual world in which they co-exist.

Place

Space transforms into place as meaning and definition are developed within a space [1,29,56]. Meaning refers to sensory and symbolic experiences that humans have in a space [55]. Thus, while a space may be a geographic area (e.g., consisting of particular latitudes, longitudes, altitudes), a place at that space might be "home" or "work" [59]. "Place-ness" renders space valuable and memorable to humans. Dourish [18] described space as geometrical arrangements structuring and enabling movement, while place denotes the ways in which settings acquire recognizable meaning through interactions. Mixed reality systems render spaces meaningful, making place (even if their setting already has place-ness).

Aura

When considering pure virtual reality systems, the concept of *presence* [50], becomes a key to their evaluation, accounting for how users are immersed in a virtual world, their sense that they are visiting a virtual place. MacIntyre et al. [40] argued against presence in the context of mixed reality systems because, in such systems, users are already present in a physical-world space. They introduced *aura*, building on Benjamin's prior essay regarding the value of art [5].

Aura describes the cultural and personal significance that a place (or object) holds for an individual, which helps to operationalize the definition of place. MacIntyre et al. [40] discuss how aura arises from significant historical, cultural, and personal aspects of a place or object and represents a relationship between a person and the place or object. Mixed reality systems potentially enhance and are enhanced by the aura of places in which they are set.

Magic Circle

Games are played in what game scholars term the *magic circle* [33,49], the temporal and physical bounds of play[2] The magic circle is a temporary geographical, virtual, or mental space within a player's world. By willingly entering into the magic circle, the game acts as an extension of everyday life where player attitudes and behaviors change, special rules apply, and new reality is created [15,42,58]. Montola et al. [P46] defined the magic circle as being bounded by space, time, and participation, and suggest that the magic circle can be expanded through pervasive games [P37]. Popular spatial mixed reality games such as *Pokèmon GO* [G8], *Zombies GO* [G16], and *Ingress* [G7] provide augmented and mixed reality experiences that are also pervasive. More event-oriented games, like *Can You See Me Now?* [P7] and *Treasure* [P6] are played in a specific bounded space at a particular time, isolating their magic circles from everyday life.

Summary

Space is a critical component of spatial mixed reality play and such play renders spaces meaningful, making place. We perceive space through not only our senses, but also through time and memory. These experiences enable us to form a mental model of the space and, eventually, transform it into a place through which we understand and relate to different aspects of our surroundings. Connecting all these concepts together helps develop a sense of what mixed reality spaces incorporate and what we should consider when selecting outdoor spaces.

[2] Huizinga's "magic circle" specifically referred to an inscribed circle used by witches for practicing magic. Salen and Zimmerman [49] appropriated that example place for game play, popularizing it as a generic game design term.

PRIOR MIXED REALITY THEORIES

Our interaction with the physical-world landscape as an information (i.e., virtual-world) landscape is still in its infancy [21]. Although our focus in this paper on spatial mixed reality play, we work from prior theories of mixed reality system design to drive the present research and, later, explain how our developed framework incorporates these prior frameworks.

Benford and Giannachi [4] describe the experience of a user in a mixed reality system in terms of *trajectories*. Trajectories are initiated through the design of the mixed reality interactions, guiding initial experience. Inevitably, users direct their experience and deviate from designed paths to establish their unique trajectories. Processes of orchestration serve to drive users back toward a canonical trajectory. Benford and Giannachi conceptualize trajectories in terms of *space*, *time*, *role*, and *interface*. Space defines the setting in which the mixed reality system is staged and informs our grounded theory coding. Time deals with the temporal structure and scale of the experience. Role deals with participants' roles in a mixed reality performance, and how these shift over time. The interfaces trajectory defines how user interfaces change during a mixed reality experience.

Lundgren et al. [39] provide a practical design framework for collocated mobile experiences, which functions as a tool to analyze mobile experiences. This framework develops four perspectives, including a spatial perspective, to support designers in asking questions of mixed reality systems. The present research builds on and extends spatial perspective and its properties of PROXIMITY, LOCATION, and MOVEMENT, providing insights into the importance of continuity of space for design and how the type of space affects experience.

Bowser et al. [P10] developed the PLACE Framework that introduces an iterative approach to prototyping and developing mixed reality application development. This approach considers four elements for mixed-fidelity prototyping where the fidelity changes with iteration. The four elements in consideration are: location, activities, collective experience, and time. Of these elements, the present research focuses on location. We aim to understand how location shapes the development of mixed reality systems and the components of space designers need to consider.

Bligh and Crook [7] identified space-affordance types for learning: impeding (e.g., learners may be inhibited by space around them), containing (e.g., the layout of a space may restrict / challenge or support / enhance learning interactions), stimulating (e.g., spaces can be used to stimulate learners' thinking and encourage physical exploration), associative (e.g., they support developing abstractions), constitutive (e.g., being part of the environment learners are located), and socially constitutive (e.g., creating a place through social interactions).

Montola et al. [P46] introduced the concept of *site-specific games*. These type of games are localized to a specific place. The authors argue that such games can provide a deeper historical experience for players even though they might be costly to develop and difficult to set up. Kristiansen [P37] noted that Montola's concept of site-specific games only focused on games dealing with local history. To widen the scope, Kristiansen [P37] conceptualized mixed-reality games as spatially-extended pervasive games and developed a model for designing site-specific games based on performance studies. This model includes the physical site of the game and the *locomotion* of the players.

Montola also introduced the concept of *site-adaptable games* [P46]. He defines them as games that can be adapted easily to a different place. Designers of such games need to take into consideration the size, duration, location infrastructure, and the role of place in the gameplay to successfully adopt games to new locations. [P54] Similarly, Flanagan [P24] introduced the concept of *location-free games*.These are games that can be moved from one location to another without any noticeable changes. In these games, players might be asked to visit places or perform actions that are described generically (e.g., dance on a bench) [P46].

Ejsing-Duun [P22, P23] undertook a design-based research approach to identify prerequisites for location-based games (LBGs) through a review of previous research and existing LBGs. The author argued that when playing an LBG, navigation between *play* and *ordinary*, *authenticity* and *fiction*, and *physical* and *digital* is at the core of the gameplay. The author was engaged in playing and analyzing a number of LBGs and noted that games relate to specific locations in different ways. Furthermore, the analysis revealed that LBGs can be location-free, site-relative, and site-adaptable.

Hinske et al. [P29] introduced four dimensions that contribute to players' experiences in mixed reality games. The *physical* dimension is experienced when players interact with tangible objects in the physical reality. *Mental* experience is stimulated by mental and intellectual challenges. The *social* dimension is experienced when players interact and communicate with other players. The last dimension is the *immersion* of players into a game. The author argues that the potential to fully realize these dimensions is higher in mixed reality games than in physical and virtual reality.

Summary

While most theories [4, P10, P22, P23, P29] include space as a prominent dimension of mixed reality design, they do not focus on how spaces should be chosen. Other prior research (e.g., [P22, P23, P38, P46]) has emphasized location and attempted to categorize mixed reality systems based on how they relate to space, they fail to compare types of mixed reality spaces. The current research focuses only on mixed reality space and proposes a universal framework for efficient categorization of mixed reality spaces and how each can affect the design of mixed reality games and play.

METHODOLOGY

We conducted a qualitative study to identify the main research domains around mixed reality systems in order to investigate the ways in which space and place have been used in location-based mixed reality games. We undertook a grounded theory approach [25–27], starting with open coding on the research domain of each paper, followed by a second, focused round of open coding on the use of space.

Grounded theory is a process of generating theory based on empirical qualitative data [25–27]. Similar to any research method, grounded theory procedures include sampling participants, collecting data, analyzing data, reviewing relevant literature, and reporting results [31]. However, grounded theory begins with collecting data in order to build up categories and form a theory [32], rather than starting from a hypothesis. Grounded theory data can come from many sources, including interviews, video recordings, survey data, books, and scientific papers [14]. Alongside the iterative process of collecting data, *open coding* is performed to develop initial concepts. This process will result in the development of categories which will eventually form a theory [32].

Our iterative process started with identifying, retrieving, and reviewing mixed reality literature. Based on the abstract of each paper, an open coding and ranking process was performed, resulting in emergent initial concepts. Axial coding was then conducted, followed by selective coding, leading to the final categories.

Search Strategy

A key component of the grounded theory approach is to collect a relevant corpus of data. Previously, Carter et al. [12] performed a grounded theory analysis of game-related research in the past 10 years of CHI conferences to identify distinct research paradigms. We follow a similar technique to come up with categories and acquire relevant papers. In order to identify a comprehensive sample of this literature, we focus on two primary venues where high-quality mixed reality research has been published: the *Proceedings of the ACM Conference on Human Factors in Computing Systems* (CHI) and the *Proceedings of the International Symposium on Mixed and Augmented Reality* (ISMAR). In addition to using a set of developed search criteria on these proceedings, we add additional works from relevant scholarly sources, including the *Proceedings of the Annual Symposium on Human-Computer Interaction in Play* (CHI PLAY). We also consider a set of commercial games.

In order to identify relevant papers for this literature review, we used the following search strings on the ACM Digital Library (DL)[3] for CHI to identify papers relating to mixed and augmented reality:

```
(((Title:mixed reality*) or
(Abstract:mixed reality)) and
(PublicationTitle:SIGCHI Conference on
Human Factors in Computing Systems)) and
PublishedAs:proceeding)
```

[3] http://dl.acm.org

```
(((Title:augmented reality*) or
(Abstract:augmented reality)) and
(PublicationTitle:SIGCHI Conference on
Human Factors in Computing Systems)) and
PublishedAs:proceeding)
```

The "mixed reality" search identified 40 total papers and the "augmented reality" search identified 88 papers. Of these, 2 were duplicates, so 126 papers were obtained.

We included papers from the ISMAR proceedings, which was more challenging than using the ACM DL. We tried a number of programs: Zotero,[4] Publish or Perish,[5] Papers,[6] and IEEE Xplore.[7] The results obtained from Zotero contained no abstract, while results from Publish or Perish and Papers identified fewer papers. IEEE Xplore was the most effective. We used the following search string:

```
(("Document Title":mixed reality)
OR "Abstract":mixed reality)) AND
(Refined by:(Publisher:  IEEE), (Content
Type:  Conference Publications), AND
(Publication Title:  ISMAR 2002, 2004,
2006, 2008-2015, ISMAR-AMH 2009-2013,
ISMAR-MASH'D 2014).
```

We specify the publication year range from 1979 to 2015. The search resulted in a total of 177 results, which included proceedings frontmatter, cover image credits, and workshop whitepapers; we removed these, ending up with 117 peer-reviewed papers.

Procedure

The research process included four phases, which are outlined in Figure 1 and described below.

Phase 1: Open Coding for Research Domain

Our first step was to identify the research domains of the resulting papers prior to further filtering. Based on the abstracts of each of the 243 papers, open coding was performed to cluster papers which share common domains in mixed reality research. From this, 9 categories of research domains emerged.

Phase 2: Filtering and Open Coding on Space Usage

The second phase of the process focused on the use of space in mixed reality. During the Phase 1 coding process, each paper was assessed for its *use of space* and rated by one researcher on a scale of 0 to 5, with 5 being the most relevant. The rating of each paper reflects the relevance to our research and its insight into the use of and selection of space for the described mixed reality system. To determine the ranking of each paper, we reviewed the titles, abstract, and keywords of each paper based on the following characteristics:

- the words "mixed reality", "augmented reality", or "outdoor" appeared and

[4]http://zotero.org
[5]http://www.harzing.com/resources/publish-or-perish
[6]http://papersapp.com
[7]http://ieeexplore.ieee.org

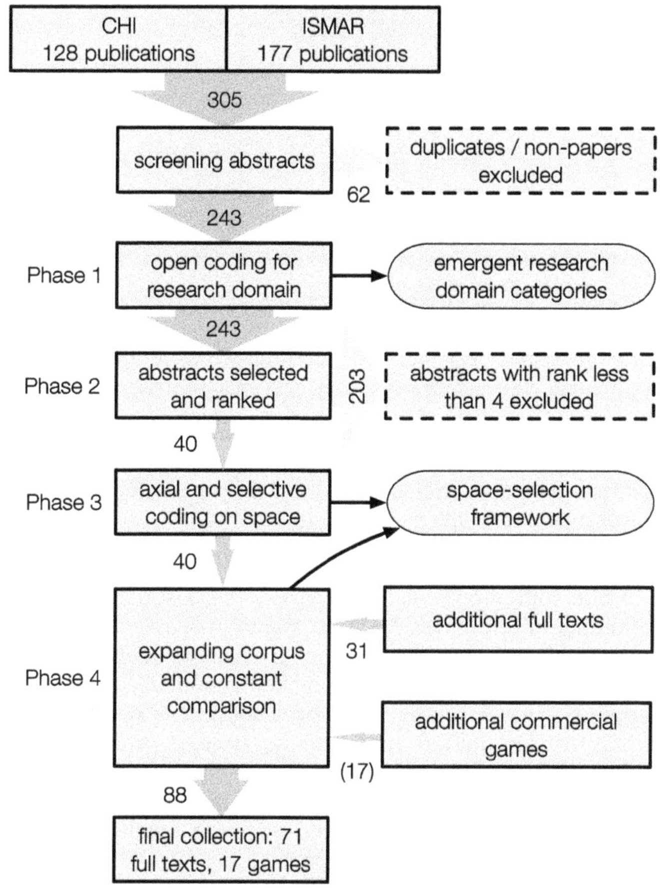

Figure 1. Process of acquiring and filtering papers and games. Phase identifiers are connected to this process; Phase 2 involved filtering, while Phase 4 involved adding to the corpus. Phases 1 and 3 occur between the filtering blocks.

- the design, assessment, or evaluation of outdoor mixed reality system was the main topic.

While one researcher rated all of the papers, a second researcher independently rated a subset of 20 of the papers to establish inter-rater reliability (IRR) [28]. Due to the nature of the data, we used a Pearson correlation to calculate IRR; the result was an acceptable 0.75.

In order to investigate the ways in which space and place have been used in location-based mixed reality research, we focused on the papers that were highly likely to provide insight about mixed reality spaces. Thus, papers with ratings of 4 and 5 were selected for further study, which resulted in a total of 40 papers. As we analyzed these, we engaged in further open coding, looking for common properties of outdoor mixed reality spaces in order to define concepts and categories.

Phase 3: Axial and Selective Coding on Space Usage

Axial coding was conducted to explore how the emergent concepts and categories were related in order to refine the final categories. While re-reading the selected papers, we undertook an iterative process of analyzing the relationship between the research domains and properties of outdoor mixed

rating	CHI	ISMAR	additional
5	15	7	31
4	13	5	
3	19	24	
2	16	41	
1	20	17	
0	43	23	
total	126	117	31

Table 1. Number of papers from each source by rating. Papers rated 4 or 5 were included in the analysis.

reality space. Through axial coding, we developed two axes of categories: space continuity and specificity requirements.

Finally, selective coding was conducted on the axial codes, removing and combining categories. The resulting two axes of codes developed are described in the Space-Selection Framework section of the paper.

Phase 4: Expansion of Corpus and Constant Comparison

While studying the selected papers, we also came across a number of references that were found to be relevant but were not published in either CHI or ISMAR. We added these papers to the corpus in order to make the collection more comprehensive. A survey paper by Thomas [P65] was used to find relevant outdoor mixed reality systems. We also manually identified all relevant CHI PLAY papers, collecting three papers from the three years of that conference (2014–2016). In reading the additional papers, we found that the axial codes readily applied to the new papers.

In addition to peer-reviewed articles, a number of existing mixed reality games were collected for the purpose of comparison. Because mobile platforms offer the technology needed for mixed realities, many commercial systems are developed for them. We focused on the two most popular mobile app stores: the Apple App Store for the mobile iOS operating system and Google Play for Android. To identify mixed reality games, we used two search strings: `("mixed reality games")` and `("augmented reality games")`. We selected 17 games that were ranked 4 or 5 stars and categorized them with the framework. The selected games are referenced in the Ludography.

RESULTS

We present the results of our grounded theory analysis, which develops a space-selection framework. We also cover further observations from the papers surveyed.

Space-Selection Framework

We explored the finalized papers and grouped them based on the space(s) in which the described mixed reality game was staged or played. We attempted to determine the size of locations in which mixed reality systems were deployed. However, this proved challenging because many papers only describe the name or type of space, but not the actual size of the location.

We developed an axial coding scheme for space usage in mixed reality. On one axis is space continuity and on the other is specificity requirements for deploying the system. Figure 3 shows how each paper and game was categorized in the framework.

Space Continuity

Based on the literature we reviewed, we consider the boundaries (or lack thereof) of the physical-world region in which a mixed reality can be experienced. It is worth noting that we are not discussing size, but how boundaries are organized. This resulted in four classifications of space continuity: individual spaces, isolated spaces, continuous spaces, and ubiquitous spaces. The spectrum of of space continuity types is described below and in Figure 2; Figure 3 shows how the data fit into the framework.

- **Individual Spaces** offer mixed reality experiences in one bounded location, defined by the developer in advance. A user does not need to move outside of the individual space to any other location to experience mixed reality. Most indoor mixed reality experiences take place in individual spaces (e.g., Scorpiodome [P45]), but outdoor mixed realities with well-defined boundaries may also be individual.
- Systems that develop **Isolated Spaces** connect together multiple individual spaces without mixed reality in between them. As the user moves from one location to another on a definite route, possibly returning to earlier spaces, s/he experiences mixed reality at each individual space. Developing an isolated space does not imply that users move through the individual spaces sequentially, although some experiences do work this way. An example is the Westwood Experience [P70], where specific story events happen at discrete locations around a city, but not in between.
- Similar to isolated spaces, **Continuous Spaces** provide users with mixed reality experiences along a route, but in this case this experience is continuous. While there may be points at which more substantial, individual-space-style events occur, the user is experiencing the virtual world along the way (e.g., *PAC-LAN* [P53]).
- **Ubiquitous Spaces** are large-scale and feature poorly defined or undefined boundaries (possibly including anywhere in the world). Ubiquitous spaces allow users to experience mixed reality continuously in all directions. The user does not need to follow a route and can move around freely to explore the environment. *Can You See Me Now?* [P7] is played over multiple city blocks and is an example of a ubiquitous space. *Pokèmon GO* [G8] is another example, as it can be played in any space, as long as the player's location can be determined.

Specificity Requirements

As a second axis, we consider the specificity requirements for the researched spatial mixed realities, which accounts for how generic or specific a space needs to be to support the intended experience, including technological requirements. Specificity requirements leverage affordance theory and space versus place, building on the prior frameworks discussed earlier that we connect here. These include open space, templated space, and place, described as follows:

type	number	example
university	7	Forgotten Valley [P57]
town / city	5	*Can You See Me Now?* [P7]
indoor	4	Alice's Adventures [43]
historical sites	2	The Augurscope [P59]
amusement park	1	Thrill Laboratory [P60]
cemetery	1	Voices of Oakland [P20]

Table 2. Types of places observed in the data. Some papers reported on specific places in which the mixed reality experience was held; we present them here in descending order of prevalence. An example is provided for each.

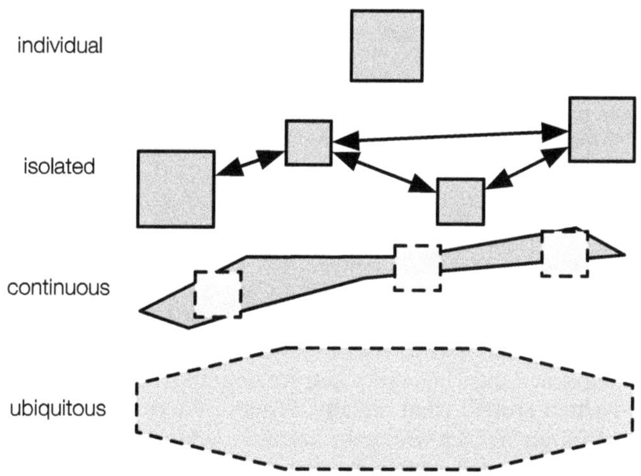

Figure 2. Graphical representation of the space continuity types found in the literature. Individual spaces are self-contained, with definite boundaries. Isolated spaces are each self-contained and experienced in a sequence. Continuous spaces are like isolated spaces, but with mixed reality along a path. Ubiquitous spaces have poorly defined or no boundaries. This style of diagram can easily be used by designers to specify boundaries in their own spatial mixed realities.

- **Open Space** mixed reality games do not *require* any particular affordances or constraints in the physical environment. These games can be experienced anywhere, although the particulars of each mixed reality instance will vary, dependent on where the experience is located. In these games, the physical world may function for users as a "found object" [11, 36], ready to be leveraged as part of the mixed reality experience (e.g., affordances for hiding, sprinting, or moving carefully may be different from space to space). Examples include *AR Soccer* [G5], which can be played anywhere. Prior frameworks do not identify open space – even location-free games [P22–P24] put requirements on space.

- Many mixed reality games that can be deployed without a specific place rely on **Templated Space**. A templated space may be created anywhere that specific requirements (e.g., location data sources, locations with specific affordances, technology support) are met. *Can You See Me Now?* [P7] is a good example: the game can be played in different geographic locations by modifying it to fit to the location, but does rely on those locations to have GPS blind spots, be urban, etc. *Pokèmon GO* [G8] and *Ingress* [G7] are other good examples, since they rely on a populated database of places of interest. While the developers of *Pokèmon GO* and *Ingress* have substantial databases of places of interest, resulting in near-ubiquitous coverage, the games are not playable in locations where a database is not available. Prior frameworks identify site-adaptable games [P22, P23, P46], site-relative games [P22, P23], and location-free games [P22–P24], which are all played in templated spaces.

- Other mixed reality experiences rely on a specific **Place**. They develop an experience that is unique to a specific location owing not only to the templated space there, but also unique characteristics, such as aura. In the Westwood Experience, the tour ends with a grave of a specific person, which is unique [P70]. The experience cannot be replicated in a different geographic location. Archeoguide relies on the ancient site where the Olympic Games started [P68]. *Operation: Citadel* is set in and around the historic Halifax Citadel, providing history about that location [P71]. Place-based systems are custom-built to incorporate the characteristics of their setting, which is unique. While not directly invoking the notion of place, prior frameworks have identified site-specific games [P37, P46], which are equivalent.

Additional Observations

Some other observations came out of our grounded theory analysis. None of the papers in our original dataset discussed the physical size of space. As an additional data point, for those systems that use places, we provide insight into the type of place on Table 2. Most common (unsurprisingly, given the focus on academic papers) are universities, followed by urban locations.

DISCUSSION

Based on our study of 71 papers and 17 games through this research, we develop insights to help mixed reality game designers select mixed reality spaces or make mixed reality experiences more meaningful.

Space-Selection Framework Observations

Working from Figure 3, we note that some combinations of continuity and specificity are null sets and one is impossible.

Place-based systems are the fewest, likely due to the need to deeply invoke the human value of a place. Likewise, it is not surprising that there are no ubiquitous place-based systems, as it would be challenging to develop systems that evoke the uniqueness of an unbounded space. At the same time, it is notable that there are no individual or continuous place-based systems; there is no reason such systems cannot exist, but none were observed in the review. Many of these systems are in the storytelling domain and describe tours of places, which is why they are isolated.

Unsurprisingly, templated space is the most commonly observed type specificity. We expect templated spaces balance the needs of having a certain physical environment with the ability to constrain the design space for a mixed reality.

Open spaces, like places, make up a small number of collected systems; most open-space systems are games. Open

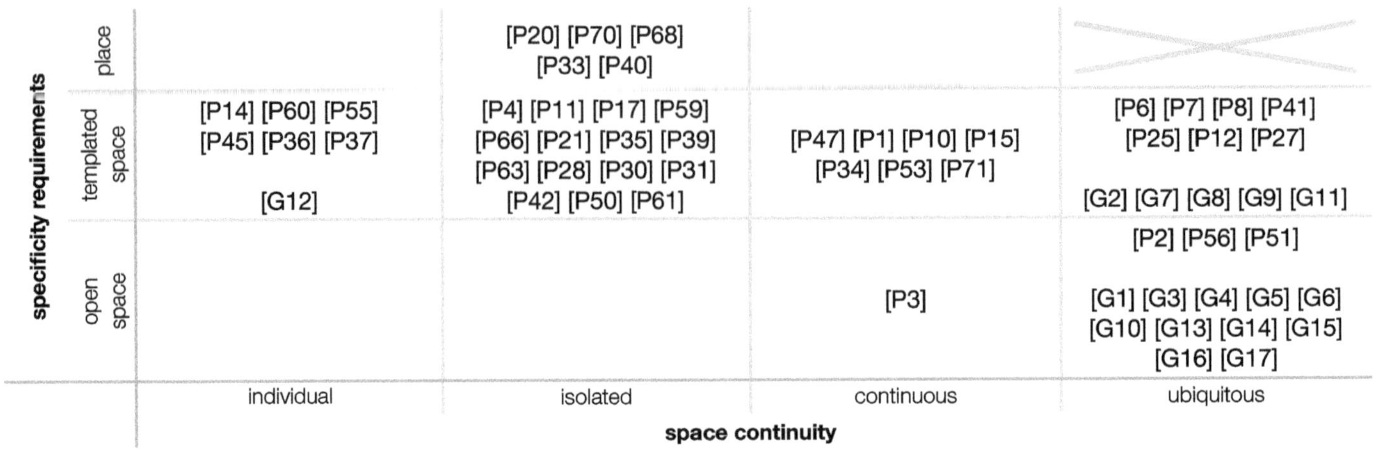

Figure 3. Application of axial codes to the data. Note that the majority of mixed reality games use templated space, which enables them to be run in many different spaces. All reviewed papers that used place were isolated; all of these systems created a specific experience that was run in a specific order.

spaces are challenging to design for, since the designer does not know, in advance, where the user will be or what physical affordances s/he will have access to.

Finally, we note that almost all observed games have ubiquitous continuity. This is likely due to the fact that more specific specifications would limit the market for purchasers of such games.

Considerations in Creating and Using Places

A space transforms into a place as the space acquires meaning [55]. Any spatial mixed reality has the potential to transform a space into a place, regardless of the starting status of the setting. Space-based experiences are potentially more challenging to design on the physical side, owing to lack of specificity, especially in the case of open-space-based systems. At the same time, they have fewer requirements than place-based experiences that will need to leverage the human value of a place.

Authentic places are not always available for mixed reality creation. Places can be constructed, transposed, or evoked through the careful use of the virtual worlds of mixed reality. One example of constructing a place was in Alice's Adventures [43], where developers created a physical model where a user is immersed to experience the story of *Alice in Wonderland*. In San Francisco<->Baghdad, Levine *transposed* a place into a local space by connecting locations in Baghdad that had been bombed to locations in San Francisco [35]. The designer's intention was to provoke a sense of presence in a remote place, which lends meaning to the local space, transforming it. Finally, the prototype Voices of Oakland [P20] used a cemetery to develop users' understanding of a battlefield. The grave sites function as meaningful stand-ins for the historic event, even though the event took place elsewhere.

Mixed realities set in meaningful places can leverage a place's aura to transform participants' understanding of that place. Storytelling and exploration support were the major research domains that contained place-based mixed realities found in the present research. Many such systems draw participants into the history of a specific location. The Westwood Experience [P70] emphasizes the fact that narrative should be carefully tailored to the actual environment. This research suggested that, in case of storytelling, the narrative should be written around what already exists in the real world, instead of simply a place where the narrative is located. The selection of place and narrative development go hand-in-hand. Further, the mixed reality experience of the television series *The Walking Dead* would have not have been as immersive if the tour was not performed in the same city on which the story is based [P39]. Nilsson's [44] project about writer Astrid Lindgren was situated in places where the writer was inspired. They selected the location around the theme "this was where it happened." Archeoguide [P68] uses the ancient site where the Olympic Games started. This place was selected because it was the birthplace of the Olympics Games.

Selecting space for mixed reality games poses significant challenges to designers. Davidson et al. [P19] discussed five of these challenges; dealing with uncertainty, hybrid architectures, hefting domains, configuration, and orchestration. It is important to note that as space size, complexity, layout and boundaries change, uncertainty also changes and, in some cases, might increase.

Value of the Physical World

Farman [21] points out that while mixed realities provide embodied [17] experiences, they must be better than a well-made documentary on the same topic. Place-based mixed realities must do more than simply provide information, otherwise, a documentary suffices. Thus, interaction with *both* the virtual and physical reality is essential, as is tapping into aura.

Thomas and Piekarski [53] keenly observed that while operating outdoor augmented reality applications that are not registered to the physical world, visual information from the physical world becomes irrelevant and merely a backdrop. Hence, they moved from developing augmented reality to developing

Virtual Reality Quake, which can be played at any location and does not use the physical world.

Safety Considerations

Insights from Ballagas' [3] work on *REXplorer*, a pervasive game for tourists, and Barkhuus et al.'s *Treasure* [P6], suggested that there should be a balance between immersion and safety. As mixed reality experiences happen in physical locations, too much immersion in the virtual world can make a user unsafe as they focus more on the virtual world at the expense of the physical.

As the physical-world boundaries of a mixed reality experience expand, the level of risk increases with it. The design of a mixed reality game in terms, of its space continuity and layout, has significant implications for safety. Ubiquitous and continuous spaces are potentially the most dangerous, since there are no imposed boundaries on where users engage with the system and, thus, unsafe space (e.g., automobile roads and parking lots) may be a part of the mixed reality space. On the other extreme, individual spaces can be constructed so that the user only operates in mixed reality in safe areas. Isolated spaces enable the designer to build mixed realities over large areas, but disengage the user between them. Such systems enable safe design, since the designer can ensure that players reach safe areas for interaction, and then move between them without distraction. Further, physical space can be reconfigured to ensure safety (e.g., by setting up barriers).

Regardless of space continuity, a key UI concern for designers should be identifying to the user s/he can disengage from the virtual world to facilitate safety in the physical world. We note that *Pokèmon GO* [G8], with its ubiquitous continuity, now requires that the user tap "OK" to clear a modal dialog that states: "Remember to be alert at all times. Stay aware of your surroundings." prior to playing. A balance between immersion and continuity of spaces should be considered carefully when designing mixed reality games.

Technology and Space

A variety of modalities now exist to support creating mixed realities. The means of rendering virtual world information perceptible as well as tracking and communicating with users is now an immense design space. While the technologies that support mixed reality games are rapidly improving, issues with tracking and networking remain and need to be considered in design, especially when they interact with space.

For outdoor applications, especially games, the combination of GPS and electronic compass is the most widely used means of tracking users [P63]. These technologies can reduce the specificity needs of a physical space. Studies show that in a location-aware game played in an urban area had GPS error that ranged from 4m to 106m, with a mean of 12.4m and a standard deviation of 5.8m [P25]. The impact of inaccuracy can be very high, which directly impacts the mixed reality experience and places constraints on its design. This uncertainty is caused by limitations of wireless communications, especially in urban areas. To reduce this uncertainty, designers need to carefully select locations that can provide players with a higher reliability. For example, the Situated Multimedia Learning Arts Learning Laboratory (SMALLab), a portable templated mixed-reality environment, used a combination of RFID and motion capture technologies to achieve accuracies within a few centimeters [6].

Work by Chalmers and Galani [13], further developed by Benford et al. [P7], recommended *seamful design*, especially in light of the inaccuracy of location tracking. Because tracking and networking technologies are unreliable, the designer must address the seams of developed mixed reality games. Location tracking is heavily impacted by availability of satellites, which is dependent on space [60] and/or augmentations available in the built environment (e.g., fiducials, ultrasonic pingers [9]), which become part of a templated space. Designers can ignore, work around, and/or exploit seams as intentional design components.

Other systems aim to work around seams in mixed realities through templated space. CityViewAR [P40] is designed to overcome the limitations in tracking accuracy by encouraging users to move to known locations where they can have a better AR experience. They also recommend building applications *around the content* that is the main focus of the user experience and have specific viewpoints to present augmented reality data so that interaction is not destroyed due to lack of GPS or other technological limitations.

Display modality is another consideration while selecting space for mixed reality experiences [51]. If a handheld device is the display, then the colors and/or textures of the physical background might not be problematic. However, for see-through and head-mounted displays, the background colors and luminance of the environment onto which virtual information is displayed make a big difference. These constraints serve to increase the specificity requirements for a physical space. Various studies shed light on the design of interfaces for head mounted displays that include recommendations on color choice and drawing style [38], optimal font size [47], and assistance in visual search [47]. A key concern in developing augmented reality, which incorporates 3D information into views of the physical world, is lighting and shadows. Often, the degree of realism of virtual objects in outdoor lighting environments makes a big difference for augmented reality experiences, so space selection must properly account for lighting conditions, which are potentially variable [51,52].

DESIGN IMPLICATIONS

The developed framework provides insights into possibilities and constraints of space selection. Based on developing the framework, we highlight specific design implications for spatial mixed reality play.

Knowing Existing Place

It is critical that designers be aware of the potential for existing aura in a space, which may not be immediately obvious. This prior aura may impact how players experience play, negatively or positively influencing the experience. This can be challenging or impossible to analyze in ubiquitous space, but play in tighter scopes can be analyzed in advance.

Considerations Making Place

Space transforms to place through well-designed mixed reality play. When working in established places, the designer needs to consider how developed new meaning interacts with existing place-ness. The design may conflict, co-exist, or even amplify the existing meaning in the place.

Analyze Continuity

Designers need to consider the continuity of their spatial mixed realities. Play can stay in one location, expand discretely or continuously in one direction or in all directions. Designing for individual spaces can benefit from being designed on-site, which helps designers personalize the experience, gain further insights, and promotes creativity by leveraging affordances of the environment. When designing for an isolated space, it can be beneficial to set up play around known landmarks. The surrounding landmarks help maintain player immersion while moving from one individual space to another.

Consider Safety and Technology

Safety considerations and resource needs increase as continuity expands. Individual and isolated spaces might require less resources and safety measures. If the target space is ubiquitous, start prototyping with individual spaces and more towards isolated, continuous and then to ubiquitous. Moving from individual to ubiquitous also falls in line with the recommendations of Bowser et al. [P10] who recommends to prototype mixed reality games in place that are actually the final locations of the game.

For non-individual spaces, reliability of player tracking becomes challenging because of technological limitations. Designers are recommended to select locations that provide higher reliability of tracking technology (e.g., urban canyons for better GPS reception, use alternative tracking such as RFID). However, incorporating these limitations as part of the game play can help overcome these challenges as well [P7]. It is important to select locations that do not interfere with user interfaces of the game (e.g., see-through HMDs do not perform well in bright sunlight).

A CALL TO ACTION: REPLICATION AND REPORTING

While researchers strive to create new systems and evaluate them in the HCI literature, it is also important to consider replicability.

- When replicating mixed reality game research, developers need to consider place, but when systems are space-based, they can be moved from one location to another, especially when these are open-space systems.
- When reporting on template-based space systems, a template description is essential.
- Diagrams with physical-world anchors are ideal for reporting on space continuity (see Figure 2).

Overall, we call for better reporting of space usage in mixed reality games research. Few of the reviewed papers provided sufficient insights to reproduce the research performed, yet information on space size and space template information could have easily been provided. Further, such information would assist readers in understanding what they can take away from the presented research and limits of that research. Thus, we encourage future researchers to ensure that their work makes available maps/layouts, boundaries, size descriptions, and template descriptions for the physical components of mixed realities.

CONCLUSION

Selecting a space in which to set a mixed reality requires careful planning and balancing of number of variables. In this paper, we acquired, filtered, and deeply evaluated research that reports on its use of space. From this, we developed a framework that identifies mixed reality spaces spaces along two axes: space continuity and space specificity.

Space continuity defines the scope of a mixed reality experience, affects the affordances and constraints the physical world imposes, and may impact its safety. The continuity of space drives the need for virtual data that is linked to a physical-world location: the larger and more continuous the space, the greater the need for virtual world data and connectivity.

The specificity of mixed reality space describes how important qualities of the physical world are for experience. Effectively describing space specificity can support replication in research and design. Developing systems that can be built onto open space is challenging, as the affordances and constraints may be unknown. Templated spaces are versatile and enable the designer to create specific experiences without the need of an exact place. Places can help to drive narrative and mutually develop meaning for the mixed reality and the source place. While authentic places may be unavailable for use as mixed realities, when such technologies are introduced to extant places, a new authenticity is gained.

We expect the present research to be of value to mixed reality designers and researchers as they select space and make place. In addition, designers will find the framework useful in characterizing potential locations for setting mixed reality games and support understanding the design trade-offs of using particular locations. Researchers should find that the framework enables them to better describe their own games, supporting replicability and reporting.

ACKNOWLEDGEMENTS

This material is based upon work supported by the National Science Foundation under Grant No. IIS-1619273.

REFERENCES

1. John A. Agnew and David N. Livingstone. 2011. *The SAGE Handbook of Geographical Knowledge*. SAGE Publications Ltd., London, UK.
2. Ronald T. Azuma. 1999. The Challenge of Making Augmented Reality Work Outdoors. In *Mixed Reality: Merging Real and Virtual*. Springer-Verlag, 379–390.
3. Rafael Ballagas, André Kuntze, and Steffen P. Walz. 2008. Gaming Tourism: Lessons from Evaluating REXplorer, a Pervasive Game for Tourists. In *Proceedings of Pervasive Computing (Lecture Notes in Computer Science)*, Jadwiga Indulska, Donald J. Patterson, Tom Rodden, and Max Ott (Eds.), Vol. 5013. Springer, Berlin, Heidelberg, 244–261. DOI: http://dx.doi.org/10.1007/978-3-540-79576-6_15
4. Steve Benford and Gabriella Giannachi. 2011. *Performing Mixed Reality*. MIT Press, Cambridge, Massachusetts, USA.
5. Walter Benjamin. 1969. The work of art in the age of mechanical reproduction. In *Illuminations*, Hannah Arendt (Ed.). Schocken Books, New York, New York, USA. Translated by Harry Zohn from the 1935 essay.
6. David Birchfield, Harvey Thornburg, M. Colleen Megowan-Romanowicz, Sarah Hatton, Brandon Mechtley, Igor Dolgov, and Winslow Burleson. 2008. Embodiment, multimodality, and composition: Convergent themes across HCI and education for mixed-reality learning environments. *Advances in Human-Computer Interaction* 2008 (2008).
7. Brett Bligh and Charles Crook. 2017. Learning Spaces. In *Technology Enhanced Learning*, Erik Duval, Mike Sharples, and Rosamund Sutherland (Eds.). Springer, Cham, Switzerland, 69–87.
8. Elizabeth M. Bonsignore, Derek L. Hansen, Zachary O. Toups, Lennart E. Nacke, Anastasia Salter, and Wayne Lutters. 2012. Mixed Reality Games. In *Proceedings of the ACM 2012 Conference on Computer Supported Cooperative Work Companion (CSCW '12)*. ACM, New York, NY, USA, 7–8. DOI: http://dx.doi.org/10.1145/2141512.2141517
9. Gaetano Borriello, Matthew Chalmers, Anthony LaMarca, and Paddy Nixon. 2005. Delivering Real-world Ubiquitous Location Systems. *Commun. ACM* 48, 3 (March 2005), 36–41. DOI: http://dx.doi.org/10.1145/1047671.1047701
10. Roger Caillois. 1961. *Man, Play and Games*. University of Illinois Press, Urbana, Illinois, USA. Translated by Meyer Barash from the 1958 *Les jeux et les hommes*.
11. Paul M. Camic. 2010. From trashed to treasured: A grounded theory analysis of the found object. *Psychology of Aesthetics, Creativity, and the Arts* 4, 2 (2010), 81–92. DOI: http://dx.doi.org/10.1037/a0018429
12. Marcus Carter, John Downs, Bjorn Nansen, Mitchell Harrop, and Martin Gibbs. 2014. Paradigms of Games Research in HCI: A Review of 10 Years of Research at CHI. In *Proceedings of the First ACM SIGCHI Annual Symposium on Computer-human Interaction in Play (CHI PLAY '14)*. ACM, New York, NY, USA, 27–36. DOI: http://dx.doi.org/10.1145/2658537.2658708
13. Matthew Chalmers and Areti Galani. 2004. Seamful Interweaving: Heterogeneity in the Theory and Design of Interactive Systems. In *Proceedings of the 5th Conference on Designing Interactive Systems: Processes, Practices, Methods, and Techniques (DIS '04)*. ACM, New York, NY, USA, 243–252. DOI: http://dx.doi.org/10.1145/1013115.1013149
14. Juliet M. Corbin and Anselm Strauss. 1990. Grounded theory research: Procedures, canons, and evaluative criteria. *Qualitative Sociology* 13, 1 (1990), 3–21. DOI: http://dx.doi.org/10.1007/BF00988593
15. Chris Crawford. 1984. *The Art of Computer Game Design*. Osborne/McGraw-Hill, Berkeley, California, USA.
16. Sebastian Deterding, Dan Dixon, Rilla Khaled, and Lennart Nacke. 2011. From Game Design Elements to Gamefulness: Defining "Gamification". In *Proceedings of the 15th International Academic MindTrek Conference: Envisioning Future Media Environments (MindTrek '11)*. ACM, New York, NY, USA, 9–15. DOI: http://dx.doi.org/10.1145/2181037.2181040
17. Paul Dourish. 2001. *Where the Action Is: The Foundations of Embodied Interaction* (1st ed.). MIT Press, Cambridge, Massachusetts, USA.
18. Paul Dourish. 2006. Re-space-ing Place: "Place" and "Space" Ten Years on. In *Proceedings of the 2006 20th Anniversary Conference on Computer Supported Cooperative Work (CSCW '06)*. ACM, New York, NY, USA, 299–308. DOI: http://dx.doi.org/10.1145/1180875.1180921
19. Michael Epstein and Silvia Vergani. 2006. History Unwired: Mobile Narrative in Historic Cities. In *Proceedings of the Working Conference on Advanced Visual Interfaces (AVI '06)*. ACM, New York, NY, USA, 302–305. DOI: http://dx.doi.org/10.1145/1133265.1133327
20. Hauke Ernst and Martin Faust. 2002. DERIVE: A Distributed Platform for Mixed Reality Interaction. In *CHI '02 Extended Abstracts on Human Factors in Computing Systems (CHI EA '02)*. ACM, New York, NY, USA, 570–571. DOI: http://dx.doi.org/10.1145/506443.506488
21. Jason Farman. 2013. *Mobile interface theory: Embodied space and locative media*. Routledge, New York, New York, USA.
22. Steven Feiner, Blair MacIntyre, Tobias Hollerer, and Anthony Webster. 1997. A Touring Machine: Prototyping 3D mobile augmented reality systems for exploring the urban environment. In *ISWC '97: Proceedings of the 1st IEEE International Symposium on Wearable Computers*. IEEE Computer Society, 74–81.

23. Dedre Gentner and Albert L. Stevens. 1983. *Mental Models*. Lawrence Earlbaum Associates, Hillsdale, New Jersey, USA.

24. James J. Gibson. 2014. *The Ecological Approach to Visual Perception* (classic ed.). Psychology Press, New York, New York, USA.

25. Barney G. Glaser. 1978. *Theoretical Sensitivity: Advances in the Methodology of Grounded Theory*. The Sociology Press, Mill Valley, California, USA.

26. Barney G. Glaser. 1998. *Doing Grounded Theory: Issues and Discussions*. The Sociology Press, Mill Valley, California, USA.

27. Barney G. Glaser and Anselm Strauss. 1967. *The Discovery of Grounded Theory: Strategies for Qualitative Research*. Aldine Publishing Company, Chicago, Illinois, USA.

28. Kilem Li Gwet. 2014. *Handbook of Inter-Rater Reliability: The Definitive Guide to Measuring the Extent of Agreement Among Raters* (4th ed.). Advanced Analytics, LLC, Gaithersburg, Maryland, USA.

29. Steve Harrison and Paul Dourish. 1996. Re-place-ing Space: The Roles of Place and Space in Collaborative Systems. In *Proceedings of the 1996 ACM Conference on Computer Supported Cooperative Work (CSCW '96)*. ACM, New York, NY, USA, 67–76. DOI: http://dx.doi.org/10.1145/240080.240193

30. Jeffrey Hightower and Gaetano Borriello. 2001. Location Systems for Ubiquitous Computing. *Computer* 34, 8 (2001), 57–66. DOI: http://dx.doi.org/10.1109/2.940014

31. Rashina Hoda, James Noble, and Stuart Marshall. 2011. Grounded Theory for Geeks. In *Proceedings of the 18th Conference on Pattern Languages of Programs (PLoP '11)*. ACM, New York, NY, USA, 24:1–24:17. DOI: http://dx.doi.org/10.1145/2578903.2579162

32. Nathan Hook. 2015. Grounded Theory. In *Game Research Methods*, Petri Lankoski and Staffan Björk (Eds.). ETC Press, Pittsburgh, Pennsylvania, USA, 309–320.

33. Johan Huizinga. 1955. *Homo Ludens: A Study of the Play-Element in Culture* (translated from the 1944 German ed.). Beacon Press, Boston, MA, USA. Translator unknown.

34. David H. Jonassen and Philip Henning. 1996. Mental models: Knowledge in the head and knowledge in the world. In *ICLS '96: Proceedings of the 1996 International Conference on Learning Sciences*. International Society of the Learning Sciences, 433–438.

35. Paula Levine. 2003. Shadows from another place: Transposed space. *Media in Transition* 4 (2003), 1–21.

36. Lucy R. Lippard. 1971. Marcel Duchamp. In *Dadas on Art: Tzara, Arp, Duchamp, and Others*, Lucy R. Lippard (Ed.). Dover Publications, Inc., 139–154.

37. Wei Liu, Adrian David Cheok, Charissa Lim Mei-Ling, and Yin-Leng Theng. 2007. Mixed Reality Classroom: Learning from Entertainment. In *Proceedings of the 2nd International Conference on Digital Interactive Media in Entertainment and Arts (DIMEA '07)*. ACM, New York, NY, USA, 65–72. DOI: http://dx.doi.org/10.1145/1306813.1306833

38. Mark A. Livingston, Joseph L. Gabbard, J. Edward Swan II, Ciara M. Sibley, and Jane H. Barrow. 2013. Basic perception in head-worn augmented reality displays. In *Human Factors in Augmented Reality Environments*, Weidong Huang, Leila Alem, and Mark A. Livingston (Eds.). Springer, New York, New York, USA, 35–65.

39. Sus Lundgren, Joel E. Fischer, Stuart Reeves, and Olof Torgersson. 2015. Designing Mobile Experiences for Collocated Interaction. In *Proceedings of the 18th ACM Conference on Computer Supported Cooperative Work & Social Computing (CSCW '15)*. ACM, New York, NY, USA, 496–507. DOI: http://dx.doi.org/10.1145/2675133.2675171

40. Blair MacIntyre, Jay David Bolter, and Maribeth Gandy. 2004. Presence and the aura of meaningful places. *Presence: Teleoperators and Virtual Environments* 6, 2 (2004), 197–206.

41. Paul Milgram and Fumio Kishino. 1994. A taxonomy of mixed reality visual displays. *IEICE Trans. Information Systems* E77-D, 12 (1994), 1321–1329.

42. Markus Montola. 2005. Exploring the edge of the magic circle: Defining pervasive games. In *Proceedings of Digital Arts and Culture*.

43. M. Nakevska, Jun Hu, G. Langereis, and M. Rauterberg. 2012. Alice's adventures in an immersive mixed reality environment. In *2012 IEEE International Symposium on Mixed and Augmented Reality (ISMAR)*. 303–304. DOI: http://dx.doi.org/10.1109/ISMAR.2012.6402585

44. Susanna Nilsson, Mattias Arvola, Anders Szczepanski, and Magnus Bng. 2012. Exploring Place and Direction: Mobile Augmented Reality in the Astrid Lindgren Landscape. In *Proceedings of the 24th Australian Computer-Human Interaction Conference (OzCHI '12)*. ACM, New York, NY, USA, 411–419. DOI: http://dx.doi.org/10.1145/2414536.2414601

45. Don Norman. 2013. *The Design of Everyday Things: Revised and Expanded Edition* (2013 ed.). Basic Books, New York, New York, USA.

46. Remo Pillat, Arjun Nagendran, and Robb Lindgren. 2012. A Mixed Reality System for Teaching STEM Content Using Embodied Learning and Whole-body Metaphors. In *Proceedings of the 11th ACM SIGGRAPH International Conference on Virtual-Reality Continuum and Its Applications in Industry (VRCAI '12)*. ACM, New York, NY, USA, 295–302. DOI: http://dx.doi.org/10.1145/2407516.2407584

47. Helge Renkewitz, Verena Kinder, Mario Brandt, and Thomas Alexander. 2008. Optimal font size for head-mounted-displays in outdoor applications. In *2008 12th International Conference Information Visualisation*. IEEE, 503–508.

48. Katie Salen and Eric Zimmerman. 2004a. *Rules of Play: Game Design Fundamentals*. MIT Press, Cambridge, MA, USA, Chapter Defining Games, 70–83.

49. Katie Salen and Eric Zimmerman. 2004b. *Rules of Play: Game Design Fundamentals*. MIT Press, Cambridge, MA, USA, Chapter The Magic Circle, 92–99.

50. Martijn J. Schuemie, Peter van der Straaten, Merel Krijn, and Charles A. P. G. van der Mast. 2001. Research on Presence in VR: A Survey. *Cyberpsychology and Behavior* 4, 2 (April 2001), 183–201.

51. Hitesh Nidhi Sharma, Zachary O. Toups, Igor Dolgov, Andruid Kerne, and Ajit Jain. 2016. Evaluating Display Modalities Using a Mixed Reality Game. In *Proceedings of the 2016 Annual Symposium on Computer-Human Interaction in Play (CHI PLAY '16)*. ACM, New York, NY, USA, 65–77. DOI: http://dx.doi.org/10.1145/2967934.2968090

52. Bruce Thomas, Ben Close, John Donoghue, John Squires, Phillip De Bondi, Michael Morris, and Wayne Piekarski. 2000. ARQuake: An outdoor/indoor augmented reality first person application. In *Proceedings of the Fourth International Symposium on Wearable Computers (ISWC'00)*. 139–146. DOI: http://dx.doi.org/10.1109/ISWC.2000.888480

53. Bruce H. Thomas and Wayne Piekarski. 2003. Outdoor Virtual Reality. In *Proceedings of the 1st International Symposium on Information and Communication Technologies (ISICT '03)*. Trinity College Dublin, 226–231. http://dl.acm.org/citation.cfm?id=963600.963645

54. Marjaana Träskbäack and Michael Haller. 2004. Mixed Reality Training Application for an Oil Refinery: User Requirements. In *Proceedings of the 2004 ACM SIGGRAPH International Conference on Virtual Reality Continuum and Its Applications in Industry (VRCAI '04)*. ACM, New York, NY, USA, 324–327. DOI: http://dx.doi.org/10.1145/1044588.1044658

55. Yi-Fu Tuan. 1975. Place: An Experiential Perspective. *Geographical Review* 65, 2 (1975), 151–165. DOI: http://dx.doi.org/10.2307/213970

56. Yi-Fu Tuan. 1977. *Space and Place: The Perspective of Experience*. University of Minnesota Press, Minneapolis, Minnesota, USA.

57. Dimitrios Tzovaras, Konstantinos Moustakas, Georgios Nikolakis, and Michael G. Strintzis. 2009. Interactive Mixed Reality White Cane Simulation for the Training of the Blind and the Visually Impaired. *Personal Ubiquitous Comput.* 13, 1 (Jan. 2009), 51–58. DOI: http://dx.doi.org/10.1007/s00779-007-0171-2

58. Friedrich von Borries, Steffen P. Walz, and Matthias Böttger. 2007. *Space Time Play: Computer Games, Architecture and Urbanism: The Next Level*. Birkhäuser Architecture, Basel, Switzerland.

59. Changqing Zhou, Pamela Ludford, Dan Frankowski, and Loren Terveen. 2005. An Experiment in Discovering Personally Meaningful Places from Location Data. In *CHI '05 Extended Abstracts on Human Factors in Computing Systems (CHI EA '05)*. ACM, New York, NY, USA, 2029–2032. DOI: http://dx.doi.org/10.1145/1056808.1057084

60. Jean-Marie Zogg. 2007. *Essentials of Satellite Navigation - Compendium*. Technical Report GPS-X-02007-C. u-blox AG.

EXTENDED BIBLIOGRAPHY

1. Anupriya Ankolekar, Thomas Sandholm, and Louis Yu. 2013. Play It by Ear: A Case for Serendipitous Discovery of Places with Musicons. In *Proceedings of the SIGCHI Conference on Human Factors in Computing Systems (CHI '13)*. ACM, New York, NY, USA, 2959–2968. DOI: http://dx.doi.org/10.1145/2470654.2481411
2. Benjamin Avery, Wayne Piekarski, James Warren, and Bruce H. Thomas. 2006. Evaluation of User Satisfaction and Learnability for Outdoor Augmented Reality Gaming. In *Proceedings of the 7th Australasian User Interface Conference - Volume 50 (AUIC '06)*. Australian Computer Society, Inc., Darlinghurst, Australia, Australia, 17–24. http://dl.acm.org/citation.cfm?id=1151758.1151759
3. Benjamin Avery, Bruce H. Thomas, Joe Velikovsky, and Wayne Piekarski. 2005. Outdoor Augmented Reality Gaming on Five Dollars a Day. In *Proceedings of the Sixth Australasian Conference on User Interface - Volume 40 (AUIC '05)*. Australian Computer Society, Inc., Darlinghurst, Australia, Australia, 79–88. http://dl.acm.org/citation.cfm?id=1082243.1082254
4. Rafael Ballagas, André Kuntze, and Steffen P. Walz. 2008. *Pervasive Computing: 6th International Conference, Pervasive 2008 Sydney, Australia, May 19-22, 2008 Proceedings*. Springer Berlin Heidelberg, Berlin, Heidelberg, Chapter Gaming Tourism: Lessons from Evaluating REXplorer, a Pervasive Game for Tourists, 244–261. DOI: http://dx.doi.org/10.1007/978-3-540-79576-6_15
5. E. Barba. 2014. A theory of meaning for Mixed Reality walking tours. In *Mixed and Augmented Reality - Media, Art, Social Science, Humanities and Design (ISMAR-MASH'D), 2014 IEEE International Symposium on*. 43–50. DOI: http://dx.doi.org/10.1109/ISMAR-AMH.2014.6935437
6. Louise Barkhuus, Matthew Chalmers, Paul Tennent, Malcolm Hall, Marek Bell, Scott Sherwood, and Barry Brown. 2005. Picking Pockets on the Lawn: The Development of Tactics and Strategies in a Mobile Game. In *Proceedings of the 7th International Conference on Ubiquitous Computing (UbiComp'05)*. Springer-Verlag, Berlin, Heidelberg, 358–374. DOI: http://dx.doi.org/10.1007/11551201_21
7. Steve Benford, Andy Crabtree, Martin Flintham, Adam Drozd, Rob Anastasi, Mark Paxton, Nick Tandavanitj, Matt Adams, and Ju Row-Farr. 2006. Can you see me now? *ACM Transactions on Computer-Human Interaction (TOCHI)* 13, 1 (2006), 100–133.
8. Steve Benford, Martin Flintham, Adam Drozd, Rob Anastasi, Duncan Rowland, Nick Tandavanitj, Matt Adams, Ju Row-Farr, Amanda Oldroyd, and Jon Sutton. 2004. Uncle Roy All Around You: Implicating the city in a location-based performance. *Proceedings of the 2004 ACM SIGCHI International Conference on Advances in Computer Entertainment Technology* (2004).
9. Frank Biocca, Arthur Tang, Charles Owen, and Fan Xiao. 2006. Attention Funnel: Omnidirectional 3D Cursor for Mobile Augmented Reality Platforms. In *Proceedings of the SIGCHI Conference on Human Factors in Computing Systems (CHI '06)*. ACM, New York, NY, USA, 1115–1122. DOI: http://dx.doi.org/10.1145/1124772.1124939
10. Anne E. Bowser, Derek L. Hansen, Jocelyn Raphael, Matthew Reid, Ryan J. Gamett, Yurong R. He, Dana Rotman, and Jenny J. Preece. 2013. Prototyping in PLACE: A Scalable Approach to Developing Location-based Apps and Games. In *Proceedings of the SIGCHI Conference on Human Factors in Computing Systems (CHI '13)*. ACM, New York, NY, USA, 1519–1528. DOI: http://dx.doi.org/10.1145/2470654.2466202
11. Barry Brown, Ian MacColl, Matthew Chalmers, Areti Galani, Cliff Randell, and Anthony Steed. 2003. Lessons from the Lighthouse: Collaboration in a Shared Mixed Reality System. In *Proceedings of the SIGCHI Conference on Human Factors in Computing Systems (CHI '03)*. ACM, New York, NY, USA, 577–584. DOI: http://dx.doi.org/10.1145/642611.642711
12. Liselott Brunnberg and Oskar Juhlin. 2003. Motion and Spatiality in a Gaming Situation - Enhancing Mobile Computer Games with the Highway Experience. In *Proceedings of Interact 2003*.
13. Volkert Buchmann, Mark Billinghurst, and Andy Cockburn. 2008. Directional Interfaces for Wearable Augmented Reality. In *Proceedings of the 9th ACM SIGCHI New Zealand Chapter's International Conference on Human-Computer Interaction: Design Centered HCI (CHINZ '08)*. ACM, New York, NY, USA, 47–54. DOI: http://dx.doi.org/10.1145/1496976.1496983
14. Fred Charles, Marc Cavazza, Steven J. Mead, Olivier Martin, Alok Nandi, and Xavier Marichal. 2004. Compelling Experiences in Mixed Reality Interactive Storytelling. In *Proceedings of the 2004 ACM SIGCHI International Conference on Advances in Computer Entertainment Technology (ACE '04)*. ACM, New York, NY, USA, 32–40. DOI: http://dx.doi.org/10.1145/1067343.1067347
15. Adrian David Cheok, Kok Hwee Goh, Wei Liu, Farzam Farbiz, Sze Lee Teo, Hui Siang Teo, Shang Ping Lee, Yu Li, Siew Wan Fong, and Xubo Yang. 2004. Human Pacman: A Mobile Wide-area Entertainment System Based on Physical, Social, and Ubiquitous Computing. In *Proceedings of the 2004 ACM SIGCHI International Conference on Advances in Computer Entertainment Technology (ACE '04)*. ACM, New York, NY, USA, 360–361. DOI: http://dx.doi.org/10.1145/1067343.1067402
16. Enrico Costanza, Andreas Kunz, and Morten Fjeld. 2009. *Human Machine Interaction: Research Results of the MMI Program*. Springer Berlin Heidelberg, Berlin,

Heidelberg, Chapter Mixed Reality: A Survey, 47–68. DOI: http://dx.doi.org/10.1007/978-3-642-00437-7_3

17. Paul Coulton, Kate Lund, and Andrew Wilson. 2010. Harnessing Player Creativity to Broaden the Appeal of Location Based Games. In *Proceedings of the 24th BCS Interaction Specialist Group Conference (BCS '10)*. British Computer Society, Swinton, UK, UK, 143–150. http://dl.acm.org/citation.cfm?id=2146303.2146325

18. Andy Crabtree, Steve Benford, Tom Rodden, Chris Greenhalgh, Martin Flintham, Rob Anastasi, Adam Drozd, Matt Adams, Ju Row-Farr, Nick Tandavanitj, and Anthony Steed. 2004. Orchestrating a Mixed Reality Game 'on the Ground'. In *Proceedings of the SIGCHI Conference on Human Factors in Computing Systems (CHI '04)*. ACM, New York, NY, USA, 391–398. DOI: http://dx.doi.org/10.1145/985692.985742

19. Drew Davidson, Heather Kelley, and Julian Kcklich. 2007. *Space time play: computer games, architecture and urbanism: the next level*. Springer Science & Business Media.

20. Steven Dow, Jaemin Lee, Christopher Oezbek, Blair Maclntyre, Jay David Bolter, and Maribeth Gandy. 2005. Exploring Spatial Narratives and Mixed Reality Experiences in Oakland Cemetery. In *Proceedings of the 2005 ACM SIGCHI International Conference on Advances in Computer Entertainment Technology (ACE '05)*. ACM, New York, NY, USA, 51–60. DOI: http://dx.doi.org/10.1145/1178477.1178484

21. Steven Dow, Manish Mehta, Annie Lausier, Blair MacIntyre, and Micheal Mateas. 2006. Initial Lessons from AR FaÇAde, an Interactive Augmented Reality Drama. In *Proceedings of the 2006 ACM SIGCHI International Conference on Advances in Computer Entertainment Technology (ACE '06)*. ACM, New York, NY, USA, Article 28. DOI: http://dx.doi.org/10.1145/1178823.1178858

22. Stine Ejsing-Duun. 2011. *Location-Based Games: From Street to Screen*. Ph.D. Dissertation. Aarhus University.

23. Stine Ejsing-Duun. 2016. Participatory urbanism: Making the stranger familiar and the familiar strange. In *The Oxford Handbook of Innovation*, Citizen Media, Public Spaces: Diverse Expressions of Citizenship, and Dissent (Eds.). Routledge.

24. Mary Flanagan. 2007. Locating play and politics: Real world games & activism. *Leonardo Electronic Almanac* 16, 2-3 (2007), 1–13.

25. Martin Flintham, Steve Benford, Rob Anastasi, Terry Hemmings, Andy Crabtree, Chris Greenhalgh, Nick Tandavanitj, Matt Adams, and Ju Row-Farr. 2003. Where On-line Meets on the Streets: Experiences with Mobile Mixed Reality Games. In *Proceedings of the SIGCHI Conference on Human Factors in Computing Systems (CHI '03)*. ACM, New York, NY, USA, 569–576. DOI: http://dx.doi.org/10.1145/642611.642710

26. Chris Furmanski, Ronald Azuma, and Mike Daily. 2002. Augmented-reality visualizations guided by cognition: Perceptual heuristics for combining visible and obscured information. In *Mixed and Augmented Reality, 2002. ISMAR 2002. Proceedings. International Symposium on*. IEEE, 215–320.

27. Anton Gustafsson, John Bichard, Liselott Brunnberg, Oskar Juhlin, and Marco Combetto. 2006. Believable Environments: Generating Interactive Storytelling in Vast Location-based Pervasive Games. In *Proceedings of the 2006 ACM SIGCHI International Conference on Advances in Computer Entertainment Technology (ACE '06)*. ACM, New York, NY, USA, Article 24. DOI: http://dx.doi.org/10.1145/1178823.1178852

28. Iris Herbst, Anne-Kathrin Braun, Rod McCall, and Wolfgang Broll. 2008. TimeWarp: Interactive Time Travel with a Mobile Mixed Reality Game. In *Proceedings of the 10th International Conference on Human Computer Interaction with Mobile Devices and Services (MobileHCI '08)*. ACM, New York, NY, USA, 235–244. DOI: http://dx.doi.org/10.1145/1409240.1409266

29. Steve Hinske, Matthias Lampe, Carsten Magerkurth, and Carsten Röcker. 2007. Classifying pervasive games: on pervasive computing and mixed reality. *Concepts and technologies for Pervasive Games-A Reader for Pervasive Gaming Research* 1, 20 (2007).

30. T. Hollerer, S. Feiner, and J. Pavlik. 1999. Situated documentaries: embedding multimedia presentations in the real world. In *Wearable Computers, 1999. Digest of Papers. The Third International Symposium on*. 79–86. DOI: http://dx.doi.org/10.1109/ISWC.1999.806664

31. Christian Jacquemin, Wai Kit Chan, and Mathieu Courgeon. 2010. Bateau ivre: an artistic markerless outdoor mobile augmented reality installation on a riverboat. In *Proceedings of the international conference on Multimedia*. ACM, 1353–1362.

32. Alexander Kan, Bernd Ploderer, and Martin Gibbs. 2014. Mixed Reality Stories: How Creative Writers Integrate Virtual and Physical Realities. In *Proceedings of the 26th Australian Computer-Human Interaction Conference on Designing Futures: The Future of Design (OzCHI '14)*. ACM, New York, NY, USA, 115–118. DOI: http://dx.doi.org/10.1145/2686612.2686628

33. J. Keil, M. Zollner, M. Becker, F. Wientapper, T. Engelke, and H. Wuest. 2011. The House of Olbrich; An Augmented Reality tour through architectural history. In *2011 IEEE International Symposium on Mixed and Augmented Reality - Arts, Media, and Humanities*. 15–18. DOI: http://dx.doi.org/10.1109/ISMAR-AMH.2011.6093651

34. SeungJun Kim and Anind K. Dey. 2009. Simulated Augmented Reality Windshield Display As a Cognitive Mapping Aid for Elder Driver Navigation. In *Proceedings of the SIGCHI Conference on Human*

Factors in Computing Systems (CHI '09). ACM, New York, NY, USA, 133–142. DOI: http://dx.doi.org/10.1145/1518701.1518724

35. Boriana Koleva, Ian Taylor, Steve Benford, Mike Fraser, Chris Greenhalgh, Holger Schnädelbach, Dirk vom Lehn, Christian Heath, Ju Row-Farr, and Matt Adams. 2001. Orchestrating a Mixed Reality Performance. In *Proceedings of the SIGCHI Conference on Human Factors in Computing Systems (CHI '01)*. ACM, New York, NY, USA, 38–45. DOI: http://dx.doi.org/10.1145/365024.365033
36. Martijn J.L. Kors, Gabriele Ferri, Erik D. van der Spek, Cas Ketel, and Ben A.M. Schouten. 2016. A Breathtaking Journey. On the Design of an Empathy-Arousing Mixed-Reality Game. In *Proceedings of the 2016 Annual Symposium on Computer-Human Interaction in Play (CHI PLAY '16)*. ACM, New York, NY, USA, 91–104. DOI: http://dx.doi.org/10.1145/2967934.2968110
37. Erik Kristiansen. 2009. *Computer Games for the Real World: Designing a Design Method for Site-specific Computer Games*. Ph.D. Dissertation. Performance Design, Department of Communication, Business and Information Technologies, Roskilde University.
38. Erik Kristiansen and Olav Harslf. 2015. *Engaging Spaces: Sites of Performance, Interaction, and Reflection*. Museum Tusculanum Press.
39. Isaac Kulka, Blair MacIntyre, Maribeth Gandy, and Jay David Bolter. 2012. Plants and zombies: Two use cases for on-location panorama viewing in handheld mobile AR. In *Mixed and Augmented Reality (ISMAR-AMH), 2012 IEEE International Symposium on*. 103–104. DOI: http://dx.doi.org/10.1109/ISMAR-AMH.2012.6484002
40. G. A. Lee, A. Dnser, Seungwon Kim, and M. Billinghurst. 2012. CityViewAR: A mobile outdoor AR application for city visualization. In *2012 IEEE International Symposium on Mixed and Augmented Reality - Arts, Media, and Humanities (ISMAR-AMH)*. 57–64. DOI: http://dx.doi.org/10.1109/ISMAR-AMH.2012.6483989
41. Kyong Joon Lee, Sang Chul Ahn, and Hyoung-Gon Kim. 2006. Using a Mobile Device As an Interface Tool for HMD-based AR Applications. In *Proceedings of the 2006 ACM SIGCHI International Conference on Advances in Computer Entertainment Technology (ACE '06)*. ACM, New York, NY, USA, Article 7. DOI: http://dx.doi.org/10.1145/1178823.1178833
42. Fotis Liarokapis, Stella Sylaiou, David M Mountain, and others. 2008. Personalizing Virtual and Augmented Reality for Cultural Heritage Indoor and Outdoor Experiences.. In *VAST*. Citeseer, 55–62.
43. Craig A. Lindley. 2005. Game Space Design Foundations for Trans-reality Games. In *Proceedings of the 2005 ACM SIGCHI International Conference on Advances in Computer Entertainment Technology (ACE '05)*. ACM, New York, NY, USA, 397–404. DOI: http://dx.doi.org/10.1145/1178477.1178569
44. Sus Lundgren and Staffan Björk. 2005. Forces, Clashes and Remnants: A Model for Event-driven Iterative Multidisciplinary Game Design. In *Proceedings of the 2005 ACM SIGCHI International Conference on Advances in Computer Entertainment Technology (ACE '05)*. ACM, New York, NY, USA, 326–329. DOI: http://dx.doi.org/10.1145/1178477.1178538
45. G. Metaxas, B. Metin, J. Schneider, G. Shapiro, W. Zhou, and P. Markopoulos. 2005. SCORPIODROME: An Exploration in Mixed Reality Social Gaming for Children. In *Proceedings of the 2005 ACM SIGCHI International Conference on Advances in Computer Entertainment Technology (ACE '05)*. ACM, New York, NY, USA, 229–232. DOI: http://dx.doi.org/10.1145/1178477.1178514
46. Markus Montola, Jaakko Stenros, and Annika Waern. 2009. *Pervasive games: theory and design*. Morgan Kaufmann Publishers Inc.
47. Ann Morrison, Antti Oulasvirta, Peter Peltonen, Saija Lemmela, Giulio Jacucci, Gerhard Reitmayr, Jaana Näsänen, and Antti Juustila. 2009. Like Bees Around the Hive: A Comparative Study of a Mobile Augmented Reality Map. In *Proceedings of the SIGCHI Conference on Human Factors in Computing Systems (CHI '09)*. ACM, New York, NY, USA, 1889–1898. DOI: http://dx.doi.org/10.1145/1518701.1518991
48. Wafaa Moussa, Jean-pierre Jessel, and Emmanuel Dubois. 2006. Notational-based prototyping of mixed interactions. In *Proceedings of the 5th IEEE and ACM International Symposium on Mixed and Augmented Reality*. IEEE Computer Society, 229–230.
49. Stéphane Natkin and Chen Yan. 2006. User Model in Multiplayer Mixed Reality Entertainment Applications. In *Proceedings of the 2006 ACM SIGCHI International Conference on Advances in Computer Entertainment Technology (ACE '06)*. ACM, New York, NY, USA, Article 74. DOI: http://dx.doi.org/10.1145/1178823.1178910
50. Susanna Nilsson, Mattias Arvola, Anders Szczepanski, and Magnus Bng. 2012. Exploring Place and Direction: Mobile Augmented Reality in the Astrid Lindgren Landscape. In *Proceedings of the 24th Australian Computer-Human Interaction Conference (OzCHI '12)*. ACM, New York, NY, USA, 411–419. DOI: http://dx.doi.org/10.1145/2414536.2414601
51. Jason Orlosky, Kiyoshi Kiyokawa, and Haruo Takemura. 2013. Management and manipulation of text in dynamic mixed reality workspaces. In *Mixed and Augmented Reality (ISMAR), 2013 IEEE International Symposium on*. IEEE, 1–4.
52. F. Pankratz, A. Dippon, T. Coskun, and G. Klinker. 2013. User awareness of tracking uncertainties in AR navigation scenarios. In *Mixed and Augmented Reality (ISMAR), 2013 IEEE International Symposium on*. 285–286. DOI: http://dx.doi.org/10.1109/ISMAR.2013.6671807

53. Omer Rashid, Will Bamford, Paul Coulton, and Reuben Edwards. 2006. PAC-LAN: The Human Arcade. In *Proceedings of the 2006 ACM SIGCHI International Conference on Advances in Computer Entertainment Technology (ACE '06)*. ACM, New York, NY, USA, Article 33. DOI: http://dx.doi.org/10.1145/1178823.1178864

54. Josephine Reid. 2008. Design for Coincidence: Incorporating Real World Artifacts in Location Based Games. In *Proceedings of the 3rd International Conference on Digital Interactive Media in Entertainment and Arts (DIMEA '08)*. ACM, New York, NY, USA, 18–25. DOI: http://dx.doi.org/10.1145/1413634.1413643

55. Derek Reilly, Mohamad Salimian, Bonnie MacKay, Niels Mathiasen, W. Keith Edwards, and Juliano Franz. 2014. SecSpace: Prototyping Usable Privacy and Security for Mixed Reality Collaborative Environments. In *Proceedings of the 2014 ACM SIGCHI Symposium on Engineering Interactive Computing Systems (EICS '14)*. ACM, New York, NY, USA, 273–282. DOI: http://dx.doi.org/10.1145/2607023.2607039

56. Christian Reimann. 2005. Kick-real, a Mobile Mixed Reality Game. In *Proceedings of the 2005 ACM SIGCHI International Conference on Advances in Computer Entertainment Technology (ACE '05)*. ACM, New York, NY, USA, 387–387. DOI: http://dx.doi.org/10.1145/1178477.1178562

57. Christian Reimann and Volker Paelke. 2005. Adaptive Mixed Reality Games. In *Proceedings of the 2005 ACM SIGCHI International Conference on Advances in Computer Entertainment Technology (ACE '05)*. ACM, New York, NY, USA, 302–305. DOI: http://dx.doi.org/10.1145/1178477.1178532

58. Christian Sandor, Arindam Dey, Andrew Cunningham, Sebastien Barbier, Ulrich Eck, Donald Urquhar, Michael R Marner, Graeme Jarvis, and Sang Rhee. 2010. Egocentric space-distorting visualizations for rapid environment exploration in mobile mixed reality. In *Virtual Reality Conference (VR), 2010*. IEEE, 47–50.

59. Holger Schnädelbach, Boriana Koleva, Martin Flintham, Mike Fraser, Shahram Izadi, Paul Chandler, Malcolm Foster, Steve Benford, Chris Greenhalgh, and Tom Rodden. 2002. The Augurscope: A Mixed Reality Interface for Outdoors. In *Proceedings of the SIGCHI Conference on Human Factors in Computing Systems (CHI '02)*. ACM, New York, NY, USA, 9–16. DOI: http://dx.doi.org/10.1145/503376.503379

60. Holger Schnädelbach, Stefan Rennick Egglestone, Stuart Reeves, Steve Benford, Brendan Walker, and Michael Wright. 2008. Performing Thrill: Designing Telemetry Systems and Spectator Interfaces for Amusement Rides. In *Proceedings of the SIGCHI Conference on Human Factors in Computing Systems (CHI '08)*. ACM, New York, NY, USA, 1167–1176. DOI:http://dx.doi.org/10.1145/1357054.1357238

61. Hitesh Nidhi Sharma, Zachary O. Toups, Igor Dolgov, Andruid Kerne, and Ajit Jain. 2016. Evaluating Display Modalities Using a Mixed Reality Game. In *Proceedings of the 2016 Annual Symposium on Computer-Human Interaction in Play (CHI PLAY '16)*. ACM, New York, NY, USA, 65–77. DOI: http://dx.doi.org/10.1145/2967934.2968090

62. Masayuki Takemura and Yuichi Ohta. 2002. Diminishing head-mounted display for shared mixed reality. In *Proceedings of the 1st International Symposium on Mixed and Augmented Reality*. IEEE Computer Society, 149.

63. Yuichiro Takeuchi and Ken Perlin. 2012. ClayVision: The (Elastic) Image of the City. In *Proceedings of the SIGCHI Conference on Human Factors in Computing Systems (CHI '12)*. ACM, New York, NY, USA, 2411–2420. DOI: http://dx.doi.org/10.1145/2207676.2208404

64. F. Tecchia, G. Avveduto, M. Carrozzino, R. Brondi, M. Bergamasco, and L. Alem. 2014. [Poster] Interacting with your own hands in a fully immersive MR system. In *Mixed and Augmented Reality (ISMAR), 2014 IEEE International Symposium on*. 313–314. DOI: http://dx.doi.org/10.1109/ISMAR.2014.6948466

65. Bruce H. Thomas. 2012. A Survey of Visual, Mixed, and Augmented Reality Gaming. *Comput. Entertain.* 10, 1, Article 3 (Dec. 2012), 33 pages. DOI: http://dx.doi.org/10.1145/2381876.2381879

66. Kathleen Tuite, Noah Snavely, Dun-yu Hsiao, Nadine Tabing, and Zoran Popovic. 2011. PhotoCity: Training Experts at Large-scale Image Acquisition Through a Competitive Game. In *Proceedings of the SIGCHI Conference on Human Factors in Computing Systems (CHI '11)*. ACM, New York, NY, USA, 1383–1392. DOI:http://dx.doi.org/10.1145/1978942.1979146

67. Shinji Uchiyama, Kazuki Takemoto, Kiyohide Satoh, Hiroyuki Yamamoto, and Hideyuki Tamura. 2002. MR Platform: A Basic Body on Which Mixed Reality Applications Are Built. In *Proceedings of the 1st International Symposium on Mixed and Augmented Reality (ISMAR '02)*. IEEE Computer Society, Washington, DC, USA, 246–320. http://dl.acm.org/citation.cfm?id=850976.854992

68. Vassilios Vlahakis, Nikolaos Ioannidis, John Karigiannis, Manolis Tsotros, Michael Gounaris, Didier Stricker, Tim Gleue, Patrick Daehne, and Almeida. 2002. Archeoguide: An Augmented Reality Guide for Archaeological Sites. *IEEE Computer Graphics and Applications* 22, 5 (2002), 52–60. DOI: http://dx.doi.org/10.1109/MCG.2002.1028726

69. Steffen P. Walz (Ed.). 2010. *Toward a Ludic Architecture: The Space of Play and Games*. ETC Press, Pittsburgh, PA, USA.

70. Jason Wither, Rebecca Allen, Vids Samanta, Juha Hemanus, Yun-Ta Tsai, Ronald Azuma, Will Carter, Rachel Hinman, and Thommen Korah. 2010. The westwood experience: connecting story to locations via

mixed reality. In *Mixed and Augmented Reality-Arts, Media, and Humanities (ISMAR-AMH), 2010 IEEE International Symposium On*. IEEE, 39–46.

71. Daniel Yule, Bonnie MacKay, and Derek Reilly. 2015. Operation Citadel: Exploring the Role of Docents in Mixed Reality. In *Proceedings of the 2015 Annual Symposium on Computer-Human Interaction in Play (CHI PLAY '15)*. ACM, New York, NY, USA, 285–294. DOI:http://dx.doi.org/10.1145/2793107.2793135

LUDOGRAPHY

1. Augmented Pixels, Inc. 2013. *Reality Hoops*. Game [iOS]. (01 January 2013). Augmented Pixels, Inc., Palo Alto, CA, USA.
2. Games4All, Ltd. 2016. *SpecTrek Light*. Game [Android]. (01 January 2016). Games4All Ltd, Birmingham, West Midlands, UK.
3. Geo AR Games Limited. 2016. *Sharks in the Park*. Game [iOS]. (01 January 2016). Geo AR Games Limited, Wellington, New Zealand.
4. Jakks Pacific, Inc. 2015. *Max Tow Truck*. Game [Android]. (01 January 2015). Jakks Pacific, Inc., Malibu, CA, USA.
5. Laan Consulting Corp. 2010. *AR Soccer*. Game [iOS]. (01 January 2010). Laan Consulting Corp, Brooklyn, NY, USA.
6. Lemondo Ltd. 2012. *Fly Hunter*. Game [iOS]. (01 January 2012). Lemondo Ltd., Tbilisi, Georgia.
7. Niantic, Inc. 2012. *Ingress*. Game [Android]. (15 November 2012). Niantic, Inc., San Francisco, CA, USA.
8. Niantic, Inc. 2016. *Pokèmon GO*. Game [iOS]. (06 July 2016). Niantic, Inc., San Francisco, CA, USA.
9. Nordau Creative LTD. 2016. *Kazooloo AR*. Game [Android]. (01 January 2016). Nordau Creative LTD, Tel Aviv, Israel.
10. Pop Culture Software, LLC. 2011. *RCvCar*. Game [iOS]. (01 January 2011). Pop Culture Software, LLC, Cortlandt Manor, NY, USA.
11. RocketChicken Interactive Inc. 2013. *CodeRunner*. Game [iOS]. (01 January 2013). RocketChicken Interactive Inc., Vancouver, British Columbia, Canada.
12. Tore Knabe. 2012. *Bowmaster AR*. Game [iOS]. (01 January 2012). Tore Knabe, Berlin, Germany.
13. Useless Creations Pty Ltd. 2013. *Puppy Dog Fingers*. Game [iOS]. (01 January 2013). Useless Creations Pty Ltd, Victoria, Australia.
14. Useless Creations Pty Ltd. 2015a. *Aliens Everywhere*. Game [iOS]. (01 January 2015). Useless Creations Pty Ltd, Victoria, Australia.
15. Useless Creations Pty Ltd. 2015b. *Dinosaurs Everywhere*. Game [Android]. (01 January 2015). Useless Creations Pty Ltd, Victoria, Australia.
16. Useless Creations Pty Ltd. 2016. *Zombies GO*. Game [Android]. (01 January 2016). Useless Creations Pty Ltd, Victoria, Australia.
17. WowWee Group Limited. 2013. *Foam Fighter*. Game [iOS]. (01 January 2013). WowWee Group Limited, Tsim Sha Tsui, Hong Kong.

Anarchy or Order on the Streets: Review Based Characterization of Location Based Mobile Games

Paula Alavesa, Minna Pakanen, Hannu Kukka, Matti Pouke and Timo Ojala
Center for Ubiquitous Computing,
90014 University of Oulu, Finland
[firstname.lastname@oulu.fi]

ABSTRACT
Location based mobile games have traditionally relied on implicit codes of conduct, legal ordinances, common social norms, or community emergent rules. However, these games are becoming increasingly popular and enforcing these implicit or explicit restrictions has become difficult. In this paper, we present a critical and systematic review of both commercial and non-commercial location based mobile games. We list selected characteristics of the games and highlight their connection to the affordances and restrictions on urban game arenas. We also demonstrate the feasibility of our characterization by applying it to two recent location based mobile games, *Pokemon GO* [53] and *Street Art Gangs* [4].

Author Keywords
Location based mobile games; game design; pervasive games

ACM Classification Keywords
H.5.m. Information interfaces and presentation (e.g., HCI): Miscellaneous.

INTRODUCTION
All games impose a certain level of restriction to gameplay. Especially multiplayer games require a consistent set of rules and mechanics to ensure well-balanced and enjoyable gameplay. Restrictions on gameplay can be as light as a suggested storyline, to which the players can either adapt or choose to ignore; or there can be very strict rules, where the players are actively monitored and banned for *e.g.* cheating or exploiting game mechanics. In this paper, we focus on rules and restrictions outside conventional gameplay. We discuss *pervasive games* where the physical world overlaps with the boundaries of gameplay i.e. the *magic circle* [29]. Orchestrators of pervasive games have actively attempted to steer clear of imposing too many rules or regulations, and many guidelines for setting up pervasive games aim at minimizing rules and suggesting that players simply 'play fair' [50]. However, the recent success of commercial games like *Ingress* [30] and *Pokemon GO* [53] have shown that better-defined restrictions need to be applied when masses engage in gameplay.

Our focus is on a specific type of pervasive games, so-called location based mobile games (LBMGs). Substantial changes have taken place in pervasive games and LBMGs from the beginning of the century until today. Previously, orchestration, e.g. organizing and up keeping the game events, was considered inseparable from pervasive gameplay. It was further viewed as a part of the social complexity of pervasive games, and even considered beneficial for mixed reality experiences [17, 36, 73]. However, the level of orchestration per player has decreased when moving from the early *first generation* pervasive games to the *second generation*, making it possible to host games on global scale. In second generation games, it is no longer a requirement to have human intervention on the streets or do manual updates on game servers. Much of this has been automated in a way that orchestration per player is significantly lower. Specialist hardware has become largely unnecessary, as games can be deployed on smart phones and tablets. Some commercial games, such as *Pokemon GO*, are continuous and ongoing, because the games no longer need to be orchestrated events, which further adds to the player's (Figure 1) freedom on choosing when and where to play [39, 53].

Figure 1. Players on city streets. LBMGs combine true mobility of computing to the infrastructure and social possibilities of hybrid cities [66].

In this paper, we conduct a systematic review on location based mobile games, with a focus on understanding the types

CHI PLAY '17, October 15–18, 2017, Amsterdam, Netherlands

ACM ISBN 978-1-4503-4898-0/17/10$15.00
https://doi.org/10.1145/3116595.3116614

of applied affordances and restrictions. We identify the main features in LBMGs and further define the scope of the restrictions applied in games in relation to current theories and concepts [19, 21, 34, 42, 66, 67]. We conclude with discussion on our findings and further demonstrate the feasibility of our characterization by applying it to two recent location based mobile games, commercial *Pokemon GO* [53] and noncommercial academic *Street Art Gangs* [4].

BACKGROUND

On the Importance of Rules

A rule is not merely a suggestion on how to play the game. The rules of a game are there to be obeyed and they truly define the game: rules frame what is possible in the game, yet limit possibilities. In traditional video games, rules rarely need to be explicitly stated, as they are already built into the game mechanics and enforced on the player. Conversely, guidelines for pervasive games often suggest trying to avoid rules: the game is designed to facilitate play, much like a toy would. Toys do not usually have instructions or rules on how to use them correctly. They rely on users (for example children) to find imaginative ways of engaging and playing with them, and developing their own sets of rules when needed [2, 37].

The relationship between the rules of video games and pervasive games is somewhat reminiscent of the relationship between the rules of video games and traditional games such as board games: just like traditional games, pervasive games are played in the physical world [18, 28, 50, 51]. The physical world as an environment imposes certain laws and restrictions derived from everyday life in a society, and other basic rules such as the 24-hour daily rhythm, or the inability of human beings to fly unassisted, apply. Other restrictions emerge from the play itself. The idea of minimal rules of play in pervasive games stems from *ludology*, *i.e.* the notion that people are playful by nature, and everyday life already has elements and hints of this playfulness. Therefore, an orchestrated event that takes place in everyday life will intrinsically display play-like or game-like qualities [37, 50].

The question of how this relates to contemporary pervasive games, however, remains open. Can a LBMG developer rely on the player community refining their own set of rules and regulations while still following social norms, established laws, and staying safe? Furthermore, the intensity of the game can make players endure outdoors conditions they would not usually tolerate [4, 72], and the distraction to reality can lead to potentially dangerous situations [49, 63].

Why to Implement a Restriction and Why Not?

Emergence happens when player actions result in unpredicted second order of events, but the game itself stays rational and acceptable [69]. The rationale behind designing emergent game systems is that these systems empower the players, and give them a higher level of freedom of expression than a more restricted game system would. In pervasive games, there will always be a degree of emergence due to the freedom of players to interact with their environment, even in unpredictable ways [36, 50]. Location based mobile games have traditionally been very allowing for game emergence [38]. *Geocaching* is perhaps one of the most well-known examples. Player interaction and game narrative are both emergent and the only fixed items are location coordinates and the physical caches. However, even *Geocaching* has restrictions. The visibility of personal information amongst the geocacheers is restricted, as participants use game IDs. Furthermore, volunteers review the suggested new caches [18, 55]. These so-called *community emergent rules* or *restrictions* have taken a while to become established. While such rules may or may not emerge serendipitously from gameplay or the community, they are always an integral part of the game and cannot be ignored when designing a game.

For a player, the experience of successful play is composed of the ability to create a strategic path that complements the actions of other players and respects the rules of the game [37]. Therefore, successful gameplay requires a balance between player interaction, player control, and rules. In the context of human computer interaction, the player control could also be called player affordance. As discussed previously, this balance can emerge naturally after some time, i.e. players themselves can attempt to balance an unbalanced set of rules. However, relying on these self-emerging rules may lead to a situation where a majority of the player base has already given up and quit the game. Hence, it is important for a game developer or designer to implement a concise set of rules thoughtfully and clearly. However, implementing restrictions on gameplay requires resources, both during development and after deployment. Furthermore, updates may be needed to account for unforeseen exploitation by players. The lack of resources is particularly relevant in research based games, as researchers should be able to concentrate on observing the game instead of supervising it.

Generally, there is an asymmetrical tie between the rules of a game and the actual realized game: It is impossible to predict the outcome of the game only by knowing the rules [37]. This is especially true for pervasive games. Even though there are guidelines for developing and running a successful pervasive game [10, 17 , 36, 37, 39, 55], there are no guidelines specifically targeting the affordances and restrictions of LBMGs. The requirements, especially the technical ones, have been mapped [57] and ethical considerations especially on the use of player location in gameplay have been addressed [48], but no thorough assessment of the specifics of various types of LBMGs have been made. In this paper, we address this knowledge gap by first conducting a survey of modern LBMGs and then introducing a characterization of games and the affordances and restrictions in game space and play. Although phrase rules is a very common way to describe limitations in gameplay, we instead use restrictions, as those relate to both limiting or controlling as well as the act of limiting and controlling.

METHOD

We conducted a two-step review of non-commercial and commercial LBMGs. First, an initial mapping study identified the range of LBMGs. Then, a systematic review focused on selected 30 games shown in Table 1.

A Mapping Study of LBMGs

An initial review of known non-commercial and commercial LBMGs was conducted within a three-week period 5th – 26th August 2016. The information of LBMGs and their affordances and restrictions was retrieved from academic publications as well as commercial application repositories such as Google Play store and Apple App Store. The keywords used in the search were "location based mobile game" and "location-aware game".

Game	Year	Description of the game	Affordances and Restrictions	Developer motivation	Source
Geocacheing	2000 **	Single player, noncompetitive, unlimited timespan, high attendance, undefined timespan, global	High freedom of movement, locations physically fixed, non-linear emergent stories, ethical guidelines to lessen environmental impact, entwines with daily life	Noncommercial	[23, 55]
Botfighters	2001 **	Multiplayer, competitive, long timespan, global (across few countries)	High freedom of movement, nonlinear paths, locations used are the players' physical location, entwines with daily life	Commercial (Research)	[65]
URAAY	2003 **	Collaborative, noncompetitive, long timespan (two weeks), high attendance, local	Low freedom of movement, linear path, linear story, self-reported positioning	Commercial (Research)	[13]
Mogi	2003 **	Multiplayer, competitive, long timespan, high attendance, local	High freedom of movement, wide area around locations, possible to see other players' location data, entwines with daily life	Commercial	[43]
Pacmanhattan	2004 **	Multiplayer, competitive, players have different roles, low attendance, short timespan (10 min-1 h), local	Low freedom of movement, nonlinear paths, but restricted area, self-reported positioning, possible to see other players' location data	Noncommercial (Student work)	[56]
Treasure	2005 *	Collaborative, competitive, short timespan, low attendance, local	High freedom of movement, fixed locations on an unilineal path, possible to see other players' location data	Noncommercial (Research)	[6]
Prosopopeia	2005 **	Multiplayer, competitive, low attendance, long timespan, local	High freedom of movement, strong storyline forced linear paths, entwines with daily life	Noncommercial (Research)	[35]
Hitchers	2006 *	Multiplayer, competitive, long timespan, high attendance (47), global (across six countries)	High freedom of movement, nonlinear paths, players can change the locations, entwines with daily life	Noncommercial (Research)	[20]
Feeding Yoshi	2006 *	Multiplayer, collaborative, low attendance, long timespan (7 days), local	High freedom of movement, wide area around locations, possible to see other players' location data, entwines with daily life	Noncommercial (Research)	[10]
MobiMissions	2006 **	Multiplayer, photo-blogging game, competitive, low attendance, long timespan (5 weeks), local	High freedom of movement, nonlinear paths, players can change the locations, non-linear emergent stories, no direct contact facilitated for players, game-time outside school hours, entwines with daily life	Noncommercial (Research)	[26]
RexExplorer	2007 **	Single player or team play, noncompetitive, low attendance, short timespan, local	Nonlinear story, self-reported positioning used in some parts	Noncommercial (Engage visitors to a site)	[8]
Momentum (Prosopopeia 2)	2008 *	Multiplayer, competitive, low attendance, long timespan (36 days), local	High freedom of movement, strong storyline forced linear paths, some physically fixed locations, entwines with daily life	Noncommercial (Research)	[36]
EyeSpy	2009 *	Multiplayer, storytelling and photo-blogging game, competitive, low attendance, long timespan (2 weeks), local	High freedom of movement, nonlinear paths, players create the locations, entwines with daily life	Noncommercial (Research)	[11]
Parallel Kingdom	2009 **	Multiplayer (Massively Multiplayer Online Role Playing Game), competitive, high attendance, undefined timespan, global	High freedom of movement, nonlinear paths, locations are linked to the players' locations, entwines with daily life	Commercial	[58, 59]

Game	Year	Description of the game	Affordances and Restrictions	Developer motivation	Source
PanOULU conqueror	2009 **	Multiplayer, competitive, high attendance (96 players), long timespan (weeks), local	Fixed locations (Wi-Fi hotspots), no fixed paths, entwines with daily life	Noncommercial (Research)	[71]
Blowtooth	2010 *	Single player, noncompetitive, low attendance, short timespan, local	Moving locations (bluetooth on devices), no fixed paths	Noncommercial (Research)	[40, 44]
Frequency 1550	2011 *	Collaborative, low attendance, competitive, co-located gameplay, short timespan (one day), local	Linear path at some assignments, otherwise content tied to areas and locations, high story content and necessary assignments	Noncommercial (Education)	[3]
Itography Item Hunt	2011 **	Multiplayer, competitive, leaderboard, players explore close by areas and collect items, based on Foursquare, high attendance, undefined timespan, global	High freedom of movement, fixed coordinates for locations, no paths, entwines with daily life	Commercial	[32, 33]
FreshUP	2011 **	Collaborative, low attendance, competitive, co-located gameplay, long timespan (2-4 weeks), local	High freedom of movement, fixed coordinates for tasks, no paths, entwines with daily life	Noncommercial (Education, research)	[74]
Zombies, run!	2012 **	Single player, noncompetitive, high attendance, undefined timespan, global	High freedom of movement, GPS mode is not necessary, linear story, entwines with daily life	Commercial	[64]
Ingress	2012 **	Multiplayer, competitive, regional leaderboard, high attendance, undefined timespan, global	High freedom of movement, fixed coordinates for locations, no paths, entwines with daily life	Commercial	[30]
Free All Monsters	2011 * 2015 *	Multiplayer, collaborative, competitive, high attendance, relies on player authored content, undefined timespan, global	High freedom of movement, nonlinear paths, players create locations ("monsters") and routes, entwines with daily life	Commercial (Research)	[45, 46]
YourWayYourMission	2013 *	Collaborative, small attendance (23), competitive, co-located gameplay, long timespan (7 days), local	High freedom of movement, nonlinear paths, players create locations ("missions") and routes, entwines with daily life	Noncommercial (Research)	[16]
GPS Tycoon	2014 **	Multiplayer, competitive, leaderboard, players buy and explore close by areas on a map, high attendance, undefined timespan, global	High freedom of movement, in game possibility for faking player location, in came warning on playing while driving, entwines with daily life	Commercial	[25]
Street Art Gangs	2015 **	Multiplayer, competitive, players can attack each other, leaderboard, players know each other, low attendance, long timespan, local	High freedom of movement, fixed coordinates for locations, no paths, intense gameplay, entwines with daily life	Noncommercial (Research)	[4]
School Scene Investigators	2015 *	Collaborative, low attendance, augmented reality, co-located gameplay, short timespan, local	High freedom of movement, somewhat linear story, QR code locations	Noncommercial (Education, research)	[14]
Gossip at palace	2015 *	Single player or collaborative, noncompetitive, low attendance, short timespan, local	High freedom of movement, somewhat linear story, QR code locations	Noncommercial (Engage visitors to a site)	[62]
Landlord – Real Estate Tycoon	2015 **	Multiplayer, competitive, market for popular locations, based on Foursquare, high attendance, undefined timespan, global	High freedom of movement, players can see each other's real first names, fixed locations, no paths, entwines with daily life	Commercial	[60]
SoundPackman	2016 *	Single player or collaborative teamplay, noncompetitive, sound is central game element in avoiding ghosts and finding berries, short timespan, global	dynamically created but fixed coordinates for locations ("berries"), no linear paths, intense gameplay	Noncommercial (Research)	[15]
Pokemon GO	2016 **	Multiplayer, competitive, high attendance, player names used, undefined timespan, global	High freedom of movement, fixed coordinates for locations, in came warning on driving and playing, no paths, entwines with daily life	Commercial	[53]

* The year of a paper publication
** The year the game was published or piloted

Table 1. Characteristics of the reviewed LBMGs.

Characteristic		N		N		N
Player investment	*Low investment*	17			*High investment*	13
Number of players	*Few players*	17			*Unlimited number of players*	13
Commerciality	*Noncommercial*	20			*Commercial*	10
Timespan	*Short timespan*	8	*Long timespan*	13	*Undefined timespan*	9
Use situation	*Edge of the magic circle*	9			*Daily-life*	21
Competitiveness	*Noncompetitive*	7			*Competitive*	23
Gameplay type	*Single-player*	4	*Multiplayer*	18	*Player vs. player*	8

Table 2. LBMG characteristics and their frequency in reviewed games.

A search in Google Scholar returned 463 publications, while Google web search returned millions of hits, of which we included only web pages updated in 2015-2016. Furthermore, we inspected games referred in a review and a book on pervasive games [51, 39]. As a rule, the publications chosen for closer inspection had to describe a specific game. The games themselves had to fulfill two conditions: 1) they had to be played on a mobile phone or handheld device, and 2) they had to utilize player location in the game mechanics.

Some games, especially commercial ones, have not been evaluated academically or the results of such evaluations have not been published. To review such games, we installed and played the available commercial games. In these cases, the year of publication and the time of accessing a commercial game can differ notably. We focused our review on games played in urban outdoor settings, but also included some games played in vast indoor areas such as *Blowtooth* [39] played in an airport terminal and *FreshUp* played on a campus [74].

Systematic Review of LBMGs

26 games were selected from the mapping study for the thorough review as they fulfilled our conditions. We then conducted a second systematic review on 9th-13th September 2016. We used the same search and selection criteria as in the initial study. As a result, the selection of games included in the thorough review expanded to 30. Although the list of games is not exhaustive, we believe it provides an adequate basis for our analysis.

The level of pre-game and on-game orchestration distinguishes first- and second-generation LBMGs [39]. Some first-generation games deployed earlier this century were included in the analysis despite their requirement for special hardware. This was done in order to have a reference point in evolution of current pervasive games. We considered carefully whether to include games that utilized self-reported positioning and eventually decided to include *Uncle Roy All around You* (*URAAY*) [13] and *PacManhattan* [56], as these games present a specific case on the freedom of movement for the player.

CHARACTERISTICS OF LBMG GAMES AND GAM PLAY

In our review (Table 2), we first identified three overall themes for each game: description, affordances and restrictions, and developer motivation. In-depth inspection of revealed seven recurrent game characteristics that can affect the amount of required restrictions: 1) *player investment*, 2) *number of players*, 3) *commerciality of the game*, 4) *timespan*, 5) *use situation*, 6) *competitiveness*, and 7) *gameplay type*. We further identified three dimensions of affordances and restrictions that were either enforced or suggested to players: *on freedom of movement*, *on player interaction*, and *on interaction with the environment or the game*.

Game characteristics

Player investment can be either financial or time effort. The investment in game increases over time, so many games with unlimited or very long timespans, or games based on a leveling system, will have to take this in consideration. Furthermore, although we characterize games with research or educational motivation for developers as having low player investment, the incentive the players get from participating, whether it is learning or a reward, can affect player investment even when a game has a short duration.

Number of players: A coarse characterization is that in pervasive games, there exists a linear correlation between the number of players and the need for more extensive and intricate restrictions. To draw an analogy to more traditional video games, a game of solitaire requires far fewer rules than, say, a massively multiplayer online role-playing game such as *World of Warcraft*. Similarly, a pervasive game with a large number of concurrent users such as *Pokemon GO* [53] will require more rules and restrictions to gameplay than a game such as *YourWayYourMission* [16], which imposes far fewer limitations. Many current LBMGs designed to be expandable like *SoundPackman, Ingress* or *Landlord – Real Estate Tycoon* are or can be played globally, which allows having a nearly unlimited number of players. We believe that this characteristic is somewhat related to user acceptance and a direct consequence of the number of downloads. However, for academic games the *number of players* is a more suitable characteristic than the number of downloads.

Commerciality: Legal and ethical issues differ between research prototypes and commercial games. Furthermore, the level of sophistication level can vary. Where research prototypes can be unpolished yet still be able to serve their purpose, commercial products need to be polished in order to satisfy their users. Some commercial games are purely commercial, although there are games where the authors express both academic and commercial interests as their motivation, such games we categorized commercial (Table 2). It is notable though that the commerciality of a game is not a Boolean variable.

Timespan: Games mature over time, and emergent rules become guidelines. An example of this is *Geocaching*. Further, games that have long or unlimited timespans have more time to develop issues that affect the gameplay. These games must present a more sophisticated user experience and require a lower level or orchestration in order to remain viable. Games with undefined timespan also tend to be quite slow paced, despite having competitive elements (e.g. *Landlord Real Estate Tycoon* or *GPS tycoon* [60, 25]).

Use situation: LBMGs entwined with daily life have to apply further restrictions in addition to local laws and rules of conduct. The actual use situation in location-based games is more complex than mere safety issues while playing amongst traffic, for example. Generally, pervasive games are characterized as ongoing and a part of the daily life [44]. This is not though true for those LBMGs that are played as a short tournament and therefore situate closer to edge of the magic circle, where the separation between game and everyday life is more defined.

Competitiveness: The goal of a game can be winning by *e.g.* beating or outmaneuvering others. However, LBMGs can have other forms of rewards such as increased fitness or learning. A game can be classified as competitive if it involves direct or mediated confrontation or competition between players, even if this is implemented simply as a leaderboard in a single player game. This feature relates closely to *game type* described in the following and further to the characteristics of the game space on *Player-player Interaction* introduced in the following section.

Gameplay type: This characteristic directly affects the level of interactivity amongst players, hence it is presented here as a separate characteristic from *Competitiveness*, despite their close relation.

The set of characteristics listed in Table 2 are used to create an overview of the LBMGs. This overview provides a better understanding of the underlying links between game characteristics and the three categories for affordances and restrictions i.e. the characteristics of gameplay. We illustrate these links in Figures 2-4 with simple visualizations of the range of limitations set for a player by a particular dimension of affordances and restrictions. Typical ways to implement the dimension and example games are shown below the range.

Characteristics of LBMG gameplay

The game characteristics affect the characterization of the affordances and game mechanics and therefore game-play. Game characteristics are somewhat set based on the purpose and context of a game. The characteristics of game mechanics and play are subject to design and development. In the following, we go through the characteristics of LBMG gameplay as well as introduce relevant theories.

Affordances and Restrictions on Freedom of Movement

Mobile devices offer limited modalities for interaction in mobile gaming hence interaction with physical environment has high relevance [57]. However, mobile devices, wireless connectivity and positioning have shaped the perception of physical environment, which in turn has led to the reconfiguration of the urban space. It is no longer considered stable, but in constant flux as it is created and shaped by people passing through [42]. The shaping of space can be described through the concept of embodiment, where the space is shaped especially via the mobile device mediated sensory mapping of people and space. Implacement is the transformation of space into place. According to Farman [21], "*Implacement locates our situated nature and our sense of proprioception with others and with objects in a space*". The complexity of thus formed place can result in displacement [21], which has certainly been observed in pervasive games [12, 4]. In LBMGs displacement can be enhanced by the inaccuracies and latencies in connections, cognitive attention, and positioning. The characteristics of modern space and both the resulting implacement and displacement give dimensions to the players' freedom of movement. The freedom of movement is one of the most obvious non-rules in location-based games (Figure 2), possibly because previous research has shown that players prefer autonomous orienteering instead of preconceived paths [7].

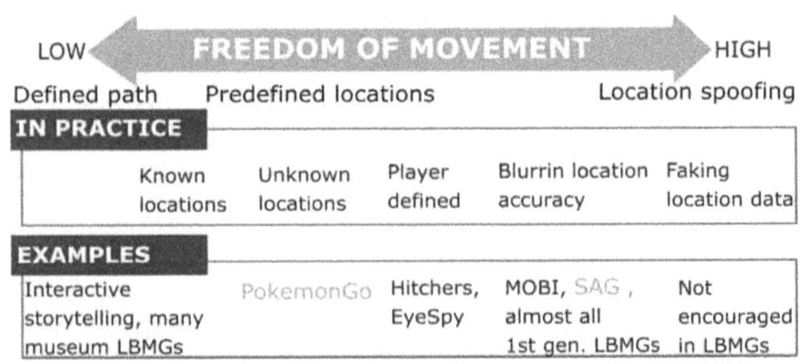

Figure 2. Levels of freedom of movement in LBMGs.

The freedom of movement was the most transparently reported feature in the reviewed games. Location based games oftentimes feature predefined targets or significant locations, which the players are allowed to reach in any given order. The game can also take place in a restricted area, e.g.

a town or a building. This is often not an implemented rule, but a necessity especially with many research based LBMGs, where restricting the observable area saves resources and removes the requirement to rely on an outside source for global positioning data [20]. We consider players having close to full freedom of movement if there are random explorable locations in a game, but also if players are allowed to shift their non-physical entity (e.g. avatar) or change their location inside game area. Few location-based games have preconceived paths for movement, which typically take place in museums or historical sites. These types of games can be considered similar to interactive storytelling.

It was noticeable that in many of the reviewed games, a strong storyline defined the paths players are allowed to take. The closer a game is to interactive storytelling, the more restricted the allowed paths become. For instance, in location based live action role-playing games (LARPs) such as *Momentum* and *Prosopopeia,* player paths are more restricted [35, 36]. Conversely, in a game like *Hitchers* that only has a hint of a backstory, players can freely drop to any location inside an undefined game area. In the commercial game *Parallel Kingdom* [59], a role-playing game saturated with fictional story content, players can move freely inside a small area on the game map and travel without having to move physically, but widening the game area requires moving on the physical streets, as well. *Zombies Run* [64] has a strong backstory, yet players are free to choose where and when they run.

Affordances and Restrictions on Player-player Interaction

Player-player interaction can take many forms in LBMGs, such as observing other players' location data, observing other players game stats, psychological battle, or bullying. We drew influence from the social interdependence theory [19, 34] to characterize a game as *individualistic* when individuals have no effect on others, *cooperative* when individual actions promote the goals and actions of others or *competitive* when individual actions obstruct the goals and actions of others [54]. However, we regard this dimension also a feature of the game space, as the affordances for interaction are offered by the game itself. Uncompetitive single player games do not often have to implement heavy restrictions or rules, as the need is typically created by the interaction with other people/players. Such games are isolated experiences where players' achievements are hidden from other players. Once a game has a real-time leaderboard, the game becomes competitive. In many location-based games where direct observation of fellow players is not possible or is prevented, the players find a way by using indirect means of observing other players such as real-time leaderboards or public logs [4, 55, 43]. On the streets, the possibility for players to be able to keep an eye on each other and especially competing players can prevent rule breaks.

In games having multiple types of player-player interactions (Figure 3) are available, we observe an interesting transition from co-located (or co-located collaborative) games and games that have player-player interference e.g. in-game battle (Figure 2). We suggest that multiple modalities of interaction afford greater freedom for interacting with other players [54].

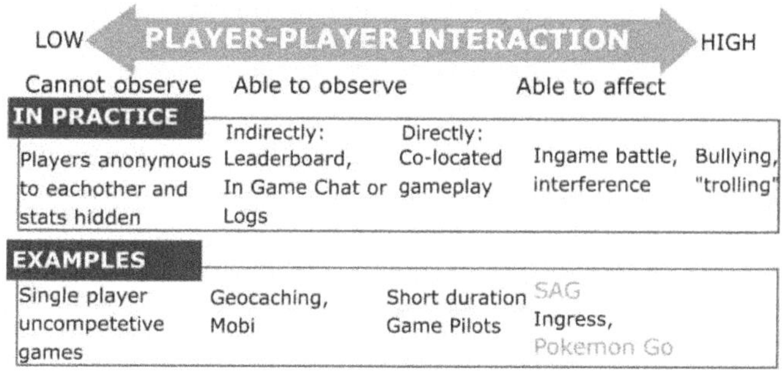

Figure 3. Levels of player-player interaction in LBMGs.

Affordances and Restrictions on Interaction with the Environment or the Game Space

In characterizing interaction with the environment or the game space, we drew inspiration on De Souza e Silva's definition of hybrid spaces [67]. Hybrid reality games utilize city infrastructure and are by definition social (Figure 4). This is especially true for games that have urban outdoor spaces as game arenas, as these spaces are full of opportunities and obstacles, which can even prove dangerous. As we have seen with *Pokemon GO* and other pervasive games, player behavior may even require the attention of local authorities [71, 55, 63].

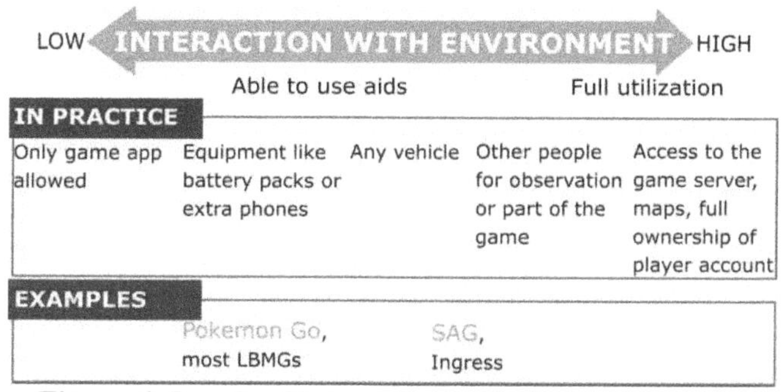

Figure 4. Levels of interaction with the environment including the game itself.

Players have the lowest amount of freedom in interacting with their environment when they can only play the game via a dedicated game application or an online interface. This kind of setup brings the game closer to a well-defined magic circle [29, 49], which is familiar from traditional videogames. The highest amount of freedom in *Interaction with the environment*, we consider to be the ability to not just utilize any tools or privileges the players have but a total ownership of their player accounts and ability to access the game server. Even if there currently are no games designed to give players this kind of freedom or let alone allow it, it is important when considering the potential of LBMGs to recognize the extremes.

DISCUSSION

There is a need for guidelines for applying restrictions on LBMGs. Often, the game developer's solution to abuse is to rely on the community to observe and report unwanted behavior [30, 31]. This approach has also been adopted by small LBMGs originating from academic research [4]. What we noticed and what we are communicating in this paper is that characterizing LBMGs is not as simple as dividing the games into commercial and noncommercial academic games. Furthermore, due to variations in LBMGs the affordances and restrictions designed into the game should relate to game characteristics and the motivation of the game developers. In the following, we show the viability of our characterization by two examples: a well-known commercial LBMG *Pokemon GO* [53] and research based *Street Art Gangs* (*SAG*) [4], where the research data is available to us.

Example 1: *Pokemon Go*

Pokemon GO (Figure 5) can be characterized as commercial, global and having very high attendance, low orchestration per player and undefined timespan. Its game play involves both exploration and battle [53]. Players collect experience, items, and fantastic creatures known as Pokemon from physical world locations. Pokemon are collected (or *captured*) using expendable items known as Pokeballs, which the player 'throws' at a creature once it appears on their mobile phone screen. After capture, Pokemon can be trained and made to fight in battle arenas known as Gyms. The game is distributed globally and has been installed from Google Play Store on estimate 50-100 million times. The game received a wide audience and enjoyed instant popularity after its launch in July 2016. *Pokemon GO*'s game characteristics are presented in Figure 5.

Pokemon GO players have high freedom of movement (Table 1). The game has fixed coordinates for Pokemon and other relevant locations, but there are no preconceived linear paths. Furthermore, in some locations players can use various devices (available as in-app purchase) to attract Pokemon to a location of their own choosing. The in-game battle system adds an element of interference between players, but the players do not need to be co-located in order to battle.

After the global launch, a new restriction was implemented in an early update. It disabled the use of external applications for visualizing the locations of hidden Pokemon on a map. Furthermore, the intensity of gameplay has already resulted in instances of people injuring themselves while playing [63]. Therefore, another restriction, an interruption to the game-play in a form of a pop-up notification, was implemented to make it more difficult to play while driving.

Figure 5. Approximate characterization of Pokemon GO. The blue line visualizes the game characteristics found in Table 2.

Currently, Niantic, responsible for such games as *Pokemon GO* and *Ingress*, is still fighting the disadvantages of hosting their games to a big audience by having to monitor the use of third party software used to cheat in the game. Further, instead of a simple ban of a player account, the punishment is built into the game in a subtler way, which means making the game more frustrating or harder to play for the cheating player and negating the some of the advantage they gain from cheating [7]. This shows that more sophisticated means of restricting LBMG gameplay are not only needed but are already in use.

Example 2: Street Art Gangs

SAG [4] is a research prototype that can be characterized as uncommercial and local with small attendance, some required orchestration and long timespan. It is a game where teams of players play for a restricted amount of time and compete for the ownership of the town, or points. In *SAG*, recruited players *conquered* locations by using their mobile device to 'spray paint' a virtual *tag* on buildings or landmarks, for example. Players were also able to *interrupt* competing players while they were attempting to conquer a location, which can be considered as an in-game battle system. The game uses fixed location coordinates, but there are no preconceived paths of movement for the players. The game area was restricted to 0.11-0.26 km^2 and game hours were limited to daytime. As such, players had plenty of opportunities to observe each other during the game and report any abuse.

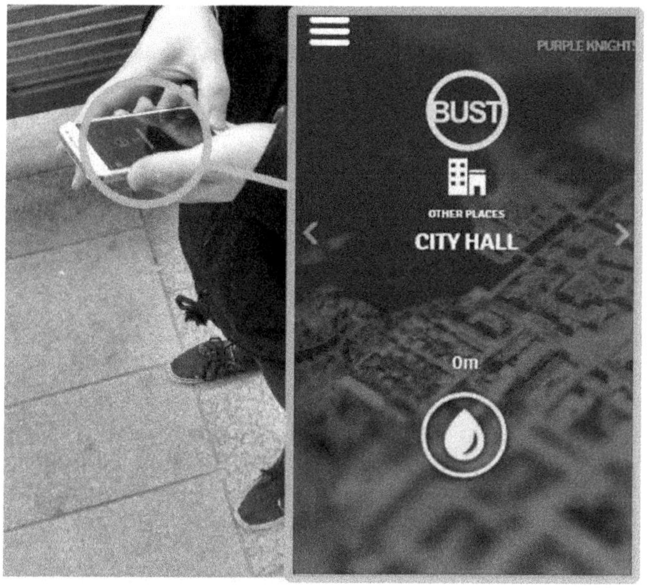

Figure 6. *SAG* player on the city streets.

Participating players (Figure 6) knew they were taking part in a study.

Unlike *Pokemon GO, SAG* 's characteristics are mostly at the left side of our characterization of LBMGs (Figure 7). They clearly affect the affordances and restriction in gameplay, e.g. the players were allowed to use any vehicle, motorized or otherwise. This was done to encourage community emergent rules. Researchers imposed one rule on their young players during orientation: "Do not neglect schoolwork or other responsibilities during the gameplay". Authors reported that participants recruited their friends from time to time to observe competing players at the streets. Players also utilized the game app's leaderboard to see how they were doing in comparison to competing teams, even when they were outside the actual game area.

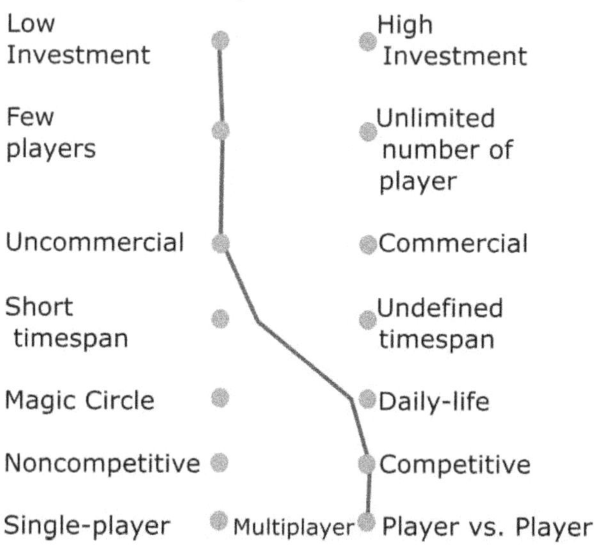

Figure 7. Approximate characterization of Street Art Gangs. The blue line visualizes the game characteristics found in Table 2.

LBMGs Expanding What Is Considered Traditional Gaming

Pervasive games are by definition games that aim at expanding the boundaries of traditional gaming. The three expansions defined by Montola are spatial, temporal and social [51]. De Souza e Silva's characteristics for hybrid reality games (urban pervasive games) are mobility, sociability and spatiality [67]. She replaced Montola's *temporal* with *mobility,* a shift that reflects the divide between the old and the more recent location based or pervasive games, i.e. the true mobility provided by the advances in mobile and ubiquitous technologies. These resemble our characterization although the temporal expansion is mentioned as a game characteristic (Timespan) and the spatial and social expansion are presented in our three characteristics of the game space. The expansion of the game space is intrinsic to pervasive games hence we extended our characterization of the restrictions outside the boundaries of what can currently be found in games. Therefore, our study helped us to recognize some ideas for future development of provocative LBMGs. We noticed that there does not appear to be LBMGs, where the players are allowed, without punishment, to utilize their environment for gameplay. The highest possible level of freedom of movement is still unattained as well. This opens an opportunity for designing games where the core game mechanics are developed around the idea of tinkering with player stats or location spoofing. We note that games with self-reported player locations [13] have already done this, but these games have not utilized both positioning with a smart phone and being able to self-report a location, shifting between the two. When it comes to player-player interaction, games allowing psychological battle between players are also scarce in LBMGs, albeit there is witty insult fighting or roasting in other medias. Of course, there are ethical considerations when such games are played in the city streets, therefore also a requirement for designing specific restrictions for gameplay. Further, our research revealed that while there are beneficial location based educational games and exergames, the full potential of LBMGs in societal and mobility training [1, 47, 70] has been largely unexplored. The upside of utilizing busy urban settings for games is that they can help people discover and see their city in new ways, they can encourage new social interactions to occur, and they can result in e.g. health benefits as players become more physically active [1, 47, 70].

Limitations and Future Work

The game characteristics discussed in this paper are derived from the reviewed games. This can be considered both as a weakness in the review methodology and as a strength due to the extensive selection of games. Further, many reviewed reports and papers do not directly mention the restrictions or rules of gameplay; hence, the records of implemented affordances and restrictions are not complete, but the wide scope of games complements this.

Noncommercial academic prototypes have different requirements and ethical considerations to commercial

LBMGs. The presented affordance and restriction categories should be refined to better account for these differences, with special focus on "interaction with the environment". This is likely to reveal new aspects of so-called *hybrid reality games* [67], where communication and interaction via and with city infrastructure is a defining quality. Some of the hypothesized factors affecting the required number of implemented rules were left out of this inspection due to insufficient material, for example regarding the role of a player motivation or player type (e.g. socializers vs. griefers) [5, 9]. For instance, would the dominant player type in a specific game have an effect on how much rules are needed for players to stay in the game. This does though provide an interesting target for future research. Social motivation is important in LBMGs [9, 41] and one could speculate that the recruitment of players for experimental LBMGs favors the socializer. Furthermore, as the number of players increase, does the number of social players diminish in relation to other player types with other motivation for playing. Will this increase cheating and further add to the amount of implemented restrictions on gameplay?

We also considered using the story content or simplicity of the game mechanics as defining characteristics. However, *Timespan* and *Game type* cover these characteristics. Complex, narrative heavy games can also be multiplayer games. Games with strong backstory like *Zombies Run* [64] or educational games located in museums can have quite simple game mechanics. The narrative seems to affect most at the point where a game moves from simple interactive storytelling to location based LARP. It is not always that straightforward however illustrated by the example of *Geocaching* [23], a game with simple game mechanics can encourage emergence of narrative. One could also argue that the ratio between the number of locations used in the game per player should be a LBMG characteristic. However, the number of used locations can be dynamic or player defined, and often is not reported at all. The *Number of players* included in the characterization has causality with both the amount of locations and the scale of the game area.

The characterization presented in this paper could benefit from a more thorough validation, which would in turn provide a scale between values in the characterization (Figure 5. Figure 7.) and make it possible to develop a more precise metrics for characterization.

CONCLUSION

Implementing and applying restrictions and rules can be considered as a specific form of orchestration. However, as games have evolved and the level of overall orchestration in LBMGs has diminished, the effort on orchestration has shifted from keeping the game up and running to monitoring the players to preventing them from breaking the rules, thus the number of implemented restrictions has increased. This has happened both as the old games like *Geocaching* have aged and as the new commercially viable games like *Pokemon GO* have appeared.

We conducted a systematic review of a wide range of LBMGs to analyze the characteristics and the rules and restriction of 30 games. We further created characterization of the games and affordances and restriction in gameplay. The purpose was to entwine the LBMGs characteristics closely into the design process and aid in understanding the close association between the characteristics and the player affordances in LBMGs. Hopefully, this will benefit the design process of future games and guide on the road to maturity for the current games.

ACKNOWLEDGEMENTS

This work has been supported by the Open Innovation Platforms spearhead project (A70202) and the Open City Model as Open Innovation Platform project (A71143) funded by the ERDF and the City of Oulu under the Six City Strategy program, and the COMBAT project (293389) funded by the Strategic Research Council at the Academy of Finland.

REFERENCES

1. Judith Ackermann and Ilaria Mariani. 2015. Re-thinking the Environment through Games. Designing Location Based Mobile Games in Higher Education for Environmental Awareness. *Innovation in Environmental Education: ICT and intergenerational learning*: 73.
2. Ernest Adams. 2014. *Fundamentals of Game Design*. New Riders Publishing.
3. Wilfried Admiraal, Jantina Huizenga, Sanne Akkerman, and Geert Ten Dam. 2011. The concept of flow in collaborative game-based learning. *Computers in Human Behavior* 27, 3: 1185–1194.
4. Paula Alavesa and Timo Ojala. 2015. Street Art Gangs: location based hybrid reality game. In *Proceedings of the 14th International Conference on Mobile and Ubiquitous Multimedia*, 64–74. http://doi.org/10.1145/2836041.2836047
5. Suen de Andrade e Silva. 2013. Social play or social cheating? Another face of sociability in social network games. *First Monday*, 18, 7.
6. Louise Barkhuus, Matthew Chalmers, Paul Tennent, Malcolm Hall, Marek Bell, Scott Sherwood, and Barry Brown. 2005. Picking pockets on the lawn: the development of tactics and strategies in a mobile game. In *International Conference on Ubiquitous Computing*, 358–374.
7. Brian Barret. Instead of Banning Cheaters, Pokémon Go Trolls Them Hard. *WIRED*. Retrieved July 20, 2017 from https://www.wired.com/2017/05/pokemon-go-cheaters-shadowban/
8. Rafael Ballagas, André Kuntze, and Steffen P. Walz. 2008. Gaming Tourism: Lessons from Evaluating REXplorer, a Pervasive Game for Tourists. In *Pervasive Computing: 6th International Conference, Pervasive 2008 Sydney, Australia, May 19-22, 2008*

Proceedings, 244–261. https://doi.org/10.1007/978-3-540-79576-6_15

9. Richard Bartle. 1996. Hearts, clubs, diamonds, spades: Players who suit MUDs. Journal of MUD research 1, 1: 19.
10. Marek Bell, Matthew Chalmers, Louise Barkhuus, Malcolm Hall, Scott Sherwood, Paul Tennent, Barry Brown, Duncan Rowland, Steve Benford, Mauricio Capra, and Alastair Hampshire. 2006. Interweaving mobile games with everyday life. In *Proceedings of the SIGCHI Conference on Human Factors in Computing Systems*, 417–426.
11. Marek Bell, Stuart Reeves, Barry Brown, Scott Sherwood, Donny MacMillan, John Ferguson, and Matthew Chalmers. 2009. EyeSpy: supporting navigation through play. In *Proceedings of the SIGCHI Conference on Human Factors in Computing Systems*, 123–132.
12. Steve Benford, Andy Crabtree, Martin Flintham, Adam Drozd, Rob Anastasi, Mark Paxton, Nick Tandavanitj, Matt Adams, and Ju Row-Farr. 2006. Can you see me now? *ACM Trans. Comput.-Hum. Interact.* 13, 1: 100–133.
13. Steve Benford, Will Seager, Martin Flintham, Rob Anastasi, Duncan Rowland, Jan Humble, Danaë Stanton, John Bowers, Nick Tandavanitj, Matt Adams, Ju Row-Farr, Amanda Oldroyd, and Jon Sutton. 2004. The Error of Our Ways: The Experience of Self-Reported Position in a Location-Based Game. In *UbiComp 2004: Ubiquitous Computing*, Nigel Davies, Elizabeth D. Mynatt and Itiro Siio (eds.). Springer Berlin Heidelberg, 70–87. http://dx.doi.org/10.1007/978-3-540-30119-6_5
14. Denise M. Bressler. 2015. School scene investigators: a collaborative AR game for middle school science inquiry. In *Mobile Media Learning*, Christopher Holden, Seann Dikkers, John Martin and Breanne Litts (eds.). ETC Press, 87–99.
15. Thomas Chatzidimitris, Damianos Gavalas, and Despina Michael. 2016. SoundPacman: Audio augmented reality in location-based games. *2016 18th Mediterranean Electrotechnical Conference (MELECON)*: 1–6. https://doi.org/10.1109/MELCON.2016.7495414
16. Ling Chen, Gencai Chen, and Steve Benford. 2013. Your Way Your Missions: A Location-Aware Pervasive Game Exploiting the Routes of Players. *International Journal of Human–Computer Interaction* 29, 2: 110–128. http://doi.org/10.1080/10447318.2012.694790
17. Andy Crabtree, Steve Benford, Tom Rodden, Chris Greenhalgh, Martin Flintham, Rob Anastasi, Adam Drozd, Matt Adams, Ju Row-Farr, Nick Tandavanitj, and Anthony Steed. 2004. Orchestrating a mixed reality game "on the ground." In *Proceedings of the SIGCHI Conference on Human Factors in Computing Systems*, 391–398.
18. Chris DeLeon. 2013. Rules in Computer Games Compared to Rules in Traditional Games. Proceedings *of DiGRA 2013: DeFragging Game Studies*: 1–1.
19. Morton Deutch. 1949. A Theory of Co-Operation and Competition. *Human Relations* 2, 2: 129–152. https://doi.org/10.1177/001872674900200204
20. Adam Drozd, Steve Benford, Nick Tandavanitj, Michael Wright, and Alan Chamberlain. 2006. Hitchers: designing for cellular positioning. In *International Conference on Ubiquitous Computing*, 279–296.
21. Jason Farman. 2011. Mapping and Representations of Space. In *Mobile Interface Theory: Embodied Space and Locative Media* (1st ed.). Routledge, 35–55.
22. Foursquare for Developers. Retrieved September 16, 2016 from https://developer.foursquare.com/
23. Geocaching. Geocaching. *Geocaching*. Retrieved August 22, 2016 from https://www.geocaching.com/play
24. Gabriel Ghinita and Mihai Maruseac. 2015. Disseminating Location Privacy Threats and Protection Techniques through Capture-the-Flag Games (Vision Paper). In *Proceedings of the 2nd Workshop on Privacy in Geographic Information Collection and Analysis*, 1–4.
25. Rasiel Suarez. 2014. *GPS Tycoon*. Rasiel Suarez. Game [Android]. September 2014. Played August 2016.
26. Lyndsay Grant, Hans Daanen, Steve Benford, Alastair Hampshire, Adam Drozd, and Chris Greenhalgh. 2007. MobiMissions: the game of missions for mobile phones. In *ACM SIGGRAPH 2007 educators program*, 12.
27. Alison Harvey. 2006. The liminal magic circle: Boundaries, frames, and participation in pervasive mobile games. *Wi: Journal of the Mobile Digital Commons Network* 1, 1.
28. Steve Hinske, Matthias Lampe, Carsten Magerkurth, and Carsten Röcker. 2007. Classifying pervasive games: on pervasive computing and mixed reality. *Concepts and technologies for Pervasive Games-A Reader for Pervasive Gaming Research* 1: 20.
29. Johan Huizinga. 1955. *Homo Ludens: A Study of the Play Element in Culture*. Routledge & Kegan Paul, London, United Kingdom.
30. Ingress FAQ. Retrieved August 5, 2016 from http://www.ingressportal.com/w/wp-content/uploads/2012/12/IngressFAQ.pdf
31. Ingress Help. Retrieved August 5, 2016 from https://support.ingress.com/hc/en-us

32. Itography-The Policy. Retrieved September 13, 2016 from http://www.itography.com/policy
33. Itography. 2011. *Itography Item Hunt*. Game [Android]. (September 2011). Itography. Played September 2016.
34. David W. Johnson. 2003. Social interdependence: interrelationships among theory, research, and practice. *American psychologist* 58, 11: 934.
35. Staffan Jonsson, Markus Montola, Annika Waern, and Martin Ericsson. 2006. Prosopopeia: experiences from a pervasive Larp. In *Proceedings of the 2006 ACM SIGCHI international conference on Advances in computer entertainment technology*, 23.
36. Staffan Jonsson and Annika Waern. 2008. The art of game-mastering pervasive games. In *Proceedings of the 2008 International Conference on Advances in Computer Entertainment Technology*, 224–231.
37. Bo Kampmann Walther. 2011. Towards a theory of pervasive ludology: reflections on gameplay, rules, and space. Digital Creativity 22, 3: 134–147. http://doi.org/10.1080/14626268.2011.603734
38. Bo Kampmann Walther. 2005. Atomic actions -- molecular experience: theory of pervasive gaming. *Comput. Entertain.* 3, 3: 4–4.
39. Vlasios Kasapakis and Damianos Gavalas. 2015. Pervasive gaming: Status, trends and design principles. *Journal of Network and Computer Applications* 55: 213–236. http://doi.org/10.1016/j.jnca.2015.05.009
40. Ben Kirman, Conor Linehan, and Shaun Lawson. 2012. Blowtooth: a provocative pervasive game for smuggling virtual drugs through real airport security. *Personal and Ubiquitous Computing* 16, 6: 767–775.
41. Maja Klausen. 2014. Re-enchanting the city: Hybrid space, affect and playful performance in geocaching, a location-based mobile game. Journal of Urban and Cultural Studies 1, 2: 193–213.
42. Henri Lefebvre. 1991. *The production of space*. Oxford Blackwell.
43. Christian Licoppe and Yoriko Inada. 2006. Emergent Uses of a Multiplayer Location-aware Mobile Game: the Interactional Consequences of Mediated Encounters. *Mobilities* 1, 1: 39–61. http://doi.org/10.1080/17450100500489221
44. Conor Linehan, Ben Kirman, Shaun Lawson, and Mark Doughty. 2010. Blowtooth: pervasive gaming in unique and challenging environments. In *CHI '10 Extended Abstracts on Human Factors in Computing Systems*, 2695–2704.
45. Kate Lund, Paul Coulton, and Andrew Wilson. 2011. Free All Monsters!: a context-aware location based game. In *Proceedings of the 13th International Conference on Human Computer Interaction with Mobile Devices and Services*, 675–678.
46. Kate Lund, Paul Coulton, and Andrew Wilson. 2015. Revealing the Participation Inequality in Mobile Location Based Games. *Comput. Entertain.* 11, 3: 1–13.
47. Charlotte Magnusson, Annika Waern, Kirsten Rassmus Gröhn, et al. 2011. Navigating the world and learning to like it: mobility training through a pervasive game. In *Proceedings of the 13th International Conference on Human Computer Interaction with Mobile Devices and Services*, 285–294.
48. Donald McMillan, Alistair Morrison, and Matthew Chalmers. 2013. Categorised ethical guidelines for large scale mobile HCI. In *Proceedings of the SIGCHI Conference on Human Factors in Computing Systems*, 1853–1862.
49. Markus Montola. 2005. Exploring the edge of the magic circle: Defining pervasive games. In *Proceedings of DAC*, 103.
50. Markus Montola. 2011. A ludological view on the pervasive mixed-reality game research paradigm. *Personal Ubiquitous Comput.* 15, 1: 3–12.
51. Markus Montola, Jaakko Stenros, and Annika Waern. 2009. *Pervasive games: theory and design.* Morgan Kaufmann Publishers Inc.
52. Donald A. Norman. 1999. Affordance, conventions, and design. *interactions* 6, 3: 38–43.
53. Niantic Labs. 2016. *Pokémon GO*. Game [Android, iOS]. (July 2016). Niantic. Played July-August 2016.
54. De Liu, Xun Li, and Radhika Santhanam. 2013. Digital Games and Beyond: What Happens When Players Compete. *Mis Quarterly* 37, 1: 111–124.
55. Carman Neustaedter, Anthony Tang, and Tejinder K. Judge. 2013. Creating scalable location-based games: lessons from Geocaching. *Personal and Ubiquitous Computing* 17, 2: 335–349. http://doi.org/10.1007/s00779-011-0497-7
56. Pac Manhattan. Retrieved August 25, 2016 from http://www.pacmanhattan.com/about.php
57. Volker Paelke, Leif Oppermann, and Christian Reimann. 2008. Mobile location-based gaming. *Map-based Mobile Services*: 310–334.
58. Ashish Patro, Shravan Rayanchu, Michael Griepentrog, Yadi Ma, and Suman Banerjee. 2012. The anatomy of a large mobile massively multiplayer online game. *SIGCOMM Comput. Commun. Rev.* 42, 4: 479–484.
59. PerBlue. 2008. *Parallel Kingdom*. Game [Android, iOS]. (October 2008). PerBlue. Played August 2016.
60. Reality Games LTD. 2015. *Landlord – Real Estate Tycoon*. Game [Android, iOS]. (2015) Reality Games LTD. Played August 2016.
61. Josephine Reid, Erik Geelhoed, Richard Hull, Kirsten Cater, and Ben Clayton. 2005. Parallel worlds:

immersion in location-based experiences. In CHI'05 extended abstracts on Human factors in computing systems, 1733–1736.

62. Irene Rubino, Claudia Barberis, Jetmir Xhembulla, and Giovanni Malnati. 2015. Integrating a location-based mobile game in the museum visit: Evaluating visitors' behaviour and learning. *Journal on Computing and Cultural Heritage (JOCCH)* 8, 3: 15.

63. Maeve Serino, Kyla Cordrey, Laura McLaughlin, and Ruth L. Milanaik. 2016. Pokémon Go and augmented virtual reality games: a cautionary commentary for parents and pediatricians. *Current opinion in pediatrics* 28, 5: 673–677.

64. Six to Start. 2012. *Zombies, Run!* Game [iOS, Android, AppleWatc]. (February 2012). Six to Start. Played August 2016.

65. Olli Sotamaa. 2002. All the World's A Botfighter Stage: Notes on Location-based Multi-User Gaming. In *Proceedings of the Computer Games and Digital Cultures Conference.*

66. Adriana de Souza e Silva. 2006. From cyber to hybrid mobile technologies as interfaces of hybrid spaces. *Space and culture* 9, 3: 261–278.

67. Adriana de Souza e Silva. 2009. Hybrid Reality and Location-Based Gaming: Redefining Mobility and Game Spaces in Urban Environments. *Simulation & Gaming* 40, 3: 404–424. http://doi.org/10.1177/1046878108314643

68. Jaakko Stenros. 2012. In defence of a magic circle: the social and mental boundaries of play. In *Proceedings of DiGRA Nordic 2012 Conference: Local and Global–Games in Culture and Society.*

69. Penny Sweetser. 2008. *Emergence in games*. Cengage Learning.

70. Masaru Tateno, Norbert Skokauskas, Takahiro A. Kato, Alan R. Teo, and Anthony P.S. Guerrero. 2016. New game software (Pokémon Go) may help youth with severe social withdrawal, hikikomori. *Psychiatry Research* 246: 848–849. https://doi.org/10.1016/j.psychres.2016.10.038

71. Juha Tiensyrjä, Timo Ojala, Toni Hakanen, and Ossi Salmi. 2010. panOULU conqueror: pervasive location-aware multiplayer game for city-wide wireless network. In Proceedings of the 3rd International Conference on Fun and Games, 157–165.

72. Johanna Ylipulli, Anna Luusua, Hannu Kukka, and Timo Ojala. 2014. Winter is coming: introducing climate sensitive urban computing. In Proceedings of the 2014 conference on Designing interactive systems, 647–656.

73. Daniel Yule, Bonnie MacKay, and Derek Reilly. 2015. Operation Citadel: Exploring the Role of Docents in Mixed Reality. In *Proceedings of the 2015 Annual Symposium on Computer-Human Interaction in Play*, 285–294.

74. Raphael Zender, Richard Metzler, and Ulrike Lucke. 2014. FreshUP—A pervasive educational game for freshmen. *Special Issue on Pervasive EducationSpecial Issue on The Social Car: Socially-inspired Mechanisms for Future Mobility Services* 14: 47–56. http://doi.org/10.1016/j.pmcj.2013.09.003

Escaping Together: The Design and Evaluation of a Distributed Real-Life Escape Room

Hanieh Shakeri[1], Samarth Singhal[1], Rui Pan[1], Carman Neustaedter[1] and Anthony Tang[2]
[1]School of Interactive Arts and Technology, Simon Fraser University, Surrey, BC, Canada
[2]Dept. of Computer Science, University of Calgary, Calgary, AB, Canada
hshakeri@sfu.ca, samarths@sfu.ca, ruip@sfu.ca, carman@sfu.ca, tonyt@ucalgary.ca

ABSTRACT
In real-life escape rooms, players try to escape a locked room by solving a series of puzzles. Currently, escape rooms involve collocated collaboration; however, there is potential for them to be distributed. We explored the design of a distributed escape room that connected two distance-separated rooms through audio/video links and shared artifacts. We evaluated it with pairs of participants to explore the design factors that affected player experiences. Results show that an audio connection created feelings of social presence. Video links augmented this connection to help players share knowledge and artifacts, however, showing less over the video feed created curiosity. Players expected a parallel setup between artifacts and puzzles in the rooms, despite the rooms being designed to vary in similarity and how closely players needed to collaborate. These results suggest directions for the design of audio connections to represent remote players, video feeds for sharing artifacts and promoting curiosity, and the use of both similar and dissimilar artifacts as a part of puzzles.

Author Keywords
Escape rooms; distributed collaboration; awareness.

ACM Classification Keywords
H.5.3 [Information Interfaces and Presentation]: Group and Organization Interfaces – CSCW.

INTRODUCTION
Real-life escape rooms are a new genre of game based on live-action role-playing games, treasure hunts, and online escape rooms [47,52]. Players are locked in a series of rooms and must solve puzzles in order to escape. Some include programmatically controlled doors or lights, computers, or sensors [47,52]. Escape rooms have been found to be a potential avenue for co-workers or friends to explore and enhance their collaboration skills, socialize with others, and build team morale [47,52]. Thus, they could be used by researchers or designers to explore a range of social and technical questions, depending on how they are constructed [52]. This is akin to the way alternate reality games (ARGs) have been used to explore social questions around trust, learning, and relationship building [1,6,9,10] and technical questions around connectivity and device usage [2,5]. For example, escape rooms could be used to study or improve relationship dynamics such as between co-workers, family or friends [52]. They could also augment educational programs for teaching workplace skills [52]. However, given their relative infancy, we know little in terms of how to effectively design escape rooms.

Real-life escape rooms typically involve collocated play where groups of players must be in the same physical location together in order to participate [52]. Yet, in reality, co-workers may be distributed around the world. This distance-separation means that they do not have many opportunities to practice their collaboration skills or participate in team building activities with remote colleagues, though it could be highly valuable [50]. Similarly, many family members or friends live apart and do not have opportunities to perform shared activities together over distance [46]. Distributed escape rooms offer one potential solution to these problems. By distributed escape room, we are referring to an escape room that connects two or more rooms over distance where players participate as a team, despite being in different locations.

The challenge, however, is that it is not clear how to best design distributed escape rooms to produce an enjoyable experience. We do not know: 1) what kinds of video and audio connectivity should be used to join the rooms; 2) how artifacts should be connected across the rooms; and, 3) if and how puzzles should be designed to support independent and joint work. To explore these points, we iteratively designed a distributed escape room called *Escaping Together* that connects two distance-separated rooms. We specifically explored three ways of connecting the rooms: video/audio connections, shared artifacts, and puzzle design. Next we conducted an exploratory study of Escaping Together with pairs who played in the distributed escape room—one partner in each of the rooms. Our goal was to understand if and why participants felt a sense of social presence with their partners; how play manifested in the rooms; how partners worked together or apart from each other; and, to what extent the design of the rooms affected

CHI PLAY 2017, October 15–18, 2017, Amsterdam, The Netherlands.

ACM ISBN 9978-1-4503-4898-0/17/10...$15.00.
https://doi.org/10.1145/3116595.3116601

these behaviors. By social presence, we refer to the feeling that one's partner is present and with you in the room [7].

Our results show that participants strongly valued the audio link to connect with their partner, while stationary and mobile video links periodically augmented this connection. In contrast to prior research on workplace collaboration (e.g., [22,32]), seeing only part of the remote room over video was valuable as it created curiosity in players who wondered what the remote room was like. Players' expectations of collaboration affected their approaches to puzzles. Participants imagined the escape room environment to offer a parallel setup between rooms; in contrast, the escape room did not always require joint work and artifacts were sometimes different. These results suggest that distributed escape rooms require ways of providing social presence through audio that is decoupled from video; video feeds for sharing artifacts where it can be valuable to show limited viewpoints in order to increase curiosity; and, a mixture of puzzles and artifacts where some are similar and others are not. Similar artifacts and shared puzzles may help create feelings of social presence, while dissimilar ones may help create feelings of intrigue.

RELATED WORK

Escape Rooms

Real life escape rooms are a new genre of game that have evolved from live-action role playing games, treasure hunts, and online escape rooms where players try to free an avatar by solving puzzles [47,52]. Many different types of escape rooms exist in various facilities around the world where themes vary [47]. Depending on the escape room, players solve logic puzzles, spatial or mechanical puzzles, and word or math puzzles [47]. A survey of proprietors of 175 escape room facilities around the world found that 13% have an open model where players solve puzzles in no particular order, 37% have a sequential model where puzzles are designed in a linear sequence, and 45% have a path-based model where there are multiple sequential paths of puzzles [47]. Escape rooms are played by corporate groups, adult friends or family, and young adult friends [47]. A study of collocated players in an escape room showed that escape rooms provide players with opportunities to practice collaboration skills such as communication, situation awareness, and conflict resolution; however, the design of escape rooms can restrict such behaviors [52]. We build on this work to explore distributed escape rooms.

Pervasive Games and Social Play

Escape rooms are similar to pervasive games—games that move beyond computers to take place on mobile or other ubiquitous devices. Alternate reality games (ARGs) are a type of pervasive game that blends game play with real life [3,4,17,36,41], often as a form of transmedia storytelling [8,9,10]. Escape rooms are similar in that they include a theme that bridges real life and an alternate reality, though the level of orchestration in them and attempts to blur real life and the game is arguably less than ARGs.

Distributed collaboration has been studied in several ARGs and pervasive games with a focus on exploring trust in strangers [1,6], creating and utilizing a sense of community [43,44,49], and privacy in public spaces [56]. Studies of these games and others have shown that distributed collaboration can help players to learn [9], create shared understanding [55], increase player motivation [43,44,48], and cause reflections on society and technology [1,4,5,6]. Collaboration can be aided through the development of leadership and roles [54,65] and digital tools that connect people across space and time [44,45,54,65]. In particular, this may involve online forums if play is asynchronous [54,65]. When play is synchronous, audio links have been found to make partners feel especially close to one another while video is difficult to use to support fine-grained collaborative tasks over distance [56]. Our study builds on this work to explore how distributed escape rooms should be connected and how collaboration should be supported.

Researchers have also studied social presence and emotions during game play more generally. Studies have found that social presence (sometimes called spatial presence) is higher when people play against other humans as compared to strangers or computer opponents [23,58]. Feelings of strong social presence have been linked to player enjoyment of games [58] and higher arousal levels have been linked to playing with a friend [38]. Higher levels of social presence can be achieved between distributed players when they are working towards collaborative goals [16,62]. We measure social presence in our escape room and explore puzzles that support joint work and independent work to understand their tradeoffs in distributed escape rooms.

Distributed Collaboration

Researchers have extensively explored the topic of distributed collaboration as it relates to teamwork amongst small groups in a work setting. This is similar to what occurs in escape rooms, with the addition of a work environment and focus. Situation awareness includes information about what is happening around oneself and how that information can be used now and in the future [18,29]. It helps collaborators establish joint goals [18,29]. When people collaborate, they maintain a sense of workspace awareness: knowledge of the actions of others in a shared workspace [25,26]. This awareness allows collaborators to coordinate their actions and move into and out of closely-knit groupwork [25,26,63,64]. Tightly coupled work is when partners need to frequently wait or interact with others, or loosely coupled work when partners work independently for long periods of time [60].

Team cognition refers to the execution of coordinated behaviors amongst team members where team members are aided by awareness, communication [11,21,30], and common ground [11], including ongoing knowledge of what team members are doing [11,18]. Group communication and team dynamics are important factors for determining how well teams perform at a given task

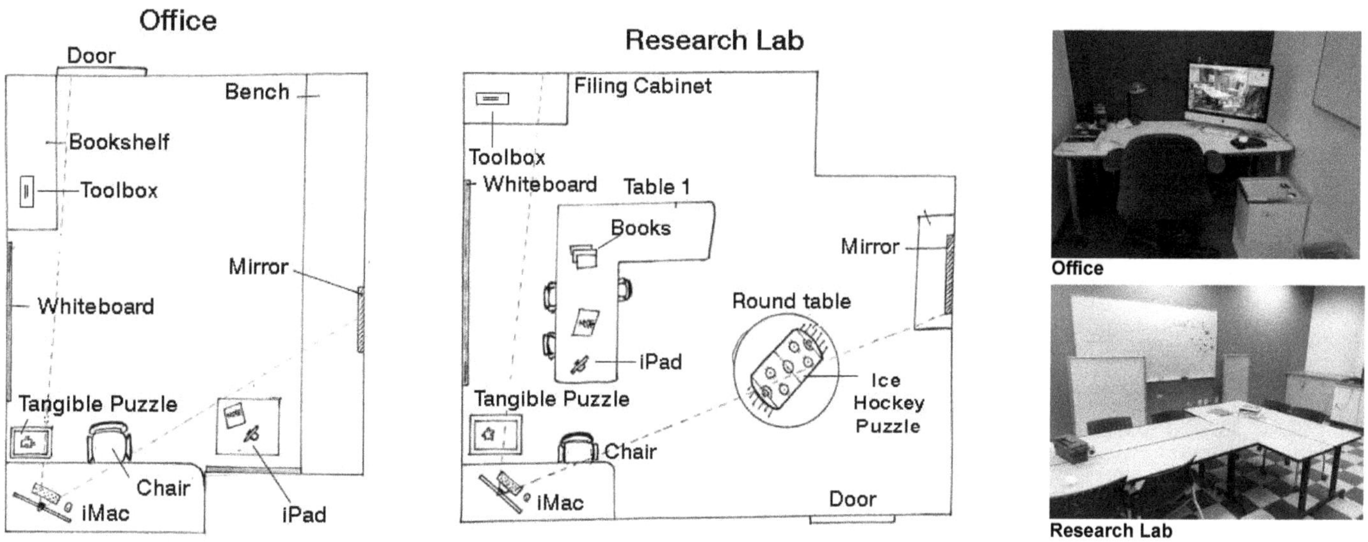

Figure 1. The distributed escape room: an office connected to a research lab.

[15,31]. Collaborators also typically develop a shared mental model—a shared mental representation of their situation, which includes knowledge of the tools available to them, the goal of their task, and what other team members know [13,28,39,40]. Shared mental models are valuable in situations where team members all work in similar roles [11]. We explore these ideas as part of teamwork in distributed escape rooms, noting when and how players maintain awareness and shared mental models.

Distributed Collaboration Puzzles and Tasks

Studies of workplace collaboration over distance have often included elements similar to what one would see in a distributed escape room. For example, partners typically work in two different locations and share a visual workspace of some form [51]. Video or audio systems aid communication and collaboration. Within the space, partners solve a puzzle or perform a task as a pair or group, where many studies have followed a helper/worker situation (e.g., [24,34,35]). In these studies, the worker completes the task with knowledge shared by the helper.

We know that sketching interfaces [35], a view of unmediated hand gestures [34], and immediate visual feedback of collaborators' actions [24] are valuable and aid situation and workspace awareness in shared digital workspaces containing video and audio connections. Collaborators value a stationary overview camera [22,32] along with mobile cameras [57]. Stationary cameras are sometimes even preferred over head-mounted cameras [22], though head-mounted cameras can provide collaborators with proactive assistance [32]. We build on these explorations to explore video and audio communication within a distributed escape room to understand when and how video and audio connections are used between partners. Here the difference is that people are participating in a game under time constraints with specific design elements that may be different than workplace and study settings. Players are also working to solve complex puzzles that are more varied and challenging than one would find in typical controlled experiments of distributed collaboration. This makes it unclear if and how findings from distributed collaboration in the aforementioned studies apply to distributed escape room play and design where there is a larger focus on enjoyment rather than getting 'work' done.

DISTRIBUTED ESCAPE ROOM DESIGN

We designed a distributed real-life escape room called Escaping Together to let partners play in interconnected escape rooms over distance. The goal was to allow players to share the experience together, feel social presence over distance, collaborate to mutually exit their locked rooms, and have an enjoyable experience. Escaping Together contained two rooms, one for each partner. Naturally, there are many ways to design a distributed escape room, e.g., multiple rooms, multiple players in each room, etc. We chose what we felt was a base case for exploring distributed escape rooms. Future work could expand on our model.

We designed our distributed escape room to fit an academic espionage theme where one room was a professor's office and the second room was the research lab of the professor (Figure 1). As part of the theme, players were told that one of them had failed a class and so they were trying to break into the professor's office and research lab in order to try and figure out how to change the grade. Grading sheets were somewhere in one of the two rooms. Players could talk to each other and see what was occurring in the other room through an audio and video connection (e.g., Google Hangouts) running on both a tablet and a computer in the room. Players were told that as soon as they entered the rooms, the doors would be auto-locked because there was unauthorized access detected. They were given 45 minutes to escape their respective rooms before an alarm would sound. They could ask for three hints as a team during their play by 'phoning a friend' (the researchers).

Table 1. Puzzle descriptions and goals.

Puzzle	Description	Goal	Type of Artifacts	Answer
1: Mirror	Each room had its own spatial puzzle where partners had to figure out a lock code using a mirror and whiteboard (Figure 2).	Have players start by exploring their own room and seeing what objects were in it.	**Similar** – both rooms had a mirror and whiteboard but they contained different numbers on the whiteboard.	**Different** – each room had a unique answer.
2: Grade Sheet	An Ottendorf cipher using a student grade sheet and books.	Have players work more closely together to achieve the same answer, while still giving them the chance to work independently.	**Similar** – both rooms had a grade sheet and books, but the contents were different.	**Same** – solving the cipher in both rooms produced the same numeric code.
3: Hockey Table	'Worker plus helper' puzzle where one partner uses an information sheet to tell the other where to position players on a table hockey game (Figure 3).	Force players into tightly-coupled work.	**Different** – one room had a table hockey game, one room had an information sheet.	**Same** – solving the puzzle produces a single numeric code used in both rooms.
4: Table Puzzle	A tangible computing jigsaw puzzle [53]. Players placed physical puzzle pieces on a digital table and moved them around. Pieces from both tables were shown on a computer screen in each room (Figure 4).	Have participants jointly come up with the final solution to their rooms to escape together.	**Similar** – each partner had different pieces of the same puzzle.	**Same** – each partner produced two numbers that, when joined, were the final numeric code to the rooms' locks.

We focused on exploring three ways of providing connectedness to the players—different aspects of the rooms that were used to create feelings of social presence and a shared experience between players across the rooms. The three elements we explored were: 1) ***Audio and Video Links:*** an audio connection and mobile and stationary video feeds; 2) ***Artifacts:*** a mixture of shared and non-shared artifacts across the rooms, including both computational and non-computationally enhanced objects; and, 3) ***Puzzles:*** a mixture of puzzles where some required tightly coupled collaboration and some could be solved independently.

1. Audio and Video Links

We included two types of video feeds between the rooms as a means to help players feel connected over distance and share their experiences (e.g., helping each other on puzzles or sharing their enjoyment of the room) along with an audio link associated with one of the video links. The first video feed was a mobile (tablet-to-tablet) connection, and the second video feed was a stationary (computer-to-computer) connection. Looking at one room's tablet showed the view from the other room's tablet. Similarly, looking at one room's computer showed the view from the other room's computer. We felt this mapping would make the video connections easily understandable.

We included the tablet as we anticipated that people would want a video feed that they could move around to show different parts of the escape room and engage in camera work as part of the experience; this builds on prior work on distributed collaboration [20,22,32,33]. Each tablet was on a stand so it could be easily positioned and set down, as opposed to having to hold it continuously. We included the computer as we anticipated that players would value seeing a static view of the entire workspace, akin to the benefits found for stationary displays in remote collaboration tasks [22,32]. Dashed lines in Figure 1 show the captured area of the stationary cameras.

We pilot-tested different video and audio configurations where we changed the starting location of the tablets and the locations of the computers to see their effects. We found that it was better to have the mobile and stationary cameras in different locations so that players would use them at different points in time. Having them in the same location meant the mobile camera rarely moved. We brainstormed the use of a head-mounted camera, but decided against it as we felt that, similar to other research, it would be less valuable for fine-grained tasks like puzzle solving and large amounts of camera movement could be awkward [33,56].

2. Artifacts

The rooms contained various artifacts that were needed to solve the escape room puzzles. We selected objects for each room that we felt fit the theme, style of the rooms, and the puzzles. For example, objects included puzzle pieces with motion tracking, books, a small travel bag, etc. Thus, objects were a mixture of computational and non-computational. We chose three types of artifacts:

a) ***Duplicate artifacts*** - the same artifact was found in both rooms (e.g., the exact same book was in each room). We included them to see how connected participants would feel when given the opportunity to work on their own (using their own object) or help out their partner (since the needed object was the same).

b) ***Similar artifacts*** - the same type of object was in both rooms but with different content or information (e.g., a different book in each room). We included them, again, to see how connected participants would feel, this time with similar but slightly different objects. This could allow them to work on their own or help their partner in a loosely coupled fashion by talking about their objects.

c) ***Different artifacts*** - completely different objects in each room (e.g., a toolbox in one room, a bag in the other room). Our goal was to create intrigue by having completely different objects be a part of the puzzle. Participants could not always assume that they needed to use the same object at the same time and they would likely want to converse about the different objects in each room.

Across all three object types, our goal was to learn how the objects would be used, shared, or referred to over the video and audio links. We placed some objects out of camera view in the rooms so that players would need to utilize the mobile camera to share them. While some objects were not computationally-enhanced, we used them to further understand how computational objects that had similar properties might be designed. Table 1 describes the puzzle-specific artifacts as part of our puzzle descriptions.

3. Puzzles

We designed a series of four puzzles for each room that players needed to solve in a *sequential order*; thus, while clues may be visible puzzles at any point in time, the puzzles had to be solved in a linear fashion in order to escape. We felt that a sequential path would be most straightforward for players to understand as a first time experience in distributed rooms. This also reflects the style of play found in escape rooms within our region of North America, though we recognize that escape rooms around the world vary and sometimes include multiple paths [47].

Figure 2. Puzzle 1 with a mirror and whiteboard.

Figure 3. Hockey table in the 'research lab' room.

Figure 4. Puzzle 4 containing interconnected playing boxes (left) and an on-screen visual (right).

Table 1 shows details for our puzzles. We included puzzles where the goal was to enable loosely coupled collaboration or individual work (Puzzles 1 & 2), as well as puzzles that required close coordination and consultation between partners, in an effort to force collaboration to be tightly coupled (Puzzles 3 & 4). While past research has shown that collaborative work increases feelings of social presence [16,62], we wanted to understand how differences in collaborative work would affect player experience and enjoyment in the escape room. We conducted pilot tests with three pairs to assess the difficulty of our puzzles. Our goal was to make the escape room somewhat easier to complete than typical commercial escape rooms (10-20% success rate) so that, when conducting a study, nearly all the players would experience each of the puzzles and be able to compare their thoughts on each. We reduced the difficulty of our puzzles as a result of pilot testing.

EXPLORATORY STUDY

We conducted an exploratory study of Escaping Together to understand if and why participants felt a sense of social presence with their partners; how play manifested in the rooms; how partners worked together or apart from each other; and, to what extent the design of the rooms—the audio/video links, artifacts, puzzles—affected behaviors.

Participants

We recruited seventeen groups of players, including a total of 34 people (21 female). All teams included two people who were self-selected as partners, representing co-workers, friends, or family members. Of these participants, 27 were aged 19-25, three were 26-30, one was 31-35, and one was 41-50. 20 of 34 participants had played at least one escape room prior to the study. Most of the participants were undergraduate or graduate students.

Method

First, players individually completed a questionnaire that asked for demographic information and their experience with escape rooms. Second, we explained the rules of the escape room, which included telling players that they could use anything that was present in the rooms to solve the puzzles, including computers, but could not open any additional applications beyond what was already running. This included the video connection and software running our tangible puzzle. Next, we described the storyline to the players and then brought each player to his or her own room. Players were randomly assigned to one of the rooms. Players did not see the other person's room in-person.

Once players entered the room, they had 45 minutes to escape. After playing, participants individually completed a post-study questionnaire that had them rate the difficulty of each puzzle, the strength of their team work and individual work for each puzzle, their enjoyment while completing each puzzle, and their sense of social presence with their partner. We defined social presence for them as "the feeling that your partner was present and with you in the room" [7]. Next, we jointly interviewed participants to understand their experience. Interviews lasted 20 to 40 minutes. We asked them questions about what they enjoyed the most, what they enjoyed the least, how they used the video and audio communication system, what was valuable or challenging with it, and how and when they collaborated.

Audio Communication

We varied the audio link that was available to connect the two rooms during the study because it was unclear what the effects would be of having the microphone/speakers on a mobile vs. stationary device. We enabled the microphone/ speakers on the tablet for half of the participants, and enabled them on the computer for the other half.

Data Collection and Analysis

We observed all sessions from a remote video feed in a separate room and kept notes about participant behaviors. We recorded the interviews and fully transcribed all audio. We recorded videos of all the study sessions and reviewed them to compare participant activities to their responses in the interview questions. We coded video transcripts of the study sessions noting distinct behaviors. We used inferential and descriptive statistics to compare the responses on the post-study questionnaire. We performed open and axial coding on the transcribed interviews and our observational notes to draw out categories of results. We conducted a selective coding process where we discussed and explored our coding categories as a team of three researchers to converge on what we felt were the design aspects of the distributed escape room that were most critical to the way in which players behaved and collaborated. These emerged as situational awareness through audio and video, sharing artifacts, expectations around collaboration, and puzzle structures.

Next we present our results where we first present players' general reactions to the escape room along with a quantitative analysis of their experience. Following this, we explore the qualitative themes uncovered in our analysis. We caution that our study entailed a largely exploratory approach where we iteratively prototyped a distributed escape room with purposeful and thoughtful elements and tried it out with participants. Thus, our study was not a carefully controlled laboratory study with varying conditions that might allow us to draw out clear cause and effect relationships while reducing confounds such as learning effects. Instead, through observations, interviews, and questionnaire responses, we thematically draw out what we feel really matters when it comes to the design of distributed escape rooms based on the observed and reported actions and feelings of participants.

Table 2. Median/range ratings for each puzzle.

Puzzle	Team	Individual	Partner	Difficulty	Enjoyment
1 Mirror	4 (1 to 5)	3 (1 to 5)	4 (2 to 5)	3 (1 to 5)	4 (2 to 5)
2 Book	4 (2 to 5)	3 (1 to 5)	4 (2 to 5)	3 (1 to 5)	5 (2 to 5)
3 Hockey	5 (3 to 5)	4 (1 to 5)	4 (1 to 5)	3 (1 to 5)	5 (2 to 5)
4 Jigsaw	4 (1 to 5)	3 (1 to 5)	4 (1 to 5)	4 (1 to 5)	4 (2 to 5)

GENERAL REACTIONS AND EXPERIENCES

Seven teams were able to escape and the mean time for completion was 34±7 minutes (range 23 to 42 min) out of a total possible 45 min. This represents a 41% completion rate. Five teams ran out of time on the final puzzle, four ran out of time on the 3rd puzzle, and one team did not make it past the 2nd puzzle. Thus, 12 of 17 teams worked on all four puzzles to varying extents. Median times (and ranges) spent on puzzles for teams that completed them were (in seconds): Puzzle 1, 600s (220-1448s); Puzzle 2, 575s (180-1740s); Puzzle 3, 750s (240-1560s); and, Puzzle 4, 330s (210-580s). Thus, Puzzle 3 typically took the longest.

Based on the post-study questionnaires, Escaping Together was enjoyable for players and created a sense of social presence. The median rating of enjoyment by players individually (1-Not at all enjoyable to 5-Very enjoyable) was 5 with a range from 3 to 5. The median rating for having feelings of social presence with one's partner (1-Low to 5-High) was 4 with a range of 2 to 5.

Table 2 shows the median ratings and ranges for a series of questions about each puzzle where we have only included data for the 12 teams (n=24 participants) that attempted all puzzles. Column 2 shows scores for how well the participant felt they worked as a ***team*** on the puzzle; Column 3 shows how well the participant thought s/he worked on the puzzle as an ***individual***; Column 4 shows how well the participant thought his/her ***partner*** worked on the puzzle; Column 5 shows the perceived ***difficulty*** of the puzzle; and, Column 6 shows how much the participant ***enjoyed*** the puzzle. All were rated from 1-Low to 5-High.

We found a statistically significant difference in scores for how well they worked as a ***team*** across all four puzzles based on Friedman's test, $\chi 2(2)=17.79$, $p=0.0005$. Post hoc analysis with Wilcoxon signed-rank tests was conducted with a Bonferroni correction applied, resulting in a significance level set at $p < 0.0125$. Significant differences were found between Puzzles 1 and 3, and Puzzles 3 and 4; *thus, players felt they worked best as a team for Puzzle 3, compared to Puzzles 1 and 4.* This likely reflects the strong need for tightly coupled work in Puzzle 3. We did not find any statistically significant differences in ratings of their individual work across all four puzzles (based on Friedman's test, $\chi 2(2)=0.8$, $p=0.849$) or their partner's individual work (based on Friedman's test, $\chi 2(2)=1.37$, $p=0.711$). Thus, *participants generally felt that their individual performance, as well as their partner's did not vary across puzzles.*

We found statistically significant differences in scores for the difficulty of puzzles based on Friedman's test, $\chi 2(2)=9.63$, $p=0.022$. Post hoc analysis with Wilcoxon signed-rank tests was conducted with a Bonferroni correction applied, resulting in a significance level set at $p < 0.0125$. Significant differences were found between Puzzle 1 and Puzzle 2 only. We did not find significant differences for enjoyment of the puzzles (based on a Friedman's test, $\chi 2(2)=6.46$, $p=0.0913$).

Next we describe a series of themes that emerged in our qualitative analysis as critical design factors for distributed escape rooms. These themes provide elaboration on when, why, and how participants felt they worked well or did not work well with their partner, and how the various ways we designed the rooms appear to have affected play.

CONTINUOUS AWARENESS THROUGH AUDIO

First, participants told us that the audio link played a pivotal role in creating a sense of presence with one's partner and maintaining situation and workspace awareness of what was happening in each room. This was a result of its location and ubiquity throughout most of the room (e.g., sound could be detected and heard from nearly anywhere). Our observations showed that audio was used far more consistently throughout all of the teams' sessions than the video link. The audio link allowed players to stay in contact with each other while moving around and working freely. They would verbally describe what they were trying, make comments about things they noticed in the room, and answer questions from their partner—most often while they were *not* looking at the video feeds. In this way, the audio link provided situation awareness of what each person was doing, but only if they chose to verbally describe it. Some teams held a conversation nearly continuously throughout their entire session. As Team 3 described, this constant communication created a strong sense of presence.

"There wasn't really a lot of moments of silence. Even when we were like doing different tasks, we kept the conversation up, so I felt like she was actually there instead of only talking to each other when we were doing. Like when we were trying to solve something, in the process we were still communicating constantly and therefore it feels like you're right there." - P6

We observed that some participants stopped talking with each other because they were trying to focus on their own tasks. Participants told us that, in these situations, they did not know what their partner was working on and many assumed it was a continuation of what they had last heard, even if this was not accurate. Only when something important arose, such as one partner figuring out how to solve part of a puzzle, did participants start to talk again.

In some cases, descriptions of one's activity over the audio link raised confusion and did not suffice since players were not always looking at a video feed to see what was being referred to. The video display was not always close by them, but audio could be captured and heard anywhere.

In cases where audio was present on the computer, we observed that players gravitated towards the desk area with the computer, and made use of the stationary camera more than the portable one. When audio was present on the tablet, players in the office would often work near the table that the tablet was placed on. In some cases, they even sat on the floor next to it. Consider Team 1:

P1 and P2 collected the artifacts in the rooms and carried them so they were all next to the desk with the stationary camera and audio source. P2 even carried the hockey table over to the desk—he had to lift it at an awkward angle and you could see the strain in his face. After moving the objects, P1 and P2 remained seated at the desks nearly their entire time in the room.

As can be seen, the audio source was a magnet for players' location in the rooms. What was most surprising about this behavior was that the audio connection picked up audio anywhere in the room, and the speakers were loud enough that it could similarly be heard from anywhere. Thus, the desire to be 'next to' the audio source was very strong despite its accessibility throughout the room. In fact, nearly all participants said that the audio made them feel like their partner was 'right there'; thus, it was the strongest representation of the remote person. For example, P20 said he felt a lack of togetherness with his partner whenever he had to move away from the stationary audio source.

SHARING OBJECTS AND CREATING INTRIGUE

Participants described the role of the video as being secondary in nature where it augmented the audio link, though this did not diminish its importance. Video was selectively used in order to communicate information that was visually shareable. This is similar to studies of workplace collaborations [22,24]. For example, we observed that teams would use one or both of the video links to show objects in the room that they thought were important (e.g., books, the hockey table, the digital puzzle pieces). This allowed them to know how similar the two rooms were and if the same artifacts were present.

"For the book one, we can show each other which book. We would be like, oh we only have one in common!" –P3

Participants told us that this process usually worked for sharing basic information, such as what objects looked like, but it was somewhat inefficient or unworkable for complex information associated with the puzzles (e.g., numbers on pages, detailed writing). In these cases, the audio link had to be used to describe the object or how to use it.

When puzzles involved loosely coupled or individual work, we found that participants most often ignored the video feeds and went for long periods of time (e.g., in the order of minutes) not looking at them. Thus, unlike studies of workplace collaboration [24], immediate visual feedback of a collaborator's activities was not as important for completing the task since participants sometimes wanted to explore their own ideas for solving a puzzle and cared less about seeing their partner's approach. The time pressures of the room meant that they could not linger and watch their partner. Like studies of workplace collaboration [22,32], the stationary camera helped give team members an overview of what was in each room, though it was difficult in practice to see the entire room given camera angles and the shape and size of the rooms. This meant that what was on or off-camera mattered. Consider Team 1:

Upon completion of Puzzle 2, P1 found the lock on a bag in her room and applied the combination in order to open it.

P2 figured the lock he was looking for was likely similar to P1's so he started looking around his room for it. P2 told P1 that he was still looking for his lock but having problems finding it. The camera was positioned in such a way that the lock was not visible, so P1 could not help in locating the lock despite trying to look at the video feed.

Conventional wisdom based on the related work would suggest that seeing an entire room as part of an overview would be extremely valuable [22,32]. However, in contrast, a constrained view of the remote room helped create curiosity. We observed this as all groups engaged in conversations at varying points in time where they asked questions about what was in both rooms. They wondered how the two rooms might be similar or different and what artifacts were in the remote room. They also spent large amounts of time sharing the view of objects over the mobile video link. For example, Puzzle 3 required the use of a toy hockey rink in the research lab and a list of player positions in the office. Because the objects were so different, many participants said they felt additional curiosity and excitement as they wanted to know details about the object in the other room. Consider Team 15:

P30 was very interested in seeing the hockey table and repeatedly asked P29 to show her different views of it with the mobile video camera. They were trying to solve Puzzle 3 by moving players into different positions. After each set of movements was complete, P30 asked P29 to see the result in spite of P29's verbal descriptions.

Some participants told us that they liked that not everything could be seen in both rooms. The placement of artifacts outside of the camera view meant the room was more mysterious. In this way, the low-fidelity video view (a small portal on a screen) of the remote location forced participants to imagine what the room looked like in detail.

"I think not being able to see each other's full room actually made the experience better." – P8

Despite the intrigue that came with different objects in each room, players said that they enjoyed the escape room more when they were able to use the same types of items together at the same time; they felt it increased feelings of playing *with* their partner. For example, this included the digital puzzle pieces for Puzzle 4 that were progressively revealed as each puzzle was solved—creating sporadic feelings of connectedness each time a new piece was found—and the book in Puzzle 2 that was the same in each room and used for the Ottendorf cipher. For example, P3 said that having the book in common made her feel less alone. This was also the case with the mirrors in Puzzle 1.

EXPECTATIONS OF COLLABORATION

One of the most engaging aspects of the room's design was the extent of participants' knowledge of how much or how little collaboration was needed to solve the puzzles and how much they needed to work together. From a theoretical perspective, they were grappling with knowing how much of a shared mental model they needed to have. Each puzzle had varying degrees of collaboration, but participants were not aware of that ahead of time. As a result, participants said that the lack of knowledge created curiosity and sometimes tension. From our observations, we saw that participants tended to assume that the rooms were providing a "parallel" setup. Then, as they worked, participants adapted their attempts to solve the puzzles by shifting between ideas relying on a shared mental model of the situation to those involving individual mental models. For example, we observed that they would start out by talking with their partner to come to an agreement on how to solve a puzzle, and, then when realizing this may not be the correct way to solve it, they would begin working on their own. By observing partners' conversations, we saw that participants began to realize the rooms were related but not necessarily parallel.

"The whole collaborative part was really interesting. It's just that I found that I thought it would be a lot more collaboration involved because first two [puzzles] was mostly just individual." – P20

This challenge came out most strongly for the first two puzzles since they were designed to support individual or loosely coupled work. In the first puzzle many teams initially thought that each mirror would hold the code for the lock in the *other* room rather than their own. Thus, they assumed they needed to use the video feed to solve the puzzle. Teams tried to solve the puzzle in this way using the tablet's camera to share the whiteboard writing. This was often a long process that did not yield the correct puzzle solution. Similarly in the second puzzle, participants expected the puzzle to require a large amount of verbal exchanges. The most commonly observed idea was that the numbers would have to be combined across rooms in some way and that partners would have to tell the remote person their numbers over the audio link. Consider Team 11:

For Puzzle 1, P21 and P22 attempted to show each other their whiteboard markings over the mobile video link. P22 copied the numbers from the video link on to his whiteboard in order to come up with the solution. This did not work, however, since the markings and solutions were meant to be separate for each room. For Puzzle 2, P21 and P22 talked over the audio link to share their cipher numbers with one another. Here they tried, again, to link the numbers together. This time they were trying to use a series of math operations between the sets of numbers in each room.

The idea that tightly coupled collaboration was always required was so strong that some teams even tried 'extra hard' to work together, even though they did not necessarily have to. For example, in Puzzle 2, some players had a more difficult time finding the book for the Ottendorf cipher so instead of continuing to look for it, they read the numbers from their own puzzle sheet to their partner over the audio link, who would then use *their* copy of the book to figure out the answer to the puzzles in both rooms. This was possible, but not necessary, as the book for the cipher was the same in both rooms.

THE REALITY OF THE PUZZLE STRUCTURES

Once players altered their perception that all puzzles would involve closely knit teamwork, the degree to which the puzzles were *actually* interwoven across the two locations affected play considerably. That is, the reality of collaboration, rather than the perception of it, affected play. Our analysis revealed that the puzzles designed to support loosely coupled work allowed participants to work individually, if they wanted to, and build on their individual confidence and abilities. Yet they could still ask their teammate for help, since the puzzles were similar. The puzzles designed to support tightly coupled work forced the teammates to collaborate closely and feel as though they were really 'in' the escape room with their partner. The mixed level of collaboration across the four puzzles was a factor that many players said increased their enjoyment of the distributed escape room.

"It's kind of a change to both have puzzles that only you can figure out. There's a sense of achievement, personal achievement, in that. Then also to collaborate when you do need help. Kind of like having a hint system but with your team." – P10

The downside of having varying degrees of collaboration meant that players were not always synchronized in terms of which puzzles they were working on. For Puzzle 1, partners for 6 of the 17 teams solved the puzzle at approximately the same time because they worked together. Of the remaining 11 teams, four partners helped and waited for their partner to solve the puzzle before moving ahead, and seven teams either did not help at all, or tried to help while concurrently moving ahead. In Puzzle 2, 7 of 17 teams finished at approximately the same time, and only one teammate waited to help their partner. The time pressure of the rooms caused some of the players to continue on their own. Because the remote partner was relatively small in the video feed and they could easily be off camera, our observations showed it was easy for participants to forget about them at times. The lack of synchronization that resulted became highly problematic and meant that even though one partner could help the other solve his or her puzzle (given the similarity), they did not. The last two puzzles forced tightly coupled collaboration; however, a lack of synchronization on Puzzle 2 sometimes meant that partners had to wait for each other in order to start Puzzle 3. This created confusion if one person tried to start Puzzle 3 on their own.

P33 and P34 progressed independently until P33 reached Puzzle 3 and could not move ahead. At this point, they began to collaborate more as P34 tried to help P33 catch up and move through Puzzles 1 and 2. Both found a bag in their rooms and assumed they should be used in the same way; however, in reality, this was not the case as P34's bag was used later on since she was ahead in the puzzles. P33 and P34 became noticeably frustrated and they could not continue without a hint.

It was evident that partners became confused in terms of situation awareness. They could see what their partner was doing over the video link and hear them, but they did not always understand this information, again, because it lacked detail to see exactly what the person was doing. Participants said that this coupled with trying to understand their own puzzle created feelings of panic and tension. For some players, this created a lack of enjoyment at times. For example, P19 said that he felt nervous when his partner moved ahead, as he did not know what she was doing. While he could see her over the video link, she worked in a very focused manner on her own puzzle and did not explain it to him. On the other hand, participants said they felt less nervous when they could work closely with their partner.

DISCUSSION AND CONCLUSIONS

The goal of our study was to understand what factors are important for the design of distributed real-life escape rooms to create an enjoyable collaborative experience for players where they feel like they are participating in a shared experience with remote partners. We now describe the design factors that we feel are most important where the factors raise important questions for researchers and designers who may create distributed escape rooms or other technology-supported distributed social activities for team building exercises, entertainment, or as research tools to explore social or technical research questions.

Audio for Presence and Awareness

First, audio was a very critical component of the distributed escape room. This is how participants 'felt' the embodiment of their remote partner—that person's representation in the remote space—and gathered a large amount of situation awareness; it was not because of the video feed. This is similar to the use of video streaming for distributed location-based games [56], yet unlike a lot of research on video-mediated workspaces (e.g., [22,24,25,35]). The reality is that players in the escape room were so focused on solving puzzles and their own efforts to do so that they did not often look at a video feed as it relates to focusing on the remote partner while performing crucial steps for the puzzles. The video feed was typically only helpful when tightly coupled work was needed, e.g., solving interconnected puzzles or when seeking help, sharing ideas, or sharing objects. Audio was lightweight because it did not involve camera work or staying in a single position, though many people did like to try to stay close to the audio source.

This raises design opportunities for thinking about ways of providing social presence in distributed escape rooms through the use of audio that is decoupled from video. For example, one may consider supporting social presence through various forms of spatialized audio or varying acoustics in order to connect people over distance. Similar approaches have been explored for other contexts (e.g., [42,48]). These findings also mean that if distributed escape rooms are going to be used as part of education or training setups more broadly that participants in them will likely focus heavily on the use of audio at the expense of video. This may or may not be desired, depending on the situation.

Video to Create Curiosity

Second, even though audio was clearly the most important connector between the rooms, video still played an important role. The stationary and mobile video connections were a means for communicating about specific items, especially when there was a low level of similarity between artifacts for a puzzle. The stationary camera also provided an overview of the space, similar to studies of distributed workplace collaboration [22,32]. Yet what was different, given the focus on entertainment in escape rooms, was the value that came from *not* being able to see everything in the remote room over the video links. This helped create curiosity and wonder in terms of what was in the remote room. Our results also suggested little need for additional cameras, such as ones that might provide first person views of the remote location, since players spent little time looking at their video feeds. The only instance where such cameras might be valuable is if puzzles require a large degree of tightly coupled work.

While studies of workplace collaborations suggest camera views that are of a high fidelity and offer both an overview and close-up view [22,32], our results point to different design needs for video feeds in distributed escape rooms. Here we see that a balance is required. On one hand, video links are clearly needed to gather situation awareness and share artifacts. On the other hand, video links that provide limited viewpoints can create curiosity, which is likely valuable in escape rooms as it could lead to excitement and enjoyment for some players who want additional mystery. We suggest distributed escape rooms offer players a mixture of both worlds by providing video feeds, but leaving the display of some information somewhat ambiguous. We achieved this, somewhat unexpectedly, with overviews that did not show the entire room. Other design solutions are certainly possible, such as partially obscuring portions of the video feed, providing low-resolution video, or by progressively revealing video feeds as players progress through the escape room. This area is certainly ripe for further research and design exploration. Designers should also consider that while some players might value the additional mystery and intrigue that comes from ambiguous video views, other players could find them frustrating and this might impede enjoyment.

Expectations and Perceptions

Third, it was very clear that participants' expectations of how much they should collaborate with each other strongly affected play. Thus, the structure of the puzzles and the room's artifacts (both computational and not) played a strong role in the experience. Players came to the escape room imagining a parallel setup where artifacts and puzzles would be the same. Yet, we had designed the escape rooms to vary in this respect and allow players to practice a variety of collaborative skills, including both loosely and tightly coupled work and the gathering of awareness information to aid this understanding and groupwork. This created tensions around synchronization and made it hard to maintain situation and workspace awareness because the actions of others became confusing. Some players liked the intrigue that this experience created, but others preferred the situations where the puzzles were tightly coupled and the artifacts were similar across rooms. Like past research [16,62], participants felt strong feelings of social presence and participants said this came from working on puzzles together and collaborating.

Overall we suggest that distributed escape rooms should focus on puzzles designed for collaborative efforts with a mixture of artifact types. Some artifacts should be designed to be connected and shared across rooms, in order to promote such collaboration. Other artifacts should be dissimilar as a means to create intrigue. With dissimilar artifacts comes a need for technology that can allow players to share details about the objects between rooms. There is also a need for players to understand whether or not the experience across rooms, including the design of puzzles, is parallel or not and if teamwork is needed. Our video tools were somewhat primitive for supporting such sharing and knowledge acquisition. Future technologies might allow the remote user to explore the remote space and objects on his or her own using, for example, multiple cameras, pan and zoom capabilities, etc. One might also imagine more futuristic setups such as the use of mixed reality displays or 360-degree video connections that might allow players to virtually 'visit' the other room and allow them to temporarily see objects for sharing and conversation. There are also likely many other ways of realizing these design goals. The emphasis we make here is on designs that allow exploration while not necessarily requiring the help of the local player since he or she may be working on their own efforts and may not want to engage in camera work that might come with supporting remote viewing setups.

Limitations and Future Work

Our study is limited in that we only explored one type of distributed escape room with only pairs of individuals. We also only tested two types of video feeds. Our escape room was simpler and easier to escape than many commercial escape rooms (given the completion rate). This was appropriate for a study exploring the topic, yet it is not clear if such completion rates would affect player perceptions of enjoyment, difficulty, social presence, and teamwork. Future work should continue explorations of distributed escape rooms with additional numbers of players and rooms, the inclusion of different audio and video setups, and the use of additional interconnected computational artifacts. Our results suggest directions for each of these design investigations.

ACKNOWLEDGMENTS

We thank NSERC for funding this research.

REFERENCES

1. Ben Bedwell, Holger Schnädelbach, Steve Benford, Tom Rodden, and Boriana Koleva. 2009. In support of city exploration. In Proceedings of the SIGCHI Conference on Human Factors in Computing Systems

(CHI '09). ACM, New York, NY, USA, 1171-1180. DOI=10.1145/1518701.1518879

2. Marek Bell, Stuart Reeves, Barry Brown, Scott Sherwood, Donny MacMillan, John Ferguson, and Matthew Chalmers. 2009. EyeSpy: supporting navigation through play. In Proceedings of the SIGCHI Conference on Human Factors in Computing Systems (CHI '09). ACM, New York, NY, USA, 123-132. DOI=10.1145/1518701.1518723
3. Steve Benford, S., & Gabriella Giannachi. Performing Mixed Reality, The MIT Press (2011).
4. Steve Benford, Gabriella Giannachi, Boriana Koleva, and Tom Rodden. 2009. From interaction to trajectories: designing coherent journeys through user experiences. In Proceedings of the SIGCHI Conference on Human Factors in Computing Systems (CHI '09). ACM, New York, NY, USA, 709-718. DOI=10.1145/1518701.1518812
5. Steve Benford, Andy Crabtree, Martin Flintham, Adam Drozd, Rob Anastasi, Mark Paxton, Nick Tandavanitj, Matt Adams, and Ju Row-Farr. 2006. Can you see me now?. ACM Trans. Comput.-Hum. Interact. 13, 1 (March 2006), 100-133. DOI=10.1145/1143518.1143522
6. Steve Benford, Andy Crabtree, Stuart Reeves, Jennifer Sheridan, Alan Dix, Martin Flintham, and Adam Drozd. 2006. The Frame of the Game: Blurring the Boundary between Fiction and Reality in Mobile Experiences. In Proceedings of the SIGCHI Conference on Human Factors in Computing Systems (CHI '06), ACM, New York, NY, USA, 427-436. DOI=10.1145/1124772.1124836
7. Frank Biocca, Chad Harms, and Judee K. Burgoon. 2003. Toward a More Robust Theory and Measure of Social Presence: Review and Suggested Criteria, Presence, Vol. 12(5), Octoboer 2003, 456-480.
8. Elizabeth Bonsignore, Vicki Moulder, Carman Neustaedter, Derek Hansen, Kari Kraus, and Allison Druin. 2014. Design tactics for authentic interactive fiction: insights from alternate reality game designers. In Proceedings of the SIGCHI Conference on Human Factors in Computing Systems (CHI '14). ACM, New York, NY, USA, 947-950. DOI=10.1145/2556288.2557245
9. Elizabeth Bonsignore, Kari Kraus, Amanda Visconti, Derek Hansen, Ann Fraistat, and Allison Druin. 2012. Game design for promoting counterfactual thinking. In Proceedings of the SIGCHI Conference on Human Factors in Computing Systems (CHI '12). ACM, New York, NY, USA, 2079-2082. DOI=10.1145/2207676.2208357
10. Elizabeth Bonsignore, Derek Hansen, Kari Kraus, Amanda Visconti, June Ahn, and Allison Druin. 2013. Playing for real: designing alternate reality games for teenagers in learning contexts. In Proceedings of the 12th International Conference on Interaction Design and Children (IDC '13). ACM, New York, NY, USA, 237-246. DOI=10.1145/2485760.2485788
11. John M. Carroll, Mary Beth Rosson, Gregorio Conertino, and Craig H. Ganoe. 2006. Awareness and teamwork in computer-supported collaborations. *Interacting with computers* 18.1 (2006): 21-46.
12. Nancy J. Cooke, Jamie C. Gorman, Jasmine L. Duran, Amanda R. Taylor. 2007. Team cognition in experienced command-and-control teams. Journal of Experimental Psychology 13, 3 (September 2007), 146–157.
13. Janis A. Cannon-Bowers, Eduardo Salas, and Sharolyn Converse. 1993. Shared mental models in expert team decision making. In Individual and Group Decision Making: Current Issues, N. J. C. Jr, Ed. Earlbaum Associates, Hillsdale, NJ, USA, 221–246.
14. Mauricio Capra, Milena Radenkovic, Steve Benford, Leif Oppermann, Adam Drozd, and Martin Flintham. 2005. The multimedia challenges raised by pervasive games. In Proceedings of the 13th annual ACM international conference on Multimedia (MULTIMEDIA '05). ACM, New York, NY, USA, 89-95. DOI=10.1145/1101149.1101163
15. Daradoumis, T., and Marques, J. M. 2002. Distributed cognition in the context of virtual collaborative learning. In Journal of Interactive Learning Research, Vol. 13, 135–148.
16. Yvonne A. W. De Kort and Wijnand A. Ijsselsteijn. 2008. People, places, and play: player experience in a socio-spatial context. Comput. Entertain. 6, 2, Article 18 (July 2008), 11 pages.
17. Christy Dena. Transmedia Practice: Theorizing the Practice of Expressing a Fictional World across Distinct Media and Environments, PhD Thesis, School of Letters, Art and Media Department of Media and Communications Digital Cultures Program, University of Sydney, Australia (2009).
18. Mica R. Endsley and Debra G. Jones. 2011. What is Situation Awareness? In Designing for Situation Awareness. CRC Press, 13-30.
19. Elliot E. Entin and Daniel Serfaty. Adaptive team coordination. Human Factors 41, 2 (June 1999), 312–325.
20. Omid Fakourfar, Kevin Ta, Richard Tang, Scott Bateman, and Anthony Tang. 2016. Stabilized Annotations for Mobile Remote Assistance. In Proceedings of the 2016 CHI Conference on Human Factors in Computing Systems (CHI '16). ACM, New York, NY, USA, 1548-1560.
21. Stephen M. Fiore and Eduardo Salas. 2004. Why we need team cognition. In Salas and Fiore, Team

Cognition: Understanding the Factors that Drive Process and Performance, 1st ed. American Psychological Association, Washington, DC, USA, 235–248.

22. Susan R. Fussell, Leslie D. Setlock, and Robert E. Kraut. 2003. Effects of head-mounted and scene-oriented video systems on remote collaboration on physical tasks. In Proceedings of the SIGCHI Conference on Human Factors in Computing Systems (CHI '03). ACM, New York, NY, USA, 513-520.

23. Brian Gajadhar, Yvonne de Kort, and Wijnand IJsselsteijn. 2008. Influence of social setting on player experience of digital games. In CHI '08 Extended Abstracts on Human Factors in Computing Systems (CHI EA '08). ACM, New York, NY, USA, 3099-3104.

24. Darren Gergle, Robert E. Kraut, Susan R. Fussell. 2013. Using Visual Information for Grounding and Awareness in Collaborative Tasks, Human–Computer Interaction, Vol. 28, Iss. 1.

25. Carl Gutwin and Saul Greenberg. 2002. A Descriptive Framework of Workspace Awareness for Real-Time Groupware. Comput. Supported Coop. Work 11, 3 (November 2002), 411-446. DOI=10.1023/A:1021271517844

26. Carl Gutwin and Saul Greenberg. 2004. The importance of awareness for team cognition in distributed collaboration. In Salas and Fiore (eds), Team Cognition: Understanding the Factors that Drive Process and Performance, 1st ed. American Psychological Association, Washington, DC, USA, 177–201.

27. Derek Hansen, Elizabeth Bonsignore, Marc Ruppel, Amanda Visconti, and Kari Kraus. 2013. Designing reusable alternate reality games. In Proceedings of the SIGCHI Conference on Human Factors in Computing Systems (CHI '13). ACM, New York, NY, USA, 1529-1538.

28. Jun He, Brian S. Butler, and William R. King. 2007. Team Cognition: Development and Evolution in Software Projects, Journal of Management Information Systems, Vol. 24, No. 2 (Fall, 200), 261-292.

29. Christian Heath and Paul Luff. 1992. Collaboration and Control: Crisis Management and Multimedia Technology in London Underground Line Control Rooms, Journal of Computer Supported Cooperative Work, Vol. 1, No. 1, ACM, 24-48.

30. James Hollan, Edwin Hutchins, and David Kirsh. 2000. Distributed cognition: Toward a new foundation for human-computer interaction research. ACM Transactions on Computer-Human Interaction 7, 2, 174–196.

31. Edwin Hutchins, E. 1991. The social organization of distributed cognition. In Perspectives on Socially Shared Cognition, L. Resnick and J. Levine, Eds., 1st ed. American Psychological Association, 283– 307.

32. Steven Johnson, Madeleine Gibson, and Bilge Mutlu. 2015. Handheld or Handsfree?: Remote Collaboration via Lightweight Head-Mounted Displays and Handheld Devices. In Proceedings of the 18th ACM Conference on Computer Supported Cooperative Work & Social Computing (CSCW '15). ACM, New York, NY, USA, 1825-1836.

33. Brennan Jones, Anna Witcraft, Scott Bateman, Carman Neustaedter, and Anthony Tang. 2015. Mechanics of Camera Work in Mobile Video Collaboration. In Proceedings of the 33rd Annual ACM Conference on Human Factors in Computing Systems (CHI '15). ACM, New York, NY, USA, 957-966.

34. David Kirk, Andy Crabtree, and Tom Rodden. 2005. Ways of the hands. In Proceedings of the ninth conference on European Conference on Computer Supported Cooperative Work (ECSCW'05), Hans Gellersen, Kjeld Schmidt, Michel Beaudouin-Lafon, and Wendy Mackay (Eds.). Springer-Verlag New York, Inc., New York, NY, USA, 1-21.

35. David Kirk and Danae Stanton Fraser. 2006. Comparing remote gesture technologies for supporting collaborative physical tasks. In Proceedings of the SIGCHI Conference on Human Factors in Computing Systems (CHI '06), Rebecca Grinter, Thomas Rodden, Paul Aoki, Ed Cutrell, Robin Jeffries, and Gary Olson (Eds.). ACM, New York, NY, USA, 1191-1200.

36. Boriana Koleva, Ian Taylor, Steve Benford, Mike Fraser, Chris Greenhalgh, Holger Schnädelbach, Dirk vom Lehn, Christian Heath, Ju Row-Farr, and Matt Adams. 2001. Orchestrating a mixed reality performance. In Proceedings of the SIGCHI Conference on Human Factors in Computing Systems (CHI '01). ACM, New York, NY, USA, 38-45. DOI=10.1145/365024.365033

37. Conor Linehan, Ben Kirman, Shaun Lawson, and Mark Doughty. 2010. Blowtooth: pervasive gaming in unique and challenging environments. In CHI '10 Extended Abstracts on Human Factors in Computing Systems (CHI EA '10). ACM, New York, NY, USA, 2695-2704. DOI=10.1145/1753846.1753853

38. Mandryk, R.L., Inkpen, K., Calvert, T. 2006. Using Psychophysiological Techniques to Measure User Experience with Entertainment Technologies. In Behaviour and Information Technology (Special Issue on User Experience, vol. 25 no. 2, 141-158. DOI=10.1080/01449290500331156.

39. John E. Mathieu, Gerald F. Goodwin, Tonia S. Heffner, Eduardo Salas, and Janis A. Cannon-Bowers. 2000. The influence of shared mental models on team process and performance. Journal of Applied Psychology 85, 2, 273–283.

40. Susan Mohammed, Richard Klimoski, and Joan R. Rentsch. 2000. The measurement of team mental models: We have no shared schema. Organizational Research Methods 3, 2 (April 2000), 123–165.
41. Mark Montola, Jaakko Stenros, and Annika Waern. 2009. Pervasive Games Theory and Design: Experiences on the Boundary Between Life and Play, Morgan Kaufmann.
42. Shohei Nagai, Shunichi Kasahara, and Jun Rekimoto. 2015. Directional communication using spatial sound in human-telepresence. In Proceedings of the 6th Augmented Human International Conference (AH'15). ACM, New York, NY, USA, 159-160.
43. Carman Neustaedter, Anthony Tang, and Judge K. Tejinder. 2010. The role of community and groupware in geocache creation and maintenance. In Proceedings of the SIGCHI Conference on Human Factors in Computing Systems (CHI'10). ACM, New York, NY, USA, 1757-1766.
44. Carman Neustaedter, Anthony Tang, and Tejinder K. Judge. 2013. Creating scalable location-based games: lessons from Geocaching. Personal Ubiquitous Comput. 17, 2 (February 2013), 335-349. DOI=10.1007/s00779-011-0497-7
45. Carman Neustaedter and Tejinder K. Judge. 2012. See it: a scalable location-based game for promoting physical activity. In Proceedings of the ACM 2012 conference on Computer Supported Cooperative Work Companion (CSCW'12). ACM, New York, NY, USA, 235-238.
46. Carman Neustaedter, Carolyn Pang, Azadeh Forghani, Erick Oduor, Serena Hillman, Tejinder K. Judge, Michael Massimi, and Saul Greenberg. 2015. Sharing Domestic Life through Long-Term Video Connections. ACM Trans. Comput.-Hum. Interact. 22, 1, Article 3 (February 2015), 29 pages. DOI=http://dx.doi.org/10.1145/2696869
47. Scott Nicholson. 2015. Peeking Behind the Locked Door: A Survey of Escape Room Facilities, White Paper, http://scottnicholson.com/pubs/erfacwhite.pdf
48. Shannon O'Brien and Florian "Floyd" Mueller. 2007. Jogging the distance. In Proceedings of the SIGCHI Conference on Human Factors in Computing Systems (CHI'07). ACM, New York, NY, USA, 523-526. DOI=10.1145/1240624.1240708
49. Kenton O'Hara. 2008. Understanding geocaching practices and motivations. In Proceedings of the SIGCHI Conference on Human Factors in Computing Systems (CHI'08). ACM, New York, NY, USA, 1177-1186. DOI=10.1145/1357054.1357239
50. Gary M. Olson and Judith S. Olson. 2000. Distance Matters, Human Computer Interaction, Vol. 15, 139-178.
51. Jiazhi Ou, Xilin Chen, Susan R. Fussell, and Jie Yang. 2003. DOVE: drawing over video environment. In Proceedings of the eleventh ACM international conference on Multimedia (MULTIMEDIA '03). ACM, New York, NY, USA, 100-101.
52. Rui Pan, Henry Lo, and Carman Neustaedter. 2017. Collaboration, Awareness, and Communication in Real-Life Escape Rooms. In Proceedings of the 2017 Conference on Designing Interactive Systems (DIS'17). ACM, New York, NY, USA, 1353-1364. DOI: https://doi.org/10.1145/3064663.3064767
53. Rui Pan, Carman Neustaedter, Alissa N. Antle, and Brendan Matkin. 2017. Puzzle Space: A Distributed Tangible Puzzle for Long Distance Couples. In Companion of the 2017 ACM Conference on Computer Supported Cooperative Work and Social Computing (CSCW'17 Companion). ACM, New York, NY, USA, 271-274. DOI: https://doi.org/10.1145/3022198.3026320
54. Tamara Peyton, Alyson L. Young, and Wayne Lutters. 2013. Playing with leadership and expertise: military tropes and teamwork in an arg. In Proceedings of the SIGCHI Conference on Human Factors in Computing Systems (CHI '13). ACM, New York, NY, USA, 715-724. DOI:10.1145/2470654.2470755
55. Jason Procyk and Carman Neustaedter. 2014. GEMS: the design and evaluation of a location-based storytelling game. In Proceedings of the 17th ACM conference on Computer supported cooperative work & social computing (CSCW'14). ACM, New York, NY, USA, 1156-1166. DOI=10.1145/2531602.2531701
56. Jason Procyk, Carman Neustaedter, Carolyn Pang, Anthony Tang, and Tejinder K. Judge. 2014. Exploring video streaming in public settings: shared geocaching over distance using mobile video chat. In Proceedings of the SIGCHI Conference on Human Factors in Computing Systems (CHI'14). ACM, New York, NY, USA, 2163-2172.
57. Irene Rae, Bilge Mutlu, and Leila Takayama. 2014. Bodies in motion: mobility, presence, and task awareness in telepresence. In Proceedings of the SIGCHI Conference on Human Factors in Computing Systems (CHI'14). ACM, New York, NY, USA, 2153-2162.
58. Ravaja, N., Saari, T., Turpeinen, M., Laarni, J., Salminen, M., & Kivikangas, M. (2006). Spatial Presence and Emotions During Video Game Playing: Does It Matter with Whom You Play? Presence: Teleoper. Virtual Environ., 15(4), 381–392. https://doi.org/10.1162/pres.15.4.381
59. Paul M. Salmon, Neville A. Stanton, Guy H. Walker, Daniel P. Jenkins, and Laura Rafferty. 2010. Is it really better to share? Distribution situation awareness and its implications for collaborative system design.

Theoretical Issues in Ergonomics Science. 11:1-2, 58-83.

60. Tony Salvador, Jean Scholtz, and James Larson. 1996. The Denver model for groupware design. SIGCHI Bull. 28, 1 (January 1996), 52-58. DOI=10.1145/249170.249185

61. Stacey D. Scott, M. Sheelagh T. Carpendale, and Kori M. Inkpen. 2004. Territoriality in collaborative tabletop workspaces. In Proceedings of the 2004 ACM conference on Computer supported cooperative work (CSCW'04). ACM, New York, NY, USA, 294-303. DOI=10.1145/1031607.1031655

62. Márquez Segura, E., & Isbister, K. (2015). Enabling Co-Located Physical Social Play: A Framework for Design and Evaluation. In R. Bernhaupt (Ed.), Game User Experience Evaluation (pp. 209–238). Cham, Switzerland: Springer International Publishing.

63. John C. Tang. 1991. Findings from observational studies of collaborative work. International Journal of Man-Machine Studies. 34, 2, 143-160.

64. Anthony Tang, Melanie Tory, Barry Po, Petra Neumann, and Sheelagh Carpendale. 2006. Collaborative coupling over tabletop displays. In Proceedings of the SIGCHI Conference on Human Factors in Computing Systems (CHI'06), Rebecca Grinter, Thomas Rodden, Paul Aoki, Ed Cutrell, Robin Jeffries, and Gary Olson (Eds.). ACM, New York, NY, USA, 1181-1190. DOI=10.1145/1124772.1124950

65. Alyson L. Young, Tamara Peyton, and Wayne G. Lutters. 2013. Understanding situated action in ludic ecologies. In Proceedings of the 6th International Conference on Communities and Technologies (C&T'13). ACM, New York, NY, USA, 100-109. DOI=http://dx.doi.org.proxy.lib.sfu.ca/10.1145/2482991.2483000

Elements of Gameful Design Emerging from User Preferences

Gustavo F. Tondello
HCI Games Group
Games Institute
University of Waterloo
gustavo@tondello.com

Alberto Mora
Estudis d'Informàtica,
Multimedia i Telecomunicació
Universitat Oberta de Catalunya
amoraca@uoc.edu

Lennart E. Nacke
HCI Games Group
Games Institute
University of Waterloo
lennart.nacke@acm.org

ABSTRACT
Several studies have developed models to explain player preferences. These models have been developed for digital games; however, they have been frequently applied in gameful design (i.e., designing non-game applications with game elements) without empirical validation of their fit to this different context. It is not clear if users experience game elements embedded in applications similarly to how players experience them in games. Consequently, we still lack a conceptual framework of design elements built specifically for a gamification context. To fill this gap, we propose a classification of eight groups of gameful design elements produced from an exploratory factor analysis based on participants' self-reported preferences. We describe the characteristics of the users who are more likely to enjoy each group of design elements in terms of their gender, age, gamification user type, and personality traits. Our main contribution is providing an overview of which design elements work best for what demographic clusters and how we can apply this knowledge to design effective gameful systems.

ACM Classification Keywords
H.1.2. User/Machine Systems: Human Factors; K.8.0 Personal Computing: Games.

Author Keywords
Gamification; Gameful Design; Games User Research; User Types; Game Design Elements

INTRODUCTION
Research on gameplay motivations has shown that players have diverse personal preferences regarding how and what they play [20, 33, 44]. Researchers have developed player type models [20, 27] or gamer motivation scales [43, 44] to capture the diverse styles of play exhibited by different players. This information has been increasingly used in gamification—using game design elements in non-game contexts [14]—to model user behaviour and design more engaging gameful systems.

CHI PLAY '17, October 15–18, 2017, Amsterdam, Netherlands

ISBN 978-1-4503-4898-0/17/10...$15.00

DOI: https://doi.org/10.1145/3116595.3116627

Gameful systems are effective when they help users achieve their goals. This often involves educating users about topics in which they lack knowledge, supporting them in attitude or behaviour change, or engaging them in specific areas [10]. To make gameful systems more effective, several researchers have attempted to model user preferences in these systems, such as user typologies [40], persuasive strategies [31], or preferences for different game elements based on personality traits [21]. Nevertheless, none of these models have studied elements used specifically in gameful design. To select design elements that can appeal to different motivations, designers still rely on player typologies—such as Bartle's player types [3, 4] or the BrainHex player types [27]—or classifications of game elements—such as the gamer motivation profile [43].

However, the applicability of these models in gamification has not been supported by empirical evidence as of yet. All of them were developed by asking participants about their experiences when playing games. Hence, they cannot be transferred one-by-one to gameful applications. Tondello et al. [40] have studied correlations between several design elements used in gameful design with the HEXAD user types. However, they have not proposed a classification of gameful design elements. Thus, we still lack a conceptual framework of design elements commonly used in gamification. The purpose of the current study was to fill this gap. Therefore, we propose a new conceptual framework for classifying gameful design elements based on participants' self-reported preferences to understand user behaviour in gamification. While the HEXAD framework [40] describes psychological characteristics of the users, this work proposes a novel way to organize gameful design elements.

To operationalise the proposed framework, we asked participants about how much they enjoy 59 design elements frequently used in gameful systems (gathered from a literature review). Next, we conducted an exploratory factor analysis to cluster these design elements into eight groups. We adopt a conceptual definition of *element* similar to that employed by Deterding et al. [14]. Thus, we consider that 'gameful design elements' are the building blocks that are characteristic to gameful systems—meaning elements that are found in many (but not necessarily all) gameful systems—and play a significant role in the emerging user experience with the system. Additionally, Deterding and colleagues suggest that gamification and gameful design are coincident concepts, framing the same extension of the phenomena through different intentions. Hence, these gameful design elements could be applied interchangeably in both gamification and gameful design.

Moreover, after establishing a model of gameful design elements, we further analyzed the data to find patterns that could potentially be used to inform gameful design. Therefore, we also present results that depict the overall participant's preferences for each group of design elements, as well as the relationship between the design element groups with the HEXAD user types, personality traits, age, and gender.

This contribution is important to human-computer interaction (HCI) and gamification because it presents the first conceptual framework of design elements constructed in the specific context of gameful design and based on user preferences. Gamification researchers and practitioners have relied—until now—on models that were previously created in the context of games, assuming that they would be generalizable to gamification without empirical evidence. Our work enables future studies and industry applications to be built upon a model empirically constructed and validated specially for gamification.

Furthermore, current gameful design practice often involves selecting design elements from a list to try and recreate patterns found in games, with little guidance regarding how each design element affects the user experience [13, 25, 28]. Design elements are usually classified by their motivational significance or structural characteristics [13], but these classifications do not help designers choose the best pattern to solve specific user needs. As a result, designers often rely on some combination of a small subset of design elements, such as points, badges, and leaderboards, simply because these are the easiest elements to implement. Therefore, a better understanding of the effects of each design element is needed to foster the utilization of a broader variety of elements selected to solve specific needs. Our work contributes with the fulfillment of this need by presenting a novel classification of gameful design elements based on user preferences, thus allowing designers to better understand the potential effect of each element on user enjoyment and make more informed design decisions.

RELATED WORK

Researchers in HCI and games have been studying different motivations and playing styles for over a decade and representing them in player typologies. Hamari and Tuunanen [20] conducted a systematic review of these models to investigate their commonalities. The authors note that massively multiplayer online (MMOs) and other types of online games are more frequently covered than other genres. This compromises the generalizability and applicability of these models. Furthermore, they compared all the analyzed models and suggested that they could be synthesized in five key dimensions: *achievement*, *exploration*, *sociability*, *domination*, and *immersion*.

One of the oldest player type models is Bartle's player types [3]. He studied what players desired from multi-user dungeons (MUDs) based on a discussion between dozens of senior players and identified four player types on two axes that express the player's desire to interact with or act on the virtual world or other players: *achievers* (acting on the world), *explorers* (interacting with the world), *socialisers* (interacting with other players), and *killers* (acting on other players). Bartle later extended the model by adding a third dimension [4]: implicit or explicit (i.e., whether the player actions are automatic and unconscious or considered and planned). Bartle's model is frequently used by gamification practitioners because of its simplicity. However, it was never empirically validated nor was it intended to be used outside of the domain of MUDs.

Based on a factor analysis of questions inspired by the original Bartle's player types, Yee [42, 44] identified three main components of player motivation with ten sub-components: *achievement* (advancement, mechanics, competition), *social* (socializing, relationship, teamwork), and *immersion* (discovery, role-playing, customization, escapism). More recently, Yee [43] expanded on his previous work by conducting a factor analysis with over 140,000 participants and developed a 'gamer motivation profile' composed of 12 dimensions grouped in 6 clusters: *action* (destruction and excitement), *social* (competition and community), *mastery* (challenge and strategy), *achievement* (competition and power), *immersion* (fantasy and story), and *creativity* (design and discovery). This recent proprietary investigation intended to capture player motivations towards many different games and was empirically supported by factor analysis. However, a standard assessment tool is not publicly and readily available.

With a different approach, the first 'demographic game design' model (DGD1) [7] tried to include a wider perspective regarding player types by adapting the Myers-Briggs type indicator (MBTI) [26] to games. The second 'demographic game design' model (DGD2) [5] explored the hardcore to casual dimension, different skill sets, and the preference for single and multiplayer gameplay. These two models served as a base on which the BrainHex player typology was built. BrainHex [5, 27] is a top-down player typology, which takes inspiration from neurobiological player satisfaction research [6], previous typology approaches, discussions of patterns of play, and the literature on game emotions to build seven archetypes denoting distinct experiences of play. The seven BrainHex archetypes (and their associated player motivations) are: *achiever* (completion), *conqueror* (challenge), *daredevil* (excitement and risk), *mastermind* (strategic reasoning), *seeker* (exploration and curiosity), *socialiser* (social interactions), and *survival* (frightening experiences). BrainHex supplements existing research with a diverse array of player types. However, initial empirical investigation on its psychometric properties has shown low reliability scores [9].

While these models are often used for personalizing gameful systems, they were built for games. However, in gameful design, only elements of games are included in non-game applications. Therefore, there is no evidence of the generalizability of game motivation models to gameful design because users might experience game elements embedded into applications differently than how they are experienced in games. Consequently, recent works have proposed new models specifically built to explain user preferences in gameful systems.

In the context of gamification, Marczewski [22] built on the literature about player types and self-determination theory in games [38, 39] to create the user types HEXAD model, which classifies distinct user preferences. The six HEXAD user types (and the motivation they represent) are: *philanthropist* (altruism), *socialiser* (relatedness), *free spirit* (autonomy), *achiever* (competence), *player* (rewards), and *disruptor* (change).

Additionally, Ferro et al. [17] studied personality models and player types. The goals were to find the similarities between them and to relate them to different game design elements. Their work grouped personality traits, player types, and game elements into five categories: *dominant*, *objectivist*, *humanist*, *inquisitive*, and *creative*. Jia et al. [21] studied the relation between the five-factor model (FFM) personality traits [19] and individual gamification elements and found several significant correlations. Orji et al. [31] studied the relation between the FFM personality traits and several persuasive strategies used in gamification and found significant correlations. Barata et al. [1, 2] studied data regarding student performance and gaming preferences from a gamified university-level course and identified different patterns in student behaviour, which the authors suggested could be used in future gamified education projects to tailor the course to different students.

Although these models provide useful insights about user experience with gameful systems, they do not provide detailed information about user's preference for different gameful design elements. In this regard, Tondello et al. [40] tested the correlation of each HEXAD user type with 32 game elements commonly used in gamification. Their results provide a starting point to understand the user's relation with gameful design elements. However, they did not develop a model to cluster different design elements together, nor studied how different factors (such as gender, age, or personality) affect user's preferences for different design elements. Therefore, the present study will advance the extant literature on this topic by proposing a framework of gameful design elements and studying which factors influence users' preferences towards them.

With a different approach, some authors have proposed taxonomies or classifications of gameful design elements based on other specific criteria. Phillips et al. [34] suggested a taxonomy of videogame rewards based on prior literature and focus group studies. Rapp [36] also discussed the classification of videogame rewards, based on an ethnographic study of World of Warcraft [8], and discussed potential applications of his model to gameful design. While both these models provide valuable information that can inform the design of rewards systems in gamification, they are limited to a specific design element, whereas our work is broad and encompasses dozens of design elements (including rewards), without diving into details regarding any of them. Differently, Exton and Murray [16] suggested a taxonomy of gameful design elements based on a theoretical evaluation of their motivational properties. Each element was classified according to their envisioned potential to afford either type of motivation descried by self-determination theory [38]: competence, autonomy, or relatedness. Robinson and Bellotti [37] proposed a preliminary taxonomy of gamification elements based on how much anticipated commitment was expected from the user. However, none of these taxonomies consider different user preferences as we do in our contribution.

It is also noteworthy that despite the existing literature on user preferences in gamification and games, most gameful design methods do not take user preference in consideration as part of their process [24, 25]. One explanation for the lack of consideration for user preferences in design methods might be the difficulty of translating the existing models directly into design guidance. Nonetheless, several studies have shown that user preferences can significantly affect the effectiveness of instrumental game systems (e.g., [10, 30, 31, 32]); therefore, we can expect that this will also happen in gameful systems. Our work will contribute to the improvement of design methods by providing a classification of gameful design elements that will help designers better understand user preferences and translate this information into design guidance.

METHODOLOGY

The process of creating a framework of gameful design elements followed these steps:

1. **Survey design**: a literature review to create a list of gameful design elements commonly employed in gamification;
2. **Data collection**: an online survey to understand participants' preferences for the elements in the list;
3. **Factor analysis**: a principal component analysis to cluster the elements into groups according to user preferences;
4. **Component interpretation**: an analysis of the composition of each cluster to interpret and label them;
5. **Hierarchical clustering**: a hierarchical cluster analysis to further cluster the element groups into high level constructs.

Survey Design

We compiled a list of gameful design elements for the survey by conducting an informal literature review of both academic and non-academic sources. By also reviewing non-academic sources, we purposefully included design elements that are frequently used by practitioners, but have not been examined in HCI studies yet. Thus, we provide the first study of how these elements relate to other elements that have already been investigated and how they explain user preferences.

The final list contains 59 gameful design elements. Academic sources included Tondello et al. [40] (56%), Jia et al. [21] (14%), and Ferro et al. [17] (19%). The inclusion criterion was peer-reviewed publications that contained a list of design elements used in the specific context of gamification, thus excluding publications in the context of gaming. Non-academic sources included lists of gamification elements from the following resources: Gamified UK [23] (73%), Yu-kai Chou Gamification [12] (34%), Enterprise Gamification [15] (29%), Werbach and Hunter [41] (27%), and Zichermann and Cunningham [45] (24%). The inclusion criteria were publications that contained a list of design elements used in the specific context of gamification and were published by authors who have been consistently listed in one of the top 100 positions in Rise's Gamification Gurus Power 100 board[1]. The numbers in brackets refer to the percentage of the 59 surveyed elements that were identified in each source; they add up over 100% because many elements appeared in more than one source.

[1]https://www.rise.global/gurus

The process of creating the list of design elements consisted on reviewing the selected sources one by one and adding all the elements described in the source with enough details to understand how they are applied. Additionally, before being added to the list, each new element was compared with the elements already in the list for similarities in their name or description. Elements that were considered similar in the researchers' judgment were merged together, whereas each different element was added as a new entry. We have provided the complete list in the appendix. It includes information about the source for each element and their descriptions as presented in the survey.

Survey Instrument

The survey was deployed as an online instrument between February and March 2017 using the *LimeSurvey* software. All questions were in English and were grouped as follows:

User types: The 24-items HEXAD user types scale [40].

Preferred gameful design elements: We asked how much participants enjoyed the 59 different design elements commonly used in gamification on a 5-point Likert scale.

Personality: The 10-items Big 5 [19] personality traits scale (BFI-10) [35].

Demographic information: Participant's country, language, age, gender, education, and gaming habits and preferences.

The survey could be completed anonymously and, prior to the decision to participate, participants were presented with an online informed consent form. In addition, the long question groups (user types and gameful design elements) had attention check questions (e.g., "Please select '3' in this item to show us that you are carefully reading all questions.") to verify if participants were reading all the items with attention.

Participants

We recruited participants by email (in both academic and non-academic environments), social networks (Facebook, Twitter, and Reddit), and online gaming forums. Participants were required to be at least 15 years old to participate and were not offered a direct remuneration, but they were offered an opportunity to enter a draw to win one of two $50 prizes.

In total, 196 participants completed the survey. However, we discarded eight participants who did not complete all question groups or failed to select the correct answer in at least one of the attention check items. Therefore, the final dataset contained 188 responses (124 men, 53 women, 4 transgender, 3 non-binary, and 4 did not indicate their gender). Participants' age ranged from 15 to 71 ($M = 26.7$, $SD = 9.7$) and were skewed towards younger participants (with 74% of participants being 30 or less), possibly because of the topic of the survey being more appealing to a younger audience. Participants were distributed geographically as follows: 60.6% from North America, 25.5% from Europe, 5.3% from South America, 4.8% from Oceania, 2.7% from Asia, and 1.1% from Africa. However, 98.9% of participants reported having a very good or native understanding of English. Therefore, we operate under the assumption that lack of English proficiency was not a detriment to our study.

Participants' scores in the HEXAD user types followed a similar distribution as previous reports [23, 40], with the following means and standard deviations: Free Spirit: 23.1 (2.8); Philanthropist: 22.8 (3.6); Achiever: 22.4 (3.4); Player: 21.1 (4.0); Socialiser: 18.3 (4.8); and Disruptor: 15.4 (4.6).

RESULTS

In this section, we first present the exploratory factor analysis used to cluster the gameful design elements into eight groups. Next, we describe the characteristics of each group and their average scores in the participant sample. Finally, we analyze how the independent variables (user type scores, personality traits, gender, and age) influence the element groups' scores. All analyses were conducted in SPSS 23 (IBM, 2015).

Exploratory Factor Analysis

We employed a principal component analysis (PCA) to cluster the 59 surveyed gameful design elements into groups. PCA is a standard method for creating groupings in data based on the covariance and correlation of items. This allowed us to establish a classification and analyze user preferences with a more manageable number of categories.

Since our investigation was exploratory, the first step was to evaluate if all the included gameful design elements could be successfully grouped into clusters because we had no prior theory to justify the inclusion or exclusion of each element. A PCA requires variables to be at least partially correlated between themselves to be able to reduce the number of components. Thus, we first analyzed the correlation matrix between all 59 variables and removed variables with only three or less relevant correlations. We considered correlations with $r >= .3$ as relevant, as suggested by Field [18] (p. 648). Moreover, we also performed an initial PCA and noted the variables that appeared isolated in one of the components—meaning variables that were the only item loading highly in one of the components—and removed them. We performed this procedure three times, until we found no more variables to remove.

After the removal process, we had removed a total of ten variables from the analysis (16.9%): *Non-linear gameplay*, *Anonymity*, *Anarchic gameplay*, *Tutorials*, *Loss aversion*, *Time pressure*, *Scarcity*, *Aura effect*, *Protection*, and *Virtual worlds*. This means that these variables could not be clustered with any other of the variables in the dataset.

For the final dataset with the remaining 49 variables, the Kaiser-Meyer-Olkin measure verified the sample adequacy for the analysis, $KMO = .77$ (a good sample size, according to Field [18]). Moreover, Bartlett's test of sphericity was significant ($\chi^2{}_{1176} = 3486.2, p < .001$), indicating that the correlations between items were sufficiently large for PCA.

We used parallel analysis and Velicer's minimum average partial (MAP) test to determine the number of components to retain in the final analysis because these procedures are validated and, hence, more adequate than a simple eigenvalues inspection [29]. The analyses suggested we should retain eight components. Moreover, we used an Oblimin rotation because we expected that some elements could appear in more than one component. Table 1 presents the final structure matrix.

	Components							
Gameful design elements	**1**	**2**	**3**	**4**	**5**	**6**	**7**	**8**
Social comparison or pressure	.821							
Leaderboards	.801							
Social competition	.789							
Social networks	.720							
Social status	.716							
Guilds or teams	.668						-.430	
Friend invite	.647						-.420	
Social discovery	.617						-.419	
Trading	.536						-.388	
Scarlet letter	.527	.377					-.414	-.381
Glowing choice		.819						
Beginner's luck		.695						
Signposting		.626						
Anchor juxtaposition		.561						
Power-ups or boosters		.555						
Humanity hero		.516	.371			-.395	-.363	
Personalization		.511			-.427			
Free lunch		.488						-.390
Mystery box			.700					
Easter eggs			.673					
Theme			.625					
Narrative or story			.485					-.361
Access				.632				
Lotteries or games of chance				.580				
Boss battles	.371			.547				
Challenges			.401	.490				
Avatar					-.761			
Customization					-.761			
Points				.361	-.604			-.352
Virtual economy				.376	-.446			
Levels or progression						-.620		
Meaning or purpose						-.584		
Progress feedback						-.539		-.358
Learning			.404			-.459		
Knowledge sharing							-.680	
Gifting	.475						-.657	
Innovation platforms							-.651	
Development tools							-.625	
Administrative roles							-.568	
Voting mechanisms							-.496	
Exploratory tasks			.457				-.487	
Creativity tools					-.399		-.456	
Meaningful choices						-.391	-.448	
Badges or achievements								-.830
Certificates								-.736
Collection								-.594
Rewards or prizes				.389	-.381			-.530
Unlockable or rare content			.436					-.506
Quests					-.366	-.438		-.494
Internal reliability (α)	.874	.787	.736	.668	.696	.674	.844	.771
Eigenvalues	9.077	4.164	3.123	2.577	2.154	1.855	1.769	1.694
% of variance	18.524	8.498	6.374	5.260	4.397	3.785	3.610	3.457

Notes. Extraction method: Principal component analysis. Rotation method: Oblimin with Kaiser normalization.
The components were labelled: (1) socialization, (2) assistance, (3) immersion, (4) risk/reward, (5) customization, (6) progression, (7) altruism, (8) incentive. For improved visualization, the factor loadings < .36 (absolute values) are suppressed.

Table 1. Exploratory factor analysis (structure matrix) of the gameful design elements.

Field [18] (p. 644) recommends considering factor loadings greater than .36 as significant for a sample size of 200 and an *alpha* level of .01. Thus, we calculated the scores and internal reliability coefficients for each component using all the gameful design elements that loaded higher than .36 in the component. All components showed adequate reliability with $\alpha >= .674$ (see Table 1).

Component Interpretation

After completing the PCA, we analyzed the composition of each component to interpret and label them. First, two researchers interpreted the component structure matrix independently. Next, both compared their interpretations, discussed similarities and divergences, and agreed on a label for each component. We labelled the eight components as follows:

1: **Socialization.** All elements in this component correspond to some form of social interaction, including both collaborative, competitive, and entirely social interactions.

2: **Assistance.** All elements in this component correspond to the user receiving some sort of aid for their progression, either from the system or from other users.

3: **Immersion.** The highest loading elements in this component are related to immersion and curiosity. This component includes elements related with a narrative or story and elements related with exploration and unpredictability.

4: **Risk/Reward.** The highest loading elements in this component are related to challenges, gambling, and the rewards that come from winning. Thus, this component represents the expectation of winning economically or socially valuable prizes both from challenges and lotteries.

5: **Customization.** The highest loading elements in this component are related to three different ways of customizing one's own experience: (1) customizing the user's avatar or experience, (2) automatic personalization, or (3) redeeming freely chosen goods with virtual currency or points.

6: **Progression.** The elements in this component are related to progression and meaning. Thus, this component represents the will to be involved in meaningful goals and to feel one is progressing towards achieving them.

7: **Altruism.** All elements in this component correspond to diverse ways of making a useful contribution, either to the system or to other users, including sharing knowledge or goods, contributing to improve the system, and collaborating with other users.

8: **Incentive.** All elements in this component correspond to incentives or rewards that the user might receive, such as badges, achievements, collectible items, and rewards.

Table 2 presents the descriptive statistics for the eight groups of gameful design elements. We calculated the mean and standard deviation based of the original 5-point Likert scale responses to all the items that loaded higher than .36 in each component. Overall, *immersion* and *progression* are the groups of design elements that score higher in user preferences, whereas *socialization* and *assistance* are the groups that score lower. However, the difference is not extensive: there is only a 1.15-point difference out of 5.0 (23%) in the difference between the highest and the lowest scoring groups.

For greater precision in the correlation analyses, we also computed participants' standardized scores for each one of the eight components as part of the PCA using the regression method. Standardizing the linear regression model generates scores for each component with a mean of zero and a standard deviation of 1.0. We used the scores calculated with this method for all subsequent correlation analyses.

Table 2 also shows the bivariate correlations of the eight groups between themselves. There is a moderate correlation between *socialization* and *altruism*, which is explained by the fact that both are related to social interactions. The difference is that the focus of the former is on the interactions themselves, whereas the latter is more focused on making a contribution, which can be directed at other users, but also at the system. There are also significant, but weaker correlations between *socialization* and *incentive*; *assistance* and *customization*; *assistance* and *incentive*; *immersion* and *altruism*; *customization* and *incentive*; and *altruism* and *incentive*. It is noteworthy that *incentive* showed the highest number of correlations (four).

Factors that Influence User Preferences

To understand which factors influence user preferences for each one of the eight gameful design element groups, we analyzed how the participant's user type scores, personality traits, age, and gender influenced their scores for each group.

			Correlations (r)							
Components	**Mean**	**SD**	**1**	**2**	**3**	**4**	**5**	**6**	**7**	**8**
1- Socialization	3.15	0.71	–							
2- Assistance	3.02	0.68	.042	–						
3- Immersion	4.17	0.46	.065	.008	–					
4- Risk/Reward	3.60	0.56	.143	.029	.003	–				
5- Customization	3.92	0.53	.069	.157 *	.078	.055	–			
6- Progression	4.16	0.46	.147	.056	.103	.088	.071	–		
7- Altruism	3.57	0.54	.281 **	.050	.164 *	.033	.150	.101	–	
8- Incentive	3.78	0.53	.157 *	.172 *	.132	.121	.199 *	.131	.174 *	–

* $p < .05$. ** $p < .01$.

Table 2. Descriptive statistics for the groups of gameful design elements and bivariate correlations between them.

Components	Correlations (r)					
	Free Spirit	Philanthropist	Achiever	Player	Socialiser	Disruptor
1- Socialization	.003	.104	.283**	.263**	.480**	.125
2- Assistance	.126	.112	-.015	-.016	.190*	.025
3- Immersion	.406**	.170*	.394**	.053	.100	.165*
4- Risk/Reward	.120	.084	.361**	.247**	.026	.183*
5- Customization	.117	-.019	-.070	.130	-.069	.006
6- Progression	.013	.170*	.186*	.104	.072	.084
7- Altruism	.149	.377**	.179*	.143	.227**	.093
8- Incentive	.030	.024	.056	.351**	.103	.003

* $p < .05$. ** $p < .01$.

Table 3. Bivariate correlations between the groups of gameful design elements and the HEXAD user types.

Components	Correlations (r)				
	Extraversion	Agreeableness	Conscientiousness	Neuroticism	Openness
1- Socialization	.323**	.067	.029	-.144	-.027
2- Assistance	.316**	.106	.040	.046	.147
3- Immersion	.035	.119	.019	.119	.140
4- Risk/Reward	.086	-.077	.068	-.030	-.019
5- Customization	.035	.000	-.154	.145	.306**
6- Progression	.031	-.080	.079	.044	-.044
7- Altruism	.002	.015	.053	.092	.084
8- Incentive	.107	.052	-.136	.194*	.019

* $p < .05$. ** $p < .01$.

Table 4. Bivariate correlations between the groups of gameful design elements and the Big 5 personality traits.

User Types

Table 3 presents the bivariate correlations coefficients between the groups of gameful design elements and participant's user type scores. The results lead to the following interpretation:

1. **Socialization** elements are strongly preferred by *socialisers*. In addition, *achievers* and *players* also show a moderate preference for these elements.
2. **Assistance** elements only show a weak preference by *socialisers*. Other than that, the user type scores do not influence the preference for receiving aid.
3. **Immersion** elements are strongly preferred by *free spirits* and *achievers*. Moreover, *philanthropists* and *disruptors* also show a weak preference for these elements.
4. **Risk/Reward** elements are moderately preferred by *achievers* and *players* and slightly preferred by *disruptors*.
5. **Customization** elements' preferences do not seem to be affected by the participant's user type scores at all.
6. **Progression** elements are only marginally preferred by *achievers* and *philanthropists*.
7. **Altruism** elements are strongly preferred by *philanthropists*. Additionally, there is a moderate preference by *socialisers* and a lighter preference by *achievers*.
8. **Incentive** elements are strongly preferred by *players*.

Personality Traits

Table 4 presents the bivariate correlation coefficients between the groups of gameful design elements and participant's personality traits scores. Results show that *extraversion* can partly explain the preferences for *socialization* and *assistance*, *openness* can partly explain the preference for *customization*, and *neuroticism* can partly explain the preference for *incentive*. However, these correlations are only moderate in strength.

Age and Gender

Table 5 presents the relationship between the groups of gameful design elements and the participant's age and gender. The results suggest that preferences for *risk and reward*, *customization*, *altruism*, and *incentive* decrease slightly with age. *Socialization* and *immersion* also seemed to slightly decrease with age, while *assistance* seemed to slightly increase with age, but the effects were not significant. Finally, the preference for *progression* was the most stable irrespective of age.

We only analyzed the data for the two main genders (female and male) because the number of participants who self-identified with other genders was too small to allow us to conduct statistical tests. Women scored significantly higher than men in *assistance*, *immersion*, *customization*, and *incentive*. On the other hand, men scored significantly higher in *socialization* and *altruism*. These results suggest that men tend to be more sociable and collaborative in gameful systems, whereas women tend to be more immersed in the narrative, customize their experience more often, and are generally more willing to receive aid.

Components	Age (r)	Female		Male		T-test			Mean Differences		95% CI	
		M	SD	M	SD	t	df	p	M	SD	lower	upper
1- Socialization	-.138	-0.366	1.027	0.205	0.941	-3.269	148	.001	-0.571	0.175	-0.915	-0.226
2- Assistance	.113	0.628	0.856	-0.287	0.944	0.508	148	.000	0.915	0.166	0.587	1.243
3- Immersion	-.137	0.369	0.949	-0.076	0.952	2.596	148	.010	0.446	0.172	0.106	0.785
4- Risk/Reward	-.150 *	0.020	0.969	-0.016	0.995	0.201	148	.841	0.036	0.178	-0.316	0.388
5- Customization	-.186 *	0.311	1.008	-0.136	0.984	2.499	148	.014	0.447	0.179	0.094	0.801
6- Progression	-.004	0.165	1.000	-0.073	1.004	0.312	148	.192	0.238	0.181	-0.120	0.595
7- Altruism	-.175 *	-0.246	0.922	0.130	0.977	-2.168	148	.032	-0.376	0.174	-0.719	-0.033
8- Incentive	-.162 *	0.233	0.965	-0.112	1.002	1.930	148	.055	0.346	0.179	-0.008	0.700

* $p < .05$.

Table 5. Bivariate correlations between the groups of gameful design elements and age and independent samples T test between the groups and gender.

Hierarchical Clustering

To verify if the groups of gameful design elements could be further clustered into higher level categories, we performed a hierarchical cluster analysis. This is important to understand how the groups relate to each other. The results demonstrate that the eight groups of gameful design elements can be further clustered into three high-level motivational categories (see Table 6). Figure 1 shows the resulting dendrogram.

Categories	Groups	Notes
INDIVIDUAL MOTIVATIONS	3- Immersion 6- Progression	This represents the user's interest in their own experience within the system.
EXTERNAL MOTIVATIONS	4- Risk/Reward 5- Customization 8- Incentive	This represents the user's interest in earning external incentives and tailoring the system to them.
SOCIAL MOTIVATIONS	1- Socialization 2- Assistance 7- Altruism	This represents the user's interest in relatedness and social interactions.

Table 6. High level categories of gameful design elements.

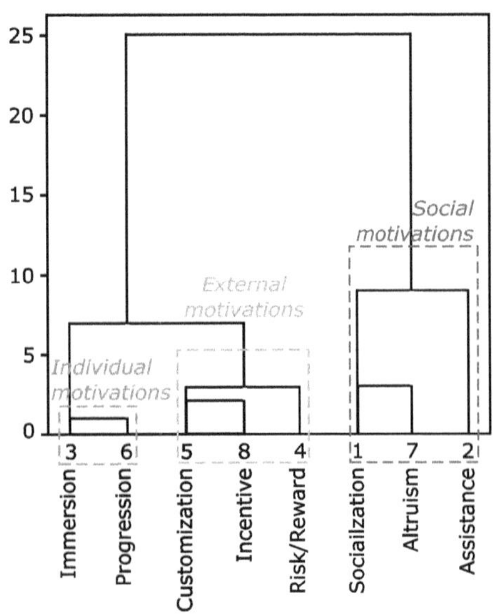

Note. Ward linkage; squared Euclidean distance.
The dendrogram shows how the groups can be hierarchically clustered according to their proximity in participants' responses.

Figure 1. Dendrogram of the groups of gameful design elements.

DISCUSSION

The findings from this study show that 49 of the most frequently used gameful design elements can be grouped into eight principal components according to user preferences. In addition, we showed that 10 out of the 59 elements included in our survey could not be grouped with any other. The overall difference between the components regarding user preferences is not extraordinary but still pronounced, with approximately 20% difference between the lowest and the highest scoring groups. Moreover, by analyzing how the participants' gender, age, user types, and personality traits influenced their scores in each group, we established a clear model of user preferences:

1. **Socialization** elements are preferred by men, socialisers, and extroverts.
2. **Assistance** elements are preferred by women and extroverts.
3. **Immersion** elements are preferred by women, achievers, and free spirits.
4. **Risk/Reward** elements are preferred by younger achievers and players.
5. **Customization** elements are preferred by younger women who are more open to experiences.
6. **Progression** preferences are not clearly explained by any of studied variables, although achievers and philanthropists tend to enjoy them more than others.
7. **Altruism** elements are preferred by younger men, philanthropists, and socialisers.
8. **Incentive** elements are preferred by younger players, who score higher on neuroticism.

Categories of Gameful Design Elements

By looking at how the gameful design elements were classified in eight groups and three categories and comparing this model with prior literature on gaming motivations, we can understand how the users' experiences with gameful applications have remarkable differences in comparison with games. Artificially constructed challenges are at the heart of game design. Therefore, game-oriented models, such as Yee's gamer motivation profile [43], demonstrate players' preferences for different types of challenges, such as action, social, achievement, or creativity. Similarly, only socialization and immersion are present in both Hamari and Tuunanen's [20] proposed dimensions and our framework, and only socialization and exploration are present in both the BrainHex [27] and our framework, whereas the remaining motivations in those models refer to types of game challenges that are not common in gamification. Differently, the challenges faced by the user in a gameful application are usually real-world tasks, not artificially created tasks. Thus, gameful applications often aim to support the user in overcoming these natural challenges. Consequently, the groups of gameful design elements reflect different approaches to offer this support to users instead of creating different types of artificial challenges. In the following, we interpret the categories of design elements that emerged from our analysis with regard to this notion of natural compared to artificial challenges.

Individual Motivations

Both groups in this category include elements aimed at supporting the user at the individual level so they can successfully achieve their goals. *Immersion* enables users to have a more engaging experience, to feel that they are part of something bigger than themselves. On the other hand, *progression* helps users track their completed steps and plan the next ones towards achieving their goals. Thus, both design elements contribute to increasing the user's self-efficacy (i.e., their belief in their own abilities) within a gameful system.

External Motivations

These groups include elements aimed at providing external incentives for carrying out the activities that make up part of the gameful system. In this sense, *incentive* is the category that most clearly identifies different types of external incentives that are frequently used as sources of extrinsic motivation.

In contrast, *risk and reward* are harder to interpret as a group of gameful design elements. The elements in this group seem diverse, such as access to exclusive features, games of chance, and challenges. However, Caillois [11] has previously described this combination involving both games of skill and chance (*agôn* and *alea* in Caillois's play style classification). In this case, both types of game represent different means by which players can feel empowered to overcome the limitations that they face in real life. In games, every player has an equal chance of winning by either improving the skills required by the game or or via chance. Thus, winning is the feeling that users seek when facing challenges or lotteries. Even when the games are based on skill, there is still gambling involved, as winning depends as much on one's own skill as on the chance of facing an opponent which is less skilled. Hence, the thrill of the unexpected is also present, although in a different format than that of the games of chance, which depend solely on luck.

Finally, *customization* might also not seem like an obvious external motivation. However, the elements included in this group are means for the user to make the system work in their favour. Therefore, they empower users to modify the external factors that influence their ability to achieve their goals.

Social Motivations

The groups in this category include the elements that allow users to interact with others while carrying out their activities in the gameful system. Thus, *socialization* enables users to interact with each other, collaborate in carrying out their tasks, or compare themselves with others. *Altruism* allows users to feel they are part of something meaningful and make a contribution to a worthy cause. And finally, *assistance* allows users to receive aid from other users or from the system, thus, helping them alleviate any difficulty that they might experience in carrying out their tasks by themselves.

Comparison with prior Frameworks of Gamification Elements

Our framework differs significantly from prior frameworks of gamification elements because it is the first approach to classify design elements based on user preferences. Robinson and Bellotti [37] suggested a model with six categories of gamification elements based on their role in the user experience. In comparison, only socialization and incentives are present in both their framework and ours, whereas the remaining categories are quite different. Exton and Murray [16] merely attributed to each element a potential to afford different types of motivation, without any organization in categories; therefore, our approach is remarkably different from theirs. Finally, Phillips et al. [34] and Rapp [36] focused exclusively on classifying rewards and incentives in games; thus, their works provide a more in-depth look into the design elements that are part of the *incentives* group in our framework. Since each one of these frameworks focused on different classification criteria, they are complementary and each one of them can contribute important information to the gameful design process. Remarkably, our framework is the first one to consider different user preferences in its construction, whereas the existing frameworks focus on different structural or motivational aspects without accounting for individual user differences.

Usage of the Framework

We have previously noted that most gameful design methods do not consider user preferences as part of their process. To address this issue, we suggest several possible usage scenarios for this framework. In a general approach, understanding the different groups of design elements and the overall characteristics of the users who are more likely to enjoy the elements from each group will allow gameful designers to create applications that can be potentially more attractive for the target user base. By understanding how different design elements appeal to different users, and which elements are similar in terms of user preferences, designers will be better equipped to employ a variety of elements instead of always relying on the same small subset of elements. Additionally, by knowing the characteristics of a product and of the population, marketing and customer relations can be better planned and directed.

Furthermore, this framework could be used to tailor the gameful experience for each particular user by adapting the system with the design elements that the user is more likely to enjoy. For this purpose, user preferences could be profiled automatically, by logging the frequency of user interaction with different activities. Alternatively, the user could be invited to answer a survey aimed at computing a preference score for each one of the eight groups. By knowing how the elements are grouped together, it is possible to assess an individual's preference for each one of the eight groups by asking them only about the elements that more strongly represent the group (i.e., the elements with the highest loading coefficients for each

	1- Socialization	2- Assistance	3- Immersion	4- Risk/Reward
1	Social comparison	Glowing choice	Mystery box	Access
2	Leaderboards	Beginner's luck	Easter eggs	Lotteries
3	Social competition	Signposting	Theme	Boss battles
4	Social networks	Anchor juxtaposition	Narrative/Story	Challenges
α (3 items)	.875	.691	.624	.475
α (4 items)	.840	.703	.651	.525

	5- Customization	6- Progression	7- Altruism	8- Incentive
1	Avatars	Levels/Progression	Knowledge sharing	Badges/Achievements
2	Customization	Meaning/Purpose	Gifting	Certificates
3	Points	Progress feedback	Innovation platforms	Collections
4	Virtual economy	Learning	Development tools	Rewards/Prizes
α (3 items)	.671	.550	.610	.727
α (4 items)	.653	.563	.684	.725

Table 7. Top loading gameful design elements per group and internal reliability of subscales using only the top three or four elements per group.

component). Depending on the degree of accuracy desired, we suggest using three or four gameful design elements for each group to compute an overall individual preference score for the group. Table 7 demonstrates that the internal reliability remains above .60 for most groups even if only three or four elements are used. Therefore, by asking an individual about their preferences using a list of 24 (three per group) or 32 (four per group) gameful design elements, it is possible to estimate their preference for any one of the 49 studied elements with a reasonable degree of accuracy.

Moreover, the assessment of an individual's preference for elements of each group can also inform HCI research intended to study the mechanisms and effects of different elements. By understanding that different participants might have different dispositions to enjoy diverse gameful design elements, participants' scores in each group of design elements might be used as a control variable for the effects being studied.

Limitations

While our study design was valid and our results were significant, we had a few minor limitations. First, all measures were self-reported and, thus, subject to participants' level of understanding of the statements in the survey and their awareness of their own preferences toward diverse gameful design elements. Furthermore, the use of short scales is subject to acquiescence issues. This could be an issue because we used a short 10-items BFI scale due to the already considerable length of our survey. Nonetheless, the BFI-10 has been validated by several studies. Thus, we consider that our survey was adequate for the goals of our study, which were to explore possible factors that might influence user preferences without testing any particular hypothesis. Therefore, the findings from this study should represent an invitation for future research that could verify specific claims in focused studies.

Moreover, although our sample size was sufficient to perform the statistical analyses, our study was an exploratory pilot, aimed at constructing an initial conceptual framework of gameful design elements. Therefore, we intend to conduct additional studies with larger and more diverse samples to verify our findings and confirm the validity of our framework.

Finally, we did not observe participants' behaviour when interacting with gameful systems to verify if their scores in each one of the groups of gameful elements would predict their real behaviour. Hence, future studies will need to investigate the relationship between an individual's self-reported preferences and their actual behaviour in gameful systems.

CONCLUSION

The current study investigated user preferences for gameful design elements frequently employed in gamification. It is the first exploratory study to investigate design elements specifically used in gameful systems, instead of trying to generalize previous work in games user research to gamification. Specifically, this paper contributes to the HCI and gamification communities by presenting a novel model of eight groups of gameful design elements in three categories: *individual motivations* (immersion and progression); *external motivations* (risk/reward, customization, and incentives); and *social motivations* (socialization, altruism, and assistance).

Additionally, we have described the defining characteristics of each group and the gameful design elements that compose them. We also explained the typical characteristics of the users who are more likely to prefer each group. Finally, we have proposed different ways in which this framework can be used to inform gameful design. This can be achieved either by automatically profiling user preferences by observing their behaviour, or by explicitly asking users about their preferences toward a reduced set of elements and extrapolating their preferences for the remaining elements.

These findings extend our understanding of user preferences in gamification and will enable researchers and practitioners to design better tailored gameful systems in the future.

ACKNOWLEDGMENTS

This research was funded by the CNPq, Brazil, SSHRC (895-2011-1014, IMMERSe), NSERC (RGPIN-418622-2012), CFI (35819), Mitacs (IT07255), and Agència de Gestió d'Ajuts Universitaris i de Recerca (Generalitat de Catalunya) through the Industrial Doctorate programme 2014-DI-006 in collaboration with Grupo ICA Barcelona.

REFERENCES

1. Gabriel Barata, Sandra Gama, Joaquim Jorge, and Daniel Gonçalves. 2016. Studying student differentiation in gamified education: A long-term study. *Computers in Human Behavior* (2016). DOI: http://dx.doi.org/10.1016/j.chb.2016.08.049
2. Gabriel Barata, Sandra Gama, Joaquim A.P. Jorge, and Daniel J.V. Gonçalves. 2014. Relating gaming habits with student performance in a gamified learning experience. In *Proceedings of the first ACM SIGCHI annual symposium on Computer-human interaction in play - CHI PLAY '14*. ACM, New York, NY, USA, 17–25. DOI: http://dx.doi.org/10.1145/2658537.2658692
3. Richard Bartle. 1996. Hearts, Clubs, Diamonds, Spades: Players who suit MUDs. *Journal of MUD Research* 1, 1 (1996).
4. Richard Bartle. 2005. Virtual Worlds: Why People Play. *Massively Multiplayer Game Development* 2, 1 (2005).
5. Chris Bateman, Rebecca Lowenhaupt, and Lennart E Nacke. 2011. Player Typology in Theory and Practice. *Proceedings of DiGRA 2011* (2011).
6. Chris Bateman and Lennart E Nacke. 2010. The Neurobiology of Play. In *Proceedings of Futureplay 2010*. ACM, Vancouver, BC, Canada, 1–8. DOI: http://dx.doi.org/10.1145/1920778.1920780
7. Chris Mark. Bateman and Richard Boon. 2006. *21st Century Game Design (Game Development Series)*. Charles River Media.
8. Blizzard Entertainment. 2004. World of Warcraft. Game [Windows/OS X]. (2004).
9. Marc Busch, Elke Mattheiss, Rita Orji, Peter Fröhlich, Michael Lankes, and Manfred Tscheligi. 2016. Player Type Models – Towards Empirical Validation. In *Proceedings of the 2016 CHI Conference Extended Abstracts on Human Factors in Computing Systems*. ACM. DOI:http://dx.doi.org/10.1145/2851581.2892399
10. Marc Busch, Elke Mattheiss, Rita Orji, Andrzej Marczewski, Wolfgang Hochleitner, Michael Lankes, Lennart E. Nacke, and Manfred Tscheligi. 2015. Personalization in Serious and Persuasive Games and Gamified Interactions. In *Proceedings of the 2015 Annual Symposium on Computer-Human Interaction in Play - CHI PLAY '15*. ACM, 811–816. DOI: http://dx.doi.org/10.1145/2793107.2810260
11. Roger Caillois. 1961. *Man, Play, and Games*. University of Illinois Press.
12. Yu-kai Chou. 2017. Yu-kai Chou: Gamification & Behavioral Design. (2017). http://yukaichou.com/
13. Sebastian Deterding. 2015. The Lens of Intrinsic Skill Atoms: A Method for Gameful Design. *Human-Computer Interaction* 30, 3-4 (2015), 294–335. DOI:http://dx.doi.org/10.1080/07370024.2014.993471
14. Sebastian Deterding, Dan Dixon, Rilla Khaled, and Lennart E Nacke. 2011. From Game Design Elements to Gamefulness: Defining "Gamification". In *Proceedings of the 15th International Academic MindTrek Conference*. ACM, ACM, Tampere, Finland, 9–15. DOI: http://dx.doi.org/10.1145/2181037.2181040
15. Enterprise Gamification. 2017. Gamification Design Elements. (2017). http://enterprise-gamification.com/mediawiki/index.php?title=Gamification_Design_Elements
16. Geraldine Exton and Liam Murray. 2014. Motivation: A Proposed Taxonomy using Gamification. (2014). http://hdl.handle.net/10344/4279
17. Lauren S. Ferro, Steffen P. Walz, and Stefan Greuter. 2013. Towards personalised, gamified systems: an investigation into game design, personality and player typologies. In *Proceedings of the 9th Australasian Conference on Interactive Entertainment: Matters of Life and Death - IE '13*. 1–6. DOI: http://dx.doi.org/10.1145/2513002.2513024
18. Andy Field. 2009. *Discovering Statistics Using SPSS* (3rd ed.). Sage Publications, London, UK.
19. Lewis R Goldberg. 1993. The structure of phenotypic personality traits. *American Psychologist* 48, 1 (1993), 26. DOI:http://dx.doi.org/10.1037/0003-066X.48.1.26
20. Juho Hamari and Janne Tuunanen. 2014. Player types: A meta-synthesis. *Transactions of the Digital Games Research* 1, 2 (2014). http://todigra.org/index.php/todigra/article/view/13
21. Yuan Jia, Bin Xu, Yamini Karanam, and Stephen Voida. 2016. Personality-targeted Gamification: A Survey Study on Personality Traits and Motivational Affordances. In *Proceedings of the 34th Annual ACM Conference on Human Factors in Computing Systems - CHI '16*. DOI: http://dx.doi.org/10.1145/2858036.2858515
22. Andrzej Marczewski. 2015. *Even Ninja Monkeys Like to Play: Gamification, Game Thinking & Motivational Design*. CreateSpace Independent Publishing Platform.
23. Andrzej Marczewski. 2017. User Types in Gamification. SlideShare. (Feb 2017). https://www.slideshare.net/daverage/gamification-player-types-talk-2017
24. Alberto Mora, Daniel Riera, Carina González, and Joan Arnedo-Moreno. 2017. Gamification: a systematic review of design frameworks. *Journal of Computing in Higher Education* (23 May 2017). DOI: http://dx.doi.org/10.1007/s12528-017-9150-4
25. Benedikt Morschheuser, Karl Werder, Juho Hamari, and Julian Abe. 2017. How to gamify? A method for designing gamification. In *Proceedings of the 50th Annual Hawaii International Conference on System Sciences (HICSS)*. IEEE, Hawaii, USA. DOI: http://dx.doi.org/10125/41308
26. Isabel Briggs Myers. 1962. *The Myers-Briggs Type Indicator*. Consulting Psychologists Press, Palo Alto, CA.

27. Lennart E Nacke, Chris Bateman, and Regan L Mandryk. 2014. BrainHex: A Neurobiological Gamer Typology Survey. *Entertainment Computing* 5, 1 (2014), 55–62. DOI:http://dx.doi.org/10.1016/j.entcom.2013.06.002

28. Scott Nicholson. 2014. A RECIPE for Meaningful Gamification. In *Gamification in Education and Business*, Torsten Reiners and Lincoln C. Wood (Eds.). Springer, 1–20. DOI: http://dx.doi.org/10.1007/978-3-319-10208-5

29. Brian P O'Connor. 2000. SPSS and SAS programs for determining the number of components using parallel analysis and Velicer's MAP test. *Behavior Research Methods, Instruments, & Computers* 32, 3 (2000), 396–402. DOI:http://dx.doi.org/10.3758/BF03200807

30. Rita Orji, Regan L. Mandryk, Julita Vassileva, and Kathrin M. Gerling. 2013. Tailoring persuasive health games to gamer type. In *Proceedings of the SIGCHI Conference on Human Factors in Computing Systems - CHI '13*. 2467–2476. DOI: http://dx.doi.org/10.1145/2470654.2481341

31. Rita Orji, Lennart E. Nacke, and Chrysanne DiMarco. 2017. Towards Personality-driven Persuasive Health Games and Gamified Systems. In *Proceedings of the SIGCHI Conference on Human Factors in Computing Systems*. ACM. DOI: http://dx.doi.org/10.1145/3025453.3025577

32. Rita Orji, Julita Vassileva, and Regan L. Mandryk. 2014. Modeling the efficacy of persuasive strategies for different gamer types in serious games for health. *User Modeling and User-Adapted Interaction* 24, 5 (2014), 453–498. DOI: http://dx.doi.org/10.1007/s11257-014-9149-8

33. Nicole Peever, Daniel Johnson, and John Gardner. 2012. Personality & Video Game Genre Preferences. In *Proceedings of The 8th Australasian Conference on Interactive Entertainment: Playing the System*. ACM, 20. DOI:http://dx.doi.org/10.1145/2336727.2336747

34. Cody Phillips, Daniel Johnson, Peta Wyeth, Leanne Hides, and Madison Klarkowski. 2015. Redefining Videogame Reward Types. In *Proceedings of the Annual Meeting of the Australian Special Interest Group for Computer Human Interaction*. ACM, 83–91. DOI: http://dx.doi.org/10.1145/2838739.2838782

35. Beatrice Rammstedt and Oliver P. John. 2007. Measuring personality in one minute or less: A 10-item short version of the Big Five Inventory in English and German. *Journal of Research in Personality* 41, 1 (2007), 203–212. DOI: http://dx.doi.org/10.1016/j.jrp.2006.02.001

36. Amon Rapp. 2017. From Games to Gamification: A Classification of Rewards in World of Warcraft for the Design of Gamified Systems. *Simulation & Gaming* 48, 3 (2017), 381–401. DOI: http://dx.doi.org/10.1177/1046878117697147

37. David Robinson and Victoria Bellotti. 2013. A preliminary taxonomy of gamification elements for varying anticipated commitment. In *Workshop on Designing Gamification: Creating Gameful and Playful Experiences*.

38. Richard M. Ryan and Edward L. Deci. 2000. Self-determination theory and the facilitation of intrinsic motivation, social development, and well-being. *The American Psychologist* 55, 1 (2000), 68–78. DOI: http://dx.doi.org/10.1037/0003-066X.55.1.68

39. Richard M. Ryan, C. Scott Rigby, and Andrew Przybylski. 2006. The motivational pull of video games: A self-determination theory approach. *Motivation and Emotion* 30, 4 (2006), 347–363. DOI: http://dx.doi.org/10.1007/s11031-006-9051-8

40. Gustavo F. Tondello, Rina R. Wehbe, Lisa Diamond, Marc Busch, Andrzej Marczewski, and Lennart E. Nacke. 2016. The Gamification User Types Hexad Scale. In *Proceedings of the 2016 Annual Symposium on Computer-Human Interaction in Play - CHI PLAY '16*. ACM, Austin, TX, USA. DOI: http://dx.doi.org/10.1145/2967934.2968082

41. Kevin Werbach and Dan Hunter. 2015. *The Gamification Toolkit: Dynamics, Mechanics, and Components for the Win*. Wharton Digital Press, Philadelphia, PA.

42. Nick Yee. 2006. Motivations for Play in Online Games. *CyberPsychology & Behavior* 9, 6 (dec 2006), 772–775. DOI:http://dx.doi.org/10.1089/cpb.2006.9.772

43. Nick Yee. 2015. Gamer Motivation Model Overview and Descriptions. Quantic Foundry. (Dec 2015). http://quanticfoundry.com/2015/12/15/handy-reference/

44. Nick Yee, Nicolas Ducheneaut, and Les Nelson. 2012. Online gaming motivations scale: development and validation. In *Proceedings of the 2012 ACM annual conference on Human Factors in Computing Systems - CHI '12*. ACM, New York, New York, USA, 2803. DOI: http://dx.doi.org/10.1145/2207676.2208681

45. Gabe Zichermann and Christopher Cunningham. 2011. *Gamification by Design: Implementing game mechanics in web and mobile apps*. O'Reilly.

Curiously Motivated: Profiling Curiosity with Self-Reports and Behaviour Metrics in the Game "Destiny"

Mike Schaekermann[1], Giovanni Ribeiro[1], Guenter Wallner[2], Simone Kriglstein[3], Daniel Johnson[4], Anders Drachen[5], Rafet Sifa[6], Lennart E. Nacke[1]
[1]University of Waterloo, Waterloo, ON, Canada
[2]University of Applied Arts Vienna, Vienna, Austria
[3]Vienna University of Technology, Vienna, Austria
[4]Queensland University of Technology (QUT), Brisbane, Australia
[5]Digital Creativity Labs, University of York, York, UK
[6]Fraunhofer IAIS, Sankt Augustin, Germany
{mschaeke, gio.rib}@uwaterloo.ca, guenter.wallner@uni-ak.ac.at, simone.kriglstein@tuwien.ac.at, dm.johnson@qut.edu.au, anders.drachen@york.ac.uk, rafet.sifa@iais.fraunhofer.de, lennart.nacke@acm.org

ABSTRACT
Identifying player motivations such as curiosity could help game designers analyze player profiles and substantially improve game design. However, research on player profiling focuses on generalized personality traits, not specific aspects of motivation. This study examines how player behaviour indicates constructs of curiosity-related motivation. It contributes a more discriminating operationalization of game-related curiosity. We derive a curiosity measure from established self-report survey methodologies relating to social capital, behavioural activation, obsessive/harmonious passion, and BrainHex player types. We present the results of a cross-sectional study with data from 1,745 players of *Destiny*—a popular shared-world first-person shooter (FPS) game. Behaviour metrics were paired with four curiosity factors: 'social' curiosity, 'sensory/cognitive' curiosity, 'novelty-seeking' curiosity, and 'explorative' curiosity. Our findings provide key insights into the relationships between players curiosity and their in-game behaviour. We infer curiosity-related motivational profiles from behaviour metrics, and discuss how this may impact game design and player-computer interaction.

Author Keywords
Games; Personality; Curiosity; Motivation; Behaviour.

ACM Classification Keywords
H.1.2. User/Machine Systems: Human Factors; K.8.0 Personal Computing: Games.

CHI PLAY '17, October 1518, 2017, Amsterdam, Netherlands

ACM ISBN 978-1-4503-4898-0/17/10...$15.00
https://doi.org/10.1145/3116595.3116603

INTRODUCTION
Video games and their virtual worlds are great sandboxes for the investigation of human behaviour. How people play a digital game can reveal things about their character, their personal attitudes, and even their motivations in life. Curiosity is a form of intrinsic motivation that plays a central role in many aspects of human behaviour. Beyond that, curiosity is a concept frequently used by game designers, because it drives player engagement and keeps people deeply involved with a game. For instance, in 2012 renowned game designer Peter Molyneux designed an experimental game [G1] which specifically revolved around the concept of curiosity. Players had to collectively dig through layers of small cubes, to discover the 'story' surrounding the giant cube that contained them. Early research into digital games indicated the possibility of constructing personality profiles from observations of a player's in-game behaviour [50, 54, 55]. However, the exact role different facets of curiosity play in digital game behaviour has not yet been studied, even though the satisfaction of appetitive motives such as curiosity is an integral component of player engagement [23, 26]. More broadly, curiosity has been identified as a motivational factor drawing people into playing today's most successful online games, such as the online shared-world shooter *Destiny* [G5]. In these online games, curiosity may manifest itself in many forms, including seeking information or experiences [63], and social curiosity [56] about other players.

However, there has not yet been an empirical attempt to measure the extent to which different components of curiosity (e.g., social, spatial, cognitive, sensory) affect an individual player's behaviour. To address this gap in the literature, we analyzed data from 1,745 players of the online shared-world shooter *Destiny*. The data was collected as part of a larger survey designed to measure social capital, behaviour activation, obsessive and harmonious passion, and different player types. These measures were not originally designed to assess curiosity as a construct in itself, but they each incorporated data with strong connections to the concept of curiosity. Based on our review of 'curiosity' concepts, we systematically selected all curiosity-related items from the relevant subscales used in the survey and used these to derive and assess a measure of player curiosity. We then conducted an exploratory factor analysis (EFA) to derive a multi-factor measure of game-related curiosity. Since we logged player identification tokens during self-reports, we were able to correlate behaviour metrics—obtained via telemetry—with the self-report scores. After establishing the relationship between self-reported curiosity factors and tracked behavioural data, we conducted multiple regressions to test how well motivational profiles could be inferred from in-game behaviour. We were able to demonstrate meaningful behavioural correlates with the curiosity-related motivational factors we had identified. For example, those with so-called 'completionist' tendencies (e.g., 'achievers' whose aim is to complete every task in the game) showed the strongest correlations with our metrics of exploration (see table 3) but also showed stronger tendencies toward obsessive engagement. In contrast, 'curious' players were more likely to exhibit a more harmonious, balanced attitude to playing the game (see table 2). In other words, it didn't seem to take over their lives.

These findings (and other connections we were able to establish between motivational factors and in-game behaviour) deepen our understanding of the ways in which different manifestations of curiosity are reflected in digital gaming behaviour. They constitute a significant first step toward a more differentiated operationalization of curiosity in games, which may in turn support the modelling of implicit user curiosity based on observations of user behaviour in virtual worlds. Besides these essential new findings, we contribute novel methodologies, specifically related to curiosity, which advance the study of motivational drivers for playing games. First, we propose a multi-factor scale to measure aspects of curiosity in online games (derived from established scales of motivation and player types). Second, we identify behavioural indicators in a large-scale online game dataset for a key group of game-related motivations. Third, we provide evidence that profiles of motivation and player types may be inferred from the logging and processing of in-game behaviour data, thus laying the foundation for automated player motivation classification—a result with potential applications well beyond the world of online gaming. The present study is the first to correlate intrinsic motivation aspects and player personality with behaviour metrics in a shared-world, online first-person shooter game. Compared to previous work on constructing player personality profiles from observations of in-game behaviour [6, 50, 55, 64], we contribute to the human-computer interaction (HCI) and player experience communities a novel analysis of the relationships between self-reported motivation and player personality, with a focal point on curiosity, as well as observations of in-game behaviour, backed by a large sample of 1,745 online players of the game *Destiny*.

RELATED WORK

Curiosity Research

Traditionally, the fields of philosophy and psychology [3, 4, 25, 40, 42] have investigated the nature, origins, and effects of curiosity—the inherent human appetite for new information. In the early 1950s, Berlyne [3, 4] formalized curiosity research through a series of experiments linking stimulus complexity and novelty to the reward value of exploratory behaviour. Building on these early findings, Loewenstein [25] operationalized curiosity in his *information gap* theory as the *perceived ability and desire to close a gap in one's knowledge.*

Curiosity in HCI and Games

Malone [27] developed design heuristics which suggested that computing systems should (a) provide an optimal level of informational complexity through novelty and surprise, and (b) offer ways to make users' knowledge structures more 'complete, consistent, and parsimonious'. HCI researchers have extended Malone's work, leveraging curiosity to enhance user activities in interactive systems. For example, Law et al. [22] employed curiosity as an incentive mechanism to increase crowd worker retention in an audio transcription task. Wilson et al. [60] used curiosity to increase correctness in end-user programming, and Wainer et al. [57] guided users' attention toward email inbox items using curiosity-inducing verbal stimuli. For digital games, Sedano et al. [45] identified curiosity as one of the key factors which arouse and sustain player engagement in pervasive game applications. Nacke et al. [28] developed BRAINHEX, a neurobiological gamer typology survey distinguishing a 'curiosity-driven' SEEKER type—explicitly linked to Malone's definition of curiosity—from six other player archetypes. In a review of techniques to integrate curiosity and uncertainty into game design, To et al. [51] discussed five game-related curiosity types, tying established constructs to Costikyan's theory of uncertainty in games [11].

Links Between Curiosity and other Motivations to Play

Given that curiosity is defined as 'an appetite for information' [25], it can manifest itself in many different forms. Curiosity is naturally interrelated with other human impulses, such as social interaction and general experience-seeking. While some works on social dynamics in online gaming [16, 24] highlight the relevance of social curiosity in large online gaming communities implicitly, Vella et al. [56] explicitly characterize games as a *site of intersection between social exploration and relationship maintenance*. Yee et al. [63] developed a three-factor scale to measure motivations for online gaming, distinguishing between IMMERSION, SOCIAL, and ACHIEVEMENT motivations. The authors identified positive links between IMMERSION motivation and intrinsically motivated exploration of a game's virtual world. Notably, one of the four items in the IMMERSION subscale [63] directly asked about the importance of *exploring the world just for the sake of exploring it*. An inverse relationship was found between this kind of exploration and the ACHIEVEMENT motivation. Schmitt and Lahroodi [44] highlighted the 'passion' aspect of curiosity as a desire that can become obsessive, at times demanding impulsive gratification *against our will and better judgment*. Indeed all four curiosity factors reported by the present study show significant positive correlations with the Obsessive passion subscale, demonstrating a link between curiosity in general as a motivator and obsessive attachment.

Analysis of In-Game Behaviour

Behavioural analytics in game development, just as in other academic fields, combines the study of behaviour, data mining, and data visualization; to take three examples [2, 12, 49]. This research domain is referred to as 'game analytics' [17]. Early work in this field is less than a decade old and focuses on how behavioural telemetry can improve the utility of user testing in major commercial games [19]. A second line of investigation has examined the games found on social networks such as *Facebook*, which put substantial amounts of information about the players into the hands of game companies for the first time [29]. A third avenue has emerged, concerned with the ever-growing numbers of games played on mobile phones as a key new element in the game industry, where the dominant free-to-play business model relies on sales made inside the games and is thus heavily dependent on behavioural analytics to optimize the monetization process [2, 48]. A fourth theme has recently started focusing on behavioural analysis in virtual reality. The latest advances in the field focus on creating efficient techniques for rapid analysis, stealth assessment through evidence-centred design (ECD) and machine learning algorithms for prediction, profiling, and adaptation. Research in behavioural data mining has led to a better understanding of human behaviour, learning, engagement, and interaction in games [48, 47].

Inferring Player Psychology from In-Game Behaviour

Following the introduction of behavioural tracking, there have been some attempts to correlate in-game behaviour with various psychometric self-report scales [6, 50, 55, 64]. This interests academia and industry because it allows us to draw inferences about why patterns of behaviour in very large sample cohorts occur as they do—some games in the mobile space have dozens and even hundreds of millions of players. There is, however, limited knowledge publicly available on this aspect of research, and evidence currently to be found in the public domain is highly fragmented and inconclusive. For example, Yee et al. [64], van Lankfeld et al. [55], and Spronck et al. [50] looked at this problem through the lens of personality research, leveraging the Five-Factor Model [14] to infer personality traits from behaviour metrics in the role-playing games *World of Warcraft* [G4], *Neverwinter Nights* [G3], and *Fallout 3* [G2] respectively. Differentiating their work from these studies, Canossa et al. [6] posited that *personality is a construct that attempts to describe what people might choose to do, while motivation attempts to infer why they do it*. They then explored correlations between behaviour metrics in the game *Minecraft* [G6] and different aspects of motivation—including a single-factor construct of curiosity (measured by the Reiss Motivation Profiler [41]) for a selected player sample. In comparison, our work uses a much larger sample and builds a player-specific curiosity scale based on empirically robust factors.

RESEARCH QUESTIONS

As discussed above, curiosity is related to other types of motivation, such as the desire for social interaction or simple fun-seeking, and it may be reflected in the expression of different player preferences. Although it has been widely accepted as a key factor driving player behaviour, there is no game-specific instrument measuring different elements of curiosity. Several scales exist, but they are designed for measuring curiosity outside of games [40, 42] while our objective in this study is to contribute to a much more nuanced view of game-related curiosity.

We propose a methodology that we believe could inform a more differentiated operationalization of curiosity in games. Building on widely adopted instruments of player motivation and typology, we generate a survey scale that investigates social, spatial, cognitive, and sensory aspects of curiosity in the context of digital games, and which at the same time refers back to player motivation and personality as fundamental anchor points. Thus, our study aims to answer two research questions:

RQ1: What curiosity factors can be derived from the previously adopted survey scales?

RQ2: Can we infer self-reports of curiosity from player behaviour data in the game world?

USE CASE: DESTINY

Destiny [G5] is a popular shared-world first-person shooter, released in September 2014, with almost 30 million players as of Q1 2016[1]. The game is set in what the developers describe as a 'mythic science-fiction' world. All the game's activities generate player rewards, including in-game currencies, weapons, and armour. The reward a player receives for an activity is usually randomly determined and some rewards are only available on completing specific tasks. The authors chose *Destiny* for use in the current study for multiple reasons. The high number of active players, the diversity of data available regarding players' in-game behaviour, and the wide range of activities for players to engage in, render *Destiny* a useful medium for research into game-related human behaviour. Moreover, *Destiny* lends itself particularly aptly to the study of curiosity, because it tracks the degree to which players try out new things and explore the game world. These activities are aggregated in a metric called the *Grimoire* score. This score rises whenever the player performs certain actions for the first time (e.g. creating a character of a certain class and race, discovering a new location, or performing certain tasks). The *Grimoire* score is shared across all of a player's characters and thus provides an objective proxy measure of a player's tendency toward exploratory behaviour spanning a broad range of possible types of interaction.

The game has two basic modes: player-versus-environment (PvE) and player-versus-player (PvP). In PvE mode, players can engage in 'story missions' (up to 3 players cooperating), 'strikes' (3 players cooperating against large numbers of enemies), or 'raids' (which involve up to 6 players cooperating in longer, more difficult sequences of gameplay and which require high levels of collaboration). Additionally, players can choose (in groups of up to 3 players) to go 'on patrol', which involves traveling to a particular planet and attempting to complete various objectives as they become available ('on patrol' games include 'public events' which occur semi-regularly and generally require collaboration between larger

[1] `http://tinyurl.com/activision-report-Q1-2016`

numbers of players for their completion). Outside of specific mission-type objectives, players in *Destiny* can choose to focus on finding collectible items of various types. In PvP, *Destiny* offers many modes in which players compete (and cooperate) with other players. Some PvP modes involve players competing individually, while others require two teams (of 2 to 6 players). The objectives in PvP modes include gaining the most kills, and securing objectives and territory (e.g. capturing zones and seizing relics, or the defence of the same). In addition to the standard PvP modes, *Destiny* offers highly competitive, time-limited events (e.g. *Iron Banner* or *Trials of Osiris*) that offer players particularly valuable rewards. In both PvE and PvP, *Destiny* offers players 'quests' that require a sequence of activities and game objectives to be completed, in return for specific rewards.

DATA ACQUISITION AND PROCESSING

The present study combines two separate sets of data: (1) Survey data collected by the authors containing demographic information and self-reports about motivation and player types from 3,542 *Destiny* players. (2) Data on in-game behaviour obtained from *Destiny* server logs.

Survey Data

Our online survey was advertised in relevant *Destiny* player forums in the spring of 2016 and collected self-reported data from *Destiny* players. The survey comprised six sections. In the first section, we asked for demographic information: gender (96% male), age (M = 25 years; SD = 7.4), country of residence (the majority of respondents were from the United States of America, United Kingdom, Australia, Canada, New Zealand, Sweden, and Germany), experience with playing video games (57% reported to be *very experienced*), as well as average (M = 34.8 hours; SD = 25.5) and maximum (M = 58.8 hours; SD = 30.7) weekly playing time during the previous year. The second section asked for information related to *Destiny*, specifically the preferred platform to play the game, the player identification (ID), and the amounts of play time, as well as the respondents' team preferences: did they prefer playing *Destiny* with strangers, gaming friends, or real-life friends? The remaining four sections corresponded to existing psychometric scales of motivation and player typology (described below).

Social Capital. The SOCIAL CAPITAL scale [59] is an established 10-item instrument in games research [10, 52, 56, 65]. It asks about the degree to which individuals tend to engage in two different types of social interaction, referred to as *bridging* and *bonding* in the target activity (in this case, playing *Destiny*). Williams [59] describes *bridging* as an inclusive aspect of social capital which occurs when individuals from different backgrounds create new ties across the boundaries of existing social networks. In contrast, *bonding* is described as an exclusive aspect of social capital in which strongly-tied individuals, such as close friends, provide substantive support for one another. All items in the SOCIAL CAPITAL instrument are scored on a five-point Likert-type scale ranging from 'strongly disagree' to 'strongly agree'.

Obsessive/Harmonious Passion. The OBSESSIVE/HARMONIOUS PASSION scale [37, 53] used in our survey has ten items. Five of these measure the level of *harmonious* passion for an object or activity—in our case, harmonious passion (or engagement) with *Destiny*—while the other five items measure the level of *obsessive* engagement with the same object or activity. 'Harmonious passion' equates to the *autonomous* internalization of an activity into a person's identity (i.e., the person has freely chosen the activity with attached contingencies and the activity 'harmonizes' with other areas of their life. The activity does not, for example, stop them from going to work in the morning or doing the washing up). In contrast, 'obsessive passion' results from a *controlled* internalization of an activity into a person's identity (people feel compelled to engage in it) with the result that the activity conflicts with other aspects of day-to-day life [53]. The OBSESSIVE/HARMONIOUS PASSION scale is a widely adopted instrument for the study of player engagement in digital games [35, 36, 37, 58]. All items in the instrument are scored on a seven-point Likert-type scale ranging from 'do not agree' to 'strongly agree'.

Behavioural Activation System. The BEHAVIOURAL INHIBITION AND ACTIVATION SYSTEM (BIS/BAS) instrument [7] was developed to assess individual differences in the sensitivity of two different motivational systems: the behavioural activation system (BAS) which regulates appetitive motives causing humans to approach something desired (e.g., rewards), and the behavioural inhibition system (BIS) which regulates aversive motives causing humans to move away from something unpleasant (e.g. punishments). For compactness, we included only the FUN-SEEKING and REWARD RESPONSIVENESS subscales of the BAS section (which we collectively refer to as BEHAVIOURAL ACTIVATION or BAS in the following). All items in the scale are scored on a four-point Likert-type scale ranging from 'very false for me' to 'very true for me'. The BIS/BAS instrument has been used in many studies to evaluate player engagement with games [30, 34, 38, 39].

BrainHex. The BRAINHEX instrument [28] is a 21-item player typology survey, inspired by research results in neurobiology, and used to distinguish between the following seven archetypes of players: SEEKER (enjoys exploration), SURVIVOR (aroused by fear), DAREDEVIL (thrilled by risk taking), MASTERMIND (strategic problem solver), CONQUEROR (excited by defeating difficult challenges), SOCIALIZER (likes the interaction with other players), and ACHIEVER (motivated by long-term achievements). The BRAINHEX instrument has been successfully used to analyze player personality and motivation in recent studies [5, 21, 32, 33]. All items in the BRAINHEX instrument are scored on a three-point Likert-type scale with response items of 'I hate it!', 'It's okay', and 'I love it!'.

We chose these four scales for our study because they are widely adopted tools for the study of player motivation and preferences (cf. [5, 10, 21, 34, 35, 38, 56, 58]), covering a broad range of human motivations with connections to different aspects of game-related curiosity. Examples of these mo-

Parent Scale	#	Survey Item	F1	F2	F3	F4
BRIDGING SOCIAL CAPITAL	1	Interacting with people in *Destiny* makes me interested in things that happen outside of my town.	**.80**	.21	.09	.06
	2	Interacting with people in *Destiny* makes me want to try new things.	**.62**	.32	.10	.18
	3	Interacting with people in *Destiny* makes me interested in what people unlike me are thinking.	**.73**	.13	.10	.15
	4	Talking with people in *Destiny* makes me curious about other places in the world.	**.79**	.16	.10	.09
HARMONIOUS PASSION	5	The new things that I discover with this game allow me to appreciate it even more.	.22	**.63**	.18	.10
	6	This game allows me to live a variety of experiences.	.25	**.68**	.08	.15
BAS FUN-SEEKING	7	I'm always willing to try something new if I think it will be fun.	.11	.07	.05	**.52**
	8	I crave excitement and new sensations.	.08	.11	.12	**.59**
BRAINHEX SEEKER	9	Exploring to see what you can find.	.11	.11	**.58**	.12
	10	Wondering what is in an unexplored area.	.09	.10	**.73**	.07
SS loadings			2.33	1.08	0.97	0.74
Cronbach's alpha			.86	.67	.61	.50

Table 1. Summary of exploratory factor analysis results for the curiosity-related survey items. Factor loadings over .40 are written in boldface. F1 = SOCIAL CURIOSITY; F2 = SENSORY/COGNITIVE CURIOSITY; F3 = EXPLORATIVE CURIOSITY; F4 = NOVELTY/FUN-SEEKING CURIOSITY (reprinted from [43])

tivations include 'tendencies toward social interaction with other players across the boundaries of existing social networks' [59], 'the formation of harmonious connections to a game by gaining new experience' [53], 'behavioural activation induced by novelty-seeking' [7], and 'inclinations toward curiosity-driven exploration of the game world' [28]. We highlight the specific connections between individual subscales and game-related curiosity below, when we describe the process of constructing a multi-factor scale for curiosity in games. For the complete survey text, we refer the reader to the supplementary material of this paper.

RQ1: Toward Four Factors of Curiosity

The four self-report 'base' scales in our survey were developed to measure constructs other than curiosity (as discussed above). However, a closer look at the semantics of the survey items and their design objectives revealed that specific items in each of these scales do in fact interrogate constructs of curiosity. Following up on this observation, we examined whether it was possible to construct a multi-factor 'curiosity' scale using survey items from these 'base' scales' existing motivation and player types. For this purpose, we extracted the ten curiosity-related survey items from the SOCIAL CAPITAL, OBSESSIVE/HARMONIOUS PASSION, BEHAVIOURAL ACTIVATION, and BRAINHEX instruments, and performed an exploratory factor analysis (EFA) on these to examine their latent factor structures. In deriving a joint factor structure from item sets with different response scales, we follow a common methodology from personality psychology [1, 13, 61]. The precise wording of the items selected can be found in Table 1, and we will direct the reader to the specific positions when discussing the individual item groups.

Social Capital. In the design considerations for the SOCIAL CAPITAL instrument, Williams [59] points out that the BRIDGING subscale is intended to measure the effects of social interaction on tendencies toward *interacting with people outside the local area, trying new things, and being curious about differences in others and different parts of the world.* We selected the first four items of the BRIDGING subscale, which address specific facets of curiosity, asking about the effect of social interaction with other players in the game on the desire to explore new things and places and to learn about people unlike oneself (Table 1, items 1 to 4).

Harmonious Passion. The connection between game-related curiosity and the design considerations of the HARMONIOUS PASSION subscale from the OBSESSIVE/HARMONIOUS PASSION instrument was highlighted by Przybylski et al. [35], who stated that modern games are designed to offer players *meaningful choices that continuously balance their boundless curiosity against a finite pool of resources and talent.* We selected items three and five from the HARMONIOUS PASSION subscale, given their semantic relatedness to sensory and cognitive curiosity (Table 1, items 5 and 6).

BAS Fun-Seeking. Evaluating the BIS/BAS instrument, Carver et al. [7] report a statistically significant correlation between the BAS FUN-SEEKING subscale and the NOVELTY-SEEKING subscale of the Tridimensional Personality Questionnaire (TPQ) [8]. In this context, the construct of novelty-seeking, as measured by the TPQ, is defined as a tendency toward *exploration in pursuit of potential rewards* [7]. We decided to include only the first and last item of the four-item FUN-SEEKING subscale in our factor analysis because they are the only ones directly to address the concept of novelty-seeking (Table 1, items 7 and 8).

BrainHex Seeker. One of the seven BRAINHEX player archetypes is referred to as the SEEKER type. The authors characterize this player type by stating that the typical SEEKER is *curious about the game world and enjoys moments of wonder* [28]. A strong connection is established between the BRAINHEX SEEKER type on the one hand and Lazzaro's *Easy Fun* [23] and Malone's 'curiosity' [27] on the other hand. Lazzaro's *Easy Fun* refers to explorative play supported by aesthetic experiences and ambiguity or incompleteness of information. It could, therefore, be interpreted as 'cognitive curiosity', according to Loewenstein's classification [25]. Malone's concept of curiosity entails both sensory and cognitive components. We included items one and three from the BRAINHEX SEEKER subscale in our analysis, since they interrogate a tendency toward explorative behaviour in games (Table 1, items 9 and 10).

RQ1: Results

After selecting the ten curiosity-related survey items, we conducted a maximum likelihood EFA on the ten items with orthogonal rotation (varimax) to determine whether the ten items could be grouped into multiple independent factors. The Kaiser-Meyer-Olkin (KMO) measure verified the sampling adequacy for the analysis, KMO = .83 [18].

All KMO values for individual items were $> .7$, which is well above the acceptable minimum of .5. Bartlett's test of sphericity, $\chi^2(45) = 2,757$, $p < .001$, indicated that correlations between items were sufficiently large for EFA. We ran an initial principal component analysis (PCA) to obtain eigenvalues for each component in the data. Four components had eigenvalues above Kaiser's criterion of 1.0 and in combination explained 71% of the variance. Given the large sample size, and the convergence of the scree plot and Kaiser's criterion on four components, we retained these four factors (F1 to F4) in our final analysis.

Table 1 shows the factor loadings after rotation. The oblique rotations oblimin and promax yielded the same factor structure as had been extracted using the orthogonal varimax rotation, indicating a stable pattern of four largely independent factors. Factor F1 had a high reliability, Cronbach's $\alpha = .86$, whereas factors F2 and F3 had moderate reliabilities with α values of .67 and .61 respectively. Factor F4 had relatively low reliability, $\alpha = .50$. However, Kline acknowledges that, for psychological constructs like curiosity, Cronbach's α can, realistically, be expected to be below .7 because of the diversity of the constructs being measured [20]. That said, our findings with respect to F4 should be interpreted with caution.

The four factors, extracted in the EFA, precisely reflect the four different subscales from which we extracted the survey items: BRIDGING SOCIAL CAPITAL (F1), HARMONIOUS PASSION (F2), BRAINHEX SEEKER (F3), and BAS FUN-SEEKING (F4). This is evidence that the four item groups measure four different factors of curiosity. In reference to the semantic connections between the items in each of the curiosity subscales, we refer to the following factors (F1-F4) in the remainder of this paper: F1 as SOCIAL CURIOSITY, F2 as SENSORY/COGNITIVE CURIOSITY, F3 as EXPLORATIVE CURIOSITY, F4 as NOVELTY-SEEKING CURIOSITY. Figure 1 shows an overview of the four curiosity factors determined through factor analysis and some of the behaviours correlated with those factors.

RQ2: Correlating Self-Reports and Behavioural Data

Destiny tracks thousands of behavioural features about individual players. However, in any work attempting to correlate in-game behaviour with psychological factors, an initial challenge lies in isolating those behaviours with the most predictive potential [2, 48]. There are two approaches to such an analysis: either a 'bottom-up', exploratory approach where high numbers of variables are correlated with the self-report scores, or a 'top-down' approach where hypotheses are used to define which behaviours to work with. While the exploratory approach can result in over-featuring and false positives, the top-down approach is exclusive, ignoring behaviours not included in the hypotheses. Hence, in this study,

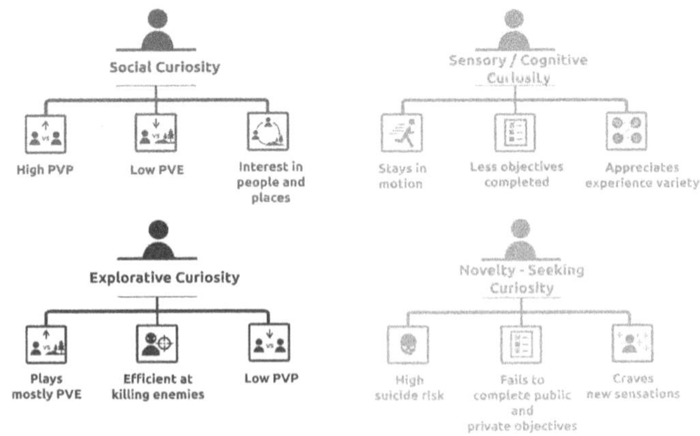

Figure 1. The four curiosity factors and their correlated game behaviours emerging from the Destiny dataset (reprinted from [43]).

a combined approach was used, where an initial set of behavioural metrics was selected based on related work and theory, and these metrics were then used to formulate a series of hypothesized correlations of curiosity factors. The correlations were then inspected in a range of related behaviours in Destiny that fit the curiosity factors. Furthermore, we included data from both gameplay options in *Destiny* (e.g., PvE and PvP play), and from across the spectrum of activities in the game, including rates of objective completion, performance, and exploration.

This process resulted in 42 variables that were used in the analysis process. Some of the metrics were specific to PvE (5) or PvP (15) game modes, though the majority were aggregates across these two modes (22), for example, the *Grimoire* score. For compactness, we summarize all behaviour metrics in the table in the supplementary material of this paper. The relevant table provides a short description of each metric, as well as the mean and standard deviation for each. To account for different play durations, certain variables were normalized as a function of time.

Data Cleaning and Filtering

To filter out survey participants who were answering without reading the questions, two validation questions were inserted into the survey asking participants to select specific answers. Discarding all incomplete entries and those with incorrect answers to the validation questions reduced the original set of 3,542 submissions to 1,745 valid survey responses.

Survey responses were deduplicated on a per-player-ID basis, retaining only the most recent entry for each set of duplicates. Subsequently, survey and behavioural data were matched based on player ID. Participants who had not entered a player ID at all or whose ID could not be matched to behavioural data were excluded. This cleaning procedure resulted in 1,267 unique entries, combining survey responses and behavioural metrics for each individual player.

In a final processing step, we removed outliers from the data set, following principles of Sifa et al. [49]. This was done by iterating over all 42 behaviour metrics and 60 survey items (i.e., 102 variables in total) and marking as outliers all values that were outside the 1st-99th percentile range. To limit the outlier removal process to a reasonable extent, variables which had more than 2.5% of the values in the aforementioned range were not included in the process. All entries containing at least one outlier value in any one of the 102 variables were discarded. This process resulted in 932 entries used for data analysis.

Correlations

After extracting the four self-report curiosity factors in the first step of our analysis, we examined the correlations between these and the 42 behavioural metrics.

Since all survey items were scored on Likert-type ordinal scales, we opted for Spearman's ρ as a non-parametric correlation coefficient. Given that each of the four extracted curiosity factors (F1-F4) was composed of survey items from just one instrument in each case, we adopted the scoring schemes from the corresponding 'parent' instrument. Consequently, no additional hybrid scoring scheme had to be created for our newly extracted curiosity subscales. Following the procedure described by Yee et al. [64], we used the analytic method developed by Sherman and Funder [46] to address the increased risk of experiment-wise error in large correlation tables. This technique answers whether the observed number of significant correlations in the data set is significantly higher than the number of correlations one would expect to find by chance.

RQ2: RESULTS

In the cross-correlation of behaviour metrics and self-report scores, we observed a total of 286 statistically significant correlations, ($p < .05$), where only 35 would be expected by chance [46]. Similarly, in the cross-correlation of all self-report scores, we observed 133 statistically significant correlations ($p < .05$), where only 7 would be expected by chance. The probabilities of these numbers of observed correlations were both $p < .001$, providing strong evidence that the observed correlations—as a whole—are not random.

Due to space limitations, we do not discuss every significant correlation in the following, but instead try to identify meaningful clusters of correlations and highlight particularly strong relationships. A complete listing of all correlations between curiosity factors and behaviour metrics is in Table 2.

	Curiosity			
Behaviour Metric	CSoc	CSens	CExp	CNovS
		Total		
Activities Entered–	.02–.02		**–.07***	–.03
Objectives Compl.	**–.07***	**–.15*****	.00	**–.17*****
Resurr. Performed	**.08***	**.10****	–.02	**.08***
Resurr. Received	**.11*****	**.10****	–.04	**.13*****
Orbs Dropped	.04	.02	.05–.01	
Orbs Gathered	**.14*****	.05–	.03	.01
Kills Deaths Ratio–	.03	.00	**.12*****	–.05
Kills Deaths Assists–	.03	.00	**.11*****	–.05
Kills–	.05–.01		**.11*****	**–.07***
Deaths	.01–.02		**–.10****	.02
Assists–	.02–.03		**–.08***	.01
Suicides	**.14*****	**.17*****	.03	**.14*****
Ability Kills–	.02	.00	**.09****	–.06
Precision Kills–	.03	.01	**.08***	–.05
Most Precision Kills	**.13*****	**.08****	**.06***	.06
Avg. Kill Distance	.01–	.04	.01–.01	
Max. Kill Distance	**.16*****	**.09****	.06	**.09****
Longest Kill Spree	**.09****	**.07***	**.13*****	.04
Avg. Lifespan–	.01	.02	**.10****	–.02
Longest Single Life	**.14*****	**.14*****	.02	**.10****
Grimoire Score	**.20*****	**.14*****	**.08***	.04
PvE Play Time Ratio	.00	.06	**.12*****	.02
		PvE		
Activities Cleared	**–.12*****	**–.09****	**–.07***	.02
Court of Oryx Attempts	**–.09****	.01	.03	**–.07***
Court of Oryx Compl.	**–.08***	.01	.03	**–.07***
Public Events Joined	**–.09****	–.01	.05	**–.12*****
Public Events Compl.	**–.09****	–.02	.05	**–.12*****
		PvP		
Activities Won	**.13*****	.05	.06	.03
Zones Captured	**–.10****	**–.12*****	.03	**–.10****
Zones Neutralized	**–.12*****	**–.12*****	–.04	**–.08***
Relics Captured	**.07***	.06–	.06	.04
Close Calls–	.01	.04–	.04–.01	
Defensive Kills–.03		**–.12*****	.01	**–.09****
Domination Kills–.03		**–.07***	.04–.03	
Offensive Kills	.00–	.05	.05–.02	
Avg. Score per Kill–	.06	.02	.03–.05	
Avg. Score per Life–	.02	.03	.03–.04	
Best Game Score	**.15*****	**.12*****	.04	.02
Combat Rating	.01	.00	.06	.01
Score	**.14*****	.05–	.02–.01	
Team Score	**.13*****	.03–	.03–.03	
Win Loss Ratio	**.08***	–.03	.03–.04	
Cronbach's α	.86	.67	.61	.50

Table 2. Correlations between behavioural metrics and self-report scores. Note: Spearman coefficients $p < .05$ are written in boldface. $^{*}p < .05$; $^{**}p < .01$; $^{***}p < .001$. Abbreviations: CSoc = SOCIAL CURIOSITY; CSens = SENSORY/COGNITIVE CURIOSITY; CExp = EXPLORATIVE CURIOSITY; CNovS = NOVELTY-SEEKING CURIOSITY (reprinted from [43]).

Correlations among self-report scores

As expected, curiosity factors were not perfectly correlated, but were strongly positively correlated with the respective subscales from which they were extracted: SOCIAL CURIOSITY (F1) was strongly correlated with BRIDGING SOCIAL CAPITAL, $\rho(930) = .91$, $p < .001$, SENSORY/COGNITIVE CURIOSITY (F2) was strongly linked to the HARMONIOUS PASSION scale, $\rho(930) = .87$, $p < .001$, EXPLORATIVE CURIOSITY (F3) showed a strong relationship with the BRAINHEX SEEKER type, $\rho(930) = .85$, $p < .001$, and NOVELTY-SEEKING CURIOSITY strongly related to the BAS FUN-SEEKING scale, $\rho(930) = .84$, $p < .001$.

We found strong positive correlations between SOCIAL CURIOSITY and BONDING SOCIAL CAPITAL, $\rho(930) = .48$, $p < .001$, HARMONIOUS PASSION, $\rho(930) = .46$, $p < .001$, and the BRAINHEX SOCIALIZER type, $\rho(930) = .42$, $p < .001$. NOVELTY-SEEKING CURIOSITY was positively linked to BAS REWARD RESPONSIVENESS, $\rho(930) = .42$, $p < .001$. Correlations of the same directionality and of similar strength were found for the corresponding 'base' scales, BRIDGING SOCIAL CAPITAL and BAS FUN-SEEKING. These correlations are displayed in Table 3.

	Curiosity				Social Capital		BAS		Passion		BrainHex						
	CSoc	CSens	CExp	CNovS	Bri	Bon	Rew	FunS	Obs	Har	Seek	Surv	Dare	Mast	Conq	Soc	Ach
Mean	13.2	10.2	1.4	6.3	34.9	28.2	17.4	12.0	14.1	24.1	1.9	1.0	2.0	2.0	1.9	0.3	1.7
St. Dev.	4.1	2.0	0.9	1.2	8.5	10.3	2.0	2.3	7.2	5.7	1.3	1.4	1.1	1.1	1.3	1.6	1.6
CBri	1.00																
CHar	**.43*****	1.00															
CSeek	**.24*****	**.26*****	1.00														
CNovS	**.25*****	**.25*****	**.19*****	1.00													
Bri	**.91*****	**.51*****	**.25*****	**.30*****	1.00												
Bon	**.48*****	**.31*****	**.10****	**.12*****	**.49*****	1.00											
Rew	**.23*****	**.32*****	**.16*****	**.42*****	**.31*****	**.19*****	1.00										
FunS	**.27*****	**.24*****	**.19*****	**.84*****	**.30*****	**.16*****	**.44*****	1.00									
Obs	**.23*****	**.33*****	**.11*****	**.10****	**.29*****	**.16*****	**.23*****	**.14*****	1.00								
Har	**.46*****	**.87*****	**.24*****	**.25*****	**.55*****	**.38*****	**.33*****	**.23*****	**.33*****	1.00							
Seek	**.28*****	**.29*****	**.85*****	**.22*****	**.28*****	**.11****	**.16*****	**.21*****	**.10****	**.28*****	1.00						
Surv	**.12*****	**.12*****	**.15*****	**.12*****	**.15*****	.02	**.17*****	**.12*****	**.08***	**.14*****	**.22*****	1.00					
Dare	**.16*****	**.21*****	**.30*****	**.27*****	**.20*****	**.12*****	**.23*****	**.27*****	**.17*****	**.21*****	**.31*****	**.20*****	1.00				
Mast	**.17*****	**.12*****	**.20*****	**.23*****	**.20*****	**.17*****	**.14*****	**.21*****	.05	**.13*****	**.19*****	**.13*****	**.25*****	1.00			
Conq	**.20*****	**.14*****	**.16*****	**.16*****	**.23*****	**.17*****	**.14*****	**.17*****	.00	**.14*****	**.15*****	**.10****	**.23*****	**.31*****	1.00		
Soc	**.42*****	**.30*****	**.26*****	**.23*****	**.47*****	**.28*****	**.18*****	**.25*****	**.11*****	**.31*****	**.32*****	**.19*****	**.26*****	**.21*****	**.23*****	1.00	
Ach	**.15*****	**.20*****	**.26*****	**.08***	**.20*****	**.13*****	**.17*****	**.09****	**.23*****	**.21*****	**.21*****	**.06***	**.19*****	**.19*****	**.11****	**.19*****	1.00
Cronbach's α	.86	.67	.61	.50	.90	.92	.69	.69	.86	.78	.60	.29	.19	.41	.35	.35	.58

Table 3. Descriptive statistics and cross-correlation of self-report scores. Spearman coefficients $p < .05$ are written in boldface. $^{*}p < .05$; $^{**}p < .01$; $^{***}p < .001$. Abbreviations: CSoc = SOCIAL CURIOSITY; CSens = SENSORY/COGNITIVE CURIOSITY; CExp = EXPLORATIVE CURIOSITY; CNovS = NOVELTY-SEEKING CURIOSITY; Bri = BRIDGING SOCIAL CAPITAL; Bon = BONDING SOCIAL CAPITAL; Rew = BAS REWARD RESPONSIVENESS; FunS = BAS FUN-SEEKING; Obs = OBSESSIVE PASSION; Har = HARMONIOUS PASSION; Seek = BRAINHEX SEEKER; Surv = BRAINHEX SURVIVOR; Dare = BRAINHEX DAREDEVIL; Mast = BRAINHEX MASTERMIND; Conq = BRAINHEX CONQUEROR; Soc = BRAINHEX SOCIALIZER; Ach = BRAINHEX ACHIEVER (reprinted from [43]).

Curiosity subscale scores and behaviour metrics correlations
In the following, we highlight selected clusters of correlations between the curiosity factor scores and behavioural metrics. Results are grouped by the curiosity sub-scale.

SOCIAL CURIOSITY was positively linked to *Grimoire* score (strongest correlation among all curiosity factors, $\rho(930) = .20$, $p < .001$), the number of resurrections performed, the number received, the number of orbs gathered, and the overall score, team score, best game score, and win-loss ratio in the group of PvP performance metrics. It was also the only curiosity factor that was positively linked to the number of relics captured in the PvP game mode. Negative correlations were observed between SOCIAL CURIOSITY and the number of objectives completed, public events joined and completed, including *Court of Oryx* events, and the number of zones captured and cleared.

SENSORY/COGNITIVE CURIOSITY also showed positive correlations with *Grimoire* score, the number of resurrections performed, the number received, the longest single life, and the best game score. Inverse relationships were found between SENSORY/COGNITIVE CURIOSITY and the number of objectives completed, activities completed, zones captured and neutralized, and 'defensive' and 'domination' kills in the category of PvP metrics.

EXPLORATIVE CURIOSITY was positively correlated with the relative time spent in the PvE game mode, performance metrics such as kills/deaths ratio, number of kills, longest kill spree, and average lifespan. It was the only curiosity factor that did not show any significant correlations with the number of resurrections performed, the number received, or any other of the PvP metrics. Negative correlations were observed between EXPLORATIVE CURIOSITY and the number of activities entered, activities completed, deaths and assists.

NOVELTY-SEEKING CURIOSITY showed positive correlations with the number of resurrections performed, the number received, suicides committed, maximum kill distance, and longest single life. Negative correlations were observed between NOVELTY-SEEKING CURIOSITY and the number of objectives completed, the number of kills, and also with the number of public events joined and completed, including *Court of Oryx* events, the number of zones captured and neutralized, and 'defensive' kills in the PvP category. We found no other significant correlations between this curiosity factor and any of the other behaviour metrics.

Predicting Self-Reports from Behaviour

RQ2 asks how well self-reports of 'curiosity' and associated player motivations and preferences can be inferred from observing player behaviour in the game world. Our main objective was thus not to describe the influence of individual predictor variables but instead to evaluate how well motivational profiles could be inferred from in-game behaviour. To this end, we adapted the procedure from Yee et al. [64] and conducted multiple regressions, one for each of the curiosity factors. For each factor, we selected the 20 strongest behavioural indicators, using these as predictor variables to infer the self-report score. We again split the report of our regression results into the four curiosity factors. For replicability, we classify effect sizes according to Yee et al. [64], who follow Cohen's notion that an R of .30 is a medium effect, while an R of .10 is a small effect [9].

Curiosity Factor	R	Adj. R^2	STE	F	p
Social	.32	.08	3.93	4.96	<.001
Sensory/Cognitive	.26	.05	2.54	3.30	<.001
Explorative	.24	.04	0.88	2.91	<.001
Novelty-Seeking	.26	.05	1.15	3.28	<.001

Table 4. Multiple regressions on the CURIOSITY factors (reprinted from [43]).

The results for the regression models of the four curiosity factors are shown in Table 4 (including R, adjusted R^2, residual standard errors (STE), F values, and p values). All of the multiple regressions yielded results deemed significant, suggesting that behaviour metrics can indeed be used to construct statistically significant models for inferring curiosity. The model for SOCIAL CURIOSITY had a 'medium' effect, while the other three models had 'close-to-medium' effects.

DISCUSSION

We matched self-reports of player motivation and preferences with a detailed set of behavioural observations for 932 individual players as identified by their player IDs (after outlier removal). Compared to previous work examining how in-game behaviour correlates with player personality or motivation as a whole, the present study contributes a building block toward a new operationalization of player curiosity (indeed, of various specified aspects of player curiosity) by constructing a scale based on reliable psychometric measures.

Expression of Curiosity in Games. The four factors emerging from our factor analysis reflect distinct aspects of game-related curiosity. SOCIAL CURIOSITY (F1) asks about the degree to which social interaction with other players in the game leads to curiosity about people unlike oneself, as well as new activities and places in the real world. In contrast, SENSORY/COGNITIVE CURIOSITY (F2) relates to the internal world of the game and assesses how strongly a player associates experience variety with game appreciation. EXPLORATIVE CURIOSITY (F3) measures individual differences in attitudes toward exploring the game world. Finally, NOVELTY-SEEKING CURIOSITY (F4) identifies the degree to which behavioural activation is induced by the motive of novelty-seeking.

Correlating our self-reported factors of curiosity many behaviour metrics, we identified meaningful behavioural correlates for many of these constructs (RQ2). The exploration of these results will be grouped by the curiosity subscale.

SOCIAL CURIOSITY was significantly positively correlated with measures logically expected to increase when playing with other players, such as resurrections performed, resurrections received, and orbs gathered. It was also the factor which displayed the most positive significant correlations with measures of performance in the PvP game mode, such as activities won, win/loss ratio, game score, highest game score, and team score. Conversely, negative correlations observed between social curiosity and every PvE behaviour metric, from number of objectives completed to public events completed indicated a lower interest in activities that take place in heavily single-player game modes. Furthermore, players high in social curiosity also displayed a propensity for having longer maximum kill distances, single life duration, and better *Grimoire* scores overall. This pattern of results may have been generated because an inclination toward social curiosity leads to more time spent in PvP and therefore more practice with a harder game mode. This in turn may lead to more opportunities to raise *Grimoire* scores in PvP. Designers of such shared-world games seeking to attract the patronage of players motivated by social curiosity should thus focus on enhancing opportunities for text and speech communication between players.

SENSORY/COGNITIVE CURIOSITY was significantly negatively correlated with many measures of performance in PvP, a game mode which frequently involves staying in one place to defend zones, while the opposition does not have far to move in their attempts to capture zones. These negatively correlated measures included zones captured, zones neutralized, and defensive kills. This may be because positive associations between variety and fun may lead these players to move around the map more during PvP games, leading to more 'best game scores' and correspondingly less time spent on geographically fixed objectives. Players motivated by sensory/cognitive curiosity also displayed significant positive correlation with longest single life, and significant negative correlation with objectives completed. These two results may be because variety-seeking distracts from objective completion, inadvertently leading to longer lives because activities are left before their relatively more difficult denouements. Game designers catering towards players motivated by this curiosity factor should consider game modes which favour fast movement and require less strategy, while at the same time providing regular opportunities for new activities.

EXPLORATIVE CURIOSITY was reflected in higher ratios of play time spent in the PvE game mode, which facilitates an exploration-driven playing style. Players driven by explorative curiosity also displayed significant positive correlations with measures of combat efficiency such as kills to deaths ratio, kills/deaths assists, longest kill spree, and total kills. This may be because a preference for exploring new areas may lead to more encounters with enemies and therefore more experience with, and chances to, kill enemies. Being the only curiosity factor not significantly correlated with PvP metrics or with the use of resurrections indicates a lower level of interaction with other players, potentially positioning players driven by explorative curiosity as opposite to those motivated by social curiosity. Designers seeking to cater to explorative players should design large game worlds which hide the content of unexplored areas as far as possible. Providing significant rewards for explorative behaviour in new areas would enhance the experience of these players. Lower interest in other players displayed by gamers driven by explorative curiosity could inform the design of privacy settings, allowing players more options in their interactions with other players.

NOVELTY-SEEKING CURIOSITY was significantly positively correlated with suicides and resurrections received which may mean that seeking novelty leads to an increased danger of accidental deaths, in turn necessitating a higher rate of resurrections. A belief that novelty is related to fun may also result in a player joining and completing fewer public events, as well as completing fewer objectives. This may be because seeking novelty distracts from the fixity of completing objectives. Games designed to cater to these players should concentrate on shorter and more varied objectives as well as environments which are highly differentiated and distinctive.

Player Motivations Related to Curiosity. We also showed that statistically significant regression models can be constructed for each of the four factors of self-reported curiosity we investigated, suggesting that nuanced profiles of curiosity and associated player motivations and preferences can be inferred merely from observing a player's behaviour in the *Destiny* game world (RQ2). This is particularly useful for the construction of implicit user models incorporating curiosity-related motivation. Being able to infer such profiles of curiosity and associated motivation implicitly from behaviour logs has direct relevance not only to games, but HCI research as a whole, taking into account the field's long-standing interest in personalization and interface customization [15, 31].

Design Implications. Our findings suggest ways in which designers of interactive systems can cater to different aspects of curiosity. One could match mission rewards to correlated game behaviours, matching the primary curiosity profile of the user. For example, by offering a player-interaction animation as a reward to a SOCIAL CURIOSITY player and PvE gear to EXPLORATIVE CURIOSITY players. Moreover, the insight that 'completionist' attitudes show a resemblance to curiosity—with a few decisive differences—in how they manifest in digital gaming behaviour, implies that design decisions should be made with care to ensure the system matches the intended user preferences. In addition to interface customization, the ability to infer motivational profiles (without the need for time-consuming self-reporting measures) lends itself to the enhancement of team matching and recommender systems by inserting these profiles into the calculation of similarity between users.

While we focus on game-related curiosity in this work, we note that being able to measure different aspects of curiosity through behaviour data would afford a wealth of applications to designers of interactive systems of many different types. Novelty-seeking on shopping websites, social curiosity on dating platforms and social network sites, or cognitive and sensory curiosity on music and movie streaming services, are a few examples of different curiosity types that could be leveraged in non-gaming contexts.

Limitations and Future Research Directions

There are three main limitations to our study. First, we only collected data from one game, which limits generalizability and applicability of our results to other games and genres. However, many multiplayer games do feature a combination of competitive and cooperative actions in a shared world with the possibility of various rewards upon completion.

Second, while the correlation coefficients between behaviour metrics and self-reports may appear low at $\rho = .34$, statistically significant yet low effect sizes are not uncommon in correlational studies with large sample sizes involving psychological factors. Our correlation coefficients are not strikingly different from those found in previous work—some published at CHI—with similar research parameters [62, 64].

Third, we are aware that players experience and express multiple types of curiosity in a single play session. The low correlation in some parts of this study may be due to this multiplicity. These natural cycles in player emotion and engagement may correlate with the different activities we describe. Investigating temporal patterns in how profiles of player motivation and personality evolve over time would be a worthy research goal for future work. Unfortunately, our dataset did not allow us to obtain further insights on temporal patterns because all metrics were cumulative values, aggregated over the entire lifetime of a user account.

Other future research directions may address the limitations of cross-sectional approaches, which do not permit conclusions about the causality of the observed relationships between variables. For example, based on our results, we do not know whether explorative behaviour leads to strong performance in the game, or if strong performance is an outcome more likely to coincide with curiosity-driven exploration.

CONCLUSION

Our findings provide important empirical evidence of the differing aspects of curiosity that motivate the video game play in our chosen game. Additionally, we would argue that the robustness of our methodology represents a solid foundation for assessing self-reported measures of curiosity, which in turn may facilitate yet more granular player experience research in the future. In particular, we were able to predict all four curiosity factors from behaviour metrics. This points the way to a promising opportunity for game designers seeking to improve team-matching and recommender systems. It also opens up potentially very fruitful avenues for research into player well-being. Perhaps most significantly, our findings suggest a breadth of applicability. Curiosity, after all, is not a factor just in the playing of cooperative video games. It could be justly regarded as one of the core motivations animating people's online experiences as a whole. The ability to measure it, as we suggest we have been able to do in this paper, differentially and in a more detailed fashion than achieved thus far, might be leveraged in a host of non-game settings, including commercial and social websites.

ACKNOWLEDGMENTS

We thank all the participants and Bungie, Inc. who generously provided us with the telemetry data needed to conduct this study. Thank you to our graphic designer Marim Ganaba for her illustrations. Part of this work was conducted in the Digital Creativity Labs (www.digitalcreativity.ac.uk), jointly funded by EPSRC/AHRC/InnovateUK under grant no EP/M023265/1. Lennart Nacke thanks NSERC Discovery (RGPIN-418622-2012), SWaGUR, SSHRC (895-2011-1014, IMMERSe), Mitacs (IT07255), and CFI (35819) for funding his research team.

REFERENCES

1. Anton Aluja, scar Garca, and Lus F. Garca. 2004. Replicability of the three, four and five Zuckerman's personality super-factors: exploratory and confirmatory factor analysis of the EPQ-RS, ZKPQ and NEO-PI-R. *Personality and Individual Differences* 36, 5 (4 2004), 1093–1108. DOI: http://dx.doi.org/10.1016/S0191-8869(03)00203-4
2. Christian Bauckhage, Anders Drachen, and Rafet Sifa. 2015. Clustering Game Behavior Data. *IEEE Transactions on Computational Intelligence and AI in Games* 7, 3 (9 2015), 266–278. DOI: http://dx.doi.org/10.1109/TCIAIG.2014.2376982
3. D. E. Berlyne. 1954. A Theory of Human Curiosity. *British Journal of Psychology. General Section* 45, 3 (8 1954), 180–191. DOI: http://dx.doi.org/10.1111/j.2044-8295.1954.tb01243.x
4. D. E. Berlyne and J. Slater. 1957. Perceptual curiosity, exploratory behavior, and maze learning. *Journal of Comparative and Physiological Psychology* 50, 3 (1957), 228–232. DOI: http://dx.doi.org/10.1037/h0046603
5. Marc Busch, Elke Mattheiss, Rita Orji, Peter Fröhlich, Michael Lankes, and Manfred Tscheligi. 2016. Player Type Models: Towards Empirical Validation. In *Proceedings of the 2016 CHI Conference Extended Abstracts on Human Factors in Computing Systems - CHI EA '16*. ACM Press, New York, New York, USA, 1835–1841. DOI: http://dx.doi.org/10.1145/2851581.2892399
6. Alessandro Canossa, Josep B. Martinez, and Julian Togelius. 2013. Give me a reason to dig: Minecraft and psychology of motivation. In *2013 IEEE Conference on Computational Intelligence in Games (CIG)*. IEEE, 1–8. DOI: http://dx.doi.org/10.1109/CIG.2013.6633612
7. Charles S. Carver and Teri L. White. 1994. Behavioral inhibition, behavioral activation, and affective responses to impending reward and punishment: The BIS/BAS Scales. *Journal of Personality and Social Psychology* 67, 2 (1994), 319–333. DOI: http://dx.doi.org/10.1037/0022-3514.67.2.319
8. C. Robert Cloninger. 1987. A systematic method for clinical description and classification of personality variants. A proposal. *Archives of general psychiatry* 44, 6 (6 1987), 573–88. http://www.ncbi.nlm.nih.gov/pubmed/3579504
9. John M. Cohen. 1988. *Statistical Power Analysis for the Behavioral Sciences* (2 ed.). Routledge, London. https://books.google.ca/books?id=2v9zDAsLvA0C
10. Emily Collins and Jonathan Freeman. 2013. Do problematic and non-problematic video game players differ in extraversion, trait empathy, social capital and prosocial tendencies? *Computers in Human Behavior* 29, 5 (9 2013), 1933–1940. DOI: http://dx.doi.org/10.1016/j.chb.2013.03.002
11. Greg Costikyan. 2013. *Uncertainty in Games*. The MIT Press, Cambridge, MA.
12. Benjamin Cowley and Darryl Charles. 2016. Behavlets: a method for practical player modelling using psychology-based player traits and domain specific features. *User Modeling and User-Adapted Interaction* 26, 2-3 (6 2016), 257–306. DOI: http://dx.doi.org/10.1007/s11257-016-9170-1
13. Laura J. Dancer and Stephen A. Woods. 2006. Higher-order factor structures and intercorrelations of the 16PF5 and FIRO-B: Information exchange article. *International Journal of Selection and Assessment* 14, 4 (2006), 385–391. DOI: http://dx.doi.org/10.1111/j.1468-2389.2006.00360.x
14. John M. Digman. 1990. Personality Structure: Emergence of the Five-Factor Model. *Annual Review of Psychology* 41, 1 (1 1990), 417–440. DOI: http://dx.doi.org/10.1146/annurev.ps.41.020190.002221
15. Nicolas Ducheneaut, Ming-Hui Wen, Nicholas Yee, and Greg Wadley. 2009. Body and mind: a study of avatar personalization in three virtual worlds. In *Proceedings of the 2009 SIGCHI Conference on Human Factors in Computing Systems - CHI '09*. ACM Press, New York, New York, USA, 1151. DOI: http://dx.doi.org/10.1145/1518701.1518877
16. Nicolas Ducheneaut, Nicholas Yee, Eric Nickell, and Robert J. Moore. 2006. "Alone together?" Exploring the Social Dynamics of Massively Multiplayer Online Games. In *Proceedings of the 2006 SIGCHI Conference on Human Factors in Computing Systems - CHI '06*. ACM Press, New York, New York, USA, 407. DOI: http://dx.doi.org/10.1145/1124772.1124834
17. Magy Seif El-nasr, Anders Drachen, and Alessandro Canossa. 2013. *Game Analytics*. Springer London, London. DOI: http://dx.doi.org/10.1007/978-1-4471-4769-5
18. Henry F. Kaiser. 1974. An index of factorial simplicity. *Psychometrika* 39, 1 (3 1974), 31–36. DOI: http://dx.doi.org/10.1007/BF02291575
19. Jun H. Kim, Daniel V. Gunn, Eric Schuh, Bruce Phillips, Randy J. Pagulayan, and Dennis Wixon. 2008. Tracking real-time user experience (TRUE): a comprehensive instrumentation solution for complex systems. In *Proceedings of the 2008 SIGCHI Conference on Human Factors in Computing systems - CHI '08*. ACM Press, New York, New York, USA, 443. DOI: http://dx.doi.org/10.1145/1357054.1357126
20. Paul Kline. 1999. *The handbook of psychological testing* (2 ed.). Routledge, London.
21. Michael Lankes, Wolfgang Hochleitner, Daniel Rammer, Marc Busch, Elke Mattheiss, and Manfred Tscheligi. 2015. From Classes to Mechanics: Player Type Driven Persuasive Game Development. In *Proceedings of the 2015 Annual Symposium on Computer-Human*

Interaction in Play - CHI PLAY '15. ACM Press, New York, New York, USA, 595–600. DOI: http://dx.doi.org/10.1145/2793107.2810316

22. Edith Law, Ming Yin, Joslin Goh, Kevin Chen, Michael A. Terry, and Krzysztof Z. Gajos. 2016. Curiosity Killed the Cat, but Makes Crowdwork Better. In *Proceedings of the 2016 SIGCHI Conference on Human Factors in Computing Systems - CHI '16*. ACM Press, New York, New York, USA, 4098–4110. DOI: http://dx.doi.org/10.1145/2858036.2858144
23. Nicole Lazzaro. 2008. The four fun keys. *Game Usability: Advancing the Player Experience* (2008), 315–344.
24. Christopher Lee, Peta Wyeth, Daniel Johnson, and Joshua Hall. 2015. Flow during Individual and Co-operative Gameplay. In *Proceedings of the 2015 SIGCHI Annual Symposium on Computer-Human Interaction in Play - CHI PLAY '15*. ACM Press, New York, New York, USA, 103–107. DOI: http://dx.doi.org/10.1145/2793107.2793142
25. George Loewenstein. 1994. The psychology of curiosity: A review and reinterpretation. *Psychological Bulletin* 116, 1 (1994), 75–98. DOI: http://dx.doi.org/10.1037/0033-2909.116.1.75
26. Thomas W. Malone. 1980. What makes things fun to learn? heuristics for designing instructional computer games. In *Proceedings of the 1980 ACM SIGSMALL Symposium and the first SIGPC Symposium on Small Systems - SIGSMALL '80*. ACM Press, New York, New York, USA, 162–169. DOI: http://dx.doi.org/10.1145/800088.802839
27. Thomas W. Malone. 1982. Heuristics for designing enjoyable user interfaces: Lessons from computer games. In *Proceedings of the 1982 SIGCHI Conference on Human Factors in Computing Systems - CHI '82*. ACM Press, New York, New York, USA, 63–68. DOI: http://dx.doi.org/10.1145/800049.801756
28. Lennart E. Nacke, Chris Bateman, and Regan L. Mandryk. 2014a. BrainHex: A neurobiological gamer typology survey. *Entertainment Computing* 5, 1 (1 2014), 55–62. DOI: http://dx.doi.org/10.1016/j.entcom.2013.06.002
29. Lennart E. Nacke, Matthias Klauser, and Paul Prescod. 2014b. Social Player Analytics in a Facebook Health Game. In *Proceedings of HCI Korea (HCIK '15)*. Hanbit Media, Inc., South Korea, 180–187. http://dl.acm.org/citation.cfm?id=2729485.2729512
30. Lennart E. Nacke and Craig Lindley. 2008. Boredom, Immersion, Flow - A Pilot Study Investigating Player Experience. In *IADIS Gaming 2008: Design for Engaging Experience and Social Interaction*, Eleonore T Thij (Ed.). IADIS, IADIS Press, 103–107.
31. Oded Nov and Ofer Arazy. 2013. Personality-targeted design: theory, experimental procedure, and preliminary results. In *Proceedings of the 2013 conference on Computer supported cooperative work - CSCW '13*. ACM Press, New York, New York, USA, 977. DOI: http://dx.doi.org/10.1145/2441776.2441887
32. Rita Orji, Regan L. Mandryk, Julita Vassileva, and Kathrin M. Gerling. 2013. Tailoring persuasive health games to gamer type. In *Proceedings of the 2013 SIGCHI Conference on Human Factors in Computing Systems - CHI '13*. ACM Press, New York, New York, USA, 2467. DOI: http://dx.doi.org/10.1145/2470654.2481341
33. Rita Orji, Julita Vassileva, and Regan L. Mandryk. 2014. Modeling the efficacy of persuasive strategies for different gamer types in serious games for health. *User Modeling and User-Adapted Interaction* 24, 5 (12 2014), 453–498. DOI: http://dx.doi.org/10.1007/s11257-014-9149-8
34. Emmanuel M. Pothos, Gavin Perry, Philip J. Corr, Mervin R. Matthew, and Jerome R. Busemeyer. 2011. Understanding cooperation in the Prisoners Dilemma game. *Personality and Individual Differences* 51, 3 (8 2011), 210–215. DOI: http://dx.doi.org/10.1016/j.paid.2010.05.002
35. Andrew K. Przybylski, C. Scott Rigby, and Richard M. Ryan. 2010. A motivational model of video game engagement. *Review of General Psychology* 14, 2 (2010), 154–166. DOI: http://dx.doi.org/10.1037/a0019440
36. Andrew K. Przybylski, Netta Weinstein, Richard M. Ryan, and C. Scott Rigby. 2009. Having to versus Wanting to Play: Background and Consequences of Harmonious versus Obsessive Engagement in Video Games. *CyberPsychology & Behavior* 12, 5 (10 2009), 485–492. DOI: http://dx.doi.org/10.1089/cpb.2009.0083
37. Catherine F. Ratelle, Robert J. Vallerand, Genevive A. Mageau, Franois L. Rousseau, and Pierre Provencher. 2004. When Passion Leads to Problematic Outcomes: A Look at Gambling. *Journal of Gambling Studies* 20, 2 (1 2004), 105–119. DOI: http://dx.doi.org/10.1023/B:JOGS.0000022304.96042.e6
38. Niklas Ravaja. 2009. The Psychophysiology of Digital Gaming: The Effect of a Non Co-Located Opponent. *Media Psychology* 12, 3 (8 2009), 268–294. DOI: http://dx.doi.org/10.1080/15213260903052240
39. Niklas Ravaja, Mikko Salminen, Jussi Holopainen, Timo Saari, Jari Laarni, and Aki Jrvinen. 2004. Emotional response patterns and sense of presence during video games. In *Proceedings of the third Nordic conference on Human-computer interaction - NordiCHI '04*. ACM Press, New York, New York, USA, 339–347. DOI: http://dx.doi.org/10.1145/1028014.1028068
40. Thomas Reio Jr., Joseph Petrosko, Albert Wiswell, and Juthamas Thongsukmag. 2006. The Measurement and Conceptualization of Curiosity. *The Journal of Genetic Psychology* 167, 2 (6 2006), 117–135. DOI: http://dx.doi.org/10.3200/GNTP.167.2.117-135

41. Steven Reiss and Susan M. Havercamp. 1998. Toward a comprehensive assessment of fundamental motivation: Factor structure of the Reiss Profiles. *Psychological Assessment* 10, 2 (1998), 97–106. DOI: http://dx.doi.org/10.1037/1040-3590.10.2.97

42. Britta Renner. 2006. Curiosity About People: The Development of a Social Curiosity Measure in Adults. *Journal of Personality Assessment* 87, 3 (10 2006), 305–316. DOI: http://dx.doi.org/10.1207/s15327752jpa8703{_}11

43. Mike Schaekermann. 2017. Resources Licensed under Creative Commons CC BY 4.0. (2017). https://cs.uwaterloo.ca/~mschaeke/cc/

44. Frederick F. Schmitt and Reza Lahroodi. 2008. The Epistemic Value of Curiosity. *Educational Theory* 58, 2 (5 2008), 125–148. DOI: http://dx.doi.org/10.1111/j.1741-5446.2008.00281.x

45. Carolina I. Sedano, Teemu H. Laine, Mikko Vinni, and Erkki Sutinen. 2007. Where is the answer?: the importance of curiosity in pervasive mobile games. In *Proceedings of the 2007 Conference on Future Play - Future Play '07*. ACM Press, New York, New York, USA, 46. DOI: http://dx.doi.org/10.1145/1328202.1328211

46. Ryne A. Sherman and David C. Funder. 2009. Evaluating correlations in studies of personality and behavior: Beyond the number of significant findings to be expected by chance. *Journal of Research in Personality* 43, 6 (12 2009), 1053–1063. DOI: http://dx.doi.org/10.1016/j.jrp.2009.05.010

47. Valerie J Shute. 2011. Stealth assessment in computer-based games to support learning. *Computer games and instruction* 55, 2 (2011), 503–524.

48. Rafet Sifa, Christian Bauckhage, and Anders Drachen. 2014. The Playtime Principle: Large-scale cross-games interest modeling. In *2014 IEEE Conference on Computational Intelligence and Games (CIG)*. IEEE, Dortmund, Germany, 1–8. DOI: http://dx.doi.org/10.1109/CIG.2014.6932906

49. Rafet Sifa, Anders Drachen, Christian Bauckhage, Christian Thurau, and Alessandro Canossa. 2013. Behavior evolution in Tomb Raider Underworld. In *2013 IEEE Conference on Computational Intelligence in Games (CIG)*. IEEE, Toronto, Canada, 1–8. DOI: http://dx.doi.org/10.1109/CIG.2013.6633637

50. Pieter Spronck, Iris Balemans, and Giel van Lankveld. 2012. Player Profiling with Fallout 3. *Proceedings, The Eighth AAAI Conference on Artificial Intelligence and Interactive Digital Entertainment* (2012), 179–184.

51. Alexandra To, Safinah Ali, Geoff Kaufman, and Jessica Hammer. 2016. Integrating Curiosity and Uncertainty in Game Design. In *Proceedings of 1st International Joint Conference of DiGRA and FDG*. Dundee, Scotland, 1–16. http://ato1120.github.io/To_CuriosityAndUncertainty.pdf

52. Sabine Trepte, Leonard Reinecke, and Keno Juechems. 2012. The social side of gaming: How playing online computer games creates online and offline social support. *Computers in Human Behavior* 28, 3 (5 2012), 832–839. DOI: http://dx.doi.org/10.1016/j.chb.2011.12.003

53. Robert J. Vallerand, Cline Blanchard, Genevive A. Mageau, Richard Koestner, Catherine Ratelle, Maude Léonard, Marylne Gagné, and Jose Marsolais. 2003. Les passions de l'âme: On obsessive and harmonious passion. *Journal of Personality and Social Psychology* 85, 4 (2003), 756–767. DOI: http://dx.doi.org/10.1037/0022-3514.85.4.756

54. Giel van Lankveld, Sonny Schreurs, Pieter Spronck, and Jaap van den Herik. 2010. Extraversion in games. In *International Conference on Computers and Games*. Springer, 263–275.

55. Giel van Lankveld, Pieter Spronck, Jaap van den Herik, and Arnoud Arntz. 2011. Games as personality profiling tools. In *2011 IEEE Conference on Computational Intelligence and Games (CIG'11)*. IEEE, 197–202. DOI: http://dx.doi.org/10.1109/CIG.2011.6032007

56. Kellie Vella, Daniel Johnson, and Leanne Hides. 2015. Playing Alone, Playing With Others: Differences in Player Experience and Indicators of Wellbeing. In *Proceedings of the 2015 SIGCHI Annual Symposium on Computer-Human Interaction in Play - CHI PLAY '15*. ACM Press, New York, New York, USA, 3–12. DOI: http://dx.doi.org/10.1145/2793107.2793118

57. Jaclyn Wainer, Laura Dabbish, and Robert Kraut. 2011. Should I open this email?: inbox-level cues, curiosity and attention to email. In *Proceedings of the 2011 SIGCHI Conference on Human Factors in Computing Systems - CHI '11*. ACM Press, New York, New York, USA, 3439. DOI: http://dx.doi.org/10.1145/1978942.1979456

58. Chih-Chien Wang and Yi-Shiu Chu. 2007. Harmonious Passion and Obsessive Passion in Playing Online Games. *Social Behavior and Personality: an international journal* 35, 7 (1 2007), 997–1006. DOI: http://dx.doi.org/10.2224/sbp.2007.35.7.997

59. Dmitri Williams. 2006. On and Off the 'Net: Scales for Social Capital in an Online Era. *Journal of Computer-Mediated Communication* 11, 2 (1 2006), 593–628. DOI: http://dx.doi.org/10.1111/j.1083-6101.2006.00029.x

60. Aaron Wilson, Margaret Burnett, Laura Beckwith, Orion Granatir, Ledah Casburn, Curtis Cook, Mike Durham, and Gregg Rothermel. 2003. Harnessing curiosity to increase correctness in end-user programming. In *Proceedings of the 2013 SIGCHI Conference on Human Factors in Computing Systems - CHI '03*. ACM Press, New York, New York, USA, 305. DOI: http://dx.doi.org/10.1145/642611.642665

61. Stephen A. Woods and Claire Hardy. 2012. The higher-order factor structures of five personality inventories. *Personality and Individual Differences* 52, 4 (3 2012), 552–558. DOI: http://dx.doi.org/10.1016/j.paid.2011.11.001

62. Tal Yarkoni. 2010. Personality in 100,000 Words: A large-scale analysis of personality and word use among bloggers. *Journal of Research in Personality* 44, 3 (6 2010), 363–373. DOI: http://dx.doi.org/10.1016/j.jrp.2010.04.001

63. Nick Yee, Nicolas Ducheneaut, and Les Nelson. 2012. Online gaming motivations scale: development and validation. In *Proceedings of the 2012 SIGCHI Conference on Human Factors in Computing Systems - CHI '12*. ACM Press, New York, New York, USA, 2803. DOI: http://dx.doi.org/10.1145/2207676.2208681

64. Nick Yee, Nicolas Ducheneaut, Les Nelson, and Peter Likarish. 2011. Introverted elves & conscientious gnomes: the expression of personality in world of warcraft. In *Proceedings of the 2011 SIGCHI Conference on Human Factors in Computing Systems - CHI '11*. ACM Press, New York, New York, USA, 753. DOI: http://dx.doi.org/10.1145/1978942.1979052

65. Zhi-Jin Zhong. 2011. The effects of collective MMORPG (Massively Multiplayer Online Role-Playing Games) play on gamers online and offline social capital. *Computers in Human Behavior* 27, 6 (11 2011), 2352–2363. DOI: http://dx.doi.org/10.1016/j.chb.2011.07.014

LUDOGRAPHY

1. 22Cans. 2012. Curiosity What's Inside the Cube? Game [iOS, Android]. (11 2012).
2. BethesdaGameStudios. 2008. Fallout 3. Game [PC, PS3, Xbox 360]. (10 2008).
3. BioWare. 2002. Neverwinter Nights. Game [PC]. (6 2002).
4. BlizzardEntertainment. 2004. World of Warcraft. Game [PC]. (11 2004).
5. Bungie. 2014. Destiny. Game [PS3, PS4, Xbox 360, Xbox One]. (9 2014).
6. Mojang. 2011. Minecraft. Game [PC, Smartphone, PS3, PS4, PS Vita, Xbox 360, Xbox One, Wii U]. (11 2011).

Age-Based Preferences and Player Experience: A Crowdsourced Cross-sectional Study

Max V. Birk[1], Maximillian A. Friehs[2], & Regan L. Mandryk[1]
[1]University of Saskatchewan
Saskatoon, SK, Canada
{firstname.lastname}@usask.ca
[2]University of Trier
Trier, Germany
s1mafrie@uni-trier.de

ABSTRACT
We tend to treat the 18-55 demographic of gamers as a monolithic and homogenous group, even though the older ones witnessed the entire rise of the videogame and the younger ones were born into a world with MMORPGs. We present a cross-sectional study of 2747 crowdsourced players aged 18-55 and conduct linear regressions of age on several measures of play habits, preferences, and play experiences. Our results show a consistent pattern that with increasing age, preferences, play motive, play style, identification as a gamer, and player experience shift away from a focus on performance and towards a focus on completion, choice, and enjoyment. We situate our results in developmental psychology, which suggests that as we age, we exhibit an increased focus on goals that prioritize emotional regulation and relationships and less on the acquisitions of new skills. Our work provides new insights into the large and core demographic of gamers.

Author Keywords
Age; player experience, motivations; player styles.

ACM Classification Keywords
K.8.0 [Personal Computing]: General - Games.

INTRODUCTION
When asked to imagine a 'gamer', stereotypes suggest that we should visualize a teenage nerd playing alone; however, market research suggests otherwise. The 2016 Essential Facts report of the US-based Entertainment Software Association (ESA) states the average age of game players is 35; furthermore, only 27% of game players are under 18 years old; 29% are 18-35, 18% are 36-49, and 26% are 50 or older [22]. There are developers who design for the particular needs of the very young demographic (e.g., Sesame Street Games; Sesame Workshop) and there are also games targeted at the growing demographic of older adult gamers (e.g., Bingo Blingo; joju games)). A recent report by the Nielsen Norman Group notes that mobile game penetration has been strongest among these same young Millennials and older consumers [65]. Similarly, there are many researchers who study play motivations and experiences specifically of children (e.g., [23]) or older adults (e.g., [27,61]), but developers, researchers and marketing experts tend to treat the range in between as a monolithic and homogenous group [12,21,29,31,52].

This is true in other media as well; for example, Nielsen ratings – the primary ratings system for television– use 18-49 year olds as a target demographic because although they watch less television overall, they drive trends in purchasing [47]. In some ways, 18-55 year-olds can be considered as a homogenous group – they are out of public school and not yet into retirement; they are classified as adults and have all of the privileges (e.g., driving, smoking, drinking alcohol) and responsibilities (e.g., voting, being subject to incarceration) that comes with adulthood; and they are into a period of child rearing and child bearing if they choose that path.

Although there is homogeneity in 18-55 year-olds, there are also differences. In the year that current 55 year-olds were born (1962), the Cuban Missile Crisis took place, the Beatles released their first single, and the FCC first authorized the television remote control. In contrast, in the year that current 18-year olds were born (1999), the impeachment trial and acquittal of Bill Clinton took place, Eminem released his first major album, and the TV series *Survivor* aired before most of them saw their first birthdays. In terms of digital games, 1962 was the year that *Spacewar!* was developed by Steve Russell, and the world was still 15 years away from the North America Release of the Atari. In contrast, 1999 was the year that Everquest (a classic Massively-Multiplayer Online Role-Playing Game: MMORPG) was released, not to mention the *eighth* installment in the Final Fantasy series.

There are clearly vast differences in the historical, cultural, technological, and game experiences of an 18-55 year-old demographic, yet we tend to treat them as a single group in games user research. Researchers have little understanding of how age differentiates the play experiences of this core demographic that comprises the largest proportion of current game players. Without an understanding of the habits, preferences, and experiences of 18-55 year olds, researchers cannot understand how gamers transition from young adults into older players, designers cannot effectively optimize game design for a portion of this group (e.g., new parents), and we risk making false assumptions based on misguided biases.

CHI PLAY '17, October 15–18, 2017, Amsterdam, Netherlands

ACM ISBN 978-1-4503-4898-0/17/10…$15.00
https://doi.org/10.1145/3116595.3116608

To better situate our understanding of play experience across this 18-55 year-old demographic, we conducted an analysis using 11 different studies with data from 3041 participants. Each study had a similar structure, recruitment methods, and context. More importantly, in each study, the same player demographic variables and the same self-reported player experience measures were collected.

Our results show a clear trend away from performance-related preferences and experiences toward completion-related ones with increasing age. As age increases, there is:

- An increasing preference for casual and puzzle games and a declining preference for performance-related games.
- A decline in performance as a motive to play.
- An increase in completion-focused player styles like achiever, mastermind, and seeker, and a decline in performance-focused player styles like conqueror, survivor, and daredevil.
- A decline in the identification as a 'gamer'.
- An increase in enjoyment, effort, and tension and greater satisfaction of autonomy, relatedness, and presence.
- A decline in competence (which normally co-varies with other experiential factors), which is partially explained by an accompanying decline in experienced intuitive control.

We further unpack this effect of declining competence, showing that its importance in predicting enjoyment, relative to autonomy and relatedness, declines significantly with age, and also that it takes less experienced competence to translate into similar enjoyment with increasing age.

The pattern that emerges suggests a shift of individual preferences over age away from performance and toward completion and an appreciation of choice and experience. Although most of the known results in games research are generated using data from this core demographic of 18-55 year-old gamers, treating this monolithic group as homogenous – simply because they all live in the range between children and older adults – is naïve. Over this age range, our cognitive and emotional abilities change, and we exhibit an increased focus on goals that prioritize emotional stability and relationships and less on the acquisitions of new skills. In this paper, we characterize the effects of these changes on what drives us to play games, and how we experience them.

RELATED WORK

To understand how play experience might be affected by age, we provide a background on theories and measures of player experience and on player typologies. We describe the relationship between age and motivation, and present findings from research on video games in different age groups.

Play Experience and Motivation

Play experience has been investigated using different theories and techniques, e.g., flow [63], engagement [15], and physiological measures [38]. The shared goal between theories and practical approaches is to understand what a player experiences under varying circumstances.

Self-Determination Theory (SDT) [54], a general theory of motivation, has been applied to games [53] and has shown a theoretically-grounded connection between in-game experiences and the resulting motivation to play [53]. SDT proposes that players are intrinsically motivated to play when three needs are satisfied: Competence – experiencing mastery over a challenge; Autonomy – engaging in a game under one's own volition; and Relatedness – experiencing meaningful relations to other players or in-game objects. The satisfaction of those three needs is commonly measured using the Player Experience of Need Satisfaction scale (PENS) [53]. SDT has been used to investigate the role of need satisfaction in different game styles, e.g., exergames [46], or serious games [67]. Other research has investigated how need satisfaction derived from different game-elements – e.g., avatar customization [12], game narratives [7], or game difficulty [4] – contributes to the intrinsic enjoyment of playing.

Enjoying a task because of the task itself and not because of a separable outcome, is the definition of intrinsic motivation [51]. Intrinsic motivation is crucial to games because it is predictive of the time invested in playing [12], the enjoyment experienced as a result of playing [53], and the effort people are willing to invest into a game [53]. Intrinsic motivation has also been shown to be predictive of purchase intentions [32], making the concept relevant for the games industry.

Individual Differences and Play Preferences

To understand and predict how players feel about a game, research has considered differences in play experience itself [35], e.g., the difference between playing a world builder and playing a first-person shooter (FPS), and individual differences [44,69], e.g., whether a player enjoys competing against another player or prefers to explore a world.

Player typologies provide a categorization of differences between a player's play style, and their genre preferences. For example, Bartle's [8] player typology suggests that players can be divided into achievers, killers, explorers, and socializers. The BrainHex model [44] integrates and extends Bartle's model by proposing seven different player types: *Conquerors* are challenge focused; *Daredevils* seek thrill and risk; *Survivors* enjoy escape and terrifying scenes. *Masterminds* enjoy strategizing and puzzles; *Seekers* are discovery and exploration focused; *Achievers* aim for completion; and *Socializers* thrive most during social-interaction.

Taking a data driven approach, Yee [68] identified achievement, immersion, and social, as three components of player motivation in World of Warcraft (Blizzard, 2004). The model was recently extended to have a more nuanced and generalizable categorization of players by revamping the old categories and adding the new categories of action, mastery, and creativity to the existing model [69].

De Grove et al. [31] suggest a theory-driven approach building on Social Cognitive Theory (SCT) [6]. SCT states that behaviour is motived by processing the implication of an action, e.g., evaluating the benefits of playing games. Based on SCT, three types of expected outcomes when playing are suggested: game-internal, i.e., *performance, agency, narrative, sociability,* game-external, i.e., *pastime, escapism*, and normative outcomes, i.e., *moral self-reflection*. The authors also include *habit* to account for less conscious behaviour.

What we like to play and how we like to play contribute to the quality of our play experiences. But beyond individual differences of play style, research suggests that play experience itself differs based on our age.

Theories of Age and Motivation

Because of the duration of longitudinal studies – i.e., studies that observe the same pool of people over time – understanding how age affects motivation and experience is a difficult topic to study. This is compounded in the domain of digital experience by the additional difficulty that events in different decades affect the beliefs and experiences of the people who live through them, e.g., people who were born pre-mobile phones have a unique relationship to communication technologies [26]. Therefore, researchers rely on theoretical models, often evaluated using cross-sectional studies – i.e., studies that look at different slices of a larger demographic group at a single point in time – to understand age-related differences in experience.

For example, one theoretical model, Socio-emotional Selectivity theory (SES) [16], explains why people tend to focus on emotional regulation goals and relatedness as they age, rather than the acquisition of a new skill. SES Theory suggests two distinct motives: those related to the regulation of emotions and those related to the acquisition of knowledge, and that our motive for knowledge declines and our motive for emotional stability increases as we age.

In line with SES, Self-Determination Theory [50] shows that older adults derive more pleasure from intrinsically-motivating work compared to younger adults, whereas younger adults are more prone to be motivated by extrinsically-motivating stimuli, such as rewards [36,37,66]. Over time, people start to gain intrinsic motivation by integrating extrinsically-motivating stimuli into their self-view, which implies that older people will find a task that was once only extrinsically motivating to be intrinsically motivating and enjoyable.

In sum, how motivated we are to engage in an activity and how we experience that activity, changes over the lifespan.

Digital Game Experience and Age

Historic events, present technology, or the zeitgeist of a period in time affect preferences and experiences [25,49]. Therefore, to understand play experience of different age groups, e.g., children [23], or older adults [27], we need to understand the context in which they grew up.

Ferguson and Olson [23], for example, investigated the motivations for children's game play and found three distinct categories: fun/challenge, social/relatedness and catharsis/autonomy, corresponding to the three basic needs described in Self-Determination Theory [54]. However, these motivations can change with age: fantasy motivations are particularly strong in younger children [28], whereas competition and challenge-related motives are stronger in older children and adolescents [62]. In the context of games, Scharkow et al. [57] showed that young people generally sought more gratification from playing; this is in line with the aforementioned results that younger adults are more motivated by external stimuli, such as rewards [36,37,66].

There is a large body of work on the experience of older adults with digital technologies. For example, older adults tend to underestimate their knowledge and competence with computers [40] and report less self-efficacy and media competence in general [1,55]. In terms of performance in computer-related tasks, senior adults show declines due to slower processing speeds and an over-all decline in cognitive functions [19,64]. However, these declines can be alleviated by experience with technology, as experience can either preserve the original skill or can help to develop compensatory skills. Selection-Optimization-Compensation (SOC) theory [5] describes the successful aging process and how aging adults can minimize their losses while maximizing their gains. In line with SOC, video games have been shown to delay physical [27] and cognitive decline [2] for seniors.

In addition to performance differences, there are differences in genre preference with age: older adults tend to prefer more casual games [58]. De Shutter and Vanden Abeele [59] showed that seniors use games to interact with their loved ones; similarly, Quandt et al. [48] used interviews among seniors to show that they have a strong interest in the social aspect of gaming. These results are in line with socio-emotional theory, which states that relatedness and emotional contact become more important as aging progresses [16].

Taken together, these theories demonstrate that digital game researchers should consideration of age-related differences. However, the focus of digital game studies on a specific demographic (e.g., children, older adults) leaves a gap in our understanding of the habits, preferences, and experiences of digital gamers in the middle of life, i.e., aged 18 to 55 years.

METHODS

We conduct a meta-analysis of data gathered over eleven different studies. Each study had its own research intention; however, similarities in how the studies were conducted allow us to aggregate the data into a single analysis to investigate the effects of age on player-centric traits and play experience. In each study, we recruited participants using Amazon Mechanical Turk, and used the same validated scales to assess play experience, i.e., PENS, and IMI, and player-centric traits, i.e., BrainHex and DGMS. We describe how we gathered and treated the data from these studies for analysis.

Participants

Over eleven different studies, we recruited 3041 (mean-age=32.07, SD=9.666) participants using the crowdsourcing platform, Amazon Mechanical Turk (AMT), a broker between requesters, i.e., entities who offer Human Intelligent Tasks (HIT), and workers, i.e., people who complete the HITs. For each study, we obtained ethical approval from the University of Saskatchewan's behavioural research ethics board, and participants were asked to provide informed consent prior to beginning the experiment.

Instruments

To assess experience and player-centric traits we used well-established, validated scales – PENS, IMI, BrainHex, and DGMS – that have been used in the context of games before [4,12,30,45,53]. PENS and IMI assess a self-reported player experience in a defined state, i.e., after playing a game. While state questionnaires provide insights into a players momentary experience, BrainHex and DGMS measure a player's more time stable traits, e.g., individual play preferences or common motives to play. In combination, trait and state questionnaires allow us to understand momentary experiences through the lens of individual differences.

PENS: Need Satisfaction of *competence, autonomy*, and *relatedness*, as well as *presence* and *intuitive control* as experienced during play were measured using the Player Experience of Need Satisfaction Scale (PENS, [53]) Each of the constructs were measured using a Likert-scale.

IMI: *Interest-enjoyment* – e.g., "I enjoyed this game very much.", *effort-importance* – e.g., "I put a lot of effort into this game.", *perceived competence* – e.g., "I'm pretty skilled at this game", and *tension-pressure* – e.g., "I felt tense while playing the game.", were measured on a Likert scale with the Intrinsic Motivation Inventory (IMI, [41]). The IMI has been used in games research before [53].

BrainHex: We used the BrainHex questionnaire to measure the preferred style of players [44]. Although BrainHex is intended to produce a type, it can also be used to express the degree of affiliation with a particular style of play, as was done by [45]. In our dataset, we have a rating of affiliation with the following player types: *Conquerors*, *Achievers*, *Daredevils, Survivors, Masterminds*, *Seekers*, *Socializers*. In ten studies, constructs were measured using the procedure described by [44]; in one case, a 4-pt scale was used.

DGMS: In 4/11 studies (n=604), we also collected the Digital Game Motivation Scale (DGMS) [31], which describes the different motives of people to play games. Based on social cognitive theory, the instrument measures the game-external motives of *pastime* and *escapism*, the normative motive of *moral self-reaction* (i.e., the evaluation that playing games is a valuable activity), the non-conscious behavioural motive of *habit*, and the game-internal motives of *agency*, *believability*, *involvement*, and *social* on a Likert scale.

Genre Preferences: We asked participants to select which genre they enjoyed playing from a list of common genres and to identify clusters of genre preferences we used K-means clustering, similar to clustering and dimension reduction approaches as used by DeGrove et al. [31] and Mandryk and Birk [39]. We identified three clusters: Casual-Puzzlers – who play only casual and puzzle games; Adventurers– who enjoy action games, FPSs, adventure, (Massively Multiplayer) Role Playing Games, and strategy games; and Comprehensives – who play a broad range of games, enjoying the same games as the Casual-Puzzlers and Adventurers combined, plus platform games, and simulations. Music games, Beat 'em ups, Sport games, and Vehicle Simulations were removed from further analysis, because they did not help differentiate clusters. To compare how frequently participants played a genre, we calculated genre percentage by age group.

Self-identification as a Gamer: We asked all participants to rate their self-identification as a gamer on a 10-point scale. We describe how this one-item scale significantly correlates with a 60-item validated scale on gamer self-identity in [39].

Datasets & Game Descriptions

Datasets for this study were sourced from eleven different studies. We first ensured that all experiential data, i.e., IMI and PENS, was collected after play sessions of a minimum length of 1 min, and a maximum length of 5 min. In the case of repeated-measure study designs that exposed one participant to the same game multiple times, we averaged the experiential constructs for that study. In one study, we induced a state of social exclusion in half of the participants; however, only participants who were not exposed to social exclusion were included in the dataset used in this study.

Instrument Scaling: In 9/11 studies, the measures were collected on a 5-pt Likert scale. In two studies, the data were collected on a 7-point scale. We used standardized scores to address this issue (discussed in the next section).

Data Processing & Outlier Removal

Participants were excluded from further analysis based on the following criteria: Surveys with zero variance between items, showed ratings of ±3SD in more than 2 questionnaires, answered more than 2 attention test questions (questions in which the correct answer is given in the question text – e.g., "click expert if you are reading this") incorrectly, or spent considerably less time on 2 questionnaires (-1SD) than the rest of the sample. We did not exclude people for spending more time filling in the questionnaires. Overall, 294 participants were removed, leaving 2747 in our analysis.

Data for each scale was standardized [24] using mean and standard deviation from the original datasets (i.e., for that particular study). Standardization was done to assure comparability of data independent of the number of levels in the Likert-scale, and to better account for differences between datasets due to the game used, the context of the study, the time of year, or other possible sources of variance. Creating standard scores for each original dataset before combining the datasets for analysis assured that the relative experience for each study was kept intact; creating standard scores based on the combined dataset would have been misleading, because the resulting standard scores would have been relative to the mean of the combined dataset, and not the mean of the original dataset. For each construct, we removed outliers (+-3SD) and treated the remaining data as missing data for further analysis. Outlier were removed after participants were excluded and scores were standardized.

For player experience measures, we split the overall dataset into two datasets, based on the game used. For five of the studies, we used a Match 3 game, and combined these into one dataset (n=1332, mean age = 31.49, SD = 8.349; 42.6%

female, 0.8% missing). We decided to combine data for previous studies featuring the Match-3 game, because the experience playing Match-3 is comparable between studies and measured variance cannot be attributed to different game mechanics. To further increase generalizability, we compared the Match-3 data with combined measures of the other casual games used, which had more diverse game mechanics.

The other dataset (n=1415, mean age = 30.92, SD = 8.035; 42.6% female, 0.8% missing) was comprised of data from a variety of other casual games, including an infinite runner [12], a side-scroller [13], a game of mini-games [11], and a narrative-based interactive story game [14].

For both datasets combined, the majority of our sample identifies as white (65.9%), followed by Hispanic/Latino (11.5%) and Asian (8.9%). 55.9% of our sample stated a household income lower than $45,000 per year. A Bachelor's degree was the most common educational level (33%), followed by at least 1 year of collage education (22.3%), an Associate Degree (13.3), and a Master's degree or higher (9.7%).

Analyses

All statistical analyses were performed using SPSS 24.0 (IBM, 2016). We report linear regressions, with age as the predictor of the dependent measure. Moderated and mediated regressions were performed using the Process Macro 2.16 by Hayes [33]. A moderation analysis tests the interacting effect of a third variable, i.e., the moderator, on an established relationship between a predictor variable and an outcome variable. A mediation analysis tests the mediating influence of a third variable, i.e., the mediator, on an established relationship between a predictor variable and an outcome variable. All beta values are presented as standardized beta scores.

RESULTS

We characterize the sample, and then establish a foundation of play preference across the sample by presenting system and genre preferences. Further, we present player-centric traits and motives to give insight into what drives people of different ages to play. Finally, we present data on play experience to explore how experience changes over age.

Characterizing the Sample

As shown in Figure 1, there was a non-normal distribution of age (Kolmogorov Smirnov: $p<.05$), skewed toward the young. Figure 1 shows a fairly even distribution of females and males, with a very slight skew towards females in the older ranges and males in the younger ranges. Finally, Figure 2 shows play frequency of the sample, revealing that the majority of players in every age group play every week or more.

System and Genre Preferences

In line with previously shown data [22,58], system preference data in our sample shows that personal computer and mobile use is stable over the age range (PC: beta=.00049, p=.672; mobile: beta=-.002, p=.112), whereas console use significantly decreases over the age range (beta=-.012, $p<.001$, R^2=.748); see Figure 3. The decreased use of consoles with increasing age is not surprising, considering that consoles only became popular in the 1990s.

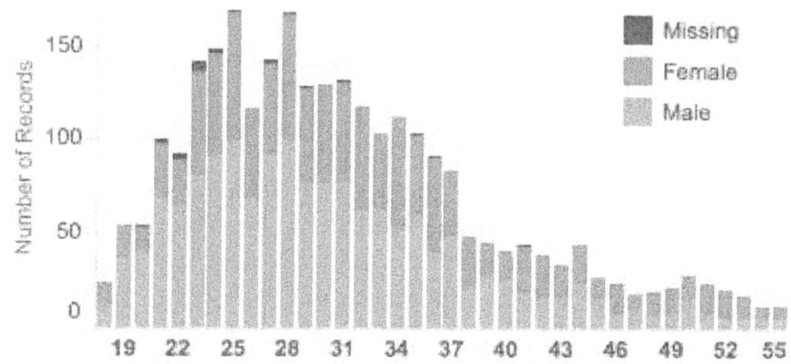

Figure 1. Histogram of the sample colour-coded by gender.

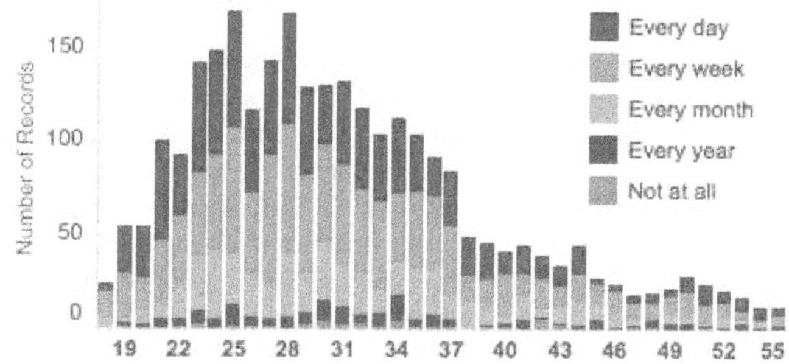

Figure 2. Histogram of play frequency by age group, colour-coded by play frequency.

Genre preference data shows that membership in the Comprehensive Cluster declines in popularity with increasing age (beta=-.008, $p<.001$, R^2=.756,). A similar decline in membership is revealed for the Adventurers Cluster (beta=-.009, $p<.001$, R^2=.747). The Casual-Puzzler Cluster, however, increases in membership with increasing age (beta=.0051, $p<.001$, R^2=.366); See Figure 3. The results suggest that with increasing age, there is an increasing interest in games that don't require an intense commitment. The increasing preference (with age) for games that are less based on reaction time, require less time commitment, and are usually easier to control can be explained in part by a lack of exposure to these types of activities in younger years, but also a lower interest in competition [69], and a focus on activities that provide more meaningful fulfillment than hedonic pleasure [16].

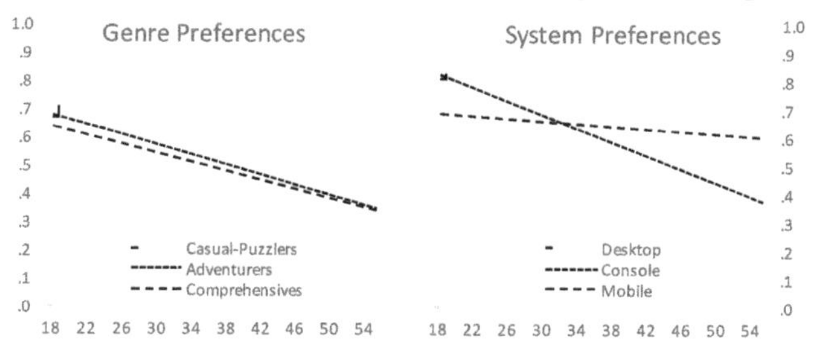

Figure 3. Genre and system preferences by age groups.

Player-centric Traits and Play Motives

The BrainHex questionnaire showed that with increasing age, people self-identify more with completion-focused play styles – i.e., achiever, mastermind, and seeker, and decreasingly with performance-focused traits – i.e., conqueror, daredevil, survivor. Self-identifying as a social player – i.e., a socializer – also declines over the life-span. This result may be partially described by the tendency of younger people to engage in social behaviour online, whereas older people may still rely on offline interaction primarily to fulfill their need to feel related to others [26].

In Figure 4, we can clearly see the increase of completion-based focused traits, and the decline of performance-focused traits. Our BrainHex results further supports that trend seen in the genre preferences that with increasing age comes an increasing preference for challenges that can be reasonably completed and not challenges that are complex, require quick reaction times, or result in overly frustrating experiences, e.g., frequently dying in a difficult game.

Play Motives

Motives from the DGMS (see Table 1) show that most game-internal motivations decline with increasing age. Specifically, the narrative, performance, and sociability motives decline; whereas, agency stays stable. Habit, an indicator for non-conscious behaviour, also declines with increasing age. Moral, an indicator of the evaluation that playing games is a valuable use of time, declines with increasing age. Finally, the two game-external factors, escapism and pastime, don't change significantly with increasing age.

Self-Identification: Self-Identifying as a gamer decreases with increasing age (beta=-.215, R^2=.046, p<.001). This trend could be related to people identifying more with their career and family roles and less with their hobbies as they age [16] or because of the specific time frame we sample – we unpack this issue further in the general discussion.

Experience Data

Self-reported experience included need satisfaction during game play, and intrinsic motivation, operationalized as experienced enjoyment, effort, tension, and competence as a result of playing a Match 3 game or one of the other games.

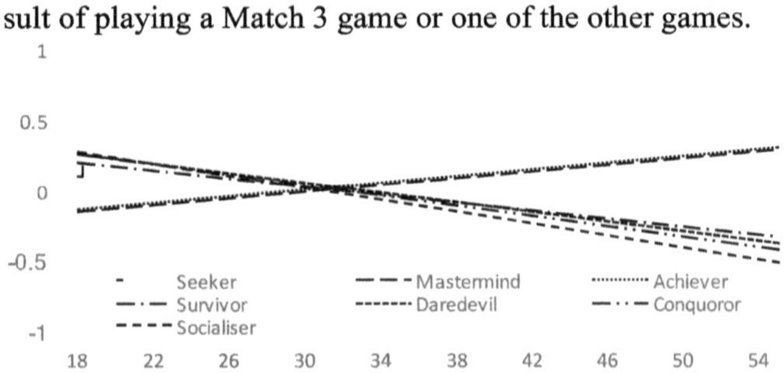

Figure 4. BrainHex regression lines by age group.

BrainHex	beta	R-sq	p
Seeker	0.007	0.03	0.003
Mastermind	0.012	0.011	<.001
Achiever	0.012	0.012	<.001
Survivor	-0.014	0.013	<.001
Daredevil	-0.017	0.02	<.001
Conquoror	-0.018	0.022	<.001
Socialiser	-0.021	0.028	<.001

DGMS	beta	R-sq	p
Habit	-0.010	0.007	0.040
Moral	-0.018	0.021	<.001
Agency	-0.008	0.004	0.139
Narrative	-0.016	0.016	0.002
Escapism	0.001	0.000	0.866
Pastime	-0.007	0.004	0.145
Performance	-0.015	0.017	0.001
Social	-0.020	0.027	<.001

Table 1. Beta, R2, and p-value for BrainHex and DGMS. Significant results are displayed with a grey background.

Player Experience of Need Satisfaction

Figure 5 shows need satisfaction for the Match 3 dataset and also for all other games combined; we find that experienced need satisfaction as a result of play increased for autonomy, relatedness, and presence with increased age. The experience of intuitive control, however, decreases with increasing age; see Table 2. It is not surprising that controls are experienced as being more intuitive for younger people, considering the age at which people in our sample were introduced to devices like mice, keyboards, and game controllers, and are thus likely to have internalized common control schemas.

Our data show that experienced satisfaction of competence does not change with age. The Match 3 game is rather simple, and outcome is partially based on the luck of the falling colours. The other games were rather simple and also not particularly challenging. Therefore, it is not surprising that competence shows only a small and statistically insignificant decrease with increasing age.

Intrinsic Motivation Inventory

Figure 5 shows data from the IMI for the Match 3 dataset and also for all other games combined. For both datasets, we see that Interest-Enjoyment, Effort and Tension-Pressure increase with increasing age for both datasets.

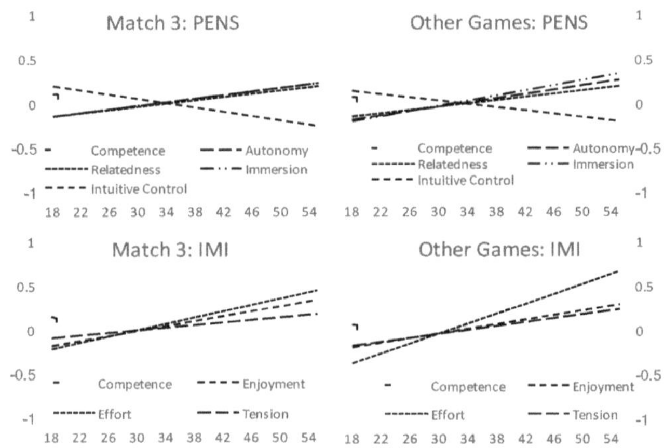

Figure 5. PENS and IMI regression lines for Match 3 and all other games combined over age.

	Match 3			Other Games		
	beta	R-sq	p	beta	R-sq	p
	PENS					
Competence	-0.005	0.000	0.130	-0.004	0.000	0.340
Autonomy	0.010	0.010	0.000	0.012	0.010	< .001
Relatedness	0.009	0.010	0.000	0.009	0.010	0.010
Presence	0.010	0.010	0.000	0.014	0.010	< .001
Intuitive Control	-0.012	0.010	< .001	-0.009	0.010	0.010
	IMI					
Interest-Enjoyment	0.014	0.014	< .001	0.013	0.010	< .001
Effort-Importance	-0.014	0.020	< .001	-0.003	0.060	< .001
Competence	0.018	0.010	< .001	0.028	0.000	0.420
Tension	0.007	0.000	0.040	0.011	0.010	0.010

Table 2. Experience Data (PENS, IMI) split by Match 3 and other games.

With increasing age, players invested more effort into the gameplay, and also derived greater enjoyment from it. They also experienced a trend of increasing experienced tension.

In the case of IMI data, perceived competence decreases in both datasets, but only significantly for the Match 3 data; see Table 2. Experienced competence decreases with increasing age; this is the trend in all measures of competence (see Figure 5), but is significant for Match 3 games and the IMI. We further unpack the results related to competence.

Unpacking Competence

The results related to declining competence raise three questions: the difference in the results for the PENS and IMI scales, the mediating influence of intuitive control on competence, and the question of how competence can decline with increasing age, but enjoyment can increase.

Why were Results Different for Competence in PENS and IMI? Although competence declined with increasing age in all cases, it was only significant for IMI in the Match 3 dataset. As both PENS and IMI measure perceived competence, why do the results differ? To address this, we considered the individual items in the questionnaires. The IMI has five items that all center around the player's perceived competence, using terms like "competence", "performance", being "good at", and "skill" (with one reverse-coded item), whereas PENS has three items that touch on the player feeling "competent", "capable and effective", and that their "ability to play the game is well matched with the game's challenge". This last item in particular assesses a more complex aspect of perceived competence in that it requires an assessment of what the game offered and how well the player was equipped to deal with the challenge offered. This difference in the items in the PENS version of competence should be reflected in the internal consistency of the scale relative to the IMI. We checked in the three largest studies in our dataset and found that Cronbach's alpha was always higher for IMI Competence than for PENS Competence (N=488: α_I=.88, α_P=.79; N=174: α_I=.85, α_P=.78; N=99: α_I=.86, α_P=.64). Furthermore, the PENS alpha fell below the established threshold of 0.8 for the reliability of a questionnaire [24]. Thus is it likely that IMI gives the more reliable and consistent measure of Competence. The subsequent analyses thus all use experienced competence as measured by the IMI.

Does Intuitive Control Mediate the Effect of Age on Competence? When Ryan et al. [53] introduced intuitive control to PENS, they described the experience of intuitive control as a potential antecedent of competence. To determine whether the decline in experienced competence over age can be explained by the decline in the experience of intuitive control, we conducted a mediation regression model [33] of age on competence with intuitive control as a mediator. We used both datasets combined. As shown in Figure 6, there is a total negative effect of age on competence, which remained a significant direct effect even after intuitive control was included as a mediator in the model, although the beta value dropped from -.008 to -.004. The bootstrapped confidence intervals for intuitive control as a mediator did not include zero [33], suggesting a partial mediation. That is, some of the variance in declining competence can be explained by declining intuitive control, but not all of it. Hence, age is the explaining factor for the decline in perceived competence, but the perceived intuitiveness of the controls also affect competence, i.e., unintuitive controls further lower perceived competence.

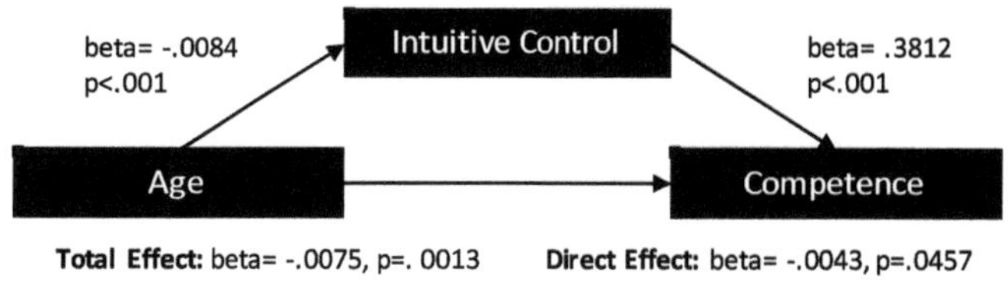

Figure 6. Mediation graph for Age on Competence, mediated by Intuitive Control – beta- and p-values are included.

How can Experienced Competence Decline over Age while Enjoyment Increases? In most player experience research, experienced competence is either a predictor of enjoyment (e.g., [53]) or at least varies in tandem with enjoyment (e.g., [43]). This is supported by Self-Determination Theory, which suggests that the satisfaction of competence leads to intrinsic motivation [54]. In our sample, competence declines over age, whereas enjoyment increases. These results suggest that as people age from 18 to 55, the satisfaction of competence becomes a less important predictor of enjoyment (relative to, for example relatedness and autonomy) and/or that it takes less satisfaction of competence to result in the same amount of enjoyment. We explored these two options.

The first explanation (importance) would be reflected in significantly declining beta values of competence in a regression of competence, autonomy, and relatedness on enjoyment for increasing ages. As such, we conducted a linear regression with competence, autonomy, and relatedness as three predictors of enjoyment, separately for each age on our combined dataset. Figure 7 shows the standardized beta values over age for these 38 regressions, and clearly shows that the weight placed on competence decreases over age (as does relatedness), whereas autonomy increases over age. This decrease in the importance of competence is significant (p=.045). It is important that the three predictor terms were entered into a single model as this result demonstrates that the relative weight of competence, in the presence of autonomy and relatedness, decreases in terms of the prediction of enjoyment. As such, we can assume that the relative importance of competence in predicting enjoyment decreases.

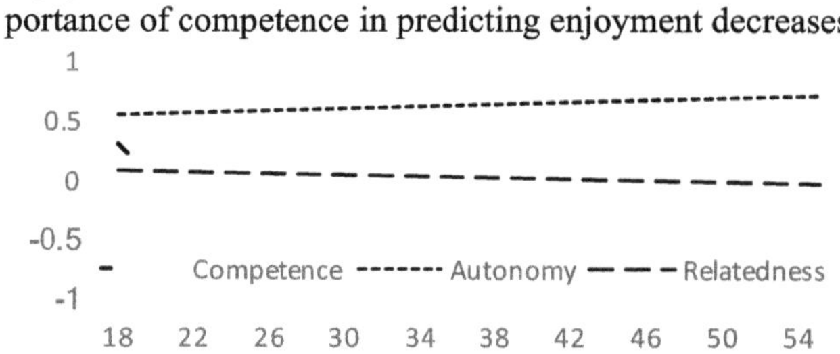

Figure 7. Regression lines for the beta-values from a multiple regression of Competence, Autonomy, and Relatedness on Enjoyment over age.

The second explanation (that it takes less satisfaction of competence to yield enjoyment) would be revealed through a significant moderation. We conducted a moderated regression [33] with age as a predictor of enjoyment, moderated by competence. Results reveal that both age ($p<.001$) and competence ($p<.001$) were significant predictors of enjoyment and that the moderation was also significant ($p<.05$), showing that there is an interaction between age and competence in predicting enjoyment. The moderation results revealed that although competence predicted enjoyment significantly for each age range, the prediction became shallower (i.e., beta value decreased) with increasing age ($\beta_{younger}$=.453; β_{middle}=.416; β_{older}=.380) – that is, it takes less satisfaction of competence to yield the same enjoyment with increasing age.

DISCUSSION

In this section, we summarize our results, explain our findings through the lens of game preferences, motives and play styles, and through the lens of prior experience. Further, we distinguish the effects of prior experience from the effects of aging. Finally, we present limitations and future work.

Summary of Results

Our results show a clear trend over the range of the 18 to 55 year-old demographic away from performance-related preferences toward completion-related preferences. We show that as age increases, there is an increasing preference for casual games and puzzle games and a decreasing preference for performance-related games. This trend is also reflected in play style and motives to play – with increasing age, performance as a motive to play decreases, completion-focused player styles like achiever, mastermind, and achiever increase, and performance-focused player styles like conqueror, survivor, and daredevil decline. Both the social motive (drive to play) and the socializer play style decline significantly with age. Furthermore, the identification as a 'gamer' declines with age.

Experience data also aligns with this trend; we reveal that with increasing age, people derive greater experienced enjoyment, effort, and tension from play. The increase in game enjoyment with age is also reflected in the increased satisfaction of autonomy, relatedness, and presence. However, competence (which generally co-varies with the other IMI factors) does not increase, and in some cases significantly declines with increasing age. Furthermore, this decrease in competence is partially explained by an accompanying decline in the experience of intuitive controls – both competence and control are related to the player's experience of their own performance during play. We further unpack this effect of declining competence, showing first that its importance in predicting enjoyment (relative to autonomy and relatedness) declines significantly over age, and that less satisfaction of competence translates into the same amount of enjoyment as age increases.

The pattern that emerges suggests a shift of individual differences and preferences over age away from performance in terms of play motive, play style, identification as a gamer, and player experience. As players shift away from performance, they shift toward completion in terms of play style and are appreciative of experience, valuing choice and experiencing more intrinsic motivation during play. These findings can be explained by existing theories of emotional, and cognitive changes over age.

Explanation for Findings

Older age groups identify less as gamers than younger age groups – a trend that doesn't come as a surprise, considering that the older generation was in their teens when the Atari was released in 1977 and were well into careers and child-rearing years when the original Sony PlayStation was released in 1995. In contrast, the low-end of our age range were all born years after the release of the PlayStation. In addition to age, differences in exposure affect what people like, what motivates them to play, and how they experience games.

Preferences, Styles, and Motives

Scharkow et al. [57], for example, showed that younger people have a stronger preference for most game genres than older adults, with the exception of card games and simulations. On a similar note, Bilgihan et al. [9] found statistical evidence that the older generation focuses more on strategic gaming whereas the younger generation tends to affiliate more with action games. Our sample supports these findings, showing that the older generation tend to get categorized in the Casual-Puzzler cluster and less in the Adventurer and Comprehensive clusters, while the younger generation shows the opposite. Considering that puzzle and casual games often build on known concepts (e.g., a digital version of an existing card game) or use a common puzzle mechanic (e.g., Match 3), the preference of older adults might be explainable by psychological theories that suggest that with increased age, people prefer familiar tasks and experiences [3,6,16]. The classic theory of mere-exposure [71] states that we develop preferences because of mere familiarity, which increases exposure and further increases familiarity in a positive feedback loop. For example, playing cards will increase your preference for cards and likely make you play more cards. Considering that older age groups had more exposure to puzzle games than to FPS and RPG games, the familiarity principle may partially explain their preferences. These results are also in-line with research showing that highly-practiced processes stay accessible later on in life [18].

Models of personality (e.g., Big-Five [42]), models of play style [44], and player archetypes [20] have been used to understand individual differences between players. De Schutter & Malliet [60] categorized senior adults into five types of players: *time wasters* (only casual games), *freedom fighters* (free to play a game and avoid work), *compensators* (playing games as a result of a deficiency), *value seekers* (to learn a lot from games) and *ludophiles* (people who had been gamers for their whole life). Other approaches have focused on the self-ascribed motives of players to engage in play. Using a large sample of more than 239,000 players, Yee et al. [69], showed that the competition motive declines over age; based on the same data source, [69] showed that interest in playing with others declines over age, except for co-located, cooperative games played with friends.

Our results show that there is a trend over age: younger ages see themselves more as performance and competition oriented, whereas older ages show a decline for the same constructs and see themselves more as completion-focused. The relationship between completion- and performance-focused play preferences confirms and extends Yee's findings by showing that it isn't just that competitive and performance traits decline over age, but that completion traits increase.

We also show that game-internal motives for play decline over age. Older ages seem to be less interested in the high-standards and technologies that the AAA market drives. For example, sophisticated social systems (as was done in, for example, Eve Online; CCP Games, 2003), are less likely to appeal to older ages. These results seem to highlight an opportunity for game developers to create games for this demographic that have a lower social demand, stay away from a heavy narrative, and are easy to access – similar to many casual games that are already released on the market.

Experiences

The consistent pattern of performance versus completion related games for younger and older age groups leads to the question of how experience is affected. The casual games used in all eleven studies allow us to investigate how different age groups experience a casual game. As individual differences suggest, we can show that older people experience more need satisfaction and higher levels of enjoyment, effort, and tension, whereas competence and the intuitiveness of control decline over age groups. Our results are in line with previous results that show that competence is in part a function of being able to control the game [10,43,53]. Furthermore, there are theories that help explain our findings.

Socio-emotional selectivity (SES) theory [16] argues that people focus on emotional regulation and relatedness centric goals as they age, rather than the acquisition of a new skill. Older age groups might experience the game as more satisfying, because they have a tendency to perceive events as emotionally more positive than younger age groups. SES theory would also suggest that older adults are aware of their decline in cognitive and physical abilities, consequentially they rate themselves as less competent. Our sample only extended to age 55, however, and does not access people experiencing the more drastic age-related decrements in cognition and physical ability [56].

How much does cognitive decline over the age represented in our sample affect performance? We don't evaluate game performance in this study, but based on prior research, we know that the decline of ability is often compensated for through knowledge. For example, Horn & Cattell [34] suggested that a lack of one ability (e.g., age-related decrease of reaction time) is often compensated for in experience and knowledge (e.g., remembering the spawn time of important items on a FPS map). As a result, self-perceived performance might decline, but other mechanisms might be in place that prevent declines in actual performance over this age range.

Digital Exposure versus Effects of Aging

As noted previously, the digital experiences of this age range differ quite dramatically. It is not surprising that the control schemes of games are experienced as less intuitive with increasing age, as people in the older end of the age range likely remember learning to use a mouse well into their adulthood, whereas the younger end of the range never lived in a world where the mouse was not a standard input device. Our sample represents a truly interesting group in terms of their exposure to digital technologies. The older group was born the year that Spacewar! was programmed, witnessed the rise of the arcade, the invention of home gaming, personal computing, mobile phones, and the Internet – all technologies that were already present when the youngest group was born.

Throughout, we have alluded to these differences in exposure to technology as potential sources of the changes in preference and experience that we see over the age range. Research supports the prospect of exposure to technology-driving differences in the experience of it. For example, older adults report less competence and self-efficacy with technology [1,40,55], but that exposure to technology and intergenerational contact can decrease anxiety and increase perceived competence about technology use [17]. And it isn't just subjective experiences that can be offset by exposure – performance differences related to general cognitive and age-related decline in functioning have been shown to be offset by experience [19,64].

Some researchers have suggested that differences between younger adults and older adults may fade over time if controls don't change drastically because the older adults will have played games their whole lives [60]. This argument around 'digital natives' as older adults makes sense from our perspective as researchers in 2017; however, history suggests that the next 50 years will bring about technological changes that we can't even begin to imagine now. As such, there will likely be future papers written about how our young cohort, born in 1999, are disadvantaged users of technology in their older years as they were not exposed to some unimaginable future technologies until well into their adulthood.

We previously situated our results in theories that explain cognitive and emotional changes over age. Here, we have described how exposure could contribute to the source of the differences. Although it is unclear whether our results should be attributed to changes in age or differences in exposure to games and digital technology in general – and is most likely a combination of both – the likelihood of future technological development implies that this pattern will continue for future cohorts of 18-55 year olds.

Limitations and Future Work

Our work provides new insights on the differing preferences, motives, play styles, and experiences of people in the 18-55 year-old age bracket. Although we are careful in the use of our terminology throughout, we would like to make explicit some of the limitations of the study and the care that must be taken when interpreting the results.

First, our results demonstrate trends in aggregate. Although performance-driven motives decrease in general over age, this does not imply that a 40-year old cannot have a higher performance motive than a 20-year old player. As with all population estimates, data of the different groups is made up of overlapping distributions. The individual difference within an age bin is much larger than the differences between neighbouring bins. Although the results do reflect the general trends over the sample, we must be careful not to overgeneralize with these types of findings to stereotype or pigeonhole individual people.

Second, we present a cross-sectional sample, which allows us only to draw conclusions about differences in age bins taken from the current population. It does not, however, allow us to draw conclusions about changes over time, i.e., the lifespan, which would require longitudinal studies that investigate change in a single cohort over multiple years. This limitation makes it impossible to determine whether the results can be attributed fully to changes as a result of the aging process or whether they can also partially be attributed to changes in digital exposure in the different age ranges of our participants.

Third, the results that we present are small but significant trends. The figures show how the slopes of the lines are not generally drastic, which is to be expected as peoples' habits and preferences don't change instantly, but slowly over a range of years. Even small slopes, however, show a big difference over a range of ages as big as 18-55.

Fourth, we present results from an age range between 18 and 55 who participated in studies playing casual games, which are preferred by older age groups. Replicating the results with a different genre would be valuable.

Finally, the number of participants in each age bin is not equivalent. While our findings are well supported by prior findings and grounded in literature, it would be of interested to have equally sized age-groups to investigate more nuanced differences. Similarly, it would also be of interest to increase the age range towards young children and seniors, which are both not covered in the current study.

CONCLUSIONS

The current core demographic of 18 to 55 year-olds is a particularly interesting group because of the diversity of their historical exposure to digital technologies in general and games in particular. The older range of this group witnessed the entire rise of the videogame – from a research prototype in an MIT lab to a world in which a game that lives on your smartphone supports the networked online play of more than 50 million daily active users [70]. The younger range were already born into a networked world of downloadable content and multiplayer coop modes. Although there are clear differences in the digital exposure of this group, we tend to treat them as a monolithic and homogenous group in games user research.

In this paper, we consider the play preferences, styles, and motives of 2747 players in this age range. Furthermore, and unique to other work in this area, we investigate differences in standard measures of play experiences that were gathered in the context of eleven similar experiments. Our results show a consistent pattern that with increasing age, preferences, play motive, play style, identification as a gamer, and player experience shift away from a focus on performance and towards a focus on completion, choice, and enjoyment. Our findings can also be explained by socio-emotional selectivity theory, which suggests that as we age, we exhibit an increased focus on goals that prioritize emotional stability and relationships and less on the acquisitions of new skills. We provide new insights into the player experience of this core demographic of gamers.

ACKNOWLEDGEMENTS

We would like to thank NSERC and SWaGUR for funding. We would like to thank members of the Interaction Lab at the University of Saskatchewan for support, and in particular those who were involved in the collection of the datasets that we used in this study: Jason Bowey, Matthew Miller, Shelby Thompson, Cher Atkins, and Benjamin Buttlar.

REFERENCES

1. Ignacio Aguaded-Gomez, Ramon Tirado-Morueta, and Angel Hernando-Gomez. 2015. Media competence in adult citizens in Andalusia, Spain. *Information Communication & Society* 18, 6: 659–679. https://doi.org/10.1080/1369118X.2014.985244

2. J.A. Anguera, J. Boccanfuso, J.L. Rintoul, O. Al-Hashimi, F. Faraji, J. Janowich, E. Kong, Y. Larraburo, C. Rolle, E. Johnston, and A. Gazzaley. 2013. Video game training enhances cognitive control in older adults. *Nature* 501, September: 97–101. https://doi.org/10.1016/j.biotechadv.2011.08.021.Secreted

3. Catherine M Arrington, Erik M Altmann, and Thomas H Carr. 2003. Tasks of a feather flock together: similarity effects in task switching. *Memory & Cognition* 31, 5: 781–789. https://doi.org/10.3758/BF03196116

4. Alexander Baldwin, Daniel Johnson, and Peta a. Wyeth. 2014. The effect of multiplayer dynamic difficulty adjustment on the player experience of video games. *Proceedings of the extended abstracts of the 32nd annual ACM conference on Human factors in computing systems - CHI EA '14*: 1489–1494. https://doi.org/10.1145/2559206.2581285

5. Paul B Baltes. 1997. On the Incomplete Architecture of Human Ontogeny - Selection, Optimization, and Compensation as Foundation of

Developmental Theory. *American Psychologist* 52, 4: 366–380. https://doi.org/10.1037/0003-066X.52.4.366

6. Albert Bandura and Albert Bandura. 1989. Human agency in social cognitive theory. *The American psychologist* 44, 9: 1175–84. https://doi.org/10.1037/0003-066x.44.9.1175
7. Tom Baranowski, Richard Buday, Debbe I. Thompson, and Janice Baranowski. 2008. Playing for Real. Video Games and Stories for Health-Related Behavior Change. *American Journal of Preventive Medicine 34*, 74–82. https://doi.org/10.1016/j.amepre.2007.09.027
8. Richard Bartle. 1996. Hearts, Clubs, Diamonds, Spades: Players who suit MUDs. *Journal of MUD research* 6, 1: 39. https://doi.org/10.1007/s00256-004-0875-6
9. Anil Bilgihan, Cihan Cobanoglu, Khaldoon Nusair, Fevzi Okumus, and Milos Bujisic. 2013. A quantitative study exploring the difference between gaming genre preferences. *The Computer Games Journal Candlemas* 2, September 1995: 19–40. Retrieved from www.computergamesjournal.com
10. Max Birk and Regan L Mandryk. 2013. Control your game-self: effects of controller type on enjoyment, motivation, and personality in game. *Proceedings of the SIGCHI Conference on Human Factors in Computing Systems - CHI '13*: 685–694. https://doi.org/10.1145/2470654.2470752
11. Max V. Birk, L. Mandryk, Regan, Jason Bowey, and Benjamin Buttlar. 2015. The Effects of Adding Premise and Backstory to Psychological Tasks. *CHI'15 Workshop "Researching Gamification: Strategies, Opportunities, Challenges, Ethics"*.
12. Max V Birk, Cheralyn Atkins, Jason T Bowey, and Regan L Mandryk. 2016. Fostering Intrinsic Motivation through Avatar Identification in Digital Games. In *CHI '16*, 207–213. https://doi.org/10.1145/2858036.2858062
13. Max V Birk, Regan L Mandryk, Matthew K Miller, and Kathrin M Gerling. 2015. How Self-Esteem Shapes our Interactions with Play Technologies. *Proceedings of the 2015 Annual Symposium on Computer-Human Interaction in Play - CHI PLAY '15*: 35–45. https://doi.org/10.1145/2793107.2793111
14. Jason Bowey and Regan L. Mandryk. 2017. Those are not the Stories you are Looking For: Using Text Prototypes to Evaluate Game Narratives Early. In *Proceedings of the 2017 Annual Symposium on Computer-Human Interaction in Play.*
15. Jeanne H Brockmyer, Christine M Fox, Kathleen A Curtiss, Evan McBroom, Kimberly M Burkhart, and Jacquelyn N Pidruzny. 2009. The development of the Game Engagement Questionnaire: A measure of engagement in video game-playing. *Journal of Experimental Social Psychology* 45, 4: 624–634 ST–The development of the Game Engageme. Retrieved from http://www.sciencedirect.com/science/article/pii/S0022103109000444
16. Laura L. Carstensen, Derek M. Isaacowitz, and Susan T. Charles. 1999. Taking Time Seriously: A theory of Socioemotional Selectivity. *American Psychologist* 54, 3: 165–181. https://doi.org/10.1037//0003-066X.54.3.165
17. Puay Hoe Chua, Younbo Jung, May O. Lwin, and Yin Leng Theng. 2013. Let's play together: Effects of video-game play on intergenerational perceptions among youth and elderly participants. *Computers in Human Behavior* 29, 6: 2303–2311. https://doi.org/10.1016/j.chb.2013.04.037
18. Fergus I M Craik and Ellen Bialystok. 2006. Cognition through the lifespan: Mechanisms of change. *Trends in Cognitive Sciences 10*, 131–138. https://doi.org/10.1016/j.tics.2006.01.007
19. Sara J Czaja, Joseph Sharit, Sankaran Nair, and Mark Rubert. 1998. Understanding sources of user variability in computer-based data entry performance. *Behaviour & Information Technology* 17, 5: 282–293. https://doi.org/10.1080/014492998119355
20. Anders Drachen, Rafet Sifa, Christian Bauckhage, and Christian Thurau. 2012. Guns, swords and data: Clustering of player behavior in computer games in the wild. In *2012 IEEE Conference on Computational Intelligence and Games, CIG 2012*, 163–170. https://doi.org/10.1109/CIG.2012.6374152
21. Nicolas Ducheneaut, Mh Wen, Nicholas Yee, and Greg Wadley. 2009. Body and Mind: A Study of Avatar Personalization in Three Virtual Worlds. *Proceedings of the SIGCHI Conference on Human Factors in Computing Systems*: 1151–1160. https://doi.org/10.1145/1518701.1518877
22. ESA Entertainment Software Association. 2016. 2016 Essential Facts About the Computer and Video Game Industry. *Media.*
23. Christopher J. Ferguson and Cheryl K. Olson. 2013. Friends, fun, frustration and fantasy: Child motivations for video game play. *Motivation and Emotion* 37, 1: 154–164. https://doi.org/10.1007/s11031-012-9284-7
24. Andy Field. 2013. *Discovering statistics using IBM SPSS statistics*. Sage.

25. Stuart Fischoff, Joe Antonio, and Diane Lewis. 1998. Favorite Films and Film Genres As A Function of Race , Age , and Gender. *Journal of Media Psychology* 3, 1: 1–25.

26. Deborah Kirby Forgays, Ira Hyman, and Jessie Schreiber. 2014. Texting everywhere for everything: Gender and age differences in cell phone etiquette and use. *Computers in Human Behavior* 31: 314–321. https://doi.org/10.1016/j.chb.2013.10.053

27. Kathrin Gerling, Ian Livingston, Lennart Nacke, and Regan Mandryk. 2012. Full-body motion-based game interaction for older adults. *Proceedings of the 2012 ACM annual conference on Human Factors in Computing Systems - CHI '12.* https://doi.org/10.1145/2207676.2208324

28. Paul E. Greenberg, Tamar Sisitsky, Ronald C. Kessler, Stan N. Finkelstein, Ernst R. Berndt, Jonathan R T Davidson, James C. Ballenger, and Abby J. Fyer. 1999. The economic burden of anxiety disorders in the 1990s. *Journal of Clinical Psychiatry* 60, 7: 427–435. https://doi.org/10.4088/JCP.v60n0702

29. Mark D. Griffiths, Mark N. O. Davies, and Darren Chappell. 2004. Online computer gaming:a comparison of adolescent and adult gamers. *Journal of adolescence* 27: 87–96. Retrieved July 26, 2017 from http://www.sciencedirect.com/science/article/pii/S0140197103000952

30. Frederik De Grove, Johannes Breuer, Vivian Hsueh Hua Chen, Thorsten Quandt, Rabindra Ratan, and Jan Van Looy. 2017. Validating the Digital Games Motivation Scale for Comparative Research Between Countries. *Communication Research Reports* 34, 1: 37–47. https://doi.org/10.1080/08824096.2016.1250070

31. Frederik De Grove, Verolien Cauberghe, and Jan Van Looy. 2014. Development and Validation of an Instrument for Measuring Individual Motives for Playing Digital Games. *Media Psychology* 3269, December: 1–25. https://doi.org/10.1080/15213269.2014.902318

32. Juho Hamari. 2017. Why do players buy in-game content ? An empirical study on concrete purchase motivations. *Computers in Human Behavior* 68: 538–546. https://doi.org/10.1016/j.chb.2016.11.045

33. Andrew F Hayes. 2013. *Introduction to mediation, moderation, and conditional process analysis: A regression-based approach.* Guilford Press.

34. John L. Horn and Raymond B. Cattell. 1967. Age differences in fluid and crystallized intelligence. *Acta Psychologica* 26: 107–129. https://doi.org/10.1016/0001-6918(67)90011-X

35. Daniel Johnson, Lennart E. Nacke, and Peta Wyeth. 2015. All about that Base: Differing Player Experiences in Video Game Genres and the Unique Case of MOBA Games. In *Proceedings of SIGCHI 2015*, 2265–2274. https://doi.org/10.1145/2702123.2702447

36. Ruth Kanfer and Phillip L. Ackerman. 2004. Aging, Adult Development, and Work Motivation. *Academy of Management Review 29*, 440–458. https://doi.org/10.5465/AMR.2004.13670969

37. Dorien T A M Kooij, Annet H. De Lange, Paul G W Jansen, Ruth Kanfer, and Josje S E Dikkers. 2011. Age and work-related motives: Results of a meta-analysis. *Journal of Organizational Behavior* 32, 2: 197–225. https://doi.org/10.1002/job.665

38. Regan L. Mandryk, Kori M. Inkpen, and Thomas W. Calvert. 2006. Using psychophysiological techniques to measure user experience with entertainment technologies. *Behaviour Information Technology* 25, 2: 141–158. https://doi.org/10.1080/01449290500331156

39. Regan L Mandryk and Max V Birk. 2017. Habits and preferences of players as a context for the design of game-based digital mental health interventions. *Journal of Medical Internet Research (in press).*

40. Jean-Claude Marquié, L. Jourdan-Boddaert, and Nathalie Huet. 2002. Do older adults underestimate their actual computer knowledge? *Behaviour & Information Technology* 21, 4: 273–280. https://doi.org/10.1080/0144929021000020998

41. Edward McAuley, Terry Duncan, and Vance V Tammen. 1989. Psychometric properties of the Intrinsic Motivation Inventory in a competitive sport setting: a confirmatory factor analysis. *Research quarterly for exercise and sport 60*, 48–58. https://doi.org/10.1080/02701367.1989.10607413

42. Robert R. McCrae and Oliver P. John. 1992. An Introduction to the Five Factor Model and Its Applications. *Journal of Personality* 60, 2: 175–215. https://doi.org/10.1111/j.1467-6494.1992.tb00970.x

43. Mitchell McEwan, Daniel Johnson, Peta Wyeth, and Alethea Blackler. 2012. Videogame control device impact on the play experience. *Proceedings of The 8th Australasian Conference on Interactive Entertainment Playing the System - IE '12* 18: 1–3. https://doi.org/10.1145/2336727.2336745

44. Lennart Nacke, Chris Bateman, and Regan L. Mandryk. 2011. BrainHex: Preliminary results from

a neurobiological gamer typology survey. *Lecture Notes in Computer Science (including subseries Lecture Notes in Artificial Intelligence and Lecture Notes in Bioinformatics)* 6972 LNCS: 288–293. https://doi.org/10.1007/978-3-642-24500-8_31

45. Rita Orji, Regan L Mandryk, Julita Vassileva, and Kathrin M Gerling. 2013. Tailoring persuasive health games to gamer type. *Proceedings of the SIGCHI Conference on Human Factors in Computing Systems - CHI '13*: 2467–2476. https://doi.org/10.1145/2470654.2481341

46. Wei Peng, Jih-Hsuan Lin, Karin A Pfeiffer, and Brian Winn. 2012. Need Satisfaction Supportive Game Features as Motivational Determinants: An Experimental Study of a Self-Determination Theory Guided Exergame. *Media Psychology* 15, 2: 175–196. https://doi.org/10.1080/15213269.2012.673850

47. Jeanine Poggi. 2014. NBC Chief Wants Peacock to Be Judged By 18-to-49 Viewership | Special Report: TV Upfront - AdAge. Retrieved April 14, 2017 from http://adage.com/article/special-report-tv-upfront/nbc-chief-peacock-judged-18-49-viewership/292531/

48. Thorsten Quandt, Helmut Grueninger, and Jeffrey Wimmer. 2009. The Gray Haired Gaming Generation. *Games and Culture* 4, 1: 27–46. https://doi.org/10.1177/1555412008325480

49. Ignacio Redondo and Morris B. Holbrook. 2010. Modeling the appeal of movie features to demographic segments of theatrical demand. *Journal of Cultural Economics* 34, 4: 299–315. https://doi.org/10.1007/s10824-010-9127-x

50. Richard Ryan and Edward Deci. 2002. Self-determination theory: An organismic dialectical perspective. *Handbook of Self-Determination Research*, 3–33. https://doi.org/citeulike-article-id:10086705

51. Richard Ryan and Edward L. Deci. 2000. Intrinsic and Extrinsic Motivations: Classic Definitions and New Directions. *Contemporary educational psychology* 25, 1: 54–67. https://doi.org/10.1006/ceps.1999.1020

52. Richard M. Ryan, C. Scott Rigby, and Andrew Przybylski. 2006. The Motivational Pull of Video Games: A Self-Determination Theory Approach. *Motivation and Emotion* 30, 4: 344–360. https://doi.org/10.1007/s11031-006-9051-8

53. Richard M. Ryan, C. Scott Rigby, and Andrew Przybylski. 2006. The Motivational Pull of Video Games: A Self-Determination Theory Approach. *Motivation and Emotion* 30, 4: 344–360. https://doi.org/10.1007/s11031-006-9051-8

54. Richard M Ryan and Edward L Deci. 2000. Self-determination theory and the facilitation of intrinsic motivation, social development, and well-being. *The American psychologist* 55, 1: 68–78. Retrieved April 5, 2017 from http://www.ncbi.nlm.nih.gov/pubmed/11392867

55. Timothy A Salthouse. 1990. Influence of experience on age differences in cognitive functioning. *Hum Factors* 32, 5: 551–569.

56. Timothy A Salthouse. 2009. When does age-related cognitive decline begin? *Neurobiology of Aging* 30, 4: 507–514. https://doi.org/10.1016/j.neurobiolaging.2008.09.023

57. Michael Scharkow, Ruth Festl, Jens Vogelgesang, and Thorsten Quandt. 2015. Beyond the "core-gamer": Genre preferences and gratifications in computer games. *Computers in Human Behavior* 44: 293–298. https://doi.org/10.1016/j.chb.2014.11.020

58. Bob De Schutter. 2010. Never Too Old to Play: The Appeal of Digital Games to an Older Audience. *Games and Culture* 6, 2: 155–170. https://doi.org/10.1177/1555412010364978

59. Bob De Schutter and Vero Vanden Abeele. 2010. Designing meaningful play within the psycho-social context of older adults. In *Proceedings of the 3rd International Conference on Fun and Games - Fun and Games '10*, 84–93. https://doi.org/10.1145/1823818.1823827

60. Bob De Schutter and Steven Malliet. 2014. The older player of digital games: A classification based on perceived need satisfaction. *Communications* 39, 1: 67–88. https://doi.org/10.1515/commun-2014-0005

61. Bob De Schutter and Vero Vandenabeele. 2015. Meaningful Play in Elderly Life. *58th annual conference of the International Communication Association "Communicating for Social Impact"*, November. Retrieved from https://lirias.kuleuven.be/bitstream/123456789/270075/3/De Schutter_VandenAbeele_2008_Meaningful Play in Elderly Life.pdf

62. John L. Sherry, Kristen Lucas, Bradley Greenberg, and Ken Lachlan. 2006. Video Game Uses and Gratifications as Predictors of Use and Game Preference. In *Playing Computer Games: Motives, Responses, and Consequences*. 213–224. https://doi.org/10.4324/9780203873700

63. Penelope Sweetser and Peta Wyeth. 2005. GameFlow: a model for evaluating player enjoyment in games. *Computers in Entertainment*

(CIE). Retrieved April 5, 2017 from http://dl.acm.org/citation.cfm?id=1077253

64. Joseph J. Thompson, Mark R. Blair, and Andrew J. Henrey. 2014. Over the hill at 24: Persistent age-related cognitive-motor decline in reaction times in an ecologically valid video game task begins in early adulthood. *PLoS ONE* 9, 4: e94215. https://doi.org/10.1371/journal.pone.0094215

65. Julia Valchanova. 2016. Finding (and Acting on) the White Spaces in Mobile Gaming. Retrieved April 14, 2017 from http://www.nielsen.com/us/en/insights/news/2016/finding-and-acting-on--the-white-spaces-in-mobile-gaming.html

66. M Vansteenkiste, B Neyrinck, C P Niemiec, B Soenens, H De Witte, and A Van den Broeck. 2007. On the relations among work value orientations, psychological need satisfaction and job outcomes: A self-determination theory approach. *Journal of Occupational and Organizational Psychology* 80: 251–277. https://doi.org/10.1348/096317906x111024

67. Pieter Wouters, Christof van Nimwegen, Herre van Oostendorp, and Erik D. van der Spek. 2013. A meta-analysis of the cognitive and motivational effects of serious games. *Journal of Educational Psychology* 105, 2: 249–265. https://doi.org/10.1037/a0031311

68. Nick Yee. 2006. Motivations for play in online games. *Cyberpsychology & behavior : the impact of the Internet, multimedia and virtual reality on behavior and society* 9, 6: 772–5. https://doi.org/10.1089/cpb.2006.9.772

69. Nick Yee. 2016. The Gamer Motivation Profile: What We Learned From 250,000 Gamers. In *Proceedings of the 2016 Annual Symposium on Computer-Human Interaction in Play*, 2. https://doi.org/10.1145/2967934.2967937

70. Sheila Yu. 2017. Tencent releases Q4 2016 and annual results - TechNode. Retrieved April 14, 2017 from http://technode.com/2017/03/23/tencent-releases-q4-2016-and-annual-results/

71. Robert B. Zajonc. 2001. Mere Exposure: A Gateway to the Subliminal. *Current Directions in Psychological Science* 10, 6: 224–228. https://doi.org/10.1111/1467-8721.00154

Beyond Addiction: Positive and Negative Parent Perceptions of Minecraft Play

Jane Mavoa[1]
jmavoa@student.unimelb.edu.au

Marcus Carter[2]
marcus.carter@sydney.edu.au

Martin Gibbs[1]
martin.gibbs@unimelb.edu.au

[1]Microsoft Research Centre for Social NUI
Computing & Information Systems
The University of Melbourne

[2]Digital Cultures Research Group
Department of Media and Communications
The University of Sydney

ABSTRACT
Parent perceptions of game play have a crucial role in forming the context in which children engage with digital games. However, little empirical information is known about these perceptions. The current study addresses this gap by describing a detailed analysis of open text responses by parents about their views on the popular game Minecraft. We show that parents are able to identify a broad range of both positive and negative outcomes associated with the game. We situate these observations within historical discourses about the role of screen media in children's lives, and the way that play itself is valued. Combining the insights from our data with these broader perspectives informs scholars interested in children's digital play and points to design implications.

Author Keywords
Minecraft; parents; children; digital games; attitudes.

ACM Classification Keywords
K.8.0 [Personal Computing]: General – *Games.*

INTRODUCTION
Digital gaming is a prominent part of contemporary childhoods with the vast majority of children, including the very young, now playing some form of digital game(s) regularly [4,40]. However, digital gaming is a form of screen time and occurs in a cultural context where 'screen time' was rated by the Australian public as the top child health concern ahead of obesity, family violence and suicide [41]. It follows then that digital gaming is a part of childhood that is understood to be something that requires careful monitoring and restriction by parents [57]. Despite the existence of generic, non-context sensitive guidelines for parents about managing 'screen time' [1], digital play does not occur in social or cultural isolation. Rather, children's engagement with technologies that facilitate digital play is surrounded, and informed, by the attitudes and behaviours of influences within the home, school and wider community [15,44,55]. One crucial variable surrounding the play experience of children is the way that parents perceive the digital games their children play [22].

This paper contributes empirically grounded insight into how Minecraft play is perceived by parents of children aged 3-12 years. Our analysis is based on open-text responses to open-ended questions. This is in contrast to much existing literature regarding parent attitudes toward gaming, which asks parents to select the degree to which they endorse pre-set statements about digital games. This paper therefore contributes a rich account of the positive perceptions of Minecraft play, alongside parental concerns. We discuss possible design implications arising from the predominantly instrumental valuing of digital games among parents apparent through our analysis. Beyond this, we also offer insight into the context of children's Minecraft play via parent attitudes. We situate our findings within broader historical and contemporary discourses surrounding the digitally mediated play of children. This perspective will be of interest to scholars studying child-player experience in its own right, in line with Carter et al.'s notion of the '*practice*' paradigm of games research within HCI [5, p.33].

Parent influence on child-player experience
Parent views about new forms of 'screen time' and internet use are emerging in the literature [7], and these attitudes have been found to be related to the amount of 'screen time' children engage in via differential mediation strategies [8]. Hiniker et al. [20] in their interviews with parents of children aged one to five years, found that negative perceptions of screen media use by children were dominant. Specifically, parents identified screen time as something requiring limits and monitoring in order that it does not displace time spent on non-screen based activities. Ito et al. [22], describing the findings from an ethnographic study of media use in families, notes that parents influence the user experience of children through a number of mechanisms. These include the provision (or not) of screen-based devices, location and time limits on use, and content-based restrictions. Ito et al. provide numerous examples

CHI PLAY '17, October 15–18, 2017, Amsterdam, Netherlands

ACM ISBN 978-1-4503-4898-0/17/10$15.00
https://doi.org/10.1145/3116595.3116638

from interview data illustrating the close link between attitudes toward media and these parent-led impacts on the experience of child media users.

Existing research about attitudes towards digital games in particular suggests that parents vary in the value they attribute to digital games. Some studies report both positive and negative perceptions associated with digital games by parents [3,25,37]. Others find more negative associations [26,27,56]. For example, Wartella et al. [56] found that parents rated 'video games' less favourably than television, computers and mobile devices in terms of perceptions of how they contribute to behaviour or learning and Kousari and Mehrabi [26] in their interviews with Iranian parents found a dominance of concern about negative effects of digital games on children's concentration, learning and 'real-life' behaviour. Kutner et al. [27] found, through focus groups with parents of adolescent boys, that displacement of time away from school work and physical activity were primary concerns.

Schott and van Vught [45] looked at parent attitudes to Grand Theft Auto IV and found that the overwhelming parental framing of the game was in terms of its moral bearings and parent concern about violence. Concerns about 'screen time' in general also frame attitudes toward gaming in particular, with parents in Sobel et al's. sample noting that even Pokémon Go, while virtuous in terms of implications for physical activity, was "*still screen time*" [46, p. 1489]. Anxieties about addiction and obsession in relation to digital games are additional concerns among parents [13,22,50]. On the other hand, Nikken et al. found parents in their sample were more likely to agree with statements about the positive effects of 'video games', though parents with a lack of personal experience of digital gameplay were more likely to endorse negative statements [39]. Part of the reason for these differences in findings could be due to the types of information gathered. In some of these studies parents were only asked about negative effects, and many relied on set questions and rating scales which precludes participant generated themes.

Literature on mediation strategies in relation to gaming provides evidence of the link between parent attitudes and child player experience. Following Nikken and Jansz's 2006 study [38] examining the ways that parents think about and mediate children's digital play, several authors have consistently found that parents who hold predominantly negative attitudes toward the effects of digital games are more likely to use restrictive mediation strategies [13,26,44,47]. Restrictive mediations strategies include limiting children's gaming time, and restricting play to certain titles. Conversely, parents who hold more neutral or positive views are more likely to co-play with their children and to apply fewer restrictions on gaming [26,39,44,47].

Stephen et al. [53] took an ecological approach to their study involving families with young children aged four and five years, which aimed to "*identify features of the home environment that make a difference to playing and learning with technological resources*" [p. 151]. They found family perspectives on the "*efficacy of technology as an educative tool*" [p. 157] were a crucial factor in shaping the lived experience of children with digital games via the degree, and type of encouragement offered to children and provision of particular games in favour of others. Relatedly, other work has shown that parents of children aged zero to five years make game purchasing decisions either on their own or in consultation with their child, whilst children rarely are solely responsible for purchase decisions and parents tend to select games that they perceive as educational [32].

Whilst our study does not draw specific links between mediation strategies and attitudes, it does provide a comprehensive description of those attitudes, in relation to Minecraft, beyond those illuminated via pre-set Likert scale questionnaires which inform the bulk of existing studies on parent perceptions and attitudes in relation to digital games.

Minecraft

Minecraft [34] serves as a particularly useful case study in examining children's gaming and related behaviours and attitudes. The game is hugely popular, particularly with children [14,28]. Minecraft is notably different to other mega successful gaming titles however, because of its perceived virtues. These benefits include the popular proposition that Minecraft offers educational and cognitive benefits [19,21]. The game is also frequently likened to Lego, which is commonly understood to be beneficial to children beyond instances of play [49].

However, Minecraft is, in its purest form, played via a screen. Therefore, it is also subject to the same concerns mentioned earlier about 'screen time'. Furthermore, the game is represented in media as being 'addictive' [23], potentially dangerous [36] and not as 'educational' as some claim [29]. These "*discursive dichotomies*" [8, p. 40] surrounding the game make it well suited to investigations of parent attitudes, as the lack of clear consensus leaves parents with the task of forming their own constructions and attitudes about the game. We sought parent perspectives on the game Minecraft as part of a larger survey about children's gaming and other screen media use [33].

METHOD

Participants and Procedure

The survey from which the current data was drawn, aimed to capture a mix of quantitative and qualitative information about the digital gaming habits of children. It was advertised via randomly selected primary schools and early learning centres (ELC's) in Metropolitan Melbourne. After initial contact with schools and ELC's yielded low rates of participation, an amendment to ethics approval was made to also allow for recruitment via word of mouth and social media. Parents and caregivers of children aged between 3 and 12 years completed the survey. The survey advertisement informed potential participants that questions would be about digital games such as Minecraft and 'screen time'. Further background provided in The Plain Language Statement indicated that we were also interested in hearing from parents of children who did not play digital games.

The project was approved by the Human Research Ethics Committee of The University of Melbourne, the Victoria Department of Education and Training, and Catholic Education Melbourne. The survey was open between November 2015 and May 2016 (this included a six week school holiday period when recruitment was paused).

Instrument and Measures

Data was collected using the REDCap (Research Electronic Data Capture) survey tool [54] hosted on The University of Melbourne data centre infrastructure. Questions began with basic demographic information related to the child, then asked about general gaming, followed by a set of Minecraft specific questions, YouTube use, general screen time, and finally basic parent demographic questions [33].

Data Analysis

In one section of the survey parents were asked: 'Do you think there are any good things about your child playing Minecraft?' and 'Do you have any concerns about your child playing Minecraft?' If parents answered 'yes' to either of these questions, they were then presented with an open text box and asked 'What sort of good things are there about your child playing Minecraft?' and/or 'What concerns you about your child playing Minecraft?'

The text responses were analysed using a constructionist grounded theory approach [6]. The responses were coded in an online rich-text collaborative analysis tool called Saturate.app [48]. Codes were applied at the sentence level and emerged initially from subject matter (for example, the code 'addiction' was given to any response mentioning addiction). Then on subsequent readings, codes were also applied to categorise observations of the way that responses related to one another, or represented some position on a subject (for example, the code 'time displacement' was given to responses that mentioned Minecraft detracting from any one of a range of other pursuits). Multiple codes were attached to individual single sentences as required. During this phase, detailed memos were made as a way of both unpacking the meaning of individual codes as well as situating them within the broader body of responses. The first author initially coded all responses, and validity was established via regular meetings between all authors where data and coding were reviewed and discussed in detail.

RESULTS

We will first present some quantitative information from the survey as a way of contextualising the responses reviewed in detail subsequently. A total of 755 completed responses were received to the survey. Respondents were predominantly between 36 and 45 years of age (67% of responses were from this age range), and most were university educated (75% of the sample). Table 1 presents descriptive statistics of the portion of the sample who had indicated that their child played digital games (n=665). Statistically significantly more boys than girls had played Minecraft in the last month (54% of boys [95% CI: 49.1%, 59.2%] vs 32% of girls [95% CI: 27%, 38.4%]), p = <.001. Older children in the sample were significantly more likely to have played Minecraft than those in the 3-5-year-old group, with only 11% [7.4%, 16.4%] of the youngest children having played in the last month compared to 53% [46.6%, 59.8%] of 6-8-year-olds and 68% [61.8%, 74.3%] of 9-12-year-olds, p = <.001.

		Male	Female	Total
	Minecraft	n (% of gender in age group)		n (% of age group)
Age Group	Play			
3-5	No	96 (83%)	92 (96%)	188 (89%)
	Yes	20 (17%)	4 (4%)	24 (11%)
	Total	116	96	212
6-8	No	39 (30%)	69 (69%)	108 (47%)
	Yes	92 (70%)	31 (31%)	123 (53%)
	Total	131	100	231
9+	No	44 (31%)	26 (32%)	70 (32%)
	Yes	97 (69%)	55 (68%)	152 (68%)
	Total	141	81	222
		n (% of gender in total sample)		n (% of whole sample)
Total	No	179 (46%)	187 (68%)	366 (55%)
	Yes	209 (54%)	90 (32%)	299 (45%)
	Total	388 (58%)	277 (42%)	665

Table 1. Descriptive statistics of the survey sample including proportions of children in each age and gender group who had played Minecraft in the past month. Responses from participants who indicated their child did not play any digital games are not included.

Positives Associated with Minecraft

91.4% (n=244) of parents of children who played Minecraft answered 'yes' to the question: 'Do you think there are any good things about your child playing Minecraft?' and 8.6% (n=23) answered 'no'. A total of 236 responses were entered in answer to 'What sort of good things are there about your child playing Minecraft?

Below we present categories of positive factors associated with Minecraft. Each is described, with the number of occurrences given in brackets next to category title. Typical examples from the data are given in italics after each description. The response numbers are given in round brackets after each example.

Creativity/Imagination (n=158)

Creativity was the most frequently mentioned positive and was often mentioned in a standalone manner but was also linked to concepts of design or construction, problem solving and spatial ability. 10 responses mentioned Minecraft in relation to Lego. 8 of these made direct links specifically with the 'creativity' of Lego. Imagination was also mentioned frequently, often in conjunction with talk of 'creativity'. Imagination appeared to be constructed as more of a repository to be drawn on in the process of being productively creative. "*creative thinking*" (10); "*creativity in building*" (14); "*It is much like Lego in the way that it is Creative*" (13); "*being very creative, using his imagination*" (17)

Social (n=59)

A range of social aspects of Minecraft play were mentioned. Some comments talked about this in a standalone manner, with 'social' or 'interaction' being construed as desirable in their own right. However, many more mentioned collaboration, cooperation, communication or teamwork. These particular responses speak more to the productive gain associated with social interaction, in terms of working effectively with others toward an end. Fourteen specifically mentioned play between siblings. Of these, the most common words used to talk about play between siblings were collaboration, cooperation, communication and interaction. Four of these also mentioned that the children enjoyed playing Minecraft together. Two responses mentioned 'being part of a community' and three talked about learning via social interaction in or around the game, either between friends or siblings. "*Teaches her to be creative and to work with other people on a project*" (33); "*being part of a virtual 'community'*" (40); "*We use it to spend time together*" (79); "*The thrill of being like his big brother*" (234)

Problem Solving (n=32)

Problem solving was mentioned frequently and either referred to as a way of thinking (often tied to creativity), or as a skill that could be taught and involved a series of steps. "*Creative problem solving*" (80); "*teaches problem solving skills*" (84)

Learning/Literacy/Mathematics (n=31)

Six responses mentioned the child either learning new vocabulary through playing Minecraft, comprehension skills or benefit to 'language' without further explanation. Ten responses mentioned reading specifically. Seven of these said that Minecraft offered practice and increase in reading ability. Three mentioned the game being an incentive to read, either in game text, Minecraft texts outside the game or texts related to aspects of the game. Seven respondents talked about mathematics, either in terms of Minecraft 'developing', 'teaching' or 'aiding' mathematical concepts. Seven respondents mentioned that Minecraft had triggered their child to seek out information about things that the game had sparked interest in. This also led to conversations about these interests. "*has also learnt new words about food, building materials and nature and mostly asks us there meaning or can figure them out due to the visual pictures*" (101); "*Encourages him to do research and read more to understand game mechanics*" (2)

Spatial Skills (n=22)

Spatial aspects of the game were described in varying ways including spatial awareness, 3D orientation, spatial creativity, spatial dexterity, spatial reasoning and spatial relationships. "*Digital spaciality* (sic)" (183); "*creative spatial play*" (35)

Digital Literacy (n=19)

Varying forms of digital literacy were mentioned including: hardware skills – typing, using mouse; software skills – skills used to produce new content (coding, mods) and skills used to find out information (using Google to find out how to do something in the game). "*mouse/keyboard*" (224); "*screen dexterity*" (180); "*learning to code through mods*" (54)

Planning/Strategy/Tactics (n=18)

Planning was mentioned either in a standalone manner or in relation to creativity, strategy or tactics. This suggests acknowledgement of the game-like elements of Minecraft. In this way, planning is not necessarily a purely procedural process but involves cognitive flexibility in the face of immediate obstacles provided by the game that threaten the success of the longer term objective. Some responses talked about planning as being a social process where children communicated with siblings, friends or parents about what they wanted to achieve in the game and how to go about doing this. "*building planning skills and putting creative plans into action*" (118); "*Planning and tactics*" (224)

Resource knowledge/Management (n=17)

Nine respondents said that Minecraft had contributed to learning about stones, elements and so on. Six of these spoke about knowledge gain directly from the game, while three also said that the game had triggered an interest in geology that had led to the child investigating the topic further outside the game. Twelve respondents mentioned that the game gave an understanding of where 'things' (food, wood, and other resources) come from. "*Learning ie chop trees to get wood*" (188); "*understanding of where materials come from*" (55)

Enjoyment (n=17)

Enjoyment was talked about in relation to specific elements that children liked, which were often linked to other codes. For example, enjoyment associated with creativity. Others mentioned enjoyment in its own right. These responses are unique in that they refer to a state of being that is valuable in and of itself, rather than a benefit actively tied to productivity either within the game or in other aspects of the child's life. "*Talk, laugh, have fun*" (17); "*shared enjoyment and connecting with friends*" (167); "*She really enjoys creating the animals and building houses*" (232)

Play (n=17)

Play was mentioned in varying ways: as creative or exploratory play, or as social, collaborative or cooperative play. Just one comment mentioned the game being a space for a child to play in (without mentioning the type or function of play). Therefore play was primarily talked about in terms of its purpose, or in terms of its quality. "*Fosters creative, imaginative play*" (30);"*playing as a team with others, communicating with others*" (236); "*creativity in making a world to play in*" (39)

Self-esteem/achievement/mastery/social capital (n=12)

These responses relate to the child gaining a sense of achievement, accomplishment or sense of mastery. Or, a gain in confidence, self-esteem or a feeling that they possess a degree of expertise in the game. Three of these responses stated that the child had relative weaknesses in other areas of their lives and that the child's Minecraft knowledge/expertise had provided a counterpoint to these. This was linked to improved social status where children's Minecraft knowledge was valued by peers. "*mastery in a controllable environment*" (62); "*Significant ego boost for my child because he is very good at minecraft (eg. school mates ring him at home for advice)*" (126); "*Gaming is something she can feel good at unlike school where she struggles*" (70)

Concerns About Minecraft Play

46.8% (n=125) of parents of children who played Minecraft answered 'yes' and 53.2% (n=142) answered 'no' to the question: 'Do you have any concerns about your child playing Minecraft?' A total of 124 responses were entered in answer to 'What concerns you about your child playing Minecraft?' The same format is used to discuss concerns about Minecraft play as in the previous section.

Time (n=48)

Concerns about time fall into those to do with:

a) *Too much* time spent on the game or too much 'screen time'. Some comments in this category did not elaborate on why too much time spent on screens or on Minecraft was a bad thing. It is commonly understood that 'screen time' is potentially harmful if done 'too much'.

b) *Time displaced* away from other pursuits. Responses made specific mention of time spent playing Minecraft taking time away from other pursuits that are commonly seen as valuable by parents, such as school work, reading, physical activity, and playing outside.

c) The *need to monitor and regulate* the amount of time children spend on Minecraft. Several comments said that the child would prefer to play Minecraft to the exclusion of these other activities if given the opportunity. This was mentioned 17 times and often included statements that children would keep on playing indefinitely if time restrictions were not in place. Seven parents said that children were only allowed to play on weekends, and others said that children were only allowed to play for a certain amount of time, or after completing other activities such as homework.

d) Ten responses mentioned that one of the things that Minecraft displaces time away from is activities that are done *outside*. Three talked about outside activities as involving physical activity, or stress relief by exposure to nature. Four responses said that the child not being outdoors was a concern in itself without explanation about why being outside was beneficial.

"*Amount of screen time*" (85); '*too much time on screen, less time for play and study*" (97); "*If I didn't stop the time she was playing I'm sure she would play for a lot longer*" (113); '*She should be outdoors*" (87); "*I would rather him play outdoors than fixed to a screen*"(101)

Cyber safety (n=30)

A range of concerns related to safety were reported. These centred on children playing with unknown people on online servers. Most responses in this group stated that 'being online' or 'playing with strangers' was concerning without explaining why/how. Three responses specifically talked about grooming and predation. Six others said that concern was about their child being exposed to the inappropriate behaviour (swearing, bullying, cruelty to animals, meanness) of other players. Two responses said that they were worried that they did not know enough about how to block content or to how to tell if their child had overridden parental controls. "*Interactions with unknown adults, grooming children*" (25); "*encountering harmful behaviours of other human players*" (52); "*playing with unknown persons, not being able to be up to date on dangers /warnings about games and what to look out for as parent*" (40)

Addiction and Obsession (n=27)

The vast majority of these used the word addictive or addicted as matter of fact, plainly understandable terms that did not require further explanation. This indicates that the word 'addiction' is commonly understood, and is readily applied to children's gaming. Many comments seemed to define addiction as a child having a desire to play Minecraft for longer than parents would like. Mention of negative behaviours after being asked to stop playing, or if denied limitless access to the game, were also mentioned several times in relation to addiction. Some responses talked about children being obsessed with the game, including talking excessively about the game and this being unpleasant for parents who have little interest in Minecraft. "*Addiction!*"(11); "*It appears to be quite addictive*" (84); "*Addictive nature/desire wanting to play more than allocated*" (42); "*Obsessed with talking about Minecraft with parents to point of parental frustration.*" (77)

Violence (n=20)

The majority of comments mentioning violence talked about children either partaking in or witnessing violence or aggression toward in-game characters. Inferred consequences of this were rarely mentioned explicitly. Though, two raised the possibility that the child would learn that such behaviour was acceptable in realms outside of the game. One postulated a possible link between a child's talk of suicide and Minecraft. Other parents talked about their own personal reactions to the violence in the game, effectively expressing a proxy dislike of certain gameplay elements because of the anti-social, unacceptable place these things have in broader culture and the strong negative emotion these acts elicit in adults. "*I do get concerned as to the culture of other users (school, friends) perhaps being more 'violent' and him thinking by 'association' with the game that this is acceptable despite my husband and my reminder to not be violent/aggressive*" (3); "*We have heard him refer rather flippantly to 'killing himself' on Minecraft in the past. In moments of great upset or drama for him in real life, he will say he wants to kill himself.*" (104); "*Will sometimes switch to survival on other peoples devices, I find this quite gruesome and violent*" (63)

Physical ill effects (n=16)

Displaced time away from physical activity was mentioned 11 times. The majority of these said lack of activity was concerning on its own, though one specifically mentioned the game being "*a contributing factor to childhood obesity*" (13). Five responses said that negative effects on eyesight were concerning, one said posture, and one said "*brain function and fatigue*"(76). "*Too much screen time - not enough physical activity*"(102); "*Not good for his eyes*"(48)

Behaviour (n=14)

These responses talked about the attribution of problematic behaviours displayed by children in relation to Minecraft play, or rather the cessation of play. Most of these responses talked about undesirable behaviours occurring when children were asked to stop playing, or when told they could not play. Some also mentioned that conflict arose between siblings or friends during the course of play. Two comments also talked about frustration as a concerning aspect of the game. "*We have noticed that she often becomes quite irritated and displays poorer behaviors on the days she plays this particular game*" (121); "*after a couple of hours both kids usually end up fighting and moody and tantrums fly*" (125); "*Gets addicted then angry when taken away*"(98); "*when they get frustrated they can become mean to the other players or destroy some of their buildings in anger*" (108)

DISCUSSION

In keeping with earlier research on parent attitudes toward screen media in general [3,25,37,42] parents recognise a wide range of both positive and negative aspects of Minecraft play. The game is not constructed in a single unified manner by individuals. In fact, there are some elements that are perceived in wholly opposite ways by different parents. The degree of violence in the game, for example, is perceived to be relatively low by some parents, and high by others. This discrepancy also reflects the fact that Minecraft offers so many different modes of play which have implications for the way the game is experienced in terms of content and sociality.

Despite this variety, there were some ideas that dominated in this sample. Minecraft as 'creative' but also as time consuming and detracting from 'reality', were pronounced trends across the sample. This dichotomous construction of the game is in keeping with historical trends in relation to perceptions of screen based media in the lives of children. For example, in introducing their observational studies about children's engagement with television between 1958 and 1960, Schramm et al., note: "*On the one hand, it is argued that television keeps children at home and gets the family to do things together. On the other hand…it encourages withdrawal from reality and makes addicts*" [27, p. 5]. Our study has shown such "*discursive dichotomies*" [9, p. 5] persist in a technological and cultural context markedly different to the one Schramm et al. wrote about in 1961.

Furthermore, the current study provides evidence that parents consider play in terms of its potential to contribute to the development of their child. Specifically, parents spoke about this particular game contributing to the development of creativity, problem solving, planning and collaboration (among a range of other skills). This replicates the findings of Marsh et al., in relation to parents' self-reported app purchase decision making. Parents of children aged zero to five years old in that study most frequently cited motivation for app purchase as: "*to support their learning*" and "*to encourage play and creativity*" [19, p.12]. The preponderance of functional benefits mentioned by parents in our sample further highlights the popular construction of children's play as productive.

Related to this idea of childhood as production, is the way that children feature in government campaigns aimed at economic growth. The Australian government is currently trying to increase the number of children, particularly female children, who will go on to have careers in the fields of Science, Technology, Engineering and Maths (STEM) [9]. Digital play is presented in popular media [52] as a gateway to STEM fields, and indeed there is literature to suggest this link is valid [16]. Our data indicate that parents see Minecraft as a form of digital play particularly well suited to the development of STEM skills. The most frequently mentioned benefits parents identified in relation to Minecraft were creativity and problem solving. These skills also feature strongly in the Victorian STEM Education State Plan document [10]. Educators also talk about '21st century learning' as a means of overcoming the perils of automation. Again, 'creativity and collaboration' are proposed as the means through which children will have hope at future employment [2].

Turning now to the concern parents had about Minecraft play, there was a strong sense throughout our data that the 'screen' or the game, exists in a state of constant competition with all of the other things that parents want their children to do. Minecraft is construed as so appealing to children that it dominates their thinking. It causes constant struggle on the part of parents to direct children's attention to other activities (homework, being outside, socialising, playing) in the pursuit of balance, and variety. In some instances there's almost a sense of resentment toward the game for being so alluring. Relatedly, this data confirms that digital gaming as a form of 'screen time' is commonly understood to be something that requires active limitation. So, parents are clearly in a position where they are charged with the difficult task of maximising the putative benefits of digital play whilst at the same time minimising the putative harms associated with 'too much' play via screen.

Another prominent feature of the responses about concerning aspects of Minecraft play was talk of cyber safety. Such concerns fit into well-established discourse about screen media in general and preconceived norms about video games. As Willet [57] notes, high-profile risks such as contact with unknown people "*have strengthened the discursive construction of children as vulnerable in relation to their media use, and the home environment as a place for extra safety measures*" [p. 1063].

It is worth noting here that elsewhere in the survey from which the current data is drawn, only 11% of parents indicated that they ever co-played Minecraft with their children, and only 13% indicated that their child ever played Minecraft online with other people not known to them. Therefore, it appears that these concerns are indeed less about direct experience or observation of children's gameplay, but rather, are heavily influenced by normative representations of what parents should be concerned about. Whilst education about safety in online spaces is crucial, there is a risk that progress in forming evidence-based guidelines for parents around digital play may be hindered by reliance on the protectionist ethos of previous waves of recommendations that do not adequately account for the lived experiences of children with online media, including online games [30,35].

Paying greater attention to parent attitudes and their antecedents is one means by which researchers can contribute to reducing this risk. Increasing parental gaming literacy is one possible means to do this. Parental mediation of children's digital play is likely to be influenced by "parents' prior experience with and knowledge of video games" [13,24]. Schott and van Vught [45] found that parent perceptions of the game Grand Theft Auto IV were drastically altered after just a short period of playing the game. They propose that "*little direct knowledge of games as a played activity...might be responsible for the misconstruction of the moral and ethical frameworks governing game worlds*" [p.2]. Parents reported that the experience of playing the game gave them knowledge about the context and consequences of in-game actions, and also about the complexities of moral decision making that the game required.

It should be noted that constructions of digital play and its value are likely to be class-bound [22,39]. Whilst our analysis did not explicitly delineate different class structures during analysis, the sample did consist predominantly of parents with university level education (a marker of middle-class status). Willet [57] notes that providing children opportunities to play digital games that cater to middle class definitions "*achievement*" constitutes "*good parenting*" [p. 1063]. Further research, with more attention given to the class status of participants, would provide valuable insight into the way that digital games are viewed across a population.

Design Implications

Based on their findings, Schott and van Vught [45] recommend that efforts aimed at reducing harm associated with digital games should consist of "*educating the public and supporting parents in learning about digital games*" [p.10]. We concur with this approach and suggest that in practice this could occur on a range of levels including policy, regulation and education (via schools as part of digital citizenship curricula for example). Game designers could also consider ways to enhance the gaming literacy of parents through features that increase the likelihood of co-play, or otherwise encourage parents to display an active interest in their children's gaming, beyond monitoring for inappropriate content and time spent playing. Some developers of game apps designed for young children currently include such features. When opening a Sago Mini app for example, a 'for parents' icon appears. When selected, a detailed explanation of the game appears including a section titled 'to talk about' where suggested prompts for co-use are included (for example, parents are told to ask questions like: 'what do you think the character will do next?' and so on) [43]. Games aimed at older children, including Minecraft, tend to not include such explicit parent-involvement features. There is no literature explicitly directed to parents on the game's primary website, and Minecraft contains no tutorial or internal "*help*" to players [12,31]. In order to play the game, even in the less challenging 'creative' mode where the process of 'crafting' items is not central, and there is no threat element, a degree of gaming literacy is required. Whilst this may provide opportunity for child-led instruction and an empowering variation on standard power dynamics between parent and child (as mentioned in several of the comments in the current study), such a 'bare-bones' framework could act as a barrier to the involvement of parents who may not have personal repertoires of gaming experience to draw upon [38] nor an intrinsic interest in digital gaming as a medium [51].

One game that has successfully facilitated co-play between parents and children is Pokémon Go. Based on survey data and interviews with guardians of children playing Pokémon Go in public spaces, Sobel et al., [50] suggest that beyond the effect of the game requiring physical activity to be played (and therefore countering concern about gaming leading to inactivity), the game also has "*simple gameplay mechanics*" that allow for focus on content and play rather than technical aspects [p. 1491]. This, combined with a range of other design features outlined by Sobel et al, led to shared enjoyment of the game parents and children and point to design elements that could foster co-play, and therefore increased parental gaming literacy.

Recognition of the common construal of digital games, in this case Minecraft, as 'addictive' and difficult for children to stop playing points to other possible design considerations. One factor sometimes associated with the game's 'addictive' qualities is the assertion that there is no end to the game [17]. Indeed, two responses in our study explicitly mentioned this in describing difficulties associated with getting children to switch tasks. Such conflict surrounding transitions away from screen media were documented by Hiniker et al. [20]. They found that parents of children aged one to five noted smoother transitions away from 'screen time' when aided by technology, for example, by a movie ending without an auto-play feature presenting further content. Hiniker et al., suggest that screen based media technologies could include: prompts to set time limits at the outset of engagement; pop-up prompts at natural time breaks asking whether the child wishes to continue; asking the child how many more minutes she would like to keep using the technology; and the presentation of a 'two-more-minutes' warning/prompt. Whilst the participants in Hiniker et al., predominantly engaged with movie and television content, we propose that the design features they suggest are equally applicable to open-world, sandbox games such as Minecraft. Designing natural breaks in game play and consideration of the ethical implications of games designed to foster limitless engagement should also inform future games for children [18].

We have shown, using Minecraft as an example, that parents value play that involves opportunity for problem solving and creativity. Marsh et al., [32] provide a range of suggestions, based on their observational studies of zero to five year old children, for design that fosters creativity. They recommend: open-ended games where the focus is on process rather than outcome; embedded meaningful problem-solving, critical and abstract thinking tasks; prompts in the form of questions or statements that stimulate play or experimentation; opportunities for creation of content within or surrounding the game, particularly co-creation involving parents or siblings; and the promotion of linkage between in-game and in 'real life' play activities.

CONCLUSION

We have provided comprehensive, qualitative empirical insight into the specific ways parents of young children perceive and interpret the game Minecraft. This represents a significant contribution to the literature because it considers, in detail, one of the most influential variables associated with the lived experience of children in relation to digital games. Research that aims to maximize the benefits, and reduce the harms associated with children's use of digital games, needs to take into account the myriad of contextual factors that surround any one child's gameplay, including the views of parents. We have shown that parents particularly value digital play opportunities that allow for creativity and problem solving, while they are also concerned about the amount of time children spend gaming and contact with unknown people during online play. Game designers should therefore consider ways to ensure games designed for children allow ample opportunity for player directed creativity, but within time bound parameters. Increasing parent gaming literacy will also aid in positive outcomes for children by reducing the risk of longstanding negative popular discourse about digital games clouding perceptions of the reality of children's everyday gaming practices.

ACKNOWLEDGMENTS

Author 1 gratefully acknowledges the support of the Microsoft Social NUI Research Centre and funding in the form of an Australian Postgraduate Award.

REFERENCES

1. AAP Council on Communications and Media. 2016. Media and Young Minds. *Pediatrics* 138, 5: 00–00.
2. Michael Anderson. 2017. Forget the 3Rs: modern schools need to embrace the 4Cs. *The Sydney Morning Herald*. Retrieved April 13, 2017 from http://www.smh.com.au/comment/forget-the-3rs-modern-schools-need-to-embrace-the-4cs-20170306-gurr8h.html
3. Jeroen Bourgonjon, Martin Valcke, Ronald Soetaert, Bram de Wever, and Tammy Schellens. 2011.

Parental acceptance of digital game-based learning. *Computers & Education* 57, 1: 1434–1444. https://doi.org/10.1016/j.compedu.2010.12.012

4. Jeffrey Brand. 2015. Digital Australia 2016 DA16 Final.pdf. Retrieved July 30, 2015 from http://www.igea.net/wp-content/uploads/2015/07/Digital-Australia-2016-DA16-Final.pdf
5. Marcus Carter, John Downs, Bjorn Nansen, Mitchell Harrop, and Martin Gibbs. 2014. Paradigms of Games Research in HCI: A Review of 10 Years of Research at CHI. In *Proceedings of the First ACM SIGCHI Annual Symposium on Computer-human Interaction in Play* (CHI PLAY '14), 27–36. https://doi.org/10.1145/2658537.2658708
6. K Charmaz. 2008. Constructionism and the Grounded Theory Method. In *Handbook of Constructionist Reserach*, J Holstein and J Gubrium (eds.). The Guilford Press, New York, 397–412.
7. Stephane Chaudron. 2015. *Young Children (0-8) and digital technology: A qualitative exploratory study across seven countries*. Publications Office of the European Union. Retrieved October 14, 2016 from http://publications.jrc.ec.europa.eu/repository/handle/111111111/33897
8. Drew P. Cingel and Marina Krcmar. 2013. Predicting media use in very young children: The role of demographics and parent attitudes. *Communication Studies* 64, 4: 374–394. https://doi.org/10.1080/10510974.2013.770408
9. Commonwealth of Australia. 2016. Embracing the digital age. *National Innovation and Science Agenda*. Retrieved August 16, 2016 from http://www.innovation.gov.au/page/embracing-digital-age
10. Department of Education and Training Victoria. 2017. VicSTEM. Retrieved April 14, 2017 from http://www.education.vic.gov.au:80/about/programs/learningdev/vicstem/Pages/default.aspx
11. Kirsten Drotner. 2005. Mediatized childhoods: Discourses, dilemmas and directions. In *Studies in modern childhood*, Jens Qvortrup (ed.). Palgrave Macmillan UK, 39–58. https://doi.org/10.1007/978-0-230-50492-9_3
12. Sean C. Duncan. 2011. Minecraft, Beyond Construction and Survival. *Well Played* 1, 1: 1–22.
13. Lina Eklund and Karin Helmersson Bergmark. 2013. Parental mediation of digital gaming and internet use. 63–70. Retrieved July 19, 2017 from http://www.diva-portal.org/smash/record.jsf?pid=diva2:622130
14. ETonline. 2015. Kids' Choice Awards 2015: The Winner's List. *Entertainment Tonight*. Retrieved April 28, 2015 from http://www.etonline.com/awards/161880_kids_choice_awards_2015_the_winner_s_list/
15. Elisabeth Gee, Sinem Siyahhan, and Anna Montana Cirell. 2016. Video gaming as digital media, play, and family routine: implications for understanding video gaming and learning in family contexts. *Learning, Media and Technology* 0, 0: 1–15. https://doi.org/10.1080/17439884.2016.1205600
16. Isabela Granic, Adam Lobel, and Rutger C. M. E. Engels. 2014. The benefits of playing video games. *The American Psychologist*, 1: 66.
17. Lisa Guernsey. 2012. An "Educational" Video Game Has Taken Over My House. *Slate*. Retrieved October 23, 2015 from http://www.slate.com/articles/technology/future_tense/2012/08/minecraft_teachers_love_the_game_but_as_a_parent_i_m_worried_my_kids_are_addicted.2.html
18. Tristan Harris. 2017. The Need for a New Design Ethics. Retrieved April 13, 2017 from http://www.tristanharris.com/the-need-for-a-new-design-ethics/
19. Nance Haxton. 2015. Teachers should embrace Minecraft as classroom tool: research. *ABC News*. Retrieved July 8, 2015 from http://www.abc.net.au/news/2015-07-07/minecraft-successful-classroom-tool-research-shows/6602078
20. Alexis Hiniker, Hyewon Suh, Sabina Cao, and Julie A. Kientz. 2016. Screen Time Tantrums: How Families Manage Screen Media Experiences for Toddlers and Preschoolers. In *Proceedings of the 2016 CHI Conference on Human Factors in Computing Systems* (CHI '16), 648–660. https://doi.org/10.1145/2858036.2858278
21. Mimi Ito. 2015. Why Minecraft Rewrites the Playbook for Learning. *Boing Boing*. Retrieved June 8, 2015 from http://boingboing.net/2015/06/06/why-minecraft-rewrites-the-pla.html
22. Mizuko Ito, S Baumer, Matteo Bittanti, danah boyd, Rachel Cody, B Herr Stephenson, Heather Horst, Patricia Lange, D Mahendran, K Martinez, C Pascoe, D Perkel, L Robinson, C Sims, and L Tripp. 2009. *Hanging Out, Messing Around, and Geeking Out: Kids Living and Learning With New Media*. MIT Press, Cambridge, MA, USA. Retrieved June 20, 2017 from https://mitpress.mit.edu/books/hanging-out-messing-around-and-geeking-out
23. J Jenkins. 2015. Should parents ever worry about Minecraft? *BBC News*. Retrieved May 15, 2015 from http://www.bbc.com/news/magazine-32051153
24. Hee Jhee Jiow, Sun Sun Lim, and Julian Lin. 2017. Level Up! Refreshing Parental Mediation Theory for Our Digital Media Landscape. *Communication Theory* 27, 3: 309–328. https://doi.org/10.1111/comt.12109

25. Joan Ganz Cooney Centre. 2017. Joan Ganz Cooney Center - Infographic: Parents on How Digital Games Affect Family Life. Retrieved May 30, 2017 from http://www.joanganzcooneycenter.org/2017/05/26/infographic-parents-on-how-digital-games-affect-family-life/
26. Masoud Kousari and Meghdad Mehrabi. 2017. Parental Mediation of Children's Video Game Experiences: Iranian Parents' Strategies of Mediation. *IAU International Journal of Social Sciences* 7, 1: 1–14.
27. Lawrence A. Kutner, Cheryl K. Olson, Dorothy E. Warner, and Sarah M. Hertzog. 2008. Parents' and Sons' Perspectives on Video Game Play: A Qualitative Study. *Journal of Adolescent Research* 23, 1: 76–96. https://doi.org/10.1177/0743558407310721
28. Derrik J. Lang. 2015. "Minecraft" most streamed video game in YouTube's history. Retrieved May 26, 2015 from http://www.nhregister.com/arts-and-entertainment/20150524/minecraft-most-streamed-video-game-in-youtubes-history
29. Jun Lee and Robert Pasin. 2014. We're ruining our kids with Minecraft: The case for unstructured play. *Quartz*. Retrieved May 15, 2015 from http://qz.com/311035/were-ruining-our-kids-with-minecraft-the-case-for-unstructured-play/
30. Sonia Livingstone, Kjartan Ólafsson, Ellen J. Helsper, Francisco Lupiáñez-Villanueva, Giuseppe A. Veltri, and Frans Folkvord. 2017. Maximizing Opportunities and Minimizing Risks for Children Online: The Role of Digital Skills in Emerging Strategies of Parental Mediation. *Journal of Communication* 67, 1: 82–105. https://doi.org/10.1111/jcom.12277
31. Esther MacCallum-Stewart. 2013. Diggy Holes and Jaffa Cakes: The rise of the elite fan producer in video-gaming culture. *Journal of Gaming & Virtual Worlds* 5, 2: 165–182. https://doi.org/10.1386/jgvw.5.2.165_1
32. Jackie Marsh, Lydia Plowman, D Yamada-Rice, J Bishop, J Lahmar, F Scott, A Davenport, S Davis, K French, M Piras, S Thornhill, P Robinson, and P Winter. 2015. *Exploring Play and Creativity in Pre-Schoolers' Use of Apps: Final Project Report*. Retrieved October 5, 2016 from http://techandplay.org/reports/TAP_Final_Report.pdf
33. Jane Mavoa, Marcus Carter, and Martin Gibbs. 2017. Children and Minecraft: A survey of children's digital play. *New Media & Society* Under Review.
34. Mojang. 2011. *Minecraft*.
35. Bjorn Nansen, Kabita Chakraborty, Lisa Gibbs, Colin MacDougall, and Frank Vetere. 2012. Children and Digital Wellbeing in Australia: Online regulation, conduct and competence. *Journal of Children and Media* 6, 2: 237–254. https://doi.org/10.1080/17482798.2011.619548
36. Jennifer Newton. 2016. German police rescue Swiss boy from attic of a man he met online. *Mail Online*. Retrieved November 24, 2016 from http://www.dailymail.co.uk/news/article-3662235/German-police-rescue-12-year-old-Swiss-boy-attic-paedophile-met-playing-Minecraft-online.html
37. D Niemyer. 2016. Four employed, middle-class, suburban mothers' understanding and acceptance of the learning potential of videogames. Sam Houston State University, Texas. Retrieved July 19, 2017 from https://search.proquest.com/openview/efdceb5ee9a12963ddcca7a4ef009089/1?pq-origsite=gscholar&cbl=18750&diss=y
38. Peter Nikken and Jeroen Jansz. 2006. Parental mediation of children's videogame playing: a comparison of the reports by parents and children. *Learning, Media and Technology* 31, 2: 181–202. https://doi.org/10.1080/17439880600756803
39. Peter Nikken, Jeroen Jansz, and Sanneke Schouwstra. 2007. Parents' Interest in Videogame Ratings and Content Descriptors in Relation to Game Mediation. *European Journal of Communication* 22, 3: 315–336. https://doi.org/10.1177/0267323107079684
40. Ofcom. 2015. Children and parents: Media use and attitudes report 2015. Retrieved October 4, 2016 from http://stakeholders.ofcom.org.uk/market-data-research/other/research-publications/childrens/children-parents-nov-15/
41. Anthea Rhodes. 2015. Australian child health poll. Retrieved December 16, 2015 from https://www.childhealthpoll.org.au
42. Victoria Rideout and Henry J. Kaiser Family Foundation. 2007. *Parents, Children & Media: A Kaiser Family Foundation Survey*. Henry J. Kaiser Family Foundation.
43. Sago Sago Toys Inc. Sago Mini. Retrieved July 20, 2017 from https://sagomini.com/apps/
44. Violetta K. Schaan and André Melzer. 2015. Parental Mediation of Children's Television and Video Game use in Germany: Active and Embedded in Family Processes. *Journal of Children and Media* 9, 1: 58–76. https://doi.org/10.1080/17482798.2015.997108
45. Gareth Schott and Jasper van Vught. 2013. Replacing preconceived accounts of digital games with experience of play: When parents went native in GTA IV. *Transactions of the Digital Games Research Association* 1, 1. Retrieved August 27, 2015 from http://todigra.org/index.php/todigra/article/view/5
46. Wilbur Schramm, Jack Lyle, and Edwin B. Parker. 1961. *Television in the lives of our children*. Stanford University Press, Stanford.

47. Wonsun Shin and Jisu Huh. 2011. Parental mediation of teenagers' video game playing: Antecedents and consequences. *New Media & Society* 13, 6: 945–962. https://doi.org/10.1177/1461444810388025

48. Jonathan Sillito. 2013. *Saturate*. Retrieved June 17, 2016 from http://www.saturateapp.com/

49. Genevieve Smith. 2016. Lego Is the Perfect Toy. *Science of Us*. Retrieved December 13, 2016 from http://nymag.com/scienceofus/2016/12/lego-is-the-perfect-toy.html

50. Kiley Sobel, Arpita Bhattacharya, Alexis Hiniker, Jin Ha Lee, Julie A. Kientz, and Jason C. Yip. 2017. It Wasn'T Really About the PokéMon: Parents' Perspectives on a Location-Based Mobile Game. In *Proceedings of the 2017 CHI Conference on Human Factors in Computing Systems* (CHI '17), 1483–1496. https://doi.org/10.1145/3025453.3025761

51. Constance Steinkuehler. 2016. Parenting and Video Games. *Journal of Adolescent & Adult Literacy* 59, 4: 357–361.

52. STEM Video Game Challenge. 2017. Teachers and parents | STEM Video Game Challenge | Australia. Retrieved April 14, 2017 from https://www.stemgames.org.au/teachers-and-parents

53. Christine Stephen, Olivia Stevenson, and Claire Adey. 2013. Young children engaging with technologies at home: The influence of family context. *Journal of Early Childhood Research* 11, 2: 149–164. https://doi.org/10.1177/1476718X12466215

54. Vanderbilt. 2016. *REDCap*. Vanderbilt University, Nashville. Retrieved December 2, 2016 from https://redcap.healthinformatics.unimelb.edu.au/index.php?action=help

55. Elizabeth A. Vandewater. 2013. Ecological approaches to media and children. In *The Routledge international handbook of children, adolescents and media*, Dafna Lemish (ed.). London ; New York : Routledge, 2013., 46–54.

56. Ellen A. Wartella, Victoria Rideout, Alexis R. Lauricella, and Sabrina Connell. 2014. *ParentingAgeDigitalTechnology.REVISED.FINAL_.2014.pdf*. Northwestern University. Retrieved May 14, 2015 from http://web5.soc.northwestern.edu/cmhd/wp-content/uploads/2014/03/ParentingAgeDigitalTechnology.REVISED.FINAL_.2014.pdf

57. Rebekah J. Willett. 2015. The discursive construction of "good parenting" and digital media – the case of children's virtual world games. *Media, Culture & Society*: 0163443715591666. https://doi.org/10.1177/0163443715591666

Bilingual SpeechBlocks: Investigating How Bilingual Children Tinker with Words in English and Spanish

Juliana Nazare*
MIT Media Lab
Cambridge, USA
juliana@media.mit.edu

Anneli Hershman*
MIT Media Lab
Cambridge, USA
anneli@media.mit.edu

Ivan Sysoev
MIT Media Lab
Cambridge, USA
isysoev@media.mit.edu

Deb Roy
MIT Media Lab
Cambridge, USA
dkroy@media.mit.edu

ABSTRACT
Many children in the United States speak a language other than English in the home, yet the literacy learning mobile apps and games available do not reflect the country's growing number of bilingual children. Furthermore, to the authors' knowledge, none of these apps provide open-ended, constructionist literacy learning opportunities for young bilinguals. In response, we created Bilingual SpeechBlocks, a version of the constructionist literacy learning app SpeechBlocks, for young children who speak both Spanish and English. We discuss the design considerations and examine the affordances of this app when tested with bilingual children, in comparison to the original monolingual app. From our observations, this version of the app enables new modes of wordplay and engagement for bilingual children and their families. This work has implications for how open-ended designs can foster bilingual literacy learning by encouraging language differentiation through exploration and providing natural opportunities for family co-engagement.

ACM Classification Keywords
H.5.m Information interfaces and presentation (e.g. HCI): Miscellaneous

Author Keywords
Bilingualism; mobile app and game design for children; constructionism; early literacy learning

CHI PLAY '17, October 15-18, 2017, Amsterdam, Netherlands

ACM 978-1-4503-4898-0/17/10...$15.00
DOI: https://doi.org/10.1145/3116595.3116616

Figure 1: The main screen of the Bilingual SpeechBlocks app (BSB).

INTRODUCTION
As 22% of school-aged children in the United States speak a language other than English at home and the number of bilingual speakers is predicted to continue growing [36], bilingualism is an increasingly important focus in the U.S. educational system, especially when it comes to learning to read and write. Additionally, as educational technology, such as learning apps for mobile devices, becomes more prevalent in homes throughout the world, it is extremely important to develop high quality educational content for these technologies that are child-interest driven and contextually relevant [43]. Yet despite these trends, there are very few high quality early learning apps that are being developed for bilingual children and their families [20]. In response to this disconnect, we created Bilingual SpeechBlocks (BSB) (Figure 1), a constructionist literacy app that provides an open-ended canvas for children to explore the phonetic rules of both Spanish and

*These authors contributed equally to this work.

English. BSB is a variation of the original SpeechBlocks app, which we will refer to as monolingual SpeechBlocks (MSB). MSB is a self-expressive literacy app that specifically focuses on helping children explore the phonetic rules of English [39]. In this paper, we will use the word app to refer to a game designed for a mobile device.

Our Motivation and Purpose

The creation of BSB was inspired by Pearson et al.'s research [29, 28]. They found that when bilingual children were given an assessment in one language, their rate of vocabulary learning was half that of monolingual children, but when they were given an assessment in both of their languages, their rate of vocabulary was equivalent to monolingual children's. Thus, it is important to consider the languages a child is exposed to when designing literacy learning experiences because bilingual children's language and literacy abilities are distributed among two languages [18, 21, 33]. This research made us question whether MSB was unintentionally impeding upon bilingual children's word play simply through providing a solely monolingual experience.

The particular design of BSB was further motivated by research on how bilingual children learn to read and write, especially for languages with similar orthographies such as Spanish and English [10, 38]. This research suggests that it is important for children to distinguish between the phonetic rules of the different languages they speak [10, 8, 38, 24].

In light of this research, we see an opportunity for educational apps and games to help bilingual children improve both their Spanish and English language abilities. Thus, we decided to create BSB so that Spanish and English-speaking bilingual children can explore the alphabetic principles of their two languages side by side. Rather than create a tool for translation, we opted to create a tool that could facilitate differentiation between the orthographies of English and Spanish, an important milestone for bilingual children [13]. The purpose of this paper is to examine how incorporating two languages into the design of SpeechBlocks may change bilingual children's nature of word play and engagement within the app. We do this by presenting the design decisions of BSB and sharing some observations from our exploratory pilot study with the app.

BACKGROUND

Bilingualism and Learning

Bilingualism is an important issue in the United States educational system, as growing up bilingual in an English-speaking school system has both advantages and disadvantages in terms of learning. According to a report by the U.S. Department of Education [31], the number of school-age children in the United States who speak a language other than English in the home grew dramatically from 9% to 20% between 1979 and 2007. Of those children, 75% spoke Spanish in the home and spoke English with difficulty. On average, it takes two to three years for these children to reach their monolingual peers' conversational abilities and five to seven years for them to be on par with their monolingual peers in academic performance [7]. However, this may differ depending on their exposure to English before entering school. Hammer et al. [15] demonstrated that children who were exposed to both Spanish and English at home had stronger English abilities upon entering Head Start (a nationwide early childhood education program in the United States), while children who were exposed to and communicated in only Spanish before entering Head Start had stronger Spanish abilities.

English-Spanish bilingualism has many advantages. Fluency in both languages can help with better semantic, phonological, and grammatical awareness [3, 4, 5, 6], as well as enhanced creativity and stronger academic performance [14]. It can also help support children's psychological development and social development (i.e. identifying with others in their communities) [26]. Therefore, the research suggests that bilingual education has many developmental and academic advantages for children who are exposed to both languages at an early age.

Despite all of the academic advantages of bilingualism, there are also many challenges that bilingual children face while learning to read and write in their two languages. When bilingual children are reading a word in one language, researchers have observed that they activate their lexical knowledge in both of their languages [37]. In particular, Spanish and English have partially overlapping orthographies [37]. Thus, negative transfer between the two languages tends to occur during spelling or word recognition tasks for bilingual Spanish-English speaking children [10, 8]. The problem which occurs is that, despite their overlapping orthographies, Spanish and English follow different spelling-sound correspondences. Durgunoğlu [10] explains that, when trying to spell a word in English, children may systematically use the sounding out strategy, which is effective in Spanish, but is much less effective for English, which has a less-transparent orthography. In contrast, children may also use common English consonant clusters when spelling in Spanish (e.g. scuela for *escuela*, stoy for *estoy*, different for *diferent*) and interchange sounds between English and Spanish, such as confusing the letters "i" and "y" (e.g. spelling happily as "hapali") [10]. Research by Simpson [38] shows similar findings for bilingual Spanish-English first graders, who tend to make errors in their English writings by using Spanish phonetic rules for invented spellings of English words (e.g. spelling bee as "vi" and tree as "tri").

Due to this negative transfer of knowledge between languages, literacy teachers may worry about bilingual students confusing their two languages [10]. In response, research by Ortiz [25] and Cummins [8] both stress the crucial role that teachers play in not only understanding the benefits and limitations of cross-linguistic transfer, but also in explicitly teaching strategies to help children differentiate between writing in Spanish and English [24]. Therefore, it is important for bilingual children to understand how to differentiate between the phonetic rules of each language as they develop their reading and writing skills.

Family Co-Engagement in Literacy Learning

Acquiring oral language can be described as a "social dance" between parents and children [16]. The next step, developing literacy skills, is ideally also a collaborative learning experience facilitated by a feedback loop between the child and the parent, where both are learning how to communicate with the other. Digital technology has the potential to support family co-engagement in literacy learning activities. However, most digital literacy tools fail to include this collaborative experience. In fact, in a recent survey of popular children's literacy learning apps, researchers found that for every literacy app that promotes a collaborative experience, there are 85 that do not [43].

Many parents are eager to be part of their children's learning experience as both collaborators and role-models [32, 30]. Additionally, studies have found that children's comprehension improves when parents engage in media-rich learning experiences (e.g., watching educational television) together with their children, in part because the parents discuss and contextualize the on-screen scenarios [40]. When only one language is spoken in the home and that language is different from that of the media-rich learning experience, it makes it much harder for parents to co-engage. Bilingual learning experiences, such as bilingual literacy apps, may help to address this problem.

Constructionism and Literacy Technology

The majority of educational apps on the market prescribe to the instructionist paradigm of delivering literacy lessons, where the main mode of interaction is directed, such as dragging and dropping letters to spell a predefined word [43]. However, research suggests that these structured, rewards-based games do not always lead to the best learning outcomes for children [17]. In contrast to this, activities focused on creation help children to develop a deeper understanding [34], especially in relation to reading development. One proponent of this in the field of literacy learning is Maria Montessori, who believed that children should learn writing, the literary form of creation, before reading [23]. This idea that child-centered, creative environments facilitate deeper learning among children also lies at the core of Papert's [27] constructionist approach to learning.

The goal of constructionist, or design-based, learning environments is to create an open space which allows for learners to find projects that are personally engaging and intellectually interesting rather than instructor-directed learning activities. Resnick, Bruckman, and Martin [34] proposed two principles of design-based learning that contribute to rich learning experiences: personal connections, which increase relatedness and motivation; and epistemological connections, which encourage new ways of thinking through the iterative design process. Similarly, work by Gee [12] on educational games, suggests that significant learning occurs through doing, exploring, and creating; where experiential learning through contextualizing the material lends itself to a deeper understanding by applying knowledge to solve problems, rather than just memorizing facts. We believe this is especially pertinent for language and literacy learning, where it is important for educational technology to allow children to explore the phonetic rules of a language rather than only creating and memorizing sight words.

One such app that we believe follows the constructionist principles of exploration and creation to produce personally meaningful learning moments is MSB. MSB is an open-ended literacy app where children explore alphabetic principles through manipulating letter blocks [39]. This original version of the app is the foundation for which BSB is built upon. In MSB, children can blend and segment phonemes into real and nonsense words by dragging letter blocks apart and pulling them together [39]. There are no correct combinations of letters, no extrinsic rewards, and contingent interactions have immediate auditory feedback. Words from a "word drawer" and letters from a "letter drawer" act as scaffolds that children can use and remix [39]. However, MSB is monolingual, specifically focusing on helping children explore the phonetic rules of English.

Bilingual Literacy Learning Mobile Apps

Smartphones are increasingly ubiquitous in American homes. In the span of just two years from 2011 to 2013, the percent of children ages zero to eight years old with access to a smartphone and/or tablet has increased from 52% to 75% [22]. Though there are reasons to be concerned about too much screen time for children, parents are also beginning to see educational apps as a part of their children's learning experience. Vaala, Ly, and Levine [43] stated that Hispanic families, in particular, see strong educational potential in media, including apps, for their children's learning.

Like MSB, most of the popular educational mobile apps are focused on children's language and literacy skills in one language. In a survey of the 183 most popular educational apps on the market, only 13 apps included features and techniques to help children learn a second language [43].

Upon review of popular bilingual literacy learning apps, we could not find any apps that allowed bilingual Spanish and English speaking children to explore the alphabetic principles of their two languages side by side. However, there are a few apps that help these children develop their abilities in one of their languages, while allowing them to use their other language to provide context. For example, Endless Spanish [19], in addition to using verbal and pictographic cues in Spanish to convey a word's meaning, provides the oral translation of the word in English so that the learner can use their English understanding to provide context. Rosetta Stone Kids Lingo Word Builder [35] helps reinforce early reading skills in English while simultaneously introducing oral skills in Spanish. Montessori Letter Sounds [1] allows children to play with letter sounds in Spanish while listening to the instructions in English.

Furthermore, all of the apps mentioned above followed some version of the instructionist mode of delivering literacy lessons, providing word and/or sentence-level puzzles with defined answers that children are tasked with solving. In general, there are very few constructionist, or self-expressive early literacy learning apps available on the market [17, 43] and, to the authors' knowledge, this list dwindles to zero when searching for a constructionist bilingual literacy app. Given the literature on the importance of early exposure to multiple languages for bilingual children and the benefits of constructionist learning apps, we believe that there should be more development of constructionist bilingual literacy apps for young children and families.

DESIGN

Design Questions

We developed BSB to serve as a platform for bilingual children's open-ended Spanish and English wordplay. We will use this paper to examine the following design questions: What are the different affordances of the two designs for bilingual children and their families during play? Is the bilingual version more personally meaningful for children? And lastly, how engaged are children when using BSB versus MSB? Finally, we will discuss the implications and limitations of the design and share our plans for future research with the BSB app.

Overview of Design

As mentioned above, BSB builds off of the original SpeechBlocks app by allowing children to create words in both Spanish and English. This literacy app follows the same constructionist approach to dual-language learning by encouraging the exploration of the alphabetic principles of the two languages through manipulating letter blocks (see Figure 2). When letter blocks or combinations of these blocks are tapped, put together, or pulled apart, they are pronounced. There is a line in the middle of the screen (midline) that separates the Spanish and English halves of the canvas.

Children can create words in either half of the canvas, and then drag that word to the other half to hear how the pronunciation of the same word changes between languages. Just like regular SpeechBlocks, there is no right or wrong combination of letters (children can create both real and nonsense words), no extrinsic rewards, and contingent interactions have immediate feedback [39]. Both English and Spanish words from the "word shelf" and letters from the "letter shelf" act as scaffolds that children can use and remix.

As previously mentioned, this is not a translation tool, rather it is an open canvas where children can explore the phonetic rules of each language and differentiate between them. This design decision to focus on differentiation was informed by the research that bilingual children struggle with negative transfer between the two languages when learning to read and write [10, 8, 24]. Therefore, we created an environment where children could immediately hear the differences in pronunciation of the same orthography between the two languages and compare the sounds.

Specific Design Considerations

Segmentation of the Canvas and Dual Voices

The BSB canvas is separated into two halves: A Spanish half and an English half (Figure 2A). When a child taps on a word in the Spanish half of the canvas, a voice synthesizer reads out the word in a Latin American Spanish pronunciation; when a child taps on a word in the English half of the canvas, a voice synthesizer reads out the word in an American English pronunciation. Both voice synthesizers used were built by Ivona Software[1] and the English synthesizer was modified in the original SpeechBlocks app to handle a set of phonemic edge-cases (e.g. AC is pronounced /ac/ instead of treated as the abbreviation of "air conditioner"). The midline provides

[1]https://www.ivona.com/us/about-us/voice-portfolio/

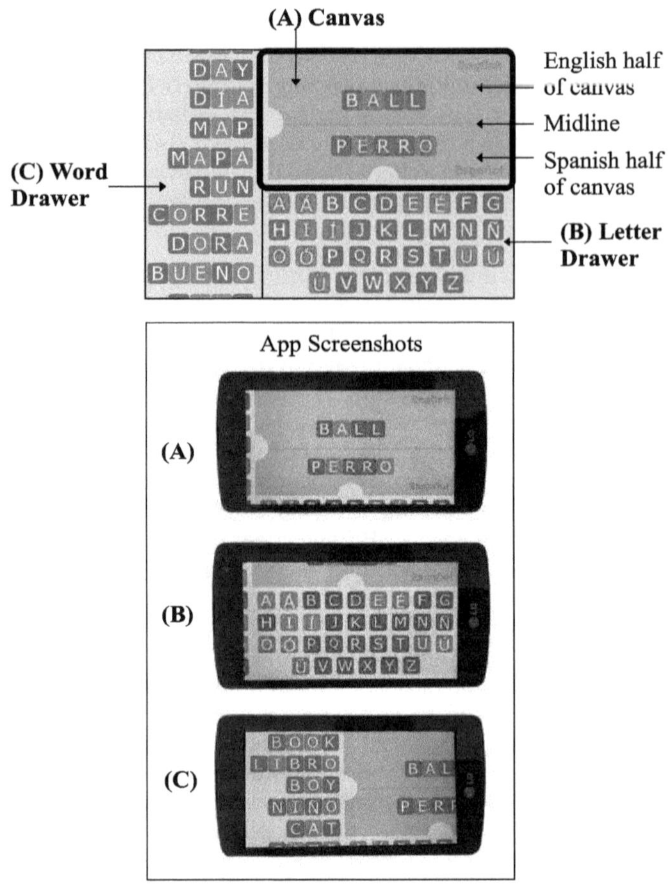

Figure 2: Diagram of the Bilingual SpeechBlocks App. **(A)** The Bilingual SpeechBlocks canvas, **(B)** the Bilingual SpeechBlocks letter drawer, and **(C)** the Bilingual SpeechBlocks word drawer.

the ability for children to toggle between both languages in the same space in order to make an immediate comparison between how a word, real or nonsense, is pronounced in the two languages. This is the most distinctive feature of BSB.

Addition of Spanish Letters

There are 33 letter-blocks in the letter drawer (see Figure 2B). Twenty-six of these blocks represent letters used in both the Spanish and English writing systems. The seven remaining blocks represent letters that are unique to Spanish. They are Ñ, Á, É, Í, Ó, Ú, and Ü. As in MSB, the letter-blocks are arranged in alphabetical order [39]. The letters with accents follow directly after the corresponding letter without an accent. Since both English and Spanish are alphabetic languages with overlapping orthographies, we decided to use only one drawer for both languages.

One design decision that was made is, when a letter in the letter drawer is tapped, only its Spanish pronunciation is read aloud. This is because we wanted to keep the pronunciation of letters in the letter drawer constant and all of the letters are pronounceable in Spanish but not in English. Additionally, Spanish has a more regular letter-to-sound mapping [37],

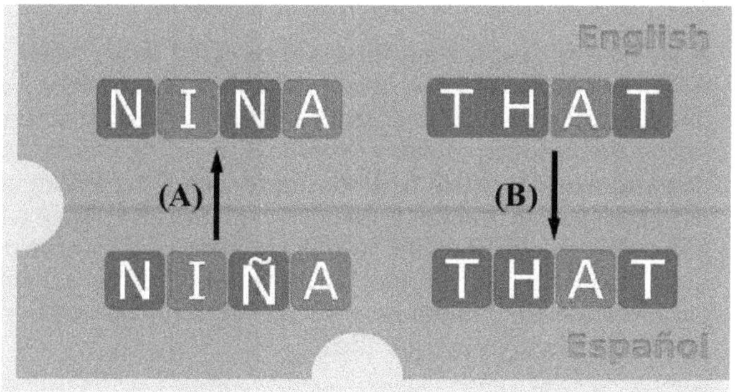

Figure 3: Letter transitions from one half of the Bilingual SpeechBlocks canvas to the other. **(A)** The "Ñ" becomes an "N" (the most similar English letter) as the word "NIÑA" is moved from the Spanish to the English half of the canvas. **(B)** The "TH" digraph splits apart into two letter-blocks as the word "THAT" moves from the English to the Spanish half of the canvas.

making it the more natural choice. We thus decided to position the letter drawer underneath the Spanish half of the BSB canvas to keep its location consistent with both the Spanish pronunciation of the letters in the drawer and the design of MSB.

While we recognize that, in Spanish, the entire word is usually written and then the accent added to one of the vowels if needed, we decided to put the letters with accents on their own letter-blocks. This was in order to (1) give the accented letters equal importance as the non-accented letters to inspire children to tinker with all of the letter-blocks and (2) to maintain the same word-construction system (i.e. side-to-side concatenation) in both languages.

Letter Transitions

Since the accented letters are only found in the Spanish writing system and not the English system, we implemented slight animations to these letter-blocks when they transition from the Spanish canvas to the English canvas across the midline. For these accented letters (Ñ, Á, É, Í, Ó, Ú, Ü), the accent is removed when the block touches the English half of the canvas, turning into the English letter most similar to it (N, A, E, I, O, U). The accent returns if the block crosses back into the Spanish half, but only if the original block had an accent when it was brought onto the canvas from the letter or word shelf (see Figure 3A).

Additionally, the letter blocks change slightly when they are used to represent digraphs. A digraph is a combination of two letters that can be represented by one sound, and that sound is different than the sounds of either of the two letters by themselves. In MSB and BSB, common digraphs are represented by the two letters appearing as one block (however, these can still be pulled apart). There are several digraphs present in BSB for Spanish (LL, RR, and CH) and English (SH, TH, PH, and CH). As these digraphs differ between Spanish and English (with the exception of CH), when a digraph crosses the language line, it appears to split into two blocks, and each letter is pronounced separately (see Figure 3B).

The slight animation in our design as a word crosses the midline allows the user to distinguish between the words or letters that have different orthographies between the two languages. As indicated by the research, Spanish and English have overlapping orthographies [37] and, therefore, we decided to let the speech synthesizers audibly pronounce the differences between the two languages for all words and letters, yet only visually animate the words and letters that change orthographies between the languages as they cross the midline.

Addition of Spanish Words

There are 45 words in the word drawer; 22 Spanish words and 23 English words (see Figure 2C). With the exception of three words related to the bilingual (Spanish-English speaking) children's character Dora the Explorer[2], all of these words were selected from the Spanish and English short forms of the MacArthur-Bates Communicative Development Inventories (CDI) [11]. The CDI forms have common words that parents can use to assess the vocabulary development of their children in the home, and the words on these forms represent vocabulary words that are frequently heard in the child's environment [6]. Since the main interaction in BSB is largely based on auditory feedback from the app, it was important to choose words that the child would have previous exposure to (e.g. water or *agua*), rather than focus on words that are typically taught in early literacy instruction, such as consonant-vowel-consonant (CVC) words (e.g. pop or bat).

There were a couple of design considerations when selecting scaffolding words. First, the words cannot exceed five letters in length due to space constraints of the word drawer. Second, words that would produce drastically different sounds in Spanish or English (e.g. ball, *niño*, *perro*) were more favorable than words with similar sounds in the two languages. Third, special attention was given to choosing words that contained the different digraphs in each language. Lastly, a majority of the selected words had to be present in both Spanish and English CDI forms so that both translations of these words could be placed next to each other on the word shelf. Since BSB is not a translation tool, this was done to make sure that the support and scaffolding provided by the word drawer was approximately equivalent for both languages.

METHODOLOGY

Initial Play-Test

Before conducting an exploratory pilot study, we play-tested BSB and MSB with two Spanish-English bilingual children (one female and one male, ages 6 and 8 years old) at an after-school tutoring program in the Greater Boston area. Each child played a version of the SpeechBlocks app (in randomized order) for approximately ten minutes while the researchers

[2] `http://www.nickjr.com/dora-the-explorer/`

took observational notes of engagement during play. The following week, children were given the other version of the app to play for another ten minutes. Their parents were not present in the room during the play sessions. When each child was finished, they were asked for their feedback on the two versions of the app.

There were many limitations of play-testing SpeechBlocks in this context. First, the availability of time and space at the after-school program was limited. Second, there were many distractions present in the room while children were playing with the app. Third, the amount of time children could play varied depending on how much homework they had to complete. Lastly, having multiple play sessions for each child proved problematic, as children's attention spans and interest varied across the play sessions. As a result, we revised the study procedure for our pilot study, which is outlined below.

Participants

We conducted a small exploratory pilot study (which we will refer to for the remainder of this paper as the "study") with seven bilingual children at an after-school program for families in the Greater Boston area. There were three female and four male children that participated, ranging in age from 5 to 9 years old (average age of 7 years old). Children between the ages of 5 and 9 have vastly different literacy skills. However, given that the open-ended and responsive nature of both MSB and BSB allows children to make any simple or complex words they desire, we believe that these apps are appropriate for a wide age range. All of the children in this pilot study were from low socioeconomic status neighborhoods, had parents who immigrated from Latin America, used Spanish as the primary language of communication with their parents, and were the first generation in their family to receive K-12 education in the United States. Quantitative analysis was conducted for the seven children in the pilot study. However, all nine children's play (the seven children from the pilot study and two children from the initial play-test), was used for the qualitative, observational analysis.

Pilot Study Procedure

The study session took about 30 minutes per participant, and the children worked individually with two researchers in a small teacher's lounge in their public school. For the seven children who received the standardized study procedure, their parents were given the option to be present in the room with their child and the researchers during the study. Since children have varying levels of bi-literacy, we conducted a pre-assessment of children's phonemic decoding skills for both Spanish and English nonsense words. For this pre-assessment, we adapted 24 words from the TOWRE-2 standardized assessment [42] and read them to the students in a randomized order, pronouncing each word using English and Spanish phonetic rules. The child had to determine whether the word was being pronounced in Spanish or English. This assessment allowed us to ensure that every child in the study had a baseline knowledge of differentiating between Spanish and English pronunciations. All seven children scored above the baseline cutoff of 50% on the pre-assessment for both Spanish and English (average English score was 89%, average Spanish score was 87%), and thus were included in the study.

After the pre-assessment, the child received either MSB or BSB (in a randomized order). The app was introduced by one researcher, who demonstrated the app's basic functions (using the drawers, creating words, segmenting words, and deleting words). When BSB was introduced, the researcher used the same instructions, but also explained that there was a line that the child could drag the word across to hear the word pronounced in the other language. Children played with each version for 5 minutes. We provided phones with the SpeechBlocks apps pre-installed.

During play, the phones were instrumented to record every finger tap and interaction that occurred within the app. These data logs provided a level of detail that allowed us to recreate the child's play session by completely reconstructing everything that happened on the child's screen. We used these logs to analyze what words the child constructed, the word and letter components that the child used to make these words, how many times the words were tapped and heard by the child, and, for BSB, what language(s) the child heard these words in.

We also took observational notes of engagement during play, noting any signs of frustration, excitement, boredom, and any dialogue that occurred throughout the play sessions. After children played with both versions of the app, we conducted a feedback questionnaire, recording data on their experiences and preferences.

The self-expressive nature of SpeechBlocks allows children to make personally meaningful words [39]. We identified personally meaningful words through qualitative analysis. Children's expressions of intent and reactions of excitement or self-efficacy around the words they made were recorded through our observational notes and the feedback questionnaire. We used the log data to code for personally meaningful words which are typically names, sentences, or expressions rather than nonsense words or objects [39].

RESULTS

We used a two-tail paired-sample t-test to determine whether the differences between the two conditions (MSB and BSB) were statistically significant and used the Clopper-Pearson method to compute 95% confidence intervals for the questionnaire responses. We examined both user-created words, meaning words that contain at least one letter-block that originated in the letter drawer, and system-created words, meaning words that contain only words and parts of words that originated as pre-assembled words in the word drawer.

Differences in Modes of Interaction

We looked at the two main modes of interaction in MSB and BSB: (1) Creating words by splitting or merging existing words or by adding letter blocks to existing words and (2) tapping on words to hear them pronounced in a given language. There was no significant difference in the total number of words that each child played with. However, on average,

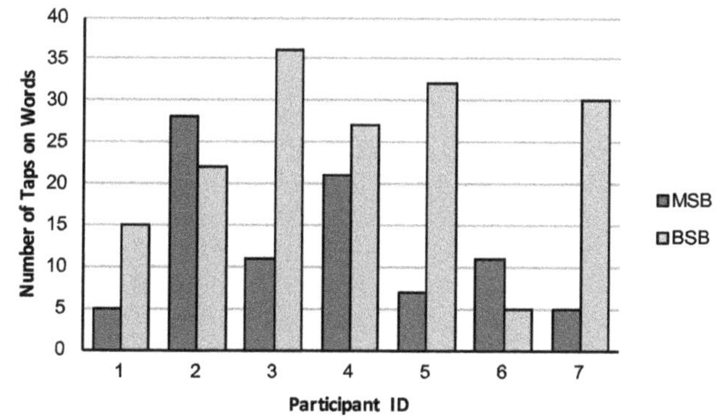

Figure 4: Comparison of the number of taps participants made on words in Monolingual SpeechBlocks (MSB) and Bilingual SpeechBlocks (BSB).

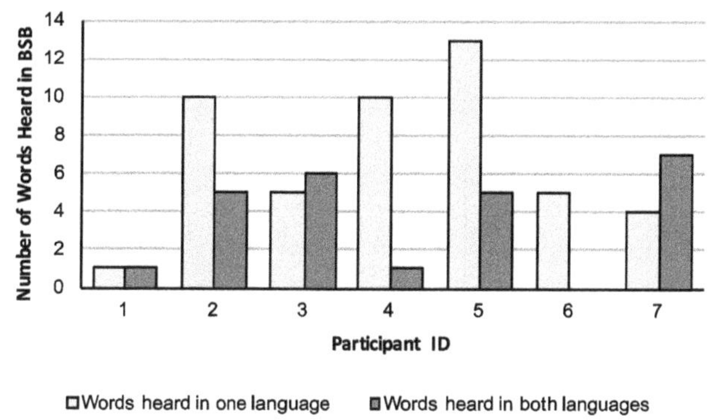

Figure 6: Comparison of the words participants heard in one language (either Spanish or English) and the words they heard in both languages (Spanish and English) during play with Bilingual SpeechBlocks (BSB).

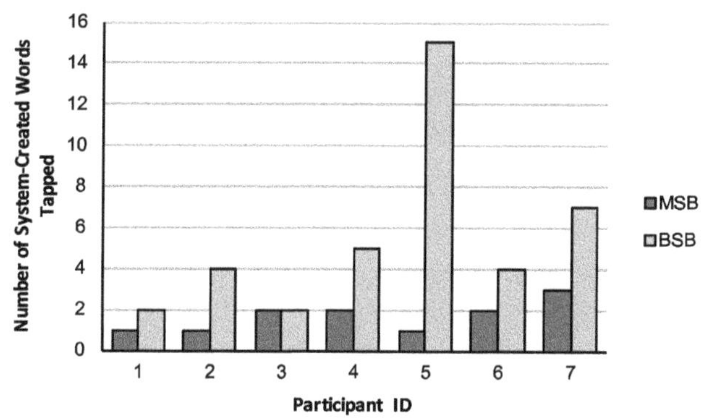

Figure 5: Comparison of the number of system-created words participants tapped in Monolingual SpeechBlocks (MSB) and Bilingual SpeechBlocks (BSB).

children tapped on words 1.9 times more in BSB than MSB (Figure 4). Moreover, they tapped on system words 3.25 times more in the BSB condition than MSB (Figure 5). Although these differences were not significant, due to the small sample size (n=7) we still find these results noteworthy.

The difference in number of taps resulted from children frequently tapping on the words to hear them in both languages, as they dragged the words across the midline. They exhibited this behavior with 34% of words they tapped on in BSB (see Figure 6). These observations indicate that BSB introduced a new affordance of playful interaction for children: comparing and contrasting pronunciations of the words in two languages. This affordance is important in light of the previously mentioned findings regarding negative transfer for bilingual children. In this way, the nature of children's wordplay changed because the BSB design included the ability to hear words pronounced in two different ways (Spanish and English), and children seemed to use this feature often.

Indications of Personal Meaningfulness

Personally meaningful words tend to be names, sentences, and expressions. We manually annotated the number of times a proper noun such as a child's name, character name (e.g. the character name "kingkong"), or name of an object (e.g. the name of the game "minecraft"). Sentences (e.g. "I love my mom" which was counted as one word), and expressions (e.g. *mamá*, meaning "mom" in Spanish) were also annotated as personally meaningful words. There was no significant difference between the number of personally meaningful words created in MSB and BSB.

However, qualitatively, the researchers observed that the nature of how some children created their personally meaningful words seemed tied to which side of the canvas they were constructing the word on. For example, one child who speaks English with her sister at home continually spelled words on the English half of the app and then moved the words over to the Spanish half to see how they were pronounced in Spanish. However, when the child wrote her own name, it was the only word she created on the Spanish canvas.

Researchers also observed that a few children who only spoke Spanish at home tended to create words on the Spanish half of the canvas and then moved over to the English half. One such child made almost all of his words in the Spanish canvas, but then decided to try and recreate his name in the English canvas. Halfway through his name, the speech synthesizer pronounced the first six letters of his name, which made up a real word when pronounced in English, but not when pronounced in Spanish. The child was very confused and exclaimed, "What?!", possibly because he had never heard the first half of his name pronounced in English before. He then proceeded to check that he was spelling his own name correctly. One possible reason for these observations is that the ability to make a word that can be pronounced in either language created an interesting dynamic that may be reflective of the child's personal identification with one language or another, as well as how a child categorizes certain concepts or words.

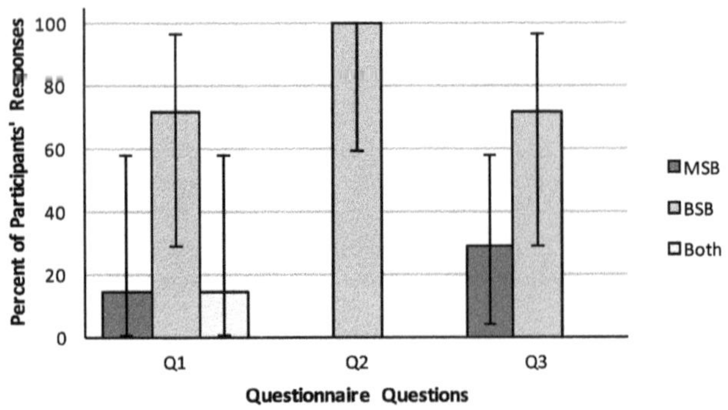

Figure 7: Percentage of participants that chose Monolingual SpeechBlocks (MSB), Bilingual SpeechBlocks (BSB), or both versions in their end-of-study feedback questionnaire responses. **(Q1)** Which version of the game was your favorite? **(Q2)** If you had to play this game again, which version of the game would you like to play again? **(Q3)** If you were playing this game at home, which version of the game would you like to play? For all three questions, the participants were presented with three options: Monolingual SpeechBlocks (MSB), Bilingual SpeechBlocks (BSB), or both versions.

Children's Engagement

To examine children's engagement, data on finger taps was used to determine children's sustained interaction within the app, and both MSB and BSB had sustained engagement, or taps, throughout the play sessions for all seven children. We posed three questionnaire questions to understand how the children perceived their experiences, serving as proxies for what experiences they found engaging during their play. When asked which version of the app was their favorite, 71% of children said BSB was their favorite version (Q1 in Figure 7). Additionally, when asked which version of the app they would rather play again, 100% of the children said that they would rather play BSB again than MSB (Q2 in Figure 7) and when asked which version they would like to play at home, 71% of children said that they would like to play BSB at home (Q3 in Figure 7). This suggests that these children may have perceived their experiences with BSB as more engaging than MSB. Note that due to our small sample size, we cannot establish the Q1 and Q3 results with confidence and a further study with a larger sample size needs to be conducted in order to understand whether these trends will be replicable.

DISCUSSION

Engagement and Funny Voices

As shown in the results, children seemed to perceive their experiences with BSB as more engaging. One possible reason for this is that the nature of wordplay is different in the BSB version than the MSB version. These new affordances may have influenced children to perceive their experience with BSB as more engaging. Children used BSB to spell words in one language and then hear how they are pronounced in another. The children did not seem to be confused by the changed pronunciation when the word crossed the midline. Instead, the unexpectedness of the pronunciations seemed to result in what we call a "funny voices" effect, which, according to observation notes, seemed to engage children and expose them to how a familiar word is differentiated between the two languages. This observation is similar to research by Tarone [41] and Bell [2], which encourages teachers to use funny voices to increase student interest and participation in language learning. Children seemed to especially appreciate the effect of the funny voices for nonsense words. For example, when asked to explain why she liked BSB, one child said she really liked being able to tap and have the app say any word she wanted in Spanish and English. She then elaborated that it was especially fun to mix up the words and hear the funny voices.

The ability for children to explore with these funny voices incorporated a playful, humorous nature into the app that research shows helps children learn [34, 12]. For example, the English word "ball" sounds like "baye" when pronounced in Spanish. This effect encourages children to explore how a word sounds in both languages, an important aspect of language differentiation for bilingual learners [10, 8]. These funny voices may have also made the interactions within BSB more memorable, influencing children to perceive that they were more engaged and made cooler words when playing with BSB than with MSB.

Stories

While playing with the bilingual version, there was one child who shared a personal story that was directly prompted by the design of BSB. During his play session with BSB, he spelled out his last name in the Spanish canvas and then removed the "s" from his name when he moved it to the English side. He then proceeded to tell the researcher a story about how when his family moved to the United States, they dropped the "s" in their last name. The dual-language nature of BSB is likely to be especially powerful for bilingual children because it pronounces personally relatable words, like names, in the child's home language.

This example and the qualitative examples of children's discussions around the words they created in BSB (see Results) present implications for the design and development of bilingual literacy apps, just as, if not more specifically than monolingual apps, to be open-ended. Each child has a unique level of bi-literacy, using a different combination of their languages for varying contexts (e.g. school, home, friends). It is important that the design remains open-ended to account for these variations and allow children to express themselves using both languages in their repertoire.

Family Co-Engagement

One observation that we did not initially account for in our study design was the level of co-engagement of Spanish-speaking parents during the BSB condition. We observed and coded three main types of parental engagement during the sessions: asking questions, sharing stories, and co-engaging in play. We define "asking questions" as questions that were initiated by the parent, addressed to the child, and referred to either the app or the child's play. We define "sharing stories" as parent-initiated conversations addressed to either the child or researchers about personal anecdotes or experiences related to the app or play. We define "co-engaging in play" as the parent interacting with the child and/or the app (verbally communicating or physically tapping on the app) in order to effect the play that happens on the screen.

Upon review of our observation notes, parents tended to co-engage more and share stories during their children's BSB play sessions, and not engage during their children's MSB play. Parents' interactions with their children were mainly in Spanish. In two particular cases, while the children played with MSB, their mothers were on their own personal phones. However, in both cases, when the children played with BSB, their mothers put down their personal phones and co-engaged with their children in playing with the app. For example, one of the mothers asked her son "What's another word? What does *mapa* mean in English?" The other mother asked her daughter what the meanings of some of the words she created were. This began a conversation between the two of them in Spanish about what the child was creating with the app.

After hearing BSB pronounce a Spanish word, another mother immediately leaned over to look at what her daughter was doing and told the researcher, "It is very interesting. For me, I didn't learn (how to write in) my own language. So it's (BSB) very interesting." The mother and daughter then proceeded to play together and make new words with the game.

As shown in the results, when asked which version of the app they would rather play again and why, all of the children preferred BSB. One child replied that BSB was her favorite because she could play it with her mother. Another said that he enjoyed BSB more than MSB because he could "translate things" for his mother using the app. From these observations, we saw that Spanish-speaking parents were more attentive when their child was playing with BSB.

Given the importance of family co-engagement in children's learning, the active participation of parents during BSB play sessions may help improve children's learning when using the bilingual vs. the monolingual version of SpeechBlocks. The open-ended nature of the SpeechBlocks design coupled with the bilingual features of the BSB app, seemed to encourage organic interactions between parents and children around their creations. This may have important implications for the design of future bilingual literacy apps to incorporate ways for parents to naturally co-engage with their children, and is an area of future study for BSB.

Implications for Design of Bilingual Learning Apps

This work presents implications for the design of children's bilingual learning apps and games. Our results and examples highlight the importance of an open-ended and evidence-based design that is informed by how bilingual children learn literacy skills. By accounting for children's varying levels of biliteracy through the open-endedness of our design, we found new affordances for children to express themselves in both languages. Additionally, the dual-language design of BSB was informed by the research on how children differentiate between overlapping orthographies. Our results showed that children differentiated between the pronunciation of words by tapping to hear them in both languages. Therefore, it is important for designers to consider how bilingual children learn literacy skills—which is different than learning a second language—and incorporate this research into how they design learning apps for bilingual children. As there is a lack of apps that specifically target bilingual children's literacy learning, we hope that this work can serve as a starting point for designers and developers to create apps for this growing population.

Limitations and Future Directions

Some of the limitations of the design were already addressed above in the design section of this paper. However, we also note some limitations to the exploratory pilot study. First, the study was conducted completely in English, which may have introduced a priming effect, influencing the children to create more English words for both conditions. For example, both researchers involved in conducting the study were native English speakers, and spoke to the children and parents in English. The assessments and instructions were all conducted in English, priming the child to respond in English, even when talking about BSB and the ability to make words in English or Spanish.

Second, the study was conducted at the children's school, which was an English-speaking school (not bilingual), and despite some of the Spanish-speaking parents being present, this may have influenced the children through a context effect. It is common for bilingual children to separate who they use each language with, and where they use each language [9]. When these contexts mix, for example, when a teacher tries to speak with a bilingual child in their home language at school, it can often confuse children and, especially for younger children, they may actually abstain from speaking in their home language at school [9]. It is possible that conducting this study at the children's English-speaking school could have influenced them to make more English words than Spanish words due to the English-dominant nature of the context.

In order to understand whether these language limitations influenced the words children made, we would like to continue this research by conducting a study where half of the participants receive the study procedure in English and half receive it in Spanish. Additionally, we plan to conduct a similar pilot in the home setting or a language neutral setting, rather than the children's school.

Another language limitation was that we only examined the difference between a monolingual English version of the app and a bilingual (Spanish-English) version of the app for bilingual Spanish-English speakers. In order to understand the true affordances of a bilingual app over a monolingual app (instead of just a monolingual English app), we would need to also create a monolingual Spanish version of SpeechBlocks. To continue this research, it would be important to see if similar trends were found for the bilingual version of SpeechBlocks compared to both monolingual versions (English and Spanish, respectively), in order to determine if it was the introduction of both languages in one canvas, or simply that children preferred one language over the other in different contexts.

Lastly, another limitation is that we did not design the study to examine the extent to which parents co-engaged during their children's play with SpeechBlocks. Although one of the affordances of both MSB and BSB is that the immediate, auditory feedback is intended to encourage social engagement along with providing feedback to the child, we did not expect there to be so much interest from the parents. Since research shows that parental involvement in children's learning is an important part of children's reading development, a future direction for this work would be to design the next pilot study to accurately measure parents' reactions and levels of co-engagement.

CONCLUSION

In response to the lack of open-ended literacy learning apps for bilingual children, we created BSB to provide a constructionist environment for children to explore the foundations of literacy by tinkering with letter-to-sound mappings in both Spanish and English. We designed, built, and ran an exploratory pilot study of the app with seven bilingual children between the ages of 5 to 9 years old. Overall, children seemed to be engaged while playing both versions of SpeechBlocks. However, BSB presented different affordances than MSB, namely that the ability for children to differentiate between Spanish and English changed the way they tapped on words in order to hear familiar words pronounced in "funny voices" and increased engagement with system-created words. Additionally, BSB presented opportunities for parents to co-engage with their children while playing with the app.

As a next step of this work, we want to see whether these affordances of BSB will be present in a larger sample of bilingual children. We aim to conduct further studies that address our limitations and use standardized assessment measures to study whether BSB can serve as a neutral platform to assess children's ability to differentiate between two languages. We hope that this work will be the first of many open-ended apps to be designed and tested for bilingual children's literacy learning.

ACKNOWLEDGEMENTS

The authors thank Marc Exposito, Cristian Jara Figueroa, Sneha Makini, Katherine McConachie, Mina Soltengheis, Lisette Soto, and Soroush Vosoughi for their helpful comments, Meredith Rowe for inspiration and guidance, Leah Gregory for assistance running the study, and the families who participated in the study.

REFERENCES

1. Edoki Academy. 2015. *Montessori Letter Sounds - Phonics in English, Spanish, French, German & Italian.* App Store. (22 October 2015). Edoki Academy, Paris, France. Played January 2017.
2. Nancy Bell and Anne Pomerantz. 2015. *Humor in the classroom: A guide for language teachers and educational researchers.* Routledge.
3. Ellen Bialystok. 1986. Factors in the growth of linguistic awareness. *Child Development* 57, 2 (1986), 498–510.
4. Ellen Bialystok. 1988. Levels of bilingualism and levels of linguistic awareness. *Developmental psychology* 24, 4 (1988), 560.
5. Ellen Bialystok. 1992. Attentional control in children's metalinguistic performance and measures of field independence. *Developmental Psychology* 28, 4 (1992), 654.
6. Ellen Bialystok. 1997. Effects of bilingualism and biliteracy on children's emerging concepts of print. *Developmental psychology* 33, 3 (1997), 429.
7. Jim Cummins. 1979. Cognitive/academic language proficiency, linguistic interdependence, the optimum age question and some other matters. *Working Papers on Bilingualism Toronto* 19 (1979), 197–202.
8. Jim Cummins. 2008. Teaching for transfer: Challenging the two solitudes assumption in bilingual education. In *Encyclopedia of language and education*. Springer, 1528–1538.
9. Una Cunningham-Andersson and Staffan Andersson. 2004. *Growing up with two languages: A practical guide.* Routledge.
10. Aydin Yücesan Durgunoğlu. 2002. Cross-linguistic transfer in literacy development and implications for language learners. *Annals of Dyslexia* 52, 1 (2002), 189–204.
11. Larry Fenson, Elizabeth Bates, Philip S Dale, Jeffrey P Hartung, Stephen J Pethick, Judy Snitzer Reilly, J Steven Reznick, and Donna J Thal. 1996. *The MacArthur communicative development inventories.* Singular publishing Group, Incorporated.
12. James Paul Gee. 2005. Good video games and good learning. In *Phi Kappa Phi Forum*, Vol. 85. The Honor Society of Phi Kappa Phi, 33.
13. Fred Genesee, Elena Nicoladis, and Johanne Paradis. 1995. Language differentiation in early bilingual development. *Journal of child language* 22, 03 (1995), 611–631.
14. Kenji Hakuta and Rafael M Diaz. 1985. The relationship between degree of bilingualism and cognitive ability: A critical discussion and some new longitudinal data. *Children's language* 5 (1985), 319–344.
15. Carol Scheffner Hammer, Shelley Scarpino, and Megan Dunn Mavison. 2011. Beginning with language: Spanish-English bilingual preschoolers' early literacy development. In *Handbook of Early Literacy Research*, Susan B Neuman and David K Dickinson (Eds.). Vol. 3. The Guilford Press, New York, NY, Chapter 8, 118–134.
16. Betty Hart and Todd R Risley. 1999. *The social world of children: Learning to talk.* Paul H Brookes Publishing Co.
17. Kathy Hirsh-Pasek, Jennifer M Zosh, Roberta Michnick Golinkoff, James H Gray, Michael B Robb, and Jordy Kaufman. 2015. Putting education in "educational" apps: Lessons from the science of learning. *Psychological Science in the Public Interest* 16, 1 (2015), 3–34.

18. Erika Hoff. 2013. *Language development*. Cengage Learning.
19. Originator Inc. 2015. *Endless Spanish*. Google Play Store and App Store. (May 2015). Originator Inc., San Carlos, CA. Played January 2017.
20. June Lee and Brigid Barron. 2015. Aprendiendo en Casa: Media as a Resource for Learning among Hispanic-Latino Families. A Report of the Families and Media Project. *The Joan Ganz Cooney Center at Sesame Workshop* (2015).
21. Jeannette Mancilla-Martinez, Barbara Alexander Pan, and Shaher Banu Vagh. 2011. Assessing the productive vocabulary of Spanish–English bilingual toddlers from low-income families. *Applied Psycholinguistics* 32, 02 (2011), 333–357.
22. Common Sense Media and Victoria Rideout. 2013. *Zero to eight: Children's media use in America*. Common Sense Media.
23. Maria Montessori. 1917. *The Advanced Montessori Method...* Vol. 1. Frederick A. Stokes Company.
24. Victoria A Murphy and Maria Evangelou. 2016. *Early childhood education in English for speakers of other languages*. British Council London.
25. A Ortiz. 2006. Descripción del proceso de desarrollo de la lectoescritura adelantado por maestros de grado transición y primero elemental en un colegio bilingüe de Bogotá. *Universidad de los Andes* (2006).
26. Amado M Padilla, Kathryn J Lindholm, Andrew Chen, Richard Durán, Kenji Hakuta, Wallace Lambert, and G Richard Tucker. 1991. The English-only movement: Myths, reality, and implications for psychology. *American Psychologist* 46, 2 (1991), 120.
27. Seymour Papert. 1987. Computer criticism vs. technocentric thinking. *Educational researcher* 16, 1 (1987), 22–30.
28. Barbara Zurer Pearson, Sylvia Fernández, and David K Oller. 1995. Cross-language synonyms in the lexicons of bilingual infants: One language or two? *Journal of child language* 22 (1995), 345–345.
29. Barbara Zurer Pearson, Sylvia C Fernández, and D Kimbrough Oller. 1993. Lexical development in bilingual infants and toddlers: Comparison to monolingual norms. *Language learning* 43, 1 (1993), 93–120.
30. Ashley M Pinkham and Susan B Neuman. 2012. Early literacy development. *Handbook of Family Literacy* 2 (2012), 23–37.
31. Michael Planty, William Hussar, Thomas Snyder, Grace Kena, Angelina KewalRamani, Jana Kemp, and Rachel Dinkes. 2009. *The condition of education 2009*. Technical Report.
32. Esther Prins and Barbara Van Horn. 2012. Adult learning in family literacy: Special considerations for women learners. *Handbook of Family Literacy* 2 (2012), 166–180.
33. Sean F Reardon and Claudia Galindo. 2007. Patterns of Hispanic students' math skill proficiency in the early elementary grades. *Journal of Latinos and Education* 6, 3 (2007), 229–251.
34. Mitchel Resnick, Amy Bruckman, and Fred Martin. 1996. Pianos not stereos: Creating computational construction kits. *interactions* 3, 5 (1996), 40–50.
35. Ltd. Rosetta Stone. 2014. *Rosetta Stone Kids Lingo Word Builder - English Reading and Spanish Speaking Ages 3 - 6*. App Store. (6 May 2014). Rosetta Stone, Ltd., Arlington, VA. Played January 2017.
36. Camille Ryan. 2013. *Language use in the United States: 2011*. Technical Report. United States Census Bureau.
37. Ana I Schwartz, Judith F Kroll, and Michele Diaz. 2007. Reading words in Spanish and English: Mapping orthography to phonology in two languages. *Language and Cognitive Processes* 22, 1 (2007), 106–129.
38. JM Simpson. 2005. A look at early childhood writing in English and Spanish in a bilingual school in Ecuador. *Bilingual education in South America* (2005), 99–115.
39. Ivan Sysoev, Anneli Hershman, Susan Fine, Claire Traweek, and Deb Roy. 2017. SpeechBlocks: A Constructionist Early Literacy App. In *Proceedings of the 2017 Conference on Interaction Design and Children*. ACM, 248–257.
40. Lori Takeuchi and Reed Stevens. 2011. The new coviewing: Designing for learning through joint media engagement. *The Joan Ganz Cooney Center at Sesame Workshop* (2011).
41. Elaine Tarone. 2000. Getting serious about language play: Language play, interlanguage variation and second language acquisition. In *Social and cognitive factors in second language acquisition: Selected proceedings of the 1999 Second Language Research Forum*. Cascadilla Press Somerville, MA, 31–54.
42. Joseph K Torgesen, Richard K Wagner, and Carol A Rashotte. 2012. *TOWRE-2: Test of word reading efficiency* (2 ed.). Pro-Ed.
43. Sarah Vaala, Anna Ly, and Michael H Levine. 2015. Getting a read on the app stores: A market scan and analysis of children's literacy apps. *The Joan Ganz Cooney Center at Sesame Workshop* (2015).

Using Serious Game Analytics to Inform Digital Curricular Sequencing: What Math Objective Should Students Play Next?

Zhongxiu Peddycord-Liu
North Carolina State University
zliu24@ncsu.edu

Christa Cody
North Carolina State University
cncody@ncsu.edu

Sarah Kessler
North Carolina State University
skessle@ncsu.edu

Tiffany Barnes
North Carolina State University
tmbarnes@ncsu.edu

Collin F. Lynch
North Carolina State University
cflynch@ncsu.edu

Teomara Rutherford
North Carolina State University
taruther@ncsu.edu

ABSTRACT

This paper applied serious game analytics to inform digital curricular sequencing in a longitude, curriculum-integrated math game, ST Math. When integrating serious games into classrooms, teachers may have the flexibility to change the order of math objectives for student groups to play. However, it is unclear how teacher decisions, as well as the sequencing of the original curricular order affect students. Moreover, few researchers have applied data-driven methods to inform content ordering in educational games, where the nature of educational content and student behaviors are different from many e-learning platforms. In this paper, we present a novel method that suggests curricular sequencing based on the prediction relationship between math objectives. Our results include specific design recommendations for ST Math, and general data-driven insights for digital curricular design, such as the pacing of objectives and the ordering of math concepts. Our method can potentially be applied to data from a wide range of games and digital learning platforms, enabling developers to better understand how to sequence educational content.

ACM Classification Keywords

H.5.2. User Interfaces: Evaluation/methodology; K.3.1. Computer-assisted instruction(CAI); K.8.0. Personal Computing: Games

Author Keywords

Serious Games; Serious Game Analytics; Digital Curricular

INTRODUCTION

The rapid growth of the serious game industry allows us to collect longitudinal gameplay data at large scale. These data capture learners' in-game behaviors and choices that go beyond information collected from traditional, shorter-term experimental trials. Such user-interaction data can offer new insights for HCI research, as it help us understand large-scale user interactions, and enable data-driven methods that inform game design in a scalable, efficient, and automatic manner.

Serious game analytics [21] (also called Game Learning Analytics [10]) is an emerging field that captures the potential of user-interaction data in serious games. This research grounds game design in students' learning and performance on targeted skills, whereas traditional game analytics [9] focuses on player enjoyment. In learning analytics we analyze data to understand and improve learning in a wide range of digital environments beyond games. These fields share similar and potentially transferable methods, but have different primary purposes. More research is needed to verify the applicability of these methods across these research domains.

This paper applies serious game analytics to evaluate the content sequencing in a year-long supplemental digital mathematics curriculum–Spatial Temporal (ST) Math. Educational research has shown that mathematics is inherently hierarchical–early mathematics skills are needed for later mathematics [8, 28]. Due to this hierarchical nature, children tend to follow a certain trajectory as early skills build upon each other to form a more complex understanding of mathematics [6]. Thus, in serious games that aim to help children develop complex interdependent skills of this type over a long timespan, math objective sequencing is an important design consideration to evaluate.

We designed a novel method to understand curricular sequencing by modeling the potential predictive relationships between objectives. We demonstrated this method on gameplay logs from 1,565 3rd graders from 17 schools and 78 classrooms during the 2012-2013 school year. Students completed different sets of objectives and often did so in unique orders depending upon their classroom structure and individual needs. Based on our new data-driven predictive models, we determined specific recommendations for curricular improvements, including the appropriate location of objective groups, the content that could

CHI-PLAY '17, October 15–18, 2017, Amsterdam, Netherlands

ACM ISBN 978-1-4503-4898-0/17/10...$15.00
DOI: https://doi.org/10.1145/3116595.3116620

be used to prepare for objectives, the pacing and the ordering of objectives, and re-design of game puzzles. Our method can potentially be applied to data from other serious games and e-learning environments that are intended to be used over a long timespan.

RELATED WORK

Serious Game Analytics and Game Design

In recent years, there has been increasing interest in applying data mining and data analytics to serious games. Increasingly, researchers have showed that serious game analytics is powerful, and can help discover how gameplay patterns relate to game design. Horn et al.[16] clustered players' action traces, and gained insight on how game mechanics can impact students' reflection on their gameplay, which impacted learning. Harpstead and Aleven [13] applied learning curve analysis from educational data mining to a physics game. By predicting students' error rates, they discovered an unforeseen short-cut strategy where students succeeded in using a game mechanism, but without a deep understanding of the physics principles. Similarly, Hicks et al.[15] applied a zero-inflation model to compare user-created content in a programming game. They found that the mechanisms of the game's different content creation tools directly impacted the aesthetics, affordances, and educational value of user-created content. Hicks and colleagues [14] also applied survival analysis and interaction networks to evaluate data from a physics game, and found problem spots where students frequently dropped out due to rough difficulty/complexity progression. These papers demonstrate that serious game analytics can help game designers better achieve their educational goals. Such data-driven insight may not be gained from traditional control-trial studies.

Data-driven Method for Curricular Design

There has been a growing interest in using data-driven approaches to inform curricular design, especially the sequencing of educational content.

At the skill granularity, researchers have informed educational content sequencing through mining prerequisites between skills. Chen et al. [4] applied Structural Expectation Maximization to learn the optimal Bayesian network structures that represent skill prerequisites using students' performance from textbook exercise for an English Proficiency test. Chen et al. [5] applied Association Rule Learning on the same educational context, which assumed that one skill is a prerequisite for another if the probabilities of mastering skill A given that B is mastered, or not mastering skill A given that B is not mastered, were both above a certain threshold. However, these methods require a significant amount of effort to map skills to educational content. This mapping process also faces the risk of expert blind-spots–pedagogical organization based on "the structure of the domain rather than the learning needs of novices." [25]

At the problem set granularity, Doroudi et al. [7] assigned each student's activity trajectory to violations of sequencing constraints, and compared how different sequencing constraints affected performance. However, it is difficult to design similar constraints for curricula with longer time spans and more varied content. Vuong et al. [30] applied binominal tests in all possible pair-wise relationships among curriculum units in an intelligent tutor. The binominal test compared the performance on unit A between students who mastered and had not mastered unit B, and deemed unit B as a prerequisite of unit A when significance was found in the test. Although this work created a heatmap describing the existence and strength of relationships, it lacked analysis of the meaning and implications of these relationships.

At the course granularity, Ochoa, Yang et al. and Moretti [26, 32, 24] applied data-driven methods on high-level data such as enrollment, web-mined course descriptions, and online ratings to inform the selection and sequencing of college courses. At the system granularity, Pechenizkiy et al. and Pechenizkiy and Toledo [27] designed conceptual frameworks for the cyclic process of curriculum mining and designing.

However, little work has applied data-driven methods to the curricular sequencing in serious games. In this paper, we focused on the problem-set granularity. ST Math implemented a pre-designed curriculum, but the sequence of students playing math objectives (problem sets) varied in practice. Our challenges were to analyze objective trajectories that varied both in length and sequence over long time-spans, and to derive meaningful data-driven insights for this serious game environment, where the nature of learning and play may differ from other e-learning technologies.

ST MATH AND DATA

ST Math

ST Math is designed to act as a supplemental program to a school's existing mathematics curriculum. In ST Math, mathematical concepts are taught through spatial puzzles within various game-like arenas. ST Math games are structured at the top level by objectives, which are broad learning concepts. Within each objective, individual games teach more targeted concepts through presentation of puzzles, which are grouped into levels for students to play. Students start by completing a series of training games on the use of the ST Math platform and features. They are then guided to complete the first available objective in their grade-level curriculum, such as "Multiplication Concepts." Students can only see this objective. and must complete a pre-test before beginning the content. Once students have completed the pretest, they can start the first sub-objective (game). Games represent scenarios for problem-solving using a particular mathematical concept, such as finding the right number of boots for X animals with Y legs. Each game contains between one and ten levels, which follow the same general structure of the game, but with increasing difficulty. Figure 1 illustrates the hierarchy of ST Math content and examples.

As with many games, students are given a set number of 'lives' per level. Every time they fail to complete a puzzle correctly, they lose one life. If all of their lives for a given level are exhausted, then they will be required to replay the level before they can move on to new content. Once a student has passed a level, they can elect to replay it at any time. Once a student has passed every level within an objective, then they

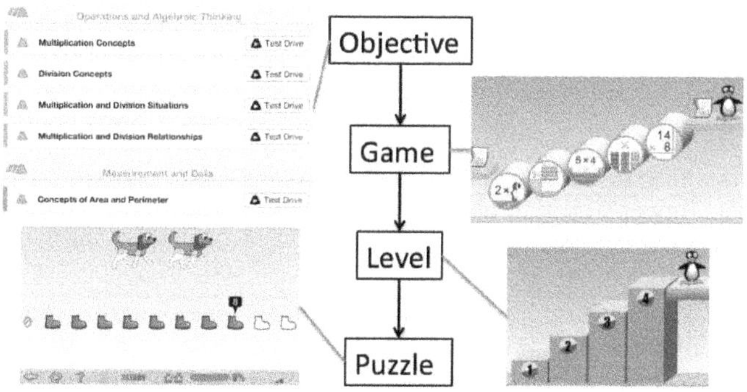

Figure 1. ST Math Content and Examples

will be permitted to take the objective-level post-test. The objective pre- and post-tests consist of 5-10 multiple choice questions related to the objective, and are parallel in both the question format and the content's difficulty. Students cannot progress to the next objective until they have completed the latest objective's post-test.

Participants and Data

MIND Research Institute, the developer of ST Math, collected and provided to the researchers gameplay data from 1,565 3rd grade students during the 2012-2013 school year. These students came from 17 schools and 78 classrooms. Among these students, 50.7% were male (2.9% NA), 80.7% were eligible for free/reduced lunch program (2.8% NA), 84.8% were hispanic or latino (2.8% NA), and 66.2% were English Language Learners (ELLs) (2.8% NA), and 10.9% were noted as having a disability (2.1% NA). For each attempt at a level (level attempt), ST Math logged the student's ID, timestamp, and the number of puzzles completed.

For the purpose of this analyses, we filtered out three types of level attempts: students' elective replay on previously passed levels (1.69%), level attempts from default objectives where all students completed less than 25% of the objectives' levels (0.54%), level attempts from 15 optional objectives provided by ST Math, and the last default objective (3.12%). We filtered out optional objectives because very few students attempted them. We filtered out the last default objective because it was a "challenge" level with spatial puzzle games that were not designed to teach math concepts. After filtering, students attempted(completed 25% levels) an average of 15.82 default objectives (sd=8.07, 95% CI: [15.42, 16.22]), with 371 students from 51 classes completing at least 25% of levels from each of the 26 default objectives. All of the remaining data (94.65%) from 1,565 students were included in the analyses.

Objective Sequencing in ST Math

The 3rd grade's pre-designed curriculum contains 27 default objectives in a particular order, as shown in Table 2. Teacher activities are the root cause of the variance in the order of objectives played by students. A teacher can separate his/her class into groups, and reorder objectives in the curriculum for each student group. For example, if some students missed the first class, a teacher can put them in a separate group, and assign what the rest of the class are currently playing first, and the missed objectives later. A teacher can also allow certain students to 'skip' an objective, which means playing the next objective before completing the current objective. Meanwhile, students can revisit skipped (allowed by teacher) objectives at any time. This causes variance in the order of objectives played by individual student.

METHOD

We first extracted objective sequences as the order of objectives that students played throughout the year. Each objective occurred only once in the sequence, representing where most of the students' effort (level attempts) occurred. For example, if a student attempted the first level of objective A, and was 'skipped' by the teacher to objective B, completed all levels in objective B, and went back to complete the rest of the levels in objective A, then objective B is ordered before objective A because most of the gameplay happened before objective A. Note that without teacher-allowed 'skipping,' a student cannot play the next objective until they have completed the latest objective's post-test. Thus, except for the rare skipping case, a student cannot complete two objective simultaneously.

Table 1 reports the statistics from objective sequences. Our data have over a hundred different objective sequences, with few sequences occurred in high frequencies. This was largely due to the nature of sequencing in ST Math–players followed a pre-designed curriculum order, with variance introduced by individual activities.

Next, we sought to understand the relations between math objectives, and to provide data-driven insight on the role and ordering of objectives. The first step was to select a single feature to measure student learning from an objective. We used percentage of levels completed within an objective, multiplied by the objective performance. We defined ***objective performance*** to be the average performance across the given objective's levels, and a level's performance as the average ***level attempt performance*** prior to and including the first attempt that passed the level. A ***level attempt performance*** is the percentage of puzzles a student completed before losing all lives on a single attempt of a level. The number ranges from two to four lives depending upon the number of questions in the level and their difficulty. Prior research has shown that this measurement can be used to predict normalized gains on the students' 2012 and 2013 state math test scores [20]. These tests provide standardized measurements for students' math ability outside this game environment. We chose to not use the

Table 1. Statistics of the Sequence of Objectives 3rd Grade Students Played in ST Math

N	#Students Played≥N Objs	#Diff. Orders Students Played the First N Objs	#Students in the Top 5 Most Frequent Order
5	1414	107	550,214,89,69,37
10	1104	194	322,131,64,54,28
15	876	205	263, 74, 48, 39,22
20	595	156	186,47,41,24,20
26	371	84	129,34,30,20,19

Table 2. A Description of Objectives in the Curriculum and Objectives with Predictive Power Over Each From Regression Analyses

SO1O-Place Value Concept	Represent three digit numbers as flower petals in group of 1,10,100
SO1P-Place Value Bundles	Represent three digit numbers as flower petals in group of 1,10,100; Addition of numbers to form building blocks in unit of 10s and Hundreds
SO2-Order & Compare Whole Number	Locate number on number line; Compare number with/out help of items and number line; Round numbers up and down on number line
SO1Y-Add & Subtraction w Regrouping	Add and subtract three-digit numbers represented as flower petals, as numbers with flower petals, and as numbers with flower petal animations; Regroup flower petals in calculation.
SO28-Division Concept	Divide countable objects into X groups equally
SO29-Division	Calculate simple division; Present answer through objects, building blocks, and number line
SO5-Lines & Angles	Match types of angles with English name; Identify parallel and perpendicular lines from given lines
SO2I-Shapes	Match 2D shape objects with English name; Identify edge numbers for shapes, objects, and shape's English name; Draw shapes with pins and a rubber band; find shape pairs with same number of edges
SO2J-Shape Attributes	Identify number of edges, vertices, faces in 3D geometry
SO8-Algebraic Expressions & Equations	Represent equation with objects; separate numbers and units objects into equal groups; Identify missing operations from equation
SO9-Functional Relationship	Find X when split N into X groups of Y objects; Fill in missing number of linear pattern (e.g. 2,4,?,8) with/out help of countable objectives
SO2S-Fraction Concepts	Split bar into equal areas; Adding parts of pie chart; Represent fraction with bar or pie chart; And represent pie chart as fraction
SOB-Fraction Addition & Subtraction	Represent fraction's denominator and numerator as parts of robot, slices of pie chart; Add and subtract with these countable objects; Locate calculation result on number line with unit 1
SOC-Fraction Addition & Subtraction L1	Add and subtract fractions without countable objects; calculate on fractions greater than 1
SOD-Money & Decimals	Recognize money unit and coins; Compare money amount; Add, subtract, and find combinations of paper money and coins equal to certain amount
SOE-Measurement	Compare weight of items using balance and scale; measure with ruler; Translate between hours and minutes, and between inch and foot, and specify the answer on number line
SO3C-Concepts of Area and Perimeter	Calculate perimeter and area of 2D shapes presented with/out square grid or fill in calculation formula; Identify 2D shapes for given perimeter and area; Select grids based on difference of 2D shape area and given number
SO3D-Volume & Weight	Order objects' weight using balance and scale; Indicate volume of a given 3D object in cubic
SOG-Addition & Subtraction to 10,000	Calculate multi-digit addition and subtraction; Represent answer on number line or unit block; Fill in missing digit given the result of a multi-digit addition and subtraction
SO3M-Number Patterns	Identify or fill in linear pattern (e.g. 10, 20, 30, 40) with help of building block;Use data-table representation for addition, subtraction, multiplication test
SOI-Multiplication of Multiple Digit	Use building block (grid) to represent multiplication; Calculate multi-digit multiplication with 2 dimensional representation of building block
SOJ-Fraction & Decimal Equivalence	Add and subtract fraction&decimal, present result in 10-by-10 grid; Locate fraction&decimal on number line of unit 1; Represent decimal as formula of fraction addition; Use coins to present dollars in decimal number
SOK-Outcomes	Distinguish whether countable object is "impossible", "unlikely", "likely" or "certain" to be picked from a jar and from lucky wheel
SOL-Using Data & Graph	Present numbers of objects in bar chart and pie chart, and read number from the charts

pre- and post-tests in ST Math in this analysis due to a their lack of precision. The pre- and post-tests contain 5-7 multiple choice questions, so a lucky guess and a mistake could cause a 14-20% change in score. The pre and post-tests also have missing data (11.8% in pre- or post- test) and ceiling effects (19.0% achieved full pre-test scores).

In the second step, it was necessary to focus on the most influential objectives. To do so, for each objective (we refer to as goal objective), we conducted linear regression analyses to find which prior objectives were most predictive of its objective performance. To avoid over-fitting, the first step was to filter the objectives included in the regression. To do so, we applied Spearman Correlation for each goal objective, against all the objectives that happened before it. To ensure there were enough observations, we applied a power test, and filtered out objective pairs with fewer than 30 observations. This step left us 430 correlations for 26 goal objectives. Given the fact that all objective performances were influenced by a student's general math ability, our correlation table had an average value of 0.39. Thus, we decided to apply linear regression with only those objectives with a correlation of at least 0.39. This resulted in considering only 189 of the 430 possible objectives-goal pairs.

In the third step, we applied stepwise mixed effect linear regression for each goal objective, as:

$$P_g = \beta_0 + \beta_1 M + \beta_2 I_g + C \sim N(0, \sigma^2) + \sum_{i=1}^{k} \beta_i P_{gi} \quad (1)$$

Each regression included only the students who attempted the goal objective. The dependent variable P_g is the percentage of levels completed, multiplied by the averaged objective performance of the goal objective g. Betas are coefficients for independent variables, derived from the regression. M is the state math test in 2012, which measured students' general math ability prior to playing ST Math. It was also necessary to include classroom C as a random effect to account for students' being taught by different teachers, especially given the importance of teachers in deciding upon the objective ordering of their classes and groups in classes. The position of objective j in each student's objective sequence is denoted by I_g. We assumed there is a linear relationship between how many objectives students played in ST Math, and the ability to perform well in the same game environment. $P_{g1} - P_{gk}$ describe the k objectives found from the previous step: happened before goal objective g in a sufficient number of sequences (at least 30 and passed the power test for correlation), correlated with g (r>0.39), and were independent of each other (VIF<1.5). Based on our outcome measurement of learning, P_{gi} is 0 if the student did not do an objective i before the goal objective. We also used a stepwise process to automatically add or remove variables based on AIC (Akaike information criterion). This process helped select variables that had the most predictive power for goal objectives, under the influence of student's general math ability, classrooms, and the sequential position of the goal objective. This step also avoided overfitting through cross-validation.

After applying the Benjamini-Hochberg Correction for multiple statistical tests, a total of 96 predictor objectives were found to be statistically significant predictors for the 26 goal objectives. The coefficients had an average standardized beta of 0.12, with 92 coefficients being positive. Figures 2 and 3 display the results, as discussed in the following subsections.

RESULTS AND INTERPRETATION

This section presents the results from two angles: categorization of objectives, and categorization on objective pairs. These categorizations were interpreted in relation to our research goal–what data-driven insight we can provide to inform the design of digital curricular sequencing.

Categorization of Objectives

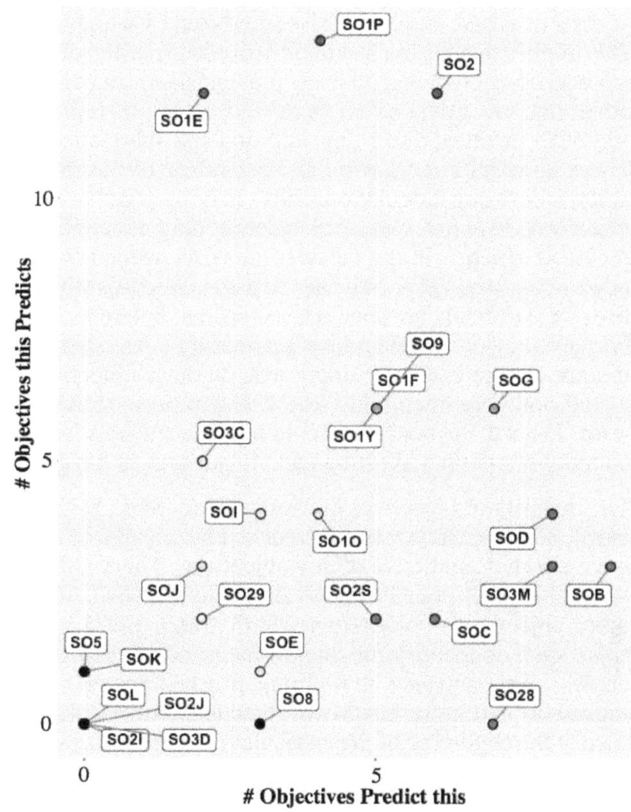

Figure 2. Objectives, and the # of objectives they predict, and the # of objectives that predict them.

Figure 2 is a plot of the predictive power and predictability of objectives, categorized by k-means clustering. Objectives in Group Dark Blue predicted a high number of other objectives. These objectives also occurred early in the pre-designed curriculum, which suggests that they captured basic skills needed in the later objectives. Objectives in this group could be used as early indicators of later performance. For example, if a student skipped or performed poorly on these basic objectives, the teacher may consider intervening to prevent poor performance in later objectives.

Objectives in Group Red were predicted by a high number of other objectives. This implies that playing objectives in this group required math skills learned from many other objectives. For example, games in SOD:"Money and Decimal" required students to compare, add, and subtract money in the form of both paper money and coins. Performing these tasks required a variety of math skills including unit transformation, calculation, number comparison, and a preliminary understanding of fractions and decimals, because coins represent fractions of a dollar. Additionally, three objectives in this group (SO3M:"Number Patterns," SOD:"Money and Decimals," and SOB:"Fraction Addition & Subtraction") were among the top five most difficult, in that students took the most attempts to pass levels within these objectives. This indicates that foundational skills may be especially important for these objectives, and struggle within them may indicate to teachers that students lack prerequisite knowledge.

Objectives in the Group Green both predicted a high number of objectives and were themselves predicted by a high number. This implies that the math skills covered in these objectives are more advanced (depend on many prerequisites), and useful (as other objectives depend on them). For example, both SO1Y and SOG involved multi-digit addition and subtraction tasks. These tasks required a solid understanding of numbers and units, and strong calculation skills. Playing puzzles in these objectives, in return, enhanced understanding on numbers and provided practice in the calculation skills needed for many other objectives. This indicates that the Green Group objectives were difficult, but should be completed before moving on because they could affect later performance. In other words, if some students weren't doing well on these objectives, we would not recommend that teachers skip these students forward. Instead, the teachers should help the students learn this material rather than allowing them to advance in the game.

The majority of objectives in Group Black (SOL, SO5, SO2I, SO2J, SO3D, SOK) were not predicted by any objectives, and were also not predictive of any objectives. This implies that these objectives practiced math skills that were isolated from other objectives. For example, SO5, SO2I, SO2J involved tasks such as identifying shapes, faces, edges and types of angles. This suggests that Group Black objectives can be moved around more flexibly in the curriculum, and may be used at the beginning of the curriculum to familiarize students with the ST Math system.

Categorization of Objective Pairs

Figure 3 presents the prediction relationship between objective pairs, symmetrically along the X=Y line to show complete information of an objective when reading from a row or column. A grey color shows a ***symmetrical relationship***: when X is attempted first, X predicts Y; when Y is attempted first, Y predicts X. A blue or red color shows an ***asymmetrical relationship***: one objective predicts another if attempted first, but not vise versa.

Within asymmetrical relationships, a light blue or red shows a ***curriculum-order asymmetrical relationship***: the objective attempted first and which predicts the other, is also ordered earlier in the curriculum. This relationship may exist because either the later-ordered objective was not chosen as a predictor of the earlier-ordered objective, or because we simply do not have enough data (failed power-test) to tell so. For either reason, this relationship suggests keeping the current ordering of the objective pairs in the curriculum.

On the other hand, a dark blue or red shows a ***non curriculum-order asymmetrical relationship***: the objective attempted first and which predicts the other is ordered later in the curriculum. This relationship implies that students who completed more levels and performed better in the later-ordered objective before attempting the earlier-ordered objective performed better in the earlier-ordered objective. These relationships are the most interesting as they may suggest potential changes to the existing curriculum. Below sections categorize the 20 ***non curriculum-order asymmetrical relationships*** we found based on their implications for curriculum design.

Suggesting more Practice on Certain Skills (8/20)

This group includes: SOG: "Addition & Subtraction to 10,000," predicted SO1F, SO9, SOB, and SOD; SOI: "Multiplication of Multiple Digit" predicted SOB and SOC; SO1Y: "Addition & Subtraction with Regrouping" predicted SO2; and SOJ: "Fraction & Decimal Equivalence" predicted SOE: "Measurement." One explanation is that these predictor objectives aimed to intensively practice a specific skill, such as multi-digit addition. These skills were needed in the earlier objectives they predicted. For example, SOJ:"Fraction & Decimal Equivalence" predicted SOE:"Measurement," where the predictor SOJ practiced the understanding and transformation between fractions and decimals. This skill was needed in SOE, where many games required students to place certain minutes on a number line of unit hours, or certain inches in a number line of unit feet. A solid understanding of fractions and decimals gained from SOJ may help transforming minutes and inches as fractions of hours and feet. However, the relationship is asymmetrical because the predicted objectives were not designed for enhancing the specific calculation skills in the predictor objectives. Thus, they were not the major influencers of the performance and completion of their predictors.

Although relationships in this group do not necessarily suggest that these calculation-based objectives should be moved earlier in the curriculum, these relationships imply that the performance and completion of many objectives could be improved if there were more practice on certain calculation skills beforehand.

Suggesting more Applicable Examples (4/20)

This group includes: SOD: "Money & Decimals," predicted SO8, SO2S; and SO3C: "Concepts of Area and Perimeter," predicted SO29, SOB. One explanation is that tasks in SOD and SO3C contained examples and practical scenarios for the more conceptually challenging objectives they predicted. For example, SOD practiced the recognition, comparison, and calculation of money units such as dimes, quarters, and dollars. Because coins are fractions of a dollar, these tasks provided examples for SO2S: "Fraction Concepts." Another example is SO3C practiced calculating area and perimeter for a given square grid or highlighting areas in a square grid for a given area and perimeter. These tasks were practical scenarios to practice addition, multiplication, and division at small-scale, with the help of countable squares. Thus, SO3C predicted

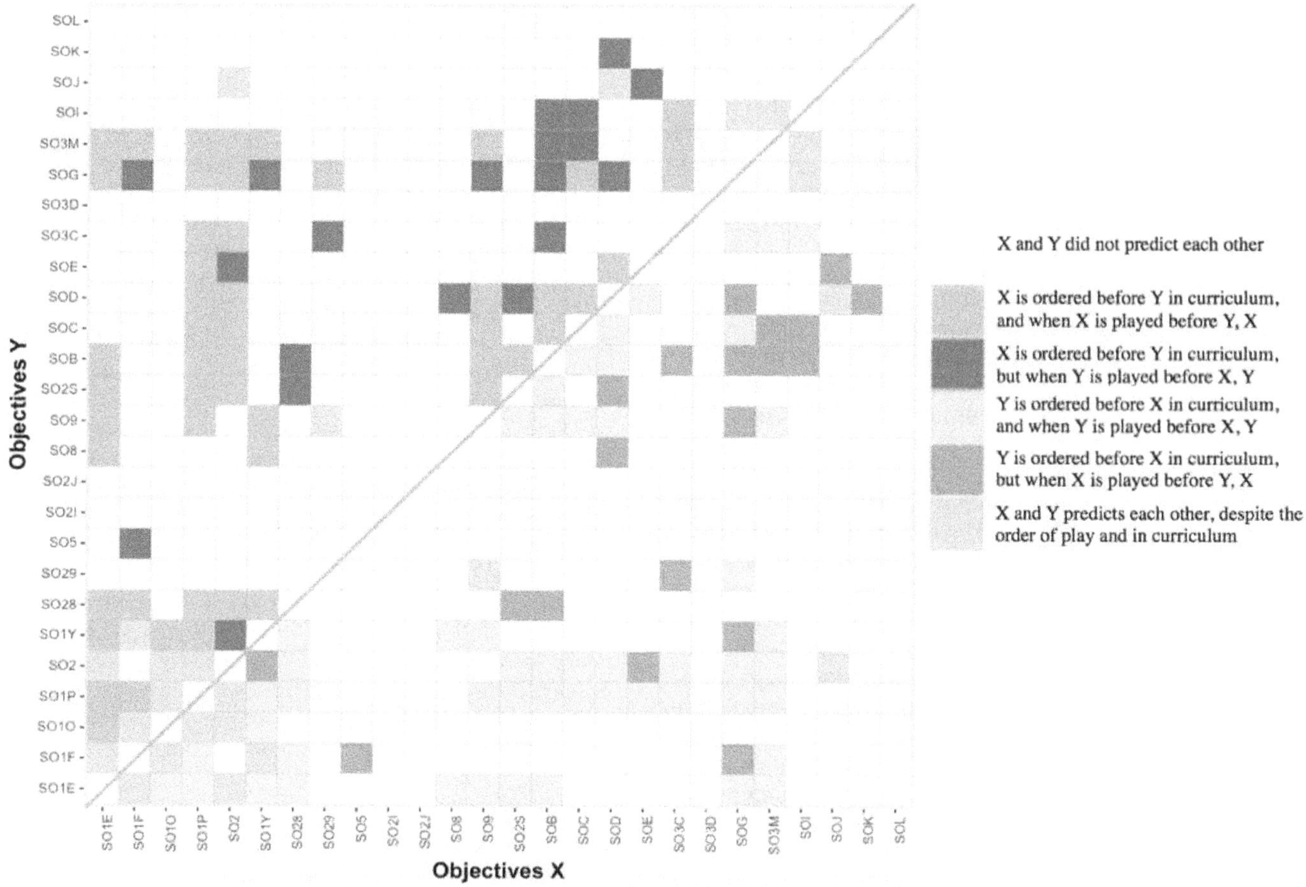

Figure 3. Pairwise Relationship between Objectives. This figure is symmetric across the X=Y line (so light pink = light blue; dark pink = dark blue) Light pink/blue relationships are expected because the curriculum is sequenced purposefully. Dark pink/blue relationships are surprising, since a later curricular item predicts performance on an earlier item if attempted early

SO29 and SOB. Relationships in this group suggest that performance and completion for some conceptually difficult objectives can be improved with more applicable, simplistic examples beforehand [2].

One interesting result is that although SOD: "Money / Decimals" predicted SO2S:"Fraction Concepts," the addition and subtraction of fractions predicted SOD (curriculum-order symmetrical relationship). This may be because the later levels in SOD required more complicated calculations. For example, some tasks asked students to add dimes and quarters to a double-digit amount in dollars, which could be helped by practice on fraction addition, and on the transformation between fractions and decimals (as SOD and SOJ predicted each other). These levels contained much harder tasks than other levels in SOD, as we found that these four levels in SOD cost students an average of 5.14 attempts to pass, whereas the other 12 SOD levels cost an average of 1.71 attempts. Thus, there may be a benefit in splitting SOD. An example would be moving the earlier levels for recognizing and comparing coins before fractions so these levels could serve as practical scenarios for using fractions, and moving the harder levels after or as levels within fraction calculation objectives.

Suggesting Reordering of Teaching Math Concepts (2/20)
SO2S: "Fraction Concept" and SOB: "Fraction Addition and Subtraction" predicted SO28: "Division Concept." Although it is conventionally believed that division should be taught before fractions, with prior research finding that division predicts fractions skills (e.g., [19, 1], there may be reasons why the specific actions within these objectives of ST Math produced the opposite order. SO2S and SOB presented fractions as countable parts of a divisible object, such as slices of a pie or groups of bricks. Manipulating these objects' parts may help students develop a better understanding of division through partitioning items into groups in a familiar way with smaller numbers [22]. This relationship is asymmetrical because games in the fraction objectives generally involved the addition and subtraction of divisible objects, which were too simple to involve division calculations.

Suggesting a Change in Game Design (2/20)
SOG: "Addition and Subtraction within 10,000" predicted SO1Y: "Addition and Subtraction with Regrouping." It could be that if a student practiced SOG and became more proficient with calculations, s/he may have more working memory to perform the extra counting and regrouping tasks in SO1Y [17]. In SO1Y, digits were presented as petals in groups of one, 10,

and 100. In the majority of tasks, students needed to count and regroup petals during calculation, with some counting above 10. In certain tasks, students also needed to present their calculation results in the format of petals. On the other hand, SOG practiced calculation with more traditional presentations, such as the numbers themselves, number lines, or building blocks marked with one, 10, or 100. SOG also did not require students to regroup objectives during calculation or to count over 10.

This relationship suggests that counting and regrouping petals during the calculation process may be ineffective and distracting. This is evidenced by the pre- and post-test scores. Recall that the pre- post-tests in ST Math consist of parallel questions (same problem type with different numbers). In both SO1Y and SOG, The tests ask student to choose the correct answer when adding or subtracting multi-digit numbers. In SO1Y: "Addition and Subtraction with Regrouping," the average pre- and post-test scores were 0.64 and 0.66; in SOG: "Addition and Subtraction within 10,000," they were 0.66 and 0.73–a much higher learning gain. It could be that students experienced the split-attention effect defined by Chandler and Sweller[3], because students spent their limited working memory resources mentally integrating two sources of informations (e.g., number and petals). Also, this relationship is not symmetrical (SO1Y does not predict SOG), which could be because the performance and completion of SO1Y reflected more about the difficulties encountered in counting and regrouping petals, than in the calculation shared with SOG. This difficulty and ineffectiveness of regrouping and counting petals is also evidenced by statistics from SO1P (Place Value Bundles using petals). SO1P had the second lowest level attempt performance among all 26 objectives, and only a 0.03 gain from pre- to post-test.

Another relationship that suggests a change in game design is SOE: "Measurement," which negatively predicted SO2: "Comparing Whole Numbers." One likely explanation is that the number line was presented differently in these two objectives. In SOE, the number line was represented by a ruler, scaled for time units and for imperial and metric length units. This means that in SOE, a number line can be one centimeter, 60 minutes, or 12 inches. On the other hand, SO2 presented the number line as metric units. Because young students often do not have an accurate understanding of the number line [12], introducing conflicting number lines may create misconceptions and interfere with their number line knowledge. This hypothesis is evidenced by the performance statistics in SO2. The first level of SO2, which requires students to locate an integer on a number line, took students an average of 5.5 attempts to pass, whereas the rest of the levels in SO2 (some contained similar tasks of a locating number on number line) only took students an average of 1.5 attempts to pass, with the max being 2.6 attempts. This relationship suggests that using different units on the same presentation of a number line may be confusing, and similar practices on unit conversion should be moved after students have developed a concrete understanding of the number line.

Suggesting a Change in Pacing (2/20)

SO3M: "Number Patterns" negatively correlated with objectives SOB: "Fraction Addition Subtraction L1" and SOC: "Fraction Addition and Subtraction I and II." It could be due to the pacing in the most common sequence, in which SO3M was played before SOB and SOC. The majority, 293 out of 360 students who played SO3M before SOB, played in a sequence "SO28 SO3M SO29 SO9 SO2S SOB SOC." SOB and SOC required calculation in conceptually difficult topic in third grade curricular–fractions. SO3M contained difficult tasks, such as asking students to find or complete number patterns of 3-6-9-12, or performing multi-digit multi-step addition, subtraction, and multiplication using a new data-table representation. As compared to the pre-designed curriculum in Table 2, these three relatively difficult concepts, division, number patterns, and fractions, were spaced too close to each other. Thus, it could be that students get mentally overloaded when too many difficult concepts and different number representations are packed together. This relationship suggests that teachers should vary the pacing accordingly and take breaks between difficult concepts [31]. For example, teachers can allow students to play simpler objectives that offer more concrete examples or practical scenarios to prepare for the upcoming difficult concepts. Teachers can also assign objectives in the Group Black described in in previous, as they practiced concepts that are isolated from other objectives.

Unclear (2/20)

SO5: "Lines and Angles" predicted SO1F: "Multiplication Concepts." One possible explanation is that SO1F was introduced very early in the curriculum, with few objectives beforehand to explain its variance in performance and completion. SO5 required selecting the right names for angle types and distinguishing parallel and perpendicular lines; it is a simple objective that could be captured by general skills, such as memorization, that helped predict SO1F. Another unclear relationship is that SOK: "Outcomes" predicted SOD: "Money." SOK dealt with probability problems. It could be that the presentations in SOK closely resembled lucky wheels and lottery jars, which both relate to money, but the relationship is still unclear.

DISCUSSION AND CONCLUSION

This paper presents a novel method that informs curricular sequencing in a serious game, taking advantage of the variance in the order of objectives that students played. We applied this method to ST Math gameplay data from 1,565 3rd graders. Our results include specific design recommendations for ST Math, and general data-driven insights for digital curricular design, such as the pacing of objectives and the ordering of math concepts. The method itself, and some of these data-driven insights can inform design for digital curricular design in other serious games and e-learning platforms.

From a technical perspective, the growth of educational games and other e-learning platforms enables a large amount of data collection. This in turn has facilitated the use of innovative analytical methods that reveal user behavior patterns, which go beyond traditional experimental trials. However, data analytics, although informative, can make it easier to find statistically-significant results that may not be grounded in theory, and simply arise because of the sheer volume of available data. Therefore, when analyzing any large data set such as ST Math, we want to ensure that our analyses help uncover educationally relevant results. From the education literature, researchers have identified some early skills that predict later mathematics skills. For example, the general knowledge of the meaning and magnitude of numbers, is highly predictive of later mathematics achievement, including number line representation and calculation fluency [18]. These skills are in turn predictive of skills such as fractions [1, 19]. We believe that our data-driven work on discovering predictive relationships can be leveraged to discover more learning trajectories[29], as well as to make practical sequencing recommendations that may not have been apparent from a purely top-down approach.

From a practical perspective, this analysis helps guide one crucial decision when integrating serious games into a classroom: what objective should students play next? When applying digital curriculum in classrooms, teachers may be given the flexibility of reordering and skipping math objectives. However, it is unclear whether teachers are aware of the impact of objective selection and sequencing[11]. Molin [23] also suggested that teachers not only have a limited time to prepare and play a game for game-based learning, but are seldom engaged with game designers in making decisions on content ordering. Thus, our method can help teachers to become more aware of how their local decisions may affect students' longer-term performance. This motivates future work on designing a user interface to notify teachers of the likely impact of individual ordering decisions. It is possible that there exists some optimal pathway through which students should experience a given game. Unfortunately, our method could not be used to find the optimal path in present context, as our data have too much variance both in objective selected and those completed. In future work, we plan to develop quantitative metrics to compare individual paths against better orderings and to relate those variances to performance.

Serious game designers can use our method and its data-driven insights to evaluate the sequencing and predictive relationships within their games. Many of our results are applicable beyond ST Math. For example, we found that counting objects during calculation distracted students, which implies that game designers should avoid designing 'extra' interactions that split students' attention during problem solving. Other results may be limited to ST Math's unique design characteristics. For example, fraction puzzles used countable parts of a divisible objects, such as divided pie charts, which helped students to understand division. Such a predictive relationship may or may not hold in games that use different representations. To assess the impact of differences between game environments, game designers can follow the same analytical procedure, and redefine performance variables and performance-associated mixed effects based upon their user-interaction data. Our method can potentially be applied to similar data outside of the serious games domain, where content is presented under varying sequences over a long time span.

One limitation of this work is that there are many factors outside of the system, such as varying instructional methods, that may affect learning and performance. We sought to control these factors by adding random effect distributions for individual classrooms. We also worked with domain experts to interpret the results, and examined the candidate predictive relationships by playing the games. Future work could collect qualitative data on teachers' understanding of these data-driven insights and the effects of their applications in classrooms.

ACKNOWLEDGEMENT
This work was supported by NSF grant IUSE #1544273 "Evaluation for Actionable Change: A Data-Driven Approach" Teomara Rutherford, Tiffany Barnes & Collin F. Lynch Co-PIs.

REFERENCES
1. D. Bailey, R. Siegler, and D. Geary. 2014. Early predictors of middle school fraction knowledge. *Developmental Science* 17, 5 (2014), 775–785.
2. S. Bokosmaty, J. Sweller, and S. Kalyuga. 2015. Learning geometry problem solving by studying worked examples: Effects of learner guidance and expertise. *American Educational Research Journal* 52, 2 (2015), 307–333.
3. P. Chandler and J. Sweller. 1992. The splitâĂŘattention effect as a factor in the design of instruction. *British Journal of Educational Psychology* 62(2) (1992).
4. Y. Chen, J. Gonzalez-Brenes, and J. Tian. 2016. Joint discovery of skill prerequisite graphs and student models. In *Proceedings of the 9th International Conference on Educational Data Mining (EDM).*
5. Y. Chen, P. H. Wuillemin, and J. M. Labat. 2015. Discovering Prerequisite Structure of Skills through Probabilistic Association Rules Mining. In *Proceedings of the 8th International Conference on Educational Data Mining (EDM).*
6. D. Clements and J. Sarama. 2014. *Learning and teaching early math: The learning trajectories approach.* Routledge.
7. S. Doroudi, K. Holstein, V. Aleven, and E. Brunskill. 2016. Sequence matters, but how exactly? A method for evaluating activity sequences from data. In *Proceedings of the 9th International Conference on Educational Data Mining (EDM).*
8. G. Duncan, C. Dowsett, A. Claessens, K. Magnuson, A. Huston, P. Klebanov, L. Pagani, L. Feinstein, M. Engel, and J. Brooks-Gunn. 2007. School readiness and later achievement. *Developmental Psychology* 43, 6 (2007), 1428.
9. M. S. El-Nasr, A. Drachen, and A. Canossa. 2016. *Game analytics.* Springer London Limited.
10. M. Freire, A Serrano-Laguna, B. M. Iglesias, I. Martinez-Ortiz, P. Moreno-Ger, and B.

Fernandez-Manjon. 2016. Game learning analytic: Learning analytics for serious games. *Learning, Design, and Technology* (2016).

11. J. Galant. 2013. Selecting and sequencing mathematics tasks: Seeking mathematical knowledge for teaching. *Perspectives in Education* 31(3) (2013), 34–48.
12. D. Geary, M. Hoard, L. Nugent, and J. Byrd-Craven. 2008. Development of number line representations in children with mathematical learning disability. *Developmental Neuropsychology* 33, 3 (2008), 277–299.
13. E. Harpstead and V. Aleven. 2015. Using empirical learning curve analysis to inform design in an educational game. In *Proceedings of the 2015 Annual Symposium on Computer-Human Interaction in Play (CHI PLAY)*. ACM, 197–207.
14. D. Hick, M. Eagle, E. Rowe, J. Asbell-clarke, Edwards T., and Barnes T. 2016. Using game analytics to evaluate puzzle design and level progression in a serious game. In *Proceedings of the 6th international conference on learning analytic and knowledge (LAK)*.
15. D. Hicks, Z. Liu, and T. Barnes. 2016. Measuring gameplay affordances of user-generated content in an educational game. In *In Proceedings of the 9th international conference on educational data mining (EDM)*.
16. B. Horn, A. K. Hoover, J. Barnes, Y. Folajimi, G. Smith, and C. Harteveld. 2016. Opening the black box of play: Strategy analysis of an educational game. In *In Proceedings of the 2016 Annual Symposium on Computer-Human Interaction in Play (CHI PLAY)*. ACM, 142–153.
17. I. Imbo, A. Vandierendonck, and E. Vergauwe. 2007. The role of working memory in carrying and borrowing. *Psychological Research* 71, 4 (2007), 467–483.
18. N. Jordan, J. Glutting, and C. Ramineni. 2010. The importance of number sense to mathematics achievement in first and third grades. *Learning and Individual Differences* 20, 2 (2010), 82–88.
19. N. Jordan, N. Hansen, L. Fuchs, R. Siegler, R. Gersten, and D. Micklos. 2013. Developmental predictors of fraction concepts and procedures. *Journal of Experimental Child Psychology* 116, 1 (2013), 45–58.
20. Z. Liu, C. Cody, T. Barnes, C. Lynch, and T. Rutherford. 2017. The Antecedents of and Associations with Elective Replay in An Educational Game: Is Replay Worth It?. In *Proceedings of the 10th International Conference on Educational Data Mining (EDM)*.
21. C. S. Loh, Y. Sheng, and D. Ifenthaler. 2015. *Serious game analytics. Methodologies for performance, measurement, assessment, and improvement*. Springer, Cham, Switzerland.
22. T. Martin and D. Schwartz. 2005. Physically distributed learning: Adapting and reinterpreting physical environments in the development of fraction concepts. *Cognitive Science* 29, 4 (2005), 587–625.
23. G. Molin. 2017. The role of the teacher in game-based learning: A review and outlook. In *In serious games and edutainment applications*. Springer International Publishing, 649–674.
24. A. Moretti, J. Gonzalez-Brenes, and K. McKnight. 2014. Data-driven curriculum design: Mining the web to make better teaching decisions. In *Proceedings of the 7th International Conference on Educational Data Mining (EDM)*.
25. M. Nathan, K. Koedinger, and M. Alibali. 2001. Expert blind spot: When content knowledge eclipses pedagogical content knowledge. In *Proceedings of the 3rd International Conference on Cognitive Science*.
26. X. Ochoa. 2016. Simple Metrics for Curricular Analytics. In *Proceedings of the 1 st Learning Analytics for Curriculum and Program Quality Improvement Workshop*.
27. M. Pechenizkiy and P. A. Toledo. 2014. Learning to teach like a Bandit.. In *Proceedings of the 7th International Conference on Educational Data Mining (EDM)*.
28. G. Ramani and R. Siegler. 2011. Reducing the gap in numerical knowledge between low-and middle-income preschoolers. *Journal of Applied Developmental Psychology* 32, 3 (2011), 146–159.
29. R. Shavelson and A. Kurpius. 2012. Reflections on learning progressions. In *Learning progressions in science*. Springer, 13–26.
30. A. Vuong, T. Nixon, and B. Towle. 2011. A method for finding prerequisites within a curriculum. In *Proceedings of the 4th International Conference on Educational Data Mining (EDM)*.
31. B. Witzel and P. Riccomini. 2007. Optimizing math curriculum to meet the learning needs of students. *Preventing School Failure: Alternative Education for Children and Youth* 52, 1 (2007), 13–18.
32. Y. Yang, H. Liu, J. Carbonell, and W. Ma. 2015. Concept graph learning from educational data. In *Proceedings of the 8th International Conference on Web Search and Data Mining*. ACM.

Wearable Learning: Multiplayer Embodied Games for Math

Ivon Arroyo
Worcester Polytechnic Institute
Worcester, MA
iarroyo@wpi.edu

Matthew Micciollo
Worcester Polytechnic Institute
Worcester, MA
mmicciolo@wpi.edu

Jonathan Casano
Ateneo de Manila University
Manila, Philippines
jonathancasano@gmail.com

Erin Ottmar
Worcester Polytechnic Institute
Worcester, MA
erottmar@wpi.edu

Taylyn Hulse
Worcester Polytechnic Institute
Worcester, MA
trhulse@wpi.edu

Ma. Mercedes Rodrigo
Ateneo de Manila University
Manila, Philippines
mrodrigo@ateneo.edu

ABSTRACT
We present a new technology-based paradigm to support embodied mathematics educational games, using wearable devices in the form of SmartPhones and SmartWatches for math learning, for full classes of students in formal in-school education settings. The Wearable Learning Games Engine is web based infrastructure that enables students to carry one mobile device per child, as they embark on math team-based activities that require physical engagement with the environment. These Wearable Tutors serve as guides and assistants while students manipulate, measure, estimate, discern, discard and find mathematical objects that satisfy specified constraints. Multi-player math games that use this infrastructure have yielded both cognitive and affective benefits. Beyond math game play, the Wearable Games Engine Authoring Tool enables students to create games themselves for other students to play; in this process, students engage in computational thinking and learn about finite-state machines. We present the infrastructure, games, and results for a series of experiments on both game play and game creation.

Author Keywords
Wearable learning; embodied cognition; educational games; mathematics; computational thinking; tutoring systems.

ACM Classification Keywords
Human Factors; Design

1. INTRODUCTION
This project is rich in the foundational constructs of learning sciences and technologies research with several movable and exciting parts. From embodied active math learning experiences to collaborative game-based learning experiences, the project engages students with mobile technologies to support math learning, as well as game creation to promote computational thinking.

A growing body of research in math education and cognitive science describes the important role of embodiment, object manipulation and motion while learning mathematics [3-5, 22, 29]. Embodied learning involves the combination of movement and gestures with higher-order cognitive activities, such as analyzing and evaluating. By grounding students through physical movement and gesture, abstract concepts can become more concrete. We ground our research on Activity Theory, which poses that consciousness and activity, including the body and environment, are all interconnected within the same system [28]. This means that any artifacts used in activity, such as physical objects, tools, or technology, are also part of the same system. In learning environments, these tools mediate that activity system and can be used to enhance learning.

At the same time, recent technologies have become more tangible, sharable and even wearable. There is potential for these new technologies to redefine the way that teachers and students interact among themselves, the content, and technological artifacts, for a shared experience that improves learning through rich interactive discourse. The benefits of technology in education in particular are well known by now: Computers are good at instantly processing large amounts of data, providing students more agency and choice, allowing for self-paced trajectories through the content, providing just-in-time support and also helping teachers with assessment [7]. However, technologies that support embodied experiences are only now starting to emerge [23, 30-31, 34]. Embedding innovative, engaging, and effective high-quality embodied technologies in K-12 mathematics classrooms has the promise of improving support given to individual students, while motivating them in STEM, via rich experiences that blends technology into classroom culture. This research article introduces a new way of learning mathematics via wearable/mobile technologies that can integrate active physical play and

CHI PLAY '17, October 15–18, 2017, Amsterdam, Netherlands

ACM ISBN 978-1-4503-4898-0/17/10…$15.00
https://doi.org/10.1145/3116595.3116637

math-rich experiences, facilitating shifts in both learning and affective outcomes. We present two series of studies that explore the feasibility of using wearable and mobile technologies for game playing and game creation, in the context of schools.

We first describe paper-based pilot studies that have iteratively driven the development of this technology. Second, we present the "Wearable Learning Games Engine" infrastructure. Third, we present results from research studies that investigated how these games, where players are supported by mobile devices, can yield gains in math achievement as well as affective gains (appreciation of math and comfort while solving math problems). Last, we present results of a recent study of students themselves creating their own embodied math games, switching their role from problem solvers to "problem posers". This required students to think at a high level of abstraction, engage in computational thinking skills, and learn to specify the role of mobile devices as guides and helpers to the players, defining the behavior of the mobile devices at each step of the game, as finite-state machines.

1.1 Background Research

Educational games are at the forefront of learning technologies, and game-based curricula is implemented to foster engagement and motivation, provide communities of learning, and enhance performance [17, 20, 24]. Technology-based education games range in structure from individual practice to fully immersive, multi-player environments. Drill and practice games are more feasible to introduce into the classroom and integrate into a traditional curriculum [25]. Immersive adventure games such as Quest Atlantis [11] have a socially-responsive design and student-driven storyline played across individuals and entire classrooms.

Learning technologies for mathematics in particular have design features that benefit students more than traditional paper-based activities including immediate and adaptive feedback, dynamic interactions aligned with mathematical rules, as well as the potential for detailed formative assessment [7, 14, 25]. All together this makes for a richer, more interactive, and more informative learning environments for both teachers and students.

More recently, some have argued that mathematics learning environments should be more embodied [1, 5, 28]. The idea of embodied learning involves the creation, manipulation, and sharing of meaning through engaged interaction with artifacts [18]. Students may be guided to encounter, discover, rehearse, and ultimately investigate new perceptuo-motor schemas. A general objective of embodied learning is for learners to develop cognitive resources that presumably undergird specialized forms of human practice, such as solving mathematics problems by productively struggling with mathematical content during an activity with corresponding physical movement, rather than merely repeating numbers or operations [1-2]. Embodied learning is also based on the constructivist tradition of promoting passages from non-symbolic interaction to symbolic representation [9, 12]. Further, this work builds on the Theory of Situated Learning first proposed by Lave and Wenger [26] as a model of learning in a community of practice. Situated learning argues that learning should not be viewed as simply the transmission of abstract and decontextualized knowledge from one individual to another, but a social process whereby knowledge is co-constructed, situated in a specific context and embedded within a particular social and physical environment. Still, we consider that the theory most aligned with this research is Activity Theory [28], which emphasizes the interaction between people, artifacts, and social groups. Activity Theory highlights the importance of leveraging life-relevant connections available within the physical space and considering policies and norms related to learners' physical bodies, physical spaces and objects, and the importance of co-design with children and teachers. Activity Theory has already been used as a theoretical framework for other embodied technologies for science education, research that is co-occurring at the same time as ours [16].

Embedding mathematics in their everyday activities, games and lives encourages students to find mathematics everywhere –transmitting the idea that math can be reached and experienced with their hands and full bodies as much as their mind. One way this has been achieved has been through research using technology-based games in museums, especially scavenger hunts. For instance, Drake et al. [19] show two examples of how wearable devices can be appropriated for use in school settings. These examples focus on instances where students turned activity trackers into objects of inquiry using data from familiar activities. Similarly, Tsai & Sung [37] extend, preserve, and integrate the museum experience with visitors' personal and social lives, via mobile apps can enhance visitors' museum experiences via scavenger hunts. These scavenger hunts are based on individual experiences in informal settings, however, our work involves team-based and formal education settings and uses this ecological perspective to integrate students, teachers, physical objects and school spaces with learning math, playing math, creating math and growing together as a community of practice.

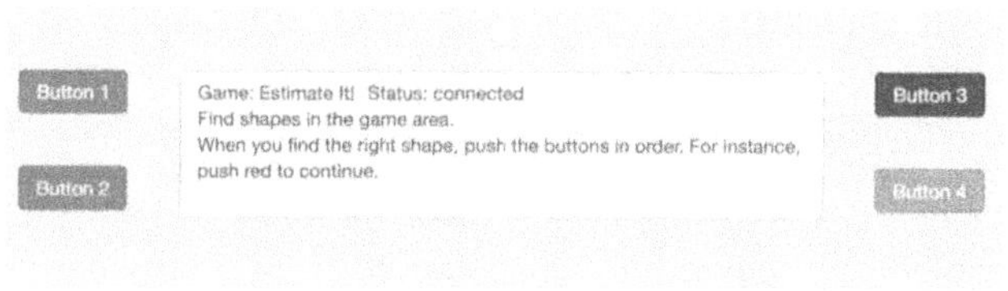

Figure 1. What students can see on their mobile device as they begin to play *EstimateIT!*

Regarding wearability, technological devices are becoming more portable and wearable (e.g. iWatch, Samsung's SmartWatch, Google Glass). The outstanding benefits of mobile technologies are: light, easy to wear or carry, and the capability to track physical activity, location information and, thanks to Near Frequency Communication (NFC) also interact with objects. These characteristics make mobile technologies appealing for a variety of social purposes, such as education and health. For instance, Chiu & Liu [15] studied SmartWatches for older adults for fall detection and medication reminder applications. The Google Glass was used for simulation-based training to record actions and later analyze, showing that it can be integrated into simulation-based training and debriefing, not interfering with the simulation experience [40]. Some applications of mobile devices to education imply carrying one device. For instance, Google Expeditions enables students to take virtual field trips by hooking a cell phone in low-cost cardboard glasses.

2. THE WEARABLE LEARNING TECHNOLOGY

The technology explained next may be wearable or not --we have experimented with students wearing cell phones in armbands, and also created a client App for an Android-based SmartWatches. It is not conclusive yet what would be the best mode of carrying a device, and this might well depend on the characteristics of the game being played. Regardless of whether it is wearable (watch) or carried (cell phone), the assumption is that there is one easy-to-carry mobile device per student available, one per student-player.

2.1 The Wearable Learning Games Engine

The core of the software is a remote java-based web-server, which alternatively can run locally on the teacher's computer. The Wearable Games Engine plays the following roles: (1) communicates with the devices; (2) maintains the state of individual players and games; (3) aids the teacher in the general functioning of activities (start the game, verify progress, determine the winner); (4) allows management of classes and allows the teacher to specify teams of students; (5) keeps track of individual and team progress; (6) allows the creation of new games through an authoring tool.

It is important to note that a variety of games can be created with this infrastructure that make use of these same mechanisms. This goes beyond scavenger hunts, as will be shown later in Section 4.

When the Wearable Learning App in the SmartPhone or SmartWatch is launched and a student joins an active game, the device opens a web-socket communication and handshakes with the web-server, which returns the first "state" of the game. The Web Server connects to a database that keeps track of students, games, devices, and gathers a history (a log) of student events.

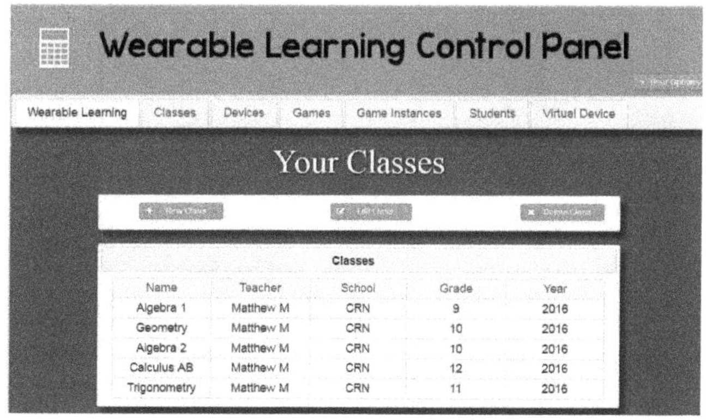

Figure 2. Control Panel for teachers to create, edit and delete classes, students, teams and start games (or create games).

Teachers have a web-based Control Panel available to them, the so-called *Wearable Learning Control Panel* (Figure 2), an HTML-based interface accessible from any web-browser. This tool allows teachers to log in to manage games, students and classes, as teachers might have more than one class of students working on the same games activity at different times. Teachers can create accounts, access and modify their own classes, students and devices. The data is persistent and remains stored in a remote location (database server). In the future, this control panel will also allow students to log in to create/enter their own games --for the time being, it is only teachers that can login.

2.2 The Games

Math Games involve multiple players and require players to have an Andriod-based SmartPhone or SmartWatch running an App. The first role of the mobile device is to maintain game flow –to give instructions to the player on what he/she should do, keep pace of the game; the second role is to provide feedback and support (e.g. 'that was incorrect; try again, or push the black button for a hint').

Behind the scenes, each game is specified as a finite-state machine (FSM), in that every output and text displayed on the device at any point of time is defined as a unique "game state". Figure 1 shows the first state of the *EstimateIT!* Game displayed on the phone, which all students see after joining that game. Note a FSM is an abstract machine defined as being in one of a finite number of states (an output state) and having transitions between states that correspond to events (input events, button presses, or NFC scans). The machine can be in only one state at a time, called the 'current state', which is the state the player is in at this time.

Transitions between states correspond to student inputs, such as colored button presses. The player's current state changes from one state to another after a specific event or

Figure 3. Everyday Geometric Objects tagged with Color Codes for EstimateIT! to be played

condition is triggered, called a transition event. For instance, in the game described later called *EstimateIT!*, students push buttons for a few purposes: to "continue" to the next instruction (e.g. push any colored button to continue), to ask for help ("push the black button if you need a hint"), or to communicate that they have found a specific object (Each object in the game has been tagged with a 4-color "bar code" that needs to be entered by the student when the sought object is found, such as Red-Green-Blue-Red, see Figures 3-4). These tags identify and are attached to objects so that students can match and integrate the real world to the current state of the game -- from small geometric shapes to windows, sections of a playground/climber, depending on the game. Games may use NFC tags to identify objects, however, note this also makes the creation of new games (e.g., by teachers) somewhat harder than plain color sequences.

Within the game-creation authoring tool, states are represented as circles or boxes (Figures 5 and 6), and events connect states via directed arrows [27]. The authoring tool allows to specify games in graphical form (State Machine view) or in pull down menu mode (Create Game States view). This is only accessible to teachers (and researchers) for the time being, but will be accessible to student accounts in the near future.

2.3 Collaboration and Cooperation

When students play, they may work individually or in teams. The game might have been set up to involve 'collaboration', implying that every member of the team gets exactly the same math question/challenge on each player's device (everybody is given the same assignment or problem to solve) or 'cooperation' [36] implying that different people within the team get complementary roles and different assigned objects to find. In this case, the smartphones are semi-synchronized for people in the team so that individual players cannot move beyond certain states unless every person in the team has gotten there. We called this the "stall for team" condition of a game state, which implies that neither watch in the team can transition to the following game state until all students in the team have finished a specific task (i.e., the team cannot move on to the next stage until every person has solved the math challenge, opening up possibilities for peer help/support by team members). We consider this an innovative way to encourage peer support and collaboration.

3. GAME PLAYING

One of the major games developed for this infrastructure is *EstimateIT!*™, a measurement estimation and number sense game for 4th–6th grade students [33]. The game is a Scavenger Hunt where students search for objects hidden around a physical space. Level 1 involves the search of geometric shapes and measurement estimation through team-based cooperation, where teams are given individual tasks to complete to help their team succeed; this may involve helping each other as more expert team players finish first. For example, the display could show the following message to a player: *"Find a cube with a 6 inch side"*. When pushing the hint button: "*I am a volume with 6 equal faces: use your 12-inch dowel to estimate my height"*. In level 1, one player in the team may look for a cube, while another looks for a cylinder. Game dynamics changes in Level 2, when every member on the team works together to find the same object. In the end, the team who finds all correct objects first wins the game.

3.1 *EstimateIT!* Scavenger Hunt Pilots

An initial usability study included students in grades 4-7 who played a few different variations of the *Estimate It*

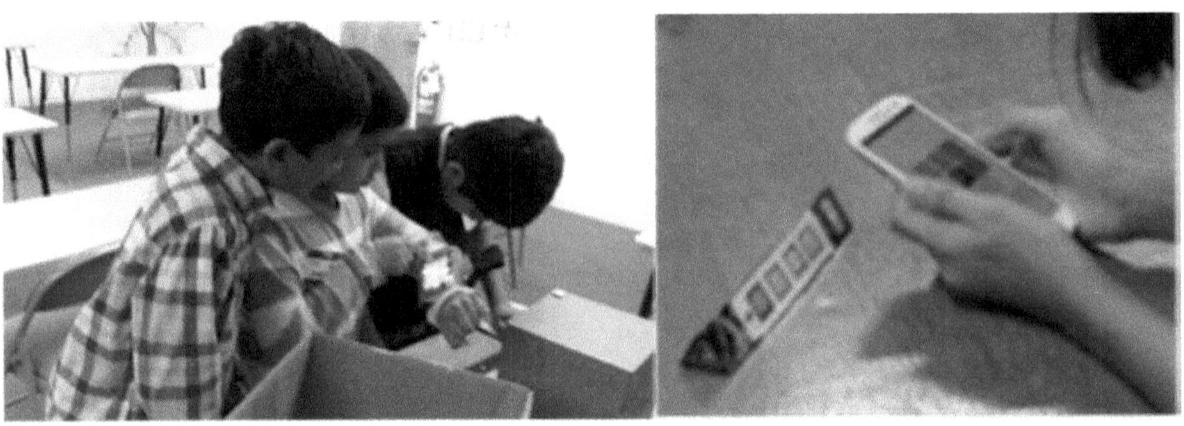

Figure 4. Students Playing EstimateIT! Left: a team discussing an object; Right: a student considering a triangular prism

Scavenger Hunt game. The game was designed as a motivational tool for students to practice measurement/geometry and develop estimation skills outside the classroom in a real world environment.

We carried several usability studies that led to the creation of this technology. We summarize the major findings of these initial qualitative studies, with the first pilot study involving index cards, outdoors in a public park. Participants were given a stack of color-coded index cards with 25 clues, which corresponded to objects/shapes on the playground/climber on index cards, such as *"Find a rectangle 2' wide by 14" long"*. Objects and parts of the climber were marked with stickers. Participants were given fixed time to find as many stickers as possible, using the index cards, and to place the stickers on the corresponding card. The total number of correctly placed stickers determined the winner. The second study involved students in a school gymnasium wearing an initial version of the technology-enhanced game, which used Arduino-lilypads devices sewn on sweatshirts and a flat LED display that showed text [8]. This electronic sweatshirt allowed students to move freely (this initial wearable technology did not use Wifi capabilities, and behavior was hard-coded in the Arduino mini-processor device). The objective of the game was to find shapes and volumes that satisfied measurement constraints on the playground or gym. Clues were given by the LED display on their sleeve instead of using index cards, like the first study. In these first studies, players had many tools available to support their problem solving: tape measure, carpenters square, calculator, pencil, paper.

Results from questionnaires, interviews and observations from this first iteration of active math game pilots indicated a benefit of wearable technology compared to paper stickers/index cards in a variety of aspects: (a) the wearable aspect affords freeing students' hands to use measurement tools; (b) access to which measurement tools could help or hinder gameplay, especially for math estimations; (c) technology can scaffold/support students by providing hints/help at key moments, to guarantee individual progress and game flow; (d) a centralized "games engine" that delivers questions should allow easy creation of questions/hints and games via game authoring tools; (e) technology should provide flexibility to form student teams to collaborate, and possibility to synchronize watches/devices for team members; (f) assessing correctness automatically via RFID/NFC tags or similar input mechanism instead of matching stickers on cards manually would improve game accuracy and game flow; (g) technology allows for multiple solutions, as several tags/objects could be correct answers to the

Measured Variable	Pretest Mean (SD)	Posttest Mean (SD)	% Increase
MCAS Standardized 7-item Test (min=0; max=1)	0.65 (0.22)	0.70 (0.23)	+5%
Self-confidence in ability to do math (min=1; max=5)	4.37 (0.50)	4.67 (0.41)**	+6%
Liking of Mathematics (min=1; max=5)	4.55 (0.89)	4.64 (1.15)	+2%

a. ** Significant paired-samples t-test difference, $p<0.005$

Table 1. Cognitive and Affective Outcomes for thirteen (13) 9-10 year old students in the USA, Before and After Playing *Estimate IT!*

different questions; (h) possibility of "personalization" of question difficulty to a child's ability level, at the edge of their knowledge, via adaptive problem/challenge selection, similar to intelligent tutoring systems; (i) possibility of logging students' actions and mistakes for teacher assessment/progress reports for detection of gaps and challenging problems. These results helped to inform the "Wearable Learning Games Engine" creation, and set a precedent for the studies that followed.

3.2 *EstimateIT!* Study in the United States

We implemented the *Estimate It!* game within a group of thirteen fourth grade students during May 2015, using an initial version of the Wearable Learning Games Engine over WiFy on a local server. The main goal of the study was to understand the feasibility of the game as an artifact that could engender mathematics learning.

As part of the activity, students wore cell phones strapped to their forearms via armbands, and because students were organized in teams, they had to both cooperate and collaborate in different levels of the game --watches were semi-synchronized so that students had to coordinate with each other and neither of the team members could succeed without the other members.

The study itself included a math pretest and posttest of geometry and measurement items from the Mathematics section of the Massachusetts Standardized Test for 4th grade (9-10 year olds), and an affective pretest and posttest survey to measure math appreciation and self-efficacy in doing math. Learning objectives included measurement and estimations, geometrical shapes and volumes. Students were given an unmarked 12" dowel as their only measurement tool. This imprecise tool gave students further opportunities to estimate, as they found the heights and widths of volumes around the space.

Measured Variable	Posttest Mean (SD)	N
Lecture-Only	8.06 (1.77)	17
Game-Only	8.44 (2.14)	18
Lecture + Game	9.93 (1.12)*	17

a. * Significant independent-samples t-test difference, $p<0.05$

Table 2. Cognitive outcomes for fifty three (53) 9-10 year old students After playing *Estimate IT!* as part of math class, in schools in the Phillipines.

Post-game survey results revealed that students enjoyed playing the game, though they found the questions and hints to be too simple and wanted more of a challenge, even though the material was supposed to match their grade level according to National Standards. This shows that an adaptive feature that could select more advanced math questions as students continue to succeed with no errors would give students the possibility to meet the edge of their ability level. Despite of this, scores on the mathematics post-test improved by 5% compared to the pre-test, after 20 minutes of play. There was also improvement in affective outcomes from pretest to posttest: mathematics liking, as well as mathematics self-concept increased after the intervention, with self-confidence in their ability to solve math problems improving significantly (see Table 2). These results are encouraging given the low number of students in the study and for an intervention lasting for about half of a regular math class session. The reasons for this boost in self-efficacy are still a matter of further study.

3.3 *EstimateIT!* in the Philippines

This study was carried out in two schools in the Naga province in the Philippines, using a new App that was child-friendly (it involved dragging the corresponding colors of the bar code instead of pushing buttons, which made it easier for children to keep track of what colors they had already entered as part of the sequence of colors; last, a gesture was required to indicate 'submit'). One major objective of this study was to analyze the feasibility of implementation to a much harder deployment target, by adjusting the technology to be feasibly implemented in the developing world, where the school's Internet connection may be slow or intermittent. The main idea was to establish a local server on the teacher's computer. Thus, the Games Engine was refactored to handle ad-hoc network connections, which allowed the client devices to connect to the teacher's computer directly. This computer acted as a hotspot, without the need of a continuous Internet Connection to a remote server [13], nor the use of a router. In addition, besides the technical feasibility of implementing the game in a classroom in the Philippines with about 20 elementary school students playing math games in teams against each other, the study attempted to understand the role of the math games themselves to either introduce or review mathematics concepts.

Participants were 53 students from two math classes in the Philippines (N=27 from School 1 and N=26 from School 2). Both groups were equally mixed in gender, male and female. Students in each school were assigned to one of three conditions with nine students each (one group had 8); groups were balanced in ability level according to school grades. All groups answered a demographics questionnaire before the start of the test and were randomly assigned to one of three conditions: a lecture-only group, a lecture-plus-game group, and a game-only group. The lecture-only group was given a lecture. The lecture-plus-game group was given the same lecture and then played *Estimate It!*. The game-only group played *EstimateIT!* but did not see the lecture. All groups were asked to answer a post-test after being exposed to their corresponding method of instruction. The post-test consisted of 14 math questions that measured their understanding of geometric shapes, math sense and estimation. Table 2 presents the means and standard deviation of the post-test scores for each group.

We used an independent t-test to measure significant differences in the scores of (1) the lecture-only group against the game-only group and (2) the lecture-only group against the lecture-plus-game group. Results suggest that there is no significant difference between the posttest scores of the lecture-only group versus the game-only group. However, the lecture-plus-game group did perform significantly better in the math posttest than the lecture-only group. The lecture-plus-game also did better than the game-only group. These results indicate that the game *EstimateIT!* seems to be a better teaching tool for practicing and reviewing mathematics material, than for introducing new material or preparation for learning. More importantly, given that the groups receiving *EstimateIT!* obtained the highest means in post-test scores, results show that the game and the technology in general are a *feasible* technology-based game to be implemented in schools, and that it is an activity conducive to student math learning, at least boosting the teaching/learning potential of a lecture covering the same material.

The students also responded to open-ended questions asking them about their experience of the game in general. We report the data in terms of varying percentages and frequencies, as there were some students who wrote answers that did not actually answer the questions given. Generally, the students seemed to really liked this active embodied math game. When asked if the game was fun, N=30 out of the 32 students who responded said yes (93%), citing reasons such as physicality (e.g. "the game not only makes me learn, it also makes me exercise"), and social interaction (e.g. "it's fun because I'm playing with my friends"). N=31 students (86% of those responding) said they would prefer playing the *EstimateIT!* game over usual classroom instruction. Fourteen (14) of the 24 students who responded (58%) answered "nothing" when asked what they liked the least about the game. Regarding the "wearability" aspect, twenty (20) students said they would like a smartphone (cell phone) for this type of game and only 2 students said they would rather play it on a SmartWatch. Some students asked if the game is available for download in the app/play store. This suggests student experience in general was extremely positive.

3.4 Teacher Acceptance Study

After being presented with a demo of the framework, the Embodied Cognition game and the technology, as well as a video of students from the previous study playing *EstimateIT!*, eight (8) teachers in the Philippines were invited to answer a debriefing questionnaire that used a 5-point scale, with possible responses going from "Strongly Disagree" (1) to "Strongly Agree" (5). Questions were derived from the criteria described by Whitton [38] for effective educational design of game-based learning applications (see Table 3). Items relevant to the purpose of the experiment were re-constructed into questions. Table 3 shows the results of the expert evaluation. The specific questions in Whitton's instrument are presented in Table 3. Follow-up questions asking what aspects the evaluators liked the most/least about the game, as well as their insights on its advantages/disadvantages over current teaching methods were also included.

Table 3 shows that teachers really liked the technology that supported game play. They generally strongly agree that the *EstimateIT!* game supports active learning, engenders engagement, is appropriate and aligned with the curriculum and is fit for classroom use.

We asked teachers to answer open-ended questions for a deeper understanding of the debriefing questionnaire scores. Overall, they think the idea of embodied math games supported by technology is promising. According to them, *EstimateIT!* seemed like a great way to compete with the smartphone apps and cellular phones that hinder students from paying attention, and actively participating in discussions. Although there are rules that prohibit bringing these gadgets inside the classroom, they reported they would often catch students secretly sending text messages and playing games in their phones. Some of the teachers reported they could foresee these cell-phone embodied games could bring their students to full and active participation. The teachers also said that they found the process of implementing games in the classroom seemed relatively easy. Some of them went on to say that if the game is found to be effective for student outcomes, they would want to use it in place of the lecture. Some teachers provided their contact numbers and asked to be contacted when the game becomes available for download. The results of this expert evaluation validates that the framework makes the system fit cultural expectation of Philippine teachers in terms of feasibility and ease of use.

4. GAME CREATION

The idea of co-designing games with teachers and students, for younger students to use, aligns with the community focus of our grounding Activity Theory. However, there are added benefits to the generation of games. First, as a way for students to deepen their understanding of mathematics concepts, thinking about math questions from a "problem posing" perspective [6, 35] instead of a problem solving perspective; second, as a way to have students engage in the abstract and systematic thinking, also called computational thinking [39], which implies a high level of precision in the specification of a solution to a problem, a multiplayer math game in this case, which has contemplated all possible movable parts, such as temporal restrictions (what happens first and later), conditional restrictions (what happens only in specific situations, and what are the consequences of a condition), concurrency issues (e.g. states of players in the game might depend on the states of other players in the game, not only of the previous states of this same player).

This would imply having students conceive and specify multi-player math games, as well as define the behavior of the mobile devices as finite-state-machines, which act as supports to the players (both supporting game flow and support when gamers get stuck). We decided to allow student and teachers to define new games as finite state machines (FSMs), as these provide a simple way to explain computer behavior in the same way that we may think about world phenomena, as a series of actions and reactions. The behavior of FSMs can be observed in many devices that perform predetermined sequences of actions depending on external events e.g., vending machines that dispense products when coins are deposited; elevators and traffic lights that change state as cars or people are waiting.

We carried out a study to analyze the feasibility that students themselves might be able to create games for other students to play, and their ability to define games with a high level of precision. This was an exploratory study, attempting to answer the following question: *"Could high school students grasp the idea of designing a multiplayer math game (with mobile devices as supports for each player), using finite-state machines as a mechanism to specify the behavior of the mobile devices to individual players, at each step of the game?"*.

Some key aspects that make this game design endeavor challenging are: a) multiple perspective taking involved in a multi-player math game for a full class of students (i.e. different teams' and players' perspective); b) differentiating the game itself and its rules from the behaviors of the mobile devices that support/guide the players; c) addressing concurrency issues involved in the synchronization of the mobile devices of multiple players; d) the requirement of high precision in both the specification of the games, and the specification of the behavior of the mobile devices for each player, at different points of time, among others.

Fifty four (54) sixteen-year-old students from a high school in Massachusetts were involved in this "game design" study, three (3) classes of students with eighteen (18) students each. A survey was given to the students to take after they had played *EstimateIT!* and after they had

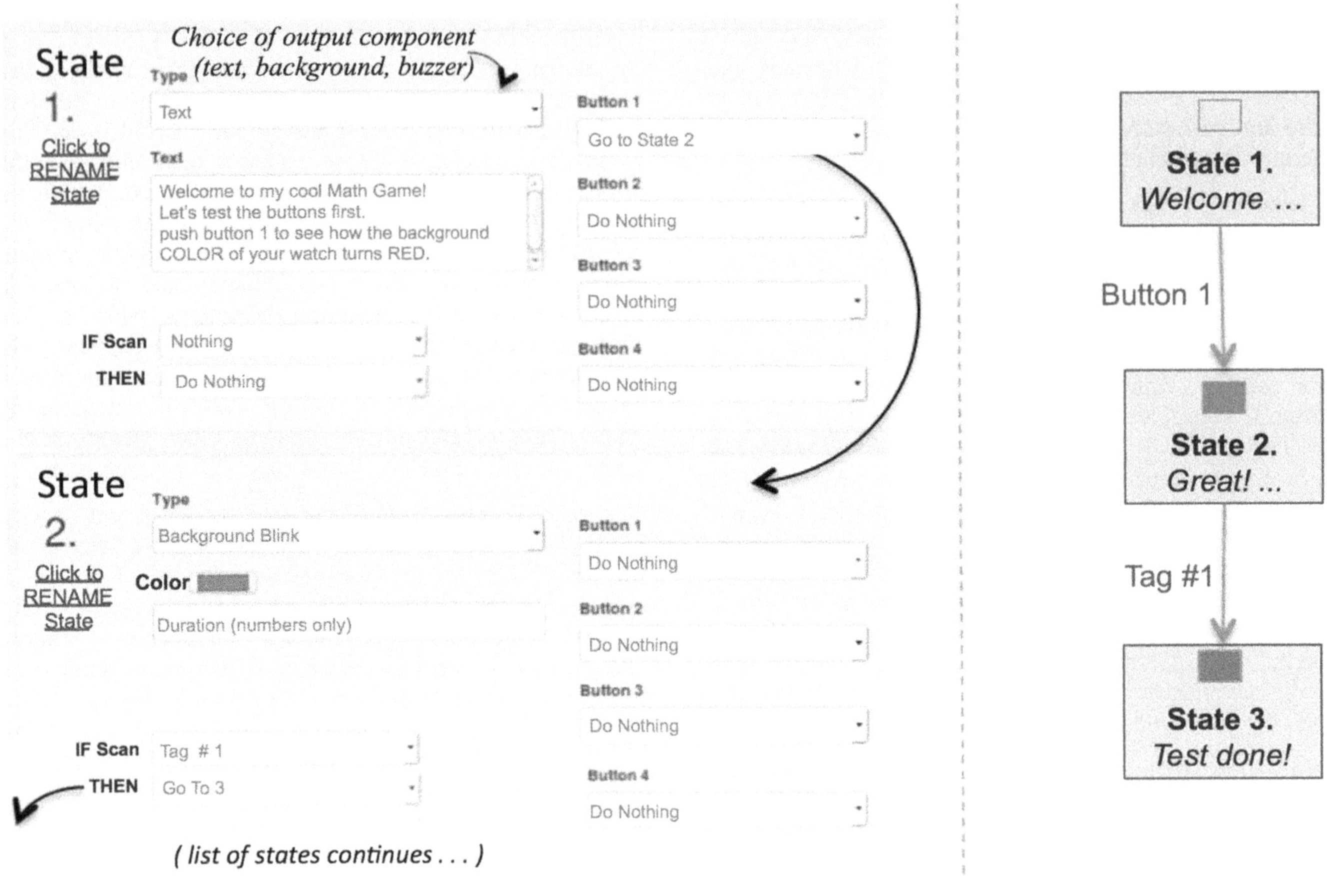

Figure 5. This interface design shows how we designed that game creators would alternate between two views: the "Create Game States" view (left) and the "Finite State Machine" view (right) as they create their own active math games; they program the behavior of mobile devices this way, so that they supports game flow, pace the game, assess success of challenges, as well as provide cognitive support when students need it.

redesigned their game to be state-based like *EstimateIT!* They were asked questions such as "was it hard to redesign your game?", and "how much do you know about state machines?" . Students worked on a variety of activities during three one hour sessions, in three consecutive days in 2017. Students in each class were divided in two groups (red and blue). Students in the blue group (N=9) played *EstimateIT!* in a classroom, with the purpose of having students understand the role that mobile devices could play as guides and scaffolds in a math game. After this, a small presentation was given to the students explaining how the game they just played works as well the system behind it powering it. Lastly, they were given a small homework assignment to complete an online survey about their experience. During this same day, the so-called *red* group of each class (N=9), instead designed math games in another classroom. Students did the opposite activity on day 2, with some students playing first and some students creating math games first. The students were given the following constraints to follow when designing their math game: a) The game you design must be playable by 4-6th graders (9-12 year olds); b) The game has to teach students some math concept appropriate for their age; c) The game must be multiplayer, meaning that the game should works for at least 6 simultaneous players; d) They should make sure the game is active by getting the students to move around, at least to some extent.

Student teams were given drawing pads and markers to plan out their design (3 teams of 3 students per red/blue team per class). At the end of the class period, teams presented their games to each other. After that they were then given a small homework assignment, which was to write a two-page explanation of how the game they created worked. They were allowed to include figures, pictures or diagrams and were asked "what was challenging" and "what did you like about it?". During the second day, the activities of the sub-groups were reversed: the students that played "Estimate It" the previous day would now be in the classroom designing games and vice versa. By the end of day 2, every team had both played *EstimateIT!* and designed some multiplayer active math game.

Day three was completely different than day one and two in that the main groups of eighteen were no longer split up in subgroups. Instead, the entire group redesigned the games they had created on either days one or two to include mobile devices, similarly to *EstimateIT!*. The first ten minutes of the session consisted of giving a 10-minute presentation that summarized the idea of finite state machines, how the cell phone and server interacted, and how actually the *EstimateIT!* game was specified as a state-machine, from start to finish, with states as outputs and button presses as inputs and transitions between states.

Students proceeded to redesign their games to include cell phones, and specified the behavior of these as state-machines. After they were done redesigning their games, they presented their new games to each other. Similarly to the previous days, students were given another small homework assignment. This included writing a two-page explanation of how they adapted their game to be more like *EstimateIT!* what was challenging about it, what did you like about it, and a survey about their experience this day.

4.1 Results to the Game Design Survey

This section shows the results of the survey after students created the games and specified them as state machines. Because the survey was not clearly compulsory to students, and provided as homework, out of the 54 students that participated in the study, only 31 answered the survey of the last day. Still we consider the results are valuable and are a reasonable sample of what students thought. These results are summarized in Table 4.

Some of the questions shown in Table 4 evaluated the difficulty or ease of creating games to teach or practice mathematics. A high percent (87%) of the students who answered the survey found the task of designing a math game for others to play easy. Almost every person who answered the survey (94%) found the game created by their t eam during days 1-2 was not very similar (in terms of design and playability) as *EstimateIT!*, which was clear as their games targeted different math topics, and did not use technology to support the player.

Other questions regarded the challenge they might face in understanding and using finite-state machines as a language to specify the behavior of player devices. In a question regarding how hard it was to determine the underlying state-based definition of the mobile devices for *EstimateIT!*, a majority of students (87%) found it easy to determine the underlying state-based design of that game they played. When asked how similar the game they designed the first or second day was to *EstimateIT!* by the end of the the third day, after redesigning their game to include the technology, a large majority (84%) found it easy to redesign their game to include mobile devices for player support by the end of the third day, and most students (84%) found it straightforward to adapt their game to the demonstrated state-based design. This is encouraging, as this specification in the form of a state-transition diagram is the method that the authoring tool would require to input as a next step in the Wearable Learning Games Engine web site, for them to program the mobile devices to behave as the game creators wanted, to support the players of their games.

Last, some questions asked the student about previous knowledge of finite-state machines, in case they already knew about them. Most students (84%) said they did not know anything about state machines before the study. This knowledge apparently grew during the study, as most students (77%) perceived they knew more and felt they understood the concept of state machines after the study.

	Active Learning Support	Strongly Agree	Agree
1	The game encourages exploration, problem-solving,	78%	22%
2	The game provides opportunities for collaboration.	100%	0%
3	The game provides opportunities to test ideas and gain	90%	10%
4	The game provides opportunities for practice and	100%	0%
5	Game goals are aligned with the subject's learning	90%	10%
	Engenders Engagement		
1	Goals of the game are clear and achievable.	72%	28%
2	The game supports a high level of interactivity.	79%	21%
3	The game stimulates curiosity and puzzlement.	100%	0%
4	The game establishes the application of estimation in	90%	10%
5	Game levels are appropriate and challenging.	90%	10%
	Appropriateness		
1	Game goals are aligned with the curriculum.	39%	61%
2	Game goals are aligned with the subject's learning	39%	61%
3	A game-based approach is applicable for teaching	78%	22%
4	The game could be played within the allotted class	78%	22%
	Classroom Use		
1	I think the game will help students learn estimation.	100%	0%
2	I think my students will find this game fun.	100%	0%
3	I think I would use this game in my classes.	100%	0%
4	I would recommend this game to my colleagues.	100%	0%

Table 3. Expert Evaluation: Responses of eight (8) teachers. Neutral, disagree and strongly disagree not shown (=0%)

A detailed analysis of students' games finite-state machines, including errors and difficulties they might have faced, is still pending. However, after an initial analysis and design of a coding scheme for such qualitative productions, we can say that students managed to generate an extremely large variety of games, targeting not only geometry but also expressions, number lines, equations, and several other concepts using a myriad of playground games. Some of those games included Capture The Flag, Relay Races, Walking Number Lines, Multiplication Grids to be Traversed, and many others going beyond scavenger hunts. These young game authors managed to provide flexibility in games design that the researchers had not been able to achieve, requiring minor functionality beyond what the Wearable Games Engine already provides. The games designed by students involved a large variety of student interactions also: teams against other teams, individuals against the teacher, and individuals against each other, and combinations of the above. Rich data was collected in the form of videos that capture their group discussions that still remains to be analyzed.

5. DISCUSSION AND CONCLUSIONS

It seems reasonable that students would acquire more positive attitudes and perceptions of math due to the

Survey Question (min=1; max=4)	Mean (SD)	MODE
How much did you know about state machines BEFORE you started? (1=Nothing; 4=A lot)	1.65 (0.91)	1 (Nothing)
How much do you feel you know about state machines NOW? (1=Nothing; 4=A lot)	2.94 (0.81)	3 (Do know)
After looking at Estimate It, how difficult was it to determine its underlying state based design? (1=Easy; 4=Hard)	1.71 (0.78)	1 (Easy)
How difficult was it to adapt your game to a state based design? (1=Easy; 4=Hard)	1.74 (0.82)	1 (Easy)
How difficult was it for you to design a math game given the set of constraints during day 1? (1=Easy; 4=Hard)	1.84 (0.73)	2 (Sort of Easy)
How similar was the game you designed to Estimate It, by the end of the FIRST day you created the math game? (1=Not Similar; 4=Very Similar)	1.35 (0.71)	1 (Not Similar)
How similar was the math game you designed to Estimate It, by the end of TODAY, after redesigning the game ? (1=Not Very Similar; 4=Very Similar)	1.94 (0.73)	2 (A bit similar)

Table 4. Means, Standard deviations and Modes of High School Students' Survey Responses about Creating Mathematics Games as Finite State-Machines

physical engagement and game components of the activities, because of its game-like nature. The interesting finding is that this excitement is paralleled with knowledge gains, especially when preceded by a short lecture. Future research should regard the analysis of the learning mechanisms and the contribution of motion and physical involvement using *EstimateIT!* as a testbed game. A variety of cognitive factors might be attributable to learning gains, for instance (1) visual imagery as students read the math description of the object to search for; (2) manual measurement procedures that involve comparisons between candidate physical objects and measurement tools (e.g. partitioning and unitizing) while using the 12" dowel in this case; (3) mental computations simultaneously performed with the manual measuring procedures while analyzing the object; (4) rounding procedures, as the measurements are inexact, students are forced to estimate up or down; (5) general problem solving, planning solutions and strategizing on how to proceed with the search; (6) right on time scaffolding via hint requests when the challenge is high; (6) right on time feedback when the incorrect object is scanned/input, allowing for revision of their work or seeking help; (7) team-based discussion and argumentation with peers, especially upon conflict or disagreement. We are ready to start using these mobile devices to collect a myriad of detailed data about students actions, including videos of students solving problems as they play and detailed logs of students actions to understand the mechanisms (both physical and mental) that mediate performance and learning within these technology-facilitated embodied games.

This research has also shown that it is feasible, at least for students of a technical high school, to create and define a diverse set of physically active math games, engage in computational thinking, perceive they learn about finite-state machines, and reach a design level where their multi-player games can be entered into the Wearable Learning platform. While this stage would require another step in which students may encounter challenges, students' state-machine diagrams closely resembled the actual diagrams we created ourselves when defining *EstimateIT!*. Given that the authoring tool is now ready for student use, our future work will go the extra step of having students enter their state-machines into the authoring tool and then playing their each others' games on mobile devices.

This work is a contribution to the field of educational games and embodied learning technologies, demonstrating the feasibility of the creation of smart contexts for education [10], wearable technologies that take an ecological perspective to formal learning environments. It is one of the first feasible learning technologies created that incorporate full classrooms of collaborating students, multiplayer games, active learning, mobile devices, and an alignment to the actual curriculum in mathematics education in formal school settings. As many have stated [21], implementing novel mobile technologies activities in real schools is not easy. We have come up with infrastructure that makes it feasible, and engenders learning and engagement. Students enjoy playing embodied math games aided by mobile devices; they learn target math skills addressed in the process; they are able to create games that combine physical play with mathematical concepts, and they develop a deeper understanding of mathematics and computational thinking. All of this while embedded within current curricula, classrooms and teaching practices.

Acknowledgements

This research was funded by NSF awards #1647023 and #1652579. Any opinions, findings, conclusions or recommendations expressed in this paper are those of the authors and do not necessarily reflect the views of NSF.

REFERENCES

1. Abrahamson, D. (2009). Embodied design: constructing means for constructing meaning. Educational Studies in Mathematics, 70(1), 27-47.
2. Abrahamson, D., Howison, M. (2010) Embodied artifacts: coordinated action as an object-to-think-with. Annual meeting of the American Educational Research Association (AERA), Denver, CO.
3. Abrahamson, D., Sánchez-García, R. (2016). Learning is moving in new ways: The ecological dynamics of mathematics education. *Journal of the Learning Sciences*, *25*(2), 203-239.
4. Alibali, M.W., & Nathan, M.J. (2012). Embodiment in Mathematics Teaching and Learning: Evidence From

Learners' and Teachers' Gestures. *Journal of the Learning Sciences, 21*(2), 247-286.

5. Antle, A. N., Corness, G., & Droumeva, M. (2009). What the body knows: Exploring the benefits of embodied metaphors in hybrid physical digital environments. *Interacting with Computers*, *21*(1), 66-75.
6. Arroyo, I, Schapira, A., Woolf, B.P. (2001). Authoring and sharing word problems with AWE . Proceedings of the International Conference on Artificial Intelligence in Education. IOS Press.
7. Arroyo, I., Woolf, B. P., Burelson, W., Muldner, K., Rai, D., & Tai, M. (2014). A multimedia adaptive tutoring system for mathematics that addresses cognition, metacognition and affect. *International Journal of Artificial Intelligence in Education, 24*(4), 387-426.
8. Arroyo, I., Zualkernan, I.A., & Woolf , B.P. (2011). *Hoodies and Barrels: Using a Hide-and-seek Ubiquitous Game to Teach Mathematics*. 11th IEEE International Conference on Advanced Learning Technologies (ICALT), Athens, Georgia.
9. Bamberger, J., & Disessa, A. (2003). Music as embodied mathematics: A study of a mutually informing affinity. *International Journal of Computers for Mathematical Learning*, *8*(2), 123-160.
10. Barab, S. A., & Plucker, J. A. (2002). Smart people or smart contexts? Cognition, ability, and talent development in an age of situated approaches to knowing and learning. *Educational psychologist*, *37*(3), 165-182.
11. Barab, S., Thomas, M., Dodge, T., Carteaux, R., & Tuzun, H. (2005). Making learning fun: Quest Atlantis, a game without guns. *Educational technology research and development*, *53*(1), 86-107
12. Bruner, J. S. (1966). *Toward a theory of instruction* (Vol. 59). Harvard University Press.
13. Casano, J., Tee, H., Agapito, J.L., Arroyo, I., Rodrigo, M.T (2016) *Migration and Evaluation of a Framework for Developing Embodied Cognition Learning Games*. The 15th ACM SIGGRAPH International Conference on Virtual-Reality Continuum and its Applications in Industry (VRCAI 2016).
14. Cayton-Hodges, G. A., Feng, G., & Pan, X. (2015). Tablet-based math assessment: what can we learn from math apps?. *Educational Technology & Society*, *18*(2), 3-20.
15. Chiu, C., & Liu, M. (2014). An innovative teaching model research affect the elder smart watch usage efficacy. *Gerontechnology*, *13*(2).
16. Clegg, T., Norooz, L., Kang, S., Byrne, V., Katzen, M., Velez, R., Plane, A., Oguamanam, V., Outing, T., Yip, J., Bonsignore, E., Froehlich, J. (2017) *Live Physiological Sensing and Visualization Ecosystems: An Activity Theory Analysis*. Computer Human Interaction Conference (CHI 2017).
17. Devlin, K. (2011). Mathematics education for a new era: Video games as a medium for learning. CRC Press.
18. Dourish, P. (2001). Where the action is: The foundations of embodied interaction. Cambridge, MA: MIT Press.
19. Drake, J., Cain, R., & Lee, V. R. (2017). From wearing to wondering: Treating wearable activity trackers as tools for inquiry. In *I. Levin & D. Tsybulsky (Eds.), Optimizing STEM Education With Advanced ICTs and Simulations*. Hershey, PA: IGI Global.
20. Gee, J. P. (2003). What video games have to teach us about learning and literacy. *Computers in Entertainment (CIE)*, *1*(1), 20-20.
21. Grotto, Lozano, Muldner, Burleson, Walker (2016). Lessons Learned from In-School Use of rTAG: A Robo-Tangible Learning Environment. CHI 2016, San Jose, CA.
22. Howison, M., Trninic, D., Reinholz, D., Abrahamson, D., (2011) The mathematical imagery trainer: from embodied interaction to conceptual learning, Proceedings of the SIGCHI Conference on Human Factors in Computing Systems, ACM, pp. 1989-1998 , New York, NY.
23. Johnson, K., Pavleas, J., & Chang, J. (2013). *Kinecting to mathematics through embodied interactions*. Computer, 46(10), 101-104.
24. Kafai, Y. B., & Kafai, Y. B. (1995). Minds in play: Computer game design as a context for children's learning. Routledge.
25. Ke, F. (2008) . A case study of computer gaming for math: Engaged learning from gameplay?
26. Lave, J., Wenger, E. (1991). *Situated learning: Legitimate peripheral participation*. Cambridge: Cambridge University Press.
27. Micciollo, M. (2017) *Physical Games for Learning II*. Major Qualifying Project. Worcester Polytechnic Institute.
28. Nardi, B. A. (1996). Context and consciousness: Activity theory and human-computer interaction. Cambridge, MA: MIT Press.
29. Nemirovsky, R., Tierney, C., & Wright, T. (1998). Body motion and graphing. *Cognition and Instruction,16*(2), 119-172.
30. Ottmar, E., Landy, D., & Goldstone, R. L. (2012). Teaching the perceptual structure of algebraic expressions: Preliminary findings from the pushing symbols intervention. In Miyake, N., Peebles, D, & Cooper, R.P. (Eds). *Proceedings of the Thirty-Fourth Annual Conference of the Cognitive Science Society,*

Sapporo, Japan (pp. 2156-2161). Pasadena, CA: Cognitive Science Society.

31. Ottmar, E., Landy, D., Weitnauer, E., & Goldstone, R. (2015) Graspable mathematics: Using perceptual learning technology to discover algebraic notation. In M. Meletiou-Mavrotheris, K. Mavrou, & E. Paparistodemou (Eds.), *Integrating Touch-Enabled and Mobile Devices into Contemporary Mathematics Education* (pp. 24-48). Hershey, PA: IGI Global.

32. Reinholz, D., Trninic, D., Howison, M., & Abrahamson, D. (2010). It's not easy being green: embodied artifacts and the guided emergence of mathematical meaning. In *Proceedings of the thirty-second annual meeting of the North-American chapter of the international group for the psychology of mathematics education (PME-NA 32)* (Vol. 6, pp. 1488-1496). Columbus, OH: PME-NA.

33. Rountree, W. L. (2015). *Redesigning Traditional Children's Games to Teach Number Sense and Reinforce Measurement Estimation Skills Using Wearable Technology.* Masters Thesis in Interactive Media and Game Development. Worcester Polytechnic Institute.

34. Silva, M. J., Ferreira, E., Andrade, V., Nunes, O., & da Luz Carvalho, M. (2015, November). Embodied education: Senses, emotions, and technology. In *Computers in Education (SIIE), 2015 International Symposium on* (pp. 32-37). IEEE.

35. Silver (1994) On Mathematical Problem Posing. For the Learning Mathematics. FLM Publishing Association.

36. Slavin, R. E. (1980). Cooperative learning. *Review of Educational Research, 50*(2), 315-342.

37. Tsai, H.; Sing, K. (2012) Mobile Applications and Museum Visitation. *Computer*. 45 (4), pp. 95-98.

38. Whitton, N. (2009). *Learning and teaching with computer games in higher education. Game-based Learning Advancements for Multi-Sensory Human Computer Interfaces: Techniques and Effective Practices.* Thomas Connally, Mark Stansfield and Liz Boyle Eds. Information Science Reference, Hershey-New York.

39. Wing, J.M., Computational thinking. *Communications of the ACM*, 2006. 49(3): 33-35.

40. Wu, T., Dameff, C., & Tully, J. (2014).Integrating Google Glass into simulation-based training: experiences and future directions. *Journal of Biomedical Graphics and Computing, 4*(2).

A Mixed Method Approach for Evaluating and Improving the Design of Learning in Puzzle Games

Monica Visani Scozzi
University College London
London, UK
monica.visani@gmail.com

Ioanna Iacovides
The Open University
Milton Keynes, UK
jo.iacovides@open.ac.uk

Conor Linehan
University College Cork
Cork, Ireland
conor.linehan@ucc.ie

ABSTRACT
Despite the acknowledgment that learning is a necessary part of all gameplay, the area of Games User Research lacks an established evidence based method through which designers and researchers can understand, assess, and improve how commercial games teach players game-specific skills and information. In this paper, we propose a mixed method procedure that draws together both quantitative and experiential approaches to examine the extent to which players are supported in learning about the game world and mechanics. We demonstrate the method through presenting a case study of the game *Portal* involving 14 participants, who differed in terms of their gaming expertise. By comparing optimum solutions to puzzles against observed player performance, we illustrate how the method can indicate particular problems with how learning is structured within a game. We argue that the method can highlight where major breakdowns occur and yield design insights that can improve the player experience with puzzle games.

Author Keywords
Games; Learning Curves; Breakdowns; Player Experience, Evaluation Methods; Games User Research.

ACM Classification Keywords
H.5.3 Information interfaces and presentation (e.g., HCI): Miscellaneous ; K.8.0. General: Games.

INTRODUCTION
One of the primary concerns of Games User Research (GUR) is to develop processes through which to evaluate and improve the player experience. Many GUR methods have been developed, from using heuristic review to identify critical issues, [e.g. 22] to using physiological measures in play-testing [e.g. 30]. However, while learning (defined here as learning 'how to play and progress') is often referred to within GUR methods, there is no established procedure intended specifically for identifying problems with how player learning is structured within commercial games, and for offering evidence-based solutions to these problems. This paper outlines and demonstrates a method appropriate for doing just that.

Many researchers, designers and commentators have argued that learning is a necessary part of all gameplay, from the understanding of game controls and interfaces, to working out solutions for in-game puzzles and challenges [i.e. 14, 15, 23]. Indeed, without developing expertise and an appropriate understanding of the game world, players will not be able to experience deeper levels of involvement such as flow [40]. However, empirical studies of learning in games focus almost exclusively on measuring the effects of game-playing on educational outcomes [7], and much more rarely on how to support learning 'how to play and progress' through design and scaffolding.

Recent work has started to address this issue, such as Linehan and colleagues [25], who examined puzzle games from a structural perspective. Through doing so they developed a set of "learning curves", which illustrated how commercially successful games are designed to introduce different skills to players and provide them with space to practice those skills. However, missing from their analysis was an observation of how players reacted to those designed curves.

Another relevant strand of research has examined gameplay in terms of the *breakdowns* experienced during play [19, 20]. This research has established processes for identifying points at which problems occur in gameplay, and for identifying the different strategies players adopt in an attempt to overcome those problems (i.e. examining how players achieve *breakthroughs*). Individual strategies can be used to diagnose the type of problems experienced by players and point to specific types of solutions. While this research provides a rich picture of how involvement is influenced by learning during play, it could be argued that such an in-depth approach would be too time consuming to adopt in a typical game development context.

We aim to build upon previous work around learning in games by presenting a mixed method approach for evaluating the player experience in commercial games from a learning perspective. We demonstrate our approach through a case study of *Portal*, a puzzle game, where we carried out an in-depth observational study with 14 players of varying expertise. Recordings of gameplay were used to

CHI PLAY '17, October 15–18, 2017, Amsterdam, Netherlands

ACM ISBN 978-1-4503-4898-0/17/10…$15.00
https://doi.org/10.1145/3116595.3116628

compare optimal performance to observed performance, while think-aloud and interview data helped to provide further insights into player experiences. We discuss specific levels and mechanics that players struggled with, before concluding with a consideration of design implications and a discussion of how our approach could be adopted to evaluate and improve the design of learning in both commercial and educational video games.

RELATED WORK

In this section, we present a brief literature review, which argues that learning is fundamental to the experience of playing a game. We discuss existing research on how to design games that players learn from consistently, and on methods that focus on evaluating learning in games. In addition, we consider existing methods used for evaluating player experience, and argue that there is an opportunity to improve our practice around the design and evaluation of learning throughout gameplay.

Learning & gameplay

Researchers, designers and commentators have long recognized learning as a core component of the experience of playing games [9, 15, 20, 25]. Through play, players learn to master interface controls, game rules and mechanics. Additionally, there is broad agreement that enjoyment of games depends largely on how well the challenges presented to players match their level of skill [e.g. 1, 6, 40], where games that are too difficult or too easy can lead to negative experiences [1, 38]. Thus, it is important to ensure, through design, that players have developed the necessary skills and information to complete the challenges that the game presents. In other words, we need to carefully design how the game teaches players.

Designing for learning in games

We are only beginning to see research that teases out how to design games to ensure that players are effectively and efficiently equipped with the necessary skills and understanding to complete in-game tasks and challenges. For example, Linehan et al. [26] present a summary of features found useful for the design of learning in games. Games benefit from the inclusion of a hierarchy of short, medium and long-term goals [38]. Long, complex tasks should be broken down into short, simple components that are trained individually before being chained together [14, 15, 23]. Players should be required to demonstrate competence at simple tasks before advancing to more complex tasks. Games should provide immediate feedback in a context appropriate manner [27, 28, 29].

It has also been argued that the *pacing* of challenges is central to player's ability to learn game-specific skills [8, 9, 13]. Pacing refers to the trajectory of difficulty over time as players advance through the game. Similarly, it is generally agreed that games should present challenges that are matched to the player's individual skill level, and that playing games is fun only if a sufficient proportion of the game challenges are mastered by the player [e.g. 1, 6, 15, 39, 40].

The challenge of designing learning progression in games is related to that of tutorial design [see 3]. Some games, such as *Portal*, incorporate all instructions and rehearsal into the general narrative of game play. Others use explicit tutorial segments and instructional materials. Either way, the same basic questions exist – when should new skills be introduced, how much help is necessary, what strategies ensure that players learn and master skills? Andersen et al., [3] carried out a study with 45,000 participants, where they questioned the "added value" of tutorials to game engagement and progression. Through investigating eight different designs, they found that tutorials have clear benefits in more complex games, while being less useful in simpler games. Thus, the authors were able to demonstrate the importance of providing structure to the skills and information learned in a game (i.e., using tutorials versus not) and for learning to be carried out through game play – and that the effect is pronounced in games that are more complex. We argue, based on an understanding of instructional design, that these concepts generalise to all game design, rather than applying simply to tutorials.

Linehan et al. [25] suggest that pacing is managed particularly effectively in commercially successful and well-regarded puzzle games. By analysing the structure of successful games, they found that each of the main skills are introduced separately through a simple puzzle that requires little more than the basic performance of the new skill. After this introduction, a number of puzzles are presented in which the player is given the opportunity to practice that skill and to integrate it with previous ones. From the point at which a new skill is introduced, puzzles increase in complexity up until the point at which the next new skill is introduced. These are useful principles around which to design learning curves in games, and match very closely with guidelines for the design of special education programmes [26]. However, missing from their analysis was an observation of how players reacted to those designed curves. It would be useful to understand whether this structured approach genuinely facilitated a satisfying experience for players. The current study will look at that question more closely.

Evaluating learning in games

The majority of research that examines games in the context of learning focuses on the use of games as educational tools and the gamification of virtual learning environments. Within the context of education, there has been a more recent focus on examining not just learning outcomes but how well a game is able to facilitate the process of learning. Many of these involve data mining, learning analytics and modelling techniques. For instance, Harpstead et al. [16], present an analysis of an educational game, which involved knowledge component modelling and empirical learning curve analysis. By combining statistical modelling with player performance data (from game logs), the authors provided insights into problems with game design and developed suggestions for improving the game to ensure that students were learning what they were supposed to.

Other examples include Andersen at al. [2] who developed the Playtracer method, where multidimensional scaling is used to produce visualisations of how groups of players move through a game, and Owen et al [32] who present the ADAGE (Assessment Data Aggregator for Game Environments) protocol for tracking players interactions and the leveraged machine learning, data mining and statistical methods to assess learning within play.

Outside of formal education, there has also been a focus on investigating the process of learning within commercial games, where researchers have examined the problems that players encounter and how to overcome them [4, 24, 35]. For instance, Iacovides et al. [18, 20] build upon work by Sharples [37] to introduce the notion of gameplay breakdowns and their converse, breakthroughs. Breakdowns and breakthroughs are described as occurring in relation to player *action* (e.g. problems with the controller vs performing a new attack); *understanding* (e.g. not knowing what to do next vs figuring out a solution a puzzle); and *involvement* (e.g. getting frustrated vs experiencing satisfaction). Their findings highlight how progress achieved without learning is less satisfying to players, suggesting a close relationship between involvement sand learning [20].

Similar work [19] illustrates how players adopt different strategies in an attempt to overcome breakdowns such as *Experiment* or *Stop & Think*: While this line of research has led to a better understanding of how players learn through overcoming breakdowns and achieving breakthroughs, the mainly qualitative approach adopted is particularly time-consuming to apply and may not be appropriate within a game development context.

Games User Research methods

The research discussed so far has all set out, from an academic perspective, to understand how to best facilitate and assess learning in games, and how to understand and recognize player's problem-solving behaviours. In parallel, much research effort has been devoted to the development of methods for evaluating and improving the player experience, particularly in relation to commercial games. These methods are intended to be used within the game development process and fall broadly under the term of Games User Research (GUR). We argue that, while learning is a key component of the games user experience, existing GUR methods do not take full advantage of recent scholarship on the design and evaluation of learning in games.

User testing is the most common GUR method [5, 21], and involves the direct observation of players as they play. Due to time and resource limitations, user testing often involves relatively small numbers of participants. Observations are typically supplemented with "think-aloud" data (where players are asked to verbalise what they are thinking during play), interviews, questionnaires [21, 33] and/or physiological measurement [30, 41].

Game analytics have also been used to inform GUR, where player behaviour within the game is tracked e.g. metrics such as total playtime, damage dealt per player, etc. [13]. Analytics are used frequently in the context of online games, where the data can be used to continuously refine and redevelop the game. However, as Seif el-Nasr et al. [36] note, there are significant challenges in using analytics for guiding game design; the designer must already know which metrics and which behaviours are important to track, and must invest significant work in interpreting fluctuations in those metrics across players. Thus, while game analytics can be helpful for highlighting points in games where players typically experience difficulties, additional methods are required to examine what exactly it is that players are struggling with and how to overcome those problems.

Similarly, while existing quantitative methods for examining learning progression in educational games [e.g. 2, 16, 32] may prove useful in a commercial GUR context, those methods often require access to large data sets and are arguably less appropriate for earlier prototypes. While there are circumstances where such an analysis has been conducted on a smaller number of players e.g. [17 – where the findings were also triangulated with qualitative data], these approaches still require the application of advanced statistical techniques, such as a hierarchical clustering, and so can be rather complex.

Another GUR method is heuristic evaluation, where games are reviewed according to a checklist of design guidelines [22]. Examples of heuristics include: "The game's interface should be intuitive and easy to use" [39] and "The game is paced to apply pressure without frustrating the players. The difficulty level varies so the players experience greater challenges as they develop mastery" [11]. While heuristic evaluations are quick and cost-effective, they are not based on observed player performance. In addition, they do not normally provide an in-depth focus to on player learning.

An exception to this is the Game Approachability Principles (GAP), a heuristic-based method that most closely matches the aims of the current study. GAP is presented by Desurvire and Wiberg [12] as a set of heuristics for considering learning within tutorials and initial game levels e.g. "Scaffolding failure prevention: player provided with help to meet goals of game". The authors found that a combination of a GAP review with usability testing was particularly effective, where the former helped to uncover approachability issues and the latter was useful for providing more detail on playability issues. However, while the principles were derived from general learning theories, they were not based on empirical studies of how players learn in games. In addition, the focus on applying them to tutorials and initial stages of the game neglects the fact that learning occurs throughout the entire experience of play.

While a combination of GUR methods can provide useful examination of various aspects of the player experience, very few approaches have attempted to evaluate gameplay comprehensively from a learning perspective. This is despite the fact that learning is a significant aspect of engagement and deeper forms of involvement such as 'flow' [10]. By overlooking the importance of learning, we are missing an opportunity to gain valuable design insights that could be used to improve the overall player experience.

In summary, the current paper brings together research on how to best design learning in games, with research on how to evaluate learning in games, and, presents it as a useful addition to existing methods for Games User Research. In the next sections, we describe the step-by-step process for evaluating player learning, and present a case study how we applied our method to the puzzle game *Portal*. *Portal* was chosen since it was previously analysed in detail in [25] and is generally considered a very well-designed game.

A METHOD FOR EVALUATING LEARNING DESIGN IN GAMES

In this section, we outline a step-by-step process for identifying problems with the design of learning in games.

Step 1: Chart learning curve of the game

The first step is to create a record of the ideal solution to each puzzle in the game. A list must be created that outlines each action necessary to solve each individual puzzle. In a game development context, designers would be able to supply this information. Next, this list is used to chart the trajectory of complexity across subsequent puzzles (i.e., the pacing or learning curve). In order to chart 'complexity,' we use a basic functional definition provide by Linehan et al. [25]. Puzzles that require more actions from the participant are considered more complex than those that require fewer actions. Complexity data is represented on a line chart to chart the trajectory of complexity over progression in the game (see Optimal actions, Fig. 1).

Step 2: Recruit participants, analyse player expertise

In line with existing user testing approaches, small numbers of participants are recruited. The group must also contain sub-sets of players that range in terms of their expertise. Player expertise is measured through a short questionnaire, which establishes familiarity with the game series (if appropriate); frequency of play (how often they play); breadth of experience (the range of genres they play and platforms they use) and gaming history (how long have they been playing games for). Based on results of this questionnaire, players are divided into novice, intermediate and expert categories. This classification is essential, since players with different skill levels are likely to have a range of learning needs. Analysis of player performance will not be useful without knowing their level of expertise. Also, note that the behaviour of novices is probably the best indication of the quality of learning design in a game, since their abilities are derived purely from the observed interactions with the game, and not by information learned in previous play-throughs.

Step 3: Gameplay is recorded in a rich, multi-modal manner

Participants must play the game or game sections that you are interested in. While they do so, it is necessary to record their performance and experience of playing. Many different approaches have been taken in GUR, but for the purposes outlined in this paper it is necessary to record (i) data on all player interactions with the game, allowing for quantitative analysis of player performance, and (ii) data on player experience in terms of how they solve the problems presented by the game e.g. concurrent or retrospective think aloud to allow for more in-depth qualitative analysis.

Step 4: Analyse participant performance

Whether player performance was recorded automatically through data logs (ideal) or manually through video recordings (more time intensive), performance data for each participant is extracted and represented on the same graphs from step 1. In this way, the performance of each player can be compared with the optimum solution. In addition, statistical means should be created for each player type (novice, intermediate, expert) and represented on the graphs.

Step 5: Identify game sections where problems have arisen

A well-designed game builds competence in players gradually and methodically, so that players are never presented with challenges that are significantly beyond their ability. Thus, a competent player is one who, when presented with a puzzle, regularly comes to the solution efficiently. Conversely, a player lacking in competence, who hasn't fluently learned the appropriate skills, will regularly face breakdowns in their gameplay and demonstrate problem-solving behaviour that resembles trial and error. A well-designed game should generally elicit competent behaviour from participants, as this is evidence of the player learning and applying skills effectively. The graphs that emerge from step 4 will identify sections of the game (or individual puzzles) where there is a consistent and large divergence between the ideal solution and the performance of players. These are the sections that must be investigated further.

Step 6: Conduct qualitative analysis of those problems

A detailed qualitative analysis of data relating to the problem sections of the game is carried out. The process follows a 'critical incidents' methodology, gathering data from multiple sources to understand the player experience relative to that one event. To facilitate coding, a table is created for each player who experienced difficulties in the problem section. The table lists the actions the player carried out (observed from the video) and any relevant think aloud and post-play interview quotes. The analysis is deductive, utilising categories from previous research, where separate columns are used to code *breakdowns* [20] and *strategies* [19]. Breakdowns are categorised as relating to *action* (when a player fails to execute an action successfully), *understanding* (when the player is confused what to do next or is suffering from a misunderstanding and *involvement* (when they appear bored or frustrated). Breakdowns are classified as *'major'* when recurring across multiple players or when they significantly obstacle player progress (e.g. the player 'dies' or is stuck for an extended time period). All other instances are *'minor'* breakdowns. Strategies are coded

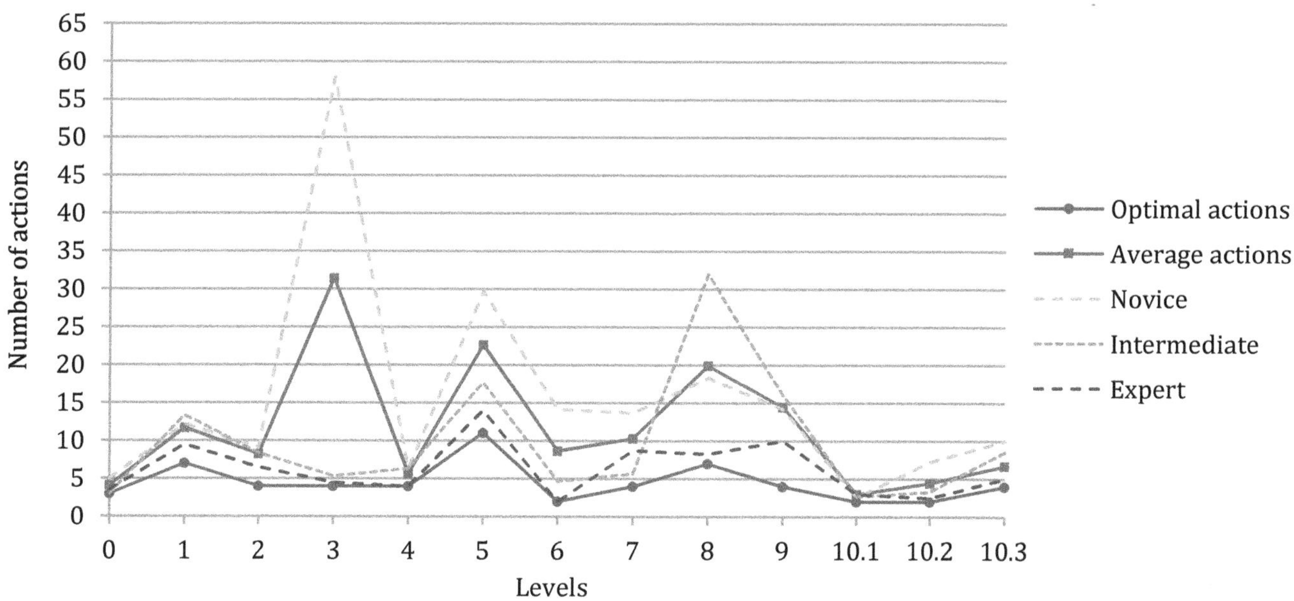

Figure 1: Action curves for (1) Optimal (minimum number of actions); (2) average actions across groups; (3) average actions for novices; (4) average actions for intermediates; (5) average actions for experts.

as *Trial & Error (*where a player carries out an action to see what, if anything will happen); *Experiment* (where the player has an informal theory about what will happen when they try something), *Stop & Think* (gameplay is suspended to reflect or consult external resources); *Take the Hint* (when the player decides to follow guidance provided within the game); and *Repetition* (when the same actions are practiced or repeated by the player several times).Through examining sets of tables related to each problem section within a the game, a deeper understanding can be developed of where difficulties are occurring and why.

Step 7: Develop design recommendations

After considering the causes of major breakdowns as part of the qualitative analysis, design recommendations can be distilled and discussed with the developers as suggestions for improving the learning design of the game.

CASE STUDY

Participants were asked to play a single-player puzzle videogame, *Portal* [42]. The game employs a 3D first-person perspective, where players have to overcome a variety of puzzles in self-contained 'test chambers' using portals to create pathways e.g. between the player and an otherwise inaccessible platform. The levels often contain visual hints on the ground and walls, while the voice of a robotic AI called GLaDOS (Genetic Lifeform and Disk Operating System), initially guides the player (though she becomes increasingly malicious as the game progresses). The game gradually introduces mechanics to the player, progressing from initial levels, where the test chamber setup controls the portals, into more complex levels, where the player is then able to shoot one portal type (blue), and eventually allowed to shoot both types (blue and orange). Simple instructions sheets regarding the controls were provided to players.

Step 1: Chart learning curve of the game

The optimum solutions for *Portal* were taken from Linehan et al. [25] where, a list has been published of all actions necessary to solve each puzzle in the game. These data were used to chart the optimal learning curve (see Fig. 1).

Step 2: Recruit participants, analyse player expertise

Fourteen participants were recruited from a university participant pool (5 female, 9 male, average age 25.1 years). All participants reported playing games at least once a week, and were recruited on the basis that they were familiar with games involving a first-person perspective (mainly FPS games) and playing with console controllers. Volunteers who played infrequently and solely on mobiles or tablets were excluded to minimise action breakdowns due to a lack of familiarity with controls. Based on their prior gaming experience and familiarity with the *Portal* series [42, 43], as evidenced by filling in a short questionnaire, participants were classified as 'Experts' if they had completed *Portal* before (N = 4); 'Intermediates' if the player had some exposure to *Portal*, or had completed *Portal 2* only (N = 3); 'Novices' if they had never or barely played either game (N = 7). Players are referred to by expertise and number e.g. PI08 is Player Intermediate 08.

Step 3: Gameplay is recorded in a rich, multi-modal manner

The study was setup in a professional UX laboratory, like a living room, with a TV and sofa. The game was played on an Xbox 360 console, with a wired controller. A video camera captured a recording of the participant, and the console connected to a recording facility to capture game footage. Microphones were used to record comments, and Media Express software for capturing all inputs.

Participants played the game for 40 minutes and asked to explain what they were doing and thinking whilst playing. A researcher was present to prompt them if they became silent. After the session, participants were asked to how much they agreed with the statement "I have enjoyed the game". The majority were positive, with 9/14 selecting 'strongly agree' and 3/14 selecting 'agree' and only 2/14 selecting 'neutral'. A short interview (10-15 minutes) then took place after the session where players were asked to review instances where they appeared to be struggling and asked to discuss these in more detail.

Step 4: Analyse participant performance

Figure 1 includes the optimal learning curve for *Portal* [25], showing the minimum number of actions required for each level. In addition, the figure displays the overall player performance curve (the total average actions per player who completed each level); and the player performance curves for each group (average actions for Novices, Intermediates and Experts). We focus on the first 10 levels of the game as less than two players from each group had progressed beyond this point within the 40-minute session.

The optimal curve indicates that *Portal* is a relatively well-designed game in that player behaviour appears to follow the general pattern of the optimal curve. However, it is clear there are some large discrepancies between optimal and average performance, particularly in relation to group expertise. While Experts tend to mirror the optimal action curves very closely (which is not surprising in this context as they were all very familiar with the *Portal* series), the discrepancies between the optimal and average curves indicate that Novices are struggling with Levels 3, 5 and 6 while Intermediates had difficulties in Level 8.

Step 5: Identify game sections where problems have arisen

We suggest that large discrepancies between the curves can serve as evidence of problems with how the game was designed to support learning. Levels 3, 5, 6 and 8 (see Table 1) showed the largest differences between optimal and average performance for particular groups so they were selected for further analysis.

	Total Average		Novice		Intermediate		Expert	
	Mean (SD)	N	Mean (SD)	N	Mean (SD)	N	Mean (SD)	N
L.3 [4]	31.4 (36.9)	14	58 (36)	7	5.33 (2.3)	3	4.5 (1)	4
L.5 [11]	22.6 (19)	14	29.7 (25.6)	7	12.7 (2.1)	3	14 (4.1)	4
L.6 [2]	8.64 (9)	14	14.1 (9.8)	7	4.7 (4.6)	3	2 (0)	4
L.8 [7]	19.9 (13.8)	12	22 (6.8)	5	32 (21.3)	3	8.3 (1)	4

Table 1: Total average and group actions for Levels 3, 5, 6, 8 with optimal actions in []

Step 6: conduct qualitative analysis of those problems

The quantitative analysis made clear that there were significant issues that required investigation in levels 3, 5, 6 and 8. Video, think aloud and interview data were analysed in terms of breakdowns that occurred and the strategies players adopted (as outlined above).

Strategies players employ when experiencing breakdowns

The pattern of strategies employed by players experiencing major breakdowns was relatively consistent and serve as a clear indicator of when they were struggling. Gameplay primarily consisted of *Trial & Error* and *Experiment* strategies as players tried to understand the game world and rules. When experiencing difficulty, players often resorted to a combination of *Trial & Error* actions e.g. firing portals at different objects in the room, and *Repetition*, when they repeated the same action several times. In addition, the think-aloud indicated when they were forming incorrect hypotheses during *Experiment*, such as thinking that creating a blue portal in a different part of the wall would change the location of the exit. Occasionally, players would *Stop & Think* where they would become inactive in the game and reflect on what they were doing or looked at menus and external resources for further hints. If a player didn't initially *Take the Hint* (in the form of visual in-game clues) but then went back to inspect them, this was seen as further evidence that they were struggling. In the subsections below, each level is introduced before examining the nature of the breakdowns experienced.

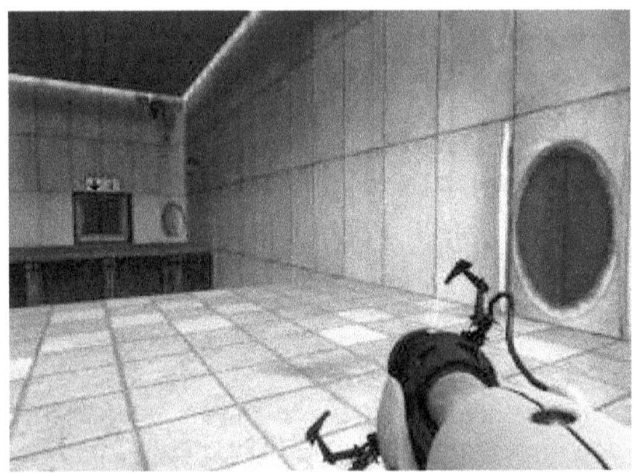

Figure 2: Level 3

Level 3: Entering and exiting different coloured portals

At the entrance of this L-shaped level, a pit separates the player from a middle floor with a fixed orange portal at the end. Around the corner from the middle floor another pit that separates this section from the exit on a higher floor. The optimal solution requires 4 steps: firing a blue portal close to the entrance; walking through it to exit out the orange portal on the middle floor (a); firing a blue portal near the distant exit (b); and walking into the orange portal to exit from the blue portal on the other side (Fig. 2). Novice players struggled with this level, taking an average of 58 actions to complete it (SD = 36), which is 14.5 times the minimum number of actions required (see Table 1).

In the previous level, a new mechanic was introduced in the form of a portal gun that allowed players to create blue portals. While all players were able to use the gun to reach the middle floor, once they were there, the majority of novices started to iterate the same set of actions. For example, PN07 reached the middle floor, commented "No idea where I am", then turned, looked through orange portal, and fired a blue portal next to it. Here the player starts to repeat the sequence of 'fire blue'+'enter blue', soon realising that those actions always led to "the same place". Similarly, PN11 repeatedly fires and enters a blue portal, noting "wherever I make a portal it still leads to the same place". Some players also tried shooting portals in each of the lateral walls, thinking that changing the entrance of the portal would lead to a different exit e.g. PN05 explains he "tried open portals on all the walls, and it just took me around in a circle".

PN01 and PN05 experienced further confusion when they thought they had encountered another character in the game. However, this is actually their own avatar, which can be viewed due to the way the portals are lined up e.g. PN05: "I can follow her. I am sure she can get me there", entered and exited the portals several times: "I am following this woman, but she is going in circles", before eventually realising "Oh no, that's my reflection, she's me". Another indication of difficulty in this level was that several of them suspended gameplay to look up the controls of the game to see if they were neglecting possible actions.

Level 3: Summary of main issues

Novice players seemed to be experiencing a major understanding breakdown around how the portals work. While these players frequently entered the blue portals they created, they only occasionally entered the fixed orange portal – not seeming to realise it could be both exit and entrance e.g. PN01 "it's blue when I enter, orange when I get out". Though all players eventually managed to complete the level, for some this was accidental as they did not understand how they reached the exit. For instance, PN07 wonders aloud "I went the right way, it seems, I think … but I don't know how I did it" while PN04 utters a surprised "Oh. How did that happen? … this is completely random". The breakdowns experienced and the fact some players could progress without gaining this knowledge suggests that the learning design of the level could be improved, at least for novices.

Level 5: More trouble with portals

Level 5 (Fig. 3) presents the player with a large room which contains a door activated by two buttons (each of which require a cube), two raised platforms facing each other and a pit which contains another cube. The door gives access to a second room and closes after the player walks past it. In the second room, a new orange portal is visible through a glass ceiling of the room above. The optimal solution requires 11 steps: firing a blue portal under the first cube in the pit; entering the blue portal within the pit; picking up the cube on the platform with the orange portal; placing the cube on one of the buttons; entering the blue portal again to go back up to the platform; firing a new blue portal on the platform opposite; entering the orange portal; picking up the second cube; placing the second cube on the remaining button; going through the door into the second room and shooting a new blue portal into the wall; entering the portal to exit out of the orange portal visible through the glass. Novices players were also seen to struggle with this level, taking an average of 29.7 actions to complete it (SD = 25.6), which is 2.7 times the minimum number of actions required (Table 1).

Figure 3: Level 5

The main reason for the large action count within this level is due to the fact some of the players were still suffering from a major understanding breakdown concerning how the portals worked. For instance, PN05 explains "I thought maybe if I try this wall, maybe a portal will lead me to here [platform with the cube]" suggesting that he believes the orange portal is only for exiting and that it can perhaps be controlled by changing where the blue portal is fired. After accidentally backing in to the orange portal, the player is able to grab the second cube "Ok, I got it" but again, does not seem to be able to explain why.

PN04 follows a similar strategy to one observed in level 3, shooting at different panels to "see whether there is a hidden area in the wall that will lead to that place, the one where the other cube is". After some time, when the player has created a blue portal on the ledge she wants to get to, she turns around and realises she can go through the orange portal exclaiming "Oh, this is how it works!". However, when asked to elaborate on what happened she seems a little unsure: "I don't know how to explain it but its' like you need to have one portal in one place and another one pointing to that so it creates a doorway and that's how it works". PN07 also struggled, though after he reaches the platform via the orange portal has a breakthrough: "Doh! I had to do the double portal thing again", remembering that you can go "back and forth through the fixed portal".

Level 5: Summary of main issues

While this level was more complex than Level 3, as indicated by the higher optimal action count, these examples show how a major breakdown in understanding that begins in an earlier level will influence later gameplay.

Level 6: Introducing High Energy Pellets

In Level 6 players encounter a new mechanic in the form of the High Energy Pellet (HEP) emitter which produces a fast-moving energy ball which the players must direct using the portal gun. Energy pellets eventually dissipate, and when they do the receiver emits a new one. The level composes of a HEP emitter on the ceiling, an inactive orange portal opposite to it, a receiver to the right of the inactive orange portal and a vertical scaffold activated by a HEP hitting the receiver (Fig. 4). The optimal solution requires 2 steps: fire a blue portal on the ceiling above the receiver (to guide the HEP to it); walk onto the scaffold which will then rise to the exit. Most of the novice players struggled with this level, taking an average 14.1 actions to complete it (SD = 9.8), 7.1 times the minimum actions required (Table 1).

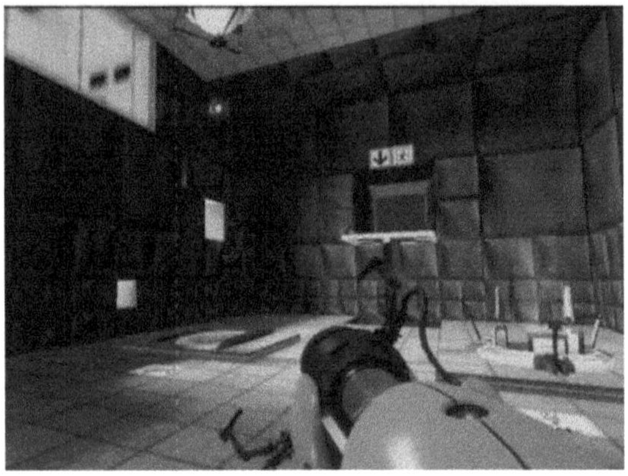

Figure 4: Level 6

When entering Level 6, players are introduced to the HEP by GLaDOS who states, "While safety is one of many Enrichment Center goals, the Aperture Science High Energy Pellet, seen to the left of the chamber, can and has caused permanent disabilities, such as vaporization". However, while some participants realised straight away that the HEP would be dangerous (e.g. PN11: "ok, so I can't touch that thing") others ended up dying, sometimes more than once, by walking right up to the pellet and coming into contact with it. For instance, PN01 struggled with the GLaDOS voiceover: "I didn't understand anything about the voice that was talking to me" as did PN07: "Not sure what they are referring to here". PN12 seemed to ignore the voiceover altogether and mistakenly assumed "I thought I had to collect the pellet, because I thought it was similar to the blue trigger" [referring to picking up the portal gun in a previous level].

Apart from experiencing an understanding breakdown regarding the nature of the HEP, there was further confusion about how to solve the puzzle. Most players quickly realised they could not create portals on black walls, but then resorted to shooting at both the emitter and receiver objects and the closed orange portal (e.g. PN01, PN05, PN11, PN12, PI14). In addition, PN05 initially thought that portals could "only open on the ground" while PN01 only realises it's possible to shoot portals in the ceiling when trying to shoot the emitter and accidentally creating a portal nearby: "I opened a door... Ah I got it".

Level 6: Summary of main issues

While some players did look at the hints available in the game, including those at the start of the level and on the ground, none of the players who struggled seemed to notice the red light emanating from the emitter that pointed up towards the ceiling, which acts as a cue of for positioning a blue portal. Instead, they adopted strategies such as PN12 who walked on top of the receiver and looked directly up to fire a portal directly above. The breakdowns experienced in this level suggest the information provided by GLaDOS was not clear to some players and that some of the cues provided were not salient enough.

Figure 5: Level 8

Level 8: Issues with perspective

In Level 8, the Test Chamber floor is covered by lethal water and presents an inactive portal on a platform on the left, and a horizontal scaffold on the right. On the left, there is a HEP emitter and a fixed orange portal on a platform, and on the right a receptacle on the wall, which will activate the immobile scaffold (Fig. 5). The level requires a minimum of 7 actions: shoot blue portal opposite the HEP dispenser; after the HEP passes through, create a new blue portal opposite the receptacle to activate the scaffold; once activated, shoot a blue portal in the wall nearby the entrance; travel through the portal to exit out of the fixed orange portal; create a blue portal above the scaffold and wait for it to appear; go through the orange portal; ride scaffold and proceed to exit. Intermediate players had difficulties with this this level, needing an average of 32 actions to complete it (SD = 21.3), which is 4.6 times the optimal number of actions required. Some novices also struggled here, requiring an average of 22 actions (SD = 6.8) to complete the level (Table 1).

The main breakdown in this level (experienced by players PI08, PI14 and PN11) originates from the central perspective of the chamber, which provides the illusion that the HEP receiver is located opposite the orange portal. P108 was able to quickly realise a solution to the problem but decided to look through the orange portal to figure out exactly far away the receptacle is on the other side. Unfortunately, this strategy leads to her dying twice and spending a large amount of time trying to count how many panels away the receptacle is e.g. "one, two, three, four..." before she successfully locates a portal opposite it. PI14 describes this level as "horrible" noting "it was the angle that was the problem"; their reaction to the level could be seen as an instance of a potential involvement breakdown. PN11 noted the same difficulty though was able to overcome it stopping for a moment and taking a different perspective: "I feel I am looking at this by the wrong angle {moves}. Oh! The machine is here! That makes a lot more sense".

Level 8: Summary of main issues
As in Level 6, a subtle red flare is projected by the receptacle onto the opposite wall that could have helped with portal positioning. However, the cue was again missed and the initial perspective the players encounter made this a particularly frustrating experience for some as it provided an obstacle to realising the solution to the puzzle.

Step 7: Develop design recommendations

Through considering the causes of breakdowns as part of the qualitative analyses, there are three main areas where the design could be improved to support learning:

1. Understanding of how portals work (Levels 3 & 5)
The Developer Commentaries [44] show that a design decision was made to force players to enter the orange portal in Level 3 by making it a fixed entrance. Despite this attempt, the fact that players could progress in this level without fully understanding how the portals operated caused a major breakdown. This is evidenced through observations of exactly the same errors being made in Level 5. This breakdown seems to stem from Level 0, where players didn't understand they could see themselves in portals and continues through subsequent levels. Potential solutions could involve locating a mirror in the room where the player starts so they see their reflection before they see themselves in a portal, providing them with a gun that can shoot both blue and orange portals in Level 2, or changing the map in Level 3 from a "L-shape" to an "I-shape" to reduce the complexity of the level.

2. Making cues more salient (Levels 6 & 8)
There may be some scope to make GLaDOS's voiceover clearer for the introduction to Level 6, but, in general, players learned relatively quickly that the HEPs were dangerous. The main issue in this level related to the fact that many did not attempt to shoot a portal in the ceiling until they had exhausted other options. Though hints were provided, these were perhaps a little too abstract, while the red light (provided to cue players to shoot above the receiver) was unfortunately not obvious. The same is true for Level 8, where again the red light pointing from the receiver to the opposite wall was rather faded (as Fig. 8 indicates). These issues suggest that the designers may need to alter the saturation and luminosity of the red light to make it more salient on console versions where television resolution could reduce the visibility of the cue and prevent players from achieving an understanding breakthrough that could help them in later levels. Unfortunately, these difficulties could be beyond developer control as in the case of playing the Xbox version of *Portal*, where the "quality of the graphics has been downsized to meet the restricted game size of Microsoft's XBLA service" [31]. Nevertheless, the use of red colour on grey walls creates an accessibility barrier for certain types of colour blindness and colours could be chosen with this in mind. Another option would be to provide players with substitute palettes on the whole game.

3. The issue of perspective (Level 8)
Level 8 was designed to teach the redirection technique [44] and players appeared at ease in grasping the concept. However, in addition to the fact that the red-light cue was not very visible, the perspective players were provided with when walking into the level mislead them to think that the receiver was located closer to the orange portal that it was. The design of Level 8 could be altered by moving the entrance point to force player to gain a different perspective when they enter the chamber, thus increasing their chances of figuring out the correct solution to the puzzle.

DISCUSSION

This paper represents an effort to devise a comprehensive evidence-based method for identifying problems with how learning is structured within commercial games, and for offering evidence-based solutions to these problems. The approach is based on a mixing of two strands of contemporary research on learning in games; one quantitative and behavioural, the other qualitative and experiential. The method consists of seven steps:

1. Chart learning curve of the game
2. Recruit participants, analyse player expertise.
3. Gameplay is recorded in a rich, multi-modal manner.
4. Analyse participant performance.
5. Identify game sections where problems have arisen.
6. Conduct qualitative analysis of those problems.
7. Develop design recommendations.

The method presented directly builds on previous work by Linehan et al. [25] and Iacovides et al. [19] by combining a learning curve analysis with work on gameplay breakdowns into a comprehensive method for evaluating how games teach players game-specific skills and information. While existing GUR methods recognise the importance of learning design to the player experience, and include some evaluation criteria that relate to learning e.g. [12], we suggest that the method we propose is particularly capable of detecting subtle problems with player understanding (across the whole experience of playing a game) and providing clear solutions to those problems. The method also fits seamlessly the type of small-scale user test frequently undertaken in early development phases, without requiring the large-scale data acquisition and advanced statistical or visualisation techniques that are involved in analytics approaches [e.g. 2, 16, 17, 32]. The approach could be used throughout the development process – from being applied to evaluate learning difficulties around key game mechanics in low fidelity prototypes to evaluating the impact of specific design elements within more developed versions.

Linehan et al. [25] suggest that *Portal* is a well-designed game, as it strictly follows a set of instructional design principles based firmly in the behavioural education literature (see [26]). Our evaluation of *Portal* provides new empirical evidence to support this claim, as players generally solved puzzles in an efficient manner, readily demonstrating the appropriate application of skills learned within the game. Furthermore, participants generally reported enjoying playing it. However, our analysis did also reveal a small number of issues, where large deviations between curves indicated areas where the game could be improved upon, particularly for novice players.

Part of the process we outline was to recruit participants who varied in terms of their expertise. This helped to ensure that we took into account the needs of different types of players. Indeed, it could be argued that the behaviour of novice players is the most informative in terms of assessing the quality of learning design in a game. However, it is important to also recruit more experienced players to understand whether performance improves on repeated play-throughs. Finding that experts perform only marginally better than novices would indicate significant issues with how the learning process is supported.

Furthermore, expertise can be hard to classify [19, 24]. We settled on a combination of questions to assess participants that related to not just how often they play, but what genres and platforms and for how long they had played. Nevertheless, some who were novices managed to complete more of the game within the play sessions than intermediates i.e. they showed more competence at solving the puzzles despite having less general experience. Researchers and practitioners need to be clear about the criteria they use to classify their participants while the area would benefit from clear guidelines about how to do so.

Limitations

This method is presented as useful in the context of puzzle games. While we only evaluated *Portal*, the method should be applicable to other games that have a set of features that allow them to benefit from a structured analysis. For example, puzzles with 'optimum' solutions which are can be compared to player behaviour. This may not be the case with simulation-based games that have multiple outcomes, or games that reward player creativity. While not impossible, it would be more difficult to plot the curves in a more 'open world' that gives agency to players to choose the order in which they encounter puzzles and challenges.

Additionally, due to the inclusion of rich qualitative data, the method is only appropriate for using with a relatively small number participants. While that may increase the chances of the method falling prey to idiosyncrasies in play testing populations, the same can be said of most small-scale user testing scenarios. An extreme outlier could be removed if a particular participant was seen to skew the results but the general aim of similar GUR approaches is to highlight and reduce potential player experience issues rather than produce statistical generalizations about frequencies and populations.

Future work

Where a large divergence between the optimum curve and that achieved by players, we suggest that difficulty should be reduced to avoid the risk of players becoming frustrated and deciding give up on the game. Conversely, in puzzles where player performance followed the curve very closely, gameplay is arguably too easy and may become boring. Ideally then, there should be some distance between the optimal and player curves. The crucial question for further research is, how much distance should there be between the optimal and average observed curves? This question has repeatedly obsessed game design researchers, as evidenced through large quantities of theoretical and empirical work on concepts such as 'flow' 'immersion' 'appropriate challenge', with a recent focus on using learning analytics. We are yet to see a unifying theory of learning design in games, but the current paper does provide a method through which those questions can be asked and answered of specific games.

In addition, the data collected can provide some insight into player engagement. Though there was little evidence of major involvement breakdowns within this study, observational, think aloud and interview data could indicate when players are becoming frustrated or bored with a section of the game [e.g. see 19]. A focus on real-time involvement would be particularly important to carry out when applying the method as part of the game development process.

While have presented our work as a case study to illustrate how our approach can be implemented in practice, further research is also required to examine how applicable it is to other games and genres. Furthermore, it would be useful to apply the method within the context of game development to validate the process and to assess feasibility in practice. Other studies could also carry out a comparative analysis with other GUR methods to explore how effective the approach is in terms of the quantity and quality of design issues it is able to uncover.

CONCLUSION

We present a mixed method approach to uncovering problems with how player learning is supported in games. The method is based in recent academic research on designing and evaluating learning in games. A case study is presented, where the method is applied to *Portal*. Issues are identified with a small number of the puzzles in that game, and explored through an in-depth qualitative analysis. While more work is required to examine the feasibility of using this method within an ongoing game development process, this paper represents an initial attempt at a comprehensive evidence-based method for identifying problems with how learning is structured within games, and for offering clear evidence-based solutions to these problems.

ACKNOWLEDGMENTS

We thank all the volunteers who took part in both studies. This research was supported by the EPSRC funded CHI+MED project (EP/G059063/1).

REFERENCES

1. Justin T. Alexander, John Sear and Andreas Oikonomou. 2013. An investigation of the effects of game difficulty on player enjoyment. *Entertainment*

Computing, 4, 53–62. http://dx.doi.org/10.1016/j.entcom.2012.09.001

2. Erik Andersen, Yun-en Liu, Ethan Apter, François Boucher-genesse, and Zoran Popovi. 2010. Gameplay Analysis through State Projection. Proceedings of the 5th International Conference on the Foundations of Digital Games - FDG '10, ACM Press, 1–8. http://dx.doi.org/10.1145/1822348.1822349
3. Erik Andersen, Eleanor O'Rourke, Yun-En Liu, Rich Snider, Jeff Lowdermilk,David Truong, Seth Cooper, and Zoran Popovic. 2011. The impact of tutorials ongames of varying complexity. In *Proc. CHI '12*, ACM Press, 59-68.
4. Fran. C. Blumberg, Sheryl F. Rosenthal and John D. Randall. 2008. Impasse-driven learning in the context of video games. *Computers in Human Behavior*, 24(4), 1530-1541. http://dx.doi.org/10.1016/j.chb.2007.05.010
5. Emily Brown. 2010. The life and tools of a games designer. In *Evaluating User Experience in Games: Concepts and Methods*, Regina Bernhaupt (ed.). Springer London, 73-87. http://dx.doi.org/10.1007/978-1-84882-963-3_5
6. Paul Cairns, Anna L. Cox, and Imran Nordin, I. 2014. Immersion in digital games: a review of gaming experience. In *Research in Handbook of Digital Games*, Marios C. Angelides and Haryy Agius (eds.). IEEE/John Wiley and Sons, 339-361. http://dx.doi.org/10.1002/9781118796443.ch12
7. Marcus Carter, John Downs, Bjorn Nansen, Mitchell Harrop and Martin Gibbs. 2014. Paradigms of games research in HCI: a review of 10 years of research at CHI. In *Proceedings of the 1st ACM Conference Computer-Human Interaction in Play* (CHI PLAY '14), 27-36. http://dx.doi.org/10.1145/2658537.2658708
8. Alessandro Canossa. 2009. *Play-Persona: Modeling Player Behavior in Computer Games.* Copenhagen, Danish Design School Press.
9. Daniel Cook. 2007. The Chemistry of Game Design. *Gamasutra.* Retrieved April 14, 2017 from: http://www.gamasutra.com/view/feature/129948/the_chemistry_of_game_design.php?print=1
10. Mihaly Csikszentmihalyi. 1990. Flow: The psychology of optimal performance. New York: Harper and Row.
11. Heather Desurvire and Charlotte Wiberg. 2009. Game Usability Heuristics (PLAY) for Evaluating and Designing Better Games: The Next Iteration. In *Proceedings of the 3d International Conference on Online Communities and Social Computing: Held as Part of HCI International 2009*, OCSC '09, 557–566. http://dx.doi.org/10.1007/978-3-642-02774-1_60
12. Heather Desurvire and Charlotte Wiberg 2010. User Experience Design for Inexperienced Gamers: GAP - Game Approachability Principles. In *Evaluating User Experience in Games: Concepts and Methods*, Regina Bernhaupt (ed.). Springer London, 131-147. http://dx.doi.org/10.1007/978-1-84882-963-3_8
13. Anders Drachen, Magy Seif El-Nasr, and Alessandro Canossa. 2013. Game Analytics – The Basics. In *Game analytics: Maximizing the value of player data*, Magy Seif El-Nasr, Anders Drachen and Alessandro Canossa (eds.). London, UK: Springer-Verlag, 13–40. http://dx.doi.org/10.1007/978-1-4471-4769-5_2
14. James P. Gee. What Video Games Have to Teach us about Literacy and Learning. 2004. New York: Palgrave Macmillan.
15. James P. Gee. 2005. Learning by Design: Good video games as learning machines. *E–Learning, 2*, 5-16. http://dx.doi.org/10.2304/elea.2005.2.1.5
16. Erik Harpstead and Vincent Aleven. 2015. Using Empirical Learning Curve Analysis to Inform Design in an Educational Game. In *Proceedings of the 2015 ACM on Computer-Human Interaction in Play* (CHI PLAY '15), 197-207. http://dx.doi.org/10.1145/2793107.2793128
17. Britton Horn, Amy K. Hoover, Jackie Barnes, Yetunde Folajimi, Gillian Smith and Casper Harteveld. 2016 Opening the Black Box of Play: Strategy Analysis of an Educational Game. In *Proceedings of the 1st ACM Conference Computer-Human Interaction in Play* (CHI PLAY '16), 142-153. http://dx.doi.org/10.1145/2967934.2968109
18. Ioanna Iacovides, James C. Aczel, Eileen Scanlon, Will I.S Woods. 2011. What can breakdowns and breakthroughs tell us about learning and involvement experienced during game-play? In *Proceedings of the 5th European Conference of Game-based Learning*, 275-281, Academic Publishing Limited.
19. Ioanna Iacovides, Anna L. Cox, Ara Avakian and Thomas Knoll. 2014. Player strategies: Achieving breakthroughs and progressing in single-player and cooperative games. In *Proceedings of the 1st ACM Conference Computer-Human Interaction in Play* (CHI PLAY '14), 131-140. http://dx.doi.org/10.1145/2658537.2658697
20. Ioanna Iacovides, Anna L. Cox, Patrick McAndrew, James C. Aczel and Eileen Scanlon. 2015. Game-play breakdowns and breakthroughs: Exploring the relationship between action, understanding and involvement. *Human Computer Interaction*, 30 (3-4), 202-231. http://dx.doi.org/10.1080/07370024.2014.987347.
21. Katherine Isbister and Noah Schaffer. 2008. *Game Usability: Advancing the Player Experience.* Morgan Kaufman.
22. Christina Koeffel, Wolfgang Hochleitner, Jakob Leitner, Michael Haller, Arjan Geven and Manfred

Tscheligi. 2010. Using heuristics to evaluate the overall user experience of video games and advanced interaction games. In *Evaluating User Experience in Games: Concepts and Methods*, Regina Bernhaupt (ed.). Springer London, 233-256. http://dx.doi.org/10.1007/978-1-84882-963-3_13

23. Raph Koster. 2005. *Theory of fun for game design.* Scottsdale, AZ: Paraglyph Press.
24. Andrew J. Latham, Lucy L. M. Patston and Lynette J. Tippett. 2013. Just how expert are "expert" video-game players? Assessing the experience and expertise of video-game players across "action" video-game genres. *Frontiers in Psychology*, 4, Article 941. http://dx.doi.org/10.3389/fpsyg.2013.00941
25. Conor Linehan, George Bellord, Ben Kirman, Zachary H. Morford, Bryan Roche. 2014. Learning curves: analysing pace and challenge in four successful puzzle games. In *Proceedings of the 1st ACM Conference Computer-Human Interaction in Play* (CHI PLAY '14), 27-36, 181-190. http://dx.doi.org/10.1145/2658537.2658695
26. Conor Linehan, Ben Kirman, Shaun Lawson, & Gail. C. Chan. 2011. Practical, appropriate, empirically-validated guidelines for designing educational games. In *Proceedings of the SIGCHI Conference on Human Factors in Computing Systems*, CHI '11, 1979-1988. http://dx.doi.org/978-1-4503-0267-8/11/05
27. Geoffrey R. Loftus and Elizabeth F. Loftus. 1983. *Mind at Play: The Psychology of Video Games*. New York, NY: Basic Books.
28. David B. Malouf. 1987. The effect of instructional computer games on continuing student motivation. *Journal of Special Education, 21*, 27-38. http://dx.doi.org/10.1109/1177/002246698802100406
29. Merrilea J. Mayo. 2007. Games for science and engineering education. *Communications of the ACM, 50* , 31-35. http://dx.doi.org/10.1145/1272516.1272536
30. Pejman Mirza-Babaei and Lennart Nacke. 2014. Introducing the biometric storyboards tool for games user research. *Games Media Entertainment* (GEM), IEEE, 1-7. http://dx.doi.org/10.1109/GEM.2014.7048098
31. MobyGames (nd). Portal: Still Alive (Xbox). Retrieved April 14 2017 from: http://www.mobygames.com/game/portal-still-alive
32. Elizabeth Owen, Dennis Ramirez, Allison Salmon, and Richard Halverson. 2014. Capturing Learner Trajectories in Educational Games through ADAGE (Assessment Data Aggregator for Game Environments): A Click-Stream Data Framework for Assessment of Learning in Play. *American Educational Research Association Annual Meeting*: 1–7.
33. Randy J. Pagulayan, Kevin Keeker, Dennis Wixon, Ramon L. Romero and Thomas Fuller. 2002. User-centered design in games. In *The human-computer interaction handbook: Fundamentals, evolving technologies and emerging applications*, Julia A. Jacko & Andrew Sears (eds.). Mahwah, NJ: Lawrence Erlbaum Associates, Inc, 883-906).
34. Caroline Pelletier and Martin Oliver. 2006. Learning to play in digital games. *Learning, media and technology*, 31, 329-342. http://dx.doi.org/10.1080/17439880601021942
35. William Ryan and Martin A. Siegel. 2009. Evaluating interactive entertainment using breakdown: Understanding embodied learning in video games. In *Proceedings of Digital Games Research Association*, (DIGRA '09).
36. Magy Seif El-Nasr, Heather Desurvire, Bardia Aghabeigi, Anders Drachen. 2013. Game analytics for game user research, Part 1: A workshop review and case study, *Computer Graphics and Applications*, IEEE 33 (2), 6-11. http://dx.doi.org/10.1109/MCG.2013.26
37. Mike Sharples. 2009. Methods for evaluating mobile learning. In *Researching Mobile Learning: Frameworks, Tools and Research designs*, Giasemi Vavoula, Norbert Pachler, Agnes Kukulska-Hulme (eds.). Oxford: Peter Lang Verlag, 17–39.
38. William Swartout, and Michal Van Lent. 2003. Making a game of system design. Communications of the ACM, 46, 32-39. http://dx.doi.org/10.1145/792704.792727
39. Penelope Sweetser, Daniel M.Johnson and Peta Wyeth. 2012. Revisiting the GameFlow model with detailed heuristics. *Journal of Creative Technologies*, 3.
40. Penelope Sweetser and Peta Wyeth. 2005. GameFlow: A Model for Evaluating Player Enjoyment in Games. *ACM Computers in Entertainment*, 3(3), Article 3A. http://dx.doi.org/10.1145/1077246.1077253
41. Chek Tien Tan, Tuck Wah Leong and Songjia Shenan. 2014. Combining think-aloud and physiological data to understand video game experiences. In *Proceedings of the SIGCHI Conference on Human Factors in Computing Systems* (CHI '14), 381-390. http://dx.doi.org/10.1145/2556288.2557326
42. Valve Corporation. 2007. *Portal.* Valve Corporation.
43. Valve Corporation. 2011. *Portal 2.* Valve Corporation.
44. Valve Corporation. 2007. *Portal: Developers Commentaries.* Retrieved April 14 2017 from: https://www.youtube.com/watch?v=2TBIfsPGeQ

Diegetic Connectivity: Blending Work and Play with Storytelling in Serious Games

Nicole Lane
Massachusetts Institute of Technology & Ithaca College
Lexington, MA USA
Nicole.Lane@ll.mit.edu

Nathan R. Prestopnik
Ithaca College
Ithaca, NY USA
nprestopnik@ithaca.edu

ABSTRACT
In this exploration of serious game design, we posit that, too often, fun and play require compromise in terms of task. Addressing this challenge, we articulate a story-driven approach to single-player serious game design called "diegetic connectivity," where task, mechanics, and story are tightly bound through conceptual relationships and aesthetic presentation. To explore the challenges and opportunities of this approach, we present a purpose-built second language acquisition (SLA) game called *Arena*, and discuss results from a preliminary mixed-methods study directed at motivation, engagement, and task outcomes. Finally, we discuss some of the critical aspects of diegetic connectivity, as well as opportunities for future research.

Author Keywords
Gamification; Serious Games; Game Design; Diegesis; Story; Mechanics; Task; Second Language Acquisition

ACM Classification Keywords: K.8.0 Games

INTRODUCTION
Gamification – the use of game elements in non-game contexts – can be a powerful way of motivating, engaging, and promoting desired behaviors in players [1]. Because of its usefulness and versatility, gamification has made its way into a variety of disciplines and contexts, from educational games and citizen science to marketing and politics.

A common approach to gamification is the application of points, badges or leaderboards to non-game tasks. There have been many successful games that use such methods, e.g. *fold.it*, *Phylo*, *Cropland Capture*, and *EyeWire* among others. However, this approach is not without limitations.

Points and achievements are just one element of game design. They are metrics for noting progress more than fostering motivation and engagement per se [2]. In addition, points are most often used to foster competition in games designed around communities of players. However, Bartle [3] noted four player types, only two of which were especially social in nature. Too strong a focus on progress metrics and competitive communities can make it easy to overlook other engaging game design tools like story, aesthetics, and variable rewards [4, 5]. Yet these are powerful ways to make gamified experiences feel, for lack of a better term, like "real games."

In this research, we propose an alternative approach to gamification that eschews "metric" and competition focused design in favor of "diegetic connectivity," where story, world, and aesthetic presentation tightly bind mechanics to purposeful tasks and vice versa. We posit that a story-focused mindset can help designers to overcome the non-trivial challenge of integrating complex, tedious tasks with play, resulting in beneficial outcomes such as enhanced player motivation, engagement, and task performance. This approach may be especially useful in single-player, entertainment-focused games directed at players who remain unmotivated by points, badges, leaderboards, and communities. This suggests the first of two overarching research questions:

RQ1: *How can we characterize approaches to gamification that go beyond "metrics" to motivate and engage participants in meaningful, single-player experiences?*

We are interested in exploring this question both conceptually and practically. The second half of this paper describes the design and evaluation of a "serious game," *Arena*, built with diegetic connectivity in mind. *Arena* is a second language acquisition (SLA) game set in a science fiction universe. Our exploratory evaluation of *Arena* is loosely directed at a second research question, drawing upon a mix of qualitative and quantitative data to show both the limits and opportunities of the diegetically connected approach to serious game design:

RQ2: *How does diegetic connectivity influence motivation and engagement in terms of play and task?*

CONCEPTUAL DEVELOPMENT

Gamification
The term "gamification" is controversial, having gained a reputation as "exploitationware" in the eyes of some designers [2]. The term sometimes disparagingly refers to competitive scoring "metrics" such as points, thinly layered

CHI PLAY '17, October 15–18, 2017, Amsterdam, Netherlands

ACM ISBN 978-1-4503-4898-0/17/10. . . $15.00
DOI: https://doi.org/10.1145/3116595.3116640

onto otherwise unaltered tasks, and this approach is often criticized as ineffective or even malicious [2, 6, 7].

Not surprisingly, many researchers have coined new terms to capture design thinking that is about more than just metrics and tasks [7], including "meaningful play" [8], "games with a purpose" [9], "serious games" [7], and more. These terms are highly contextualized, but describe approaches, often including additional elements such as story, that may enhance player engagement, improve task outcomes, or prolong play [6, 7, 10, 11].

The term "serious game" is of particular interest to us, denoting "the design of full-fledged games for non-entertainment purposes," [6]. The phrase "full-fledged" captures something qualitatively different about this term vs. the metric and competition focus of "gamification." It encompasses a more complete perspective, including story and aesthetics, possibly in a single-player context.

On the other hand, the word "serious," derived from the military traditions of sand table simulation [12], implies that potentially "unserious" aspects of game design – zany characters, dramatic stories, and fantastic worlds – need not apply. Yet modern entertainment video games, "full-fledged" games, specifically draw upon these playful elements to create fun and motivating experiences. As designers, we consider such tools to be essential.

Neither "gamification" nor "serious games" fully articulates our real intent: to produce full-fledged entertainment experiences that nonetheless accomplish something practical. We want to produce "real games," the kind that might find success in the mainstream game marketplace. This is no small feat, made more difficult by our desire to inject concrete tasks, likely to be difficult or uninteresting, into otherwise enjoyable games. Tasks, laden with detailed requirements, rules, and controls, can often spoil play. However, we see story as a subtle and powerful tool for bridging this challenging divide.

Diegetic Connectivity

We use the term "diegetic connectivity" to describe our approach to serious game design, a mindset more than a model. Diegetic connectivity helps us to understand how a "full-fledged" serious game is really a set of relationships between task, mechanics, and story. Story is our critical tool in this approach. It is used to strengthen every relationship in the game, making each one meaningful and cohesive.

Task: The Serious Objective

Serious games are organized around tasks: real world, "serious" objectives that are the important outcomes of the system. Tasks are rarely seen as inherently motivating or engaging, else why bother to build a game? It is the *combination* of task and play that provides an extra incentive to achieve real world outcomes [1, 6, 7, 11, 13].

The challenge of task is to find ways to mitigate that which is demotivating in order to enhance what is motivating. One tool for this is mechanics, the rules that define how players work toward game or task objectives [4].

Mechanics: The Rules of Play

Many, though not all, game mechanics capitalize on a short-term neurocognitive process called reinforcement learning (the so-called "dopamine loop"), which enhances engagement through dopamine release and uptake in the brain [14-16]. Reinforcement learning relies upon environmental triggers to inspire curiosity and motivate players to act in anticipation of variable rewards. A player's ability to reinvest such rewards into the game creates endogenous value [4], propelling players through additional such trigger-action-reward-reinvestment cycles [14]. One goal of designing for this process is to help players achieve a "flow state," [17] where the passage of time is forgotten and immersion is complete [4, 5].

Game rewards are valuable to players only insomuch as 1) they have real meaning outside the game *or* 2) the game itself is designed so that it creates endogenous value, making rewards meaningful inside the world of the game [4]. Points, badges, and leaderboards have real world meaning for some players – those who enjoy competition or have an intrinsic interest in the task. For many others, however, these metrics have no real world value. All too often, they are also not contextualized to the game world in a way that gives them endogenous value.

Story: Meaning, Context, and Value

A good story includes an interesting narrative, fascinating characters, and vivid worlds, structured to entertain and evoke emotion through plot, character arcs, and rising/falling action [18]. Crafting a compelling story is a non-trivial art form, and so story is an often overlooked tool for serious game design, especially in the realm of so-called "gamification." Yet stories are fundamental to human nature, and story is a mechanism through which games can inspire curiosity, fulfill emotional needs, create meaningful connections, and foster intrinsic motivation [10, 19-22]. One additional compelling aspect of story is fantasy, the evocation of, "mental images of physical objects or social situations that are not actually present," [19].

In serious games, fantasy comes in two varieties: exogenous and endogenous [23]. Endogenous fantasy tightly binds task to story. For example, in a physics learning game, players might be asked to perform real fuel calculations in order to launch a rocket. Exogenous fantasy is a less integrated approach, where fantasy content is used primarily as feedback for unrelated tasks. For example, players might add 2+2 in order to launch the rocket [10]. Endogenous fantasy is generally considered to be more motivating than exogenous fantasy.

Connections: Diegesis

Diegesis is a term that is used to draw distinction between things that are of the story and things are not [24-26]. Any game element that is rooted in the story world is considered diegetic; similarly, anything that is not part of this world is considered non-diegetic, instead existing as part of the "real" world of the player. In film and television, diegesis is often explained with an audio example. The on-screen radio playing a classic hit is diegetic because the characters in the scene can hear it; it is part of the story world. The bombastic film score, set in time to the screen action, is non-diegetic; it is not part of the story world at all [27].

In games, diegesis can be expanded to include other elements. For example, a health bar hovering over an enemy spaceship is non-diegetic, a mechanism for conveying feedback to a player. The same feedback could be conveyed diegetically by instead showing increasing amounts of smoke and fire as the enemy ship takes damage. Interestingly, the health bar can be transformed into diegetic feedback through clever use of story. By, for example, granting the player an augmented reality heads-up display, the health bar feedback can be made part of the story world and its existence cohesively justified.

We see diegesis as useful for addressing three design challenges in serious games: 1) justifying the existence of tasks inside a play environment, 2) creating endogenous value for rewards, and 3) incentivizing task outcomes through mechanics.

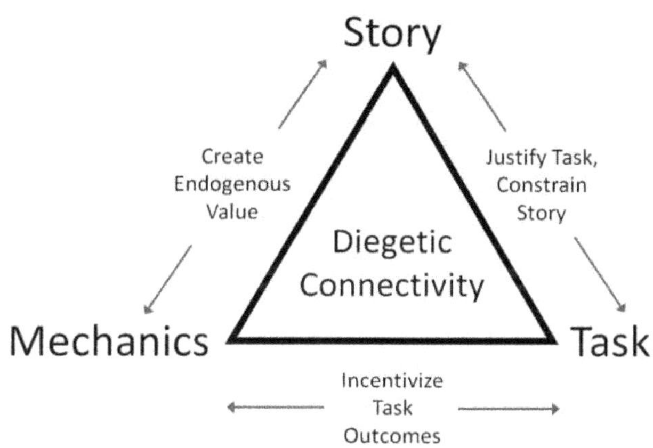

Figure 1. Diegetic connectivity is a perspective on serious game design where story is used to cohesively connect disparate aspects of the game to improve player motivation, engagement, and task outcomes.

Story can help tasks to feel seamlessly integrated into the world of the game. Designers can provide reasons for the task to exist and justifications for why it should be undertaken through clever use of narrative structure, characters, and the game world itself. At the same time, task necessarily shapes story. For example, a citizen science game featuring a taxonomic classification task could present this as a repair activity, where the player must restore damaged records in a ruined archive [28].

Story is also a tool for creating endogenous value, especially for mechanic-driven variable rewards. Unlocking new chapters of the story itself can be one type of reward, but other opportunities abound: the player avatar might be upgraded and enhanced in ways that connect meaningfully to the story and world, a game economy can be developed where players may purchase or trade items, or action-oriented mechanics like exploration and combat may provide story-justified moments of excitement and intrigue. Connections between story and mechanics abound in well-designed entertainment games. In serious games, story can also be used to forge connections between mechanics and task. For example, story-driven quests could encourage players to exercise second language reading comprehension skills in conversations with other game characters.

Connections between task, mechanics, and story can be made in many ways, including through textual explanation. However, aesthetics, the visuals and sound of a game, are especially noticeable to players [4], and we view this presentational layer as especially important for forging diegetic connections. Visual motifs and themes such as character and world design, iconography, and even the details of menus and feedback all help to convince players that tasks are an integral part of the story, far more than just busywork to be completed in order to "get on with the fun."

Outcomes: Motivation and Engagement

We see diegetic connectivity as important, not just because it has the potential to smoothly integrate tasks into single-player, entertainment-oriented serious games, but also because this approach may actually enhance player motivation and engagement, as well as task outcomes.

There is a spectrum of motivation, ranging from extrinsic to intrinsic. Extrinsically motivated individuals are moved to act because of some desirable outcome, while intrinsically motivated individuals act for the pleasure and satisfaction that the action itself provides [19]. Intrinsic motivation is often viewed as the more compelling of the two, though more difficult to create due to its highly individual, contextualized nature from person to person [29].

Psychological research has demonstrated that purely extrinsic rewards can have a negative effect on intrinsic motivation [30, 31], potentially negating the effectiveness of "metric" based scoring mechanisms in serious games. Alternatively, the more intrinsically motivated a player is to do a task, the more likely desired goals will be met [19, 30].

Motivation is usually seen as a necessary pre-requisite for engagement [32, 33], which is equally important in games, serious or not. Engaged individuals that are fully involved demonstrate a certain persistence to work through spontaneous difficulties (not found in individuals that are not engaged), and exhibit "higher levels of sustained interest in the activity or the instructional content of the activity," [19, 21, 34].

Diegetic connectivity creates opportunities to foster task engagement by raising and then satisfying player curiosity, an instinctual human behavior arising from a desire to seek information that will reduce uncertainty [35]. Stories in games raise dramatic questions, and thus curiosity, by providing places, situations, skills, and characters that players know little or nothing about. Uncertainty has been noted as an important motivating element of games [36], normally mitigated only after effort by the player to overcome challenges and obstacles of various kinds [4], including mechanically induced obstacles that also increase dopamine release and uptake [14-16]. By tightly integrating task, mechanics, and story, we anticipate enhanced player uncertainty, curiosity, motivation, and engagement, not only with respect to the non-task aspects of serious games, but also with respect to tasks themselves.

System Overview

Empirically studying diegetic connectivity will be a long-term, multi-faceted process for us. Starting out on this avenue of research, we developed a purpose-built serious game, *Arena*, and conducted a preliminary mixed-methods study directed at user perceptions of our design approach, motivation, engagement, and short-term learning effects. In this section, we describe the design of *Arena*. In the next, we describe our exploratory study methods and findings, as well as some of the future work they point to.

Arena is an SLA game set in the distant future, an age of space colonization and technological advancement. The game takes place on a colony planet where the local language is Spanish. This world is controlled by a local crime family who use a dangerous AI technology, the *Spider*, to cement their hold on power.

Figure 2. Language is an important part of *Arena* from its first moments. Here, menu choices show Spanish and English, e.g. "About Arena" changes to "Sobre Arena" when selected.

Players take on the role of Brock Springer, a military officer who is called from Earth to help his sister Emily. Emily's husband has been murdered and her life is in jeopardy. She needs Brock's help.

We selected the details of our story and world carefully, drawing upon our understanding of both task and mechanics. From a standpoint of task, we wanted a game environment that could deliver modern Spanish while still leveraging the motivational qualities of fantasy [19]. In terms of mechanics, we also wanted the creative freedom to include common entertainment game mechanics such as combat, but in a way that felt fun and exciting, rather than out of place or even uncomfortable, as in a more contemporary setting. Finally, we wanted a world that could be presented through aesthetics in a visually dramatic way. We wanted to forge diegetic connections using visuals and sound whenever possible. A futuristic science-fiction setting and plot allowed us to accomplish these goals.

Task: Spanish Language Vocabulary Matching

Arena's task is vocabulary matching, a mini-game that begins when players converse with non-player characters (NPCs). Conversations contain English passages that further the game narrative and world of *Arena*. Spanish words appear in each passage, and players must translate them in a timed matching game. Diegetically, we justify this matching mechanic with the *Spider* story element: Brock is suffering the side effects of a parasitic AI embedded in his brain. This *Spider* makes him physically stronger, but also weakens his mind. He is losing his knowledge of Spanish, and the player must help him "remember" his fading vocabulary.

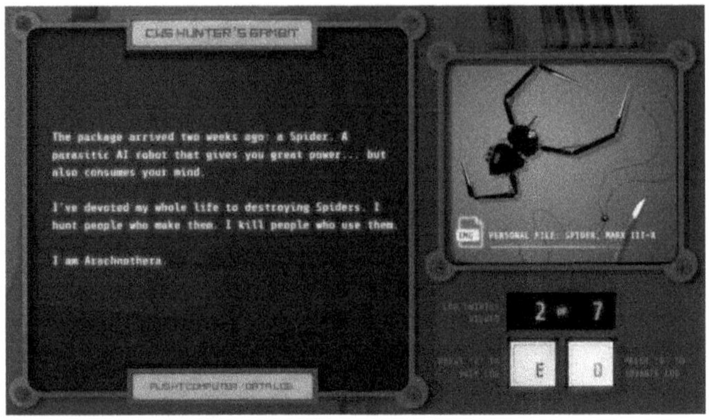

Figure 3. The *Spider* is a critical story element, used to justify both language activities and play mechanics.

Though not a task per se, players also encounter additional vocabulary passively as they explore. This vocabulary is presented through titles and in some game art assets, understandable through context clues but requiring no active work from the player. These words are diegetic, e.g. the label "puerta cerrada" (locked door), and players may choose to cognitively engage with them or not.

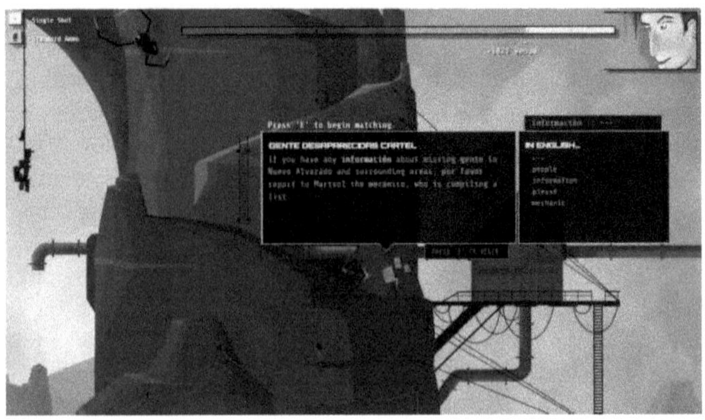

Figure 4. Vocabulary is typically presented in diegetically motivated matching tasks, e.g. story plus mechanics.

We included these two modes for language interaction to explore how story alone vs. story and mechanics together can motivate players to engage with tasks in a diegetically connected serious game.

Figure 5. Some vocabulary is presented only in passing, e.g. story only. Here, the phrase "puerta cerrada" (locked door) is presented without an associated activity.

Arena's task is based upon Psycholinguistic SLA theory, which suggests that individuals learn a second language through goal-based, communicative activities. Success is dependent on authentic encounters with a comprehensible form of the target language. Players must be exposed to the target language within contexts where they can negotiate meaning through rich interactions [37, 38]. In this way, task underpins all our decisions about conversations and communication goals in *Arena.*

Mechanics: The Spider and Venom

Players must balance the physical power of the *Spider* against the need to communicate in Spanish. This balance is accomplished by managing a critical game resource: venom. Venom reduces the time given during vocabulary matching tasks, making them more challenging. It is gained when players use the *Spider*, diegetically representing the *Spider's* increasing hold on Brock.

Figure 6. The Spider can be deployed to explore narrow crawl spaces, jump over chasms, and more.

The *Spider* is represented by a drone device that the player can deploy into the game world. The *Spider* can do things that Brock cannot, such as accessing small areas or fighting enemies. It can also be upgraded to become more powerful.

Figure 7. The Spider is also used to fight enemies in combat, clearing the way for further exploration. Using the Spider increases Venom, an important game resource.

The *Spider's* abilities have endogenous value in the context of *Arena's* world. They allow the player to clear obstacles more quickly and for less venom cost. When these rewards are used wisely and venom is managed correctly, the player can take fun liberties with the *Spider*. However, if venom or rewards are mismanaged, Brock may completely lose his memory, and the game will end in defeat.

METHODS

"Diegetic connectivity" is a complex design mindset that can be operationalized and studied in a wide variety of ways. Recognizing this, we use the remainder of this paper to report a preliminary and exploratory empirical evaluation of *Arena*. Our intention is not to make strong claims about the diegetic connectivity approach, but rather to illustrate its use and to elaborate upon its potentials and challenges.

For this exploratory investigation, we recruited a small number of participants to play *Arena* and respond to a series of questionnaires about their experience. We also administered Spanish pre- and post-tests to evaluate task outcomes (learning effects) after exposure to the game.

Participants

Participants (n=30) were recruited from computer science courses at a mid-sized undergraduate liberal arts college in the northeastern United States. 17 participants were male, and 12 were female. Ages ranged from 18 to 25, with a mean and median age of 21.

Given our interest in gamers as potential beneficiaries of single-player experiences like *Arena*, we recruited from computer science courses in anticipation that these participants might identify as gamers. Many computer science students are passionate about games, pursuing this interest both as gamers and as student game developers [39]. We asked participants to respond to the statement "I consider myself a gamer" in our demographic survey. 12 participants agreed strongly with this statement, 13 somewhat agreed, and 5 did not agree at all.

Environment and Equipment

This study was run in one of two quiet computer labs reserved for the purpose. Participants were brought to one of the labs in small groups (between 1 to 5 participants at a time); they participated in the study individually and at their own pace. The lab computers were 2013 iMacs running OSX Yosemite version 10.10.5, with a 2.7 GHz Core i5 processor and 8 GB of memory. *Arena* is a browser-based game built with the *Phaser* Javascript game engine API. It was run in the Google Chrome browser for this study.

Procedure

Participants took a demographic survey and a Spanish pre-test to evaluate their familiarity with a targeted set of Spanish vocabulary words. Following these initial surveys, participants played *Arena* for about 20 minutes. Language activities in the game were instrumented to capture player performance for later analysis.

After play, participants took a game experience survey to capture their reactions. We asked a variety of open-ended response questions about *Arena* and also adapted the Game Experience Questionnaire from IJsselsteijn et al. [40] and the NASA Task Load Index (NASA-TLX) [41], which measures mental demand, temporal demand, performance, effort, and frustration on a scale from 0 to 100. This initial evaluation reports primarily on the qualitative responses.

Following the game experience survey, participants were asked to take a Spanish language post-test with the same vocabulary as the pre-test taken before playing *Arena*. We also report on this short-term learning outcome data.

LIMITATIONS

We acknowledge a number of important limitations to this study. It was conducted under controlled conditions, and with a small sample, imposing artificiality and limited statistical power. In addition, our design is quasi-experimental; we are not comparing *Arena* to other serious games or other language-learning activities. As such, we can say little about diegetic connectivity as compared to other design approaches. As such, we report our findings primarily as a baseline for future inquiry.

In the future, we see many possibilities for manipulating and studying various diegetic approaches in *Arena*. For example, we foresee adjusting the game's mechanics, task structure, and story presentation, thereby enabling us to dissect and study the various relationships that make up a diegetically connected game. We also hope to compare various versions of *Arena* – on user experience and task outcomes – to other serious games. And we recognize that our current analysis of learning effects in *Arena* is limited; the effects we report in this study are short term, based upon a limited test vocabulary. In future work, we expect to measure learning effects (and their decay) over time, introduce listening comprehension exercises, and explore the usefulness of *Arena* as a supplement to other instruction. In short, we see this current study as the beginning of long-term exploration, and report it as such.

RESULTS

We asked participants about 1) what aspects of *Arena* influenced their interest in playing, either positively or negatively, 2) what aspects of *Arena* influenced their interest in learning Spanish, either positively or negatively, 3) whether they would continue to play and why, 4) suggestions for improvement, 5) feelings of fatigue during play, and 6) if they had any additional comments.

Note that these questions do not ask specifically about task, mechanics, or story because were interested in collecting open feedback from players to inductively explore the impact of different *Arena* elements. All the same, several themes related to diegetic connectivity strongly emerged.

Player Experience: Story, Mechanics & Aesthetics

Participants noted the importance of story, mechanics, and aesthetics in terms of motivation and engagement. These elements of *Arena* are, of course, easily noticed; it is still useful to acknowledge that players viewed them as an overwhelmingly positive influence on their play experience.

Example Statements About Story, Mechanics, and Aesthetics	
1.	STORY: The story of the game really interested me, and kept me wondering how things would progress throughout the game. The NPCs were fun-looking and added to the atmosphere of the world, which overall made the experience really nice.
2.	STORY: The story was interesting! I'm curious to find out what happened to his [the player character's] sister's husband.
3.	MECHANICS: The mechanics were pretty fun as well. I enjoyed becoming the spider and fighting enemies to unlock a new level.
4.	MECHANICS: The leveling up of the ammo system made me want to continue playing to see what kind of ammo I could get in the future.
5.	AESTHETICS: The environment was absolutely gorgeous. The sound design was very engaging, and the environment as a whole was quite immersive.
6.	AESTHETICS: The game art was really, really amazing, I kept wanting to look at all of it and it really set the sci-fi mood of the game. The music also piqued my interest because it was very intense, and it made me want to play and find out what was the mystery/action.

Table 1: Story, mechanics, and aesthetics were seen as important individual elements of the *Arena* play experience.

Players specifically noted how story enhanced their sense of wonderment and curiosity, driving them to continue exploration and play. Players also referenced the role of variable rewards, e.g. reinforcement learning, as a mechanism for motivating their actions in the game. Unsurprisingly, visuals and sound were seen as an important aspect of the overall experience. They were noted as motivators because of the way they created a sense of immersion, atmosphere, and mystery.

Player Experience: Task

Virtually all participants expressed interest in learning a second language (40% were somewhat interested, 43% interested, and 10% extremely interested), suggesting that second language learning is generally considered desirable and worthwhile. However, 20 participants (67%) indicated that they were not currently learning a second language, and only 4 participants (13%) indicated that they were. 6

participants (20%) did not answer this question. For our participants, then, the desirability and perceived benefits of learning a second language did not seem to translate into concrete action. It is beyond the scope of this study to understand exactly why this is, but we do suggest that the mismatch between perceived value and concrete action is fertile ground for a game such as *Arena*; we designed *Arena* specifically to explore how playful diegetic connections might impact this player-learner "enthusiasm gap."

Example Statements About Task Contextualized by Story	
1.	I have attempted to learn Spanish on multiple different occasions in the past with very little success. I have taken Spanish classes and also used Rosetta stone, but my lack of interest has always prevented me from really getting into it and putting in the effort required. This game had a really nice environment that was fun to explore, so it captured my attention more than something like a lesson or a virtual exercise does.
2.	There was some kind of reason behind why the character needed to know Spanish.
3.	[Arena] increased my interest [in learning Spanish] with the need to defeat that arrogant spider.
4.	The conversations were great to help understand and learn Spanish.
5.	Being story driven definitely was a key part. Additionally, gaining an understanding allowed me to progress more efficiently (actual reward for learning). I also wanted to continue along with the game itself and that meant successfully understanding what the words meant.

Table 2: Players perceived how story contextualized the Spanish language tasks in the game, giving them purpose and presenting them in a way that made coherent sense within the world of the story.

Story had three strong impacts: 1) it enhanced curiosity, 2) it captured attention, and 3) it created meaning. For some players, the world and environment of *Arena* felt qualitatively different from typical learning environments, enhancing motivation and engagement. For others, the story established concrete goals and activities, with similar results. Story, in addition to making the *game* better, seemed to make the *task* better as well.

Example Statements About Task Contextualized by Mechanics	
1.	The fact that every time I missed a word brought me closer to 'dying' in the game made me want to know more of the Spanish.
2.	Blending Spanish words into the English text makes their meaning easy to figure out using context, which I found helpful.
3.	The Spanish mechanic felt like it fit within the game, and didn't feel forced; sure, I was learning stuff, but it still felt like a normal game.
4.	There was a sense of punishment within the game when you were wrong and there was a will to learn (or memorize) the words in order to succeed.

Table 3: Players also perceived how game mechanics (rewards, punishments, and rules of play) contextualized the Spanish language tasks, giving them endogenous value within the world of the game.

Psychological effects such as reinforcement learning and reward loops also gave players an enhanced feeling that the task itself had value; the task was the mechanism by which they could make progress and participate in enjoyable play activities as they unlocked progress in the world, e.g.:

Example Statements About Reward and Punishment Mechanics	
1.	Gaining an understanding [of language] allowed me to progress more efficiently (actual reward for learning). I also wanted to continue along with the game itself and that meant successfully understanding what the words meant (punishment for being wrong could lead to game over).
2.	I never really saw the effects of venom, but I assumed it was bad from the tutorial text so I was motivated to learn the Spanish needed to get 100% on all the Spanish interactions and reduce venom.
3.	The leveling up of the ammo system made me want to continue playing to see what kind of ammo I could get in the future.

Table 4: *Arena* includes several interconnected reward and punishment systems, including venom (a resource that must be managed) and weapon upgrades. These systems are tied to task in various ways, and are also framed by the story and world of the game.

In many comments, participants indicated that the relationships between story, task, and mechanics in *Arena* were critical for fostering engagement with the game. Furthermore, these relationships also enhanced engagement with the task, giving it purpose (e.g. "There was some kind of reason behind why the character needed to know Spanish.") and meaning (e.g. "I also wanted to continue along with the game itself and that meant successfully understanding what the words meant.").

In their comments, participants also discussed how the *cohesiveness* of the experience was important. *Arena* felt "unobtrusive," and like a, "normal game." Participants also recognized *Arena* for its "fun," "atmosphere," "education," and "interactivity," and for its ability to overcome the difficulties of learning a second language. This is the blending effect of diegetic connectivity, a mindset that gives designers permission to forge playful and entertaining connections between otherwise disparate elements.

Learning Effects

Pre- and post-tests were used to capture participant knowledge of 23 vocabulary words that appear in *Arena*. Recall our interest in story and mechanic driven tasks vs. story only tasks. 16 words were included in "story plus mechanics" tasks. The remaining 7 words were shown to players in passing, usually as part of pop-up information bubbles providing information about the story and world.

The pre- and post-tests asked participants to type a Spanish translation for a provided English word. Participants were reassured that they need not use special characters (e.g. ñ, á, é, í, ó, ú, etc.) so as to avoid confounds from using US standard keyboards. Words were randomized to avoid ordering effects.

Example Statements About Work and Play in *Arena*

1. Arena taught Spanish in an unobtrusive way that is part of the gameplay rather than just sitting down and learning from flashcards. I liked that the language learning aspect seemed more conversational than memorizing.
2. The atmosphere of the game was a lot more intriguing than most educational games. It took a different approach going for a thriller sort of game rather than a game plot for young children.
3. The story was pretty interesting, as was the prospect of being able to learn Spanish in a way that was actually fun, unlike most language learning games.
4. I found the story engaging, which made the game easy to continue playing.
5. I did like this game and it did increase my willingness to learn Spanish, simply because playing five minutes of it made me feel it has the potential to be more educational and interactive than any high school class I ever took.
6. Learning another language has always been of interest. The problem, however, is that it's never been one of my strong suits (simply memorization / classroom doesn't work for me). Video games seemed like a great alternative to try.
7. I thought that it was a very interesting game that matched learning and entertainment nicely. Learning new languages have been difficult for me and I thought it would be a fun new way to try and learn.

Table 5: The connections between story, mechanics, and task, including the way these are presented through aesthetics, create a whole greater than the sum of the parts. Many participants reflected upon the way games like *Arena* can go beyond traditional educational tools to contextualize learning activities in new and engaging ways.

We used a coding process to produce a final grade for each test, akin to coding techniques used in content analysis [42]. Three coders individually graded the language pre- and post-tests, coding answers as correct (1) or incorrect (0).

Test	Judgments	# Disagreements	Rate of Disagreement
Pre-Test	690	32	4.6%
Post-Test	667	17	2.5%

Table 6: Rate of disagreement for language test grading.

Disagreements were resolved using a "majority rules" approach, where the final grade per word was assigned based on the grade given by the two raters who agreed.

We used paired two-sample t-Tests to investigate whether there was a significant difference in the mean grades for pre- and post-tests for "story only" words and "story plus mechanics" words. One participant failed to submit a post-test and was omitted from analysis.

t-test: Paired Two Sample for Means (Story plus Mechanics)

	Pre-Test	*Post-Test*
Mean	3.483	5.035
Observations	29	29
t Stat	-4.396	
P(T<=t) two-tail	0.000	

Table 7: Players actively interacted with 16 words in diegetically motivated translation activities (story plus mechanics). The difference in means from pre- to post-test was significant to $p < 0.000$, showing a strong short-term learning effect.

We found a significant learning effect ($p<0.000$) for words in the story plus mechanics category.

t-Test: Paired Two Sample for Means (Story Only)

	Pre-Test	*Post-Test*
Mean	0.931	0.793
Observations	29	29
t Stat	2.117	
P(T<=t) two-tail	0.043	

Table 8: Seven words were diegetically motivated, contextualized, and seen by players, but were not actively interacted with or translated in an activity (story only). The difference in means from pre- to post-test was not significant, showing no learning effect for these words.

We found no learning effect for story only words, suggesting that story alone does not effectively incentivize players to engage cognitively with pedagogical information. Active engagement through mechanics is important.

This seemingly trivial finding – that active engagement with the language is obviously preferable to passive exposure – nonetheless has important implications for diegetic game designers. The goal of diegetic connectivity is the smooth and cohesive blending of story, mechanics, and task, but our (admittedly limited) findings about learning suggest that many tasks, in order to be effective, must also be interruptive. Is it true, then, that task must inevitably spoil play? Or can task interruptions be managed or reframed such that they enhance engagement and promote a state of "flow" [4, 5, 17]? An earlier version of *Arena* helps shed light on such questions.

DISCUSSION

Diegesis and Task: A Four Quadrant Matrix

Our first vision for *Arena* was more radically diegetic than the version we explored in this current study. It was designed around a fully Spanish-speaking world where all game content was delivered in Spanish. Players were granted diegetically-justified translation tools to assist them in navigating this unfamiliar information space.

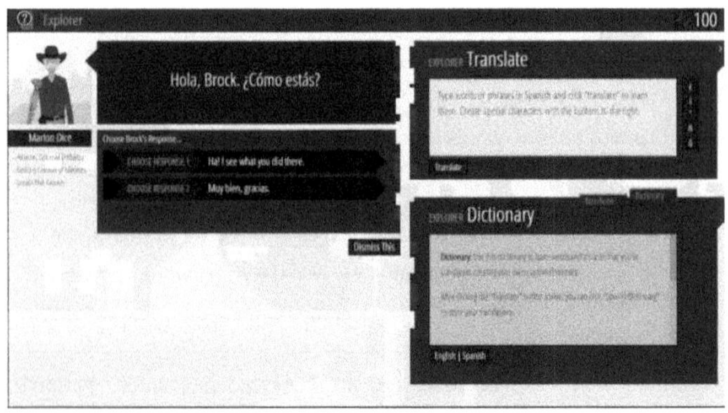

Figure 8. In our first polished version of *Arena*, players interacted with NPCs almost entirely in Spanish. A translation tool called the *Explorer* helped them to make sense of the language… for a cost.

In this early version, we wanted to create a feeling of being "dropped" into a Spanish speaking world, forced to contend with the complexities of language just as one might when living abroad [43]. This approach would create many incentives to work actively and deeply with the target language, in terms of both game mechanics and cognitive engagement. This would lead – we thought – to enhanced motivation and improved task outcomes. However, through several rounds of informal play testing, we began to see some of the costs of full immersion, especially the cognitive load imposed on players. The full translation activity was fatiguing, spoiling the fun of the game. It incentivized players to skip through language activities and undermined *Arena's* learning intent [44].

We changed our approach in the version of *Arena* reported here, creating a complex diegetic justification – the *Spider* – in order to deploy a simpler (but more artificial) vocabulary matching task. We relied upon diegetic connections to make this activity feel like a natural part of the game world. The task was greatly simplified and less of an interruption, but presenting it to players was a challenge. We were forced to craft an explanation of the *Spider*, including the harm it does to Brock's language abilities and the ways this harm is translated into game mechanics and task.

We presented this backstory in its entirety at the beginning of the game, when many other details about task, story, and mechanics are competing for player attention. This resulted in confusion for players, e.g.:

Example Statements About Usability in *Arena*	
1.	I would definitely make sure that the player had a firm grasp of how to play the game before tossing them into the activities. Also maybe the first few Spanish activities could be a little bit easier so that the player has a bit more time to fully understand what they are supposed to do.
2.	I found the directions for the matching gameplay a bit confusing. I would also like the option to read a piece of dialogue more than once.

Table 9: Many players noted that the instructions for language matching (the task) were complicated and hard to remember.

Such comments reinforce the importance of good usability in computer games [e.g. 45, 46]. They also underscore the challenges inherent to crafting successful relationships between story, mechanics, and task. In addition to creating a believable narrative with emotional impact, diegetic connectivity should produce intuitive functionality at all levels. *Arena* succeeds in many ways, but falls short here.

This struggle ultimately suggested that a more formal understanding of the relationships the task and the rest of the game would be beneficial. We see the possibility of mapping such relationships on two axes: diegetic complexity and task complexity, with various design trade-offs resulting for each combination of diegetic justification and task design.

Low complexity approaches in both axes, like our "story only" approach in the reported version of *Arena*, may be straightforward to justify. Popups that require no active engagement feel very natural and easy to players, just like a purely entertainment-oriented game. However, these seemed to foster too little active engagement (at least in *Arena*) to be successful. Designs with lower diegetic complexity but higher task complexity (our "immersive" translation approach from the earlier version of *Arena*) or lower task complexity but higher diegetic complexity (our "story plus mechanics" approach) may have greater potential for success, depending on their specific implementation, but require further study. Implementations that are complex in both axes run severe risks of overwhelming players and losing their interest.

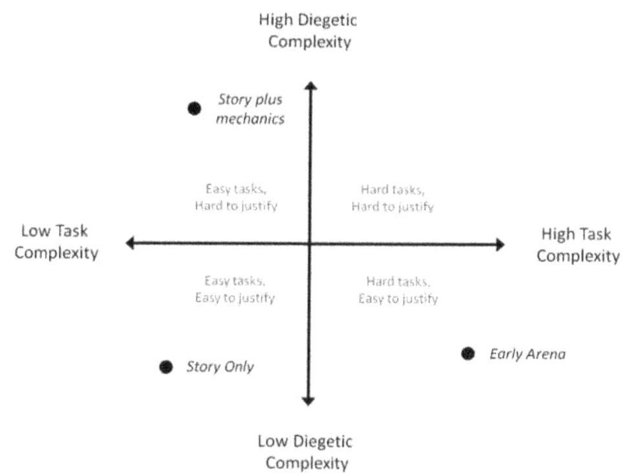

Figure 9. Different diegetic justifications and task implementations may produce different experiences and outcomes for serious game players. This may be further moderated by the task "genre," e.g. citizen science tasks to produce data may benefit from low task complexity and low diegetic complexity, while learning activities may benefit from higher task complexity.

Task as Motivator

Zhang and von Dran [47] note the importance of "motivators" and "satisfiers" in web and other interactive experiences, suggesting that some features are necessary in order to satisfy user expectations, while others are truly motivating, encouraging users to actively engage with a system. In serious game design, it is sometimes tempting to think of task as something other than a motivator – perhaps even as a demotivator – especially for entertainment minded designers. The entire premise of a serious game, after all, is to convince players to undertake mundane, challenging, or uninteresting activities by promising a playful, fun experience in return.

Our work with *Arena* shows that this view is mistaken. Tasks can, indeed, be motivators, and serious game designers should recognize the task as something unique and special about the systems they design, e.g.:

Example Statements About Language Learning as Motivating	
1.	It reminded me the importance of learning another language.
2.	The fact that it was a game where you could learn or improve on a new language.
3.	I'd still like to learn another language.

Table 10. Several participants commented on their interest in learning a second language, showing how the task itself can be a motivator, even if its difficulty is a deterrent to engagement outside of play.

This is to say that diegetic connections should not be thought of as a tool for tricking players or hiding the task from them. Rather, diegetic connectivity is an approach that gives designers a way to acknowledge both the motivating power of the task as well as the limits of that power.

Aspects of a task that seem demotivating, difficult, or boring can be streamlined and diegetically justified in a way that helps to make them feel palatable and even fun; aspects that are already seen as interesting can be foregrounded, used to recruit players and enhance the cachet of the experience. This is true of contexts beyond second language acquisition: the altruistic impulses and inspirations of citizen science, the insights gained from persuasive games, or the pride of contributing to human computation-oriented "games with a purpose."

CONCLUSION

In this paper, we explored how story can help to overcome some of the difficult challenges presented by the synthesis of task and play in serious game design. Our approach, dubbed "diegetic connectivity," highlights the importance of strong, story-oriented connections between task and mechanics to immerse players in game worlds that feel cohesive and fun, more akin to commercial entertainment than typical "gamified" experiences.

Our language learning game, *Arena*, was designed with these connections in mind, and we used an exploratory, mixed-methods study to unpack the player experience and task outcomes. Though our work here is preliminary, we nonetheless found that in *Arena*, diegetic connections did indeed seem to enhance players' self-reported motivation and engagement. Furthermore, quantitative analysis showed how this approach could produce successful task outcomes, while simultaneously raising questions about task design and diegetic presentation.

As a loosely organized approach or way of thinking, diegetic connectivity remains subject to the whims and preferences of individual designers, and there is much work to be done in terms of refinement and study of this approach to serious game design. We see many opportunities to formalize the diegetic connectivity model for serious game design across a wide spectrum of task-oriented experiences, especially when it comes to defining some of the most critical relationships between story, mechanics, and task.

ACKNOWLEDGMENTS

Many thanks to the student team responsible for designing, developing, and studying *Arena*: Kaitlyn Balogh, Jack Banta, Bernardo Simoes Lage Gomes Duarte, Maria 'Belen' de la Cruz, Geneva Faraci, Ethan Fletcher, Nicole Lane, João Gama Vila Nova, Chiara Marcario, Claire Riley, Jeff Rosen, Evan Sobkowicz, Kizito Umanakwe, Yanming 'Jimmy' Wang, Trevor Wheeler, Ian Weise, Joe Yull, and Noah Zheutlin. Thanks also to Prof. Chris Hromalik, Spanish language domain expert, and Jian Tang, PhD, for their valuable advice and assistance.

REFERENCES

1. Lee, J.J. and J. Hammer, *Gamification in Education: What, How, Why Bother?* Academic Exchange Quarterly, 2011. **15**(2).
2. Bogost, I. *Persuasive Games: Exploitationware.* Gamasutra: The Art and Business of Making Games 2011.
3. Bartle, R., *Hearts, clubs, diamonds, spades: Players who suit MUDs.* Journal of MUD research, 1996. **1**(1): p. 19.
4. Schell, J., *The Art of Game Design: A Book of Lenses.* 2008, Burlington, MA: Elsevier, Inc. 483.
5. Rogers, S., *Level Up:The Guide to Great Video Game Design.* 2010, Chichester, West Sussex, UK: John Wiley and Sons Ltd.
6. Deterding, S., *Gamification: designing for motivation.* interactions, 2012. **19**(4): p. 14-17.
7. Deterding, S., et al., *From game design elements to gamefulness: defining "gamification"*, in *Proceedings of the 15th International Academic MindTrek Conference: Envisioning Future Media Environments.* 2011, ACM: Tampere, Finland.
8. Salen, K. and E. Zimmerman, *Game design and meaningful play.* Handbook of computer game studies, 2005. **59**.
9. von Ahn, L., *Games with a purpose.* Computer, 2006. **39**(6): p. 92-94.
10. Garris, R., R. Ahlers, and J. Driskell, *Games, Motivation, and Learning: A Research and Practice Model.* Simulation & Gaming, 2002. **33**(4): p. 441-467.
11. Deterding, S., et al., *Gamification. using game-design elements in non-gaming contexts*, in *CHI 2011, Extended Abstracts on Human Factors in Computing Systems.* 2011, ACM: Vancouver, BC, Canada.
12. Halter, E., *From Sun Tzu to Xbox: War and Videogames.* 2006, New York: Thunder's Mouth Press.
13. Hamari, J., J. Koivisto, and H. Sarsa. *Does gamification work? - A literature review of empirical studies on gamification.* in *47th Hawaii International Conference on System Sciences.* 2014. IEEE.
14. Eyal, N., *Hooked: How to Build Habit-Forming Products.* 2014, New York, NY: Penguin Group. 242.
15. Howard-Jones, P., et al., *Toward a Science of Learning Games.* Mind, Brain, and Education, 2011. **5**(1): p. 33-41.
16. Koepp, M.J., et al., *Evidence for striatal dopamine release during a video game.* Nature, 1998. **393**: p. 266-268.
17. Csikszentmihalyi, M., *The Psychology of Optimal Experience.* 1990: Harper Perennial.
18. Vogler, C., *The Writer's Journey.* 2007, Saline, MI: McNaughton & Gunn, Inc.
19. Malone, T.W. and M. Lepper, *Making learning fun: A taxonomy of intrinsic motivations for learning.* Aptitude,

learning, and instruction: Vol. 3. Cognitive and affective process analyses, ed. R. Snow and M. Fair. 1987, Hills-Dale, NJ: Erlbaum.

20. Pichert, J.W. and R.C. Anderson., *Taking different perspectives on a story.* Journal of educational psychology, 1977. **69**(4).
21. Malone, T.W., *What makes things fun to learn? heuristics for designing instructional computer games*, in *Proceedings of the 3rd ACM SIGSMALL symposium and the first SIGPC symposium on Small systems*. 1980, ACM: Palo Alto, California, United States.
22. Prensky, M., *Computer games and learning: Digital game-based learning.* Handbook of computer game studies, 2005. **18**: p. 97-122.
23. Rieber, L.P., *Seriously considering play: Designing interactive learning environments based on the blending of microworlds, simulations, and games.* Educational Technology Research and Development, 1996. **44**: p. 43-58.
24. De Freitas, S. and M. Oliver, *How can exploratory learning with games and simulations within the curriculum be most effectively evaluated?* Computers & Education, 2006. **46**(3): p. 249-264.
25. Galloway, A.R., *Gaming: Essays On Algorithmic Culture (Electronic Mediations)*. 2006: University of Minnesota Press.
26. Stam, R., R. Burgoyne, and S. Flitterman-Lewis, *New vocabularies in film semiotics*. 1992, London: Routledge.
27. Alten, S.R., *Audio in media*. 9 ed. 2011, Boston, MA: Wadsworth, Cengage Learning.
28. Prestopnik, N. and J. Tang, *Points, stories, worlds, and diegesis: Comparing player experiences in two citizen science games.* Computers in Human Behavior, 2015. **52**: p. 492-506.
29. Deci, E.L., *Effects of externally mediated rewards on intrinsic motivation.* Journal of Personality and Social Psychology, 1971. **18**(1): p. 105-115.
30. Deci, E.L., R. Koestner, and R.M. Ryan, *Extrinsic rewards and intrinsic motivation in education: Reconsidered once again.* Review of educational research, 2001. **71**(1): p. 1-27.
31. Deci, E.L., R.M. Ryan, and R. Koestner, *The pervasive negative effects of rewards on intrinsic motivation: Response to Cameron.* Review of Educational Research, 2001. **71**(1): p. 43-51.
32. Saeed, S. and D. Zyngier, *How motivation influences student engagement: A qualitative case study.* Journal of Education and Learning, 2012. **1**(2): p. 252.
33. Alrashidi, O., H.P. Phan, and B.H. Ngu, *Academic Engagement: An Overview of Its Definitions, Dimensions, and Major Conceptualisations.* International Education Studies, 2016. **9**(12): p. 41.
34. Schlechty, P.C., *Shaking up the schoolhouse: How to support and sustain educational innovation.* 2001, San Francisco, CA: Jossey-Bass.
35. Gottlieb, J., et al., *Information-seeking, curiosity, and attention: computational and neural mechanisms.* Trends in cognitive sciences, 2013. **17**(11): p. 585-593.
36. Costikyan, G., *Uncertainty in Games*. Playful Thinking, ed. G.L. Jesper Juul, William Uricchio. 2013, Canbridge, Massachussetts: The MIT Press. 141.
37. Gass, S.M., *Changing views of language learning*, in *Change and continuity in applied linguistics: Selected papers from the annual meeting of the British Association of Applied Linguistics*, H. Trappes-Lomax, Editor. 2000, British Association of Applied Linguistics.: Edinburgh, UK. p. 51-67.
38. Petersen, M., *Computerized Games and Simulations in ComputerAssisted Language Learning: A Meta-Analysis of Research* Simulation and Gaming, 2010. **41**(1): p. 72-93.
39. Overmars, M., *Teaching computer science through game design*, in *Computer*. 2004. p. 81-83.
40. IJsselsteijn, W., et al. *Characterising and measuring user experiences in digital games.* in *International conference on advances in computer entertainment technology*. 2007.
41. Hart, S.G. and L.E. Staveland, *Development of NASA-TLX (Task Load Index): Results of empirical and theoretical research.* Advances in psychology, 1988. **52**: p. 139-183.
42. Weber, R.P., *Basic Content Analysis*. Quantitative Applications in the Social Sciences, ed. M.S. Lewis-Beck. 1990, Newbury Park, CA: SAGE Publications, Ltd.
43. Polanyi, L., *Language learning and living abroad: stories from the field*, in *Second Language Acquisition in a Study Abroad Context*, B.F. Freed, Editor. 1995: Amsterdam: Benjamins. p. pp. 271-291.
44. Prestopnik, N., *Games, Stories, and Language: Motivating Second Language Acquisition With Play.* International Journal of Designs for Learning, 2016. **7**(3): p. 72-87.
45. Febretti, A. and F. Garzotto, *Usability, playability, and long-term engagement in computer games*, in *CHI '09 Extended Abstracts on Human Factors in Computing Systems*. 2009, ACM: Boston, MA, USA.
46. Pinelle, D., N. Wong, and T. Stach, *Heuristic evaluation for games: usability principles for video game design*, in *Proceedings of the SIGCHI Conference on Human Factors in Computing Systems*. 2008, ACM: Florence, Italy.
47. Zhang, P. and G.M. von Dran, *Satisfiers and dissatisfiers: A two-factor model for Website design and evaluation.* Journal of the American Society for Information Science and Technology, 2000. **51**(14): p. 1253.

Towards Designing Technology for Classroom Role-Play

Amy Shannon Cook
Carnegie Mellon University
Pittsburgh, USA
amyshann@andrew.cmu.edu

Steven P. Dow
University of California San Diego
San Diego, USA
spdow@ucsd.edu

Jessica Hammer
Carnegie Mellon University
Pittsburgh, USA
hammerj@cs.cmu.edu

ABSTRACT
Classroom role-play is an interactive learning technique with a long history of success, but current attempts to augment it with technology limit the very interactions that make this technique successful. For example, digital role-play games often engage individual students at a computer, rather than creating rich social interactions among students. In order to design interactions that better support the core aspects of classroom role-play, we conducted interviews with teachers; we also interviewed role-play gamers to discover how traditional RPG techniques and technology can be used to enhance classroom role-play. In this paper we 1) explore the reasons instructors choose role-play for learning, such as giving students practice opportunities; 2) identify barriers to instructors using classroom role-play activities, such as time constraints and student discomfort; 3) report issues around integrating technology, such as the benefit of reducing cognitive load and the threat of distraction; and 4) highlight two areas where insights from role-playing games can inform the design of interactive learning systems for classroom role-play: by providing methods for emphasizing *group success* over individual achievement and by preserving the *spirit of the experience*.

Author Keywords
Role-play games; classroom role-play activities; interactive learning; educational technology design.

ACM Classification Keywords
K.3.1 Computer Uses in Education: Collaborative learning.

INTRODUCTION
Role-play has been used in classrooms across a variety of disciplines to create opportunities for interactive learning [2,14]. While role-play activities vary across disciplines in terms of numbers of participants, the modality of interaction, and feedback delivery [2,22], the core activity involves collaborating with peers to generate knowledge. According to the ICAP spectrum (interactive, constructive, active, passive) introduced by Chi et al. [6], classroom role-play activities would be an interactive learning activity.

Effective interactive learning activities must support learners in *generating* knowledge and in *collaborating* with peers. However, there are known challenges in each of these areas. For example, novice learners may not generate accurate or productive learning materials [12], and may be hesitant to contribute to a collaboration [4]. Additionally, facilitating role-play activities requires expertise [3] and there are few resources available for teachers to practice.

Instructors have tried two strategies to solve these challenges: introducing *game rules* [10,18] and using *technology tools* [28]. Game rules are often modeled after analog role-playing games (RPGs), while technology tools typically allow participants to role-play online, e.g. via Skype. When used individually, each of these strategies addresses some of the issues around classroom role-play. However, when game rules *and* technology tools are introduced at the same time, they do not always support the generative and collaborative elements that make classroom role-play effective. For example, students might be asked to pretend to be an ethnographer in *Everquest*, an MMORPG [7]. While the student certainly learns about conducting social science research from the game, they are no longer interacting with their peers in real life. Additionally, this screen-based format excludes embodied forms of role-play.

Our goal in this paper is to explore how insights from role-playing games can provide an alternate vision for designing supportive technology for classroom role-play activities, while still taking the constraints and challenges of the classroom setting into account. To understand the interaction between technology, role-playing, and the classroom context, we conducted 15 interviews with role-play gamers who use digital tools to support their play practice, and with instructors who use technology or role-play in the classroom. We used their insights to elicit design implications for systems to support classroom role-play as an interactive learning activity.

Through these interviews, we 1) explore reasons why instructors chose to use classroom role-play (rather than other pedagogical strategies), such as providing an opportunity to practice skills and giving students a "vicarious experience" [10]. We then 2) identify barriers to instructors using classroom role-play activities, such as time constraints and student discomfort. Taken together, these

CHI PLAY '17, October 15-18, 2017, Amsterdam, Netherlands

ACM ISBN 978-1-4503-4898-0/17/10...$15.00
https://doi.org/10.1145/3116595.3116632

motivations and barriers define opportunities for improving classroom role-play. Next, we 3) report additional opportunities and constraints to be considered when supporting role-play with technology, such as the benefit of reducing cognitive load and the threat of distraction. Finally, we 4) highlight and discuss two areas where insights from role-playing games can support the design of effective interactive learning systems for classroom role-play, namely by providing methods for emphasizing *group success* over individual achievement and by preserving the *spirit of the experience*.

RELATED WORK

We review the literature on classroom role-play as an interactive learning activity, consider the challenges around designing and implementing classroom role-play, and examine existing solutions used to meet these challenges.

Classroom Role-Play

Many instructors have attempted role-playing activities as a strategy for bringing interactive learning into the classroom. In classroom role-playing activities, students take on the role of a character who exists in a fictional situation, using a set of rules to interact with other role-players and with the fictional situation [14]. For example, in language learning role-play, one student might take on the role of a shopper at a store, while another could play the clerk from whom they are trying to purchase something; rules for the scenario might include speaking exclusively in the target language or using specific vocabulary words.

Interactive role-play has a well-established history of being used and researched in disciplines such as geography, foreign languages, health studies, social work, religious studies, science, drama, education, psychology, social sciences, philosophy, English literature, environmental science and engineering, tourism and hospitality, ethics, economics, marketing, political science and information technology [2,14]. Across this broad range of domains, classroom role-play activities share certain core features, such as participants acting out the role of a character. The activities typically take place during class, which has a scheduled start and end time; everyone is in the classroom at the same time. However, there are also significant differences between role-playing activities as typically adopted in different learning domains. Critical axes of difference include the *number of participants*, the *modality of interaction*, and *feedback delivery*. In language learning, classroom role-play activities are typically one-on-one and verbal, as with the shopper and clerk. Feedback typically happens infrequently and is only given by the instructor. In contrast, role-play in design classrooms is often a group activity in which students embody a user or other stakeholder during the activity and often give feedback to each other after the activity [5,22]. For example, students might act out an exchange between a user and a service provider when designing a new service.

Challenges of interactive learning activities

In the ICAP framework introduced by Chi et al [6], interactive learning techniques ask students to *generate* novel learning-related materials and to *collaborate* in engaging with those ideas. Interactive learning techniques optimize student learning because they allow students to engage deeply in activities such as co-creation [6].

Classroom role-play activities at their best can embody these principles of interactive learning. When a student is portraying a character, the student's words or actions *generate* changes in the fictional situation in ways that depend on the rules of the activity in question. For example, in a role-play activity designed to teach climate change, students take on the role of a delegation from different countries to negotiate matters of geography, economy, and politics as they relate to climate change [17]. Students participating in this activity must generate arguments and reasoning to advance the negotiations in their country's favor. They also *collaborate* with other students by reacting to the changes those students introduce to the shared fiction. For example, in the same climate change example, students might portray a government official, industry leader, or civil society member of their delegation. The delegation members collaborate with each other to form their position, but they also collaborate with students from other delegation teams by negotiating with them [17].

While the generative and collaborative nature of role-play produces its strengths as an interactive learning activity, these strengths also introduce challenges. For example, because learners are not yet domain experts, the learning-related content they generate may not be accurate or productive. Without some method of feedback on their generated material, students may reinforce their own misconceptions [12]. A second set of challenges has to do with the collaborative aspects of the activity. For example, varying levels of psychological ownership make it more difficult for students to respond meaningfully to each other's contributions as opposed to operating essentially independently [4].

Teachers also face challenges around independently designing and facilitating high-quality interactive learning activities [6]. Teachers are not typically experts in role-play; facilitating role-play activities is itself a skill [3]. Maintaining the collaborative and generative nature of the activity without special training or skills is difficult. Even if they have the expertise, designing role-play activities is a time-consuming process [17].

Existing approaches to improving classroom role-play

Instructors commonly use two strategies to respond to these challenges: introducing *game rules* that help students participate effectively, and introducing *technology tools* that keep the activity on track. However, when game rules *and* technology tools are introduced at the same time, they do not always support the generative and collaborative elements that make classroom role-play effective.

When introducing *game rules* to classroom role-play activities, instructors typically build on analog role-playing games (RPGs), including both tabletop and live-action play. RPG methods can help support students in generating learning-relevant material and in reflecting on that material in ways that connect it to desired learning outcomes. For example, a Brazilian educator asked students to create an RPG based on a work of fiction, and use the game to encourage literary analysis and reflection [11]. RPG methods can also structure student collaboration. For example, Turkington's live-action scenario *Against the Grain* has four players but only three chairs, giving certain characters a very literal seat at the negotiating table while someone must always be excluded [26].

Using RPGs in education can offer a range of benefits [10]. However, integrating these benefits into classroom role-play activities is not automatic. For example, Resnik & Wilensky designed role-play activities to help learners explore decentralized systems, but participants neither sustained the role of a character nor collaborated with other players during play [11]. Additionally, existing RPGs often need to be adapted for the classroom environment. For example, the RPG *Ars Magica* directly engages with medieval history, but is not designed to be played in the length of a class or at classroom scale [9]. Finally, existing RPGs may not address the specific topics that instructors hope to teach. To design one's own RPG is difficult, particularly if it is meant to address a complicated subject or change players' attitudes [17,23]. While instructors who are expert role-players may be able to navigate these issues, most instructors are not trained in role-playing, nor are they expected to be.

Existing strategies for incorporating *technology tools* into classroom role-play focus on using online communication technologies to perform traditional role-play activities. Bringing classroom role-playing activities online can have benefits for instructors and students. For example, conducting language learning role-play over Skype can reduce student performance anxiety when generating contributions to the role-play activity [28]. Text-based role-plays can allow students to participate asynchronously and produce an artifact for instructors to review. However, these strategies are most useful for one-on-one, verbal role-playing and do not support physical or tangible role-plays such as the ones often used in design classrooms. Additionally, some implementations (e.g. Skype role-playing) make it more difficult to role-play in groups due to technological constraints. Finally, existing technology to support classroom role-play does not incorporate insights from RPGs, but simply allows current classroom role-play practices to be performed digitally.

RPG techniques and technology are sometimes used in the classroom *together*, but often in ways that are not aligned with classroom role-play as an activity. For example, the gamified classroom is based on RPG elements such as levels, character statistics, and quests [20]. However, the gamified classroom is meant to incentivize student participation in a range of activities rather than supporting classroom role-play. Digital RPGs, including both single-player CRPGs and multi-player MMORPGs, have been used to teach a range of subjects including history and science [10], and role-play activity within these technological forms can be beneficial for learning [24]. However, with digital RPGs, students often interact with the simulated environment or with computer-controlled characters rather than generating novel material or interacting with one another.

We seek to design technological systems that support classroom role-play as it is currently practiced, and that actively support the generative and collaborative interaction of classroom role-play activities. Our goal in this paper is to build on insights from role-playing games and from instructors who use classroom-role play to provide an alternate vision for designing supportive technology for classroom role-play activities.

METHODS

To better understand how RPGs could inform the design of interactive learning experiences, we conducted open-ended interviews with instructors and game-players with a range of experience in RPGs and classroom instruction. We sought to answer the following key research questions: what parallels exist between interactive learning environments and RPGs, how can the expertise of role-play gamers and instructors inform system designers, and what

#	Job and/or Experience	Education?	RPG?
P1	Design Professor, Improv Actor	X	X
P2	Role Play Researcher		X
P3	RPG Designer		X
P4	Role Player, Sex-Ed Teacher	X	X
P5	University IT Support, Role Player	X	X
P6	German Professor, Role Player	X	X
P7	Role Player		X
P8	Computer Science Professor	X	
P9	Chinese Professor	X	
P10	Improv Professor	X	X
P11	University Teacher Support Center	X	
P12	Theater Teacher	X	X
P13	Design Professor, Role Player	X	X
P14	Improv Instructor	X	X
P15	Design Professor, RPG Designer	X	X

Table 1: List of participants and relevant experience

potential benefits and challenges emerge when technology is introduced to the activity?

Participants

Fifteen people participated in this study (9 male, 6 female). We recruited participants with experience in RPGs and/or high school or college-level classroom instruction (see Table 1). We began by reaching out to professors at our university who used role-play in their classes, and by contacting colleagues who had experience with RPGs. We then asked each participant to recommend others with relevant expertise, defined as those who had used role-play or in-class technology in a class they taught, those who had played RPGs consistently as an adult, or those with work experience in a university technology support department. For participants with experience both as an instructor and as a role-play gamer outside of an academic context, we separated their comments for analysis based on the specific experience they were describing at the time.

Procedure

Interviews were conducted either in person or online using Google Hangouts and lasted 30-60 minutes. All interviews were video recorded. Participants were asked questions about their background and experience using role-play, specific examples of role-play activities they had participated in or used in a classroom, and how they had used technology during class or during role-play. We asked participants to share what they felt were the benefits and challenges of role-play, and the benefits and challenges to using technology either during class or during an RPG.

Analysis

All interviews were transcribed from the video recording. One researcher coded all reasoning about classroom activity design or game design into one or more of four categories: reasons to role-play, reasons not to role-play, reasons to use technology, and reasons not to use technology. Within each category, a team of three researchers iteratively sorted the quotes until patterns emerged using bottom-up coding.

FINDINGS

Our qualitative analysis revealed a shared set of reasons to use or not use role-play, and a shared set of reasons to use or not use technology, despite the variety in participants' experiences. All the reasons from our data are listed in Tables 2, 3, & 4.

How Role-Playing can Support Interactive Learning

Table 2 lists the reasons participants gave for using role-play, which reflect Chi & Wylie's discussion of the benefits of interactive learning. For example, not only did all participants, including role-play gamers, identify *learning* as a key aspect of role-play activities, but they also recognized that *interactivity* was an essential aspect of role-play. Participants described co-creation activities provided by role-play, such as collaboratively participating in the creation of a shared reality (coded as *shared fiction* and *freedom/play*). Participants also recognized the importance of co-inferring, and valued that other role-players impacted how they understood the role-play experience (coded as *social interaction*). From a learning perspective, participants saw role-play as providing opportunities to have experiences they otherwise might not (*vicarious experience*), to practice skills in authentic contexts (*practice*), and to grow as human beings (*personal growth*). Instructors were concerned with innovation in the classroom (*disrupt class*), and role-players saw opportunities to form long-term relationships (*investment* and *vulnerability*). Building on these insights, we identify two aspects of interactive learning where insights from role-players can help instructors deepen the role-play activities they are already using.

Practicing and Managing Interactivity

Instructors used role-play activities as a chance for students to practice domain-specific skills interactively and, where possible, in an authentic context. For example, language instructors described role-play as "the only time the student can really produce something using the things they have learned" (P9) and as a chance to "freely speak in a

Code	Explanation
Shared Fiction	creating a story collaboratively through role-play
Vicarious Experience	experiencing something through role-play that one would not encounter under normal
Practice	using role-play to practice a skill or learning goal
Social Interaction	connecting with others through role-play
Freedom/Play	exploring the limitless nature of role-play; role-play for the sake of enjoyment
Personal Growth	self-improvement as a result of role-play
Disrupt Classroom	using role-play to create a new, unusual classroom interaction
Investment	dedication to the role-play story or group
Vulnerability	discovering or expressing vulnerability through role-play

Table 2: Reasons Why Study Participants Used Role-Play in Classrooms or in Games

language" (P6). Role-play provided a reason for students to *produce* language, and to *interact* with their peers, which precisely fits Chi & Wiley's criteria for interactive learning. These instructors faced few barriers in using role-play activities for interactive language practice. Role-play exercises were found in their textbooks, were standard procedure for other instructors they knew, and were designed to teach targeted lessons. This was not just the case for language instruction. For example, P4 used role-play activities in a sex education class to practice handling difficult sexual situations; these activities were a formal part of the curriculum.

The majority of classroom role-play activities described by participants did not incorporate RPG elements, even when the instructor was also an expert role-player. However, RPG expertise sometimes helped instructors generate novel interactive learning experiences in domains without extensive formal support for role-play. For example, P5 described an instructor who adapted Emily Short's game *San Tilapian Studies* [21] for an American History survey course. The game asks players to imagine artifacts that might be found in the museum of a fictional country, collaborate to find evidence of the artifact's validity, and discuss what that evidence might mean for their imagined artifact. By changing the game materials to reference early American artifacts that the course was targeting, students were able to practice "thinking historically" and "historical interpretation" in an interactive way.

Beyond adapting games to specific domains, role-players can also contribute deep expertise in organizing and managing interactivity. RPGs provide structures for interaction that go beyond simple turn-taking or free-for-all participation, such as the rotating player roles in *Polaris* [15] and the bidding system in *Prime Time Adventures* [27]. Role-players described interactive participation as a skill in its own right, which in turn can be supported by game rules. Instructors can both adapt specific interactive organization systems of RPGs for their own role-play activities and help students practice interactive co-creation as a core skill.

Building and Maintaining Relationships
Instructors perceived role-play activities as useful for "warming up to the other people in the class" and serving as an "ice breaker" (P1). Ice-breaking role-play activities might not convey domain-specific content, but could still help students comfortably participate in other learning activities. However, instructors did not prioritize the social interactions that occurred *during* role-play activities, even though these interactions are essential for interactive learning [6]. Role-players, on the other hand, saw RPGs as ways to improve their social and communication skills. Specific skills mentioned include reading emotions, making eye contact, teamwork, listening, empathy, awareness of others' social signals, and treating others with respect. These skills were practiced by "interacting with another human being," and experimenting with different behaviors using both "logical steps" and "emotional responses" as guides (P4). Role-players recognized that communication skills are necessary first steps to engage in the conversations required for co-inference and collaboration.

RPGs also transformed players' relationships with one another from individualistic to collective. For example, one participant described the core of improvisation as "you are with other people, those people are the most important people on stage. Your job is to make them look brilliant" (P14). This participant prioritized shared brilliance over producing an individually brilliant performance. Role-players also emphasized the RPG group as a "steady group of 4 or 5 people" (P4) that would form a social bond by coming together on a regular basis to play the game. Role-players talked about the difficulty in finding new RPG groups after moving to a new city, or using RPGs as a way to develop new friendships. This emphasis on collective success can be educationally productive, particularly for deeper interactive learning activities like co-creation.

Challenges for Bringing Role-Play into Classrooms
Participants gave fewer reasons for not using role-play than for any of the other categories. We did not separate these reasons into individual codes, but we discuss three themes that were commonly mentioned by participants.

Fitting the Learning Context
Participants remarked that some lessons or courses were not conducive to being taught with role-play activities. For example, both language instructors in our sample believed that role-play worked better in their beginning language classes than in advanced courses. "In the advanced class, they are supposed to [...] not only learn the language, but also the content itself. For some students, although they are okay with the language, they probably don't know the content. [...] so when they come up with a role-play, I just don't find it is really satisfying from my point of view" (P9). While classroom role-play succeeds in helping students practice language skills, instructors believe it is less effective at teaching cultural topics that students are unfamiliar with. Practices from RPGs could enhance classroom role-play activities, helping students develop awareness of and sensitivity to deeper cultural issues.

Overcoming Time Constraints
Two participants mentioned time as an inhibiting factor to using role-play in a classroom. Initially, a role-play activity requires up-front effort to plan. "I think the main constraint is time and planning a well-planned, coherent activity" (P6). An instructor's expertise would influence how much time they needed to design, adapt, or implement a role-play activity. Role-play also takes time during the class session, which could discourage some instructors from attempting to use this technique. P1 said that particularly in large classrooms, there often was not time to see everyone's role-play presentation.

Code	Explanation
Shared Experience	using technology to share an experience with a large group of people
Reduce Cognitive Load	using technology to make a task easier
Affordances of Technology	taking advantage of specific functions or experiences that particular technology provides
Simulated Experience	simulating an experience with technology that would be difficult to experience in real life
Record of Play/Class	creating a digital record of what occurred during a game or class session

Table 3: Reasons Why Study Participants Used Technology in Classrooms or during Role-Play

Providing Equal Access for Students with Reservations

Finally, three participants mentioned that students or players often have reservations about role-play that can limit the success of such an activity. When commenting on tabletop RPGs, P3 acknowledged that "people's comfort in a RP situation isn't uniform." Similarly, in classroom role-play, students "feel lost because they have never done certain things before" (P6). "They are nervous. I think that is actually the major barrier is they are still some of them uncomfortable, a bit shy with themselves" (P1).

How Technology Can Support Role-Play in Classroom Settings

As we have seen, there are challenges to using role-play activities in the classroom, even when the instructor might find it educationally beneficial. However, our participants had insight into ways that technology could mitigate some of these concerns (see Table 3). We discuss three examples.

Affordances of Technology: Dissemination of Activities

While role-play activities might not fit all learning content, often the greatest barrier to implementing a role-play activity in class is the time required to create and plan the activity. Technology can help role-play activity designers disseminate activities to instructors for adaptation or adoption. For example, the instructor who adapted *San Tilapian Studies* for an American History course was able to do so because the rules are freely available online.

Reduce Cognitive Load

Instructors used technology to reduce the cognitive effort spent on resource management outside of class, such as data collection and efficient grading. "The technology that supports a large class is really aimed at efforts to help the instructor manage more efficiently, so grading" (P11). Instructors did not use technology to encourage or enhance student interaction, or to lower their cognitive load *during* class when interactions might occur. Role-players, on the other hand, were focused on lowering the cognitive load spent on non-interactive elements of the game during play, to allow more interaction to occur. In some games, players might need to be simultaneously attending to die rolls (P2), map placement of characters (P5), verbal narration and time (P13), and complex mathematical calculations (P15) in order to figure out their next move. By using technology to keep track of game elements, as well as to create additional screen real estate during online games (P5), players were able to keep track of the game without a large cognitive burden. Players also used tablets and other technology to reference game rules (P13, P5), historical facts (P15), or other relevant information (P7) in real time. This freed players from having to remember all the rules to a complex game and allowed them to focus on the more important aspects of play – the interactions among players. Technology that supports student interactions during classroom role-play can help make implementing interactive learning activities more feasible for instructors.

Record of Play/Class

Instructors often use technology to provide students with a record or model of expert behavior. For example, P8 said "I always have Python open, and I write lots of code while I lecture." The code written by the instructor during lecture is available to students after class. Instructors also used technology to provide students with another way to participate in class. One instructor supported ESL students by telling them "if you do not feel like you can participate verbally in class, you can participate by writing" down their observations and emailing the instructor (P15). In one tabletop role-playing game, the players created an in-game wiki to detail "people that we met", "things that happened to this character when we weren't around", and to "signal the people running the game" of their preferred storylines (P15). Both instructors and role-players used the records of the experience to promote equal access to the game or class session. Those who may have felt reservations about fully participating in role-play or class were given an opportunity to interact with the record of the activity in a less threatening, lower-risk way.

Challenges of Using Technology

Both instructors and role-players described ways that technology could help them improve their role-playing (see Table 4). However, both groups also identified new challenges that technology introduced.

Functional and Logistical Problems

Instructors were highly concerned with technology failing, citing experiences with technology that was "buggy" (P6), had "technical issues" (P13), or had "bandwidth problems" (P5). They had strong beliefs that "they're going to break down at some point" (P11). Even technology that didn't break down generated logistical problems, like teaching students how to use new software (P8) and students

Code	Explanation
Negative Attention	when technology use causes a distraction or division of attention, or when the distraction has a negative effect on the culture of the environment
Diminishing the Experience	when technology use detracts from the overall experience in ways other than causing a distraction or division of attention
Functional Problems	when the technology breaks down, or when users expect the technology to break down
Logistical Barriers	overhead or logistical issues that make implementing technology difficult

Table 4: Reasons Why Study Participants Did Not Use Technology in Classrooms or during Role-Play

forgetting to bring clickers to class (P11). Several instructors described selecting low-tech learning activities specifically to avoid "the different things that could go wrong" (P6). By contrast, role-players saw technology primarily as an opportunity – even when describing technology going astray. For example, P5 described a game in which players tried to use Twitter to emulate the high-school rumor mill. The game managers realized Twitter was too public a venue for this record of play. "The majority wasn't really comfortable using their actual Twitter accounts for that traffic" (P5). P5 approvingly described how the group adopted a different solution, and remained interested in using Twitter in play.

Technology as a Distraction

Instructors saw students using digital devices as reducing their attention to the course material. These concerns were often framed dramatically, for example as "their brains getting sucked out of their heads" (P8). Instructors were also concerned about the distracting effects on other students. When one student becomes distracted by technology, "three or four heads around them go down on their phones" (P8). Role-players' concerns centered on preserving a shared experience. Technology might "break the illusion" of the shared imaginary world (P2) or "take the emotion out of it" (P3). Even positive interactions with technology – e.g. simplifying interactions with rules – could be understood as "checking out" of the communal experience (P5). However, role-players saw the problem of distraction as one that could be mitigated with social agreements. For example, P5 identified specific situations where technology would be particularly damaging: "if there's costumes involved, if there's real spaces involved." In these situations, P5 "very, very rarely brought out any type of device."

DISCUSSION: IMPLICATIONS FOR INTERACTIVE LEARNING

Our findings illuminate the reasons why instructors use role-play activities in the classroom, and allow us to identify two areas where insights from RPGs can support the design of effective interactive learning systems. We offer concrete suggestions for using RPG techniques to implement these suggestions.

Support Group Cohesion

In order for co-inferring and co-creation to occur, students need to interact in productive and meaningful ways. The interaction itself is the cause of learning. However, instructors often focus on individual learner's performance, rather than on the progress of the class as a whole. While students participate in the role-play interactively, the focus is on improving a student's individual performance. In contrast, role-players primarily see RPGs from a group perspective. Whether that means finding the right people to play with, or helping fellow role-players become valued contributors, role-players' concerns focus on the interactions among team members.

This difference also manifests in the way instructors and role-players talk about technology. When instructors talked about technologies to lower cognitive load, they described possible benefits for *themselves as instructors* (e.g. efficient grading) and for *individual students* (e.g. increasing accessibility for ESL learners). Role-players, on the other hand, wanted to make game tasks easier to benefit everyone. For example, in a game with complicated rules about sharing resources, one player created a spreadsheet to track what the group had access to (P15). By replacing complicated calculations with a single number, this player reduced wait times for the entire group and allowed them to spend more time interacting.

Focusing more on group cohesion during classroom role-play could help encourage interactive learning. Many educational settings involve sustained group work, particularly for project-based learning (e.g. [8]). The quality of a team affects how much participants learn [13]. However, creating a cohesive team is complex and takes time; before teams can perform at a high level, they must establish shared goals, resolve interpersonal conflicts, and take full responsibility for their shared work [25].

The RPG literature offers three concrete ways to support group cohesion that can be adapted to interactive learning systems. First, RPGs give participants the power to affect a single, shared, imaginary world [16]. When players have to come to a consensus about the shared imaginary space, they must respect or at least acknowledge one another's conclusions. Interactive learning systems can encourage students to reach consensus during their interactions and provide support for both expressing opinions and resolving disagreements. Second, RPGs have developed many different systems for managing multiple people's contributions to a single shared imaginative space [9]. One common approach is to give each person's character different necessary skills, and divide up power such that every player has limited ability to make decisions. This requires and provokes contributions from everyone that build on other people's contributions. Contribution management options can be incorporated into an interactive learning system. Third, in RPGs players have to agree that their characters should stay together during the story [9]. Game participants are explicitly putting characters in relationship to one another, which helps people see why they might engage rather than withdraw. Interactive learning systems can draw attention to relationships among students and among students' characters in a classroom role-play activity. By drawing on role-players' insights about group-first RPGs, classroom role-play activities can be designed to create cohesive groups for learning - and they can utilize technologies that help role-play activities support groups, not just individuals.

Preserve the Spirit of the Experience

One concern raised by role-players - a concern that instructors did not share - was that technology might damage the "spirit of the game." By this, role-players mean a set of norms and expectations that allow players to feel comfortable, playful, and invested in participating. Role-players consider this to be a framework or scaffold that supports and encourages player interaction. Role-players perceive this state as fragile, requiring attention and care from all players to maintain. Instructors, on the other hand, did not talk about creating a classroom culture to support interactive, participatory learning, even if the instructor had experience with role-play.

Again, this difference manifested in participants' approach to technology. Both role-players and instructors talked about using technology for recording their activities. However, they had very different purposes for recording. Role-players wanted to use recordings to re-enter the imaginative space of the game, such as by using a wiki to remind them what happened in the game (P15). In designing recording methods, they carefully thought through how the recording and retrieval process would make players feel and if it would encourage or discourage interaction (P5). Instructors, on the other hand, saw recording as a way of capturing expert behavior for students to reference. For example, P8 wanted to use recording to model code design, while P1 wanted to model how to give helpful feedback. Although role-players and instructors saw similar reasons to role-play, they focused on capturing different aspects of the experience.

This difference also informed participants' ideas about recording and privacy. Role-players, who expect to share their game experience only with those they have chosen, were concerned about intrusiveness and privacy. When talking about recording, they were interested not just in how the record was captured, but also in how it was displayed and shared after its creation. For example, in the Twitter game described previously, the game managers used "big sticky post-it notes on the wall, that people would just write on with their fake twitter handles" instead of requiring people to post publicly on their real Twitter account (P5). Instructors, on the other hand, expressed no concern for whether or not students considered records intrusive, and had no qualms about sharing records with researchers outside the classroom – perhaps because the classroom context by default involves sharing with relative strangers.

Affect matters in learning environments, as do shared norms such as attitudes to failure [29], and we believe that many instructors are already aware of this. However, instructors in our sample did not identify role-play as a way to construct and maintain shared norms, or as a way to affect learners emotionally. This belief was also reflected in their attitudes toward technology.

The RPG literature offers two concrete ways to preserve the spirit of the experience. Some role-playing games use ritual to establish the boundaries of play and model the desired experience during the game. For example, *Polaris* asks players to begin the game by speaking a key phrase. "Long ago, the people were dying at the end of the world." The game text also suggests other ritual elements to add, such as lighting a candle or playing a piece of music to evoke feelings of loss and grief [15]. Second, token systems such as those used in *The Quiet Year* [1] can encourage players not just to follow games rules, but also to express their emotions in a way that promotes the spirit of the game. These insights present an opportunity to increase instructors' sensitivity to the experiential qualities of role-play activities and help instructors use supportive technology more effectively, such as considering the context and intrusiveness of classroom recordings and how students might feel both about reviewing them and about having the recordings exposed to others.

Classroom Context and Content

Classroom differences can affect the design of role-play and/or technology interventions. For example, different domains may value certain benefits of role-play more than others. Social interaction might be particularly important for language learning as students practice language skills with each other, while vicarious experience might be more important in the design classroom because it helps learners take on the perspective of stakeholders.

Class size also has an impact, just as role-play game design differs at different scales. For example, tabletop games are typically designed for small groups (usually 3-8 players), while some live-action games can accommodate up to several thousand. Classes at different scales would be implementing games that draw on different design communities and different design principles. Some large classes might choose to break into small groups, while others might choose to stay together. This decision could be affected by the physical classroom layout, such as a lecture hall with fixed seating that does not allow students to split into groups, as well as by the instructor's learning goals.

Other factors such as access to technology, students' prior experiences, and instructor training with technology or role-play could also affect how technology and RPGs impact a classroom environment. Students enter a class with different kinds of literacy. They might have strong technical literacy and easy access to technology; strong game literacy and knowledge about a wide variety of genres and game mechanics; and/or strong role-play literacy that enables them to embody a character during improv. These prior experiences could impact the choices an instructor makes when bringing technology and role-play into a class. For example, in a class where students are technically literate but not role-play literate, an instructor might choose a game with a strong technology component that would support their burgeoning role-play skills. These and other factors of classroom context can be explored in future work.

Implications for System Design

It is important to support classroom role-play before, during, and after the role-play activity. Instructors described challenges around *planning* and *preparing for* role-play activities; *facilitating* and *monitoring* play; and *reviewing* and *providing feedback* after the role-playing finished. Role-players also see preparation for play (e.g. constructing game artifacts) and after-play activities (e.g. discussing what happened in the game) as critical for the group dynamics and the construction of a shared experience.

Systems for classroom role-play, therefore, can begin with methods for guiding instructors in creating and finding activities. During the role-play activity, systems might provide better real-time monitoring and feedback capacity, particularly in ambient or subtle ways that do not disrupt the spirit of the experience. After the role-play activity, systems might share back a record of the activity for asynchronous participation by less-engaged students or for experts to provide feedback. Other ways of supporting students might involve reducing performance anxiety, scaling the number of students who can participate actively in a given role-play, and reducing their cognitive load when interacting with the rules (rather than the learning content) of the classroom role-play activity.

The obvious stakeholders are the instructor and the student, but our findings suggest that systems also need to support the *group*, which might include only students or might include students and instructors role-playing together.

Systems for classroom role-playing *in groups* need to support group decision-making, information exchange, evaluation of group rather than individual outcomes, and group meaning-making. They also need to capture data for presentation to the instructor that is relevant at the *group* and not only at the *individual* level. Before the role-play activity, group-based systems can support the development of group identity and group construction of what a shared experience might look like. After role-playing, group-based systems might support debriefing and reflection on the shared activity *within the group itself*, as well as feedback exchange between role-playing groups.

Limitations

Our study included a limited number of participants and relied primarily on interviews. We chose to conduct interviews because we wanted to understand participants' experiences with multiple open-ended domains. However, this method is limited by the particular experiences of the participants in our study and the constrained amount of time we could spend with each interviewee. Our instructor interviews did not cover the full range of disciplines in which teachers use role-play in class, such as simulations used in medical training and education.

FUTURE WORK

We chose to only conduct interviews in our initial exploration of this research space. In future studies, we would use additional methods to gather more comprehensive data. Future studies could conduct observations of role-play in different settings to collect behavioral data that can further inform system design. Future studies could draw from principles of body storming [19], where designers role-play to design for people, which could also provide design guidelines for systems supporting role-play games.

CONCLUSION

We conducted an interview study with 15 participants with a range of experience with role-playing and classroom instruction to understand if and how role-play might inform interactive learning systems. We found that role-players have insights about supporting group cohesion and preserving the spirit of the experience that could positively impact how interactive learning is implemented. We also examined how role-play gamers' perspectives on technology can help address many of the challenges of using role-play during class. These insights connecting interactive learning and RPGs can benefit both communities as it is explored further.

ACKNOWLEDGMENTS

The research reported here was supported in part by a training grant from the Institute of Education Sciences (R305B150008). Opinions expressed do not represent the views of the U.S. Department of Education.

REFERENCES

1. Avery Alder. 2013. The Quiet Year. Retrieved from http://buriedwithoutceremony.com/the-quiet-year/
2. EK Armstrong. 2003. Applications of role-playing in tourism management teaching: An evaluation of a learning method. *Journal of Hospitality, Leisure, Sport and Tourism* .... Retrieved March 19, 2016

from http://citeseerx.ist.psu.edu/viewdoc/download?doi=10.1.1.603.1204&rep=rep1&type=pdf

3. Allan Baumer and Brian Magerko. 2009. Narrative development in improvisational theatre. *Joint International Conference on Interactive Digital Storytelling*: 140–151. Retrieved April 14, 2017 from http://link.springer.com/chapter/10.1007/978-3-642-10643-9_19
4. Ina Blau and Avner Caspi. 2009. What type of collaboration helps? Psychological ownership, perceived learning and outcome quality of collaboration using Google Docs. *Proceedings of the Chais conference on instructional technologies research*. Retrieved February 6, 2017 from http://telem-pub.openu.ac.il/users/chais/2009/noon/1_1.pdf
5. Marion Buchenau and Jane Fulton Suri. 2000. Experience prototyping. *Proceedings of the conference on Designing interactive systems processes, practices, methods, and techniques - DIS '00*, ACM Press, 424–433. http://doi.org/10.1145/347642.347802
6. MTH Chi and R Wylie. 2014. The ICAP framework: Linking cognitive engagement to active learning outcomes. *Educational Psychologist*. Retrieved March 19, 2016 from http://www.tandfonline.com/doi/abs/10.1080/00461520.2014.965823
7. A Delwiche. 2006. Massively multiplayer online games (MMOs) in the new media classroom. Retrieved September 16, 2014 from http://scholar.google.com/scholar?cluster=5832740351102013769&hl=en&oi=scholarr#0
8. Matthew W. Easterday, Daniel Rees Lewis, Colin Fitzpatrick, and Elizabeth M. Gerber. 2014. Computer supported novice group critique. *Proceedings of the 2014 conference on Designing interactive systems - DIS '14*, ACM Press, 405–414. http://doi.org/10.1145/2598510.2600889
9. Jessica Hammer and Kaitlin Heller. 2012. Playing History: How Ars Magica Players Develop Historical Literacy. *Meaningful Play*. Retrieved October 29, 2016 from http://meaningfulplay.msu.edu/proceedings2012/mp2012_submission_7.pdf
10. Jessica Hammer, Alexandra To, K. Schrier, S. Bowman, and Geoff Kaufman. Role-playing Games and Learning. In *The Handbook of RPG Studies*.
11. Carlos Klimick, Eliane Bettocchi, and Rian Rezende. 2016. The Incorporeal Project: Teaching through Tabletop RPGs in Brazil. *Analog Game Studies*.
12. Marilyn Kourilsky. 1993. Economic Education and a Generative Model of Mislearning and Recovery. *The Journal of Economic Education* 24, 1: 23–33. http://doi.org/10.1080/00220485.1993.10844776
13. Heng-Yu Ku, Hung Wei Tseng, and Chatchada Akarasriworn. 2013. Collaboration factors, teamwork satisfaction, and student attitudes toward online collaborative learning. *Computers in Human Behavior* 29, 3: 922–929. http://doi.org/10.1016/j.chb.2012.12.019
14. J. Lean, J. Moizer, M. Towler, and C. Abbey. 2006. Simulations and games: Use and barriers in higher education. *Active Learning in Higher Education* 7, 3: 227–242. http://doi.org/10.1177/1469787406069056
15. Ben Lehman. 2011. These are our games: Polaris. Retrieved March 25, 2016 from http://www.tao-games.com/polaris/
16. M Montola. 2009. The invisible rules of role-playing: the social framework of role-playing process. *International journal of role-playing*. Retrieved November 7, 2016 from http://www.ijrp.subcultures.nl/wp-content/uploads/2009/01/montola_the_invisible_rules_of_role_playing.pdf
17. Melissa Paschall and Rolf Wüstenhagen. 2012. More than a game: Learning about climate change through role-play. *Journal of Management Education* 36, 4: 510–543. Retrieved April 14, 2017 from http://journals.sagepub.com/doi/abs/10.1177/1052562911411156
18. Mike Pearl. At This Danish School, LARPing Is the Future of Education. *VICE*. Retrieved March 1, 2016 from http://www.vice.com/read/at-this-danish-school-larping-is-the-future-of-education-482
19. Dennis Schleicher, Peter Jones, and Oksana Kachur. 2010. Bodystorming as embodied designing. *interactions* 17, 6: 47. http://doi.org/10.1145/1865245.1865256
20. Lee Sheldon. 2011. *The Multiplayer Classroom: Designing Coursework as a Game*. Cengage Learning. Retrieved March 1, 2016 from https://books.google.com/books?hl=en&lr=&id=qYMLAAAAQBAJ&pgis=1
21. Emily Short. 2012. San Tilapian Studies (a casual narrative entertainment for 30-40 players). *Wordpress*. Retrieved March 24, 2016 from https://emshort.wordpress.com/2012/08/30/san-tilapian-studies-a-casual-narrative-entertainment-for-30-40-players/

22. Kristian T. Simsarian. 2003. Take it to the next stage: the roles of role playing in the design process. *CHI '03 extended abstracts on Human factors in computing systems - CHI '03*, ACM Press, 1012–1013. http://doi.org/10.1145/765891.766123
23. Stephen Slota, Kevin Ballestrini, and Mark Pearsall. 2013. Learning Through Operation LAPIS— A Game-Based Approach to the Language Classroom. *The Language Educator*, 36–38. Retrieved from http://practomime.com/pdf/tle_art.pdf
24. Constance Steinkuehler. 2006. The Mangle of Play. *Games and Culture* 1, 3: 199–213. Retrieved April 14, 2017 from http://journals.sagepub.com/doi/abs/10.1177/1555412006290440
25. BW Tuckman. 1964. Personality structure, group composition, and group functioning. *Sociometry*. Retrieved March 24, 2016 from http://www.jstor.org/stable/2785659
26. Moyra Turkington. 2016. War Birds. Game.
27. Matt Wilson. 2004. Primetime Adventures | Dog Eared Designs. Retrieved March 25, 2016 from http://www.dog-eared-designs.com/primetime-adventures/
28. Yen-Chen Yen, Huei-Tse Hou, and Kuo En Chang. 2015. Applying role-playing strategy to enhance learners' writing and speaking skills in EFL courses using Facebook and Skype as learning tools: a case study in Taiwan. *Computer Assisted Language Learning* 28, 5: 383–406. http://doi.org/10.1080/09588221.2013.839568
29. JE Zins. 2004. *Building academic success on social and emotional learning: What does the research say?* Retrieved March 24, 2016 from https://books.google.com/books?hl=en&lr=&id=MuDGDHCb_iwC&oi=fnd&pg=PR7&dq=student+emotion+learning&ots=oGcyn8OEA_&sig=nMY95f5g-BkM1DW7up9Hplq1aHo

Understanding Engagement within the Context of a Safety Critical Game

Jennefer Hart[1], Ioanna Iacovides[1], Anne Adams[1], Manuel Oliveira[2] and Maria Magroudi[2]

[1]Institute of Educational Technology,
The Open University, Milton Keynes, UK
{jennefer.hart, jo.iacovides,
anne.adams}@open.ac.uk

[2]HighSkillz,
London, UK
{manuel.oliveira,
maria.magroudi}@highskillz.com

ABSTRACT
One of the most frequent arguments for deploying serious games is that they provide an engaging format for student learning. However, engagement is often equated with enjoyment, which may not be the most relevant conceptualization in safety-critical settings, such as law enforcement and healthcare. In these contexts, the term 'serious' does not only relate to the non-entertainment purpose of the game but also the environment simulated by the game. In addition, a lack of engagement in a safety-critical training setting can have serious ethical implications, leading to significant real-world impacts. However, evaluations of safety-critical games (SCGs) rarely provide an in-depth consideration of player experience. Thus, in relation to simulation game-based training, we are left without a clear understanding of what sort of experience players are having, what factors influence their engagement and how their engagement relates to learning. In order to address these issues, this paper reports on the mixed-method evaluation of a SCG that was developed to support police training. The findings indicate that engagement is supported by the experience *situational relevance,* due to the player's experience of *real-world authenticity, targeted feedback mechanisms* and *learning challenges.*

Author Keywords
Serious Games; Game Based Learning; Engagement; Player Experience; Business Simulation; Safety Critical; Police Training.

ACM Classification Keywords
H.5.m. Information interfaces and presentation (e.g., HCI): Miscellaneous; K.8.0. General: Games.

ACM ISBN 978-1-4503-4898-0/17/10…$15.00
https://doi.org/10.1145/3116595.3116633

INTRODUCTION
The term serious games i.e. games that are used for purposes other than pure entertainment [13] is a wide reaching one that has been applied to a vast array of games that have been used for within education, advertising, training across a range of domains [6; 13]. In relation to training specifically, games have gained increasing popularity in the recent years and have been advocated as promising technologies for the support of training within sectors such as education, the emergency services, the military and healthcare [36; 44]. Many of these games can be described as safety-critical games (SCGs) since they are used to support training in domains where mistakes can have grave psychological or physical consequences in the real-world settings (e.g. law enforcement, firefighting, healthcare etc.).

While there are many reasons why serious games can support effective learning e.g. through providing authentic contexts and safe environments [11; 43], the perception that they are engaging is perhaps the most prevalent [e.g. 2; 21]. However, in relation to SCGs specifically, there are surprisingly few studies that examine the wider player experience and the factors that influence it. This is despite widespread consensus that engagement is a necessary part of learning [14; 22; 30; 41] and without a comprehensive understanding of how engagement and learning can be supported, there is a significant risk that an SCG will not be successful in achieving its aims.

Engagement is a complex construct and it has been conceptualized in a variety of ways. Within HCI, the emphasis has primarily been on "enjoyment", which usually describes positive cognitive and affective appraisal of a game experience [31]. Similar, within game-based learning, there is a desire to harness the motivational power of games [25] through promoting intrinsic motivation [30] and providing the "fun factor" [45]. However, as Bogost [6] notes, the "serious" component of a serious game sometimes relates to the nature of the content and, in the case of SCGs, fun and positive affect may not be the most appropriate concepts to have in mind when considering what sort of player experience you want learners to have and how best to support their engagement.

In this paper, we describe the results of an evaluation of a SCG that focused on training police officers to take initial witness accounts from children. Through doing so, our research aims to provide an in-depth exploration of the factors that influence engagement with game-based safety-critical training.

RELEVANT WORK

Within this section, we first provide an overview of how engagement has been conceptualized within the field of HCI and games, as well as in relation to game-based learning. We then discuss the literature on safety-critical games and player experience evaluation. Finally, we provide some background to the project by providing a brief explanation of police training and then introduce the SCG developed.

Engagement and learning in Games

Mekler et al. [31] indicate that there has been a primary focus on enjoyment within studies examining player experiences. In their review of the literature, they note that the focus of evaluations is generally on the positive affective and cognitive appraisal of the game experience. While there are different ways to conceptualize engagement (e.g. in relation to immersion [8], flow [10] and presence [41]), it is generally described as existing on a continuum where players can be more or less involved depending on the exact nature of their experience [7; 9].

There are also many ways to assess engagement, including such as the Immersion Experience Questionnaire [24] and a scale to measure flow [42]. However, both these examples focus on understanding very specific aspects of the gameplay experiences; the IEQ emphasizes cognitive involvement and the flow scale relates to identifying an extreme experience rather than more general engagement. Another example is the Game Experience Questionnaire [32], which was designed to provide a comprehensive evaluation of the player experience. While Cairns et al [9] point out that validation work on the GEQ has not been published they also suggest the scale covers wider aspects of the gaming experience (e.g. negative affect such as frustration). They also note it has been widely applied, including in the context of educational games [e.g. 27].

In terms of the relationship between games and learning, it has long been argued that games are intrinsically motivating [30], where they are able to engage learners through a combination of fantasy, rules/goals, sensory stimuli, challenge, mystery and control [14]. Despite the acceptance that games can provide motivating experiences, designers of educational games still face a challenge in relation to effectively blending (presumably 'boring') learning with engagement and 'fun' with, as evidence by use of the term 'serious games'. There has been research looking at frameworks that can support this process [e.g. 19] while other work has argued that, rather than how intrinsic the 'fantasy' is within a game, learning content needs to be tightly coupled with core game mechanics in order to ensure that players will experience both engagement and successful learning [17]. In the context of education and training, the risks of not considering the overall player experience are significant; if players do not find the game to be engaging, then learning is unlikely to result and the main purpose will not be achieved.

Safety critical games

The risk of providing an unsuccessful learning experience is especially severe within the area of safety-critical training. In these contexts (including domains healthcare, emergency services, crisis management etc.), the potential consequences of providing inadequate training could result in significant physical or psychological harm being caused to people in the real world. Though there are some exceptions [see 40 for a different approach], the majority of SCGs attempt to provide mimetic (rather than abstracted) simulations of practice due to a desire to provide realistic learning experiences within a 'safe' space [44] and to increase the chances of transferring learning outside of the game [43]. Game elements are usually used to convey different forms of information to players as a way of indicating progress and providing feedback on performance. Arguably, these sorts of games are quite different to serious games that are more abstract (e.g. that occur in a fantasy world) and which are less focused on supporting procedural forms of learning. However, despite the emphasis on safety-critical scenarios, engagement with SCGs is still sometimes considered as being about 'enjoyment', yet there are surprisingly few studies that examine the player experience in any real depth.

For instance, Di Loreto, Mora & Divitini [12] when providing an overview of serious games for crisis management highlight the importance of the "fun factor" in stimulating motivation to play and state that "a serious game is a way of providing participants with a fun experience from which they can learn more about themselves and their interaction with their world" (p 352). While the literature suggests that factors such as the level of realism, which is usually interpreted as graphical fidelity [e.g. 28, 40, 44] and feedback [e.g. 11; 18] are noted as being important to learning within a simulation-based context, it is unclear how they relate to the experience of engagement. Without a deeper understanding how these concepts relate to each other, there is a risk that learners will not spend the time and energy necessary to deeply engage in training when they are not requested to as part of an evaluation study.

With regard to police training, there are some examples of games that have been developed including one for dealing with accident investigations [4]. A 3D training environment was created for the Dubai Police force, involving a traffic accident scenario where officers are able to practice procedures such as placing traffic cones, photographing the scene etc. While they did find significant learning effects between those who used a game and a control group (who did not play the game), they did not look at comparing engagement between the game produced and any existing forms of training (as this did not exist). Additionally, they choose to focus on presence by adapting an existing questionnaire [35] to measure the subjective experience felt by the participants of 'being there' in the accident scene." [P.340; 4]. However, beyond looking at differences between novice and experts, it is unclear why they chose this measure. Since the focus of the scale is mainly on the experience of spatial habitation (which does not necessarily relate to engagement [9]) the findings do not provide much insight into whether learners actually found the game to be engaging. Though some open-ended comments were collected from participants, these do not appear to have been reported in detail. In addition to the fact that a comparison could not be made to any other type of training, it is thus quite hard to establish what it is about the game that led to learning and what factors influence player engagement.

In another example, Linssen et al. [28], present a preliminary evaluation of Loiter (LOItering Teenagers, an Emergent Role-play) a game that focused on training Dutch police officers in the interpersonal skills required for street interventions. In this case the emphasis was less on training officers to follow certain procedures and more on supporting the development of social interaction skills (including verbal responses and physical stance). The developers sought to represent feedback to players in the form of "thought bubbles" (that represent how game characters are reacting to the player) and flashbacks relating to previous actions. While the mechanisms appear to be an interesting way to make the effects of player actions more explicit, they did not lead to improvement in learning measures. The authors also mention they asked player to rate their experience on a number of Likert scales, but unfortunately little information is supplied about what scales were used, and the results are not presented. Some brief information is provided about open-ended comments, which suggested the game wasn't very challenging. A further investigation into the overall player experience and how players engaged with the game may have yielded further insight into ways to improve the game and establishing how best to support player learning.

These studies indicate that engagement is often not given a significant amount of attention in the context of safety-critical games. Questions remain about what player experiences with these games actually involve and what factors seem to contribute to engagement. In order to further explore these issues, we present an evaluation of a game that was created for the UK police force to support the training of new officers in taking an initial account from a child witness.

Background to project

The Child Interview Simulator (CIS) was developed as a serious game to support the training of new UK police recruits in collecting initial witness accounts from children. In addition to learning, the trainees develop the necessary confidence to relate to children, which previously has only come from experience. The CIS provides an interactive scenario where one assumes the role of an officer that needs to interview a nine-year-old boy, who allegedly witnessed a woman being attacked on his way home from school. The diagram in Figure 1 shows an overview of story structure, which consists of two distinct episodes. The first episode requires the trainee to take an 'initial account' from the child at their home, whilst the second episode takes the trainee through the process of how to conduct a full ABE (Achieving Best Evidence) interview with the child.

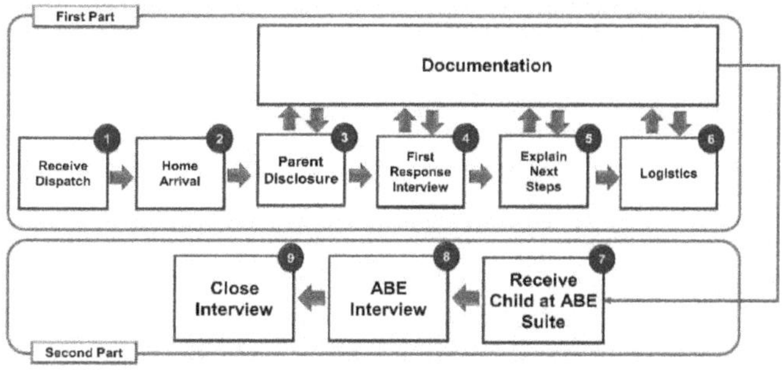

Figure 1. Story structure overview

The police domain and thus the police training experience have traditionally been driven by both empirical and experiential knowledge [33, 34]. In designing and evaluating this game we have taken insights from both the gaming and criminology literature to inform the development process. Police training is set within a safety-critical context where our focus is the training of new police officers. Engagement with learning is critical since it must lead to an embedded understanding for the police that will influence life and death decision making. To achieve effective real-world understanding the game must engage the learners in acquiring both tacit knowledge, and formal procedural knowledge.

The game was co-created with a multidisciplinary team (experts in child interviewing, police trainers, experienced police officers, game developers and academic researchers). An agile development approach was adopted, with iterative releases of the game that used storyboards, interactive mock-ups and subsequent software prototypes until the final version was produced.

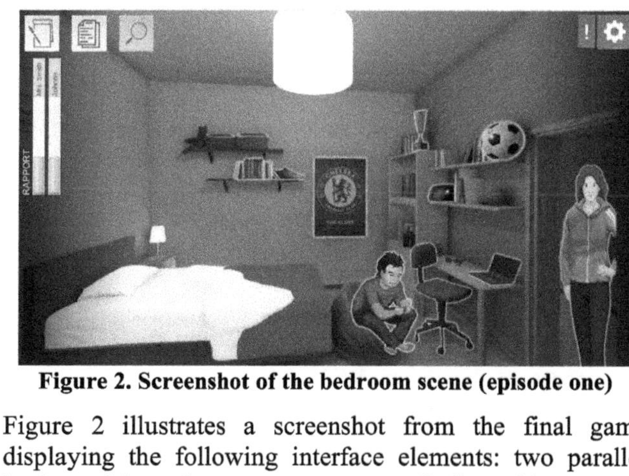

Figure 2. Screenshot of the bedroom scene (episode one)

Figure 2 illustrates a screenshot from the final game displaying the following interface elements: two parallel horizontal bars that represent rapport (indicated by a green feedback bar that moves up or down depending on the players interactions); a notepad icon, where players can refer to past conversations they have had; an ABE form icon, which players are prompted to complete during their conversations; and the observe icon, which allows players to return to the room from the conversation menu. When entering the conversation mode, this scene is partially covered by the menu that enables players to ask questions about various topics via multiple-choice options. Different interactive objects are highlighted (with a white border), that invite players to observed these by clicking on them (thus opening up further dialogue options).

At different development stages, formative testing and validation was carried out that focused on different aspects such as game mechanics, interface design, and the dialogue engine. For example, testing was carried out to ensure that players would be able to interpret the emotions displayed by the characters [29], as this is a significant part of rapport building. The feedback collected at different stages yielded important insights that shaped many aspects of the SCG, including the storyline, aesthetics, content, dialogue and the mechanics. Further examples of these insights include:

- In an initial exploratory workshop, participants were shown existing games and interactive mock-ups with both 2D and 3D visual experiences. The conclusion was that the environment would benefit from the realism of 3D, but with the requirement of non-verbal communication cues (that associated with the emotional state of the child), would be easier to interpret with 2D.
- To contribute to rapport building, the game allows for the exploration of the environment by inviting closer observation, as a way of uncovering topics of interest to discuss with the different characters. The testing of the game demonstrated that the initial themes of football and electronic games needed to be extended as trainees had different backgrounds and required other clues to trigger their curiosity.
- The player needs to be mindful of building and maintaining rapport with the characters in the story, as this will unlock particular story branches and responses from the characters. It soon became clear that players had a low tolerance of convoluted story plots where the actions in one scene would impact on the outcomes much later in the game.
- Between each scene in a scenario, players are given detailed feedback on their performance along three dimensions (interview skills, rapport building and process). An assessment on each learning outcome was also given (fulfilled, partially fulfilled and fail), but feedback from the users indicated that it was necessary to provide further hints in the assessment of what to do differently when an outcome was not achieved.
- The dialogue interface was seen as crucial for the success of the game. With the release of the first full featured prototype, it was evident that interface difficulties created poor usability. A complete redesign of the interface was carried out, resulting in a simpler and more intuitive interaction flow.

METHOD

This research forms part of a larger Randomized Control Trial (RCT) within the UK, currently being conducted to elicit knowledge acquisition specific to collecting first accounts from child. As the RCT aims to collect quantitative data from over 100 participants, this aspect of the research is ongoing and will be reported in a later publication. The focus of this paper is on evaluating the overall player experience of the game, where data has been collected from a total of 65 participants. A mixed methods approach was adopted, that involved questionnaires and focus groups. The questionnaires provide background to the qualitative findings, which provides the main focus of the analysis.

Participants

Data was collected from a total of 65 new recruit police officers across two different UK police forces that were currently on their 13-16-week 'Initial Police Learning and Development Programme' (IPLDP). There were slightly more male (54%) to female participants, with 81% falling below the age of 35, and just under half (49%) having obtaining a university level degree. Just over half the participants (52%) did not consider themselves as gamers.

Design Plan

Quantitative data was captured at two key points during the IPLDP, the first just after a 3-5 day witness interview-training course (the length depended on the force) and then again after interacting with the simulation. Although the interview training did not focus specifically on collecting first accounts from children, it provided the closest type of face-to-face training, so was used as a baseline for comparison. All UK police officers and staff are provided with a wide variety of online-learning training courses that are accessed via a Managed Learning Environment (MLE), maintained by the National Centre for Applied Learning Technologies (NCALT). Training involves a mix of mandatory and self-selected online training courses, which forms a large part of the IPLDP student training.

Qualitative data was captured post-interaction with the simulation through eight focus groups (which varied in number N=5-18) following a semi-structured interview guide. These typically lasted between 20-25 minutes and were led by one of the authors. Questionnaire data was collected via an online survey tool, while the qualitative data was audio recorded for later transcription, and took place within two police force training centers.

Measures

Two short questionnaires were used to capture participant's attitudes towards their different training methods. The first asked participants to rate the value of four types of training, *Face-to-face, Role-based, Online* and *Game-based* using a 5-point Likert scale (1=low, 5=high). This was administered just after students received the witness training, and then again after they interacted with the game. The second questionnaire was the 'in-game' concise 14-item version of the Game Experience Questionnaire (GEQ) scale [32], which measures seven components (*competence, sensory & imaginative immersion, flow, tension, challenge, negative affect,* and *positive affect)*. The same questionnaire was used to compare participants' experiences of the 3-5 day witness interview training with their experience of CIS. Although this questionnaire is aimed at player experience, using the same questions (with slight alteration) enabled us to compare the traditional face-to-face training, with game-based training. The concise version of the GEQ was selected to avoid questionnaire fatigue through having participants fill the GEQ multiple times. Additional questionnaires from the user experience field [26; 37] were collected post-interaction to capture usability, utility and overall quality.

The focus groups were guided by a series of around 12 open questions that acted as prompts to guide discussion. Questions focused on capturing five key areas, *Learning, Usefulness, Relevance* and *Engagement*, along with the general *Likes and Dislikes*.

QUANTITATIVE ANALYSIS

Quantitative questionnaire data was collected from participants and analyzed using excel and SPSS.

Quantitative Findings

Quantitative data was collected from participants, where they were asked to rate the value of different forms of training they had experienced. The Interview-Witness training consisted of both *Face-2-Face* and *Role-based* training, while police *Online* training forms a fundamental part of the wider IPLDP training program. The online training is used to support classroom training, where students take at least 5 or more courses per week, depending on the force requirement. Out of the 65 participants who took part in the focus groups, 45 also filled in questionnaires just after the Interview-Witness training, and just after the Simulation Game-based training. Since not all participants had prior experience of game-based training, only 24 of the 45 provided value ratings for this approach.

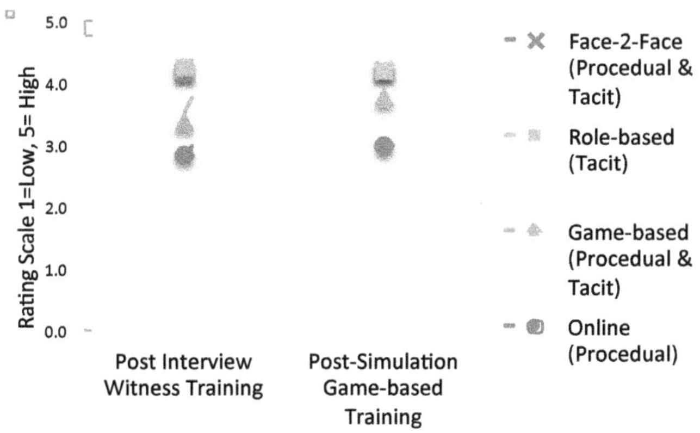

Figure 3. Value mean ratings comparing 4 different training methods between post-interview and post-game.

Participants' ratings for the value of *Face-to-Face training* (N=45) showed no change between post interview (M=4.2, SD=0.88) and post game assessment (M=4.2, SD=0.9). Similarly little difference was found for the *Role-based* training (N=45) post-interview (M=4.3, SD=0.86) and post game (M=4.2, SD=0.75). Ratings for both *Face-to-Face* and *Role-based* training were generally higher than the two technology based training *(Online* or *Game-based)*. However, the *Game-based* training (N=24) showed an increase in ratings post interview (M=3.4, SD=0.88) to post game (M=3.8, SD=1.07) after participants had interacted with the game, where a slight increase was also found for the *Online* training ratings (N=45) from post interview (M=2.8, SD=1.03) to post game (M=3.0, SD=1.17), see Figure 3.

The same 45 participants, also provided responses to the 14-item 'in-game' GEQ questionnaires for both the interview-witness training and game-based training (see Table 1). A paired-samples t-test was conducted to evaluate the difference between the witness training and game-based training ratings for each of the seven components within the GEQ. There were significant differences for 2 (out of 7) components; *'Flow'* t (44)=-3.8, $p < .001$, $d=0.57$, and *Negative Affect* t (44)=2.24, $p < .05$, $d=0.33$. No significant differences were found for the remaining 5 GEQ components, *Competence* t (44)=1.3, $p = .111$, $d=0.19$, *Sensory & Imaginative Immersion* t (44)=-1.1, $p = .283$, $d=-0.16$, *Tension* t (44)=-1.7, $p = .093$, $d=-0.26$, *Challenge* t (44)=1.6, $p = .111$, $d=0.24$, and *Positive Affect* t (44)=-0.29 $p = .775$, $d=-0.43$.

Five Items from in-game GEQ	Witness Training	Game-based Training
Flow**	M= 2.3, (SD= 0.89)	M= 2.9, (SD= 0.98)
Negative Affect*	M= 2.1, (SD= 0.82)	M= 1.8, (SD= 0.83)
Competence	M= 3.5, (SD= 0.66)	M= 3.4, (SD= 0.69)
Sensory	M= 3.4, (SD= 0.83)	M= 3.6, (SD= 1.00)
Tension	M= 1.8, (SD= 0.77)	M= 2.0, (SD= 0.99)
Challenge	M= 3.5, (SD= 1.01)	M= 3.2, (SD= 0.93)
Positive Affect	M= 3.3, (SD= 0.64)	M= 3.3, (SD= 0.72)

**Sig - p < 001, *Sig - p <05

Table 1. Interview & game-based training GEQ comparison

Participants rated the game higher for *Flow*, indicating they found it more absorbing than the witness training, which was rated significantly higher for *Negative Affect*. Thus, CIS was experienced as more likely to hold attention, while the more traditional face-2-face witness training was viewed as being more boring and tiresome.

User experience ratings for the game-based training were also collected from the same 45 participants: *Usability* (M=2.9. SD=1.4), *Utility* (M=3.2, SD=1.4), and *Overall Quality* (M=3.1, SD=1.5) The ratings were all above average, indicating the CIS provided a reasonable user experience, with some areas for improvement, e.g. usability issues with the ABE form, text clarity, cross-force relevance (in relation to dispatch procedures) and problems with scrolling without using mice (as identified from the qualitative comments).

Overall the quantitative findings identified that the game-based training was more engaging that the interview witness training, as indicated by two of the components (*Flow* and *Negative Affect*) within the GEQ questionnaire. The value ratings (Fig 3.) for game-based learning also saw the largest increase (as compared to other forms of training) after participants interacted with the game. While these are useful indicators, these findings do not explain what aspects of the in-game player experience contributed to player engagement and why.

QUALITATIVE ANALYSIS

The qualitative data gathered from the focus groups aimed to unpick the factors and reasons behind participants' positive quantitative ratings through addressing the following research question: What factors influence engagement with game-based training in a safety-critical setting?

Qualitative data was collected from eight focus groups (involving 65 participants in total, including the 45 participants who completed the questionnaires) where the analysis involved in two stages; top-down and bottom-up coding. Two researchers were involved in developing the codes in order to increase the reliability of the findings [1, 5] – due to the interpretative nature of the analysis, inter-rater coding was not carried out [see 5].

In the first stage, the data was analyzed and coded using a thematic analysis. The themes were pre-defined by insights drawn from the literature e.g. engagement, usefulness etc. Key quotes from the data were categorized according to these initial themes (top-down analysis). The second stage, took a grounded theory approach [16] to analyze the sub-set of the data identified during the first stage. An open coding approach was taken where the data was cross-referenced across the coding groupings to identify new categories for the quotes (bottom-up analysis). The coding was guided by the frequency and fundamentality approach [1]. In summary, the initial analysis of open-ended data put an emphasis on those issues that occurred frequently or those that were deemed in this safety critical context to be of fundamental importance. The approach followed quality guidelines for research [20] and allowed the analysis to maintain links to existing literature knowledge whilst uncovering new themes that were novel to this project [1].

Qualitative Findings

The qualitative findings identified that safety-critical engagement appeared to result from experiencing ***situational relevance*** via ***real-world authenticity, targeted feedback mechanisms***, and ***learning challenges***. We discuss how situational relevance cuts across each of the other three themes. (Please note, each participant quote is labeled by number and focus group e.g. P1, F2 refers to Participant 1, Focus group 2).

Real-world authenticity

Within safety-critical settings there is a particular emphasis on learning authentic and relevant procedures. In police settings, for example, players must engage with key procedural knowledge as this will be tested in court-cases to justify that they have had the right training and know the correct legal processes. The findings identified that many of the players compared this game with current online police training – although there is no current police training for collecting 'initial accounts' from children specifically – which they described as generally focusing more on procedural knowledge and processes. Players valued the way in which the gameplay was able to represent a more authentic situation, as it related to both the tacit skills of dealing with people, as well as learning about how to apply the correct police procedures. Typical online approaches focus the police officer on accurately stepping through the procedures, but without supporting tacit understanding:

"It was really current... the {current online training} I find some of them are ancient, and cause they don't seem real life to me I don't take anything from them" [P11, F 7]

During the development process, one of the key aims was to ensure that a realistic scenario was provided, which included police verification of visual images used within the game. Police experts were also involved to help create and verify the conversation dialogue. Qualitative findings identified that players engaged with the game due to its relevance to reality. In particular it was found that the authenticity provided by the gameplay created learning points and deepened engagement, leading to reflections on how players would later replicate (or not) this behavior within a real-world setting:

"It's the scenario, like you are sat in the police car at the beginning, you have to check the log, you have to call the operator... we've not actually done anything like [that], and it makes you think...what would I actually do on the job" [P7, G5]

Players particularly valued moments where they saw how the gameplay could transfer to real-life activities that they would be likely to encounter outside of the game. Again, their engagement was supported through realistic narratives and character responses within the gameplay:

"I liked you could ask too many questions ... they (the child) just get a bit bored of you... its like realistic in that sense" [P9, G5]

Some of the trainees were aware of barriers when engaging in the activity of talking to children, especially within this safety-critical context of child interviewing. A key finding was that not only did the trainees positively engage with the game, but felt it would impact significantly on their future practice:

"I do feel a little more prepared for going out there and speaking to children" [P5, F1]

In particular, the players noted specific learning points that would guide future practice suggesting that the game could have a longer term impact on their confidence:

"I am fairly confident interacting with children... So I am okay with that side, but the legislation bit, ... that's where the computer will give you the confidence..." [P8, F3]

Their engagement was also evidenced by comments indicating reflections on how they would apply specific learning points in future situations:

"I was thinking as I was going through, if I was to speak to a child now, I would change my type of questioning" [P8, F5]

The findings suggest that the game was able to support engagement through allowing players to take on a particular role and reflect on how this could impact actual practice. While they were aware they where playing a character within the game, they were also able to consider how their in-game identity related to their real-world identity; as one trainee explains:

"You learn to play the game, and you also develop a sort of skill base you can take to reality [P8, F3]

Feedback Mechanisms

Within safety-critical contexts such as policing, the concept of 'wasting time' is not only frowned upon but almost viewed as a dereliction of duty. A game for training can be seen as an inherent distractor, where gameplay could be viewed as wasting valuable time. To counteract this, yet still engage the player, relevant in-game feedback mechanisms were used explicitly to facilitate learning and as a way to make continual references to real-world practice.

In-game mechanisms were used to focus the learners' attention on specific learning points. Players noted the value of these learning points especially when poor procedural decisions within the game resulted in negative consequences. Many of these pathways resembled real life decisions, and players recognized that wrong decisions caused problems later, thus helping to embed their understanding. One example was when players failed to check the correct information (i.e. the address) in the log before making a house call, which results in them being attacked by an axe murder. It is interesting to note that although this was recognized as being somewhat unlikely, the procedural learning point was perceived as relevant and thus reinforced and remembered.

"I got to the door, and I was like I don't even know which flat I'm supposed to be visiting, and it just made me think then, now when I go to a job, I need to know exactly where I going and what I'm going into" [P8, F1]

This particular quote highlights that for engagement in gameplay, the relevance of the learning point was more important than that of a realistic narrative.

In addition, the placing of interactive objects within the gameplay environment was intended to inspire realistic curiosity for potential police officers and provide prompts for discussion with the characters. Whilst interacting with these objects achieved the in-game objective, we also found that this mechanism inspired players to see themselves as investigative police officers looking for 'clues' within the environment:

"Clues in like the trophies, football, you could click on it and it tells them what they're interested in..." [P6, F2]

Again, these sorts of examples show that the players are engaged in the narrative and immersing themselves in the role they are playing.

One of the key learning points of this game (that is critical for police when collecting a first account from a child) was for players to focus on the tacit skills of building trust and understanding the characters. This formed an important part of gameplay, where the players' attention was focused on the need to establish rapport through various feedback mechanisms. For example, by observing (through clicking on) various objects within the environment the officer can find topics of interest to communicate with the different characters prior to questioning, thus simulating being observant and picking up clues in the real-world. Through, selecting various topics of interest the police officer gains the child's attentions and respect (if the appropriate questions are selected). Again it was the real-world relevance of this gameplay activity that made it engaging for the police trainees.

"Having a look around the room... that's what you do when you normally go into a room... you look around" [P 7, F 2]

To focus player attention on this learning more explicitly and to provide in-game feedback a Rapport Bar (the green level that increased or decrease according the players' gameplay – see Figure 2) was used to show the players' current rapport levels. This mechanism provided valuable in-game feedback that changed as a result of objects and responses, thus focusing attention on developing tacit social skills. Comments showed that the rapport bar increased player interest and aided motivation:

"You were conscious of that green bar, so it kept you alert the whole time" [P10, F7]

Even in cases where the player found the gameplay less interesting, the feedback provided by the Rapport Bar was able to positively influence involvement by providing a counterbalancing focus for attention and further stimulation:

"Cause you do want that green bar to go up, even if you're bored you want that bar to go up" [P4, F5]

In addition, this stimulating of attention also seemed to motivate some players to think more deeply about their learning through their gameplay, thus indicating a continued sense of engagement:

"You've got like a target, you concentrate on that green bar, and I thought... I've got to think about my answers here..." [P2, F4]

Learning challenges

The final theme concerns how engagement related to experiencing relevant learning challenges within the game. The players talked about the relationship between frustration and learning, which once they had overcome, produced a rewarding experience. When making decisions within the game, players were able to engage in safety-critical learning through the feedback mechanisms and different storylines (e.g. when they were faced with an axe murderer after following incorrect procedures). Arguably, engagement and learning were successfully woven together, as players became aware of their responsibility and took ownership for their learning journey by putting effort into the game:

"It does make you think... because it makes people actually do their own research" [P11, F1]

Similarly, players were able to clearly identify engagement as the pathway to successfully learning from the game. Several players also stated that while this was not a simple process, they valued the learning that resulted from overcoming challenges in the game:

"You have to engage in it to do well ... people may find that frustrating but ultimately you're forcing that person to learn" [P9, F8]

For some this engagement was a simple relationship between feedback mechanisms reinforcing what they did and didn't know. The feedback produced at the end of each scene would indicate if players had missed something, thus creating a further challenge for them to engage in:

"I just wanted to get all my stars but the thing that got me down was the process that I didn't know, but then it got me dead annoyed... but it made sense"[P8, F7]

For others, the gameplay could produce a deeper more dynamic interaction between engagement, ownership and motivation, thus highlighting the value of sustained learning:

"It makes it more memorable... cause you can actually refer it back to the game, I would remember it" [P12, F8]

Ultimately the game was able to generate effective engagement that incited learner reflections around key learning points:

"Gaining your rapport. It's common sense, if you think about it but you don't always think about it." [P2, F7]

DISCUSSION

Engagement is frequently provided as a rationale for the use of serious games. However, within the context of games that provide safety-critical training, the literature lacks a clear understanding of what sort of experiences players are having and what factors influence their engagement. In this paper, we explore these questions through presenting the player experience evaluation of a SCG that aims to train new police recruits in obtaining 'initial accounts' from child witnesses. A mixed-methods approach was used that captured quantitative survey data on usability and game experience, while qualitative findings provided a deeper understanding of player engagement through identifying the factors that influence engagement and potentially learning.

The quantitative value ratings suggest that players preferred game-based learning to online-training, while the UX ratings suggested that the game was able to provide a reasonable user experience that was unlikely to get in the way of deeper levels of engagement. The GEQ results also indicated that participants found a 45-minute play session with CIS to be more absorbing than the 3-5 day training events, as well as being less boring and tiresome. While these results do suggest the game was somewhat engaging when compared to other forms of training, the qualitative findings were able to provide more in-depth insights into the experiences of players and how intrinsically learning and engagement were intertwined. In the context of SCGs engagement appears to be less about 'enjoyment' and more about the relevance of the game to players. The findings illustrate how situational relevance was supported through providing real-world authenticity, targeted feedback mechanisms, and learning challenges.

In relation to real world authenticity, previous research has investigated how the level of realism can influence learning [e.g. 38]. However, the focus tends to be on the level of graphical fidelity - with a consideration of whether higher realism can improve learning or even distract novices due to creating additional complexity [e.g. 39]. During the development phase, testing suggesting that 2D animation would be more effective in a safety-critical context, as it enabled players to focus more specifically on learning points. Furthermore, the qualitative findings indicated that relevance was more important than realism for engagement. Through providing a scenario based on the real world, the players were able to relate their gameplay experience to their practice. The authenticity of the game narrative may have helped players narrow the gap between their virtual and real-world identities (through adopting what Gee [15] refers to as a 'projective identity') where they could reflect on their own learning.

In addition, the relevance of the learning points seemed to be more important to players than attempting to provide them with a completely realistic environment. For instance, the fact that players would encounter an axe-murderer if they did not check the address properly was not a particularly realistic outcome but it did provide a valuable learning point that emphasized the value of following particular procedural steps.

These learning points were also facilitated through feedback mechanisms that helped to focus a player attention on the relevance of both tacit and procedural learning. Feedback is seen as an important way to support learning in games [18], though these findings also illustrate how feedback can support engagement through indicating in-game progress. While the rapport bar is obviously not something that exits outside of the game, it was able to provide relevant real-time feedback on player actions that they could use to progress in the game. In addition, the interactive objects also supported engagement by prompting players to explore the environment and think about how they could create rapport with the other characters.

Feedback mechanisms are also closely linked to the learning challenges provided within the game. Players were required to try and build rapport and carry out the correct procedures, in order to effectively collect an initial witness account from the child. As in real-life, they had to engage in decision making, where their actions could result in different consequences. While wrong decisions may have caused short-term frustration, this also led to a stronger embedding of learning as players were provided with information about how to improve their performance. Challenge is generally seen as important for facilitating engagement in games [14; 30, 31], but also plays a role in learning, where, for example, Iacovides et al [22] illustrate the ways in which breakdowns provide opportunities for players to develop deeper understanding. While the feedback is the CIS may have challenged players, arguably this led to more rewarding experiences in the longer term where players learned how to improve their performance not online within the game, but in the real-world setting.

Through a combination of creating authentic experiences, delivering informative feedback and providing learning challenges the game was able to effectively engage players and create an absorbing learning experience. Both engagement and learning appeared to result from the merging of procedural tasks and tacit in-game feedback-mechanisms (e.g., active objects, rapport bar), which were interwoven with decision-making within the storyline (e.g. selecting appropriate questions, paying attention to information). In relation to creating a game within a safety-critical context, it is particularly important to ensure that relevance related to each of the three factors outlined – where engagement appeared to result from how players valued their in-game experiences for informing their practice as police officers.

Design implications

In relation to developing an engaging SCG, we suggest adopting a 3-step design approach: (1) identify the contextual relevant learning points (both tacit and procedural) for the game, (2) create relevant scenarios to represent those learning points and then (3) develop game mechanisms that produce and guide players through the scenario and key learning points. To ensure relevance, key stakeholders should be involved throughout the process and iterative testing will need to be carried with experts and members of the target population. This process can help to ensure that authentic experiences are provided along with informative feedback and appropriate learning challenges.

Based on our experience, we present the following design recommendations for guiding players through key learning points within an SCG (step 3):

Avoid assumptions about the gaming literacy of the target population: while the popularity of gaming has increased within society, not all trainees will be familiar with gaming controls and mechanics. The initial dialogue system had to be replaced, as it was too complicated for those who did not regularly play computer games. The audience for SCGs is likely to consist of people who have different degrees of familiarity with games. If basic controls can be mastered by non-gamers easily, then a much wider proportion of the target audience will be likely to experience engagement.

Players welcome complexity, but ensure sufficient support to solve the challenges: although players accept responsibility for wrong decisions that lead to failure, the learning experience does not terminate with completion of the narrative. It is important to adequately support reflection concerning mistakes through providing sufficient insight as to how to perform better next time, thus mitigating the short-term frustration. Doing so will help to ensure that players find feedback relevant and understand how it relates to their real-world practice. In some cases, this will be a matter of careful calibration, but in others, it may require a redesign of the narrative.

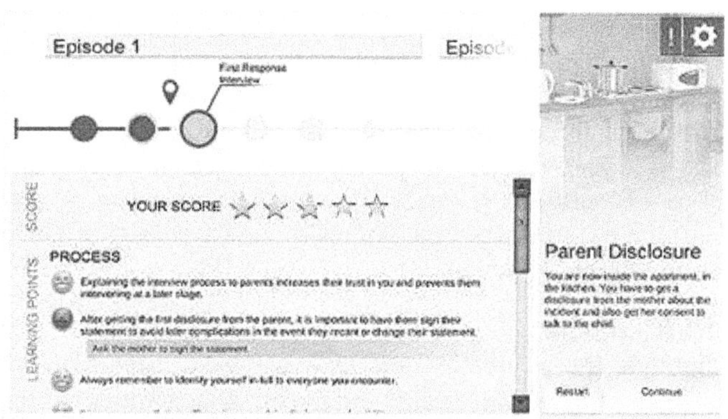

Figure 4: Feedback after one of the in-game scenes

Keep scoring as simple as possible: initially performance was represented by an overall score, decomposed further into the three dimensions (interview skills, rapport building and following process). However, players had difficulties interpreting the feedback so this was replaced with a simpler system (see Figure 4) that provided clearer feedback for what players needed to go back and focus on.

Limitations and future work

One of the main limitations of the study relates to the lack of equivalent police training in the collection of first accounts from children, which means direct comparisons could not be made with non-game based training. However, it is important that when developing novel approaches that at least a relative comparison is made, so we looked instead to more general forms of witness training.

Another potential limitation concerns the fact that we did not explicitly consider the impact of prior gaming experience outside of development testing. While engagement may have been influenced by how players identified as gamers [23], this was not something that seemed to come out of the focus groups. However, future research could be carried out to explicitly focus on the influence of prior gaming experience on engagement and learning within a SCG.

In addition, we did not report any measures of learning within this paper, as the work is still ongoing. This research forms part of a larger body of current work that investigates the effectiveness of game-based training, involving a full randomized-control-trial that will collect knowledge ratings from over 100 participants. Instead we focus on understanding player engagement as a necessary component of the wider learning experience.

This research has created great interest within the police, with possibilities of developing further police-related game-based simulations that focus on a range of topics e.g. dealing with vulnerable people, online grooming, stop and search. There is also further potential to adapt the current prototype to achieve different learning goals. Additionally, there has been interest in the wider 'blue-light' (i.e. ambulance, fire-brigade) and disaster recovery contexts. The aim would be to develop a suite of game-based training packages that provide a cost-effective, engaging and effective approach that compliments current training needs. This would then provide further opportunities to examine player engagement and learning across a range of SCGs. The main three areas that require further research are 1) how to effectively design games for learning across a range of safety critical settings; 2) how best to evaluate any learning has occurred and 3) to examine the role of SCGs in future training practices.

CONCLUSION

Through the evaluation of CIS, we have been able to explore the factors related to player engagement in the context of games used for safety-critical training. While engagement is important to consider in relation to serious games in general, it has further ethical considerations for SCGs, where a lack of engagement and inadequate training could have severe consequences in the real world. These findings highlight how engagement is supported by experiencing situational relevance, due to a focus on real-world authenticity, targeted feedback mechanisms, and learning challenges. We also present a summary of a three-step design approach, which emphasizes the importance of incorporating both procedural and tacit learning points, and consider specific design recommendations for developing engaging SCGs.

ACKNOWLEDGMENTS

This work was jointly funding by an initiative between the College of Policing and the Higher Education Funding Council for England (HEFCE). Special thanks to Lancashire Constabulary and Thames Valley Police who contributed in the co-development of game and evaluation.

REFERENCES

1. Anne Adams, Peter Lunt and Paul Cairns. 2008. A qualitative approach to HCI research. In: Cairns, Paul and Cox, Anna eds. *Research Methods for Human-Computer Interaction. Cambridge*, UK: Cambridge University Press, 138–157.
2. António Andrade, David Gouveia, Paula Escudeiro and Carlos Vaz de Carvalho. 2014. Can SME Managers Learn from Games? In *Proc. Interacción '14*, ACM Press, Article No. 96, doi:10.1145/2662253.2662349
3. Jeffrey M. Beaubien and David P. Baker, 2004. The use of simulation for training teamwork skills in health care: How low can you go? *Quality and Safety in Health Care,* 13, i51–i56. doi: 10.1136/qshc.2004.009845
4. Ahmed Binsubaih, Steve Maddock, and Daniela Romano. 2006. A serious game for traffic accident investigators. *Interactive Technology and Smart Education*, 3(4), 329-346. doi: 10.1108/17415650680000071
5. Anne Blandford. 2013. Semi-structured qualitative studies. In: Soegaard M, Dam RF (eds) *The encyclopedia of human-computer interaction*, 2nd edn. The Interaction Design Foundation, Aarhus. Retrieved April 14th 2017: http://www.interaction-design.org/encyclopedia/semi-structured_qualitative_studies.html
6. Ian Bogost. 2007. *Persuasive games: The expressive power of videogames*. Cambridge, MA: The MIT Press.
7. Jeanne H. Brockmyer, Christine M. Fox, Kathleen A. Curtiss, Evan McBroom, Kimberly M. Burkhart, and Jacquelyn N. Pidruzny. 2009. The development of a Game Engagement Questionnaire: A measure of engagement in video game-playing. *J Exp Soc Psychol.* 45, 4, 624-634, doi: Horg/10.1016/j.jesp.2009.02.016
8. Emily Brown and Paul Cairns. 2004. A grounded investigation of game immersion. In *Proc. CHI 2004*, ACM Press, 1279-1300, doi: 10.1145/985921.986048
9. Paul Cairns, Anna L. Cox, A. Imran Nordin. 2014. Immersion in Digital Games: Review of Gaming Experience Research. In MC Angelides and H. Agius, *Handbook of digital games*, Wiley-Blackwell, 339-361.
10. Jenova Chen. 2007. Flow in games (and everything else). *Communications of the ACM*, ACM Press, 50 (4), 31-34, doi: 10.1145/1232743.1232769
11. David Crookall. 2010. Serious games, debriefing, and simulation/gaming as a discipline. *Simulat Gaming*, 41, 898–920, doi: 10.1177/1046878110390784
12. Ines Di Loreto, Simone Mora, Monica Divitini. 2012. Collaborative serious games for crisis management: an overview. In *Proc. IEEE 21st International WETICE*, doi: 10.1109/WETICE.2012.25
13. Simon Egenfeldt-Nielsen, Jonas H. Smith, and Susana P. Tosca. 2008. *Understanding video games: the essential introduction*. New York and London: Routledge.

14. Rosemary Garris, Robert Ahlers and James E. Driskell. 2002. Games, motivation, and learning: A research and practice model. *Simulat Gaming*, 33(4), 441–467, doi: 10.1177/1046878102238607
15. John Paul Gee. 2004. *What video games have to teach us about literacy and learning*. New York: Palgrave Macmillan.
16. Barney G. Glaser and Anslem. L. Strauss , 2009. *The Discovery of Grounded Theory: Strategies for Qualitative Research*. Transaction publishers.
17. M.P. Jacob Habgood and Shaaron E. Ainsworth. 2011. Motivating children to learn effectively: Exploring the value of intrinsic integration in educational games. The *J Learn Sci,* 20, 169–206. doi: http://dx.doi.org/10.1080/10508406.2010.508029
18. Nina, Haferkamp. Nicole C. Kraemer, Conor Linehan, and Massimiliano Schembri. 2011. Training disaster communication by means of serious games in virtual environments. *Entertainment Computing*, 2 (2), 81-88, doi: http://doi.org/10.1016/j.entcom.2010.12.009
19. Joshua V. Hall, Peta Wyeth and Daniel Johnson. 2014. Instructional objectives to core-gameplay: a serious game design technique. In *Proc. CHI PLAY'14*, ACM Press, 121–130, doi: 10.1145/2658537.2658696
20. Karen L. Henwood and Nick F. Pidgeon. 1992. Qualitative research and psychological theorizing. *Brit J Psychol*, 83(1), 97-111, doi: 10.1111/j.2044-8295.1992.tb02426.x
21. Geoffrey Hookham, Keith Nesbitt, and Frances Kay-Lambkin. 2016. Comparing Usability and Engagement between a Serious Game and a Traditional Online Program. In *Proc, of the Australasian Computer Science Week Multiconference*. 54. ACM, doi: 10.1145/2843043.2843365
22. Ioanna Iacovides, Anna L. Cox, Patrick McAndrew, James Aczel, and Eileen Scanlon. 2015. Game-play breakdowns and breakthroughs: exploring the relationship between action, understanding, and involvement. *Human–computer interaction*, 30, 3-4, 202–231, doi:10.1080/07370024.2014.987347
23. Ioanna Iacovides, Patrick McAndrew, Eileen Scanlon and James Aczel. 2014. The gaming involvement and informal learning framework. *Simulat Gaming*. 45 (4-5), 611-626, doi: 10.1177/1046878114554191
24. Charlene Jennett, Anna L. Cox, Paul Cairns, Samira Dhoparee, Andrew Epps, Tim Tijs, Alison Walton. 2008. Measuring and defining the experience of immersion in games. *Int. J. Hum-Comput St*, 66, 641-661, doi: http://doi.org/10.1016/j.ijhcs.2008.04.004
25. John Kirriemuir, Angela Mcfarlane. 2004. *Literature Review in Games and Learning*. A NESTA Futurelab Research report - report 8. 2004. <hal-00190453> Retrieved April 14th 2017 : http://hal.archives-ouvertes.fr/docs/00/19/04/53/PDF/kirriemuir-j-2004-r8.pdf
26. Talia Lavie and Noam Tractinsky. 2004. Assessing dimensions of perceived visual aesthetics of web sites. *Int. J. Hum-Comput St* studies, 60(3), 269-298, doi: 10.1016/j.ijhcs.2003.09.002
27. Effie Lai-Chong Law and Xu Sun. 2012. Evaluating user experience of adaptive digital educational games with activity theory, *Int. J. Hum-Comput St*,70, 478–497, doi: 10.1016/j.ijhcs.2012.01.007
28. Jeroen Linssen, Mariët Theune, Thomas de Groot, and Dirk Heylen. 2015, Improving social awareness through thought bubbles and flashbacks of virtual characters. In *Proc. International Conference on Intelligent Virtual Agents*, 250-259. Springer International Publishing, doi: 10.1007/978-3-319-21996-7_25
29. Maia Margoudi, Jennefer Hart, Anne Adams and Manuel Oliveira .2016. Exploring Emotion Representation to Support Dialogue in Police Training on Child Interviewing. In: *Serious Games JCSG' 16*, Lecture Notes in Computer Science 9894, Springer, 73–86.
30. Thomas W. Malone 1981. Toward a theory of intrinsically motivating instruction. *Cognitive Sci*, 5(4), 333–369, doi: 10.1016/S0364-0213(81)80017-1
31. Elisa D. Mekler, Julia Ayumi Bopp, Alexandre N. Tuch, Klaus Opwis. 2014. A systematic review of quantitative studies on the enjoyment of digital entertainment games. In *Proc. CHI 2014*, ACM Press, 927-936, doi: 10.1145/2556288.2557078
32. Karolien Poels, Yvonne de Kort, and Wijnand A. IJsselsteijn. 2007. D3.3 : *Game Experience Questionnaire: development of a self-report measure to assess the psychological impact of digital games*. Technische Universiteit Eindhoven. Retrieved April 14th 2017: https://pure.tue.nl/ws/files/21666952/Fuga_d3.3.pdf
33. Lawrence Sherman and Richard A Berk. 1984. The specific deterrent effects of arrest for domestic assault. *Am Sociol Rev*, 49(2), 261-272.
34. Lawrence Sherman and David Weisburd. 1995. General deterrent effects of police patrol in crime "hot spots": a randomized, controlled trial. *Justice Quarterly,* 12(4), 625-648, doi: 10.1080/07418829500096221
35. Mel Slater. 1999. Measuring Presence: A Response to the Witmer and Singer Questionnaire, *Presence: Teleop Virt*, 8(5), 560–566, doi: 10.1162/105474699566477
36. Tarja Susi, Mikael Johannesson and Per Backlund. 2007. *Serious Games - An overview*. Technical Report HS- IKI -TR-07-001, School of Humanities and Informatics, University of Skövde, Sweden. Retrieved April 14th 2017: http://www.diva-portal.org/smash/get/diva2:2416/FULLTEXT01.pdf

37. Alistair Sutcliffe and Jennefer Hart. 2017. Analyzing the Role of Interactivity in User Experience. *Int J Hum-Comput Int*, 33(3), 229-240, doi: 10.1080/10447318.2016.1239797

38. Breen Sweeney and Anne Adams. 2009. Virtual world users evaluated according to environment design, task based and affective attention measures. In *Proc. BCS HCI 2009,* 1-5 Sept 2009, Cambridge, UK.

39. Jay Shiro Tashiro, and David Dunlap. 2007. The impact of realism on learning engagement in educational games. In *Proc. Future Play* '07, 113-120, ACM Press, doi: 10.1145/1328202.1328223

40. Zachary O. Toups, Andruid Kerne, William A. Hamilton, W. A., and Nabeel Shahzad. 2011. Zero-fidelity simulation of fire emergency response: improving team coordination learning. In *Proc. CHI '11,* ACM Press. 1959-1968, doi: 10.1145/1978942.1979226

41. Vicki Trowler. 2010. *Student engagement literature review.* Lancaster University, The Higher Education Academy.

42. David Weibel and Bartholomäus Wissmath. 2011. Immersion in computer games: The role of spatial presence and flow. *Intl. Journal of Computer Games Technology*, Article no. 6.

43. Nicola Whitton. 2014. *Digital Games and Learning: Research and Theory*. London, UK: Routledge.

44. F. Michael Williams-Bell, Bernadette Murphy, Bill Kapralos, Andrew Hogue and Elizaeth, J. Weckman. 2015. Using Serious Games and Virtual Simulation for Training in the Fire Service: A Review. *Fire Technol.* 51(3), 553-584. doi:10.1007/s10694-014-0398-1

45. Brian Winn. 2007. Design, play, and experience: A framework for the design of serious games for learning. In R. E. Ferdig (ed.), *Handbook of research on effective electronic gaming in education, Vol. III, Information Science Reference*, Hershey, 1010–1024.

Those are not the Stories you are Looking For: Using Text Prototypes to Evaluate Game Narratives Early

Jason T. Bowey and Regan L. Mandryk
Department of Computer Science, University of Saskatchewan
Saskatoon, SK, Canada, S7N 5C9
{firstname.lastname}@usask.ca

ABSTRACT
In game design, evaluation is important to do early and often; however, evaluating game narratives early in development is an open problem. We don't know how the evaluation of a game narrative will be affected when it is experienced outside of the context of the game's mechanics and graphics. In this paper, we test the plausibility of using a text-based narrative prototype, by evaluating player experience and narrative experience in two studies using different game genres. In both studies, we compare the narrative evaluation of low- and high-fidelity graphics, but in study 1 (N=78), we kept interaction mechanics intact, and in study 2 (N=124), we removed game interaction in the text prototype. We observed no significant differences in player experience or narrative engagement in either study, indicating that text-based narrative prototypes could be an effective playtesting tool for game studios to integrate into their development cycle early.

Author Keywords
narrative; digital games; transportability; prototyping

ACM Classification Keywords
K.8.0 [Personal Computing]: General - Games.

INTRODUCTION
Game evaluation is an important component for a game's eventual critical and commercial success, and as such, should be done early in the development lifecycle and often throughout [31]. Some aspects of games are evaluated easily early in development (e.g., basic mechanics and procedures); however, other aspects are more difficult to evaluate outside of the context of a complete prototype (e.g., accessibility, balance) [17]. Because of the benefits of early evaluation, methods have been proposed for play-testing prototypes of games under development, such as physical prototypes [17] or low-fidelity digital prototypes [17]. Furthermore, researchers have been exploring how the fidelity of the prototype affects the player's experience of the game mechanics and have shown that the evaluation of core mechanics in low-fidelity prototypes of casual games is reliable [19]. Although games user research (GUR) tends to focus on methods that evaluate a game's mechanics and dynamics [25] [26], there are other factors that contribute to play experience – such as narrative experience – that are less well understood or represented in GUR.

CHI PLAY '17, October 15–18, 2017, Amsterdam, Netherlands

ACM ISBN 978-1-4503-4898-0/17/10...$15.00
DOI: https://doi.org/10.1145/3116595.3116636

The evaluation of game narratives is an important aspect of playtesting because incoherent, inconsistent, or boring stories can result in poor critical and commercial reception of a game. In a series of blog posts, interviews, and talks [37,38,50], Bioware, a game studio praised for their successful merging of game and narrative, discuss how they employ narrative prototypes to evaluate the story early in a development process in which the writing team is well integrated with the development team. Bioware partially attribute their critical and commercial success of narrative-based games to this early evaluation and the integration of the different teams. In a counter-example, a blog post-mortem of the game *Destiny* [7], developed by Bungie [44], revealed that the game narrative was rebooted just months before the original release date, leading to delays, and a story that was criticized by reviewers for its vague plot, thin characters, and opaque dialogue. These examples lend support to the idea that narratives should be evaluated early in the development lifecycle of a game.

Questions around the process of early evaluation of game narratives are being asked by games user researchers in both academia and industry. At the 2016 GamesUR Summit [23], there was a panel on the evaluation of narratives that questioned whether or not they could be evaluated early and what effects there might be from evaluating narratives in isolation from the completed game. However, there is little guidance for game designers on the effects of evaluating narratives on prototypes; games user researchers do not currently understand the effects of evaluating an interactive narrative early in the design process – that is, outside of the context of a completed game. For example, will a game narrative be experienced differently if it is disconnected from the immersive and transportative aspects of completed games, such as the high-fidelity graphics? Will a game narrative be experienced differently if disconnected from the control scheme used to interact with the game's mechanics?

In this paper, we ask how game narrative evaluation is affected when embedded in early game prototypes. Specifically, we systematically investigate how the game narrative evaluation is affected if it is disconnected from the high-fidelity graphics of a completed game (study 1) and the mechanics used to control interaction (study 2).

In a first study, we investigated the player experience differences in a narrative-based game with low-fidelity graphics (LoFi) and high-fidelity graphics (HiFi). All other aspects of the games (i.e., interaction and game control) were kept consistent between the two versions to avoid confounding factors that might cause differences in experience. The game used was similar to an interactive narrative, e.g., *The Stanley Parable* [18] We found no statistically-significant differences on any experiential measures and no interactions between a median split of how transportable a player tends to be and fidelity on any experiential measure.

In a second study, we used an adventure game that included more non-narrative interaction (i.e., fighting, running, and shooting). Furthermore, we did not mirror all of the controls and interaction as we did in study 1, but rather prototyped only a very minimal amount of game interaction to replicate a situation closer to what would be seen in industry when games are under development. We also added measures of narrative engagement and transportation. Again, we found no statistically significant differences on experiential measures or narrative engagement. There were also no significant interactions between player transportability and fidelity on any measure. We did, however, see a minor difference in the transportation of players, which showed that players were slightly more transported when playing the LoFi version rather than the HiFi version, consistent with ideas suggested in the literature for other types of narrative immersion, such as Avatar Identification [13].

Our results showed that there were no significant differences in player experience or narrative engagement as a result of playing a narrative prototype as opposed to the full game. These results hold regardless of whether or not the game interaction itself was prototyped and in two different game genres. There was a small positive effect on experienced transportation in the narrative prototype of study 2. Our results suggest that text prototypes of game narratives can be used early in the development of a game, increasing the likelihood of integrating narrative development with system development, and maximizing a game narrative's chance for a successful reception.

RELATED WORK

We first present player and narrative experience, then discuss iterative development and prototyping in games.

Player Experience

Research in studying how players experience games is primarily rooted in psychology. In particular, a common model used as a basis for explaining player experience is needs satisfaction, which is part of the larger theory called Self-Determination Theory (SDT) [42]. SDT explains intrinsic motivation, i.e., doing something for the pure desire to do it, as opposed to being driven by the promise or threat of external rewards [42]. When engaging with an activity, such as a game, an individual's intrinsic motivation to engage in the activity can be broken down into four dimensions: interest-enjoyment, effort-importance, perceived competence, and the amount of tension-pressure felt during the activity. [36] The building blocks that lead to the experience of intrinsic motivation are based on our basic psychological needs: competence, autonomy, and relatedness. In using needs satisfaction in the specific context of play, Ryan et al. added two additional constructs: intuitive controls and immersion-presence [42].

Narrative Experience

Researchers have recently begun extending constructs and ideas from media *psychology* into the realm of digital games [13,22]. For the purposes of this paper, we will distinguish between narrative engagement, experiences which pertain primarily to the game's narrative [8] and narrative immersion, which depend more strongly on non-narrative game elements to create an immersive experience.

Narrative Immersion

Two types of narrative immersion have been used in the context of games: Identification [24] and Transportation [11]. Both types of immersion involve a similar cognitive process in players: a deep immersion into the narrative aspects of the game in which the player loses awareness of the outside world.

A state of immersion through Identification involves the creation of a connection between the player and a character in the game so that the player loses awareness of their outside self, experiencing the game from a different point of view [13]. There are three main ways a player can identify with a character [32]: *similarity identification* - identifying through perceived physical similarities with a character; *embodied presence* - seeing the narrative world through the perspective of a character; and *wishful identification* - when a player sees a character as a desirable version of themselves. Previous work has shown that aspects of player experience, e.g., enjoyment, are predicted by the amount of Identification [4,5] experienced.

Transportation is often described using a traveler metaphor, in which the player is so immersed in the narrative world of a game that they lose sense of their physical surroundings [22]. Transportation is facilitated through the interaction and presentation of the game (i.e., the depth, complexity, and attractiveness of the narrative world) but also through the personality trait *Transportability*, which has been shown to reliably predict transportation [12].

Narrative Engagement

The Narrative Engagement Scale was created by drawing items from a wide selection of narrative measures to create four new subscales measuring narrative-specific experiences: narrative understanding, attentional focus, narrative presence, and emotional engagement [8].

Iterative Development in Interfaces and Games

We describe the iterative cycle (design, development, and evaluation) of interactive systems and games.

Prototyping

In interactive systems and interface design, it is common practice to start with LoFi prototypes and iteratively work up to HiFi versions [1,21]. This process allows designers to quickly explore a wide array of different design directions and possibilities, throwing out those ideas that didn't work without losing a significant amount of time and effort. Various types of prototyping methods have been used, each with varying levels of fidelity: paper prototypes [14], digital mockups and wireframes [28], and interactive prototypes [16]. There is also research that directly compare prototypes of varying fidelity that have found no difference in the number of usability problems between prototyping fidelity [10,47,48], and that users tended to prefer working with a computer prototype compared to a paper prototype [45].

Game designers have used similar approaches to prototype their ideas because games can be seen as a specific type of interactive system. However, previous work has argued that there is more to test in a game than usability, such as playability, which requires game designers to use slightly different prototyping methods [20]. Fullerton describes two levels of fidelity in prototyping: physical paper prototypes and digital prototypes, as well as various tools to create them [17]. Game designers often prototype by starting with simple LoFi assets, such as capsules for characters and boxes for objects in the environment. Previous work has shown that playtesters find the same amount of usability issues in LoFi and HiFi graphic levels [29].

Evaluation

As mentioned, both interface and game designers follow an iterative design strategy. Part of this iterative process is the notion that the product starts at a LoFi stage and increases in fidelity through iteration, but the other essential part of this iterative cycle is the evaluation component that feeds into the next iteration of design.

For interfaces, evaluation may include formal usability inspections [27] heuristic evaluations [27] and cognitive walkthroughs [27] to name a few examples. For games, a different type of user testing can be required because of the increased interaction, which can lead to different kinds of bugs and design problems, often unforeseen by developers. Evaluation strategies have been created for games that have adapted strategies used in interface design – for example heuristic evaluation [40] and usability testing [26], whereas others are more unique to games, such as analytics [15] and playtesting [17]. More advanced playtesting approaches have used modelling techniques to evaluate experience using physiological data [33,34], biometric storyboards [39], and analysis of facial expressions [46]. Additionally, specific tools have been created or adapted from other areas to empirically measure various aspects of players and player experience in games [12,22,32,36,43].

The main idea behind iterative evaluation is for designers to test their current prototype with users to make sure they like it and are able to use it in the intended way. These goals differ for games and interfaces, but the common thread is that users test the prototype and designers use the feedback to make it better. This process is repeated throughout the entire design and development process with quick bursts of development and testing and updating the design to make the product better and easier to use [30].

INDUSTRY APPROACHES TO GAME NARRATIVES

Because industry practices are rarely published in academic venues, and development processes can be a closely guarded secrets for game studios, there is not a large amount of publicly-available information regarding the actual processes that studios use to prototype, test, and integrate narrative structures into their games. To gain knowledge on how some prominent companies do this, we searched for blog posts written by developers and game designers, post-mortem analyses of games, and conference talks (e.g., Game Developer's Conference – GDC) to try to piece together the kinds of processes and systems that are used to evaluate narratives.

Bioware, a studio well-known for their use of narrative structures in their games, seems to be the most forthcoming about their narrative design process, though there are only a few public resources that give an indication of what they do. Combing through the statements and interviews indicate three important development practices that demonstrate their commitment to producing excellent game narratives: 1) the close integration of their quality assurance (QA) team with the development team, 2) their use of narrative prototyping to iteratively test and develop game narrative, and 3) the merging of story design and system design.

Across several blog posts, team leads at Bioware have discussed several important QA practices that the studio has embraced over the years to improve their final products, in both narrative and design. In one such post [37], a QA lead talked about how the QA department plays an increasingly important role in the development cycle, moving away from reactionary to proactive involvement in the development process from the beginning. QA leads began attending designer and programmer meetings to be more informed about the game, and the QA team was eventually split into two separate disciplines – Tech, which supported the programmers, and Design, which supported designers and writers. In another post [38], the lead describes the role QA has at Bioware compared to other large studios and reiterates the integration of QA with development.

In 2007 at The Australian Game Developers Conference, a lead writer for Bioware, Mike Laidlaw, gave a presentation describing the early part of the production process for a Bioware game. [49] Laidlaw noted that the writers are part of the design process from day one, as a part of the design team. He also describes three phases of development the team undergoes: prototyping – exploring ideas, setting, and story work; pre-production – systems, pipelines, and story arcs are defined; and production – "a flood of content".

Laidlaw further describes the writing process for their game *Mass Effect* [2] from early-stage prototyping to late-stage integration. In the early-stage prototyping, the writing team designed the dialogue system and tested how players would interact with it, the tone and shape of the game was formed, and the ESRB rating was decided so the writers knew what type of content to create. In the next phase, the game story was written by the writing team. The written content was then iteratively tested using a LoFi narrative prototype, to test for technical issues with the story content. The end result of the narrative prototyping stage was a playable level with full dialogue in text format. This allowed for major rewrites, because the content was text, which was cheap to rewrite as needed. After this initial prototyping phase, the text was passed to QA, who looked for plot holes, bugs, and inconsistencies. From there, the text moved to voiceovers, cinematics, and integration into the game.

Integrated Development of Story and System

A talk at GDC 2015 [50] discussed Bioware's process of melding story with game systems in the production of *Dragon Age: Inquisition* [3]. The design team split in half to explore different design techniques. The first team created narrative content and the second team designed standalone systems. What they found was that the narrative team's content scaled poorly, and the system team's content had a disconnected impact. The main conclusion was that story and technical systems developed separately cause problems and dissonances in the final product. The solution was to develop story and systems together, in tandem.

Bungie's Destiny [7] is an example of a game that was received poorly by players due to the separation of narrative and system teams. The details of what led to the game's lukewarm reception after the large pre-release hype are fuzzy, but the general idea is documented in a post-mortem of the game [44]. After three years of development, and only months before the game was initially supposed to be released, the lead writer put together the 'supercut' for the game – a video that included the game's cinematics and major story points, and showed it to the studio's leadership. The senior staff at Bungie were not satisfied with the story and scrapped it, deciding to start from scratch. The result was a hacked together story, criticized by reviewers for its vague plot, thin characters, and opaque dialogue. Furthermore, there were system elements that could not be scrapped as too much development had gone into them and it was too close to release, so they did not hang together well with the final version and seemed to be disconnected.

Fans blamed *Destiny's* [7] poor reception on its lackluster story, which can likely be attributed to the separation of the development of story and game systems, the same problem Bioware found with *Dragon Age: Inquisition* [3]. That the leadership had not seen the story and cinematics prior to their completion, combined with a mindset that they could develop and implement a full story within the restrictions of existing game systems as a final touch, rather than a fundamental part of the game, resulted in a poorly constructed and inconsistent narrative experience.

The important part of this is that game studios with successful narrative games, such as Bioware, are successful because of how the story is integrated into their process. They develop the story early on, in parallel with the other game systems. The story and game need to fit well together without creating inconsistencies between them and in order to achieve that, iterative testing of these two systems together early and throughout development is important. Many studios, like Bungie, developed these two branches separately, which led to miscommunication between departments and an inconsistent, dissonant narrative experience, even though the game mechanics were innovative and well designed.

CONSTRUCTING A NARRATIVE PROTOTYPE

In this paper, we conducted two studies in which we created a LoFi narrative prototype based off of a finished HiFi game. In this section we will document the process we used to construct our narrative prototypes.

The first step was to write the overall story, conveying through text the information that would normally be understood from the visuals. The goal was to try to get the same information across as would be in the final game.

The second step was to simulate player actions and game mechanics using a simple text interface. Player actions refer to simple things like "Walk over to the computer". Game mechanics refer to interactions such as combat, in which the player has a wider range of options and the interaction is more complex. For these types of game mechanics, we presented options to the player, but in a very simplified version, (e.g., "Attack").

The final step is to implement the narrative. We used a simple tool [41] that we customized to convert a game script (scene descriptions and character dialogue) into an interactive system. Our tool allowed us to display the text in a game-like environment – we displayed the character portraits alongside their dialogue in study 2, but not in study 1 – and use mouse and keyboard controls to move through the prototype. However, a different medium-fidelity tool (e.g., PowerPoint) could just as easily have been used to achieve the same functionality.

STUDY 1

Using Bioware's narrative prototypes as inspiration, we wanted to systematically measure how effective such a technique is for narrative games, and the feasibility of using it as an iterative development tool. That is, we wanted to determine how the player experience of the narrative could be evaluated early in the development lifecycle. In particular, we wanted to know whether a text-based version of a game would result in reduced player experience, when compared to the same game with high-fidelity graphics.

To investigate this, we used the above-mentioned process to create a text-based version of an existing research game and compared the LoFi text version with the HiFi graphical version. We performed a between-subjects experiment and collected measures of experience, in-game behavioural motivation, and demographic surveys to assess player traits.

Figure 1: Screenshots for LoFi (left) and HiFi(right) versions

Game Design

We created *Space Adventure*, a narrative game involving an accident on a space ship; participants play the game from the perspective of the ship's Captain and explore different rooms through a surveillance system to discover the events that occurred on board. The game was implemented in C# using the Unity Game Engine.

Space Adventure is played in a full 3D game environment similar to immersive narrative-based commercial games (Figure 1). Players started by designing their customized avatar: they were given the choice to select sex, hairstyle, hair colour, shirt, shirt colour, pants, and pants colour. The player moved around the inside of a spaceship, experiencing the game's narrative and optionally discovering the backstory that led to the events in the game.

Narrative/Procedure

In the game, the player awakens after the ship's engines had crashed. One of the ship's soldiers instructs the player about the controls for moving around the environment, before guiding the player to investigate the cause of the failure. First, players are introduced to the *Surveillance Room* where they can access various cameras around the ship to view footage from different rooms of the ship, shown to the player through a text-based description. They then teleport to the *Hacking Room*, which is necessary in the game to unlock the cameras one at a time for viewing in the *Surveillance Room*. The game primarily consists of players teleporting back and forth between the *Hacking Room* and the *Surveillance Room* throughout the narrative, unlocking a camera in the *Hacking Room*, then viewing a piece of the story by looking through the camera in the *Surveillance Room*, then teleporting back to hack the next camera. This is done eight times throughout the narrative, each time revealing a different piece of the story. In addition, while in the *Hacking Room*, the player can unlock more of the game's backstory by optionally hacking a console each time they return to the room. Pressing the right arrow key reveals more information about the backstory one word at a time, which is revealed while the player-character is waiting to gain access to the next camera in the surveillance room. Once a console is hacked, the player teleports back to the surveillance room and the cycle continues.

Using cameras as a narrative technique allowed us to guide participants through a narrative from a local point of action, reducing the need for navigation through the virtual world. After hacking the last console, participants could either escape the ship right away by pressing a button, or alternately run down the hallway to escape the ship.

Controls, Interface, and Versions

Participants controlled the avatar using 'W' to move forward, 'A' to rotate the avatar to the left, and 'D' to rotate the avatar to the right. A 3rd-person camera was positioned in a fixed location directly behind the avatar.

We included a heads-up-display (HUD) on which players could hack and teleport by clicking on the *hacking* and *teleport* buttons, using the left mouse button when the options were available (see Figure 1). A mini-map was provided in the bottom right corner with highlighting of the current room so the player could see where the fictional camera was looking (see Figure 1).

We used two versions of the game: the HiFi version as described, and a text-based LoFi version (See Figure 1).

Participants and Deployment Platform

We recruited participants by telling them that they would be evaluating a game under development. We had 81 participants (48% female) with an average age of 22 (SD = 15.9) participate in our study through Amazon Mechanical Turk (MTurk), a platform that acts as a broker between parties offering a range of *Human Intelligence Tasks* (HITs) and paid workers. Participants received $6 USD as compensation and the study took on average 40 minutes (15 minutes of gameplay). Although it has been shown that MTurk is a reliable research tool [35], we measured the time spent per questionnaire to evaluate task performance and ensured that participants were attentive despite the online setting. As a compliance check, we removed participants who spent less than 1.5 seconds per item on two or more questionnaires, as these participants likely did not carefully read and consider the questions. Three participants were detected and removed using this filter, leaving a total of 78 participants to be used in the final analysis ($N_{low\text{-}fidelity}$=40, $N_{high\text{-}fidelity}$=38).

Ethical Compliance

Ethical approval was obtained from the *University of Saskatchewan* behavioural ethics board; participants were asked to give informed consent at the beginning and debriefed on the experiment at the end. To comply with ethical guidelines, the HIT was only made available to workers in the USA who were older than 18. Also, only workers with an approval rate above 90% were offered the HIT as a means of quality control. After the experiment, we asked participants to respond to simple questions about the story to ensure that the experiment was understood.

	Low-Fidelity		High-Fidelity		Low-Trans		High-Trans		CONDITION			TRANSPORTABILITY			CONDITION*TRANSPORTABILITY		
	Mean	SD	Mean	SD	Mean	SD	Mean	SD	F	p	ß	F	p	ß	F	p	ß
Enjoyment	4.88	1.35	4.30	1.73	4.00	1.65	5.20	1.08	2.82	0.10	0.60	19.26	0.00	0.01	1.59	0.21	0.75
Effort	5.44	1.27	5.53	1.27	4.99	1.33	5.97	0.93	0.23	0.64	0.92	13.36	0.00	0.04	0.04	0.84	0.94
Tension	3.14	1.52	2.81	1.21	2.79	1.33	3.29	1.42	0.95	0.33	0.83	3.97	0.05	0.47	0.95	0.33	0.83
Competence	5.09	1.19	4.90	1.41	4.67	1.18	5.37	1.29	0.33	0.57	0.91	6.72	0.01	0.25	0.50	0.48	0.89
Autonomy	3.93	1.44	3.40	1.46	3.28	1.47	4.20	1.33	2.55	0.12	0.63	11.87	0.00	0.06	2.01	0.16	0.69
Relatedness	4.07	1.40	3.93	1.34	3.79	1.28	4.27	1.40	0.14	0.71	0.93	3.04	0.09	0.57	0.51	0.48	0.89
Presence	4.48	1.39	3.99	1.66	3.50	1.36	5.05	1.23	2.08	0.15	0.68	28.85	0.00	0.00	0.00	0.96	0.95
Intuitive Controls	5.74	1.09	5.61	0.94	5.32	1.03	6.00	0.88	0.22	0.64	0.92	8.33	0.01	0.16	0.10	0.75	0.94
Similarity ID	3.31	1.56	3.73	1.56	2.85	1.30	4.21	1.52	2.43	0.12	0.65	19.61	0.00	0.01	0.21	0.65	0.92
Embodied Presence	4.02	1.67	3.47	1.77	2.85	1.42	4.69	1.52	1.88	0.14	0.72	30.33	0.00	0.00	0.03	0.85	0.95
Wishful ID	3.07	1.50	3.12	1.40	2.58	1.24	3.64	1.45	0.09	0.76	0.94	12.18	0.00	0.06	0.57	0.45	0.89
Motivation	0.95	0.13	0.94	0.18	0.91	0.21	0.97	0.16	0.10	0.75	0.94	2.48	0.12	0.64	0.25	0.62	0.92

Table 1: Study 1 results – Means and SD for Low-Fidelity and High-Fidelity conditions, as well as F, p, and ß values from a Multivariate Analysis of Variance (MANOVA) for Condition, Transportability, and the interaction.

Measures

In this section we present the measures used for study 1. Unless otherwise specified, all items were presented to participants using a 7-point Likert scale.

Needs Satisfaction (i.e., competence, autonomy, relatedness, presence, intuitive controls) was measured using the Player Experience of Needs Satisfaction Scale (PENS, [43]). Participants rated their agreement to a series of statements, e.g., "I feel competent at the game". (Cronbach's alpha = .75, .85, .65, .94, .712).

Enjoyment, Effort, and Tension were measured using the Intrinsic Motivation Inventory (IMI, [36]), e.g., "I enjoyed the game very much." (Cronbach's alpha = .94, .85, .85).

Identification was measured using the Player Identification Scale (PIS, [32]). Participants reflected on their experience and answered several questions on how they identified with the character they played. The PIS consists of three subscales: *similarity identification, embodied presence, and wishful identification.* (Cronbach's alpha = .95, .96, .91).

Transportability is a personality trait that describes an individual's susceptibility to become transported into a narrative world. The transportability scale [12] was presented prior to playing the game to measure this trait. Participants rated their tendency to become transported on a series of items, (e.g., "I have vivid images of the events in the story") (Cronbach's alpha = .93). High- and low- transportability were calculated using a median split.

Motivation was measured using the in-game behavioural measurements from the hacking terminals. At each terminal, the player could reveal the backstory, but could leave the task at any time with no negative consequences to the game. We calculated the motivation score by combining the number of words revealed in each terminal and normalizing the score to an overall average percentage. The purpose of this measure was to get an idea of how much effort participants put into the task, since as crowd workers they could primarily be motivated by the money rather than the task.

Results

The purpose of this study was to investigate differences in player experience of narrative-based games with high or low graphic fidelity. Based on previous research [19] that investigated the experiential effects of HiFi and LoFi casual games, we expected there to be no main effects by condition on any measure. Also, because the game was primarily an interactive narrative, we expected there to be significant differences on all dependent measures between participants who rated high and low in transportability. Based on this, we came up with the following hypotheses:

H1: There will be no differences in any game experience measures due to graphical fidelity.

H2: There will be significant differences in experiential measures between high and low transportable participants.

We conducted an a priori power analysis using [6] to ensure that we recruited enough participants to find medium to large effect sizes, if they existed. We performed the test expecting an effect size of 0.33, a significance level of 0.05, a ß of 0.8, and two different groups in our between-subjects experiment design. We decided that medium-large effect sizes were sufficient, because we only need to show that any differences between dependent measures are quite small, rather than statistically identical. The power analysis suggested a sample size of 37 participants per group, which we rounded up to 40. For all of our analyses, we use $p < .05$ as a threshold for accepting statistical differences, and ß > .80 as a threshold for accepting statistical similarities.

Differences in Experiential Measures

We conducted a multivariate analysis of variance (MANOVA) in SPSS 24 using all of the dependent measures and using both condition and a median split of transportability as between-subject factors. We used the application g*Power [6] to calculate the post-hoc power for each of the analyses performed and derived the ß values. We present the means and standard deviations for both factors, as well as the F, p, and ß values for both factors and the interactions in Table 1.

Effects of Fidelity. There were no significant differences between conditions for any experiential measure, and the ß values were sufficiently high enough to determine that there were no differences between competence, intuitive controls, relatedness, effort, tension, wishful identification, and behavioural motivation. Autonomy, presence, enjoyment, similarity identification, and embodied presence did not have a high enough post-hoc statistical power to say there was no difference, but their non-significant differences were still very small (about 0.5 points on a seven-point Likert scale). These results support H1, with the exception of the measures that didn't have enough statistical power to determine that there was no difference.

Effects of Transportability. There were significant differences between players with high and low transportability for all dependent measures, except for relatedness ($p=.09$) and motivation ($p=.12$). With the exception of these two non-significant differences, our results support H2.

Additionally, there were no significant interactions between fidelity condition and transportability, showing that the lack of differences between the LoFi and HiFi versions did not depend on the transportability of the players.

Study 1 Discussion

Our results suggest that for a short narrative game, player experience does not change very much between a LoFi prototype and a HiFi version with the same story and interactions. The narrative immersion measures of identification were also not statistically different.

Because the goals of this study were to compare play experience between different levels of graphic fidelity, our measurements were primarily focused on measures of play experience, such as need satisfaction and game enjoyment. We decided to include avatar identification as a measure of narrative immersion, but we did not specifically evaluate the players' experience of the narrative itself.

We also decided in this study to keep the controls consistent between the two versions – the game interaction was made as similar as possible by minimizing the necessary navigation and exploration in the HiFi condition and making the interaction in the hacking mini-game identical between conditions. As a result, the HiFi game was essentially an interactive narrative rather than a complete polished game. While this means the results are not generalizable to games in general, the game we created was fairly representative of a particular genre of narrative-based games, which are often focused on following a story and being present in a 3D world (e.g., walking simulators, such as *The Stanley Parable* [18]). Furthermore, we know that the lack of game interaction or control did not confound our results.

While the results from study 1 indicate that graphic fidelity may not be as important to certain kinds of games, the short play time is not enough to make a general claim. What we can say, however, is that in a short amount of time playing this type of game, graphic fidelity had very little to do with the overall play experience and narrative immersion. This indicates that this type of LoFi text interface could be useful for game developers when designing and testing game narratives early in development, before graphics and mechanics are fully implemented.

In our second study, we addressed the limitations from study 1 to help generalize to commercial narrative games.

STUDY 2

In study 1 we showed that measures of experience remain similar when comparing LoFi and HiFi graphics. We made several changes in study 2. First, we included measures of narrative engagement and removed PENS [43] to reduce the study complexity and shift the focus to narrative experience. We kept the IMI as a means of replicating the results from study 1 and understanding effects on experience. Second, we added simple, controlled game mechanics to generalize our results beyond an interactive narrative. Third, we made the LoFi version with simplified game controls to test if the fidelity of game interaction affects experience.

Game Design

We created a simple, 2.5D fantasy game with 5 main levels: A prologue, three levels, each with a single unique game mechanic, and an epilogue. The prologue showed a Princess running through a forest, chased by the shadow of a dragon, accompanied by text setting up the story. The first level used sword-based combat, the second level was an infinite runner, and level 3 used a shooting mechanic. The epilogue was a conversation to complete the narrative arc. The game was built initially to study sexism in games [5] however, a neutral version was used in the present study.

Narrative/Procedure

The underlying narrative of the game followed a damsel-in-distress trope. The player took on the role of a knight character on a quest to rescue a Princess captured by an evil wizard. In the prologue, the Princess's kidnapping is shown, and the premise of the story is described to the player through text scrolling across the screen. In level 1, the Knight is investigating the forest where the Princess was last seen when he runs into a woman trapped in a cage in the middle of a bandit camp. The knight fights off the bandits and rescues the prisoner from her prison. The woman, named Victoria, thanks him, but runs off into the forest, prompting the knight to follow her to learn what happened to the Princess. In level 2, the Knight runs along a forest path, trying to catch up to Victoria to find out where the Princess was taken. Catching up to her, she promises to lead him to the wizard's castle if he rescues her village from a bandit raid. In level 3, the knight sits outside the village walls with a crossbow and must shoot bandits, while avoiding the villagers, as they run out through the main gate one at a time. Once the Knight has killed enough bandits, Victoria leads him to the wizard's castle, as promised. In the epilogue, the Knight and Victoria arrive at the castle only to find it abandoned, with Victoria claiming that "The Princess is another castle", before deciding to permanently join the Knight in his quest to find the Princess.

Low-Fidelity Version

The LoFi version of the game follows the same story with identical dialogue as the HiFi version (Figure 2). As place-

Figure 2: LoFi (top-left), HiFi Level 1 (top-right), Level 2 (bottom-left), and Level 3 (bottom-right) Screenshots

holders for gameplay mechanics, this version used simple text-based interactions to simulate the actions the player undertook in the HiFi version. For example, the knight fighting off the bandits was replaced with player text options such as "Perform sword slash" and the infinite runner level had options such as "Dodge to the left" or "Jump over the fallen tree" to provide players with high-level actions to replace the actions taken in the HiFi condition (see Video Figure). Unlike in study 1, the game controls in the LoFi version were not intended to be comparable to the HiFi version and were more representative of what might be possible to prototype very early in the development of a game, when the details of the mechanics are still being developed.

Participants, Deployment, and Ethics

We used identical deployment methods as with study 1, except we chose to recruit 125 participants (46.8% female), one of which was removed using the outlier filter from study 1 ($N_{low\text{-}fidelity}$=65, $N_{high\text{-}fidelity}$=59). The study took an average of 19 minutes to complete (10 minutes of gameplay), and participants were compensated $5 USD.

Measures

Player Experience was measured as in study 1 using the Enjoyment, Effort, Tension, and Perceived Competence subscales from the Intrinsic Motivation Inventory. Because our goal with this study was to further investigate narrative experience, we chose to leave out PENS [43].

Transportability and *Identification* were measured using the same scales as in study 1 [22,32] (Cronbach's alpha = .94, .94, .96, .91 for ID_{sim}, ID_{emb}, ID_{wish} and transportability).

In addition, we added the following measures in study 2.

Transportation was measured using the Transportation Scale [22] which measures an individual's transportation into a narrative world during their experience with a particular narrative (e.g., "I wanted to learn how the narrative ended"). Transportation is indicative of the quality of a narrative that is experienced (Cronbach's alpha = .83).

Narrative Engagement was measured using the Narrative Engagement Scale (NES, [8]), which measures four aspects of narrative engagement: *narrative understanding* - reverse coded items to measure the understanding of the narrative, e.g., "I had a hard time recognizing the thread of the story", *attentional focus* - reverse coded items asking participants about how well they were able to mentally focus on the story, e.g., "I had a hard time keeping my mind on the game", *narrative presence* - how strongly they felt present in the narrative, e.g., "At times during the game, the story world was closer to me than the real world", and *emotional engagement* - how emotionally connected they felt to the events of the story, e.g., "The story affected me emotionally". To maintain consistency across the four subscales, results from narrative understanding and attentional focus are presented reversed, so for all four a higher value refers to stronger narrative engagement (Cronbach's alpha = .79, .89, .75, .82).

In the results and discussion below, we distinguish between player experience, *narrative engagement,* and *narrative immersion* as discussed in the related work section.

Results

We conducted an identical analysis as was done with study 1. We present the means and standard deviations for both independent factors, as well as the F, p, and ß values from the MANOVA by condition, a median split of transportability, and the interaction between the two in Table 2.

Differences in Experiential Measures

Play Experience. In terms of play experience, there was enough statistical power to assert that there were no signifi-

	Low-Fidelity		High-Fidelity		Low-Trans		High-Trans		CONDITION			TRANSPORTABILITY			CONDITION TRANSPORTABILITY		
	Mean	SD	Mean	SD	Mean	SD	Mean	SD	F	p	ß	F	p	ß	F	p	ß
Enjoyment	4.93	1.41	4.76	1.28	4.43	1.31	5.25	1.26	0.96	0.33	0.83	13.12	0.00	0.04	0.00	0.98	0.95
Effort	5.35	1.06	5.58	1.16	5.08	1.09	5.83	1.01	1.01	0.32	0.83	15.06	0.00	0.02	0.80	0.38	0.85
Tension	2.37	1.24	2.25	1.06	2.25	0.96	2.37	1.32	0.29	0.59	0.92	0.25	0.62	0.92	3.48	0.07	0.53
Competence	5.58	0.79	5.75	0.81	5.47	0.78	5.85	0.78	1.03	0.31	0.82	7.17	0.01	0.23	0.01	0.92	0.95
Similarity ID	3.48	1.42	3.06	1.37	2.84	1.24	3.71	1.44	4.00	0.05	0.48	13.92	0.00	0.04	0.33	0.57	0.91
Embodied Presence	3.83	1.60	3.64	1.65	3.02	1.35	4.43	1.56	1.12	0.29	0.82	28.42	0.00	0.00	1.21	0.27	0.80
Wishful ID	4.02	1.47	3.52	1.54	3.18	1.34	4.36	1.47	5.33	0.02	0.35	23.35	0.00	0.00	0.26	0.61	0.92
Transportation	4.59	0.88	4.37	0.89	4.05	0.84	4.91	0.72	4.28	0.04	0.46	40.47	0.00	0.04	0.00	0.96	0.95
Narrative Understanding	5.11	1.05	5.02	0.87	4.85	1.12	5.28	0.73	0.42	0.52	0.91	6.18	0.01	0.29	0.41	0.52	0.91
Attentional Focus	4.90	1.20	4.82	1.12	4.58	1.27	5.13	0.98	0.32	0.57	0.91	7.54	0.01	0.21	0.08	0.77	0.94
Narrative Presence	4.15	1.47	3.90	1.33	3.48	1.26	4.56	1.34	1.90	0.17	0.71	22.14	0.00	0.00	0.05	0.83	0.95
Emotional Engagement	3.75	1.49	3.50	1.51	3.01	1.25	4.23	1.48	1.83	0.18	0.72	25.04	0.00	0.00	0.68	0.41	0.86

Table 2: Study 2 results – Means and SD for Low-Fidelity and High-Fidelity conditions, as well as F, p, and ß values from a Multivariate Analysis of Variance (MANOVA) for Condition, Transportability, and the interaction

cant differences between conditions for enjoyment, effort, tension, and competence.

Narrative Engagement and Immersion. There was enough statistical power to assert that there were no significant differences between narrative understanding, attentional focus, and embodied presence. Narrative presence and emotional engagement were also not statistically different and had a relatively high power but didn't meet the threshold of 0.8 (ß=0.71 and ß=0.72, respectively) to accept the null hypothesis.

There was, however, a significant difference between the LoFi and HiFi versions in terms of transportation ($p=.04$, $\eta^2_p=.034$), similarity identification ($p=.05$, $\eta^2_p=.03$), and wishful identification ($p=.02$, $\eta^2_p=.04$), although the actual difference between means were small (less than 0.5 on a seven-point Likert scale). An independent-samples t-test showed no significant differences in the transportability between the groups ($t_{22}=0.18$, $p=.859$), this shows the differences cannot be explained by random assignment to the game versions. The results showed that experienced transportation was slightly higher in the LoFi version than the HiFi version.

Effects of Transportability. Comparing high and low transportability revealed similar results as in study 1 – there were significant differences between highly-transportable and low-transportable players for all dependent measures, with only experienced tension failing to reach significance. Additionally, there were no significant interactions between condition and transportability, showing that the lack of differences between the LoFi and HiFi versions did not depend on the transportability of the players.

Study 2 Discussion

The main interpretation of results is very similar to study 1. For all of the measures of play experience there were no significant differences between conditions, indicating that LoFi narrative prototypes can be used to assess the game narrative in early stage development. Furthermore, there were no significant differences in experienced narrative engagement, showing that the quality of the narrative could be assessed outside of the context of the full game experience (i.e., HiFi graphics and game interactions).

Interestingly, the two measures of immersion, transportation and identification, were two of the exceptions to this pattern, though the differences were very small in terms of the big picture of overall experience. This could be an indicator that for story immersion, while the story itself is important, there are other factors beyond the story that go into it, such as the presentation of the narrative world and the interaction with and presentation of different characters.

DISCUSSION

In this section, we will discuss the implications of our results, industry use cases and how game studios could integrate narrative prototypes into their existing design processes. We will also discuss the limitations of our studies and future opportunities.

Implications of Results

While we did see similarities between many measures of player experience and narrative immersion, these similarities were often not significantly similar, and in some cases were significantly different.

From a practical point of view, the most useful result from a narrative prototype is the narrative engagement. In Study 2, we showed that level of fidelity had no effect on narrative understanding and attentional focus, and narrative presence and emotional engagement were very similar between the conditions. This shows that the addition of visual graphics and game mechanics had very little effect on how well participants understood the narrative, the level of focus they placed on the story, their presence in the narrative, and the emotional engagement they felt from the story. These four measures suggest that early testing of a story in a text-based format would be useful for game designers to test for these particular narrative properties early in the story's conception, since they appear to be fairly independent from the game mechanics and visuals.

Industry Use Cases

There are two different situations in which the ideas underlying our proposed narrative prototypes could be used and applied to game studios. The most obvious, and the main motivation for this paper, is a tool to be integrated into the iterative design process that most game studios now use.

A second application for narrative prototyping is to cheaply evaluate game ideas before committing to a project. While more study is needed to be able to confidently say that our technique would apply across games of different types and genres, our results show that, at least for a certain type of narrative game, we can get similar levels of narrative experience from a simple, text-based narrative compared to a complete experience. This would allow game studios to create fast and cheap prototypes for several story-based games in a short amount of time and quickly test them with users to get a feel for which game, or games, would be the best to invest further resources into.

How to Integrate Prototypes into the Design Process

Here, we discuss how a narrative prototype could be embedded in the iterative design process of games, based on the current use of LoFi prototypes, and using our understanding of industry practices. In our approach, we adhere to the following three guidelines for effectively making use of a narrative prototype: close integration with the current state of the game, iterative testing and feedback, and increasing fidelity over time.

A lesson Bioware learned from working on *Dragon Age: Inquisition* [3], and the lesson Bungie learned with *Destiny* [7], is the need for story to be developed in tandem with the game itself. If the narrative team doesn't consider how players will interact with the game, and if the game designers don't consider the game narrative while developing their content, they may introduce dissonances between the narrative and the game. The goal, then, is to match the narrative prototype with the game's current level of development. This is similar to the goal of interactive system prototypes in which the fidelity of the sketch or prototype should match the maturity of the idea [9].

Early on in the development cycle, the narrative prototype would be similar to the text-based prototypes used in our studies. The goal would be to test and evaluate the story, looking for narrative dissonances, plot holes, and travel through branching and fold-back story structures. As the story is tested and refined, the game would be developed in parallel, constructing LoFi versions of the systems and interactions. As the game gets fleshed out, the narrative prototype should slowly add in the assets and mechanics as they become available (for example, how we added the static character image in study two). This stage can also be used to test multiple options with users (e.g., different avatars or character personalities). As a game level gets constructed, the descriptions in the narrative prototype could be replaced by the actual level, placing the prototype inside the level, with the tester now focusing more on the dialogue, and ensuring the setting makes sense with that version of the story. As mechanics get developed, e.g., a sword attack, these can also be added to the prototype, replacing the early-stage text-based interactions. The goal with iteratively developing the story in this way is to always be aware of how the story fits with the game and vice versa. By always testing the latest version of the story, game developers have a better chance of finding dissonances between the two, as with *Destiny* [7], as early as possible, instead of waiting until the game is nearing completion.

Limitations and Future Opportunities

In both studies, the two conditions differed in graphical fidelity and interaction. While we tried to minimize differences in terms of game interaction for study 1, there were still slight differences due to the closely-coupled nature of graphics and interaction. We argue that this prioritizes external validity, as both conditions represent a snapshot in the development timeline of a game. In study 2, we iterated on this closely-coupled aspect, further differentiating the interaction between conditions. The design choice of representing the mechanics as simple text options is representative of how such a prototype would be created early in a game's development, with no access to graphics or systems.

A second limitation of our work is that both games we used in the studies were already developed and the narrative prototypes were developed after the games, rather than before as would happen in a real-world use case.

A third limitation is that our games – although enjoyed by participants according to the means – were representative of what a small, indie studio would create as a demo and not what a triple-A studio would generate. Because the goal is for the fidelity of the narrative prototype to match the maturity of the game's development, we don't see this as a potential source of error; however, higher-fidelity narrative prototypes may yield different play experiences than their game-based counterparts of commercial quality.

Finally, participants were only exposed to the game for a short time (ten to fifteen minutes). Our results show no significant difference in play experience between the LoFi and HiFi versions, but we speculate that with a significantly longer play session, differences may emerge, due to a lack of visual stimulation in the LoFi versions over a long period of time. Short sessions are ideal for playtesting, however, which fits the use case of our prototyping method.

Future Work

We would like to expand on the ideas in this paper and more deeply consider narrative prototyping. In both of our studies, we used games we had created. While this gave us an advantage in having control over every aspect of their design, the experiences were short and were not comparable to commercial game in terms of content and quality. The next step would be to replicate study 2 with an off-the-shelf narrative game, such as *The Stanley Parable* [18]. This would increase the generalizability of our results, showing that narrative prototypes can be effective on commercial games with complex content and interactions, built by professional writers. Second, we would like to document the processes we describe in the paper by iteratively developing a game using narrative prototyping, to test the feasibility of the method in practice. Finally, the narrative prototypes we used are focused on early-stage narrative evaluation and, to some extent, character dialogue. We would like to expand on this idea and look at creating different types of narrative prototypes, focusing on specific aspects of story development, such as world building, designing character personalities, and evaluating procedurally-generated narratives.

CONCLUSIONS

Iterative development and evaluation is important for all types of interactive systems, including interfaces and games. While iterative methods have become common practice for most game designers, the integration of game narratives early in development is still new and unfamiliar to many developers. We proposed using text-based narrative prototypes as a means to iteratively test and develop game narratives, allowing writers to work closely and in parallel with the designers of the game systems. Through two studies, we compared high and low levels of graphic fidelity and player interaction with game mechanics and show that all experiential measures are not affected by playing the narrative prototype. Our findings provide evidence that narrative prototyping could feasibly be used by game studios to quickly and cheaply evaluate game ideas before committing development resources to them and to more closely integrate their narrative design into existing iterative development processes.

ACKNOWLEDGEMENTS

We thank NSERC and the UofS for funding.

REFERENCES

1. Michael Arent, Jonathan Arnowitz, and Nevin Berger. 2007. Acknowledgments. In *Effective Prototyping for Software Makers*. Elsevier, xxvii--xxviii. https://doi.org/10.1016/b978-012088568-8/50000-x
2. Bioware. 2007. *Mass Effect*. Game [Xbox 360, PC, PlayStation 3]. (16 November 2007) Electronic Arts..
3. Bioware. 2014. *Dragon Age: Inquisition*. Game [Xbox360, Xbox One, PlayStation 3, PlayStation 4, PC]. (18 November 2014) Electronic Arts.
4. Max V. Birk, Cheralyn Atkins, Jason T. Bowey, and Regan L. Mandryk. 2016. Fostering Intrinsic Motivation through Avatar Identification in Digital Games. *CHI'16* 55: 207–213. https://doi.org/10.1145/2858036.2858062
5. Jason T. Bowey, Ansgar E. Depping, and Regan L. Mandryk. 2017. Don't Talk Dirty to Me: How Sexist Beliefs Affect Experience in Sexist Games. In *Proceedings of the 2017 CHI Conference on Human Factors in Computing Systems.*
6. Axel Buchner. G*Power.
7. Bungie. 2014. *Destiny*. Game [Xbox 360, Xbox One, PlayStation 3, PlayStation 4]. (9 September 2014). Activision.
8. Rick Busselle and Helena Bilandzic. 2009. Measuring narrative engagement. *Media Psychology* 12, 4: 321–347. https://doi.org/10.1080/15213260903287259
9. Bill Buxton. 2010. *Sketching user experiences: getting the design right and the right design*. Morgan Kaufmann.
10. Michael B Catani and David W Biers. 1998. Usability evaluation and prototype fidelity: Users and usability professionals. In *Proceedings of the Human Factors and Ergonomics Society Annual Meeting*, 1331–1335.
11. Katheryn R Christy and Jesse Fox. 2016. Transportability and presence as predictors of avatar identification within narrative video games. *Cyberpsychology, Behavior, and Social Networking* 19, 4: 283–287.
12. S Dal Cin, M P Zanna, G T Fong, and B Gibson. Narrative persuasion and overcoming resistance. https://doi.org/10.1037/e633872013-232
13. Jonathan Cohen. 2001. Defining Identification: A Theoretical Look at the Identification of Audiences with Media Characters. *Mass Communication & Society* 4, 3: 245–264. https://doi.org/10.1207/S15327825MCS0403
14. Jianming Dong. 2004. Book Review: Paper prototyping-The fast and easy way to design and refine user interfaces, by Carolyn Snyder. *International Journal of Human-Computer Interaction* 17, 2: 287–288. https://doi.org/10.1207/s15327590ijhc1702_10
15. Magy Seif El-Nasr, Anders Drachen, and Alessandro Canossa (eds.). 2013. *Game Analytics*. Springer London. https://doi.org/10.1007/978-1-4471-4769-5
16. Daniel Engelberg and Ahmed Seffah. 2002. A Framework for Rapid Mid-Fidelity Prototyping of Web Sites. In *Usability*. Springer {US}, 203–215. https://doi.org/10.1007/978-0-387-35610-5_14
17. Tracy Fullerton and Christopher Swain. 2008. The Structure of Games. In *Game Design Workshop*. Elsevier, 26–48. https://doi.org/10.1016/b978-0-240-80974-8.50008-7
18. Galactic. Cafe. 2013. *The Stanley Parable*. Game [PC]. (17 October 2013). Galactic Café.
19. Kathrin M Gerling, Max Birk, Regan L Mandryk, and Andre Doucette. 2013. The Effects of Graphical Fidelity on Player Experience. In *Proceedings of International Conference on Making Sense of Converging Media - {AcademicMindTrek} {\textquotesingle}13*. https://doi.org/10.1145/2523429.2523473
20. Jose González Sánchez, Natalia Padilla Zea, and Francisco Gutiérrez. 2009. From usability to playability: Introduction to player-centred video game development process. *Human centered design*: 65–74.
21. John D Gould and Clayton Lewis. 1985. Designing for usability: key principles and what designers think. *Communications of the {ACM}* 28, 3: 300–311. https://doi.org/10.1145/3166.3170
22. Melanie C Green and Timothy C Brock. 2000. The Role of Transportation in the Persuasiveness of Public Narratives. *Journal of Personality and Social Psychology* 79, 5: 701–721. https://doi.org/10.1037//0022-3514.79.5.701
23. Adams Greenwood-Ericksen and Juliana Goriounov. 2016. Assessment of Responses to Narrative in Games.
24. Dorothée Hefner, Christoph Klimmt, and Peter Vorderer. 2007. Identification with the Player Character as Determinant of Video Game Enjoyment. *Entertainment Computing - ICEC 2007* 4740, March 2016: 39–48. https://doi.org/10.1007/978-3-540-74873-1_6
25. Robin Hunicke, Marc LeBlanc, and Robert Zubek. 2004. MDA: A formal approach to game design and game research. In *Proceedings of the AAAI Workshop on Challenges in Game AI.*
26. Katherine Isbister and Noah Schaffer. 2015. *Game usability: Advancing the player experience*. CRC Press.

27. Michael J Kahn and Amanda Prail. 1994. Formal usability inspections. In *Usability inspection methods*, 141–171.

28. Maarten van de Kant, Stephanie Wilson, Mathilde Bekker, Hilary Johnson, and Peter Johnson. 1998. PatchWork: A software tool for early design. In *CHI 98 Conference Summary on Human Factors in Computing Systems*, 221–222.

29. Barbara Köhler, Juan Haladjian, Blagina Simeonova, and Damir Ismailović. 2012. Feedback in low vs. high fidelity visuals for game prototypes. In *Proceedings of the Second International Workshop on Games and Software Engineering: Realizing User Engagement with Game Engineering Techniques*, 42–47.

30. Craig Larman. 2004. *Agile and iterative development: a manager's guide*. Addison-Wesley Professional.

31. Ben Lewis-Evans. 2012. Finding Out What They Think: A Rough Primer To User Research, Part 1.

32. Jan Van Looy, Cédric Courtois, Melanie De Vocht, and Lieven De Marez. 2012. Player Identification in Online Games: Validation of a Scale for Measuring Identification in MMOGs. *Media Psychology* 15, 2: 197–221. https://doi.org/10.1080/15213269.2012.674917

33. Regan L Mandryk and M Stella Atkins. 2007. A fuzzy physiological approach for continuously modeling emotion during interaction with play technologies. *International journal of human-computer studies* 65, 4: 329–347.

34. Regan L Mandryk, Kori M Inkpen, and Thomas W Calvert. 2006. Using psychophysiological techniques to measure user experience with entertainment technologies. *Behaviour & information technology* 25, 2: 141–158.

35. Winter Mason and Siddharth Suri. 2011. Conducting behavioral research on Amazon's Mechanical Turk. *Behavior Research Methods* 44, 1: 1–23. https://doi.org/10.3758/s13428-011-0124-6

36. Edward McAuley, Terry Duncan, and Vance V Tammen. 1989. Psychometric Properties of the Intrinsic Motivation Inventory in a Competitive Sport Setting: A Confirmatory Factor Analysis. *Research Quarterly for Exercise and Sport* 60, 1: 48–58. https://doi.org/10.1080/02701367.1989.10607413

37. Tulay Tetiker McNally. 2013. Part 1: The End of the Dark Ages for QA in game development.

38. Tulay Tetiker McNally. 2013. Part 4: "Adopt, Adapt and Improve" - Agile QA BioWare Style.

39. Pejman Mirza-Babaei, Lennart E Nacke, John Gregory, Nick Collins, and Geraldine Fitzpatrick. 2013. How does it play better?: exploring user testing and biometric storyboards in games user research. In *Proceedings of the SIGCHI conference on human factors in computing systems*, 1499–1508.

40. David Pinelle, Nelson Wong, and Tadeusz Stach. 2008. Heuristic evaluation for games: usability principles for video game design. In *Proceedings of the SIGCHI Conference on Human Factors in Computing Systems*, 1453–1462.

41. Pixelcrushers. Dialogue System. http://www.pixelcrushers.com/dialogue-system/

42. Richard M Ryan and Edward L Deci. 2000. Self-determination theory and the facilitation of intrinsic motivation, social development, and well-being. *American Psychologist* 55, 1: 68–78. https://doi.org/10.1037/0003-066x.55.1.68

43. Richard M Ryan, C Scott Rigby, and Andrew Przybylski. 2006. The Motivational Pull of Video Games: A Self-Determination Theory Approach. *Motivation and Emotion* 30, 4: 344–360. https://doi.org/10.1007/s11031-006-9051-8

44. Jason Schreler. 2015. The Messy, True Story Behind The Making Of Destiny.

45. Reinhard Sefelin, Manfred Tscheligi, and Verena Giller. 2003. Paper prototyping - what is it good for? In *{CHI} {\textquotesingle}03 extended abstracts on Human factors in computing systems - {CHI} {\textquotesingle}03*. https://doi.org/10.1145/765891.765986

46. Chek Tien Tan, Sander Bakkes, and Yusuf Pisan. 2014. Inferring player experiences using facial expressions analysis. In *ACM International Conference Proceeding Series*.

47. Robert A Virzi, Jeffrey L Sokolov, and Demetrios Karis. 1996. Usability problem identification using both low-and high-fidelity prototypes. In *Proceedings of the SIGCHI Conference on Human Factors in Computing Systems*, 236–243.

48. Michael E Wiklund, Christopher Thurrott, and Joseph S Dumas. 1992. Does the fidelity of software prototypes affect the perception of usability? In *Proceedings of the Human Factors and Ergonomics Society Annual Meeting*, 399–403.

49. 2007. AGDC: BioWare Charts Writing For Mass Effect. Retrieved April 13, 2017 from http://www.gamasutra.com/view/news/106358/AGDC_BioWare_Charts_Writing_For_Mass_Effect.php

50. 2015. GDC: See how BioWare melded story with systems to make Dragon Age.

Adapting Cognitive Task Analysis to Elicit the Skill Chain of a Game

Britton Horn
Northeastern University
Boston, Massachusetts
bhorn@ccs.neu.edu

Seth Cooper
Northeastern University
Boston, Massachusetts
scooper@ccs.neu.edu

Sebastian Deterding
University of York
York, United Kingdom
sebastian.deterding@york.ac.uk

ABSTRACT
Playing a game is a complex skill comprising a set of more basic skills. These skills commonly map onto the main mechanics of the game, and build and depend on each other in a nested learning hierarchy, which game designers have modeled as *skill chains* made of *skill atoms*. For players to optimally learn and enjoy a game, it should introduce skill atoms in the ideal sequence of this learning hierarchy. However, game designers typically construct and use hypothetical skill chains based solely on design intent, theory, or personal observation, rather than empirical observation of players. This risks creating incomplete or suboptimal progression designs. In response, this paper presents an adapted cognitive task analysis method for eliciting the empirical skill chain of a game. A case study illustrates and critically reflects the method. While effective in foregrounding overlooked low-level skills required by a game, its efficiency and generalizability remain to be proven.

ACM Classification Keywords
H.5.m Information interfaces and presentation: Miscellaneous; K.8.0 Personal Computing: General: Games

Author Keywords
cognitive task analysis; game atoms; learning hierarchy; skill atoms; skill chains

INTRODUCTION
Like cooking, driving, and many other everyday activities, playing a video game is a complex skill [60]. *Complex skills* integrate a network of more basic skills: driving, for instance, requires independently mastering braking, steering, and switching gears, but also integrating and fluently switching between them [49]. These constituent basic skills hang together in a *learning hierarchy*: the logical order in which they build and depend on each other and therefore, in which they are ideally learned. For instance, we have to learn counting before we can learn addition and subtraction, and it is easier to learn these before multiplication [26, 4, 64]. Identifying the learning hierarchy of a to-be-taught complex skill is therefore a key task of instructional design, as it directly informs what learning goals to pursue, what outcomes to assess, and what tasks and material to present in what order to optimally support learning [35].

We find the very same need in entertainment and serious game design. No matter if designers want to create good tutorials and level progressions for a game [48, 8]; balance level difficulty or procedurally generate levels that fit player skills [45]; create educational games whose mechanics train targeted capacities [23]; or gamefully restructure everyday activities [21] – they are faced with the question what component skills a given game entails or ought to entail, and in what order the game should introduce these to players. More colloquially, if games are learning machines we enjoy to master [27, 42], it stands to reason they benefit from a well-designed sequence of learning.

Unsurprisingly, game design has developed a range of formal models that describe games as nested networks of game atoms or loops which revolve around specific actions or skills [21]. One particularly popular model, developed by Dan Cook, describes games as *skill chains*, directed graphs of *skill atoms* or core loops that logically build on each other – mirroring learning hierarchies in everything but name [14]. Likewise, there are many design methods such as *Rational Level Design* for prospectively deriving optimal level progression sequences from a given atom model [47, 48].

However, these models and methods provide little if any guidance how to reliably deduce the skill chain or learning hierarchy of a given game. Models are either sketched as blueprints for a new game or based on a designer's or researcher's individual reading of a game. Scarcely any game research methods exist to empirically deduce the skill chain of a game from actual player experience, or assess to what extent the skills and ideal sequencing order predicted by a model matches the actual skills it requires from players, or their actual learning hierarchy. This risks overlooking essential skills, not introducing them to players or introducing them in a suboptimal sequence.

In instructional design, cognitive task analysis (CTA) is a well-established family of methods to identify the skills and knowledge involved in a given task based on empirical observation and interviewing of experts [16, 13]. This includes methods for eliciting and modeling learning hierarchies [63,

CHI PLAY '17, October 15–18, 2017, Amsterdam, Netherlands

ACM ISBN 978-1-4503-4898-0/17/10...$15.00
DOI: https://doi.org/10.1145/3116595.3116640

35], which makes CTA an ideal candidate for identifying the learning hierarchies or skill chains of games. Although CTA techniques have existed for decades, to our knowledge, they haven't been adopted in games research and design for this purpose. Hence, this paper presents an adapted cognitive task analysis method for extracting the skill chain of a game from empirical gameplay. Akin to prior work on method development [36], we conducted a case study in a mode of critical *reflective practice* [54], continually documenting and reflecting on our method design process to assess its utility, identify future improvements, as well as surface more general issues in eliciting the knowledge and skills involved in playing a particular game.

The next section reviews existing work in games research related to modeling and identifying the component skills of games and introduces CTA. We then lay out our adapted CTA method, including its underlying rationale and a concrete step-by-step procedure for interested users. Our case study – using the method to identify the skill chain of the human computation game *Paradox* – illustrates the method in use and provides material for emerging observations and challenges. We discuss the contribution and limitations of the presented work and derive ramifications for future research.

BACKGROUND

Formal Modeling of Games

Doug Church [11] initiated contemporary work on "formal abstract design tools": developing grammars and tools to describe, analyze, and design the structural components of a game (for recent reviews, see [2, 22]). Following Almeida and da Silva [2], one can roughly distinguish (a) broad models like the MDA framework [34], (b) collections of descriptive terms and patterns (e.g. [6]), (c) design guidelines such as playability heuristics [41], and (d) modeling languages and tools of the core *mechanics* of a game, such as Machinations [22, 1]. Game mechanics describe the "core verbs" or "methods" by which players change the game state, such as moving, shooting, or trading [56]. They form part of *game atoms* [43] or *game loops* [57] – feedback loops between player input (invoking a particular mechanic, e.g. shooting), rules processing (e.g. adjudicating whether the shot hit), and computer output. A game atom is the smallest indivisible functional unit of a game. However, games are usually composed of nested networks of interlinked atoms: In a cover shooter, the "shooting" atom is part of a larger "defeating enemies" atom, which also entails a "cover" atom and may connect to an "upgrading atom," etc.

Skill Chains

As noted, game atom modeling is highly similar to modeling the learning hierarchies of complex skills. Both capture nested relations of basic to complex capacities, mechanics here, skills there – with one crucial difference: most game atom models concern themselves with a *synchronic overview* of the *game* and how the outputs of one atom (e.g. in-game resources like health or experience points) feed into others [2, 22]. They do not capture the *diachronic sequence* in which *players* (ought to) acquire proficiency in each atom. The exception is the *skill atom model* first articulated by Cook [14] and since extended

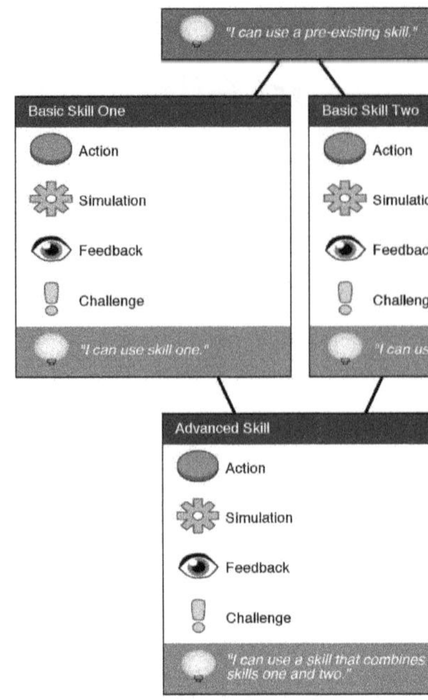

Figure 1. An example skill chain.

by Deterding [21]. It expressly models game mechanics and their relation from the perspective of player learning. A skill atom describes a game loop between player and game comprising five elements:

1. *action*: the player invoking a mechanic (e.g. shooting);
2. *simulation*: the game processing the action according to rules and changing its internal game state (adjudicating whether the shot hit, changing the location and health score of the hit enemy);
3. *feedback*: the game informing the player (displaying an animation of the hit enemy);
4. *challenge*: the parameters that make executing this particular action differently easy or difficult; and
5. *synthesis*: the player incorporating the feedback, adjusting their mental model of the game state and improving the skill(s) required to master this particular atom (e.g. fast hand-eye coordination to aim and shoot).

Skill atoms exist in nested *skill chains*: directed graphs of the order in which skills build on each other and in which players necessarily or ideally acquire them [14]. For instance, a player has to know how to *equip* a gun before learning how to *aim* and *shoot* with it. Skill chains bottom out in *pre-existing skills*: capacities game designers can assume players already bring to the game. Most PC games assume that players know how to move and click a mouse, for instance. Figure 1 presents a simple skill chain of one pre-existing skill, two basic skills, and one advanced skill that builds on them. Figure 2 shows a skill chain for the game *Tetris*.

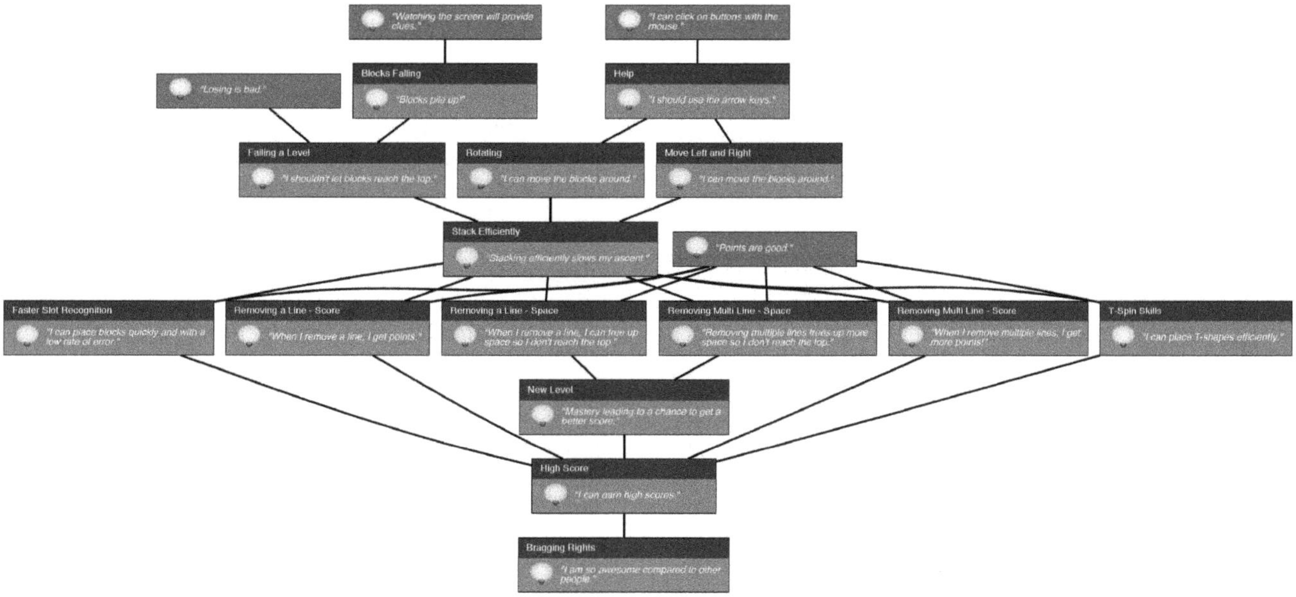

Figure 2. Skill chain for *Tetris*, taken and simplified from Cook [14].

Cook's model has found rich practical application, particularly in applied game design. For instance, Echeverría and colleagues [23] used it to improve an educational physics game. They analyzed which physical concepts the game ought to teach and which concepts it actually incorporated as skill atoms. Redesigning the game to incorporate previously missing skill atoms led to statistically significant learning improvements. Deterding's [21] method for gameful design similarly uses skill atoms to tease out the latent 'mini-games' of existing real-life activities and then redesign these to make them more explicitly and enjoyably game-like.

While not using Cook's [14] explicit articulation, Rational Level Design (RLD) [47, 48] has brought game atom analysis to broad use in entertainment game design, chiefly for difficulty balancing. Following flow theory [17], RLD assumes that players have an optimal or "flow" experience when the difficulty of challenges presented matches players' skill. As player skill grows over time, games have to increase difficulty in lockstep to avoid frustrating or boring players. This raises the question how to systematically design the *difficulty curve* of a game – the rate at which it increases difficulty. To this end, RLD suggests to identify (a) the atoms of a given game and (b) the parameters which affect the challenge of each game atom. For instance, the difficulty of "shooting" may be affected by parameters like enemy distance and speed. Designers should then craft a level sequence that systematically (a) introduces and involves new mechanics and (b) varies and increases the difficulty of the parameters of each atom. RLD essentially translates a synchronic map of game atoms into a recipe for diachronic level progression. However, RLD is chiefly interested in *difficulty* as an *aggregate effect* of the number of atoms involved and the configuration of their parameters. Unlike skill chains, it doesn't concern itself with logical or pragmatic dependencies – how skills build on each other.

Methods for Atom Identification

Either way, both skill chain mapping and RLD require means to elicit the actual skill atoms a game consists of. Cook [14], Echeverría [23] and Deterding [21] are notably silent about how they arrived at the skill atoms and chains they discuss. Where they mention the underlying process, it essentially bottoms out in "expert evaluation". This is a common issue of formal game analysis methods: most are some form of expert interpretation whose content and quality hinges on the unvalidated and tacit expertise of the reviewer. Guidance only concerns the format of the presented result, not the review process, leading to low replicability [44]. RLD [47, 48] similarly provides no method how to initially identify the atoms of a game and its parameters. Only once designers prototype actual levels based on hypothesized atoms and parameters does RLD loop in playtesting to assess the *actual* difficulty of each level as a player fail rate. From there, RLD focuses on iteratively understanding and tweaking the impact of atom parameters (enemy speed and distance) on difficulty. It offers no similar process to identify the game atoms themselves.

Existing playtesting and game user research methods are likewise of little help. No matter if based on player self-report, observation, psychophysiological measures, game telemetry, or a mixture thereof, they revolve around capturing constructs of player *experience* (like flow or immersion) and how game features affect these [5, 19, 24, 10, 39]. Closest to our concerns are heuristic analyses of game approachability – how easy a game is to learn [20] – and methods to balance game difficulty [33]. Yet again, both revolve around approachability or difficulty as aggregate results, not the underlying required skills. For example, Linehan and colleagues [45] charted difficulty curves for four popular puzzle games by coding Let's Play videos for the number of actions required to solve a given level and when the game required a new skill. This provides an aggregate measure of difficulty and a description of the sequence in which skills are introduced by the game, but not the *learning* sequence in which these build on each other and *should* be introduced to players. The same holds for applied game design [50, 65]. A number of recent methods support the capture of a given game's game and learning mechanics, but chart them in the actual game design sequence, not the ideal learning sequence [3, 9].

A final source of potential methods is recent work merging intelligent tutoring systems with educational games. Butler and colleagues [8] for instance present a system for automatic game progression design for a game teaching fractions. The system models the algorithm required to solve all possible basic fraction problems, generates a large number of game levels, assesses each level's complexity on the number and kind of involved solution features (substrings of the total algorithm required to solve it), and serves players levels matching their measured mastery of solution features. While promising, this approach by definition only works for skills that are easily formalized into an algorithm, and offers no means of empirically identifying what skills a game requires and therefore needs to formalize. Harpstead and Aleven [29] use empirical learning curve analysis, a performance data analysis method from intelligent tutoring systems, to evaluate how well hypothesized models of player skills predict player success in an educational game. While this method does help assess whether there are hidden, non-modeled skills, again, it provides no means to empirically develop initial models.

In summary, skill atom chains formally model the component mechanics and skills of a game and their logical dependencies. Thus, they lend themselves readily to map a game's learning hierarchy. Current game user research, applied gaming, and intelligent tutoring research provide no reliable empirical method to identify the learning hierarchy or skill chain of a given game – the *actual* skills a player needs to acquire to master a game, and the *actual* order in which they build on each other and therefore *should* be introduced. Existing methods are limited to either (a) charting what mechanics a given game practically includes and introduces in what order (rather than *should* include or sequence to match the empirical learning hierarchy), (b) generating, testing, and optimizing level progression in terms of difficulty given an initial model, or (c) testing the statistical fit of a given model.

Cognitive Task Analysis

Faced with the same question – how to identify the skills involved in a domain – instructional design has developed a cluster of methods called Cognitive Task Analysis (CTA). CTA involves a variety of interview, observation, and modeling techniques to elicit and describe the knowledge and skills experts use to solve complex tasks [15]. CTA is the currently prevalent method for determining how people solve complex problems and for eliciting their learning hierarchies, forming the bedrock of any instructional design [35]. Recent systematic reviews suggest that basing instruction on CTA has strong positive effects on learning outcomes [62].

That said, there is no one single CTA. With over 100 CTA techniques available [15], choosing an appropriate method is challenging. A review by Wei and Slavendy [63] distinguishes four families of CTA methods and derive guidelines when to apply which: (1) more informal *observations and interviews* are advisable when the domain in question is very broad, ill-defined, or ill-understood; (2) more rigorous *process tracing* captures the actual steps and involved knowledge and skills of performing a given task through think-aloud or stimulated recall techniques, and is advised when exemplary tasks are easily identified; (3) *conceptual techniques* generate structured representations of domain concepts and their relations and are used to either analyze and represent data collected through other techniques, or when the domain in question mainly involves conceptual knowledge; (4) computer simulations testing *formal models* are used when task models already exist and quantitative predictions or measures are required. Combining multiple techniques is generally recommended to reduce errors and improve validity.

No matter what technique, CTA generally involves an iterative five-step process [13]:

1. *Collect preliminary knowledge to identify learning goals, tasks and subjects*: The analyst familiarizes themselves with the domain and desired learning outcomes to identify tasks to analyze and experts to recruit through e.g. document analysis, observation, or initial interviews.
2. *Identify knowledge types*: The analyst determines what kind of knowledge and skills the given tasks comprise and therefore, what specific elicitation, analysis and representation techniques are best suited (e.g., cooking a meal is a highly sequential task involving lots of tacit skills around preparation techniques, suggesting close observation and a flow chart as a representation).
3. *Apply focused knowledge elicitation methods*: The analyst uses the chosen techniques to elicit the knowledge and skills involved in the observed tasks. These typically involve some form of verbal report by the expert to surface covert cognitive processes.
4. *Analyze and verify data*: The analyst codes the generated data following the chosen method and produces initial representations of the involved skills and knowledge. Data and representations are cross-checked with the involved experts for potential errors and unclear points, and compared and contrasted between multiple elicitations to arrive at a final, integrated model.
5. *Format results for intended application*: The analyst prepares a formal presentation of the resulting model depending on the intended purpose of the CTA.

ADAPTING CTA FOR SKILL CHAIN ELICITATION

Given the maturity of CTA as a means for eliciting the skills involved in a given task, we decided to develop an adapted CTA method to identify the skill chain of a game. We were especially encouraged in this as the skill atom model frames gameplay as a learning process of moving through an implicit learning hierarchy [14], and CTA is recommended specifically to identify learning hierarchies [35]. For each of the five steps of CTA methods, we will first explain why we chose specific techniques and adaptations. We will then give idealized step-by-step instructions for our final procedure to allow easy replication.

Method Development and Rationale

1. Collect preliminary knowledge to identify learning goals, tasks and subjects. In the case of game analysis, domain and learning goals are determined by the game in question and what counts as successfully completing it. The task is naturally a stretch of gameplay, which should be long enough for players to demonstrate the skills in question without putting undue hardship on subject or analyst. Depending on the size of the game, analysts may therefore want to focus on a particular aspect or stretch of the game. For instance, to analyze end-game raiding in an online role-playing game, which players often only access after dozens or hundreds of hours of gameplay, it may be advisable to focus on the first half an hour of an exemplary raid.

In terms of subject recruitment, most CTA techniques rely on subject matter experts. However, especially basic, low-level gameplay (like using controls) is a highly automated skill [12] that experts are rarely able to consciously explicate. A proven technique for foregrounding these skills is comparing novice and expert performance [55]. We conclude that unless the focus is on 'high-end' gameplay (such as end game raiding), recruiting a diverse set of expert *and* novice players of the game in question is a preferable strategy. As regards sample size, CTA gives no hard recommendations beyond recruiting more than one expert [13]. Given most CTA techniques are qualitative suggests adopting sampling criteria from qualitative research paradigms, most notably theoretical saturation: data collection should cease when additional data doesn't challenge the developed model anymore. Since a recent meta-analysis of qualitative interview methods suggest theoretical saturation is typically reached at around 12 or more participants [28], we chose 12 participants as our lower bound.

2. Identify knowledge types: Playing any game is a well-defined task that usually involves complex problem-solving with a wide variety of required skills and knowledge types [12], suggesting a process tracing technique [63]. Given our particular interest in skills, we chose Seamster and colleagues' [55] skill-based CTA (SBCTA) as a starting point. SBCTA combines a number of specific techniques to identify five types of cognitive skills that capture the range of skills required by video game play well: *automated* (e.g. hand-eye coordination), *procedural* (e.g. how to open menus), *representational* (mental models like predictions of enemy movement patterns), *decision-making*, and *strategies*. Seamster and colleagues and Wei [63] suggest to elicit automated and procedural skills through process tracing combined with verbal reports such as think-aloud. However, gameplay is highly cognitively involving, making parallel think-aloud problematic [31]. We therefore chose to use *stimulated recall*, likewise a common process tracing technique in CTA [16]. Here, the subject is video-recorded while performing the task in question. Afterwards, the analyst replays the video to the subject, stopping the video at relevant moments to ask the subject to explicate their thoughts and decision-making processes at the recorded time. This method allows the subject to perform tasks without interruption in a more natural setting while also cueing fresh memories and double-checking recall against actual recorded behavior, reducing false memories and post-rationalization [18]. For these and other reasons, variants of stimulated recall have been in active use in game research for some time [52, 7, 37, 38]. Following SBCTA, *representational* and *decision-making* skills are captured through the critical decision method [40] and error analysis, focused interview probing of moments in task performance when subjects made decisions or errors. Finally, *strategy* skills are likewise elicited with structured interview probing on decision points and/or scenarios [55].

3. Apply focused knowledge elicitation methods: Each subject is video-recorded playing the gameplay stretch investigated. Since gameplay occurs both on and in front of the screen, both should be captured and merged into a single picture-in-picture or picture-next-to-picture video file for replay and analysis [52, 59]. We decided to instruct players to think-aloud while they play *to the extent possible*, since think-aloud data provides additional cues and checks on the player's memory during stimulated recall [58, 61]. To elicit representational and decision-making skills via critical decisions and errors, the analyst watches the unfolding play and makes time-stamped notes on these incidents for focused follow-up. Indicators for relevant incidents are moments such as the player taking additional time to figure something out; struggling, pausing, or making errors; expressing an "aha" moment verbally or through body language; making a decision; or deviating from expected gameplay.

The play session is followed by a video-aided recall session that is also recorded. These generally follow a semi-structured interview pattern of initial scripted questions to elicit the subject's thinking at a given point, followed up by further, more open probing [46]. Concretely, we decided to show the player the record of each point in gameplay marked by the interviewer, and ask them (a) what elements of the game they interacted with or paid attention to, (b) what they were thinking at this point, and (c) why they took the action they took. These questions try to elicit procedural and automated knowledge around low-level gameplay as well as representational decision-making and strategy skills. Finally, subjects are asked what aspects of the game made it more or less difficult to complete the particular game goal at that point in order to identify the "challenge" component of the skill atom.

4. Analyze and verify data: Following standard procedures for stimulated recall analysis [52], the recall session record is transcribed as a structured, time-coded script of (a) the recall dialogue and (b) recorded gameplay and think-aloud verbalizations it refers to. To conduct analysis and cross-check transcripts against video data, we suggest using a computer-aided qualitative data analysis (CAQDA) software that can code and display text and video data. As skill atoms already prescribe a clear unit of analysis, we adopted a directed qualitative content analysis method [32]: each unit of the first transcript is parsed for any *actions* the player takes in the game at that point. These actions are then contextualized in the video record and transcript to assess whether it forms part of a skill atom, meaning it involves some *simulation*, *game feedback*, *challenge*, and player *synthesis*.

The *simulation* portion of a coded atom can be determined by observing audiovisual feedback indicating a game state change, or additional knowledge of the game itself. *Feedback* is determined by observing the audiovisual record of gameplay and analyzing a subject's statements directly after an action is performed to see what feedback (if any) they noticed and (rightly or wrongly) interpreted as a result of their action. *Challenge* is explicitly derived from subject's statements about what makes a given moment of gameplay hard or easy to master, and implicitly from moments of pausing or failures at performing a given action. *Synthesis* can be derived from moments where the player explicitly voices a particular "aha" moment or demonstrates newly competent performance of an action. Each instance showcasing all five elements is coded as a skill atom. A second pass through the transcript codes for further instances of the identified skill atoms or their components, e.g. additional dimensions of challenge.

Dependencies between atoms in the skill chain are discovered through (a) analyzing the transcript for the sequence in which players showed or reported to learn a given atom, and (b) subsequent logical challenging whether the observed sequence expresses a necessary dependency or not. After analyzing the first transcript, transcripts of additional subjects are coded for the already-identified and additional skill atoms, also revising or refining prior skill atoms as needed.

5. Format results for intended application: Wei and Slavendy recommend conceptual CTA techniques such as visual diagramming to articulate and present the structure of knowledge of a domain [63]. Cook [14] already provides a visual diagramming language for skill chains, which we chose to adopt. Interestingly, skill chains parallel the graphical structure of concepts maps, a common conceptual tool for diagramming results of a CTA [51]: both are constructed of nodes representing a specific concept and edges connecting nodes that represent their relationships. We took this as convergent support for our choice. We programmed a script to automatically generate a visualization from a simple JSON file. True to the iterative nature of CTA [13], we found it useful to already sketch and iteratively revise and refine a draft diagram skill chain in parallel to data analysis.

Method Procedure

The following is a streamlined set of instructions for replicating the final methodology of our adapted CTA.

1. Identify analysis goals, tasks and subjects. Determine which game and particular aspect of its gameplay you wish to map as a skill chain. Choose a portion of gameplay that requires players to learn and/or demonstrate mastery of the focused aspect and does not overburden subjects – assume that interview sessions last at least double the time of the recorded gameplay stretch plus 20 minutes of briefing and debriefing. Unless you focus on a particular audience or gameplay aspect (e.g. end-game content), recruit a diverse pool of 12+ subjects that involves both novices and experts at the game.[1]

2. Elicit knowledge. Instruct subjects to play the selected stretch of gameplay, verbalizing what is going through their head as they do so. During gameplay, audiovisually record both on-screen game events and off-screen player activity and take notes including time stamps on critical moments when players (a) seem to make a decision; (b) struggle, pause, or make an error; (c) express an "aha" moment; or (d) deviate from expected gameplay. After the play session, replay the video recording to the subject. Fast forward to and play each critical moment you noted and ask the subject to verbalize (a) what game elements they were paying attention to or interacting with, (b) what was going through their mind at that point, (c) why they took the action they took, and (d) what aspects of the game made it more or less difficult to complete the particular game goal at that point.

3. Analyze data. Transcribe all stimulated recall sessions with time codes, noting (a) the recall dialogue and (b) recorded gameplay and think-aloud verbalizations it refers to. Upload video data and transcript to a CAQDA software that can display and code both. For analysis, parse each unit of the first transcript for *actions* the player takes. Contextualize each action in the video recording and transcript to determine whether it forms part of a skill atom comprising:

- an *action*,
- *simulation* or rule processing and game state change, based on recorded game screen feedback,
- game *feedback*, based on recorded game feedback and subject statements directly after an action indicating whether they (in)correctly perceived a game state change as feedback on their action,
- dimensions of *challenge*, based on subject statements about what makes a given moment of gameplay hard or easy, as well as play pauses or failures at performing a given action,
- moments of *synthesis* where the player voices insight into or demonstrates competent enactment of some required knowledge or skill connected to the action.

Code each instance showcasing all five elements as a skill atom and label it based on the main synthesis knowledge or skill. Cross-validate player-derived *simulation* with the actual game rules, code, and/or game designer to ensure these aren't player misconceptions. In a second pass, code the transcript for further instances of the identified skill atoms or their components. After identifying skill atoms, parse the transcript for *dependencies* between atoms expressed in when and/or what order players showed or reported to learn a given atom. Challenge each derived dependency by questioning whether the documented order is an incidental result of the game's design, or a logically necessary dependency. After analyzing the first transcript, code transcripts of additional subjects for

[1]Our results indicate a smaller n of 5+ may be sufficient, see below.

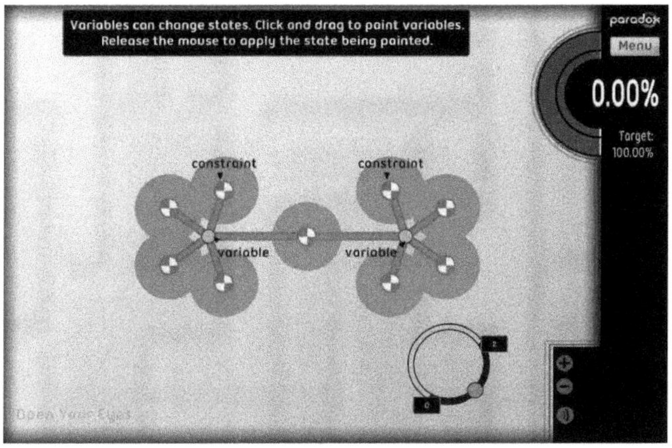

Figure 3. A screenshot of the game *Paradox* analyzed in our case study.

already-identified and additional skill atoms, iteratively revising or refining prior skill atoms and re-coding prior transcripts as needed.

4. Visualize skill chain. Already during data analysis, draft a first skill atom list and skill chain diagram as a reference and cross-check for coding. Once all transcripts are analyzed and have informed the draft skill chain, draw up a final clean skill chain diagram using the provided script[2].

CASE STUDY

Game and background

We developed and tested the above CTA method by eliciting the skill chain of the human computation game (HCG) *Paradox* (Figure 3). This was part of a larger project aimed at developing automatic level progression algorithms for HCGs that crowdsource scientific tasks like classifying images of galaxies. Notably, HCGs suffer from poor player retention at least partially due to poor progression design: instead of sequencing tasks in an order matching the learning curve of players, they predominantly serve tasks at random, risking both player frustration and boredom [53]. To inform machine learning algorithms that would automatically assess the difficulty of each task in *Paradox*, we wanted to get a grounded understanding of what component skills are required to play the game and thus, how difficult each *Paradox* task would be, depending on what skills it required (akin to [8]). *Paradox* was designed to crowdsource software verification, checking how many given conditions a given piece of code could satisfy. Each level or task presents players with a visualization of an underlying code piece as a graph of variables (displayed as nodes that can take different states) and conditions pertaining to variables (visualized as edges). Players can manually click individual variables to change their states or use various "brushes" to select subsets of variables to be modified. Different brushes trigger different approaches to modifying variables, from simple brushes that immediately set all to a certain value, to brushes that run specific optimization algorithms. The player's goal is to configure variables so that the highest possible number of conditions are satisfied. To complete a level, a player must reach a given target score or percentage of satisfied conditions. In general, it is not known in advance whether the target percentage of conditions (let alone all conditions) of a level can be satisfied.

[2]Available at http://github.com/crowdgames/skillchain.

Procedure, Observations and Reflections

In the following, we report on how we concretely implemented our method step by step and what generally relevant observations we made for that step.

Identify analysis goals, tasks and subjects. To make sure subjects were exposed to the same gameplay, we used a stable local version of *Paradox*[3] that featured seven tutorial levels introducing gameplay, followed by a fixed series of 20 challenge levels, which were generally larger, more open-ended and more difficult than the tutorials. Levels were chosen to cover a range of level sizes and likely solution strategies. Tutorial levels were gated: players had to complete a level by reaching its target score before being able to proceed to the next tutorial level. In contrast, players were able to skip challenge levels without completing them if they desired. We asked participants to play the game for 30 minutes, immediately followed by a 30 minute stimulated recall session. Gameplay length was determined by estimating how long players typically take to get through the tutorial and five challenge levels, which we assumed sufficient for novice players to acquire and demonstrate basic gameplay skills and for expert players to be challenged in the breadth of their expertise.

To record at least 12 subjects (ensuring theoretical saturation [28]), we recruited 15 subjects, preparing for a number of no-shows. We recruited 5 "expert" subjects who had played *Paradox* extensively in the past and 10 "novice" players who had never seen *Paradox* before, otherwise aiming for maximum diversity in gender, age, and socio-economic background.

Observations and Reflections. *Novices are more valuable than experts.* Interestingly, novices proved much more valuable for discovering low-level interface and gameplay skills than expert players. Indeed, analyzing expert gameplay only added minor refinements to the emerging skill chain. This somewhat contradicts standard CTA philosophy to rely on experts, but may be at least partially due to the relatively simple gameplay of *Paradox* or the fact that expert traces were analyzed last.

Quick saturation. We identified the vast majority of skill atoms during analysis of the first five recall transcripts, with subsequent transcripts adding only about one additional skill atom (3 percent of all codes) each. This suggests that future analyses may work sufficiently with a smaller number of subjects than we used – although this has to be tested with larger, more complex games.

Recognize and bracket shortcuts. At the conclusion of the first three recall sessions, we noticed that players heavily relied on the so-called optimizer brush. This brush automatically maximized satisfied conditions in a given graph area. While

[3]http://paradox.centerforgamescience.org/

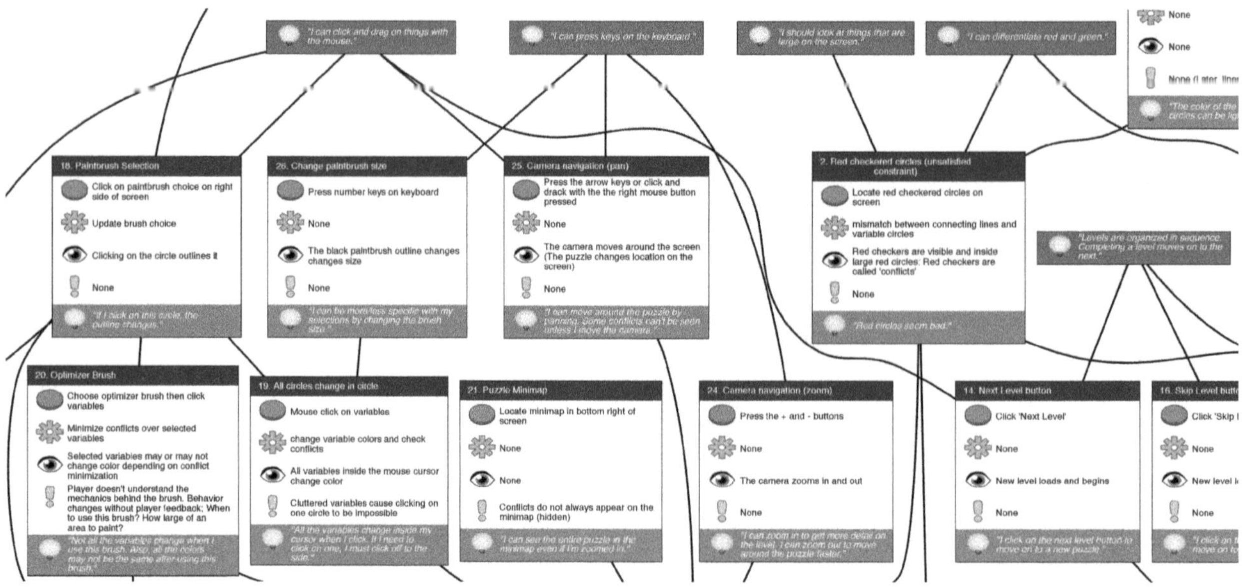

Figure 4. Detail of *Paradox* skill chain produced by our method.

generating a good first score, the global maximum of possible satisfied conditions cannot usually achieved with the optimizer; it requires deeper analysis and probing of the total graph. However, since the optimizer brush was introduced early on in the tutorial and was enough to complete early tutorial levels, novices tended to learn the heuristic to simply use the brush to clear each level, rather than learning how the constraint satisfaction mechanic worked and how to manually analyze and manipulate the graph. Hence, they would often become frustrated in later challenge levels when the brush alone didn't suffice, and were not able to switch to manual optimization. (One participant even said that the optimizer felt "like cheating" because it would do all the work without players understanding how.) In terms of CTA, this highlights that the availability of "power tools," "exploits," or "shortcuts" as part of the analyzed task can prevent certain procedural skills from being actively performed and thus made observable. Observed tasks should therefore ideally be trialled in advance of actual analysis to check for and eliminate undesired shortcuts. In our case, we later on manipulated the game and restricted two novices and one expert from using the optimizer brush at all, requiring them to manipulate each variable of a level individually. This helped discover particular skill atoms for novices as well as challenge features of graph layouts we hadn't observed before.

Elicit knowledge and analyze data. We began stimulated recall sessions with novice players as we assumed that their play would feature many critical moments foregrounding basic *Paradox* skills which expert players had already perfected and would therefore be hard to notice. Gameplay sessions were captured using *Morae*[4], which allows to make categorized notes during screen and camera recording that are logged on the recording timeline. We used this to log critical moments we would then replay to subjects to stimulate recall after the play session. Stimulated recall sessions were recorded with *Camtasia Studio*[5], as this program allowed to display and screen capture play session video and audio in addition to the camera video and audio of analyst and subject conversing. Stimulated recall sessions were transcribed and coded using *MaxQDA*[6].

Observations and Reflections. *Skill dependencies are unclear and confounded by level design.* We found it hard to identify clear dependencies between skill atoms and to disentangle (a) the order in which the game's progression design required certain skills, (b) the order in which players developed insights, and (c) the ideal learning hierarchy in which both should occur. Instead, the order in which the game tutorial introduced skill atoms strongly shaped player perceptions and analyst coding: both tended to state that the order in which the game presents skill atoms is the order in which players learned them. This indicates a strong limitation in using qualitative analysis of fixed games with fixed progressions for eliciting skill chains. Ideally, players would be exposed to a randomized multivariate ordering of skill atoms to observe which order empirically produces the fastest learning gains.

Strategy skills are unvalidated. In alignment with Seamster and colleagues' [55] hierarchy of cognitive skills, we found *strategies* to sit at the 'highest' level of our skill chain. The distinction between procedural and strategy skills is fuzzy. We found a good indicator for strategy skills to be that players consciously identified different approaches or composite applications of procedural skills and chose between them based on context. For example, players chose from what location to begin solving *Paradox* levels and in which order to move through the graph depending on level geometry. Sometimes a player would work from the periphery to the center, other times a player would choose to start in an area that had the

[4]https://www.techsmith.com/morae-features.html

[5]https://www.techsmith.com/camtasia.html
[6]http://www.maxqda.com/

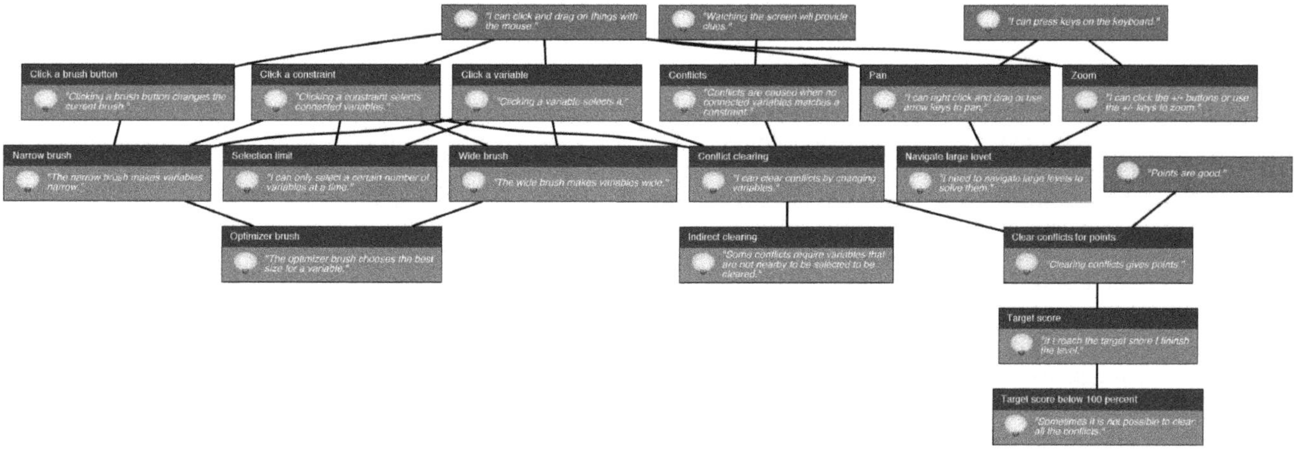

Figure 5. Simplified *Paradox* skill chain hand-authored by one of the game's designers.

most conflicts, and players would generally verbalize that and why they chose this particular strategy. That said, it is hard to tell from our data whether and how optimal any of these strategies in a particular context actually are. (Notably, the same holds for CTA, which simply assumes that expert practice is self-validated as best practice.) It would be good to triangulate our qualitative data with quantitative data on the relative performance of different strategies, in the same way players and teams in eSports analyze the performance of different characters or items[7].

Also, conceptual CTA techniques focus on mapping the cognitive skills and knowledge of a task rather than individual strategies, meta-strategies, and conditions when to employ them [63]. To a certain extent, one could argue that the three strategy skill atoms we mapped are really on the skill atom "choosing optimal strategies". Hence, CTA may be less apt at analyzing and visualizing strategies and strategy-heavy games.

Visualize skill chain. A detail of the final skill chain we created for *Paradox* can be seen in Figure 4. The full skill chain is given as supplementary information. To assess the produced skill chain, we asked one of the designers of *Paradox* to draw a skill chain based off of their understanding of the skills necessary for the game, which can be seen in Figure 5.

Observations and Reflections. *Skill chain analysis surfaces low-level and pre-existing skills.* While both designer and CTA-derived skill chain covered the same basic mechanics, the CTA-generated chain is far more detailed and comprehensive. First, it entails many required pre-existing skills. For instance, we discovered that the game was not accessible for people with blue-yellow and green-red color blindness, who had difficulty recognizing the color-coded states of the variables. Second, comparing novice and expert gameplay brought to light that experts used certain low-level skills that were not explicitly conveyed to players in the tutorial and therefore not used by novice players. One example is changing brush sizes. Because expert players had explored *Paradox* and its interface more deeply, they had discovered how to change the brush size, which allowed them more control over the variables selected. This observation arguably demonstrates the most direct value of our method: the tutorial, based on the designers' hypothetical skill chain, overlooked parts of the actual empirical skill chain of players – quite possibly since designers are expert players who therefore have difficulty recognizing the low-level, highly automated skills they possess but novices don't. That said, it is an open question whether the same insights could not be generated more efficiently through standard usability and playability testing.

Skill chains run together in a core mechanic. Interestingly, unlike the designer-generated skill chain, the CTA-generated chain eventually runs together in one central node, "efficiently reduce number of conflicts", which then branches out into strategies for achieving such efficient reduction. Discussions with the game's designers and our own gameplay experience suggest that this central node is indeed the "core mechanic" of *Paradox* [56]. We take this as further validation of our method and find it suggestive for formal game analysis more broadly: core mechanics or loops are the graph-theoretically most central nodes in which all dependencies and subskills run together.

Skill chains remain flat. Overall, the skill chain we elicited had a flat, "pancake" quality: it consists of many fundamental skills around using the interface without many dependencies between or beyond them. The same flat structure can be seen in Cook's skill chain of *Tetris* [14], while the skill chain of *Pac-Man* shows greater depth [25]. This may be due to many things: the relative simplicity of *Paradox* and *Tetris* compared to a greater gameplay depth of *Pac-Man*; the subjectivity of involved analysts; or the general complexity of the underlying genre. It is worth noting that all published uses of skill atoms cover relatively simple puzzle and action games. Hence, it is an open question whether (a) different game genres and more complex games would produce different skill chains, and whether (b) skill chain mapping is feasible or productive for

[7]See e.g. https://www.dotabuff.com/heroes/winning

more complex games or whether graphs become too unwieldy to be of much use.

DISCUSSION

Reflecting on our case study, we think it warrants the conclusion that our method worked: we were able to elicit a skill chain from gameplay that roughly mapped the understanding of one of the game's designers, identified the correct "core loop", and produced useful design insight. Particularly, it surfaced a range of overlooked prerequisite and low-level skills that had eluded the designer's attention and made the game more challenging to learn and play for novices. A second main observation vis-à-vis CTA is that observing novices learning how to play a game proved potentially more valuable than observing smooth expert performance.

That said, our case study also surfaced a series of major challenges and limitations. First, it is unclear whether standard usability and playability testing methods wouldn't be more efficient in producing the same insights into overlooked low-level gameplay skills. Although our case study suggests that skill chains can be elicited with a smaller (5+) n than we used, the method remains quite involved, using about 10 hours per subject (1 interview, 6 transcription, 3 analysis). Likewise, it is unclear how approachable our method is for designers and game researchers. In future work, we would therefore like to run method variants with other analysts to assess ease of use, approachability, perceived efficacy, and outcomes, and to trial the method with smaller n's and with direct video analysis that doesn't rely on transcription.

Now standard playability and usability testing don't provide learning hierarchies to inform e.g. level design or procedural content adaptation or generation. However, this arguable main differentiator of our method – identifying the dependencies between skills – also proved the most elusive. Actual ideal dependencies were hard to ascertain, and the resultant skill chain featured little depth. We assume this is partially due to the simplicity of *Paradox* and the fact that the game's actual fixed progression sequence strongly biased observation. In future work, we would therefore want to use process tracing on experimental variations of skill sequencing, and replicate our method with more complex games, which brings us to a further limitation: We tested the method with a very simple puzzle game. It is unclear whether it would work with different genres or more complex games. Action games rich in automated 'twitch' skills may prove harder to analyze, and 'big' games like the MMORPG *EVE Online* may involve so many skill atoms that eliciting them in short gameplay sessions or mapping them in a single chain could prove unwieldy.

A final challenge and limitation concerns strategy skills. While we could elicit a number of emergent strategies actively used by players, our method cannot speak to how empirically optimal these strategies actually are. Here, combinations of our qualitative analysis and quantitative game analytics would be useful. Indeed, we view novel mixed method combinations of qualitative 'thick data' methods like CTA with 'big data' analytics to be a highly promising future direction, as many data-driven methods of tutorial or progression design and analysis [60, 8, 30] in turn lack exactly the specificity and insight into what particular skills to analyze for or generate from that qualitative data provides.

CONCLUSION

Like designing good instruction, designing an enjoyable, easy to learn game requires understanding what skills the game's mechanics require, how these build and depend on each other, and thus, in what order to introduce them to players. Learning hierarchies in instructional design and skill chains in game design are common formal models to map these relations. Yet where instructional design can rely on cognitive task analysis to empirically identify the learning hierarchy of a task, game design so far relied on expert interpretation to identify the skill chains of games. Given that experts are typically blind to the full range of tacit skills they have mastered, this risks overlooking crucial skills that novices need to be taught. In this paper, we therefore developed and presented an adapted cognitive task analysis method to elicit a game's skill chain from empirical player observation and interviewing. The method combines stimulated recall interviews on targeted stretches of gameplay with directed qualitative content analysis of the generated data. We demonstrated and critically reflected on the method through a case study use on the game *Paradox*. The skill chain elicited for *Paradox* with our method indeed proved aligned with but more comprehensive than a designer-crafted skill chain produced without empirical player observation. Specifically, it included critical missing pre-requisite and low-level skills.

While principally effective in our case study, the method also showed major limitations and open questions regarding its efficiency, generalizability across genres and more complex games, and ability to reliably elicit skill dependencies, and validity of captured emergent player strategies, which we hope to address in future applications with replications and mixed method approaches.

ACKNOWLEDGEMENTS

This work was supported by a Northeastern University TIER 1 grant and partly conducted in the Digital Creativity Labs (digitalcreativity.ac.uk), jointly funded by EPSRC/AHRC/InnovateUK under grant no. EP/M023265/1. This material is based upon work supported by the National Science Foundation under grant no. 1652537. We would like to thank the University of Washington's Center for Game Science for initial *Paradox* development.

REFERENCES

1. Ernest Adams and Joris Dormans. 2012. *Game Mechanics: Advanced Game Design*. New Riders, Berkeley, CA.
2. Marcos Silvano Orita Almeida and Flavio Soares Correa da Silva. 2013. A Systematic Review of Game Design Methods and Tools. In *ICEC 2013*, J.C. Anacleto (Ed.). Springer, 17–29.
3. Sylvester Arnab, Theodore Lim, Maira B. Carvalho, Francesco Bellotti, Sara De Freitas, Sandy Louchart, Neil Suttie, Riccardo Berta, and Alessandro De Gloria. 2015. Mapping learning and game mechanics for serious games

analysis. *British Journal of Educational Technology* 46, 2 (2015), 391–411.

4. Melissa Baralt, Roger Gilabert, and Peter Robinson. 2014. An introduction to theory and research in task sequencing and instructed second language learning. *Task sequencing and instructed second language learning* (2014), 1–50.
5. Regina Bernhaupt. 2010. User Experience Evaluation in Entertainment. In *Evaluating User Experience in Games: Concepts and Methods*, Regina Bernhaupt (Ed.). Springer London, London, 3–7.
6. Staffan Björk and Jussi Holopainen. 2005. *Patterns in Game Design*. Charles River Media, Boston, MA.
7. Joceran Borderie and Nicolas Michinov. 2016. Identifying Flow in Video Games: Towards a New Observation-Based Method. *International Journal of Gaming and Computer-Mediated Simulations (IJGCMS)* (2016).
8. Eric Butler, Erik Andersen, Adam M Smith, Sumit Gulwani, and Zoran Popovic. 2015. Automatic Game Progression Design through Analysis of Solution Features. *Chi'15* (2015), 2407–2416.
9. Maira B. Carvalho, Francesco Bellotti, Riccardo Berta, Alessandro De Gloria, Carolina Islas Sedano, Jannicke Baalsrud Hauge, Jun Hu, and Matthias Rauterberg. 2015. An activity theory-based model for serious games analysis and conceptual design. *Computers and Education* 87 (2015), 166–181.
10. Judeth Oden Choi, Jodi Forlizzi, Michael Christel, Rachel Moeller, MacKenzie Bates, and Jessica Hammer. 2016. Playtesting with a Purpose. *Proceedings of the 2016 Annual Symposium on Computer-Human Interaction in Play - CHI PLAY '16* (2016), 254–265.
11. Dough Church. 1999. Formal Abstract Design Tools. (1999).
12. D. B. Clark, E. E. Tanner-Smith, and S. S. Killingsworth. 2016. Digital Games, Design, and Learning: A Systematic Review and Meta-Analysis. *Review of Educational Research* 86, 1 (2016), 79–122.
13. Richard E. Clark, D. Feldon, Jeroen JG van Merriënboer, Kenneth Yates, and Sean Early. 2008. Cognitive task analysis. *Handbook of research on educational communications and technology* 3 (2008), 577–593.
14. Daniel Cook. 2007. The chemistry of game design. `http://www.gamasutra.com/view/feature/1524/the_chemistry_of_game_design.php`. (2007).
15. Nancy J Cooke. 1994. Varieties of knowledge elicitation techniques. *International Journal of Human-Computer Studies* 41, 6 (1994), 801–849.
16. Beth Crandall, Gary Klein, and Robert Hoffman. 2006. *Working Minds: A Practitioner's Guide to Cognitive Task Analysis*.
17. Mihaly Csikszentmihalyi. 1990. *Flow: the psychology of optimal experience*. Harper and Row, New York.
18. Nicholas P. Dempsey. 2010. Stimulated Recall Interviews in Ethnography. *Qualitative Sociology* 33, 3 (2010), 349–367.
19. Heather Desurvire and Magy Seif El-Nasr. 2013. Methods for Game User Research: Studying Player Behavior to Enhance Game Design. *IEEE Computer Graphics and Applications* 33, 4 (2013), 82–87.
20. Heather Desurvire and Charlotte Wiberg. 2015. User Experience Design for Inexperienced Gamers: GAP – Game Approachability Principles. In *Game User Experience Evaluation*, Regina Bernhaupt (Ed.). Springer, London, 131–147.
21. Sebastian Deterding. 2015. The lens of intrinsic skill atoms: a method for gameful design. *Human-Computer Interaction* 30, 3-4 (2015), 294–335.
22. Joris Dormans. 2012. *Engineering Emergence: Applied Theory for Game Design*. PhD Thesis. Universiteit van Amsterdam.
23. Alejandro Echeverría, Enrique Barrios, Miguel Nussbaum, Matías Améstica, and Sandra Leclerc. 2012. The Atomic Intrinsic Integration Approach: A structured methodology for the design of games for the conceptual understanding of physics. *Computers & Education* 59, 2 (2012), 806–816.
24. Magy Seif El-Nasr, Anders Drachen, and Alessandro Canossa (Eds.). 2013. *Game Analytics: Maximizing the Value of Player Data*. Springer, London. 815 pages.
25. firecorth. 2013. Game Design Alchemy the Second. (2013).
26. Robert M Gagne. 1968. Presidential address of division 15 learning hierarchies. *Educational psychologist* 6, 1 (1968), 1–9.
27. James-Paul Gee. 2003. *What Video Games Have to Teach Us About Learning and Literacy*. Palgrave Macmillan, New York.
28. Greg Guest, Arwen Bunce, and Laura Johnson. 2006. How Many Interviews Are Enough?: An Experiment with Data Saturation and Variability. *Field Methods* 18, 1 (2006), 59–82.
29. Erik Harpstead and Vincent Aleven. 2015. Using Empirical Learning Curve Analysis to Inform Design in an Educational Game. In *CHI Play 2015*. 197–207.
30. Erik Harpstead, Thomas Zimmermann, Jose J Guajardo, Ryan Cooper, Tyson Solberg, and Dan Greenawalt. 2015. What Drives People : Creating Engagement Profiles of Players from Game Log Data. (2015), 369–379.
31. Jettie Hoonhout. 2008. Let the Game Tester Do the Talking: Think Aloud and Interviewing to Learn About the Game Experience. In *Game Usability: Advice from the Experts for Advancing the Player Experience*, Katherine Isbister and Noah Schaffer (Eds.). Morgan Kaufmann, Amsterdam et al., 65–78.

32. Hsiu-Fang Hsieh and Sarah E Shannon. 2005. Three approaches to qualitative content analysis. *Qualitative health research* 15, 9 (Nov 2005), 1277–88.

33. Robin Hunicke. 2005. The case for dynamic difficulty adjustment in games. *Proceedings of the 2005 ACM SIGCHI International Conference on Advances in computer entertainment technology - ACE '05* (2005), 429–433.

34. Robin Hunicke, Marc LeBlanc, and Robert Zubek. 2004. MDA: A Formal Approach to Game Design and Game Research. In *Papers from the 2004 AAAI Workshop "Challenges in Game Artificial Intelligence"*, Dan Fu, Stottler Henke, and Jeff Orkin (Eds.). AAAI Press, Menlo Park, Ca, 1–5.

35. David H. Jonassen, Martin Tessmer, and Wallace H. Hannum. 1998. *Task Analysis Methods for Instructional Design*. Routledge.

36. Rilla Khaled and Gordon Ingram. 2012. Tales from the front lines of a large-scale serious game project. In *Proceedings of the SIGCHI Conference on Human Factors in Computing Systems*. ACM, 69–78.

37. David Kirschner and J Patrick Williams. 2013. Experts and Novices or Expertise? Positioning Players through Gameplay Reviews. In *DiGRA 2013: DeFragging Game Studies*. DiGRA, Snowbird, UT.

38. D. Kirschner and J. P. Williams. 2015. Measuring Video Game Engagement Through Gameplay Reviews. *Simulation & Gaming* 45, 4-5 (2015), 593–610.

39. J. Matias Kivikangas, Guillaume Chanel, Ben Cowley, Inger Ekman, Mikko Salminen, Simo Järvelä, and Niklas Ravaja. 2011. A review of the use of psychophysiological methods in game research. *Journal of Gaming & Virtual Worlds* 3, 3 (2011), 181–199.

40. G. A. Klein, R. Calderwood, and D. MacGregor. 1989. Critical decision method for eliciting knowledge. *IEEE Transactions on Systems, Man, and Cybernetics* (1989).

41. Christina Koeffel, Wolfgang Hochleitner, Jakob Leitner, Michael Haller, Arjan Geven, and Manfred Tscheligi. 2010. Using Heuristics to Evaluate the Overall User Experience of Video Games and Advanced Interaction Games. In *Evaluating User Experience in Games*, Regina Bernhaupt (Ed.). Springer, London, 233–255.

42. Raph Koster. 2004. *A Theory of Fun for Game Design*. Paraglyph Press, Scottsdale, AZ.

43. Raph Koster. 2013. *Theory of fun for game design*. O'Reilly Media, Inc.

44. Petri Lankoski and Staffan L Björk. 2015. Formal analysis of gameplay. In *Game Research Methods: An Overview*, Petri Lankoski and Staffan L Björk (Eds.). ETC Press, Pittsburgh, PA, 23–36.

45. Conor Linehan, George Bellord, Ben Kirman, Zachary H Morford, and Bryan Roche. 2014. Learning Curves: Analysing Pace and Challenge in Four Successful Puzzle Games. In *CHI Play'14*. 181–190.

46. John Lyle. 2010. Stimulated recall: a report on its use in naturalistic research. *British Educational Research Journal* 29, 6 (2010), 861 878.

47. Chris McEntee. 2012. Rational Design: The Core of Rayman Origins. `http://www.gamasutra.com/view/feature/167214/rational_design_the_core_of_.php`. (2012).

48. Luke McMillan. 2013. The Rational Design Handbook: An Intro to RLD. (2013).

49. Jeroen J. G. van Merriënboer, Richard E. Clark, and Marcel B. M. de Croock. 2002. Blueprints for complex learning: The 4C/ID-model. *Educational Technology Research and Development* 50, 2 (2002), 39–61.

50. Lennart Nacke, Anders Drachen, and Stefan Gobel. 2010. Methods for Evaluating Gameplay Experience in a Serious Gaming Context. *International Journal of Computer Science in Sport* 9, 2 (2010).

51. Joseph D Novak and Alberto J Cañas. 2008. The theory underlying concept maps and how to construct and use them. (2008).

52. Jori Pitkanen. 2015. Studying thoughts: Stimulated recall as a game research method. In *Game Research Methods*, Petri Lankoski and Staffan L Björk (Eds.). ETC Press, 117–132.

53. Anurag Sarkar, Michael Williams, Sebastian Deterding, and Seth Cooper. 2017. Engagement Effects of Player Rating System-Based Matchmaking for Level Ordering in Human Computation Games. In *FDG'17*. ACM Press, New York.

54. Donald A Schon. 1984. *The reflective practitioner: How professionals think in action*. Basic books.

55. Thomas L. Seamster, Richard E. Redding, and George L. Kaempf. 2000. A skill-based cognitive task analysis framework. In *Cognitive task analysis*, Jan Maarten Schraagen, Susan F. Chipman, and Valerie L. Shalin (Eds.). Lawrence Erlbaum, Mahwah, NJ, 135–146.

56. Miguel Sicart. 2008. Defining game mechanics. *Game Studies* 8, 2 (2008), 1–14.

57. Miguel Sicart. 2015. Loops and Metagames: Understanding Game Design Structures. In *Foundations of Digital Games*.

58. M. W. Someren, Y. F. Barnard, and J. a. C. Sandberg. 1994. *The think aloud method: a practical approach to modelling cognitive processes*. Academic Press.

59. Reed Stevens, Tom Satwicz, and Laurie McCarthy. 2008. In-Game, In-Room, In-World: Reconnecting Video Game Play to the Rest of Kids' Lives. In *The Ecology of Games: Connecting Youth, Games, and Learning*, Katie Salen (Ed.). MIT Press, Cambridge, MA, 41–66.

60. Joseph J Thompson, Mark R Blair, Lihan Chen, and Andrew J Henrey. 2013. Video Game Telemetry as a Critical Tool in the Study of Complex Skill Learning. *PLoS ONE* 8, 9 (2013), e75129.

61. Bonnie L Tjeerdsma. 1997. A comparison of teacher and student perspectives of tasks and feedback. *Journal of teaching in physical education* 16, 4 (1997), 388–400.

62. Colby Tofel-Grehl and David F. Feldon. 2013. Cognitive Task Analysis–Based Training. *Journal of Cognitive Engineering and Decision Making* 7, 3 (2013), 293–304.

63. June Wei and Gavriel Salvendy. 2004. The cognitive task analysis methods for job and task design: review and reappraisal. *Behaviour & Information Technology* 23, 4 (2004), 273–299.

64. Richard T White and Robert M Gagné. 1974. Past and future research on learning hierarchies 1. *Educational psychologist* 11, 1 (1974), 19–28.

65. Pieter Wouters, Erik D. van der Spek, and Herre van Oostendorp. 2009. Current practices in serious game research: A review from a learning outcomes perspective. In *Games-Based Learning Advancements for Multi-Sensory Human Computer Interfaces: Techniques and Effective Practices*, Thomas Connolly, Mark Stansfield, and Liz Boyle (Eds.). IGI Global, Hershey, PA, 232–250.

Leveraging Design Patterns to Support Designer-Therapist Collaboration When Ideating Brain Injury Therapy Games

Jinghui Cheng*, Dorian Anderson†, Cynthia Putnam*
DePaul University
Chicago, IL, USA
*{jcheng13, cputnam}@cdm.depaul.edu,
†dorian.c.anderson@gmail.com

Jin Guo
University of Notre Dame
Notre Dame, IN, USA
jguo3@nd.edu

ABSTRACT
Many therapists who work with patients who have had a brain injury (BI) include games to ameliorate boredom associated with repetitive rehabilitation exercises. However, designing effective, appropriate, and engaging games for BI therapy is challenging. Following a user-centered approach we created GaPBIT (**Ga**me Design **P**atterns for **BI T**herapy), a prototype tool that leveraged design patterns to support designer-therapist collaboration when ideating games for BI therapy. We observed the use of GaPBIT in six game ideation workshops that involved game designers and therapists. The tool effectively facilitated collaboration in the interdisciplinary teams. Findings also suggested that information tools like GaPBIT support but do not replace informative collaboration among designers and subject-matter experts (i.e., therapists in our study). We argue that our findings and research methodology generalize to other domains where communication and collaboration among interdisciplinary design teams are imperative for designing 'successful' games; i.e. games that meet the varied goals among stakeholders.

Author Keywords
Game design; game design patterns; brain injury; therapy; serious games; games for health; stakeholder collaboration.

ACM Classification Keywords
H.5.2. Information interfaces and presentation (e.g., HCI): User Interfaces (User-centered design); K.4.2. Computers and Society: Social Issues (Handicapped persons/special needs); K.8.0. Personal Computing: Games.

INTRODUCTION
Brain injuries (BI) are a major public health issue affecting many societies worldwide [39]; approximately 6.4 million children and adults in the United States live with a lifelong disability as a result of a BI [9]. The causes of BIs include traumatic incidents (e.g. car accident, falling), loss of oxygen to the brain, and cerebral vascular accidents (i.e. stroke) [10,47]. Depending on the causes and nature, a BI can result in impairments affecting both physical and cognitive abilities, which in turn, lead to diverse recovery paths. As a result, therapists need to customize rehabilitation treatments to meet each patient's individual needs and unique goals.

Many BI rehabilitation treatments require repetitive activities to reinforce practice and learning. Motivation to engage in repetitive activities is a common challenge in BI therapy [6,23,24]. To overcome this challenge, many therapists include games in their sessions; therapists use varied combinations of commercial off-the-shelf (COTS) games designed for the general public and games that are specifically designed for BI therapy [5,41,42]. However, currently available games have many limitations for this population. On one hand, COTS games are often too difficult and have too steep a challenge ramp for many who have had a BI [16,32,43]. On the other hand, games designed specifically for rehabilitation have often failed to achieve a proper balance between player experience and therapeutic efficacy [12,48]. Consequently, designing effective, appropriate, and engaging games for BI therapy is a challenging and important area for exploration.

In our previous work involving interviews with game designers who focused on games for health (i.e. serious games embedded with health-related goals), we found that designers described very user-centric approaches to their work, emphasizing early involvement of target players. [17]. The designers' 'player-centered' efforts, however, did not always ameliorate many of the challenges they met in their work. For example, several interviewees expressed frustration when consolidating different mindsets and motivations with subject matter experts (e.g. therapists in the context of BI therapy games) [17]. Specifically, subject matter experts were described as narrowly focused on the purposeful goals of the game, while the game designers often lacked knowledge about the context in which the game would be played. The interviewees voiced a need for tools to support collaboration among designers and subject-matter experts when ideating games for health [17].

To address these challenges in the context of games for BI rehabilitation, we created and evaluated a prototype tool, GaPBIT (**Ga**me Design **P**atterns for **B**rain **I**njury **T**herapy),

CHI PLAY '17, October 15-18, 2017, Amsterdam, Netherlands

ACM ISBN 978-1-4503-4898-0/17/10…$15.00
https://doi.org/10.1145/3116595.3116600

that leveraged the game design patterns we identified in our previous work focused on BI therapy [18]. Design patterns, originating from Christopher Alexander's work in architecture [3], document reusable design concepts that have successfully solved recurring problems in a certain realm. Particularly, game design patterns explore reusable concepts in the design of gameplay [7,30]. In the context of serious games (i.e., games designed to convey a purposeful goal in addition to entertainment), game design patterns have been advocated as an effective tool to support design ideation and facilitate communication among game designers and other stakeholders [25,29,34].

We created and iterated the design of the GaPBIT prototype with the involvement of professional games-for-health designers. We then explored GaPBIT's ability to support collaboration in the conceptual design process through six game ideation workshops (i.e., exploratory case studies of use); the workshops included both game designers and therapists who had worked with patients who had BIs. The primary contribution of this project is twofold. First, communication and collaboration challenges among designers and subject matter experts are common and critical in serious game design but are not well addressed in the literature. This project directly targets this limitation. Second, through this project we demonstrated that tools leveraging design patterns are promising techniques for bridging designer-expert collaboration. These techniques and our research methodology generalize to other domains where communication and collaboration among interdisciplinary design teams are imperative for success.

RELATED WORK

In this section, we discuss related work in three key areas: (1) serious games for BI therapy, (2) game design patterns, and (3) game design tools.

Serious Games for BI therapy

Researchers have investigated COTS games for BI rehabilitation on various gaming platforms, including Nintendo Wii [20,35], Sony Play Station [49], Microsoft Xbox [40], and web-based games [50]. Research has identified that many COTS games can provide an engaging experience for patients with BIs; some have been found effective at addressing therapeutic goals (e.g. [40]). Researchers and practitioners have also created games designed specifically for BI therapy. Much of the recent work in this area leveraged commercially available hardware (e.g. low-cost webcams [13] and Xbox Kinect [33]); some focused on providing adjustable parameters to accommodate diverse patient needs (e.g. [1]).

However, cases cited in literature have identified that currently available games have limitations in BI therapy. Beyond the too-challenging aspects of COTS games [43], some games also provide negative feedback that is inappropriate for this group of players [32]. Further, some COTS games require players to go through lengthy setup and/or cutscenes (non-interactive video clips) that take up valuable time during a therapy session [16]. As a result, therapists use COTS games with only a small portion of their patients; i.e., those who have demonstrated higher physical and cognitive abilities [42]. Meanwhile, games specifically created for BI therapy have often overly focused on therapeutic effects at the cost of player experience [11,12,48].

To address these issues, researchers have generated design guidelines for BI therapy games aimed at balancing therapeutic efficacy and engaging gameplay. For example, Flores et al. [21] generated a list of design criteria for stroke rehabilitation games focused on both rehabilitation and entertainment. Many have also argued that a successful collaboration between subject matter experts and game designers is crucial for creating engaging and therapeutically effective games [12,21]. Our work builds on research in this area by focusing on how conceptual and information tools can support games-for-health design.

Game Design Patterns

Design patterns are a collection of solutions that have successfully solved recurring problems in corresponding contexts [3]. Based on Christopher Alexander's concept, design patterns: (1) are capable of supporting communication of design knowledge and fostering creativity; (2) should contain context, the problem, and a solution to capture the invariant design knowledge; (3) should be interconnected and organized hierarchically; and (4) need to be iterated during design practice to realize their value [2,3]. The concept of design patterns has been adopted in many fields, including software engineering [14,22] and interaction design [8,19].

Applying the concepts of design patterns and pattern language in the design of gameplay has been discussed in the general game development community since the early 2000s [30]. Björk and Holopainen [7] accomplished the most comprehensive work in this field. Through an examination of common game mechanics, existing games, and game design methods, they generated a set of over 200 game design patterns organized into 11 broad categories. Thus, their patterns constituted a comprehensive common language of game design that could arguably be used to analyze and design games.

Researchers have also explored patterns in serious game design; most focused on educational games [26,29,34]. For example, Huynh-Kim-Bang et al. [26] investigated how game design patterns can help balance fun and learning elements, as well as support the collaboration between game designers and non-designers (e.g. teachers) in creating educational games. By analyzing 25 serious games and related literature, the authors provided more than 30 patterns focused on educational game design. Marne et al. [34] also investigated design patterns as a collaboration space to facilitate communication among game designers and non-designer stakeholders of educational games.

Very few studies have investigated design patterns for rehabilitation games. Goude et al. [25] mapped the general game design patterns established by Björk and Holopainen with taxonomy of common stroke rehabilitation tasks. Through analyzing data about the use of commercial games in BI therapy, our previous work has also investigated a set of game design patterns specifically focused on design considerations when addressing therapeutic goals in BI rehabilitation [18]. This paper directly builds and expands our previous research on BI therapy game design patterns.

Game Design Tools

It is a notable challenge that game designers lack conceptual and computer-aided design tools to support their ideation, communication, and documentation of game design ideas [17,37]. Attempting to address these issues, researchers have created software tools. For example, Karakaya et al. [27] developed a game ideation tool called 'Sketch-It-Up!' that affords the ability for game designers and other stakeholders to explore and communicate ideas. More closely related to our work, in his master's thesis Kuittinen [31] embedded Björk and Holopainen's game design patterns in a software tool for Computer-Aided Game Design (CAGE). In doing so, he intended to support designers to select appropriate patterns by providing a visual representation of the inter-relationships among the patterns. While preliminary, Kuittinen's work demonstrated an early effort to incorporate game design patterns in a tool.

More recently, researchers have also explored requirements for game design tools. For example, Nelson and Mateas [38] conducted job shadowing and interviews with three teams of independent game designers and identified requirements for a game design tool aimed at helping designers explore the interactions of game mechanics. Reviewing current and proposed game design approaches, Almeida and Silva [4] also identified a list of 14 general requirements for game design tools. Their requirements specified that a game design tool must: (1) define a formal structure for a collection of design concepts (e.g. game design patterns); (2) provide a software system to support the use and extension of this collection; and (3) consider both the designer's perspective and the player's perspective [4]. We followed these requirements in this project.

In our literature review, we did not find previous research focused on tools for therapy-centered game design. Our work addresses this gap by exploring meaningful ways to incorporate BI therapy game design patterns in design tools.

BRAIN INJURY THERAPY GAME DESIGN PATTERNS

GaPBIT leveraged a BI therapy pattern language we created in previous work that emerged from analyzing COTS game usage by therapists in BI rehabilitation. Following a data-driven approach, we identified 25 BI therapy game design patterns based on a large dataset about COTS game use in BI therapy [18]. These patterns were organized into two groups: (1) *efficacy-centered* patterns that focus on enforcing the effectiveness of games at addressing BI therapy goals and (2)

Efficacy-Centered Patterns

Game Rules Patterns
- Fine Control
- Minimalist Task
- Optimal/Adjustable Pace
- Step by Step
- Unpredictable Events

Physical Mechanics Patterns
- Change Hands
- Integrated Standing Duration
- Moving Different Body Parts
- Self-Paced Weight Shifting
- Weight Shifting to the Extremes

Perception Patterns
- Focus and Distraction
- Three-Dimensional Space

Social Patterns
- Collocated Multiplayer
- Turn-Based Multiplayer

Experience-Centered Patterns

Challenge Patterns
- Multiplayer Competition
- Optional High-Level Challenge

Progress Patterns
- Advancing
- Optimistic Performance Evaluation

Learn and Master Patterns
- Adjustable Speed
- Gentle Challenge Ramp
- Minimized Distraction
- Pick up and Play

Theme Patterns
- Age Appropriate Theme
- Enabling Theme
- Familiar Theme

Figure 1. Summary of BI therapy game design patterns

experience-centered patterns that focus on fostering in-game experience of patients who have had a BI. We further divided each pattern group into sub-categories; Figure 1 lists the patterns we had identified.

Each pattern in the library contains (1) a name, (2) a category, (3) (for efficacy-centered patterns) a set of associated therapeutic goals, (4) a problem statement describing conflicts in design, (5) a solution proposed to resolve the problem, (6) example COTS games exhibiting this pattern to help users understand the pattern, and (7) a list of related patterns. While COTS games have limitations in use for people with a BI, it's beneficial to leverage COTS games for two reasons. First, there are very few games specifically for BI therapy that represent good game design. And second, COTS games are widely available so users of the patterns are either already familiar with them, or could easily get access to them to better understand the patterns. For details about efficacy-centered patterns, see [18]. In the following section, we provide one example experience-centered pattern.

Experience-Centered Pattern Example

The pattern ***Optional High-Level Challenge*** is a *Challenge Pattern* that focuses on a game challenge structure to avoid intimidating patients with limited abilities and at the same time engage patients with better abilities.

Problem: Because of the wide range of physical and cognitive effects of BIs, it is difficult to identify a "right" level of challenge to accommodate a range of patients who have had a BI.

Solution: Provide regular challenges throughout the play but occasionally give the player optional higher-level challenges. The high-level challenges should NOT be associated with the progress of the game; instead, they should provide appropriate incentives (e.g. bonuses) to encourage players to accomplish them and avoid frustration.

Example game – Wii Fit 'Penguin Slide': Players stand on a platform (about 2 inches high) and shift weight from side to side; this movement controls an iceberg on-screen so that a penguin character can slide to catch fish jumping from the water. Blue and green fish (easier to catch) provide lower points. Red fish are very difficult to catch and provide the highest points, but are optional (non-frustrating) challenges.

Anti-example game – Wii Fit 'Balance Bubble': A player avatar stands in a bubble suspended in a river. Players shift weight on the balance platform to control the speed and direction of the bubble to follow the river's path; the goal is to reach the finish line while avoiding the riverbank and obstacles. If a player hits an obstacle the game resets; some obstacles are extremely difficult to avoid (especially for many BI patients) resulting in a frustrating experience.

(The pattern document also included additional example games and specified the related patterns.)

BUILDING THE GAPBIT PROTOTYPE

Based on the structure of the BI therapy game design patterns, we created the initial user interface with paper wireframes (line drawings illustrating functionality and information hierarchy) and then progressed to web-based interactive versions. The concept of GaPBIT focused on allowing users to browse the pattern library via different views and providing structural and visual information for them to understand the patterns. In the following sections, we describe our user-centered design iteration process and the current interaction design of GaPBIT.

User Study Methods

We evaluated and iterated the interaction design through user studies with six professional games-for-health designers. During the studies, we first asked participants to complete four tasks using a think-aloud protocol; the tasks included identifying appropriate design patterns for a scenario and looking for specified information. After task completion, participants were asked to provide detailed feedback about the browsing features and the information provided in the patterns. Finally, we debriefed the participants about their experience using the prototype.

Design Iteration and User Feedback

All six participants completed the four tasks. Based on participants' feedback, we made several functional and visual modifications to enhance the design. First, we improved navigation among interconnected patterns by including links that allowed users to navigate to: (1) patterns addressing the same therapy goals; (2) patterns of the same category; and (3) related patterns. Second, we included background information about game design for BI therapy and added a narrated video to provide an introduction. Third, we added a "*My Saved Patterns*" function that allows users to save patterns to a personalized library and retrieve the saved patterns.

All of our participants expressed excitement about the tool concept. For example, a designer focused on board games that address adolescent sexual health issues said, "*I totally love it. ... You are providing multiple pathways to shake loose deeper ideas, I think it really helps getting past the surface.*" Participants also commented on the potential communication value of the tool; e.g. a designer who created iPad games addressing young adults' health issues mentioned, "*I think the potential here is not only for designers, but also for therapists to think about games – to have words to talk about why games might be useful for a particular brain injury. ... Once you have these terms, they are very powerful in communicating with other people.*"

Current GaPBIT Interaction Design

The current version of GaPBIT is available at: http://gametherapy.cstcis.cti.depaul.edu:8888. The home-page of GaPBIT provides background about game design for BI therapy and indicates three main functions of the system: (1) browse game design patterns focusing on therapy goals (i.e. efficacy-centered patterns); (2) browse game design patterns focusing on player experience (i.e. experience-centered patterns); and (3) visit the user's personalized library and retrieve the saved patterns. For each pattern browsing function, the system provides different views that organize the patterns according to their names, therapy goals (for efficacy-centered patterns), categories, and interrelations among the patterns.

Users can find detailed information by clicking on the patterns in the browsing interfaces. The detailed pattern information page includes the pattern's name, category, a brief definition, the problem and solution descriptions, and the example games. The tool also provides graphs and textual descriptions explaining how each example game realized the pattern; additionally, each game included comments from the therapists who previously used it in therapy. As illustrated in Figure 2, users are able to navigate from the detailed pattern information page to the connected patterns and save patterns to their library.

EXPLORATORY CASE STUDIES USING GAPBIT

To understand how the BI therapy patterns and the GaPBIT prototype could support ideation and designer-therapist collaboration in realistic design situations, we conducted six game ideation workshops in which game concepts were conceived. Following the workshops, we invited both game designers and therapists who were not involved in the workshops to evaluate the resulting game concepts.

Methods

The workshops were designed as quasi-experimental case studies guided by three hypotheses. Hypothesis 1: GaPBIT facilitates collaboration among designers and therapists; Hypothesis 2: GaPBIT will lead to game concepts that are better perceived by both designers and therapists; and Hypothesis 3: GaPBIT is especially effective at supporting novice designers who have less established ideation methods. In the following sections, we describe our methods

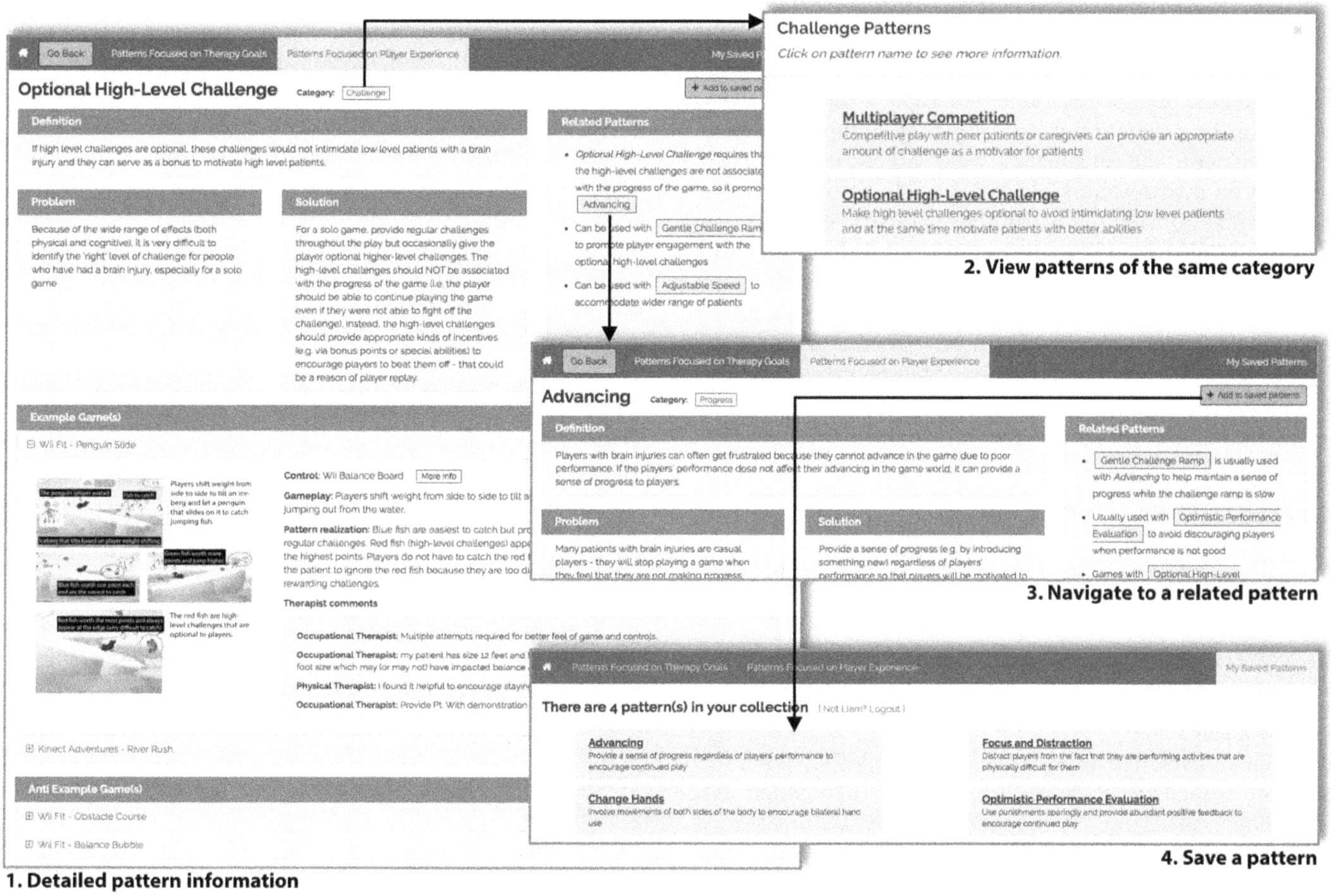

Figure 2. Example user interaction paths in the detailed pattern information page

for: (a) the game ideation workshops; (b) evaluation of the game concepts produced in the workshops; and (c) our data analysis procedures.

Game Ideation Workshops

In the game ideation workshops, we asked participants to conceive a game concept for a given BI therapy scenario and create a two-page written game design pitch to illustrate the concept and gameplay. The workshops included three conditions: (1) a designer working with a therapist (*Condition DT*); (2) a designer using the GaPBIT prototype (*Condition DG*); and (3) a designer working with a therapist while using the GaPBIT prototype (*Condition DTG*). Two workshops were held in each condition; one included a professional designer and the other included an undergraduate game design student from DePaul University. A total of six game designers participated in the workshops. Four therapists who focused on BIs participated in *Conditions DT* and *DTG*; one was an occupational therapist (OT) and three were physical therapists (PT). Table 1 summarizes our case study design.

For each workshop, we began with an introduction about game design for BI therapy. In *Conditions DG* and *DTG*, we also provided a brief tutorial of the GaPBIT prototype. We then presented the game design requirements, which described a fictional female patient who had a stroke in her 50s and was focused on improving her standing, walking, attention, and concentration abilities; the requirements also specified several hobbies (e.g. doll collector) of the patient prior to injury. Workshop participants were then asked to create a game on any platform (either digital or non-digital). We observed the design sessions from a soundproof room behind a one-way mirror. Workshop sessions were video recorded and were limited to 90 minutes. After the sessions, we debriefed the participants about their experience; debrief interviews were also video recorded and later transcribed.

Condition	Case	Participants
DT	PD+T	Professional Designer + Therapist
	SD+T	Student Designer + Therapist
DG	PD+G	Professional Designer + GaPBIT
	SD+G	Student Designer + GaPBIT
DTG	PD+T+G	Professional Designer + Therapist + GaPBIT
	SD+T+G	Student Designer + Therapist + GaPBIT

Table 1. Game ideation workshop experimental design

Game Concept Evaluation Sessions

We asked three professional game designers and three therapists (one PT, one OT, and one recreational therapist) to evaluate the game concepts created during the workshops;

evaluators were not involved in the workshop sessions. We framed the evaluation criteria so that the designer evaluators focused on player experience outcomes while therapists focused on the therapeutic value; see Table 2 for a summary of foci in the evaluation criteria for both groups. For each game concept, the evaluators were asked to rate each criterion on a five-point scale and provide an overall score from zero to ten. To mitigate order effects, we counterbalanced the design pitches using a randomized Latin Square [28]. After evaluation, we debriefed the evaluators to discuss the factors associated with the potential success of those game design concepts. Each evaluation session lasted for an hour; all were conducted over the phone and audio-recorded.

For Designer Evaluators	For Therapist Evaluators
• Game goal is clear	• Effective for the therapy goals
• Feedback is relevant	• Difficulty level is appropriate
• Mechanics are innovative	• Theme is appropriate
• Theme is appropriate	• Suitable for in-patient therapy
• Theme is unique	• Suitable for at-home therapy
• Game is re-playable	

Table 2. Foci of criteria for evaluating the design pitches

Data Analysis

We used an inductive approach in data analysis [15]. For the ideation workshop sessions, one author first coded the workshop videos in 10-second increments to identify predominant activities and events in each time slice and created a codebook. Two other authors then used the codebook and each deductively analyzed three workshop videos. We calculated the percentage of time increments in which the participants' activities were categorized in each theme. We then evaluated inter-rater reliability on these percentage values between the codebook generator and the blind coders using Intraclass Correlation Coefficient (ICC) Model 2 [36,46]. Additionally, the game design pitches were shared and discussed among all authors after the ideation workshops to identify common themes. Two authors also inductively coded the debrief interviews and combined their results.

Findings

In this section we present several categories of findings that include: (1) game concepts created during the workshops and their evaluation results; (2) designer-therapist conversation during the workshops; (3) high-level design phases that emerged when we analyzed the workshops; (4) a detailed description of an example workshop session; and (5) workshop participant feedback.

Findings 1: Game Concepts and Their Evaluation Results

Although we asked the participants to consider both digital and non-digital games, all design pitches focused on digital games. Among the four cases using GaPBIT, participants incorporated between four and ten game design patterns in the game concepts. In the following sections, we summarize each design concept.

Game Concept PD+T

Participants designed a Kinect game concept in which the player explores an enchanted garden maze and catches dolls that came to life from the player's collection; during the gameplay, a mystery storyline unveils. The player is required to step to navigate the maze and moves his/her arms to catch dolls and solve various puzzles. The dolls have different behaviors, providing various physical and cognitive challenges. Players and/or therapists can also adjust required movements, the amount of visual and auditory stimulation, and maze complexity level.

Game Concept SD+T

Participants designed a concept involving a series of mini-games/activities; each requires either Wii controllers or the Dance-Dance Revolution controller to play. Example activities include a racing game in which the player shifts weight to steer and accelerate and a tower defense game in which the player steps in different directions to move the cursor and place structures. Some activities allow players or therapists to adjust the required movements.

Game Concept PD+G

The professional designer used GaPBIT to create a concept based on adult coloring activities. Players are required to stand and use a baton paintbrush to complete images on a big screen by adding textures and colors. The images were curated to the player's taste and interest. Upon full or partial completion of an image, an animation effect activates based on the player's work. At the start of the game, players can adjust the boundaries of play space based on their range of motion.

Game Concept SD+G

The student designer used GaPBIT to design a concept that uses the Wii Fit balance board in which the player experiences the growth of a flower. The game starts with the player shifting weight to allow a bud to gather sunlight; more complex mechanics that involve arm movements to control the leaves are introduced as the game progresses and the flower grows. The game also provides different adjustable modes, imposing various levels of challenges.

Game Concept PD+T+G

Participants used GaPBIT to create a concept using the Wii Fit balance board in which players cycle in increasingly complex environments, collecting items to unlock new areas to explore. The player is required to shift weight side to side to pedal and to steer using a stand that resembles a bicycle handle supporting two Wii remote controllers. Players or therapists are able to adjust the required movements, the amount of visual and auditory stimulation, and the speed of the game.

Game Concept SD+T+G

Participants used GaPBIT to create a concept involving a series of Wii mini-games based on activities in Yellowstone National Park. Example mini-games include: Log-Balancing, in which the player shifts weight to keep the avatar on a wooden log while crossing a river; and Bird

Watching, in which the player shifts weight to move binoculars looking for a certain kind of bird and holds the position to take a picture. Each mini-game introduces additional movements and puzzles as it progresses. Players or therapists can adjust the required movements and the amount of visual and auditory stimulation in the game.

Game Concepts Evaluation Results

Table 3 summarizes the average overall score (out of ten) that the designer and therapist evaluators gave for each game concept. Overall, the highest scores were achieved in *Condition DTG* (use of GaPBIT) and in *Concept PD+T*.

The therapist evaluators rated the game concepts created in *Condition DTG* as the highest. They felt those two concepts were particularly suitable for inpatient use (an average score of 4.7 out of 5 on that criterion) because they both presented a wide variety of adjustable physical and cognitive challenges. *Concept SD+G* was rated as the lowest by the therapist evaluators because of its oversimplified theme and inability to provide adequate challenge for target patients; e.g., one evaluator said, "*I think there is just not enough in the game. It might be nice for a very low-level patient who is just starting to work on their standing balance, but it seems like that the target group is higher level than that.*"

Conversely, designer evaluators rated *Concept SD+G* the highest; they praised its minimalist design and the metaphor of growth in the game. For example, one evaluator said, "*It's pretty elegant. It's not terribly complex but it does feel complex enough to be engaging. ... And the metaphor of growth is very nicely embedded.*" *Concept SD+T*, on the other hand, was considered the least impressive among the designer evaluators mainly because it lacked innovative elements (the criteria "the mechanics are innovative" and "the theme is unique" were rated as 1.7 and 1.3 out of 5, respectively) and did not have a coherent theme.

	Condition DT		Condition DG		Condition DTG	
Case	PD+T	SD+T	PD+G	SD+G	PD+T+G	SD+T+G
Therapist Evaluators	7.7	6.7	7.0	5.7	8.0	8.0
Designer Evaluators	6.3	4.3	6.0	7.3	6.3	6.0
Combined	7.0	5.5	6.5	6.5	7.2	7.0

Table 3. Average overall score for each game idea

Findings 2: Designer-Therapist Conversation

We examined the designer-therapist conversation during the workshops through video coding. Recall, we coded the workshop videos in 10-second increments and evaluated inter-rater reliability using ICC2. In this and the following sections, we only report on themes in which inter-rater correlation was considered statistically significant based on F-test with an alpha level of .05 [36].

Observed Events Among Therapists and Designers

When a therapist was involved (*Conditions DT* and *DTG*), we identified several prominent events during the conversation between the designer and the therapist; those events were attributed to the individual participants and included: (1) asked a question to acquire information; (2) suggested a game design idea; and (3) voiced disagreement or concern about the other party's opinions. During sessions when GaPBIT was used (*Condition DTG*), therapists provided more game design suggestions and both the therapist and the designer voiced considerably less disagreements or concerns (see Figure 3 and Figure 4).

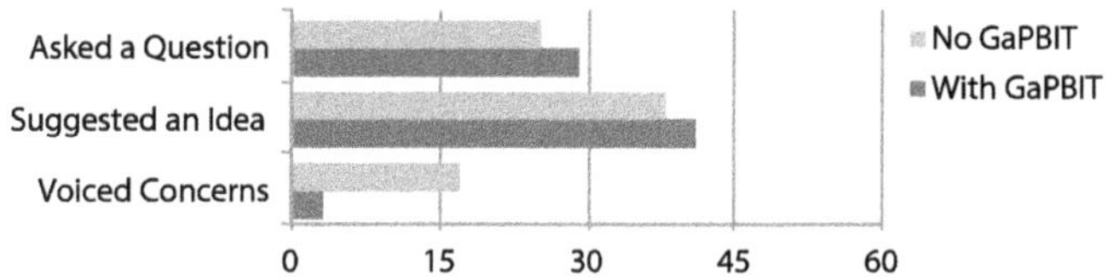

Figure 3. Counts of designer conversation events

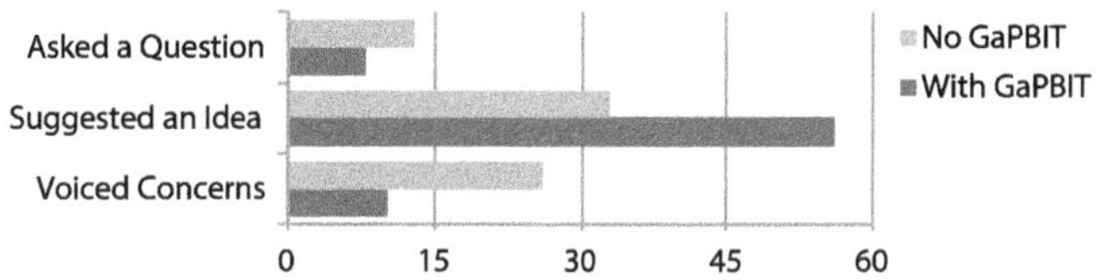

Figure 4. Counts of therapist conversation events

Further, when GaPBIT was not used, the discussion around disputable issues was often intense. E.g., in *Case PD+T* the participants had a heated discussion about adjusting the game's challenge level after the designer wrote, "*the maze will start simple and get more challenging*":

Therapist: Does that statement there mean that we can change the variables for the maze? ...

Designer: [hesitantly] Well, if the complexity could be changed, then it would probably be a procedurally generated maze. I don't know how that'd work...

Therapist: I mean the maze can get a little harder each level. That's fine. But maybe in one level, as far as the cognitive layers we've been discussing ...

Designer: Well, as far as the actual mechanics, you could go with something that is completely flexible, but then I'm essentially giving you a toolbox and say, "put it together." Then you'll have to be the game designer and determine the challenge. Alternatively, we could say we design a learning curve that we decide would make a good puzzle. But it is what it is. I mean it's possible to do it either way, but I think it'd put a big burden and take a lot of time for a therapist to set it up.

Therapist: Well. I am just thinking it would be nice like when she is on level one and she needs to find five dolls in ten minutes, and it is taking her six minutes to get the first one. ... So it would be nice if I could pause it and change the objectives a little bit. Or if she's been super distracted all the birds that fly by, I can get rid of some of those things. ...

Eventually, both compromised and agreed to include only some adjustable variables. In *Condition DTG*, we did not witness this type of intense discussion. This suggested that the design patterns presented as part of the GaPBIT prototype helped both designers and therapists realize potential issues early, resulting in more efficient discussion. We also observed that the patterns presented in GaPBIT facilitated discussion of game concepts. For example, in *Case PD+T+G* participants discussed how to incorporate several design patterns:

Therapist: Since she [the patient] is a cycler, maybe we can use some platform that she can hold on to, allowing her to stand and shift weight side to side to mimic that.

Designer: Yeah. With "*Moving Different Body Parts*", I think we can integrate the balancing with the hand motion to pick things up, to collect things. … And it also goes with "*Self-Paced Weight Shifting*". … I think the motivation to continue playing would be that you go farther and you see new things, instead of like you are trying to beat a certain distance. …

Therapist: Yeah. And just in terms of "*Focus and Distraction*" and increasing the level of difficulty, it could be just about the setting. She could start out in a very non-busy area and go to more maybe…

Designer: Like a meadow into a forest, then into a city.

Therapist: Yeah. And sound-wise too.

Discussion Topics Among Therapists and Designers

We identified eight major categories of topics that emerged from the designer-therapist conversation:

- *BI therapy practices*: Participants discussed general goals and typical practice of BI therapy.
- *Target player attributes*: Participants discussed target player attributes from the scenario; attributes included physical and cognitive abilities, and/or taste and interest.
- *Game – High-level concerns*: Participants discussed high-level design considerations for the proposed game. E.g., in Case SD+T+G, during an early stage of design the therapist said, "*We need to keep it simple, being able to customize without taking too much time*"
- *Game – Platform/controller*: Participants discussed which game platform and/or controller to use.
- *Game – Fictional layer*: Participants discussed the game's genre, theme, and/or story. E.g., in Case PD+T, the designer proposed the enchanted garden idea and expressed willingness to include a storyline, then the therapist suggested the idea of using a garden maze to promote problem solving.
- *Game – Core mechanics*: Participants discussed the core mechanics of the game (i.e. the essential play activities players perform repeatedly in a game [44]).
- *Game – Features/variations*: Participants elaborated the game design idea and discussed the game's additional features. E.g., in Case PD+T+G, the designer suggested the idea to use music as an indirect reward: "*It could be that the music plays with more instruments if you go faster – as a 'non-essential' reward for moving faster.*"
- *Design patterns*: When participants used GaPBIT, they discussed which design patterns to choose and how to incorporate the patterns in their game.

Findings 3: GaPBIT Use in Design Phases

The concept of design phases emerged from analysis of the workshop sessions. We found that each design session included three high-level phases. The first was an *Exploration* phase. All design sessions started with participants reading the requirements document. The participants then explored the problem and solution spaces of game design through discussion and/or using the GaPBIT prototype. Initial discussion topics were usually about BI therapy practices and the target player attributes; discussion then shifted to topics about high-level game design considerations, the game's platform or controller, and its core mechanics. Next came the *Elaboration* phase. When a core concept of the game is settled (indicated either in written notes or verbal discussion), participants took extensive notes and focused on expanding the game's core mechanics and theme; the discussion topics covered all categories and were mainly focused on the game's fictional layer and its features and variations. Last, the design process moved into a *Finalization* phase when participants started writing the design pitch. While mostly focused on typing and editing, participants also refined their design ideas during the finalization phase.

The GaPBIT prototype was used most frequently in the *Exploration* phase (See Figure 5), in which participants explored various design patterns and regularly "saved" patterns into their library; when a therapist was involved (*Condition DTG*), GaPBIT helped frame the discussion about the high-level design considerations and the game's core mechanics. Particularly, participants focused on examining the patterns' problem and solution descriptions and explored related patterns to identify the most relevant ones and paid less attention to the example games in this phase. In the *Elaboration* and *Finalization* phases, participants revisited their saved patterns, especially the example games included in each pattern, to seek clarification and inspiration for game design ideas. The discussions about the game's features and variations were usually shaped by patterns in GaPBIT. Figure 6 summarizes the average percentage of time participants spent using different GaPBIT functionalities in the three design phases.

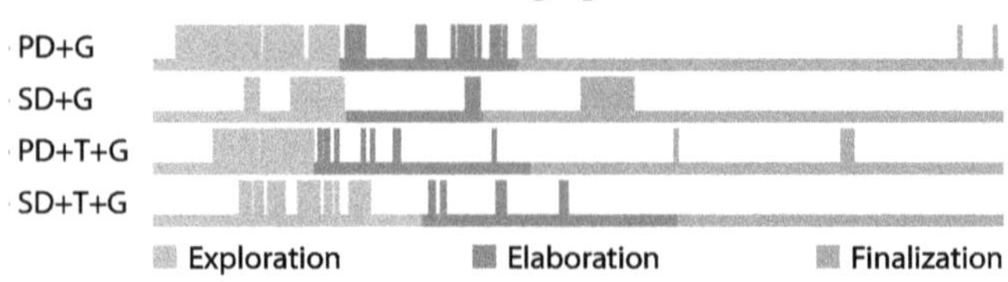

Figure 5. Frequency of GaPBIT use by phase. Each vertical bar indicates a 10-second increment in which GaPBIT is used.

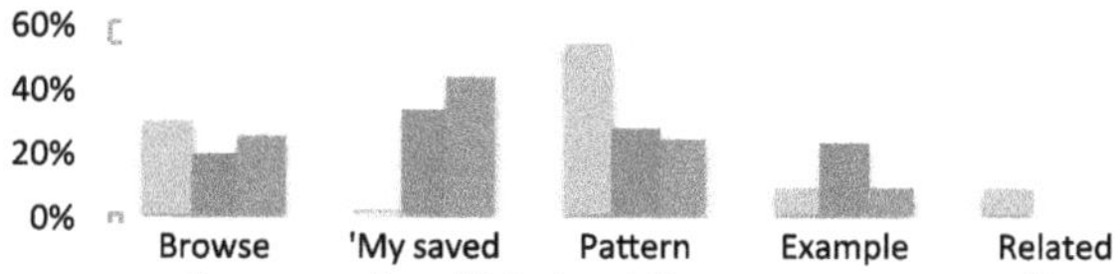

	Browse patterns	'My saved patterns' list	Pattern descriptions	Example games	Related patterns
Exploration	30%	1%	53%	9%	8%
Elaboration	18%	33%	27%	22%	0%
Finalization	25%	43%	23%	8%	0%

Figure 6. Average percentage of time spent on GaPBIT functionalities by design phase

Findings 4: Example Case SD+T+G

To illustrate how participants approached game concept design during the workshops, we provide the details of an example workshop case: *SD+T+G*. The designer involved in this case was a junior-year undergraduate student in the game design program at DePaul University. He worked with an occupational therapist who had used video games in therapy. Figure 7 and Figure 8 illustrate their ideation workshop timeline.

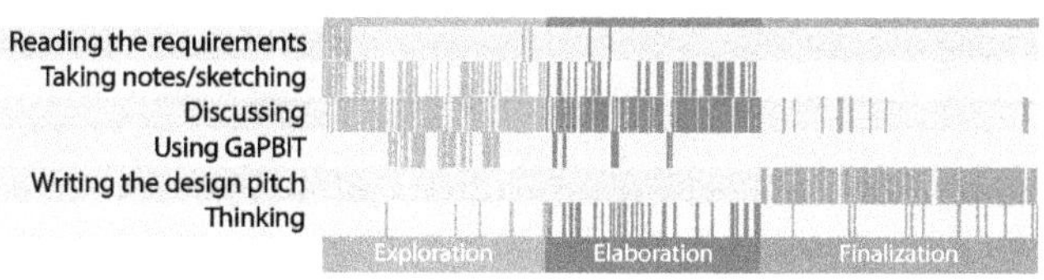

Figure 7. Major activities of participants in *Case SD+T+G*

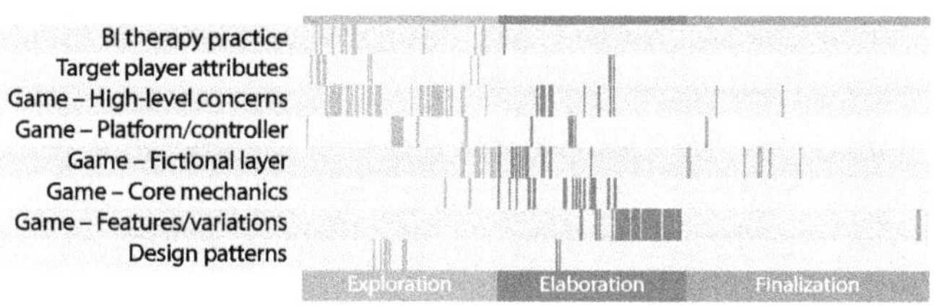

Figure 8. Discussion topics in *Case SD+T+G*

At the beginning of the *Exploration Phase*, both participants read the design requirements; the designer took notes about the target player and therapy goals. Then the designer asked about the therapist's typical practice if he was working with a patient like the target player. The therapist brought up several high-level issues very early in the exploration phase; e.g., "*We need to keep it simple, and also being able to customize without taking too much time.*"

After discussing these issues, they used GaPBIT to explore the resolutions. They browsed, discussed, and saved 11 game design patterns in GaPBIT. During this process, they were mostly focused on pattern descriptions and related patterns and did not explore the example games. Based on these patterns, the therapist suggested using the mini-game format to support adjustable features: "*Maybe for our game, we can have two pathways: standing only and arm use only. Then the therapist can decide which one is more appropriate. If there is a set of mini-games, then we can divide them up into different games.*" The participants then agreed upon the platform, the main theme, and the core mechanics of the game: a Wii game that includes activities happening in national parks.

In the *Elaboration Phase*, they first used GaPBIT to explore several example games in the patterns they saved. Based on this exploration, they discussed and settled on six mini-games within the national parks theme. They elaborated each mini-game to include different difficulty modes and other adjustable features. During this process, they revisited the design patterns they saved in GaPBIT to get clarifications and inspiration; they also extensively explored the example games associated to their saved patterns for ideation of game mechanics. The designer took extensive notes to record the ideas emerged during the discussion.

During the *Finalization Phase*, the participants focused primarily on typing and editing the game design pitch. They occasionally discussed to clarify or confirm the ideas they previously generated.

Findings 5: Workshop Participants' Feedback

During debrief, participants in all conditions stated that they were satisfied with their game ideation process. However, the reasons for satisfaction varied. In *Condition DT*, participants valued the interaction with someone from an unfamiliar field to bring in different perspectives. For example, the therapist from *Case PD+T* mentioned, "*It's nice to talk to someone in a completely different field because you can bounce ideas off of each other and get a different point of view.*"

In *Condition DG*, the designers felt that GaPBIT was useful at helping them explore game design ideas and understand the needs in BI therapy. For example, the professional designer in *Case PD+G* mentioned, "*I came with the idea very early on and I think from the tool I got just enough support without being overwhelmed.*" The student designer in *Case SD+G* also said, "*When making games I don't often think about players who have a disability. So the tool did help me single out the things I am looking to the needs of this particular group.*"

In *Condition DTG*, participants commented on the common language GaPBIT provided to support collaboration. For example, the therapist from *Case SD+T+G* said: "*I think the tool did open up that communication where you have two experts in very different areas trying to come up with something that they have to work together on. It captured a lot of the terms we use and the goals that we have. So I think it helped the game designer talk in our terms.*" The designer from *Case PD+T+G* mentioned: "*The tool acts as a checklist. So it helps to have someone else view it and also to hear their understanding of how each thing could be addressed.*"

DISCUSSION AND CONCLUSION

In this paper, we explored how GaPBIT, a tool incorporating game design patterns supported conceptual design of games for BI therapy and facilitated collaboration among designers and subject matter experts. We frame our discussion in the next sections by reflecting on our three hypotheses. We conclude with additional implications of our study and discuss limitations and future work.

GaPBIT Supported Ideation and Collaboration

There is rich evidence to support Hypothesis 1, that GaPBIT facilitates collaboration among designers and therapists. We found that GaPBIT facilitated the game ideation process and helped to support an efficient discussion among the workshop participants. Our results indicated that GaPBIT was able to help establish an early mutual understanding that resulted in fewer conflicts and disputes between our designer and therapist participants. Participants also employed the pattern language embedded in GaPBIT when discussing their game design ideas. Further, in debrief interviews participants indicated that they appreciated the communication scaffolding provided by GaPBIT.

Tools Could Not Substitute Collaboration

Hypothesis 2, that GaPBIT will lead to game concepts that are better perceived by both designers and therapist, was only partially supported. The most highly rated games by therapists were those that included GaPBIT, a designer and a therapist, indicating that the use of GaPBIT led to games with more predicted therapeutic value. However, there were no salient patterns among the designer evaluators. Particularly, there was a substantial discrepancy between therapist and designer evaluators on *Concept SD+G*, designed without the input from a therapist. These results suggested that information tools like GaPBIT should only be considered as a supportive channel and should not substitute collaboration with subject matter experts.

Characteristics of the six game concepts also indicated that the therapists provided valuable information about the needs in BI therapy during the game ideation process. While the two concepts designed without a therapist (*Condition DG*) embodied a more artistic quality, the concepts designed with a therapist (*Conditions DT* and *DTG*) integrated more challenging physical and cognitive activities. Further, allowing players and/or therapists to adjust game features was commonly desired by therapists [5,42]. GaPBIT was able to communicate this need through certain patterns (e.g. *Optional High-Level Challenge*); however, the adjustable features were more emphasized and contained more details with therapists' input.

Novice Designers May Need More Scaffolding

Hypothesis 3, that the GaPBIT prototype is especially helpful for novice designers, was also partially supported. On one hand, when used with a therapist, GaPBIT helped student designers achieve considerably higher scores from both designer and therapist evaluators; for experienced designers however, the scores for *Concepts PD+T* and *PD+T+D* are similar. On the other hand, novice designers exhibited difficulty in absorbing the complexity of information provided by the therapists, resulting in games that had less coherent themes and gameplay. Notably, both game concepts designed by student designers working with a therapist (*Game Concepts SD+T* and *SD+T+G*) adopted a mini-game structure; *Concept SD+T* exhibits considerable incoherence. The student designer from *Case SD+T* mentioned in debrief, "*At first we wanted to focus on one game. But it's hard to do too much in one activity. ... [The therapist] just prodded a lot of different considerations you have to worry about.*" These results indicated that while GaPBIT and the design patterns were helpful for novice designers who have less established ideation methods, more scaffolding is needed for students to consider coherent design concepts in extremely complex contexts, such as the context of games for BI therapy.

Conclusion: Game Design as a Reflective Process

The results of this study supported previous findings that games-for-health designers tend to explore both the problem and the solution spaces somewhat equally [17]. Particularly, participants spent much of the *Exploration* phase to examine the current BI therapy practice and the target player's attributes. Further, the participants' approach echoed Schön's concept of "reflection-in-action" [45]; i.e., designers constantly engage in critical, reflective thinking to adjust and refine their design concepts in an unfolding situation. Even with the limited time provided in the ideation workshops, participants still performed multiple mini-iterations through the three design phases. Reflective thinking and adjustment manifested as a major activity in the *Exploration* and *Elaboration* phases; and in the *Finalization* phase, participants still refined their design when new information and/or clarification emerged.

In this study, we demonstrated that tools incorporating game design patterns are promising techniques to support reflective design process of BI therapy games. These techniques are critical for domains in which there are collaboration challenges among designers and subject matter experts. As such, we argue that our research methodology used in this study generalizes to other domains to support design in interdisciplinary teams; e.g. other types of games for health such as games aimed at ameliorating challenges for children with autism.

Limitations and Future Work

While the small sample size of the ideation workshop sessions afforded detailed exploration, conducting a larger-scale study might support quantitative analysis of our three hypotheses. Further, although somewhat realistic, our ideation workshops did not duplicate real-world game design situations that involve more complex issues, such as budget, time, and market constraints. Additionally, this study focused solely on the creation of initial game concepts. Further research exploring how patterns and tools could support evolvement of fully developed games in real-world game design contexts would be valuable.

ACKNOWLEDGEMENTS

We thank all the participants and acknowledge the grant from the DePaul University Research Council.

REFERENCES

1. Gazihan Alankus, Amanda Lazar, Matt May, and Caitlin Kelleher. 2010. Towards customizable games for stroke rehabilitation. In *Proceedings of the 28th international conference on Human factors in computing systems CHI '10*, 2113–2122. https://doi.org/10.1145/1753326.1753649
2. Christopher Alexander. 1979. *The Timeless Way of Building*. https://doi.org/10.1080/00918360802623131
3. Christopher Alexander, Sara Ishikawa, and Murray Silverstein. 1977. *A Pattern Language: Towns, Buildings, Construction*. https://doi.org/10.2307/1574526
4. Marcos S O Almeida and Flávio S C Silva. 2013. Requirements for game design tools: A Systematic Survey. In *Proceedings of SBGames 2013*, 277–284.
5. Jan-Henk Annema, Mathijs Verstraete, Vero Vanden Abeele, Stef Desmet, and David Geerts. 2010. Videogames in therapy: a therapist's perspective. In *Proceedings of the 3rd International Conference on Fun and Games - Fun and Games '10*, 94–98. https://doi.org/10.1145/1823818.1823828
6. Aimee L Betker, Ankur Desai, Cristabel Nett, Naaz Kapadia, and Tony Szturm. 2007. Game-based exercises for dynamic short-sitting balance rehabilitation of people with chronic spinal cord and traumatic brain injuries. *Physical therapy* 87, 10: 1389–1398. https://doi.org/10.2522/ptj.20060229
7. Staffan Björk and Jussi Holopainen. 2004. *Patterns in game design*. Charles River Media.
8. Jan O. Borchers. 2001. A pattern approach to interaction design. *AI & Society* 15: 359–376. https://doi.org/10.1007/BF01206115
9. Brain Injury Association of America. Quick Facts About Brain Injury. Retrieved March 17, 2015 from http://www.biausa.org/bia-media-center.htm
10. Brain Injury Association of America. About Brain Injury. Retrieved March 24, 2015 from http://www.biausa.org/about-brain-injury.htm
11. Richard Buday. 2015. Games for Health: An Opinion. *Games for Health Journal* 4, 1: 38–42. https://doi.org/10.1089/g4h.2014.0083
12. Richard Buday, Tom Baranowski, and Debbe Thompson. 2012. Fun and Games and Boredom. *Games for Health Journal* 1, 4: 257–261. https://doi.org/10.1089/g4h.2012.0026
13. J. W. Burke, M. D. J. McNeill, D. K. Charles, P. J. Morrow, J. H. Crosbie, and S. M. McDonough. 2009. Optimising engagement for stroke rehabilitation using serious games. *The Visual Computer* 25, 12: 1085–1099. https://doi.org/10.1007/s00371-009-0387-4
14. Frank Buschmann, Regine Meunier, Hans Rohnert, Peter Sommerlad, and Michael Stal. 1996. *Pattern-Oriented Software Architecture, Volume 1: A System of Patterns*. Wiley, John & Sons, United Kingdom.
15. Kathy Charmaz. 2014. *Constructing Grounded Theory*. SAGE Publications Ltd.
16. Jinghui Cheng and Cynthia Putnam. 2015. Therapeutic Gaming in Context: Observing Game Use for Brain Injury Rehabilitation. In *Proceedings of the 33rd Annual ACM Conference Extended Abstracts on Human Factors in Computing Systems - CHI EA '15*, 1169–1174. https://doi.org/10.1145/2702613.2732697
17. Jinghui Cheng, Cynthia Putnam, and Jin Guo. 2016. "Always a Tall Order": Values and Practices of Professional Game Designers of Serious Games for Health. In *Proceedings of the 2016 Annual Symposium on Computer-Human Interaction in Play - CHI PLAY '16*, 217–228. https://doi.org/10.1145/2967934.2968081
18. Jinghui Cheng, Cynthia Putnam, and Doris C Rusch. 2015. Towards Efficacy-Centered Game Design Patterns For Brain Injury Rehabilitation: A Data-Driven Approach. In *Proceedings of the 17th International ACM SIGACCESS Conference on Computers & Accessibility*, 291–299. https://doi.org/10.1145/2700648.2809856
19. Andy Dearden and Janet Finlay. 2006. Pattern languages in HCI : a critical review. *Human-Computer interaction* 21, January 2015: 49–102. https://doi.org/10.1207/s15327051hci2101
20. Judith E Deutsch, Arielle Brettler, Caroline Smith, Jamie Welsh, Roshan John, Phyllis Guarrera-Bowlby, and Michal Kafri. 2012. Nintendo Wii Sports and Wii Fit Game Analysis, Validation, and Application to Stroke Rehabilitation. *Topics in Stroke Rehabilitation* 18, 6: 701–719. https://doi.org/10.1310/tsr1806-701
21. Eletha Flores, Gabriel Tobon, Ettore Cavallaro, Francesca I. Cavallaro, Joel C. Perry, and Thierry Keller. 2008. Improving patient motivation in game development for motor deficit rehabilitation. In *Proceedings of the 2008 International Conference in Advances in Computer Entertainment Technology - ACE '08*, 381–384. https://doi.org/10.1145/1501750.1501839
22. Erich Gamma, Richard Helm, Ralph E. Johnson, and John Vlissides. 1995. *Design patterns: elements of reusable object-oriented software*.
23. José-Antonio Gil-Gómez, Roberto Lloréns, Mariano Alcañiz, and Carolina Colomer. 2011. Effectiveness of a Wii balance board-based system (eBaViR) for balance rehabilitation: a pilot randomized clinical trial in patients with acquired brain injury. *Journal of neuroengineering and rehabilitation* 8, 30: 1–9. https://doi.org/10.1186/1743-0003-8-30

24. José Antonio Gil-Gómez, José Antonio Lozano, Mariano Alcañiz, and Sergio Albiol Pérez. 2009. Nintendo Wii balance board for balance disorders. In *2009 Virtual Rehabilitation International Conference, VR 2009*, 213. https://doi.org/10.1109/ICVR.2009.5174251

25. Daniel Goude, Staffan Björk, and Martin Rydmark. 2007. Game design in virtual reality systems for stroke rehabilitation. *Studies in Health Technology and Informatics* 125: 146–148.

26. Benjamin Huynh-Kim-Bang, John Wisdom, and Jean-Marc Labat. 2010. Design Patterns in Serious Games: A Blue Print for Combining Fun and Learning. *Project SE-SG*. Retrieved March 7, 2014 from http://seriousgames.lip6.fr/DesignPatterns/designPatternsForSeriousGames.pdf

27. Bulut Karakaya, Camilo Garcia, Daniel Rodriguez, Manoj Nityanandam, Nadia Labeikovsky, and Theyab Al Tamimi. 2009. Sketch-it-up! Demo. In *Entertainment Computing–ICEC 2009*, 313–314. https://doi.org/10.1007/978-3-642-04052-8_49

28. Donald Keedwell and József Dénes. 2015. *Latin squares and their applications*. Elsevier2015.

29. Sebastian Kelle, Roland Klemke, and Marcus Specht. 2011. Design patterns for learning games. *International Journal of Technology Enhanced Learning* 3, 6: 555–569. https://doi.org/10.1504/IJTEL.2011.045452

30. Bernd Kreimeier. 2002. The Case For Game Design Patterns. *gamasutra.com*. Retrieved from http://www.gamasutra.com/view/feature/132649/the_case_for_game_design_patterns.php?print=1

31. Jussi Markus Kuittinen. 2008. Computer-Aided Game Design. University of Jyväskylä.

32. B. Lange, S. Flynn, and A. Rizzo. 2009. Initial usability assessment of off-the-shelf video game consoles for clinical game-based motor rehabilitation. *Physical Therapy Reviews* 14, 5: 355–363. https://doi.org/10.1179/108331909X12488667117258

33. Belinda Lange, Chien-Yen Chang, Evan Suma, Bradley Newman, Albert Skip Rizzo, and Mark Bolas. 2011. Development and evaluation of low cost game-based balance rehabilitation tool using the Microsoft Kinect sensor. In *Annual International Conference of the IEEE Engineering in Medicine and Biology Society*, 1831–1834. https://doi.org/10.1109/IEMBS.2011.6090521

34. Bertrand Marne, John Wisdom, Benjamin Huynh-kim-bang, Jussieu Paris, and Jean-marc Labat. 2012. A Design Pattern Library for Mutual Understanding and Cooperation in Serious Game Design. In *Intelligent Tutoring Systems*. Springer, Berlin Heidelberg, 135–140. https://doi.org/10.1007/978-3-642-30950-2_18

35. Nelson J McClanachan, Janelle Gesch, Nampech Wuthapanich, Jennifer Fleming, and Suzanne S Kuys. 2013. Feasibility of gaming console exercise and its effect on endurance, gait and balance in people with an acquired brain injury. *Brain injury* 27, 12: 1402–8. https://doi.org/10.3109/02699052.2013.823654

36. Kenneth O. McGraw and S. P. Wong. 1996. Forming inferences about some intraclass correlations coefficients. *Psychological Methods* 1, 1: 30–46. https://doi.org/10.1037/1082-989X.1.4.390

37. Katharine Neil. 2012. Game design tools: Time to evaluate. In *Proceedings of 2012 DiGRA Nordic*. Retrieved from http://www.digra.org/wp-content/uploads/digital-library/12168.46494.pdf

38. Mark J Nelson and Michael Mateas. 2009. A requirements analysis for videogame design support tools. In *Proceedings of the 4th International Conference on Foundations of Digital Games - FDG '09*, 137–144. https://doi.org/10.1145/1536513.1536543

39. World Health Organization. 2015. Projections of mortality and causes of death. Retrieved June 6, 2016 from http://www.who.int/healthinfo/global_burden_disease/projections/en/

40. Jessica M Paavola, Kory E Oliver, and Ksenia I Ustinova. 2013. Use of X-box Kinect Gaming Console for Rehabilitation of an Individual with Traumatic Brain Injury: A Case Report. *Journal of Novel Physiotherapies* 3, 1: 1–6. https://doi.org/10.4172/2165-7025.1000129

41. Cynthia Putnam, Jinghui Cheng, Feng Lin, Sai Yalla, and Stephanie Wu. 2016. "Choose a Game": Creation and Evaluation of a Prototype Tool to Support Therapists in Brain Injury Rehabilitation. In *Proceedings of the 2016 CHI Conference on Human Factors in Computing Systems - CHI '16*, 2038–2049. https://doi.org/10.1145/2858036.2858258

42. Cynthia Putnam, Jinghui Cheng, and Gregory Seymour. 2014. Therapist Perspectives: Wii Active Videogames Use in Inpatient Settings with People Who Have Had a Brain Injury. *Games for Health Journal* 3, 6: 366–370. https://doi.org/10.1089/g4h.2013.0099

43. D Rand, R Kizony, and P L Weiss. 2004. Virtual reality rehabilitation for all : Vivid GX versus Sony PlayStation II EyeToy. In *Proceedings of the 5th International Conference Series On Disability, Virtual Reality and Associated Technologies (ICDVRAT)*, 87–94.

44. Katie Salen and Eric Zimmerman. 2004. *Rules of play: game design fundamentals*. MIT Press, Cambridge, MA, USA.

45. Donald A. Schön. 1984. *The Reflective Practitioner: How Professionals Think in Action*. Basic Books.

46. Patrick E. Shrout and Joseph L. Fleiss. 1979. Intraclass correlations: Uses in assessing rater reliability. *Psychological Bulletin* 86, 2: 420–428. https://doi.org/10.1037/0033-2909.86.2.420

47. Jonathan M Silver, Thomas W McAllister, and Stuart C Yudofsky. 2011. *Textbook of traumatic brain injury*. American Psychiatric Publishing, Inc, Arlington, VA, USA.

48. Debbe Thompson, Tom Baranowski, Richard Buday, Janice Baranowski, Victoria Thompson, Russell Jago, and Melissa Juliano Griffith. 2010. Serious Video Games for Health: How Behavioral Science Guided the Development of a Serious Video Game. *Simulation & gaming* 41, 4: 587–606. https://doi.org/10.1177/1046878108328087

49. G. Yavuzer, a. Senel, M. B. Atay, and H. J. Stam. 2008. "Playstation eyetoy games" improve upper extremity-related motor functioning in subacute stroke: A randomized controlled clinical trial. *European Journal of Physical and Rehabilitation Medicine* 44, 3: 237–244.

50. Samantha Zickefoose, Karen Hux, Jessica Brown, and Katrina Wulf. 2013. Let the games begin: a preliminary study using attention process training-3 and Lumosity™ brain games to remediate attention deficits following traumatic brain injury. *Brain injury : [BI]* 27, 6: 707–16. https://doi.org/10.3109/02699052.2013.775484

Predicting Player Experience without the Player An Exploratory Study

Christian Guckelsberger[1,*], Christoph Salge[2,3], Jeremy Gow[1], and Paul Cairns[4]

[1]Computational Creativity Group, Goldsmiths, University of London, London, UK
[2]Adaptive Systems Research Group, University of Hertfordshire, Hatfield, UK
[3]Game Innovation Lab, New York University, New York, US
[4]Department of Computer Science, University of York, York, UK
[*]Corresponding author. Email: c.guckelsberger@gold.ac.uk

ABSTRACT
A key challenge of procedural content generation (PCG) is to evoke a certain player experience (PX), when we have no direct control over the content which gives rise to that experience. We argue that neither the rigorous methods to assess PX in HCI, nor specialised methods in PCG are sufficient, because they rely on a human in the loop. We propose to address this shortcoming by means of computational models of intrinsic motivation and AI game-playing agents. We hypothesise that our approach could be used to automatically predict PX across games and content types without relying on a human player or designer. We conduct an exploratory study in level generation based on empowerment, a specific model of intrinsic motivation. Based on a thematic analysis, we find that empowerment can be used to create levels with qualitatively different PX. We relate the identified experiences to established theories of PX in HCI and game design, and discuss next steps.

ACM Classification Keywords
H.5.m. Information Interfaces and Presentation (e.g. HCI): Miscellaneous

Author Keywords
Player Experience; Procedural Content Generation; Models of Intrinsic Motivation; AI Players; Empowerment

INTRODUCTION
Procedural content generation (PCG) holds great advantages for modern video games: By algorithmically creating levels, as in *Spelunky* [57, 58], or other elements such as characters and music, game developers can satisfy the players' demand for richer and more detailed content, while keeping production costs and time manageable [52]. Adding new content like quests or weapons procedurally allows designers to create open-ended games, and increase their replay value [49]. Moreover, PCG can be used to adapt content to individual players [45], and has been proposed as a game mechanic in itself [9].

CHI PLAY '17, October 15–18, 2017, Amsterdam, Netherlands.

ACM ISBN 978-1-4503-4898-0/17/10 . . . $15.00
DOI: https://doi.org/10.1145/3116595.3116631

PCG algorithms require formal guidelines about the desired content characteristics. A procedurally generated level should without doubt be *playable*, i.e. there must be a way for the player to succeed or fail, or to experience the whole content instance and not just a small part of it. Content should also be *novel* and *typical* (cf. [38]): a generated quest for instance should be different from existing quests, but still fit the game under consideration. However, nobody would care about a level, character or as a consequence even the overall game, if the content in question did not lead to a desired experience. *Player experience* (PX) substantially determines the *value* of a content instance, and consequently its acceptance and replayability (cf. [46]). The key challenge for PCG arising from this is to evoke a certain PX, when we have *no direct control over the content* which gives rise to that experience.

We argue that established methods in human computer interaction (HCI) and PCG do not address the challenge of predicting PX in PCG sufficiently. HCI's methods rely on human players and thus come with strong time and cost constraints. Dedicated PCG approaches either still involve human players for machine-learning predictive models of PX, or require designers to hand-craft such models based on explicit knowledge of the game's semantics. Any present approach relies on people, and is unlikely to scale when new elements are introduced to the game which might invoke new, unanticipated experiences. The challenge of assessing PX in PCG is thus somewhat paradoxical: can we evaluate PX independently of the players themselves, and of designers' knowledge as proxies to PX? Furthermore, can we specify a predictive model of PX which works across games without constant human involvement?

In this paper, we propose such a general, automatic approach to assess PX based on *computational models of intrinsic motivation*, and evaluate it qualitatively. More specifically, we suggest to predict PX from intrinsic motivation quantities calculated on game state samples from AI players. Our approach is independent of players and of designers' knowledge about the meaning of game tokens, and could thus work across different games and content facets. We support our proposal with an exploratory study based on *empowerment* [27], one specific model of intrinsic motivation. We conduct a thematic analysis of player think-alouds while playing procedurally generated levels of an (in)finite runner game. Formally, empowerment quantifies an agent's potential and perceivable influence on their environment in a given state. We find that using empowerment in our generic procedure allows the creation of levels that elicit qualitatively different PX. We relate our results to theories of PX in game design and HCI, and outline the next steps towards a full, quantitative proof-of-concept.

THE CHALLENGE OF ASSESSING PX IN PCG

PX describes the personal, transient and dynamic qualities an individual player experiences from interacting with a game [54]. Amongst these manifold experiences are competence, autonomy, control, immersion, presence, flow, engagement, relatedness, challenge, tension, curiosity, and affect.

HCI and PCG assess PX for different reasons, and HCI's instruments are not applicable to PCG straight away. In HCI, PX is evaluated e.g. to give directions at key points of game development, or to infer more general insights about how people interact with games. Crucially, PX is usually assessed on very *few* conditions, and *after* the player has experienced them. Denisova and Cairns [14] for instance bias participants with two explanations about a game's AI for the same game, and measure the effect of these conditions on their immersion. HCI researchers rely on rich subjective [5, 8, 54] feedback and objective data [30] from players to make detailed and reliable judgements. However, the speed of evaluation is limited by the participants' game-playing and information processing capacity. In addition, certain devices might be expensive to use, and participants want to be paid, thus imposing costs.

The goals and requirements in PCG are typically very different. HCI's instruments could still be applied when PCG is used as a tool during development (cf. [12]), and generated content is carefully curated by designers for the final game. However, the full power of PCG, especially for replayability, can only be unleashed when PCG is used in the shipped game, either offline before-, or online during play. In this scenario, usually *many* content instances must be assessed *before* they are experienced by a player. Each instance can be considered one experimental condition resulting from e.g. different parameter combinations in the generator. Speed is of prime importance, and HCI's traditional subjective and objective approaches do not scale. Acquiring explicit feedback from the player is rarely an option, as it is either too obtrusive, e.g. when using questionnaires, or too imprecise, e.g. when asking for binary preference ratings.

These shortcomings impose a bottleneck on PCG development: to guarantee a particular PX, designers are forced to keep their generators within tight constraints. In *Spelunky*, some *experiential control* is retained by predefining *experiential chunks* [46] during development, i.e. rooms that can be individually experienced by the player. These rooms are then procedurally arranged in a grid during runtime (cf. [58]). In other cases, generators are kept simple by relying on small grammars or noise-based algorithms [49]. These constraints make the *explicit* [12] prediction of player experience obsolete, but they considerably limit the *expressive range* [47] of generators, and thereby the actual benefits of PCG in practice.

Researchers in PCG aim to realise the benefits of less constrained and more complex generative approaches by using predictive models of PX that only require minimal human involvement. Yannakakis and Togelius [56] survey related work in their *experience-driven PCG* framework. A predictive model is essentially a mapping from game content to experiential qualities. We demonstrate the breadth and shortcomings of existing approaches by distinguishing two extreme means to establish this mapping. They belong to the classes of *model-based* and *theory-driven* approaches, respectively.

Recent *model-based* approaches reduce the dependency on players drastically by using player feedback only once for the *training* of a machine-learning model [49], which can then be applied over and over. Guzdial, Sturtevant and Li [19], for instance, create a predictive model of player enjoyment, difficulty and visual aesthetics for *Infinite Mario Bros.* [35] levels, a clone of *Super Mario Bros.* [31]. They use a convolutional neural network and player feedback to automatically extract content features that correlate with the targeted experiences.

Some *theory-driven* approaches are entirely independent of the player, but rely on designers instead: guided by their intuition and/or some qualitative theory, the designers must manually establish a functional mapping between content or gameplay features and experiential qualities [12]. While Yannakakis and Togelius [56] only consider approaches based on *static* game content, we explicitly include *simulation-based* approaches [52] in this category, where *gameplay* features are extracted from the simulation of human play with AI agents. Togelius, De Nardi and Lucas [51] predict a player's enjoyment of racing game tracks based on AI player's learning progress, performance variation and difference in driving speed. Sorenson, Pasquier and Di Paola [48] determine challenge in platformer levels similar to *Super Mario Bros.* [31] based on static level features such as gap size, the player's maximum jump length and the presence of enemies. Recently, Khalifa et al. [24] go one step further and present a more general model of player enjoyment for any game level encoded in the *Video-Game Description Language* [44]. Their model is based on both static level features like the presence of harmful sprites and gameplay features including the score difference of AI players.

Current approaches to predict PX in PCG thus still involve human players or designers at some point. We argue that this dependency renders them inflexible and imprecise: they are likely to fail as soon as new game elements are introduced or present elements are changed. This is commonplace during development, e.g. to balance a game. Adding the *Berserker* power-up to a battle scene in *Doom* [22] for instance is likely to change the player's experience drastically, but this correlation would not be reflected in a previously trained model. With present *model-based* approaches, we would have to acquire new feedback from players each time the game is changed. The *theory-driven* approach in contrast is constrained by the designers' anticipation skills. PX strongly depends on the *interaction* of game elements, and identifying all possible interactions and every possible situation can be very complex. We expect designers to not anticipate a substantial part of these interactions, making their hand-crafted models imprecise. The same inflexibility applies when manually crafting gameplay metrics to gather human player feedback *implicitly* [12].

PX can be assessed based on algorithmic prediction mechanisms, or by gathering explicit and/or implicit designer and player feedback. In this section, we have shown exhaustively (cf. [12]) that there is no means to assess PX in PCG in a sufficiently precise and unobtrusive way without constraining the power of the content generator. In summary, the identified challenge of assessing PX in PCG is twofold: we have to assess PX independently of human players, while not relying on designers' knowledge about a game's semantics.

PREDICTING PX WITH INTRINSIC MOTIVATION MODELS

We propose to compensate for human feedback in the prediction of PX with computational models of intrinsic motivation. Being *intrinsically motivated* means to engage in "an activity for its inherent satisfactions rather than for some separable consequence" [39]. We could easily be mislead to consider games as intrinsically motivating because players act on game-internal goals, in contrast to external rewards such as a prize in an e-sports competition. However, this does not go far enough, as acting on such game-internal goals is not necessarily inherently satisfying and can still be considered a separate consequence from the player's perspective. We can most clearly observe intrinsic motivation in games without apparent goals, or when goal pressure is particularly low. In *Skyrim* [21] for instance, there is no time pressure to complete goals in terms of quests in the main storyline. Despite this, players do not become passive but explore the world and the skill-crafting system. The goals which determine this behaviour are then shaped within the players. The reason why most games are considered intrinsically motivating even in the presence of strong goal pressure is that these goals are designed to align with the players' intrinsic motivations: it is more common e.g. to find quests about exploring the world and gaining power than quest that would require one to stay in a boring place and do nothing. This concept of intrinsic motivation is what Pavlas et al. refer to as *autotelic experience* [33], and constitutes an important factor in many other theories of PX [40, 13, 1].

Given the concept's omnipresence in PX theories, we consider the use of *computational models* of intrinsic motivation a natural fit to predict PX. We adopt a strict, formal definition of intrinsic motivation put forward by Oudeyer and Kaplan [32]. Here, a motivation as basis for an agent's actions only depend on the "collation or comparison of information from different stimuli [...] independently of their semantics" [32]. Goals must therefore not only be generated from within the agent, but must also not refer to anything outside. We thus only need to know about a player's interaction with the game, but not about the meaning of game tokens. How game tokens affect our motivational values depends on the specific computational model under consideration. The independence of sensor semantics allows us to apply a model across different games and content types. In contrast to existing work, we use an AI agent to reproduce human play, and do not depend on actual players.

Shaker [45] has recently also proposed to embrace models of intrinsic motivation in PCG, but her focus is fundamentally different. She suggests reinforcement learning as an approach to content generation, and intrinsic motivations as reward signals to support the generation of novel and diverse content. While her generative system is driven by intrinsic rewards, she proposes to estimate PX based on the traditional methods outlined earlier, and relies on player feedback.

We describe our approach here informally and as it was employed in our later study. It comprises three consecutive steps.

1. Recording state samples

Our primary concern is to determine players' typical experience of a game. As basis for our prediction, we consequently have to record a state sample that closely resembles the *typical states* that players would pass through in our game. While only few will discover all the secrets in *Doom* [22], every player will engage in the major battles. At the same time, we have to identify *inaccessible states*: while the game parameters could realise many potential states, a player only perceives a small subset. We cannot determine these typical and accessible states from the static game content, but have to use playouts. PCG's time constraints enforce a *simulation-based approach* [52], i.e. we sample from the play of AI controllers.

2. Calculating intrinsic motivation quantities

We do not use models of intrinsic motivation to steer behaviour, but leverage the quantities underlying decision-making as predictors of human PX. To calculate these quantities efficiently, we condense the information in our sample to what is required by the model used. For our study, we only need to retain the visited states, but not their order. We then calculate our motivational quantity on every state in the sample.

3. Aggregating quantities into experience prediction

We finally aggregate the previously calculated, raw motivational quantities into a scalar *experience prediction*, which could eventually inform the experimenter or be used e.g. in the objective function of a content generator. We normalise the quantities across different content instances to allow for comparison. We aggregate all values of a playout in the mean.

A more detailed but generic description of our approach must take the specific requirements of other models of intrinsic motivation into account, and is yet to come. We believe that different models can be used to predict the effect of different types of content on PX. A model of curiosity, for instance, could be employed on *decorative content* [46] such as sound and visuals. For our exploratory study, we use a specific model of intrinsic motivation, *empowerment*, to predict the effect of *functional content* [46] in the form of level structure on PX.

EMPOWERMENT

Empowerment [27] is an information-theoretic quantity, defined over the relationship between the actuators and sensors of an artificial agent. Informally, empowerment measures the influence of an agent's actions on its environment (controllability), and the extent to which the agent can perceive this influence afterwards (observability). In short, it quantifies *an agent's potential, perceivable influence on the world.*

We have chosen empowerment for several reasons: It has already been briefly investigated in HCI to quantify the impact of uncertainty in manual control [53]. Interfaces with reduced empowerment were correlated with feelings of frustration, providing us with a preliminary connection between the formal model and user experience. Crucially, *empowerment maximisation* has been hypothesised as proxy for behaviour in

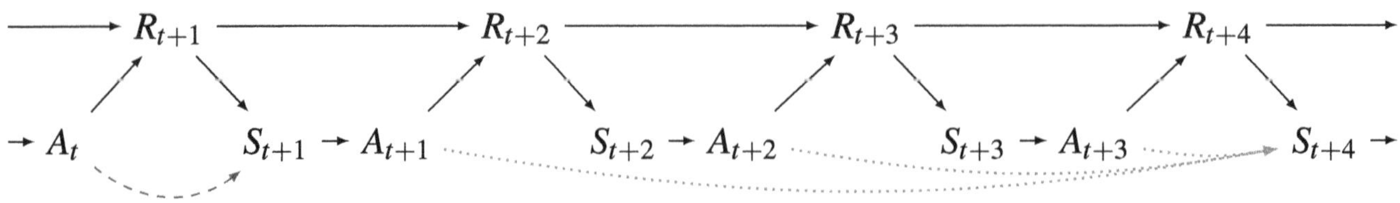

Figure 1: Causal Bayesian network of the perception-action loop of a memoryless agent unrolled in time, with the agent's sensors S, actuators A and the rest of the world R. The blue, dashed line represents the anticipation of follow-up states from $t \to t+1$. The red, dotted lines represent 3-step empowerment at time $t+1$.

animals and humans [27, 37, 17]. Some argue that "understanding games is approaching a phase where it is close to understanding the psychology of individual life experiences in general" [50], and we believe that empowerment could relate to such experiences. Empowerment maximisation has already been used to drive the behaviour of general game-playing agents [3] and non-player characters [18]. The agents successfully identified latent game features, leading to meaningful behaviour in the absence of explicit goals [3]. This leads us to believe that empowerment might also influence how people play and consequently experience games.

At the centre of the empowerment definition is the interpretation of an agent's embodiment as an information-theoretic communication channel. For any arbitrary separation between an agent and a world R we can define the sensors S and actuators A as random variables whose states allow for the in- and outflow of information to the agent, respectively. This interaction with the world is usually described as a perception-action loop, which can be analysed by means of a causal Bayesian network as in Figure 1. Here, arrows imply causation between random variables: the agent's actions A only depend on its sensor input S, which in turn is determined by the rest of the system R. The latter is affected by the preceding system state and the agent's actions. Games can be understood as similar feedback systems [41], where R corresponds to the partially observable game state that the player influences and perceives with their available actions A and their senses S, respectively.

The causal probability distribution $p(S_{t+1}|S_t,A_t)$ represents the (potentially noisy) communication channel between a sensor state and actions at time t, and the future sensor states at $t+1$. In a game, this distribution is reflected in the player's *forward model*. Empowerment $\mathfrak{E}_{s_t}$ in a given state $S_t = s_t$ is defined as the *channel capacity*, i.e. the maximum potential flow of information that could possibly be induced into the future sensor state by a suitable choice of actions. More generally, we consider a sequence of actions $A_t^n = (A_t,\dots,A_{t+n-1})$ corresponding to a lookahead of n. With *n-step empowerment* we can then quantify the amount of information an agent can potentially inject into its sensor n steps in the future:

$$\mathfrak{E}^n_{s_t} = \max_{p(a^n_t)} I(S_{t+n}; A^n_t = (A_t,\dots,A_{t+n-1})|S_t = s_t) \qquad (1)$$

The term being maximised represents the mutual information between the actuator and future sensor states, given the current sensor state s_t. Cover and Thomas [10] treat the information-theoretic notions in depth. For simplicity, we have defined empowerment for discrete interactions in time and space, but continuous implementations exist (cf. [43] for a survey).

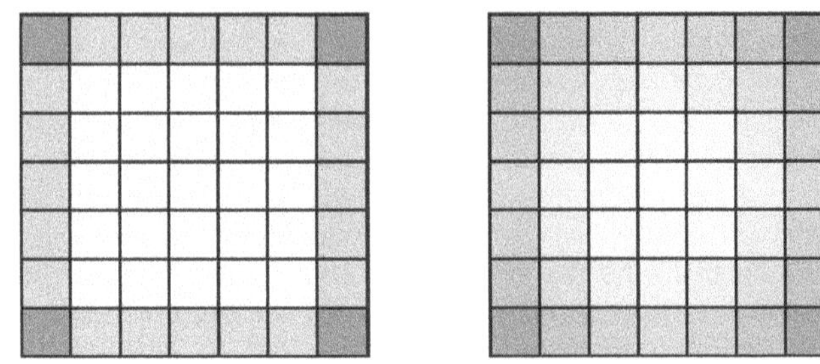

(a) n=1 (b) n=3

Figure 2: n-step empowerment of an agent at different positions in a gridworld, surrounded by walls. The agent can move north, east, south, west and idle, but it cannot go beyond the boundaries. The agent's sensor captures its position. Darker values indicate lower empowerment.

The red, dotted line (·····) in Figure 1 represents an agent's 3-step empowerment at $t+1$. Figure 2 illustrates empowerment and the difference between lookaheads in a simple gridworld surrounded by walls. The agent can sense its absolute position. It can idle or move north, east, south, and west, but it cannot cross the worlds' boundaries. There is no uncertainty about the consequences of actions. In this deterministic scenario, empowerment is proportional to the number of distinct states an agent can reach within the next n steps. For $n = 1$, it is very distinguished and low at the edges and in the corners, reflecting the impact the walls have on the agent's mobility. The larger lookahead ($n = 3$) produces a smooth reachability gradient. Empowerment is highest in the middle where the agent can access the most states in the specified time frame.

Empowerment has been hypothesised as driving principle in decision-making [27, 37, 17], i.e. animals and humans might choose their actions depending on the expected empowerment of the future situations that these actions might lead to. In our exploratory study, we want to quantify empowerment on game states, and consequently look at the player's *state-expected empowerment*. For the calculation of state-expected empowerment, we consider the action-expected empowerment for all available actions in the current state s_t, weighted by the probability that the player is going to choose these actions:

Figure 3: The *RoboRunner* testbed: a deterministic, one-button (in)finite runner game.

$$E[\mathfrak{E}^n]_{s_t} = \sum_{a_t} p(a_t|s_t) \sum_{s_{t+1}} p(s_{t+1}|s_t,a_t)\ \mathfrak{E}^n_{s_{t+1}} \tag{2}$$

This definition accounts for the possibility of noise in the agent's local dynamics, i.e. the player's forward model: a player might not be sure about the consequences of their actions, or the action outcomes might objectively be uncertain. Figure 1 shows the two stages in the calculation of 3-step state-expected empowerment at time t: the agent first anticipates which states its actions might yield at $t+1$ (- -), and then calculates 3-step empowerment for each state (·····).

Empowerment comes with several important properties. It is *local*, i.e. the agent's knowledge of the local dynamics $p(S_{t+1}|S_t,A_t)$ is sufficient to calculate the quantity. Its information-theoretic formulation makes empowerment *domain-independent* and *universal*, i.e., it can be applied to every possible agent-world interaction. Finally, empowerment is *task-independent*, i.e., it is not evaluated in regard to a specific external goal or reward, but determined by the agent's embodiment in the world. Empowerment can thus be calculated for any interaction of a player with a game, independent of the meaning of game states. Furthermore, we do not need to know about the game's complete mechanics or parameters, but only about how the player's actions affect what they can perceive. Existing studies demonstrate that empowerment is not restricted to single-player games [16, 18], and can deal with uncertainty and dynamic game worlds [42].

EXPLORATORY STUDY

Our overall goal is to predict PX with computational models of intrinsic motivation. This study represents the first step towards a proof-of-concept based on empowerment as one particular model used with our generic approach. While empowerment formally translates to an agent's potential and perceivable influence over the environment, we cannot assume the same experience for a human player. In order to conduct a quantitative study based on established, reliable HCI instruments for a full proof-of-concept, we first have to explore the aspects of PX to which empowerment potentially pertains.

Method

We approach this study as an instance of an *experiential vignette* [20] where the goal is to manipulate explicitly the response of players by providing them different games to play, but the data is analysed qualitatively in order to explore the concepts in play around the manipulation. For this reason, only modest numbers of participants are required. Different conditions here are given by different level instances of an (in)finite runner game. Our hypothesis is that levels with low mean state-expected empowerment evoke qualitatively different experiences than levels with high values. We conduct a *thematic analysis* [6] on player think-alouds to find out which experiences the different conditions give rise to. We decided against a more quantifiable approach such as content analysis, as the goal was not to see how often people engaged in a set of previously known experiences, but to explore the range of yet unknown experiences that people have in response to our manipulation. Given ambiguity and noise in the think-aloud data, we only coarsely state the frequency of specific experiences.

We have evaluated two conditions, given by levels with low- and high mean state-expected empowerment. We refer to these conditions by *low* and *high*. We have chosen a mixed experimental design, in which the two conditions are evaluated within subjects, while two instantiations of the same condition are considered between subjects. The levels were procedurally generated, and, due to stochasticity in the generator, can vary locally despite having the same mean state-expected empowerment. The goal of our mixed design was to balance effects of these within-condition differences on PX. Each participant first had to complete one of two tutorial levels with medium state-expected empowerment to familiarise with the game. We thus evaluated 8 level combinations (2 instances $\times$ 2 conditions $\times$ 2 tutorials), presented in balanced order.

Testbed: RoboRunner

Participants were asked to play different levels of *RoboRunner* (Figure 3), a simple game from the infinite runner genre specifically developed for this study. The goal is to drive a yellow robot from the left to the right of a space station. In order to reach the end of the level, the robot has to jump across chasms. The game has one implicit and one explicit action: the robot will drive to the right automatically with constant speed, while the player can invoke jumps only when the robot is on the floor. While *RoboRunner* has all characteristics of an infinite runner, our levels are in fact finite to ensure that all participants experience the same content.

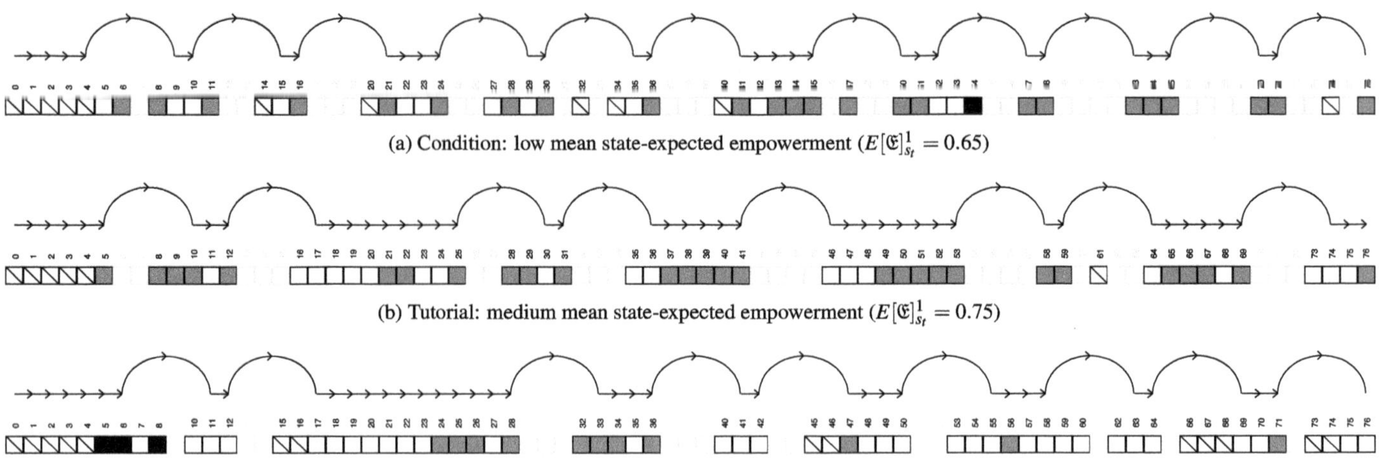

(a) Condition: low mean state-expected empowerment ($E[\mathfrak{E}]^1_{s_t} = 0.65$)

(b) Tutorial: medium mean state-expected empowerment ($E[\mathfrak{E}]^1_{s_t} = 0.75$)

(c) Condition: high mean state-expected empowerment ($E[\mathfrak{E}]^1_{s_t} = 0.85$)

Figure 4: Left third of three levels used in the study, with different mean 1-step state-expected empowerment. Striked-through modules represent irrelevant states. The AI play trajectory is shown above. Each level starts and ends with a 5-module safety zone.

We have chosen this particular testbed for several reasons. Infinite runners are, despite their simplicity, very popular. Our participants have likely seen or played similar games before, and we have assumed that they can thus familiarise with our testbed more easily. Due to its linear nature, *RoboRunner* allows us to determine the relevant states the player is going to pass through with little ambiguity: while the player can jump at different positions, there are no alternative routes to reach the end of the level. The simple controls and linearity also eased the task to create an AI controller which resembles human play. The game appears continuous in time and space to the player, but it is composed of modular blocks and can consequently be treated as discrete in space to simplify our analysis. *RoboRunner* is deterministic, i.e. only the player causes changes to the game state. Each state is thus fully characterised by the player's position, and we can visualise the whole state space at once. Furthermore, the game's low complexity allows us to develop a level generator without biases prior to the evaluation with an objective function.

Participants

The study was completed by eight participants (5 male, 3 female). Six were aged between 25-34, and two belonged to age groups 18-24 and 35-44, respectively. They were all native speakers, and most were recruited from our local MSc and PhD games programmes. We can thus presume a good video game playing experience, supported by a reported average of 16.25 hours of video game playing per month ($sd = 5.29$). Their experience is critical, as making progress in our levels is essential for rich and representative responses in the think-aloud. The participants were incentivised with chocolates.

Materials

We have generated and selected our levels in a two-stage process. We first procedurally generated level candidates over the whole range of possible instances with a genetic algorithm, to avoid any design bias from the authors. We employed a simple AI player to determine if a level is generally playable, and to find all accessible states that a human player could possibly experience. To increase the human-likeness, the controller realises a *reaction time constraint*, i.e. our AI player could not jump from the same module in which it landed. We then calculated the player's state-expected empowerment (Equation 2) for each state of the current genotype, except for the inaccessible states. The first- and last five modules of the level were considered unchangeable to form a "safety zone" for the player, and were also excluded from the calculation. Together, these states were labelled *irrelevant*. We then aggregated all quantities in the mean to form our experience prediction. The fitness of each level was determined from the distance of this prediction to a target mean.

In a second step, we selected the stimuli for our evaluation from the generated candidate levels. We observed that levels with a mean state-expected empowerment below 0.65 had very short platforms and large gaps, and were thus almost unplayable. Levels with a mean state-expected empowerment above 0.95 in contrast had almost no gaps, and did not represent typical examples of an infinite runner. We consequently picked three values from the *playable and typical range*: 0.65 for our *low* condition, 0.85 for *high*, and 0.75 for our tutorial level. We generated two instances of each condition and the tutorial level to balance for local structural differences that may affect PX. We ended up with eight unique level combinations. Figure 4 shows the left third of an instance of each level type with a trajectory of our AI player. Modules with brighter hues indicate higher state-expected empowerment for an agent in that position. Irrelevant states are crossed-through.

For an example consider the small platform at position 47 in Figure 4a. State-expected empowerment here is lower, as only jumping would allow the agent to get on solid ground and perform more actions in the future. The opportunity to hit the small platform is reflected in the higher value at position 42, as this is where the agent would have to jump to hit the platform.

Procedure

The experiment was run individually under lab conditions. Each participant was assigned one level combination, starting with the tutorial and followed by the conditions in balanced order. They were introduced to *RoboRunner*, and asked to play the tutorial level to get familiar with the game and controls. They were then prompted to play the two remaining levels until completion, or for at most five times, while thinking aloud. After completing both conditions, we asked them:

- Did you spot any differences between the levels?
- Did they feel different while playing?
- Which level did you enjoy more, and why?

This interview was structured to consist of only these three questions. The entire session lasted about 25 minutes per participant, and was recorded on audio.

Results

The thematic analysis was jointly conducted by the authors, following the procedure by Braun and Clark [6]. We first exhaustively transcribed the think-alouds, and familiarised ourselves with the data. In an iterative process, we then assigned codes and clustered them into themes that occurred across participants. A code dictionary was used between the authors to ensure consistency. The targeted interview data was analysed similarly to the think-aloud. However, because interview data is more reflective by nature, it also gave the opportunity to interpret some of the more immediate responses generated by the think-aloud data. This informed the development of the thematic analysis. Our results show how structural differences, based on empowerment, correlate with PX. We identified six major themes: *challenge*, *involvement*, *attention and engagement*, *learning* and *emotions*.

Physical & Cognitive Challenge

The players consistently considered *low* as more *challenging*:

> Ouh god it's tricky! I see, yes! God is that ...! (1)

Figure 4 shows that *low* has smaller platforms and more gaps than *high*. Players were sensitive to how these structural differences affected them, allowing us to distinguish two types of challenge: *physical challenge* addresses the player's physical limitations to interact with the game, affecting the speed and accuracy of actions [11]. *Cognitive challenge* in contrast is based on the player's cognitive capacities, and the speed and accuracy of problem solving [11]. In *RoboRunner*, the avatar's speed and the level layout determine how often the player has to jump and judge distances to succeed, influencing both physical and cognitive challenge and making them hard to separate. An exception is given by short platforms as around position 47 in Figure 4a: here, the player has to jump on- and off quickly, while the immanent gap makes further reasoning unnecessary. Participants described their struggle in terms of reaction time:

> This is tricky, because you feel like you should jump in the middle, and I suspect when I jump on the middle one, I won't jump off in time. (2)

Players experienced *cognitive challenge* in the levels' demand for *spatial reasoning* and *planning*:

> My spatial reasoning, to determine whether or not I can actually make that [jump]. So, it feels like the biggest question it is asking me is whether my judgement of the distance, *pause*, whether I should jump sooner or later. It makes me question my ability to do that. (3)

> If you chose the wrong thing, you would be left in a situation where you had to jump and land in a hole. So you wouldn't jump at the earliest opportunity. (4)

> The small platforms are those that are challenging, because you have to bounce off them really quickly, and measure your distance appropriately so you don't fall down the gaps, which I've now done 5 times! (5)

Both types of challenge were increased by decision pressure:

> The second one (*low*), it felt like [the gaps] were a lot smaller, and less frequent, so there wasn't so much of a challenge of 'I have to make this decision now'. (6)

Involvement

Participants described the experience of being *actively involved* or being *passive*, depending on the frequency with which they had to take action to succeed in the game. Almost all participants considered themselves as more passive in *high*:

> The [*low* condition] seemed to have less of those really short platforms, and they had longer stretches of where you just didn't, didn't jump. So I kind of waited. (7)

They however preferred *low* for being more involving:

> Cause this one (*high*) has like too many ... where you're just not jumping. It's got quite a loong platform. So it's kind of, just less interesting, than hard games. (8)

A lack of threats did not discourage all participants from acting, with some jumping wildly on a long stretch without gaps:

> Oh, I'm trying to do a double for fun. And another! (9)

Attention and Engagement

Almost all participants talked about *attention* in terms of *concentration* and *focus*. More than half of them had to *concentrate* harder while playing *low*, expressed explicitly and through interrupted speech:

> Yeah, I'm having to concentrate a lot harder (pause) than before. And I'm, and I'm, ..., och, I'm keeping doing that. I'm keeping falling down this one. (10)

While statements on concentration were rather unspecific, participants reported on their *focus* with respect to the game elements. They e.g. focused on jumping, while blocking out the game's visuals or details of the level structure:

> I don't know if the gaps were set on random or not. I was so focussing on jumping, I wasn't actually looking at the sizes of them. I think maybe, *pause*, the spaces changed in the game as well. (11)

In more focussed situations, players also expressed a stronger *engagement*. The majority of participants were *determined* to succeed and willing to *re-engage*:

> I'm gonna make these lives count. Now it's personal! (12)

Some participants described their engagement as "being on a roll", "zoning in" and as "flow":

> [*Low* is] a tougher game that you get into flow quite easily, because you're quite focused on just jumping over the obstacles. (13)

Learning

Almost all participants referred to the concept of *learning*. They talked about remembering mistakes and the level structure for their next attempt:

> And the gaps are, the gaps are, *pause*, whoops! Oh no, that was an error! (robot dropped into gap) I'm gonna remember, I'm gonna remember the end now. (14)

The majority of participants touched on their *performance* and *progress* without being asked explicitly, and by relating back to previous attempts:

> I felt like it (*low*) was quite hard, but I feel like, even though it is frustrating to constantly die playing a level, I feel like I would've gotten there eventually. (15)

Emotions

Our impression of engagement is supported by the players' varied expression of emotions. Almost everyone expressed *pleasure* when succeeding in the game and *disappointment* when failing, but some were also *angry*, *tense* and even *anxious*. They were particularly upset when failing at the same position repeatedly:

> So, cause I know what's coming now, I played it enough times, *pause*, I kind of, *pause*, bloody hell! (16)

This previous quote also expresses some *tension*. The feeling of tension was usually followed by relief:

> Sh! Uh oh oh oh, oh! Oh no! Ah! *Deep breath, exhaling*. Puh! Release now, I'm really upset! (17)

Some participants even expressed some *anxiety* from anticipating and assessing upcoming situations in the game:

> It's this little one that gives me the heebie-jeebies. (18)

As is common in thematic analysis, the themes are intended to stand alone as broad qualitative descriptions of the data. The method is not designed to look more causally at links between the themes but future work will exam the links explicitly.

DISCUSSION

Altering game levels based on empowerment does not only yield different structural outcomes; the preceding analysis supports our hypothesis that it also evokes qualitatively different experiences in human players. We have reported our results independently of established PX theories. We now make up for this and address potential connections between empowerment and PX theories both in game design and HCI. We selected the theories based on the formal interpretation of empowerment, and related them to the results of our exploratory study.

Empowerment & PX in Game Design

Empowerment resonates with several theories on game design. Salen and Zimmerman describe *play* in the most general sense as *"free movement within a more rigid structure"* ([41], p. 304). This rigid structure emerges from the interplay of game rules and content, and is explored and exploited in play. Such exploitation however requires the player to become aware of the structure's boundaries. Formally, empowerment quantifies an artificial agent's perceivable influence on the environment in terms of controllability and observability, and thus allows to trace the boundaries of an agent's rigid world structure and to identify latent game features [3]. To engage in play, human players might employ a similar metric to trace the structure imposed on them: When talking about challenge in our study, players referred to particularly constrained areas (Quote 4, 5).

The notion of play as free movement within a rigid structure is strongly related to a player's *control* in a game. *Super Mario Bros.*'s [31] creator Shigeru Miyamoto puts *Tegotae*, a satisfaction coming from being in control, at the core of their games design [34]. He explains "if the player jumps from a high place, the amount of time they stay in the air needs to be just right, or else they'll feel disconnected from the experience". The player's empowerment would be high on the ground, and drop to zero while being in the air. We thus hypothesise that empowerment correlates with *Tegotae* as PX. The player who jumped around wildly on a long stretch might have probed their *Tegotae* in a situation where they are otherwise just passively pushed forward by the game mechanics (Quote 9).

Salen and Zimmerman also deem *outcome uncertainty* essential for meaningful play: "If the outcome of the game is completely predetermined – then any choices a player makes are meaningless, because they do not impact the way that the game plays out" ([41], p. 174). Caillois [7] directly relates outcome uncertainty to enjoyment. Empowerment measures the consequences of a player's action sequences, and could thus, given a sufficiently large lookahead, quantify the player-distinguishable game outcomes. In practice however, this lookahead is bound by the available computational resources. Empowerment is then restricted to the near future and captures the richness of intermediate rather than terminal game states. Outcome uncertainty however is also influenced by noise in the player's actions: it can be crucial whether a given action leads to one distinct outcome, or to a set of different possible outcomes with equal probability. This noise might be inherent to the game content and rules, but it might also only exist in the agent's local model of the game dynamics. Our testbed is deterministic, but players were uncertain about their reaction times and spatial reasoning (Quote 2, 3). As an agent-centric measure, empowerment captures both types of noise.

Empowerment & PX in HCI

These design theories are supported by empirical studies in HCI. Abuhamdeh, Csikszentmihalyi and Jalal [1] for instance show that greater *outcome uncertainty* leads to an increase in enjoyment. This effect was mediated by *suspense*, which also shows in our participant's *tension* in *low* (Quote 17).

Perceivable control as in *Tegotae* is also considered an important element in many theoretical models of *engagement*, e.g. *cognitive absorption* [2], *flow* [13], and *immersion* [23]. Some of our participants said to "be on a roll", "zoned in" and in "flow" (Quote 13). Nevertheless, we focus on the more immanent relationship between empowerment and players' *perceived control*. Strictly speaking, empowerment does not directly correspond to control; it relates more to *effectance*, which can be considered a part or precondition of control. Klimmt, Hartmann and Frey define effectance as the experience of "receiving immediate, direct feedback on one's action and of influencing the game world" [26]. They empirically link effectance to game enjoyment, but their experiment is limited to situations where available actions are expected to, but do not affect the current state. In our study, the player who exercise their effectance by jumping wildly clearly enjoyed themselves (Quote 9). Empowerment additionally differs from control in that it also quantifies how the game constrains the *availability* of actions, but this was not the case in *RoboRunner*.

The players' perceived *challenge* represents the strongest theme in our study. Challenge is an element of many PX theories, and there is general agreement that being optimally challenged leads to stronger enjoyment [25]. In our study, most participants preferred *low*, the levels that were also generally considered more challenging. Optimal challenge is also an element in theories of immersion [11] and flow [13], and it might not be a coincidence that our participant said to be "in flow" for *low* (Quote 13). Malone [29] has related challenge to a player's uncertainty, and our participants mentioned their uncertainty in spatial reasoning when talking about challenge (Quote 3). Poels et al. [36] show that challenge can also trigger negative emotions such as tension, disappointment or anger, and our study supports their claim (Quote 16 –18). Our participants also appeared to talk more about their *attention* and *learning* as a result of cognitive challenge (Quote 10, 14).

We finally relate empowerment to *Self-Determination Theory* (SDT), a popular theory of intrinsic motivation which has also been applied to PX [40]. SDT is formed of several subtheories; *Cognitive Evaluation Theory* highlights the critical role of a person's *competence* and *autonomy* in intrinsic motivation. Ryan, Rigby and Przybylski [40] relate these arguably loosely defined concepts to enjoyment in games. In-game autonomy is "the degree of choice one has over the sequence of actions, or the tasks and goals undertaken" [40]. Competence in contrast is defined as a player's "need for challenge and feelings of effectance" [40]. We believe that empowerment relates to autonomy in that it quantifies the availability of actions in different game states, and relates to competence in terms of effectance as discussed earlier.

MOVING FORWARD

Our exploratory study highlights the next steps for a strong proof-of-concept on employing computational models of intrinsic motivation to predict PX. Empowerment as one particular model evokes qualitatively different PX and thus qualifies as a candidate for future studies. However, we cannot tell yet whether the identified relationships, e.g. between empowerment and challenge, will persist beyond our very minimal testbed, and if the direction of the observed effects remains. The most important step thus is to investigate if our approach *generalises*. In our next study, we will validate the identified relationships across different game genres and reward structures based on quantitative player feedback.

We furthermore have to *discriminate the PX* that empowerment directly relates to rather than mediating effects. Many experiences have been described in terms of other, more fine-grained ones, such as effectance as part of control, or different types of challenge [15]. We have to use players' quantitative feedback to identify which experiences empowerment correlates with strongest. We must also consider the effect of player skill on experience. Ultimately, we want to compile a list of intrinsic motivation models, mapped to the types of PX they are best suited to predict in different game genres.

The accuracy of our prediction is strongly influenced by how closely the behaviour of our AI agents resembles human play. A truly general, human-independent predictor of PX must be complemented with an accurate, *general model of player behaviour*. We can consider the challenge of automatically predicting PX as an iterative refinement process: on the one hand, the prediction of PX requires us to make general game-playing agents more human-like. On the other hand, our models of intrinsic motivation might provide insights on how players experience and consequently act in games, which could contribute to developing more human-like AI players. General game-playing agents are not truly general yet [4], and research on making AI agents more human-like still has some way to go. Luckily, we can separate these two sides in the lab: for our next study, we will record the play traces of human players, use them as basis for our prediction, and relate the outcome to their quantitative feedback on PX.

The experience of individual participants in our study varied strongly within a level. In order to clearly separate experimental conditions in cases where participants will unlikely complete them, we have to ensure more homogeneity of experience within conditions. We can realise this by not collating all motivational values into an average, but preserving the time of experienced states and fitting the intrinsic motivation quantities to a function, e.g. a constant. We plan to use this *time-series approach* for content generation in future studies.

We have focussed on predicting a player's *typical experience* in a video game, but suggest to adopt this approach for two more scenarios. On the one hand, we can learn a model from the behaviour of one individual or use player persona models [28] to predict the experience of one person or a small group of players for the generation of *custom-tailored content*. On the other hand, we can move from individual pieces of content to analysing the entire content generator. We suggest to take Smith and Whitehead's concept of *expressive range* analysis [47] further and calculate the "*experiential range*" of a given generator, i.e. all experiences it can potentially give rise to, given possible parameter configurations.

CONCLUSION

PCG yields many advantages for modern video games, and we believe that assessing the player's experience of procedurally generated content represents an important and interesting challenge for HCI research. We have argued that neither the rigorous methods to assess PX in HCI, nor the specialised methods developed by PCG researchers are sufficient, because they rely on a human in the loop. We proposed to solve this paradoxical challenge with computational models of intrinsic motivation. We hypothesise that these models could be used to automatically predicting PX across different games and content types without relying on a human player or designer.

As a first step towards a proof-of-concept, we conducted a qualitative, exploratory study in level generation based on empowerment. A thematic analysis allowed us to identify correlations between empowerment and *challenge*, *involvement*, *attention and engagement*, *learning* and *emotions*. After relating our findings to established PX theories, we think that these experiences are more mediating effects of empowerment, while empowerment might be more directly related to *effectance*, *(outcome) uncertainty* and *perceived control*. The most important next step is to investigate the generality of our claims, and the predictive power of empowerment in respect to the identified experiences. We hope that our findings encourage researchers to examine the relationship between other models of intrinsic motivation and PX. While empowerment might be most suitable for predicting PX arising from *functional content* [46], other models are likely to account for the impact of *decorative content* [46], e.g. sounds and visuals, too.

We have motivated our approach with the tough challenges that PCG imposes on present methods for assessing PX. However, our proposal is not limited to PCG. We do not think that our approach is going to match the precision of traditional HCI instruments; nevertheless, its speed and potential flexibility could be used in *creativity support tools* to quickly assess game designers' hand-crafted content without interrupting their workflow, or to propose alterations to their content in a *co-creative* manner [55]. This could guide designers to convey the experiences they envisaged, and to create better games.

ACKNOWLEDGEMENTS

CG, JG and PC were supported by EPSRC grant EP/L015846/1 (IGGI). CS is funded by the EU Horizon 2020 programme under the Marie Sklodowska-Curie grant 705643. Many thanks to Gillian Smith, Julian Togelius and our anonymous reviewers for very valuable feedback.

REFERENCES

1. S. Abuhamdeh, M. Csikszentmihalyi, and B. Jalal. 2015. Enjoying the Possibility of Defeat: Outcome Uncertainty, Suspense, and Intrinsic Motivation. *Motiv. Emot.* 39, 1 (2015), 1–10.
2. R. Agarwal and E. Karahanna. 2000. Time Flies When You're Having Fun: Cognitive Absorption and Beliefs About Information Technology Usage. *MIS quarterly* (2000), 665–694.
3. T. Anthony, D.l Polani, and C. L. Nehaniv. 2014. General Self-Motivation and Strategy Identification: Case Studies Based on Sokoban and Pac-Man. *IEEE T-CIAIG* 6, 1 (2014), 1–17.
4. P. Bontrager, A. Khalifa, A. Mendes, and J. Togelius. 2016. Matching Games and Algorithms for General Video Game Playing. In *Proc. Conf. AIIDE*.
5. E. A. Boyle, T. M. Connolly, T. Hainey, and J. M. Boyle. 2012. Engagement in Digital Entertainment Games: A Systematic Review. *Computers in Human Behavior* 28, 3 (2012), 771–780.
6. V. Braun and V. Clarke. 2006. Using Thematic Analysis in Psychology. *Qualitative Research in Psychology* 3, 2 (2006), 77–101.
7. R. Caillois. 1961. *Man, Play and Games*. University of Illinois Press.
8. P. Cairns, A. Cox, and A. I. Nordin. 2014. Immersion in Digital Games: Review of Gaming Experience Research. *Handbook of Digital Games* (2014), 337–361.
9. M. Cook, M. Eladhari, A. Nealen, M. Treanor, E. Boxerman, A. Jaffe, P. Sottosanti, and S. Swink. 2016. PCG-Based Game Design Patterns. *arXiv preprint arXiv:1610.03138* (2016).
10. T. M. Cover and J. A. Thomas. 1991. *Elements of Information Theory*. Wiley-Interscience.
11. A. Cox, P. Cairns, P. Shah, and M. Carroll. 2012. Not Doing But Thinking: The Role of Challenge in the Gaming Experience. In *Proc. ACM Conf. CHI*. 79–88.
12. R. Craveirinha, N. Barreto, and L. Roque. 2016. Towards a Taxonomy for the Clarification of PCG Actors' Roles. In *Proc. ACM Conf. CHI Play*. 244–253.
13. M. Csikszentmihalyi, S. Abuhamdeh, and J. Nakamura. 2014. Flow. In *Flow and the Foundations of Positive Psychology*. Springer, 227–238.
14. A. Denisova and P. Cairns. 2015. The Placebo Effect in Digital Games: Phantom Perception of Adaptive AI. In *Proc. ACM Conf. CHI Play*. 23–33.
15. A. Denisova, C. Guckelsberger, and D. Zendle. 2017. Challenge in Digital Games: Towards Developing a Measurement Tool. In *Proc. ACM Conf. CHI*.
16. C. Guckelsberger and D. Polani. 2014. Effects of Anticipation in Individually Motivated Behaviour on Survival and Control in a Multi-Agent Scenario with Resource Constraints. *Entropy* 16, 6 (2014), 3357–3378.
17. C. Guckelsberger and C. Salge. 2016. Does Empowerment Maximisation Allow for Enactive Artificial Agents?. In *Proc. Conf. ALIFE*. 704–711.
18. C. Guckelsberger, C. Salge, and S. Colton. 2016. Intrinsically Motivated General Companion NPCs. In *Proc. IEEE Conf. CIG*. 150–157.
19. M. Guzdial, N. Sturtevant, and B. Li. 2016. Deep Static and Dynamic Level Analysis: A Study on Infinite Mario. In *Experimental AI in Games Workshop*, Vol. 3.
20. M. Hudson and P. Cairns. 2014. Interrogating Social Presence in Games with Experiential Vignettes. *Entertainment Computing* 5, 2 (2014), 101–114.
21. id Software. 2011. *The Elder Scrolls V: Skyrim*. Game [Windows, PlayStation 3/4, Xbox 360/One]. (11 Nov 2011). Bethesda Game Studios.
22. id Software. 2016. *Doom*. Game [PC/PS4/XBoxOne]. (13 May 2016). id Software, Richardson, USA.
23. C. Jennett, A. L. Cox, P. Cairns, S. Dhoparee, A. Epps, T. Tijs, and A. Walton. 2008. Measuring and Defining the Experience of Immersion in Games. *Human Computer Studies* 66, 9 (2008), 641–661.

24. A. Khalifa, D. Perez-Liebana, S. M. Lucas, and J. Togelius. 2016. General Video Game Level Generation. In *Proc. Conf. Genetic and Evolutionary Computation*.
25. M. Klarkowski, D. Johnson, P. Wyeth, M. McEwan, C. Phillips, and S. Smith. 2016. Operationalising and Evaluating Sub-Optimal and Optimal Play Experiences through Challenge-Skill Manipulation. In *Proc. ACM Conf. CHI*. 5583–5594.
26. C. Klimmt, T. Hartmann, and A. Frey. 2007. Effectance and Control as Determinants of Video Game Enjoyment. *Cyberpsychology & Behavior* 10, 6 (2007), 845–848.
27. A. S. Klyubin, D. Polani, and C. L. Nehaniv. 2008. Keep Your Options Open: An Information-Based Driving Principle for Sensorimotor Systems. *PloS one* 3, 12 (2008), 1–14.
28. A. Liapis, C. Holmgård, G. N. Yannakakis, and J. Togelius. 2015. Procedural Personas as Critics for Dungeon Generation. In *Proc. European Conf. Applications of Evolutionary Computation*. 331–343.
29. T. W. Malone. 1981. Toward a Theory of Intrinsically Motivating Instruction. *Cognitive science* 5, 4 (1981), 333–369.
30. L. E. Nacke. 2013. An Introduction to Physiological Player Metrics for Evaluating Games. In *Game Analytics*. Springer, 585–619.
31. Nintendo R&D4. 1985. *Super Mario Bros.* Game [NES]. (13 September 1985). Nintendo, Kyoto, Japan.
32. P.-Y. Oudeyer and F. Kaplan. 2008. How Can We Define Intrinsic Motivation?. In *Proc. Conf. Epigenetic Robotics*. 93–101.
33. D. Pavlas, F. Jentsch, E. Salas, S. M. Fiore, and V. Sims. 2012. The Play Experience Scale: Development and Validation of a Measure of Play. *Human Factors* 54, 2 (2012), 214–225.
34. A. Perry. 2016. 'Tegotae' is essential to Nintendo's philosophy on video games – here's what it means. `http://www.techinsider.io/tegotae-is-essential-to-nintendos-philosophy-2016-7`. (2016). [Online; accessed 21-July-2016].
35. M. Persson. 2010. *Infinite Mario Bros.* Game [Cross-Platform/Java]. (2010).
36. K. Poels, Y. De Kort, and W. Ijsselsteijn. 2007. It Is Always a Lot of Fun!: Exploring Dimensions of Digital Game Experience Using Focus Group Methodology. In *Proc. ACM Conf. Future Play*. 83–89.
37. D. Polani. 2009. Information: Currency of Life? *HSFP Journal* 3, 5 (2009), 307–316. Issue 3.
38. G. Ritchie. 2007. Some Empirical Criteria for Attributing Creativity to a Computer Program. *Minds and Machines* 17, 1 (2007), 67–99.
39. R. M. Ryan and E. L. Deci. 2000. Intrinsic and Extrinsic Motivations: Classic Definitions and New Directions. *Contemp. Educ. Psych.* 25, 1 (2000), 54–67.
40. R. M. Ryan, C. S. Rigby, and A. Przybylski. 2006. The Motivational Pull of Video Games: A Self-Determination Theory Approach. *Motiv. Emot.* 30, 4 (2006), 347–363.
41. K. Salen and E. Zimmerman. 2004. *Rules of Play: Game Design Fundamentals*. MIT Press.
42. C. Salge, C. Glackin, and D. Polani. 2014a. Changing the Environment Based on Empowerment as Intrinsic Motivation. *Entropy* 16, 5 (2014), 2789–2819.
43. C. Salge, C. Glackin, and D. Polani. 2014b. Empowerment – an Introduction. *Guided Self-Organization: Inception* (2014), 67–114.
44. T. Schaul. 2013. A Video Game Description Language for Model-Based or Interactive Learning. In *Proc. IEEE Conf. CIG*. 1–8.
45. N. Shaker. 2016. Intrinsically Motivated Reinforcement Learning: A Promising Framework for Procedural Content Generation. In *Proc. IEEE Conf. CIG*. 1–8.
46. G. Smith. 2014. Understanding Procedural Content Generation: a Design-Centric Analysis of the Role of PCG in Games. In *Proc. ACM Conf. CHI*. 917–926.
47. G. Smith and J. Whitehead. 2010. Analyzing the Expressive Range of a Level Generator. In *Proc. 2010 Workshop on PCG in Games*. 1–7.
48. N. Sorenson, P. Pasquier, and S. DiPaola. 2011. A Generic Approach to Challenge Modeling for the Procedural Creation of Video Game Levels. *IEEE T-CIAIG* 3, 3 (2011), 229–244.
49. A. Summerville, S. Snodgrass, M. Guzdial, C. Holmgård, A. K. Hoover, A. Isaksen, A. Nealen, and J. Togelius. 2017. Procedural Content Generation via Machine Learning. *arXiv preprint arXiv:1702.00539* (2017).
50. J. Takatalo, J. Häkkinnen, J. Kaistinen, and G. Nyman. 2010. Presence, Involvement, and Flow in Digital Games. In *Evaluating User Experience in Games. Concepts and Methods*, R. Bernhaupt (Ed.). Springer, 23–46.
51. J. Togelius, R. De Nardi, and S. M. Lucas. 2007. Towards Automatic Personalised Content Creation for Racing Games. In *Proc. IEEE Symp. CIG*. 252–259.
52. J. Togelius and N. Shaker. 2015. The Search-Based Approach. In *Procedural Content Generation in Games*, N. Shaker, J. Togelius, and M. J. Nelson (Eds.). Springer, 17–30.
53. D. Trendafilov and R. Murray-Smith. 2013. Information-Theoretic Characterization of Uncertainty in Manual Control. In *Proc. 2013 IEEE Conf. Systems, Man, and Cybernetics*. 4913–4918.
54. J. Wiemeyer, L. Nacke, C. Moser, and F. Mueller. 2016. Player Experience. In *Serious Games*, R. Dörner, S. Göbel, W. Effelsberg, and J. Wiemeyer (Eds.). Springer, 243–271.
55. G. N. Yannakakis and C. Alexopoulos. 2014. Mixed-Initiative Co-Creativity. In *Proc. Conf. FDG*.
56. G. N. Yannakakis and J. Togelius. 2011. Experience-Driven Procedural Content Generation. In *IEEE Trans. Affective Computing*. 147–161.
57. D. Yu. 2008. *Spelunky*. Game [PC]. (21 December 2008). Mossmouth.
58. D. Yu. 2016. *Spelunky*. Boss Fight Books.

Comparing Effects of Dynamic Difficulty Adjustment Systems on Video Game Experience

Dennis Ang, Alex Mitchell
National University of Singapore
Singapore
dennis@u.nus.edu, alexm@u.nus.edu

ABSTRACT

Dynamic Difficulty Adjustment (DDA) is used by game designers to adaptively balance game challenge against player skill during play. While many DDA implementations exist, few comparative empirical studies, if any, have been done. This study investigates the effects of DDA systems on player experience through 3 conditions: no DDA, system-oriented ramping DDA (rDDA) and player-oriented DDA (pDDA). The presence of DDA was found to produce better overall game experiences. However, we found that players in the rDDA condition experienced less self-consciousness and more transformation of time but a lower sense of control compared to the players in the pDDA condition. Our findings provide new insight into DDA, demonstrating that while DDA systems can provide superior game experiences, specific drawbacks reduce their effectiveness. These considerations are of interest to interactive system designers, extending beyond games to areas where these types of adaptive systems have beneficial applications (e.g. physiotherapy or learning).

Author Keywords
Video game; player experience; dynamic difficulty adjustment; challenge; skill; player-oriented.

ACM Classification Keywords
H.5.m. Information interfaces and presentation (e.g., HCI): Miscellaneous.

INTRODUCTION

The notion of a video game is constantly evolving; what used to be confined to the arcade space can now be found in a wide range of platforms ranging from handheld devices to consoles or personal devices. Video games are playing an increasingly larger role in our lives; we collectively spend more than 3 billion hours a week on gaming [22:6].

CHI PLAY '17, October 15–18, 2017, Amsterdam, Netherlands
© 2017 Association for Computing Machinery.
ACM ISBN 978-1-4503-4898-0/17/10…$15.00
https://doi.org/10.1145/3116595.3116623

Video games are no longer used just for entertainment. As the impact of games reaches out into the real world, the invisible boundaries separating the real world and the game become increasingly blurred [5]. The application of video game concepts extends into other domains such as education [7] and healthcare [13]. Practitioners of these domains are exploring the use of games as means to help people face challenging processes such as learning and physiotherapy. Similarly, serious game research integrates game design findings with other research areas such as cognitive and motor learning, and rehabilitation science to tap into the motivation and engagement resulting from game play [20].

While software design seeks to increase productivity by simplifying processes and making tasks easier, video game design purposefully includes carefully crafted obstacles within the game that serve to challenge the player [25]. By overcoming these obstacles, players address the challenge as part of the gameplay process [27]. Although challenge in video games can come in a variety of forms, they can be broadly classified into two categories: explicit challenges that the game designer directly designs for, and implicit challenges that indirectly emerge from the game design. In this paper, we are interested in studying the explicit challenges that can be directly controlled through design.

One of the methods game designers use to more efficiently tackle difficulty in games is through the design of systems that allow for the regulation of the game challenge during the game session. This dynamic difficulty adjustment (DDA) mechanism can allow the game system to handle the difficulty adjustment on behalf of the game designer. An alternative method of DDA implementation was proposed by Chen [6]: instead of allowing the game system to make the difficulty adjustment, as is the case in traditional system-oriented DDA, Chen's player-oriented DDA (pDDA) implementation allows the player to take control of the difficulty adjustment process, as demonstrated in his game *flOw*. The use of such DDA systems does not entirely replace the need for game balancing. However, it reduces the time required for game designers to achieve the balance in difficulty, and often does so with greater accuracy [15].

This paper explores how the player experience is altered by (1) the presence of and (2) the type of DDA systems employed in a game. This research provides a unique contribution to existing literature by demonstrating that the mere presence of minimalistic player-oriented or system-oriented DDA systems in games can provide superior player experience in general. The findings also add to the existing literature, or lack thereof, by surfacing specific drawbacks in both types of DDA systems that reduce their effectiveness in enhancing player experience.

The findings of this paper will be of interest to game designers who utilize difficulty mechanics in their game design process. In the broader context, system designers can use these insights to inform their designs of systems that need to cater for users with varying skill levels, involve task flows with varying task difficulty, or facilitate activities that involve volatile user skill during the activity itself.

RELATED WORK

Dynamic Difficulty Adjustment in Video Games

Current research on DDA systems focuses on the development or study of artificial intelligence systems which automatically adjust the challenge level based on player performance [11,14,30].

Few studies have been done to examine the impact of DDA systems on the player experience. One such study by Baldwin, Johnson and Wyeth [1] investigates the effects of a multiplayer DDA (mDDA) system on player experience and performance through a subjective survey and objective biometric measure. Their preliminary analysis indicated an improvement in some areas of the subjective player experience when mDDA is present, particularly for assisted players [1].

Another study by Smeddinck, Mandryk, Birk, Gerling, Barsilowski and Malaka [28] investigated how the modality of difficulty choices impact player experience of needs satisfaction in casual games. They found that the mode of difficulty choices (menu-based, embedded or automatic) had an impact on perceived autonomy but no other player experience measures were affected.

While these studies suggest that DDA systems have the capability of altering player experience, little is known about how the experiences of different DDA systems compare against each other.

Video Game Experience

Researchers have long been fascinated with what makes video games so captivating, interesting and enjoyable [21,26]. Some existing studies try to measure video game experience in the separate conceptual dimensions of immersion, engagement, enjoyment or presence [3,23].

Other studies such as those by Brown and Cairns [4] conceptualize engagement and presence as degrees of immersion. Brown and Cairns present immersion as a range – with engagement as the first stage of immersion followed by engrossment and finally presence or total immersion; enjoyment is conceptualized as a possible result of immersion.

Given these varying and potentially conflicting treatments of these concepts, it remains unclear whether these concepts are distinct from one another.

Flow in Video Games

Scholars studying video game experience often rely on the multi-dimensional construct from Flow [10:15], a broader theory of intrinsic motivation. Flow is described by Csikszentmihalyi [9] to be the state of optimal or "peak" experience.

One of the important preconditions to enter this optimal experience or Flow state is a balance between activity challenge and skill. Similarly, in DDA systems the focal point is to attain the "sweet spot" for the game challenge and the player skill in order to improve the player experience. The multi-dimensional construct of Flow should thus be an integral measure in player experience, particularly for the current study focusing on DDA systems.

The related literature points toward the difficulties and problems of using such multi-dimensional constructs. For example, Smeddinck et al. [28] discussed the similarities of Flow concepts with the concepts from self-determination theory (SDT), another motivational theory. Their study used the *Player Experience of Needs Satisfaction* (PENS) questionnaire that assesses SDT instead of Flow.

However, there is an important distinction to be made between the measures for SDT and Flow. As Smeddinck points out, Flow is a process variable while SDT measures are focused on the pre-process or needs. For this study, we are interested in how DDA system improve the process (player experience) during the game, rather than the pre-processes or post-processes (motivations or needs satisfaction) to play the game. Thus, Flow is the logical measure (as opposed to the need for competence, autonomy, and relatedness) to adopt to measure the wholesome player experience in the context of this study. In adapting the concept of Flow to video games, Sweetser and Wyeth [32] constructed the GameFlow model that consists of eight core elements: concentration, challenge, player skills, control, clear goals, feedback, immersion and social interaction. The first seven of these elements are based on the conditions and characteristics of Flow. Each of the core elements is assigned a set of criteria, which can be used to evaluate player enjoyment in games. While the GameFlow framework is useful as a set of general heuristics in evaluating Flow in video games via content analysis methods [31], the framework is not designed for use in experiments.

Few studies have manipulated Flow in video games through experiments. An experimental study conducted by Nacke and Lindley [24] utilized three different game conditions to induce immersion, boredom and flow through level designs specifically for First-Person Shooter (FPS) combat mechanics in a single-player video game. Nacke and Lindley's conditions were rated by their participants through a game experience questionnaire; the results show that the boredom condition scored the lowest on challenge, immersion, and flow while the flow condition scored highest on flow, challenge, and tension. Another study conducted by Keller and Bless [17] adapted the computer game *Tetris* (1985) into different versions suitable for representing the conditions of boredom, adaptive and overload in order to assess the different dimensions of Flow experiences in a single-player context. The study achieved higher performance, lower time estimates, perceived fit of skills and higher involvement and enjoyment in the adaptive condition compared to the boredom and overload conditions [17].

Such studies, though few in number, have demonstrated the successful manipulation and measurement of Flow in quantitative experimental contexts using a variety of customized scales.

While many researchers have operationalized custom Flow measures for their studies, one common Flow scale has been validated and used in several domains including games [2,19]. The Jackson and Marsh's Flow State Scale (FSS) [16] operationalizes Flow into nine subscales that measure challenge-skill balance, action-awareness merging, clear goals, unambiguous feedback, concentration on task at hand, sense of control, loss of self-consciousness, transformation of time and autotelic experience. These nine measures closely match the conditions and characteristics of Flow as defined by Csikszentmihalyi [9,10].

It is important to emphasize that the use of the multi-dimensional construct of Flow together with other conceptualized dimensions of player experience is problematic as these concepts are not internally heterogeneous. Examples of secondary dimensions of player experience that overlap with the dimensions of Flow include (1) competence with challenge-skill balance and (2) immersion or engagement with action-awareness merging or loss of self-consciousness. Accordingly, this study focuses exclusively on Flow as a measure of player experience and adopts the Jackson and Marsh subscale constructs to examine the dimensions of an optimal game experience as understood in Flow theory.

RESEARCH PROBLEM

Current literature on DDA in video games focuses on system-oriented DDA implementations in which the game system determines the appropriate difficulty level for the player based on artificial intelligence algorithms or heuristics of player performance [11,24,33]. However, we found no empirical studies that have investigated the effects of player-oriented DDA on the player experience. In addition, the discussion and understanding of the Flow experience in the context of video games remain largely theoretical and has not been extensively tested through empirical studies.

As such, the literature reveals a lack of empirical understanding of the comparative effects of different DDA implementations on the player experience. Thus, this study is interested in exploring (1) how the presence of DDA in single-player video games affects the Flow state, as well as (2) how the player experience might differ when a game uses player-oriented DDA implementations as compared to non-player-oriented counterparts.

We do this by comparing three different experimental conditions with each other. First, a control condition in which no DDA implementation exists (no DDA). Second, a system-oriented ramping DDA in which the difficulty automatically rises based on player performance (rDDA). Third, a player-oriented DDA in which the player is given direct manipulation over the difficulty level (pDDA).

HYPOTHESES

Although Csikszentmihalyi's [10] initial research on Flow over a broad spectrum focuses more towards real life challenges such as those faced by athletes and artists, the concept of Flow has been applied to the domain of video games as well [8,31,32].

For example, in *Tetris* (1985), the game gets harder as the player successfully addresses more challenges in the game. The challenge given to the player in *Tetris* is to place as many stackable odd shaped blocks, which "fall" at an increasingly faster pace from the top of the game board, in rows on the game board itself before any one piece touches the top of the board, at which point the game will end. The player can address this challenge by forming complete rows using the blocks, and by doing so trigger a "clear" that removes the completed rows from the board, providing more board space, and therefore allowing the player to continue with the game for a longer period of time.

Despite the ever-increasing challenge, players are willing to play the video game again and again. One possible reason for this is that the player finds the game experience a reward in itself and that the player is willing to play the game again to once again enter the optimal experience state of Flow [31].

Through effective DDA implementations, video games are able to achieve a better balance of challenge and skill. As such, the player would then theoretically be able to enter a state of Flow or an optimal experience much faster and for longer periods of time, improving the overall game experience. To test the theoretical assumption that DDA implementations result in an improved game experience, we formulate our first set of hypothesis as follows:

Hypothesis 1 (H1): *Players in the no DDA condition will experience less (i) Challenge-skill Balance, (ii) Action-Awareness Merging, (iii) Clear Goals, (iv) Unambiguous Feedback, (v) Concentration on Task at Hand, (vi) Sense of Control, (vii) Loss of Self-consciousness, (viii) Transformation of Time and (ix) Autotelic Experience compared to players in the (a) ramping DDA condition and (b) player-oriented DDA condition.*

Chen suggests that "player-oriented DDA offers an active mechanic for players to control their in-game Flow experience" [6] in which players would be able to choose to play at a more difficult level as they start feeling bored and at an easier level if they perceive the difficulty to be too high for them. Theoretically, this additional control by the player that is not present in system-oriented DDA implementations should result in better Flow for the player. However, Chen also warns that when such DDA choices are not embedded into the gameplay, the frequent choices become potential interruptions to the Flow experience as the player has to pull out from the game immersion and make the choice with regards to the adjustment of the game difficulty level.

We consciously made a design decision to use an implementation of pDDA in which the difficulty choice is not embedded into the game mechanics as Chen recommends. This is to test whether a minimalistic implementation of the pDDA implementation is sufficient to significantly alter the player experience; this implementation will also amplify the effects of the disruption highlighted by Chen to give us a clearer understanding of the game experience drawbacks of using such implementations.

Thus, considering Chen's suggestions, we hypothesize that pDDA can result in a superior Flow experience compared to system-oriented ramping DDA, with the exception of the dimension of concentration on task at hand. We hypothesize that this one dimension will be lower, as disruption may take place when the player has to shift attention away from the game and make a decision to press a keyboard button in order to increase or decrease the difficulty level. Formally, the second set of hypotheses is as follows:

Hypothesis 2 (H2): *Players in the player-oriented DDA condition will experience (i) more Challenge-skill Balance, (ii) more Action-awareness Merging, (iii) more Clear Goals, (iv) more Unambiguous Feedback, (v) less Concentration on Task at Hand, (vi) more Sense of Control, (vii) more Loss of Self-consciousness, (viii) more Transformation of Time and (ix) more Autotelic Experience compared to players in the ramping DDA condition.*

METHOD

A fully counter-balanced single factor within-subjects design was employed to test the hypotheses. The single factor of DDA system had 3 levels; no DDA, rDDA, and pDDA. The full counter-balancing on the design results in a total of six orders of treatments.

Participants

30 participants, 16 male and 14 female ranging in age from 19 to 35 years (M=24.80, SD=3.38) took part in the experiment. Each participant was randomly assigned to one of the six orders of treatments in the fully counter-balanced design. All participants were volunteers who were not given any form of reimbursement for participating in the experiment.

Half of the participants identified as gamers. The gamers have an average gaming experience of 9.8 years (Mdn=10, Mode=5, SD=4.49) and spend an average of 3.4 hours a day on playing video games (Mdn=3, Mode=3, SD=1.50).

All except one participant have played variations of *Tetris* before the experiment session. Most participants identified themselves as a beginner (n=12) or novice (n=12) *Tetris* players. The remaining participants (n=6) identified as intermediate *Tetris* players. No participant identified as an expert *Tetris* player.

Apparatus

The physical apparatus for the experiment consisted of a computer running the Windows operating system as well as hardware used for input, which includes a keyboard and a mouse. Three different variations of classic *Tetris* were created to use as the software apparatus for each of the conditions being tested. The *Tetris* variations used the same 7 pieces that appear in the original *Tetris* game. They also used a bag-style randomizer to generate the pieces. As such, all 7 pieces are guaranteed to appear every 7 turns and there will never be 3 consecutive pieces of the same kind.

The difficulty aspect manipulated in the variations is constrained to only the falling rate of the Tetris blocks. While several other alternatives have been considered in the design of the apparatus such as manipulating the block type pool, or the frequency of the block types, these manipulations may interfere with the findings (e.g. the dimension of clear feedback). All variations start off with a base speed at which the pieces drop one row per second. In the variations with DDA, each increase of the difficulty level will reduce the drop interval by a compounded 30%.

We implemented keyboard controls for the game: left and right arrow keys to move the piece left or right, up arrow key to rotate a piece and down arrow key to move the piece downwards by one row. Tapping once on the spacebar key resulted in the current piece immediately dropping to the bottom of the board.

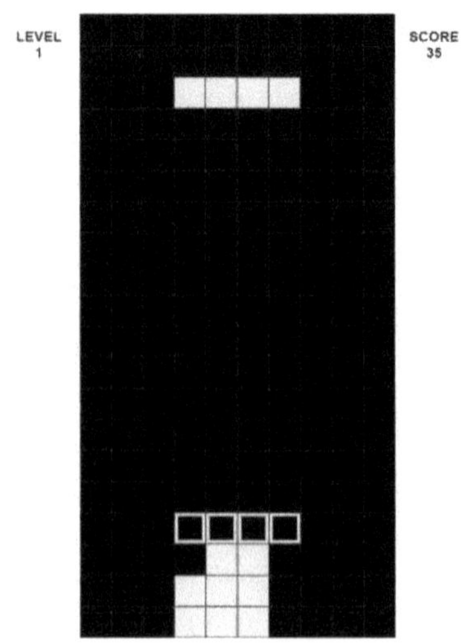

Figure 1. Screenshot of in-game experiment user interface

We also chose to use a minimalistic representation of the *Tetris* interface (see Figure 1) with the standard board size of 10 columns by 20 rows. This was done to reduce the potentially confounding effects of visual aesthetics on the player experience and was controlled for by standardizing this visual format across all experiment conditions.

In the no DDA condition, the drop rate of the tiles remained constant throughout the game session. In the rDDA condition, the drop rate increased by one difficulty level for every 10 lines cleared. In the pDDA, the drop rate decreases or increases by one difficulty level each time the player taps on the Z or X button respectively on the keyboard.

Additional software apparatus in the form of a digital experimental environment facilitated the display of the game conditions as well the automatic logging of data from the demographic questionnaire and post-questionnaires. The environment was hosted on a local Apache web server setup and displayed using the Google Chrome browser in full-screen mode.

For participant privacy, no identity-revealing data was collected. Instead, a pre-assigned unique participant identification number was tagged to all relevant data sets.

Measures

In order to measure the player's game experience, we utilized all sub-scales from the Flow State Scale (FSS) [16] measured on a 5-point Likert scale (1=Strongly Disagree, 5=Strongly Agree) to comprehensively measure several major dimensions of the player's Flow experience within the game.

The subscales consist of 9 constructs as defined by Jackson and Marsh [16] each consisting of 4 items. The internal consistency of all sub-scales for each of the three points of administration during the experiment were found to be acceptable, indicating that the items used for each of the constructs produce similar scores: *challenge-skill balance* ($\alpha_1 = .82$, $\alpha_2 = .90$, $\alpha_3 = .90$), *action-awareness merging* ($\alpha_1 = .83$, $\alpha_2 = .92$, $\alpha_3 = .83$), *clear goals* ($\alpha_1 = .90$, $\alpha_2 = .89$, $\alpha_3 = .85$), *unambiguous feedback* ($\alpha_1 = .70$, $\alpha_2 = .86$, $\alpha_3 = .74$), *concentration on task at hand* ($\alpha_1 = .88$, $\alpha_2 = .81$, $\alpha_3 = .75$), *sense of control* ($\alpha_1 = .88$, $\alpha_2 = .77$, $\alpha_3 = .89$), *loss of self-consciousness* ($\alpha_1 = .85$, $\alpha_2 = .86$, $\alpha_3 = .83$), *transformation of time* ($\alpha_1 = .84$, $\alpha_2 = .72$, $\alpha_3 = .88$) and *autotelic experience* ($\alpha_1 = .83$, $\alpha_2 = .94$, $\alpha_3 = .88$) in which the task at hand for the context of this study refers to the playing of the *Tetris* game.

Procedure

After participant consent was obtained, the participant was seated facing the computer screen and a digital demographic questionnaire was administered. Then, participants were put through a practice session of *Tetris* to reduce learning effects as well as familiarize them with the interface and controls of the game. Participants were only allowed to proceed when they had demonstrated an understanding of the basic controls (moving the pieces) as well as the game mechanics (placing down blocks and clearing lines) during the practice session.

Instructions pertaining to the experiment task were displayed on the screen after the practice session. The experiment task given to the participant was to play a variation of the *Tetris* game given the appropriate instructions on the screen for a total of five minutes before filling in the FSS questionnaire followed by a manipulation check questionnaire. The task procedure was repeated three times for each DDA variation in the order of treatment that was randomly assigned to the participant. Once all three variations have been played, and the respective FSS questionnaires and the manipulation check questions had been administered, the participant was debriefed and dismissed.

Manipulation Checks

Manipulation checks were conducted after each experiment condition. This was done through three simple 'true' or 'false' questions which checked if the participants were consciously aware that (1) the game difficulty could not change, (2) the game system could automatically change the difficulty during the game, and (3) the participant could change the game difficulty during the game.

Manipulation for the no DDA variation was successful if the participant answers 'true' to only the first question. Manipulation for the rDDA variation was successful if the participant answers 'true' to only the second question. Finally, for the pDDA variation, the manipulation was considered successful if the participant answers 'true' only the last question. The manipulations of all game sessions were verified to be successful.

RESULTS

A one-way within-subjects multivariate analysis of variance (MANOVA) was used to evaluate the effect of the three conditions (no DDA, rDDA, and pDDA) on nine dependent variables (FSS measures). Significant differences were found among the three conditions on the dependent variables, $\Lambda = .14$, $F(18,100) = 9.33$, $p < .001$, $\eta_p^2 = .63$. Within-subjects univariate analyses of variance (ANOVAs) for each dependent variable were conducted as follow-up tests to the MANOVA.

		H1 no DDA vs.		H2 pDDA vs rDDA
		(a) rDDA	(b) pDDA	
Challenge-skill Balance	(i)	Less*	Less*	-
Action-awareness Merging	(ii)	Less*	Less*	-
Clear Goals	(iii)	-	-	-
Unambiguous Feedback	(iv)	-	-	-
Concentration on task at hand	(v)	Less*	Less*	-
Sense of Control	(vi)	More^	-	More*
Loss of self-Consciousness	(vii)	Less*	-	Less^
Transformation of Time	(viii)	Less*	Less*	Less^
Autotelic Experience	(ix)	Less*	Less*	-

Table 1: Summary of hypotheses testing based on results from within-subjects univariate ANOVAs. Supported hypotheses are indicated with (*). Hypotheses with an inverse relationship of what was hypothesized indicated with (^). Hypotheses that are not supported are indicated with a (-).

The results of the hypotheses based on the follow-up ANOVAs are summarized in Table 1. The detailed statistics are reported in the relevant sections below.

Challenge-skill Balance

Mauchly's Test indicated that the assumption of sphericity has been violated, $X^2(2) = 6.02$, $p = .049$. Therefore, degrees of freedom were corrected using Huynh-Feldt estimates of sphericity ($\varepsilon = .88$). The mean scores for challenge-skill balance were significantly different, $F(1.77, 51.23) = 29.36$, $p < .0005$, $\eta_p^2 = .50$.

Post-hoc pairwise comparisons using the Bonferroni correction revealed that challenge-skill balance was significantly lower for participants in the no DDA ($M = 2.67$, $SD = .58$) compared to the rDDA ($M = 3.60$, $SD = .66$) and pDDA ($M = 3.80$, $SD = .71$). Hypothesis 1(i) was supported. The comparisons also revealed that challenge-skill balance was not significantly different for participants in the pDDA condition compared to the rDDA condition. Hypothesis 2(i) was not supported.

Action-awareness Merging

Mauchly's Test indicated that the assumption of sphericity has not been violated, $X^2(2) = 4.14$, $p = .126$. The mean scores for action-awareness merging were significantly different, $F(2, 58) = 11.00$, $p < .0005$, $\eta_p^2 = .28$.

Post-hoc pairwise comparisons using the Bonferroni correction revealed that action-awareness merging was significantly lower for participants in the no DDA condition ($M = 2.79$, $SD = .60$) compared to the rDDA($M = 3.43$, $SD = 1.04$) and pDDA ($M = 3.43$, $SD = .81$) conditions. Hypothesis 1(ii) was supported. The comparisons also revealed that action-awareness merging was not significantly different for participants in the pDDA condition compared to the rDDA condition. Hypothesis 2(ii) was not supported.

Clear Goals

Mauchly's Test indicated that the assumption of sphericity has been violated, $X^2(2) = 11.97$, $p = .003$. Therefore, degrees of freedom were corrected using Greenhouse-Geisser estimates of sphericity ($\varepsilon = .74$). The mean scores for clear goals were not significantly different, $F(1.48, 43.03) = .476$, $p = .623$, $\eta_p^2 = .50$. There was no significant difference in clear goals between the no DDA ($M = 4.05$, $SD = .67$), rDDA ($M = 4.08$, $SD = .77$) and pDDA ($M = 4.15$, $SD = .61$) conditions. Hypothesis 1(iii) and Hypothesis 2(iii) are not supported.

Unambiguous Feedback

Mauchly's Test indicated that the assumption of sphericity has been violated, $X^2(2) = 8.83$, $p = .012$. Therefore, degrees of freedom were corrected using Huynh-Feldt estimates of sphericity ($\varepsilon = .825$). The mean scores for unambiguous feedback were not significantly different, $F(1.65, 47.82) = 1.26$, $p = .289$. There was no significant difference in unambiguous feedback between the no DDA ($M = 3.91$, $SD = .50$), rDDA ($M = 4.06$, $SD = .63$) and pDDA ($M = 3.98$, $SD = .50$) conditions. Hypothesis 1(iv) and Hypothesis 2(iv) are not supported.

Concentration on Task at Hand

Mauchly's Test indicated that the assumption of sphericity has been violated, $X^2(2) = 6.86$, $p = .032$. Therefore, degrees of freedom were corrected using Huynh-Feldt estimates of sphericity ($\varepsilon = .88$). The mean scores for concentration on task at hand were significantly different, $F(1.63, 47.65) = 18.89$, $p < .0005$, $\eta_p^2 = .39$.

Post-hoc pairwise comparisons using the Bonferroni correction revealed that concentration on task at hand was significantly lower for participants in the no DDA condition ($M = 3.29$, $SD = .70$) compared to the rDDA ($M = 4.03$, $SD = .67$) and pDDA ($M = 4.08$, $SD = .50$) conditions. Hypothesis 1(v) was supported. The comparisons also revealed that concentration on task at hand was not significantly different for participants in the pDDA condition compared to the rDDA condition. Hypothesis 2(v) was not supported.

Sense of Control

Mauchly's Test indicated that the assumption of sphericity has not been violated, $X^2(2) = .49$, $p = .783$. The mean scores for sense of control were significantly different, $F(2, 58) = 15.45$, $p < .0005$, $\eta_p^2 = .35$.

Post-hoc pairwise comparisons using the Bonferroni correction revealed that sense of control was significantly higher for participants in the no DDA ($M = 3.75$, $SD = .73$) compared to the rDDA condition ($M = 3.25$, $SD = .59$). As the relationship was an inverse of what was hypothesized, Hypothesis 1(vi)(a) was not supported. There was no significant difference in sense of control between no DDA and pDDA ($M = 3.95$, $SD = .87$) conditions. Hypothesis 1(vi)(b) was not supported. The comparisons also revealed that sense of control was significantly higher for participants in the pDDA condition compared to the rDDA condition. Hypothesis 2(vi) was supported.

Loss of Self-Consciousness

Mauchly's Test indicated that the assumption of sphericity has been violated, $X^2(2) = 9.50$, $p = .009$. Therefore, degrees of freedom were corrected using Huynh-Feldt estimates of sphericity ($\varepsilon = .81$). The mean scores for loss of self-consciousness were significantly different, $F(1.63, 47.12) = 13.71$, $p < .0005$, $\eta_p^2 = .32$.

Post-hoc pairwise comparisons using the Bonferroni correction revealed that loss of self-consciousness was significantly lower for participants in the no DDA ($M = 3.17$, $SD = .72$) compared to the rDDA ($M = 3.88$, $SD = .82$). Hypothesis 1(vii)(a) was supported. There was no significant difference in loss of self-consciousness between no DDA and pDDA ($M = 3.38$, $SD = .69$) conditions. Hypothesis 1(vii)(b) was not supported. The comparisons also revealed that the challenge-skill balance was significantly lower for participants in the pDDA condition compared to the rDDA condition. As the relationship was an inverse of what was hypothesized, Hypothesis 2(vii) was not supported.

Transformation of Time

Mauchly's Test indicated that the assumption of sphericity has not been violated, $X^2(2) = 2.67$, $p = .263$. The mean scores for transformation of time were significantly different, $F(2, 58) = 15.90$, $p < .0005$, $\eta_p^2 = .37$.

Post-hoc pairwise comparisons using the Bonferroni correction revealed that transformation of time was significantly lower for participants in the no DDA (M = 2.95, SD = .74) compared to the rDDA (M = 3.86, SD = .72) and pDDA (M = 3.50, SD = .96). Hypothesis 1(viii) was supported. The comparisons also revealed that transformation of time was significantly lower for participants in the pDDA condition compared to the rDDA condition. As the relationship was an inverse of what was hypothesized, Hypothesis 2(viii) was not supported.

Autotelic Experience

Mauchly's Test indicated that the assumption of sphericity has been violated, $X^2(2) = 13.476$, $p = .001$. Therefore, degrees of freedom were corrected using Greenhouse-Geisser estimates of sphericity ($\varepsilon = .72$). The mean scores for autotelic experience were significantly different, $F(1.45, 41.97) = 20.50$, $p < .0005$, $\eta_p^2 = .41$.

Post-hoc pairwise comparisons using the Bonferroni correction revealed that autotelic experience was significantly lower for participants in the no DDA (M = 2.95, SD = .55) compared to the rDDA (M = 3.83, SD = .87) and pDDA (M = 3.82, SD = .64). Hypothesis 1(ix) was supported. The comparisons also revealed that autotelic experience was not significantly different for participants in the pDDA condition compared to the rDDA condition. Hypothesis 2(ix) was not supported.

DISCUSSION

The main findings from our study are:

- DDA systems alter the game experience in a positive way. Several dimensions of what constitutes an optimal experience, or Flow, have been demonstrated to be worse off in the absence of DDA.
- Ramping DDA systems can impact the game experience negatively. The study specifically demonstrates how players can experience a significantly diminished sense of control with such systems;
- Player-oriented DDA systems, on the other hand, give players a better sense of control compared to ramping DDA. Our study also reveals that the use of such DDA systems could come with certain game experience tradeoffs. Specifically, the study demonstrates how such systems can result in higher self-consciousness and lower alteration of one's perception of time.

DDA and Overall Game Experience

Both of the DDA implementations we tested resulted in general improvements to the players' game experience, with each dimension being either similar or better compared to the implementation with no DDA, with the exception of the dimension of sense of control which fared the worst in the rDDA condition. This suggests that designers should consider DDA systems as a viable strategy to bolster experience through the manipulation of difficulty based on certain indicators, of which game performance was used in this study.

Clear Goals and Unambiguous Feedback

We hypothesized that the players would perceive clearer goals and less ambiguous feedback in both DDA conditions compared to the no DDA condition as the additional feedback that the participants get in the DDA conditions (e.g. the visual feedback that the game level changed) may positively impact these two dimensions. However, these two dimensions did not differ in the DDA condition compared to the no DDA condition.

These non-differences may be attributed to some limitations of our experiment. The game we used, *Tetris*, is a straightforward game with simple goals. In fact, this was a deliberate choice we made when selecting a game for experiment use. While a more complex game may affect the clear goals and unambiguous feedback measures, such games introduce a wide range of variables that becomes difficult to account for and may confounded the results. An example of such additional complexity is the presence of a narrative.

All participants except one had prior experience with at least one variation of *Tetris* outside of our experiment. Furthermore, the simplicity of the game we used restricted the possible goals that participants had. These restricted goals were further clarified through the experiment procedure as participants were put through a practice session in order to reduce the effect of uncertainty of the game controls and mechanics on the game experience.

As a result, it is likely that participants in all conditions had a clear sense of what they wanted to do or achieve as well as what to look out for to gauge their game performance for the game sessions that followed.

System-oriented Adjustment Systems

The system-oriented rDDA implementation demonstrated a robust performance in positively affecting game experience compared to having no DDA at all. However, our study clearly demonstrated an important drawback that is present when using rDDA implementations. Such implementations diminish the sense of control a player has, not only when compared a system with pDDA, but also when compared a system with no DDA. This finding indicates that system designers should be cautious when using system-oriented adjustment systems. A lack of sense of control, which can negatively impact the user experience, could be amplified to the point where it degrades the overall experience.

Player-oriented Adjustment Systems

The pDDA implementation performed better than the no DDA condition and was almost evenly matched compared to the rDDA implementation. While pDDA gave players a better sense of control compared to rDDA, this sense of control was not significantly different compared to having no DDA. Interestingly, our study shows that pDDA did not significantly affect the player's concentration on task at hand. Furthermore, the study revealed specific side effects of the pDDA approach: increased self-consciousness and increased consciousness of time.

Increased Self-consciousness

The increased concern for the self that is present in the pDDA condition could be due to the participants' self-evaluation during the game session. It is plausible that in the act of making the game difficulty choice, participants consciously go through an evaluation of their current performance, the result of the evaluation driving their decision to make the choice to change the difficulty to either a higher or lower level. If so, it is likely that this evaluation is the source of concern for how one is doing at that point of time, explaining the higher self-consciousness of players in the game sessions in the pDDA condition.

Increased Consciousness of Time

The study shows that the participants in pDDA did not experience as much transformation of time compared to the rDDA condition. The difficulty in the game apparatus is tied to the concept of time; the faster the piece falls, the harder the game gets. As such, a possible explanation of the increased consciousness of time can be attributed to the perceptive evaluation of whether pieces are falling faster or slower after the player has made a game difficulty choice. In making such a choice, the player might become more, if not fully, aware of time in relation to how fast a piece used to fall before a given game difficulty choice was made, and how fast it is falling after the difficulty choice.

Limitations and Practical Significance

Our study compares ramping and player-oriented DDA implementations with each other as well as with a no DDA implementation. It does not address other popular DDA implementations such as adaptive DDA, also known as auto-difficulty adjustment [34]. The main difference between ramping DDA and adaptive DDA is that ramping DDA allows for the game difficulty to automatically rise depending on player performance, while adaptive DDA allows for the difficulty to automatically either rise or fall depending on player performance. However, we have specifically picked DDA implementations that were minimal in order to test whether bare-bones implementations of DDA could result in a superior player experience compared to no DDA at all, which our study had achieved. Game designers can use this information to make an educated choice on their DDA strategies in their future game designs.

Our participant pool did not contain any self-identifying experts. As such, the findings may not be representative of the experience of experts using systems that implement dynamic adjustment. While the effects on expert user experience may differ, our findings are still useful in signaling the need for careful consideration of the potential effects of implementing dynamic adjustment mechanics in system design.

While participants were informed as part of the experiment brief that they would be playing different versions of Tetris, they were not informed beforehand what the specific differences in the versions were. However, the instructions for the controls that were displayed just before each game session, particularly for the pDDA condition, may have given participants an expectation of the type of DDA in the game session that followed immediately. To reduce the potential placebo effect [12], in addition to the manipulation checks, we made sure that the difficulty changes were perceptually noticeable through prior pilot studies.

We consciously omitted or minimized several aspects of the game design that could drastically change the player experience. These aspects include the presence of a narrative, as well as visual and audial aesthetics. In many games, these components are present either individually or sometimes all together. These components may interact with DDA implementations and alter the game experience. While our investigation is limited to only the role of DDA implementations, we were able to provide an in-depth analysis of the effects of DDA on the player experience despite being unable to describe the role of the controlled components.

There are aspects of this study that may apply beyond games. Serious game designers or even system designers can utilize the comparative results of the user experience with no DDA and DDA systems to make design choices for systems, especially those with the aspect of difficulty or challenge, that have greater real-world implications. Such systems can be applied to the domain of health and education, improving therapy experience for patients and improving learning systems that not only balance the challenge of the learning activity with student ability but also allow the learner to better enjoy the challenge.

However, we acknowledge that the findings may have limited generalizability, as designers from related domains should also consider the presence of exogenous goals or potential confounding factors that may be present in drastically different game types (e.g. 3D environments in first person shooters) that might complicate the play experience.

Future Work

Following our discussion, we propose four directions for future work. First, to examine the role of DDA within systems that are much more complex than the simplistic systems we used for this experiment. Future work might look at games with several concurrent game goals, such as in open sandbox games, or systems in which underlying state is hidden, obscured or abstracted might impact the unambiguous feedback dimension. Other questions that invite investigation include exploring how narrative and aesthetics might interact with DDA implementations to alter the player experience. The current study used the original bag-style randomization algorithm, which has been shown to significantly differ in terms of perceived difficulty from other randomization algorithms [29], Future work can explore the use of these alternative methods of difficulty manipulation for dynamic difficulty adjustment during a game session to alter the player experience, such as the dynamic swapping of block choosing algorithm during game play based on player performance.

Second, it would be valuable to investigate factors that might mitigate the drawback of the lack of a sense of control in the context of system-oriented adjustment systems. One possible exploration of this would be to make use of a narrative to negate the drawback of a DDA system; if the system-oriented difficulty choice is justified or cloaked under the guise of a narrative, the effects of the drawback could potentially be reduced.

Third, an interesting next step would be to probe the nuances of pDDA implementation. In the context of this study, we implemented player-oriented DDA in a very raw sense of simply providing the player with direct controls (keyboard buttons) that change the difficulty level. Player-oriented DDA warrants more research in design techniques and comparative studies to expand the role of player-oriented design on systems. Chen's [6] recommendation of embedding the pDDA mechanic within the game is worth looking into as it suggests that the way in which pDDA is implemented might affect player experience.

Fourth, the ramifications of the potential differences induced in player experience in a single player context should be considered in relation to existing literature on multiplayer game play. For example, co-operative game play has been found to result in greater autotelic experience and flow compared to single player gameplay [18]. However, this might not hold true with certain DDA strategies. In particular, with pDDA strategies the sense of control that a player has in cooperative gameplay could be compromised should multiple players of the game have control over the difficulty adjustment of the game.

CONCLUSION

Game designers often use a technique known as dynamic difficulty adjustment (DDA) to match player skill with game challenge. According to Flow theory, DDA should allow the player to enter the optimal experience state [31]. However, several types of DDA implementations exist, and each of these implementations could result in a different player experience.

To understand how DDA impacts the player experience, we carried out an experimental study to examine (1) how the presence of DDA affects the player experience compared to the non-presence of DDA; and (2) how a traditional system-oriented DDA compares against a player-oriented DDA in terms of player experience.

We found that the presence of DDA improves the overall player experience. Aside from sense of control, all other experience constructs were on par with or better when a DDA system is present. Only the dimension of sense of control in the rDDA condition fared worse compared to the no DDA condition.

In addition, we found that both system-oriented DDA and player-oriented DDA had different strengths and drawbacks. The system-oriented ramping DDA condition resulted in players having the least sense of control while players in the player-oriented DDA condition had the highest sense of control out of the three conditions. However, players in the system-oriented ramping DDA condition were less self-conscious and experienced a greater transformation of time compared to the player-oriented DDA condition.

The study provides empirical support for Csikszentmihalyi's Flow theory [10] in the context of DDA systems and games. We also documented the experimental method towards the successful manipulation of DDA systems to affect the Flow experience in a controlled environment, and validated the use of Jackson and Marsh's [16] Flow State Scale in the context of video game research.

Our work provides insight into how the presence of DDA, and the use of specific variations of DDA, can affect player experience. We identified the potential player experience benefits and drawbacks of employing these DDA variations. This allows designers of games and similar systems, where there is a need to consider the difficulty or challenge of the activity and the skill of the user or player, to make informed decisions when considering the impacts of the choice of DDA mechanisms in their system design on the user experience.

REFERENCES

1. Alexander Baldwin, Daniel Johnson, and Peta A. Wyeth. 2014. The Effect of Multiplayer Dynamic Difficulty Adjustment on the Player Experience of Video Games. *CHI '14 Extended Abstracts on Human Factors in Computing Systems*, ACM, 1489–1494. http://doi.org/10.1145/2559206.2581285

2. Patricia Belchior, Michael Marsiske, Walter L Leite, Anna Yam, Kelsey Thomas, and William Mann. 2016. Older Adults' Engagement During an Intervention Involving Off-the-Shelf Videogame. *Games for Health Journal* 5, 3: 151–156.

3. Jeanne H Brockmyer, Christine M Fox, Kathleen A Curtiss, Evan McBroom, Kimberly M Burkhart, and Jacquelyn N Pidruzny. 2009. The development of the Game Engagement Questionnaire: A measure of engagement in video game-playing. *Journal of Experimental Social Psychology* 45, 4: 624–634.

4. Emily Brown and Paul Cairns. 2004. A Grounded Investigation of Game Immersion. *CHI '04 Extended Abstracts on Human Factors in Computing Systems*, ACM, 1297–1300. http://doi.org/10.1145/985921.986048

5. Gordon Calleja. 2010. Digital games and escapism. *Games and Culture* 5, 4: 335–353.

6. Jenova Chen. 2006. Flow in Games.

7. Thomas M Connolly, Elizabeth A Boyle, Ewan MacArthur, Thomas Hainey, and James M Boyle. 2012. A systematic literature review of empirical evidence on computer games and serious games. *Computers & Education* 59, 2: 661–686.

8. Ben Cowley, Darryl Charles, Michaela Black, and Ray Hickey. 2008. Toward an Understanding of Flow in Video Games. *Comput. Entertain.* 6, 2: 20:1–20:27. http://doi.org/10.1145/1371216.1371223

9. Mihaly Csikszentmihalyi and Isabella Selega Csikszentmihalyi. 1992. *Optimal experience: Psychological studies of flow in consciousness*. Cambridge university press.

10. Mihaly Csikszentmihalyi. 2014. Toward a psychology of optimal experience. In *Flow and the foundations of positive psychology*. Springer, 209–226.

11. Alena Denisova and Paul Cairns. 2015. Adaptation in Digital Games: The Effect of Challenge Adjustment on Player Performance and Experience. *Proceedings of the 2015 Annual Symposium on Computer-Human Interaction in Play*, ACM, 97–101. http://doi.org/10.1145/2793107.2793141

12. Alena Denisova and Paul Cairns. 2015. The Placebo Effect in Digital Games: Phantom Perception of Adaptive Artificial Intelligence. *Proceedings of the 2015 Annual Symposium on Computer-Human Interaction in Play*, ACM, 23–33. http://doi.org/10.1145/2793107.2793109

13. Ann DeSmet, Debbe Thompson, Tom Baranowski, Antonio Palmeira, Maïté Verloigne, and Ilse De Bourdeaudhuij. 2016. Is Participatory Design Associated with the Effectiveness of Serious Digital Games for Healthy Lifestyle Promotion?: A Meta-Analysis. *J Med Internet Res* 18, 4: e94. http://doi.org/10.2196/jmir.4444

14. Arend Hintze, Randal S Olson, and Joel Lehman. 2016. Orthogonally Evolved AI to Improve Difficulty Adjustment in Video Games. *European Conference on the Applications of Evolutionary Computation*, Springer, 525–540.

15. Robin Hunicke. 2005. The case for dynamic difficulty adjustment in games. *Proceedings of the 2005 ACM SIGCHI International Conference on Advances in computer entertainment technology*, ACM, 429–433.

16. Susan A Jackson and Herbert W Marsh. 1996. Development and validation of a scale to measure optimal experience: The Flow State Scale. *Journal of Sport and Exercise Psychology* 18: 17–35.

17. Johannes Keller and Herbert Bless. 2008. Flow and regulatory compatibility: An experimental approach to the flow model of intrinsic motivation. *Personality and Social Psychology Bulletin* 34, 2: 196–209.

18. Christopher Lee, Peta Wyeth, Daniel Johnson, and Joshua Hall. 2015. Flow During Individual and Co-operative Gameplay. *Proceedings of the 2015 Annual Symposium on Computer-Human Interaction in Play*, ACM, 103–107. http://doi.org/10.1145/2793107.2793142

19. Li Li, Rongrong Chen, and Jing Chen. 2016. Playing Action Video Games Improves Visuomotor Control. *Psychological Science* 27, 8: 1092–1108.

20. Keith Lohse, Navid Shirzad, Alida Verster, Nicola Hodges, and HF Machiel Van der Loos. 2013. Video games and rehabilitation: using design principles to enhance engagement in physical therapy. *Journal of Neurologic Physical Therapy* 37, 4: 166–175.

21. Thomas W Malone. 1981. Toward a theory of intrinsically motivating instruction. *Cognitive science* 5, 4: 333–369.

22. Jane McGonigal. 2011. *Reality is broken: Why games make us better and how they can change the world.* Penguin.

23. Alison McMahan. 2003. Immersion, engagement and presence. *The video game theory reader* 67: 86.

24. Lennart E. Nacke and Craig A. Lindley. 2010. Affective Ludology, Flow and Immersion in a First-Person Shooter: Measurement of Player Experience. *CoRR* abs/1004.0248: 4. Retrieved from http://arxiv.org/abs/1004.0248

25. Randy J. Pagulayan, Kevin Keeker, Dennis Wixon, Ramon L. Romero, and Thomas Fuller. 2003. User-centered Design in Games. In *The Human-computer Interaction Handbook: Fundamentals, Evolving*

Technologies and Emerging Applications, Julie A. Jacko and Andrew Sears (eds.). L. Erlbaum Associates Inc., Hillsdale, NJ, USA, 883–906.

26. Marc Prensky. 2001. Fun, play and games: What makes games engaging. *Digital game-based learning* 5: 1–5.

27. Andrew Rollings and Ernest Adams. 2003. *Andrew Rollings and Ernest Adams on game design*. New Riders.

28. Jan D. Smeddinck, Regan L. Mandryk, Max V. Birk, Kathrin M. Gerling, Dietrich Barsilowski, and Rainer Malaka. 2016. How to Present Game Difficulty Choices?: Exploring the Impact on Player Experience. *Proceedings of the 2016 CHI Conference on Human Factors in Computing Systems*, ACM, 5595–5607. http://doi.org/10.1145/2858036.2858574

29. Katharina Spiel, Sven Bertel, and Fares Kayali. 2017. Not Another Z Piece!": Adaptive Difficulty in TETRIS. *Proceedings of the 2017 CHI Conference on Human Factors in Computing Systems*, ACM, 5126–5131. http://doi.org/10.1145/3025453.3025721

30. Rhio Sutoyo, Davies Winata, Katherine Oliviani, and Dedy Martadinata Supriyadi. 2015. Dynamic Difficulty Adjustment in Tower Defence. *Procedia Computer Science* 59: 435–444.

31. Penelope Sweetser, Daniel Johnson, Peta Wyeth, and Anne Ozdowska. 2012. GameFlow Heuristics for Designing and Evaluating Real-time Strategy Games. *Proceedings of The 8th Australasian Conference on Interactive Entertainment: Playing the System*, ACM, 1:1–1:10. http://doi.org/10.1145/2336727.2336728

32. Penelope Sweetser and Peta Wyeth. 2005. GameFlow: A Model for Evaluating Player Enjoyment in Games. *Comput. Entertain.* 3, 3: 3–3. http://doi.org/10.1145/1077246.1077253

33. Rodrigo Vicencio-Moreira, Regan L. Mandryk, and Carl Gutwin. 2015. Now You Can Compete With Anyone: Balancing Players of Different Skill Levels in a First-Person Shooter Game. *Proceedings of the 33rd Annual ACM Conference on Human Factors in Computing Systems*, ACM, 2255–2264. http://doi.org/10.1145/2702123.2702242

34. Chang Yun, Dvijesh Shastri, Ioannis Pavlidis, and Zhigang Deng. 2009. O' Game, Can You Feel My Frustration?: Improving User's Gaming Experience via Stresscam. *Proceedings of the SIGCHI Conference on Human Factors in Computing Systems*, ACM, 2195–2204. http://doi.org/10.1145/1518701.1519036

A Framework and Taxonomy of Videogame Playing Preferences

Gustavo F. Tondello[1,2], **Rina R. Wehbe**[1,2], **Rita Orji**[1,4], **Giovanni Ribeiro**[1], **Lennart E. Nacke**[1,2,3]
[1]HCI Games Group, Games Institute, [2]Cheriton School of Computer Science, [3]Drama and Speech Communication, Stratford Campus, University of Waterloo
[4]Faculty of Computer Science, Dalhousie University
gustavo@tondello.com, rina.wehbe@uwaterloo.ca, rita.orji@dal.ca, ggsribei@uwaterloo.ca, lennart.nacke@acm.org

ABSTRACT
Player preferences for different gaming styles or game elements has been a topic of interest in human-computer interaction for over a decade. However, current models suggested by the extant literature are generally based on classifying abstract gaming motivations or player archetypes. These concepts do not directly map onto the building blocks of games, taking away from the utility of the findings. To address this issue, we propose a conceptual framework of player preferences based on two dimensions: *game elements* and *game playing styles*. To investigate these two concepts, we conducted an exploratory empirical investigation of player preferences, which allowed us to create a taxonomy of nine groups of game elements and five groups of game playing styles. These two concepts are foundational to games, which means that our model can be used by designers to create games that are tailored to their target audience. In addition, we demonstrate that there are significant effects of gender and age on participants' preferences and discuss the implications of these findings.

ACM Classification Keywords
H.1.2. User/Machine Systems: Human Factors; H.5.m. Information Interfaces and Presentation (e.g. HCI): Miscellaneous; K.8.0. Personal Computing: Games

Author Keywords
Games User Research; Game Elements; Player Types.

INTRODUCTION
Understanding how players differ in their preferences for various game elements and playing styles has many practical uses. For example, game designers can use this information to better target their ideas towards specific groups of players or towards broader audiences, whereas marketers can better understand their target players and direct their communication efforts accordingly.

CHI PLAY '17, October 15–18, 2017, Amsterdam, Netherlands

ISBN 978-1-4503-4898-0/17/10...$15.00
DOI: https://doi.org/10.1145/3116595.3116629

For this purpose, several researchers have suggested models of player types or gaming motivations. These models are generally based on conceptual analysis, psychographic methods, or behavioural analysis [17]. However, researchers Hamari and Tuunanen [17] have noted that most of these approaches suffer from similar limitations. First, most of them were based on or were inspired by Bartle's original work [2], which suffers a number of limitations. Bartle conducted a qualitative and conceptual study of multi-user dungeons (MUD) players to classify them in types. However, his work was never empirically validated nor intended to be used outside of the context of MUDs. Nevertheless, it inspired and became the foundation of most of the posterior attempts to create player typologies for multiple genres. Consequently, many of the proposed models are limited in the number and types of motivational factors considered because most constructs are similar or derivatives of Bartle's four types. Another issue is that most studies were limited to online games or massively multiplayer online games (MMOs). This makes it difficult to transfer insights to other game genres or contexts. Finally, many models attempt to classify players in distinct types [3, 24]. This can be misleading because they try to segment players in dichotomous categories. This approach might not adequately represent reality because humans are complex and players usually display a combination of distinct preferences in variate degrees, instead of a single category of preferences.

To address these issues, we present a novel conceptual framework and an associated taxonomy of videogame play preferences. Rather than using Bartle's taxonomy or one of its derived works as a building block, we devised a new framework based on existing game design literature. We considered player preferences from the point of view of two distinct constructs in our conceptual framework: *game elements* and *game playing styles*. Game elements are the activities that players engage with in games, such as resource management, exploration, or combat. Game playing styles, on the other hand, refer to the different ways by which players interact with the game and with other players, instead of the activities that players do. Hence, we studied game playing styles such as team-based play, competitive play, solo play, and e-sports. Next, we created a new taxonomy by analyzing players' preferences from empirical data related to a broad range of game elements and playing styles. This way, we explored diverse elements and styles that were never previously investigated.

Our work contributes to the human-computer interaction (HCI) and games user research (GUR) communities by developing a new conceptual framework and taxonomy for understanding player preferences and hence, addressing the shortcomings of prior works. Moreover, we demonstrate that participants' gender and age significantly influence their preferred elements and play styles. Our framework is applicable for designing and studying a broader category of games, game elements, and playing styles and is grounded on solid empirical evidence. Therefore, it can be used to inform the design of more engaging games because it helps designers understand which elements and playing styles players usually enjoy when playing together. Furthermore, detailed information about the target audience of a game is necessary because of an increasing interest in the design of *serious games* (i.e., games that serve a main purpose other than entertainment, such as health, education or fostering awareness to a cause). Particularly, for serious games it is important to understand how players are motivated by different gaming elements and styles, so the game can achieve its instrumental purpose for distinct players.

The remainder of this work is organized as follows. First, we review the existing literature on player typologies and preferences. Next, we introduce our player preferences framework and the results of an empirical study in which we analyzed participants' self-reported preferences towards 66 game elements and 20 game playing styles to devise a taxonomy or player preferences. Finally, we discuss the implications of our findings and the potential applications of the framework.

RELATED WORK

Player Typologies and Preferences

In the last decade, researchers in games and HCI have been studying different game play motivations and playing styles and representing them in player typologies. Bartle's original player types for MUDs [2] are based on two axes that express the player's desire to interact with or act on the virtual world or other players: ACHIEVERS (acting on the world), EXPLORERS (interacting with the world), SOCIALISERS (interacting with other players), and KILLERS (acting on other players). Bartle later extended it by adding a third dimension [3]: implicit/explicit (i.e., whether the player actions are automatic and unconscious or considered and planned). Thus, each of the four original types was split in two subtypes. The implicit subtypes are respectively OPPORTUNISTS, HACKERS, FRIENDS, and GRIEFERS. The explicit sub-types are respectively PLANNERS, SCIENTISTS, NETWORKERS, and POLITICIANS.

Bartle's research is a cornerstone of player typology with many researchers building off the ideas; however many researchers also expanded on it by proposing their own models. Based on a factor analysis of questions inspired by Bartle's player types, Yee [35, 38] identified three main components of player motivation with ten subcomponents: ACHIEVEMENT (advancement, mechanics, competition), SOCIAL (socializing, relationship, teamwork), and IMMERSION (discovery, role-playing, customization, escapism). His analysis provides a solid base for understanding player motivation, but it is limited because of its focus on one specific game genre (Massively Multiplayer Online Role-Playing Games—MMORPGs).

Bateman and Boon [4] contributed research to provide a wider perspective regarding player types by adapting the Myers-Briggs Type Indicator (MBTI, [23]) to games. Their first demographic game design model (DGD1) proposed the player styles CONQUEROR, MANAGER, WANDERER, and PARTICIPANT. The second demographic game design model (DGD2, [5]) explored the hardcore to casual dimension, different skill sets, and the preference for single and multiplayer gameplay. Following this work, the BrainHex [5, 24] was developed, which is a top-down player typology that takes inspiration from neurobiological player satisfaction research [6], previous player typologies, discussions of patterns of play, and the literature on game emotions to build seven archetypes denoting distinct experiences of play. The BrainHex archetypes are: ACHIEVERS (goal-oriented and motivated by completion); CONQUERORS (enjoy struggling against strong opponents); DAREDEVILS (motivated by excitement and risk taking); MASTERMINDS (enjoy solving puzzles and devising strategies); SEEKERS (motivated to explore the game world); SOCIALISERS (enjoy interacting with other people); and SURVIVORS (enjoy frightening experiences in games).

Busch et al. [11] conducted a validation of the BrainHex model and argued for an improvement of its psychometric properties, based on poor results of factor, stability, and internal consistency analyses. Despite lack of empirical validation, the BrainHex is increasingly gaining researchers' attention; it has been used by several studies for investigating player motivation and personalization of games. For example, Orji et al. [26] used BrainHex to tailor persuasive health games to different player types and Birk et al. [8] used BrainHex to model player motivation in a social network game.

Hamari and Tuunanen [17] conducted a systematic review of player type models to investigate their commonalities. The authors note that MMOs and online games are more frequently covered than other genres in several of these studies, therefore compromising the applicability of these models outside of the multiplayer domain. Furthermore, they compared all the analyzed models and suggested that they could be synthesized in five key dimensions of play motivations: *achievement*, *exploration*, *sociability*, *domination*, and *immersion*.

More recently, Yee [36] expanded on his previous work by conducting a factor analysis with over 140,000 participants and developed a *gamer motivation profile* composed of 12 dimensions grouped into six clusters: ACTION (destruction and excitement); SOCIAL (competition and community); MASTERY (challenge and strategy); ACHIEVEMENT (competition and power); IMMERSION (fantasy and story); and CREATIVITY (design and discovery). Yee's recent proprietary investigation intends to capture player motivations towards a large variety of games and is empirically supported by factor analysis. It is also noteworthy that it intends to classify different elements that foster different playing motivations, instead of trying to classify players in types. Unfortunately, a standard assessment tool is not publicly and readily available.

While all these prior player preference models provide useful insights towards understanding different player motivations, most of them are limited by the lack of empirical validation, unavailability of a standard assessment tool, or are only suitable for a specific game or genre. In addition, they fail to consider different elements of play that have surfaced more recently, such as body movement-controlled games, and different styles of play, such as electronic sports, streaming, or casual games. The present work aims to fill this gap, by researching player preferences using a wider scope and providing new information based on the analyzed data.

Player Preferences Based on Game Features

Several authors have investigated how players' perceived values and identification with game characters, avatars, and objects increase motivation and enjoyment in digital games. For example, Birk et al. [7] revealed that avatar customization stimulates player identification, leading to increased autonomy, immersion, invested effort, enjoyment, and positive affect. Livingston et al. [21] interviewed twenty *World of Warcraft* [9] players with the goal of investigating what kind of value their game characters provided. Tondello et al. [32] and Toups et al. [33] built on their work to examine why players value and collect a diversity of game objects, including but not limited to characters. While these frameworks can help explain part of a player's preferences for different games, they are limited to one of the many aspects that define a game (their characters or objects). In contrast, our work aims to study a more generic and broad player preferences framework.

Player Preferences Based on Personality Factors

Besides models of player motivation, there is growing evidence within the HCI and GUR communities that personality factors also influence player motivation and preferences. Yee [37] investigated the relation of the five-factor personality traits [16] with the different motivations in the Gamer Motivation Profile, thus establishing a bridge between personality factors and player preferences. Similarly, Jeng and Teng [19] found a relation between personality traits and preferences for different playing styles. Likewise, Peever et al. [28] found significant correlations between personality traits and players' preferences for particular game genres. Moreover, McMahon et al. [22] investigated the relation of the five-factor personality traits with the player types of the DGD1 model. Finally, Zeigler-Hill and Monica [39] identified several significant associations between the BrainHex archetypes and the HEXACO personality traits [20]. Moreover, Orji et al. [27] studied the relation between the five-factor personality traits and several persuasive strategies used in the context of serious and persuasive games. They noted that extraversion, agreeableness, and openness are the three personality traits that predict most of the variance in the effectiveness of different persuasive strategies.

With a different approach, Ryan et al. [30] and Przybylski et al. [29] built a motivational model of video game engagement based on self-determination theory (SDT) [12]. They discovered that competence, autonomy, relatedness, presence, and intuitive controls are good predictors of player enjoyment and engagement. Their player motivation model can explain why a game is successful; however, it does not account for different player preferences.

These studies suggest that personality traits might only partly explain player preferences for different games. For example, if two games are successfully designed to equally satisfy players' psychological needs or appeal to the same personality traits, it is common for a player to still prefer one game over the other and it is not clear (from available research) what attributes make some players prefer one game over the other. Therefore, a new conceptual framework, which specifically describes player's preferences, might be more suited to explain the whole range of player motivations and play styles.

Concurrently, Ferro et al. [13] conducted a literature review and proposed a theoretical model that encompasses and suggests relationships between personality traits, player types, and game elements and mechanics. Their work identifies five combinations of these constructs: DOMINANT (which refers to players who are self-serving and want to make themselves visible), OBJECTIVIST (focus on achievement), HUMANIST (focus on social engagement), INQUISITIVE (focus on exploration and discovery), and CREATIVE (focus on creativity). The novelty of their work consists in the attempt to combine personality traits, player types, and game elements in a general model. However, their suggested model is only theoretical and still lacks empirical validation.

A FRAMEWORK OF PLAYER PREFERENCES

One of the goals of studying player types or preferences is to inform game design decisions. However, none of the approaches described in the related literature has attempted to identify the relationship between the motivational factors or player types and the elements or atoms used in the construction of games. For example, once one considers the motivation for achievement, it is not clear exactly what are the game mechanics or dynamics that afford this kind of experience. Therefore, we propose a new conceptual framework of player preferences, which is based on the elements used in the design and construction of games. Consequently, our framework will be directly applicable to informing game design.

The issue with existing attempts to describe player preferences is that they consider only high level factors, such as achievement, socialization, or immersion. Nevertheless, game designers must work on more detailed and finer levels of abstraction. They often need specific details about the building blocks that are actionable in game design. Therefore, designers and researchers have used several terminologies to describe the building blocks of games. For example, Brathwaite and Schreiber [10] refer to *game atoms* as the parts that make a game. These atoms include: the game *state* and *views*, the *players* and the elements that represent them (e.g., avatars or tokens), the *mechanics* (relating to the rules of the game), the *dynamics* (relating to the emerging patterns of play once mechanics are set in motion by players), the *goals*, and the *theme*. Schell [31], on the other hand, refers to the parts of a game as *game elements*. The author classifies elements into four types: the *mechanics* are the procedures and rules of the game, the *story* is the sequence of events that unfolds in the game, the *aesthetics* is how the game looks and feels, and the *technology* is the set of materials and interactions that make the game possible (which might be digital or not). Another approach to game design is the MECHANICS, DYNAMICS, and AESTHETICS (MDA) framework [18]. It introduces three distinct game components: MECHANICS are the smallest components of a game, DYNAMICS are the run-time behaviour of the mechanics interacting with the player, and AESTHETICS are the emotional responses or experiences evoked in the player.

Considering these diverse views on game design, we must establish what is the adequate granularity level for a conceptual framework of player preferences. We have already mentioned that we do not consider looking only at high level constructs an adequate approach because it would not explain which are the smaller building blocks that designers should use to foster different types of experiences. However, looking at the game mechanics (which represent the smallest granularity level) is also not helpful because mechanics are just generic building blocks, which are employed to build many types of dynamics and are often subject to several operationalizations. For example, a game mechanic like a token on a board might be used to build several different dynamics, such as a racing game, a strategy game, or a game of chess. Therefore, we contend that a player preferences framework must map constructs on an intermediate granularity level, which many game design methods refer as *dynamics*. This approach will allow us to classify player preferences in a level that can be used to inform game design by translating them to dynamics such as resource management, combat, puzzles, or racing. Therefore, we devised our conceptual framework of player preferences based on the classification of the intermediate granularity elements employed in the building of games. Nonetheless, there are many approaches to game design, which sometimes employ different terminologies, and our framework is not based on any of them in particular. Hence, we decided to employ the more generic terminology *game elements* (instead of dynamics) to refer to the mid-level building blocks of games that we classify in our research.

In addition to the elements that make part of a game, there are also different modes or styles or play. One example is the preference for single or multiplayer gameplay. These game playing styles are orthogonal to the game elements and can be combined with them in a variety of ways. For example, if we consider a game element such as combat, players can experience single player combat (player against the game's artificial intelligence), team-based multiplayer combat (several players teamed against the game's artificial intelligence), or competition-based multiplayer combat (players competing against other players). Choosing among the potential styles of play is also an important game design decision. This is why we include *game playing styles* as the second dimension of our framework.

A TAXONOMY OF GAME ELEMENTS AND GAME PLAYING STYLES

After defining a conceptual framework of player preferences, we created a taxonomy of game elements and game playing styles based on an empirical study, which we describe in this section.

Methodology

We conducted this study to understand participants' preferences for diverse game elements and game playing styles.

Survey Design

To create the lists of game elements and game playing styles for our survey, we consulted several titles from the game design literature [1, 10, 15, 31]. However, we did not find lists that we could use because the literature usually focuses on high level motivations or aesthetics or on low level game mechanics, but we needed a list of elements described in an intermediate granularity level. Therefore, we conducted a brainstorming between three player experience researchers to create lists of game elements and game playing styles. The brainstorming followed an informal process to generate intermediate level elements from the high or low level elements found in the literature and the researchers' experience. Initially, one researcher consulted the mentioned literature with the goal of listing intermediate level elements that could represent the high level elements found in the literature with more details, as well as intermediate level elements that could summarize the low level game mechanics described in the literature. Next, the three researchers reviewed and discussed this initial list of game elements and game playing styles and brainstormed additional elements that they felt were missing from the list, based on their experience with games. The final lists contains 66 game elements and 20 game playing styles. We have provided the complete lists in the appendix, which includes information about each item's descriptions as presented in the survey.

Survey Instrument

The survey was deployed as an online instrument between February and March 2017 using the *LimeSurvey* software version 2.50+ (LimeSurvey, 2016). All questions were in English and were grouped as follows:

Preferred game elements: We asked how much participants enjoyed the 66 different game elements in a 5-point Likert scale. The elements were presented in randomized order.

Preferred game playing styles: We asked how much participants enjoyed 20 different game playing styles in a 5-point Likert scale. The styles were presented in randomized order.

Other: Additional questions, unrelated to the current study.

Demographic information: Participant's country, language, age, gender, education, and gaming habits and preferences.

The survey could be completed anonymously and allowed participants to skip any question. Prior to the decision to participate, participants were presented with an online informed consent form. In addition, all the long question groups (such as game elements and game playing styles) had attention check questions (e.g., "Please select '3' in this item to show us that you are carefully reading all questions.") to verify if participants were reading all the items with attention.

Participants

We recruited participants by email (in both academic and non-academic environments), social networks (Facebook, Twitter, and Reddit), and online gaming forums. Participants were required to be at least 15 years old. Study volunteers were not offered a direct remuneration, but instead were offered an opportunity to enter a draw to win one of two $ 50 prizes.

In total, 196 participants completed the survey. However, we discarded eight participants who did not complete all question groups or failed to select the correct answer in at least one of the attention check items. Therefore, the final dataset contained 188 responses (124 men, 53 women, 4 transgender, 3 non-binary, and 4 did not inform their gender). Participants' ages ranged from 15 to 71 ($M = 26.7$, $SD = 9.7$) and were skewed towards younger participants (with 74% of participants being 30 or less), possibly because the topic of the survey was more appealing to a younger audience.

Participants were distributed geographically as follows: 60.6% from North America, 25.5% from Europe, 5.3% from South America, 4.8% from Oceania, 2.7% from Asia, and 1.1% from Africa. However, 98.9% of participants reported having a very good or native understanding of English. Therefore, we operate under the assumption that lack of English proficiency was not a detriment to our study.

Analytic Procedure

In the following subsections, we will present the results of the data analysis procedures that led us to devise a taxonomy of game elements and game playing styles. First, we conducted an exploratory factor analysis to construct the taxonomy. Following the successful factor analysis, we conducted a correlation analysis to determine how the independent variables (gender and age) influence the groups' scores. All analyses were conducted in SPSS 23 (IBM, 2015). We present the details of each of these analyses.

We employed a principal component analysis (PCA) to cluster the surveyed game elements and game playing styles into groups. PCA is a standard method for creating groupings in data based on the covariance and correlation of items. This allowed us to establish a taxonomy and analyze players preferences with a more manageable number of categories. Since our investigation was exploratory and we included game elements and playing styles in our survey through brainstorming, we had no prior theory to justify their inclusion or exclusion from the taxonomy. Therefore, the first step was to evaluate if all the included elements and playing styles could be successfully grouped into clusters. A PCA requires variables to be at least partially correlated between themselves to be able to reduce the number of components. Thus, we first analyzed the correlation matrix between all variables and removed variables with only three or less relevant correlations. We considered correlations with $r >= .3$ as relevant, as suggested by Field [14] (p. 648). Moreover, we also performed an initial PCA and noted the variables that appeared isolated in one of the components (variables that were the only item with a high loading in one of the components and did not have a high loading in any other component) and also removed them. We performed this procedure iteratively, until we found no more variables to remove.

Moreover, we used parallel analysis and Velicer's minimum average partial (MAP) test to determine the number of components to retain in the final analyses because these procedures are validated and, hence, more adequate than a simple eigenvalues inspection [25]. Furthermore, we employed an Oblimin rotation because we expected that the components could partially overlap. Finally, we considered factor loadings greater than .36 as significant, following Field's [14] (p. 644) recommendation for a sample size of 200 and an $\alpha = .01$.

After completing the PCA, we analyzed the composition of each component to interpret and label them. To achieve this, four researchers independently interpreted the structure matrices. Next, they compared their interpretations by discussing similarities and divergences, and came to an agreement on a representative label for each component.

Finally, to understand which factors influence user preferences for each one of the groups in the taxonomy, we analyzed how the participant's gender and age influenced their scores for each group. We included only the genders 'male' and 'female' in the analysis because we did not have enough data points in the remaining categories to perform a statistical analysis. For these correlation analyses, we computed participants' standardized scores for each component as part of the PCA using the regression method. Standardizing the linear regression model generates scores for each component with a mean of zero and a standard deviation of 1.0.

Game Elements

On completion of the analytic procedure to identify the variables that were useful for the PCA, we removed six game elements from the analysis (9.1%): *fixed rewards*, *performance-based rewards*, *random rewards*, *open progression*, *horror*, and *stealth play*. This means that these variables could not be clustered with any of the other variables in the dataset. For the final dataset with the remaining 60 variables, the Kaiser-Meyer-Olkin measure verified the sample adequacy for the analysis, $KMO = .70$ (a good sample size, according to Field [14]). Moreover, Bartlett's Test of Sphericity was significant ($\chi^2_{1770} = 5085.1, p < .001$), indicating that the correlations between items were sufficiently large for PCA. The final results of the PCA revealed nine components. Table 1 presents the final structure matrix.

All components showed adequate reliability with $\alpha >= .665$, except for component 9, which showed a lower reliability of $\alpha = .555$ (see Table 1), but still acceptable. Furthermore, component 9 showed one significant variable (*drawing or painting*) with a positive sign, whereas all other significant variables were negative. This means that participants who said they enjoy all the other significant elements in this component are very unlikely to also enjoy drawing or painting. Thus, this element was not considered as part of this component.

Component Interpretation

We labelled the nine components as follows:

1. **Strategic resource management:** represents several dynamics of resource management, construction, or strategic gameplay.
2. **Puzzle:** includes diverse types of puzzles.
3. **Artistic movement:** includes several types or artistic expression (such as music or painting) or body movement.

	Components								
Game Design Elements	**1**	**2**	**3**	**4**	**5**	**6**	**7**	**8**	**9**
4X (explore, expand, exploit, and exterminate)	.775								
Impersonal power	.749								
Management simulation	.746								
Unit building	.728								
Production management	.704								
Territorial conquest	.663							.409	
Turn-based strategy	.635								
Wargame	.607							.598	
Construction	.569					.375	.396		
Turn-based combat	.521								-.393
Real-time strategy	.483							.379	-.379
Sales management	.479			-.429					
Board game	.445			-.383					
Spatial puzzle		.818							
Logic puzzle		.771							
Strategic escape		.756							
Maze		.668							
Tile-matching puzzle		.531	.460						
Dancing			.811						
Singing			.723						
Music			.706						
Exergaming			.695						
Drawing or painting			.566						.392
Platforms		.421	.473					.368	
Sports				-.684				.383	
Sport tournaments				-.682				.363	
Gambling				-.637					
Cards				-.613					
Trivia				-.488					
Trading				-.482		.478			
Action-adventure					.665			.370	
Adventure		.469			.609				
Fantasy					.579				
Role-playing					.570				
Science-fiction					.540				
Avatar					.432	.384			
Completion					.418	.379			
Exploration					.413				
Collecting						.704			
Crafting						.683			
Currency						.664			
Resource harvesting	.392					.571			
Equipment management						.513			
Reality-bound							.748		
Open world							.636		
Interactive story					.450		.588		
Life simulation							.511		
Shooting								.727	
Detonation								.725	
Real-time combat								.721	
Combat								.721	
Fighting								.695	
Racing				-.415				.632	
Rushed escape								.627	
Vehicle simulation								.610	
Parkour			.382					.548	
Obstacle running			.400					.478	
Pre-determined progression			.372						-.543
Skill trees						.400			-.521
Character power					.404	.439			-.510
Internal reliability (α)	.878	.804	.812	.761	.770	.763	.665	.882	.555
Eigenvalues	8.651	5.572	4.604	4.105	2.735	2.546	2.097	1.980	1.665
% of variance	14.418	9.286	7.673	6.841	4.558	4.243	3.496	3.300	2.775

Notes. Extraction method: Principal component analysis. Rotation method: Oblimin with Kaiser normalization.
Principal components were labelled: 1-strategic resource management, 2-puzzle, 3-artistic movement, 4-sports and cards, 5-role-playing, 6-virtual goods, 7-simulation, 8-action, 9-progression. For improved visualization, the factor loadings $< .36$ (absolute values) are suppressed.

Table 1. Exploratory factor analysis (structure matrix) of the game design elements.

4. **Sports and cards:** includes dynamics related with sports, cards, and gambling.
5. **Role-playing:** represents several dynamics which support role-playing, such as fantasy or science fiction, avatars, and exploration.
6. **Virtual goods:** includes dynamics of acquisition, collection, and use of virtual goods or resources.
7. **Simulation:** represents the means by which players can simulate scenarios inspired by real life.
8. **Action:** includes diverse dynamics related with action, excitement, and fast-paced play.
9. **Progression:** represents means of progressing towards accumulating power or learning.

Table 2 presents the descriptive statistics for the nine groups of game elements. Overall, *role-playing* and *simulation* are the groups that scored higher in player preferences, whereas *sport and cards* and *artistic movement* are the groups that scored lower. There is a 1.37-point difference out of 5.0 (27%) in the difference between the highest and the lowest scoring groups.

Table 2 also presents the bivariate correlations of the nine groups between themselves. There is only one significant moderate correlation between *puzzle* and *artistic movement*.

Factors that Influence Player Preferences

Table 3 shows that women scored significantly higher than men for *puzzle*, *artistic movement*, and *virtual goods*, whereas men scored significantly higher for *strategic resource management*, *sports and cards*, and *action*. Regarding age, only the preferences for *role-playing* and *progression* seem to significantly decrease with age.

Game Playing Styles

On completion of the analytic procedure to identify the variables that were useful for the PCA, only one variable (5%) was removed from the analysis: *Casual gaming*. This means that the preference for casual gaming stands alone, not grouped with any other styles of playing. For the final dataset with the remaining 19 variables, $KMO = .82$ (meaning that the sample size was great for the analysis, according to Field [14]). Moreover, Bartlett's test of sphericity was significant ($\chi^2{}_{171} = 1047.0, p < .001$), indicating that the correlations between items were sufficiently large for PCA. The final results of the PCA revealed four components. Table 4 presents the final structure matrix. All components showed a good reliability with $\alpha >= .698$, except for component 3, which showed a lower $\alpha = .582$, but still acceptable.

Component Interpretation

We labelled the four components as follows:

1. **Multiplayer:** includes several types of multiplayer interactions (collaborative or competitive).
2. **Abstract interaction:** represents individual playing styles in which the player feels less directly immersed in the game, by playing for example from an isometric or a top-down view.
3. **Solo play:** represents individual playing styles in which the player might be more directly immersed in the game, by playing from a third-person view and freely moving around the game world.
4. **Competitive community:** represents several ways in which players can interact with others in a community, such as streaming, competing in e-sports, or co-located play.

Components	Mean	SD	Correlations (r) 1	2	3	4	5	6	7	8	9
1- Strategic resource management	3.60	0.68	–								
2- Puzzle	3.65	0.73	-.033	–							
3- Artistic movement	3.02	0.70	-.030	.254 **	–						
4- Sports and Cards	2.94	0.64	.155	.032	.131	–					
5- Role-playing	4.31	0.47	-.038	.114	.008	-.063	–				
6- Virtual goods	3.87	0.49	.119	.080	.023	.016	.126	–			
7- Simulation	4.00	0.60	.116	.063	.041	.001	.032	.103	–		
8- Action	3.42	0.64	.090	.046	.015	.087	.082	.054	.075	–	
9- Progression	3.88	0.56	.131	-.007	-.011	.109	.104	.026	-.067	.095	–

** $p < .01$.

Table 2. Descriptive statistics for the groups of game elements and bivariate correlations of the groups between themselves.

Components	Female M	Female SD	Male M	Male SD	t-test t	t-test df	t-test p	Mean Difference M	Mean Difference SD	Age (r)
1- Strategic resource management	-0.280	1.025	0.123	0.969	-2.290	143	.024	-0.403	0.176	.034
2- Puzzle	0.353	0.910	-0.147	0.982	2.921	143	.004	0.500	0.171	.017
3- Artistic movement	0.412	1.052	-0.178	0.921	3.429	143	.001	0.590	0.172	-.018
4- Sports and Cards	-0.276	0.892	0.154	1.028	-2.441	143	.016	-0.430	0.176	.005
5- Role-playing	0.243	1.047	-0.088	0.985	1.845	143	.067	0.331	0.179	-.216 **
6- Virtual goods	0.222	0.953	-0.148	0.952	2.176	143	.031	0.370	0.170	-.141
7- Simulation	0.186	0.871	-0.076	1.057	1.463	143	.146	0.262	0.148	-.021
8- Action	-0.602	1.019	0.374	0.729	-6.580	143	.000	-0.976	0.148	-.396 **
9- Progression	0.070	1.102	0.012	0.958	0.328	143	.744	0.059	0.179	.008

** $p < .01$.

Table 3. Independent samples t-test between the groups of game elements and gender and correlations with age.

Game Playing Styles	Components 1	2	3	4
Chatting	.783			.387
Raids	.779			
Teams	.759			.439
Voice-over	.728			.471
Massive multiplayer online (MMO)	.702			
Multiplayer online battle arena (MOBA)	.629			.423
Isometric view		.789		
Top-down view		.761		
Controlled movement		.741		
Third-person view		.539	.414	
Player vs. environment			.730	
Free movement			.706	
Soloing			.693	
Streaming	.590			.707
eSports	.457			.667
First-person view				.651
Watching				.647
Co-location or couch co-op				.621
Player vs player	.484			.599
Internal reliability (α)	.872	.698	.582	.857
Eigenvalues	5.365	2.196	1.744	1.332
% of variance	28.234	11.558	9.179	7.011

Notes.
Extraction method: Principal component analysis. Rotation method: Oblimin with Kaiser normalization. Principal components were labelled: 1-multiplayer, 2-abstract interaction, 3-solo play, 4-competitive community. For improved visualization, the loadings $< .36$ (absolute values) are suppressed.

Table 4. Factor analysis (structure matrix) of the game playing styles.

Table 5 presents the descriptive statistics for the groups. We also included *casual play* because the PCA showed that it cannot be grouped with other styles, but rather it represents a distinct player preference on its own. Overall, *solo play* is the highest scoring group, whereas *multiplayer* and *competitive community* are the lowest scoring groups. The difference between the highest and the lowest scoring groups is 1.06 points out of 5.0 (21%). Finally, Table 5 also presents the bivariate correlations of the five game playing styles between themselves. The only significant correlation occurs between *multiplayer* and *competitive community*, demonstrating that these two playing styles are strongly correlated.

Components	M	SD	Correlations (r) 1	2	3	4	5
1- Multiplayer	3.11	0.86	–				
2- Abstract interaction	3.46	0.67	.123	–			
3- Solo play	4.17	0.52	.066	.080	–		
4- Competitive community	3.11	0.86	.359 **	.103	.047	–	
5- Casual play	3.28	1.12	.071	.135	-.072	-.076	–

** $p < .01$.

Table 5. Descriptive statistics for the groups of game playing styles and bivariate correlations of the groups between themselves.

Factors that Influence Player Preferences

Table 6 presents the results of the t-test of the groups' scores between genders, as well as the correlations with age. Women scored significantly higher than men only for *casual play*, whereas men scored significantly higher for *multiplayer* and *competitive community*. The difference was not significant for *abstract interaction* and *solo play*. Regarding age, the preferences for *solo play* and *competitive community* seem to significantly decrease with age, whereas the preference for *casual play* seems to significantly increase with age.

Game Elements vs Game Playing Styles

There are several significant correlations between the groups of game elements and game playing styles (see Table 7). Figure 1 summarizes the final player preferences model emerged from the data, which consists on the combination of the two taxonomies (game elements and game playing styles) and the correlations between them found in the data.

Components	Female M	SD	Male M	SD	t-test t	df	p	Mean Difference M	SD	Age (r)
1- Multiplayer	-0.261	1.1232	0.181	0.913	-2.628	154	.009	-0.442	0.168	-.125
2- Abstract interaction	-0.169	1.022	0.101	0.988	-1.584	154	.115	-0.270	0.170	.111
3- Solo play	-0.043	1.167	0.008	0.911	-0.301	154	.764	-0.051	0.171	-.156 *
4- Competitive community	-0.517	0.874	0.254	0.967	-4.823	154	.000	-0.772	0.160	-.237 **
5- Casual play	3.623	1.096	3.138	1.096	2.689	174	.008	0.484	0.180	.157 *

* $p < .05$. ** $p < .01$.

Table 6. Independent samples t-test between the groups of game playing styles and gender and correlations with age.

Components	1- Multiplayer	2- Abstract interaction	3- Solo play	4- Competitive community	5- Casual play
1- Strategic resource management	.093	.360 **	.034	.079	.055
2- Puzzle	.105	.157	.209 *	.154	.123
3- Artistic movement	-.002	.184 *	-.318 **	.017	.232 **
4- Sports and cards	.268 **	.149	-.227 **	.246 **	.236 **
5- Role-playing	.019	.166 *	.367 **	-.065	.137
6- Virtual goods	.182 *	.039	.257 **	.143	.095
7- Simulation	.093	-.177 *	.141	-.137	.025
8- Action	.368 **	.171 *	.301 **	.478 **	-.226 **
9- Progression	-.038	.349 **	-.017	-.021	-.041

* $p < .05$ ** $p < .01$.

Table 7. Bivariate correlations between the groups of game design elements and the groups of game playing styles.

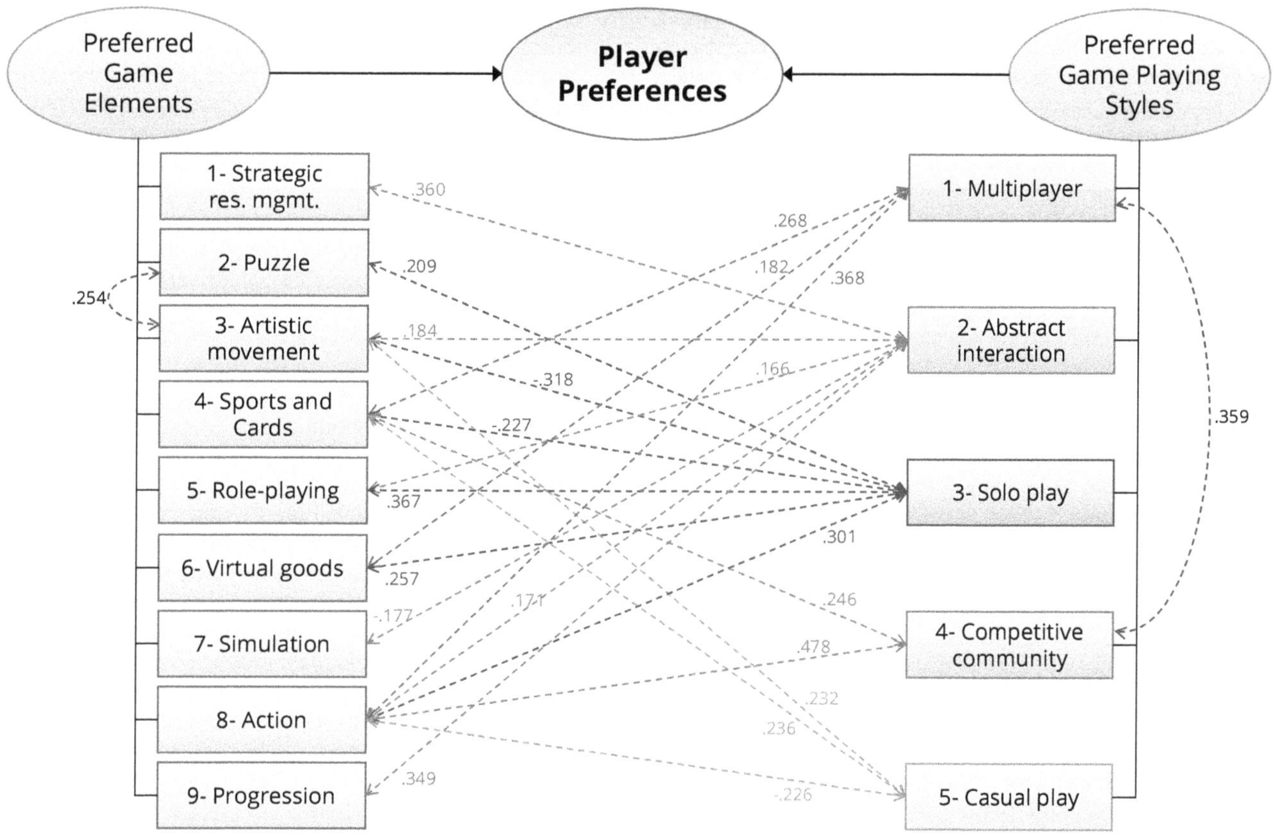

Figure 1. The final player preferences model that emerged from the data. The dashed lines represent the significant correlations (*r*).

DISCUSSION

We contribute to the GUR community by proposing a novel conceptual framework of player preferences linking game elements and game playing styles. Without reservation, we demonstrate that there are discernible patterns of player preferences, which can be used by designers and researchers to inform game design and evaluation. For instance, one of the patterns identified by our study is the relationship between game elements and game playing styles, such as 'action, multiplayer, and competitive community' or 'solo play and role-playing'. Furthermore, our results show that players' gender and age significantly influence their preferred game elements and playing styles.

Designers can benefit from our findings by using them to inform the creation of tailored games, which might be more successful in engaging the targeted players. For example, a game studio might screen its target audience and find that players enjoy some of the strategic resource management elements, such as unit building and production management. Thus, it is likely that these players will also enjoy all other elements from the same group. Therefore, designers can focus on integrating additional elements from this group, such as territorial conquest and turn-based strategy, to create a game that is strongly appealing to the target players. In addition, designers can assume that these players will likely enjoy the abstract interaction style of play because it is positively correlated with strategic resource management. Similarly, researchers can use the taxonomy to better understand and identify mediating factors of player experience. For example, a researcher studying player experiences in action games might measure participants' preferences for these kind of elements, then verify if the difference in participants' preferences for action elements influences their experiences.

Furthermore, these findings are important for serious games because they are usually meant to engage a broad player audience into achieving an instrumental goal. However, if a player does not enjoy the game, it will be difficult to achieve the goals. By better understanding player preferences, designers can better tailor their serious games to their target audience, or focus on the elements and playing styles that are enjoyed by a larger number of players.

Factors of Influence in Player Preferences

Regarding the differences observed in participants' overall enjoyment of each group of game elements and playing styles, it is worth noting that *role-playing*, *simulation*, and *solo play* are the highest scoring groups. Therefore, game designers can use this information as a guideline to inform their ideation process because our findings show that games which employ these elements are more likely to appeal to a larger audience.

Considering the factors that influence player preferences, gender appears to be the most significant factor. Women appear to enjoy more *casual play*, as well as *puzzles*, *artistic movement*, and *virtual goods* elements. On the other hand, men appear to enjoy more *multiplayer gaming* and *competitive communities*, as well as *strategic resource management*, *sports and cards*, and *action* elements. Contrarily, *solo* and *abstract interaction* playing styles, as well as *role-playing*, *simulation*, and *progression* elements are similarly appealing to both women and men. Williams et al. [34] had previously noted that women are more motivated by social reasons, whereas men are more motivated by achievement-related reasons. Our findings present a new perspective on this topic because we have looked at game elements in more detail. Thus, we show that women are more likely to enjoy puzzles, which might be seen as one form of achievement-related motivation. In comparison, our findings demonstrate that men are more likely to enjoy multiplayer gaming and competitive communities. Therefore, we can conclude that men seem to be more attracted to the challenge of playing with or against other players, rather than the social interactions.

On the other hand, age does not explain much of the variability in player preferences, but there are some important considerations. Our findings suggest that games targeting older audiences should lean more towards casual games that are easier to learn and play. On the contrary, games focused on action elements are more likely to appeal to younger audiences.

Finally, it is possible to identify some relationships between game elements and game playing styles: (1) *action*, *sports*, and *cards* strongly favour *multiplayer* and *competitive communities*; (2) *progression* and *strategic resource management* elements strongly favour the *abstract interaction* playing style; (3) *role-playing*, *action*, and *virtual goods* favour *solo playing*; and (4) *casual gaming* occurs more frequently with *artistic movement* and *sports and cards* elements. Therefore, designers can use this information as guidelines for building more entertaining games because these combinations are more likely to appeal to their targeted player audience.

Relationship of our Framework with Related Work

We attempted to compare our taxonomy with the existing models from the literature: Yee's gamer motivation profile [36], the BrainHex [24], Hamari and Tuunanen's dimensions [17], and Ferro et al.'s categories [13]. However, we concluded that the groups identified in our taxonomy do not seem to be directly associable to the dimensions in these models. This is because our model does not identify player types or traits; it groups game elements and game playing styles according to how likely it is for players to enjoy them. Nonetheless, one question remains: how do the groups of game elements and game playing styles that we uncovered relate to the dimensions of motivations and player archetypes suggested by the extant literature? Further studies are needed to answer this question.

Limitations and Future Work

We note all measures were self-reported and, thus, subject to participants' level of understanding and their awareness of their own preferences. Moreover, the present study was exploratory, aimed at constructing an initial conceptual framework and taxonomy of player preferences. Therefore, there is room for additional studies with larger samples to verify our findings and confirm the validity of our framework and taxonomy. Furthermore, because there is currently no universal and agreed upon list of game elements, we devised our own list of game elements and game playing styles for this study. Consequently, our results are particular to the characteristics of the list we employed. Regardless, we are confident in the validity of our model as a good representation of player preferences because our list was based on the extant game design literature and encompassed a bigger variety of game elements than what has been seen in studies of player preferences so far. The goal of the presented research was to look at self-reported preferences. However, future studies could investigate the relationship between an individual's self-reported preferences and their actual behaviour.

CONCLUSION

In conclusion, we contributed a new conceptual framework and created a taxonomy of game elements and game playing styles based on an empirical investigation of player preferences. We also showed that a player's gender and age significantly influences their average preferences: women are more inclined to enjoy casual play, artistic play, puzzles, and virtual goods, whereas men are more inclined to enjoy strategy, sports, cards, action, multiplayer and competitive play. Additionally, younger players are more likely to enjoy action, role-playing, solo play, and competition, whereas older players are more likely to enjoy casual play.

The strength of the presented work stems from the fact that it is the first in the literature that explores player preferences towards the building blocks of games, instead of mapping abstract player motivations that do not translate directly into game design suggestions. Therefore, we contribute to the HCI and GUR communities by providing a practical framework, which would empower designers to create more engaging games, as well as helping researchers better understand player experiences and the effects of games on players. For example, the designers of a MMO game might use our framework with the goal of further expanding their community, by understanding what are the elements and playing styles that their players are more likely to enjoy to make more informed decisions.

Additionally, this research has implications for the design of serious games. Since our framework classifies different player preferences in a way that can be directly mapped into design decisions, it would help serious games designers to create experiences that are appealing to a broad audience or to specific groups of players. Therefore, our work will assist on creating more engaging and effective serious games.

ACKNOWLEDGMENTS

Gustavo Tondello would like to thank the University of Waterloo and the CNPq, Brazil for his funding. Rina Wehbe would like to thank the University of Waterloo and NSERC for her funding. Rita Orji would like to thank the Canadian Government Banting NSERC for her funding. This research has received funding from NSERC (RGPIN-418622-2012), SSHRC (895-2011-1014, IMMERSe), CFI (35819), Mitacs (IT07255), and SWaGUR.

REFERENCES

1. Ernest Adams and Joris Dormans. 2012. *Game Mechanics: Advanced Game Design*. New Riders, Berkeley, CA.
2. Richard Bartle. 1996. Hearts, Clubs, Diamonds, Spades: Players who suit MUDs. *Journal of MUD Research* 1, 1 (1996).
3. Richard Bartle. 2005. Virtual Worlds: Why People Play. *Massively Multiplayer Game Development* 2, 1 (2005).
4. Chris Bateman and Richard Boon. 2006. *21st Century Game Design (Game Development Series)*. Charles River Media.
5. Chris Bateman, Rebecca Lowenhaupt, and Lennart E Nacke. 2011. Player Typology in Theory and Practice. *Proceedings of DiGRA 2011* (2011).
6. Chris Bateman and Lennart E Nacke. 2010. The Neurobiology of Play. In *Proceedings of Futureplay 2010*. ACM, Vancouver, BC, Canada, 1–8. DOI: http://dx.doi.org/10.1145/1920778.1920780
7. Max V. Birk, Cheralyn Atkins, Jason T. Bowey, and Regan L. Mandryk. 2016. Fostering Intrinsic Motivation through Avatar Identification in Digital Games. In *Proceedings of the 34th Annual ACM Conference on Human Factors in Computing Systems*. ACM. DOI: http://dx.doi.org/10.1145/2858036.2858062
8. Max V. Birk, Dereck Toker, Regan L. Mandryk, and Cristina Conati. 2015. Modeling Motivation in a Social Network Game Using Player-Centric Traits and Personality Traits. In *Proceedings of User Modeling, Adaptation and Personalization*. Springer, 18–30. DOI: http://dx.doi.org/10.1007/978-3-319-20267-9_2
9. Blizzard Entertainment. 2004. World of Warcraft. Game [Windows/OS X]. (2004).
10. Brenda Brathwaite and Ian Schreiber. 2009. *Challenges for Game Designers*. Charles River Media, Boston, MA.
11. Marc Busch, Elke Mattheiss, Rita Orji, Peter Fröhlich, Michael Lankes, and Manfred Tscheligi. 2016. Player Type Models – Towards Empirical Validation. In *Proceedings of the 2016 CHI Conference Extended Abstracts on Human Factors in Computing Systems*. ACM. DOI:http://dx.doi.org/10.1145/2851581.2892399
12. Edward L Deci and Richard M Ryan. 1985. *Intrinsic Motivation and Self-Determination in Human Behavior*. Plenum, New York and London.
13. Lauren S. Ferro, Steffen P. Walz, and Stefan Greuter. 2013. Towards personalised, gamified systems: an investigation into game design, personality and player typologies. In *Proceedings of the 9th Australasian Conference on Interactive Entertainment: Matters of Life and Death - IE '13*. 1–6. DOI: http://dx.doi.org/10.1145/2513002.2513024
14. Andy Field. 2009. *Discovering Statistics Using SPSS* (3rd ed.). Sage Publications, London, UK.
15. Tracy Fullerton. 2008. *Game Design Workshop: A playcentric approach to creating innovative games* (2nd ed.). Morgan Kaufmann, Burlington, MA.
16. Lewis R Goldberg. 1993. The structure of phenotypic personality traits. *American Psychologist* 48, 1 (1993), 26. DOI:http://dx.doi.org/10.1037/0003-066X.48.1.26
17. Juho Hamari and Janne Tuunanen. 2014. Player types: A meta-synthesis. *Transactions of the Digital Games Research* 1, 2 (2014). http://todigra.org/index.php/todigra/article/view/13
18. Robin Hunicke, Marc LeBlanc, and Robert Zubek. 2004. MDA: A Formal Approach to Game Design and Game Research. In *Workshop on Challenges in Game AI*. 1–4. DOI:http://dx.doi.org/10.1.1.79.4561
19. Shih-Ping Jeng and Ching-I Teng. 2008. Personality and motivations for playing online games. *Social Behavior and Personality: an international journal* 36, 8 (2008), 1053–1060. DOI: http://dx.doi.org/10.2224/sbp.2008.36.8.1053
20. Kibeom Lee and Michael C. Ashton. 2004. Psychometric Properties of the HEXACO Personality Inventory. *Multivariate Behavioral Research* 39, 2 (2004), 329–358. DOI:http://dx.doi.org/10.1207/s15327906mbr3902_8
21. Ian J Livingston, Carl Gutwin, Regan L Mandryk, and Max Birk. 2014. How players value their characters in World of Warcraft. In *Proceedings of the 17th ACM conference on Computer Supported Cooperative Work & Social Computing*. ACM, 1333–1343. DOI: http://dx.doi.org/10.1145/2531602.2531661
22. Nicole McMahon, Peta Wyeth, and Daniel Johnson. 2012. Personality and Player Types in Fallout New Vegas. In *Proceedings of the 4th International Conference on Fun and Games (FnG '12)*. ACM, 113–116. DOI: http://dx.doi.org/10.1145/2367616.2367632
23. Isabel Briggs Myers. 1962. *The Myers-Briggs Type Indicator*. Consulting Psychologists Press, Palo Alto, CA.
24. Lennart E Nacke, Chris Bateman, and Regan L Mandryk. 2014. BrainHex: A Neurobiological Gamer Typology Survey. *Entertainment Computing* 5, 1 (2014), 55–62. DOI:http://dx.doi.org/10.1016/j.entcom.2013.06.002
25. Brian P O'Connor. 2000. SPSS and SAS programs for determining the number of components using parallel analysis and Velicer's MAP test. *Behavior Research Methods, Instruments, & Computers* 32, 3 (2000), 396–402. DOI:http://dx.doi.org/10.3758/BF03200807
26. Rita Orji, Regan L. Mandryk, Julita Vassileva, and Kathrin M. Gerling. 2013. Tailoring persuasive health games to gamer type. In *Proceedings of the SIGCHI Conference on Human Factors in Computing Systems - CHI '13*. 2467–2476. DOI: http://dx.doi.org/10.1145/2470654.2481341

27. Rita Orji, Lennart E. Nacke, and Chrysanne DiMarco. 2017. Towards Personality-driven Persuasive Health Games and Gamified Systems. In *Proceedings of the SIGCHI Conference on Human Factors in Computing Systems*. ACM. DOI: http://dx.doi.org/10.1145/3025453.3025577

28. Nicole Peever, Daniel Johnson, and John Gardner. 2012. Personality & Video Game Genre Preferences. In *Proceedings of The 8th Australasian Conference on Interactive Entertainment: Playing the System*. ACM, 20. DOI:http://dx.doi.org/10.1145/2336727.2336747

29. Andrew K Przybylski, C Scott Rigby, and Richard M Ryan. 2010. A motivational model of video game engagement. *Review of general psychology* 14, 2 (2010), 154. DOI:http://dx.doi.org/10.1037/a0019440

30. Richard M. Ryan, C. Scott Rigby, and Andrew Przybylski. 2006. The motivational pull of video games: A self-determination theory approach. *Motivation and Emotion* 30, 4 (2006), 347–363. DOI: http://dx.doi.org/10.1007/s11031-006-9051-8

31. Jesse Schell. 2008. *The Art of Game Design: A Book of Lenses*. Morgan Kaufmann, Burlington, MA.

32. Gustavo F Tondello, Rina R Wehbe, Zachary O Toups, Lennart E Nacke, and Nicole K Crenshaw. 2015. Understanding Player Attitudes Towards Digital Game Objects. In *Proceedings of the 2015 Annual Symposium on Computer-Human Interaction in Play - CHI PLAY '15*. ACM, London, United Kingdom. DOI: http://dx.doi.org/10.1145/2793107.2810292

33. Zachary O. Toups, Nicole K. Crenshaw, Rina R. Wehbe, Gustavo F. Tondello, and Lennart E. Nacke. 2016. "The Collecting Itself Feels Good": Towards Collection Interfaces for Digital Game Objects. In *Proceedings of the 2016 Annual Symposium on Computer-Human Interaction in Play - CHI PLAY '16*. ACM, Austin, TX, United States. DOI: http://dx.doi.org/10.1145/2967934.2968088

34. Dmitri Williams, Mia Consalvo, Scott Caplan, and Nick Yee. 2009. Looking for gender: Gender roles and behaviors among online gamers. *Journal of Communication* 59, 4 (2009), 700–725. DOI: http://dx.doi.org/10.1111/j.1460-2466.2009.01453.x

35. Nick Yee. 2006. Motivations for Play in Online Games. *CyberPsychology & Behavior* 9, 6 (2006), 772–775. DOI: http://dx.doi.org/10.1089/cpb.2006.9.772

36. Nick Yee. 2015. Gamer Motivation Model Overview and Descriptions. Quantic Foundry. (Dec 2015). http://quanticfoundry.com/2015/12/15/handy-reference/

37. Nick Yee. 2016. Gaming Motivations Align with Personality Traits. Quantic Foundry. (Jan 2016). http://quanticfoundry.com/2016/01/05/personality-correlates/

38. Nick Yee, Nicolas Ducheneaut, and Les Nelson. 2012. Online gaming motivations scale: development and validation. In *Proceedings of the 2012 ACM annual conference on Human Factors in Computing Systems - CHI '12*. ACM, New York, New York, USA, 2803. DOI: http://dx.doi.org/10.1145/2207676.2208681

39. Virgil Zeigler-Hill and Sean Monica. 2015. The HEXACO model of personality and video game preferences. *Entertainment Computing* 11 (2015), 21–26. DOI:http://dx.doi.org/10.1016/j.entcom.2015.08.001

The Effects of Navigation Assistance on Spatial Learning and Performance in a 3D Game

Colby Johanson, Carl Gutwin, and Regan L. Mandryk
Department of Computer Science, University of Saskatchewan
Saskatoon, SK, Canada
{firstname.lastname}@usask.ca

ABSTRACT
Navigation in 3D game environments is often difficult for novices, who may get lost and be unable to reach game objectives. Many games provide navigation assistance (e.g., mini-maps, directional markers, or glowing trails); however, there is a risk that players will become reliant on an aid and fail to develop a mental model of the map. To investigate, we carried out two online studies in which people carried out training tasks with varying navigation assistance. After training, they navigated the map with assistance turned off. In both studies, we found that assistance improved training performance, but found no harmful effect of assistance on performance after it was removed, even when comparing between those who received glowing trails to follow and those who received no assistance. We show that navigation assistance in 3D games is effective, and that it does not necessarily harm development of a novice's spatial learning.

Author Keywords
Game navigation; navigation aids; guidance hypothesis.

ACM Classification Keywords
K.8.0 [Personal Computing]: General - Games.

INTRODUCTION
There are many skill differences between novices and experts in 3D games, including targeting, evading enemy attacks, understanding weapon capabilities, and the ability to memorize and navigate the game map [27,48]. Map knowledge – knowing one's own location as well as knowing game locations and routes – can dramatically affect play experience: whereas experts quickly learn where resources and enemies are located [43], novices find themselves continually lost and unable to get to objectives.

Spatial abilities in games are of particular interest because unlike many game skills, learning and navigating 3D environments is something that people do in the real world throughout their lives. Even though there are individual differences in spatial ability, most people are fully able to function in the environments around them, and can easily find their way through houses, office buildings, or shopping centres. This does not appear to be the case in 3D games: Several researchers have noted the difficulty of navigating virtual environments [15,16], and there are many examples of novice players discussing difficulties with navigation, or videos making fun of their poor navigational skills. For example, a player of *Final Fantasy Online* posted in a forum:

> **Noob, Lost, Cannot find my way around the map to the point of AHHHHHHH!!!** I am super frustrated. I am a noob to the game. I am somewhere on some steps... I can get to all the levels and outside but I cannot find the Drowning Wench. [...] Once you stop laughing at how much of a moron I am for not being able to find my way out of a paper bag could someone please give me some tips or something. (forum.square-enix.com/ffxiv/threads/90497)

Problems with game navigation – that is, getting lost or not knowing how to get to an objective – can be extremely frustrating, and may contribute to a novice player's decision to quit the game. To reduce navigational difficulty, some games add directional assistance to the game environment, such as markers telling the player where to go (Figure 1), or routes drawn on the game map (Figure 2). However, these assists have one significant limitation – they only work when the desired destination is well known. There are many situations in which a player needs to adapt to changing conditions in the game and stray from the well-marked path: for example, to find an alternate route that flanks an enemy, or to look for treasure in the environment. In fact, wayfinding itself can be a compelling challenge for many players [38], and some even feel that the joy of discovery is stolen from them when an assist led them to that discovery [12].

Although providing novices with assistance can improve early performance and experience, designers may be setting players up to fail later on. There is a concern that a player will become reliant on an aid, and when they are eventually required to navigate on their own (e.g., to play competitively), they will be unable to do so. This phenomenon of players relying on external feedback is known as the *guidance hypothesis* [40,41], which suggests that greater effort during training (i.e., *intentional* learning) will lead to better retention and understanding [18].

In contrast to the guidance hypothesis, however, is research suggesting that spatial knowledge in 3D environments can be gained through *incidental* learning [2,4,23]. Incidental learning occurs simply through exposure to an environment

CHI PLAY '17, October 15–18, 2017, Amsterdam, Netherlands

ACM ISBN 978-1-4503-4898-0/17/10…$15.00
https://doi.org/10.1145/3116595.3116602

– for example, people may learn the layout of a building even if they are being led by a guide. This natural ability to learn about an environment may arise because an understanding of our surroundings was critical for the survival of early humans. There is debate about whether location learning can occur as an incidental process, however, and there are studies that point to problems in spatial learning caused by navigation aids such as GPS (e.g., [6,26,33]).

These competing theories about location learning mean that it is difficult to predict the effects of navigational assistance techniques in games. To determine both the benefits and risks of navigation assistance in 3D games, we carried out two studies in which novices completed several route-finding tasks with different forms of navigation aid, and then completed test routes without any assistance. The training tasks used one of three assistance levels: *no assistance*, *moderate assistance* (a mini-map and pop-up map with the player's current location), or *strong assistance* (a path drawn on the ground of the game world itself). The testing routes required novices to navigate un-aided to a particular landmark. Both studies used the same testing and training routes, and the same two real game environments: the "Gold Rush" map from *Enemy Territory* [42], and the "Furious Heights" map from *Quake Live* [25].

In the first study, participants completed sixteen training routes, then eight test routes, all in the same session. In the second study, participants completed sixteen routes in each of three sessions on three successive days, as well as eight test routes on the third day. In addition to the in-game navigation test, we asked participants questions to assess their knowledge of landmarks, routes, and distances on the two game maps; and we also asked them to rate their play experience after training and after testing.

Our goal in both studies was to determine whether having more assistance during training would result in poorer navigation performance and knowledge during testing (when assistance was removed). The results of both studies were surprising – in neither case did our findings agree with the predictions of the guidance hypothesis:

- Navigation assistance helped substantially when it was present: in both studies, having more assistance allowed participants to complete significantly more routes, and to complete them in significantly less time.
- There were no performance differences in testing: despite the strong effects in training, there were no significant differences in performance on the test tasks – including the number of test routes completed, the distance travelled, or the completion time – regardless of whether or not people had assistance during training.
- Subjective responses mirrored performance results: the presence of navigation assistance significantly reduced perception of effort, frustration, and mental demand. When the assistance was taken away in testing, these differences disappeared.

Our findings confirm that navigation assists substantially help novices, and adds to evidence [20] that early guidance does not necessarily hinder performance when taken away (even with strong assistance such as glowing trails). Our results can be used by game designers in several ways: first, designers should be aware of the difficulties that novices have in learning 3D game environments; second, designers can substantially improve novices' initial play experience with navigation assistance; third, navigation assistance can be used as a player-balancing mechanism for social-play situations; and fourth, taking navigation assistance away will not necessarily result in the player becoming lost.

RELATED WORK

Navigation in Real and Virtual Environments

A wide variety of research has been carried out to investigate the ways that humans learn and perform navigation in real-world environments – for example, researchers have looked at the development of spatial knowledge in children (e.g., [21]), sex differences in navigation (e.g., [9,32]), and theoretical models for navigation (e.g., [11]). One major focus in navigation research is on *wayfinding*, the process by which people orient themselves to an environment and move from place to place. Early work identified three kinds of knowledge that are important for wayfinding, and that are associated with increasing spatial understanding [45–47]:

- *Landmark knowledge* involves remembering specific objects or settings in an environment – such as a statue or a building in a city centre.
- *Route knowledge* is understanding how to navigate between specific locations, and the actions required to reproduce a specific path between them. Route knowledge often builds on landmark knowledge (e.g., by linking different landmarks together).
- *Survey knowledge* is a map-like mental representation of an environment, and is the highest form of spatial understanding. Survey knowledge allows people to navigate skillfully, estimate relative distances, and choose alternate routes to objectives.

There are two ways in which people can gain this spatial understanding of an environment [15]. First, people learn through direct exposure to their surroundings – that is, simply being in an environment and moving through it. Second, external information sources such as maps provide other forms of spatial learning. When used in an actual navigation task, maps require that users identify their own location on the map, and then translate orientations, directions, and distances from the map representation to the actual environment.

Researchers have also studied a variety of navigational tools and aids in real-world wayfinding. The most common tool is the map, and researchers have looked at several aspects of map use, such as the differences between "track-up" and "north-up" orientations [3]. Recent research has also looked at the effects of guidance systems such as GPS, and has found that people can become overly focused on the directions provided by external guidance, hindering the development of their spatial knowledge (e.g., [6,26,33]).

Navigation in virtual environments has also been extensively studied. One main interest is in whether virtual environments can be used as training simulations for real-world navigation [51], and whether spatial knowledge and wayfinding ability transfer to real environments. Researchers have also identified that navigational difficulties are common in virtual environments (e.g., [15,28]): "Virtual world navigators may wander aimlessly when attempting to find a place for the first time. They may then have difficulty relocating places recently visited. They are often unable to grasp the overall topological structure of the space" ([15], p. 166).

To combat these difficulties, previous work has also looked at a variety of navigational aids. The value of landmarks has led researchers to consider the idea of allowing users to place visual markers, having the system create a visual trail showing where users have been, or having a fixed marker to provide a consistent indication of north [15,16]. Results with these forms of assistance are mixed, however: adding a simple compass did not substantially improve navigation performance [17], and trails can quickly clutter an environment. To our knowledge, no studies have looked at the effects of navigation assistance on spatial performance once the assistance has been removed.

Incidental vs. Intentional Spatial Learning

A continuing debate concerns the relationship between spatial knowledge acquisition and intentionality. Studies indicate that at least some aspects of location learning occur automatically [2,23]. For example, one study showed that recall of word locations was unaffected by the difficulty of a concurrent task [2]. Other work, however, shows the importance of intention; studies have shown that when people focused their attention on a route through a building, they were better able to draw a map of that path [4], and that even long experience with an environment may still result in poor survey knowledge [8].

Similarly, Ehret [18] suggests that the amount of attention, repetition, and practice during training will affect the degree to which an object's location can later be retrieved from memory. Ehret suggests that because explicitly remembering locations requires effort, people will choose a lower-cost strategy when possible, impairing their learning. This phenomenon is related to the guidance hypothesis and effort-retrieval hypothesis, described further below.

Navigational Assistance in Games

From subtle signs or arrows, to obvious glowing trails, many games feature navigational aids or assistance. Two common navigational assists are compasses and mini-maps [38]. Both are used to display locational information to the player. An example is the quest marker [38,54] – icons that indicate the start, end, or intermediate goal of a quest. For example, *Skyrim* [5] (Figure 1) includes a compass at the top of the screen with markers for selected quests and icons for points of interest. Mini-maps are used similarly: *Counter-Strike: Global Offensive*'s [24] mini-map shows nearby teammates and the location of objectives.

A stronger aid that is found in games is a highlighted trail in the environment. The effect is often implemented as a smoke or particle trail along the recommended path. For example, *Fable II* [34,44] (Figure 2) and *Neverwinter* [13] have particle trails which can be turned on or off through the user interface. In other cases, the trail may be implemented diegetically: in *Skyrim*, magic users have access to a "clairvoyance" [5] spell that temporarily highlights the route to a quest marker with a smoke trail.

Figure 1. The quest marker on *Skyrim*'s compass display, showing the direction to the next objective.

Figure 2. Glowing "breadcrumb trail" in *Fable II*, showing the path to the start of the quest (or the next objective).

Skill Development in Games

Games have gained a reputation as powerful learning tools; they are able to transform novices into experts through an engaging, motivating, and enjoyable experience [19,31]. Many theories apply to learning in games. We describe Kiili's experiential gaming model, the guidance hypothesis, and the retrieval effort hypothesis.

Kiili's experiential gaming model is based on experiential learning theory [30], flow theory [10,14], and the zone of proximal development [49]. In *experiential learning theory,* a person forms a prediction based on their prior experiences and then tests those predictions on new experiences. Games provide many opportunities for players to test their ideas and predictions [19]. *Flow theory* describes a state in which one becomes so immersed in an experience that they notice nothing outside of that experience. Well-designed games are able to keep players in the flow state for long periods of time by providing challenges that are well-matched to the player's ability [19,29,31]. The *zone of proximal development* describes what a learner can accomplish if they are given some guidance. Often, the systems within a game can provide that guidance, scaffolding a player to overcome a challenge just outside their current skill level [31].

Kiili incorporates ideas from these three theories to form his experiential gaming model [29]. As it has been shown that being in the flow state benefits learning [52], Kiili proposes that the flow state can be extended with the zone of proximal development – if a player's ability is scaffolded so that they can complete challenges just outside of their ability, maximum learning will occur. Kiili's model is based on continual re-learning, and includes two phases. In the *ideation* phase, the learner generates ideas and potential solutions while in the *experience* phase, the learner tests their ideas while attempting to overcome in-game challenges. After testing, the learner can then incorporate their new experiences and generate new ideas.

The *guidance hypothesis* refers to the phenomenon where a learner starts to rely on extrinsic feedback provided by a system. The type of feedback which leads to this phenomenon is Knowledge of Results (KR) [40]. KR refers to extrinsic feedback indicating task success in response to a learner's actions [41]. A few researchers have studied whether assistance systems in games result in reliance on the assistance. For example, Gutwin et al. [20] investigated whether providing players with aim assistance in a first-person shooter (FPS) would hinder aiming ability without the assist, or affect their ability to learn other FPS skills. They found that players were not hindered in skill development for either skill when aim assist was present – in opposition to what the guidance hypothesis suggests.

The *retrieval effort hypothesis* refers to the relationship between the amount of effort involved in memory retrieval and the development of memory: "given that retrieval is successful, more difficult retrievals are better for memory than less difficult retrievals" [39]. In other words, increased effort when trying to remember should lead to a better memory of the retrieved information. This difficulty can be operationalized in many different ways, such as spacing out the time between retrievals [39], or making users use less representative symbols in a mental mapping between symbol and colour [18].

STUDY 1

We conducted an online experiment to explore whether the amount of assistance provided to a player when navigating an unfamiliar environment would affect route-finding ability and player experience, both when the assistance was present and after it was removed.

Study 1 Experimental Design

We designed and implemented a system that allowed online participants to navigate 3D environments between defined start and end points. The system could vary the amount of navigation assistance provided to the player. We investigated three levels of assistance, and implemented these in two environments from 3D first-person shooter (FPS) games.

Navigation Task

Participants were asked to navigate from a starting position to an end location in a 3D environment. The game environment and the navigation tasks were implemented using the Unity game engine and were deployed online as a browser-based WebGL game displayed on a computer monitor. For each task (also referred to as a route), participants were placed at a predefined starting point, and instructed to move to a location indicated on the map.

Both training and testing phases involved navigating a 3D environment, but there were three different interfaces used during the training phase that provided different amounts of navigation assistance. These interfaces included several elements (Figure 3): a mini-map in the top-right corner of the screen, a full-screen map that was accessed by pressing the M key, and a route path that was displayed in the game world. In training tasks, the destination location was indicated with a flag on the maps and in the environment. In testing tasks, none of the three assists were used, and the destination was indicated at the start of the task as an image of an in-game landmark (such as a tank, bars of gold, or an in-game powerup) that the player needed to reach. This destination was also marked in the environment with a flag. To ensure that any spatial learning was acquired incidentally, there was no prior indication before or during training that participants would be tested on their spatial knowledge. In both training and testing, participants had to touch the flag to complete the task. All tasks had a 90-second time limit, after which the system would move to the next route (optimal times to traverse the routes ranged from 5-25s).

Assistance Levels (Training Phase)

The assistance groups were designed to vary the amount of navigation effort required by the participant. The system had three assistance levels, from no assistance to strong assistance, as shown in Figure 3.

No Assistance. With no assistance, the player saw the normal first-person view, and had access to a full-screen pop-up map (invoked with the M key) that showed the target destination. In this condition, participants had to identify their own position on the map, plan a route to the destination, and translate directions and distances from the map view to the first-person environment.

Moderate Assistance. With moderate assistance, the interface showed an always-on mini-map in the top right corner of the screen. The pop-up map was also available. In addition to the target icon (a red flag), both maps included an icon indicating the player's current location and direction (similar to the pin icon used in Google Maps). In this condition, participants could see their dynamic progress on the map views – and if they focused on the map, there was less of a requirement to translate to the first-person view.

Strong Assistance. The strong assistance interface provided the same mini-map and pop-up map as described above, but additionally showed the path to the destination with a solid white line permanently drawn in the game environment. The line was a guide only – players could take any route they wanted. This visual effect is similar to the navigational aids

Figure 3. Left to right: Strong assist, moderate assist, and no assist, and testing UI (showing the "Gold Rush" map).

used in several commercial games (as discussed above). In this condition, players had to expend far less effort than with the other interfaces – they did not have to identify their location or plan a route, and could simply follow the white line to the destination.

3D Game Environments

We used environments from two commercial 3D first-person shooter games. From *Wolfenstein: Enemy Territory*, we used the map "Gold Rush," and from *Quake Live*, we used the map "Furious Heights." These maps were extracted from the original games and recreated in Unity.

"Gold Rush" (Figure 3) is set in a fictional town in northern Africa, and most of the routes in the map take place outside. The town has a variety of streets, walls, buildings, passages, plazas, and staircases. There are several naturalistic landmarks such as palm trees in a town square, vehicles including carts and tanks, and multi-story towers.

"Furious Heights" (Figure 4) is set in a fictional multi-level castle, and all of the routes take place indoors. The castle has multiple distinct floors, and the most obvious landmarks in the map are artificial game objects (e.g., a glowing yellow first-aid symbol) that float above the floor. This environment also features two special navigation-related game mechanics: teleporters and jump pads. Both teleporters and jump pads allow players to travel to a higher floor, but are not required to travel through the environment.

Study 1 Procedure

At the start of the study, participants were told that the study would use WebGL to render 3D environments, and that they would need a relatively fast computer to participate. They were then asked to provide informed consent, and continued through the three phases described below.

Navigation Tutorial and Random Group Assignment. Participants were instructed to complete a simple navigation task in a separate tutorial level (not used in the rest of the study). The task had them walk down a hallway, jump over a small gap, travel through a teleporter, take a jump pad to a higher level, and finally, touch a flag to proceed. This tutorial was intended to give participants a chance to check their system's performance before getting too far into the experiment, and to introduce them to the controls they would use to navigate the virtual environment and the gameplay mechanics of the teleporter and the jump pad. After the tutorial, participants completed demographic and personality trait questionnaires. They were then randomly assigned to one of three assistance groups, and one of two orders.

Training Phase. Depending on their order group, participants started with either the Furious Heights map or the Gold Rush map. They carried out eight different route tasks (as described above). After completing the eight routes, participants completed a questionnaire about their subjective experiences. This training procedure was then repeated for the second map for their order group (for a total of 16 routes).

Figure 4. "Furious Heights" environment from *Quake Live*.

Testing Phase. After completing training routes and experience questionnaires in both maps, participants moved to a testing phase that involved questions about their spatial knowledge, and four additional route tasks in each map. First, the spatial-knowledge questions asked participants to locate four landmarks and three scenes on a 2D map that was similar to the pop-up map used in the training tasks, but with no marked icons. The landmarks and scenes had all been seen previously in the training phase. Participants answered the spatial-knowledge questions for both maps, in the same order as for training. Second, participants carried out four route tasks in each map: they were shown a picture of a landmark and instructed to go to it as directly as possible, but with no navigation aids (no mini-map, no pop-up map, no route line). The landmarks that were used as destinations for these tasks had all been seen previously in the training tasks (they were either used as destinations or were on a required route); however, since starting points were different for the test tasks, none of the routes had been used previously. After the four routes in each map, participants also completed the same experience questionnaire that was used during training. Participants completed test routes and questionnaire for the two maps in the same order as used for training.

At the end of the experiment, participants completed a debrief protocol and a final questionnaire, giving them an opportunity to provide comments about the experiment.

Study 1 Measures

At the start of the study, we collected measures of prior expertise and personality traits. During the study we collected information about navigation performance, spatial knowledge, and play experience.

Navigation Performance Measures

Route completion time. The system recorded each participant's total time to complete the eight training routes in each map, and the four test routes in each map. The maximum time per route was 90 seconds.

Map review time. The system recorded the total time that participants had the pop-up map open during training.

Distance travelled. The system recorded the total 3D Euclidean distance travelled by the participant for each route (using Unity's default measuring system).

Route Completion. The system recorded the number of routes where the participant reached the destination flag within the 90-second time limit.

Spatial Knowledge Measures

Scene-to-map translation: We presented participants with three screenshots for each environment, and asked them to indicate the location of that scene by clicking on one of six labels (A-F) on a 2D map. The scenes were ones that players had seen during training (although the screenshot was taken with a wider camera angle to show more of the scene).

Landmark-image-to-map translation: We presented participants with images of four landmarks from each environment, and asked them to indicate the location of the landmark by selecting one of six labels (A-F) on a 2D map. All of the landmarks had been seen during training.

Route duration estimate: For each map, participants were shown a 2D map with a route marked on it (not one they had traversed). Based on their experience with navigating the environment, they were asked to estimate the time it would take someone to navigate that path directly.

Confidence: After each spatial-knowledge question, we asked participants to rate their confidence in their answer.

Player Experience Measures

Task-Load Index (NASA-TLX) [22]. The NASA Task-Load Index questionnaire is a widely-used [35] questionnaire to rate perceived workload when completing a task. We used the questionnaire's mental demand, performance, effort, and frustration scales.

State Anxiety (SA) [36]. We anticipated that a participant's state anxiety could differ based on our conditions. We used Marteau and Bekker's six-item questionnaire of state anxiety to measure this construct.

Perceived Map Knowledge. To measure their perceived map knowledge after training, we asked users to rate their knowledge of the layout of the map.

Prior Expertise and Personality Traits

Several factors have been shown to affect a person's navigation performance in virtual environments, such as prior experience with virtual navigation, wayfinding anxiety, and immersive tendencies [50]. To account for these individual differences, we collected the following measures.

Experience with our chosen environments. Participants rated their experience with each of the two games (*Wolfenstein: Enemy Territory* and *Quake Live*) and each of the two maps (Gold Rush and Furious Heights).

3D gaming expertise. We asked participants questions to establish their gaming expertise: how much they self-identified as a gamer, their experience with video games, their experience with keyboard-and-mouse input in games, their FPS experience, and their experience with 3D games.

Immersive Tendencies. We used the Immersive Tendencies Questionnaire (ITQ) [53] to measure participants' tendency to experience presence in virtual environments. The questionnaire consists of three subscales: *involvement* (propensity to get involved with an activity), *focus* (ability to concentrate on enjoyable activities), and *games* (how much they play games and whether they become involved enough to feel like they are inside the game).

Wayfinding Traits. We measured each participant's trait anxiety and tendency to use a "route-learning" strategy or an "orientation" strategy using Lawton and Kallai's [32] International Wayfinding Anxiety Scale and International Wayfinding Strategy Scale, respectively.

Participants and Recruitment

The experiment was deployed on Amazon's Mechanical Turk (MTurk) crowdsourcing platform. MTurk connects willing workers to paid *Human Intelligence Tasks* (HITs) – it has been used for research purposes before and has been shown to be reliable [37]. We had 42 participants complete the experiment. Participants were paid \$6 USD for completing the experiment, which took 42 minutes on average.

We randomly assigned all participants to one of the three assistance levels, balancing for self-declared gender. We excluded 12 participants from our analysis for either rating themselves too high in prior experience (moderate experience or higher) with either of the two games or maps used, or for having too low a framerate on their system (<15 FPS). This left 15 female and 15 male participants (mean age 32.7, SD=7.56, min=20, max=53). Ten participants completed each of the three assistance conditions.

Data Analyses

For each participant, we aggregated performance data from both maps. This provided mean performance measures per participant for completion time, distance travelled, and routes completed (for each of training and testing). We also aggregated each participant's scores across both maps for the three types of spatial-knowledge question (scene location, landmark location, route duration estimation).

Due to our between-subjects design, we used covariates to acknowledge trait difference in anxiety and spatial ability in our participants. Covariates were chosen based on correlation between traits and dependent measures. For the subjective measures, four covariates were included: ITQ's focus subscale, ITQ's games subscale, wayfinding anxiety, and gaming expertise. For our objective measures, five covariates were included: ITQ's focus subscale, ITQ's games subscale, orientation wayfinding strategy, gaming expertise, and gender. Note that in both studies, one-way ANOVAs showed no significant group differences in the trait measures used as covariates, indicating that random assignment did not result in one of the assistance groups having skewed levels of any trait measure.

We expected differences between assistance groups during the training phase, and so performed two multivariate analyses of covariance (MANCOVA) using only the training data – one analysis for the subjective measures of experience (with four covariates), and one for the objective measures of performance (with five covariates). To test for effects of assistance level on performance and experience in the testing phase, we similarly carried out two MANCOVAs using the dependent measures collected during testing. Alpha was set at 0.05, and all pairwise comparisons used the estimated marginal means and Bonferroni corrections.

Study 1 Results

We first look at how assistance affected participant subjective experience and performance during training, and then report whether the type of assistance used in training affected performance or experience in the testing phase (where all navigation assistance was removed). Note that because there were different numbers of tasks in training and testing, and because the actual routes involved different start and end points, it is not possible to directly compare each group's training performance to their testing performance.

Effects of Assistance Level in Training

For the performance measures, there were significant main effects of assistance level on the time taken to complete the training routes, the time spent reviewing the map, the distance travelled, and the number of routes completed within the 90-second time limit (see Table 1). Pairwise comparisons showed that participants with moderate or strong assistance spent less time completing the training routes (p_m=.038, p_s<.001), travelled less distance (p_m<.001, p_s<.001), and completed more routes within the time limit (p_m=.044, p_s=.002) compared to participants with no assistance. Furthermore, participants with strong assistance spent less time reviewing the map than participants with moderate assistance (p=.050) or with no assistance (p=.005).

For the experiential measures, there were significant main effects of assistance on effort, frustration, perceived performance, and mental demand, but not anxiety or self-rated map knowledge (Table 1). Pairwise comparisons revealed that participants experienced higher effort (p=.013), frustration (p=.002), mental demand (p=.022), and perceived performance (p=.018) with no assistance compared to strong assistance. In addition, participants experienced higher frustration (p=.043) with no assistance compared to moderate assistance. No other pairwise differences were significant.

Effects of Assistance Level in Testing

For the performance measures, there were no effects of assistance type on any measure, including completion time, distance travelled, and number of routes completed. There were similarly no main effects of assistance type on the spatial-knowledge questions, including landmark location, scene location, and route duration estimation. In addition, there were no differences in participants' confidence ratings for landmark or scene location. For experiential measures, there were also no significant effects of assistance type on any measure, including effort, frustration, perceived performance, mental demand, and anxiety (See Table 1).

Summary of Results

In training, participants who had navigation assistance spent significantly less time completing the routes, spent less time looking at the map, and travelled a shorter distance. This reduced exposure to the 3D environment, however, did not translate into reduced performance in unassisted test tasks when compared to participants who had trained with no assistance (and whose testing experience was therefore much closer to their training experience).

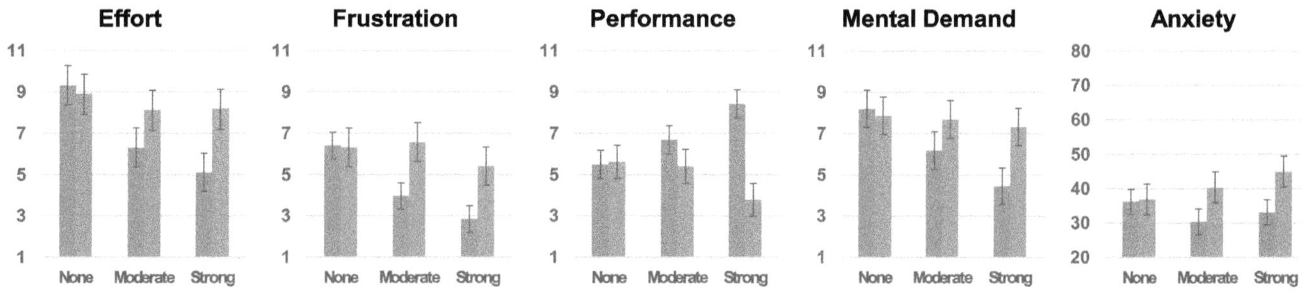

Figure 5. Experiential results after training (with assistance) and testing (with no assistance). Values are estimated marginal means, error bars are ±s.e.

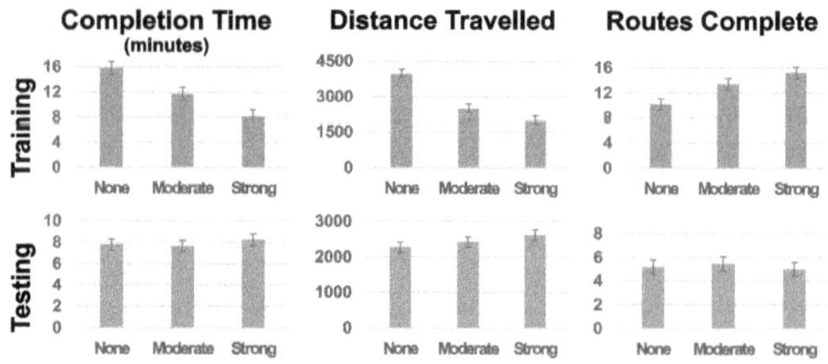

Figure 6. Descriptive statistic results for the performance measures of the 16 training routes and 8 testing routes. Values are estimated marginal means; error bars are ±s.e.

Navigation assistance also led to significantly better scores during training for perceived effort, frustration, performance, and mental demand. As with the performance measures, removing the assistance in testing did not lead to a worse experience than what was reported by participants who had trained with no assistance – we observed no differences in the subjective measures between the groups.

STUDY 2

Our first study suggested that navigation assistance helped participants during training, and did not hurt them (relative to the no-assistance group) when the aids were removed. However, the first study provided only a short training phase (eight routes in each map), and we wanted to determine whether differences might emerge if participants had more training time to learn the maps. Therefore, we conducted a follow-up study that used a much longer training period.

Study 2 Experimental Design

The second study was similar to the first but used three training sessions over three days. The study was again deployed on Amazon's Mechanical Turk, and we reproduced all aspects of the procedure described above. Participants completed the same navigation tasks for training and testing, with the same assistance levels used during training. We also used the same dependent measures.

The difference in Study 2 was the duration of training – three sessions on three consecutive days, totalling 48 navigation tasks instead of 16. The testing phase was identical to Study 1, and immediately followed the third training session.

Study 2 Participants and Recruitment

We recruited participants on MTurk using a qualification task, limited to 100 participants, in which people completed the tutorial navigation task and demographics questionnaire that we used at the start of Study 1. The qualification task took less than 5 minutes and paid $0.50 USD. The average framerate was logged during the navigation task. We excluded people from the main study if they had a framerate lower than 45 FPS (to ensure high framerates in the more graphically intense maps), or if they had moderate or greater experience with the two games and maps described above. After exclusions, 73 participants were eligible to participate in the main study.

The first day of the experiment was open to the first 50 participants who accepted the task on MTurk, and consisted of the personality trait questionnaires and a 16-route training session (as described earlier, 8 routes in each of two maps, seen in balanced order). Participants were paid $3.50 USD for completing the first day. The second day consisted only of the same 16-route training session, and participants were paid $3 USD. The final day consisted of the final 16-route training session, the same spatial-knowledge questionnaires as in Study 1, and the 8-route testing session, with the same testing routes as Study 1. Participants were paid $4.50 USD for day 3.

Of the 50 who started the multi-day study, 46 completed all three days. We excluded two participants from our analysis due to logging errors, leaving us with 44 participants (29 male, 15 female, mean age of 33.7, SD=8.68; min=20; max=59). Male and female participants were evenly distributed among the assistance groups as in Study 1. The 44 participants were randomly assigned to assistance levels: 14 had no assistance, 16 had moderate, and 14 had strong.

Study 2 Data Analyses

To evaluate the training sessions, we used a repeated measures MANCOVA – the same MANCOVA model as in Study 1 but with Day (one, two, and three) as an additional within-subjects factor. The testing session was analysed using the same statistical model as in Study 1.

Study 2 Results

Effects of Assistance Level and Day on Training

In terms of the performance measures, there were no main effects of day on the time taken to complete the training routes ($F_{2,72}$=0.73, p=.487), the time spent reviewing the map ($F_{2,72}$=0.67, p=.51), the distance travelled ($F_{2,72}$=0.72, p=.492), or the number of routes completed ($F_{2,72}$=1.6,

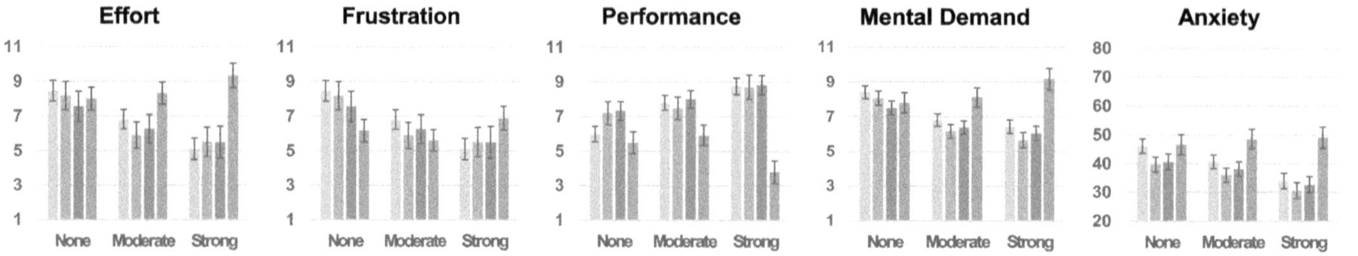

Figure 7. Descriptive statistics for subjective measures in Study 2 for day 1, 2, 3, and testing. Values are estimated marginal means; error bars are ±s.e.

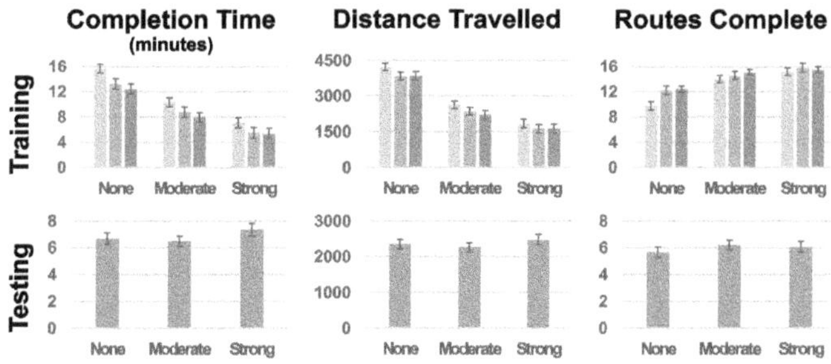

Figure 8. Descriptive statistic results for the performance measures of the 16 training routes and 8 testing routes for day 1, 2, 3, and testing. Values are estimated marginal means; error bars are ±s.e.

p=.218). There were significant main effects of assistance on the time taken to complete the training routes, the time spent reviewing the map, the distance travelled, and the number of routes completed (see Table 1). Pairwise comparisons showed that each level of assistance decreased the time spent (all p<.029) and the distance travelled (all p<.011). Furthermore, both moderate and strong assistance reduced the time spent on the map (all p<.020) and increased the number of routes completed (all p<.001). There were no significant interactions between day and assistance on time, time reviewing the map, or distance; however, a significant interaction between day and routes completed ($F_{4,72}$=3.7, p=.009, η_p^2=.169) showed that the differences between the assistance techniques were less pronounced over time.

In terms of the subjective results, there were no main effects of Day on effort ($F_{2,74}$=0.36, p=.696), frustration ($F_{2,74}$=0.36, p=.696), perceived performance ($F_{2,74}$=1.2, p=.299), mental demand ($F_{2,74}$=0.28, p=.759), anxiety ($F_{2,74}$=2.4, p=.095), or self-rated map knowledge ($F_{2,74}$=2.8, p=.066). There were significant effects of assistance level on effort, frustration, perceived performance, mental demand, and anxiety (see Table 1). Pairwise comparisons revealed that participants who trained with strong assistance experienced less effort (p=.040), frustration (p=.040), perceived performance (p=.021), mental demand (p<.001), and anxiety (p=.017) than those who received no assistance. In addition, those with moderate assistance rated their mental demand as lower than with no assistance (p=.001). There were no interactions between Day and Assistance on any of the measures.

Effects of Assistance Level on Testing

There were no significant main effects of assistance level on any of our performance measures, including time taken, distance travelled, and routes completed. There were also no main effects of assistance level on any of our spatial-knowledge questions, including landmark location, scene location, and route duration estimation. There were also no differences in confidence ratings (see Table 1). There were no significant effects of assistance on any of the subjective measures, including effort, frustration, perceived performance, mental demand, anxiety, or self-declared map knowledge (see Table 1).

		Study 1			*Study 2*		
		$F_{2,23}$	p	η_p^2	$F_{2,37}$	p	η_p^2
Effort	Train.	**5.31**	**.013**	**.316**	**3.61**	**.037**	**.163**
	Test	0.21	.812	n.s.	0.99	.381	n.s.
Frustration	Train.	**8.10**	**.002**	**.413**	**3.61**	**.037**	**.163**
	Test	0.43	.655	n.s.	0.89	.418	n.s.
Perceived Performance	Train.	**4.66**	**.020**	**.288**	**4.12**	**.024**	**.182**
	Test	1.53	.238	n.s.	2.95	.065	n.s.
Mental Demand	Train.	**4.33**	**.025**	**.274**	**12.0**	**<.00**	**.394**
	Test	0.09	.915	n.s.	1.37	.267	n.s.
Anxiety	Train.	0.60	.556	n.s.	**4.33**	**.020**	**.190**
	Test	0.80	.460	n.s.	0.14	.874	n.s.
Map	Train.	0.33	.725	n.s.	0.22	.800	n.s.
Time	Train.	**12.4**	**<.001**	**.529**	**26.6**	**<.00**	**.596**
	Test	0.33	.723	n.s.	1.02	.369	n.s.
Distance Travelled	Train.	**25.2**	**<.001**	**.696**	**57.2**	**<.00**	**.761**
	Test	1.34	.292	n.s.	0.57	.571	n.s.
Routes Completed	Train.	**8.29**	**.002**	**.430**	**16.5**	**<.00**	**.478**
	Test	0.16	.851	n.s.	0.57	.573	n.s.
Map Time	Train.	**6.64**	**.006**	**.376**	**12.9**	**<.00**	**.418**
Landmark ID	Test	0.21	.815	n.s.	0.22	.801	n.s.
LM Conf.	Test	0.42	.662	n.s.	0.04	.959	n.s.
Scene ID	Test	0.54	.591	n.s.	1.99	.152	n.s.
Scene Conf.	Test	0.13	.883	n.s.	0.17	.841	n.s.
Route Est.	Test	0.32	.730	n.s.	0.48	.241	n.s.

Table 1. MANCOVA results for the effects of assistance on the subjective and objective measures for the training session and testing session.

Summary of Results

The findings from Study 2 mirror the findings from Study 1, with the additional result that anxiety during training was higher without assistance. As Figures 7 and 8 show, the longer training period did not substantially change any of our subjective or performance measures.

DISCUSSION

Summary of Results

Our expectation, based on the guidance and retrieval-effort hypotheses, was that increased navigation effort in training would result in better spatial understanding of the map, and thus better performance during testing. However, this did not occur in either study. Although it was clear that both kinds of navigation assistance helped when they were present, we found no differences in route-finding performance when assists were removed, and no difference in spatial-knowledge questions (regardless of the duration of the training period – 16 or 48 routes). The lack of differences across assistance level is even more surprising given that the overall time in the game world for the no-assistance group was approximately double that of the strong assistance group, and 1.5 times that of the moderate group. In addition, navigation assistance improved subjective experience. When assistance was taken away during the testing session, the differences between assistance groups disappeared.

Possible Explanations for Results

There are several possible reasons why navigation assistance did not hinder route-finding performance once the assists were removed. First, it may be that incidental learning took place during training (as suggested by previous work [2,23]), even though the navigation tasks were made easier by the assistance. One mechanism for this incidental learning could be that the assistance reduced the cognitive effort of the task to the point where players could pay more attention to their surroundings. We believe it is important that players still experienced the entire route and participated in traversing it, even though they were assisted – if the assist had taken the player out of the route (e.g., by teleporting them to the destination), the opportunity for incidental learning would have been much reduced.

A second (and related) possibility is that spatial learning was somehow hindered by the no-assistance condition. It is possible, for example, that the tasks were so difficult for novices that they were outside Vygotsky's "zone of proximal development" where people learn best [49] (similar to the "flow state" in Kiili's learning model [29]). Players in the no-assist condition may have been unable to learn the maps effectively because they were overwhelmed by the basic actions of locating themselves on the map, recognizing landmarks, and understanding the relationships between the pop-up map and the first-person view of the game world.

Implications for Game Designers

The use of assistance did not have a significantly negative effect on performance in the test tasks – even despite the large differences in training time. This finding has intriguing consequences for utilizing route guidance as an assistance technique in games.

Skill Development Considerations

Some games are better candidates for navigational assistance than others. There are many games that require players to operate in the same environment many times, so players must become familiar with the maps if they want to succeed.

Skill assists have been investigated previously to improve player balancing [7,48], but a common concern is that providing assistance will result in player reliance. Our results add to increasing evidence that some degree of assistance does not necessarily reduce learning. For example, Gutwin et al. [20] found that providing aim assistance to novices did not hinder the development of either aiming skill or overall FPS abilities. When games require many skills, providing assistance in one area (and thus reducing effort overall) can allow players to improve in other areas. For example, navigation assistance in an FPS game could free the player to work on skills such as aiming, movement, or monitoring audiovisual cues [27].

It is even possible that providing dynamic skill assistance can enhance learning. Kiili's [29] experiential gaming model proposes that a balanced game that facilitates the player reaching a flow state will result in the strongest learning. This corresponds to Anderson and Bischof's suggestion that guidance gradually be removed as a learner gains expertise [1]. Gradual removal of the assist would also reduce the sharp drop in experience measures that we observed between training and testing.

There are still likely to be cases in which providing a strong assist for a particular skill results in a dependency on the assist. Further research is required to determine when and where this effect appears.

Implementation Considerations

We chose our assistance techniques because they are already used extensively in games. The augmented (moderate-assistance) map works if the player has time to study it, and the glowing trail works if the destination is known to the system. The trail allowed participants to reach a higher level of performance in less time than the augmented map, so it may be worthwhile to consider implementing it in more games. In games where destinations are not known (or where there are many possible destinations), it is not clear how well this method will work.

Assistance could be made context-sensitive: for example, if a player has no weapons or is low on health, the game could show a trail to the nearest weapon or the nearest health pack. A player's role in a team game could also determine which routes are visualized for that player (e.g., a trail to a wounded player for a medic role). Finally, for scenarios in which navigational assistance is not possible, or where the player chooses to turn off the aids [12,38], it appears that the use of even strong assistance early in a player's experience will not significantly affect their long-term performance.

CONCLUSIONS AND FUTURE WORK

3D game navigation is difficult for novices. Games can provide visual assistance for wayfinding, but there is a risk that players will become overly reliant on these assists and fail to develop independent spatial understanding. We investigated the benefits and potential risks of navigation assistance through two online studies. We found that having assistance helped significantly when it was turned on – and when it was turned off, navigation performance did *not* suffer. This work provides new evidence that navigation assistance is a valuable tool to help novices deal with the complexities of 3D games, and that incidental learning of 3D game environments can occur, even with strong assistance.

In our future work, we plan to examine several issues raised by our experiments. First, we will look in more detail at whether navigation assistance acts as a scaffold that can improve learning (by putting players in a flow zone or zone of proximal development). Second, we will test other kinds of navigation assistance and other game environments to see if our results hold in different settings. Third, we will develop versions of the assist that gradually disappear, to see if this further improves spatial knowledge. Fourth, we will test our techniques in actual play settings, to see if navigation assistance can improve play experience and player balancing in real games.

REFERENCES

1. Fraser Anderson and Walter F Bischof. 2013. Learning and Performance with Gesture Guides. In *Proceedings of the SIGCHI Conference on Human Factors in Computing Systems* (CHI '13), 1109–1118. https://doi.org/10.1145/2470654.2466143
2. Jackie Andrade and Peter Meudell. 1993. Short report: Is spatial information encoded automatically in memory? *The Quarterly Journal of Experimental Psychology Section A* 46, 2: 365–375. https://doi.org/10.1080/14640749308401051
3. Anthony J Aretz and Christopher D Wickens. 1992. The Mental Rotation of Map Displays. *Human Performance* 5, 4: 303–328. https://doi.org/10.1207/s15327043hup0504_3
4. Marieke van Asselen, Eva Fritschy, and Albert Postma. 2005. The influence of intentional and incidental learning on acquiring spatial knowledge during navigation. *Psychological Research Psychologische Forschung* 70, 2: 151–156. https://doi.org/10.1007/s00426-004-0199-0
5. Bethesda Game Studios. 2011. *The Elder Scrolls V: Skyrim*. Bethesda Softworks.
6. Gary E Burnett and Kate Lee. 2005. The Effect of Vehicle Navigation Systems on the Formation of Cognitive Maps. In *Traffic and Transport Psychology*. Elsevier, 407–418. https://doi.org/10.1016/b978-008044379-9/50188-6
7. Jared E Cechanowicz, Carl Gutwin, Scott Bateman, Regan Mandryk, and Ian Stavness. 2014. Improving player balancing in racing games. In *Proceedings of the first ACM SIGCHI annual symposium on Computer-human interaction in play - CHI PLAY '14*. https://doi.org/10.1145/2658537.2658701
8. William G Chase. 1983. Spatial Representations of Taxi Drivers. In *The Acquisition of Symbolic Skills*. Springer US, 391–405. https://doi.org/10.1007/978-1-4613-3724-9_43
9. Chien-Hsiung Chen, Wen-Chih Chang, and Wen-Te Chang. 2009. Gender differences in relation to wayfinding strategies, navigational support design, and wayfinding task difficulty. *Journal of environmental psychology* 29, 2: 220–226.
10. Jenova Chen. 2007. Flow in games (and everything else). *Communications of the ACM* 50, 4: 31–34. https://doi.org/10.1145/1232743.1232769
11. Jui Lin Chen and Kay M Stanney. 1999. A Theoretical Model of Wayfinding in Virtual Environments: Proposed Strategies for Navigational Aiding. *Presence: Teleoperators and Virtual Environments* 8, 6: 671–685. https://doi.org/10.1162/105474699566558
12. CherrySlurpee. 2016. CMV: Quest markers are one of the worst things to ever happen to video games, and they're ruining the concept of immersion. *Reddit*. Retrieved April 12, 2017 from www.reddit.com/r/changemyview/comments/4nnt79/cmv_quest_markers_are_one_of_the_worst_things_to/
13. Cryptic Studios. 2013. *Neverwinter*. Perfect World Entertainment.
14. Mihaly Csikszentmihalyi. 2000. *Beyond boredom and anxiety*. Jossey-Bass.
15. Rudolph P Darken and John L Sibert. 1996. Wayfinding Strategies and Behaviors in Large Virtual Worlds. In *Proceedings of the SIGCHI Conference on Human Factors in Computing Systems* (CHI '96), 142–149. https://doi.org/10.1145/238386.238459
16. Rudolph P Darken and John L Sibert. 1996. Navigating large virtual spaces. *International Journal of Human-Computer Interaction* 8, 1: 49–71.
17. Rudolph Darken and Barry Peterson. 2014. Spatial Orientation, Wayfinding, and Representation. In *Handbook of Virtual Environments*. CRC Press, 467–491. https://doi.org/10.1201/b17360-24
18. Brian D Ehret. 2002. Learning where to look. In *Proceedings of the SIGCHI conference on Human factors in computing systems Changing our world, changing ourselves - CHI '02*. https://doi.org/10.1145/503376.503414
19. James Paul Gee. 2004. Learning by design: Games as learning machines. *Interactive Educational Multimedia*, 8: 15–23.
20. Carl Gutwin, Rodrigo Vicencio-Moreira, and Regan L Mandryk. 2016. Does Helping Hurt?: Aiming Assistance and Skill Development in a First-Person Shooter Game. In *Proceedings of the 2016 Annual Symposium on Computer-Human Interaction in Play*, 338–349. https://doi.org/10.1145/2967934.2968101
21. Douglas A Hardwick, Curtis W McIntyre, and Herbert L Pick. 1976. The Content and Manipulation of Cognitive Maps in Children and Adults. *Monographs of the Society for Research in Child Development* 41, 3: 1. https://doi.org/10.2307/1165952
22. Sandra G Hart and Lowell E Staveland. 1988. Development of NASA-TLX (Task Load Index): Results of empirical and theoretical research. *Advances in psychology* 52: 139–183.
23. Lynn Hasher and Rose T Zacks. 1979. Automatic and effortful processes in memory. *Journal of Experimental Psychology: General* 108, 3: 356–388. https://doi.org/10.1037/0096-3445.108.3.356
24. Hidden Path Entertainment and Valve Corporation. 2012. *Counter-Strike: Global Offensive*. Valve

Corporation.

25. id Software. 2010. *Quake Live*. Bethesda Softworks.

26. Toru Ishikawa, Hiromichi Fujiwara, Osamu Imai, and Atsuyuki Okabe. 2008. Wayfinding with a GPS-based mobile navigation system: A comparison with maps and direct experience. *Journal of Environmental Psychology* 28, 1: 74–82. https://doi.org/10.1016/j.jenvp.2007.09.002

27. Colby Johanson and Regan L Mandryk. 2016. Scaffolding Player Location Awareness through Audio Cues in First-Person Shooters. In *Proceedings of the 2016 CHI Conference on Human Factors in Computing Systems*, 3450–3461. https://doi.org/10.1145/2858036.2858172

28. Susanne Jul and George W Furnas. 1997. Navigation in electronic worlds. *ACM SIGCHI Bulletin* 29, 4: 44–49. https://doi.org/10.1145/270950.270979

29. Kristian Kiili. 2005. Digital game-based learning: Towards an experiential gaming model. *The Internet and higher education* 8, 1: 13–24.

30. D A Kolb. 1984. Experiential learning: experience as the source of learning and development.

31. Raph Koster. 2013. *Theory of fun for game design*. O'Reilly Media, Inc.

32. Carol A Lawton and Janos Kallai. 2002. Gender differences in wayfinding strategies and anxiety about wayfinding: A cross-cultural comparison. *Sex Roles* 47, 9–10: 389–401.

33. Gilly Leshed, Theresa Velden, Oya Rieger, Blazej Kot, and Phoebe Sengers. 2008. In-Car GPS Navigation: Engagement with and Disengagement from the Environment. In *Proceeding of the twenty-sixth annual CHI conference on Human factors in computing systems - CHI '08*. https://doi.org/10.1145/1357054.1357316

34. Lionhead Studios. 2008. *Fable II*. Microsoft Game Studios.

35. I Scott MacKenzie. 2012. *Human-computer interaction: An empirical research perspective*. Newnes.

36. Theresa M Marteau and Hilary Bekker. 1992. The development of a six-item short-form of the state scale of the Spielberger State—Trait Anxiety Inventory (STAI). *British Journal of Clinical Psychology* 31, 3: 301–306.

37. Winter Mason and Siddharth Suri. 2012. Conducting behavioral research on Amazon's Mechanical Turk. *Behavior research methods* 44, 1: 1–23.

38. Felipe Pepe. 2016. The history of the Quest Compass & its dreadful convenience. *Gamasutra*. Retrieved April 12, 2017 from http://www.gamasutra.com/blogs/FelipePepe/20160412/270100/The_history_of_the_Quest_Compass__its_dreadful_convenience.php

39. Mary A Pyc and Katherine A Rawson. 2009. Testing the retrieval effort hypothesis: Does greater difficulty correctly recalling information lead to higher levels of memory? *Journal of Memory and Language* 60, 4: 437–447. https://doi.org/10.1016/j.jml.2009.01.004

40. Alan W Salmoni, Richard A Schmidt, and Charles B Walter. 1984. Knowledge of results and motor learning: a review and critical reappraisal. *Psychological bulletin* 95, 3: 355.

41. Richard A Schmidt, Douglas E Young, Stephan Swinnen, and Diane C Shapiro. 1989. Summary knowledge of results for skill acquisition: support for the guidance hypothesis. *Journal of Experimental Psychology: Learning, Memory, and Cognition* 15, 2: 352.

42. Splash Damage. 2003. *Wolfenstein: Enemy Territory*. Activision.

43. John Sweller. 1988. Cognitive Load During Problem Solving: Effects on Learning. *Cognitive Science* 12, 2: 257–285. https://doi.org/10.1207/s15516709cog1202_4

44. The Fable Wiki. 2012. Glowing Trail. *Wikia*. Retrieved April 12, 2017 from http://fable.wikia.com/wiki//Glowing_Trail

45. Perry W Thorndyke and Sarah E Goldin. 1983. Spatial Learning and Reasoning Skill. In *Spatial Orientation*. Springer {US}, 195–217. https://doi.org/10.1007/978-1-4615-9325-6_9

46. Perry W Thorndyke and Barbara Hayes-Roth. 1982. Differences in spatial knowledge acquired from maps and navigation. *Cognitive Psychology* 14, 4: 560–589. https://doi.org/10.1016/0010-0285(82)90019-6

47. Perry W Thorndyke and Cathleen Stasz. 1980. Individual differences in procedures for knowledge acquisition from maps. *Cognitive Psychology* 12, 1: 137–175. https://doi.org/10.1016/0010-0285(80)90006-7

48. Rodrigo Vicencio-Moreira, Regan L Mandryk, and Carl Gutwin. 2015. Now You Can Compete With Anyone: Balancing Players of Different Skill Levels in a First-Person Shooter Game. In *Proceedings of the 33rd Annual ACM Conference on Human Factors in Computing Systems* (CHI '15), 2255–2264. https://doi.org/10.1145/2702123.2702242

49. Lev Vygotsky. Interaction between learning and development. *Readings on the development of children* 23, 3: 34–41.

50. Szymon Walkowiak, Tom Foulsham, and Alison F Eardley. 2015. Individual differences and personality

correlates of navigational performance in the virtual route learning task. *Computers in Human Behavior* 45: 402–410.

51. David Waller, Earl Hunt, and David Knapp. 1998. The Transfer of Spatial Knowledge in Virtual Environment Training. *Presence: Teleoperators and Virtual Environments* 7, 2: 129–143. https://doi.org/10.1162/105474698565631

52. Jane Webster, Linda Klebe Trevino, and Lisa Ryan. 1994. The dimensionality and correlates of flow in human-computer interactions. *Computers in human behavior* 9, 4: 411–426.

53. Bob G Witmer and Michael J Singer. 1998. Measuring presence in virtual environments: A presence questionnaire. *Presence: Teleoperators and virtual environments* 7, 3: 225–240.

54. WoWWiki. 2016. Quest. *Wikia.* Retrieved April 12, 2017 from http://wowwiki.wikia.com/wiki/Quest

A Game of Research: Information Management and Decision-making in Daily Fantasy Sports

Donghee Yvette Wohn
New Jersey Institute of Technology
Newark, NJ, USA
wohn@njit.edu

Emma J. Freeman
New Jersey Institute of Technology
Newark, NJ, USA
ejw1887@njit.edu

Katherine J. Quehl
Yahoo!
Sunnyvale, CA, USA
katiequehl@yahoo-inc.com

ABSTRACT
In this study, we interviewed players of daily fantasy sports to understand their information management and decision-making behaviors. Due to the rapid cycle of decision-making that is required to play daily fantasy sports, we found that participants engaged in sophisticated and complex methods of information compilation and evaluation, using a wide range of digital and analog tools to help them organize vast amounts of information in a short amount of time. We contribute an account of these practices along with suggestions on how to further improve daily fantasy sports products.

Author Keywords
Fantasy sports; information seeking; decision making; daily fantasy

ACM Classification Keywords
H.5.m. Information interfaces and presentation (e.g., HCI): Miscellaneous; H.3.3 Information Search and Retrieval: Selection process

INTRODUCTION
Fantasy sports is a social game of skill [7] where participants create virtual teams based on real professional sports players. The performance of the virtual team depends on the statistical performance of the real players in actual sports games. The objective of the fantasy game is to build a virtual team that has the best performance out of a group of individuals competing with one another in leagues [27].

People compete with others at a distance to see who has the best team in a variety of different gameplay styles [27]. In some cases, the competitors all know one another and are part of a private, invite only contest. Other contests and leagues are public and open for anyone with an interest in playing. Each contest has rules, deadlines for completing certain activates, and different layouts of how wining or prizes are determined.

CHI PLAY '17, October 15-18, 2017, Amsterdam, Netherlands

ACM ISBN 978-1-4503-4898-0/17/10...$15.00
https://doi.org/10.1145/3116595.3116605

Fantasy sports players need information to help them make decisions as they play the game. This information used to be hard to obtain because it was primarily available in newspapers and specialty magazines, but the Internet has made it easier for people to have access to this information [18]. Moreover, being able to play with others online has helped increase the popularity of this sport [32].

Daily Fantasy Sports (DFS) is a relatively new form of fantasy sports game play. DFS requires people create their fantasy teams on a frequent and short-term basis to win prizes, but little is known about their decision-making process for creating team line-ups. One of the main differences separating daily from the traditional seasonal fantasy is the turnaround time on investment. Because DFS players have to make so many decisions within a short timeframe, their process of information seeking, organization, and decision-making could be very different from players of season-long fantasy sports. This makes DFS a unique context for HCI gaming research, because players play within a social system, yet have to use information resources outside of the system to inform their gaming behavior.

In this paper, we ask three key research questions aimed at understanding how people undergo this decision making process in the context of daily fantasy sports: *How do people decide which players to choose for their line-up? What resources—both social and informational—are used to make these decisions? What types of technology are used in the process?*

The contribution of this work provides insight into how people make short-term financial decisions on constantly-evolving events through their information seeking behaviors. The results also provide a set of design guidelines for online DFS services to best support their products.

ABOUT FANTASY SPORTS
The first public fantasy league was introduced in 1969 by Andy Mousalimas, who was the founder of the Greater Oakland Professional Pigskin Prognosticators League (GOPPPL) in 1963 which started the first drafting of players into a league [24]. The baseball fantasy league was started in the 1980's by sportswriter Daniel Okrent in a Manhattan restaurant named La Rotisserie Francaise which

led to the naming of the first fantasy league "rotisserie league baseball" [24].

In 1988 it was reported by "USA Today" that the participation had grown to an estimated 500,000 players [37]. In 1997 the first two Internet fantasy sites, RotoNews.com and Commissioner.com, were launched and the new favorite past time took off and running. In 2007, Chris Fargis, a professional poker player, introduced the first daily fantasy sports format through his blog called Instant Fantasy Sport [38].

Since the beginning of online fantasy leagues the number of fantasy sports participants has risen dramatically from 500,000 in 1988 to approximately 56.8 million as of 2015 according to the Fantasy Sports Trade Association [16]. According to the trade association's 2015 research it has been found that 66% of general fantasy sports participants are male; the average age is 37; and the primary fantasy sport played is football [16]. The survey also found that the number of players who play some form of daily fantasy sports has increased from 31% in 2012 to 64% in 2015, and one of the contributing factors to the growth in fantasy sports is the ability to manage teams from mobile phones. There are a variety of DFS providers including FanDuel, DraftKings, and Yahoo Fantasy Sports.

Based on work within the HCI field on gaming, fantasy sports may classified as a type of pervasive game play [22] or more broadly, pervasive play as it involves "technology-mediated, playful experiences that are interwoven throughout our everyday lives and the physical and virtual spaces we inhabit"[1]. By leveraging real-world events during sporting events, fantasy sports augments through gameplay, similar to games such as Augmented Reality Games (ARG), or Live Action Role Playing (LARP) game genres. In addition to being a pervasive game, other research has categorized fantasy sports as a type of data-driven prediction game in which data sets are used to inform playful and social interactions [12]. These categories of game play are not mutually exclusive; rather, both support and capture the multifaceted fantasy sports experience as a form of an online community. We situate our work in game research as a part of the of practice paradigm of game research, focusing on "experience and consequent interactions between users that occur as a result of interaction with the game, or as a result of entering a lusory attitude." [9]

Motivations for Playing Fantasy Sports

The motivation for playing fantasy sports crosses interdisciplinary boundaries. Dwyer and Kim [10] were able to validate three motivational dimensions: entertainment/escape, competition and social interaction. Entertainment consisted of enjoying the game play was a fun way to pass time. Escape was a motivation by using fantasy sports as a way to mentally take a break from daily rituals such as work, school, or other personal responsibilities. Social interactions in fantasy sports supported creating and maintain relationships with others through game play. Finally, those who found motivation in the competitive aspects of Fantasy Sports were driven by the need to both win and be seen as the best by his or her competitors [10].

Billings and Ruihley have conducted a series of sociologically-based studies around the motivations for playing season-long fantasy sports [4,28,29]. In their research, they identified motivations including enjoyment, arousal, escaping daily life, passing time, information seeking, fanship, demonstrating sports knowledge, helping others find information, and self-esteem.

Another study conducted by Farquhar and Meeds [15] on motivations of fantasy sports usage found additional categories of motivation to be more influential. Although entertainment/escape, competition, and social interaction were factors in motivating fantasy usage, surveillance and arousal were judged to be more important motivating qualities. Surveillance includes the process of gathering information, working with statistical data, and staying closely connected with real-world sports. Arousal motivates users to participate in fantasy sport gameplay for the trill of pursing the next big victory.

By analyzing these motivational factors among fantasy sports players, the researchers [15] developed a framework of types of players. The three most prevalent player types include 1) *Casual Players* who invest less time, money, and effort into fantasy sports, but enjoy the game for fun; 2) *Skilled players* who invest a large amount of time, money, and energy into fantasy sports (high levels of surveillance) and who feel a sense of accomplishment the more they invest into the game (arousal); and 3) *isolationist thrill-seekers* who have a high level of arousal for winning, but don't want to put in as much of the surveillance work required.

These qualities of entertainment, competition, social involvement, surveillance, and arousal all contribute to reasons why sports enthusiasts are motivated to augment their sports watching habits with fantasy sports and provide evidence that suggests that fantasy sports is a complex game that involves viewing, information gathering, and decision making, financial investment, and entertainment.

Daily Fantasy Sports

Daily Fantasy Sports is a rather recent way to participate in fantasy sports on a daily or weekend basis versus an entire season like the traditional season-long leagues. The first DFS providers began gaining traction in 2010 and have continued to grow. Building a virtual team is referred to as "crafting" or "drafting" a lineup. The ability to create/draft lineups daily and the nightly turnaround time on entry results seem to be drawing people away from the seasonal leagues over to the daily fantasy sites [26]. There are several key differences between traditional fantasy sports and daily fantasy sports. With DFS, you see quick results from your games that are played on a daily (or sometimes weekly) basis as opposed to waiting until the end of the season, which lasts multiple months. With DFS, you have the opportunity to draft a new lineup everyday versus having a lineup that is drafted at the start of the season for the entire season with very little room for trades or changes.

The second difference is social dynamics of leagues compared to contests. In leagues, individuals get to know one another through the routine interactions they have across the longer duration of time. There is a consistency in social interactions. With DFS, the competitors may or may not continue to participate each week. Also, DFS is more likely to be played against strangers than with leagues which often include friends, coworkers, and family members.

There is also a major monetary difference in league and DFS. In many cases, individuals will pay entry fees into fantasy sports contests or leagues. The winner of fantasy sports (or the top several placers) will receive a payout based on their performance. Full-season fantasy sports usually provides this compensation at the end of several months of gameplay. However, those playing DFS receive their prizes immediately after their short contest of a day or week. This provides more opportunities to win prizes, as well as more immediate returns on their entry fee, when applicable.

Although motivational factors may not differ between traditional and daily participants, the two types of fantasy play influence different media consumption, monetary commitments, and perception of fantasy game play [5]. DFS sports participants are significantly more likely to consume more fantasy sports media. Additionally, participants who played DFS are more likely to consider a higher proportion of their ability to win to be based on skill rather than chance. In part, this was due to investing into research efforts for selecting lineups.

DECISION MAKING

Shipman [32] has called for the HCI community to further study fantasy sports (which we specifically extend to DFS) as a means of understanding how entertainment-based domains focused in bridging the virtual and physical worlds are mediated by our devices, especially in terms of active and passive engagement with sporting events . One such way DFS supports active engagement between these two spaces is through making decisions as part of game play.

DFS, like traditional fantasy sports, relies on choosing sports players to create virtual teams, which are called lineups. There is an abundant amount of factors that lead people to these decisions, and oftentimes the choices involve conflict because there are too many variables [25].

Decision Support Systems (DSS), defined as interactive and technologically-mediated systems designed to support handling and management of large amounts of data to support and improve a decision process [2], have been studied in HCI in a variety of contexts including eSports, investment decision making [3,6,17,36]. Although DFS players may be pulling from different source, little is known about how they create adhoc DSS to help manage their lineups.

In the world of fantasy sports there is a plethora of both professional and collegiate sports to select from and a variety of fantasy sites that offer opportunities to experience different levels of participation as a team member in a league or as an individual contestant. The research on decision-making processes in season-long fantasy sports indicates that it is a complicated process that involves much data and data analysis [11,18].

Despite its popularity, research on fantasy sports is lacking in general [27], and with very few studies within the HCI community, but there are even more limitations on DFS studies, a relatively new genre. While DFS shares many attributes with season-long fantasy sports, the shorter daily timeframe creates a unique situation where those playing DFS need to make decisions about their lineup in shorter intervals, giving people very little time to ponder over their choices. With a limited timeframe, it is very likely that DFS players rely on heuristics to make their decisions [35]. Heuristic decision-making is different from rational decision-making in that the former is unable to make a comprehensive assessment of the factors at play due to cognitive limitations such as time and money.

Studies on full-season fantasy have shown that players focus on various attributes of the athlete [33], but it is unknown what factors influence daily fantasy sports players. Our first research question thus inquiries into understanding what informs and supports DFS players when they are putting together their lineups:

RQ1: What factors influence how people decide how to build their lineup?

INFORMATION MANAGEMENT BEHAVIORS

Several studies have explored the ways in which users seek and manage their information for leisure activities [14,19], or in everyday life [31]. However, most of the literature around fantasy sports has been within media studies, sociology, or sports marketing [18]. For DFS, more research has been conducted in the legal domain.

DFS has been criticized and is banned in certain states in the United States for being a form of gambling [20]. DFS has been the focus of a recent debate on if the model of gameplay and Daily Contests is considered a form of gaming due to some contests having an entry fee and prize model. Recent court decisions have ruled is a game of skill and exempt under the 2006 Unlawful Internet Gambling Enforcement act. While there is some degree of luck is associated with any sporting contest, in order to consistently do well in fantasy sports, players must have knowledge about the sport and the players involved. A fantasy sports user creating a lineup must have skill and knowledge of the professional players and understand the factors influencing their performance during games. As such, this skill and the knowledge is what drives the ability to win, rather than just luck, and is considered a game of skill and requires a deep understanding of sport.

Since the performance of DFS relies on the performance of actual sports players, some of that performance can be predicted through probability (statistics based on past performance) even though there will always be unforeseen chance factors that influence the outcome.

Because some proportion of future performance can be predicted by past performance, many DFS players engage in research. In particular, within the HCI community, Dzodom and Shipman [11] found full-season fantasy sports players struggle to find any given source to satisfy their information seeking needs and therefore use a variety of sources to gather and manage data informing their fantasy decisions, with over half of their survey respondents using 5 of more data sources to triangulate data.

Hirsh et al. [18] also found that players used multiple sources when playing season-long fantasy NASCAR and Football. In their research players often searched for different information based on stage of the season (i.e. drafting, game day, playoffs), and found that information seeking needs varied by task, but called for additional research on broadening the type of fantasy sports included which we aim to accomplish through researching DFS.

According to Eilers Research's *Daily Fantasy Sports Player Survey-2015*, most players spent between 10-20 hours a week doing research and RotoGrinders was the preferred research site [21]. According to RotoGrinders' website, they provide fantasy sports content, member blogs, player rankings, and discussion forums. On this site fantasy sports participants can sign up for a free or premium account. The site offers the utilization of research tools, some are free and others have fees, to aid in creating one or more lineup options across multiple sports and/or multiple fantasy sites. Under their DFS Alerts a participant can filter through all or specific sports alerts (i.e. MLB, NFL, NBA) using the desired tab of all, urgent, important and noteworthy; by doing this the participant is able to obtain updated information regarding players that they may be drafting for current and upcoming games.

Eighmey and McCord [13] were able to establish the importance of website organization and design as factors that drew consumers to become repeat visitors websites. By studying participants' usage across multi-media platforms it was found that the top uses and gratifications dimensions were entertainment and information.

Nadelson, et. al [23] found that participants engaged in "heutagogy" (self-determined learning). This type of information seeking is not lead by a set list of rules or instructions, it is free flowing according to the user. This process is seen when fantasy sports participants are deciding on which fantasy sites to participate on; which sites are trustworthy and which sites hold the most informational value. The fantasy sport player makes the determination on the path they are going to follow during their information seeking periods. The participants retrieve this information from multiple entities and make the final determination on what information is pertinent to their lineups.

Taking a sense-making approach [30] by focusing on a user-centered approach to information use, our study examined the amount of time spent collecting data, exactly what participants are researching, how they are conducting this research and why they do the research.

RQ2: What methods are being used to gather the information?

RQ3: What methods are being used to organize information?

METHOD

Recruiting Method

For our study we posted a short survey on Mechanical Turk that offered participants $1 for completing the survey and the opportunity to volunteer for interviews. Participants that wanted to volunteer for the interviews provided their email information at the end of the survey. When the survey period was closed 87 out of the 323 completed participants had volunteered; emails were sent out to participants to schedule interviews. From multiple rounds of emails sent, 14 out of 87 actually participated in the interview sessions. These participants were considered to be low spenders since more than half of them entered contests for free and out of the paying participants, $20 was the highest paid entry fee. Since we were looking for a broader spectrum of player behavior additional emails were sent out to Yahoo! Sports VIPs through a contact at Yahoo! who was unrelated to this research. In total we conducted 21 interviews where each participant was compensated in the form of a $20 gift card upon completion of the interview.

Interviews lasted from 30-45 minutes and were audio recorded with the participants' permission. The recordings were transcribed by three research assistants and double-checked for accuracy by the primary researchers. Thematic analysis [8] of the transcripts was used to develop the themes for each of our research questions.

Participant Demographics

In our study we had a total of 21 participants that were interviewed: 18 male and three female with an age range of 18 to 52. Participants were from both urban and rural regions across the United States, but mostly White in terms of ethnicity. Aside from one participant who played DFS professionally, all participants had jobs that were not related to DFS or sports. We asked them about all of the daily fantasy they played, but the interviews took place during American football season, so most of the questions focused on the context of daily fantasy football.

Participant	Sex	Age	Ethnicity	Duration playing DFS
James	M	35	White	2 years
Hector	M	44	Hispanic	25 years
Derrick	M	52	Black	4 years
Joshua	M	37	Hispanic	3 years
Luke	M	29	White	2 years
Mark	M	26	White	2 years
Peter	M	38	Mixed	10 years
Penny	F	47	White	2-3 years
Sheldon	M	35	White	3 years
Leonard	M	36	White	3-4 years
Howard	M	32	White	3 years
Stuart	M	18	White	1 month
Felix	M	24	White	2 years
Paul	M	25	Black	3 years
Donnie	M	33	White	10 years
Sarah	F	40	White	2 years
Arthur	M	49	White	2.5 years
Vic	M	34	White	2 years
Helena	F	35	White	1 year
Rollin	M	28	White	2 years
Castor	M	40	White	14-15 years

Table 1. Participant Demographics and Duration of Fantasy Sports Participation

RESULTS

General Characteristics of Players

In our study participants averaged between 5-30 hours a week conducting research to inform their lineup selections. The leading "research sites" were DFS sites, ESPN.com, Yahoo, and NFL.com. Mobile phones and laptops tied as the top devices used during their research periods, followed by tablets and desktops. The top mobile applications used were NFL and ESPN. One-third of the participants said that they receive notifications from their apps.

The top four DFS sites used by our participants were FanDuel, DraftKings, Yahoo!Sports, and SportsLine. Their entry fees spanned between $0-$5,000, though most participants spent under $20. Some of the other DFS sites that the participants frequented were: RotoViz, FootballOutsiders.com, ProFootballFocus.com, NumberFire.com, DailyFantasySportsRanking.com and NFLToday.com.

When speaking with the participants of our study, the majority stated they gained a broader experience with the sport that they were participating in. It was an added form of entertainment beyond the games that also gave the possibility of monetary gain. The participants stated that through daily fantasy sports they were able to gain a better appreciation for the sport and the players through the research they conducted prior to drafting players to their lineups.

Penny, a 47 year-old female that has been playing DFS for about 3 years, talked about how playing changed the sport for her:

> *"I think it actually gets me a little more excited as well for the game which makes watching it more fun. I do think it's a really great tool for teaching people about the game and how it works. So that's probably the most fun that I've had with it, learning about the game."*

Castor, a 40 year-old male has been playing daily and seasonal fantasy for a total of 15 years, pointed out how participating changed his outlook on sports:

> *"It's made me more appreciative and more aware than I was before in general... it's given me a better appreciation of how the game itself has evolved, not only from when I started playing fantasy sports, but how it's have changed from then to now. Even more so it's allowed me to appreciate players from other teams, other conferences and other players."*

Factors That Influence Lineup Decision-Making

Our first research question was asking about what factors influence how people decide how to build their lineup. While talking to the participants of our study we were able to see different types of factors that would drive a daily fantasy sports player to the selections that they make regarding their team lineups and site selections. Some of these factors, such as player statistics, were those already documented in the literature of traditional (season-long) fantasy sports, but others were less intuitive.

Player information (background, injuries, past performance)

Participants discussed about how different aspects of the player's background and performance influence their decisions. All participants were interested to a certain extent in objective facts related to players, such as statistics, how long they have been playing, what teams they've been on, or injury reports.

For example, Howard said that when debating with himself what player to choose, he would first go to the news, then look at player statistics before making a decision.

Similarly, Hector said:

> *"I'm looking for, you know, any type of information that could help me; from the players going up against an untested player, or there's been an injury in a key position that might help a player that's going up against that particular defense."*

While all participants relied on some numerical form of player statistics to inform their choices, those who had been playing DFS for several years or more had more elaborate, established routines that were formulaic and developed over a long period of time, based on longitudinal information. These routines were like *heuristic sequences*, in which participants had a mental model of "do this first, then this, then that."

These heuristic sequences were best exemplified by Castor, who said that he uses what he calls a "three-two system" for selecting his players. He first looks at who is still available to draft and then weighs them against who they are competing against that week. If it looks like the match will be close he goes to what he calls "task performers" who have great overall records or pick from his favorite team—in his case, the New York Giants.

Soft Traits and Personal Life

While objective facts played a major, if not the biggest role in decision-making, we noticed that participants also relied on subjective factors that may seem not directly related to physical performance. A few participants looked at "soft" characteristics of the athletes, such as drama in their personal life, perceived personality, or an emotional connection.

Peter is an avid fantasy sports player since his days in the military and he makes it a point to know his players and who they are involved with romantically, as he states it bleeds over into their professional careers. He gave the example of basketball player James Harden dating reality television star Khloe Kardashian:

> *"So for instance, people would say James Harden, very good basketball player but the reason why I stay away from him while drafting him is because he's dating a Kardashian... He's a good player, but he's one dimensional... and taken even more of a hit ever since he's been with 'that'. So you kind of have to look up certain things to see how it's affecting the player."*

Helena, a 35 year-old woman who has been playing DFS for 1 year, said, "Of course I look at the stats as far as wins versus losses, but also other things like their demeanor on the field, personalities, if I can find that information; um, you know, like their style of playing or style of teamwork." She went on to state that if she's spending a lot of time doing the research, she wants to feel an emotional connection with the players: "I mean it's like which one resonates with me; which ones do I feel are closer to; or that I feel are the ones that would be interesting for me to follow."

Two participants discussed about how they took a long-term approach to identify potentially good athletes—sometimes even years in advance—by focusing on personality. For example, Mark said he constantly looked for athletes who did not do well but had traits that he thought would make them perform better in the future:

> *"[There is] value in the lower end player... generally everyone knows who the best players in the league are so I'm trying to find the underdog so when they perform well the public won't see that coming. Like a more psychological approach to it rather than just statistical."*

Peter stated that he becomes familiar with the players before they even reach professional status by watching college sports to see how they perform in their positions. Through this, he stated that he is looking at "somebody's tendencies; how they are in the team."

Simulations

Multiple participants mentioned using statistical programs or websites to test-run their lineups. Leonard is a 36 year-old male that has been playing DFS for about 4 years. He said that uses a simulation site called DailyFantasyMirror, which he described as a "PC-like game."

Some were projecting into the future with simulations based on algorithms set by the system that they were using or as a supplement to their own algorithm that they built over years of participation.

Hector stated that he uses his own spreadsheets combined with RotoGrinder to assist him highlighting potential players from a generally developed list. He said that he uses the lineup generators about 20% of the time because they "generate lineups for me and highlight certain players. It has an essentially good algorithm."

Howard said that he thought it would be very difficult to win without running simulations because the simulations are more likely to be better than himself at identifying good players who are not big names. "What happens is you pick a few big names and you pick a few longer shots, but you usually do a so-so job," he explained.

Extenuating Criteria

While participants stated that they based their lineup decisions on statistics like prior performance, injury history and other factors that can be found across multiple sports platforms; they also stated that there were other critical factors unique to themselves that had to be met for them to decide that they were going to take the time to conduct research and create lineups and participate in any contests for that day.

Paul is a 25 year-old male that has been participating in DFS for 3 years. He stated that he enters contests every day of the week when there are games scheduled except when there are no games airing that day that he can view.

Stuart is an 18 year-old male that is new to DFS as he has only been playing for one month. He stated that his participation is based on not only what he is doing for the day but also his ability to view the games and if he has the financial means to enter.

Derrick, who has been playing DFS for 4 years, stated that his criteria for participation includes looking at the fantasy sites, the site's scoring system, correlations between the number of teams playing that day and number of contests because he only plays when there is a minimum of five teams playing. He stated that if there are less than 5 teams playing everybody's lineup looks the same so there is no real potential to get ahead or have an advantage.

Information Gathering

Our second research question asked about the methods that people used to gather their player information. Participants in our study expressed how the availability of information at any given time on their mobile devices has enhanced their involvement with daily fantasy sports and their seasonal leagues. All participants confirmed that they used a combination of methods like laptops, mobile devices, and physical newspapers to collect viable player information.

Two–thirds of the participants in the study confirmed that they utilized search engines like Google and Yahoo to do their initial player research. More than half of the participants also found it useful when their research included viewing sports networks like: ESPN, SportsCenter, NFL Network, Fox, NBC, and CBS. They stated that they viewed online game highlights, live stream fantasy sports shows and YouTube.

One-third of the participants reported that they also did some reading during their research periods. They readings included: sports articles, college and professional sports magazines, local newspapers, online sports articles and online sports magazines. Less than half of these same participants browsed through sports forums, Twitter and Reddit posts for player information and updates.

Peter summarized it to "checking on that player any which way you can. Whether it would be just Googling his name to see if anything has come up about him … basically what it's like, it's like being a full time stalker for these players."

Sports Websites

Participants stated that by having access to player information via the sports sites like ESPN, SportsCenter, NFL Network, Fox, NBC, and CBS it made the research more sports specific and gave statistical insight to the players in a team setting. It also gave the participants the opportunity to view specific player clips that are being highlighted on these sites.

Sarah, a 40 year-old female that has been participating in DFS for 2 years, informed that she and her boyfriend watch CBS, FOX and NBC sport networks to see the commentator shows and go online to do their research together.

Penny said that she goes onto NFL.com and does reading to research player stats and injury information "Hoping that something will catch my eye that will tell me 'Oh yeah this will be a really good pickup' or 'avoid this particular pick right here.'"

Fantasy Sports Websites

Websites that were specifically about playing fantasy sports also served as information portals. Participants in the study pointed out that the structure and interface ease of usage was one of the leading factors that led them to return to the same research sites during their information seeking periods. Some of the factors that were mentioned included not only the interface but also flexibility, the ability to track prior contest history, comprehensive information and lineup algorithms.

Several participants noted that compared to general sports sites such as ESPN, which required "digging around forever," fantasy sites his history of past plays and information in a single interface so he didn't have to jump from page to page.

Vic, a 34 year-old male that has been participating in DFS for 2 years and traditional for 12 years, states that Yahoo give him statistical information through their forecasts and game by game breakdowns that helps to aid him in choosing which players he will play in his lineup. "I mean everything is literally right there. And the projections; there's actually a projection, a week by week projection that updates as the season is played on how many fantasy points any player will accrue for the upcoming games."

One-third of the participants said that they received notifications on their mobile phones and laptops which led them to do further research or make modifications to their lineups. Sheldon said that he mostly received projection updates for trades and injuries. When time permitted he would read them and do further research and make changes if needed in his lineup.

While participants agreed that the design of the site was important in their preference of fantasy sports sites, they had different opinions on which sites had a better design. Some preferred sites like FanDuel that had a more simple design, whereas others preferred more information-heavy interfaces such as DraftKings.

While new and more casual players liked that fantasy sports sites were a "one-stop shop" veteran players and more competitive players said that they would prefer utilizing other platforms to get their information so that they could rely on their own judgment and experiences as opposed to the third party research tools and lineup optimizers hosted on fantasy sports sites.

Derrick, who used to use the third party site RotoGrinder but no longer did so, said that he wanted to take a proactive role in information seeking:

> *"You start to realize that this is like any other business or like any other thing in life, this is about money; this is competitive; these people are not out there to give you their tricks to sell the farm in a sense, you know; they are not there to give you their secrets. And so you are sheep sitting there listening to them and you want to move away from that and want to develop what they have developed for yourself."*

Joshua, a 37 year-old male what has been playing for 3 years, advised he has never used third party sites and explained why "No because I figure other people are doing that too so how is that going to give me an advantage."

Other People's Recommendations

While we thought that participants would be secretive about information so they could perform better than others, we surprised to find that many participants were quite open about sharing information with their friends if that could improve their performance:

Helena describes how she interweaves these factors together in her information-collecting:

> *"I would ask my friends who have been experienced in this for longer than me; which ones are good to choose for my lineup and, um, you know, which ones have performed better versus worst, like that's a big deciding point. It is all part of my research, so it definitely plays a big factor. It's like bounce ideas off each other or just brainstorm together or share something new that I might have read that looks interesting."*

Arthur, a 29 year-old male that has been participating in DFS for 2 ½ years, spoke about the discussions that he and his friends have during the season. "With my friends, sometimes we'll talk about who we like, you know, and especially about football who we think is going to beat us. Yeah we just talk about it and then kick around different strategies, maybe debate on who we think's going to do better."

Sarah plays DFS with her boyfriend and together they do the research and decide together on who they are going to put in their lineups. She spoke about how they utilize the apps on his mobile phone in conjunction with their computer to compile information regarding player to help them focus on key players and narrow down together on who they are going to play in which lineups.

Hector stated that he and his friends that play DFS communicate regularly during the season "we're into information sharing, we're looking to gain extra insight that we can. During the season we are usually complaining or gloating about performance; complaining about injuries. Complaining or gloating about a good selection."

Rollin frequently communicates with a fellow computer gamer that he has been playing with since 2005 and who introduced him to DFS: "We do have each other's phone numbers and text, also we have an application called Steam, it's like for gaming, and it's like a chat application. We are just talking about how teams play and kind of talking trash."

Social Media

Multiple participants advised that they utilized YouTube highlights to view the game play of particular players they were interested in or had in their lineups. These participants took this time to get a better understanding of how that player performed against different teams and with their fellow teammates.

Several participants used social media to listen to or read about other players' opinions. Donnie stated that he searches online reviews and frequents sports forums just reading whatever he can since he says that these are his primary sources of information regarding players. Paul stated that even though he has the NBA League Pass to watch the Sixers; he still watches YouTube on a regular basis for everything else sports related. He primarily watches highlight clips and sports shows, but he also watches a YouTube channel that stars two guys who he thinks are pretty good at giving advice on certain players and which ones to put in your fantasy league.

Deciding who to follow on social media, however, also came with its own research. Helena said that she did not want to get "blindly involved" and thus looked up statistics of DFS players who were playing live to help narrow down her choices.

Participants also used online forums, Twitter, and Reddit to gain up to the minute information on players and game stats from the commentators they were following and using this information along with other research to make their final decisions on who to play that day or for the next contest.

James stated: "Twitter is a very quick way to get up to date and accurate information from various sources out there that will help you finalizing or constructing a lineup."

Rollin said that he utilized Reddit to add to his player information seeking. "I'll go on Reddit to like read about specific players. I'll just see what's going on like anything like, any criminal charges or any injuries…family problems or a week off."

Howard spoke about his use of sports forums while researching "I'm just reading it mostly and I'm comparing it to what I got for my lineup at the moment and I make, I might make a lineup change based on what I'm reading."

Information organization and application

Our third research question asked participants about their organization methods and information application. More than half of the participants stated that they use their DFS sites for organization because it shows the contest history of which players they used and their stats. Multiple participants stated it's easier because everything is right there on the site. However, 8 participants had additional ways of organizing their player information which included saving things like posts, articles and even emails.

Spreadsheet

The most prevalent method of information organization was Excel spreadsheets (seven people).

Donnie stated that he literally saves everything that he sees as important information to his laptop's hard drive and then eventually to an external hard drive. He saves articles, posts, and Microsoft Excel spreadsheets that he systematically orders in a way that he can easily access the information at any given moment.

Derrick said that he uses Excel via an open server because as he states "it gives you more options" and for stats using his own root a matrices for calculations to aid in filtering out all the restraints each site that he uses has on players according to their rules so he can make a determination on which ones to play for a specific contest entry.

Sarah that she and her boyfriend use Excel to store their research information and believes that it aids in their strategy: "I think so, yes because we're keeping track of our players each week and I think it helps us… it's right there in front of us; it's easy to change their stats week by week and we can even keep it, you know, and put it right next to them each week."

Joshua stated that he does not save his information using Excel but he goes to different websites to review numbers and statistics of players and "those websites usually have spreadsheets full of all kinds of information that you are looking for. So they are kind of there for you, you just have to go look at them."

Email and Paper

Two people said that they utilized email to save information about players. They save news articles, stats and emails from sports sites. Helena said:

> *"It's very simple really; I mean I don't get very elaborate with it. I use just a word document where I would paste some links and I would have like specific team names and specific player names and then just have like a bunch of links under that and I could refer back to it… if it's something interesting that I figured would help me in the future, I save it. I like email it to myself and I save it in my email. I might either email myself a link or email myself like a screenshot or an actual article; like I will copy and paste the text, if it has some tables or some stats that might disappear over time. Um, so I do use email I just figure that's like the best repository for me because this way I can retrieve it in the future and I find it most convenient."*

Castor also saves emails and that this was the best method for him since he can be forgetful at times.

While most participants used some kind of digital tool to record and organize their information, Mark was an exception because when he does his research throughout the day he is writing down whatever he finds in his notebook, whether it's important or not so that he can have it as a reference point to look back on when he is doing his lineup.

DISCUSSION

We found that numerous factors influence people's decisions about how to form their lineups, but that it breaks down into three stages: information collection, assessment, and verification. The information collection phase can be both quantitative or qualitative. A quantitative approach, based on statistics, involves objective facts about the athletes that the users are interested in, including performance history. A qualitative approach is based on feelings of connectivity or self-assessments of sports players' personality and character.

After assessing this information and building a "draft" lineup, we found that many DFS players tried to verify or test their lineups by running simulations and using external tools to validate or improve their picks. These three phases formed an iterative cycle.

When it comes to informational resources and organization, it was clear that no single platform provides DFS users all the tools that they need in one place. Some were using specialty sites to help with their decision-making, such as the type of system described by Solomon [34]. However, especially for users who are more experienced DFS players, they created an ecosystem of hacked-together tools and resources to maximize their chances of winning. Also, no single information source was enough—players used a variety of sources and source types to triangulate data points and get a holistic view of the sports players they were interested in.

We also found that context matters, because players' decision to participant in a contest or not revolved around situations in their own lives such as financial means and ability to view the games, as well as game-specific situations, such as how many games were taking place in a given day.

Design Implications

Intense and casual users had different information gathering practices. Casual users liked having everything in one place, whereas players with higher stakes preferred to investigate a myriad of information. This suggests that the interface of DFS systems should be customizable so players can decide which suite of tools and/or information they want and that even if DFS sites should serve as an information portal, they could benefit from letting the players choose their information sources. At the same time, too many customization options may be overwhelming for the casual user, so the site default should be minimal and simple, with the option to add features, like widgets.

While DFS sites already archive players' past lineups, we found that the ability to archive research information was also important for players. Adding features that support systematic and searchable forms of information storage may increase engagement on the site. Incorporating bookmarking features that are commonly used in scholarly article reference systems, that enable users to save "clippings" of articles in a systematic way and be able to search one's own archive of curated information could be useful to players.

Playing DFS is arguably inherently social because one is competing with other players, but we found that for many participants, playing DFS was also a collaborative activity. Our participants—especially those whose primary motivation was not making money—were generally open to sharing information with others and, in the case of couples, made decisions together. Participants were also using social media to see others' thoughts and engage in discussions with people that they did not know. This presents an opportunity to incorporate more communication and social features into DFS sites, as current DFS sites are designed more for the individual player.

Limitations

We had some limitations in terms of sampling, as users were recruited through Mechanical Turk and the Yahoo VIP list. Thus the people we interviewed were more likely to be technically savvy than the average person.

The self-identified daily fantasy sports players that we interviewed were also most likely people who enjoyed playing, as evidenced by the fact that many had been playing fantasy sports for years. Among our participants, the least amount of time spent on research per week was five hours, reflecting intense research practices. It is unclear if this sample is representative of all DFS players, although the average time they spent doing research were similar to national surveys.

CONCLUSION

In this study, we interviewed players of daily fantasy sports to understand their information-seeking and decision-making behaviors. As a unique type of pervasive play that incorporates both real-world sporting events that augmented by data analysis, information collection, and social interactions, DFS was an unique context in which we could understand how people navigate this complexity. We found that players of DFS see being successful at DFS as not entirely up to chance and spend much time collecting and assessing information to increase their chances of winning through a variety of social and technologically-mediated research practices.

Due to the rapid cycle of decision-making that is required to play daily fantasy sports, we found that participants engaged in sophisticated and complex methods of information compilation and evaluation, using a wide range of digital and analog tools as ad-hoc decision support systems to help them organize vast amounts of information in a short amount of time. Data analysis, however, was not just about statistical modeling; we found that qualitative assessments mattered just as much as quantitative ones and that no one tool suited the needs of a player, which resulted in a wide variance of practices across individuals.

ACKNOWLEDGEMENT

This study was funded in part by the Yahoo Faculty Research Engagement Program.

REFERENCES

1. June Ahn, Elizabeth Bonsignore, Derek L. Hansen, Kari Kraus, and Carman Neustaedter. 2016. Pervasive Play. *Proceedings of the 2016 CHI Conference Extended Abstracts on Human Factors in Computing Systems (CHI EA '16)*, ACM, 3317–3324.
2. David Arnott and Graham Pervan. 2014. A critical analysis of decision support systems research revisited: the rise of design science. *Journal of Information Technology* 29, 4: 269–293. http://doi.org/10.1057/jit.2014.16
3. Pratyush Bharati and Abhijit Chaudhury. 2004. An empirical investigation of decision-making satisfaction in web-based decision support systems. *Decision Support Systems* 37, 2: 187–197. http://doi.org/10.1016/S0167-9236(03)00006-X
4. Andrew C. Billings and Brody J. Ruihley. 2013. Why We Watch, Why We Play: The Relationship Between Fantasy Sport and Fanship Motivations. *Mass Communication and Society* 16, 1: 5–25. http://doi.org/10.1080/15205436.2011.635260
5. Andrew Billings, Brody James Ruihley, and Yiyi Yang. Fantasy gaming on steroids? Contrasting fantasy sport participation by daily fantasy sport participation. *Communication & Sport*. http://doi.org/10.1177/2167479516644445
6. James Bonner and Clinton J. Woodward. 2012. On domain-specific decision support systems for e-sports strategy games. *Proceedings of the 24th Australian Computer-Human Interaction Conference on - OzCHI '12*, ACM Press, 42–51. http://doi.org/10.1145/2414536.2414544
7. Jon Boswell. 2007. Fantasy Sports: A Game of Skill That Is Implicitly Legal under State Law, and Now Explicitly Legal under Federal Law. *Cardozo Arts & Entertainment Law Journal* 25. Retrieved September

21, 2016 from http://heinonline.org/HOL/Page?handle=hein.journals/caelj25&id=1263&div=&collection=

8. V. Braun and V. Clarke. 2006. Using thematic analysis in psychology. *Qualitative research in psychology* 3, 2: 77–101.

9. Marcus Carter, John Downs, Bjorn Nansen, Mitchell Harrop, and Martin Gibbs. 2014. Paradigms of games research in HCI. *Proceedings of the first ACM SIGCHI annual symposium on Computer-human interaction in play - CHI PLAY '14*, ACM Press, 27–36. http://doi.org/10.1145/2658537.2658708

10. Brenda Dwyer and Yongjae Kim. 2011. For love or money: Developing and validating a motivational scale for fantasy football participation. *Journal of Sport Management* 25, 1: 70–83. Retrieved October 16, 2015 from http://www.humankinetics.com/AcuCustom/Sitename/Documents/DocumentItem/07 Dwyer_jsm_2009_0178.pdf

11. Gabriel S. Dzodom and Frank M. Shipman. 2014. Data-driven web entertainment: the Data collection and analysis practices of fantasy sports players. *Proceedings of the 2014 ACM conference on Web science - WebSci '14*, ACM Press, 293–294. http://doi.org/10.1145/2615569.2615649

12. Gabriel Dzodom and Frank Shipman. 2016. Data-driven Prediction Games. *Proceedings of the 2016 CHI Conference Extended Abstracts on Human Factors in Computing Systems (CHI EA '16)*, ACM, 1857–1864.

13. John Eighmey and Lola McCord. 1998. Adding Value in the Information Age: Uses and Gratifications of Sites on the World Wide Web. *Journal of Business Research* 41, 3: 187–194. Retrieved from http://www.sciencedirect.com/science/article/pii/S0148296397000611

14. David Elsweiler, Stefan Mandl, and Brian Kirkegaard Lunn. 2010. Understanding casual-leisure information needs. *Proceeding of the third symposium on Information interaction in context - IIiX '10*, ACM Press, 25. http://doi.org/10.1145/1840784.1840790

15. Lee K. Farquhar and Robert Meeds. 2007. Types of Fantasy Sports Users and Their Motivations. *Journal of Computer-Mediated Communication* 12, 4: 1208–1228. Retrieved September 23, 2015 from http://doi.wiley.com/10.1111/j.1083-6101.2007.00370.x

16. FTSA. 2016. Indusrty Demographics At A Glance. *Fantasy Sports Trade Association*, 3–5. Retrieved from https://fsta.site-ym.com/?page=Demographics

17. Amitava Ghosh and Ambuj Mahanti. 2014. An information system for investment advisory process. *Proceedings of the International Conference on Information Systems and Design of Communication - ISDOC '14*, ACM Press, 143–148. http://doi.org/10.1145/2618168.2618191

18. Sandra Hirsh, Christine Anderson, and Matthew Caselli. 2012. The reality of fantasy: Uncovering information-seeking behaviors and needs in online fantasy sports. *Proceedings of the 2012 ACM annual conference extended abstracts on Human Factors in Computing Systems Extended Abstracts - CHI EA '12*, ACM Press, 849. http://doi.org/10.1145/2212776.2212858

19. Jenna Hartel. 2003. The Serious Leisure Frontier in Library and Informtion Science: Hobby Domains. *Knowledge Organization* 30, 3/4. Retrieved from https://works.bepress.com/jenna_hartel/32/

20. Jay Caspian Kang. 2016. How the Daily Fantasy Sports Industry Turns Fans Into Suckers - The New York Times. *The New York Times Magazine*. Retrieved April 13, 2016 from http://www.nytimes.com/2016/01/06/magazine/how-the-daily-fantasy-sports-industry-turns-fans-into-suckers.html?_r=1

21. Adam Krejcik. 2015. *Daily Fantasy Sports Player Survey - 2015*.

22. Markus Montola, Jaakko Stenros, and Annika Waern. 2009. *Pervasive games: theory and design*. Elsevier/Morgan Kaufmann, Amsterdam, Boston.

23. Louis S. Nadelson, Christina M. Sias, Joshua Matyi, et al. 2016. A World of Information at Their Fingertips: College Students' Motivations and Practices in Their Self-Determined Information Seeking. *International Journal of Higher Education* 5, 1: 220–231. http://doi.org/10.5430/ijhe.v5n1p220

24. Nico Newman. 2015. History of Fantasy Sports. Retrieved April 13, 2016 from https://fantasy-sport.net/history-of-fantasy-sports/

25. John W. Payne and James R. Bettman. 2002. Preferential choice and adaptive strategy use. In *Bounded rationality: The adaptive toolbox*, G. Gigerenzer and R. Selten (eds.). MIT Press, Cambridge, MA, 123–145.

26. PDFS. 2015. What is Daily Fantasy Sports? 3–5. Retrieved from http://www.playdailyfantasysports.com/what-is-daily-fantasy-sports/

27. Richard G. Lomax. 2006. Fantasy sports: History, game types, and research. In *Handbook of Sports and Media*, Arthur A. Raney and Jennings Bryant (eds.). Lawrence Erlbaum, 416–425. Retrieved from

https://books.google.com/books?hl=en&lr=&id=SWyNAgAAQBAJ&oi=fnd&pg=PA416&dq=daily+fantasy+sports&ots=A8R10SRC88&sig=qRFQYbVCvCf8XNA8ol_WvWJZkTs#v=onepage&q=daily fantasy sports&f=false

28. Brody J. Ruihley and Andrew C. Billings. 2013. Infiltrating the boys' club: Motivations for women's fantasy sport participation. *International Review for the Sociology of Sport* 48, 4: 435–452. http://doi.org/10.1177/1012690212443440

29. Brody J. Ruihley, Andrew C. Billings, and Coral Rae. 2014. As time goes by: Deciphering the fantasy sport playing teenager. *Sport Marketing Quarterly* 23: 187–197.

30. Reijo Savolainen. 1993. The sense-making theory: Reviewing the interests of a user-centered approach to information seeking and use. *Information Processing & Management* 29, 1: 13–28. http://doi.org/10.1016/0306-4573(93)90020-E

31. Reijo Savolainen. 1995. Everyday life information seeking: Approaching information seeking in the context of "way of life." *Library & Information Science Research* 17, 3: 259–294. http://doi.org/10.1016/0740-8188(95)90048-9

32. Frank M. Shipman. 2009. Blending the real and virtual in games. *Proceedings of the 4th International Conference on Foundations of Digital Games - FDG '09*, ACM Press, 169. http://doi.org/10.1145/1536513.1536547

33. Brian Smith, Priya Sharma, and Paula Hooper. 2006. Decision making in online fantasy sports communities. *Interactive Technology and Smart Education* 4: 347–360.

34. Jacob Solomon. 2014. Customization bias in decision support systems. *Proceedings of the 32nd annual ACM conference on Human factors in computing systems - CHI '14*, ACM Press, 3065–3074. http://doi.org/10.1145/2556288.2557211

35. Amos Tversky and Daniel Kahneman. 1973. Availability: A heuristic for judging frequency and probability. *Cognitive Psychology* 5: 207–232.

36. Yunfeng Zhang, Rachel K.E. Bellamy, and Wendy A. Kellogg. 2015. Designing Information for Remediating Cognitive Biases in Decision-Making. *Proceedings of the 33rd Annual ACM Conference on Human Factors in Computing Systems - CHI '15*, ACM Press, 2211–2220. http://doi.org/10.1145/2702123.2702239

37. The History And Evolution Of Fantasy Sports. Retrieved April 13, 2016 from http://futureoffantasy.com/the-history-and-evolution-of-fantasy-sports

38. How the Daily Fantasy Sports Industry Turns Fans Into Suckers - The New York Times. Retrieved April 13, 2016 from http://www.nytimes.com/2016/01/06/magazine/how-the-daily-fantasy-sports-industry-turns-fans-into-suckers.html?_r=1

The Effects of Context-Sensitive Tutorials in Virtual Reality Games

Julian Frommel
Institute of Media Informatics
James-Franck-Ring
Ulm University, Germany
julian.frommel(at)uni-ulm.de

Kim Fahlbusch
Institute of Media Informatics
James-Franck-Ring
Ulm University, Germany
kim.fahlbusch(at)uni-ulm.de

Julia Brich
Institute of Media Informatics
James-Franck-Ring
Ulm University, Germany
kim.fahlbusch(at)uni-ulm.de

Michael Weber
Institute of Media Informatics
James-Franck-Ring
Ulm University, Germany
michael.weber(at)uni-ulm.de

ABSTRACT
Virtual reality (VR) devices have become popular in recent time due to the release of several consumer grade VR devices. Currently games are considered one of the primary use cases for VR. Game mechanics in VR games frequently work differently compared to non-VR games. However, there is no prevalent way how to teach game mechanics and game interaction to players in VR games. In this work we implemented a VR wave shooter game with two variants of a tutorial. We conducted a user study (n = 39) examining the effects of a context-sensitive tutorial on players' experience compared to a traditional instruction screen tutorial. The results show that the context-sensitive tutorial elicited higher positive emotions, lower negative emotions, and higher motivation while immersion and performance were comparable. These findings highlight that tutorials should not be seen as a separate introduction to a game but part of the overall experience as they can directly influence the players' experience.

Author Keywords
virtual reality; VR; game; tutorial; context-sensitive; player experience

ACM Classification Keywords
K.8.0. General: Games; H.5.2. User Interfaces: Evaluation/methodology

INTRODUCTION
Virtual reality (VR) has found its way into consumers' homes. Frequently, gaming is seen as one of most prevalent use cases for VR. Compared to non-VR games, there are few best practices on how to design VR games and their interaction. While there are guidelines that provide useful advice (e.g. [19]), there is little published evidence that practitioners and researchers can use to inform their design decisions. Games for VR frequently necessitate very different interaction schemes compared to traditional non-VR games. It is essential that players learn how to interact with a game and how game mechanics work. There are several ways to teach players game mechanics and game interaction. For games in general a common practice is to let players engage in tutorial levels before they start regular game play [1]. Using tutorials in VR games seems obvious as they provide a safe space for learning and exploring what might be especially important for VR games since recent research has shown that players need to get accustomed with VR devices and the input style required [24].
Some commercial games in recent years moved towards tutorials that are more context-sensitive in a way that they let players explore the game world and mechanics on their own and provide explanation just-in-time when required without interrupting the player. Andersen et al. [3] found that context-sensitive tutorials that introduce concepts close to where they are used can in some games improve engagement compared to more context-insensitive tutorials that provide all instructions upfront. In the light of the challenge of teaching game mechanics and interaction for VR games, employing context-sensitive tutorials could provide benefits. However, to our knowledge there has been no research yet examining the effects of context-sensitivity for tutorials in VR games. Studying these effects seems especially important as the domain of VR games is rather novel and there is little advice guiding researchers and practitioners developing VR games in general.

The main research question of this paper is to investigate the effects of context-sensitive design on player experience in VR game tutorials. For that purpose, in this work we compare a context-sensitive tutorial to a more traditional instruction screen tutorial regarding their effects on players' emotion, immersion, performance, and motivation. We implemented a VR wave shooter game for the HTC Vive with two different

CHI PLAY '17, October 15–18, 2017, Amsterdam, Netherlands

ISBN 978-1-4503-4898-0/17/10...$15.00
DOI: https://doi.org/10.1145/3116595.3116610

Figure 1. Different styles of tutorials are used in successful commercial games, e.g. traditional instruction screens in the *Witcher 3* [7] (a) and the VR game *Serious Sam VR: The Last Hope* [27] (b) and context-sensitive just-in-time instructions in *Half-Life 2* [25] (c) and the VR game *The Lab* [26] (d).

tutorial levels. A user study ($n = 39$) was conducted in that participants played one of the tutorials as well as a regular game play session and then reported subjective measures of their experience. The results show that the context-sensitive tutorial led to more positive emotion, less negative emotion, and higher motivation compared to an instruction screen tutorial.

RELATED WORK

Due to the increasing complexity of games, developers regularly include tutorial levels in games that are used to introduce players to the game [1]. Such tutorial levels usually contain explanations on the user interface and game mechanics [22]. Regarding user interfaces in games, Adams [1] mentions several types of interaction models. While these generally cover many types of user interfaces in non-VR games, interaction types and their effects in VR games are frequently very different [24]. Although, regular interaction such as keyboard, mouse, or gamepads can be used in VR games, other novel interaction methods might be more suitable. For example, developers are encouraged by the manufacturers of one VR head-mounted-display (HMD) to assess the usability of novel control schemes in order to avoid frustration and discomfort [19]. Similarly, the effects of interaction modes with VR games were examined in recent research [5, 10]. However, this research not only highlights the need to assess the quality and effects of interaction modes but also indicates that players are possibly unfamiliar with interaction and mechanics of VR games and need to get accustomed with them. With regard to game design in general Adams suggests that games which use interaction models that are not familiar to the player necessitate more detailed tutorials teaching the controls to the player [1]. Recently, Morin et al. [17] proposed that developers should provide tutorials if they are in doubt of the level of their users' expertise. As many players have little experience in the novel VR domain, using tutorials for games seems plausible but how they are best designed has yet to be studied.

Although the benefit of tutorials in general is largely accepted [22], there has been little research examining how differently designed tutorials affect player experience in VR games. Commercial games use very different techniques for teaching game mechanics and interaction. There are games in that instructions are provided by modal instruction screens. The regular game play is interrupted, an explanation of a game mechanic is provided as text, and players sometimes even have to explicitly confirm that they want to continue after they finished reading the instruction (see Figures 1a/1b). In some games information is provided just-in-time when players require it, e.g. through context-sensitive messages (see Figure 1c/1d). In this work we consider the latter variant as context-sensitive tutorials in a way that they provide explanations without interrupting the player and supplying necessary information by taking into account the players' behavior and current state in the game. On the other hand tutorials employing instruction screens are a more traditional approach to teaching game mechanics and interaction. Andersen et al. [3] compared context-sensitive tutorials that introduced concepts close to where they were used with context-insensitive tutorials that provide an instruction before regular game play. They found that the context-sensitive tutorials can improve engagement but this effect was only found for the most complex game. However, the authors studied regular non-VR games with regular interfaces. In this work we want to examine if the results also apply in the novel domain of VR games and if context-sensitive tutorials provide a better player experience compared to a more traditional tutorial, especially since what constitutes as a complex or simple game might be very different in comparison with regular non-VR games.

In summary, while there has been research on the effects of tutorials in games, there has been no such research in the domain of VR games, but there are still very different tutorials in commercial VR games. In this work we want to examine if the results of previous research can be replicated in this novel domain, especially as aspects such as expertise and complexity might actually be very different in VR games compared to non-VR games.

CONCEPT AND IMPLEMENTATION

In order to examine the research question, we implemented a VR wave shooter game featuring different variants of tutorials. In games of this genre the player has to defend a position by shooting enemies approaching from multiple directions. Such games have been very popular amongst the early games for consumer grade virtual reality featuring 6DOF-tracked head and hands (e.g. [2], [4], [13], [27]). Players use weapons to defend themselves against the enemies. These weapons usually are directly mapped to the controllers and their corresponding real world position. Such input generally is unique to VR and players are often not very familiar with this form of input from

Figure 2. ***MummyDefense*** **is a VR wave shooter game in which players use bow and arrow to defend themselves from approaching enemies (a). Players can dye arrows by touching colored spheres on pillars surrounding their platform as enemies require that they are hit by specifically colored arrows (b). Different items are included that help defeating specific enemies, e.g. a shield to let players defend themselves against enemies shooting projectiles (c).**

regular non-VR games what makes this genre very well suited for our research question.

MummyDefense

We implemented *MummyDefense*, a VR wave shooter game for one player on the HTC Vive. In this game players stand on a platform on which they can move around freely. Enemies are approaching the platform from all directions and are constantly damaging the player when they arrive at the platform. Players can defend themselves by shooting the enemies with bow and arrow (see Figure 2a). When players have lost all their life points they lose. If they on the other hand, defeat all waves of enemies they beat a level. There are small enemies that are defeated by one arrow as well as big enemies that have to be hit multiple times. Enemies appear in different colors and can only be defeated when players have dyed their arrow in the corresponding color. For that purpose there are four pillars on the corners of the platform that allow dyeing the arrow by touching a color sphere with the arrow (see Figure 2b). Players have access to several items: a bomb, a shield (see Figure 2c), and a healing potion. From time to time groups of small enemies approach the platform that can be easily defeated using the bomb. The players can use the shield to defend themselves from projectiles that the big enemies shoot. The healing potion can be used to refill the players life points. Using items usually involves the player pressing a specific button and performing a specific gesture, e.g. activating and aiming the shield, throwing a bomb, or making a drinking motion to activate the healing potion. These gestures were chosen in order to introduce interaction that is not usually found in regular non-VR games.

Tutorials

Two variants of a tutorial were implemented to teach the game mechanics to players. We employed a more traditional instruction screen tutorial and a context-sensitive tutorial. Both tutorials feature similarly worded text-based explanations of game mechanics. Figures 3 and 4 show how the same instruction is presented in both variants.

Instruction Screen Tutorial

We implemented an instruction screen tutorial as a more traditional form of tutorial. In our implementation the game mechanics are described in text form. For that purpose instructions are displayed on parchment floating next to the platform players are standing on (see Figure 3). The instruction screen is implemented as a plane with a fixed position and orientation. The explanations of the game mechanics are distributed on multiple parchments and players proceed to the next instruction screen by shooting a target below the parchment. This is similar to a button that players use to continue to the next instruction in other games. However, players can already practice aiming and shooting with bow and arrow. This tutorial design features two phases. Players first are presented with the phase in that they encounter the instructions and then they enter a phase in that they can practice the different mechanics. They come across the different types of enemies and can use all of the game's items. With regard to Andersen et al.'s design variants [3] this tutorial can be regarded as context-insensitive.

Context-Sensitive Tutorial

In the context-sensitive tutorial the explanations of the game mechanics are also presented one by one. However, compared to the instruction screen tutorial, explanations are not presented to the user before they can try them in the second phase on the tutorial. In this version of the tutorial both phases (instruction and practice) are combined. Players directly start in a phase in that they can encounter mechanics of the game (trial phase) and explanations are provided in speech bubbles just-in-time when a new mechanic and interaction is introduced (see Figure 4). Speech bubbles are anchored at a suitable position, e.g. at the controller when the instruction explains a new interaction. Players encounter mechanics in the same order as in the instruction tutorial.

STUDY

The aim of this study was to examine effects of different forms of tutorials on player experience in VR games. For that purpose two versions of *MummyDefense* were implemented featuring a traditional instruction screen (*InstructionScreen*

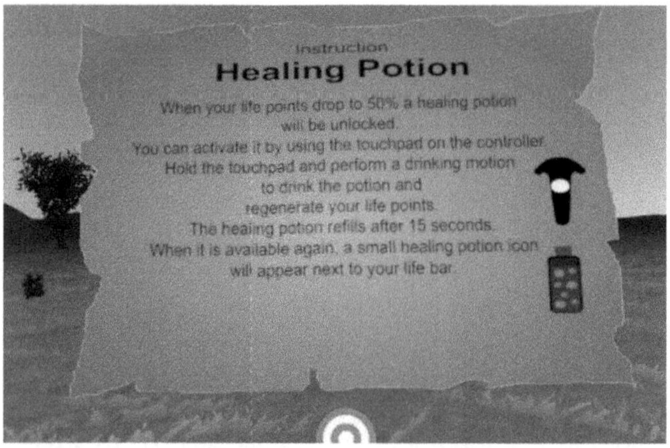

Figure 3. The traditional instruction screen was implemented for *MummyDefense* as a parchment floating on a fixed position and rotation. Instructions are presented in succession before players can practice the mechanics. After they finish an instruction, they have to confirm proceeding to the next instruction by shooting the target below the parchment.

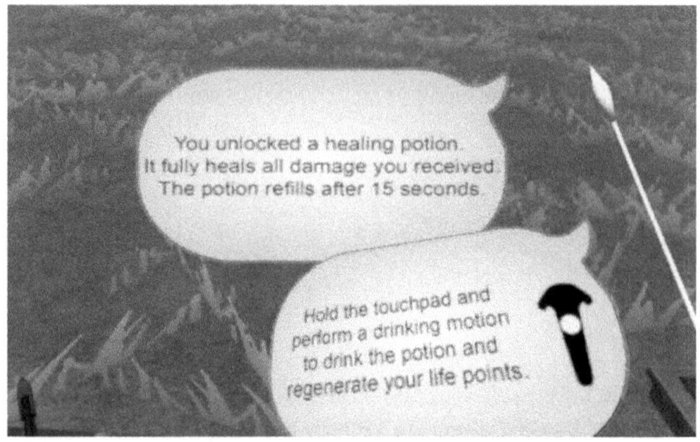

Figure 4. The context-sensitive tutorial provides information in speech bubbles just-in-time. When the player requires new information or new features are unlocked this information is shown. The speech bubbles are anchored at appropriate locations, e.g. at the controller for new controller input.

condition) and a context-sensitive tutorial (*Context-Sensitive* condition).

Participants
Overall we recruited 40 participants (14 female, 25 male, 1 not reported). One male participant was excluded from the analysis as he experienced discomfort during the study. The final sample consisted of 39 participants (14 female, 24 male, 1 not reported) with an average age of 23.56 (SD = 3.754) years. On average they reported playing video games for 6.949 (SD = 12.890) hours per week. Only 4 participants reported playing VR games regularly, i.e. 0.5 hours (2 participants), 1 hour, and 5 hours per week.

Procedure
Participants were invited into a university lab where the study took place. The study was designed as a between-subjects experiment. The participants were randomly assigned to the *Context-Sensitive* or the *InstructionScreen* condition. In the study participants played one of the tutorial variants and regular game play session of *MummyDefense* afterwards. At first, the participants were introduced to the topic of the study, stated their consent, and completed a questionnaire about their demographic background. Subsequently, the participants were introduced to the HTC Vive and *MummyDefense*. The participants were instructed that they could replay the tutorial as often as they liked but only until they decided to start the regular game. On the other hand, the players could not skip the tutorial and had to complete it at least once in order to proceed to regular game play. The duration of the tutorial phase lasted for approximately 5-10 minutes and the regular game consisted of 5 minutes game play. The game featured a level system in that difficulty increased in higher levels. Participants would have to repeat a level if they lost and proceeded to the next one if they won. After the regular game play the participants completed a questionnaire about their experience and received their compensation. The duration of the study was approximately 30 minutes and participants were compensated with 5 euros.

Measures
Several metrics were measured in our study in order to determine the effects of the tutorial variants. We measured the participants emotional state by measuring valence, arousal, and dominance via SAM [6], and the self-reported emotions joy, frustration, anger, and boredom on 7-point Likert scales. These can play an important role during learning [20] and as a result might be crucial for tutorials. Further, we measured the participants' immersion and game experience using the IEQ [14] and their intrinsic motivation using the *interest/enjoyment* subscale of the IMI [16]. We assessed the performance of the tutorial objectively by recording how far the participants progressed in the game and how many tries they required. Participants also reported their subjective opinion on the performance of the tutorial by stating their agreement to four statements: *"The tutorial helped me understand the game mechanics"*, *"The tutorial prepared me well for the game"*, *"I thought the tutorial was good with respect to content"*, and *"The tutorial taught me everything I needed to know for the game"*. Participants stated their agreement on 7-point Likert scales (1 = *strongly disagree*, 7 = *strongly agree*). Finally, participants had the chance to give qualitative feedback by supplying open-ended comments.

Results
Scores were calculated for IMI *interest/enjoyment* subscale, IEQ factors, and performance measure. Normally distributed data was analyzed using independent samples t-tests (2-tailed) while Mann-Whitney U tests were used for the analysis of data which was not distributed normally. Exact 2-tailed significances are reported for the Mann-Whitney U tests. Levene's test was used to assert that variances were equal in the groups before conducting the t-tests.

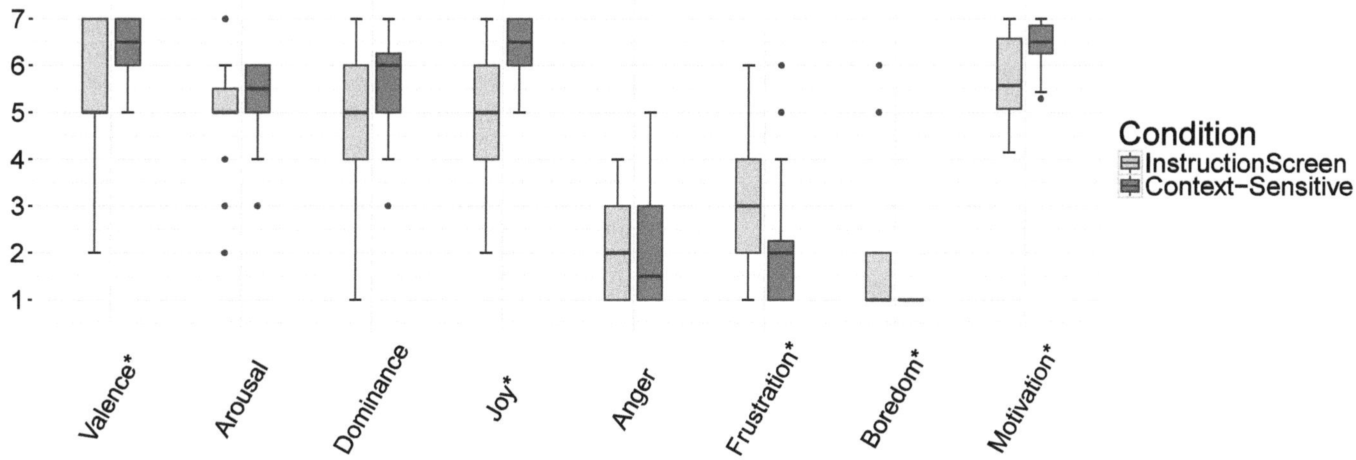

Figure 5. Boxplots for the emotion and motivation scores for both conditions. * indicates significant differences

Emotion

Results show that the *Context-Sensitive* condition elicited higher valence scores (*Mdn* = 6.50) compared to the *InstructionScreen* tutorial (*Mdn* = 5.00), ($U = 110.00$, $z = -2.378$, $p = .017$, $r = -.38$). The form of the tutorial did not affect arousal scores ($U = 163.00$, $z = -.799$, *ns*) or dominance scores ($U = 131.00$, $z = -1.701$, *ns*). Joy ratings in the *Context-Sensitive* condition (*Mdn* = 6.50) were significantly higher than in the *InstructionScreen* condition (*Mdn* = 5.00), ($U = 84.50$, $z = -3.102$, $p = .002$, $r = -.50$). The tutorial condition did not influence anger scores ($U = 168.00$, $z = -.653$, *ns*). Participants were significantly less frustrated in the *Context-Sensitive* variant of the tutorial (*Mdn* = 2.00) than in the *InstructionScreen* variant (*Mdn* = 3.50), ($U = 118.00$, $z = -2.073$, $p = .038$, $r = -.33$). Further, boredom scores were significantly lower in the *Context-Sensitive* condition (*Mdn* = 1.00) compared to the *InstructionScreen* condition (*Mdn* = 1.00), ($U = 130.00$, $z = -2.688$, $p = .008$). However, that variable was rated very low in both conditions as indicated by the medians, even constantly as 1 in the *Context-Sensitive* condition. For an overview of emotion scores see Figure 5.

Immersion

IEQ overall ratings in the *Context-Sensitive* condition (*Mdn* = 5.69) were not significantly different from ratings in the *InstructionScreen* condition (*Mdn* = 5.23), $U = 143.50$, $z = -1.307$, *ns*. Similarly there was no effect of the condition on the IEQ challenge ($t(37) = .520$, *ns*), IEQ control ($U = 142.00$, $z = -1.357$, *ns*), IEQ real world dissociation ($U = 171.00$, $z = -.536$, *ns*), IEQ emotional involvement ($U = 166.00$, $z = -.677$, *ns*), and IEQ cognitive involvement scores ($t(37) = .959$, *ns*), as well as on single item immersion measure ($t(37) = .520$, *ns*).

Motivation

Regarding the IMI *interest/enjoyment* subscale participants reported significantly higher motivation in the *Context-Sensitive* condition (*Mdn* = 6.50) than in the *InstructionScreen* condition (*Mdn* = 5.57), $U = 100.50$, $z = -2.525$, $p = .011$, $r = -.40$ (see Figure 5).

Measure	*Mdn (CS)*	*Mdn (IS)*	*U*	*z*	*p*
T1	7.00	7.00	139.50	-1.661	.101
T2	6.50	6.00	143.00	-1.416	.166
T3	6.50	6.00	149.00	-1.245	.212
T4	7.00	7.00	186,50	-.118	.993

Table 1. Medians and test statistics show that there are no significant differences between the subjective performance measures with regard to condition (CS: *Context-Sensitive*, IS: *InstructionScreen*, T1: "The tutorial helped me understand the game mechanics", T2: "The tutorial prepared me well for the game", T3: "I thought the tutorial was good with respect to content", T4: "The tutorial taught me everything I needed to know for the game").

Performance

As soon as participants completed a level they proceeded to the next level. If they lost they had to repeat the level. As participants only had 5 minutes to play the regular game of *MummyDefense* they could finish at most 2 levels while they could lose in a level multiple times before proceeding to the next one. We calculated the performance of the participants as the number of levels won divided by the number of tries. Results show that the performance scores for *Context-Sensitive* ($M = .413$, $SD = .370$) were not significantly different from scores of the *InstructionScreen* condition ($M = .300$, $SD = .414$), ($U = 148.50$, $z = -1.229$, *ns*). Participants had the chance to repeat the tutorial as many times as they wanted before they started the game. There was no significant difference in how often participants played the tutorial between the *Context-Sensitive* condition ($M = 1.35$, $SD = .489$) and the *InstructionScreen* condition ($M = 1.53$, $SD = .697$), ($U = 169.50$, $z = -.674$, *ns*). Participants stated their agreement to several statements regarding the subjective performance of the tutorial. Table 1 shows that there are no significant differences between the conditions.

	Overall		*CS*		*IS*	
	τ_b	*p*	τ_b	*p*	τ_b	*p*
Valence	.338**	.007	.336	.076	.262	.151
Arousal	.297*	.017	.104	.569	.441*	.016
Dominance	.192	.114	.107	.543	.172	.333
Joy	.348**	.005	.371	.050	.300	.092
Anger	-.282*	.024	-.088	.623	-.496**	.007
Frustration	-.294*	.015	-.111	.534	-.433*	.015
Boredom	-.407**	.002	—†	—†	-.586**	.002
Motivation	.541**	.000	.535**	.001	-.596**	.000

* significant at the .05 level (2-tailed)

** significant at the .01 level (2-tailed)

† boredom scores are constant in the *Context-Sensitive* condition

Table 2. Kendall's tau-b correlations of immersion with emotion and motivation (CS: *Context-Sensitive*, IS: *InstructionScreen*).

Experience with Games and VR

Although the data showed trends of differences regarding the weekly play time of video games (*Context-Sensitive*: M = 9.950, SD = 17.006, *InstructionScreen*: M = 3.789, SD = 4.995), this was mostly due to one outlier who reported an average play time of 80 hours per week (more than 6 times of the *SD*). An analysis after excluding this outlier mostly confirmed the reported results. The difference of boredom scores between the conditions became non-significant after excluding the outlier (U = 123.50, z = -2.625, *ns*). All other reported differences remained significant. As most of the participants (35 of 39) reported not regularly playing VR games we did not account for this variable in our analysis.

Relationship of Emotion and Motivation with Immersion

Since there was an effect of the experimental condition on emotion measures and motivation, but not on immersion we examined the relationship of these variables by calculating Kendall's tau-b correlation of these measures. There was a significant relationship of IEQ overall score with most measures (see Table 2). Immersion was positively correlated with positive emotions and motivation, but negatively correlated with anger, frustration, and boredom. Then, we divided our whole sample in two samples based on condition and calculated correlations in these subsamples. Motivation was highly correlated in both conditions. There were no significant correlations of immersion and emotional state in the *Context-Sensitive* condition, but correlation coefficients are comparably high to those in the overall sample for valence and joy scores. In the sample for the *InstructionScreen* condition immersion was positively correlated with arousal while immersion had a negative correlation with anger, frustration, and boredom.

DISCUSSION

In summary, the results show that in this study a context-sensitive tutorial in VR games elicited higher positive emotion, lower negative emotion, and higher intrinsic motivation compared to a traditional context-insensitive instruction screen tutorial. On the other hand the experimental condition did not lead to any significant differences with regard to immersion, other more specific IEQ measures such as challenge as well as subjective and objective performance of the tutorial. Overall the findings of this study confirm the previous results of Andersen et al. [3] that context-sensitive tutorials can lead to a better player experience. However, although Andersen et al. found these effects mainly for complex games, our study showed similar effects for a rather simple game in the VR games context. These findings might be evidence that in VR games well-designed tutorials might lead to an overall enjoyable player experience regardless of the complexity of the game. Thus, it seems that the relationship of the variables moderating the positive effects of well-designed tutorials on player experience require further study in the domain of VR games. However, this work provides evidence that context-sensitivity can be valuable when designing game tutorials. This is particularly important for tutorials in VR games, as VR is quite novel for games and players need to get accustomed to this new medium. When designing tutorials for VR games, it seems necessary that developers and researchers pay attention to how they design a tutorial as it not only teaches players how a game is played but also directly influences player experience.

Limitations

There are some limitations that should be considered with regard to generalizability of the results. Participants overall had very low experience with VR games. This might have resulted in a better player experience for the context-sensitive tutorial as its presentation was more novel compared to a traditional instruction screen. However, in this study we wanted to examine what tutorial is most suitable for teaching game mechanics in the new domain of VR games and, due to their novelty, VR games are new to a lot of players. Thus, a population with little experience with VR is currently close to the real population of VR game players. It seems reasonable to expect that tutorials should provide a good experience especially for novices that need a good introduction to a game and its mechanics.

The implementation of the sequencing of instruction and trial phase was different for the *Context-Sensitive* and *InstructionScreen* condition. While the *InstructionScreen* tutorial provided a complete block of instructions and a trial phase afterwards, in the *Context-Sensitive* tutorial these phases were mixed. The latter condition allowed players to explore a feature as soon as it was unlocked and explanations were provided. A similar implementation could have been chosen for the *InstructionScreen* tutorial as well, i.e. modal instruction screens are displayed when a new feature is provided. Such implementation would have provided a middle ground between the adaptivity of the *Context-Sensitive* condition and the traditional *InstructionScreen* condition. For this study we decided against such implementation as instruction screens would actually have interrupted practice phases what can negatively affect presence and emotion [9]. The effects of varying degrees of context-sensitivity should be examined in future work nonetheless.

This study compared two implementations of a player-game interaction interface and its effects on the players' experience. In our analysis we did not yet consider other player specific aspects that might have an influence on player experience such as player motivations or types [11], the theory of learning styles [8], or knowledge acquisition styles [21].

In this study we examined one game in a domain (VR games)

and specific genre (VR wave shooter). If similar effects can be expected in other VR games or even games in general has to be examined in further studies. However, it seems plausible to expect that a context-sensitive tutorial leads to an overall better player experience in VR games that feature similar interaction circumstances: 6DOF-tracking of the players' head and hands. Such setup would allow a similarly context-sensitive tutorial since information can be anchored to objects in the players' hands or the players' looking direction. In our opinion the effects should be independent of the content of the explanations that is presented as well as how the information is presented (e.g. with speech bubbles as in our study). These aspects should rather be designed to fit the style of the game.

Interplay of Emotion and Immersion

Although the experimental conditions affected several emotion measures, there was no significant effect of the experimental condition on immersion. This is surprising as one might expect that immersion is interconnected with positive emotions and experiences in games and especially in VR games. Similar to previous research [12, 18] we found positive correlations of positive emotion and immersion. When examining the relationship of immersion and emotion separately for each condition the negative correlation of immersion and the negative emotions frustration, boredom, and anger was only found for the *InstructionScreen* condition but not for the *Context-Sensitive* condition. This might be indicative that negative emotions which happen during tutorials might not influence immersion if the tutorial is designed context-sensitive. However, these assumptions currently are speculation and thus these findings highlight that the interplay of emotion and immersion requires further examination in the context of VR game tutorials.

Relationship of Performance and Player Experience

One might expect that the performance of the context-sensitive tutorial would be better as players directly had the chance to practice interaction of specific mechanics as soon as they were explained in comparison to the instruction screen which featured two more distinct phases (instruction and practice). However, contrary to our expectations there was no difference of the form of tutorial on subjective or objective performance measures. Thus, both variants of the tutorial might be equally useful with regard to how well they are actually able to teach game mechanics. However, players reported more positive emotions, less negative emotions, and higher motivation in the *Context-Sensitive* condition. This mismatch of higher positive emotions but no increased performance lies in contrast to previous research. Previous work showed a connection of learning and presence [28] while presence has been shown to be connected to positive emotions [9]. This suggests that the tutorial eliciting a better player experience should also have a better performance. This mismatch might be due to the fact that the measure of performance that we used was not ideal for measuring if players learned game mechanics. How well a tutorial prepares players for a game might not even be assessable in a rather short lab study and might have to be examined in a longer study. In a realistic game context, however, a context-sensitive tutorial might lead to a better performance in any case. Games should feature tutorials that can be skipped [1] and this study showed a better player experience for the context-sensitive tutorial. In a real game players might rather skip tutorials they experience as low fun what could lead to players missing important information and as a result could negatively affect the tutorial's performance.

Adaptivity for Tutorials

In this study the context-sensitive tutorial was implemented in a way that instruction and practice phases were interwoven. Instructions were provided just-in-time when players needed them. Such an approach could be implemented in an adaptive fashion. In previous research adaptivity is sometimes defined as an approach that is not only based on player behavior but rather reacts accordingly to the players' current emotional state or experience [15, 23, 29]. In our work we only examined the effects of providing context-sensitive tutorials in VR games based on players behavior and current state in the tutorial. However, the positive effects of a well-designed tutorial might even be greater when it reacts adaptive to the players' current emotional and motivational state. For example, the tutorial could be adapted in pace if players are frustrated or bored. For that purpose any form of recognizing the players' emotional or motivational state is necessary. We plan to explore the direction of a more player-centered adaptive approach in future work.

CONCLUSION

In this work we examined the effects of two tutorials variants on player experience in VR games. We designed and implemented *MummyDefense*, a VR wave shooter game that features several game mechanics that are unique for VR games in comparison to non-VR games. Two variants of a tutorial level were implemented: a context-sensitive tutorial that provides information about game mechanics just-in-time and a more traditional instruction screen tutorial. We conducted a user study examining the effects of these tutorials on emotion, motivation, immersion, and performance. Results show that the context-sensitive tutorial elicited higher positive emotions, lower negative emotions, and higher motivation while there was no effect on performance or immersion. While there is more work required to further examine these effects and how to incorporate the players' current emotional state, these findings indicate that developers should not regard tutorials as separate introduction levels to a game but rather as part of the overall game experience.

ACKNOWLEDGMENTS

We thank the study participants; we also thank the Carl-Zeiss Foundation for the partial funding of this work.

REFERENCES

1. Ernest Adams. 2014. *Fundamentals of game design*. Pearson Education.
2. Alzan Studios, LLC. 2016. *Holopoint*. Game [HTC Vive]. (5 Apr 2016). Alzan Studios, LLC.

3. Erik Andersen, Eleanor O'Rourke, Yun-En Liu, Rich Snider, Jeff Lowdermilk, David Truong, Seth Cooper, and Zoran Popovic. 2012. The impact of tutorials on games of varying complexity. In *Proceedings of the SIGCHI Conference on Human Factors in Computing Systems*. ACM, 59–68.
4. Blueteak. 2016. *QuiVr*. Game [HTC Vive]. (20 Dec 2016). Alvios Inc.
5. Evren Bozgeyikli, Andrew Raij, Srinivas Katkoori, and Rajiv Dubey. 2016. Point & Teleport Locomotion Technique for Virtual Reality. In *Proceedings of the 2016 Annual Symposium on Computer-Human Interaction in Play (CHI PLAY '16)*. ACM, New York, NY, USA, 205–216. DOI: http://dx.doi.org/10.1145/2967934.2968105
6. Margaret M Bradley and Peter J Lang. 1994. Measuring emotion: the self-assessment manikin and the semantic differential. *Journal of behavior therapy and experimental psychiatry* 25, 1 (1994), 49–59.
7. CD PROJEKT RED. 2015. *The Witcher 3: Wild Hunt*. Game [PC]. (18 May 2015). CD PROJEKT RED.
8. Frank Coffield, David Moseley, Elaine Hall, Kathryn Ecclestone, and others. 2004. Learning styles and pedagogy in post-16 learning: A systematic and critical review. (2004).
9. Julian Frommel, Katja Rogers, Julia Brich, Daniel Besserer, Leonard Bradatsch, Isabel Ortinau, Ramona Schabenberger, Valentin Riemer, Claudia Schrader, and Michael Weber. 2015. Integrated Questionnaires: Maintaining Presence in Game Environments for Self-Reported Data Acquisition. In *Proceedings of the 2015 Annual Symposium on Computer-Human Interaction in Play*. ACM, 359–368.
10. Jan Gugenheimer, Evgeny Stemasov, Julian Frommel, and Enrico Rukzio. 2017. ShareVR: Enabling Co-Located Experiences for Virtual Reality between HMD and Non-HMD Users. In *Proceedings of the SIGCHI Conference on Human Factors in Computing Systems (CHI '17)*. ACM.
11. Juho Hamari and Janne Tuunanen. 2014. Player Types: A Meta-synthesis. *Transactions of the Digital Games Research Association* 1, 2 (2014).
12. Laura Herrewijn, Karolien Poels, and Gordon Calleja. 2013. The relationship between player involvement and immersion: An experimental investigation.. In *FDG*. 364–367.
13. I-Illusions. 2016. *Space Pirate Trainer*. Game [HTC Vive]. (5 Apr 2016). I-Illusions.
14. Charlene Jennett, Anna L Cox, Paul Cairns, Samira Dhoparee, Andrew Epps, Tim Tijs, and Alison Walton. 2008. Measuring and defining the experience of immersion in games. *International journal of human-computer studies* 66, 9 (2008), 641–661.
15. Ricardo Lopes and Rafael Bidarra. 2011. Adaptivity challenges in games and simulations: a survey. *IEEE Transactions on Computational Intelligence and AI in Games* 3, 2 (2011), 85–99.
16. Edward McAuley, Terry Duncan, and Vance V Tammen. 1989. Psychometric properties of the Intrinsic Motivation Inventory in a competitive sport setting: A confirmatory factor analysis. *Research quarterly for exercise and sport* 60, 1 (1989), 48–58.
17. Raphaël Morin, Pierre-Majorique Léger, Sylvain Senecal, Marie-Christine Bastarache-Roberge, Mario Lefèbrve, and Marc Fredette. 2016. The Effect of Game Tutorial: A Comparison Between Casual and Hardcore Gamers. In *Proceedings of the 2016 Annual Symposium on Computer-Human Interaction in Play Companion Extended Abstracts (CHI PLAY Companion '16)*. ACM, New York, NY, USA, 229–237.
18. Lennart E Nacke and Craig A Lindley. 2010. Affective ludology, flow and immersion in a first-person shooter: Measurement of player experience. *arXiv preprint arXiv:1004.0248* (2010).
19. Oculus VR, LLC. 2016. Oculus Best Practices. https://developer3.oculus.com/documentation/intro-vr/latest/concepts/bp_intro/. (2016). Accessed: 2017-04-12.
20. Reinhard Pekrun. 2006. The Control-Value Theory of Achievement Emotions: Assumptions, Corollaries, and Implications for Educational Research and Practice. *Educational Psychology Review* 18, 4 (2006), 315–341.
21. Ray, Sheri Graner. 2010. Tutorials: Learning to play. http://www.gamasutra.com/view/feature/134531/tutorials_learning_to_play.php. (2010). Accessed: 2017-04-11.
22. Richard Rouse III. 2010. *Game design: Theory and practice*. Jones & Bartlett Learning.
23. Claudia Schrader, Julia Brich, Julian Frommel, Valentin Riemer, and Katja Rogers. 2017. Rising to the Challenge: An Emotion-Driven Approach Toward Adaptive Serious Games. In *Serious Games and Edutainment Applications*. Springer, 3–28.
24. Chek Tien Tan, Tuck Wah Leong, Songjia Shen, Christopher Dubravs, and Chen Si. 2015. Exploring Gameplay Experiences on the Oculus Rift. In *Proceedings of the 2015 Annual Symposium on Computer-Human Interaction in Play (CHI PLAY '15)*. ACM, New York, NY, USA, 253–263. DOI: http://dx.doi.org/10.1145/2793107.2793117
25. Valve. 2004. *Half-Life 2*. Game [PC]. (16 Nov 2004). Valve.
26. Valve. 2016. *The Lab*. Game [HTC Vive]. (5 April 2016). Valve.
27. Croteam VR. 2016. *Serious Sam VR: The Last Hope*. Game [HTC Vive]. (17 Oct 2016). Devolver Digital, Croteam.

28. Bob G Witmer and Michael J Singer. 1998. Measuring presence in virtual environments: A presence questionnaire. *Presence: Teleoperators and virtual environments* 7, 3 (1998), 225–240.

29. Georgios N Yannakakis and Julian Togelius. 2011. Experience-driven procedural content generation. *IEEE Transactions on Affective Computing* 2, 3 (2011), 147–161.

Evaluating the Onboarding Phase of Free-to-Play Mobile Games: A Mixed-Method Approach

Falko Weigert Petersen
Department of Communication Aalborg University
Copenhagen, Denmark
falkowp@hotmail.com

Line Ebdrup Thomsen
Department of Communication Aalborg University
Copenhagen, Denmark
let@hum.aau.dk

Pejman Mirza-Babaei
University of Ontario Institute of Technology
Oshawa, Canada
Pejman.Mirza-Babaei@uoit.ca

Anders Drachen
Digital Creativity Labs, University of York
York, United Kingdom
anders.drachen@york.ac.uk

ABSTRACT
The first few minutes of play, commonly referred to as the onboarding phase, of Free-to-Play mobile games typically display a substantial churn rate among new players. It is therefore vital for designers to effectively evaluate this phase to investigate its satisfaction of player expectations. This paper presents a study utilizing a lab-based mixed-methods approach in providing insights for evaluating the user experience of onboarding phases in mobile games. This includes an investigation into the contribution of physiological measures (Heart-Rate Variability and Galvanic Skin Conductance) as well as a range of self-reported proxy measures including: a) stimulated recall, engagement graphs, b) flow state survey and c) post-game experience questionnaire. These techniques were applied across 28 participants using three mobile Free-to-Play titles from different genres. This paper makes two important contributions to the games user research (GUR) domain: 1) evaluates different research techniques (e.g. physiological measures and experience graphs) in the context of mobile games; 2) provides an empirically based recommendation for design elements that result in high arousal.

ACM Classification Keywords
H.5.2 Information Interfaces and Presentation: User interfaces – Evaluation/ methodology

Author Keywords
Mobile Games; GUR; Games User Research; Onboarding phase; User Experience; Free-to-Play; Freemium; F2P.

INTRODUCTION
In recent years, alongside technological advancements, the Freemium business model with the Free-to-Play (F2P, FtP), revenue model has come to dominate the mobile game market [1]. F2P functions by initially offering the game to the player for free, generating revenue via in-game advertisements and purchases [2,3,4]. Although the model is attractive, due to the low financial barrier of entry for new players, developers face many challenges, such as discoverability issues caused by saturation in the F2P market across Android and iOS platforms. Moreover, the first few minutes of play, also referred to as the onboarding phase, is highly critical for F2P games. As they are also characterized by low player retention rates (i.e., most players that leave within a few minutes of play never return) [4,5]. While specific rates vary from game to game, and there are few verified data sources available on the topic, one general estimate suggests that only 28.60% of players return to a game after the first day, and retention rates drop exponentially as a function of the time since the player was last in contact with the game [6]. Many other studies (i.e., Sifa et al. [7] and Hadiji et al. [4]) also reported similar rapid attrition, however, the causes of the low retention rate in F2P mobile games varies based on factors such as competition, traffic sources, and failing to meet user expectations. There are also studies that argued one potential key issue could be poorly designed onboarding experiences (i.e., the starting experience does not foster engagement) [6,1]. For example, Seufert [1] describes the user's first session with a product as being critical in determining the player's lifetime experience with the game in question and it is therefore "worthy of the product team's attention when optimizing the user experience".

In addition to development costs, rises in User Acquisition Cost (UAC - describing the cost of acquiring new players via marketing), market research, and advertising demand that F2P games rapidly engage and retain new players in order to generate profit. Hence, the onboarding phase is arguably more critical in F2P games because players have not yet made any investment in the game, unlike premium games, where the full game is paid for in advance. The F2P revenue model will thus only generate an adequate return on investment (ROI) if users continue to play after the onboarding phases has ended.

Research addressing the onboarding phase of mobile F2P titles, and the development of evaluation frameworks

CHI PLAY '17, October 15–18, 2017, Amsterdam, Netherlands

ACM ISBN 978-1-4503-4898-0/17/10.
DOI: https://doi.org/10.1145/3116595.3125499

suitable for mobile titles, has the potential to address these challenges. There are, however, to the best of our knowledge, limited resources available for the evaluation of mobile games – including the applicability and adaptation of different user research methods in such contexts, work targeting the onboarding phases of games, or design implications of such work. This means that any attempt at investigating the onboarding phase of mobile F2P titles will need to start by considering related work for other, more documented categories of games. A more detailed description of the onboarding phase as a concept and how it is used in this paper will be described in the related work section.

The current approaches for evaluating User Experience (UX) in digital games are largely based on methods that have been adapted from other fields, repurposed in the domain of Game User Research (GUR) [8]. User research has been embraced by the game industry, as it can generate meaningful user insights, which could provide a competitive edge for game companies [9]. However, the success of conducting user research in the context of games is largely dependent on appropriately applying methods which are traditionally reserved for productivity applications to game features [10]. Approaches for evaluating player experience are grounded in a variety of fields and feature-structured research protocols. Evaluation practices vary between developers, and elements like game genre, platform, and target audience are some factors that can affect evaluation techniques throughout the development process [8].

This paper will investigate a range of UX proxy measures for evaluating the onboarding phase of F2P mobile games, including the contributions of physiological measures in evaluating small-factor gaming platforms.

RELATED WORK

Mobile games have been the target of Human-Computer Interaction (HCI) and games research, but mainly in the context of application-specific requirements or the establishment of design guidelines [11], and rarely in terms of evaluating one or more elements or factors impacting UX in mobile games. This is evident in the few references that exist on mobile games and UX. For example, Duh et al. [12] examined the lack of UX research on mobile games, and highlighted a need for research on UX and form factors in mobile games. They investigated three different games played on a mobile platform and discussed control elements such as complexity, motor skill, and interface mapping. Similarly, Engl & Nacke [13] suggested that the context of play was important for the user experience in mobile gaming, and adapted contextual models to suit the mobile situation, noting the need for further research. Moreover, Paul et al. [14] studied social aspects of mobile gaming, which identified socialization as one of the key contextual drivers in playing mobile games, and emphasized the lack of available knowledge on testing methodologies for this format.

A substantial amount of attention in GUR has been directed at exploring the use of physiological (or psycho-physiological) measures to evaluate user experience in games [15,16]. Parallel to similar developments in academia, game studios have started using physiological measures. For example, Chalfoun [17] reported on the use of physiological measures within the User Research Team at Ubisoft. Ambinder [18] reported on similar use of physiological measures – such as Heart Rate (HR), Galvanic Skin Response (GSR), and facial expressions – as possible inputs for games that respond to physiological signals.

Physiological measures require extensive knowledge to implement and can be difficult to analyze, complicating its use in comparison with other user research methods such as observation and interview. Collecting and evaluating physiological data is one out of many methods for evaluating UX, but many studies have reported the fundamental advantage of providing continuous and unconscious recordings of UX [15,19].

Despite this interest and the arguably recent rapid growth of the mobile game industry, the use of physiological measures has not been utilized for evaluation of mobile games; or, such knowledge has not yet been made available in the public domain. Furthermore, there has been little research on using physiological measures to evaluate mobile applications in general, with few exceptions. For instance, Yao et al. [20] reported on a preliminary study examining the possibility of including physiological responses for task performance testing on mobile platforms. They investigated GSR data on failed vs. successful task completions, correlating this response with simple self-reported UX measures. The results indicate that there is potential value in using physiological measures to evaluate UX in mobile applications.

It is thus unclear how well current evaluation techniques translate from large form factor PC and console games, to the smaller form factor screens of mobile phones and tablets. Furthermore, divergent use contexts and different control schemes (often solely touch-based) can also impact the insights generated via different methods, which in turn may require adaptation to suit the mobile product – similar to how user research techniques from productivity applications were modified to suit the evaluation of video games [8,19].

GUR Methods: Towards a Framework for Mobile Games

This section focuses on key related work regarding methodologies for measuring UX in mobile games.

Evaluating F2P mobile games

The existing body of literature available on F2P games is mainly focused on the revenue model [2] and the use of analytics [21], which are applied in the prediction of purchase decisions [7]. The relationships between critical acclaim and commercial success in mobile free-to-play games have also been investigated. These studies often focus on factors relevant to the success of specific games (e.g. marketing budget or strategy) [22]. Our focus, however, is to establish methods for UX evaluation of onboarding phases. The challenge is that existing literature in this particular area is sparse and largely outdated, as the mobile platform has undergone vast technological advances since its establishment as a gaming platform. For example, Korhonen [23] conducted a study comparing user testing methods (think-aloud, questionnaire, and post-session interview) with expert reviews (using playability heuristics [11]). Although the study was conducted in 2010, the device and the game used are almost incomparable with today's systems. A newer study by Alha et al. [24] also used playability heuristics to evaluate issues in games based on the F2P revenue model. However, the games studied were played through social networks, and are therefore not directly comparable with traditional mobile games. Expert review methods have also been compared to user testing, indicating that expert review is able to discover usability problems, but that user testing is able to reveal very detailed and specific usability problems, which were not adequately identified by expert review [23]. Moreover, expert reviews often suffer from experts' subjective opinions [25].

GUR Measures

When conducting GUR, selecting the right evaluation method depends on several variables (e.g., which kinds of data researchers want to collect). Questionnaires are frequently used for user testing, but often as a supplement to other methods, and can be used before, during, or after a play session. This method focuses on collecting players' self-report impressions and attitudes regarding factors including experience, engagement, and motivation [26,27]. However, the use of self-reporting measures for data collection incurs challenges such as self-selected and time-dependent biases. Hence, using questionnaires or interviews to measure UX elements suffers from the underlying problem of relying on participants' discussion decisions (they may only refer to game events that were meaningful to them) and their ability to recall their experiences of those events [28]. One way to minimize biases in interviews is by using video recordings of the participant's gameplay session to facilitate improved memory, also known as stimulated recall [28]. Another relatively new technique supporting participant memory is the use of experience graphs, where researchers instruct players to draw a curve visualizing their experience and describe it afterwards [29]. Studies show that these graphs accurately reflect overall experience, but are limited in detail [19]. The graphs also appear to address the perception issue by tying the player's impressions of play to their memory of actual in-game events, which will very likely be the issues or successes that participants may communicate to other potential players [19].

Physiological research emphasizes measurement of physiological signals, enabling the identification of associated mental processes [19]. Human experiences are theorized to be highly associated with the emotions encountered during an interaction. The use of physiological measures to identify and understand emotional reactions is common in a range of academic fields [30].

Two of the most widely used methods in academic GUR literature are Galvanic Skin Response (GSR) and Heart Rate Variability (HRV). Both are considered lightweight measures, feature portable equipment, and are seeing use in industrial contexts [18]. GSR is viewed as a reasonably robust measure of arousal if not misused or directly abused [31]. The HRV score is a widely used measure for assessing arousal by looking at the activity of the autonomic nervous system. Photoplethysmogram (PPG) sensors can be used to measure the interbeat interval (IBI) of the heart, by monitoring changes in the blood volume. IBI is than used to calculate the HRV score [32]. Although these measures have been used with both PC/console games and other media and productivity applications, they have not, to the best knowledge of the authors, been previously explored in the context of mobile games.

The Onboarding Phase in F2P Mobile Games

As discussed earlier, the onboarding phase is a critical component in the design of F2P mobile games due to their high attrition rates. Despite this, there are limited resources and research available on this topic.

A related concept in game analytics [33] is First-Time User Experience (FTUE). FTUE refers to the experience of playing a game for the first time. Available knowledge is mainly based on industry research [34,35] and aims to provide design tips on constructing the optimal FTUE, for example, via the application of design principles [36].

Chou [5] presented the Octalysis (within the domain of gamification), a theoretical framework describing eight core player motivations connected to four phases of a player's journey [5]. The first phase is Discovery, which features the player's motivation for wanting to try out the experience. The next phase is Onboarding, where players learn the rules and tools required to play the game [5]. The last two phases are Scaffolding and Endgames, which are concerned with repeated actions taken towards a specific goal, and how current players' motivation can be retained. Hence, the onboarding phase, as defined by Chou [5], begins as soon as the players download the game and ends when the players have mastered the core mechanics and fundamental skills required for the early stages of the game.

On the other hand, Seufert [1] introduces the onboarding funnel, which is an event-based graph of player churn during the initial set of game interactions. He also refers to the "onboarding period" and elaborates that it can vary from being "a very explicit sequence of levels or events" to "a more vague sequence of events employed over multiple game sessions". However, his description of the purpose of onboarding is very similar to Chou's [5], *"the purpose of the onboarding process is to introduce a new user to the product and equip the user with the knowledge necessary to interact completely with the product's feature set*" [1] (P98).

This paper adapts a definition of the onboarding phase in mobile games based on related research and available industry sources, including reviewing the onboarding of 25 top-ranked F2P mobile games available on Android and iOS App stores, as well as discussions with developers from two game studios (King and Norsfell). Based on these discussions, we tracked the onboarding phase as defined by Seufert [1]. However, we also utilized Chou's [5] definition, as we needed an end time for the onboarding phase, in order to evaluate it effectively. Chou [5] describes the end of the phase as when "users are fully equipped and they are ready to take on the journey on their own". For our purposes, the onboarding phase starts from the first time a player interacts with the game client, and lasts until the completion of a learning phase covering the core game mechanics. Using this definition we examined the onboarding phase of three different games, detailed in the following section. We determined that the onboarding phase of the games used would last around seven minutes (during which players complete the tutorial and/or learn the core mechanics). The designers at King and Norsfell (studios who developed the games in this study) validated this definition as fitting for all three games used in the studies.

EVALUATION

To investigate the contributions of different GUR methods in evaluating the mobile onboarding experience, we designed a mixed-methods experimental setup to study three different F2P titles. The games selected were *Candy Crush Jelly Saga* [37], *WinterForts* [38], and *Pogo Chick* [39]. The measures utilized include two physiological measures, HRV obtained via PPG sensors [32] and GSR, combined with self-report proxy measures related to UX and engagement: questionnaires, stimulated recall interviews, and engagement graphs. GSR and HRV were both chosen based on related literature (as discussed earlier) describing them as lightweight measures with a low level of intrusiveness that can be collected and analyzed without extensive specialized knowledge regarding physiological measures.

Setup

The experimental setup was based on a within-subject design [40] where each participant was exposed to three different mobile game onboarding phases. All test sessions were held in the same location, on weekdays between 10:00 and 19:00, with each test session lasting approximately one hour and 30 minutes. After a short introduction including information about the test session, the participant was asked to sign a consent form informing them about the purpose of the test session, their rights, and how the collected data would be handled and stored.

The Games

The participants played the onboarding phase of three different mobile games, *Candy Crush Jelly Saga*, *WinterForts*, and *Pogo Chick* (see Figure 1). Each game had unique onboarding phases, play styles, and genre features (puzzle, strategy, and arcade). Diverse genres and onboarding styles were chosen to make the sample representative of the variety available in the mobile games market, with the goal of yielding more generalizable results. These titles were also selected based on an ongoing collaboration with the developers. This was an important factor, as the study relied on input from the developers for their intended design.

Figure 1: In-game screenshots of the onboarding phases of *Pogo Chick* (Top left), *Candy Crush Jelly Saga* (Top Right), and *WinterForts* (Bottom) [41].

Participants

The participants included 21 females and seven males. The age of the participants ranged from 20-37 years (mean = 25.25; SD = 3.63). The gender inequality in our sample is due to the uneven distribution among people who volunteered to participate in the study. Participants were recruited voluntarily through email and social networks. Demographic data was collected as well as information on prior game experiences. All participants played mobile games at least 1-2 days a week and the majority considered themselves casual players. During the pre-session interview, the participants were asked if they had prior experience with the games in this study. While most participants had played earlier versions of *Candy Crush*, none had played *Candy Crush Jelly Saga*. Additionally, none of the participants had prior experience with *WinterForts* or *Pogo Chick*.

Apparatus

Participants sat in a comfortable chair while electrodes and the PPG sensor were applied. The participants were asked to rest for three minutes while a baseline for physiological measures was recorded. After the rest period, the participants were given a tablet with a running game. The participant played each game for approximately seven minutes, which represented the onboarding experience, as discussed in the previous section. To reduce the potential of carryover effects [40] affecting the data collection, a counterbalancing approach was utilized. The six different gameplay orders were assigned evenly amongst participants.

Pre-session and physiological measures

Physiological data (GSR and IBI) was recorded during the play sessions. After each session, questionnaires, interviews, and experience graphs were collected. Skin conduction levels were measured using a Bitalino sensor and the included recording and visualization software. Pre-gelled Skintact F-401C silver-silver chloride (Ag-AgCl) electrodes, were attached to the participant's ring and little fingers on the non-dominant hand, to reduce interference during play. The electrodes where disposed after each test session to reduce the potential for electrode polarization [42]. The participants reported feeling no particular hindrance from this attachment method. IBI data was recorded using a Merlin-digital Heart Rate Monitor PRO (PPG sensor) attached to participants' left earlobe. An iPad Mini 3 was used for the test sessions. The iPad was placed in a stable mount, which enabled the participant to comfortably play the three different games while allowing screen recording. The same iPad was used to ensure that every participant had the same game experience and in an attempt to control the extraneous variables that the use of different devices could add to the study. Two video cameras, a GoPro Hero3 and a Panasonic HC-V700 HD Camcorder, were used for this study. The HC-V700 HD was placed behind the participants to record the screen of the tablet. The GoPro Hero3 was placed in front of the test participant in order to record movement and other events that could have introduced bias into the collected data

Post-session and self-reported measures

The post-play sessions consisted of five steps: 1) drawing first experience graph [19]; 2) FSS questionnaire [26]; 3) stimulated recall interviews [43]; 4) drawing second experience graph; 5) PGQ questionnaire [44]. Immediately after playing each onboarding phase, the participants were asked to draw an experience graph and to subsequently explain the graph. This is a method previously used by other researchers [19] and serves as a tool for helping participants visualize and reflect upon their recent experience. The participants were provided with a pen and paper with pre-drawn X and Y axes. The participants were instructed that the x axis represented time, with the y axis symbolizing the level of experience (positive to negative), and directed to draw a graph resembling their game experience. After the participants finished drawing the first graph, they completed the FSS, a multiple choice Likert scale item questionnaire. The questionnaire was printed out and presented to the participants. Following this, participants completed a stimulated recall interview. Stimulated recall can be an alternative to think-aloud techniques, as it is conducted post-play and therefore does not disturb the collection of physiological data. Similar to the think-aloud method, participants were instructed to speak their mind during a video of their gameplay. This allowed for the participant to comment freely while the facilitators are able to ask follow up questions when deeper insight is needed. This method also enabled players to point out exactly where they had an encountered issues, as they might otherwise remember only an emotional impression (e.g., feeling annoyed or confused) without sufficient details of the interaction leading to this impression. After finishing both the FSS questionnaire and stimulated recall interview, the participants were asked to draw a second experience graph to clarify whether they had a different recollection of their experience after watching their play session. Lastly, the participants were asked to answer the PGQ, another multiple choice Likert scale item questionnaire. This approach was followed for each onboarding phase condition. Before the first test session, several pilot tests were conducted to optimize the setup and detect issues related to participant fatigue following guidelines by Bordens & Abbot [40].

DATA ANALYSIS

Data analysis consisted of multiple steps: 1) post-session processing of physiological data; 2) evaluation of the FSS and PGQ surveys; 3) explorative content coding of the post-session interviews; 4) evaluation and comparison of the experience graphs with GSR and HRV; 5) comparative and correlational analysis across the qualitative and quantitative measures. This approach was used for all three evaluated games. For the physiological measures, the recorded GSR data was first visually inspected to check for logging gaps [45]. Logging gaps were identified in the GSR data for four test sessions and were excluded from the analysis, while no logging gaps were identified in the IBI data. The next step in the GSR analysis was a normalization of the data, since skin conductance level (SCL) can vary from participant to participant and absolute GSR values are therefore not comparable between participants. GSR data was normalized using a rescaling technique that was used in similar previous analysis [15]:

$$GSR_{Normalized} = \frac{(GSR_{(t)} - GSR_{Min})}{(GSR_{Max} - GSR_{Min})}$$

In the GSR normalization above, *GSRMin* and *GSRMax* refer to the minimum and maximum GSR values in a certain time frame. *GSRt* is a GSR data point contained within the time frame [46]. After normalizing the physiological data, it was divided into smaller time windows that were based on the game design (e.g. levels for *Candy Crush*). This was done in order to identify how participants' physiological responses fluctuated throughout the play session. This furthermore provided context for the data and enabled the creation of composite graphs for both GSR and HRV for all three games. The GSR and HRV graphs were compared to the experience graphs created by the game designers and participants (an example of these graphs can be seen in Figure 2-4). This was done to investigate whether physiological data would mirror the indented design of the developers, which could then help to indicate if the onboarding design is experienced as intended.

The recordings of the test sessions were used for multiple purposes. A meaning condensation was created for the stimulated recall interviews and subsequently compared to the experience graphs drawn during the test session. The meaning condensations were then also coded through an open approach to identify emerging patterns and issues discovered during the test sessions. Recordings were also used for the second part of the physiological data analysis, examining whether peaks in GSR or HRV data was event-related or non-specific. The GSR and HRV data was normalized into seven-second time frames [46]. This allowed for the identification of small game events that caused a fluctuation in the physiological responses across participants. The game events were then identified using the screen recordings for each game and logged to determine whether similar events caused changes in arousal across different participants (see Table 1).

RESULTS

Several findings were observed throughout this study: 1) insights on events that caused arousal in the players during the onboarding phase; 2) Contribution of using physiological measures and other user research methods in a mobile game context; 3) a relationship between the proxy measure of UX (experience graph), and the physiological composite graphs; 4) a set of onboarding heuristics, which is discussed in our previous article [47].

Although physiological measures have previously been used for the evaluation of video games, no study has discussed the contribution of these measures in evaluating an onboarding phase of mobile games. One of our main goals was to investigate if mobile games had the capability to cause changes in the participant's arousal levels. The analysis of the physiological data showed that it was possible to pinpoint specific game events that caused fluctuations in the participant arousal levels. Table 1 shows events across all three games yielding the most notable increases in arousal. In *Candy Crush* Jelly Saga, the level change event caused high arousal among 24 of the participants. For *Winter Forts*, the most notable event was the appearance of the advisor character; for *Pogo Chick*, the most consistently arousing event was player death.

When comparing the physiological data (coded in table 1) to the meaning condensed interview data, it was found that the participants described their game experience on a more general level when interviewed, when compared to the physiological data. During the stimulated recall, and while explaining their experience graphs, the participants described feelings they had during specific moments. During the stimulated recall of *WinterForts*, 19 participants expressed annoyance during battles, where players were forced to wait for several minutes while the game performed all actions automatically, and 24 participants felt frustration after dying several times in *Pogo Chick*. In addition, the interview data revealed game elements that were hard to identify by the means of physiological measures. For example, during the stimulated recall, participants stated that the music added a positive element to the games (*WinterForts* 79%, *Pogo Chick* 63%, and *Candy Crush* Jelly Saga 45%). The high percentage of participants indicating this during *WinterForts*, indicates that the music contributed positively to the participant's game experience. This element would be challenging to identify if only inspecting the physiological measures.

The analysis of the physiological measures also indicates that they are event-specific and more objective than self-reported measures when evaluating mobile games, specifically the onboarding phase of these games. On the other hand, not all game elements that formed the overall user experience could be identified by the means of physiological measures alone, for example, the feeling of success that participants described after playing *Candy Crush Jelly Saga*. Furthermore, during the analysis of the physiological measures, counter-attacking was identified as a game event in *WinterForts* that caused high levels of arousal. During the stimulated recall however, it was found that a feeling of annoyance instigated by a lack of autonomy caused this change. The physiological measures used for this study demonstrated fluctuations in the arousal level of the participants, however, they do not indicate the valence (i.e., positive or negative quality) of these changes, and may be influenced by external disturbances, not related to the test sessions. This made the analysis of the physiological data time-consuming, which the literature review identified as another general drawback of using physiological measures.

Candy Crush Jelly Saga		*WinterForts*		*Pogo Chick*	
Game Events	Count	Game Events	Count	Game Event	Count
Frame Change	24	Meeting advisor	21	Death	18
Considering what move to make	20	Mining	19	Restarting after death	16
Using Special candy	17	Counter attack	15	Challenging map element	14
Level completed	14	Building roads	8	Jump without visible track	9
Chain Reaction	13	Naming fort	8	Close to dying	8
Instruction Tutorial	13	Upgrading castle	8	Exploring menus	7
Level Overview	13	Add	7	Finding balance	3
Positive feedback	13	Building workers	7	Add	2
End Level Explosions	11	Completing quest	7	Selecting new skin	2
Illegal Move	10	Browsing menus	6	Unlocking new skin	2
Level begins	9	Building solider	6	Browsing skins	1
Special Candy Creation	6	Clicking during attack	5		
Fast Move	5	Browsing quests	4		
Notification	5	Attacked by enemy	3		
External events (not game related)	3	Enemy commander	3		
Restarting level (after fail)	2	Game bug	3		
		Browsing Buildings	2		
		Browsing enemy base	1		
		Finding treasure chest	1		

Table 1: Game event identified in the physiological data (seven-second normalization) for the three evaluated games and the number of times events were identified across all participants. Each event was only counted once per participant [41].

The stimulated recall interviews and the experience graphs also generated different levels of insights. While the experience graph is more concerned with general concepts and the overall game experience, the stimulated recall interviews fostered more event-specific descriptions of how emotional responses developed, and thus provided more specific insights. Participants would often pinpoint events drawn on the graph during the interview, indicating that the recall of some of the emotions and events described during interviews may have depended on participants' ability to draw and refer to a graph. When compared with physiological measures, which can locate many events connected to specific design elements, the stimulated interview identifies fewer events, but affords more in-depth descriptions of game experience.

Combining stimulated recall interview and experience graphs with physiological measures was found to be a useful data collection method, as the data was collected post-play and thereby did not add noise to the GSR and HRV data. The stimulated recall also reminded participants of issues they might not have disclosed or remembered during their description of the experience graph.

Additionally, this approach also proved to be useful for the participants to describe playing habits, context, and how they valued playing games in general. The act of playing a game and subsequently being interviewed about their experience appeared to trigger a need for sharing details 'about their general relationship with and use of games. The participants reported: 1) usually playing with sound off to avoid disturbing their surrounding;, 2) that games helped them relax in their stressful everyday life; 3) if they could relate to the theme of the game.

- *"The chick sounds are funny, also the sound that the chick makes when I fall. Although I do not usually have the sound turned on when I play. " (P3, Pogo Chick)*
- *"I am thinking constantly and it is just a way to get away from your thoughts." (P18, Candy Crush Jelly Saga)*
- *"It was the same and I was not engaged at all. The medieval theme is not me at all." (P12, WinterForts)*

The questionnaire analysis started by investigating the reliability of the PGQ and FSS answers by calculating Cronbach's Alpha. Both the FSS and PGQ had acceptable Cronbach's alpha scores (.7 and above in all scales for both the PGQ and FSS). While analyzing the PGQ it was found that the participants rated *Candy Crush Jelly Saga* as the most positive, followed by *WinterForts*. *Pogo Chick* was rated highest on the negative game experience scale, in line with the players descriptions of feeling frustrated because of the difficulty of the game.

	Positive	Negative
Candy Crush Jelly Saga	2.27 (SD=1.19)	1.52 (SD=.94)
Pogo Chick	1.74 (SD=.95)	2.04 (SD=1.40)
WinterForts	2.08 (SD=1.40)	1.83 (SD=.99)

Table 2: Average scores for the positive and negative scales of the PGQ [41].

In addition to *Candy Crush Jelly Saga* being rated most positive in the PGQ, it also managed to get the highest Flow score, followed by *WinterForts* with the second highest, and *Pogo Chick* with the lowest FSS score.

Game	Average flow scores
Candy Crush Jelly Saga	3.84 (SD = 1.03)
WinterForts	3.11 (SD = 1.26)
Pogo Chick	3.04 (SD = 1.30)

Table 3: Average FSS score for the three tested games

In addition to coding the physiological data, GSR and HRV were also visualized by composite average graphs that showed the average experience of all participants. These composite average graphs were created for the onboarding phase of all three games and compared to the experience graphs created by the game developers, visualizing the intended experience during the onboarding phases, and the experience graphs created by the participants.

When comparing the designers' intended experience graphs to the composite player experience graphs, it was found that the two graphs for *Candy Crush Jelly Saga* matched well, in the sense that both graphs increased and decreased at the same time. This indicated that the onboarding experience of *Candy Crush Jelly Saga*, in relation to arousal and experience, follows the intended design.

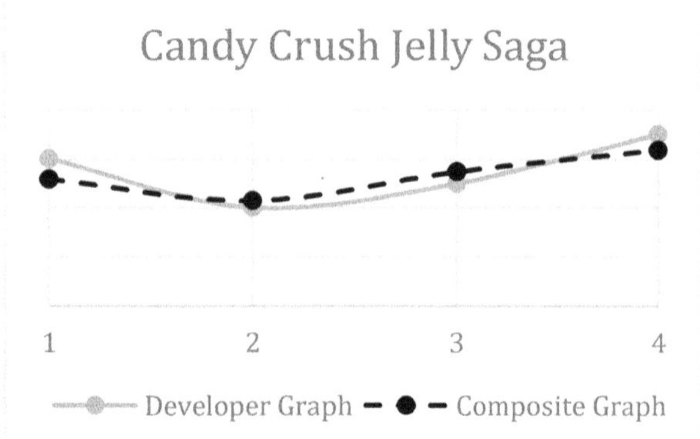

Figure 2: Comparison between designer-intended user experience graph and average player experience graph for *Candy Crush Jelly Saga*. The graphs show the experience for each of the levels that the participated played during the test session, meaning that each number on the X-axis equates to an in-game level [41].

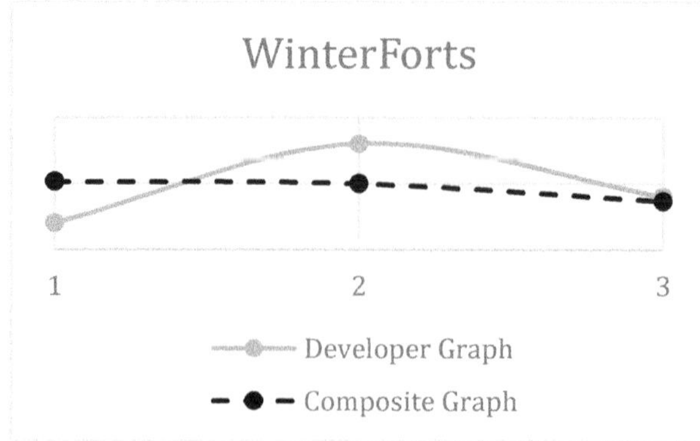

Figure 3: Comparison between designer-intended user experience graph and average player experience graph for *WinterForts*. The first point on the X-axis is the moment where the participants started playing the onboarding phase. The second point is where the tutorial ended, and the third is the end of the onboarding phase

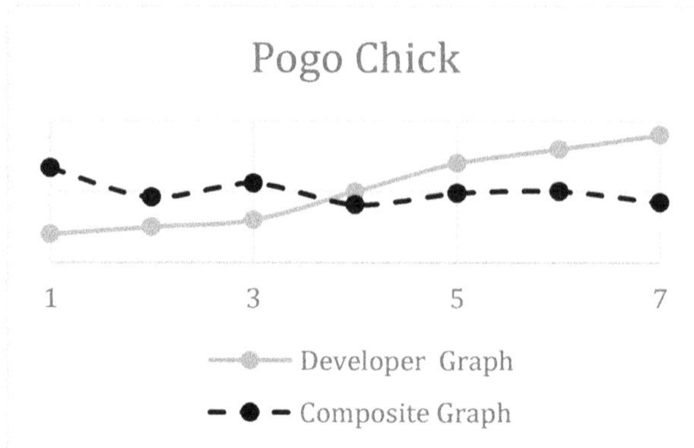

Figure 4: Developer and average player experience graph comparison for *Pogo Chick*. Points on the X-axis delineate minutes of gameplay time. This scaling was chosen due to the loosely structured nature of *Pogo Chick's* onboarding phase [41].

During the interview with the developers of *WinterForts*, it was stated that the experience of the players should increase during the course of the tutorial, as players build their fort and engage in battles with enemies and decrease when the tutorial ended. When inspecting the average graph however, it was visible that the arousal level did not increase during the tutorial phase, but follows the intended design after the tutorial ended. While analyzing the data, collected through stimulated recall and the explanations of the participant created experience graphs, it was found that this lack of engagement was caused by the highly structure tutorial phase, where participants missed the feeling of autonomy. Figure 4 shows the developer and average player experience graphs for *Pogo Chick*. The game was designed to be a challenging action game, and the goal of the designers was that the engagement should only increase during the onboarding phase. The average graph however shows that, even though the arousal level increases at several points, the overall arousal level is decreasing over time.

In addition to comparing player and designer experience graphs, a comparison between the participants' created experience graphs and the average physiological data graphs, was performed. The analysis showed that 43.4% of the participant graphs for *Candy Crush Jelly Saga* and 42% of the graphs for *Pogo Chick* had a strong visual resemblance to the physiological graphs. However, only 17.3% of the participant-created graphs shared characteristics with the average physiological graph for *WinterForts*. While inspecting the self-reported data, no common explanation could be found for this low resemblance compared to the other two games.

DISCUSSION AND CONCLUSIONS

The focus of the work presented here was to evaluate the adaption of physiological, qualitative, and self-report techniques to evaluate UX in the onboarding phase of three F2P mobile games. A number of experiences were drawn from the methodological implementation that bears importance on future work regarding the adoption of physiological measures in mobile game contexts.

Applying Physiological Measures in Mobile Games User Research

The results of this study indicate that physiological measures can be applied to evaluate mobile games, similar to PC and console game contexts [48], as well as for mobile productivity applications, though evidence for this use case is highly limited [20]. While the event-dependent activation of GSR and HRV signals appears similar to those for other game formats, it is worth noting that the arousal-related signals were generally of lower amplitude than reported for other formats [19,48]. The comparison was made by looking at the results from other studies but even though an educated guess could be made on why PC or console horror games tend to generate higher amplitude responses than F2P mobile games, it is still unknown which elements cause this disparity (e.g., screen size, sounds, genre etc.).

The mixed-methods approach used for this study showed how the techniques used could provide insights on specific game events. The engagement graphs visualized the main spikes in participants' remembered experience, and explanation provided information about the reason behind the spikes. This method relied on participant memory and ability to recall specific game events, however, this means that this technique identified arguably the most meaningful events. On the other hand, physiological measures could highlight specific game events that cause fluctuations in player arousal levels, without the need for the participants to remember the specific event, and are thereby more objective then both stimulated recall and the experience graphs [16]. The physiological measures taken alone did not, however, explain the reason behind these fluctuations in the arousal levels. The stimulated recall interviews provided insights about the participant's feelings and reasons behind specific game events, but like the experience graphs, require the participant to remember and interpret their experience. While each of these three methods alone could provide information about the onboarding phase of mobile games, and potentially be used to improve the user experience, the three methods used together can provide a more holistic picture about player's game experience. Moreover, since physiological measures represent unconscious responses, they are less contaminated by variables such as answering style or interpretation of questionnaire items. Physiological measures have previously been perceived as expensive in relation to equipment and training [48], but with today's advancements in technology and the increasing focus on smart health care, equipment has become more advanced, less intrusive, and cheaper. The rise of smart personal health care has, over the years, produced new and more capable devices, such as sports watches with GSR and PPG sensors, while still maintaining relatively high precision and minimizing intrusiveness. It was also found during the literature review, that off-the-shelf equipment enables the collection of physiological data, to be utilized in a much wider range across research fields [30].

Furthermore, during the planning phase of this project, it was decided that physiological data would be analyzed post-session. However, because GSR and HRV were relatively lightweight and easy to analyze, the data could potentially have been preliminarily analyzed while the participants complete the first experience graph and questionnaire, providing a tool for the interviewer to ask more precise probing questions during the stimulated recall interviews. Future work could investigate if this alteration of the test setup, where preliminary analysis of physiological data acts as an interview tool, could improve the setup and provide deeper and more precise information about the player experience during the onboarding phase of mobile games.

The Onboarding Phase

During the initial research for this study, poorly designed onboarding phases, amongst others, were identified as one of the main reasons for the typical high churn rate of F2P mobile games. One of the goals of this study was to create a test setup that could be used to collect FTUE data and provide game designers with a tool to improve this phase. During the analysis of the physiological data, average player arousal graphs were created and compared to the designers' intended user experience graphs, visualizing player experience. This comparison has the potential to help game designers improve the onboarding phase of their games highlighting differences between actual player arousal and the intended design. More research is needed to refine and improve this method in order to maximize the value that these graphs provide for game designers. Future studies could focus on improving the use of physiological measures and experience graphs by combining them with data analytics, which are already widely used by mobile game companies to improve their games.

The analysis of the data collected during the test sessions showed that all three games use highly diverse onboarding styles, and all three games contained some game elements that were perceived negatively by the participants (e.g., lacking autonomy in *WinterForts*, waiting times during end level explosions in *Candy Crush Jelly Saga*, and the challenging controls in *Pogo Chick*). Our methods highlighted these and several more game elements that could be improved to create an even more enjoyable onboarding experience for players and thereby potentially increase player retention rates. In general, if players are exposed to the same stimuli, comparing results across multiple players is comparatively simple; comparison can be more challenging if many different first-time experiences exist. For example, *Candy Crush Jelly Saga* presents almost identical onboarding experiences across players, whereas *Pogo Chick* opted for more variety.

Even though the techniques used provided deep information about player experience, one of the main drawbacks of the testing setup is that it used a combination of data collection techniques, which makes the test sessions relatively complex, and requires extensive planning. This complexity could potentially be problematic for small game companies without a dedicated UX or GUR department. Future studies could therefore also focus on how this method could be improved to make it more accessible for smaller organizations. This is also the case for other situations where onboarding experiences are particularly important, such as ensuring successful learning in virtual labs and educational applications. A potential reduction in complexity could be achieved by removing the two questionnaires, as the physiological measures together with experience graphs and stimulated recall interview provided a rich data source even without the two questionnaires. Another benefit of removing the two questionnaires from the test setup would be reduced length of the test sessions.

In conclusion, physiological measures can be utilized to evaluate the UX of mobile games, when supported by the qualitative measures, such as stimulated recall interviews and experience graphs, to provide insights into the impact of design on player experience. This finding thus broadly corresponds with conclusions from other game formats [49], although the focus for onboarding phases demands a particular level of detail, as high F2P attrition rates mean that mobile developers must refine action-response cycles on a literal second-by-second basis to optimize UX. The apparent relationship between the physiological measures (arousal), average player experience graphs, and self-reported engagement measures indicates a connection between physiological arousal responses, and qualitative proxy measures of engagement, which is a key UX component for F2P mobile games [33,7]. The full relationship between the measures requires additional research to explore, ideally including additional dimensions of UX, and introducing the valence dimension of physiological measures, even if these measures are not yet economically viable in industrial contexts [50,18].

LIMITATIONS

This study has only been conducted with the onboarding phases of three mobile games, and additional empirical research is thus needed in order to establish the quality of this methodological approach. By repeating the study using other genres of mobile games and even on other elements than the onboarding phase, the quality of the method can be further investigated. As for most laboratory-based user research, the sample size was also too small to draw statistical inference to the parent population of F2P mobile game players worldwide. However, combining small-scale user research with large-scale behavioral analytics [33,7] forms a potential pathway towards solving this problem. Finally, physiological measures are highly dependent on the context in which the data is collected [50,15,28]. Both setup and context will thus have an impact on the interpretation of the data; hence, further studies in different lab contexts would be useful to validate the findings presented here.

ACKNOWLEDGEMENTS

The authors extend their warmest gratitude towards the developers at King and Norsfell for their contribution to this study. We thank Samantha Stahlke for informative discussion and valuable feedback in preparing the final draft of this paper. Furthermore, we would like to thank the participants who volunteered for this study.

This project has received funding from the European Union's Horizon 2020 research and innovation programme under grant agreement No 731900. Part of this work was conducted in the Digital Creativity Labs (www.digitalcreativity.ac.uk), jointly funded by EPSRC/AHRC/InnovateUK under grant no EP/M023265/1.

REFERENCES

1 Seufert, Eric. *Freemium Economics - Leveraging Analytics and User Segmentation to Drive Revenue*. Morgan Kaufmann, Burlington, Massachusetts, 2014.

2 Alha, Kati, Koskinen, Elina, Paavilainen, Janne, Hamari, Juho, and Kinnunen, Jani. Free-to-play games: Professionals' perspectives. *In Proc DiGRA Nordic 2014* (2014).

3 ESA. *Indystry Facts*. http://essentialfacts.theesa.com/, 2016.

4 Hadiji, F, Sifa, S, Drachen, A, and Thurau, C. Predicting Player Churn in the Wild. *Player Churn in the Wild. In Proceedings of the IEEE Computational Intelligence in Games* (2014).

5 Chou, Yu-Kai. *Actionable Gamification - Beyond Points, Badges, and Leaderboards*. Lean Publishing, 2014.

6 Even, Alon. 2015/10/13/gaming-app-user-retention-only-22-return-after-one-month/ (Oct. 13, 2015).

7 Sifa, R., Hadiji, F., Drachen, A., and Runge, J.

Predicting Purchase Decisions in Mobile free to play Games. In *AAAI Artificial Intelligence in Interactive Digital Entertainment* (Santa Cruz, CA 2015).

8 White, Gareth R and McAllister, Graham. Video Game Development and User Experience. In *Game User Experience*. Springer International Publishing, Switzerland, 2015.

9 Pagulayan, R., Keeker, K., Wixon, D., Romero, R. L., and Fuller, T. User-centered design in games. In *The Human-Computer Interaction Handbook*. L. Erlbaum Associates Inc. , 2003.

10 Smeddinck, Jan David, Markus, Krause, and Kolja, Lubitz. Mobile Game User Research: The World as Your Lab? *Proceedings at CHI'13,* (April 27, 2013).

11 Korhonen, Hannu and Koivisto, Elina M, I. Playability heuristics for mobile games. In *Proceedings of the 8th conference on Human-computer interaction with mobile devices and services* (Helsinki 2006), ACM Digital Library, 9-16.

12 Duh, Henry Been-Lirn, Chen, Vivian Hsueh Hua, and Tan, Chee Boon. Playing Different Games on Different Phones: an empirical study on mobile gaming. In *Proceedings of the 10th international conference on Human computer interaction with mobile devices and services* (Amsterdam 2008), ACM Digital Library, 391-394.

13 Stephan Engl, Lennart E. Nacke. Contextual influences on mobile player experience – A game user experience model. *Entertainment Computing*, 4, 1 (2013), 83-91.

14 Paul, Sheila A, Jensen, Marianne, Wong, Chui Y, and Khong, Chee W. Socializing in mobile gaming. In *Proceedings of the 3rd International Conference on Digital Interactive Media in Entertainment and Arts* (New York 2008), ACM, 2-9.

15 Mandryk, Regan L, Atkins, M Stella, and Inkpen, Kori M. A Continuous and Objective Evaluation of Emotional Experience with Interactive Play Environments. *CHI 2006 Proceedings - Novel Methods: Emotions, Gestures, Events* (April 2006), 1027-1036.

16 Mirza-Babaei, Pejman, Long, Sebastian, Foley, Emma, and McAllister, Graham. Understanding the Contribution of Biometrics to Games User Research. (2011), DiGRA Conference.

17 Chalfoun, Pierre. Biometrics at Ubisoft Montreal (March 15, 2016).

18 Ambinder, M. Biofeedback in Gameplay: How Valve Measues Physiology to Enhance Gaming Experiences. In *Game Developers Conference* (San Francisco, CA 2011).

19 Mirza-Babaei, Pejman. *Biometric Storyboards: A Games User Research Approach for Improving Qualitative Evaluations of Player Experience*. Sussex, 2013.

20 Yao, Lin, Liu, Yanfang, Li, Wen, Zhou, Lei, Ge, Yan, Chai, Jing, and Sun, Xianghong. Using Physiological Measures to Evaluate Use Experience of Mobile Applications. In *Engineering Psychology and Cognitive Ergonomics*. Springer International Publishing, Switzerland, 2014.

21 Drachen, Anders, El-Nasr, Magy Seif, and Canossa, Alessandro. Game Analytics – The Basics. In *Game Analytics - Maximizing the Value of Player Data*. Springer, London, 2013.

22 Alha, Kati, Koskinen, Elina, Paavilainen, Janne, and Hamari, Juho. Critical Acclaim and Commercial Success in Mobile Free-to. play Games. *DiGRA/FDG '16 - Proceedings of the First International Joint Conference of DiGRA and FDG*, 13, 1 (August 2016).

23 Korhonen, Hannu. Comparison of playtesting and expert review methods in mobile game evaluation. *10 Proceedings of the 3rd International Conference on Fun and Games* (2010), 18-27.

24 Alha, K, Paavilainen, J, and Hamari, J. Domain-specific playability problems in social network games. *In proceedings of DiGRA FDG Conference*, Dundee, Scotland (2016).

25 White, Gareth R, Mirza-Babaei, Pejman, McAllister, Graham, and Good, Judith. Weak inter-rater reliability in heuristic evaluation of video games. In *CHI'11 Extended Abstracts on Human Factors in Computing Systems* (2011), ACM.

26 Jackson, Susan A. and Marsh, Herbert W. Development and Validation of a Scale of Measure Optimal Experience: The Flow State Scale. *Journal of sport & exercise psychology* (1996), 17-35.

27 Brockmeyer, Jeanne H., Fox, Christine M., Curtiss, Kathleen A., McBroom, Evan, Burkhart, Kimberly M., and Pidruzny, Jacquelyn N. The development of the Game Engagement Questionnaire. *Journal of Experimental Social Psychology* (2009), 624-635.

28 Nacke, Lennart E. Game user research and physiological evaluation. In *Game user experience evaluation.* Springer, Toulouse, 2015.

29 Bromley, Steve, Mirza-Babaei, Pejman, McAllister, Graha, and Napier, Jonathan. Playing to Win? In Quandt, Thorsten, ed., *Multiplayer: The Social Aspects of Digital Gaming*. Routledge, Oxon, 2013.

30 Silveira, Fernando, Eriksson, Brian, Sheth, Anmol, and Sheppard, Adam. Predicting Audience Responses to Movie Content from Electro-Dermal Activity Signals. *UbiComp'13, ACM international joint conference on Pervasive and ubiquitous computing September and Behavior* (September 8-12, 2013), 707-716.

31 Boucsein, Wolfram. *Electrodermal Activity*. Springer US, New York, 2012.

32 Lu, G., Yang, F., Taylor, J. A., and Stein, J. F. A comparison of photoplethysmography and ECG recording to analyse heart rate variability in healthy subjects. *Journal of Medical Engineering & Technology* (2009), 634–641.

33 Seif El-Nasr, M., Drachen, A., and Canossa, A. *Game Analytics: Maximizing the Value of Player Data*. Springer, London, 2013.

34 Mcalmont, T. Tips for a Great First Time User Experience (FTUE) in F2P Games (September 3, 2015), http://blog.gameanalytics.com/blog/tips-for-a-great-first-time-user-experience-ftue-in-f2p-games.html.

35 Higgins, Krystal. First time user experiences in mobile apps (April 15, 2012), www.kryshiggins.com/first-time-user-experiences-in-mobile-apps/.

36 Novik, David G and Ward, Karen. Why don´t people read the manual? *Departmental Papers (CS)* (2006), Paper 15.

37 King Digital Entertainment. 2016. Candy Crush Jelly Saga. Game [mobile] (Jan 6, 2016) King Digital Entertainment, Dublin, Irland. Played january 2016.

38 Norsfell Games Inc. 2014. WinterForts: Exiled Kingdom. Game [mobile] (Oct 1, 2014).Execution Labs, Montréal, Canada.Played january 2016.

39 Norsfell Games Inc. 2015. Pogo Chick. Game [mobile] (Aug 13, 2015). Norsfell Games Inc, Montréal, Canada.Played january 2016.

40 Bordens, Kenneth S. and Abbott, Bruce B. *Research Design and Methods A Process Approach*. McGraw-Hill, New York, NY 10020, 2011.

41 Accessed on 2017-07-19, Wikidot. (2017). Retrieved from http://mgur.wikidot.com/start.

42 Khawaji, Ahmad , Zhou, Jianlong, Chen, Fang, and Marcus, Nadine. Using Galvanic Skin Response (GSR) to Measure Trust and Cognitive Load in the Text-Chat Environment. In *SIGCHI Conference on Human Factors in Computing Systems* (Crossings, Seoul, Korea 2015), ACM Digital Library, 420-423.

43 Lyle, John. Stimulated recall: a report on its use in naturalistic research. *British Educational Research Journal* , Volume 29, Issue 6 (2003), 861-878.

44 Poels, Karolien, de Kort, Yvonne, and Isselsteijn, Wijnand. Identification and Measurement of Post Game Experiences. *Westminster paper* (April 2009), 109 -129.

45 Nacke, Lennart and Lindley, Craig A. Flow and Immersion in First-Person Shooters: Measuring the player's gameplay experience. In *Proceedings of the 2008 Conference on Future Play: Research* (Toronto, Ontario, Canada 2008), ACM, 81-88.

46 Mirza-Babaei, Pejman, Wallner, Günter, McAllister, Graham, and Nacke, Lennart E. Unified visualization of quantitative and qualitative playtesting data. In *CHI '14 Extended Abstracts on Human Factors in Computing Systems* (New York 2014), ACM, 1363-1368.

47 Thomsen, Line Ebdrup, Petersen, Falko Weigert, Drachen, Anders, and Mirza-Babaei, Pejman. Identifying Onboarding Heuristics for Free-to-Play Mobile Games: A Mixed Methods Approach. In *Entertainment Computing - ICEC 2016*. Springer, 2016.

48 Kivikangas, Matias J., Ekman, Inger, Chanel, Guillaume et al. Review on psychophysiological methods in game research. In *Nordic DiGRA 2010* (Stockholm 2010), Authors & Digital Games Research Association (DiGRA)., 181-199.

49 Ravaja, N, Turpeinen, M, Saari, T , Puttonen, S, and Keltikangas-Jarvinen, L. The psychophysiology of James Bond: Phasic emotional responses to violent video game events. *Emotions vol. 8* (Feb 2008), 114-120.

50 Cacioppo, John T., Tassinary, Louis G., and Berntson, Gary G. *The Handbook of Psychophysiology*. Cambridge University Press, New York, 2007.

51 Julkunen, J. 3 Things to KNow About Session-Length Restriction When Designing a Free2play Game (Februray 19, 2015), http://www.bluecloudsolutions.com/articles/mobile-gaming-sessions-now-longer/.

52 Saari, Timo, Ravaja, Niklas, Salminen, Mikko, Laarni, Jari, and Kallinen, Kari. Phasic Emotional Reactions to Video Game Events: A Psychophysiological Investigation. *Media psychology* (2006), 343-367.

CrowdChess: A System to Investigate Shared Game Control in Live-Streams

Pascal Lessel
DFKI GmbH
Saarland Informatics Campus
pascal.lessel@dfki.de

Alexander Vielhauer
Saarland University
Saarland Informatics Campus
s9alviel@stud.uni-saarland.de

Antonio Krüger
DFKI GmbH
Saarland Informatics Campus
krueger@dfki.de

ABSTRACT
Recently, gaming live-streams appeared in which the audience interacts without a streamer. These settings sometimes allow the audience to select from a set of input aggregators to mediate how individual contributions are aggregated. We developed *CrowdChess*, a system which is optimized for the live-streaming context: multiple viewers play chess together in a single game instance against an AI; they suggest moves and further select one of six aggregators to mediate their contributions. In contrast to existing approaches, *CrowdChess* allows reasoning about the quality of individual and aggregator contributions, and thus it serves as a test bed for how effectively an audience interacts in such settings. We conducted a study in a live-streaming setup (n=12) and contribute insights on the player perception of audience-driven games and show how aggregators in such a small-scale setting are used, for example, the tendency to use group-based aggregators instead of empowering an individual.

ACM Classification Keywords
H.5.m. Information Interfaces and Presentation (e.g. HCI): Miscellaneous

Author Keywords
Wisdom of crowds; input aggregation; co-presence; self-administration; audience control; audience-driven games

INTRODUCTION
User-generated live-streaming of games [6, 27] has become popular in recent years. Twitch, one of the major live-streaming platforms, was amongst the top five internet traffic generators of 2014 in the US [4], and is in the 20 top sites in the US according to Alexa traffic rank [1]. Streamers can reach many viewers in parallel, who not only watch them playing in, for example, competitive e-sport matches [3] or games for entertainment purposes ("Let's Plays") [27], but also make use of the social component of these live-streaming platforms: a real-time chat is offered that allows the viewers to chat with each other and with the streamer. While in the beginning of live-streaming this feature was used only for communication, recently it has provided viewers more influence options: games appeared that enable the audience to alter what happens in the game by entering chat commands (e.g. ChoiceChamber [28]); some live-streaming formats, for example interactive pen&paper role-playing sessions, allow the audience to alter the story by using the chat (as done for example by Rocket Beans TV [12]), and specific streams, such as "Twitch Plays Pokémon" (TPP) [9, 12, 18], allow the audience to share control over the game and play together without a streamer. Especially the latter has sparked much interest and led to a new experience on live-streaming platforms that has not yet received much scientific attention.

CHI PLAY '17, October 15–18, 2017, Amsterdam, Netherlands

ACM ISBN 978-1-4503-4898-0/17/10...$15.00
DOI: https://doi.org/10.1145/3116595.3116597

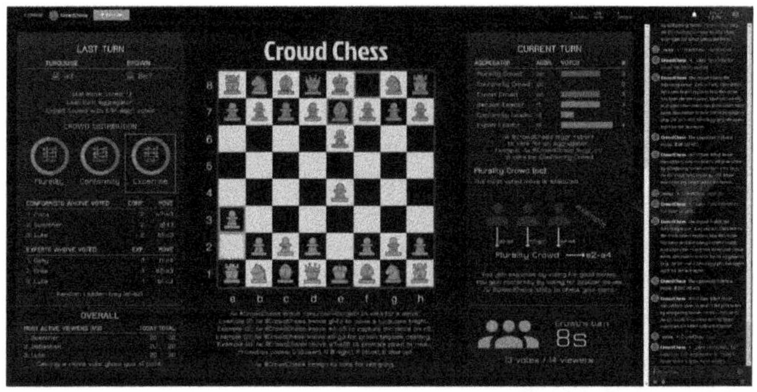

Figure 1. A screenshot of *CrowdChess* running on the live-streaming platform Beam (today called "Mixer"). Left: our video stream. Right: the channel's chat.

How to handle individual contributions is an important question in all the aforementioned examples: either all individual contributions are used and, for example, interpreted as game commands (such as in the beginning of the TPP stream) or the individual contributions are aggregated first. For the latter, polls based on a plurality voting scheme are commonly used in streams today. However, it is questionable whether this kind of aggregation is optimal, especially as investigations exist that show different approaches to input aggregation in the domain of crowd-sourcing that are more effective than a majority/plurality vote [10, 11]. First investigations in the live-streaming domain indicated that an audience which has the option to change input aggregators also selects aggregators other than majority/plurality aggregators [12]. Additionally, an analysis of the TPP phenomenon also indicates that an audience is not uniform in what they expect of such shared game control settings, and sometimes a suboptimal aggregator was selected for entertainment reasons [18].

The games used in these settings are often too complex to objectively reason whether an individual user contribution is beneficial towards the game's goal. Even though specific actions could in theory be rated (e.g., going left is faster), contextual factors and multiple sub-goals in games make a metric for assessing individual actions too complex or even impossible (e.g., in the given example, going right might earn the player an item that might help later). This makes it difficult to reason about interactions in a shared game control setting. With this paper we follow two goals: first, we scientifically investigate such a setting in more detail, and second, we want to be able to reason about the quality of individual and aggregator decisions. Towards these goals, we developed *CrowdChess*, a chess game that is designed for the live-streaming context (see Figure 1) and for audience control. *CrowdChess* should serve as a test bed for shared game control settings. We evaluated *CrowdChess* on the live-streaming platform Beam[1] with twelve participants and found that an expertise voting scheme is favored over a plurality voting scheme, that participants did not enable individual experts to decide alone and that even under time pressure, in small-scale settings, they still communicate over the chat to come to a group decision.

RELATED WORK

Gaming live-streams are relevant for research as they attract many users [6, 27] and findings here relate to several other research areas, for example, Social TV [2], crowd-sourcing [11, 29] and computer-mediated communication [30].

The current body of research mainly focuses on live-streaming usage data on these platforms [8, 21, 22] or considers the social aspects of streamers and their audience. An example of the latter is the work of Hamilton et al. [6]. The authors investigated Twitch streams under the aspect of virtual third places and found that the integrative options offered by the live-chat attract viewers, especially as this is not possible in television. The authors also elaborate on how audience integration looks today, based on interviews with several viewers and streamers. This was also investigated in the first case study of Lessel et al. [12] by analyzing a popular format on Twitch which attracts several thousand viewers regularly, and some overlap with Hamiliton et al.'s findings was reported: besides the fact that showing individual viewer contributions (e.g., viewers' self-made art) in streams is a common theme, plurality polls are also often used to find out what most of the audience wants. In another work, Lessel et al. [13] reported problems when viewer-streamer interactions happen on live-streaming platforms: a) a technological lag leading to asynchrony between chat messages entered and video content shown; b) information overload in channels where more than 150 people are active chatters and c) conveying historical information to newly joining viewers. The authors created a system for the digital card game *Hearthstone* in which they target these issues with the goal to improve the communication between viewers and streamers. They offered a direct interaction option on the video stream, and aggregations of individual viewer opinions were used to reduce the information overload. For the latter, they follow the "ballot box communication" concept [32] but also only use aggregations based on a majority scheme. The direct interaction was perceived well, but is not easy to achieve with the current live-streaming platforms. This hints that input aggregation is necessary in these settings (especially in larger streaming channels) and that simple majority/plurality voting schemes are usually used.

Audiences that interact as a group were already investigated in other domains (e.g. [20]), but investigations have also appeared recently in the live-streaming domain: "Twitch Plays Pokémon" (TPP) had the idea that the audience itself plays a game, instead of simply watching a person playing it. Every Twitch viewer could enter chat messages that were interpreted as game commands. This experiment attracted large numbers of viewers (1.1 million people entered 122 million commands, with 121,000 playing in parallel [23]). The creator recognized that forwarding every viewer command made it hard to finish the game and added an aggregator based on a plurality voting scheme, i.e., only the command entered by the largest number of participants in a time-frame was forwarded. When this aggregator was active was controlled by the audience. This feature of self-administration was frequently used [9]. The first game was finished after 16 days. Ramirez et al. [25] conclude that TPP is not comparable to the "Infinite Monkey Theorem" [31], i.e., it was not the case that the audience finished the game simply because they entered so many commands. Margel also considered TPP and reports explanations for when the audience switched to the plurality voting scheme [18], namely, when situations became too difficult, and not overcoming the obstacle would reduce the entertainment value of the stream. In their second case study, Lessel et al. also investigated TPP with a custom setup, in which several input aggregators were offered [12]. In a lab study they found that there are different reasons when specific aggregators were selected by the audience. They report that viewers still had the feeling of making no progress in the game, but the authors did not further elaborate on whether the audience objectively made progress; therefore, it is currently unclear whether the audience can pick the best input aggregator in a given situation in terms of effectiveness. With *CrowdChess* we want to provide further insights into this question.

Input aggregation is a topic that is investigated in the context of crowd-sourcing: work such as [7, 10, 11, 15] has investigated aggregation schemes for different contexts in which sometimes every input entered is used, without any aggregation, similar to the case of TPP. Other aggregators are used that build on plurality or majority voting schemes (e.g., "Vote" in [11]), weighted plurality/majority voting schemes with weights either based on the expertise of crowd-workers (which is adapted based on task performance [14]) or conformity, i.e., how similar the crowd-worker is to other workers (e.g., based on the idea of "Leader" in [11]). Furthermore, sophisticated algorithms exist that select an input without aggregating. Here, it is not the inputs that are mediated but the selection of one input source. Such approaches have been shown as relevant in the live-streaming context as well [12]. We consider these approaches to inform our selection of input aggregators and will elaborate on them in the next section.

[1] Beam has recently been rebranded to "Mixer": `https://mixer.com/`, last accessed: 31/07/2017.

CROWD CHESS

For a test bed that allows reasoning about whether an audience of gaming live-streams can effectively self-administrate, we needed a game which allows evaluations on the effectiveness of actions and is still interesting in the context of live-streaming platforms. As games usually have multiple goals, evaluating the available game actions in terms of whether they are helpful towards these goals is not trivial. For example, the game *Pokémon*, which was investigated in [12], allows various actions that cannot easily be judged as the goals the players follow might be different (e.g., catching a new Pokémon, leveling one up, defeating a certain NSC, exploring the optional area X before Y, etc.), and there is no metric that defines exactly how to calculate effectiveness here. In contrast, we decided to use the game chess. Chess software today allows for judging moves and therefore allows comparisons. In addition, the game itself has a complexity that makes playing it interesting enough to attract viewers on live-streaming platforms (e.g., on Twitch several chess channels exist that attract several hundred viewers on average[2]).

Live-streaming challenges

Gaming live-streams that aim for integrating the audience pose different challenges. One challenge is how to enable the audience to enter game inputs. Even though platforms such as Beam allow channel owners to customize their channel page with HTML input elements (such as buttons) and to programmatically listen to viewer interactions, these options are still limited. For example, it is not possible to provide a virtual representation of the chess board to allow viewers to suggest moves via direct interactions, similar to other chess games, while providing them with feedback. Using external web pages (as used in [13]) is potentially not helpful, as there is (to our knowledge) no analysis yet of how open viewers of live-streams are to switch to these during a stream. Another challenge, especially on Twitch and YouTube, is a lag [13, 33] that causes an offset between entered chat messages (which are presented for everyone in nearly real time) and the video shown in the stream (which in relation to the source is already outdated by 15-45 seconds and varies for every viewer). This makes it difficult to relate chat messages to the situation in the stream. In settings in which audience input is interpreted as game commands, this is especially problematic and needs to be considered in the underlying game concepts. Finally, using the chat (as it works in real time, in contrast to the video stream) to provide information to game situations and individual feedback poses the challenge that platforms have limitations on how many messages can be sent in a minute. Although white-listing options might be granted by platform vendors for interesting channel concepts, this cannot be assumed unconditionally. Even a white-listed channel might still be too limited to provide individuals with enough feedback, depending on the channel size. Exceeding the limits can, depending on the platform, mean that the messages are simply not sent to other viewers, or in the worst case that the sending account is banned for multiple hours.

[2]For example https://www.twitch.tv/chess, last accessed: 31/07/2017.

System overview

With respect to these challenges we created *CrowdChess*. It consists of four components: the chess engine, the aggregator system, the live-streaming integration and the user interface shown in the stream. *CrowdChess* is designed for audience vs. AI, but it can easily be adapted to allow for streamer vs. audience or audience vs. audience matches. For this first investigation, we wanted to rule out effects that might be introduced by a streamer that hosts the game (e.g., encouraging aggregator scheme changes), but we see such an investigation as an interesting next step. As chess is already partitioned into turns and does not require fast interactions, it helps to lower the impact of the lag issue mentioned before.

Chess engine and AI

We use Stockfish [26], one of the strongest open-source chess engines available, to evaluate the individual and aggregator-derived move suggestions. Besides using these results as data points for our study, we use them to inform the expertise-based aggregators (see below). This engine is too strong as an opponent to be a motivating challenge in live-streaming settings. Therefore, we use some of the engine-offered options to limit the engine's power (such as the maximal search depth for possible moves). *CrowdChess* offers 16 AI levels; the level increases (decreases) by one when the audience wins (loses). While the upper levels utilize the full capabilities of the engine, the lower levels can be easily beaten even by chess beginners.

Aggregator system

CrowdChess allows the audience to alter the way individual move suggestions are aggregated by voting for an aggregator scheme. Six different schemes are offered (and are partially based on Lessel et al.'s investigation of aggregators in their custom Twitch Plays Pokémon setup [12]) and we distinguish between two classes: those that aggregate the input (named "crowd") and those that select an individual based on certain attributes and use their move suggestion (named "leader").

- **Plurality Crowd (PC)**: A plurality vote, i.e., the move suggested by most viewers is executed. This is a common aggregator in live-streaming polls and was also available in (for example) "Twitch Plays Pokémon". In [12] the authors showed that other aggregators were used more often.
- **Expert Crowd (EC)**: A weighted plurality vote with weights based on individual expertise levels. How the expertise is calculated is not disclosed to the viewers; they can only see the rating, which is updated for every move suggestion given. Every viewer starts with an expertise of 1. A given move suggestion is evaluated by the chess engine in relation to the current board situation. This increases (decreases) the viewer's expertise by up to 2 (-2) points depending on how good (bad) the suggestion was. For this, it is considered whether the suggestion leads to the opponent's mate, to one's own mate (although other moves would have been possible), whether the viewer has missed mate in 1/2/3 turn(s) and finally, how the suggestion score relates to the score of the best possible move in the given board situation[3]. Using expertise is relevant in many

[3]For more details on the expertise and conformity algorithms see the appendix.

crowd-sourcing approaches [24] and is also interesting for our consideration. An audience having the goal to beat the chess AI should empower experts, as they are more likely to provide good move suggestions. The "expertise weighted vote aggregator" had the highest up-time in [12].

- **Conformity Crowd (CC)**: This aggregator is also a weighted plurality vote where the weights are based on the individual conformity levels. Move suggestions given by viewers are continuously compared to suggestions provided by other viewers in the same turn. Suggesting moves that were also suggested by the majority increases a viewer's conformity by up to 2 (starting at 1), depending on the uniformity among move suggestions. The level is decreased (by up to -2) when suggestions are made which only small portions of (or no one else in) the audience also made. This aggregator follows the idea introduced in Lasecki et al.'s work [11]. As soon as the "expertise weighted vote" aggregator became available, the conformity-based "crowd weighted vote" aggregator had nearly no up-time anymore in [12]. Thus, it is interesting to learn whether the CC aggregator in our setting will be used at all.
- **Random Leader (RL)**: The random leader aggregator randomly selects one of the viewers' move suggestions. Such an aggregator relates to the "Anarchy" aggregator in the original TPP, in which all commands were executed and thus all viewers could contribute something. Using the concept of "Anarchy" is possible, but seems unreasonable for a chess setting, as the chance of doing something "worse" and not being able to reverse this decision through other viewer commands, in contrast to Pokémon, is much higher. RL in contrast ensures that in theory all viewers can participate in the game independent of their conformity/expertise level, but also allows the matches to still be playable. A similar aggregator was introduced in Lasecki et al.'s work [11] and was also offered in [12], but had a low up-time there.
- **Expert Leader (EL)**: In contrast to RL, EL uses the move suggestion of the viewer with the highest expertise level. [12] has shown that the audience empowers individuals in difficult situations. In chess settings, it seems reasonable to offer an aggregator that provides the best player with full control. Similar to EC, empowering the best user seems reasonable, when the goal is to beat the AI.
- **Conformity Leader (CL)**: In contrast to EL, here the conformity level is the selection criterion. CL follows the "Legion Leader" approach of Lasecki et al. [11]. In [12] this kind of aggregator was also available (but no counterpart to EL was available in their setting) and this aggregator was used in difficult situations to provide an individual with complete control. It is interesting to see whether this aggregator is also used when EL is offered in parallel.

The selection of the active aggregator is an ongoing plurality vote. Viewers can switch their vote anytime and the one with the most votes becomes active at the end of a turn. The time left in a turn is always shown to the viewers. In the case of a draw, one of the aggregators is randomly selected. If the active aggregator provides the same value for multiple moves, one of these is also randomly selected.

Live-streaming integration

CrowdChess uses a chat bot to inform viewers about their interaction options via the channel's chat. These messages also provide insights into the current game state (e.g., whose turn it is and which piece was moved last). Especially for the aforementioned lag issue, this allows the viewers to think about the next turn, even if the video stream does not yet show the corresponding state visually. Three example messages are:

> *YOUR turn: What move should turquoise do next? Cast your votes by whispering !move <from>-<to> (e.g., /whisper @CrowdChess !move h7-h5).*
>
> *The crowd makes the following move: pawn h4 (h2-h4). Data to the left of the chess board explains how this move has been decided (using Random Leader) and what other outcomes there could have been. Remember to vote for an aggregator (e.g., /whisper @CrowdChess !aggr pc); see upper right for the acronyms.*
>
> *The opponent makes a move: pawn e4 (e2-e4).*

We require viewers to interact with *CrowdChess* via whispers. We did not want viewers—for this first exploration—to influence others merely by disclosing what they want to do, by simply displaying their vote command publicly. Such social effects were already reported by other research [16, 17, 19]; we try to reduce these effects with whispering. These whisper messages are also the primary feedback channel of *CrowdChess*. We use this channel to acknowledge that a viewer has correctly entered a move suggestion, to inform him/her that a move is not possible in the current board situation or that an ill-formed command was entered. If viewers enter commands into the chat instead of whispering, the chat bot removes the entered command from the chat and sends a message informing all users that they need to whisper.

Valid move suggestions follow the form *!move <from field>-<to field>*. This notation is used for all kinds of move suggestions in *CrowdChess* (e.g., capturing other pieces and castling) to simplify the interaction. A user is able to enter multiple move suggestions per turn, but only the last one is considered at the end of a turn. By entering *!aggr <aggregator name>* players can switch their aggregator vote. *!stats* provides the user with his/her current statistics (i.e., his/her conformity/expertise level, which aggregator he/she has currently voted for and the numbers of votes given today and overall). Entering *!resign* is treated as a special move suggestion. If the active aggregator selects this suggestion, the match ends. We implemented a queuing system to cope with the situation of having no white-listing and to avoid exceeding the limits the live-streaming platforms allow.

We use the channel description to give an overview on the command options and the aggregators. Together with the streamed interface of *CrowdChess* (see below) and the chat bot's proactive and reactive messages, viewers have three sources to learn how to use *CrowdChess*. Finally, the game is designed to run unsupervised and continuously (similar to TPP). As soon as a match is over (or no viewer is available anymore), the game restarts with an adapted AI level and thus allows for continuous playing.

Figure 2. The user interface of *CrowdChess* consists of last turn information (left), the chess board (middle) and the current turn information (right).

User interface

Figure 2 shows the *CrowdChess* user interface consisting of three thematic areas: historical information (left), the chess board (center) and the current information (right).

Historical information: The historical information shows data on the last turn (upper part) and the overall game (lower part). At the top we display the last audience and AI move. Below, we show the aggregator that was active and how many viewers wanted it in relation to all given aggregator votes. Additionally, we provide information on how many move suggestions were entered by the viewers. This area also shows, based on all provided move suggestions, which moves the aggregators' would have selected (the last active aggregator is additionally marked with a cyan box). This should help viewers to make their aggregator vote decisions (e.g., when other aggregators seem to be more suitable for individual goals). We display pie charts for the three crowd aggregators. In each chart we display the top three moves the aggregator outputs in the middle and the relative distribution of each of them in the circle. For EL and CL we display tables showing the top three most conforming/experienced viewers that entered move suggestions for the last turn, together with their current conformity/expertise level and which move they suggested. Finally, we also show which viewer would have been selected randomly by RL together with his/her move suggestion.

The area in the lower part switches every 20 seconds between showing the top nine active viewers (in groups of three), how many matches the audience/AI has won today/overall and the current AI level.

Chess board: In the center the chess board is shown together with the corresponding column letters and row numbers as these need to be entered by the viewers in their move suggestions. On the board we also highlight the last turns made in the color of the audience/the AI. Below the board, examples on how to enter move suggestions are given. It is shown how to do a normal move, how to capture pieces, how to do special moves (castling/promotion) and how to resign the game.

Current information: Information relevant for the current turn is shown on the right side. The upper part displays the aggregators' distribution by showing the different aggregator names (and their abbreviations) and how many viewers have voted for every aggregator. This is followed by a short explanation on how a viewer can switch his/her aggregator vote and a large area providing an example for every aggregator. Every 20 seconds a different aggregator is presented here (see Figure 3). With this element, viewers do not need to read the channel description to understand how aggregators work. We also give information on what expertise and conformity mean in our context, and provide the information that one's own expertise/conformity value can be queried with the *!stats* command. Below this area, we show whether the audience or the AI needs to make a move. When it is the audience's turn, we also show the remaining time. To further mitigate the lag issue, we distinguish between lag and turn time. The lag time denotes a time before the turn timer starts. The lag and turn time can be adjusted, but are fixed at run time (i.e., the audience cannot vote to set up the time by themselves). Below the time we indicate how many viewers are present and how many have entered a move suggestion.

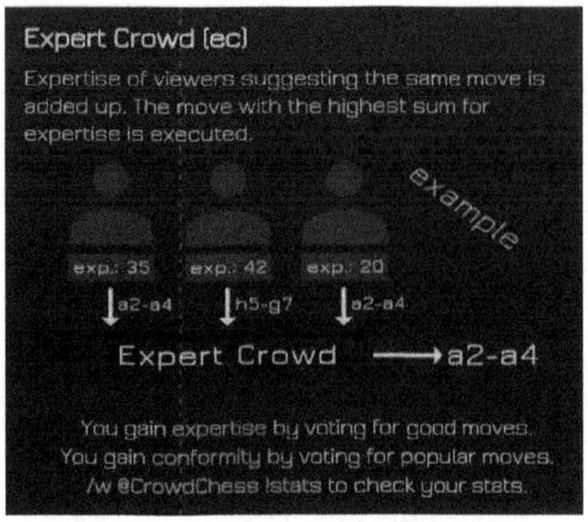

Figure 3. The explanation shown for the Expert Crowd aggregator.

STUDY

CrowdChess offers a test bed for various scenarios in the live-streaming context. In an exploratory fashion, we conducted a first study, where we were interested in how it is perceived, how the players use the aggregators and how these perform.

Method

CrowdChess is implemented to work with arbitrary live-streaming platforms. For this first test, we decided to use the platform Beam mainly because the lag is reported to be below one second. Thus, viewers would directly see moves on the streamed video and are not restricted to the chat-bot until the lag time is over. Simply launching a channel on a live-streaming platform was shown to be problematic in several related works that crawled platform data (for example [8, 34]): most of the channels on live-streaming platforms do not attract many viewers in parallel, or any viewers at all. Therefore, we advertised an event in which "you should play chess as part of a group on a live-streaming platform to beat an AI" over Facebook, chess communities and student mailing lists (consisting of computer science, media informatics and psychology students). As prerequisites, we mentioned that players should know the chess rules (but that skill level is irrelevant) and that a Beam account is necessary. During run time it was also possible that Beam users joined who were not explicitly recruited in this way. In general, this kind of advertisement is similar to the usual live-streaming case in which streamers also, for example, announce their streaming times and content via social media platforms. The event ran for 45 minutes. Before the event began, we streamed a slide with information on the event (such as that the channel description provided all necessary commands). Here, we also stated that all communication should be done over the channel's chat and not over tools such as Skype. The turn time was restricted to 60 seconds (and one second lag time), leading to 61 seconds between the opponent move being shown in the chat and the next turn of the opponent. The time restriction was to allow a faster gameplay and ensure that more moves could be carried out in the event. The AI was initially set up with a depth of five (easy) and was then set to ten (rather challenging) after the first match, to let the audience play against an easy and a harder opponent. After the 45 minutes, we provided a link to a questionnaire (which was available in English and German) for the participants via the channel's live-chat that assessed demographics, a self-assessment of one's own skill level, the perception of *CrowdChess* based on statements to be answered on 4-point scales (with the labels *disagree*, *rather disagree*, *rather agree*, *agree*) and some optional questions that allowed for free-text answers. We logged the chat messages, recorded the live-stream and persisted all interactions with our system.

Results

We clustered the results into general usage statistics, qualitative feedback, move suggestion quality and aggregator usage.

General usage statistics

18 registered users visited our channel during the experiment: 13 wrote at least one message (independent of whether it was a chat message or command) and three users remained as spectators for an average of two turns (without doing any interactions before leaving the channel); the other two users visited and left immediately. One user only entered chat messages (this user joined a few seconds before we closed the event). The remaining twelve users all entered at least one move or aggregator change command, i.e., they participated directly in the game (and will be called "players" subsequently). Nine of them used the chat to communicate (and wrote a total of 153 chat messages). The players entered 214 move suggestions (mean M=17.8, standard deviation SD=8.1, median Mdn=21), 24 aggregator commands (M=3.4, SD=2.3, Mdn=2; done by seven players) and 8 stats requests (M=1.6, SD=0.9, Mdn=1; done by five players). Two matches were finished: the first one against AI level five was won by the audience, the match against AI level ten by the AI. Ten players played both matches; two players entered player commands in the second match only. Overall, the audience played 31 chess turns. In match one (13 turns) the average number of move suggestions per turn was 7 (min=4, max=9); in the second match (18 turns) 6.8 (min=3, max=11). Table 1 shows the number of actions per player, their average expertise/conformity value and percentages on how active they were in relation to the number of turns they were on the channel. 75% of the players participated in more than 50% of their witnessed turns.

Twelve participants (7x male, 3x female, 2x no answer; 2x <19, 5x 19-25, 2x 26-32, 2x 33-39 years old, 1x no answer) finished the questionnaire and provided us with their Beam name, showing that all active players did the questionnaire. All but one (Scottish) reported to be German. The Scottish player joined the event by coincidence, while the remaining players heard about it via our advertisement. We let the participants rate their own skill level (see also Table 1) by providing them with statements that indicate different playing skills and they were sorted from lowest to highest. They either selected *"I know the chess rules, but I have not played chess much so far"* (which we denoted with inexperienced in the table) or *"I know the chess rules and I think that I can win against other casual chess players"* (some experience). The next statement *"I know the chess rules and I think that I can win against players that play chess regularly but are not chess club players"* was not selected, indicating that overall our players were not skilled chess players. Furthermore, no one reported playing chess regularly. Only four participants reported consuming live-streams and three had participated in a shared game control setting (here: "Twitch Plays Pokémon").

ID	Number of actions				Avg. expertise value	Avg. conformity value	Witnessed turns	% of witnessed turns in which the user did a player action	% of witnessed turns in which the user did any action	Skill self-assessment
	Move	Aggregator	Stats	Chat				*!move* and/or *!aggr*	any command/chatted	
01	27	6	0	8	17	13	31	87%	97%	Some experience
02	21	7	0	2	4	5	31	74%	77%	Inexperienced
03	26	0	3	18	10	11	31	84%	87%	Inexperienced
04	18	1	0	11	13	10	31	61%	65%	Some experience
05	6	2	0	10	2	3	31	26%	39%	Inexperienced
06	15	2	2	13	6	5	31	52%	71%	Some experience
07	22	0	0	0	7	11	31	71%	71%	Inexperienced
08	23	4	1	28	12	9	31	81%	97%	Some experience
09	24	2	1	61	9	7	31	81%	97%	Inexperienced
10	21	0	0	0	6	9	31	68%	68%	Inexperienced
11	8	0	0	2	3	2	23	35%	39%	Inexperienced
12	3	0	1	0	2	2	11	27%	27%	Some experience

Table 1. Player overview. As players were able to join the game later, we added indications on how active they were in relation to their witnessed turns.

Qualitative feedback

Seven participants stated they liked *CrowdChess* (three times agree, four times rather agree), leading to an average of 2.75 on the 4-point scale. Seven participants reported having fun playing it (M=2.6, only asked with a one item question) and four participants stated that it was more fun than playing "normal" chess (M=2.1). The idea of playing chess as a group was liked by half the participants (M=2.5), and five would continue to play *CrowdChess*. Potential aspects that might have impacted the perception of *CrowdChess* were:

- **Time**: No participant reported being familiar with playing chess under time pressure. Eleven participants (rather) disagreed with the statement that the turn time was too long (M=1.3) and ten disagreed with the statement that they had enough time to play and consider the historical information (M=1.3). In the free text questions, six reported that they wanted to participate in every turn and thus had insufficient time to consider all parts of the interface. As this study tried to mimic the live-streaming setting (in which visitors also simply join the channel and are confronted with it directly), we did not explain the user interface beforehand. In this study situation with a clearly communicated time limit of 45 minutes, though, participants might have thought that they needed to provide a move in every turn (which was not necessary) or found it more appealing to enter move suggestions. Concerning time, two participants suggested in the free-text answers to either add an automatic turn time adaptation (by considering how much discussion happens in the chat) or audience-based options to adjust the time. They also reported that they wanted an option to skip the remaining time, if the audience has already decided.
- **User interface**: Seven participants (rather) agreed to the statement that they like the graphical appearance of *CrowdChess* (M=2.4). Five times it was mentioned in the free-text answers that the UI is too overloaded and three times it was reported that the user's monitor (and thus the video stream window) was too small to see all elements properly.
- **Text-based interaction**: Seven participants (rather) agreed to the statement that the interaction via chat messages was acceptable (M=2.4). Four participants explicitly stated that they would rather interact directly with the chess board on the stream. This is in line with the findings of Lessel et al. [13] related to direct interaction. Nine participants (rather) agreed to the statement that they always knew how to enter a move suggestion (M=3.0). 6 syntactical incorrect and 41 invalid (with respect to the chess rules) move commands were entered, but considering who entered those, no relation to the aforementioned question was found. Even though the chat bot provided an error message via whisper in this case, this might have been overlooked.
- **Group feeling**: Two participants reported that they were frustrated because moves were executed that they assessed as worse than their move suggestions. Only five (rather) agreed to the statement that they felt part of the group (M=2.3) and six reported that they thought that their move suggestions mattered (M=2.3). Two participants suggested replacing the historical information with the current move suggestions all players have provided in the current turn to come to a better decision.

We also provided statements on the offered features: Nine participants found the chat bot messages useful (M=2.9) and nine liked to see the current aggregator distribution (M=3). Seeing examples of the aggregators in the stream was liked by seven (M=2.6), the high score list of the most active players by nine (M=2.8) and ten participants liked to see the win/loss ratio against the AI (M=3.3). Seeing which moves the active aggregator has also considered was liked by seven participants (M=2.8); what the other aggregators would have selected by six (M=2.7). Seven (rather) agreed to the statement that they understood the aggregator explanations in the stream (M=2.7), but only four (rather) agreed to the statement that they understood all components of the history (M=2.2). The aspects (time and UI) mentioned above might be explanations for this.

Eight participants were interested in the expertise (M=2.6) but only two in the conformity ratings (M=1.6). None of the participants reported using the stats request command frequently to check his/her expertise (M=1.1) or conformity (M=1.1) (also in line with the actual frequency of the *!stats* command) and only five (one) reported checking the table in the history to see the expertise (conformity) distribution. As an optional

Agg.	% best move suggestion selected	Avg. % of move suggestions better than move selected by aggregator (across all turns)	% worst move suggestion selected
PC	64.5%	13.6%	29%
CC	71%	13.1%	19.4%
EC	71%	11.7%	25.8%
RL	51.6%	24.8%	32.3%
CL	64.5%	17.8%	29%
EL	71%	15%	29%

Table 2. Aggregator performances based on all board positions (31) and all move suggestions (214).

Agg.	#Turns active (# of last active turn)	Draw wins	% best move suggestion selected	Avg. % of move suggestions better than move selected by aggregator (across all active turns)	% worst move suggestion selected
PC	7 (#16)	5	57.1%	13%	14.3%
CC	0 (-)	0	-	-	-
EC	17 (#31)	2	76.5%	14.3%	35.3%
RL	5 (#19)	5	40%	31.6%	60%
CL	2 (#2)	2	100%	0%	0%
EL	0 (-)	0	-	-	-

Table 3. Aggregator performances while active. All values are in relation to the turns in which the aggregator was active.

question we asked whether the expertise/conformity values derived by *CrowdChess* seemed plausible; while the three participants that answered this (rather) agreed for conformity (M=3.3), three (of four) participants that answered this for the expertise value rather agreed to that statement (M=2.8).

Move suggestion quality

We first analyzed the 214 move suggestions for how different they were for every turn. We counted how many groups of same move suggestions in a turn were provided and divided this by the number of all suggestions in this turn. Averaged over all turns, a number near 0 would indicate that in most turns the audience would have provided only uniform suggestions; a number near 1 would indicate that the audience only provided different move suggestions in most turns. Both would render most of the aggregators useless, but this was not an issue in our case (M=0.5, SD=0.23, Mdn=0.4). Using the chess engine, we analyzed all 214 move suggestions. Only 40% of the suggested moves would have changed the board situation in favor of the crowd. This is in line with Table 1 and the skill self-assessment. For every board position (31) we aggregated the given move suggestions by using all six aggregators regardless of which one was actually active in the turn. For the random leader aggregator, we used the suggestion of the player that was randomly selected in this turn; for the expert/conformity leaders we utilized the values that the players had at the point of time when the suggestion was made. Based on this, in 25 of 31 turns (81%) at least one aggregator provided the best result amongst the user suggestions (i.e., it selected the move suggestion that received the highest engine score). Table 2 shows the performances of the aggregators. The table represents the case without filtering situations in which the worst was the same as the best move suggestion (e.g., all move suggestions were equivalent). Column 2 of this table shows that the offered aggregators are not perfect. PC, for example, only selects the best suggestion in 64.5% of the turns. This is not surprising as this aggregator was only able to select the move when the majority of the players suggested it. Even the expert aggregators did not clearly excel here, indicating that no player (especially the ones that had a slightly higher expertise value) consistently provided better moves than other players. In column 3 we present an average value: for every turn, we checked how many move suggestions were provided that were better than the selected one. Here, the "crowd" aggregators seem to be better than the "leader" aggregators. This is explainable with the concept of the wisdom of crowds [29], i.e., that a group of people comes to a better decision compared to an individual decision. Especially in our case, in which no proficient chess players were present, this seems reasonable. Column 4 shows how often an aggregator selected the worst suggestion amongst the user votes. Overall, the performance of the random leader is (as expected) worst.

Aggregator uses

Table 2 shows only a generalized view that does not consider when an aggregator was actually activated by the audience. For example, if an aggregator outputs the best move amongst all available suggestions only 40% of the time, it does not necessarily mean that this aggregator is bad. If the audience selected this aggregator only in situations in which it outputs the best move of the available user move suggestions, this would lead to two conclusions: first, it would show that the audience is able to self-administrate itself (by knowing which aggregator is currently good) and second, that even though the overall performance of the aggregator is suboptimal, in terms of how it is used, it is optimal. We found that in 20 of 31 turns (65%), the audience indeed activated an aggregator that selects the best move amongst the user suggestions. Considering that in only 25 turns the aggregators could have provided the best outcome, this is an encouraging result. Table 3 shows how often an aggregator was active and its performance. These numbers also represent the case without filtering situations in which the worst and best move suggestion were the same.

The following results could be derived from Table 3: first, the most active aggregator was EC. This is in line with our expectation (cf. aggregator section). Interestingly, EL was never activated. It seems that the audience still wanted to empower their members to contribute something instead of simply providing one expert with the option to play alone. Another explanation might be that they were aware that no single player alone excels. Second, activating EC was a reasonable decision, as it selected the best suggestion in 13 of the 17 turns it was active. We analyzed what happened in the other four turns: two times at least one other aggregator would have provided the best result: PC for one turn and RL for the other. As choosing RL could not be accounted for as a deliberate "better" choice, this led to only one turn in which another aggregator would have provided the best result. By additionally considering how often any aggregator would have provided a better result (and not necessarily the best), one instance of RL and one instance of PC/CC/CL would have. Second, compared to Table 2, EC and CL performed (slightly) better, i.e., they seemed to be activated at the right time. Third, we had many turns (14/31) in which two or more aggregators had the same number of up-votes (draws). PC, RL and CL had most (or all) of their up-time only because they were randomly selected in such situations. This shows that the crowd was not uniform. EC instead was preferred clearly as it was active in 17 turns (with only two draw wins). EC also dominates in the second match, as PC for example was never activated after the 16th turn. This dominance was also visible in the vote distributions, as four participants wanted EC, while only two wanted other aggregators towards the end of the study (4:1:1). Fourth, the conformity-based aggregators were not really used (even though CC is about as good as EC, as shown in Table 2). As the participants also stated that they were not interested in the conformity, they either did not understand the functionality of the value itself, did not understand the aggregator, or they found the expertise-based aggregators more appealing. As seven participants stated they did not feel part of the group, they might have thought that CC and CL do not provide coherent results, as they are "outside" the group. We also checked for every aggregator how many players voted for it at least once: PC (3x), CC (1x), EC (7x), RL (3x), CL (1x), EL (0x). This again shows that CC, CL and EL were not appealing for the players and that EC dominated.

Overall, these results should be seen in the context that only seven users did aggregator switches at all. As we had a question on infrequent aggregator switches in the questionnaire (and allowed multiple selections) we could investigate this further: considering the players that never used the aggregator change command, the players with ID 10 and 12[4] reported that they did not understand the aggregators, players 03 and 11 that they had too little time and players 03 and 07 that they thought switching the aggregator would not have led to better moves and that they were satisfied with the current aggregator. Considering the players that voted for aggregators, 01, 04 and 05 reported that they had too little time, 02 and 06 that switching would not have led to better outcomes and 01, 04, 08 and 09 that they were satisfied with the current aggregator.

Participants were also asked why they did change the aggregator, and five participants responded: 06 stated that RL was more interesting as he/she had not expected to make an impact in EL and CL. 08 stated that he/she was interested in PC and EC and that the game was too fast to switch the aggregator more often. 01 reported that he/she switched "*when moves were executed that I thought were bad and a switch would favor mine*"; 09 stated "*partially, I have selected expertise, because I'm not so good myself*". 02 answered that he/she wanted to prevent a move being executed randomly. This shows that the motives for why changes happen are different. None of the participants thought that *CrowdChess* needed further aggregators, and four thought that there were too many, but the answers for which ones should be removed were inconclusive (CC (1x), EC (1x), RL (2x), CL (2x), EL (2x)).

We also considered the chat to learn which social interactions towards decision-finding happened that might be a further explanation for why the aggregator system was not used more often. 15 turns were discussed in terms of which move should be done next (the chat was used in both matches for these discussions): either by a user giving a concrete suggestion (e.g., 06: "*f8 - b5*" or 01: "*I recommend to move the queen*"), a player starting a discussion (e.g., 03: "*g8-e7?*"), a player asking for help (e.g., 09: "*suggestions from pros, please*") or discussing more general plans (e.g., 06: "*cover the e5*" or 09: "*killllllit - with the pawn?????*"). Seven players participated in these discussions. One time, a player asked which aggregator should be activated and two other players responded with their preferences. Similar to TPP [18], even in this small user base, we found trolling tendencies by one user (e.g., 06: "*we should always do the same like the AI*" or 06: "*randomize it*").

[4]Indicates the ID in Table 1.

Discussion

In this first study, we only tested *CrowdChess* with a small number of participants in an exploratory fashion (see also the limitations below). Our results should thus not be overestimated, but they already give valuable insights on how small groups of viewers interact in such a scenario: first of all, we found that the aggregators were not used by all players. As we could show, EC performed well in this setting, and the audience mainly activated this aggregator. Viewers might have voted for EC because they liked its move selection, they approved our expertise metric and/or they liked the idea of the aggregator. As no other aggregator significantly outperforms EC, we cannot decide which hypothesis should be accepted, but we will explore this further, for example with the addition of a "fake aggregator" that is purely based on the chess engine and objectively excels the other aggregators. In contrast, PC—often used in the live-streaming context—was not often favored (otherwise it would not have come to so many draws) and had no up-time later on. The conformity-based aggregators were not interesting for the audience, even though the performance of CC was slightly better than EC's. As many participants reported not feeling part of the group, this might be an explanation of why the audience had no trust in an aggregator that uses one's similarity in relation to the group. Lessel et al. [12] also reported that the conformity-based group aggregator was not interesting anymore after an expertise-based aggregator became available. The difference here is that in their experiment the expertise values were viewer-based (viewers could up-vote others) instead of computed objectively; however, both show that conformity-based aggregators are less interesting as soon as other aggregators become available. Furthermore, EL was never activated, indicating that either the audience has more trust in the "wisdom of crowds" [29], or that they simply did not want to enable one player to decide the moves alone. Both is also supported by considering that the "leader" aggregators had less up-time in comparison to the "crowd" aggregators.

From the qualitative answers, we learned that there were different reasons why participants did not vote for aggregators (more often): besides too little time, they often reported that they were already satisfied with the active aggregator or thought that other (inactive) aggregators would not perform better. This seems to be a reasonable explanation and hints that this needs to be considered in such types of audience-driven games. Not participating in something can also mean that the users agree with what is happening, and today, when polls are used in streams, the number of non-voting viewers is not considered. We also learned that there are different motivations for why aggregators should be changed. Even though EC was selected, other tendencies were also revealed that are not primarily helpful for the goal of winning the game (such as being able to contribute a move with RL in the presence of a conformity/expertise aggregator where a viewer with low conformity/expertise values has little influence). Considering TPP, this might explain why so much chaos happened there and led to the introduction of the majority-based aggregator. Although participants reported problems of time, it seems that some still had enough time to discuss moves in the chat, instead of relying on the aggregators alone. We hypothesize that this has less impact in larger channels, as work already exists that shows that the chat in larger channels is hard to maintain [6] or that the chat dynamics change [5].

For audience-driven games, our results hint that the time restriction is an issue. We will increase the turn time and will offer a *!ready* command in the future: if entered by enough players (e.g. 70% of the active players) the turn ends early. Additionally, regular chess players who are used to playing with time constraints should also be able to deal better with the time restriction in *CrowdChess*. The main issue that the participants reported with the short turn time was that they did not have enough time to understand/consider all UI elements of *CrowdChess*. In a live-streaming situation this might be different than in our study: as our participants knew that they would only play for a limited time overall, they apparently invested more in the move suggestions than in getting familiar with the interface. The chat-based interactions were treated as suboptimal and users wanted a more direct interaction. This is in line with Lessel et al. [13], in which the direct interaction with the live-stream was found to be a beneficial feature. Unfortunately, the current live-streaming platforms do not offer enough technical features to realize such an interaction that at the same time provides sufficient individual feedback. Thus, we reason that the current platforms need to improve to allow audience-driven games to truly emerge.

Our study had several limitations: first, the small number of participants, which seems acceptable for a first exploration with *CrowdChess*. Further studies will be done with more participants and we expect that a larger sample will change the dynamics that happen in the chat. Also, the selection of aggregators might be different when more users in a larger sample have trolling tendencies or want to follow their own agenda. Here, it will be interesting to see whether participants that have not voted so far start to vote to reduce the impact of such players. Second, restricting the study time to only 45 minutes meant participants were only able to play two matches and were keen on participating in both, instead of interacting with the other *CrowdChess* features. Especially the perception of such an audience-driven game might change during a longer time-span. Third, regarding the selection of our sample, only four participants had live-streaming experiences, and no one was a regular chess player. Conducting a study with chess players only, or players that are regular consumers of live-streams, might reveal different results in relation to the aggregators (for the chess group) or towards audience-driven games (for the stream viewers). Fourth, we investigated the board game chess instead of digital games. Even though we explicitly wanted to use a less complex game in terms of its game actions to evaluate aggregator decisions, it is currently unclear how these findings map to other (video) games. Nonetheless, as findings are in line with reports of TPP (e.g., such as the different player tendencies) [9, 18] and also the lab study of Lessel et al. [12] (e.g., similar up-times of the aggregators), it seems that the results can be extended to different settings. Fifth, from a technical point of view, some participants reported disconnects on Beam or refreshed their browser window. In both cases, *CrowdChess* cleared their votes and it is unclear if they were aware of this. In the future votes will be persisted briefly before they are erased.

FUTURE WORK

Besides the aspects for future work already stated throughout the paper (e.g., investigating how dynamics change in a streamer vs. audience setting) and conducting studies that overcome the mentioned limitations (e.g., a larger sample size, integrating more chess players), several further research directions can be followed with *CrowdChess*. For the aggregators, it would be interesting to see whether the usage patterns remain stable across samples (size and composition). For example, as the “Anarchy” aggregator was often used for entertainment reasons in TPP [25], it might happen that a sample of regular live-stream viewers behaves differently. The exact rationale for how we derived the conformity and expertise values was not disclosed. In upcoming studies this could be explained in detail, and different approaches on how these values are updated could be compared in respect to the viewers' perception. At the same time, effects on the viewers' perceived agency and fairness could also be considered. Another valuable direction could be to analyze the social dynamics that happen in the chat in relation to the audience size and how this affects the move suggestions and aggregator selections. This could be contrasted with a study in which an aggregator is dictated by the system (and not by the viewers) for every turn. Because of the technical situation of live-streaming platforms, the chat interaction was chosen as the primary interaction paradigm. Analyzing the viewers' perception of other input options (e.g., via an external web page) in such a context seems important as well. Taken together, such research will eventually lead to design recommendations for audience-driven games.

CONCLUSION

We presented *CrowdChess*, a game to investigate shared game control in live-streams. With it, we follow the goal to investigate the emerging experience of audience-driven games in the live-streaming context, which is not yet researched in depth. Besides elaborating on the features of *CrowdChess*, we contribute a first user study. Our results can help other researchers to inform the design of their audience-driven projects. Furthermore, we contributed insights on how a small-scale audience interacts when their goal is to win the game and aggregators are offered. We found that the audience selected an expertise-based group aggregator primarily, but did not want to let the most experienced player play alone. As discussed, *CrowdChess* can now be used to pursue a range of further research directions that will help to inform future audience-driven games.

REFERENCES

1. Alexa Internet, Inc. 2017. Top Sites in United States. (2017). http://www.alexa.com/topsites/countries/US, last accessed: 31/07/2017.
2. Pablo Cesar and David Geerts. 2011. Understanding Social TV: A Survey. *Proc. NEM Summit 2011* (2011), 94–99.
3. Gifford Cheung and Jeff Huang. 2011. Starcraft from the Stands: Understanding the Game Spectator. In *Proc. CHI 2011*. ACM, New York, NY, USA, 763–772. DOI: http://dx.doi.org/10.1145/1978942.1979053
4. Matthew DiPietro. 2014. Twitch is 4th in Peak US Internet Traffic. (2014). https://blog.twitch.tv/twitch-is-4th-in-peak-us-internet-traffic-90b1295af358, last accessed: 31/07/2017.
5. Colin Ford, Dan Gardner, Leah Elaine Horgan, Calvin Liu, a. m. tsaasan, Bonnie Nardi, and Jordan Rickman. 2017. Chat Speed OP PogChamp: Practices of Coherence in Massive Twitch Chat. In *CHI 2017 Extended Abstracts*. ACM, New York, NY, USA, 858–871. DOI: http://dx.doi.org/10.1145/3027063.3052765
6. William A. Hamilton, Oliver Garretson, and Andruid Kerne. 2014. Streaming on Twitch: Fostering Participatory Communities of Play Within Live Mixed Media. In *Proc. CHI 2014*. ACM, New York, NY, USA, 1315–1324. DOI: http://dx.doi.org/10.1145/2556288.2557048
7. Hsi-Mei Hsu and Chen-Tung Chen. 1996. Aggregation of Fuzzy Opinions Under Group Decision Making. *Fuzzy Sets and Systems* 79, 3 (1996), 279–285.
8. Mehdi Kaytoue, Arlei Silva, Loïc Cerf, Wagner Meira, Jr., and Chedy Raïssi. 2012. Watch Me Playing, I Am a Professional: A First Study on Video Game Live Streaming. In *Proc. WWW 2012 Companion*. ACM, New York, NY, USA, 1181–1188. DOI: http://dx.doi.org/10.1145/2187980.2188259
9. Harris Kyriakou. 2015. Twitch Plays Pokémon: An Exploratory Analysis of Crowd Collaboration. (2015). http://www.innqui.com/wp-content/uploads/2015/11/Twitch-Draft.pdf, last accessed: 31/07/2017.
10. Walter S. Lasecki, Christopher Homan, and Jeffrey P. Bigham. 2014. Architecting Real-Time Crowd-Powered Systems. *Human Computation* 1, 1 (2014).
11. Walter S. Lasecki, Kyle I. Murray, Samuel White, Robert C. Miller, and Jeffrey P. Bigham. 2011. Real-Time Crowd Control of Existing Interfaces. In *Proc. UIST 2011*. ACM, New York, NY, USA, 23–32. DOI: http://dx.doi.org/10.1145/2047196.2047200
12. Pascal Lessel, Michael Mauderer, Christian Wolff, and Antonio Krüger. 2017a. Let's Play My Way: Investigating Audience Influence in User-Generated Gaming Live-Streams. In *Proc. TVX 2017*. ACM, New York, NY, USA, 51–63. DOI: http://dx.doi.org/10.1145/3077548.3077556
13. Pascal Lessel, Alexander Vielhauer, and Antonio Krüger. 2017b. Expanding Video Game Live-Streams with Enhanced Communication Channels: A Case Study. In *Proc. CHI 2017*. ACM, New York, NY, USA, 1571–1576. DOI:http://dx.doi.org/10.1145/3025453.3025708
14. Jing Liu, Young-In Song, and Chin-Yew Lin. 2011. Competition-based User Expertise Score Estimation. In *Proc. SIGIR 2011*. ACM, New York, NY, USA, 425–434. DOI:http://dx.doi.org/10.1145/2009916.2009975
15. Anna Loparev, Walter S. Lasecki, Kyle I. Murray, and Jeffrey P. Bigham. 2014. Introducing Shared Character Control to Existing Video Games. In *Proc. FDG 2014*.
16. Jan Lorenz, Heiko Rauhut, Frank Schweitzer, and Dirk Helbing. 2011. How Social Influence can Undermine the Wisdom of Crowd Effect. *Proc. National Academy of Sciences* 108, 22 (2011), 9020–9025.
17. Albert E. Mannes. 2009. Are We Wise About the Wisdom of Crowds? The Use of Group Judgments in Belief Revision. *Management Science* 55, 8 (2009), 1267–1279. DOI:http://dx.doi.org/10.1287/mnsc.1090.1031
18. Michael Margel. 2014. Twitch Plays Pokemon: An Analysis of Social Dynamics in Crowdsourced Games. (2014). http://www.cs.utoronto.ca/~mmargel/2720/paper.pdf, last accessed: 31/07/2017.
19. Winter A. Mason, Frederica R. Conrey, and Eliot R. Smith. 2007. Situating Social Influence Processes: Dynamic, Multidirectional Flows of Influence Within Social Networks. *Personality and Social Psychology Review* 11, 3 (2007), 279–300. DOI: http://dx.doi.org/10.1177/1088868307301032
20. Dan Maynes-Aminzade, Randy Pausch, and Steve Seitz. 2002. Techniques for Interactive Audience Participation. In *Proc. ICMI 2002*. IEEE Computer Society, Washington, DC, USA, 15–. DOI: http://dx.doi.org/10.1109/ICMI.2002.1166962
21. Gustavo Nascimento, Manoel Ribeiro, Loïc Cerf, Natalia Cesario, Mehdi Kaytoue, Chedy Raïssi, Thiago Vasconcelos, and Wagner Meira Jr. 2014. Modeling and Analyzing the Video Game Live-Streaming Community. In *9th Latin American Web Congress*. 1–9. DOI: http://dx.doi.org/10.1109/LAWeb.2014.9
22. Karine Pires and Gwendal Simon. 2015. YouTube Live and Twitch: A Tour of User-generated Live Streaming Systems. In *Proc. MMSys 2015*. ACM, New York, NY, USA, 225–230. DOI: http://dx.doi.org/10.1145/2713168.2713195
23. Sam Prell. 2014. Twitch Plays Pokemon Final Stats: 1.1 Million Players, 36 Million Views. Internet. (2014). http://www.engadget.com/2014/03/01/twitch-plays-pokemon-final-stats-1-1-million-players-36-millio, last accessed: 31/07/2017.

24. Nguyen Quoc Viet Hung, Nguyen Thanh Tam, LamNgoc Tran, and Karl Aberer. 2013. An Evaluation of Aggregation Techniques in Crowdsourcing. In *Web Information Systems Engineering (WISE 2013)*, Xuemin Lin, Yannis Manolopoulos, Divesh Srivastava, and Guangyan Huang (Eds.). Lecture Notes in Computer Science, Vol. 8181. Springer Berlin Heidelberg, 1–15. DOI:http://dx.doi.org/10.1007/978-3-642-41154-0_1

25. Dennis Ramirez, Jenny Saucerman, and Jeremy Dietmeier. 2014. Twitch Plays Pokemon: A Case Study in Big G Games. In *Proc. DiGRA 2014*. 3–12.

26. Tord Romstad, Marco Costalba, and Joona Kiiski. 2017. Stockfish Chess. (2017). https://stockfishchess.org, last accessed: 31/07/2017.

27. Thomas Smith, Marianna Obrist, and Peter Wright. 2013. Live-Streaming Changes the (Video) Game. In *Proc. EuroITV 2013*. ACM, New York, NY, USA, 131–138. DOI:http://dx.doi.org/10.1145/2465958.2465971

28. Studio Bean. 2015. Choice Chamber. (2015). http://www.choicechamber.com, last accessed: 31/07/2017.

29. James Surowiecki. 2005. *The Wisdom of Crowds*. Anchor.

30. Crispin Thurlow, Laura Lengel, and Alice Tomic. 2004. *Computer Mediated Communication*. Sage.

31. Wikipedia Community. 2017. Infinite Monkey Theorem. (2017). https://en.wikipedia.org/wiki/Infinite_monkey_theorem, last accessed: 31/07/2017.

32. Mu Xia, Yun Huang, Wenjing Duan, and Andrew B. Whinston. 2009. Ballot Box Communication in Online Communities. *Communications of the ACM* 52, 9 (Sept. 2009), 138–142. DOI: http://dx.doi.org/10.1145/1562164.1562199

33. Cong Zhang and Jiangchuan Liu. 2015. On Crowdsourced Interactive Live Streaming: A Twitch.tv-Based Measurement Study. In *Proc. NOSSDAV 2015*. ACM, New York, NY, USA, 55–60. DOI: http://dx.doi.org/10.1145/2736084.2736091

34. Cong Zhang, Jiangchuan Liu, and Haiyang Wang. Towards Hybrid Cloud-assisted Crowdsourced Live Streaming: Measurement and Analysis. In *Proc. NOSSDAV 2016*. ACM, New York, NY, USA, Article 1, 6 pages. DOI:http://dx.doi.org/10.1145/2910642.2910644

Game & Watch: Are "Let's Play" Gaming Videos as Immersive as Playing Games?

Priscilla N.Y. Wong, Jacob M. Rigby, Duncan P. Brumby
UCL Interaction Centre
University College London, WC1E 6EA, UK
ngoi.wong.13@alumni.ucl.ac.uk, {j.rigby.14, d.brumby}@ucl.ac.uk

ABSTRACT
Let's Play videos, where players record themselves playing games, are a new and popular way of experiencing game content. To investigate the experience of watching Let's Play videos, we had 40 participants watch a video of someone playing a racing game. The same participants also played the racing game and watched footage of an actual racing event. After each media experience, participants completed a modified version of the Immersive Experience Questionnaire (IEQ). Results show that IEQ scores were highest after participants played the game, and lowest after passively watching the non-gaming content; watching the Let's Play video was in between. When watching the Let's Play video, participants who were familiar with the game had lower IEQ scores than participants who were new to the game. These results show that actively controlling a game generates a deeper immersive experience than passively watching others play — watching is not as immersive as playing.

ACM Classification Keywords
K.8.0 General: Games; H.5.m.Information Interfaces and Presentation (e.g. HCI): Miscellaneous

Author Keywords
Gaming; Let's Play; immersion; video; experience measurement

INTRODUCTION
Computer games are an extremely popular form of entertainment, and their profitability has even exceeded the film industry in recent years [7]. Surrounding these games are active on-line communities, where fans can share content for different games. A particularly popular form of fan-made content, the Let's Play video, has emerged, where gamers record themselves playing a game, often while providing a running commentary on what they are doing. These videos have grown in popularity and attract a large number of viewers on video sharing sites, such as YouTube [20]. For example, PewDiePie has the most subscribed channel on YouTube, with more than 52 million subscribers and 15 billion accumulated views since 2013 [20]. Creating a hugely successful YouTube channel with many millions of subscribers is financially rewarding. These rewards in turn encourage the production of yet more Let's Play videos [24].

Given the popularity of the Let's Play video format for sharing gaming content, we wonder what kind viewing experience they produce. This is an important question because enjoyment is linked to the quality of a media experience [32]. For example, Weibel and Wissmath [32] suggested that the quality of a gaming experience (i.e. sense of being situated and involvement in a game), directly affects enjoyment. In a similar way, this may mean that individuals' experience in Let's Play videos may have an impact on their enjoyment in the medium. In the study presented here we investigated the experience of watching Let's Play gaming videos in relation to other media experiences: actively playing the game or passively watching related, non-gaming video content.

Video-sharing sites offer a platform that allows anyone to watch and upload content. Gaming channels have become particularly popular, and their audiences can be categorised into two groups: players and non-players. An individual's experience as a player or a non-player when viewing gaming videos may be different, and it may also be an important factor in determining whether they would choose a particular medium or not. In the study presented here, we investigate whether familiarity with a game impacts the experience of watching Let's Play videos. Is it the case the only those that are already intimately familiar with a game enjoy watching others play (maybe to learn new tricks or techniques)?

In the following, we first review related prior work on understanding immersion in media experiences with different types of media (i.e., digital gaming, TV, and Let's Play videos). After this, we describe the results of a lab study that investigates the experience of watching Let's Play videos compared with other media experiences (actively playing a game, and passively watching related, non-gaming content). The contribution of this paper is in providing an empirical understanding of the gaming experience and how it is changing with the advent of new formats, such as the Let's Play gaming video.

CHI PLAY '17, October 15-18, 2017, Amsterdam, Netherlands

ACM ISBN 978-1-4503-4898-0/17/10.
https://doi.org/10.1145/3116595.3116613

RELATED WORK

Gaming, Viewing, and Immersion

Given the importance of digital gaming as an entertainment medium, prior research has been conducted to understand how games can be designed to draw people in and make them forget about their worries in their daily life [17]. Among the many established methods for measuring gaming experience, such as Game Flow [30], cognitive absorption [1] and presence [34], the concept of immersion is believed to have incorporated a more extensive and broad view in player's experience than the other constructs [17]. However, despite its advantages over the other measures, the exact meaning of immersion can be unclear. The work of Jennett et al. [17] has been highly valuable by providing a practical tool for measuring immersision through the Immersive Experience Questionnaire (IEQ), which covers several aspects of the gaming experience.

Immersion is also described as a state of high engagement [5], to an extent to which individuals feel like they are "in the game". It should be noted that immersion, and related conceptualisations of high engagement, are not exclusive to digital games, but they are also present when watching films [27] and reading literature [28]. These media involve consuming a scripted narrative, and these experiences may therefore differ from gaming because of the lack of interactivity and agency. Given that measures for immersion have been well-developed and already applied to different forms of media, we therefore chose to use a modified version of the IEQ to measure experiences in the present study. In addition, while immersion and other measures of media experiences have been explored extensively in gaming [3] and TV viewing [27], little research has been conducted on assessing immersion when viewing Let's Play videos.

Media Type and Interactivity

Modern technology offers a number of different entertainment media, such as playing video games, watching gaming footage, and watching TV [19]. Two ways in which these media are distinctive are the absence and presence of interactivity [23] and different types of media environment [14]. In a game, the player actively participates in the control of the game, whereas passively viewed media such as TV and film do not build an interactive relationship between the audience and the media. Let's Play video footage is essentially form of video entertainment that innovatively incorporates digital game elements. Its lack of interactivity naturally resembles the traditional viewing form of media, while revealing the central ideas of digital gaming in the same mediated world.

The three different types of media concerning this study are therefore characterised as follows: digital gaming, an interactive activity in gaming environment; watching Let's Play video footage, a non-interactive activity in gaming environment; and watching TV, a non-interactive activity in a non-gaming environment. These differences and similarities between these media have not been compared in previous research, as Let's Play videos are a relatively new form of entertainment. Let's Play videos provide a bridge between the interactivity of playing games and the passive entertainment enjoyed by many when watching videos.

Immersion and Different Cognitive Activities

Sense of Control

Having a sense of control in a media environment describes the ability to which a person can influence the events of a situation [18]. The different characteristics of the media types determine whether a person can exert a sense of control in a particular media environment. For instance, level of interactivity affects the ability to be in control of the events of a particular media type [14]. In interactive gaming, players are able to experience a sense of control by controlling the movement of the gaming character. However, watching a Let's play video footage and a TV clip are passive activities that sense of control is less tangible than gaming [13]. This is because audiences lack the ability to alter and make decisions about the content of the media.

It has been suggested that sense of control and gaming experience are closely linked together [18, 4]. Klimmt, Hartmann and Tilo [18] found that being in control of a game is indeed a factor affecting the enjoyment of a game, but has a complicated effect associated with how challenging the player thought the game was. Witmer and Singer [33] found that the greater the level of control a player has over an avatar, the higher the level of presence they experience. Furthermore, players, who were qualitatively interviewed in Brown and Cairns's [4] study associated the sense of control they gain during games with how immersed they subsequently feel. The authors also suggest that an immersion is experienced to a higher level of immersion if a player familiarises themselves with the controls to a point where they become "invisible". This supports Witmer and Singer's [33] finding that control and presence.

Role-taking

Role-taking, which is used interchangeably with perspective-taking, refers to a cognitive process by which an individual temporarily imagines themself as another person so as to understand their thoughts, attitudes, intentions, and behaviours in a given situation [23]. In media contexts, the term describes the extent to which a player or an audience is perceptually absorbed, cognitively motivated, emotionally affected and behaviourally engaged with the character(s). In the process of role-taking, the phenomenon of representing oneself as another person can occur to different extents according to different media environments. Cohen [9] suggested that passive visual media such as TV can lead to a low sense of role-taking when the viewer attempts to put themselves in the character's shoes. On the other hand, gaming can enable a player to achieve a higher level of role-taking, as the player actively takes on the role of the avatar, taking on the physical movement control and the mental perspective of the character. Therefore, it is possible that higher levels of interactivity in a medium can lead to higher levels of role-taking.

It has been suggested that strong role-taking could lead to an enhanced media experience. Nicovich, Boller and Cornwell [22] investigated presence experience in relation to the projection of oneself to a view of a virtual character. Their findings suggested that the ability to project oneself is important in order to experience a state of presence, suggesting that higher levels of perspective-taking can lead to an increased experience. This role-taking seems to be reinforced by the interactivity nature of the media in their study. In the design of their experiment, participants either took control of a flight simulator or they merely viewed a video of it, which controlled for a different level of perspective-taking. In the interactive media environment, where people were able to control the plane, presence experience was enhanced.

Role-taking is involved strongly in gaming because interactivity and active participation blurs the identity between the player and the character, and synchronises their roles perceptually, cognitively and motivationally [23]. Additionally, strong role-taking occurs also because interactive digital gaming requires less cognitive capacity for role-taking to occur than visual media environments. For example, watching Let's Play videos and TV as players cognitively infer the character's thoughts and perspectives while at the same time are motivated by and share goals with the in-game character. Therefore, media experience in digital gaming may differ when compared to passive visual media due to a higher degree of role-taking.

In distinguishing between media experiences in Let's Play and TV, we can consider their difference in terms of user's subjectivity in role-taking. With the perspective of the eyes of the character, first-person point of view (POV) provides a more subjective and personal experience than third person POV. It was suggested that first-person POV enhanced immersive experience when compared to third-person POV in gaming [11]. Hence, it is possible that due to a higher degree of subjectivity in perspective taking that a higher immersion is experienced. The subjectivity in Let's Play video footage is stronger than in TV due to the inherited interactive relationship between a gamer and the in-game character even though it was not a first hand experience. Conversely, traditional television viewing mostly shows objective camera shots that switch between different scenes with multiple camera angles, potentially conveying a lower sense of subjectivity in role-taking.

Game Familiarity and Immersion

The aforementioned concept suggested by Brown and Cairns [4] essentially states that the more familiar a player is with the game controls, the more immersed they can be. Cheung and Huang [8] asked the question of whether audiences who have been exposed to the game (players) would show different level of interest or react differently in viewing another person playing the game compared to those who have not (non-players). Their qualitative research found that people who had played a game themselves found it more interesting to watch pro-players play the same game [8]. However, the kinds of viewers who lacked understanding of the game showed the opposite. Therefore, prior exposure to the mechanics of a game may possibly enhance a person's experience on viewing the game.

GOALS AND HYPOTHESES

The study aims to see if three distinct media types (playing a game, watching a game, and watching TV) lead to different levels of immersion, and explores how different levels of control and role taking may affect this. Furthermore, we explore whether the level of immersion experienced when watching Let's Play videos is affected by prior familiarity with a game (i.e. having played it immediately before).

We make two main predictions concerning the effects of media type and familiarity. First, we expect that immersion scores will be proportional to the cognitive activity required across the different media types. Specifically, we expect immersion scores to be highest after participants have actively played the game, followed by watching Let's Play footage, and lowest after watching TV. This prediction is based on prior work that shows how sense of control and role-taking have been shown to affect media experiences. Second, we expect that higher familiarity with a game will lead to higher levels immersion when watching gaming footage of the same game. This is because participants will have developed a higher level of understanding of the game after playing it.

METHOD

Participants

Forty university students were recruited using opportunity sampling (9 males, 31 females). Age ranged from 18 to 24 years old ($M = 20.2$ years old, $SD = 1.63$). We asked participants about their prior experience of playing *Mario Kart Wii* and with Nintendo Wii controllers. Thirty-one of the participants said that they had played *Mario Kart Wii* before. Of these, one participant reported to be extremely familiar with the game; five participants were moderately familiar with the game; and six participants were somewhat familiar with with the game.

Design

The experiment used a 2×3 (Familiarity × Media Type) mixed factorial design. The between-subject independent variable was the participants' level of familiarity to the game *Mario Kart Wii* when they were watching the Let's Play video footage. There were two levels: high familiarity, where the participant had played the game immediately before watching the Let's Play; and low/no familiarity, where they watched the footage before playing the game. The within-subject independent variable was the media type, and there were three levels: playing *Mario Kart Wii* (Play), watching a Let's Play video footage of *Mario Kart Wii* (GamingFootage) and watching TV clip of a British Superbike Championship (TV). The dependent variable is participant's level of immersion during each media measured via questionnaire, as well as the subscales therein.

Materials

The game *Mario Kart Wii* was used in the Play condition of the experiment, played on a Nintendo Wii console. This is a racing game where in-game characters compete on various race tracks, and features an especially popular multiplayer mode. In the interests of experimental control, settings for characters and vehicles were the same for all participants. The first and easiest two tracks were selected for participants to play. Participants used the Wii remote controller with a steering wheel attachment, which allows them to manipulate in-game mechanics through gestures movements intended to simulate real-world driving.

A Mario Kart Let's Play video [2] and a British Superbike Championships 2015 [21] TV clip were sourced from YouTube and were used in the GamingFootage condition and TV condition respectively. The Let's Play footage shows a game that was played with identical the in-game characters, settings, and tracks to those in the Play condition. The TV clip shows a motorcycle racing competition from the British Superbike Championship 2015, where there were 36 motorcycle riders competing. It was selected to be similar to playing Mario Kart with motorcycles. These two videos were trimmed to around 4 minutes, which is approximately the same time it takes to play the game. All conditions were displayed on a 32 inch LCD TV.

Modified immersion questionnaire

This study adopts the Immersive Experience Questionnaire (IEQ) [17], a well-established and validated scale for measuring self-reported immersion. It has been used widely in exploring gaming experiences [6, 10, 15], and is a scale that has been applied to passive visual media as well [16, 27]. As the original IEQ [17] was created for measuring immersion in gaming, for our purposes the questions that do not apply to all the media types we used were removed. For instance, the question "Were you in suspense about whether or not you would win or lose the game?" was taken out since there are no win and lose conditions in TV watching.

This modified IEQ (see Table 1) consists of five subscales adopted from the original IEQ, measuring cognitive involvement (5 questions, Q.1-3, Q.10, Q.19), real world dissociation (6 questions, Q.4-8, Q.11), control (4 questions, Q.9, Q.13, Q.18), challenge (2 questions, Q.14-15), emotional involvement (5 questions, Q.12, Q.16-17, Q.20-21). Five questions are scored negatively (Q.5, Q.7, Q.8, Q.9, Q.16). The modified IEQ is therefore composed of 3 personal factors (cognitive involvement, real world dissociation and emotional involvement) and 2 game factors (challenge and control). Questions are answered using a 5-point Likert scale, and total immersion is computed by summing the scores.

We also added questions that ask about initial familiarity with the game used prior to the experiment, e.g. "How familiar are you with playing Mario Kart?" and "How familiar are you with playing Mario Kart with Wii controllers?". The response scales were built according to the Vagias's Likert-Type Scale [31] for measuring level of familiarity, ranged from 1 to 5 with 1 being not at all familiar and 5 being extremely familiar.

1. To what extent did the task hold your attention?
2. To what extent did you feel you were focused on the task?
3. How much effort did you put into completing the task?
4. To what extent did you lose track of time while completing the task?
5. To what extent did you feel consciously aware of being in the real world whilst completing the task?
6. To what extent did you forget about your everyday concerns?
7. To what extent were you aware of yourself in your surroundings?
8. To what extent did you notice events taking place around you while completing the task?
9. Did you feel the urge at any point to stop doing the task and see what was happening around you?
10. How much would you say your attention was focused more on your surroundings than on the task content?
11. To what extent did you feel as though you were separated from your real-world environment?
12. To what extent did you feel that the task was something you were experiencing, rather than something you were just doing?
13. To what extent did you feel as though the events in the tasks were happening according to your expectation?
14. To what extent did you find the task challenging?
15. To what extent did you find the task easy?
16. To what extent did you feel emotionally attached to the task?
17. To what extent were you interested in seeing how the task would progress?
18. To what extent did you enjoy the graphics and imagery?
19. How much would you say you enjoyed the task?
20. When interrupted, were you disappointed that the task was over?
21. Would you like to do the task again?

Table 1. Modified Immersive Experience Questionnaire.

Procedure

Participants were seated in an office. They were then asked to read the information sheet, and to sign the consent form if they agreed to take part in the study. They completed a questionnaire to collect demographic information and their prior familiarity with the game using a laptop. Participants were then required to perform three tasks: play *Mario Kart Wii* (Play); watch the Let's Play video of *Mario Kart Wii* (GamingFootage); and watch the British Superbike World Championship video (TV).

Before each session, participants were informed what to do in the tasks that followed. In the Play condition, participants were given the information about the game, e.g. they were going to play two race tracks where they had to drive 3 laps in each race track to complete the game, and that there were power-up items that assist them to win. Also, they were provided with instructions on how to use Wii controller. They were also told that they were allowed to ask questions. If participants were unclear about the controls, the experimenter explained how they worked. Once ready, participants were asked to position themselves 1.5 meters in front of the TV monitor to play. In the GamingFootage condition and the TV condition, participants were told that they would be shown a gaming video from YouTube that showed the game being played, and a short TV clip of a Superbike World Championship race. Similarly, they were asked to position themselves in front of the TV monitor. After each condition, they were also asked to fill in the modified IEQ.

Participants were exposed to the conditions one-by-one. The order of conditions was organized so that there were four different orders assigned to different participants. First, the order sequences between Play and GamingFootage sessions were arranged so that they were always shown together in order to try and expose the immediate effect of familiarity as much as possible; participants received either Play then GamingFootage order or GamingFootage then Play order. Second, the TV clip was presented either before or after the Play GamingFootage pairs in a counterbalanced manner. Therefore, the four different orders were:

1. Play - GamingFootage - TV
2. GamingFootage - Play - TV
3. TV - Play - GamingFootage
4. TV - GamingFootage - Play

At the very end of the experiment, participants were asked what they thought the purpose of the experiment was before being debriefed.

RESULTS

Data Analysis

Immersion scores were computed from the modified IEQ results by summing individual question results. Questions 5, 7, 8, 9 and 16 were scored negatively. In addition to analysing the overall immersion scores, the five subscales that compose the IEQ were also assessed separately. Results for statistical analysis of the subscales are presented in Table 3. Effects were considered significant where p values $\leq .05$.

Immersion Score

Media Types

In observing the means and among the Media Types in Figure 1, overall mean immersion score was highest for Play condition, followed by GamingFootage Condition, and lowest in the TV condition. A 2 × 3 (Familiarity × Media type) Mixed Factorial ANOVA was conducted, which showed a significant main effect of media type, $F(2,76) = 65.7, p < .001, \eta_p^2 = .634$. No significant media type * familiarity interaction effect was found, $F(2,76) = 0.89, p = .416, \eta_p^2 = .023$.

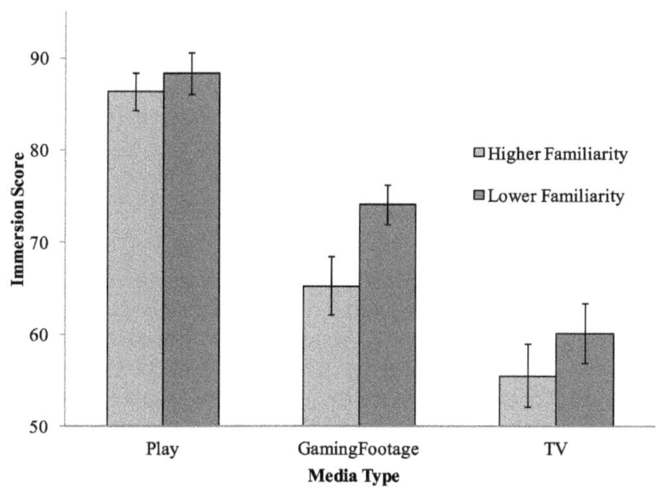

Figure 1. Mean overall immersion scores of different familiarity conditions across different Media type conditions.

Familiarity

We also wanted to see if watching a Let's Play video after playing the same game would result in a higher level of immersion than watching it before playing the game. Results of the GamingFootage condition showed a higher mean immersion score with lower familiarity than with higher familiarity (see Figure 1). A 2×3 (Familiarity × Media Type) Mixed Factorial ANOVA revealed a significant main effect of Familiarity on immersion scores, $F(1,38) = 4.23, p.047, \eta_p^2 = .10$. Two one-way ANOVA analyses were performed to determine the simple effects of Familiarity at Play and GamingFootage level. No simple effect of Familiarity at the level of Play was found, $F(1,38) = 0.415, p.523, \eta_p^2 = .011$. However, there was a simple effect of Familiarity at the level of GamingFootage, $F(1,38) = 5.44, p.025, \eta_p^2 = .125$.

Two repeated measures ANOVA analyses performed according to familiarity level suggested that there were simple effects of Media Type at both the Higher Familiarity level, $F(2,38) = 27.84, p < .001, \eta_p^2 = .594$ and Lower Familiarity level, $F(2,38) = 44.07, p < .001, \eta_p^2 = .699$. By performing paired t-tests which are shown in Figure 2, it was also found that participants were significantly more immersed in the Play condition than the GamingFootage condition at both Higher Familiarity level and Lower Familiarity level. In fact, all the paired t-tests between pairs of the three Media Type conditions were significant at both familiarity levels except for that between GamingFootage and TV at Higher Familiarity.

	Higher Familiarity		Lower Familiarity	
	$t(19)$	d	$t(19)$	d
Play VS GamingFootage	6.19**	1.38	7.02**	1.57
Play VS TV	8.23**	1.84	7.75**	1.73
GamingFootage VS TV	1.85	.413	4.47**	1.00

Table 2. Paired t-tests between Media Types in Different Levels of Familiarity. *$p < .05$. ** $p < .001$.

Subscales

IEQ Subscale Analysis

2 × 3 (Familiarity × Media Type) Mixed Factorial ANOVAs were conducted on the separate IEQ subscales, main effects of Media Type were found in all the measures (as shown in Table 3). While most subscales followed the decline pattern of the overall immersion scores with regards to media types, Challenge was the exception.

Challenge

Unlike the overall immersion score, Figure 2 illustrates that the Challenge score was highest in Play, followed by TV and then GamingFootage. Main effect of Media Type in Challenge scores was followed up by pairwise comparisons of different Media Types. Paired tests showed that there were significant differences between each of the three conditions, Play VS GamingFootage, $t(39) = 8.73, p < .001, d = 1.38$; Play VS TV, $t(39) = 5.88, p < .001, d = 0.93$; GamingFootage VS TV, $t(39) = 2.26, p = .029, d = 0.36$.

There were simple effects of Media Type at the level of Higher Familiarity, Play VS GamingFootage, $t(19) = 6.95, p <$

	Media Type		Familiarity		Media Type x Familiarity	
	$F(2,76)$	η_p^2	$F(1,38)$	η_p^2	$F(2,76)$	η_p^2
Cognitive Involvement	57.6**	.602	3.62	.087	0.771	.020
Real World Dissociation	42.4**	.527	1.92	.048	0.679	.018
Control	17.0**	.309	0.145*	.055	0.682	.018
Emotional Involvement	58.8**	.607	0.216	.040	0.412	.023
Challenge	42.2**	.526	3.58	.086	1.56	.039

Table 3. Mixed Factorial ANOVA F ratios of IEQ subscale scores by Media Type condition (Play/GamingFootage/TV) and Familiarity (Higher/Lower). $*p < .05$. $** \ p < .001$.

$.001, d = 1.55$; Play VS TV, $t(19) = 6.53, p < .001, d = 1.46$; GamingFootage VS TV, $t(19) = 2.22, p = .039, d = 0.50$. Simple effects were only found between Play and GamingFootage and Play and TV at Lower Familiarity level, Play VS GamingFootage, $t(19) = 5.60, p < .001, d = 1.25$; Play VS TV, $t(19) = 2.80, p = .011, d = 0.63$; GamingFootage VS TV, $t(19) = 1.21, p = .243, d = 0.27$.

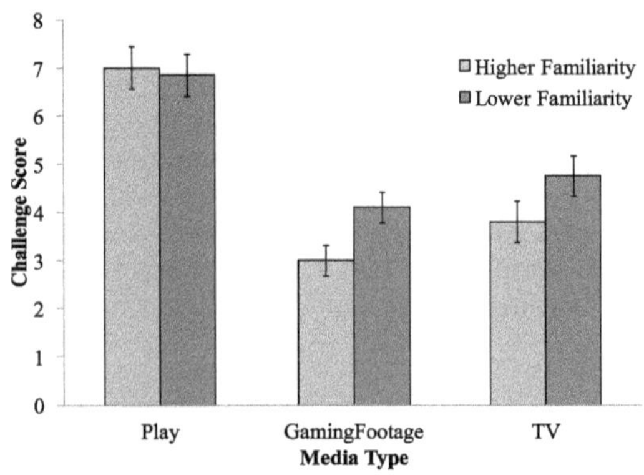

Figure 2. Challenge score means by Media Type conditions and Familiarity levels.

DISCUSSION

This study sought to understand the effect of different types of media and familiarity with the game material on immersion. The pattern of immersion was obtained as predicted – immersion was the highest when playing, then when watching Let's Play videos, and lastly when watching TV clips. However, our prediction that that being more familiar with playing the game would result in a higher immersion when watching the game was not supported by our results. In fact we found the opposite, where higher immersion when watching the Let's Play video was recorded for those who had not played the game immediately before watching than those who had. Therefore, it seems that immersion is moderated by familiarity: immersion in the Let's Play video was only different from that of the two other media types in the lower familiarity condition, but was the same as immersion in TV in the higher familiarity condition.

The first part of our results demonstrated that media types that differed in terms of their characteristics affected the immersion experienced by participants. We suspect that these differences between the conditions are effects of underlying factors including sense of control and role-taking. In line with Witmer and Singer's [33] study, the higher immersion score in game playing as compared to viewing content such as Let's Play gaming footage and TV highlights the importance of the presence of sense of control in relation to media experience. In addition, in the same sense, role-taking was found directly proportional to immersive experience, confirming Nicovich et al.[22] and Denisova and Cairns's [11] studies.

There are several factors that can be explored further in future research. In the present design, only a game with a third person POV where the whole character was shown was used. There might be more complicated effects of role-taking regarding different elements of a game. For example, role-taking in simulation video games where the characters are more realistic may be stronger as it resembles real life more and role-taking in game where first person POV is taken may also be stronger as the perspective is more subjective.

There are improvements that can be made in exploring sense of control. One's sense of control might not exist in an absolute sense but on a spectrum relative to player's skills to the medium [14]. In the present study, participants were given a certain set up of the game, for instance, engine class, character, vehicle and drift. The difficulty of the game, which is mainly governed by engine class and drift here, was set up for the participants as 150cc and manual drift respectively. These two selections are the most difficult to master compared to other options such as 50cc and 100cc for engines and automatic drift for drifts. Therefore, participants might find it less manageable and hence, less in control of the game.

The Wii controller that was provided in the Mario Kart game works by recognising gestures. Unlike traditional controllers where players manipulate character(s)'s movement by keys and control stick, Wii controller is lower in sensitivity to your responses [29] so participants might take longer and find it difficult to get used to the controls, affecting the level of immersion experienced [4]. In consideration of these factors, exploring different levels of difficulties and training participants to use the controls to different levels of proficiency in future research may reveal richer pattern of contrasts in immersive experience.

Mario Kart is a competitive multiplayer game. In our study, participants played and watched a single player game mode of Mario Kart in which the opponents where virtual agents (rather than other gamers). Having this competitive component is one of the factors that makes the game more fun as it increases one's level of adrenaline [25]. Therefore, this might also have affected participants' immersion. It is worthwhile in the future to investigate whether a game is competitive or non-competitive may affect one's immersion. Also, as the TV clip used was from the beginning of the Superbike race, most of the commentary was not aggressive, which might have a different effect on immersion compared with that of an aggressive commentary. A more aggressive commentary may have been more enjoyable than non-aggressive commentary [26].

With regard to familiarity, we predicted that higher immersion would be experienced when watching Let's Play videos immediately after playing the game. In fact, we found the opposite - immersion was higher with lower familiarity. The issue of difficulty and the interaction between controller and player could explain why the result is inconsistent with the hypothesis. This is because these factors might have affected the level of control participants subjectively perceived they had over the characters. After playing a game with high difficulty and with an unfamiliar controller, participants might perceive that the pro player has played with a greater control of the characters in the footage. Therefore, comparison between their performance and the pro player's performance might have undermined the degree of immersion in the gaming footage.

We found that participants who had played the game first had lower immersion scores when watching the gaming footage. This is in contrast to previous research, which showed that people with prior experience playing a game got more out of watching pro-players play a game [8]. However, the players studied in Cheung and Huang's [8] study must have a certain level of gaming experience. This study made the assumption that participant's level of familiarity was fully controlled by the order of Play and GamingFootage conditions. However, it is important to acknowledge that there were a number of participants who had no experience with Mario Kart prior to the game and most participants were not familiar with playing the game with Wii controllers. One experience of the game in the study is not enough to define one's familiarity level or whether he/she was a 'player' of the game or not. Hence, levels of familiarity with Mario Kart varied among participants. Therefore in future research, participants should practise on Mario Kart with Wii controllers for a period of time before taking part in the actual experiment. Moreover, it might be useful to have tracked participants' level of general knowledge of video games, familiarity with the Wii console, and with racing games, as these differences may also be confounding factors.

Moreover, Peng et al. [23] suggests that a lower cognitive requirement is needed for role-taking to take place in playing games than in viewing passive visual contents. Extracting meaning from information that is passively received requires longer cognitive process. Therefore, when participants immediately switched from playing the game to watching gaming footage, transitioning to the other media type might have created a huge contrast in cognitive requirement of role-taking, hence undermined immersion in watching gaming footage. Moreover, the gaming footage immersion at higher familiarity was not only significantly lower than that at lower familiarity, also it was as low as the TV immersion score, indicating the same high level of cognitive demand in interacting with gaming footage after the transition. Therefore, the levels of cognitive demand in role-taking might have hindered participants' immersion when switched from a highly interactive medium to a less interactive medium.

With regard to the formation of the IEQ, questions that do not fit with all media types were excluded from the original Jennett et al. IEQ [17] which resulted in having as few as two questions in the Challenge subscale. Despite large effect sizes in Challenge , the number of questions is a worrying issue regarding its representative power in the subscales or not. In particular, the Challenge score in the present study did not follow the overall immersion pattern according to different media types. Challenge score was highest in play mode, then in viewing TV and finally in viewing gaming footage This pattern gives us insight into immersion in viewing contents such as gaming footage and TV that they might have lower or greater effects on a certain dimension of immersion. Klimmt et al. [18] suggested that struggle for control (same as challenge), which is often associated with suspense, also affects one's gaming experience. This might also apply to viewing contents as well. The fact that TV resulted in a higher score than gaming footage means that it might have elicited higher excitement in individuals due to uncertainty to the content, and hence increased its competitiveness in involving individuals in its media experience compared to other media.

Limitations

Demand characteristics are one of the limitations of this study. Participants' feedback in regards to the purpose of the study showed that there might be possible bias in their response. For example, one participant stated the purpose of the study was "to assess which form of media people feel more involved with and enjoy more, particularly the difference between playing a game yourself or watching someone else." When different types of media were being put closely with one right after another, the purpose in comparing between the forms and nature of the media might become obvious. This was especially the case when both conditions, Play and GamingFootage were controlled to the same settings, characters and vehicles, revealing the obvious differences between the forms and types of media. Furthermore, another participants made a guess similar to the present hypothesis of the study, for instance, "To see if your interaction with the task/media affects how you perceive the surroundings around you. The more interactive you are with the task the less you are aware of your surroundings". Although participants did not refer directly to immersion or its correct definition, this showed a correct expectation of the pattern of the result where they might have reflected in their immersion response. Future amendments to control this confounding variable can be to insert some unrelated tasks in between the conditions, before the start of the tasks or at the end of the tasks, e.g. mathematics problems or memory tasks, to hide the purpose of the study.

Immersion in this study is a self-reported measure, the issue of demand characteristics is even more of a concern as it is easy for participant's response bias to influence the data. Besides, self-reported immersion was problematic due to issues such that participants might vary in their understanding of the questions or lack introspective ability to accurately view themselves, which would lead to inaccurate results. Direct measures such as eye tracking data could be used in future studies to control for consistency with the self-reported results.

This study did not account for the fact that viewers may not only enjoy the content of the video, but also the connection that they have with the creator of the content and the wider community of their subscribers and followers [12]. Further research that investigates how these social connection may affect people's immersion in the Let's Play videos may also be interesting.

CONCLUSION

The study reported in this paper investigated the experience of watching Let's Play gaming videos in relation to other media experiences: actively playing the game or passively watching related, non-gaming video content. Results show that the highest levels of immersion were experienced when playing a game, then viewing Let's Play footage. However, watching a Let's Play video was more immersive than watching related, non-gaming TV content. Interestingly, those who were not exposed to the game beforehand reported higher levels of immersion, suggesting that immersive experiences when watching Let's Play are moderated by familiarity.The implications of these results are that Let's Play videos should cater for audiences with differing levels of familiarity with the game, which could allow for the video producers to strategically attract wider audiences In exploring some possible limitations of our study we have also identified potential directions for future research, such as comparing first-person and third-person POV games.

ACKNOWLEDGEMENTS

This work was supported by EPSRC grant EP/G037159/1.

REFERENCES

1. Ritu Agarwal and Elena Karahanna. 2000. Time flies when you're having fun: Cognitive absorption and beliefs about information technology usage. *MIS Quarterly* (2000), 665–694.
2. BlueShadowRP. 2015. Mario Kart Wii - Mushroom Cup (150cc). (Sept. 2015). `https://www.youtube.com/watch?v=YnWnSYGlhPg`
3. Elizabeth A Boyle, Thomas M Connolly, Thomas Hainey, and James M Boyle. 2012. Engagement in digital entertainment games: A systematic review. *Computers in Human Behavior* 28, 3 (2012), 771–780.
4. Emily Brown and Paul Cairns. 2004. A grounded investigation of game immersion. In *CHI'04 Extended Abstracts on Human Factors in Computing Systems*. ACM, 1297–1300.
5. Paul Cairns, Anna Cox, and A Imran Nordin. 2014a. Immersion in digital games: review of gaming experience research. *Handbook of Digital Games* (2014), 337–361.
6. Paul Cairns, Jing Li, Wendy Wang, and A Imran Nordin. 2014b. The influence of controllers on immersion in mobile games. In *Proceedings of the SIGCHI Conference on Human Factors in Computing Systems*. ACM, 371–380.
7. Tom Chatfield. 2009. Videogames now outperform Hollywood movies. *The Guardian.* (2009). `http://www.theguardian.com/technology/gamesblog/2009/sep/27/videogames-hollywood`
8. Gifford Cheung and Jeff Huang. 2011. Starcraft from the stands: understanding the game spectator. In *Proceedings of the SIGCHI Conference on Human Factors in Computing Systems*. ACM, 763–772.
9. Jonathan Cohen. 2001. Defining identification: A theoretical look at the identification of audiences with media characters. *Mass Communication & Society* 4, 3 (2001), 245–264.
10. Anna Cox, Paul Cairns, Pari Shah, and Michael Carroll. 2012. Not doing but thinking: the role of challenge in the gaming experience. In *Proceedings of the SIGCHI Conference on Human Factors in Computing Systems*. ACM, 79–88.
11. Alena Denisova and Paul Cairns. 2015. First Person vs. Third Person Perspective in Digital Games: Do Player Preferences Affect Immersion?. In *Proceedings of the 33rd Annual ACM Conference on Human Factors in Computing Systems*. ACM, 145–148.
12. Stuart Dredge. 2016. Why are YouTube stars so popular? *The Guardian* (2016). `https://www.theguardian.com/technology/2016/feb/03/why-youtube-stars-popular-zoella`
13. Beryl Graham. 1996. Playing with yourself: pleasure and interactive art. *Fractal Dreams: New Media in Social Context* (1996), 154–79.
14. Torben Grodal. 2000. Video games and the pleasures of control. *Media Entertainment: The Psychology of its Appeal* (2000), 197–213.
15. Hayrettin Gürkök. 2012. *Mind the sheep! User experience evaluation & brain-computer interface games.* University of Twente.
16. R. Hong. 2006. Immersion in reading and films as a function of personality. *B. Sc. Thesis, Dept. of Psychology, University College London* (2006).
17. Charlene Jennett, Anna L Cox, Paul Cairns, Samira Dhoparee, Andrew Epps, Tim Tijs, and Alison Walton. 2008. Measuring and defining the experience of immersion in games. *International Journal of Human-Computer Studies* 66, 9 (2008), 641–661.
18. Christoph Klimmt, Tilo Hartmann, and Andreas Frey. 2007. Effectance and control as determinants of video game enjoyment. *Cyberpsychology & Behavior* 10, 6 (2007), 845–848.
19. Sonia Livingstone. 2002. *Young People and New Media: Childhood and the Changing Media Environment*. Sage.
20. Fred McConnell. 2014. Let's Play - the YouTube phenomenon that's bigger than One Direction. *The Guardian* (2014). `http://www.theguardian.com/technology/2014/jan/02/lets-play-youtube-pewdiepie-one-direction`

21. MotoRacingHD. 2015. British Superbikes 2015. Round 7. Thruxton. Race 1. (Aug. 2015). http://www.youtube.com/watch?v=PEn9upRn14E

22. Stef G Nicovich, Gregory W Boller, and T Bettina Cornwell. 2005. Experienced Presence within Computer-Mediated Communications: Initial Explorations on the Effects of Gender with Respect to Empathy and Immersion. *Journal of Computer-Mediated Communication* 10, 2 (2005), 00–00.

23. Wei Peng, Mira Lee, and Carrie Heeter. 2010. The effects of a serious game on role-taking and willingness to help. *Journal of Communication* 60, 4 (2010), 723–742.

24. Hector Postigo. 2016. The socio-technical architecture of digital labor: Converting play into YouTube money. *New Media & Society* 18, 2 (2016), 332–349.

25. Marc Prensky. 2001. Fun, play and games: What makes games engaging. *Digital Game-Based Learning* 5 (2001), 1–05.

26. Arthur A Raney and Anthony J Depalma. 2006. The effect of viewing varying levels and contexts of violent sports programming on enjoyment, mood, and perceived violence. *Mass Communication & Society* 9, 3 (2006), 321–338.

27. Jacob M Rigby, Duncan P Brumby, Anna L Cox, and Sandy JJ Gould. 2016. Watching movies on netflix: investigating the effect of screen size on viewer immersion. In *Proceedings of the 18th International Conference on Human-Computer Interaction with Mobile Devices and Services Adjunct*. ACM, 714–721.

28. Marie-Laure Ryan. 2001. *Narrative as Virtual Reality: Immersion and Interactivity in Literature and Electronic Media*. Johns Hopkins University Press.

29. Thomas Schlömer, Benjamin Poppinga, Niels Henze, and Susanne Boll. 2008. Gesture recognition with a Wii controller. In *Proceedings of the 2nd International Conference on Tangible and Embedded Interaction*. ACM, 11–14.

30. Penelope Sweetser and Peta Wyeth. 2005. GameFlow: a model for evaluating player enjoyment in games. *Computers in Entertainment (CIE)* 3, 3 (2005), 3–3.

31. Wade M Vagias. 2006. Likert-type Scale Response Anchors. Clemson International Institute for Tourism. *& Research Development, Department of Parks, Recreation and Tourism Management, Clemson University* (2006).

32. David Weibel and Bartholomäus Wissmath. 2011. Immersion in computer games: The role of spatial presence and flow. *International Journal of Computer Games Technology* 2011 (2011), 6.

33. Bob G Witmer and Michael F Singer. 1994. *Measuring presence in virtual environments*. Technical Report. DTIC Document.

34. Bob G Witmer and Michael J Singer. 1998. Measuring presence in virtual environments: A presence questionnaire. *Presence: Teleoperators and Virtual Environments* 7, 3 (1998), 225–240.

The Impact of Game Patterns on Player Experience and Social Interaction in Co-Located Multiplayer Games

Katharina Emmerich
Entertainment Computing Group
University of Duisburg-Essen, Germany
katharina.emmerich@uni-due.de

Maic Masuch
Entertainment Computing Group
University of Duisburg-Essen, Germany
maic.masuch@uni-due.de

ABSTRACT
Outstanding multiplayer games engage players by providing rich social interactions. Yet, it is still not clear how to purposefully design these interactions. Our paper tackles this issue by establishing a research model for social player interaction highlighting the impact of the game design, the player group, and the gaming setting. Based on that model, we investigated the influence of three particular game design patterns—*player interdependence*, *time pressure*, and *shared control*—on the interaction of players. For that purpose, we developed a co-located game to systematically test variations of those patterns. We analyzed the resulting player experience and social interaction by applying questionnaires and videotaping game play sessions. Results indicate that high player interdependence implies more communication and less frustration, whereas shared control results in less perceived competence and autonomy. Moreover, individual player characteristics also impact the social interaction.

ACM Classification Keywords
K.8.0. Personal Computing: General – Games

Author Keywords
social play; co-located gaming; player experience; game design patterns; evaluation; video annotation; communication.

INTRODUCTION
Playing digital games is not a solitary activity. Multiplayer games, both online and co-located, are very popular. For many players, the social interaction with others is the main motivator to play [13, 35, 25]. This motivational pull can be attributed to the positive impact of social interaction and communication between players. The social context is supposed to have a significant influence on players' overall experience [8] and, thus, on a game's general evaluation and success [17].

The question arises how the social interaction of players can be anticipated and purposefully designed. We assume that three main factors shape the interaction: the basic game design, the setting in which the game is played, and the composition of the player group. However, it is yet unclear to what extend these factors have impact on the social interaction, which of their sub-dimensions are relevant, and how their impact is weighted. Knowledge about the interplay of those factors is supposed to help inform future design processes to improve the experience of multiplayer games. Furthermore, it can help us to develop games that particularly focus on social interaction, for instance for the purpose of team-building processes.

CHI PLAY '17, October 15–18, 2017, Amsterdam, Netherlands

ACM ISBN 978-1-4503-4898-0/17/10...$15.00
DOI: https://doi.org/10.1145/3116595.3116606

Hence, this paper focuses on the question how the social dynamics of a game are influenced by its design patterns and contextual factors of the gaming situation. Note that we use the term *game pattern* to describe a set of specific mechanics and rules that shape the overall gameplay, like proposed in [27, 5] (not to be confused with software design patterns). As co-located gaming allows for the richest social interaction compared to distributed scenarios due to the immediacy of communication (both verbal and non-verbal), we chose this setting as a starting point for our research. Kröger et al. [19] emphasize that despite existing examples of interesting and relevant work in this area, there is still a need to focus more academic attention to it.

With this paper, we contribute to this research area by presenting a research model of social player interaction and results of a study that examines the impact of three particular game patterns: *player interdependence*, *time pressure*, and *shared control*. The model combined with the detailed methodology of our study approach is supposed to help researchers frame their own studies in the field of social player experience. Furthermore, findings of our study can be used by designers to purposefully design rich social experiences and intended interactions between players.

THE SOCIAL CONTEXT OF GAMING
The experiences emerging from playing digital games are complex and multi-faceted. Till now, several models and approaches have been proposed to break player experience down into sub-dimensions to be able to analyze its components and the relationships between those (e.g., [29, 25, 16]). In the context of multiplayer games, the social component is considered as a highly influential aspect for the overall experience, making the interplay of dimensions even more complex [8]. As soon as more than one person or artificial social entity is included in the gaming context, social-psychological effects have to be considered while examining player experience. Effects like evaluation apprehension, social learning, and emotional

contagion can significantly influence players during play [17]. To account for the interaction between players and its impact on the overall experience, the concept of *social presence* was introduced to the field of game user research. It defines the degree to which players are aware of each other and feel psychologically and behaviorally involved [9, 2].

The occurrence of social effects and the way players interact and communicate with each other is determined by a wide range of factors. In the following, we look at models that attempt to define these factors.

Determinants of the Social Experience

A common assumption in game user research is that player experience is dependent on the inter-relationship between game content, game context, and the player [18]. De Kort et al. [8] describe several sociality characteristics of game settings and group them in *social affordances* (e.g. communication, monitoring, awareness) and *objective characteristics of the game and interface* (e.g. communication channels, player representation, controls). They emphasize the role of communication, opportunities for monitoring performance and actions of the other players, as well as the relationship of players, both in-game and in real-life. Similarly, Isbister [17] highlights the impact of contextual and motivational factors in the context of social play. The work of Stenros et al. [28] points out, that even a single-player game can implicitly feature sociability in the broader gaming context (e.g., due to spectators, which is also emphasized by Tekin et al. [30]). Emmerich et al. [12] also define social aspects of a gaming session and point out six components that constitute the social context of gaming: the number of players, the real-world relationship between them, the form in which the other players are present (co-located or mediated), the presence of spectators, communication channels offered by the game, and the form of interaction imposed on players by the game (their in-game relationship). They also provide an overview of studies addressing these factors.

To integrate and arrange the social context aspects mentioned in the related work above, we propose to classify them within the following three categories:

(1) *Composition of the player group*
Comprises the number of players, their relationship to each other, individual's personality and attitudes, as well as any common history of the group.
(2) *Game patterns, mechanics, and rules*
Comprises the characteristics and features of the game, its rules, possible player actions, and the roles assigned to players. Also aspects of the interface and hardware belong to this category.
(3) *Characteristics of the environment*
Comprises the broader context of gaming in terms of environmental characteristics like the presence of spectators, the privacy of the location, and the atmosphere.

Accordingly, we summarized the models of social player experience and their related factors mentioned in the literature by integrating them into a research model for investigating social interaction in games. The result is presented in Figure 1. This model serves as the basis of our research presented in this paper. We assume that the interplay of player characteristics, game design aspects, and the setting (upper part of the model) determines players' behavior and interaction, which in turn contribute to the final player experience.

As shown by the middle part of the model, it can further be distinguished between different forms of social interaction: The interaction itself can take place either inside the game world (affecting the game state of a player, e.g. by healing another player's avatar), called *in-game interaction*, or outside the game (communication and physical interactions, e.g. talking to another player or tapping someone to attract attention), called *real-world interaction*. Although a player's behavior inside the game is limited by the system (due to rules, certain goals, and a limited range of actions a player may perform), the real-world social interaction between players can be as complex as in other real life situations. However, both forms of interaction are supposed to frame the social experience.

We assume that game mechanics and rules as well as social context factors significantly frame the interaction between players. In this context, Salen et al. [26] distinguish internally from externally derived interactions. Internally derived interactions emerge from the implemented game rules and design patterns, while externally derived interactions emerge from the players and the social playing context outside the game, which includes aspects like the relationship between players and their current mood.

This paper aims at investigating the influence of certain game patterns on players' interaction and experience. Hence, the second category of the social context in our research model—*game patterns, mechanics and rules*—and the related internally derived interaction is focused in the following. The other aspects are considered as potential influencing variables.

Impact of Game Patterns on Social Player Interaction

There is already a convenient amount of literature addressing the design of multiplayer games and social interaction in games [4, 23, 37, 24, 11, 31, 27, 21]. Such game patterns can be used both in the design process and for evaluating existing games. Hence, they are also relevant to the investigation of the impact of a game's mechanics on player interaction. Research results confirm the general assumption that social play is highly influenced by game mechanics and rules. In this context, Kröger et al. [19] present a comprehensive overview of current research related to co-located console gaming. One influential aspect of game design is the assignment of player roles and goals: Hereby it is determined whether players are supposed to interact basically competitive, cooperative or collaborative and may form teams and alliances [31, 4]. Several studies indicate that this difference has significant impact on player experience and interaction, for instance in terms of arousal, aggression, social presence, and enjoyment [12, 33, 32, 34]. Other examples of certain design patterns that can be used to further shape player interactions are player dependencies regarding abilities, shared and individual rewards, or the necessity to align actions [23, 4, 14]. Opportunities for verbal and non-verbal communication [8], as well as the design of character control [20] also shape the social context. Seif El-Nasr [27] conducted a comprehensive study analyzing

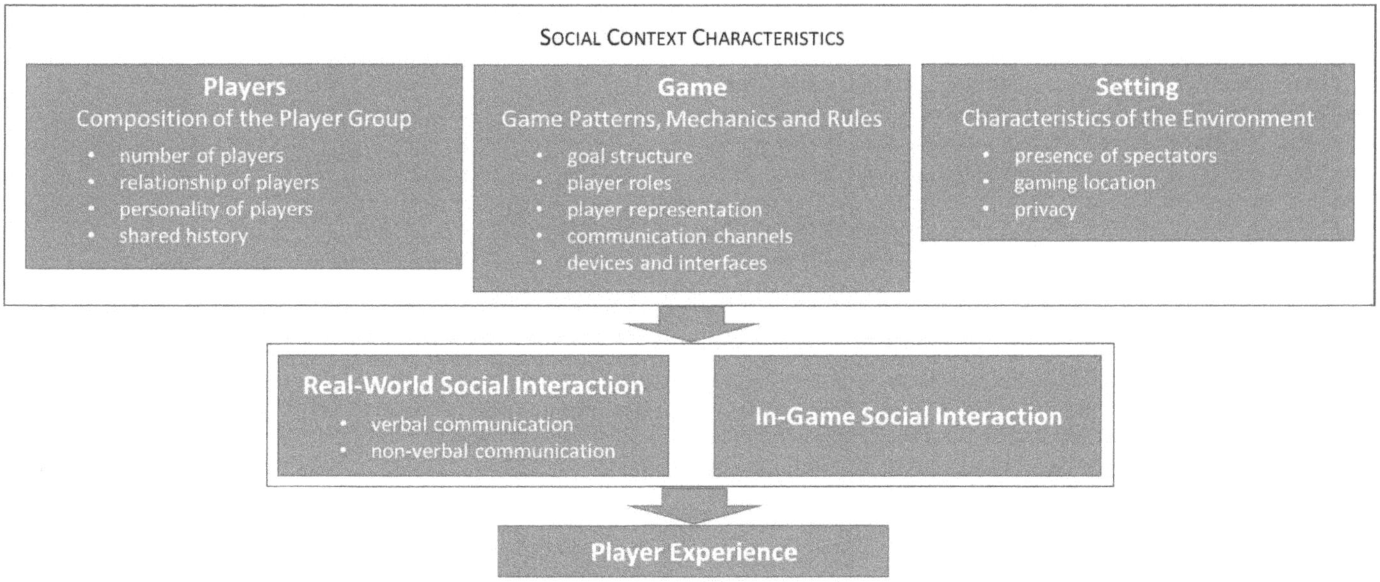

Figure 1. Our research model of social player interaction: Player characteristics, game patterns, and the gaming setting determine players' social interaction (both in-game and in the real world) and influence the player experience.

games in terms of cooperative design patterns. They found that shared puzzles and complementarity (in terms of different player roles and abilities) foster the establishment of global strategies, and that cut scenes and animations are related to common laughter and excitement.

As implied by the studies referenced above, there are a lot of game design patterns that can potentially influence social interaction, some of which have been more in the focus of research than others. We decided to pick three exemplary patterns with distinct foci to investigate their impact. The goal of this investigation is twofold: It is aimed at gaining insights how those concrete patterns influence player experience and interaction, thereby gaining new knowledge as well as reinforcing previous findings. Moreover, we want to demonstrate that those patterns can purposefully be used in game design to shape the social player experience and to foster intended social behavior of players. As first pattern, we chose *player interdependence*, which refers to the degree to which players are dependent on the other player's actions (cf. the pattern *complementarity* by Rocha et al. [24]). Second, we want to address the type of control of player characters. As indicated by Loparev et al. [20], shared control is an interesting design pattern for cooperative games, giving players simultaneous control over the same characters. Finally, we picked a pattern that is not necessarily related to multiplayer games, namely time pressure (cf. *limited ressources* mentioned by Björk et al. [5]). The impact of time pressure on player experience has recently been investigated by Yildirim [36], indicating influences on perceived flow and competence. We assume that it can also significantly shape the players' interaction.

Measuring Social Game Interaction

In order to investigate the social interaction of players, we also have to consider how it can be measured. In general, game user researchers have successfully applied different methods of the broader field of HCI, including self-reports, physiological measures, observation, and gameplay metrics [27, 1, 10]. There are several approaches to use these methods to assess social aspects of gaming (cf. [17, 27]). In terms of self-reports, several questionnaires have been developed to measure social presence [9], perceived relatedness [25], and the quality of cooperation and competition [15]. Those tools help to gain insights about how the social interaction was perceived during play. However, due to their retrospective and subjective nature, questionnaires cannot assess the concrete interactions and communication that evolve during play. Hence, another important method in this context is observation.

As shown by Seif El-Nasr et al. [27] and Bromley et al. [6] specific observation schemes can be used to assess and categorize social interaction events during play. To allow for detailed analysis, observation is often accompanied by videotaping. Bromley et al. [6] used a custom tool to directly code social interactions during play sessions based on revised categories of Voida et al. [31]: *shared awareness*, *requesting information*, *shared history*, *shared success*, *shared failure*, *team optimization*, *trash talk*, and *self-indulgence*. In a similar way, Seif El-Nasr et al. [27] present cooperative performance metrics as a result of a comprehensive study of gaming sessions: *laughter or excitement together*, *worked out strategies*, *helping*, *global strategies*, *waited for each other*, and *got in each others way*. These metrics are supposed to be related to game mechanics and events. Authors therefore suggest to apply them as a basis for video annotation of cooperative play sessions.

TESTBED GAME DEVELOPMENT

We developed a testbed game to systematically investigate the influence of game patterns on players' interaction and communication. It was designed as a collaborative, co-located multiplayer game, with simple rules to enable an easy access. We decided to focus social interaction in a collaborative game, as two of the design patterns of interest, *shared control* and *player interdependence*, require some form of cooperation of players. We did not use an off-the-shelf game, as a bespoke game allows us to vary single game design patterns and compare game versions under controlled conditions. To ensure a compelling basic game design, it was oriented towards the successful commercial game *Thomas Was Alone* [3], which is a 2D indie puzzle platformer game. The key feature is the integration of four different kinds of player characters represented by colored blocks (see Figure 2). These blocks have specific shapes and related strengths and weaknesses: The cyan block is slim, tall and has the highest jumping power, the orange one is very small with medium capabilities to jump. The other two blocks have very limited jumping power. Instead, the red block is flat and can be used as a trampoline, while the blue block is voluminous and able to float on the water, whereas all other blocks are destroyed by water contact.

In contrast to the single-player game *Thomas Was Alone*, we adapted the mechanics so that it can be played by two co-located players. The game is displayed on one single screen, and both players can simultaneously control their characters via wireless controllers. In each level, two or more of the player blocks have to be navigated to predefined target positions. To reach this goal, players have to overcome obstacles like water basins, laser barriers, and closed doors that can be unlocked by activating switches (see Figure 2). Due to their distinct shapes and abilities, the blocks can use different ways and reach different parts of the levels. If more than two blocks are present, players can switch control between the blocks anytime. A destroyed block is reset to its start position.

We used this basic game design to implement several levels to investigate the impact of the game patterns *player interdependence*, *shared control*, and *time pressure* on players' social interaction. The according level designs are described in the following subsections.

Player Interdependence

One important aspect in collaborative games is the degree of dependence between players. High interdependence can be induced by implementing complementarity (cf. [24]). Two levels were implemented, each in two versions: one version with low interdependence between players and one with a strong coupling of player actions. Players' characters are separated by a wall and cannot interact directly. In the high interdependence condition, players can use switches to open gates and activate platforms in the other player's area of the level. Thus, they have to thoroughly co-ordinate actions. In the low interdependence condition, players have to overcome the same obstacles but they can control their own level parts by switches and hence are not dependent on the other's action.

Shared Control

By default, both players have control over distinct blocks and can not take control over the blocks of their co-player. This distribution is supposed to also increase player interdependence. An alternative is the concept of shared control: In this case, all blocks can be controlled by all players simultaneously. Thus, one player could theoretically solve the game alone. On the other hand, the wider range of opportunities of action may also increase communication to co-ordinate strategies. We implemented another two levels to investigate the impact of the type of control distribution on the interaction between players. Both are complex levels including all four blocks. Each player either has control over two distinct blocks (default distributed control) or can switch between all blocks (shared control).

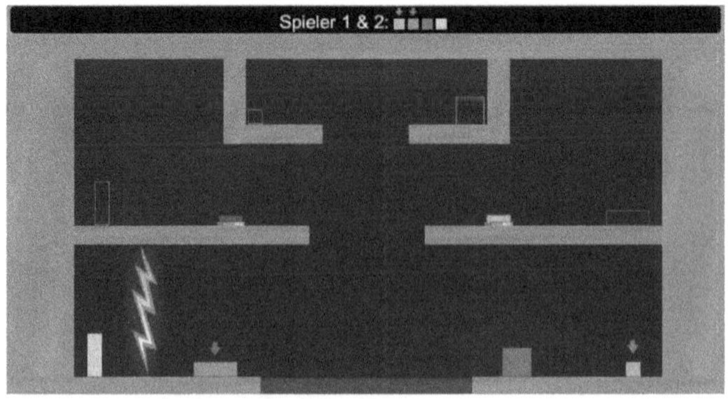

Figure 2. Screenshot of the testbed game: This level includes all four player characters (colored blocks at the bottom). To complete the level, players have to navigate all blocks to their respective destinations in the upper part of the level (indicated by the unfilled shapes of the blocks).

Time Pressure

Time pressure is supposed to influence player experience as well as the communication between players: If players are forced to make decisions quickly and do not have time for comprehensive discussions or the trying out of different strategies, they may interact and communicate differently. Hence, we wanted to test the influence of game mechanics that induce this pressure. We designed two respective levels. In the first level, water is rising from the bottom and gradually fills the screen. In the second level, a row of thorns is slowly coming down from the ceiling and thereby impends to block the only way to the level's end. In both cases, players can see that they have to act quickly to complete the level.

EVALUATION

We conducted an exploratory study to investigate the communication between players and their experience related to the different game patterns implemented in our game. We invited participants to play our game and administered questionnaires to assess player experience. Furthermore, we videotaped players during the complete gaming session to be able to analyze player communication and non-verbal interaction. We used a mixed-design. All participants played levels referring to all game patterns (i.e. *interdependence*, *time pressure*, and *shared control*), hence, game patterns are a within-subjects factor. However, they only played those level sets in one of the two conditions each (control vs. treatment condition) as between-subjects factors.

Research Questions and Hypotheses

With regard to the implemented game mechanics under investigation, we assume:

(H1) Players will communicate and interact differently in the two conditions of high and low interdependence. We expect players to communicate more and to be more focused on common strategies in the high interdependence condition.
(H2) Players will communicate and interact differently when exposed to time pressure. In case of time pressure, we expect more commanding and shorter discussions.
(H3) Players will communicate and interact differently in the two conditions of distinct character control and shared control. We expect them to communicate less when they are able to control all game characters on their own.

Study Procedure and Measures

The study took place in our gaming lab at the university. In each session, two participants had to play together. Participants could apply directly in pairs or were randomly assigned to another participant as gaming partner. An overview of the procedure is depicted in Figure 3. At first, participants were asked to fill in a questionnaire regarding demographic data, their prior experiences with digital games, their current gaming habits, and the relationship to their co-player of the study session (referring to their degree of familiarity and shared prior game experiences). The questionnaire also included three evaluative questions to rate trust, sympathy and the other's competence in relation to digital games. Furthermore, the 10 item Big Five Inventory (BFI-10)[22] was applied to assess basic personality traits on the dimensions *openness*, *conscientiousness*, *extraversion*, *agreeableness*, and *neuroticism*.

After that, the game was explained and started. It was projected on the wall and participants sat next to each other on a sofa, using wireless Xbox 360 controllers to play the game (see Figure 4). Participants were told that they were videotaped during the playing sessions. However, the camera was placed on the side so that it was not in their direct view. As intended, the majority of subjects reported that they had quickly forgotten to be videotaped and did not pay any attention to the camera while playing. In addition to the recording of players, we also captured the game screen of each session.

The game began with five short tutorial levels allowing to familiarize with the controls and to learn about the characteristics of the different blocks. Then, participants played the three level sets referring to the different game patterns *player interdependence*, *time pressure*, and *shared control*. The applied condition in each level set was randomized to avoid sequence effects and interference between level set conditions. In total, playing all levels took about 25 minutes. After each level set (i.e. every two levels), the game was paused and participants were asked to fill in questionnaires. The *Player Experience of Need Satisfaction* (PENS) questionnaire [25] was used to assess player experience in terms of the three sub-dimensions perceived *autonomy*, *competence*, and *relatedness* on a 5-point Likert scale (coded 1 - 5). Furthermore, we asked players to rate four additional aspects on a 5-point scale ranging from 1 ("not at all") to 5 ("absolutely"): (1) the *difficulty* of the two levels, (2) how much *fun* they had, (3) how satisfied they are with *their own contribution* to the completion of the levels, and (4) how satisfied they are with *their co-player's contribution*

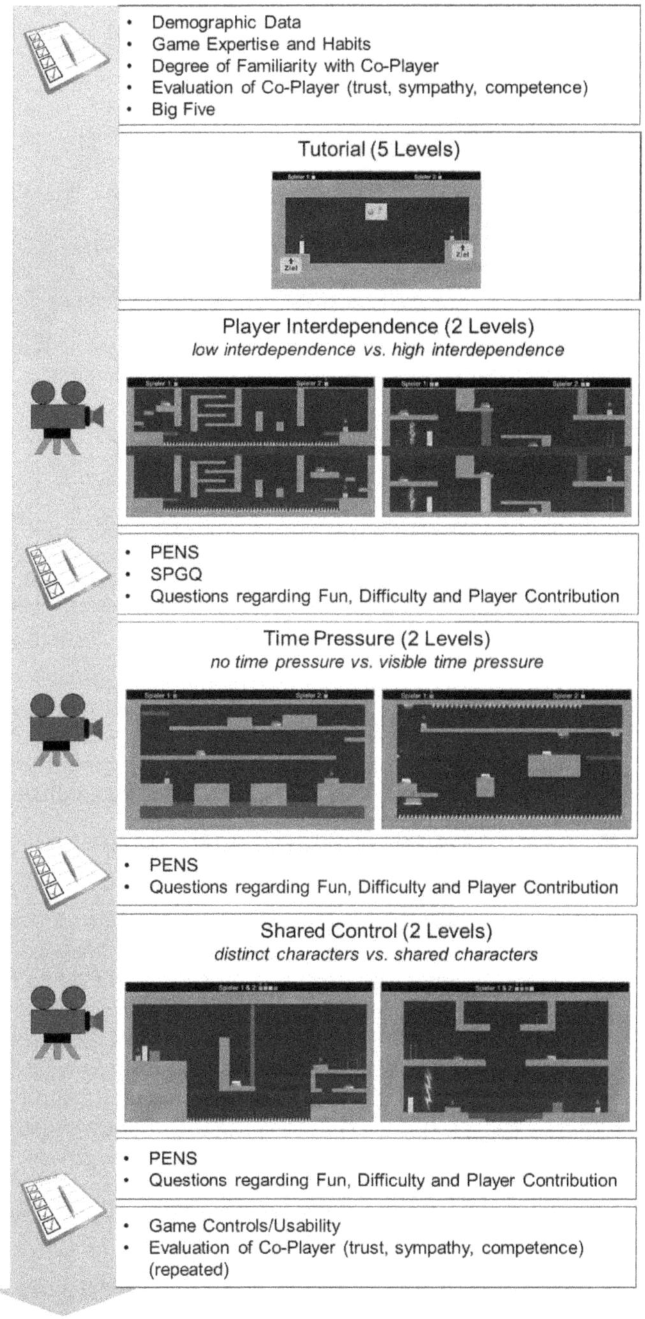

Figure 3. Overview of the study procedure, showing the sequence of gaming sessions and the applied questionnaires.

to the completion of the levels. Regarding the game pattern *player interdependence*, we were also interested in its impact on social presence. Hence, after the first level pair, the *Social Presence in Gaming Questionnaire* (SPGQ) [9] was administered to measure social presence on the three sub-dimensions *empathy*, *negative feelings*, and *behavioral engagement* on a 5-point Likert scale (coded 1 - 5).

At the end a final questionnaire was administered addressing the game's general usability and perceived quality of controls.

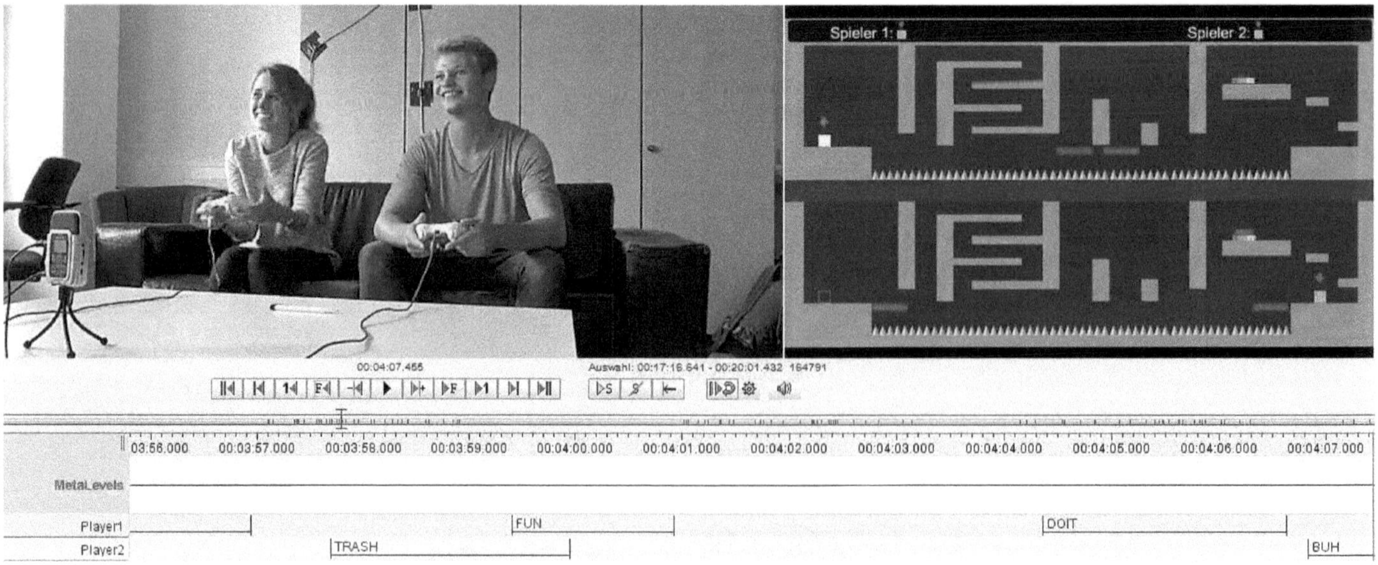

Figure 4. Example screenshot of the ELAN video annotation tool, including the videotaped gaming session (left), the corresponding screencast of the game (right), and the annotations and duration of social interaction events for each player (bottom).

Additionally, the three evaluative questions that were asked about the co-player at the beginning of the study were repeated. This way, it was tested whether the ratings of trustfulness, sympathy, and the other person's competence was influenced by having played together.

RESULTS

In sum, 50 subjects (25 gaming dyads), aged 18 to 33 ($M = 23.84$, $SD = 2.86$), took part in the experiment. Most participants were students from the local university (92 %) and the majority was familiar with digital games: 36 participants stated that they played digital games frequently, most of them several times a week ($N = 17$). Gender distribution was relatively balanced (30 females, 20 males) and there were 15 same-sex dyads as well as 10 mixed dyads. The distribution of gender, game expertise, and age in the single condition groups was balanced as well, showing no significant differences. The majority of participants stated that they were friends ($N = 29$) or even best friends ($N = 14$) with their co-player.

In general, participants expressed that they liked the game and rated fun for all level sets as very high on average (all mean values above 4 on a scale from 1 to 5). No participant reported any problems with the game's controls. Hence, the game was implemented successfully and the following analysis is not biased by usability issues or bad game design.

Iterative Annotating and Analysis of Videotaped Sessions

For the video analysis we used the tool ELAN, which is a professional tool for the creation of complex annotations on video resources [7] created by the Max Planck Institute for Psycholinguistics (The Language Archive, Nijmegen, The Netherlands)[1]. We synchronized videos of the players with the respective screencasts of the game to be able to evaluate players' communication and behavior considering their in-game behavior and game events (see Figure 4). All videotaped gaming sessions were annotated in an iterative process. First, all 25 sessions were equally distributed among two examiners. They performed the first round of annotation by analyzing their video material independently from each other based on the observation categories suggested by Bromley et al. [6] and Seif El-Nasr [27]. Social events (verbal and non-verbal communication) were marked with the abbreviation of the appropriate category (e.g. "TRASH" for *trash talk*) and with their duration. Hence, we counted each communication in form of periods (in seconds), not just single points in time, because we consider each communication act as a process. Subsequently, examiners discussed their experiences and pointed out communication events that could not properly be assigned to one of the existing categories due to semantic mismatch. Based on those insights, annotation categories were revised, resulting in the final coding scheme presented in Table 1. This was used to annotate all videos once again in a second iteration. A third examiner, who was not involved in the previous process, annotated all video material from scratch based on the supplemented scheme. Deviations between annotations from this examiner and the other two were investigated. There were little discrepancies, indicating high inter-rater reliability. Annotations that did not coincide were discussed and adjusted. The final annotations serve as the basis for our analysis of participants' social interaction. The length of all annotations of the same category was summarized for each level set.

General Indications of the Following Analysis

To investigate the impact of certain game patterns on the social interaction between players and on the player experience, results of the different experimental groups are compared. Regarding player experience measures, the requirements for parametric calculations (homogeneity of variances, normal distribution) are tested with Levene's and Kolmogorov-Smirnov

[1] http://tla.mpi.nl/tools/tla-tools/elan/

Table 1. Social interaction categories for social interaction events that were used to annotate the videotaped gaming sessions (based on the work by El-Nasr et al. [27] and Bromley et al. [6].

Category (abbreviation)	Description	Relates to (source)
Enjoying *(FUN)*	Laughing, expressing fun or pleasure, showing enjoyment due to game events	Laughter or excitement together [27]
Swearing *(BUH)*	Expressing frustration or annoyance, also as spontaneous reaction to failure in the game	— *(new)*
Commanding *(DOIT)*	Imperative call for action: telling the other player what to do (or not to do) without further explanation or discussion	— *(new)*
Strategizing *(STRAT)*	Working out strategies to overcome the games challenges; suggesting actions for both players, explaining what should be done	Worked out strategies [27]
Synchronizing Actions *(SYNC)*	Co-ordinating own actions with the other player's actions while performing them	— *(new)*
Helping *(HELP)*	Giving advise about how to control the game; hints to pay attention to some game object or event; explaining the rules and mechanics of the game	Helping [27]
Waiting *(WAIT)*	Expressing impatience while waiting for the other player to perform a certain action or to accomplish a certain goal	Waited for each other [27]
Blocking *(BLOCK)*	Pointing out that the other player retains one from doing something, e.g. by blocking her avatar's way	Got in each others way [27]
Creating Shared Awareness *(STATE)*	Exchanging information about the game's state, current game events, or the presently performed action	Shared Awareness [6]
Shared History *(PAST)*	Talking about priorly shared game experiences, relating common experiences to the current situation	Shared History [6]
Sharing Success and Failure *(SHARE)*	Celebrating group success or agreeing that failure was not an individual fault but the result of bad collaboration	Shared Success and Shared Failure [6]
Talking Trash *(TRASH)*	Insulting the other or talking the other's performance down, put the blame for failure on the other player	Trash Talk [6]
Giving Feedback *(FEEDBACK)*	Appreciating the other's contribution to the game, judging their actions or performance	Team optimization [6]
Off-topic comments *(OFF)*	Talking about something that is not related to the game or the current gaming situation	Off-topic [6]

tests. If violated, Mann-Whitney U tests or Wilcoxon signed rank tests are reported instead of independent samples t-tests for hypotheses predicting a difference. Pearson's r is calculated as effect sizes of Mann-Whitney U tests ($r < 0.3$ = weak effect, $0.3 < r < 0.5$ = medium effect, $r > 0.5$ = strong effect). For t-tests, Cohen's d is reported ($0.2 < d < 0.5$ = weak effect, $0.5 < d < 0.8$ = medium effect, $d > 0.8$ = strong effect). To test for correlations, data is analyzed using the Spearman's rank correlation coefficient (Spearman's rho) (due to a lack of normal distribution). Our video annotations are count data, thus, we investigate the effect of study condition on annotated player interaction by using a generalized linear model method. As data of dependent variables does not have a Poisson distribution due to overdispersion, we used negative binomial regression with estimated dispersion parameters. The duration of every level depended on the performance of participants and, thus, differs between sessions. Hence, we considered the variable time in play sessions as offset in the regression.

The Impact of Player Interdependence

The analysis of the annotated communication events shows significant influences of player interdependence on the behavior of players in terms of swearing (BUH) and commanding (DOIT). Negative binomial regression modeling indicates that players in the high interdependence condition spent about 70% less time on utterances of frustration or swearing than independent players ($B = -1.208$, $Exp(B) = .299$, $p < .001$). In contrast, highly interdependent players gave over twice as much DOIT commands compared to players who were not dependent on each other ($B = .777$, $Exp(B) = 2.175$, $p = .049$). Negative binomial regression modeling of the other twelve social interaction categories reveals no significant influence of player interdependence.

To investigate the impact of player interdependence on player experience, values of the PENS and the SPGQ measured after the first two study levels were analyzed. The comparison of the SPGQ sub-scales shows significant differences between the

Table 2. Mean scores and standard deviations of the PENS sub-scales for the two study conditions of each level set. Significant difference of mean values between conditions (based on Mann-Whitney U tests reported in the text) are marked by * (marginally significant) and ** (significant).

	Player Interdependence		Time Pressure		Shared Control	
	low	high	without	with	distinct	shared
PENS Dimension	M (SD)	M (SD)	M (SD)	M (SD)	M (SD)	M (SD)
Competence	3.83 (0.82)	3.86 (0.85)	3.50 (0.88)	3.68 (1.02)	4.21 (0.86)**	3.81 (0.72)**
Autonomy	3.14 (0.90)	3.32 (0.85)	3.29 (0.90)	3.13 (0.88)	3.83 (0.90)**	3.30 (1.01)**
Relatedness	4.55 (0.86)	4.58 (0.60)	4.63 (0.76)	4.45 (0.67)	4.97 (0.63)*	4.61 (0.65)*

p< .10, **p*< .05

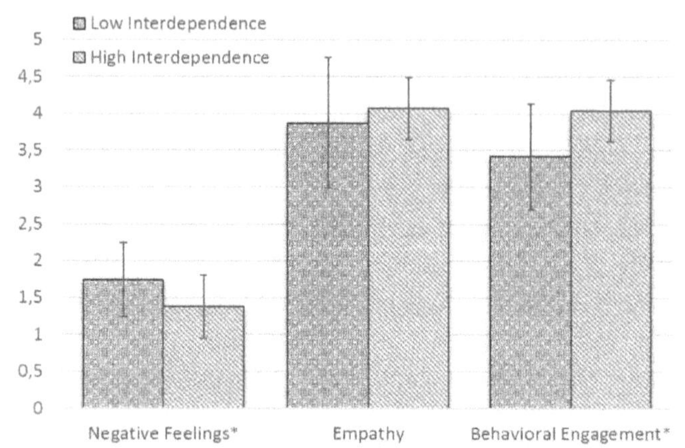

Figure 5. Results of the SPGQ compared for the low interdependence and the high interdependence condition (significant differences indicated by *).

low and the high interdependence condition (see Figure 5). Participants reported higher scores for *negative feelings* in the low interdependence condition ($M = 1.74$, $SD = 0.51$) than in the high interdependence condition ($M = 1.38$, $SD = 0.43$) according to a Mann-Whitney U test, $U = 175.0$, $p = .009$, $r = -.38$. Results also indicate that high interdependence led to higher perceived *behavioral engagement* ($M = 4.04$, $SD = 0.42$) than loose coupling ($M = 3.42$, $SD = 0.72$), $U = 146.0$, $p = .001$, $r = -.76$. The difference regarding *empathy* (high interdependence: $M = 4.07$, $SD = 0.42$; low interdependence: $M = 3.87$, $SD = 0.88$) is not significant, $t(40.55) = -1.05$, $p = .301$, $d = -.28$.

A comparison of the player experience in terms of perceived need satisfaction (PENS) shows no significant differences between conditions (all $p > .417$). Values for the dimensions *competence*, *autonomy*, and *relatedness* are fairly equal for low and high player interdependence (see Table 2). Furthermore, participants' evaluation of level difficulty, fun, and the contribution of each player does not differ significantly (all $p > .170$).

The Impact of Time Pressure

In the second level set, we varied the urgency of action by implementing time pressure. Half of the dyads played the levels with time pressure (induced by rising water and coming down thorns), the other half without it. However, the video analysis does not indicate any influence on players' communication and interaction. Measures of player experience show similar results: Mann-Whitney U tests do not indicate any significant difference between the two study conditions regarding perceived competence, autonomy, and relatedness (all $p > .420$). Mean scores of players playing under time pressure and of those who did not face time constraints are rather similar (see Table 2). The same is true for values of fun, perceived level difficulty and the evaluation of the contribution of each player to level completion (all $p > .116$).

The Impact of Shared Control

The third level set varied the control scheme of the game (distinct characters or shared characters). With regard to social communication acts, the regression analysis indicates no significant influence of control mode on the fourteen interaction categories. The analysis of the PENS sub-scales shows significant differences (see Table 2). Players in the shared control condition reported significantly less perceived competence ($U = 205.50$, $p = .042$, $r = -.28$) and autonomy ($U = 192.50$, $p = .022$, $r = -.32$). Scores for relatedness show a similar tendency, and the difference is marginally significant in this case ($U = 213.50$, $p = .061$, $r = -.26$). Furthermore, participants who could control all blocks in the shared control condition were significantly less satisfied by their own contribution to the completion of the level ($M = 4.04$, $SD = 0.84$) than players with distinct game characters ($M = 4.55$, $SD = 0.80$), $U = 194.00$, $p = .016$, $r = -.31$. Mean values regarding the contribution of the co-player, fun, and level difficulty do not differ significantly.

Further Results

We also investigated the potential confounding effect of personality and familiarity on players' communication. We analyzed the correlation of players' personality assessed by the BFI-10 and their individual communicative behavior to see whether personality traits have a basic impact on how players interact. We found only few significant correlations, all concerning the dimension *extraversion*: Extraversion correlates positively with swearing ($r(50) = .30$, $p = .039$), off-topic comments ($r(50) = .32$, $p = .028$), and trash-talk ($r(50) = .35$, $p = .015$). Furthermore, we also tested for the influence of the degree of familiarity of players on their communication by integrating the factor into the negative binomial regressions. Model fit was not improved and no significant influence was found.

Finally, we investigated whether the mutual playing experience has an impact on the evaluation of the co-player. To test this, we compared the values for trust, sympathy, and competence assessed prior gaming to the measurements at the end of the study. Wilcoxon signed rank tests expose significant differences. The evaluation of the item *my game partner can satisfactorily solve the challenges in the game* is significantly higher after the game session ($M = 4.62$, $SD = 0.64$), compared to the first evaluation at the study's beginning ($M = 3.92$, $SD = 0.94$; $z = -3.88$, $p < .001$, $r = .55$). The evaluation of *I think my game partner is likeable* shows significant differences as well ($z = -2.12$, $p = .034$, $r = -.30$): Sympathy was rated higher after the game session ($M = 4.90$, $SD = 0.30$), compared to the evaluation prior to it ($M = 4.78$, $SD = 0.55$). Ratings of trust show the same tendency, but do not differ significantly before ($M = 4.68$, $SD = 0.59$) and after the gaming session ($M = 4.80$, $SD = 0.49$; $z = -1.54$, $p < .124$).

DISCUSSION

The main goal of the study was to investigate the communication between players and their experience dependent on the different game patterns implemented in our game. Regarding our first hypothesis, results show that *player interdependence* indeed has an effect on the way players communicate. High player interdependence led to less utterances of frustration. Instead, players used more time for commands, telling the other player what to do (e.g. "Now, jump!"). Other communication events, like the coordination of common strategies, were not significantly predicted by study condition. This might be explained by the observation that players tend to cooperate and discuss level solving strategies in all levels, no matter whether they were dependent on each other. The significant increase of commands, however, indicates that players were more focused on the success of their partner if there was a high level of interdependence. Hence, results (at least partly) support hypothesis 1.

Scores of the SPGQ reveal that players have also experienced social presence differently in both conditions. High interdependence is reflected in higher values regarding behavioral engagement. Thus, the variation of player dependency was actually perceived by players, as intended by our design. Furthermore, players reported less negative feelings related to the other player when being dependent on each other. This result corresponds with the difference found for expressed frustration. Furthermore, it indicates that dependent players focused their common goal and did not blame each other for mistakes, whereas independent players experienced the levels as individual challenges. In fact, the design of the levels in the low interdependence condition may have conveyed a rather competitive atmosphere, as players had to overcome the same obstacles simultaneously and could observe the progress of the other. In this way, it was obvious who is performing better and will reach the goal first. That is a possible explanation why negative feelings like schadenfreude or envy were more likely to occur for independent players.

We did not find significant differences concerning need satisfaction or fun. However, values of the PENS sub-scales and fun ratings are very high in both conditions (above 4 with a scale maximum of 5), indicating a very positive experience overall. This might be the reason why significant differences did not manifest. Overall, results indicate that the integration of player dependencies is a suitable way to foster internally derived social interaction among players in order to enhance their social experience. Designers should be aware that the degree of player interdependence can change the way players communicate and pay attention to each other and that low interdependence can even create an atmosphere of competitiveness in collaborative games.

Regarding the other two game patterns, *time pressure* and *shared control*, the video analysis did not indicate significant influences on players' communication. Hence, hypotheses 2 and 3 are not supported by the results. Furthermore, time pressure did not influence players' experience either according to results of the questionnaires. This lack of effect surprises us, as we expected players to be affected by time pressure in some way, for instance in terms of increased arousal and less feelings of competence and autonomy due to the fact that the game urges them to react without being able to plan or discuss strategies. Results indicate that either time pressure does not significantly contribute to the emergent gameplay and player experience, or that participants did not perceive any time pressure at all. To investigate whether our implementation of time pressure worked as intended, we took another look at the videotaped sessions. Less than half of the pairs playing with time pressure did actually address this aspect in their communication (e.g. "look, the water, we have to hurry"), whereas the others did not seem to notice (or care about) the imminent threats. Hence, we cannot make a clear statement whether (and how) time pressure impacts social interaction and player experience, but will revise the game design of the corresponding levels and address this question in future studies.

Regarding the pattern *shared control*, significant differences were found for several aspects of player experience. Although the observable social interaction of players did not differ, players in the shared control condition reported lower PENS scores. Giving players communal control over all player characters led to a decrease of perceived autonomy and competence. Although it could be assumed that having more options of control will result in higher perceived autonomy, results indicate the opposite. We suggest that players in the shared control condition did not perceive the wider range of options for action, but instead missed to have exclusive control over one (or more) characters. Notionally, all actions performed by one player could be reversed by the other player in the shared control game mode. Perceived competence was also lower in this condition. Moreover, participants were also less satisfied by their own contribution to the collaboration. All findings indicate that players might have perceived the other player as being more dominant or that they had general problems to adapt to the new control scheme of switching between all blocks. Consequently, game designers who consider to implement shared control as an interesting feature should carefully account for needs of autonomy and competence, for instance by giving clear instructions how to use the feature properly and how to divide responsibilities to achieve the game's goals.

To summarize, we found effects on player interaction only for one of the three patterns under investigation. Player interdependence is supposed to be strongly connected to players' communication and interaction, whereas shared control does not impact observable communication, but has significant influence on player experience nonetheless.

We further investigated the influence of player personality and familiarity on the social interaction during play. Extraversion, a personality dimension comprising aspects of sociability and communicativeness, is positively correlated with swearing, trash-talk, and off-topic comments. This is consistent, because all these categories of communication are related to expressiveness without being dependent on the concrete game content. Those correlations indicate that player personality may contribute to the social behavior of a player. However, no other significant correlations were found, hence we assume that it is not the predominant factor determining players' social interaction during play. In terms of familiarity, we could not find any influence on social interaction events. However, other studies suggest that familiarity is an influential factor in multiplayer gaming [15]. We did not focus our study on the impact that different levels of familiarity might have on players' interaction, hence we did not recruit participants with respect to that aspect. Being randomly composed, our sample is unbalanced in terms of familiarity, including mostly friends. Therefore, low levels of familiarity are underrepresented and we cannot reasonably analyze differences between groups of high and low familiarity in our current data set. We propose that familiarity has to be considered in evaluations of multiplayer scenarios, although we did not find significant influences.

Finally, the pre- and post-game evaluations of the gaming partner indicate interesting effects on the relationship of participants: They tend to rate competence, sympathy, and trustfulness of the co-player significantly higher after the gaming session. This indicates a positive team-building effect of playing collaborative games. Generalizability of this finding is limited due to the fact that most participants already knew each other well and defined their relationship as friendship. However, it provides a promising approach for further research on how games can be applied to foster the establishment of positive relationships.

Limitations

Generalizability of results is limited due to the specific study design. We used a bespoke platformer game. Decisions regarding game genre and design were based on the application context: The game should be fun, short and easy to understand, yet rather complex in its capabilities to foster collaboration. Moreover, a bespoke implementation enabled us to investigate variations of the game in a controlled way. Thus, we consider the implemented testbed game to be a good choice for our research approach. However, it only represents one of many game genres and social settings, which might differ regarding their affordance of social interactions and possibilities to implement the game patterns. Whereas we assume that results can be transferred to games that similarly rely on players' collaboration, dexterity, and reaction, we admit that future studies should consider other game genres, slow-paced games, competitive games, and games played by more than two players. Moreover, co-located settings can be compared to remote gaming, in order to investigate the importance of communication channels and non-verbal communication. Besides, game patterns can be implemented in very different ways. Our specific implementations are just examples. The discussion of our time pressure pattern illustrates that differences (not) found between game modes have to be interpreted with respect to the specific pattern implementation. Other forms should be applied in future studies to confirm the results presented here.

Despite those limitations, we are confident that our work provides valuable insights into the interplay of game mechanics and social player interaction and presents impulses for future research endeavors.

CONCLUSION

We started off by establishing a research model for investigating social player interaction. Based on that model, we examined the impact of three specific game patterns: player interdependence, time pressure, and shared control. Our evaluation shows how slight changes in game design can significantly influence the interaction and communication between players in collaborative multiplayer games. In particular, high player interdependence implies more communication and less frustration. With respect to shared control, enabling this feature results in less perceived competence and autonomy.

Our results underline the importance of considering game patterns related to player interdependence and the control scheme in the design process of multiplayer games. In addition to the mentioned patterns, our findings indicate that individual player characteristics also impact the social interaction. Hence, to design positive social experiences, our results should motivate game designers to consider the interplay of the three factors game design, player group, and gaming setting.

We plan to apply our testbed game in future studies to investigate the impact of other game patterns on social interaction in detail, for instance the kind of feedback players are provided with (individual vs. communal) and the type of reward/penalty system. Moreover, our model is not limited to collaborative games and can also be applied to team-based and competitive games. In that context, the application of games in team-building activities can be further evaluated.

Our study methodology is supposed to serve as an inspiring example of how to assess and analyze real-world player interaction in co-located settings, moving forward the approaches of El-Nasr et al. [27] and Bromley et al. [6]. Further research should address possibilities of automated analysis of video data, as the process of annotating video material and classifying player interaction events is still very time-consuming and error-prone. Improving these aspects would allow for significant advances in that research area.

ACKNOWLEDGMENTS

We thank Ralf Berger, Benjamin Gansert, Oliver Gornik, Felix Hoppe, Anna Jedich, Sven Karsten, Christian Schlusche, and Philip Witte for their great effort in developing the testbed game and for their assistance during the evaluation.

REFERENCES

1. Regina Bernhaupt. 2010. User Experience Evaluation in Entertainment. In *Evaluating user experience in games*, Regina Bernhaupt (Ed.). Springer, London and New York, 3–7.
2. F. Biocca, C. Harms, and J. Burgoon. 2003. Towards a More Robust Theory and Measure of Social Presence: Review and Suggested Criteria. *Presence: Teleoperators and Virtual Environments* 12, 5 (2003), 456–480.
3. Mike Bithell. 2012. *Thomas Was Alone*. Game [Microsoft Windows]. (30 June 2012). Bithell. Played January 2017.
4. Staffan Björk and Jussi Holopainen. 2005. Game Design Patterns for Social Interaction. In *Patterns in game design*, Staffan Bjork and Jussi Holopainen (Eds.). Charles River Media, Hingham, Mass.
5. Staffan Bjork and Jussi Holopainen (Eds.). 2005. *Patterns in game design* (1st ed. ed.). Charles River Media, Hingham, Mass.
6. Steve Bromley, Pejman Mirza-Babaei, Graham McAllister, and Jonathan Napier. 2014. Playing to win? Measuring the Correlation Between Biometric Responses and Social Interaction in Co-Located Social Gaming. In *Multiplayer*, Thorsten Quandt and Sonja Kröger (Eds.). Vol. 3. Routledge, London and New York, 172–182.
7. Hennie Brugman and Albert Russel. 2004. Annotating Multi-media/Multi-modal resources with ELAN. In *Proceedings of the 4th International Conference on Language Resources and Language Evaluation (LREC 2004)*, M.T. Lino, M.F. Xavier, F. Ferreira, R. Costa, and R. Silva (Eds.). Paris, 2065–2068.
8. Yvonne A. W. De Kort and Wijnand A. Ijsselsteijn. 2008. People, places, and play: Player Experience in a Socio-Spatial Context. *Computers in Entertainment* 6, 2 (2008), 1.
9. Yvonne A. W. De Kort, Wijnand A. Ijsselsteijn, and Karolien Poels. 2007. Digital games as social presence technology : development of the social presence in gaming questionnaire (SPGQ). In *Proceedings of the 10th Annual International Workshop on Presence*. 195–203.
10. Heather Desurvire and Magy Seif El-Nasr. 2013. Methods for Game User Research: Studying Player Behavior to Enhance Game Design. *IEEE Computer Graphics and Applications* 33, 4 (2013), 82–87. DOI: http://dx.doi.org/10.1109/MCG.2013.61
11. Nicolas Ducheneaut and Robert J. Moore. 2004. The social side of gaming. In *CSCW '04 Proceedings of the 2004 ACM conference on Computer supported cooperative work*, Jim Herbsleb and Gary Olson (Eds.). 360. DOI:http://dx.doi.org/10.1145/1031607.1031667
12. Katharina Emmerich and Maic Masuch. 2013. Helping Friends or Fighting Foes: The Influence of Collaboration and Competition on Player Experience. In *Proceedings of Foundations of Digital Games 2013*.
13. Entertainment Software Association. 2016. Essential facts about the computer and video game industry. (2016). http://www.theesa.com/wp-content/uploads/2016/04/Essential-Facts-2016.pdf
14. John Harris, Mark Hancock, and Stacey D. Scott. 2016. Leveraging Asymmetries in Multiplayer Games. In *Proceedings of CHI PLAY 2016*, Anna Cox, Zachary O. Toups, Regan L. Mandryk, Paul Cairns, Vero vanden Abeele, and Daniel Johnson (Eds.). 350–361. DOI: http://dx.doi.org/10.1145/2967934.2968113
15. Matthew Hudson and Paul Cairns. 2014. Measuring Social Presence in Team-Based Digital Games. In *Interacting with Presence: HCI and the Sense of Presence in Computer-mediated Environments*, Giuseppe Riva, John Waterworth, and Dianne Murray (Eds.). DE GRUYTER OPEN, Warsaw, Poland. DOI: http://dx.doi.org/10.2478/9783110409697.6
16. W. A. Ijsselsteijn, W. M. van Den Hoogen, C. Klimmt, Y.A.W. de Kort, C. Lindley, K. Mathiak, K. Poels, N. Ravaja, and M. Turpeinen. 2008. Measuring the experience of digital game enjoyment. In *Proceedings of Measuring Behavior 2008, 6th International Conference on Methods and Techniques in Behavioral Research*, A. J. Spink, M. R. Ballintijn, N. D. Bogers, F. Grieco, L.W.S. Loijens, L.P.J.J. Noldus, G. Smit, and P. H. Zimmerman (Eds.).
17. Katherine Isbister. 2010. Enabling Social Play: A Framework for Design and Evaluation. In *Evaluating user experience in games*, Regina Bernhaupt (Ed.). Springer, London and New York, 11–22.
18. Dennis L. Kappen, John Gregory, Daniel Stepchenko, Rina R. Wehbe, and Lennart E. Nacke. 2013. Exploring social interaction in co-located multiplayer games. In *CHI '13 Extended Abstracts on Human Factors in Computing Systems*, Wendy E. Mackay, Stephen Brewster, and Susanne Bødker (Eds.). 1119. DOI: http://dx.doi.org/10.1145/2468356.2468556
19. Sonja Kröger and Thorsten Quandt. 2014. Get together: Console Playing as a Group Experience. In *Multiplayer*, Thorsten Quandt and Sonja Kröger (Eds.). Vol. 3. Routledge, London and New York, 147–161.
20. Anna Loparev, Walter S. Lasecki, Kyle I. Murray, and Jeffrey P. Bigham. 2014. Introducing Shared Character Control to Existing Video Games. In *Proceedings of Foundations of Digital Games 2014*. http://www.fdg2014.org/papers/fdg2014_wip_10.pdf
21. Florian Mueller, Martin R. Gibbs, and Frank Vetere. 2010. Towards understanding how to design for social play in exertion games. *Personal and Ubiquitous Computing* 14, 5 (2010), 417–424. DOI: http://dx.doi.org/10.1007/s00779-009-0268-x
22. Beatrice Rammstedt, Christoph J. Kemper, Mira Céline Klein, Constanze Beierlein, and Anastassiya Kovaleva. 2013. A Short Scale for Assessing the Big Five Dimensions of Personality. (2013). DOI: http://dx.doi.org/10.12758/mda.2013.013

23. Christian Reuter, Viktor Wendel, Stefan Göbel, and Ralf Steinmetz. 2014. Game Design Patterns for Collaborative Player Interactions. *Proceedings of DiGRA 2014* (2014). http://www.digra.org/wp-content/uploads/digital-library/digra2014_submission_39.pdf

24. Jose Bernardo Rocha, Samuel Mascarenhas, and Rui Prada. 2008. Game Mechanics for Cooperative Games. *ZON Digital Games* (2008).

25. Richard M. Ryan, C. Scott Rigby, and Andrew Przybylski. 2006. The Motivational Pull of Video Games: A Self-Determination Theory Approach. *Motivation and Emotion* 30, 4 (2006), 344–360. DOI: http://dx.doi.org/10.1007/s11031-006-9051-8

26. Katie Salen and Eric Zimmerman. 2003. *Rules of play: Game design fundamentals*. MIT Press, Cambridge, Mass.

27. Magy Seif El-Nasr, Bardia Aghabeigi, David Milam, Mona Erfani, Beth Lameman, Hamid Maygoli, and Sang Mah. 2010. Understanding and evaluating cooperative games. In *Proceedings of the SIGCHI Conference on Human Factors in Computing Systems*, Elizabeth Mynatt, Don Schoner, Geraldine Fitzpatrick, Scott Hudson, Keith Edwards, and Tom Rodden (Eds.). 253–262. DOI: http://dx.doi.org/10.1145/1753326.1753363

28. Jaakko Stenros, Janne Paavilainen, and Frans Mäyrä. 2009. The many faces of sociability and social play in games. In *Proceedings of the 13th International MindTrek Conference*, Artur Lugmayr, Heljä Franssila, Olli Sotamaa, Pertti Näränen, and Jukka Vanhala (Eds.). 82. DOI:http://dx.doi.org/10.1145/1621841.1621857

29. Jari Takatalo, Jukka Häkkinen, Jyrki Kaistinen, and Göte Nyman. 2010. Presence, Involvement, and Flow in Digital Games. In *Evaluating user experience in games*, Regina Bernhaupt (Ed.). Springer, London and New York, 23–46. DOI:http://dx.doi.org/10.1007/978-1-84882-963-3{_}3

30. Burak S. Tekin and Stuart Reeves. 2017. Ways of Spectating: Unravelling Spectator Participation in Kinect Play. In *CHI'17*, Gloria Mark, Susan Fussell, Cliff Lampe, M.C. Schraefel, Juan Pablo Hourcade, Caroline Appert, and Daniel Wigdor (Eds.). ACM, New York, NY and New York, NY, 1558–1570. DOI: http://dx.doi.org/10.1145/3025453.3025813

31. Amy Voida, Sheelagh Carpendale, and Saul Greenberg. 2010. The individual and the group in console gaming. In *Proceedings of the 2010 ACM conference on Computer supported cooperative work*, Kori Inkpen (Ed.). ACM, New York, NY, 371. DOI: http://dx.doi.org/10.1145/1718918.1718983

32. Rina R. Wehbe, Dennis L. Kappen, David Rojas, Matthias Klauser, Bill Kapralos, and Lennart E. Nacke. 2013. EEG-based assessment of video and in-game learning. In *CHI '13 Extended Abstracts on Human Factors in Computing Systems*, Wendy E. Mackay, Stephen Brewster, and Susanne Bødker (Eds.). 667. DOI: http://dx.doi.org/10.1145/2468356.2468474

33. Rina R. Wehbe and Lennart E. Nacke. 2015. Towards Understanding the Importance of Co-Located Gameplay. In *CHI PLAY '15 Proceedings of the 2015 Annual Symposium on Computer-Human Interaction in Play*, Anna L. Cox, Paul Cairns, Regina Bernhaupt, and Lennart Nacke (Eds.). 733–738. DOI: http://dx.doi.org/10.1145/2793107.2810312

34. Russell B. Williams and Caryl A. Clippinger. 2002. Aggression, competition and computer games: Computer and human opponents. *Computers in Human Behavior* 18, 5 (2002), 495–506. DOI: http://dx.doi.org/10.1016/S0747-5632(02)00009-2

35. Nick Yee. 2006. Motivations for play in online games. *Cyberpsychology & behavior : the impact of the Internet, multimedia and virtual reality on behavior and society* 9, 6 (2006), 772–775. DOI: http://dx.doi.org/10.1089/cpb.2006.9.772

36. Irem Gökçe Yildirim. 2016. Time Pressure as Video Game Design Element and Basic Need Satisfaction. In *the 2016 CHI Conference Extended Abstracts*, Jofish Kaye, Allison Druin, Cliff Lampe, Dan Morris, and Juan Pablo Hourcade (Eds.). 2005–2011. DOI: http://dx.doi.org/10.1145/2851581.2892298

37. J. P. Zagal. 2006. Collaborative games: Lessons learned from board games. *Simulation & Gaming* 37, 1 (2006), 24–40. DOI:http://dx.doi.org/10.1177/1046878105282279

The Impact of Agency and Familiarity in Cooperative Multiplayer Games

Kellie Vella
Queensland University of Technology
Brisbane, Australia
kellie.vella@qut.edu.au

Christopher James Koren
Queensland University of Technology
Brisbane, Australia
c.koren@qut.edu.au

Daniel Johnson
Queensland University of Technology
Brisbane, Australia
dm.johnson@qut.edu.au

ABSTRACT
Many online videogames make use of characters controlled by both humans (avatar) and computers (agent) to facilitate game play. However, the level of agency a teammate shows potentially produces differing levels of social presence during play, which in turn may impact on the player experience. To better understand these effects, two experimental studies were conducted utilising cooperative multiplayer games (*Left 4 Dead 2* and *Rocket League*). In addition, the effect of familiarity between players was considered. The trend across the two studies show that playing with another human is more enjoyable, and facilitates greater connection, cooperation, presence and positive mood than play with a computer agent. The implications for multiplayer game design is discussed.

Author Keywords
Video games; agency; social presence; player experience; affect; avatar; artificial intelligence.

ACM Classification Keywords
K.8.0 Personal computing: General: Games; I.2.1 Artificial intelligence: Applications and expert systems

INTRODUCTION
Multiplayer games have come a long way since Higinbotham invented *Tennis For Two* using an oscilloscope and two custom control pads [8]. The advent of high-speed broadband services has sped the development of new ways to build connection with others online, driving an increasing focus on multiplayer games. Within massively multiplayer online role-playing games (MMORPGs) alone, play has been found to generate new friendships [4] that for many players offer benefits equivalent to or better than non-gaming friendships [40], while play with existing friends enhances these relationships [29]. However, many multiplayer games also make use of computer-controlled characters (agents) to supplement or replace unavailable human players (avatars). While much work has gone into producing agents that are human-like in their decision-making [7, 11], whether this is enough to replicate the experience of playing with a human is still to be determined.

Play amongst humans has been found to generate feelings of relatedness, or warm connection with others [26]. Self-Determination Theory (SDT), argues that experiences of relatedness, as well as those of autonomy and competence result in both the intrinsic motivation to engage in that activity, and wellbeing [6]. This theory, applied to game play contexts, finds that solitary play offers greater experiences of autonomy and presence than social play [36], while social play, unsurprisingly, offers more opportunity to experience feelings of connection with others [31, 36]. There is also evidence that competitive play creates a greater opportunity to satisfy competence needs, relative to non-competitive play [15]. However, SDT is relatively unexplored in terms of gameplay featuring agents and avatars, which offer a unique means of testing the impact of social presence on the player experience.

Social presence is described as the 'sense of another through a medium' [1]. That social presence might be expected to impact on the player experience is supported by a meta-analysis finding that avatars, rather than agents, exert a stronger influence on a range of measures, such as presence, flow and enjoyment [9]. Social presence has also been found to differ in a contrast of online and co-located play [10]. In turn, play with a friend or stranger can produce different player experiences [18, 25], which may indicate the influence of social presence. Whether these effects are due to the 'bragging rights' allocated to social actors, or 'shared intentionality' - a uniquely human cognition resulting from an evolution shaped by cooperation [34], is unknown. It seems, however, that just the belief that one is playing with another human, especially a known other, can invest the relationship with a sense of social presence and from there influence the experience of play [9].

By contrasting play using avatars and agents, the current studies build on research examining how game features and social play generates differences in aspects of the player

CHI PLAY '17, October 15–18, 2017, Amsterdam, Netherlands

ACM ISBN 978-1-4503-4898-0/17/10…$15.00
https://doi.org/10.1145/3116595.3116622

experience. In addition, it takes into account the possible influence of another intersecting contextual factor: that of players' familiarity with each other. In doing so, it adds to existing research on the impact of shared experiences and cooperative interactions, such as those that may occur in computer-assisted work environments. This program of research also has implications for fields that might privilege the use of conversational agents and virtual assistants, as well as agent-supported online education.

Agency in Multiplayer Games

Being able to virtually interact with game elements via an avatar, facilitates a sense of social presence by providing players with a virtual self that can interact with other virtual selves [16]. Advancements in game technologies, however, are gradually making it harder to perceive whether another player is human- or computer-controlled; a distinction referred to as agency [23]. Given that both an avatar and an agent may be indistinguishable, an opportunity arises for researchers wishing to test whether the influence of social presence rests on the expectation of playing with a human, and if so, how this might impact the player experience.

To date, contrasts between avatars and agents have found mixed effects. An experiment using *World of Warcraft*, a MMORPG, found that greater arousal, presence and likability of the other was reported when the other player was perceived as being an avatar compared to an agent [17]. However, a more complex pattern emerged between the type of play and the agency of the other player, such that positive valence, likeability and presence were greater in cooperative play with an agent, relative to competitive play with an agent, but did not differ when play was with an avatar. This suggests that while the impact of competitive versus cooperative play with a human on a player's emotional responses or engagement with the game do not differ, play with an agent is likely to produce more benefits when play is cooperative. The impact of type of play (cooperative or competitive) in this study, may also be explained by differences in the pace and excitement of the activities used to represent it. Specifically, cooperative play entailed trading for items while competitive play was a duel with the other character. This highlights the methodological difficulties finding comparable cooperative and competitive activities for research and reinforces the need to test across a range of game mechanics.

One way this methodological challenge can be managed is to simply contrast play with an agent or avatar while they are engaged in the same task. This approach was taken in an experiment contrasting cooperative play with agents and avatars using the first-person shooter, *Payday* [14]. Play with an avatar was found associated with greater relatedness, but less flow and competence, compared to play with an agent. Recorded brainwave activity also suggested that play with humans leads to greater mentalising, in the sense that there is more consideration and evaluation of the other players' intentions. While the finding for relatedness is intuitively supported, and reinforced by research contrasting solitary and social play [31, 36], this study did not control for differences in the behaviour of avatars and agents, indicating differing levels of task load may have impacted on the findings.

In studies where these potential differences have been controlled for, some of the effects reverse. For example, an experiment contrasting competitive play in a MMORPG (*NeverWinter Nights*) where participants believed they were playing with agents or avatars (both sessions were actually played against agents to ensure consistent gameplay across conditions), found that players experienced greater presence, flow and enjoyment when the opponent was perceived to be an avatar [39]. This is also supported by studies not making use of avatars and agents. For example, an experiment contrasting competitive play of *WoodPong* in different play arrangements (using the same screen; different screens; with the computer), found that play against a co-located human led to significantly greater social presence, enjoyment and flow than did play against the computer [10]. A deception was enacted in this study, such that all conditions were in fact performed with the other participant to ensure that there was no difference across the three conditions in terms of the level of skill displayed by the opponent. Relatedly, while there is evidence that agency effects are greater when both conditions are actually human-controlled [9], there have been few comparable studies alternating this manipulation in videogame play research.

Cairns and colleagues [2], however, replicated and built on Gajadhar and colleagues' study [10] in a series of three experiments. The first was a complete replication with the addition of a measure of immersion. The second used a more modern game (*Midtown Madness 2*, a racing game), and participants played online against each other and against the computer, in the same room. The third used *Wii MarioKart* (another modern racing game), took measures of familiarity (friends or strangers), and used two conditions: online and co-located (different room/same room). This program of research found that players experienced greater immersion and social presence when play was against another human rather than when against the computer, however the increase in social presence when co-located did not lead to a significant increase in immersion. This led the authors to suggest that co-location is not as important for immersive play as is *who* one is playing against. However, it is unclear whether participants were communicating with each other or not while co-located across the three studies, and all social play was competitive.

While each of these studies indicate the impact of agency on a range of player experience measures, it is worth considering that cooperative play may have its own distinct relationship to social presence. Evolutionary anthropology has outlined the ways in which interdependence has helped form our cognition, namely the sense of shared intentionality that forms the basis of human inter-personal and inter-group relations [33, 34]. Obvious comparisons can be made between the evolution of human cooperation and contemporary cooperative gameplay, such as the need for coordination, and the sharing of resources or spoils. Whether cooperation can facilitate social presence with computer agents however, is yet to be determined.

Familiarity with Other Players

Prior relationships with a teammate or opponent can also affect the player experience, though the findings are mixed. One experiment using an ice-hockey game, *NHL 2003*, and taking both physiological and self-report measures, found that play against a friend was found to be more exciting than playing against the computer, and more fun than playing against either the computer or a stranger [18]. This is supported by another experiment finding play against a friend produced greater spatial presence, engagement, arousal (physiological and reported) and positive valence than play against a stranger [25]. It may be that playing with a friend produces greater psychological involvement than play against a stranger, as was found in Gajadhar et al.'s [10] study. However, no effect for familiarity was found in Cairns and colleagues' [2] study, discussed earlier. These studies also varied in their reporting of whether participants were able to socially interact during play, which may have its own relationship to the outcome measures above and beyond a sense of social presence. As other research has determined that friendly and unfriendly communication can impact on the player experience [27], this procedural choice may well have impacted on the findings for familiarity. Relatedly, these studies involved competitive play, and did not provide anthropomorphic agents in all instances, implying the need to test cooperative interactions across a wider range of games.

In more naturalistic settings, such as via a survey of team-based gaming communities, familiarity has been found positively correlated with both cooperative social presence, and team trust [12]. This is supported by another survey of a gaming community (*Halo: Reach*), which finds that cooperative play is typically with known others and that playing with friends offers practical advantages [19]. Specifically, the more friends that were present in a team, the less betrayal occurred; the more assistance was offered; and the greater were improvements in individual performance. It seems likely that improvements in mood should result from play such as this, however the mixed findings for player experience measures across multiple studies, and few studies contrasting the effects of familiarity and agency, suggests the need for further study.

The Current Studies

The two studies described herein extend previous research by determining the impact of cooperative play across multiple game genres (shooters, sports). The trend across the research reviewed suggests play with avatars (humans) will result in greater presence, enjoyment, and positive affect than play with agents, or computers [2, 10, 17, 18, 25, 39]. However, in some previous research differences in the behaviour of avatars and agents was not controlled, nor was the impact of social interaction during play accounted for. Relatedly, surveys of solitary and social play/games [13, 36] finds greater presence allocated to the former. Additionally, the impacts of teammate agency on autonomy is unknown, and while it may intuitively be expected that a greater sense of connection and cooperation will occur when playing with an avatar, there is little empirical evidence to support this. Thus, we ask:

RQ1: Do aspects of the player experience differ when playing cooperatively with either an avatar or an agent (agency)?

Relatedly, play against known others has been found to produce greater spatial presence, positive emotion [25], social presence [10], and fun [18] than play against strangers, while familiarity has been found to be positively associated with cooperative social presence [12]. However, other studies have found no impact of player familiarity on immersion [2], or cooperative behaviours [37]. Whether familiarity will impact on the player experience and post-play mood is still in question, as is whether familiarity might interact with the effects of playing with either an avatar or an agent. This leads to our final questions:

RQ2: Do aspects of the player experience differ when playing cooperatively with either a friend or stranger (familiarity)?

RQ3: Does familiarity interact with agency to influence aspects of the player experience?

STUDY 1

This study aimed to explore the impacts of agency and familiarity in the context of cooperative play of a first-person shooter.

Method

We employed a 2 x 2 repeated-measures mixed factorial design, with agency (agent/avatar) as the within-subjects factor, and familiarity (known/unknown) as the between-subjects factor. In most (if not all) videogames, agents are known to behave differently to humans in certain key ways that make it possible for players to recognise them [5]. In order to ensure equivalent play experiences while allowing us to compare play with agents and avatars, a deception was employed, such that play occurred with a human teammate in both conditions, but participants were told in the agent condition that they were playing with a computer-controlled character. Both players were (unknowingly) each other's agent companion for the agent condition, as well as (knowingly) each other's avatar companion in the avatar condition. The decision to have both sessions played with humans instead of agents was due to the technical limitations of the game in question, which made successfully deceiving participants unlikely if both conditions were played with agents (agents in the game display distinct behaviours that make it easy to identify them as computer-controlled). To help increase the believability of the deception, participants were told that the purpose of the study was to test a new agent with more human-like game artificial intelligence (AI) behaviours and to see how they impact on the gameplay experience.

A measure of the player's sense of being challenged, was taken for each game to check that the two games did not significantly differ in terms of task load. The order of the conditions was counter-balanced to offset any order effects.

Recruitment

Approval was granted by a university ethical review board to recruit individuals aged 17 years or older with experience playing first-person shooter games. Pairs of participants were recruited from a videogame studies course at a university, the general public via social media, and a research database of participants from prior studies. Snowball sampling techniques were also used [22]. Data collection ran from August 2014 to February 2015. Participants were provided with a free coffee voucher and could choose to enter a draw to win a AU$100 gift voucher.

Procedure

The experimental sessions took place in a computer laboratory. Friends would typically arrive together, and strangers separately. Only two participants were tested in any one session. Written informed consent was obtained prior to commencing the study. Participants were seated in adjacent booths with a partition between them (Figure 1), and were asked to not speak to each other once the experiment began. Text chat was disabled and participants wore headsets that delivered the game's audio in order to mask any sounds made by the other participant. The researcher remained present in the room. The participants first answered questions regarding demographics, their previous experience with games, and whether they knew the other participant. They then played two games in counterbalanced order (agent and avatar) for approximately ten minutes each game. Participants were told beforehand which game they were playing (agent or avatar), and were not given a specific task to perform, other than to 'enjoy the game'. Each game automatically timed out and delivered the player to the corresponding survey. The approximate total time of each session was one hour. At the end of the experiment, participants were asked to indicate whether they believed they were playing with AI or a human during the (ostensible) agent condition. Following this, participants were also debriefed regarding the deception.

Figure 1. Experimental setup for two participants

In order to minimize the impact of the researcher's social presence, and to streamline the study, we developed an application that partially automated the experimental procedure. This application loaded various stages of the study (i.e. videogame play conditions and survey measures) in a sequence based on participants' assigned experimental condition (making use of codified participant numbers). This assisted with the deception component of the study, as participants familiar with the game were not placed in the game's lobby system (where they would see other participants), but instead were routed directly to the game servers by the application. Complementing this, unique servers were launched, ensuring that the conditions were counterbalanced and linked to the correct survey.

Stimuli

The game used in this study was *Left 4 Dead 2* (*L4D2*) [35], a first-person shooter where the players are placed in a post-apocalyptic world inhabited by zombies. This game was chosen because of its AI director, which provides a level of dynamic difficulty adjustment to mitigate any differing levels of player ability. The AI director determines the pace of the game, via the number of attacking zombies, and is a direct response to how an individual performs and how well teams work together. The level chosen was 'The Parish' and involved players navigating an abandoned town while being attacked by zombies. This level was long enough to allow players to spend an entire ten-minute session without completing the level. Players were able to pick up weapons and medical packs that allowed them to defend and heal both themselves and others. At random times an event would be triggered in which the participants would be swarmed by zombies. Player health was modified to stop players from dying during the game - when their health bar dropped below a certain point it automatically topped up. As such, players did not need to start the game over, allowing them to stay with their partner at all times, consequently protecting the deception and providing a more consistent play experience to all participants.

Measures

Players were asked to indicate on a 7-point scale how experienced they were playing first person shooters, as well as with *L4D2* (from 'no experience' to 'very experienced'). Familiarity was gauged by asking players if they knew the other participant (yes/no response).

Positive post-play affect was measured with the positive affect subscale of the short 10-item version of the Positive and Negative Affect scale (PANAS). The PANAS-short form is a validated measure of affect [32]. The positive affect scale is comprised of 5 items measured on a 5-point scale, which asks participants to rate the extent to which they are experiencing a particular emotion 'right now', e.g. 'excited'. Unlike the other measures in this study which were averaged, the PANAS items were summed to produce a total score, thus the highest possible score is 25.

The in-game experiences of autonomy, competence and presence were measured with the Player Experience of Need Satisfaction Scale (PENS) [26], a validated measure. Autonomy was measured with 3 items, competence with 3 items, and presence with 9 items, examples being: 'I experience a lot of freedom in the game' (autonomy); 'I feel very capable and effective when playing' (competence); and 'When moving through the game world I feel as if I am actually there' (presence). The presence measure includes items related to spatial, emotional and narrative presence.

Challenge was measured with 3 items, created by the authors, on a 7-point scale, e.g. 'I had to put a lot of effort into the game'. Enjoyment was measured with an adaption of the Intrinsic Motivation Inventory's (IMI) interest/enjoyment subscale. The IMI is a validated measure of a participant's subjective experience of intrinsic motivation for an activity [21]. The items were adapted to read 'game' instead of 'activity'. The IMI consists of 7 items measured on a 7-point scale, an example being "I thought this was a boring game" (reversed).

Connection with teammate was measured with an adaption of the Overlap of Self, Ingroup and Outgroup Scale (OSIO) [28], a one-item, 7-point pictorial measure of circles at different distances from each other. Participants were asked to indicate which image best represented their level of connection with their teammate, with the distance between the circles indicating the degree of connection.

Cooperation was gauged by five items created by the authors measured on a 7-point scale, e.g. 'I helped my teammate', 'My teammate was supportive'.

Analyses

All analyses were carried out using SPSS 21.0. Preliminary analyses revealed that while sixty participants took part in the study, 18 revealed that they were not deceived in the agent condition and were excluded from analyses; two due to technical difficulties occurring during the play session; and one who didn't respond to over 10% of the self-report measures. The final sample was based on 39 participants (87.2% male, 5.1% female, 7.7 % unreported; between 18 to 54 years of age; M=28.05, SD=9.57). Gender distribution is comparable to that reported for first-person shooters [41].

The final sample was largely comprised of players with a high level of experience playing shooters (M=4.97, SD=1.48), and a moderate level of experience playing *L4D2* (M=3.59, SD=2.29). Twenty-three participants were familiar with the other participant (approximately 59%), while 16 participants were paired with strangers. Pearson correlations and Cronbach's alpha for the dependent measures can be found in the supplementary materials.

An ANOVA was carried out to test for any difference in task load across conditions using the challenge measure. Challenge was non-significant, $F(1,37)=.561$, $p=.459$, suggesting that task load was equivalent across conditions. The primary analysis was conducted using a combination of 2x2 mixed-factorial analysis of variance (ANOVA), and multivariate analysis of variance (MANOVA). Agency (avatar or agent) was entered as the within-subjects factor, and familiarity (friends or strangers) as the between-subjects factor. In order to address the assumptions laid out in Tabachnick & Fidell [30] regarding the inclusion of variables in MANOVA, the dependent variables were entered into separate tests based upon conceptual similarity and moderate correlation. This resulted in three separate tests: an ANOVA contrasting the levels of competence; and two MANOVAs, one containing the outcome measures of cooperation and connection, and the other, those of autonomy, enjoyment, positive affect and presence. A Bonferroni correction was applied across analyses with a revised statistical significance level of $p<.016$.

All further assumptions were satisfied as per the recommendations of Tabachnick & Fidell [30]. Follow-up tests using a series of ANOVAs were used to reveal any simple main effects. Effect sizes are reported as partial eta-squared and interpreted using Cohen's [3] criterion of small (.01), medium (.25) and large (.40) effects.

Results

The univariate analysis for the dependent variable of competence found the within-subject effect of agency non-significant, $F(1,37)=.006$, $p=.94$, $\eta_p^2<.001$. The between-subject effect (familiarity), $F(1,37)=.009$, $p=.93$, $\eta_p^2<.001$, and the interaction between familiarity and agency, $F(1,37)=2.07$, $p=.16$, $\eta_p^2 < .053$, were also non-significant.

The analysis for the combined dependent variables of cooperation and connection found the within-subjects effect of agency to be significant, $F(1,37)=9.34$, $p=.001$, $\eta_p^2=.34$. Neither the between-subjects effect of familiarity, $F(1,37)=.55$, $p=.58$, $\eta_p^2=.03$ nor the interaction, $F(1,37)=.39$, $p=.67$, $\eta_p^2=.02$, were significant. Follow-up univariate two-way ANOVAs revealed significant main effects and medium effect sizes for connection, $F=17.97$, $p<.001$, $\eta_p^2= .33$, and cooperation, $F=13.58$, $p=.001$, $\eta_p^2=.27$; indicating higher levels of cooperation and connection when participants were playing with avatars, compared to playing with agents.

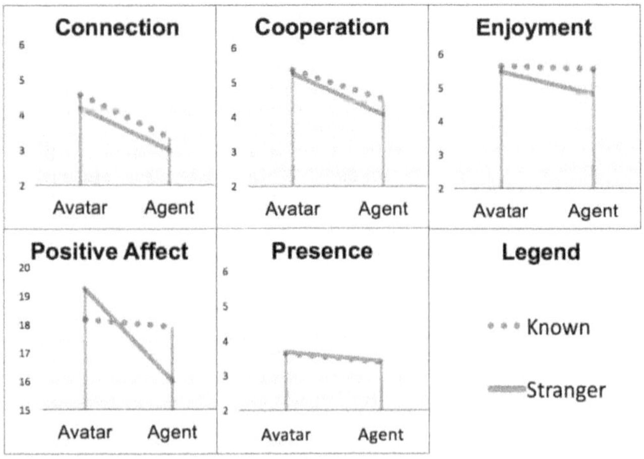

Figure 2. Study 1: Significant relationships

The analysis for the combined dependent variables of autonomy, enjoyment, positive affect and presence found the between-subject effect of familiarity to be non-significant, $F(1,37)=.86$, $p=.50$, $\eta_p^2=.09$. The within-subjects effect of agency, however, was found to be significant, $F(1,37)=8.00$, $p<.001$, $\eta_p^2=.49$, and qualified by an interaction between player agency and familiarity, $F(1, 37)=4.28$, $p=.007$, $\eta_p^2=.34$.

Follow-up univariate two-way ANOVAs revealed a significant main effect and medium effect size for agency on enjoyment, $F=11.39$, $p=.002$, $\eta_p^2=.24$, qualified by a significant interaction between agency and familiarity, $F=6.53$, $p=.016$, $\eta_p^2=.15$. Analysis of simple main effects revealed that when present with a friend no difference for playing with an avatar or an agent emerged. However, when present with a stranger, participants reported significantly higher ($p < .001$) levels of enjoyment when play was with an avatar than when it was with an agent.

A significant main effect and medium effect size for agency was also found for post-play positive affect, $F=19.61$, $p < .001$, $\eta_p^2=.35$, qualified by a significant interaction, $F=14.22$, $p=.001$, $\eta_p^2=.28$. Examination of the simple main effects again showed that when playing with friends present there was no significant difference between play with an avatar and agent. However, when playing with a stranger present, there was significantly greater ($p < .001$) positive affect reported when play was with an avatar than an agent.

A significant main effect and small effect size was found for presence, $F=6.79$, $p=.013$, $\eta_p^2=.16$, unqualified by an interaction ($F=.001$, $p=.98$, $\eta_p^2<.001$), showing higher levels of presence reported in play with an avatar than an agent. Autonomy was not found to significantly differ across conditions ($F=.009$, $p=.92$, $\eta_p^2<.001$), nor present an interaction, ($F=.076$, $p= .79$, $\eta_p^2=.002$). For all estimated marginal means and standard errors see Table 1. Figure 2 displays graphed significant relationships.

Summary

Cooperative play with an avatar produced greater post-play positive affect, presence, enjoyment, and perceptions of connection and cooperation than play with an agent (RQ1). No main effect for familiarity was found (RQ2), however, familiarity was found to qualify the impact of playing with an agent or avatar on game enjoyment and post-play mood (RQ3). This showed that the greater enjoyment and positive affect experienced when playing with an avatar (compared to an agent) was experienced only when players did not know each other.

			Study 1		Study 2	
Measure	**Agency**	**Familiarity**	**M**	**S.E**	**M**	**S.E**
Autonomy	Avatar	Known	4.20	.27	5.11	.30
		Stranger	4.31	.33	4.89	.30
	Agent	Known	4.25	.30	4.48	.31
		Stranger	4.29	.36	4.89	.31
Competence	Avatar	Known	4.91	.24	4.98	.29
		Stranger	5.17	.28	4.94	.29
	Agent	Known	5.15	.27	4.70	.28
		Stranger	4.96	.32	4.91	.28
Connection	Avatar	Known	4.57	.31	4.50	.32
		Stranger	4.19	.38	4.00	.32
	Agent	Known	3.35	.31	2.50	.31
		Stranger	3.00	.37	2.56	.31
* Cooperation	Avatar	Known	5.36	.25	4.04	.14
		Stranger	5.25	.30	4.04	.14
	Agent	Known	4.50	.28	3.01	.17
		Stranger	4.05	.33	3.11	.17
Enjoyment	Avatar	Known	5.65	.20	5.71	.25
		Stranger	5.47	.24	5.69	.25
	Agent	Known	5.55	.25	5.12	.26
		Stranger	4.80	.30	4.87	.26
Positive Affect	Avatar	Known	18.17	.75	19.17	.99
		Stranger	19.25	.89	20.28	.99
	Agent	Known	17.91	.88	17.56	.99
		Stranger	16.00	1.05	18.67	.99
Presence	Avatar	Known	3.64	.26	3.83	.30
		Stranger	3.67	.31	3.93	.30
	Agent	Known	3.39	.26	3.32	.28
		Stranger	3.41	.31	3.52	.28

Table 1. Estimated Marginal Means and Standard Errors for Study 1 and 2

*Cooperation is measured with an author-created scale (Study 1) and the CCPIG (Study 2)

In analysing our results for study 1, however, we identified a possible issue with our chosen manipulation. As discussed, within each pair, the participants knowingly acted as the cooperative partner for one another in the avatar condition and unknowingly acted as the cooperative partner for the other person in the agent condition. In other words, in the avatar condition, Person A correctly believes their cooperative partner is Person B (and vice versa), while in the agent condition Person A and Person B incorrectly believe their cooperative partner is an agent when it is actually the other person. The issue that emerges is that when Person A believes they are playing with an agent they may (for example) provide less support to the agent (which is actually Person B). Thus, Person B is potentially exposed to less supportive behaviour from their teammate in the agent condition than in the avatar condition. In summary, although our manipulation check confirmed that participants included for analysis were successfully deceived into believing they were playing with a computer-controlled partner in the agent condition, it is possible that we inadvertently introduced a confound such that partner behaviour differed between the avatar and agent conditions.

This issue would be resolved if computer agents were used as cooperative partners in all conditions and participants were deceived into believing their partner was actually a human in the avatar condition. By reversing the manipulation in this way, it is possible to guarantee that the cooperative teammate (now an agent) acts identically across conditions. However, this change comes at the cost of using a game with a diverse range of possible player behaviours. Such a deception would not be believable in *L4D2* as the range of possible actions mean that an agent can often be detected. This suggested the need (in Study 2) for a game with a narrower range of agent/avatar behaviours. In addition, while the cooperation measure used may act as a proxy for social presence, the need for more targeted measure was indicated. These limitations shaped the refinements made in Study 2.

STUDY 2

This study aimed to replicate the findings of Study 1 with three methodological changes. One, the deception utilised in Study 1 was reversed such that in both conditions participants played with an agent (game AI). Two, this necessitated the use of a game with computer agent teammates that could believably be perceived as human. The electronic sports game *Rocket League* (*RL*) was selected as the more rigid ruleset of the game made it easier to hide the limitations of game agents (i.e. agents with predictable movements/paths in first-person shooter games). Three, the cooperative subscale of the Competitive and Cooperative Presence in Gaming Questionnaire (CCPIG), replaced the author-created cooperation scale.

Method

Again, a 2 x 2 repeated-measures mixed factorial design using agency as the within-subjects factor (avatar/agent), and familiarity (known/unknown) as the between-subjects factor was employed. The order of conditions was once again counter-balanced to offset any order effects.

Recruitment

The same ethical approval and recruitment processes were used as were in Study 1, however, only males who enjoyed playing videogames and were aged between 17 and 35 years were approached, due to the research requirements of the study's funding body. Each participant was compensated AU$20 for their time. Data collection was conducted from August 2016 to September 2016.

Procedure

The experiment once again took place in a computer laboratory. Sessions were conducted with only a single pair at any given time. As per Study 1, participants were seated in adjacent booths with a partition between them (similar to Figure 1), and asked not to communicate throughout the experiment. Participants were again given headsets to wear to mask any vocalisations from their fellow participant, and in-game communication was disabled. The researcher again remained present in the room.

Participants were given a pre-game survey covering demographics, gaming experience and their relationship with their fellow participant. Participants were then given a set of instructions, and a brief two-minute session to familiarise themselves with the controls. They then played two eight-minute sessions in a counterbalanced order (agent and avatar). Participants were informed before each match who they would be playing with (agent or avatar), and asked to enjoy the game. After each session (eight minutes of play), the games were remotely ended by the researcher, and the participants given a questionnaire to reflect on the previous round. At the end of the experiment, participants were debriefed regarding the deception and compensated.

Stimuli

The study used *Rocket League* [24], a futuristic sports-action game that mixes aspects of the real-world sport soccer with fast-paced driving and physics. Gameplay consists of two opposing teams competing to hit a ball into their opponent's goal while keeping it out of their own. Eight minutes of play could result in up to ten goals being kicked, necessitating a short reset of a few seconds while the game set up a re-match. Unlike *L4D2*, *RL* presents a clear objective (the opposing team's goal), method (directing a soccer ball) and obstacles (two opponents - the computer agents of the opposing team). As such, gameplay was more linear than that of *L4D2*. Player controls were modified so that any form of communication was restricted, as was access to personal scoreboards during the match.

Measures

The measures from Study 1 were repeated, except that the five-item author-created measure of perceived cooperative play was replace with the cooperative subscale of the Competitive and Cooperative Presence in Gaming Questionnaire (CCPIG) [12]. Its twenty-five items use a 5-

point Likert scale asking the participant to 'indicate your level of agreement with the following', such as 'I felt I contributed to the team'.

Analyses

All analyses were carried out using SPSS 23.0. Forty participants took part in the study, however four participants were excluded from the analysis. Two were removed as they were confused as to which condition was which, making their responses unreliable, and another two, because they had become aware of the deception. The final sample consisted of 36 male participants, aged from 17 to 27 years old (M=19.74, SD=2.4). Preliminary analyses revealed that the sample had a high general level of experience with videogames (M=5.83, SD=1.08). and a moderate level of experience with the stimulus game (M=3.08, SD=2.02). The final sample maintained an even balance of friend and stranger pairs, as well as an equal distribution in the order of agency conditions.

The manipulation check for task load were again carried out revealed that the level of challenge across conditions were equivalent, $F(1,34)=1.504$, $p=.228$. In order to address the assumptions laid out in Tabachnick & Fidell [30], the variables were again entered into separate tests, requiring the same composition as those used previously. Additionally, the PENS presence subscale and the CCPIG's cooperative social presence subscale were identified as being non-normal. These two scales were log transformed, and the primary analyses carried out with transformed and non-transformed variables. No substantive differences in results were revealed and thus, for ease of comparison between the two studies, the results using the non-transformed variables are reported below. The Pearson correlations and Cronbach's alpha for the final dependent measures can be found in the supplementary materials.

Results

The univariate analysis for the dependent variable of competence found the within-subject effect of agency non-significant, $F(1,34)=.52$, $p=.48$, $\eta_p^2=.015$. The between-subject effect (familiarity), $F(1,34)=.06$, $p=.81$, $\eta_p^2=.002$ and the interaction between familiarity and agency, $F(1,37)=2.07$, $p=.16$, $\eta_p^2=.009$, were also non-significant.

The analysis for the combined dependent variables of cooperation and connection found the within-subjects effect of agency to be significant, $F(1,34)=32.23$, $p < .001$, $\eta_p^2=.66$. Neither the between-subjects effect of familiarity, $F(1,34)=.57$, $p=.57$, $\eta_p^2=.033$, nor the interaction, $F(1,34)=.79$, $p=.46$, $\eta_p^2=.046$, were found to be significant. Follow-up univariate two-way ANOVAs revealed significant main effects and large effect sizes for cooperation, $F=66.14$, $p < .001$, $\eta_p^2= .66$, and connection, $F=41.05$, $p < .001$, $\eta_p^2= .55$. Consistent with study 1, participants reported greater cooperation and connection in play with an avatar compared to play with an agent.

The analysis for the combined dependent variables of

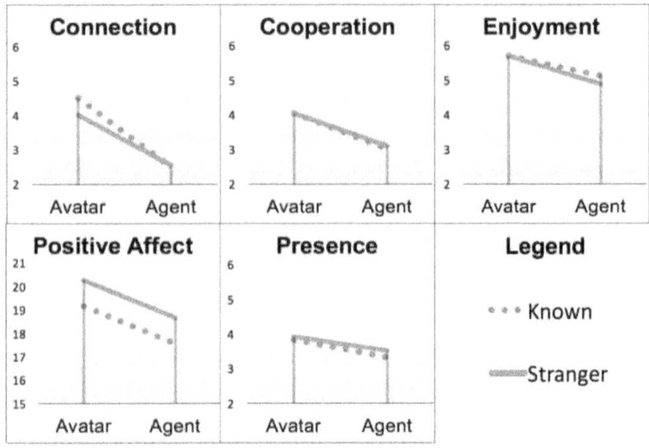

Figure 3. Study 2: Significant relationships

autonomy, enjoyment, positive affect and presence found the within-subjects effect of agency to be significant, $F(1,34)=5.153$, $p=.003$, $\eta_p^2=.40$. The between-subject effect of familiarity, however, was non-significant, $F(1,34)=.40$, $p=.81$, $\eta_p^2=.049$ and no significant interaction between player agency and familiarity, $F(1, 34)=1.30$, $p=.29$, $\eta_p^2=.14$, was displayed. Follow-up univariate two-way ANOVAs revealed significant main effects and medium effect sizes for agency on enjoyment, F=13.13, $p=.001$, $\eta_p^2=.28$; positive affect, F=15.24, $p < .001$, $\eta_p^2=.31$; and presence, F=12.60, $p=.001$, $\eta_p^2=.27$. Again, greater scores were reported in relation to play with an avatar, than an agent. Autonomy was not found to significantly differ across conditions ($F=.40$, $p=.054$, $\eta_p^2=.11$). For all estimated marginal means and standard errors see Table 1 (earlier). Figure 3 above displays graphed significant relationships

Summary

Despite reversing the terms of the deception used in Study 1, a similar pattern of results was found for Study 2. Perceived cooperative play with an avatar again produced greater post-play cooperation, connection, enjoyment, positive affect, and presence (RQ1). Also, again no main effect was found for familiarity (RQ2). Study 2, however, failed to find the interaction between familiarity and agency demonstrated in Study 1 (RQ3).

DISCUSSION

The sense of being with another person brings a level of investment that impacts on the emotional experience of a shared activity. These two studies establish that agency impacts on aspects of the player experience leading to greater cooperation, connection, enjoyment, presence (spatial, narrative, emotional), and a more positive mood when play is perceived as being with another human. The first study also found an interaction between agency and familiarity. Greater effect sizes were found in the second study for connection, cooperation, enjoyment and presence, contrasting with research suggesting that experiments where both conditions are human-controlled generate greater effects [9]. This relationship however was reversed for player enjoyment, with greater effects found in the first study. Overall, playing with a human had the greatest impact on the sense of cooperative social presence followed by a sense of connection, and positive affect. The findings for cooperation were further emphasised with the use of a more developed measure of cooperation (CCPIG - Study 2).

The greater sense of connection, and cooperation with others that play with avatars produced across a range of measures, is likely due to players being more attentive, and potentially more receptive, to cooperative actions when they believe another human is present in the game. In turn, this may be due to the higher emotional stakes created through a sense of shared risk and reward. Participants may also have chosen to act more pro-socially due to the potential for social repercussions after the experiment, given the co-located non-anonymous experimental conditions. This is partially supported by research finding cooperative play with friends encourages pro-social behaviour, and improves both individual and team performance [19]. More broadly, it is also supported by research finding that the addition of human players increases the requirements of cognitive processing [14], which in turn supports the notion of 'shared intentionality' [34]. This implies that agents do not create the same sense of connection and shared goals as does play with humans, regardless of how human-like their behaviour may be.

Both studies found that enjoyment and positive affect were greater in play with an avatar than an agent. The manipulation of the conditions across the studies (deceiving participants as to the true nature of the agent teammate in Study 1, and the avatar teammate in Study 2), demonstrates that this effect is entirely due to the belief that they are playing with a human. While it is intuitive that enjoyment and positive affect might occur simultaneously, as players who are enjoying themselves are more likely to have elevated moods, it seems that just the social presence generated by playful interactions with another can cause it. This presents a strong case for focusing on the human component of multiplayer games (and indeed, human-computer interaction), when wellbeing is the desired outcome. This research also builds on research finding greater enjoyment for playing against a human than a computer [10, 18], or an avatar against an agent [39], as well that contrasting cooperative play to solitary play [31].

Positive affect and enjoyment in Study 1, however, presented an interaction with familiarity. Only strangers experienced more enjoyment and positive affect in play with an avatar than an agent, while familiar players generated equivalent levels of enjoyment and positive affect across conditions. The most likely explanation is that co-located play with friends (or even just attending an experiment together) is enjoyable regardless of whether these friends are playing together or not. The absence of this effect in Study 2 may be explained by differences in the games used. *L4D2* offered a complex map and gameplay, as well as a modification that wouldn't allow players to die, whereas *RL* contained simpler gameplay, and short, demanding matches in which players could potentially lose to the opposing team. As such, the attentional demands of *RL's* gameplay may have detracted from the sense of social outing or the enjoyable shared experience of playing with a friend in the same room, who was engaged in the same task. However, given the size of the F value and associated small effect in Study 2, further research may be needed to confirm the absence of an interaction.

Finally, finding greater presence with avatars than agents across both studies is most likely due to the design features of multiplayer games that emphasise the sense of shared experience, which when players believe themselves to be sharing these experiences with another human brings a sense of reality or immediacy to the gameplay. This finding is in line with experimental research utilising competitive play and different game genres [17, 39], as well as experiments contrasting play against humans or against the game [2, 25]. However, it contrasts with survey results suggesting that less presence is experienced when playing games that are typically played socially compared to games that are not [13], or social play relative to solitary play [36]. It seems likely that a continuum may exist such that single-player games offer greater presence than multiplayer games with avatars, which offer more presence than multiplayer games with agents. However, further research is needed to confirm this possibility.

Feelings of competence were not found to differ across conditions suggesting that neither familiarity nor agency influence how well players feel they perform (at least in the games chosen). While this contrasts with findings that play with avatars produce less competence than play with agents [14], it may reflect the balanced level of challenge across conditions (thereby removing the opportunity for differences in feelings of competence). It is also possible that the lack of human opponents may have reduced the opportunity for feelings of achievement, as it seems likely that winning against a human creates a greater sense of competence than winning against the computer. This is supported by research finding that competitive play facilitates the satisfaction of competence needs [15].

Similarly, the null finding for autonomy may reflect that familiarity and agency do not influence feelings of freedom during play or otherwise. Alternatively, it may be due to the choice of games used. The need to constantly fend off zombie attacks in *L4D2,* as well as the short, intense matches enacted in *RL* would necessarily curtail exploration and experimentation, thus removing the possibility for greater autonomy to emerge in either condition. It is feasible that other games may allow for greater autonomy to emerge in either play with avatars or agents. Conducting studies using games with different content, pacing and mechanics will benefit this field of research.

Research Implications

As previous research has found that friendly and unfriendly communications can impact on outcomes [27], we chose to disallow communication amongst participants in order to isolate social presence from social interaction, and to protect the deception. For multiplayer gaming in which communication is typical, however, other methodologies such as field experimentation may be required to capture the impact of agency on the player experience. Alternatively, further laboratory-based research could manipulate the use of communication between teammates to isolate its effects. The two studies were also heavily weighted towards male participation. Future research could attempt recruiting a more balanced sample, or seek purely female participation to determine if the effects are generalisable to a female population. The high level of experience with game play that our participants demonstrated also raises the question of whether these results would hold with an inexperienced sample.

The use of cooperative and not competitive play was chosen to provide players with the opportunity to form feelings of connection to agents, which seemed more likely to develop with supportive characters engaged in a common task. The choice not to add a competitive play condition was largely due to concerns about player fatigue, as well as the potential to introduce confounding variables. For example, when participants are cooperating to defeat the game, they have the support of another human; but when they are competing against each other, they both lack the support of another human, and are seeking to defeat a human either directly (killing a character, beating to finish line, points etc.). This potentially creates conditions with very different task loads (greatest in direct competition), or incomparable tasks (e.g. cooperating to finish a campaign together v. competing in death match). Future research might instead consider closer examination of either type of interaction (cooperative or competitive) in isolation, or focus on team-against-team play to capture both at once.

Design Implications

While much effort has been expended creating agents with human-like decision making and behaviours, this research underscores that these are less impactful on some aspects of the player experience than is the belief that people are playing with another human. That this is effective even when communication channels are closed speaks to the influence of social presence. Rather than focus resources into creating more life-like cooperative agents for multiplayer games, this research suggests that these resources might be better used encouraging players to play together. This does not, of course, imply that agents do not serve a valuable purpose within single-player games.

Beyond encouraging players to team up, there is also value in exploring technologies that increase social presence between players. Facial recognition technology that maps facial expressions onto game avatars - such as is being explored by researchers using Oculus Rift [38] – is one such avenue. Using eye-tracking to refocus game maps on objects of joint attention may be another way in which a sense of shared intentionality between players could be reinforced, as other research suggests [20, 33]. These technologies may also be impactful in online education and online collaborative work environments in order to effect greater cohesion and presence. Relatedly, that co-located friends experience enjoyment and positive affect in the play of one game, but not another, suggests that certain gameplay mechanics foster greater social presence than others - and that this effect can be felt even when playing separate instances of the game. Further research may wish to address whether greater sense of affinity and shared experience with avatars is more likely to be produced in rich virtual environments with free-ranging gameplay than short, competitive matches in a limited field.

It is also worth considering how larger community dynamics shape the level of active participation in cooperative gameplay. The comparable levels of enjoyment and positive affect that both friends and strangers experienced when playing with each other, reinforces the importance of encouraging team-players, positive inter-personal dynamics, and relationship formation. While some of this is covered in the burgeoning field of MMORPG research [4, 29, 40], further investigation could explore how to increase such positive social connections, for example, through mentoring and support roles, or in-game rewards.

CONCLUSION

Developments in artificial intelligence and an increase in focus on multiplayer games, combined with a growing reliance on computer-mediated communication and entertainment, indicates the importance of contrasts between agents and avatars. This study shows that, in game play at least, engaging with another human is experienced as more enjoyable than play with a computer agent, as well as bringing greater presence, positive emotion, connection and cooperation. Finding enjoyment and affect to be qualified by an interaction with familiarity also demonstrates the powerful and positive impacts of being with friends and highlights a methodological consideration for researchers in this field (specifically, that playing with friends in the room may influence study conditions regardless of whether the players are directly interacting with each other). The relative newness of this field of research, however, indicates the need for further exploration across of range of settings including different game genres and other social contexts, such as team play.

ACKNOWLEDGEMENTS

We would like to thank the participants for their time, and the MindMax initiative (funded by the Movember Foundation) for partially supporting this research, Dr Paul Cairns for his input on study design, as well as Cody Phillips and Dr David Conroy for technical assistance.

REFERENCES

1. Frank Biocca, Chad Harms, Judee K. Burgoon. 2003. Toward a more robust theory and measure of social presence: Review and suggested criteria. *Presence: Teleoper. Virtual Environ.* 12, 5: 456-480. http://dx.doi.org/10.1162/105474603322761270
2. P. Cairns, Anna L. Cox, Matthew Day, Hayley Martin, Thomas Perryman. 2013. Who but not where: The effect of social play on immersion in digital games. *Int J Hum-Comput St.* 71, 11: 1069-1077. http://dx.doi.org/10.1016/j.ijhcs.2013.08.015
3. J. Cohen. 1992. A power primer. *Psychol Bull.* 112, 1: 155-9.
4. H. Cole, M. D. Griffiths. 2007. Social interactions in massively multiplayer online role-playing gamers. *Cyberpsychol Behav.* 10, 4: 575-583. http://dx.doi.org/10.1089/cpb.2007.9988
5. David Conroy, Peta Wyeth, Daniel Johnson. 2012. Spotting the difference: Identifying player opponent preferences in FPS games. In *Entertainment Computing - ICEC 2012*, M Herrlich, R Malaka, and M Masuch (eds.). Springer Berlin Heidelberg, 114-121. http://dx.doi.org/10.1007/978-3-642-33542-6_10
6. Edward L. Deci, Richard M. Ryan. 2000. The "what" and "why" of goal pursuits: Human needs and the self-determination of behavior. *Psychol Inq.* 11, 4: 227-268. http://dx.doi.org/10.2307/1449618
7. C. Delgado-Mata, J. Ibanez-Martinez. 2007. Behavioural reactive agents for video game opponents with personalities. In *Intelligent Virtual Agents, Proceedings*, C Pelachaud, et al. (eds.). 371-372.
8. Tristan Donovan. 2010. *Replay: The History of Video Games.* Yellow Ant.
9. Jesse Fox, Sun Joo Ahn, Joris H. Janssen, Leo Yeykelis, Kathryn Y. Segovia, Jeremy N. Bailenson. 2014. Avatars versus agents: A meta-analysis quantifying the effect of agency on social influence. *Human–Computer Interaction.* 30, 5: 401-432. http://dx.doi.org/10.1080/07370024.2014.921494
10. Brian Gajadhar, Yvonne De Kort, Wijnand Ijsselsteijn, *Shared fun is doubled fun: Player enjoyment as a function of social setting*, in *2nd International Conference on Fun and Games*2008, Springer-Verlag: Eindhoven, Netherlands. p. 106-117.
11. Philip Hingston, *A new design for a Turing Test for bots*, in *2010 IEEE Conference on Computational Intelligence and Games*2010, IEEE: Denmark. p. 345-350.
12. Matthew Hudson, Paul Cairns, A. Imran Nordin. 2015. Familiarity in team-based online games: The interplay between player familiarity and the concepts of social presence, team trust, and performance. In *Advances in Visual Informatics*, H Badioze Zaman, et al. (eds.). Springer International Publishing, Cham, 140-151. http://dx.doi.org/10.1007/978-3-319-25939-0_13
13. Daniel Johnson, Lennart Nacke, Peta Wyeth, *All about that base: Differing player experiences in video game genres and the unique case of MOBA games*, in *33rd Annual ACM Conference on Human Factors in Computing Systems*2015, ACM Press: Seoul, Republic of Korea. p. 2265-2274.
14. Daniel Johnson, Peta Wyeth, Madison Clark, Christopher Watling, *Cooperative game play with avatars and agents: Differences in brain activity and the experience of play*, in *33rd Annual ACM Conference on Human Factors in Computing Systems*2015, ACM Press: Seoul, Republic of Korea. p. 3721-3730.
15. Snezhanka Kazakova, Veroline Cauberghe, Mario Pandelaere, Patrick De Pelsmacker. 2014. Players' expertise and competition with others shape the satisfaction of competence needs, gaming gratifications, and contingent self-esteem in a gaming context. *Cyberpsychol Behav Soc Netw* 17, 1: 26-32. http://dx.doi.org/10.1089/cyber.2012.0413
16. Kwan Min Lee. 2004. Presence, explicated. *Communication Theory.* 14, 1: 27-50. http://dx.doi.org/10.1111/j.1468-2885.2004.tb00302.x
17. Sohye Lim, Byron Reeves. 2010. Computer agents versus avatars: Responses to interactive game characters controlled by a computer or other player. *Int J Hum-Comput St.* 68, 1-2: 57-68. http://dx.doi.org/10.1016/j.ijhcs.2009.09.008
18. Regan L. Mandryk, M. Stella Atkins, Kori Inkpen, *A continuous and objective evaluation of emotional experience with interactive play environments*, in *SIGCHI Conference on Human Factors in Computing Systems*2006, ACM: Montréal, Québec, Canada. p. 1027-1036.
19. Winter Mason, Aaron Clauset, *Friends FTW!: Friendship, collaboration and competition in Halo: Reach*, in *2013 conference on Computer supported cooperative work*2013. p. 375-386.
20. Bernhard Maurer, Michael Lankes, Barbara Stiglbauer, Manfred Tscheligi. 2016. EyeCo: Effects of shared gaze on social presence in an online cooperative game. In *Entertainment Computing - ICEC 2016: ICEC 2016. Lecture Notes in Computer Science*, G Wallner, et al. (eds.). Springer, Cham, 102-114. http://dx.doi.org/10.1007/978-3-319-46100-7_9
21. E. McAuley, T. Duncan, V. V. Tammen. 1989. Psychometric properties of the Intrinsic Motivation Inventory in a competitive sport setting: A

confirmatory factor analysis. *Res Q Exerc Sport*. 60, 1: 48-58.

22. David L. Morgan. 2008. Snowball Sampling. In *The Sage Encyclopedia of Qualitative Research Methods*, LM Given (ed.) SAGE Publications, Inc., Thousand Oaks, CA, 816-817. http://dx.doi.org/10.4135/9781412963909
23. Kristine L. Nowak, Frank Biocca. 2004. The effect of the agency and anthropomorphism on users' sense of telepresence, copresence, and social presence in virtual environments. *Presence*. 12, 5: 481-494.
24. Psyonix, *Rocket League*, 2015.
25. Niklas Ravaja, Timo Saari, Marko Turpeinen, Jari Laarni, Mikko Salminen, Matias Kivikangas. 2006. Spatial presence and emotions during video game playing: Does it matter with whom you play? *Presence-Teleop Virt*. 15, 4: 381-392. http://dx.doi.org/10.1162/pres.15.4.381
26. Richard M. Ryan, C. Scott Rigby, Andrew Przybylski. 2006. The motivational pull of video games: A self-determination theory approach. *Motiv Emotion*. 30, 4: 347-363. http://dx.doi.org/10.1007/s11031-006-9051-8
27. Mike Schmierbach, Qian Xu, Anne Oeldorf-Hirsch, Frank E. Dardis. 2012. Electronic friend or virtual foe: Exploring the role of competitive and cooperative multiplayer video game modes in fostering enjoyment. *Media Psychol*. 15, 3: 356-371.
28. Thomas W. Schubert, Sabine Otten. 2002. Overlap of self, ingroup, and outgroup: Pictorial measures of self-categorization. *Self and Identity*. 1, 4: 353-376. http://dx.doi.org/10.1080/152988602760328012
29. J. G. Snodgrass, M. G. Lacy, H. J. F. Dengah, J. Fagan. 2011. Enhancing one life rather than living two: Playing MMOs with offline friends. *Comput Hum Behav*. 27, 3: 1211-1222. http://dx.doi.org/10.1016/j.chb.2011.01.001
30. Barbara G. Tabachnick, Linda S. Fidell. 2007. *Using multivariate statistics: Fifth edition*. Allyn & Bacon, Inc.
31. Ron Tamborini, Nicholas David Bowman, Allison Eden, Matthew Grizzard, Ashley Organ. 2010. Defining media enjoyment as the satisfaction of intrinsic needs. *J Commun*. 60, 4: 758-777. http://dx.doi.org/10.1111/j.1460-2466.2010.01513.x
32. Edmund R. Thompson. 2007. Development and validation of an internationally reliable short-form of the positive and negative affect schedule (PANAS). *Journal of Cross-Cultural Psychology*. 38, 2: 227-242. http://dx.doi.org/10.1177/0022022106297301
33. M. Tomasello, M. Carpenter. 2007. Shared intentionality. *Developmental Science*. 10, 121-125. http://dx.doi.org/10.1111/j.1467-7687.2007.00573.x
34. M. Tomasello, M. Carpenter, J. Call, T. Behne, H. Moll. 2005. Understanding and sharing intentions: The origins of cultural cognition. *Behav Brain Sci*. 28, 5: 675-9. http://dx.doi.org/10.1017/s0140525x05000129
35. Valve Corporation, *Left 4 Dead 2*, 2009, Valve Corporation.
36. Kellie Vella, Daniel Johnson, Leanne Hides, *Playing alone, playing with others: Differences in player experience and indicators of wellbeing*, in *ACM SIGCHI Annual Symposium on Computer-Human Interaction in Play* 2015, ACM Press: London, United Kingdom. p. 3-12.
37. Julia Crouse Waddell, Wei Peng. 2014. Does it matter with whom you slay? The effects of competition, cooperation and relationship type among video game players. *Comput Hum Behav*. 38, 331-338. http://dx.doi.org/http://dx.doi.org/10.1016/j.chb.2014.06.017
38. M Walton. 2015. Oculus Rift hack transfers your facial expressions onto your virtual avatar. Retrieved September, 2016 from http://arstechnica.com/gaming/2015/05/oculus-rift-hack-transfers-your-facial-expressions-onto-your-virtual-avatar/
39. David Weibel, Bartholomäus Wissmath, Stephan Habegger, Yves Steiner, Rrudolf Groner. 2008. Playing online games against computer- vs. human-controlled opponents: Effects on presence, flow, and enjoyment. *Comput Hum Behav*. 24, 5: 2274-2291. http://dx.doi.org/10.1016/j.chb.2007.11.002
40. Nick Yee. 2006. The demographics, motivations, and derived experiences of users of massively multi-user online graphical environments. *Presence-Teleop Virt*. 15, 3: 309-329. http://dx.doi.org/10.1162/pres.15.3.309
41. Nick Yee. 2017. Beyond 50/50: Breaking down the percentage of female gamers by genre. Retrieved February, 2017 from http://quanticfoundry.com/2017/01/19/female-gamers-by-genre/

Social Support in eSports: Building Emotional and Esteem Support from Instrumental Support Interactions in a Highly Competitive Environment

Guo Freeman
University of Cincinnati
Cincinnati, OH, U.S.A.
guo.freeman@uc.edu

Donghee Yvette Wohn
New Jersey Institute of Technology
Newark, NJ, U.S.A.
wohn@njit.edu

ABSTRACT
In this paper we report an empirical study of how and what types of social support eSports players can experience from their gameplay. Specifically, we interviewed 26 eSports players and sought out their first-person descriptions of experiences of social support. We found that even though most players started out as strangers, the context of eSports facilitated frequent acts of helping through both tangible and intangible means within the game. Such in-game informational and instrumental support often led to emotional and esteem support, and these different types of support functions not only remained within the context of the game but also "bled" out into in-person interactions and relationships. We contribute to CSCW and HCI by both confirming and augmenting existing theories of mediated social support in this underexplored context. Our findings regarding how emotional and esteem support are built from instrumental support interactions in eSports not only provide a rich description of players' experiences in highly competitive digital environments and the consequences of their social interactions but also suggest a number of future research opportunities.

Author Keywords
eSports; social support; competitive gaming; social capital

ACM Classification Keywords
H.5.m. Information interfaces and presentation (e.g., HCI): Miscellaneous.

INTRODUCTION
HCI and CSCW researchers have noted a trend to "focus on technology that is playful and highly immersive, meaning technologies that are built around video games or leverage game design in some form." [37, p. 1088]. Online gaming, thus, has been regarded as a serious and important area of research at CHI instead of superficial leisure activities [37]. In particular, nowadays the increasing popularity of Electronic Sports (eSports) has pervaded into the youth culture and opened up opportunities for new avenues of inquiry in our field [18].

At a high level of understanding, eSports is usually perceived as a new form of digital gaming that often requires competitive and cooperative interactions between players and involves spectating [18]. In addition, eSports is situated at a unique intersection that combines recreation, interaction, task, competition, and collaboration: it is task-based with serious purposes (e.g., collaborate to complete tasks and win). It also happens in an intense fictional virtual environment that requires fast decision-making and response rate. Furthermore, many players are still amateur, practicing skills at home, without pay, for fun and challenge [24].

While some research have explored the motivations for participating and spectating eSports [5,21,22,48], the legitimacy of playing computer games as sports (e.g., [61]), and designing new interaction modality and communication/streaming technologies for this new genre of gaming [23,27,29,31], the social outcomes of eSports is often a neglected topic. The focus on interpersonal interaction is not new in studies of multiplayer online gaming (e.g., [40,60,64]), yet the tension between eSports as a new context of online gaming that especially values the competitive dynamics between human rivalries and its high demands for extensive social interactions both online and offline for building high performance teams raises interesting questions about players' experiences of social interaction consequences emerging in their eSports activities.

Therefore, in this paper we use our empirical study of how and what types of social support that eSports players can experience from their gameplay in hopes of investigating players' various interpretations and sense making of their eSports practices. Specifically, this research builds on previous studies of theories of relationship development and social support in both online and offline social spaces.

Our work makes a number of contributions to the HCI/CSCW community: Theoretically, we contribute to both confirming and augmenting existing theories of

CHI PLAY '17, October 15-18, 2017, Amsterdam, Netherlands

ACM ISBN 978-1-4503-4898-0/17/10…$15.00
https://doi.org/10.1145/3116595.3116635

mediated social support using this new dataset. While a large body of previous literature distinguishes between the different types of social support, we found that in the context of eSports, the fact that the team-emphasized, highly competitive gaming practice is a shared goal and core task makes it difficult to separate instrumental support from other types of support. Empirically, our findings regarding how informational and instrumental support serve as a basis for emotional and esteem support, as well as how players had to choose between different relationship roles so as to manage different expectations of support, provide a rich description of players' experiences in highly competitive digital environments and the consequences of their social interactions. This also suggests future research opportunities such as the tension between built-in game features and the natural emergence of social support, the role of physical presence in virtual teamwork, and how to design new sociotechnical features that better serve players' needs for social support in varied online environments.

WHAT IS ESPORTS?

eSports is multidimensional: the term "eSports" can be used to describe a large variety of different "types" of eSports ranging from a professional environment in which players compete in person in large arena settings to semi-professional and entertainment forms of eSports played online. It also involves different levels of gameplay – e.g., as professional play that is denoted by players under contract with an e-sports team/organization or as amateur or entertaining play in more traditional digital gaming. In particular, some even suggest that there is no clear differentiation between "eSports" games as opposed to "non-eSports" games: eSports is more or less a meta-game that can be played based on almost any digital game.

Therefore, in our previous work [18], we have noted that while the term of eSports is widely used, researchers do not have consensus with regard to its definition other than a high level understanding that eSports usually refers to competitive multiplayer gaming that involves spectating. Many players also tended to describe eSports using terms and concepts from traditional sports (e.g., competition and training). Specifically, we found that players' perceptions of eSports often include the following components: competition; goals/ rules; professional scene; spectators; intellectual and motor skills; governing body, and human competitors.

Following this high level understanding, in this study we refer "eSports" to a form of varied computer-mediated competitive gaming activities that attracts spectators: it involves both professional and amateur players as well as a wide range of different game titles. This diversity allows for a broader examination of eSports activities and experiences in different contexts.

THEORIZING SOCIAL SUPPORT ONLINE AND OFFLINE

In traditional social scientific studies, social support relates to "the social resources that people perceive to be available or are actually provided to them by nonprofessionals in the context of both formal support groups and informal helping relationships" [7, p.4]. It is not an existing resource but rather a form of expression that arises out of one's social structure as well as the relationships with people within that structure.

Social scientists have proposed many different types of conceptualizations of social support, depending on what the criteria for *support* are. The Social Provisions Scale, which was designed for use with general populations [9], is based on Weiss' [58] model of social provisions. This model separates assistance-related support (e.g., guidance, reliable alliance, reassurance of worth) with non-assistance-related support (e.g., attachment, social integration). This four-typology is consistent across varied psychology literature. For example, House [26] categorized social support into "an interpersonal transaction involving one or more of the following: (1) emotional concern (liking, love, empathy), (2) instrumental aid (goods or services), (3) information (about the environment), or (4) appraisal (information relevant to self-evaluation)" (p. 39). Similarly, Barrera [2] categorized social support as emotional support, instrumental support, informational support, companionate, and esteem support. He also distinguished perceived support—the belief that support is available—from actual support—the mobilization and expression of support.

Another approach is to conceptualize social support as a form of *social capital*, which separates functional aspects of support such as those identified above from structural aspects of one's social network (e.g., the size and composition such as strong vs. weak ties [54,56]). The concept of *social capital* was first introduced by Bourdieu [3] and Coleman [8] as a form of capital that is distinct from human capital (e.g., access to people with certain knowledge) or tangible capital (e.g., money): Although social capital can facilitate productive activity (as does human capital and tangible capital), it is inherently unique in that it resides in the connections between people and the potential for individuals to access resources through their social network.

Specifically, Putnam [42] articulated two different types of social capital: bridging and bonding. *Bridging social capital* refers to the potential resources that lie within interactions with weak ties (acquaintances or "friends of friends"). These weaker contacts are more likely to hold different beliefs and have access to novel information. In one of the most famous studies on the power of weak ties, Granovetter [20] found that people were more likely to report hearing about a job opportunity from a weak tie. Individuals with a more diverse network are typically higher in bridging social capital. Close ties, on the other hand, offer different types of support, namely emotional. Close ties usually have access to similar information because they share similar experiences [34], thus close ties are more likely to hold information redundant with our own. The potential to obtain resources that are typically obtained from close relationships, such as emotional support or tangible support (e.g., money) are commonly associated with *bonding social capital*.

One question, then, is to what degree these theories of social support can be applied to online social spaces, and how, if at all, those mediated environments give rise to new forms of social support. With these concerns, hundreds of studies have documented the supportive functions of online (mediated) environments in helping develop social capital and maintain relationships. One reason is that the Internet has been proven to be able to provide heightened access to social support [30] and facilitate support from both strong and weak relational ties [43,66]. Though many of the earlier arguments on technology-mediated social support focused on whether or not it was a "rich-get-richer" type of buffering effect or if it were indeed beneficial to people who would otherwise not have the support [30,47], the dialog has moved on to understanding the supportive functions of specific online features rather than conceptualizing the Internet as a whole [49]. In particular, social network sites (SNSs) have been found to play a considerable role in both maintaining and building relationships through social support functions [4,12,36]. Even the smallest of social media behaviors—such as single clicks in response to posts—can be perceived as supportive [63] and people perceive attention from strong ties as being more supportive [6].

SOCIAL SUPPORT IN GAMES RESEARCH

There has been a growing body of research that has explored social support emerging in a particular type of mediated environment: online gaming. The majority of existing studies have mainly focused on two different genres of online gaming: fantasy-based Massive Multiplayer Online Role Playing Games (MMORPGs) such as *World of Warcraft* (*WoW*) (e.g., [40]), and casual/social games such as dancing games (e.g., [15,17]), open-ended virtual worlds (e.g., [16]), and social network games (e.g., [64,65]).

Across these different genres, the consistent finding is that shared gameplay experiences generate social capital and social support among players, both online and offline. For example, in the context of MMORPGs, scholars found that the interaction itself, which includes verbal and non-verbal communication, helps develop people's sense of social support over a long period of time [44,50,60]. Kobayashi [28] also found that increased social tolerance toward other members in an online gaming environment can be transferred to offline settings, suggesting that the social support built through the game had lasting effects that were not confined within the medium in which the interaction happened. In the context of casual/social gaming (e.g., Facebook games), Wohn [62] found that even the simplest of interactions can lead to feelings of closeness and willingness to provide tangible and emotional support both inside and outside of the game, albeit, the perception being much stronger for in-game contexts. Wohn et al. [64] also found that social network games could serve different social support functions based on the structural components of the relationship—for example, for weak ties, the games served as a way to maintain relationships by providing a topic of common ground.

In addition, many studies have confirmed that collaborative dynamics in gaming can provide both social support (e.g., emotional connections among multiple players) and strategic support (e.g., knowledge gathering and sharing, player decision-making, leadership, failure) (e.g., [1,59]). In MMORPGs, collaboration-mediated social support mainly emerges in guilds and raiding. Guilds are virtual associations run by players who are natural organizers; they usually have formalized membership and rank assignments in order to encourage participation; and they involve a complicated leader-subordinate and leader–leader relationship. And aiding are large-scale, complex group activities that involve 10-40 people working together in real time to solve extreme problems [1]. As Nardi and Harris [38, p. 152] described in their ethnographic study of *WoW*, "[m]uch of the sociable non-game-related chat takes place in the guild channel. Most is informal, humorous, or downright silly… Though such messages were brief, they provided enough information so that guild mates had a sense of others' lives." Instead of merely playing alone or observing others' behavior via public communication channels, collaboration as groups makes MMORPG players engage in a more intimate forum that allows them to attach themselves to a group, to automatically follow and better understand one another, to naturally compete with other groups, and to show how they react in tense, risky, and unclear situations [35]. Collaboration is also highly generative of belongingness [33], as well as a "trusted responsibility because allowing the wrong people into a guild can ruin its social dynamics" [38, p. 152]. During this process, players come to trust (or distrust) one another.

In more casual/social games, collaboration-mediated social support can occur in small groups or in various forms. For example, Freeman et al. [16,17] discussed emotional connections between players in collaboration in dyad (e.g., virtual marriage). Such a marriage system enforces gameplay in pairs not in groups, allowing players to construct exclusively one-to-one relationship: Once married, the game automatically ties the pair together, and collaboration in dyads not only becomes part of the instrumental gameplay but also involves self-disclosure and sharing deepest feelings – the very basis for emotional connections, intimate experiences, and various types of support.

This prior body of literature provides a picture of how online gaming can support, mediate, and facilitate social support in various ways, such as through the dynamics of collaboration or shared gaming experiences. However, eSports can be distinctive from other popular online games that have been routinely studied throughout the history of multiplayer online games as it adds multiple "layers" of complexity. First, eSports gameplay occurs in highly competitive and fast-paced virtual environments. Although competition is possible in traditional multiplayer games (e.g., MMORPGs), players usually make their own progress and have individual tasks" [41]. Yet in eSports, competition is the core for the team performance with common goals and interests. As a result, eSports gaming tends to have a higher demand for skills than traditional online gaming even when people are playing the exact same game – since skills are also closely associated with the team's fame, revenue, and reputation out of the game. For example, *Counter-Strike* players' skilled expertise [45] and *League of Legends* players' in-game and out-of-game practices to pursue competitive success [11] have attracted some research attention.

Second, due to the high demand for skills and wins, eSports players are expected to engage in intensive social interactions both online and offline. How players are engaged physically in practice and play [61] as well as their out-of-game or metagame expertise [11] have been considered key to team cohesion and high performance teamwork. For example, players tend to use an array of multimodal communication tools in gameplay for the sake of synchronous information sharing and status updating as well as group decision-making. Out of the game, players also frequently communicate with one another to help either strategize the gameplay beforehand or reflect on (un)successful team performance afterwards. In addition, players often made exerted efforts to arrange face-to-face interaction, such as social gatherings in local eSports clubs, group training/team building activities, and travel to tournaments together.

Third, the sophisticated sociocultural structure of "professionalism" is likely to make studies of eSports different (and probably more complicated) than studies of non-eSports games. In addition, professionalism in eSports does not only refer to highly skilled gameplay and strategic team management [53,57] but also emphasizes the so-called "pro culture" [53]. It explains the broader structural mechanisms that make this field distinctive -- the collaborative efforts of gaming companies, players, communities, spectators, and many other stakeholders who contribute to establishing a set of stable, widely acknowledged, and abided standards [46], and the "rebuilding, rather than blurring, the boundaries between content producers and audiences" [52, p. 293].

To what degree can our existing theories of mediated social support accommodate new phenomena/practices of social support emerging in online spaces? And to what degree can these emerging practices confirm and/or argument our existing understandings of social support? We therefore use eSports as a unique context to further investigate computer-mediated social support.

METHODOLOGY

Research Questions and Data Collection

In this study we ask the following research questions: *How, if at all, do eSports players exchange social support through their team dynamics? How do the different types of social support identified in previous literature map out in the context of eSports?*

To explore these questions, data were collected as part of a larger study that examines player experiences in eSports. After consulting with two professional eSports players, we learned that eSports players usually used Facebook groups to communicate and organize events. Therefore, we searched groups with keywords related to eSports such as *eSports*, *Dota*, *Overwatch*, *League of Legends*, or *LoL* on Facebook. Then we sent requests to join the retrieved groups and posted a message on those groups who accepted our requests (N = 12) in order to recruit players who had played eSports games as part of a team and were willing to be interviewed as voluntary participants. All players who responded to our messages and agreed to participate were interviewed. As a result, 26 semi-structured in-depth interviews were conducted via text/audio/video Skype chat by the first author based on participants' modality preferences from May to July 2016.

In each interview, 23 predefined open-ended questions regarding eSports players' gaming experiences (e.g., "*Have you ever used eSports as a way to seek friends, romance or any type of close interpersonal relationship? If so, how?*") were asked and the average length of interviews was 85 minutes. Table 1 provides details about our interview participants. It should be noted that our sample includes both professional and amateur players: six participants had engaged in professional gaming in some ways (e.g., in a colleague team playing for tournaments, contracting with a professional eSports organization, running eSports-related business, and streaming to make income) and 20 (77%) self-identified themselves as amateur players. Most participants belonged to remote teams but 21 (80.8%) of them managed to meet their teammates offline at least once.

Gender	Female: 4 (15%) Male: 22 (75%)
Age	Average: 21.5 years old Oldest: 52 years old
Location	All located in the U.S
Professional players	6 (23%)
eSports games played	*League of Legends* (*LoL*), *Dota*, *StarCraft*, *Counter Strike*, *Super Smash Bros*, *Overwatch*, *SMITE*, *Hearthstone*, *Guild Wars*, *Halo*, *World of Tanks*, and *Rocket League*
Experience in eSports	Average: 3 years (max. = 15 years)

Table 1. Interviewee demographics (N =26)

Data Analysis

An in-depth qualitative analysis was conducted to code and interpret the data. This method was used to focus on first-person and narrative accounts of players' unique perceptions and understandings of their eSports activities as well as its impacts on their social life, in order to provide rich and detailed descriptions of human experience [29].

The data analysis in this study ensued the following steps: 1) the authors closely read through players' narratives to acquire a sense of the whole picture as regards their social experiences and interpersonal relationships in eSports; 2) social support emerged as a strong series of themes; 3) the authors conducted literature review on different types of social support; 4) supportive behaviors were separated into four types based on the literature; 5) the authors identified a preliminary set of narrative themes emerging in players' social experiences and interpersonal relationships in eSports for each of the four social support categories; 6) the authors iteratively discussed findings from step three and synthesized those themes to summarize the fundamental aspects of players' social experiences and interpersonal relationships in eSports.

RESULTS

In our interviews, all participants, including both professional and amateur players, expressed that they established a certain type of close interpersonal relationships with their teammates and gained somewhat support from them over time. Especially, various game elements and technological features (e.g., the very emphasis on competition and teamwork; the wide use of in-game and out-of-game multimodal communication channels; the timely action-feedback gameplay process; and the exposure to team members all over the world with diverse backgrounds) create and afford opportunities for meaningful social support that eSports players may experience. In the following sections we discuss the four themes of social support emerging in our data based on previous literature: emotional support, informational support, instrumental support, and esteem support.

Emotional Support through Mediated Friendship and Romance

All players expressed that the emotional connections to team members, either as friendship or romantic relationship, constituted significant part of the social support they gained from teamwork. Considering their life stage (e.g., mostly college students), formation of teams, and gameplay behavior (e.g., collaboration in a highly competitive environment), friendship is a natural outcome of their eSports practices. For example, one participant described how being in a college that was far away from home motivated him to seek friends in eSports, whose very focus on teamwork and collaborative play eventually built his new social circle and made him no longer lonely:

> *I have used eSports to seek friends. Take college as an example. I went to a school 11 hours away and knew no one. Went to the LOL call out meeting and now I'm friends with a lot of those guys.* (P11, amateur, male, age 19)

For these players, social relationships outside the family started to expand through eSports teamwork, and their quality has been linked to various behavioral outcomes [19]. Their team members thus become a new type of social support: adjust to new and unfamiliar environments and satisfy their growing needs for care and attachment through friendships.

Especially, some players noted that they not only sought new friendship and emotional connections but reinforced established friendship through eSports teams. For example, "*It [Playing eSports] is what really keeps my friends together. We'd all probably stay friends if we stopped playing, but I don't think we would have gotten here without gaming.*" (P22, professional, male, age 22) In this sense, continuously engaging in teamwork with friends maintained their attachment to each other instead of drifting apart due to factors such as school, family, distance, or time.

However, while all players admitted the emergence of friendship in their teams, they pointed out that teamwork did not always mediate friendship. For them, friendship was not "sought" but "happened/emerged," though it did require a great amount of emotional investment. Therefore, friendship would only emerge under a certain conditions such as supporting each other in competitions for a long time, communicating outside of the game, and shared interest. Some even talked about how winning was less important when playing with players whom they felt connected to. A few participants have shared their stories:

> *Friendships form when hardships are endured together. That's why school and sports bond people, and why gaming communities continue to get stronger.* (P14, professional, male, age 23)

> *Most if not all of your teammates start as strangers. You do eventually become real life friends. Playing competitively together builds a strong comradery between players on the team. You'll start not knowing anything about the other members on your team but can eventually exchange other information such as social media, phone numbers, and in some cases even meet up offline.* (P17, amateur, male, age 22)

> *As for how it [our friendship] happens, it usually requires more than just playing the game together - I've only made one friend that way, and it was because we were both making Hamilton references in the entire game. An unlikely shared interest.* (P20, amateur, male, age 20)

In addition, emotional supportive words and behaviors could lead to more intimate relationships in some cases. In contrast to friendship, the idea of romance may seem odd due to the highly competitive (sometimes aggressive) nature of eSports. As one player noted, "*In my opinion, the competitive mindset and dedication to the game and your team doesn't really lend itself to those types of relationships [romantic relationships]*" (P17, amateur, male, age 22). In his opinion, eSports players' focus on comradery and commitment to the team as a unity may discourage them to develop exclusively one-to-one interpersonal relationships (e.g., romance).

Surprisingly, this does not mean that it is impossible to generate romance in eSports. Five participants described how engaging in eSports teams led to a romantic relationship with their teammates; and that such a relationship was the main source for them to feel emotionally satisfied in the team. For example:

> *I met a guy who I liked from the game. It's interesting because you come to learn the personality first.* (P15, amateur, female, age 18)

> *Interestingly enough I met my current girlfriend through one of the startup online League of Legends teams. I didn't go into it thinking I wanted to pursue a relationship with this person I just thought of it as another team I could join to play on for a while. One day I mentioned that I was going to X [a university] to visit some high school friends and she said that she was going to college there so we decided to meet up at a restaurant and we hung at together for a while afterwards. We talked about it afterwards and decided that we were both willing to give the relationship a go and we've been together for a little over 2 years now.* (P5, amateur, male, age 21)

P5's account represents a typical love story of how eSports players built romantic feelings toward their teammates: Starting as online stranger, playing together and supporting each other in competitive and stressful (game-based) scenarios, communicating both online and offline, and eventually moving to an offline relationship. In this process, eSports teams were not only places where they met each other but also a start point to know each other's personality and behavioral patterns through collaborative activities.

Yet players also warned that the intense commitment and the high demand for skills in eSports could both facilitate and destroy the feeling of romance and the affiliated emotional satisfaction:

> *I spent a lot of time with my ex [girlfriend] on League before meeting more in person. But it really helped the connection by teamwork. A lot of eSports heavily emphasize teamwork and synergy. So things can get really exciting or really scary very quickly, since you spend a lot of time working together (as a team).* (P9, amateur, male, age 19)

> *Think about what would happen if you told a couple that the only way they can survive is if they work together to kill their opponent. That sure will bond or break you quick. And I do mean break. I've seen both sides. You couldn't cooperate to win, you get frustrated, and you get angry. Skill difference in those situations is a lot of the issue. In league of legends asking a diamond league player to play with a bronze player is rough. You feel like you are babysitting. It's hard for people.* (P14, professional, male, age 23)

According to P9 and P14, the very emphasis on competition and teamwork in eSports can be a double-edged sword for developing romantic relationships: On the one hand, the highly competitive environment somewhat forced players to closely collaborate with each other in order to win, which opened opportunities for inter-dependence, familiarity, and eventually intimate interpersonal relationships such as romance. On the other hand, the emphasis on seamless teamwork in fast paced game sessions could undermine such relationships by posing high stress and frustration. Players may need to sacrifice the overall benefit for their team (e.g., win) for the benefit of their one-to-one relationship (e.g., always team with their romantic partner regardless of his/her skill levels). This can generate tensions both between the romantic partners and within all the team members.

Nevertheless, players reported that they received tremendous emotional support through their friendships and/or romantic relationships emerging in eSports. Such emotional support included trust (e.g., "*I trust that they will do their best to do their role in the game while I do my best.*" P24, professional, female, age 19), respect (e.g., "*my teammates trust and respect me even when I show weakness with emotions.*" P18, amateur, female, age 18), a feeling of belongingness (e.g., "*I honestly consider them my family. And the one big thing that binds us is that we game together.*" P22, professional, male, age 22), and a sense of inclusive and promising community (e.g., "*all we want now is to be their own big group of prominent people who are valued the same as even a sports star. The community rallies behind that ideology and it's great.*" P14, professional, male, age 23).

For many players, the emotional connections that they established in the online team can be naturally transferred to the offline life, which we will further discuss in the third section. P21 (amateur, male, age 18) summarized such transition:

> *When you are in a competitive game, your players' safety becomes very important. You put your life (in game) in danger and you trust your teammate to protect you. You can tell when they try hard to protect you. That connection transfers over to real life. "This player is willing to put his characters life in danger to protect mine" is a strong 'message' on how they treat you in real life. Basically, I see a connection between in game attitude and real life attitude.*

Informational Support: A Basis for Team Dynamics and Instrumental Support

In the context of eSports, information could be loosely interpreted as knowledge about game mechanics. This knowledge was transferred through vicarious means (e.g., viewing how others play or in-game chat) or through group discussions. Some players even consider such informational support a foundation for their team dynamics, for example:

> *Collaboration could be any form of communication to help the great good of the team such as using the ingame text chat and ping system to give teammates information. Such information can help the team to take important objectives such as tower, kills, or dragons.* (P3, amateur, male, age 20).

> *People are asking questions such as which target I should take first, they are trying to find resources, or they want to know something about the game. I usually answer their questions and give them the information they want. That's how we become a community.* (P7, amateur, female, age 52)

> *In an online tournament, we often get together in a voice chat channel before playing, sharing general information, what we know about the other teams, strategize, etc. I think those sharing and conversations is the key to our success.* (P20, amateur, male, age 20)

Another example of collaborative informational support is the discussions around player selection and management for team composition. With regard to game-related tasks, teamwork allows players to combine their avatars' combat skills and pool the capabilities of different avatar classes (e.g., different champions in *LoL*). This decreases the risk of being killed and facilitates the process of avatar advancement through group efforts. Therefore, such informational support became crucial for gathering and maintaining a high performance team. Such informational support extended outside the game as well. As a professional player described,

> *I was a manager of a professional team at one point. We wanted to add a Korean player to the team. He was extremely talented but less well-known. So we wanted to bring him to represent us and to the world stage for everyone to see. There were a lot of discussions and information sharing about how we could do this, how much it would cost, what benefits and risks were for us, and how we could communicate with the player, etc.* (P26, professional, male, age 29).

In addition, both amateur and professional players used a variety of multimodal communication tools in gameplay for the sake of synchronous information sharing and status updating as well as group decision-making under extreme time pressure. Although most games already had in-game communication features, many participants chose to use a third party application such as Skype and ooVoo. Participants also preferred those that were specifically designed for gaming or watching game streaming (e.g., Discord, Curse, and Teamspeak) due to their low latency, in-game overlay (i.e., seamless integration with the gaming environment), encrypted server to client communication, and the affordance of multiple chat channels/groups. It should also be noted that informational support does not end as exchanges of knowledge or group decision-making. Rather, it functions as a mediator or precursor that leads to other types of sharing (e.g., opinions, mentoring, and resources), which ultimately generate instrumental support.

Instrumental Support In and Out of the Gameplay

Instrumental support was related to two contexts: instrumental support within the game and outside of the game. At the very baseline, players would help them out in the game, mostly through informational support, as described in the earlier section. Players were also supportive of teammates who were seeking professional careers in eSports that extended beyond game mechanics:

> *It's a close knit group of 6 of us. We'll help each other out with pretty much anything. One of our friends is trying to go pro [professional] in a game and we're all supporting him, going to his tournaments, cheering him on, doing research for him, being his practice partner (even though we all suck), etc.* (P22, professional, male, age 22)

However, players also described that the instrumental support they received was often extended to the non-gaming contexts, which contributed to their success and achievements in various situations. For example, a few players noted how the team dynamics emerging in gameplay helped team members achieve career goals not related to games:

> *Out of game, we often help one another work on personal goals and such. I often chat with my friends about ideas I have for my business and they want me to succeed, so we talk on that.* (P8, amateur, male, age 21)

> *Me and someone that plays for the organization on the team are graphic designers. I've been a graphic designer for 5 years now and he's been one for three. We ended up getting into graphic designing together and no pun intended, collaborate making pieces of art together.* (P26, professional, male, age 29)

> *I would probably say the best example is me and our mid-laner. We are in the same major and we exchange notes multiple times and helped each other try and get through the class.* (P10, amateur, male, age 19)

According to these accounts, no matter which direction a team member wanted to pursue, his or her team members enthusiastically provided a variety of instrumental support that might not be available in their regular offline social networks, including verbal encouragements ("*cheering him on*"), company ("*going to his tournaments*" "*being his practice partner*"), working together toward a goal ("*getting into graphic designing together*"), and sharing information and resources ("*exchange notes multiple times*" "*doing research for him*"). In the team, everyone was sincerely happy to see others' success and would love to assist as much as possible both online and offline.

In addition, such a willingness to support team members could be found in almost all aspects of team members' everyday life, including the mundane. This seemed to improve the quality of their offline lives in return. For some, their eSports team members carried them through what had been some "tough times" in their lives. When they encountered life issues, their team members were there to listen, calm them down, and suggest potential solutions. For example,

> *I live with one of my team members and we clean the house together, organize our bills, etc. We have perfect trust in each other, even with stuff like finances. One of our friends was in a tough financial spot and we all pitched in to help him out; we even bought him a game we knew he wanted but obviously couldn't afford.* (P22, professional, male, age 22)

Especially, many players considered supporting team members in the offline life a "natural process." For them, teamwork in the game became "*a very immediate thing to tie you to that person. Something to talk about, something in common, something that allows you to engage in a deeper conversation.*" (P7, amateur, female, age 52) This process enabled them to know each other and establish close relationships, which allowed them to project the same expectations and demands for mutual help in the game (e.g., keep team members alive and win) as well as offline (e.g., keep team members happy and help them succeed), as P17 (amateur, male, age 22) mentioned, "*since you develop a strong friendship with your teammates it's very common to go to your team when you need advice on real world issues.*"

Esteem Support: Self-improvement through Mutual Learning

Through informational and instrumental support, players gradually achieved self-improvement not as a gamer but as a young human being (in most cases) whose personality and identity was still forming.

In our interviews, players identified a few types of learning experiences that emerged in their teamwork. For example, a few players described that how they became more considerate and caring after learning to "look out" peers and pay attention to their mental states:

> *You're looking out for your peers more. I think in a way it makes you care more because you want people to be there for you too and you understand that stuff can be difficult and it's okay to help and receive help.* (P15, professional, female, age 18)

> *We are always there for a teammate when they are feeling sad or depressed. Overall, we all just look out for each other.* (P23, amateur, male, age 18)

> *The team environment is a great environment in which the more you put in, the more you get out.* (P24, professional, female, age 19)

According to them, one of the most important experiences was to learn the fact that care was a mutual activity: in order to receive help, it was important and necessary to give help. This constituted the key to win and the very basis for trust. Especially in a highly risky and fast-paced environment, players immediately experienced the outcome of helping/not helping others. This timely action-feedback process reinforced their understanding of the significance of "taking care of others" in a team.

In addition, while some may consider committing to eSports time-consuming and addicting, players regarded their engagement as an approach to achieve better time management and self-discipline. P26 (professional, male, age 29) explained,

> *I definitely valued that experience as it taught me to become disciplined in what I do. Being good at anything takes time and dedication. This has definitely made a big contribution to what I would commit in the future. Maybe this skillset is useful for pursuing a PhD. Who knows?*

For these players, their dedication to eSports was not distinctive from commitments that were required for success in any other area. Instead, through competitive and collaborating gaming, they learned about endurance, persistence, and tolerance, which would better prepare them for completing tasks in other fields.

How did this happen? A few players pointed out that understanding team members' different cultural perspectives and "*the unique experience of suffering through a defeat*" made them grow up and become better people intellectual, mentally, and emotionally:

> *I've had opportunities to meet, talk to, and become friends with hundreds of people from all around the world and gain a very great cultural perspective. I learned a great deal about live streaming and technical skills, and was able to create things that people really enjoyed.* (P2, amateur, male, age 21)

> *I think eSports provides the unique experience of suffering through a defeat in a game. I believe it strengthens the bonds between the people on your team. I believe it provides more of an impact than other sports because of the connection and closeness of your teammates.* (P17, amateur, male, age 22)

As part of a virtual team, on the one hand, players gained technical skills with regard to how to better navigate and control the system as well as how to collaborate with others; on the other hand, throughout the gaming process, they exposed to a variety of perspectives, views, and opinions from team members with diverse backgrounds. In this way, the game became a platform where they interacted with other cultures and appreciated the cultural diversity by carrying each other through tough situations (e.g., the highly intensive competition and the frustration of being defeated). As a result, they became more open-minded, tolerant, and considerate. The following quotes well summarized how teamwork in eSports was so powerful that even shaped players' mindset over time and made them whom they were today:

> *I was a really quiet person in high school and when I brought in Melee for everyone to play I was able to connect with people through that and make friends. This completely changed my life.* (P5, amateur, male, age 21)

> *I was pretty toxic when I first started. It's like, I was never at fault for my mistakes. It was always my team's fault, haha. But over the years, I've met some very different people. Now I guess I'm more open minded and accepting. Like, mistake happens, something bad happens, that's okay. I don't really blame anybody.* (P9, amateur, male, age 19)

> *I've honestly enjoyed every second I've spent playing and even just watching. It's been a great experience and I've honestly developed a lot as a person due to eSports.* (P22, professional, male, age 22)

DISCUSSION

As a new context of online gaming that focuses on competition and as a collaborative system that requires "fast and precise interaction" [23 p. 311], eSports has been considered an emerging research area at CHI [18]. In this paper we focus on players' experiences of social interaction consequences mediated by their eSports activities. We have presented in the previous section how players experienced and interpreted four main themes of social support in their gameplay. In this section we discuss how our findings confirm or augment existing theories of mediated social support.

Intertwined Social Support

While a large body of previous literature distinguishes between the different types of social support, we found that in the context of eSports, the fact that the team-emphasized, highly competitive gaming practice was a shared goal and core task made it difficult to separate instrumental support from other types of support. For example, in the case of emotional support that led to the development of relationships (e.g., romantic ones), the exchanged instrumental support played a crucial role: Many times, this type of instrumental support was phrased as "teamwork."

To some degree, it is similar to the collaboration-mediated social support in multiplayer games that has been discussed in previous game studies. Yet it is more difficult to put support-related eSports behaviors, rather than supportive behaviors in non-eSports multiplayer games, into traditional support categories due to eSports' high demand for skills, team cohesion instead of individual achievements, win, and professional context. Therefore, instrumental support makes informational and instrumental support serve as a basis for emotional and esteem support. In this sense, it is almost as if there were a hierarchy of the different types of social support in terms of how they were developed, with instrumental and informational support serving as the starting point.

The instrumental to emotional and esteem support development is also facilitated by the fact that trust could develop quickly through reciprocity. In a "normal" situation between individuals, trust gradually develops as individuals engage in reciprocal behaviors over time. Yet the highly complex eSports activities (e.g., high performance team in a time sensitive, competitive digital environments) require equally complex support for the team efficiency/success. This unique context seems to accelerate the foundation for higher-level support functions by the frequent reciprocal interactions that occur in the game. This might be the reason why players were able to determine compatibility in a relatively easier method than non-game situations. Therefore, our qualitative results extend understandings of the role of reciprocity, as previous studies have found that reciprocity contributes to both perceived emotional and instrumental support, but is stronger with instrumental [62]. Our results suggest that over time, the instrumental could even act as a mediator toward emotional and esteem support and that even in situations where reciprocity is forced upon individuals as a function of game mechanics, this could lead to other types of more meaningful support. Future research should look more into how reciprocal interactions in game contribute to instrumental support and whether or not there are differences based on certain fixed roles of the character. For example, in some games, teams need to be composed of avatars that have different skills—it is advantageous for the team to have people with diverse abilities to win the game. In other games, however, players may be equal in terms of the abilities that their characters have. Then the question becomes: Do complementary roles naturally lend themselves to more supportive functions?

At the same time, it is unclear what would happen in situations where the instrumental support lacks reciprocity. Are people who receive more help more likely to feel instrumental support than those who give it? Again, the likelihood of offering instrumental support to others could be based on a number of different motivations, so it is difficult to unpack in the current study. Moreover, certain characters are designed to give more instrumental support to others. For example, with a "healing" type character, the main function of this character is to make sure everyone remains healthy; similarly, a "tank" character is designed to soak up damage by making themselves a human shield for other team members. These character types may be seen as more altruistic or generous with instrumental support than other types of characters that do not have functions that directly benefit other characters. Future research may also take into consideration the different roles eSports players usually play, to pick apart differences between instrumental support that is a built-in game feature or naturally emerges in gameplay because of personality or social dynamics within the team.

Especially, we found that the relationships were emergent and often the meaningful ones were those that happened organically. This sheds further light on why earlier studies have found that social capital motivations lead to players becoming offline friends, but game performance-related motivations do not [10]. Our research suggests that the transition from online to offline relationship often has nothing to do with the game itself or the instrumental support related to game mechanics—rather, it is the emotional and esteem support that facilitate the desire to meet face to face.

Face to Face Still Matters

In regards to emotional support, our findings are consistent with existing scholarship on the formation and maintenance of relationships. However, unlike much of the MMORPG scholarship, the relationships of eSports players seem to bleed more into offline relationships. This is consistent with some earlier quantitative work, which found a significant association between physical proximity and bonding social capital [55].

Given that a fair number of our participants were college students, it could be that our sample is biased because they are living on or near college campuses. It is also uncertain whether or not the physical proximity is an artifact of emotional and instrumental support, or if the inherent characteristics of eSports lend itself to desire for in-person interaction. Professional eSports teams in South Korea, for example, are known for co-habitation and living a regimented lifestyle. Is the coordination or teamwork required in eSports so satisfactory that players need to be connected physically?

This raises interesting questions about the role of physical presence in virtual teamwork, which is a very unique situation given that most studies on presence has been about the feeling of (non-physical) presence in virtual worlds [25,39].

Bridging or Bonding?

Similar to how the different types of social support were difficult to isolate, we also found that the distinction of bridging and bonding social capital was very different in the context of eSports. Traditionally, the literature suggests that bridging social capital occurs through weak ties and bonding through strong ties, but in this particular context, we found that players—especially team members—could be both weak ties and still be able to provide the type of emotional support commonly found only among strong ties.

In particular, players discussed the role of bridging social capital in the development of esteem support, by being exposed to diverse perspectives and views from people who they would otherwise not encounter in their offline world. Previous studies have shown that online gaming can help with informational support for high school students [13] because they can get novel information from adults who are not part of their offline community. Yet this research may be the one of the few documentation of esteem support development in online gaming. Given the extensive literature on harassment and trolling in online games [14,51], these examples highlight yet another dimension of the positive social influences of online gaming. However, these results should also be interpreted with caution. Most of our interview participants were young men, and thus it was difficult to tease out gender differences.

CONCLUSIONS

Drawn on previous studies of theories of relationship development and social support in both online and offline social spaces, in this study we used eSports as a unique research site to examine the different types of social support exchanged between players. We found that even though most players started out as strangers, the context of eSports facilitated situations of extremely frequent acts of helping through both tangible and intangible means within the game. Such in-game informational and instrumental support often led to more emotional and esteem support, and these different support functions not only remain within the context of the game but also "bled" out into in-person interactions and relationships. When relationships became more complex, however, players had to manage different expectations of support that accompanied different relationship roles and sometimes had to make a conscious decision between choosing a relationship as a friend or lover over a relationship as a fellow competitive gamer.

We hope that these findings can contribute to a better understanding of player experiences in highly competitive and time sensitive digital environments, the structure and dynamics of those virtual teams, and the consequences of players' social interactions in such environments, in order to design and develop interactive technologies that better serve those types of collaborative systems and players' unique social needs.

It should also be noted that our data have a few limitations. All participants were volunteers recruited from Facebook groups. There was a potential bias toward players who used social media. In addition, interviews were the primary data. Therefore, our results may be particular to a selected group of eSports players. A variety of other data sources (e.g., large-scale surveys) and a broader participant population may be needed to further validate and generalize our findings.

ACKNOWLEDGEMENTS

We thank Dean Hayes and all participants. We also thank the anonymous reviewers for their useful suggestions.

REFERENCES

1. Jeffrey Bardzell, Jeffrey Nichols, Tyler Pace, and Shaowen Bardzell. 2012. Come meet me at ulduar: Progression raiding in world of warcraft. *Proceedings of the ACM 2012 conference on Computer Supported Cooperative Work - CSCW '12*: 603–612. http://doi.org/10.1145/2145204.2145296
2. Manuel Barrera. 1986. Distinctions between social support concepts, measures, and models. *American*

Journal of Community Psychology 14, 4: 413–445. http://doi.org/10.1007/BF00922627

3. Pierre Bourdieu. 1986. The forms of capital. In *Handbook of Theory and Research for the Sociology of Education*, J. Richardson (ed.). Greenwood, NY, 241–58. Retrieved from http://www.marxists.org/reference/subject/philosophy/works/fr/bourdieu-forms-capital.htm
4. Moira Burke, Cameron Marlow, and Thomas Lento. 2010. Social network activity and social well-being. *Proceedings of the 28th international conference on Human factors in computing systems CHI 10*, ACM Press, 1909–1912. http://doi.org/10.1145/1753326.1753613
5. Benjamin Burroughs and Paul Rama. 2015. The eSports Trojan Horse: Twitch and Streaming Futures. *Journal For Virtual Worlds Research* 8, 2. http://doi.org/10.4101/JVWR.V8I2.7176
6. Caleb T. Carr, D. Yvette Wohn, and Rebecca A. Hayes. 2016. [Thumbs up emoji] as social support: Relational closeness, automaticity, and interpreting social support from paralinguistic digital affordances in social media. *Computers in Human Behavior* 62: 385–393. http://doi.org/10.1016/j.chb.2016.03.087
7. Sheldon Cohen, Benjamin Gottlieb, and Lynn G. Underwood. 2000. Social relationships and health. In *Measuring and Intervening in Social Support*, Gottlieb B Cohen S, Underwood L (ed.). Oxford University Press, New York, NY, 3–25.
8. James S. Coleman. 1988. The creation and destruction of social capital: Implications for the law. *Notre Dame Journal of Law, Ethics, & Public Policy* 375: 375–404.
9. Carolyn E. Cutrona and Daniel W. Russell. 1987. The provisions of social relationships and adaptation to stress. *Advances in Personal Relationships* 1, 1: 37–67.
10. Emese Domahidi, Ruth Festl, and Thorsten Quandt. 2014. To dwell among gamers: Investigating the relationship between social online game use and gaming-related friendships. *Computers in Human Behavior* 35: 107–115. http://doi.org/10.1016/j.chb.2014.02.023
11. Scott Donaldson. 2017. Mechanics and metagame: Exploring binary expertise in League of Legends. *Games and Culture* 12, 5: 426–444.
12. Nicole B. Ellison, Charles Steinfield, and Cliff Lampe. 2011. Connection strategies: Social capital implications of Facebook-enabled communication practices. *New Media & Society* 13, 6: 873–92. http://doi.org/10.1177/1461444810385389
13. Nicole B. Ellison, D. Y. Wohn, and C. M. Greenhow. 2014. Adolescents' visions of their future careers, educational plans, and life pathways: The role of bridging and bonding social capital experiences. *Journal of Social and Personal Relationships* 31, 4: 516–534. http://doi.org/10.1177/0265407514523546
14. Jesse Fox and Wai Yen Tang. 2016. Womens experiences with general and sexual harassment in online video games: Rumination, organizational responsiveness, withdrawal, and coping strategies. *New Media & Society*: 1–18. http://doi.org/10.1177/1461444816635778
15. Guo Freeman, Jeffrey Bardzell, and Shaowen Bardzell. 2016. Revisiting Computer-Mediated Intimacy. *Proceedings of the 2016 CHI Conference on Human Factors in Computing Systems - CHI '16*, ACM Press, 4325–4336. http://doi.org/10.1145/2858036.2858484
16. Guo Freeman, Jeffrey Bardzell, and Shaowen Bardzell. 2016. Intimate experiences in virtual worlds: The interplay among hyperpersonal communication, avatar-based systems, and experiential drives. *Proceedings of iConference*: 1–10.
17. Guo Freeman, Jeffrey Bardzell, Shaowen Bardzell, and Susan C. Herring. 2015. Simulating Marriage: Gender roles and emerging intimacy in an online game. *Proceedings of the 18th ACM Conference on Computer Supported Cooperative Work & Social Computing - CSCW '15*, ACM Press, 1191–1200. http://doi.org/10.1145/2675133.2675192
18. Guo Freeman and Donghee Yvette Wohn. 2017. eSports as an emerging research context at CHI: Diverse perspectives on definitions. *CHI Extended Abstracts*, ACM Press, 1601–1608. http://doi.org/10.1145/3027063.3053158
19. Peggy C Giordano. 2003. Relationships in Adolescence. *Annual review of sociology* 29: 257–281. http://doi.org/10.1146/annurev.soc.29.010202.100047
20. Mark S Granovetter. 1973. The strength of weak ties. *The American Journal of Sociology* 78: 1360–1380. http://doi.org/10.2307/2776392
21. Mark Griffiths. 2017. The psychosocial impact of professional gambling, professional video gaming & eSports. *Casino & Gaming International* 28: 59–63.
22. Juho Hamari and Max Sjöblom. 2015. What Is eSports and Why Do People Watch It? *Social Science Research Network*, August 2016: 1–26. http://doi.org/10.1108/IntR-04-2016-0085
23. William Hamilton, Andruid Kerne, and Jon Moeller. 2012. Pen-in-hand command: NUI for real-time strategy esports. *Proceedings of the 2012 ACM annual conference extended abstracts on Human Factors in Computing Systems Extended Abstracts - CHI EA '12*, ACM Press, 1455–1456. http://doi.org/10.1145/2212776.2212483

24. William Hamilton, Andruid Kerne, and Tom Robbins. 2012. High-performance pen + touch modality interactions. *Proceedings of the 25th annual ACM symposium on User interface software and technology - UIST '12*, ACM Press, 309. http://doi.org/10.1145/2380116.2380156

25. Carrie Heeter. 1992. Being there: The subjective experience of presence. *Presence* 1: 262–271.

26. James S. House. 1981. *Work stress asnd social support.* Addison-Wesley, Reading, MA.

27. Mehdi Kaytoue, Arlei Silva, Loïc Cerf, Wagner Meira, and Chedy Raïssi. 2012. Watch me playing, i am a professional. *Proceedings of the 21st international conference companion on World Wide Web - WWW '12 Companion*, ACM Press, 1181. http://doi.org/10.1145/2187980.2188259

28. Tetsuro Kobayashi. 2010. Bridging Social Capital in Online Communities: Heterogeneity and Social Tolerance of Online Game Players in Japan. *Human Communication Research* 36, 4: 546–569. http://doi.org/10.1111/j.1468-2958.2010.01388.x

29. Yong Ming Kow and Timothy Young. 2013. Media technologies and learning in the starcraft esport community. *Proceedings of the 2013 conference on Computer supported cooperative work - CSCW '13*, ACM Press, 387. http://doi.org/10.1145/2441776.2441821

30. Robert Kraut, Sara Kiesler, Bonka Boneva, Jonathon Cummings, Vicki Helgeson, and Anne Crawford. 2002. Internet Paradox Revisited. *Journal of Social Issues* 58, 1: 49–74. http://doi.org/10.1111/1540-4560.00248

31. Alex Leavitt, Brian C. Keegan, and Joshua Clark. 2016. Ping to Win? Non-verbal communication and team performance in multiplayer games. *Proceedings of the 2016 CHI Conference on Human Factors in Computing Systems - CHI '16*, ACM Press, 4337–4350. http://doi.org/10.1145/2858036.2858132

32. Thomas R. Lindlof and Bryan C. Taylor. 2010. *Qualitative communication research methods (3rd ed.).* SAGE, Thousand Oaks, CA.

33. Thomas M. Malaby. 2007. Contriving Constraints (The Gameness of *Second Life* and the Persistence of Scarcity). *Innovations: Technology, Governance, Globalization* 2, 3: 62–67. http://doi.org/10.1162/itgg.2007.2.3.62

34. Miller Mcpherson, Lynn Smith-Lovin, and James M Cook. 2001. Birds of a Feather: Homophily in Social Networks. *Annual Review of Sociology* 27, 1: 415–444. http://doi.org/10.1146/annurev.soc.27.1.415

35. Jack Muramatsu and Mark S. Ackerman. 1998. Computing, Social Activity, and Entertainment: A Field Study of a Game MUD. *Computer Supported Cooperative Work (CSCW)* 7, 1–2: 87–122. http://doi.org/10.1023/A:1008636204963

36. Robin L. Nabi, Abby Prestin, and Jiyeon So. 2013. Facebook friends with (health) benefits? Exploring social network site use and perceptions of social support, stress, and well-being. *Cyberpsychology, Behavior, and Social Networking* 16, 10: 721–727. http://doi.org/10.1089/cyber.2012.0521

37. Lennart E. Nacke, Anna Cox, Regan L. Mandryk, and Paul Cairns. 2016. SIGCHI Games: The scope of games and play research at CHI. *Proceedings of the 2016 CHI Conference Extended Abstracts on Human Factors in Computing Systems - CHI EA '16*, ACM Press, 1088–1091. http://doi.org/10.1145/2851581.2886438

38. Bonnie Nardi and Justin Harris. 2010. Strangers and friends: Collaborative play in World of Warcraft. *International Handbook of Internet Research*: 395–410. http://doi.org/10.1007/978-1-4020-9789-8

39. Kristine L. Nowak and Frank Biocca. 2003. The Effect of the Agency and Anthropomorphism on Users' Sense of Telepresence, Copresence, and Social Presence in Virtual Environments. *Presence: Teleoperators and Virtual Environments* 12, 5: 481–494. http://doi.org/10.1162/105474603322761289

40. Tyler Pace, Shaowen Bardzell, and Jeffrey Bardzell. 2010. The rogue in the lovely black dress. *Proceedings of the 28th international conference on Human factors in computing systems - CHI '10*, ACM Press, 233. http://doi.org/10.1145/1753326.1753361

41. Nataliia Pobiedina, Julia Neidhardt, Maria del Carmen Calatrava Moreno, Laszlo Grad-Gyenge, and Hannes Werthner. 2013. On Successful Team Formation: Statistical Analysis of a Multiplayer Online Game. *2013 IEEE 15th Conference on Business Informatics*, IEEE, 55–62. http://doi.org/10.1109/CBI.2013.17

42. Robert D. Putnam. 2001. *Bowling alone: The collapse and revival of American community.* Simon & Schuster, New York, NY.

43. Stephen A. Rains, Emily B. Peterson, and Kevin B. Wright. 2015. Communicating social support in computer-mediated contexts: A meta-analytic review of content analyses examining support messages shared online among individuals coping with illness. *Communication Monographs* 82, 4: 403–430.

44. Rabindra A. Ratan, Jae Eun Chung, Cuihua Shen, Dmitri Williams, and Marshall Scott Poole. 2010. Schmoozing and smiting: Trust, social institutions, and communication patterns in an MMOG. *Journal of Computer-Mediated Communication* 16: 93–114.

45. Stuart Reeves, Barry Brown, and Eric Laurier. 2009. Experts at play: Understanding skilled expertise. *Games and Culture* 4, 3: 205–227.

46. Yuri Seo. 2016. Professionalized consumption and identity transformations in the field of eSports. *Journal of Business Research* 69, 1: 264–272. http://doi.org/10.1016/j.jbusres.2015.07.039

47. Lindsay H. Shaw and Larry M. Gant. 2002. In Defense of the Internet: The Relationship between Internet Communication and Depression, Loneliness, Self-Esteem, and Perceived Social Support. *CyberPsychology & Behavior* 5, 2: 157–171. http://doi.org/10.1089/109493102753770552

48. Max Sjöblom and Juho Hamari. 2016. Why do people watch others play video games? An empirical study on the motivations of Twitch users. *An Empirical Study on the Motivations of Twitch Users*. http://doi.org/10.1016/j.chb.2016.10.019

49. Andrew D. Smock, Nicole B. Ellison, Cliff Lampe, and Donghee Yvette Wohn. 2011. Facebook as a toolkit: A uses and gratification approach to unbundling feature use. *Computers in Human Behavior* 27: 2322–2329. http://doi.org/10.1016/j.chb.2011.07.011

50. Constance A. Steinkuehler and Dmitri Williams. 2006. Where everyone knows your (screen) name: Online games as "third places." *Journal of Computer-Mediated Communication* 11: 885–909.

51. Wai Yen Tang and Jesse Fox. 2016. Men's harassment behavior in online video games: Personality traits and game factors. *Aggressive Behavior* 42, 6: 513–521. http://doi.org/10.1002/ab.21646

52. Nicholas Thiel Taylor. 2016. Now you're playing with the audience power: The work of watching games. *Critical Studies in Mass Communication* 33, 4: 293–307.

53. T. L. Taylor. 2012. *Raising the Stakes : E-Sports and the Professionalization of Computer Gaming*. MIT Press.

54. Peggy A Thoits. 2011. Mechanisms linking social ties and support to physical and mental health. *Journal of health and social behavior* 52, 2: 145–61. http://doi.org/10.1177/0022146510395592

55. Sabine Trepte, Leonard Reinecke, and Keno Juechems. 2012. The social side of gaming: How playing online computer games creates online and offline social support. *Computers in Human Behavior* 28(3): 832–839.

56. Bert N. Uchino, John T. Cacioppo, and Janice K. Kiecolt-Glaser. 1996. The relationship between social support and physiological processes: A review with emphasis on underlying mechanisms and implications for health. *Psychological Bulletin* 119, 3: 488–531. http://doi.org/10.1037/0033-2909.119.3.488

57. Michael G. Wagner. 2006. On the Scientific Relevance of eSports. *International Conference on Internet Computing*: 437–442. http://doi.org/10.1086/290752

58. Robert Weiss. 1974. The Provisions of Social Relationships. *Doing Unto Others*, 17–26.

59. Dmitri Williams. 2006. Why Game Studies Now? Gamers Don't Bowl Alone. *Games and Culture* 1, 13: 13–16. http://doi.org/10.1177/1555412005281774

60. Dmitri Williams, Nicolas Ducheneaut, Li Xiong, Yuanyuan Zhang, Nick Yee, and Eric Nickell. 2006. From tree house to barracks: The social life of guilds in World of Warcraft. *Games & Culture* 1: 338–361.

61. Emma Witkowski. 2012. On the digital playing field: How we "do sport" with networked computer games. *Games and Culture* 7, 5: 349–374.

62. Donghee Yvette Wohn. 2016. From Faux-Social to Pro-Social: The Mediating Role of Copresence in Developing Expectations of Social Support in a Game. *Presence: Teleoperators and Virtual Environments* 25, 1: 61–74. http://doi.org/10.1162/PRES_a_00246

63. Donghee Yvette Wohn, Caleb T. Carr, and Rebecca A. Hayes. 2016. How Affective Is a "Like"?: The Effect of Paralinguistic Digital Affordances on Perceived Social Support. *Cyberpsychology, Behavior, and Social Networking* 19, 9: 562–566. http://doi.org/10.1089/cyber.2016.0162

64. Donghee Yvette Wohn, Cliff Lampe, Rick Wash, Nicole Ellison, and Jessica Vitak. 2011. The "S" in Social Network Games: Initiating, Maintaining, and Enhancing Relationships. *2011 44th Hawaii International Conference on System Sciences*, IEEE, 1–10. http://doi.org/10.1109/HICSS.2011.400

65. Donghee Yvette Wohn and Yu-Hao Lee. 2013. Players of Facebook Games and How They Play. *Entertainment Computing* 4, 3: 178–171. http://doi.org/10.1016/j.entcom.2013.05.002

66. Kevin B. Wright and Claude H. Miller. 2010. A Measure of Weak-Tie/Strong-Tie Support Network Preference. *http://dx.doi.org/10.1080/03637751.2010.502538.*

Cooperation and Interdependence: How Multiplayer Games Increase Social Closeness

Ansgar E. Depping and Regan L. Mandryk
Department of Computer Science, University of Saskatchewan
Saskatoon, SK, S7N 5C9, Canada
{firstname.lastname}@usask.ca

ABSTRACT
Games have long been used as a bonding activity; however, research on establishing and maintaining social closeness through games uses different terms, different mechanics and controls, and different contexts of use. As a result, designers have little guidance on which multiplayer game mechanics are most effective. We summarize literature on game design for social closeness into a framework with two collaborative mechanics: cooperation and interdependence. We then created four versions of an online game to independently test the effects of these game mechanics on relationship formation between paired online strangers, showing that cooperation and interdependence are two distinct factors that both can be used to improve play experience and increase social bonds. Additionally, we unpack the effect of interdependence, showing that the improved social closeness can be explained by the increase in conversational turns.

Author Keywords
Social Play, Cooperation, Interdependence, Collaboration

ACM Classification Keywords
K.8.0 [Personal Computing]: General - Games.

INTRODUCTION
Games have long been used to support social interaction: family board game nights, tabletop gaming in board game stores, and weekly poker games among friends can help us satisfy our need for relatedness [42,43] and create shared experiences that draw us closer together. Digital games are increasingly being employed to help form and maintain social relationships, with the additional advantage of assisting distributed friends and families to maintain social connections – for example, people enhance their friendship through playing social network games [51], seniors play online poker together to stay connected [47], and kids with mobility disabilities connect through online multiplayer games [17]. The Entertainment Software Association (ESA) reports that in 2016, the majority of gamers played in multiplayer mode at least weekly because they felt that video games help them connect with friends [12]. Multiplayer co-op modes are becoming increasingly common in games [34,37] and people are playing games online with both friends and strangers [12].

Research on facilitating social closeness through games suggests that multiplayer game mechanics can be used to build or strengthen relationships in various contexts. For example, in the context of supporting people with different game preferences and abilities (e.g., grandparents playing with grandchildren), Harris et al. [16] explore asymmetric games that embrace and cater to differences between players, but maintain tightly-coupled social interactions. Investigating the context of supporting distributed work teams, Depping et al. [9] show that playing a cooperative interdependent digital game can facilitate trust formation between two strangers online. And in the context of family members with caring responsibilities, Gerling et al. [14] show that playing a motion-based game with cooperative, closely-coupled game mechanics can help caregivers bond with an older adult who has motor impairments.

Although these examples all demonstrate the benefits of multiplayer game mechanics for establishing or reinforcing social closeness, we cannot compare or contrast the advantages of the different approaches taken by the different research teams. Each project uses different terms for the multiplayer aspects (e.g., asymmetry vs. complementarity), different game mechanics and controls (e.g., a shooting mechanic in a motion-controlled game vs. a puzzle mechanic in a mouse-based game), and different contexts of use (e.g., supporting existing familial relationships vs. building new work relationships). These differences mean that game designers or researchers who wish to leverage multiplayer game mechanics to facilitate social relationships have little guidance on which mechanics or approaches to choose to implement for optimizing social closeness.

In this paper, we systematically explore how multiplayer game mechanics facilitate social closeness among dyads of strangers. First, based on a literature review of multiplayer game mechanics for relationship formation and maintenance, we establish cooperation and interdependence as two distinct multiplayer game mechanics that have been successfully employed. Second, we designed a game to investigate the efficacy of these two mechanics separately and in combination, but with all other structural elements of the game remaining

CHI PLAY '17, October 15–18, 2017, Amsterdam, Netherlands
© 2017 Association for Computing Machinery.
ACM ISBN 978-1-4503-4898-0/17/10...$15.00
https://doi.org/10.1145/3116595.3116639

consistent. Third, we conducted an experiment with dyads of strangers to determine how the mechanics affect the social relationship that results from playing together. Our results show the following:

- Collaboration and interdependence are two distinct mechanics that separately influence *game enjoyment and experienced relatedness* during play.
- Similarly, collaboration and interdependence are two distinct mechanics that separately and significantly influence the *experienced social closeness* as a result of play. Furthermore, they do not interact with each other.
- We additionally determine a primary mechanism through which interdependence works – the number of conversational turns between players fully mediated the prediction of interdependence on resulting social closeness.

Fourth, we explain our results and turn to theories of interpersonal interaction to describe why these two mechanics facilitate social closeness. And finally, we discuss the implications of our results for the design of games to establish and facilitate social closeness.

Social games have the potential to help form new relationships and strengthen existing ones. We contribute to the growing body of literature that aims to understand the potential of games to strengthen the bonds between people.

RELATED LITERATURE

We reviewed literature on the benefits of multiplayer game mechanics for establishing or reinforcing social closeness.

Scope of Literature Review

To scope the review, we were specifically interested in including previous work that satisfied three conditions:

First, the primary goal of the research should be promoting or understanding social closeness, rather than it being a secondary benefit that "came for free" along with the main goal of interest. For example, we do not include multiplayer exergames in which the goal was to leverage social pressure to improve exercise adherence (e.g., [38]), or papers in which communication is more productive when using game interfaces that support simultaneous interaction (e.g., [46]).

Second, the research should be focused on games as a tool of intervention, rather than an ethnographic study of how playing games can bring people closer together. For example, we do not include work that examines how playing online games, such as World of Warcraft, helps people make friends (e.g., [7,49]) and build social capital (e.g., [55]).

Third, the research should have either built and evaluated, or analyzed collaborative games, as opposed to other forms of technology that promote social closeness. For example, we do not include in our review work on how domestic video technologies can be used to bring families together (e.g., [26,27]), how adolescents can engage in playful activities over videochat interfaces (e.g., [53]), or how grandparents can read to their kids over a distance (e.g., [2]).

Although there are important results that we draw from each of these out-of-scope areas, our intent in the systematic review was to synthesize the literature on collaborative game mechanics that facilitate social closeness.

Goal of Literature Review

As noted in the introduction, researchers that investigate the effects of collaborative play on social closeness have implemented different mechanics with different goals and have used different terminologies. For example, Harris et al. investigated "asymmetric" game mechanics in the context of intergenerational play in the game *Beam Me 'Round, Scotty!* [15,16]. Beznosyk et al. investigate "closely-coupled" play in the context of six casual games using six different mechanics [4]. Rocha et al. identify collaborative design patterns like "complementarity" and "synergies between abilities" in an analysis of existing collaborative games [40].

Our primary goal was therefore to identify the commonalities between all of these implementations so that we could identify the abstract overarching patterns that connect the existing approaches. The three aforementioned examples might use very different mechanics in very different contexts; however, what they have in common is the goal of inducing a dependency between players. Based on our review of the literature on collaborative game mechanics and their potential to facilitate social bonds, we identified two overarching mechanics: cooperation and interdependence. In the next sections, we use these two dimensions to review existing literature on social closeness through play.

Cooperation

The most prevalent idea in the literature on collaborative play is the notion of players working towards the same goal. This stands in contrast to competitive play in which players have separate or in its most extreme, opposing goals. Rocha et al. [40] identify "shared goals" and "synergy between goals" as essential design pattern in collaborative play. The "synergy between goals" pattern acknowledges that collaboration does not necessarily mean complete cooperation. It is possible for players to simultaneously pursue individual goals (leveling up one's own character) and group goals (making sure the group wins). Zagal et al. [54] describe this phenomenon as the tension between 'individual utility' and 'group utility'. Another way of thinking about cooperation is by examining conflict. Definitions of 'games', as well as design guidelines, emphasize the important of conflict [13]. Competitive and cooperative games differ in where conflict originates. Competitive games pitch players against each other and the conflict lies between the players. In cooperative games, players team up to overcome obstacles and challenges (e.g., limited time or resources) and the conflict originates between the players and the system or other groups.

The virtue of cooperation in the context of facilitating social bonds seems obvious and a matter or common sense and is often included in design frameworks [3,19]. It is therefore not surprising that every study we reviewed implicitly assumes cooperation to be the superior mechanic for facilitating social bonds. Seif El-Nasr et al. [45] investigated cooperative games like *Little Big Planet* or *Rock Band 2* to identify cooperative performance metrics. Depping et al. [9] investigated the trust facilitating properties of a cooperative puzzle game in the context of distributed teams. A number of cooperative 3D environment puzzle games have been found to effectively promote team building [6,11,30]. In the game *Operation Sting*, players share the goal of successfully performing a heist together [35,36]. Researchers found the game to have a positive effect on the social fabric of the group [35,36]. Only one study investigating the effect of a collaborative game on the players' perception of each other actually built a competitive version of the game [8]. Unfortunately, a direct comparison between cooperation and competition was not reported. The authors do, however, suggest that competition diminishes the extent to which players relate game outcomes to liking for their partner in a game [8].

The idea that games should be cooperative if they are to facilitate social closeness appears to be an assumption made by researchers and designers. Unfortunately, there has not been a direct comparison between cooperation and competition regarding their individual effects on the social bonds formed through play. Furthermore, cooperation has almost always been implemented in combination with interdependence. Without an investigation of cooperation separately from interdependence, we can only make assumptions about the effectiveness of either mechanic.

Interdependence

The second theme that emerges in the literature on collaborative play is focused on the level of dependence between players. Interdependence is a term from psychological frameworks on social and group interactions and is commonly defined as the 'degree to which group members must rely on one another to perform their task effectively' [44]. In the context of games, the 'task' can be viewed as the goal players want to achieve within the game. Rocha et al. [40] identify six design patterns in their analysis of popular collaborative games. As already discussed, 'shared goals' and 'synergies between goals' are mechanics emphasizing cooperation. The other four design patterns are: 'complementarity' (specific to roles in the game), 'synergies between abilities', 'abilities that can only be used on another player' and 'special rules for players of the same team.' All of these patterns describe game mechanics that induce dependency, i.e., a need to rely on and interact with the other players [40]. Similarly, in their analysis of the collaborative board game *Lord of the Rings*, Zagal et al. [54] suggest that 'a collaborative game should bestow different abilities or responsibilities upon the players', emphasizing the importance of interdependent play. Beznosyk et al. [4] distinguish 'closely-coupled' from 'loosely-coupled' casual games and find that closely-coupled games rated higher overall in engagement. Unfortunately, they compare different games with each other, making it hard to distinguish what effects are due to the game and what effects are due to interdependence. Their results suggest however, that interdependence has a positive effect on player experience.

In the game *Zoom* [6], each player received one picture they had to describe to the others; the group then had to arrange the order to create a coherent story. The game utilized complementary knowledge to induce dependence between the players. Findings suggested that the game was a viable tool for team building [6]. Similarly, Ellis et al. [11] designed the games *Castle Builder* and the *Tower of Babble*, which each utilized complementary knowledge in a different way. In *Castle Builder*, only a few players were familiar with the blueprint of the castle that was supposed to be built. In the *Tower of Babble*, players were required to utilize perspectives of different viewpoints to ensure the tower was being built straight. In all of these games players were bound to interact because each member had a piece of information that was required to complete the task. All of these games appeared to have positive effects on the social fabric between the players. Nasir et al. [35,36] created a game called *Operation Sting* to facilitate team building. Players each had the same knowledge, however, the actions they were able to perform were different for each player, giving them complementary roles (e.g., thief, hacker). Also utilizing complementary roles, Harris et al. [15] created the game *Beam Me 'Round, Scotty!*, a game utilizing "asymmetric" game mechanics inducing interdependence between players. The experimental design does not compare high interdependence to low interdependence; however, the participants' quotes suggest a positive impact of the interdependence that was experienced. Gerling et al. built two interdependent games to explore social play as an opportunity to connect caregiving dyads [14]. They found that dependence between players appeared to foster communication between the players.

Each of these studies used different games, mechanics and contexts to implement interdependence. The findings suggest, however, that a dependence between players and a necessity to interact and communicate could potentially facilitate social closeness. While these results seem promising, we do not know how high interdependence compares to low interdependence or how it affects social closeness when it is not confounded with cooperation.

Summary of Systematic Review

Although these examples suggest that cooperation and interdependence can promote social closeness, we cannot compare or contrast the advantages of both mechanics. While we have a rich understanding of different methods and contexts in which playing together facilitates social bonds, we have little guidance on the effects of the underlying mechanics. If we want our academic knowledge of collaborative games to effectively inform game design, we need to understand the different elements that make games so effective at reinforcing relationships. In previous studies, cooperation and interdependence have been implemented together. How the two mechanics affect relationships individually is yet unclear. Previous studies have also not systematically evaluated how the mechanics affect social bonds. Are the relationships formed through cooperation different from the relationships formed through competition? Finally, we have no knowledge about how the two mechanics interact. Common wisdom might suggest that both mechanics have to occur together in order to facilitate social closeness. Psychological theories on group work would even suggest that interdependence in combination with competition would elicit hostilities and distrust [23,24]. For game designers to be able to make informed design choices based on research, we need to look beyond the blanket term 'collaboration' and systematically disentangle and evaluate the underlying forces of collaborative play.

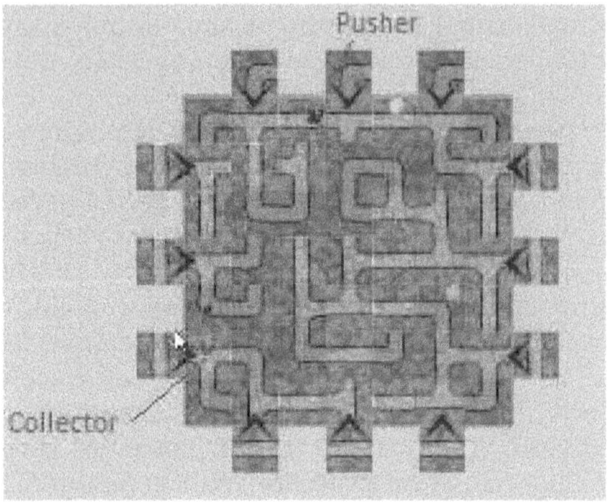

Figure 1. Labyrinth game board (cooperative, interdependent)

EXPERIMENT

We conducted an experiment to evaluate how cooperation (vs. competition) and interdependence (vs. independence) affect how players perceive the game and each other.

Game Design

We created a game in which both collaborative factors, i.e. cooperation and interdependence, could be varied independently. This resulted in a two-by-two matrix: crossing competition or cooperation with independence or interdependence resulted in four different games. In our design process, we ensured that all other structural elements of the game were identical, and that only the two game mechanics were manipulated. In the following sections, we will first describe the general design of the game, and then describe the implementation of the four versions.

Labyrinth Game

We created the game called *Labyrinth*: a networked, 2-player puzzle game implemented with the Unity Game Engine, based on a German board game of the same name. The game is a top-down 2D board-style game. The game board is comprised of tiles and the configuration of the tiles creates paths through the maze. The players control 2D avatar sprites that they can move along the paths using the arrow keys. The goal is to reach and collect gems that are positioned on the paths of the maze. The game is structured in individual puzzle 'sets'. A set starts with both players and one gem spawning in specific locations. A set lasts for a fixed period of time during which the players have to collect the gem (the set duration is different between the four versions for balancing purposes). Once the set time is up, a new set is loaded with new starting positions. If a gem is not reachable with the current configuration of the maze, the players can push rows and columns to reconfigure the maze and open new paths. Players change the maze by pressing the spacebar and walking against the wall they want to push. After a wall is pushed, the players have to wait until the wall automatically moves back to its original position before they can push another wall.

Before the multiplayer game, players completed an interactive single-player tutorial that took approximately three minutes. The tutorial used written instructions to present the rules of movement and wall pushing. Players could only progress to the multi-player experiment versions once they completed the tutorial.

Interdependence

In order to operationalize dependency or lack thereof between the players, we used two strategies: complementary roles and separate board games. Complementary roles meant that one player was only able to move walls but not collect (the '*pusher*') while the other player was only able to collect gems but not push (the '*collector*'), leading to a high level of dependency in the interdependent versions of the game. In the independent game version, each player could use both abilities. To further avoid any effect one player might have on the other player's game experience we had them play on two separate game boards in the independent games.

Cooperation

We induced cooperation by manipulating the goal of players. In the cooperative conditions, players were instructed to work together to maximize the gems they collected as a team. To reinforce this, we presented the final team score. Depending on their score, they received a crown (bronze, silver, gold, or diamond), emphasizing the struggle of the players against the game system. In the competitive conditions, players were informed that they were rivals and were to compete for the gems. To reinforce this, their scores were presented individually and the winner received a golden crown after the game, emphasizing comparison.

Game Versions

These variations resulted in four versions of the game (see video figure for audio-visual explanation):

Cooperative and Interdependent

Both players were positioned on the same game board. One was the pusher and the other was the collector. Together, they had to try to collect as many gems as possible. Each set consisted of a gem that was not reachable without pushing at least one wall; the most difficult sets required three wall pushes to reach the gem. The difficulty of the sets increased over time. The final score was the number of gems collected.

Competitive and Interdependent

Both players were positioned on the same game board. One was the pusher and the other was the collector. The collector was instructed to collect as many gems as possible. The pusher was instructed to prevent the collector from doing so. The gems were positioned in a way that made them reachable for the collector without any wall pushes. The pusher was spawned in a position that made it possible for them to rearrange the maze so that the collector's path was blocked. The collector's score was based on the number of gems they collected. The pusher's score was based on the number of gems they prevented the collector from reaching before the set timed out and a new set was loaded. A winner was declared at the end.

Cooperative and Independent

Both players solved the same maze configuration; however, they were positioned on individual game boards. Both players were capable of pushing and collecting. Players were instructed to collect as many gems as possible as a team. The final score was the sum of both players' scores.

Competitive and Independent

Both players solved the same maze configurations; however, they were positioned on individual game boards. Both players were capable of pushing and collecting. Players were instructed to collect more gems than their rival. Their final scores were compared to declare a winner.

In all versions, participants played two rounds of 5 minutes each (10 total minutes of gameplay). In the conditions with asymmetric roles, they switched roles in the second round to ensure that both players had experience with both roles. During gameplay, partners were connected over voice chat.

Measures

All responses were measured on a 7-point-Likert scale.

Interpersonal trust: Social closeness or the quality of a relationship has been measured in a variety of different ways. In the context of computer-mediated relationships, some research measures 'liking' [8,23] to describe the depth and quality of the relationship. However, the predominant construct that has reliably and authentically characterized social relationships in this context has been interpersonal trust [9,22,25,28,39,41]. To measure trust, we adopted a scale that was previously used in the context of brief initial encounters [9]. The scale consisted of 11 items that were derived from the Rempel trust scale [39] (e.g., *"I could count on my partner to be concerned about my welfare."*), the Dyadic Trust scale [28] (e.g., *"I feel that my partner can be counted on to help me."*), and the Specific Interpersonal Trust Scale [25] (e.g., *"I could expect my partner to tell the truth."*). As with previous research [9], the scale was an internally consistent measurement of trust (Cronbach's α=.922, M=5.46, SD=.93).

Intrinsic Motivation Inventory (IMI): To quantify the play experience, we measure interest/enjoyment, invested effort and pressure/tension using the IMI [32].

Player Experience of Needs Satisfaction (PENS): We used the PENS scale, which measures need satisfaction of competence, autonomy and relatedness in-game. We also measured intuitiveness of controls [43].

Conversational turns: We quantified how responsive or involved the participants were with each other by calculating the number of conversational turns in the speech signal based on the audio that we recorded during play (M=28.69, SD=19.35). Each change in who is talking is considered a turn in the conversation.

Propensity to trust: We measured general propensity to trust (trait) as proposed by Yamagichi [52]. The 6-item questionnaire asks participants to rate statements such as *"Most people are basically honest."*

Participants

The study was deployed on Amazon's Mechanical Turk (MTurk) crowdsourcing platform. MTurk connects paid workers to *Human Intelligence Tasks* (HITs) and has been shown to be a reliable research tool [31]. We recruited 138 participants, who received $3 for the 20 min study. Ethical approval was obtained from the behavioral research ethics board of our university, and participants were asked to give informed consent. To comply with ethical guidelines, the task was only made available to workers older than 18.

Procedure

We first presented participants with information about what was expected of them (a working microphone and the willingness to interact with another person for 10 uninterrupted minutes). They then completed the consent form and demographics and propensity to trust. Subsequently they performed the tutorial in which they learned the basic gameplay. Once they completed the tutorial, they progressed to matchmaking in which they were assigned a partner and then randomly assigned to a condition. They were connected over voice chat to their partner for the duration of the game. After 10 minutes of gameplay, they completed the PENS, IMI, and trust scales. Finally, there was a debriefing and an opportunity to leave comments.

Data Analyses

All analyses were performed with SPSS 24. We identified noncompliant participants based on two criteria and removed them from subsequent analysis. First we went through the comments in the debrief and the audio recordings to check if they actually had a working microphone and removed the ones who did not (N=14). Second, we checked for careless responses in the questionnaires using a response-time threshold. We removed participants who completed three or more questionnaires with an average time per item of less than 1.5 seconds (N=19). Our final dataset consisted of 105 participants. Our phonetic analysis of conversational turns required high sound quality. Despite microphone checks and careful instruction, in some cases the sound quality was not high enough to be accurately analyzed. For the analysis including conversational turns, we excluded an additional 39 participants due to poor sound; this left 66 participants for analyses involving conversational turns.

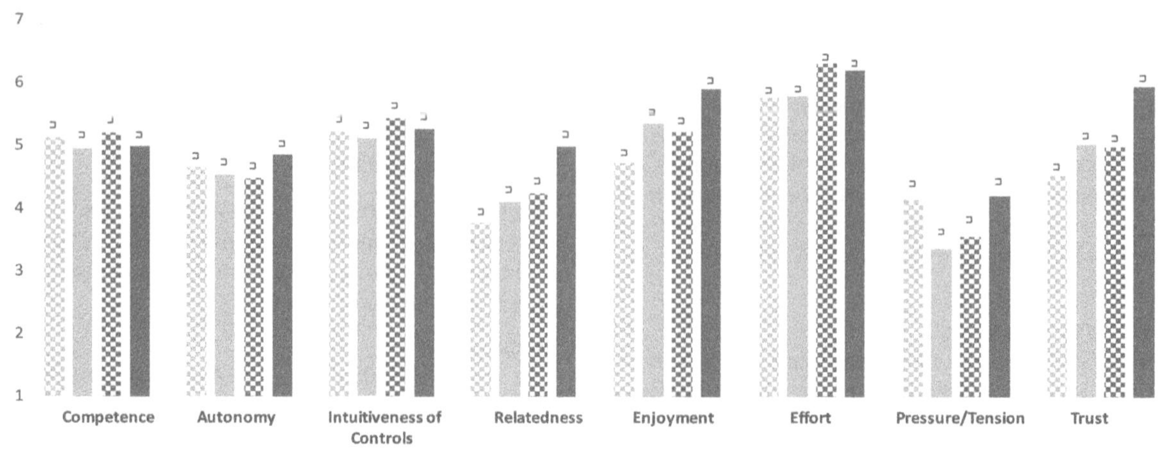

Figure 2. Means and standard errors for outcome variables. (light blue)=competition, ■(dark blue)=cooperation; (pattern)=independent, ■ (solid)=interdependent (e.g., = Cooperative and Independent).

Group vs. Individual Variables

Although our survey items were completed by individual participants, their individual ratings are subject to the experience of being in a dyad with another participant. For statistical analyses, it is important to determine whether the participants can be treated as independent cases. We conducted an inter-rater agreement (IRA) analysis [29]. The IRA was assessed using the r_{WG} index, which defines agreement in terms of the proportional reduction in error variance. It compares the observed variance on a variable over the group members to the variance drawn from a theoretical null distribution that represents complete lack of agreement [29]. We computed the multi-item r_{WG} index over all relevant constructs. Our r_{WG} index (M= .60, se= .06) was below the recommended threshold for group aggregation (.72). We therefore proceeded treating our psychometric measurements (i.e., surveys) as individual variables. Excluded from this analysis were conversational turns, which were inherently measured on a group level.

Propensity to Trust

Literature on trust formation has long acknowledged that a large factor in trust formation is someone's general propensity to trust [41,52]. To control for this, we used the participants' propensity to trust as a covariate in all subsequent models that use trust as an outcome.

RESULTS

We explore the independent and joint effects of cooperation and interdependence by answering two questions: First, do the two mechanics affect how players experience the game? Second, how do the two mechanics affect the relationship between players outside of the game?

A two-way analysis of variance with two between-subjects factors (cooperation/competition and independence/inter-dependence) was conducted to investigate the main effects and interaction of cooperation and interdependence on the dependent measures (see Figure 2). This analysis allowed us to investigate the distinct main effects of cooperation and interdependence as well as their interaction.

Player Experience

Are the games structurally similar?

The different versions of the labyrinth game employed different mechanics that changed the gameplay significantly. The changes were designed to manipulate the multi-player experience; however, we intended our manipulation to be as equal as possible to avoid confounding factors. To ensure our manipulations did not systematically vary in overall difficulty or the difficulty of the control scheme, we investigated the effect of our manipulations on the perceived competence and autonomy of players and on the intuitiveness of controls.

For perceived competence, we did not observe any significant main effects of cooperation ($F_{1,101}$=.05, p=ns, η^2=.00) or interdependence ($F_{1,101}$=.58, p=ns, η^2=.00). Neither was the interaction of the two mechanics significant ($F_{1,101}$=.00, p=ns, η^2=.00). Similarly, autonomy was not affected by cooperation ($F_{1,101}$=.08, p=ns, η^2=.00), interdependence ($F_{1,101}$=.32, p=ns, η^2=.00), or the interaction of the two mechanics ($F_{1,101}$=1.05, p=ns, η^2=.01). Finally, intuitiveness of control was also not affected by cooperation ($F_{1,101}$=.56, p=ns, η^2=.01), interdependence ($F_{1,101}$=.34, p=ns, η^2=.00), or the interaction of both mechanics ($F_{1,101}$=.01, p=ns, η^2=.00).

Based on these results, we can assume that there were no inadvertent differences in the perceived competence, autonomy, or the difficulty of the control scheme.

How were the remaining aspects of player experience affected by cooperation and interdependence?

First we investigated differences in how related the players felt during the game. The ANOVA revealed significant main effects for cooperation ($F_{1,101}$=7.08, p=.01, η^2=.07) and interdependence ($F_{1,101}$=4.19, p=.04, η^2=.04) on experienced in-game relatedness. Both mechanics increase scores in relatedness but do not interact ($F_{1,101}$=1.19, p=ns, η^2=.01).

We also investigated the effect the two mechanics have on enjoyment. Similar to relatedness, there are significant main effects for cooperation ($F_{1,101}$=4.92, p=.03, η^2=.05) and interdependence ($F_{1,101}$=8.19, p<.01, η^2=.08) on enjoyment. Both cooperation and interdependence increase the enjoyment of the game. The two mechanics do not interact in their effect on enjoyment ($F_{1,101}$=.10, p=ns, η^2=.00).

The significant main effects and the lack of interactions indicate that cooperation and interdependence are two distinct mechanics. Both appear to increase experienced relatedness and enjoyment.

We observe a significant main effect on invested effort for cooperation ($F_{1,101}$=4.33, p=.01, η^2=.06); however, there was no main effect of interdependence ($F_{1,101}$=.28, p=ns, η^2=.00). Cooperation increased invested effort over competition. The interaction of the two mechanics is also not significant ($F_{1,101}$=.68, p=ns, η^2=.01).

There were no main effects of cooperation ($F_{1,101}$=.16, p=ns, η^2=.00) or interdependence ($F_{1,101}$=.46, p=ns, η^2=.00) on experienced tension. The interaction term, however, is significant ($F_{1,101}$=5.21, p=.02, η^2=.05); the effect of interdependence on tension appears to depend on whether the players are competing or cooperating. When competing, interdependence decreases perceived tension. When cooperating, interdependence increases perceived tension.

Relationship between Players

We were most interested in how the two mechanics affect the feelings of closeness and rapport that developed between the players as a result of gameplay.

Similar to enjoyment and relatedness, we can observe two distinct main effects of cooperation ($F_{1,101}$=.12.00, p<.01, η^2=.11) and interdependence ($F_{1,101}$=13.47, p<.01, η^2=.12) on interpersonal trust after gameplay. Cooperation facilitated trust development better than competition and interdependence facilitated trust better than independence. Furthermore, there was no significant interaction between cooperation and interdependence ($F_{1,101}$=2.32, p=ns, η^2=.02).

These findings further suggest that cooperation and interdependence are two distinct game mechanics that both influence the relationship individually and do not interact.

Unpacking the Effect of Interdependence

As explained previously, interdependence is likely to affect social bonds due to the increase in interaction and communication between the agents involved. Our ANOVA results support the idea that interdependence increases trust development between the players. Theory suggests that this relationship facilitation can be explained by the degree of interaction between the players during the game.

To explore this idea, we performed a mediated regression analysis using the Process macro [18] in which we investigated whether the prediction of interdependence on trust is mediated by the number of conversational turns (controlling for an individual's propensity to trust). The regression revealed that interdependence significantly predicted the number of conversational turns (b=25.75, SE=3.005, p<.001), explaining 52% of the variance and also directly predicted trust (b=.544, SE=.227, p=.020). Conversational turns also directly predicted trust (b=.021, SE=.010, p=.038). Furthermore, when conversational turns were included in the model, interdependence was no longer a predictor of trust (b=-.017, SE=.353, p=.961), consistent with a full mediation. The indirect effect was tested using the bootstrap estimation approach with 10000 samples [18], revealing that conversational turns significantly mediated the prediction of interdependence on trust (b=.561, SE=.274, 95% CI=.1043, 1.1439). Approximately 20% of the variance in trust was explained by all predictors (R-sq= .20, including general propensity to trust).

There is no theoretical reason to assume that the number of conversational turns would mediate the effect of cooperation on trust as the theoretical underpinnings of cooperation as an effective game mechanic relate to shared goals and establishing an in-group effect (i.e., us against the game). A mediated regression supports this. Cooperation predicts trust (b=.697, SE=.231, p=.004), but not conversational turns (b=4.44, SE=4.48, p=.325). Furthermore, when the number of conversational turns is included in the model, the effect of cooperation on trust is still significant (b=.612, SE=.210, p=.005, 95% CI=.1915, 1.03).

DISCUSSION

In this section, we summarize our results, provide some theoretical background for our findings, and discuss design implications, limitations and future directions.

Summary of Results

Our results demonstrate that cooperation and interdependence each affect the relationship between players. First we established comparability between the four versions of the game. The four different versions of our game were identical in terms of the dramatic elements and visual design; we further established that the players' perceived competence, autonomy, and intuitiveness of controls did not differ between versions. Ensuring these similarities between the game versions allows us to more confidently attribute our results to the manipulations of cooperation and interdependence. Second, we reveal how cooperation and interdependence affect different aspects of player experience. As expected, both collaborative mechanics appear to increase the relatedness that players experience during the game. Similarly, both cooperating and interdependence increase game enjoyment. When considering the invested effort and the perceived tension, the two mechanics appear to have different effects. The effort players invest into the game increased when they were cooperating compared to competing. Sharing a goal with another player appears to be a key motivator to engage with the game. Interdependence between players seems to have no effect on the effort invested by players. Cooperation can also induce tension and pressure; however, only when the game is also interdependent. When players' actions do not affect each other (low interdependence), cooperating decreases the perceived tension. Third we confirm that cooperation (vs. competition) and interdependence (vs. independence) affect the relationship between players outside of the game. Similar to relatedness and enjoyment, we observe both mechanics separately affecting the interpersonal trust that developed between players. Informed by theory, we further offer a model as to how interdependence facilitates the relationship between players. As proposed by previous work, interdependent tasks increase the need for communication [10,9,23,24] and previous work in psychology has hypothesized that this increase in interaction between group members would be responsible for stronger social bonds between the group [5,21,22,24,41]. Our results confirm this hypothesis. The influence that interdependence has on interpersonal trust is fully explained by the increased number of conversational turns between the players.

Disentangling Collaborative Mechanics

Previous research has only implemented cooperation and interdependence together. This approach was enough to illustrate the potential of games to enhance social relationships. For game developers to make informed design choices, however, we need a more detailed understanding of how these different parts make collaborative games effective at establishing and reinforcing relationships. We need to look underneath the broad category of "collaboration" and start teasing out the underlying mechanics of social play. Our study is the first to disentangle two major mechanics and investigate them as separate properties of a collaborative game. We successfully demonstrate that cooperation and interdependence are in fact two separate forces shaping the players' perception of the game as well as the relationship that develops with their fellow players.

A Systematic Comparison

Looking back at existing literature, it becomes evident how much we already know about collaborative play. We have an understanding of which mechanics successful multiplayer games utilize [40,54]. Findings suggest that collaborative games can reinforce relationships between work colleagues [6,11,30], caregiver and caretakers [14], or family members of different generations [16]. What we still lack are systematic evaluations of the mechanisms that we believe are driving the beneficial effects of games on relationships. Our study systematically compares cooperation with competition as well as interdependence with independence within an otherwise identical game. This allowed us to make assertions about how strongly each mechanic influences different outcomes. What we observe is that both mechanics have medium-sized effects on the perceived relatedness, enjoyment and tension. The invested effort in the game is only affected by shared goals, but also with a medium effect size. Regarding the relationship between the players, we observe that both mechanics exhibit large effects on interpersonal trust.

The Additive Model of Collaborative Play

Our experimental approach allowed us to also investigate how the two mechanics interact with each other. As cooperative and interdependent play have so far only been implemented together, we had no knowledge about if and how the two mechanics influence each other. One reason why these two mechanics are always used together might be the idea that a dependence between players is only conducive to their relationship if they are on the same team, working towards the same goal. Social interdependence theory [24], for example, proposes that interdependence in combination with competition would lead to oppositional, negative interaction resulting in conflict and distrust. Or perhaps researchers have only used the two mechanics in tandem because they thought that the two mechanics would amplify each other's effect on social bonds if they occurred together. These models of thinking about the inner workings of collaborative play represent ideas of interactions between the two mechanics. These models, however, have never been investigated in the context of games. Our study addresses this lack of knowledge by giving evidence in support of an additive model. Our findings support the notion that cooperating and being dependent on the other player are two separate mechanics that do not interact, but instead each provide their own influence on how players experience the game and each other. Our results indicate that both individual effects are additive, leaving the cooperation plus interdependence condition to be the most effective at facilitating social closeness. Only the effect on the perceived tension/ pressure appears to adhere to a conditional model.

Theories of Interpersonal Interaction

In the following section, we look to psychological theories offering explanations as to why cooperation and interdependence in games facilitate social closeness.

Cooperation in Theory: The argument that working towards the same goal will facilitate social bonds is most commonly justified using Social Identity Theory (e.g., [11]), which argues that a large part of a person's self-concept is based on group membership [48]. As an individual can potentially identify with many different groups, an important concept within Social Identity Theory is *group saliency* [19]. When a group membership is more salient to the individual, they will likely identify more strongly with that group. Findings suggest that group saliency can be induced by a minimal set of identifiers–even randomly assigning people to a group can elicit group identification [19]. A game that pits the players together against another team or the system could therefore already be enough to create a sense of group membership reinforced by conflict, i.e., 'us vs. them'. Greater identification with a group has been linked to greater trust and cohesion among group members [1], greater individual contribution to the goals of the group [1], and increased group productivity [19].

Interdependence in Theory: The concept of task interdependence comes from psychological frameworks on group work and is usually described as the 'degree to which group members must rely on one another to perform their task effectively' [44]. Regarding the formation of trust in relationships, psychological research supports the idea that task interdependence is a requirement. Trust towards another person is only required if that person's actions affect the trustor. A person is only vulnerable to a partner if they can be potentially hurt or helped by that person. Therefore, a context of interdependence is helpful, and perhaps even necessary for two people to build a trusting relationship [41,23]. According to Social Interdependence Theory [24], if a group or dyad performs a task that is high in interdependence, their need to interact and engage with each other increases. This increased interaction and communication between group members is believed to reinforce the formation and maintenance of social relationships. Interestingly the assumption that interdependence in competitive settings would diminish social closeness was not confirmed in our study. Our results suggest that even in competition, interdependence increases relatedness, enjoyment, and interpersonal trust.

Implications for Design

Given what we have learned from our results, and the psychological theory that explains the findings, we can derive some design implications for social games with the goal to facilitate relatedness, enjoyment, and the relationship between players.

Maximizing Cooperation

Our results show that sharing a goal with the other players affects the game positively. Building on social identity theory, we can further recommend that cooperative game mechanics should be designed with group identification in mind. Designs could maximize group saliency by emphasizing group identity. In-group identification can be enhanced by pitting the in-group against an outside force, such as a challenging system or another group. Many multiplayer games have been successfully using group membership as a tool to emphasize cooperation as a game mechanic. *World of Warcraft* (WoW) introduced two factions, creating strong in-group identification (e.g. “For the Horde!”) and a clear enemy faction that players are pitched against in PvP games and ranking systems within WoW. A similar faction system was used in *Pokémon Go*. While there is little interdependence between fellow players in the same team (e.g. team Mystic), game designers used team colors, symbols, and unique Pokémon to create a sense of belonging to one particular group.

So far we have only discussed fully assured cooperation in which goals were pre-set as fully shared. In some games, however, players pursue multiple goals that might conflict. A support character in a MOBA game like *League of Legends* for example, is pursuing the individual goal to level up their own character. Their group goal, however, is to support other characters, which can result in fewer resources for them. As mentioned previously, Zagal et al. [54] describes this as the tension between individual utility and group utility. These scenarios add a level of uncertainty as the players cannot know whether the other players will act in their own best interest or what is best for the group. This uncertainty could hurt the social facilitation through the game or it could form even stronger bonds as cooperation is now a choice and thereby perceived as more meaningful. Our study has only investigated the effect of full cooperation. How conflicting goals affect the relationship between players remains to be investigated.

Maximizing Interdependence

Based on our results, we can conclude that a high level of dependency is a desirable property of a game if the goal is to strengthen the social bonds between players. We can furthermore suggest that any mechanic implemented to induce dependency between players (e.g., synergies between abilities, complementary knowledge) should be in service of increasing interaction between players. In this study, we used voice chat as a communication channel and operationalized ‘interaction’ through conversational turns. While our system configuration yielded very positive results, many games might not offer that communication channel to their players. Other games offer different means of interaction such as text chat or low bandwidth signals that signify simple massages like, for example, ‘help’, ‘danger’ or ‘missing enemy’ (as is implemented in *League of Legends)*. Research has even suggested that in-game actions can be interpreted as conversational turns [33]. Any mechanic that induces interdependence challenges the players to effectively coordinate and communicate. As a design guideline, we can recommend that any implementation of interdependence should be accompanied by a way for players to successfully send, receive and adequately interpret other players’ signals. The communication channel has to allow for signals that are rich enough in information that players can effectively overcome the coordination challenges that the game poses.

Frameworks from literature on work and organizational psychology distinguish different kinds of interdependence [23,44,50] – specifically, task interdependence and outcome interdependence [50]. Johnson and Johnson [23] define *task interdependence* as the necessity for each member to take action for other members to do any part of their work. In contrast, *outcome interdependence* is defined as the degree to which the outcomes an individual receives depend on the performance of others [23]. As outcome interdependence does not actually require interaction during the task, we would recommend implementing task interdependence. In games, this means that the dependence between players should not be an addition of scores or damage or any other resource in the game, but be derived from a need to coordinate and interact during play.

Working with Restrictions

Ideally a game should employ both mechanics in pursuit of strengthening the social bonds between players. However, some games have core mechanics that are incompatible with some of our recommendations. Some games might be inherently competitive and shared goals as a design option is unavailable. Online chess, for example, or multiplayer tower defense games are inherently zero sum paradigms that pit players against each other. Our results suggest that even competitive games can still reinforce relationships through interdependence. Other games might be entirely optimized for individual play independent of other people’s influence or cooperation. *Clash of Clans* for example, is an interesting example of an inherently single player game that still successfully generates strong bonds between their players. The core game elements of building your village and raiding other villages are competitive and independent in nature. Game designers implemented clan membership, and clan-specific success metrics and leaderboards to induce group identification and an "us vs them" mentality. Game designers also created interesting ways to induce interdependence. Because the core game elements were asynchronous and optimized for a single-player experience, game designers opted for outcome interdependence. In 'Clan Wars' (battles between two clans), individual performances were added up to clan-specific performance metrics. Clan wars also induced a need for coordination, as attack strategies have to be discussed. Another mechanic they introduced was a reinforcement system. Other clan members can send reinforcements that support the single players in their raids. These design choices are all peripheral additions that do not fundamentally change the game. They rather leverage the psychological mechanics that underlie the benefits of cooperation and interdependence (group identification, increased interaction), without actually requiring the development of a fully cooperative and interdependent game.

Limitations and Future Work

Although our findings provide insights into multiplayer game mechanics for facilitating social closeness, we acknowledge the limitations of this work.

First, we only tested our results using one specific puzzle game. Comparing our conditions in an otherwise identical game was necessary for our research questions. How well our findings translate into game genres like platformers, first-person shooters, or even board games remains unclear. The psychological frameworks would suggest that dynamics like group identification and increased interaction would have similar effects regardless of genre; however, future research should investigate if our findings hold in different genres.

Second, we only tested with a specific set of mechanics. While we believe that these mechanics are valid representations of cooperation and interdependence, we cannot exclude the possibility that other mechanics inducing cooperation and interdependence might have led to different results.

Third, we focused on establishing a new relationship between two strangers in a brief game interaction. How the results extend to relationship maintenance or to establishing relationships that are intended to be deeper (e.g., longer term) or of a different nature (e.g., romantic) is still speculative.

Fourth, we examined dyads. Extending the findings to groups would provide value for the field.

Fifth, it is important to acknowledge that cooperation and interdependence are most likely not the only game elements that facilitate social closeness. Based on theory and the predominant themes discussed in the game literature, however, we found them to be the most prevalent. Future research should further identify mechanics that can bring players closer together.

Finally, our experimental setup did not anticipate the difficulties of sound quality we encountered. While we still found effects using phonetic analysis despite our reduced sample size, future research can draw a lesson from this and instructs participants to reduce background noise (e.g. radio, TV) and use headphones to avoid echo.

CONCLUSIONS

The motivational draw of video games comes from different needs they satisfy. While games can make players feel powerful, autonomous, and explorative, they can also make players feel socially connected to other players. In 2016, 54% of the most frequent gamers played socially, to bond with friends, family, or strangers through play [12]. This need is already being acknowledged by game researchers who investigate the social potential of games, as well as by the video game industry who continue to implement more multiplayer mechanics into their games. How do we design games that effectively promote social closeness between the players? We previously had a very narrow understanding of what social play should look like. The work on social play predominantly assumed that games need to be cooperative and interdependent to facilitate social closeness. Our results demonstrate that both factors do in fact positively influence the relationship between the players. Our findings additionally widen the perception of what collaborative play can entail. The effects of cooperation and interdependence are not co-dependent, but are additive and can therefore be leveraged separately. A competitive game high in interdependence can still help two players form a connection. Similarly, shared goals and group identification alone could help players form communal bonds. The disentanglement of concepts previously only used in tandem broadens the design space that we can explore to innovate and further the use of social games. Our findings also help us better understand these mechanics. Interdependent play may only ever be as effective as the communication channels of the game allow it to be.

Forming and maintaining positive relationships between grandparents and grandchildren, caregivers and elderly caretakers, work colleagues, parents and their kids, or distributed friends can be difficult. Social games can be a powerful tool to help strengthen these bonds. The more we understand the underlying elements of social play, the more we can use games to bring people closer together.

ACKNOWLEDGEMENTS

We thank NSERC for funding, Shelby Thompson for her work on the implementation of the games, and Colby Johanson for his assistance with the online deployment. We thank the members of the Interaction Lab at the University of Saskatchewan for continued support and our participants. We would also like to thank Sigrid, Horst, Miriam, Anna-Mareike, Christoph and Luisa for being wonderful.

REFERENCES

1. Dominic Abrams, and Michael A. Hogg, 1999. *Social identity and social cognition*. Oxford: Blackwell.

2. Rafael Ballagas, Hayes Raffle, and others. 2013. Reading, Laughing, and Connecting with Young Children. In *Connecting Families*. Springer, 159–172.
3. Karl Bergström, Staffan Björk, and Sus Lundgren. 2010. Exploring aesthetical gameplay design patterns: camaraderie in four games. *Proceedings of the 14th International Academic MindTrek Conference: Envisioning Future Media Environments*. ACM.
4. Anastasiia Beznosyk, Peter Quax, Wim Lamotte, and Karin Coninx. 2012. The effect of closely-coupled interaction on player experience in casual games. In *International Conference on Entertainment Computing*, pp. 243-255. Springer Berlin Heidelberg.
5. Nathan Bos, Judy Olson, Darren Gergle, Gary Olson, and Zach Wright. 2002. Effects of four computer-mediated communications channels on trust development. In *Proceedings of the SIGCHI conference on Human factors in computing systems Changing our world, changing ourselves - CHI 02*. Association for Computing Machinery (ACM). http://dx.doi.org/10.1145/503376.503401
6. Aysun Bozanta, Birgul Kutlu, Nuket Nowlan, and Shervin Shirmohammadi. 2012. Multi User Virtual Environments and Serious Games for Team Building. *Procedia Computer Science* 15 (2012), 301--302. http://dx.doi.org/10.1016/j.procs.2012.10.086
7. Herena Cole and Mark D Griffiths. 2007. Social interactions in massively multiplayer online role-playing gamers. *Cyberpsychology, Behavior, and Social Networking* 10, 4: 575–583. https://doi.org/10.1089/cpb.2007.9988
8. Laura A. Dabbish. 2008. Jumpstarting relationships with online games. In *Proceedings of the ACM 2008 conference on Computer supported cooperative work - CSCW 08*. Association for Computing Machinery (ACM). http://dx.doi.org/10.1145/1460563.1460620
9. Ansgar E. Depping, R. L. Mandryk, C. Johanson, J.T. Bowey, SC. Thomson. 2016. Trust Me: Social Games are Better than Social Icebreakers at Building Trust. In *Proceedings of the SIGCHI conference on Human factors in computing systems Changing our world, changing ourselves - CHIPlay 2016*. Association for Computing Machinery (ACM). http://dx.doi.org/10.1145/2967934.2968097
10. Morton Deutsch. 1949. An experimental study of the effects of cooperation and competition upon group process. *Human relations* 2, no. 3: 199-231.
11. Jason B. Ellis, Kurt Luther, Katherine Bessiere, and Wendy A. Kellogg. 2008. Games for virtual team building. In *Proceedings of the 7th ACM conference on Designing interactive systems - DIS 08*. Association for Computing Machinery (ACM). http://dx.doi.org/10.1145/1394445.1394477
12. Entertainment Software Association. Essential Facts about the computer and video game industry. 2017. Retrieved April 14, 2017 form http://www.theesa.com/wp-content/uploads/2016/04/Essential-Facts-2016.pdf
13. Tracy Fullerton. 2014. *Game design workshop: a playcentric approach to creating innovative games*. CRC press.
14. Kathrin Gerling, Regan L Mandryk, and others. 2014. Designing video games for older adults and caregivers. *Meaningful Play* 2014, 16-18
15. John Harris, Mark Hancock, and Stacey Scott. 2014. Beam me' round, Scotty!: exploring the effect of interdependence in asymmetric cooperative games. In *Proceedings of the first ACM SIGCHI annual symposium on Computer-human interaction in play*, pp. 417-418. ACM.
16. John Harris, Mark Hancock, and Stacey D Scott. 2016. Leveraging Asymmetries in Multiplayer Games: Investigating Design Elements of Interdependent Play. In *Proceedings of the 2016 Annual Symposium on Computer-Human Interaction in Play* (CHI PLAY '16), 350–361. https://doi.org/10.1145/2967934.2968113
17. Hamilton A Hernandez, Mallory Ketcheson, Adrian Schneider, Zi Ye, Darcy Fehlings, Lauren Switzer, Virginia Wright, Shelly K Bursick, Chad Richards, and T C Graham. 2014. Design and evaluation of a networked game to supportsocial connection of youth with cerebral palsy. In *Proceedings of the 16th international ACM SIGACCESS conference on Computers & accessibility*, 161–168.
18. Andrew F. Hayes. 2012. PROCESS: A versatile computational tool for observed variable mediation, moderation, and conditional process modelling. Retrieved from http://www.afhayes.com/public/process2012.pdf
19. Aki Järvinen. 2009. Game design for social networks: interaction design for playful dispositions. *Proceedings of the 2009 ACM SIGGRAPH Symposium on Video Games*. ACM.
20. Keith, James and Jeff Greenberg. 1989. In-group salience, intergroup comparison, and individual performance and self-esteem. *Personality and Social Psychology Bulletin* 15, no. 4: 604-616.
21. Sirkka L. Jarvenpaa, Kathleen Knoll, and Dorothy E. Leidner. 1998. Is Anybody out There? Antecedents of Trust in Global Virtual Teams. *Journal of Management Information Systems* 14, 4 (mar 1998), 29--64. http://dx.doi.org/10.1080/07421222.1998.11518185
22. Sirkka L. Jarvenpaa, and Dorothy E. Leidner. 1998. Communication and trust in global virtual teams. *Journal of Computer-Mediated Communication* 3, no. 4: 0-0.

23. David W. Johnson, and Roger T. Johnson. 1989. *Cooperation and competition: Theory and research*. Interaction Book Company.
24. D. W Johnson and R. T Johnson. 2008. Social interdependence theory and cooperative learning: The teacher's role. In *The teacher's role in implementing cooperative learning in the classroom*. Springer, 9–36.
25. Cynthia Johnson-George and Walter C. Swap. 1982. Measurement of specific interpersonal trust: Construction and validation of a scale to assess trust in a specific other. *Journal of Personality and Social Psychology* 43, 6 (1982), 1306--1317. http://dx.doi.org/10.1037/0022-3514.43.6.1306
26. Tejinder K Judge, Carman Neustaedter, and Andrew F Kurtz. 2010. The family window: the design and evaluation of a domestic media space. In *Proceedings of the SIGCHI Conference on Human Factors in Computing Systems*, 2361–2370.
27. Tejinder K Judge and Carman Neustaedter. 2010. Sharing conversation and sharing life: video conferencing in the home. In *Proceedings of the SIGCHI Conference on Human Factors in Computing Systems*, 655–658.
28. Robert E. Larzelere and Ted L. Huston. 1980. The Dyadic Trust Scale: Toward Understanding Interpersonal Trust in Close Relationships. *Journal of Marriage and the Family* 42, 3 (aug 1980), 595. http://dx.doi.org/10.2307/351903
29. James M. LeBreton, and Jenell L. Senter. 2007. Answers to 20 questions about interrater reliability and interrater agreement. *Organizational Research Methods*.
30. Sheena Lewis, Jason B. Ellis, and Wendy A. Kellogg. 2010. Using virtual interactions to explore leadership and collaboration in globally distributed teams. In *Proceedings of the 3rd international conference on Intercultural collaboration - ICIC 10*. Association for Computing Machinery (ACM). http://dx.doi.org/10.1145/1841853.1841856
31. Winter Mason, and Siddharth Suri. Conducting behavioral research on Amazon's Mechanical Turk. *Behavior research methods* 44, no. 1 (2012): 1-23.
32. Edward McAuley, Terry Duncan, and Vance V. Tammen. 1989. Psychometric properties of the Intrinsic Motivation Inventory in a competitive sport setting: A confirmatory factor analysis. *Research quarterly for exercise and sport* 60, no. 1: 48-58.
33. Gregor McEwan, Carl Gutwin, Regan L Mandryk, and Lennart E Nacke. 2012. "I'm Just Here to Play Games": Social Dynamics and Sociality in an Online Game Site. In *Proceedings of CSCW 2012*, 549–558. https://doi.org/10.1145/2145204.2145289
34. Kirk McKeand. The 25 Best Co-Op Games Ever Made. 2015. Retrieved April 14, 2017 from https://www.rockpapershotgun.com/2015/06/18/best-coop-games/
35. Maaz Nasir, Kelly Lyons, Rock Leung, and Ali Moradian. 2013. Cooperative Games and Their Effect on Group Collaboration. In *Design Science at the Intersection of Physical and Virtual Design*. Springer Science Business Media, 502--510. http://dx.doi.org/10.1007/978-3-642-38827-9_43
36. Maaz Nasir, Kelly Lyons, Rock Leung, Anthea Bailie, and Fred Whitmarsh. 2015. The effect of a collaborative game on group work. In *Proceedings of the 25th Annual International Conference on Computer Science and Software Engineering*, pp. 130-139. IBM Corp.
37. Dennis Patrick. op Upcoming Co-Op Games of 2017. 2016. Retrieved April 14, 2017 form http://gameranx.com/features/id/86957/article/top-upcoming-co-op-games-of-2017/
38. Wei Peng and Julia Crouse. 2013. Playing in parallel: The effects of multiplayer modes in active video game on motivation and physical exertion. *Cyberpsychology, Behavior, and Social Networking* 16, 6: 423–427.
39. John K. Rempel, John G. Holmes, and Mark P. Zanna. 1985. Trust in close relationships. *Journal of Personality and Social Psychology* 49, 1 (1985), 95--112. http://dx.doi.org/10.1037/0022-3514.49.1.95
40. José Bernardo Rocha, Samuel Mascarenhas, and Rui Prada. *2008* . Game mechanics for cooperative games. *ZON Digital Games:* 72-80.
41. Ellen Rusman, Jan van Bruggen, Peter Sloep, and Rob Koper. 2010. Fostering trust in virtual project teams: Towards a design framework grounded in a TrustWorthiness ANtecedents (TWAN) schema. *International Journal of Human-Computer Studies* 68, 11 (nov 2010), 834--850. http://dx.doi.org/10.1016/j.ijhcs.2010.07.003
42. Richard M. Ryan. 1982. Control and information in the intrapersonal sphere: An extension of cognitive evaluation theory. *Journal of personality and social psychology* 43, no. 3: 450.
43. Richard M Ryan, C Scott Rigby, and Andrew Przybylski. 2006. The motivational pull of video games: A self-determination theory approach. *Motivation and emotion* 30, 4: 344–360.
44. Richard Saavedra, P. Christopher Earley, and Linn Van Dyne. 1993. Complex interdependence in task-performing groups. *Journal of applied psychology* 78, no. 1: 61.
45. Magy, Seif El-Nasr, Bardia Aghabeigi, David Milam, Mona Erfani, Beth Lameman, Hamid Maygoli, and Sang Mah. 2010. Understanding and evaluating cooperative games. In *Proceedings of the SIGCHI Conference on Human Factors in Computing Systems*, pp. 253-262. ACM,
46. Stacey D Scott, Regan L Mandryk, and Kori M Inkpen. 2002. Understanding children's interactions in synchronous shared environments. In *Proceedings of the*

Conference on Computer Support for Collaborative Learning: Foundations for a CSCL Community, 333–341.

47. Nicholas Shim, Ronald Baecker, Jeremy Birnholtz, and Karyn Moffatt. 2010. TableTalk Poker: an online social gaming environment for seniors. In *Proceedings of the International Academic Conference on the Future of Game Design and Technology*, 98–104.
48. Henri Tajfel, and John C. Turner. 2004. The Social Identity Theory of Intergroup Behavior. In Worchel and Austin (eds.), Psychology of Intergroup Relations. Chicago: Nelson-Hall.
49. Sabine Trepte, Leonard Reinecke, and Keno Juechems. 2012. The social side of gaming: How playing online computer games creates online and offline social support. *Computers in Human Behavior* 28, 3: 832–839. https://doi.org/10.1016/j.chb.2011.12.003
50. Gerben Van Der Vegt, Ben Emans, and Evert Van De Vliert. 1998. Motivating effects of task and outcome interdependence in work teams. *Group & organization management* 23, no. 2: 124-143.
51. Donghee Yvette Wohn, Cliff Lampe, Rick Wash, Nicole Ellison, and Jessica Vitak. 2011. The“ S” in social network games: Initiating, maintaining, and enhancing relationships. In *System Sciences (HICSS), 2011 44th Hawaii International Conference on*, 1–10.
52. Toshio Yamagishi and Midori Yamagishi. 1994. Trust and commitment in the United States and Japan. *Motivation and Emotion* 18, 2 (jun 1994), 129--166. http://dx.doi.org/10.1007/bf02249397
53. Svetlana Yarosh, Kori M. Inkpen, and A.J. Bernheim Brush. 2010. Video playdate: toward free play across distance. In *Proceedings of the 28th international conference on Human factors in computing systems - CHI '10*, 1251–1260. https://doi.org/10.1145/1753326.1753514
54. J. P. Zagal, Jochen Rick, and Idris Hsi. 2006. Collaborative games: Lessons learned from board games. *Simulation & Gaming* 37, 1: 24–40. https://doi.org/10.1177/1046878105282279
55. Z. Zhong. 2009. The effects of MMORPG play on online and offline social capital. *Computers in Human Behavior* 27, 6: 2352–2363. Retrieved from http://dspace.cityu.edu.hk/dspace/handle/2031/5792

Bibles and *BioShock*: Affording Religious Discussion on Video Game Forums

Lars de Wildt, Stef Aupers
KU Leuven
Leuven, Belgium
lars.dewildt@kuleuven.be
stef.aupers@kuleuven.be

ABSTRACT
This study sets forth to analyze and categorize attitudes shown by communities of players on internet forums, debating religious worldviews in games such as *BioShock* and *Assassin's Creed.* It does so in light of the theo- and technological affordances that shape these discussions through the platforms of digital games and internet forums. Is the predominance of religion in games, as noted by other scholars, actually a topic of discussion for players themselves? And if so, which games afford discussion? What attitudes are displayed? And what are the motivations behind these attitudes? A multi-method approach is presented, analyzing 91 discussions and 20 interviews; rooted in extensive familiarization with the relevant games. Research outcomes include a typology of user attitudes, part of which actively seek out enchantment in the face of secularization. These are theorized in the context of two affordances: the theological affordances of some interactive systems to invite play with religious worldviews in a secularizing world; and the technological affordances of the internet forum as a platform that affords but shapes forum discourse.

Author Keywords
Player research; online discussion platforms; games and worldview; multi-method; online communities.

ACM Classification Keywords
H.5.m. Information interfaces and presentation (e.g., HCI): Miscellaneous; H.5.3. Information interfaces and presentation: Group and Organization Interfaces---Web-based interaction; K.4.m. Computers and Society: Miscellaneous; K.8.0. Personal Computing: General---Games. General Terms: Human Factors.

ACM ISBN 978-1-4503-4898-0/17/10…$15.00
https://doi.org/10.1145/3116595.3116625

INTRODUCTION
Every day, millions of players around the world engage in fictional worlds that appear profoundly religious, incorporating religious imagery, narratives and rituals. Despite living in an age of supposed secularization, they are playing *Assassin's Creed* [93]), *Dark Souls* [36], *BioShock: Infinite* [53], or other games across genres, which draw on a variety of religious traditions. Moreover, players seldom do so in isolation: they gather online in large numbers to discuss what those games mean, within the digital affordances of an online forum: a threaded, hierarchized and pseudonymous community.

Throughout genres, games utilize religion to present worlds and rituals for players to interact with. Historical games try to quantify the political influence of church allegiances (e.g., *Civilization VI* [34]; *Europa Universalis* [73] or narrativize the power of secret religious organizations (*Assassin's Creed*). Fantasy games like *Zelda: Breath of the Wild* [70], and *The Witcher 3* [20] regularly have players deal with various gods, their shrines and those who worship them. Religion appears in the shape of oppressive theocracy in first-person shooter *BioShock: Infinite*; but as a source of hope in Fantasy RPG *Dragon Age: Inquisition* [10]. It appears in the guise of world-threatening fundamentalist terrorists in military games such as *Call of Duty 4* [52]; or as a humanizing insight into the personal background of your favourite helicopter pilot, Faridah Malik in *Deus Ex: Human Revolution* [32].

While many of these games are single-player games meant to play in isolation, players can be found online, discussing these games and their meanings to them. They do so in great numbers, on internet forums such as *Reddit* (243.6 million users), *IGN* (1.2 million) down to more select forums such as *NeoGAF* (151 thousand), which have month-long waiting lists. Other than social media, forums are pseudonymous and are overall more hierarchical, both in their chronological ordering of messages and thematised subdivisions of topics; as well as their moderation by 'mods,' who approve posts and users, enforce etiquette and police the tone of discussions. Phenomena such as "GamerGate" have shown that forums are societally and academically relevant, if only due to the (pseudo-)anonymous, semi-organized force of online gamer communities' policing of identity: the white, male, heterosexual "gamer" [14, 22, 61]. What place does religiosity take in this intersection of stereotypical identity? And how do these pseudonymous communities discuss the topic of religion in games?

LITERATURE

Outside of forums, several academic communities have been dedicated to finding and analyzing the religious heritage in digital games. Several edited volumes [30, 16, 86], dissertations [88, 75], and entire journals (the *Gamevironment* journal and Heidelberg's *Online*) carefully root out and interpret video games' reliance on religious tropes. Content analyses, especially in the context of theology or religious studies, eagerly identify religious representations in game narratives and aesthetics, finding Judaism [62], Islam [84, 85], Hinduism [72, 99] or "God" [56, 12, 96]. From a slightly different perspective, religious scholars and sociologists of religion have argued that game-design may function *as* religion. Design, it has been argued, may disclose what Huizinga called, a "magic circle, [a] temple," among other metaphors [50], which temporarily affords community-formation and collective effervescence [90, 37]; which may provide rule-structured ethical dilemmas for reflection [37, 82, 83, 98]; and, like religion, produce ultimate meaning through the "procedural rhetoric" of rituals [94, 11].

This is odd, because philosophers and sociologists of religion have long pointed to the perceived (and abundantly theorized) loss of religion as a source of meaning in secularized society as a whole. After all, Nietzsche's "God is dead" decries first and foremost the loss of the Christian god as a moral authority in which to ground a shared set of cultural beliefs and truths: a loss of orientation ("whither are we moving?") from which to make sense of morality, meaning and a world without transcendence [68, 43, 19, 97]. This "tremendous event" of god's death, which "ha[d] not yet reached the ears of men" when Nietzsche wrote in 1882 [68], finds resonance with Weber, who stresses that the disenchantment of the world [*die Entzauberung der Welt*]...

> "...destines us to realize more clearly these struggles [of meaning] after our eyes have been blinded for a thousand years by the allegedly or presumably exclusive orientation towards the grandiose moral fervor of Christian ethics" [95]

As various authors have stated, a modern world that cannot give transcendent meaning to everyday human lives is experienced as meaningless, abstract, or "alienated" [6, 60, 100; see also 47]. As a consequence, "no longer provided with pre-given and solidly grounded meaning and subjected to rationalized modern institutions," Dick Houtman and Stef Aupers argue, "modern selves find themselves plagued by nagging questions [...] 'Do I really want this?' and 'What sort of person am I, really?" [47].

Popular culture has been presented by many such sociologists as an enduring displacement (or even replacement) of religion as a ground for enchantment, belief and ultimate meaning [74, 23, 78, cf. 92]. Outside of established, institutionalized religions, individuals increasingly constitute their own systems of ultimate significance [57], in what Thomas Luckmann called "bricolage," a mixing of religious elements [58], and others have called "pick-and mix religion'' [42] or a "spiritual supermarket" [59, 3].

Some fictional texts, films, games and their worlds are particularly prone to be taken up for meaning-making [27, 92]. Markus Davidsen calls the properties of such fictions "religious affordances," after ecological psychologist James Gibson's concept of certain use-objects offering "action possibilities," i.e., "affordances" [38]. Consumers distil meaning from such texts and fictional worlds, with digital gaming worlds newly enabling "people['s] choos[ing] realities that are experienced as real, meaningful and enchanting" [3; see also 46]. *Even* when these experience appear initially in contradiction to their own (non-)religious worldviews, incorporating witches [74]; shaman and druidic worship [56]; or "Buddhist [and] Hindu stuff" into existing beliefs [45]. These experiences are not bound to pre-established or "history-based" religiosities, but can freely include "fiction-based" [27], "invented" [26], or "hyper-real" religions [77] in which individuals are inspired by fiction to construct belief systems such as 'Jediism,' 'Matrixism' (ibid.), or any number of Tolkien-inspired religions [27].

Players, meanwhile, do their own research as amateurs, in groups: as lovers of games, religion or both. More so than other media, digital games are surrounded by an enthusiastic and medium-specific "gamer culture" that relies on internet forums, community-made 'wiki'-encyclopediae and fan cultures to discuss games and what it means (for better or worse) to be a "gamer" [89, 81, 14]. When discussing games' meanings online, communities of players discuss and negotiate games' meanings within the subcultural context of game culture.

Moreover, they do so within the technological context of online forums. As has been noted [e.g., 29, 55], online forum communities bring with them the affordance of pseudonymity, which allows both recognition (of the pseudonym) and relative anonymity outside of the forum. This recognition in turn allows forum users to accumulate social capital and prestige – being able to rise even, say, to the level of moderator or administrator. Many forums have elaborate hierarchies of users, the top ranks of which can decide on the structure of forums (divisions, subdivisions and themes) and which threads and users are allowed to participate. On the other hand, the relative anonymity of pseudonymity affords users not to be nominally responsible for the content of one's post (as with platforms such as *Facebook*, which enforces the use of real names) makes it possible for niche, controversial and illegal opinions and groups to convene, making forums for many a place where "nowhere I could talk like that" [29, 14, 55, 61].

1. Reddit.com (ranked 33)	11. Rockstargames.com (ranked 3154) *single-developer
2. Gameforge (ranked 317)	12. Eurogamer (ranked 3902)
3. IGN (ranked 325)	13. Minecraftforum.net (4073) *single-game
4. Battle.net (ranked 379)	14. Giantbomb (4304)
5. Gamefaqs (ranked 496)	15. N4G (4905)
6. Gamespot (ranked 746)	16. Planetminecraft.com (4970) *single-game
7. Leageoflegends.com (ranked 770) *single-game	17. Rockpapershotgun (5382)
8. Wowhead (ranked 1557) *single-game	18. Penny-arcade forums (5604)
9. NeoGAF (ranked 2099)	18. Game-debate.com (6036)
10. Minecraft.net (ranked 2900) *single-game	20. Destructoid.com (ranked 6,045)

Table 1. First ranking of websites for popularity based on data from Alexa.

When discussing games on forums such as *Reddit*, *NeoGAF* and other platforms, gamers such as these form "interpretive communities:" groups of consumers sharing overlapping "interpretive strategies" for texts and other cultural artefacts, based on knowledge and cultural assumptions about things such as genre conventions, authorial intention, and so on in order to establish shared interpretations [35]. Interpretive communities are a helpful concept in that it helps "explain why there are disagreements and why they can be debated in a principled way:" not because games have a stable or intended meaning, but because interpretive communities offer stabilized and opposing positions from which to interpret games' meanings [35]. These communities and their opposing positions of interpretation, originate for Fish broadly in the set of cultural assumptions which allow communities of readers/consumers (in this case, players or even 'gamers') to create meanings from the game in ways that make sense to them, and on which they can agree. In some time-worn examples – such as your high school English literature class – interpretive communities can become dominant so as to render their interpretations canonical. Some examples of near-canonical interpretations include, e.g., that most of Shakespeare's sonnets address his love for a young boy; that "rosebud" represents *Citizen Kane*'s protagonist's childhood comfort (through the image of the sled); or that the child protagonist and his sister in the game *Limbo* are both bound to fruitlessly search the afterlife forever.

How do the online interpretive communities of players engage with religion? Instead of theologians, sociologists and religious scholars as interpretive communities, this paper looks at players and the game culture(s) that surround them: is the predominance of religion in games a topic of discussion for them? And what games do they actually discuss? Outside of academic analysis, again, the "gamer" which asserts himself in online communities in the 21st century as stereotypically white, heterosexual and male, and seems increasingly willing to police these boundaries [22, 54, 40]. What position does religiosity have, next to race, sexuality and gender, within this culturalized gamer identity? While earlier research indicates that players navigate religious identity and pluralism in response to religious content in games on an *individual* level [4, 80], there is little insight into how communities – in other words, gamer *cultures* – engage with such content. This paper looks at how players interpret and discuss religion in games, based on how they discuss it in large groups on public platforms, asking:

- Which games provoke discussions of their religious content on public forums?
- Which religious positions and perspectives are represented in these discussions?
- Which attitudes do players take toward the meaning of religious content in digital games?

This paper thus aims to provide a methodological contribution by providing ways in which to collect and organize forum data; as well as empirical insight into how and which players engage with religious themes in games, re-informing other and earlier (deductive) theoretical work.

METHOD

In order to answer these questions, three general methods were used. Primarily, we analyzed discussions on the five most popular video game forums. These amount to N = 91 discussion 'threads' of between 3 and 576 posts in which players from various religious and non-religious backgrounds discuss the perceived worldview of several videogames in light of their own convictions. Secondly, in order to gain further and more elaborate qualitative insight into these players, a number of forum users were approached for additional semi-structured interviews, of which N = 20 were conducted. Thirdly, the researchers became acquainted with all of the digital game titles and series mentioned throughout the research, representing an undocumented amount of hours of contact with the games' contents. The approach should be classified as multi-method [25, 65], where the first, second and third method followed each other sequentially. A constant comparative method was used throughout the process [5, 40, 45].

Forum discussions were collected based on a strict four-step selection of data. Firstly, page-ranking service *Alexa* was consulted to rank gaming websites based on traffic data. Second, websites were removed that no longer have active forums and have not archived them (e.g., *PC Gamer*, *Gamesradar*, *VG247*); as well as forums focusing on a single game or developer (e.g., *Leagueoflegends.com*, *Minecraftforum.net*, *Battle.net*), in order to exclude self-selection based on religiously-themed games – setting out instead to find out which games afford religious discussions on open forums. See Table 1 for the resulting ranking.

Alexa's rankings are based on web traffic for the entire website. Secondly, for that reason websites were re-ranked for traffic only to their forums (e.g., 'www.neogaf.com/forum/' and 'forums.penny-arcade.com' instead of the full domain), and cross-referenced with three other metrics: *MozRank*, *MozPA* and Google's *PageRank*, all of which focus on the use of backlinks, i.e., "other Web pages that have a hyperlink pointing to the company of interesting," [21] rather than page views and unique visitors.

Thirdly, data was gathered on the selected fora through a Google search deployed from a 'research browser,' i.e., an anonymized, non-personalized browser that minimizes the customization of search results based on previous search activity, according to the practices proposed by the Digital Methods Initiative [31]. Google was used to ensure all data was gathered consistently across forums, since forums' native search functions are intransparent (it is impossible to know whether results are sorted by relevance, date, 'likes,' [trending] activity, etc.), often divided (per [sub]section), and function differently between fora. Data was collected for each forum by prefixing the google string with the operator "site:" followed by the url (e.g., "site:http://www.ign.com/boards/"). The resulting search string entered for each forum's site domain on google was:

```
site:[SITEDOMAIN]+religio*+OR+spiritual*+OR+bel
ief+OR+Christ*+OR+muslim*+OR+islam*+OR+hind*
```

The reasoning behind each element is such: in order to answer how players discuss religious elements in games, threads should contain mention of either 'religion,' 'spirituality' or 'belief;' or explicitly mention one of the three major world religions (Christianity, Islam or Hinduism) or their followers. Additional religious positions (e.g., agnostic, pagan) were tried and were observed not to affect search results – despite being well-represented within discussions – and were thus deemed unnecessary for the formal search string. The wildcard '*' replaces inflections, affixes and compounds so that 'religio*' returns 'religious,' 'religion,' 'religiously,' and so on (as for 'Christ*/-ian/-ianity,' etc.).

Fourth, up to the first twenty threads were selected, ignoring those unrelated to religion (e.g., "religiously" to describe enthusiasm or addiction) and religious groups (e.g., "Hindi" to denote language, "Hindu" as geographical-cultural identifier). These were archived as PDFs and coded through inductive content analysis [48]. Informed consent was not deemed necessary [13, 64]: players posted anonymously on public forums, according to the terms and conditions for that forum's publication of their posts.

As a second method, some groups were deemed relevant but requiring more data during collection, according to a constant comparative method [5, 40, 45]. Forum users in these groups were approached for further qualitative interviews in order to gather insight into the motivations, beliefs and social positions behind their online post. In other words: to further question the person behind the forum discussant. Of the users approached, N = 20 semi-structured interviews were conducted with users from various religious backgrounds.

DISCUSSING WORLDVIEW IN VIDEO GAMES

Forum discussions are well-organized, if not always civil, conversations. As described above, when users assemble on a forum to discuss religion in games, the forum acts as a specific communicative context by both technologically mediating conversation (allowing users to register under nicknames and post in threaded conversations) as well as by enabling those users to create a culture of hierarchical, codified discussion. Long-standing forums usually have an extensive list of rules for proper etiquette, and their heterogeneous player communities put forward administrators to govern their forums.

In the context of this paper, one pertinent example of forum culture is that, on all the forums included in the data set, religious discussions were referred to as recurring, conflictual and generally unpleasant. As one user on *GameSpot* commented: "*I think it [i]s strange that most of Offtopic is religion based... either we have a LOT of curious people or we have LOTS of people that like to ruffle feathers.*" A thread about the upcoming release of *Assassin's Creed 2* on another forum, *GameFAQs*, was outright titled "*Am I the only one not looking forward to the religious arguments bound to ensue?*" Of course, in this attempt to keep people from repeating the same kinds of discussions, the thread quickly turns into a religious debate. In the same thread, another user adds that

> "They will always find something or someone to vent their anger towards. I can remember reading posts about *Doom 3* in '04, from Christians worried they were going to hell for playing a game with demons. The best thing to is ignore it. If the topic is hinting towards that, ignore it and find something else to read."

Signposting

Another general feature of these discussions of religion in games, which greatly helped us contextualize our analysis, is how adamant users are to indicate their own religious positions. Posts very frequently included a kind of 'signposting,' an announcement of that user's religion, e.g.:

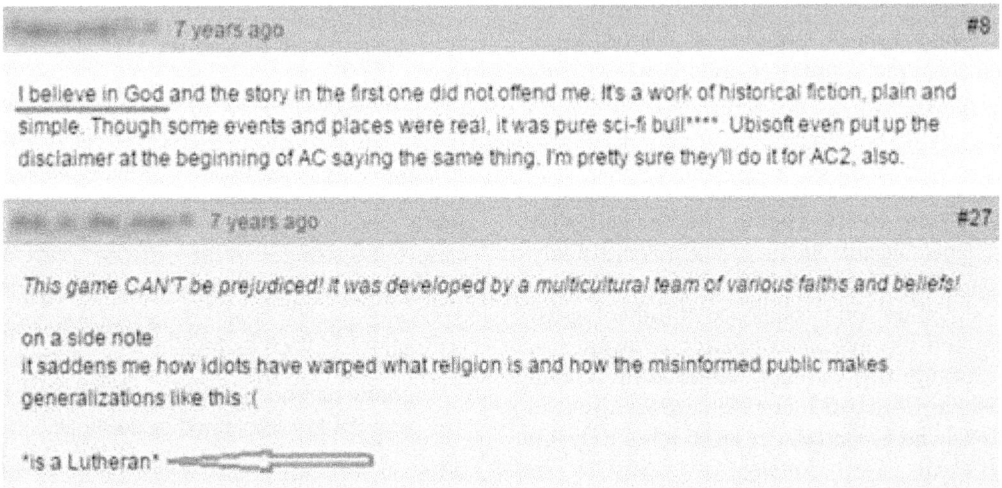

Figure 1. Two examples of anonymized users signposting their religious positions, on the GameFAQs forums.

"*I'm christian and* [...]," "*I'm devoutly religious, but seriously...,*" and equally: "*As an atheist,*" "*Full disclosure, I'm not a religious person,*" or "*That plot sounds kind of badass to be honest but I'm not a religious person so what do I know*" (See Figure 1). Such pre- and affixing of posts with the religious position of the user has two consequences: firstly, it makes it easier for readers to get an idea of what perspective is behind the post – whether those readers are other forum users or academics analyzing thousands of such posts. Secondly, it may be used as a rhetorical device to indicate nuance ("but I'm not a religious person so what do I know") or authenticity ("*I'd consider myself a pretty devout Muslim. My religion actually does affect the way I play*"); while keeping opinions segregated and entrenched, thereby enabling users to present their identities as relatively stable, while simultaneously allowing readers to freely agree with or ignore posts merely based on the position of who wrote it.

GAMES FOR DISCUSSION

Which games actually prompt religious debate? Based on the discussions found, we were able to form a list of the game series which were most frequently referred to, by coding for titles as they occurred (Table 2). Threads are ordered by the amount of discussions (forum threads) they appeared in. The bottom three game series in the table occupied a shared spot, getting an equal amount of mentions.

This indication of games serves a few purposes. First, it informs future research: it provides a list of inductively grounded case studies, as opposed to the theoretical (and often opportunistic) sampling approach taken for case studies by theologians, sociologists and other cultural researchers up to this point [e.g., 12, 64, 71]. Second, it informed, directly, our own method in this project: these games were given precedence in following content analyses, and were prioritized in order to facilitate analysis of the forum discussions below, as well as the following interviews, all the better to understand what participants were talking about.

Thirdly, the list of games gives a first insight into which game series and genres provide the opportunities for discussions of religiosity. Several types can be distinguished: Firstly, games such as *Assassin's Creed* and *BioShock* present kinds of 'alternate histories' in which religion has not lost its central role, but is combined with modern regimes and technologies; or alternatively, is traced through the ages in a narrative of 'what if,' i.e., what if secular developments had not occurred and religious orders are (secretly) in power (e.g., *BioShock: Infinite*; or the Templars in *Assassin's*

#	Game (series)	Threads (N=91)
1	Final Fantasy (Square Enix, 1987—)	27
2	Assassin's Creed (Ubisoft, 2007—)	22
3	BioShock (Irrational, 2007—)	22
4	Xeno(gears/-saga/-blade) (Takahashi, 1998—)	20
5	(Shin) Megami Tensei [2]—)	17
6	Dante's Inferno [34]	16
7	Dark Souls (FromSoftware. 2011—)	15
8	Dragon Age (BioWare, 2009—)	9
9	The Elder Scrolls (Bethesda, 1994—)	8
9	The Binding of Isaac (Edmund [64]	8
9	Devil May Cry (Capcom, 2001—)	8

Table 2. Game series and their developers, ordered by the number of appearances in unique threads.

Creed). Secondly, game series such as *Final Fantasy*, *The Elder Scrolls* (including *Skyrim*), *Dragon Age*, *Shin Megami Tensei* and *Xenogears* present fantasy worlds in which gods are often provided as reasons for magic, incentives for quests and other variably mundane interactions. Japanese fantasy (e.g., *Final Fantasy, Shin Megami Tensei, Dark Souls*) presents an especially interesting case because of its frequent reliance on imagery from world religion, used eclectically: Lucifer, Yahweh, Quetzalcoatl, Shiva and others are freely appropriated from Judaic, Christian, Meso-American, Hindu, Shinto, Egyptian and other mytho-theological traditions. Thirdly and fourthly, *The Binding of Isaac* and *Dante's Inferno* provide two outliers. While both ground their narrative basis in Christian literary intertextuality (the Bible and Dante's *Divina Commedia,* respectively), they are mechanically different: *The Binding of Isaac* is an autobiographical roguelike based on the creator's own childhood traumas with Christian parents, *Dante's Inferno* is a third-person action-adventure which possibly deserves its own classification: within the same genre, popular alternatives *God of War, Devil May Cry* and lesser-known *Viking: Battle for Asgard* provide the same 'beat them all' game-play while drawing on different (Greco-Roman, Japanese demonic, Norse) pantheons [79, 17, 24]. More importantly, what did players find 'religious' about these games, and with what attitudes did they approach this religiosity?

ATTITUDES TOWARD RELIGIOUS CONTENTS

Throughout discussions of these games we found four typical attitudes toward what they recognized as religious content in digital games. These ideal-typical attitudes will be set forth below: Rejecting, Debunking, Debating and Connecting. An overview of the types should show, first and foremost, an intensity of engagement with games' content on the axis from Rejecting to Connecting. Underlying these, are four attitudes along this axis of engagement which we wish to represent below. That is, of Rejecting as a type of disengagement with fictions that are perceived to challenge one's worldview. Debunking as a way of trivializing fiction to be 'actually' irrelevant to a non-fictional world. Debating as a mobilization of games' formal properties to support one's interpretation. As well as, finally, of Connecting as a willingness to seek out and engage with opposite worldviews through fascination, understanding and empathy.

1. Rejecting

Some users choose to reject any game that disagrees with their own worldview. Rejecters can be found on all sides and variations of belief. Rejecting a game can be vocal and total, stating for instance, that "[t]his game [*Doom*] is worthless and is satanic. Jesus died on the cross to defeat Satan and the power of Sin," or leading to personal calls to warn other believers:

> "Anyone who is a servant of CHrist [*sic*] will stay far away from this Satanic game. Be warned this game is not of God or from God but from Satan. It's seen in the advertizing and in the actual game itself.
>
> In Christ,
>
> Andrew"

Rejecters refuse to play a game when it endorses a worldview that disagrees with theirs. In a way, what fundamentally distinguishes 'rejecting' as an attitude from the second attitude below ('debunking') is that it takes the content of the game seriously, despite wishing to completely disengage with it. Rejecting is not an attitude solely for believers. One presumably atheist or agnostic forum user states:

> "All I'm saying is that I can't relate to someone who's religious, and if I'm supposed to bond with this character and 'go on a journey' with him, I just, I can't and I'm not interested in doing so."

What is difficult about rejecting as an attitude on public forums, is that because the player does not want anything to do with the game – in many cases to not even buy it based on advertising or word of mouth – they seldom speak up about it. In order to gain more insight into players rejecting games' religious contents, we contacted and actively sought out some of these forum users for further interviews.

Greg, for example, a Jehovah's witness, felt alienated by representations of atheism and (other) religions, remarking that his religious life outright "*limits what I play*:" he stays away from violence, demons, and games like *God of War* and *Devil May Cry* that feature "un-Christian" content [79, 17]. Religion, he claimed, was usually revealed in games to be "*window dressing*:" mundane, irrelevant or it simply "*turns out to be alien technology*." Ali, a Dutch-Moroccan Muslim, felt similarly that, although "*heathen content is inescapable, you'll have to deal with it if you want to play games,*" which increasingly lead him to just not play them altogether. He referred to games like *Uncharted,* which uses "*pagan symbols*" [66], the "*satanic content*" of the *Doom* series [51], and so on (Ali). This group of players further included brothers Dan and Bert, both Christian ministers, who resorted to shooting and sports games to enjoy instead. This is true for all the 'rejecters' we interviewed: while gaming is a fun activity for its challenges, game-play and story, the latter all too often proved a distracting or even distasteful contestation of their beliefs.

2. Debunking

Debunking forum posts assert that the religious content of a game is essentially hollow or trivial. For religious and non-religious players alike, debunking is the fundamental assertion that their beliefs remain unshaken, regardless of what kind of worldview a game confronts them with.

Debunking, in its simplest form, is familiar to most people – and perhaps academics studying games in particular – as "*it's just a video game*." In many examples, debunking is a way to denounce fiction as having any sway over religious beliefs: "*If a work of fiction makes you angry because in their fictional universe God maybe did not cause historical events that is pretty sad. This is coming from a religious person as well.*" By extension, another religious player noted that what

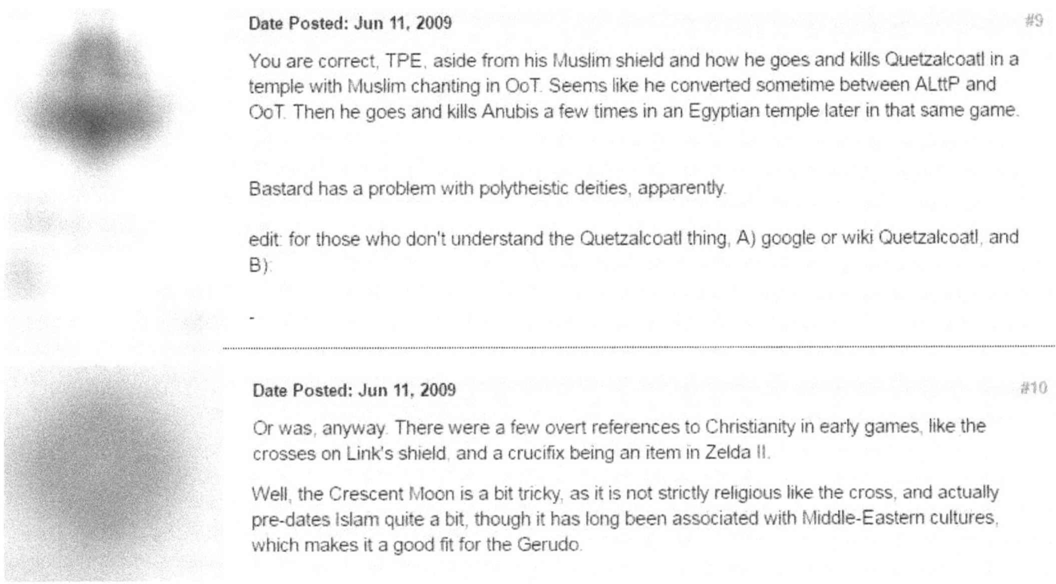

Date Posted: Jun 11, 2009 #9

You are correct, TPE, aside from his Muslim shield and how he goes and kills Quetzalcoatl in a temple with Muslim chanting in OoT. Seems like he converted sometime between ALttP and OoT. Then he goes and kills Anubis a few times in an Egyptian temple later in that same game.

Bastard has a problem with polytheistic deities, apparently.

edit: for those who don't understand the Quetzalcoatl thing, A) google or wiki Quetzalcoatl, and B):

-

Date Posted: Jun 11, 2009 #10

Or was, anyway. There were a few overt references to Christianity in early games, like the crosses on Link's shield, and a crucifix being an item in Zelda II.

Well, the Crescent Moon is a bit tricky, as it is not strictly religious like the cross, and actually pre-dates Islam quite a bit, though it has long been associated with Middle-Eastern cultures, which makes it a good fit for the Gerudo.

Figure 2. Excerpt from two anonymized users Debating Link's religiosity on IGN.com. Various abbreviations refer to different games in the Zelda series [70].

religion is 'about' is more important than works of fiction, such as *BioShock: Infinite*, in this case:

> "I'm Christian but nothing about this game bothered me [...] it's a work of fiction made for entertainment, so anyone who can have their ideals swayed by a story isn't really getting what religion is all about."

Forum users like the one quoted above essentially favour the truth-value of one text, such as the Bible or other religious writing, over another 'text' – e.g., *BioShock* – by debunking the latter as a fictional text and respecting the former as more influential to their worldview.

In its most extreme cases, the rhetoric of Debunking seeks to trivialize the relevance of religious content on the grounds that *any* fictional content is trivial. In a thread, started by a religious player asking how atheists respond to religion in games, one user responds "*Well, I don't feel affected and no one should be... because you know why?... It's just a game!... if you feel bad about a game then you have a problem...*" According to another, "*It's just all fantasy to me. I don't have a problem with it at all.*" This interpretation of actions and stories in games as, in the end, irrelevant to 'real' life is shared by Christians, as well:

> "I am pretty sure that if you realize it[']s a game and you don't go and commit crimes or live an awful life God will understand ;). The other day I was punching birds in *Crysis* and I would NEVER do that in real life :P."

In such cases, the rhetoric of debunking holds that it is absurd to regard actions and stories in video games, and all fiction by extension, as *really* having any impact on what people – and gods! – think or believe: fiction is irrelevant.

Flat theology

What differentiates the Bible from *BioShock*, for these discussants? Whereas for a large group of (religious) Debunkers, religious texts retained a special significance over video game fictions; debunking *all* fiction has further-reaching implications. For non-religious players specifically, this assertion may lead to the (proposed) idea that any game or story is entirely fictional and irrelevant – be it in the Bible or *BioShock*, the Quran or *Assassin's Creed*, the Dao de jing or *Dark Souls*. "*Fantasy fits right in with more fantasy.*" Many discussions involved debunkers comparing games' fictions to religious stories as equally fictional, and equally trivial. Such a position equates to what we henceforth call a 'flat theology.' As one user deftly put it, "*I don't really mind [religion in games], I consider Angels and Demons just the same as Trolls and pixies.*" Yet another one asserts, "*I see religious elements in games as I see them in reality: it's a bunch of myths and legends that make good stories.*"

3. Debating

Debating, as opposed to Rejecting and Debunking, can only happen when players engage explicitly with interpretations of the game. Some of the most concise statements of the rhetoric of Debating are made in reply to Debunking. One user replies to a Debunking post (which stated that "*It's just a game, don't take it too seriously*"), by expressing their dislike for such trivialization: "*You know, I don't like this. Just because something is a game/movie/show or w/e one shouldn't dismiss the message it tries to convey.*" Another user explains his own decision to take a game (*Bayonetta* [76]) seriously, when considering that even though

> "*Bayonetta* doesn't take itself seriously, [that] doesn't mean that it's not serious. [...] I know it's just a game, a good game, but the underlying themes of the game do give me a little bit of a chill when I play it."

What gave them "*a little bit of a chill*" was that "*killing angels or any religious metaphor can be a[n] offensive thing to some people,*" stressing that "*whether it's offensive or not can be subjective.*"

That interpretations of games can be 'subjective' at all is an important way in which the rhetoric of Debating differs from Rejecting and Debunking. Games, according to these users, have meaning: they can be offensive to some and fascinating to others. Debating users take games seriously by analysing them as meaningful artefacts – and engaging in vigorous debates about *what* they mean. Players freely mobilize themes and references for their arguments – e.g., "*It's filled with religious references anyway. The Ark, the Covenant, the Flood... Hell, even the game is called* Halo" [15] – as well as authorial arguments: "*I know that Darksiders has no religious undertones because the developers said it doesn't.*" Many debates concern the beliefs and opinions of game 'authors' such as Ken Levine, Hideo Kojima, or Ubisoft's 'religious disclaimer.'

An elaborate example should illustrate debates like these, by representing a part of a specific discussion on whether Link – the protagonist of the *Zelda* series [69]—) – is Catholic. The participants mount various arguments which employ both a detailed knowledge of the formal properties of *Zelda* games across the series, as well as their cultural and historical contexts (Figure 2).

The specific form of the forum is clear: messages are presented chronologically, discussants remain more or less anonymous (pseudonymous), and the discussion goes on a-synchronously. The debate continues for 36 more posts, with additional users pointing out other religious symbols in the game, including discussion of Aztec, Egyptian, Mayan, Muslim, Christian elements, as well as the game's own mythology, introduced in later games. These formal elements of the game range from visual icons to ludic elements – such as the "'Book of Magic' [item] in the first game, which had a cross on it, and is called 'Bible' [バイブル] in the Japanese version" (Figure 3). It further includes a number of narrative, musical, authorial and even paratextual or 'paraludic' sources: a large part of the initial debate surrounds a picture of Link praying to Jesus and Mary in a church, which was taken from an official Japanese guide to the game by Nintendo.

This kind of 'pop semiotics,' in which players engage in light-hearted, sometimes associative analyses of the games they play, mobilizes knowledge from both games and religion. Debates often point to a wide familiarity with games for comparison ("*I do find it interesting that basically every game that tackles religion seems anti-religion* [such as] Assassin's Creed, F[inal]F[antasy]X, Xenogears, *etc.*"). Furthermore, debates point to an extensive knowledge of religions, as well: the aforementioned discussion on Zelda touches on a range of religious topics, including the history of certain icons (the crescent moon, the cross) and the variations of feathered serpents in Mesoamerican mythologies, be they called Quetzalcoatl, Kuulkulkan or otherwise. All to either prove – or ridicule – the idea that the *Zelda* games contain religion; and the same debates occur for nearly all the games we found.

Figure 3. The "Book of Magic" item from *The Legend of Zelda* [69], called 'Bible' [バイブル] in the Japanese original.

Finally, Debating shows that no matter how formally users engage with the text, interpretations are never final, but indeed 'subjective,' as stated by the forum user above. Debaters frequently argue for entirely mutually exclusive interpretations of the same game – usually following their contrary religious beliefs. Hence, *Assassin's Creed* is at the same time a Christian game "*against the illuminaties, the knight templars and the anti-christ*" while other users argue that the game definitely "*did imply that religion is false,*" and that

> "The idea that laws do not come from Divinity but common sense and that the miracles in religious texts were accomplished due to mind control. [...] that's a VERY strong anti-religious sentiment."

The protagonist of *Assassin's Creed 2*, i.e., "*the main character of ACII (Ezio) is a damned Catholic himself,*" while yet another user stresses that the game is secular, in accordance with its historical period: "*Renaissance Italy was the period of Humanism- secular, secular, secular. They portrayed it accurately, pack up your bible and go somewhere else.*" Similarly, *BioShock: Infinite* both shows that "*societies without faith fail in the long run because of a lack of morality;*" while to other players it is "*is one big 'anti-religious' aspect.*" While the game is frequently analyzed by academics and critics as a criticism of American Protestantism, one forum user argued instead that:

> "The game does a good job of emphasizing how the core values of religion are quite beautiful [...] Love, community, redemption are all concepts the game looks at fondly [...] By the time you reach the end of the game, it's about people. Any vestiges of religious commentary are, by that point, positive."

Debating, while a more serious engagement with games' religious contents than Rejecting or Debunking, all too often devolves into a stalemate. In many cases, players such as those above end up entrenched within their own interpretation, appropriating the meanings of the games discussed according to their own religious position – and fundamentally disagreeing on their mutually exclusive interpretations of the same game.

4. Connecting

Other users actively sought to connect to other worldviews than their own. This attitude of Connecting is different from Debating in that Connecting players seek engagement with – and often get a lasting impression of – a game's religious content, rather than arguing for its agreement with their own beliefs. Opposite from Rejecting; Connecting often entails actively seeking out such games, for various reasons. One reason is that "theistic themes often make for a fantastic work of fantasy or fiction," suggesting that religious worlds just inherently represent quality to some users. Such users typically report that they "*even actively look for them,*" preferring to seek out game worlds that contain or thematise religion. Central among these reasons for Connecting is a fascination with other worldviews, in which religious characters, fantasy worlds and ritualized spaces present an escape from everyday life. Another forum user, who introduced his post stating "*Full disclosure, I'm not a religious person,*" explains:

> "I enjoy the 'lore' surrounding different religions. The sense of the unknown, the high strangeness, the savagery and difficulty in reconciling the cruelty of the world with higher ideals. People using these forces to manipulate others, and those that truly seem to have good intentions."

In this sense, religion is something not found in the 'normal,' an enchantment of the world that is fascinating precisely due to its absence from everyday experience. One agnostic forum user who displayed a Connecting attitude was Günther, whom we approached to ask what that desire for religious escapism came from. He explained finding solace in games' straightforward certainty: "*life isn't handing out feedback as willingly as a game does,*" instead "*the results of player actions in a game are far more often visible and relatable* […] *I would like for life's choices to be seen as less differentiated and nuanced.*" Indeed, as another Connecting player stated, in a lot of fantasy worlds, faith in gods just makes sense, "*since the ones* [i.e., the gods] *in video games often give good evidence that they exist, the people in those games' universes have ample reason to be theists.*" As similar qualitative research has demonstrated, "*within the boundaries of the game world, self-proclaimed atheists can safely experiment with the ultimate meanings of (religious) worldviews,*" in which gods exist unambiguously [80].

Such desire and fascination is of course not exclusive to irreligious players; and indeed religious and irreligious players alike joined discussions by stating that they came into meaningful contact with other belief systems. One forum user shares "*I'm a Taoist, and yet I enjoy RPG games and the like, many of which feature Christian themes. This doesn't bother me. The bible is filled with tales that are ripe for gaming adaptation.*" Two other examples include Geoff who came into contact with gurus and meditation as a child playing *Faxanadu* [49], which presented him with such a fascinating "*different way of thinking about religion than [he] had so far had […] being raised catholic and going to Sunday school*" that he would later "*cobble together [his] own version kind of a spirituality,*" inspired by Eastern religions, New Age and spending much of his life playing games that allowed his "b*ecoming aware of the existence of other belief systems. And that prompts a questioning of one's own belief system*" (Geoff). By comparison, Methodist-raised-turned-atheist James was reminded of the personal side of religion by playing *That Dragon, Cancer* [41], which includes the player in the designers' struggle with their fatally ill child. For James, the game's emphasis on "*struggling with religion and questioning it […] humaniz[ed] religious people […] and then creating empathy for them,*" caused him to take a more empathic look at the Christianity he had rejected in adolescence (James).

These encounters with other religious worlds and worldviews can be instructive and even convincing. Another interviewed participant explains her intriguing 'meeting' with God in *Dragon's Dogma* [18], which led her to think about her own religiosity: "*once you get to meet God, you learn God's been pulling the strings all along;*" making her wonder whether, outside of the game, "*it's possible that I'm only aware of the 'appearance' of God's non-interaction when in reality God could be intervening in a way that's not immediately discernible*" (Joan). Such thought experiments are typical among players that positioned themselves as actively connecting to other-religious content. Another interviewed participant who, despite being a convinced atheist, wrote about playing a religious Sheppard and Altaïr,[1] shared his game-induced doubt in the interview stating:

> "What if I'm wrong? What is the game trying to make me think about? Just by being on the topic of religion [it] does make me question... I constantly question my worldview and, *you know*, whether I'm right or wrong. It makes me think: is this how people in the real world use religion?"

Seeking out, trying to empathize with and understand religious worldviews can lead to games changing their players' convictions. We contacted one user who had written that "Persona 4: Golden *made me a better person,*" explaining how it helped him realize and come to terms with the fact "that I was not religious at all. That I was the 'a'-word, the one reserved for baby-eaters and neckbeards." Another user, identifying himself as a "*secular humanist*" shared in a thread on *Assassin's Creed* and atheism that "*Thinking back to playing these games I can't help but realize that they probably played at least a small portion in my deconversion. They're some of my favorite games.*" One of them, when asked in an interview to elaborate, also

[1] In *Mass Effect* [8], and *Assassin's Creed* [93], respectively.

explained that he "*deconverted*" from Christianity, aided by seeking out games which "showed me it was okay to be an atheist" (Phil). Throughout our interview, he stressed the role that games such as *Persona 4* [2], *Undertale* [91], and others played in showing him the joy of personal investment and individual choice that games can celebrate without having to rely on faith ("*religious iconography and figured are used, but they are* [...] *shown more as myth than fact, rooted in people* [...] *shown to be manifestations of human nature*" [Phil]. Using the ending to *Persona 4* as an example, he explained:

> "The people *you* gained social links from call out to you with encouragement, the music swells in just the right way, and you toss aside your glasses to see the world how it truly is -- which is what you make of it." (Phil)

In all, what makes Connecting, as an attitude toward religious representation in video games, different from the other attitudes found in online discussions, is this willingness to seek out other worldviews and connect to the way they are represented in video games. By doing so, players in many cases succeed in not just finding interest in them, but at internalizing other ways of thinking and believing – be it temporarily or lastingly.

CONCLUSION

This paper set out to inductively find and analyze how players engage with religion through the technological and theological affordances of digital games and online forums. Perhaps unexpectedly, they turn out to do so in various ways and for various reasons.

On the basis of a wide selection of 91 online discussions, several games present what could be called 'theological affordances,' that is (borrowing somewhat from Davidsen's research into "fiction-based" Tolkien-inspired religion [28]), that these games afford groups of players to discuss the religious meanings of these games, of the religions alluded to, and of the nature of religion. In this sense, the research firstly contributes an inductive list of games that, much like Gibson's and Norman's affordances suggest [38, 71], are designed to afford a certain use: the reflection on religion and ultimate meaning, even among secular consumers. Such an inductive list may serve to replace, on empirical basis, the opportunistic and theoretical sampling of case studies that have been taken within the field of games and religion.

Secondly, these forums show specific technological affordances. The specific form of chronological, a-synchronous, threaded conversations shapes discussion, e.g., by driving many players (specifically those taking 'Debating' attitudes) into entrenched positions – from which the same game can be interpreted in mutually exclusive ways: e.g., of religious and irreligious interpretive communities understanding Bibles in *Zelda* or religion in *BioShock: Infinite* as portrayed in accordance with both groups' mutually exclusive convictions. The technological affordance of pseudonymity, while turning out less relevant to the eventual analysis and theorization of the data, is present throughout, and undoubtedly influences the tone, extremity of positions and the length of the discussions when compared to other platforms (such as *Facebook* or other social media).

Finally, this paper's main contribution is in providing both the empirical basis for the ascertainment *that* players actually engage in such discussions, confirming most of the content-based work on games and religion from other disciplines; as well as providing analysis of *how* players engage in these discussions. To this end, the paper proposes four ideal-types: Rejecters who refuse to confront media which (is expected to) present other worldviews. Debunkers who trivialize the meaning of fiction and interactive systems, in many cases espousing a 'flat theology' in which all mediatized supernatural beings – whether digital or in holy texts – are equally fictional and trivial. Debaters who engage in elaborate formal discussion on properties of games and religion, mobilizing knowledge of both under the assumption that fiction is both relevant to their convictions, and has a stable meaning in accordance therewith. Connectors were recognized as those players who engaged with games to play with worldviews, in most cases by seeking out different (world-religious or fictional) worldviews as a compelling fantasy outside of agnosticism and atheism; or as a way to engage with other-religious worldviews.

In all, the research opens up possibilities for further research: outside of forums, the question still remains how players from different religious backgrounds engage differently (or similarly) with the theological and technological affordances of games. Furthermore, insight is left to be gained into how these worldviews function. What happens when players are confronted or convinced with other ways of viewing the world? Are there qualitative differences between the provision of 'ultimate meaning' by digital games; and texts such as the Bible or Quran? While empirical and theoretical work is thus left to be done, this paper provides the basis for a strange possibility: that faith and ritual may be displaced – perhaps for just a few nightly hours a week – to the realm of digital play.

REFERENCES

1. Atlus. 1987. *Megami Tensei*. Game [Famicon].
2. Atlus. 2008. *Shin Megami Tensei: Persona* 4. Game [PlayStation 2].
3. Aupers, S., & Houtman, D. 2006. Beyond the spiritual supermarket: The social and public significance of new age spirituality. *Journal of contemporary religion*, *212*, 201-222.
4. Aupers, S., & Schaap, J. 2015. Beyond Belief. Playing with Pagan Spirituality in World of Warcraft. *Online-Heidelberg Journal of Religions on the Internet*, *7*.
5. Aupers, S., Schaap, J., & de Wildt, L. 2017. Qualitative In-depth Interviews: Studying Meaning-Making and Religious Reflexivity in MMOs. in Šisler, V., Radde-Antweiler, K. & Zeiler, X. *Games, Gods and Gamers:*

Methods for Studying Video Games and Religion. London: Routledge.

6. Berger, P.L., Berger, B. & Kellner, H. 1973. *The Homeless Mind: Modernization and Consciousness*. Random House
7. Bethesda Game Studios. 1994. *The Elder Scrolls*. Game [Personal Computer]
8. Bioware. 2007. *Mass Effect*. Game [Xbox 360].
9. Bioware. 2009. *Dragon Age*. Game [PlayStation 3].
10. Bioware. 2014. *Dragon Age: Inquisition*. Game [PlayStation 3].
11. Bogost, I. 2007. *Persuasive games: The expressive power of videogames*. Cambridge: MIT Press.
12. Bosman, F.G. 2015. 'Playing God'. *Online-Heidelberg Journal of Religions on the Internet*, 7.
13. Bourgonjon, J., Wever, B.D., Soetaert, R., & Valcke, M. 2015. Players' perspectives on the positive impact of video games. *New Media and Society*, *11*, 1–18.
14. Braithwaite, A. 2014. 'Seriously, get out': Feminists on the forums and the War (craft) on women. *New Media & Society*, *16*,5: 703-718.
15. Bungie. 2001. *Halo*. Game [Xbox].
16. Campbell, H.A. and Grieve, G.P. eds., 2014. *Playing with religion in digital games*. Indiana University Press.
17. Capcom. 2001. *Devil May Cry*. Game [PlayStation 2]
18. Capcom. 2012. *Dragon's Dogma*. Game [PlayStation 3]
19. Caputo, J.D., Vattimo, G., & Robbins, J.W. 2007. *After the death of God*. Columbia University Press.
20. CD Projekt RED. 2015. *The Witcher 3: Wild Hunt*. Game [PlayStation 4].
21. Chau, M., Shiu, B., Chan, I., & Chen, H. 2007. Redips: Backlink search and analysis on the Web for business intelligence analysis. *Journal of the American Society for Information Science and Technology*, *58*(3), 351-365.
22. Chess, S., & Shaw, A. 2015. A conspiracy of fishes, or, how we learned to stop worrying about #GamerGate and embrace hegemonic masculinity. *Journal of Broadcasting & Electronic Media*, *591*, 208-220.
23. Clark, L.S., 2005. *From angels to aliens: Teenagers, the media, and the supernatural*. Oxford University Press on Demand.
24. Creative Assembly. 2007. *Viking Battle for Asgard*. Game [PlayStation 3]
25. Creswell, J. W., & Clark, V. L. P. 2007. Designing and conducting mixed methods research.
26. Cusack, C. 2010. *Invented Religions: Imagination, Fiction and Faith*, Farnham/Burlington: Ashgate.
27. Davidsen, M.A., 2014. *The spiritual Tolkien milieu: a study of fiction-based religion* (Doctoral dissertation, Leiden Center for the Study of Religion, Faculty of the Humanities, Leiden University).
28. Davidsen, M. A. 2016. The religious affordance of fiction: a semiotic approach. *Religion*, *46*,4: 521-549.
29. de Koster, W. 2010. *'Nowhere I could talk like that': Togetherness and identity on online forums.* PhD dissertation, Erasmus University, Rotterdam
30. Detweiler, C. ed., 2010. *Halos and avatars: Playing video games with god*. Westminster John Knox Press.
31. Digital Methods Initiative. 2015. The Research Browser. Video. 1 June 2015. Retrieved April 14, 2017 from https://www.youtube.com/watch?v=bj65Xr9GkJM
32. Eidos Montreal. 2011. *Deus Ex: Human Revolution*. Game [PlayStation 3].
33. Electronic Arts. 2010. *Dante's Inferno*. Game [PlayStation 3]
34. Firaxis. 2016. *Civilization VI*. Game [Personal Computer].
35. Fish, S.E. 1976. Interpreting the "Variorum." *Critical Inquiry*, *2*,3: 465-485.
36. FromSoftware. 2011. *Dark Souls*. Game [PlayStation 3]
37. Geraci, R.M. 2014. *Virtually Sacred: Myth and Meaning in World of Warcraft and Second Life*. Oxford University Press.
38. Gibson, James J. 1979. The Ecological Approach to Visual Perception. Boston: Houghton Mifflin Company.
39. Glaser, B.G. and Strauss, A.. 1967. The discovery of ground theory. *Alpine, New York*.
40. Golding, D. and Van Deventer, L. 2016. *Game Changers*. Simon and Schuster.
41. Green, R. 2016. *That Dragon, Cancer.*
42. Hamilton, M.B. 2000. An analysis of the festival for Mind-Body-Spirit. In S. Sutcliffe & M. Bowman (Eds.), *Beyond new Age: Exploring alternative spirituality* pp. 188–200. Edinburgh: Edinburgh UP.
43. Heidegger, M. 1943 [1977]. The Word of Nietzsche: 'God is Dead.' Lovitt, W. (ed.) *The Question Concerning Technology and Other Essays*. London: Garland.
44. Holton, J. A. 2008. Grounded theory as a general research methodology. *The grounded theory review*, *7*(2), 67-93.
45. Hoover, S. 2006. *Religion in the Media Age*. London, New York: Routledge.

46. Hornbeck, R.G. 2012. A pure world: moral cognition and spiritual experiences in Chinese World of Warcraft (Doctoral dissertation, University of Oxford).
47. Houtman, D., & Aupers, S. 2010. Religions of Modernity: Relocating the Sacred to the Self and the Digital. *Religions of Modernity*: pp. 1-30. Leiden: Brill.
48. Hsieh, H.F., & Shannon, S. E. 2005. Three approaches to qualitative content analysis. *Qualitative Health Research*, 15, 9: 1277–1288.
49. Hudson Soft. 1987. *Faxanadu.*
50. Huizinga, J. 1938. Homo Ludens: Proeve eener Bepaling van het Spel-Element der Cultuur [Homo Ludens: a Study of the Play-Element in Culture]. Haarlem: Tjeenk Willink.
51. Id Software. 1993. *Doom*. Game [Personal Computer].
52. Infinity Ward. 2007. *Call of Duty 4: Modern Warfare*. Game [PlayStation 3].
53. Irrational Games. 2013. *BioShock: Infinite*. Game [PlayStation 3].
54. Kafai, Y.B., Tynes, B.M. and Richard, G.T., 2016. *Diversifying Barbie and Mortal Kombat: Intersectional Perspectives and Inclusive Designs In Gaming*. Lulu Press, Inc.
55. Kollock, P., & Smith, M. (Eds.). (2002). *Communities in cyberspace*. Routledge.
56. Krzywinska, T. 2006. Blood Scythes, Festivals, Quests, and Backstories: World Creation and Rhetorics of Myth in World of Warcraft. *Games and Culture*, *1*(4, 383–396.
57. Luckmann, T. 1967. *The Invisible Religion*. Macmillan.
58. Luckmann, T. 1979. The Structural Conditions of Religious Consciousness in Modern Societies. *Japanese Journal of Religious Studies*, 121–137.
59. Lyon, D. 2000. Jesus in Disneyland: Religion in Postmodern Times. Oxford: Polity Press.
60. Marx, K. 1848 [1964]). *Economic and Philosophic Manuscripts of 1844*. New York: International Publishers.
61. Massanari, A., 2017. # Gamergate and The Fappening: How Reddit's algorithm, governance, and culture support toxic technocultures. *New Media & Society*, *19*(3), pp.329-346.
62. Masso, I.C., & Abrams, N. 2014. Locating the Pixelated Jew. In Campbell, H. A., & Grieve, G. P. (Eds.). *Playing with Religion in Digital Games*. Indiana University Press: 47-65.
63. McMillen, E. 2011. *The Binding of Isaac*. Game [Personal Computer].
64. Mo, P.K.H., & Coulson, N. 2008. Exploring the communication of social support within virtual communities. *Cyberpsychology & Behavior*, *11*(3, 371–374.
65. Morse, J.M. (2003). Principles of mixed methods and multimethod research design. In A. Tashakkori & C. Teddlie (Eds.), *Handbook of mixed methods in social & behavioral research* (pp. 189-208). Thousand Oaks, CA: Sage.
66. Takahashi, T. 1998. *Xenogears*. Game [PlayStation].
67. Naughty Dog. 2007. *Uncharted*. Game [PlayStation 3].
68. Nietzsche, F. 1882 [1974]). The gay science: With a prelude in rhymes and an appendix of songs. Kaufmann, W. (tr.). NY: Vintage.
69. Nintendo. 1986. *The Legend of Zelda*. Game [NES]
70. Nintendo. 2017. *Zelda: Breath of the Wild*. Game [Nintendo Switch].
71. Norman, D. A. 2013. *The design of everyday things*. Basic books.
72. O'Donnell, J. 2015. A Digital Devil's Saga. Representation(s) of the Demon in Recent Videogames. *Online-Heidelberg Journal of Religions on the Internet*, *7*.
73. Paradox. 2001. *Europa Universalis*. Game [Personal Computer]
74. Partridge, C. 2004. *The Re-Enchantment of the West. Volume 1: Alternative Spiritualties, Sacralization, Popular Culture, and Occulture*. London: T&T Clark International.
75. Perreault, G.P. 2015. *Sacred Space Evaders: Religious Hegemony in Gaming Journalism* (Doctoral dissertation, University of Missouri-Columbia).
76. Platinum Games. 2009. *Bayonetta*. Game [PlayStation 3].
77. Possamai, A. 2005. Religion and popular culture: A hyper-real testament. Peter Lang.
78. Santana, R.W., & Erickson, G. 2016. Religion and popular culture: Rescripting the sacred. McFarland.
79. Santa Monica Studio. 2005. *God of War*. Game [PlayStation 3].
80. Schaap, J., & Aupers, S. 2016. 'Gods in World of Warcraft exist': Religious reflexivity and the quest for meaning in online computer games. *new media & society*, 1461444816642421.
81. Shaw, A. 2010. What is video game culture? Cultural studies and game studies. *Games and culture*, 5,4: 403-424.
82. Sicart, M. 2011. *The ethics of computer games*. Cambridge, MA: MIT Press.
83. Sicart, M. 2013. *Beyond choices: The design of ethical gameplay*. Cambridge, MA: MIT Press.

84. Šisler, V. 2008. Digital Arabs: Representation in Video Games. *European Journal of Cultural Studies*, *112*.

85. Šisler, V. 2009. Video Games, Video Clips, and Islam: New Media and the Communication of Values. *Muslim Societies in the Age of Mass Consumption*, 231–258.

86. Šisler, V. Radde-Antweiler, K. & Zeiler, X. (2017) *Methods for Studying Video Games and Religion*. London: Routledge.

87. Square Enix. 1987. *Final Fantasy*. Game [NES]

88. Steffen, O. 2017. Religion in Games: Eine Methode für die religionswissenschaftliche Digitalspielforschung (Doctoral dissertation). Berlin: Reimer.

89. Steinkuehler, C.A. 2006. Why game (culture) studies now?. *Games and Culture*, *1*1, 97-102.

90. Steinkuehler, C.A., & Williams, D. 2006. Where everybody knows your (screen) name: Online games as "third places". *Journal of Computer-Mediated Communication*, *11*(4, 885-909.

91. Toby Fox 2015. *Undertale*. Game [Personal Computer].

92. Tolkien, J.R.R. 1939. *Tolkien on Fairy-Stories*. HarperCollins.

93. Ubisoft. 2007. *Assassin's Creed.* Game [PlayStation 3].

94. Wagner, R. 2012. Godwired: Religion, ritual and virtual reality. London: Routledge.

95. Weber, M. 1919. Science as a Vocation. H.H. Gerth & C. Wright Mills (Eds.), *From Max Weber: Essays in Sociology* (pp. 129–156). London: Routledge.

96. Wiemker, M., & Wysocki, J. 2014. 'When people pray, a god is born... This god is you!'An Introduction to Religion and God in Digital Games. *Online-Heidelberg Journal of Religions on the Internet*, *5*.

97. Young, J. 2014. The Death of God and the Meaning of Life. Routledge.

98. Zagal, J. P. 2009. Ethically notable videogames: Moral dilemmas and gameplay. *Proceedings of DiGRA 2009*.

99. Zeiler, X. 2014. The Global Mediatization of Hinduism through Digital Games. *Playing with Religion in Digital Games*. Indiana UP: 66–87

100. Zijderveld, A.C. 1970. The Abstract Society: A Cultural Analysis of Our Time. Doubleday.

Is My Dog "Playing" Tablet Games? Exploring Human Perceptions of Dog-Tablet Interactions

Anna Zamansky
University of Haifa
Haifa, Israel
annazam@is.haifa.ac.il

Dirk van der Linden
University of Haifa
Haifa, Israel
djtlinden@is.haifa.ac.il

Sofya Baskin
Tauber Bioinformatics Centre
Haifa, Israel
sfbskn@gmail.com

Vitaliya Kononova
Dog Training Private Practice
Krivoj Rog, Ukraine
vitaliyaolegovna@gmail.com

ABSTRACT
Playful interaction of pets with tablets is a spreading phenomenon. Thousands of videos of people giving tablets to their pets to "play" can be found online, and training schools are offering classes teaching tablet skills for dogs. While the nature of pets "playing" with tablets is yet to be fully understood, some works highlight the potential dangers of such interactions. Humans – both pet owners and pet professionals, play a pivotal role in shaping the way pets interact with technology, both in terms of promoting pet-oriented technologies, as well as posing requirements for them. This paper presents an exploratory study of human perceptions and attitudes towards playful interactions of dogs with tablets. Our results reveal mixed feelings towards this phenomenon, and awareness of the potential dangers of such interactions. Moreover, roughly half of the participants do not consider such interactions as "play", leading to further questions concerning the motivations of pet owners for exposing their pets to technology and the future of mobile apps for pet play.

ACM Classification Keywords
K.8.0; H.1.2 animal-computer interaction: perceptions of playnon-human playersdigital games

Author Keywords
animal-computer interaction, ACI, perceptions of play

INTRODUCTION
Play is one of the most natural and basic activities of almost any animal. Burghardt [5] characterizes animal play as a behavior that is not 'fully functional', i.e., including elements which do not contribute to current survival; it is performed repeatedly (but not stereotypically); is self-rewarding and is initiated when the animal is in a relaxed mode (perceives no immediate threats).

Animal-computer interaction (ACI) is a quickly expanding field promoting a *user-centric* approach to studying the interaction of animals with technologies [14]. ACI offers new exciting opportunities to study animals' playful interactions by employing digital media. Such interactions have the potential to improve animal welfare at homes, zoos and beyond by providing cognitive enrichment and physical exercise, and creating stronger bonds between humans and non-human animals [7, 19, 24, 27].

Studying dogs in the context of technology for play is particularly rewarding. Dogs are one of the most easily available companion animals; they are one of the species in which play is routinely performed by adults, including play directed at objects. Dogs have outstanding capabilities to communicate with people and study from them. Finally, their behavior is studied and understood much better than that of any other domestic animal.

One notable type of dogs' playful interactions with technology is interaction with tablets, which nowadays can be found in almost every home. This type of playful ACI is becoming more widespread: hundreds of digital games have hit the application market [17]; numerous YouTube videos featuring pets "playing" tablet games can be found (see Figure 1 for some examples). Recently several dog training centers were reported to have opened classes teaching dogs to use mobile devices, such as School for the Dogs in New York and City Dog in London [21, 18]. Dog experts are also using tablets for the cognitive development of puppies.[1]

Despite their growing popularity, the impact of interactions of pets with tablets is not yet fully understood. Attention is drawn

[1] Daniela Salvi, a dog behavior researcher and dog trainer at Accademia per lo Studio della Comunicazione con il Cane, (http://www.cani-da-assistenza.it/) told the authors in a personal communication about her use of tablets to develop cognitive abilities of puppies that are to become service dogs.

CHI PLAY 2017, October 15–18, 2017, Amsterdam, The Netherlands.

ACM ISBN 978-1-4503-4898-0/17/10 ...$15.00.
http://dx.doi.org/10.1145/10.1145/3116595.3116634

Figure 1. Cat, lizard, dog, and bonobo in tablet interactions.

in [2, 1] to potential dangers in playful interactions of dogs with tablets and it is pointed out that there are several types of possible dog-tablet interactions (enjoyment, serious hunting and overstimulating). The need for careful use of tablets in this context and better understanding of impact such "play" may have on pets is also stressed. How successful will digital games for pets become in the future? Are pet owners able to recognize the benefits, and – even more crucially, the dangers of such games for their pets? Any interaction of pets with tablets is initiated and mediated by humans; pets will only play with technological devices if humans let them. As humans play a pivotal role in the ways pets interact with technology, this leads to the need for understanding human perceptions and attitudes towards animal-computer interactions, which also holds the key to encouraging more responsible use of digital technology for pets.

This paper presents an exploratory study of human perceptions and attitudes towards playful interactions of dogs with tablets, extending some first results presented in [3]. In this study we posed the following research questions:

RQ1 : What are the common human perceptions of pets interacting with tablets? Do they interpret the interaction as "play"?

RQ2 : What are the attitudes towards pets interacting with tablets; how useful/harmful are they considered for the pet?

RQ3 : Are there differences in the attitudes of dog professionals vs. dog owners?

RQ4 : Are there differences in attitudes towards different ("good" and "bad" as identified by experts) interactions?

The rest of this paper is structured as follows. In Section 2 we review some work related to digital play in the context of animals. Section 3 presents the results of our empirical study highlighting existing perceptions and attitudes towards dog-tablet playful interactions. Section 4 provides a discussion of these results. Finally, we summarize and provide some directions for future research in Section 5.

RELATED WORK

A detailed introduction into animal cognition and the nature of animal play is provided Bekoff et al. [4] and Burghardt [5]. In this section we review some works that focus on animals' playful interactions with technological devices.

Wirman and Zamansky proposed [29] a framework for characterizing playful interactions of animals with digital devices, which is grounded in Burghardt's definition of animal play [5]. Exploiting natural play for involving animals as participants in the design process has been discussed by a.o, Westerlaken[25] and Wirman [30].

Several works have explored digital enrichment for animals kept in captivity. Webber et al. [22, 23] addressed enhancing visitors' experience of viewing animals interacting with technology. Wirman et al [28, 27] discuss the challenges of the design of touchscreen-based games for orangutans.

Several digital games have been developed with the aim of enhancing the human-animal bond, such as *Felino* for cats [24], *Metazoa Ludens* for hamsters [7], *Playing with Pigs* for pigs [9] and *CAT (Canine Amusement and Training)* [26] for dogs. Games for cognitive enrichment of stay-at-home dogs with the aim of reducing boredom and stress have also been proposed[2] [11, 15]. Pons et al [20] provides an overview and comparison of the above mentioned digital enrichment. Dog-tablet playful interactions were investigated in Zamansky et al. [2, 1], where behaviors of dogs playfully interacting with tablets were analyzed and classified into three types: (a) enjoyable, (b) serious/hunting behavior, and (c) overstimulation, providing also behavioral indications for identifying each of the interactions. For instance, tail wagging and easily switching attention from tablet to owner is an indication of enjoyable interaction, while signs of stress such as heavy panting, nose licking and nervous yawning, as well as attention fixed to screen are indications of overstimulation. Zamansky et al. [2, 1] highlight the potential dangers of dog-tablet interactions (overstimulation and even redirected aggression) and call for a more responsible exposure of dogs to tablet games. Such exposure is in the hands of humans - dog owners and professionals, which provides the motivation for an exploratory study of human perceptions and attitudes towards playful interactions of dogs with tablets, which is described next.

EMPIRICAL STUDY

Preparations

An ethogram is a catalogue of observed behaviors of an animal in a particular situation or context [13]. Ethograms are one of the main tools for understanding animal behavior in behavioral science. In this study we used the ethogram constructed in [2, 1] for dog-tablet interactions. We used the classification of [1] for identifying "good" (enjoyable) and "bad" (overstimulated) interactions of dogs with tablets. We analyzed a collection of

[2]To the best of our knowledge, the work of Geurtsen et al. [11] was the only one that used cortisol measurements for evaluation of the effect of the game on stress levels of dogs.

over 20 YouTube videos, searching for a significant number of the above mentioned behavioral indications for enjoyable versus overstimulated interactions. Figures 2 and 3 show screenshots of videos that were eventually chosen (detailed ethograms of both videos were performed independently by two of the authors, who are animal experts). Video 1 features a dog wagging its tail and easily switching attention to its owner; only the dog's nose licking behavior can be described as a very light level of motivational conflict. Video 2 is a typical example of overstimulated interaction, with the featured dog exhibiting signs of stress and overexcitement: heavy panting, nervous yawning, and fixed attention to the screen.

Figure 2. Video 1 – enjoyable interaction. See https://www.youtube.com/watch?v=ds09kba06d0

Figure 3. Video 2 – overstimulation. See https://www.youtube.com/watch?v=QvJwcXiiguc

Participant demographics

In total 276 people participated in our study. Demographic information is shown on Fig. 4. The type of participants involved in the study were either *professionals*, having a professional background in dog behavior (trainer, veterinary doctor, researcher or other dog professional), *amateurs* who hold an active interest in dog behavior (via online courses, communities, reading books, etc, regular *dog owners* with no particular background in dog behavior, and participants who *do not own a dog*.

Data Collection

The main tool of data collection was via a questionnaire administered to the participants online. In this questionnaire the participants were requested to watch the videos 1 and 2 described above. After watching each video, they were requested to answer the following questions:

1. What is the dog experiencing?
2. On a scale from 1 to 5, how useful is this experience for the dog? (1 being harmful, 5 being useful). Explain your answer.
3. What is the dog feeling?
4. On a scale from 1 to 5, how positive are its emotions? (1 being negative, 5 being positive). Explain your answer.
5. Provide any other comments you have on the interactions you have just watched.

The use of questionnaires for data collection in the animal behaviour domain has been discussed [16]; it was noted that despite threats of subjectivity, asking people about their opinions and experience has the potential to lead to valuable insights. This form of data collection is quite common in domestic animals research and is usually applied for tackling questions related to one of the following aspects: (i) a dog's living conditions, (ii) its perceived relationship with humans, (iii) personality traits, and (iv) opinions about behavioural traits and abilities. The latter seems particularly relevant in the context of our posed research questions.

Results

We first performed a qualitative analysis of answers to the open questions for both videos. We divided the analyzed phrases into three types:

1. phrases related to the dog's actions/interactions with tablet (extracted from answers to question 1 in the questionnaire)
2. phrases related to the dog's emotional/cognitive state (extracted from answers to question 3).
3. phrases from general comments on the two videos (extracted from answers to question 5).

Three of the authors independently iteratively coded the answers to the questions on dog's actions and feelings, until a manageable number of categories emerged. In discussion among all the authors the final categories presented below were decided upon and applied for data analysis. We then performed a further quantitative analysis of the obtained categories, the results of which are also presented below.

Fig. 5 presents the size of the most popular categories of the first type. 'Hunting' was the leading category for video 1. However it was mentioned in only 52% of the answers. In video 2 it is not even the leading category (only 21%),

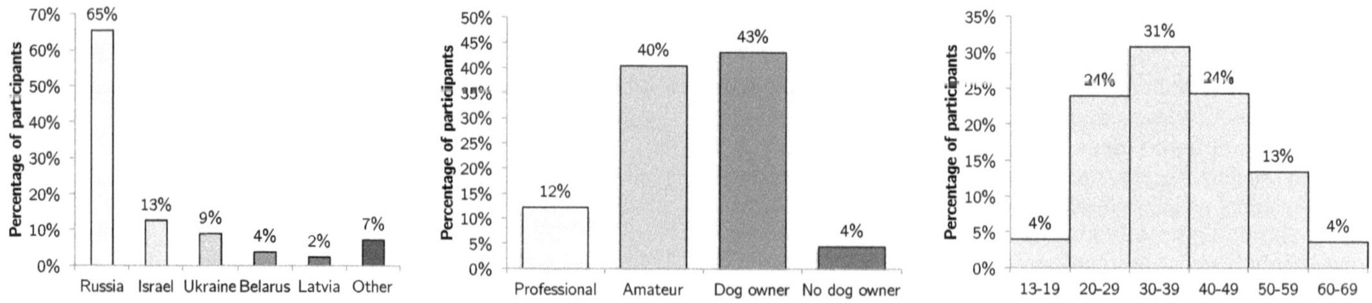

(a) Region of participant (b) Type of participant (c) Age group of participant

Figure 4. Demographic details of the 276 participants. Given are the (a) geographical origin of participants, (b) type of participant according to their knowledge of dogs and dog behavior, and (c) the age distribution of the participants.

coming second after 'digging' (this category includes also words such as 'scratching' and 'touching'). Interestingly, this category did not occur in the context of the first video. Another popular category was 'playing', coming second in the first video (28%) and fourth (15%) in the second video. Other, less popular categories included general phrases such as "working", "performing actions" and "I am not sure what the dog is doing".

Fig. 6 presents the size of the most popular categories for the second type, related to dog's emotional/cognitive state. The most popular category for the first video was 'interested'/'engaged' (49%, as opposed to only 13% in the second video). The most popular category for the second video was 'excited' (41%, as opposed to only 18% in the first video), while 'disappointed' came second (33% as opposed to 15% in the first video).

Next we used the Likert scale based answers to question 2 (how useful the experience is for the dog?) to divide explanations to positive and negative ones. The most popular explanations are shown below.

Positive responses to question 2:

1. The dog is gaining new experiences in a positive environment;
2. The dog is cognitively stimulated.
3. The dog is playing and play is always good for dogs.
4. The dog can safely satisfy its predatory instincts and fulfil its natural need for active movements.
5. It's useful for the development of quick reactions and general attentiveness of the dog.

Negative responses to question 2:

1. The dog is frustrated as it cannot reach its goal (of catching the object).
2. The dog is overexcited and if develops any further it can be harmful for its health and problematic for the owner.
3. This behavior is useless for physical or obedience training.
4. The screen may emit radiation which can damage the dog's vision.

Next for Fig. 7 we defined each participant's usefulness score of a video as the Likert scale based answer to question 2 concerning that video. Similarly, each participant's emotion score of a video is defined as the Likert scale based answer to question 4 concerning that video.

A clear distinction between the first and second video can be seen, in particular in terms of how those experienced or interested in dog behavior rated how useful the play interaction in Video 2 was, and what emotion the dog was experiencing.

Finally, we divided the phrases of the third type taken from the general comments into three categories: positive, negative and neutral reactions. Figure 8 presents the distribution of the phrases in these categories. Some examples for each of the categories are provided next.

Positive comments:

1. Such interactions enhance the dog's cognitive processes, make it follow the virtual object with its gaze, listen to different sounds.
2. Such games have great potential for cognitive stimulation and learning in dogs. But it must be adapted to each dog individually, based on its breed, character and cognitive abilities, and must involve the owner.
3. This is great for developing the dog's ability to focus and concentrate.

Neutral comments:

1. Interesting, but I have never thought of such interactions before.
2. I do not think there is damage in such interactions, but also no good may come out of it. It's better if the dog plays with actual physical toys.

Negative comments:

1. I feel extremely negatively with respect to using tablets with dogs. This is unnatural for the dog and may affect its normal behavior. For instance, when it gets used to playing with technology, it may grab a a mobile phone from owner, or when staying home alone may start to play with a gadget in an unsafe way and even get electrized! Dog owners, please take your dog out and just play with your beloved pet!

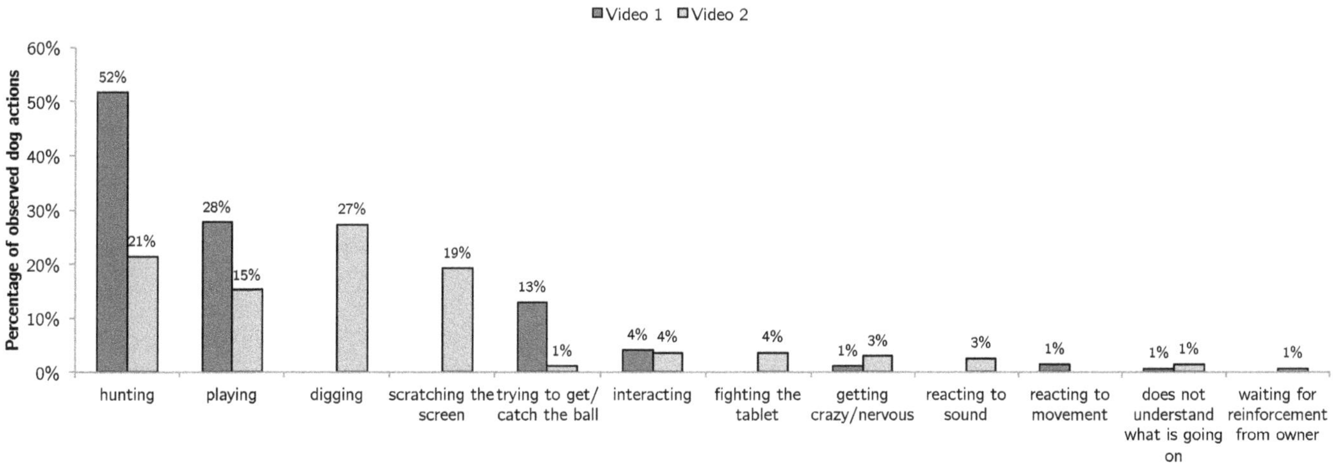

Figure 5. Categories of dog actions observed by participants in the videos.

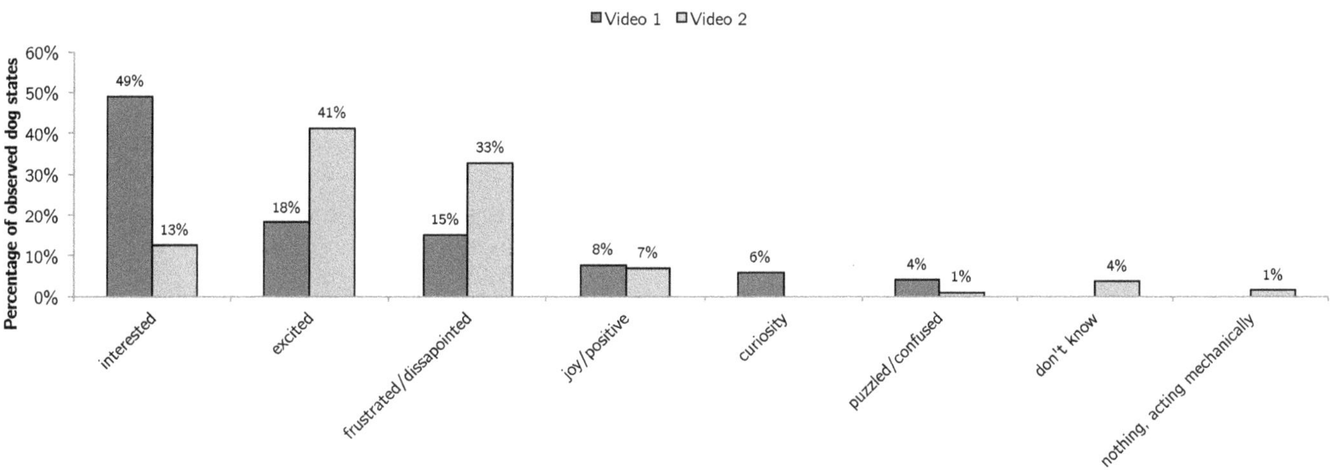

Figure 6. Categories of dog states observed by participants in the videos.

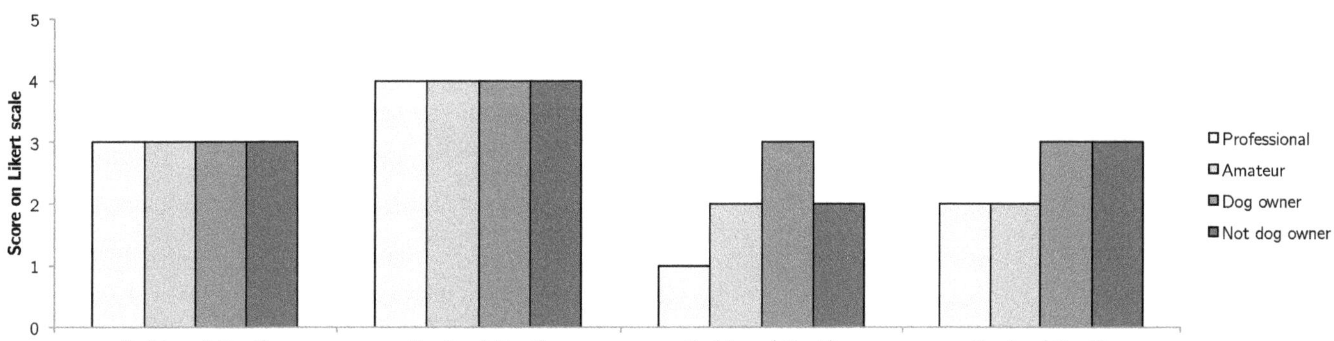

Figure 7. Median of usefulness and emotion response scores. The Likert scale range runs from 1–5, but is shown from 0 to emphasize the significantly negative score (i.e., 1) of professionals for the usefulness of Video 2's interaction.

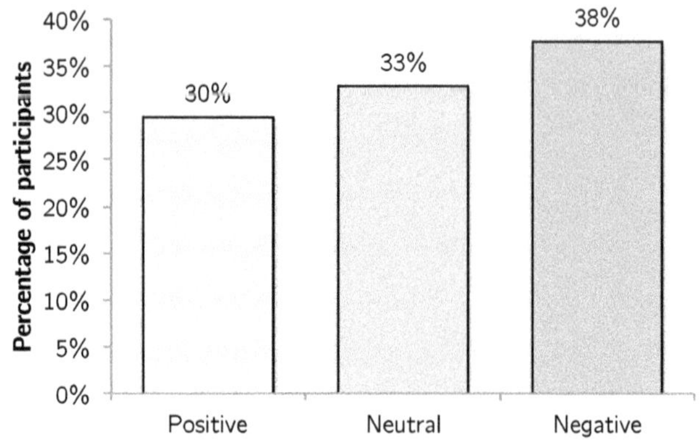

Figure 8. Distribution of general comments.

2. The lazier the dog owner, the more will his dog play with tablet.
3. This damages the dog's eyes and when playing the dog cannot control its emotions, definitely bad.
4. People who give tablets to their dogs without slowly exposing them to technology first, I suggest you go into aliens flying saucer to see how comfortable you are with new unknown technologies which you cannot even begin to understand.

For further analysing the differences in perceptions and attitudes between the two videos, we used nonparametric criterions of Spearman correlation and Wilcoxon Signed Ranks Test. Below are the most significant findings.

F1. Statistically significant positive correlations with moderate to strong effect size were found between a participant's usefulness scores of the two videos, and emotion scores for the two videos In other words, either both videos scored low, or both scored high for a given participant (Spearman correlation, two tailed, $r1 = 0.59$, $r2 = 0.75$ $p < 0.01$).

F2. Despite F1, the difference between the scores of the first and second videos was statistically significant with medium and large effect sizes [8]: video 1 scored higher both in usefulness and emotion score. The difference in scores between the two videos was significantly larger in the population of dog professionals, (Wilcoxon Signed Ranks Test, $p < 0.001$, Cohen's $D_{usefulness} = 0.74$, Cohen's $D_{emotion} = 0.83$).

F3. A statistically significant difference with a large effect size in the scores of the second video was detected between scores of professionals and scores of non-professionals, namely scores of professionals were much lower, (Wilcoxon Signed Ranks Test, $p < 0.01$, Cohen's $D = 1.05$). To address the difference in the amount of expert and non-expert participants we treated groups (iii) and (iv) of the participants as non-experts.

F4. A statistically significant difference wit a medium effect size for both videos was detected between participants aged 40-67 and participants aged 13-39: younger participants provided lower general scores than older participants, both in professional and non-professional categories (Wilcoxon Signed Ranks Test, $p < 0.01$; Spearman correlation, $p < 0.05$, Cohen's $D = 0.51$).

Threats to Validity

External validity

Number of videos: we currently only had participants assess two videos, one for enjoyable interaction and one for overstimulation. This is not sufficient to thoroughly ensure differences in observation by participants, as other factors in the videos (e.g., breed) may also affect a participant's observation. Expansion of the work incorporating more videos is a natural next step, but nonetheless, given the effect size of the findings so far the conclusions seem warranted.

Demographics of participants: The questionnaire was administered mainly via the School of Applied Ethology, whose main target population is Russian-speaking (hence the majority of participants were from Russia, Ukraine and Belarus). To provide further generalizability, we also added participants from other countries by administering an English questionnaire.

Internal validity

Expert assessment of videos: namely, the accuracy of the classification of the videos into "good" and "bad" interactions. Videos 1 and 2 were carefully selected from a large set of videos and validated independently to accurately represent the intended behavior with 2 dog experts to minimize this threat.

Translation between questionnaires: the Russian speaking participants were given a questionnaire in Russian, and responded like-wise. Other participants received a questionnaire in English, and responded in English. To ensure the same intended meaning of each element of the questionnaire remained intact we had two bilingual speakers of Russian and English independently translate and verify the questionnaire.

Erroneous interpretation of videos: To prevent erroneous (over)interpretation of the dogs' actions and states we instructed the participants to describe *what* the dog does, without interpreting it. More care to prevent misinterpretation can be taken using the approach of Hirskey-Douglas et al. [12], in which information is provided to dog owners prior to interviewing them, however it requires more active involvement of participants and is not feasible given our choice of data collection method.

DISCUSSION

One interesting finding arising from the analysis above is that the participants' view of dog-tablet interactions as "play" is not so dominant as might be expected, raising questions on the motivations for cultivating such interactions both by pet owners and companies developing digital games and gadgets for pets. The participants' neutral (for the first video) and slightly negative (for the second one) attitudes towards the benefits of dog-tablet interactions further reinforce these questions.

The popularity of the 'hunting' category, however, may be related to the nature of the digital games played in both videos: a moving virtual target chased by the dog on the screen. A choice of another type of game (i.e., logical puzzle or maze) could perhaps have resulted in a different description. The presence of 'communication with owner' category may indicate perceptions that a dog depends on its owner to interact with tablet and interpret the stimuli produced by it.

Curiously, while younger people are thought to adopt new technologies easier, F4 shows the opposite of such tendencies. F1 is also an interesting finding, which may indicate the existence of a certain prejudice among participants with respect to dog-tablet interaction, as many participants either gave low scores to both videos, or high scores to both. In other words, their pre-existing opinion on dog-tablet interaction may have impacted their judgement, irrespectively of the particular video.

While there is a need for further investigation with larger samples of participants, F3 provides an indication towards positively answering our research question RQ3. While the ability to recognize different dog behaviours and to interpret them correctly depends on one's knowledge and experience in behavioral analysis, some studies show humans do not even need to be dog owners in order to recognize dog emotional state based on barking and interpret it correctly [10]. It is therefore assumed in some theories that some canine behavioral elements (such as frequency of barking) are non-specific, i.e., their recognition and correct interpretation do not depend on knowledge and experience, and can be mastered by anyone. Is behavior of dogs towards tablets another such non-specific example? Our findings provide a starting point for exploring this question.

Concerning the last research question RQ4, both experts and non-professionals provided lower scores for the second video and so were able to differentiate between enjoyable and stressful interactions. However, the gap between the scores increases with the level of professionalism of participants. This leads to the observation that non-professionals are more prone to generalizations (such as "digital games are bad for dogs", or "tablets are useful for dogs"), while professionals are able to take a more individual approach ("while tablets may be useful for dogs, this particular dog should not be using it").

CONCLUSIONS AND FUTURE RESEARCH

Play interactions between animals and technological devices have been recently attracting attention of the HCI and game design communities, as such interactions contribute to pushing the boundaries of our understanding of digital play by placing a non-verbal, non-human user for whom play is still a natural and frequent activity.

While there is a lot of anecdotal evidence of pets playing digital games, we are only starting to explore the nature of animal-computer play interactions. Factors of animal welfare must not be disregarded, and the impact of such encounters on animals must be well understood before it is further encouraged. In this context exploring pets' encounters with technology from a human's perspective is a crucial factor as humans are the ones encouraging and shaping these interactions, as well as dictating the requirements for them.

Our preliminary results show that while many people perceive dog-tablet interaction as play, other categories such as hunting and digging were also dominant, raising questions on the motivation and benefits behind developing "games" for pets and teaching pets to "play" tablets. While the attitudes were also mixed (slightly more positive for the first video, indicating that overstimulation can be recognized even by non-experts), but a significant number of participants held strictly negative view on the benefits of such interactions. A finding worth further exploring is the correlation described above between the usefulness and emotion scores, which may indicate the existence of a certain prejudice among participants with respect to dog-tablet interaction, as many participants either gave low scores to both videos, or high scores to both. Thus, pre-existing opinions on dog-tablet interaction may impact one's judgement. Such opinions can be shaped, e.g., through education and social media, but at first they must be well understood, reiterating the need for further research on dog owners' perceptions of technology for pets.

Playful interactions of animals with technology have potential dangers, and as our exploratory findings have shown, the opinions of dog owners and professionals on these interactions are mixed. However, they also have a potential for improving animals' welfare by cognitive stimulation and enrichment, as well as physical exercise – at homes, animal shelters and zoos [7, 11, 19, 24, 27]. Exploring this potential, as well as ways to measure and analyze it seems a promising direction for future research.

We believe that animals are a fascinating user to study in the context of play, as they are the most honest type of game players: they never lie or fake their reactions. Therefore, a digital game that an animal plays and enjoys must provide stimuli that unlock appropriate play behavior of an animal player. As highlighted in literature [7, 11, 27, 6], finding and producing such stimuli is extremely challenging. It is our hope that this paper will stimulate cross-fertilization between CHI play and ACI communities on exploring different dimensions of digital play in non-human users.

Acknowledgement. We are grateful to Pavel Goldstein for his assistance with the statistical analysis of the data.

REFERENCES

1. Sofya Baskin, Sharon Anavi-Goffer, and Anna Zamansky. 2015. Serious Games: Is Your User Playing or Hunting?. In *International Conference on Entertainment Computing*. Springer, 475–481.

2. Sofya Baskin and Anna Zamansky. 2015. The player is chewing the tablet!: Towards a systematic analysis of user behavior in animal-computer interaction. In *Proceedings of the 2015 Annual Symposium on Computer-Human Interaction in Play*. ACM, 463–468.

3. Sofya Baskin, Anna Zamansky, and Vitaliya Kononova. 2016. Exploring human perceptions of dog-tablet playful interactions. In *Proceedings of the Third International Conference on Animal-Computer Interaction*. ACM, 15.

4. Marc Bekoff, Colin Allen, and Gordon M Burghardt. 2002. *The cognitive animal: Empirical and theoretical perspectives on animal cognition*. MIT press.

5. Gordon M Burghardt. 2005. *The genesis of animal play: Testing the limits*. Mit Press.

6. Marcus Carter, Sarah Webber, and Sally Sherwen. 2015. Naturalism and ACI: augmenting zoo enclosures with digital technology. In *Proceedings of the 12th International Conference on Advances in Computer Entertainment Technology*. ACM, 61.

7. Adrian David Cheok, Roger Thomas Kok Chuen Tan, Roshan Lalintha Peiris, Owen Noel Newton Fernando, James Teh Keng Soon, Imiyage Janaka Prasad Wijesena, and Janyn Yin Ping Sen. 2011. Metazoa Ludens: Mixed-reality interaction and play for small pets and humans. *IEEE Transactions on Systems, Man, and Cybernetics-Part A: Systems and Humans* 41, 5 (2011), 876–891.

8. Jacob Cohen. 1977. Statistical power analysis for the behavioral sciences (revised ed.). (1977).

9. Clemens Driessen, Kars Alfrink, Marinka Copier, Hein Lagerweij, and Irene van Peer. 2014. What could playing with pigs do to us? Game design as multispecies philosophy. *Antennae: The Journal of Nature in Visual Culture* 30 (2014), 81–104.

10. Tamás Faragó, Attila Andics, Viktor Devecseri, Anna Kis, Márta Gácsi, and Ádám Miklósi. 2014. Humans rely on the same rules to assess emotional valence and intensity in conspecific and dog vocalizations. *Biology letters* 10, 1 (2014), 20130926.

11. Annika Geurtsen, Maarten H Lamers, and Marcel JM Schaaf. 2015. Interactive digital gameplay can lower stress hormone levels in home alone dogsâĂŤA case for animal welfare informatics. In *International Conference on Entertainment Computing*. Springer, 238–251.

12. Ilyena Hirskyj-Douglas and Janet C Read. 2016. Using behavioural information to help owners gather requirements from their dogs' responses to media technology. In *Proceedings of the 30th International BCS Human Computer Interaction Conference: Fusion!* BCS Learning & Development Ltd., 42.

13. Philip N Lehner. 1998. *Handbook of ethological methods*. Cambridge University Press.

14. Clara Mancini. 2011. Animal-computer interaction: a manifesto. *interactions* 18, 4 (2011), 69–73.

15. Demi Mankoff, Anind Dey, Jennifer Mankoff, and Ken Mankoff. 2005. Supporting interspecies social awareness: using peripheral displays for distributed pack awareness. In *Proceedings of the 18th annual ACM symposium on User interface software and technology*. ACM, 253–258.

16. Ádám Miklósi. 2014. *Dog behaviour, evolution, and cognition*. OUP Oxford.

17. Conor Murphy. 2013. Chew on This: Analyzing 200 Dogs & Cats Playing with iPads. (2013). `http://www.bigfishgames.com/blog/chew-on-this-analyzing-200-dogs-cats-playing-with-ipads/`

18. Padgadget. 2014. iPad Classes for Dogs. (2014). `http://www.padgadget.com/2014/03/21/idog-clinics-use-ipad-to-teach-dogs-to-read/`

19. Patricia Pons, Javier Jaen, and Alejandro Catala. 2015a. Envisioning future playful interactive environments for animals. In *More Playful User Interfaces*. Springer, 121–150.

20. Patricia Pons, Javier Jaen, and Alejandro Catala. 2015b. Envisioning future playful interactive environments for animals. In *More Playful User Interfaces*. Springer, 121–150.

21. Team Register. 2013. iPad classes for DOGS offered in New York. (2013). `http://www.theregister.co.uk/2013/08/28/ipad_classes_for_dogs_offered_in_new_york/`

22. Sarah Webber, Marcus Carter, Sally Sherwen, Wally Smith, Zaher Joukhadar, and Frank Vetere. 2017a. Kinecting with Orangutans: Zoo Visitors' Empathetic Responses to Animals? Use of Interactive Technology. In *Proceedings of the 2017 CHI Conference on Human Factors in Computing Systems*. ACM, 6075–6088.

23. Sarah Webber, Marcus Carter, Wally Smith, and Frank Vetere. 2017b. Interactive technology and human–animal encounters at the zoo. *International Journal of Human-Computer Studies* 98 (2017), 150–168.

24. Michelle Westerlaken and Stefano Gualeni. 2014. Felino: The philosophical practice of making an interspecies videogame. (2014).

25. Michelle Westerlaken and Stefano Gualeni. 2016. Becoming with: Towards the inclusion of animals as participants in design processes. In *Proceedings of the Third International Conference on Animal-Computer Interaction*. ACM, 1.

26. Chadwick A Wingrave, Jeremy Rose, Todd Langston, and Joseph J LaViola Jr. 2010. Early explorations of CAT: canine amusement and training. In *CHI'10 Extended Abstracts on Human Factors in Computing Systems*. ACM, 2661–2670.

27. Hanna Wirman. 2014. Games for/with strangers-Captive orangutan (pongo pygmaeus) touch screen play. *Antennae* (2014).

28. Hanna Wirman, Willie Smits, Gino Yu, and Wilson Yuen. 2011. Defeated by an orangutan? Approaching cross-species gameplay. In *DiGRA 2011 Conference*.

29. Hanna Wirman and Anna Zamansky. 2016. Toward characterization of playful ACI. *interactions* 23, 4 (2016), 47–51.

30. Hanna E Wirman and Ida KH Jørgensen. 2015. Designing for intuitive use for non-human users. In *Proceedings of the 12th International Conference on Advances in Computer Entertainment Technology*. ACM, 58.

Understanding Dangerous Play: A Grounded Theory Analysis of High-Performance Drone Racing Crashes

Amirreza Barin[1], **Igor Dolgov**[2], **Zachary O. Toups**[1]
[1]Play & Interactive Experiences for Learning Lab, Dept. Computer Science
[2]Perception, Action, & Cognition in Mediated Artificial & Natural Environments Lab, Dept. Psychology
New Mexico State University, Las Cruces, New Mexico, USA
barin@nmsu.edu, id@nmsu.edu, z@cs.nmsu.edu

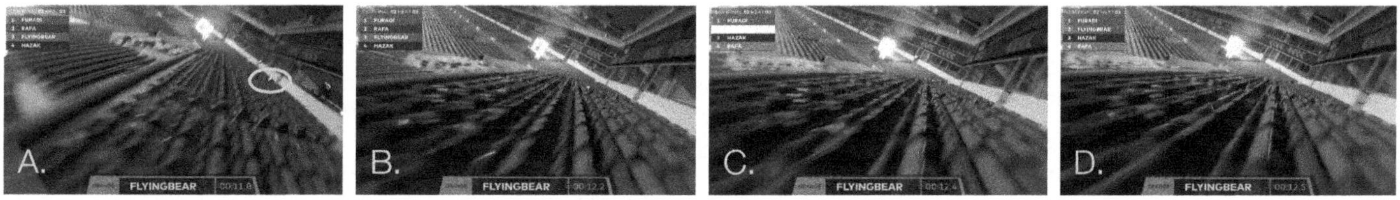

Figure 1. A crash in the Drone Racing League's Level 1 competition (Semifinal 2, Heat 3). The drones are flying over empty seats of a stadium, approaching a glowing green stand gate. Seen from the first-person view video feed from pilot FlyingBear (yellow), pilot Rafa's drone (red) hits a hard-to-spot handrail. In (A.), Rafa's drone is circled. (B.) is just before the crash. In (C.), Rafa crashes (note the leaderboard shows him eliminated). In (D.), FlyingBear begins to take action to avoid debris. Images ©2016 DRL; used with permission.

ABSTRACT
In drone racing, pilots compete on 3D race courses with quadcopter drones. A first-person view camera feed displayed through an immersive head-mounted display, gives them the sense of directly piloting the remote vehicle. The Drone Racing League (DRL) operates standardized competitions from which it produces professional video. In the present research, we analyze DRL videos to examine the reasons that high-performance drone pilots crash. The video corpus, combined with the standardization of the event, enables us to study pilot performance without interfering factors (e.g., customized drones or interfaces). We present a deep understanding of the sport of drone racing, a framework for understanding crashes, and insights into the reasons that pilots crash, exploring how the HCI community can benefit drone racing through future user interface augmentations.

Author Keywords
Drone racing; unmanned aircraft systems; UAS; first-person video; crashes; grounded theory.

ACM Classification Keywords
H.5.1 Information Interfaces and Presentation (e.g. HCI): Artificial, augmented, and virtual realities

CHI PLAY '17, October 15–18, 2017, Amsterdam, Netherlands

ISBN 978-1-4503-4898-0/17/10...$15.00
DOI: https://doi.org/10.1145/3116595.3116611

INTRODUCTION
Drone racing is a recent competitive sport in which pilots, equipped with immersive wearable displays, fly unmanned aircraft systems (UAS, i.e., drones) through complex 3D courses. Pilots don a head-mounted display (HMD) wirelessly linked to a front-facing camera mounted on their drones, providing them, and their audience, a first-person view (FPV) that creates a sense of being on the course (see video frames in Figure 1). Race courses feature many obstacles, requiring pilots to maneuver quickly and carefully. The goal of drone racing is to finish the course in the fastest time to accumulate points; crashes eliminate pilots from a race.

The sport has proliferated among enthusiasts, attracting amateurs and professionals. There are a small number of professional drone leagues, including the Drone Racing League (DRL), which are organized by companies and private investors. Interest from advertisers and media has been piqued: ESPN2, a cable network channel devoted to sports, has regularly featured the DRL since 2016 [34].

In this paper, we develop grounded theory of drone crashes. UAS, in general, experience a much higher rate of crashes than their manned counterparts [8, 20]. Documented crashes in drone racing allow scholars to closely investigate causes of pilot error and better understand drone operation under standardized, stressful conditions. Thus, it is valuable to study both human performance and interface design in this domain [9]. While preventing crashes is important for winning races, it is vital in non-recreational contexts, where drone crashes can cause significant damage to people and property.

The present research focuses on races conducted in the DRL, a professional drone racing league. While other leagues allow racers to provide their drones, DRL rules require racers to pilot a standard drone made by the DRL; there is no drone customization as a component of play. Thus, pilot skill is the primary factor in success. This provides a methodological advantage for our research in that we can study drone pilot performance and crashes using platforms with identical technology running on standardized courses.

We gathered numerous drone racing videos provided by the DRL to identify all crash events. Because these are sporting events, there are ancillary data sources for crashes (e.g., interviews with pilots, slow-motion replays, professional commentary) that help us triangulate the reasons for crashes. In this paper we present a synthesis of all of these observations to help the community understand the sport and see opportunities for design. The research covers one level of DRL racing events with 168 unique videos totaling 514 minutes. We captured a total of 18 documented crashes in the dataset. In this paper, we provide three contributions:

1. a first-of-its-kind description for the research community of the emerging sport of drone racing;
2. a framework for studying drone crashes; and
3. a grounded theory analysis to understand the reasons for crashes in drone racing.

It is our expectation that this research will form the foundation of a better understanding of drone interfaces, drone play, human performance, and opportunities to design for sports. At the same time, we present a note of caution about changing the nature of the present sport: while it may be possible to intervene and provide "better" and "safer" drone interfaces, they may not be desirable as part of this sport. However, the lessons learned can translate to non-recreational UAS domains where safety is paramount.

BACKGROUND

Prior research on drone racing is absent from the academic literature, as it is an emerging sport. However, ample attention has been paid to other UAS domains in recent decades. In this section, we briefly cover prior UAS research, elaborate on the design of UAS pilot interfaces, review visual perception research, and provide a brief history of drone racing.

Prior UAS Research

While drone racers put speed and maneuverability at a premium, most UAS not designed for this context are designed for safety above all else. So, while the standard DRL drone is bare-bones and consists of a propulsion system, a camera, and a power supply, a standard UAS is equipped with additional technologies to support tracking (e.g., Global Positioning System (GPS) sensors), stability (e.g., inertial measuring units, accelerometers), and automation (e.g., sensor-driven autopilot) [2,4,46].

Additionally, UAS systems vary greatly in terms of platform size and crew composition, often needing an on-site, "external" pilot for takeoff / landing and a remote, "internal" pilot responsible for all other phases of flight (in addition to one or more crew for commanding the mission and managing payloads, such as sensor packages) [8,20]. Wwhile drone racers pilot via an FPV camera, the majority of UAS are equipped with automation that allows pilots to simply indicate waypoints on a map and the drone flies on autopilot [2,4,5,32]. That said, findings gathered from the extant UAS literature also apply in the context of drone racing.

Unmanned aircraft have incident rates at approximately 10 times greater than their manned counterparts [8,20]. Although equipment malfunctions and weather contribute to UAS crashes and mishaps, the primary cause is pilot error [5,8,20]. Poor pilot performance occurs in various forms and often stems from lack of situation awareness [10,11] and / or high workload [9]. As with most interfaces, while pilots generally bear the blame, often suboptimal control interface design and / or training are the true source of error [31,32].

Despite these challenges, in 2016 the United States Federal Aviation Administration (FAA) issued the *Small Unmanned Aircraft Rule* (14 CFR Part 107) [45], which allowed routine civil operations of small UAS (55 pounds [~25kg] and less) in *Class G* airspace (no more than 400 feet [~120 meters] above ground level and not in the vicinity of airports or other designated areas) [45]. One of the main safety-related stipulations to this rule is that UAS pilots must effectively accomplish see-and-avoid duties, keeping well clear of all other aircraft, persons, and property, by maintaining the aircraft within visual line-of-sight throughout the flight (and occasionally scanning the sky for incoming air traffic).

In contrast, DRL pilots are not bound by such rules and fly in close proximity to each other on closed courses. While typical UAS pilots look at their aircraft during flight, DRL pilots use a fully enclosed FPV HMD, and cannot see their aircraft. Furthermore, while typical UAS pilots rely on assistive technologies to navigate, DRL pilots rely entirely on vision.

UAS Pilot Interfaces

UAS platforms vary greatly in complexity, and thus, crew composition [2,4,5,8,20,46]. Pancock et al. [32] conducted a literature review investigating UAS control stations, with special attention to their designs and capabilities. They found that that small / simple platforms typically solely require a single external pilot for all phases of flight, whereas big / complex platforms require an external pilot for takeoff and landing and an internal pilot for other phases of flight.

During manual flight, UAS pilots use common handheld remote controllers, similar to those used with radio-controlled (RC) aircraft. These devices are typically fitted with two joysticks and various other functional units, depending on the design of the specific system [32,48]. On the other hand, for automated flight, external and internal pilots utilize a computer-based setup, known as a ground control station. Most ground control stations use a laptop or desktop with mouse and keyboard input, while some include additional input modalities (e.g., touch screens, joysticks) [32]. The displays include some combination of a moving map display, a navigation display, a system health / status display, and an out-window / payload display [32,48].

Visual Perception while Piloting a UAS

Dolgov [7] notes that, when manually flying UAS, external pilots use strategies similar to tracking an object on a flat projection plane, which is based on a target's (UAS's) heading angle, optical trajectory, and optical velocity [30, 37–39]. Rather than using depth cues, which are mostly absent at the altitudes and distances at which UAS are operated, pilots use 2D planar cues that enable see-and-avoid duties. When UAS platforms are equipped with a forward-facing camera, UAS pilots can sometimes rely on an FPV out-the-window display to manually navigate the aircraft. In such systems, this mode of control is typically relied upon during takeoff and landing, whereas the remainder of flight is highly automated [2, 4, 5, 46]. In contrast, DRL pilots rely entirely on an FPV wearable display for all parts of flight.

DRL pilots are adept at executing complex tricks with their drones while maneuvering around obstacles at break-neck speeds [43]. While this is nothing new in the world of RC aircraft (whose controls are similar to those of external UAS pilots), DRL pilots accomplish these feats of control while using an FPV wearable display and, effectively, looking "through a straw." While this greatly limits situation awareness, DRL pilots can still take advantage of perceptual regularities, like depth and time-to-contact cues, as well as other information available in their optic flow, to safely and speedily maneuver their aircraft around the course.

The concept of optic flow was introduced by Gibson in the 1950s and developed over the next several decades [13, 14]. Optic flow refers to the perceived movement of the optic (visual) array (the totality of what is seen) as person moves through the environment (or the environment moves around them). While DRL pilots are controlling their aircraft remotely, they still experience optic flow via their FPV HMD. Parsimoniously, Gibson originally developed the concept of optic flow while serving as unit director for the U. S. Army's Air Force Aviation Psychology Program, where he had access to hoards of pilots. Among numerous feats of human performance demonstrated by pilots, one particular scenario that piqued his interest was the ease at which ace pilots land their jets on the deck of an aircraft carrier, a task that seems nearly impossible given the physics involved. So, Gibson reasoned that there must be information available in the optic array that allows them to achieve such high performance [13, 14].

Gibson's thinking was later empirically confirmed by Lee and others [25, 26, 41]. A property of optic flow is that the closure rate of the gap between an animal and an approaching object is directly proportional to the rate at which the retinal projection of the object grows, a variable known as Tau [23, 25, 26, 35, 41]. Tau and its derivative are used by humans and other animals for planning and executing movements and directly perceiving time to contact (TTC) with an approaching object [26, 41]. Accurate perception of Tau is essential for survival of both predatory and prey species, and requires no complex knowledge. This is best illustrated by the spectrum of non-human creatures who manage to skillfully control their locomotion during complex pursuit, avoidance, appetitive, and herding behaviors [26, 27, 29, 47].

Recently, research has shown Tau may not be the whole story and that individual and stimulus differences impact TTC judgment [19]. TTC may be better predicted by image velocity, rather than Tau [44]. While more research is needed, the mastery exhibited by drone racers while using an FPV HMD to navigate complex 3D courses favors the image velocity account. This is due to the fact that a retinal image originating from an HMD does not hold the same relationship to Tau that a bona fide retinal image does. On the other hand, image velocity is unaffected by image source.

History of Drone Racing

The convergence of a number of technologies (e.g., high-precision sensors for tracking; miniature cameras; high-resolution displays; shrinking low-power, high-performance mechanical components) has driven the proliferation of inexpensive and fast drones, leading to the new sport of drone racing. Drone racing started in late 2014 as an amateur sport in Australia. Pilots shared video via social media, which were welcomed by enthusiasts worldwide [49]. As the amateur play grew in popularity, various organizations helped cultivate it into a professional sport, resulting in a number of competitive leagues and race formats.

Professional drone racing is proliferating worldwide. There are four large U.S.-based drone leagues which provide competitions with cash prizes: the DRL,[1] the MultiGP-Drone Racing League,[2] the Drone Sports Association U.S. National Drone Racing Championships,[3] and the Aerial Sport League. Beyond the U.S., DJI, a Chinese drone maker, has just opened a similar arena to the Aerial Sport League's *Drone Sports World* entertainment complex, and the International Drone Racing Association promotes drone racing worldwide.

GROUNDED THEORY METHODOLOGY

We aim to understand the sport of drone racing, in general, and the reasons for crashes, in specific. Grounded theory analysis entails collecting a multifaceted corpus of data and coding it to derive theory [16, 17]. Similar to other research methods, grounded theory requires that researchers construct a structured network that identifies the relationships and functionalities of involved participants, data, relevant literature, and collected data [15].

Grounded theory works well to analyze relationships [6], which is important when approaching a new field with few established frameworks. The data we were able to acquire from the DRL provided multiple, overlapping perspectives: video of drone racing events, with commentary, interviews, and replays; documentation; and enthusiast websites. Crashes are hard to analyze in the wild, but the DRL videos and other documentation provide multiple perspectives that facilitate triangulation, rendering grounded theory an effective approach.

In the present research, we used ATLAS.ti Windows[4] [3] for analysis. All videos were downloaded into the software for analysis and segmentation.

[1] https://thedroneracingleague.com/
[2] http://www.multigp.com/site/index
[3] http://dronesportsassociation.com/
[4] http://atlasti.com/product/v8-windows/

Data Collection and Segmentation

In the first step, we collected information about DRL race terms and conditions, piloting rules, venue operation, official course dimensions and boundaries, drone parts, technologies, course timing systems, scoring, pilots, classes, and levels. We explored websites that report on the sport (e.g., DroneGuru[5]) and websites that sell drone parts (e.g., AtmosphericAdventures[6]) to develop a comprehensive understanding.

In the second step, we acquired our primary data source: one researcher watched and categorized all available DRL videos. Collection took place over June–October 2016. At that time, there was a substantial number of videos available from the DRL on YouTube for all races that occurred on DRL Level 1: Miami Lights (Sun Life Stadium, Miami, Florida). Additional levels were not available on any network to which the team had access. At the time of this writing, the DRL is preparing for a new round of events and is obscuring links to the researched race events.

This initial dataset consisted of 284 videos. Some of these were subsets of other videos (e.g., a clip showing only an interview segment that is part of a larger race video); we removed overlapping videos, resulting in a corpus of 168 videos totaling 514 minutes. The collected videos were all professional productions and consisted of four types:

1. comprehensive race videos that included commentary, multiple event perspectives, FPV videos from all pilots, and interviews (57 videos);
2. separate pilot interviews (34 videos);
3. advertisements for DRL events (which included information on levels beyond the first; 48 videos); and
4. instructional videos (29 videos).

The researcher watched all of the videos at least three times each and simultaneously recorded notes. In this phase, he split videos with multiple contents, mostly the race videos, into their component segments (e.g., race event, post-race interviews, commentary from racers, replays). This process produced a total of 359 documents (i.e., video segments and unsegmented videos) for further analysis.

In the analysis of the segmented dataset, we categorized videos according to content: drone crashes, pilot interviews, piloting techniques, course simulation[7] races, and advertisements. The categorized videos drove our analysis focus.

Analysis Focus

In this research, our aim was to deeply understand the sport of drone racing and identify how and why pilots crash. This focused our efforts on understanding the mechanics of the sport as well as the proximate (e.g., obstacles) and ultimate (e.g., errors in perception) causes of crashes. In the remainder of this section, we explain analysis foci; in the Results section, we describe what we learned through these foci.

[5]`http://www.droneguru.net`

[6]`http://atmosphericadventures.com/`

[7]While the other content types are self-explanatory, course simulations are video clips that explain the race course, rendered in 3D.

Understanding the Sport

The overarching goal of the present research was to understand and communicate to the community the play of drone racing. Through immersing ourselves in the data, we developed a deep understanding of drone racing play, pilot and spectator experience, and tournament and course design.

Investigating Obstacles

Through the race videos it became clear that obstacles, which are a form of skill test for pilots, are a key part of race course design and worthy of deeper investigation. We turned to the sport documentation, looked specifically at obstacles in our videos, and identified the types of obstacles that racers face. Through our analysis, we also discovered that obstacles can be official (constructed) or incidental (i.e., related to the venue, but not constructed).

Investigating Crashes

The primary driver for the present research was to investigate how and why drone racers crash. To advance this component, we identified crash events in our data, finding 18 events. From these 18 events, we identified all corroborating evidence across our dataset and linked them to the crash event. In identifying corroborating documents, the researcher took notes on the event and wrote down transcripts of all speech associated with the event. On average, there were 4–5 documents linked to each of the 18 crashes; the linked documents included interview videos, race videos, FPV videos of the crashed drone, other drones' FPV videos for this crash, notes, and transcripts.

Through the crash dataset, we sought specific information from the data, which emerged as we developed our knowledge base. We reviewed the crash dataset multiple times to develop our schema. Ultimately, we collected the following information for each crash:

- the pilots(s) involved;
- the race course and location of the crash on the course;
- the type of obstacle involved (if any); and
- environmental conditions (including ambient light).

All these attributes were not always available, but we developed as much of an understanding as we could.

Using the data points collected from the linked documents and coding them, we developed a framing to understand crashes. In some cases, we found that instructional videos were helpful in understanding the reasons for a crash. The crash analysis framework synthesizes the information collected and frames each crash in terms of the following fields:

1. **Crash Location**: Locations are on race courses, described in terms of an obstacle of that course (e.g., a particular tunnel). We have seven crash locations in our dataset.
2. **Crash Position**: The exact position in / on an obstacle where a drone crashed (e.g., the exact position of the top of a particular tunnel).
3. **Maneuver Type**: Maneuver types describe the activity the pilot was performing with the drone when it crashed (e.g.,

turning left or right, climbing). Instructional videos were especially helpful in understanding and describing maneuver types.

4. **Descriptive Reason for Crash**: Based on observation of race video and interviews, we identify the reasons for crashes.

5. **Crash Type**: We classified crashes as one of three types (described in detail later): drone-obstacle collisions, drone-drone collisions, or stall crashes. Collisions occur when the drone strikes another object; stall crashes occur due to the aerodynamics of the drone and performed maneuver.

This framing is potentially useful to analyze any drone race crash event. For each data field, there are a number of possible values. Some values are specific to our observed venue, but can be adapted or expanded as new data are collected.

RESULTS

Our results provide insight into play in the DRL and an understanding of the reasons for drone crashes in races. While our results are specific to the DRL, mostly due to the extensive number of documents we were able to acquire that were not available for other leagues or events, we expect that general understanding can be extrapolated from them.

One contribution is an account of the sport of drone racing through the lens of the DRL. In this section, we describe how the sport is played and provide a detailed description of the context of the sport as derived from our observations of videos and the sport documentation. The description here combines elements of multiple races that we observed in DRL Level 1. We describe an example race, from the data, as well as a general description of play.

Example Race

The massive [American] football stadium is devoid of spectators and a course has been configured through it: bright LED strips line the seats, walls, and columns. The lights roughly mark out a course through the concrete structure. Aside from pilots' prior experience flying course, the lights are the only indication that a pilot is on-course. Throughout, large, brightly lit open squares make the gates through which drones will fly to score points.

Up to four drones are set up on illuminated podiums at the starting line. The surface is angled forward, to ensure that drones take off flying forward, rather than up. They are in a staggered formation, minimizing the chances of collision. Smoke blows across the podiums, giving the effect that the brightly lit drones are rockets prepared for takeoff.

Nearby, in the safety of a covered VIP area, pilots prepare. They are seated in a row overlooking the stadium in large, comfortable seats. The vantage point on the empty space is irrelevant, they will be wearing fully immersive HMDs.

Radio chatter can be heard, "The course is now closed. We are clearing the area. Initiating check..."

As chatter continues on the radio, an announcer, pacing in the VIP area, says, "Alright, pilots, goggles. Arm check."

The pilots all fit their HMDs over their faces, securing straps and ensuring a comfortable fit. One-by-one they raise one hand in a thumbs up, indicating they are set. They are now fully immersed in the race: their HMD goggles show an FPV video feed from the front cameras of their resting drones. They pick up their RC controllers: bulky boxes with two thumbsticks and various switches; they prepare to race.

"Ten seconds, pilots." A female voice counts down over the PA system: "Ten, nine, eight..."

When she reaches "Three", her voice is replaced by a beep, another beep, and the starting tone.

The drones lift off, one speeding after the other. One lags behind as a commentator notes, "The start can be critical!" The race has begun.

A group of three drones bob along at high speed, their propellers sounding like a humming swarm of angry bees. They swoop over empty stands, cornering around glowing pylons and through the lit, square gates.

The pilots' "eyes" are the cameras mounted at front of the drones, experiencing the event as if flying extremely fast through a giant's stadium. Their palms sweat as they impart minute changes to the two sticks with their thumbs, tilting their drones to change their velocity and attitude.[8]

The course requires the pilots to deviate from their circular path around the bowl, sweeping out of the stands and over the field. The drones, one-by-one, drop down to where a green illuminated tunnel, normally access for spectators, is the next segment of the course. One drone swings too far, losing time.

They fly through a concrete concessions area, avoiding flying too high, lest they hit fans on the ceiling. They dodge around columns, coming to another tunnel that takes them to a spectator-queuing area. A spiral ramp takes them up a floor and another tunnel takes them back out into the bowl, where they circle over the stands again.

The final stretch aims the drones at the starting point, where they will encounter the finish box. They pick up speed as they make the final straightaway, at the end of which is a box designed to catch the drones and detect who finished first. One-by-one, the drones smack into the springy back of the box, falling to its padded floor.

Drone Racing League Play

In this section, we provide further details of play. We start from our primary data, and generalize to the sport as a whole from less rigorous observations of online sources. Our foci on understanding the sport and investigating obstacles drive our explanations.

Race Environment

DRL races take place on 3D courses inside abandoned buildings, around major landmarks, or inside stadiums. Every DRL event, called a "level" has a unique venue and title (e.g., Level 1: Miami Lights, Level 2: L.A.pocalypse). A course

[8] Attitude is the angle of the drone relative to horizon.

that passes through various parts of the venue is identified and marked out with bright lights and obstacles.

Within the race environment, a safe area for pilots is configured with a protective cover. Each pilot has a specified seat and may stand up, but they cannot leave the designated pilot area; it is unclear if this is to preserve fairness or for safety.

The drones start the race at a particular location, resting on individual podiums that are angled to enable a fast take-off. Additionally, the drones are clustered together, but spaced far enough apart to ensure that pilots do not collide immediately.

A key piece of preparation is the installation of necessary infrastructure. Infrastructure includes specifying the digital and analog network channels that are used for communicating with drones and transmitting FPV video. Cameras are located throughout the course to capture the race from multiple angles for the production of race videos.

No spectators are allowed within the DRL race environment. Similar to the DRL, a few other racing leagues utilize indoor areas, which place hard constraints on drone maneuverability, making it probable that some drones will crash. Looking beyond, we find that many organized amateur events are held in open spaces when/where other people are not present. Racers employ found objects (e.g., trees, playground equipment) as obstacles or course markers (e.g., to note where pilots should turn around). Play in open spaces can be relatively safe for the drones, but trees and other obstacles can still be dangerous.

Live audiences are rare, owing to safety and the fact that drones are hard to track visually. This contrasts sharply with automobile racing, in which crowds can safely and easily watch the large vehicles move around a 2D track [12]. Sometimes, a few spectators watch a race from a safe place, often using remote video. The video, typically a direct FPV feed or transmitted online, is often displayed on the large monitor. In some races, spectators can choose from the various drone video feeds by tuning their HMDs to the appropriate channel.

Courses

Courses are the path drones need to take around a race environment; normally, these are designed to maximize the need for skillful maneuvering. Drones are free to fly within any space in the race environment, but to be competitive they need to pick efficient lines in navigating the course. For any DRL race, the course is run by pilots one time, accumulating points by clearing obstacles and finishing quickly.

The starting line for a course includes the podiums for the drones. Each course consists of a number of obstacles, primarily gates, that drones must pass through. The courses are lit throughout; in some cases, the lights are the only marker of where the course actually is. For example, part of Level 1 involves the drones flying out across an open space toward the football field in the middle; a line of lights marks where they need to drop down and turn around to enter a tunnel.

Each course concludes with a finish box: a large, padded box with one open side to catch speeding drones. The design of the box is such that it allows drones to crash into its interior somewhat safely, supporting finishing the race as fast as possible. The box is enclosed, so drones that are stopped (or disabled from the final impact) are unlikely to escape.

All DRL courses also are designed in with 3D elements. We are able to gather some data on the design of multiple DRL courses through simulation videos. We know that they use gates, tunnels, ramps, windows, stairs and floors as paths and obstacles, and that bright LED lighting is key to making these things visible to pilots. Each course makes use of the unique affordances of the venue in which they are set.

We have the most details on the DRL's Level 1 course, Miami Lights (Figure 2). This course includes five 3D illuminated stand gates. There are also three tunnel segments that create a tight space for flying. A unique element of this course is the helix, a long spiraling ramp that rises in elevation.

Course designs take advantage of drones' unique ability to move in 3D and prioritize the ability to engage in aerial acrobatics as a core skill in the game. In any event, there is an identified course that often incorporates 3D elements. Sometimes races are set up through spaces that players cannot physically access, like flying through the windows of abandoned buildings. Due to power requirements and cost, only professional leagues are likely to use large amounts of bright lights to plot complex pathways.

Obstacles

DRL courses consist of a number of obstacles, spread throughout a course. Some are official and are configured as part of the course, others are simply characteristics of the venue (i.e., incidental obstacles).

The official obstacles in DRL levels are usually gates, tunnels, ramps, walls, windows, stairs and floors. Official obstacles in DRL Level 1: Miami Lights include:

- **Stand gates** are large square or circular frames surrounded by lights that the drones fly through to score points.
- **Tunnels** force drones into tight spaces. These tunnels are often the passageways that are used to enter or exit the bowl of the stadium. Sometimes smoke machines spread smoke inside of the tunnels, reducing visibility.
- **Louvered wall**: Pilots must fly along a wall with a repeating light pattern on it, then break away at the right time.
- **Helix**: A winding spiral ramp up which pilots must fly.

In addition, the seats, handrails, ceiling fans, and walls of the stadium serve as incidental obstacles that pilots must avoid.

For general drone racing, found objects often serve as obstacles to avoid. Inasmuch as the goal of the sport is to demonstrate acrobatic ability, obstacles serve to engage pilots in displays of skill.

Equipment

For DRL races, all equipment is standardized, so equipment customization (including drones) is *not* a component of play. DRL funds a special engineering department for developing drones, video transmission methods, radio frequency technology, and race equipment. For each pilot, normal DRL equipment includes a drone, RC controller, and HMD.

Figure 2. Overview of the DRL Level 1 Miami Lights course in Sun Life Stadium. A blue flag calls out the starting point and the course follows the bright blue line around the bowl of the stadium, into the side areas, along the louvered wall (bottom center), via the three tunnels (one near Checkpoint A, lower-left; two near Checkpoint B, lower-right), up the helix (lower-right of image), around the bowl again, and concludes with the finish box at the black Finish Line flag. Image ©2016 DRL; used with permission.

Drone. Drones are the primary technology for the DRL and the focus of its development efforts, which optimize for speed, agility, and resilience. In the present research, pilots were using Racer 2 drones, although DRL has recently released the Racer 3. DRL provides all drones for its competitions and keeps a queue of ready drones for each pilot as races progress.

Racing drones are quadcopters (4 upward facing rotors), but are configured differently from common hobby drones. Racing drone rotors form an H-shape, rather than an X-shape, to support forward speed, rather than stability. DRL drones use powerful motors and aim to be lightweight. Since they impact the finish box and crash land, in addition to normal crashes, they must have a sturdy frame and body.

The front-mounted camera is angled such that pilots can see straight ahead as the drone pitches forward during flight. The camera transmits video in real time to the pilot's HMD; the feed can be tapped into for spectating purposes.

As they are competing in races, visually tracking drones is key, both for spectators and pilots. DRL drones are covered in all sides in a grid of color-changable LEDs. During each race, a pilot's drone is set to a particular color.

Outside the DRL, drone customization is often a key component of competition and a means for pilots to distinguish themselves. Racing drones run a gamut of designs, but are almost universally small quadcopters with an FPV camera.

Controller. RC controllers are used to pilot drones and consist of two analog thumbsticks that can be pushed in any direction: the right joystick controls roll (via left-right movement) and pitch (via forward-back movement) and the left joystick controls yaw (via left-right movement) and overall throttle (via forward-back movement). Roll is the primary means to turn a drone while flying, causing the drone to tilt along its longitudinal axis by adjusting the relative power to rotors on either side. Pitch adjusts the forward / backward leaning of the drone, which enables it to fly forward or backward. Yaw is primarily useful for spinning the drone in place. As with all rotor-wing aircraft, the throttle controls how fast all props are spinning, so that, if tilted forward, the drone acquires forward and upward momentum; if level, the drone will simply go up.

This is a standard configuration for drone racers (and RC flight, in general). The overall effect is that, to fly forward, the pilot pushes both sticks forward. Typical turns are accomplished by moving the left stick to the left or right, causing the drone to bank.

The controller and drone must be set to the same radio frequency channels, which are specified for each pilot in a race.

HMD Goggles. DRL pilots wear HMD goggles that completely obscure vision of the world around them. The HMD goggles provide a raw live video feed of the drone's FPV camera, simulating sitting in a cockpit.

In the DRL, race status information is overlaid on the live video feed to each racer. The overlay provides a leaderboard in the corner, which indicates each pilot's relative position and whether or not any have crashed. This is accomplished with special software and a repeater device.

Infrastructure

A key part of any race is setting up infrastructure. All course designers must be careful about ensuring that the radio bands needed for transmitting to and from drones are interference free. In addition, the DRL includes substantial infrastructure for live mixing of video feeds and for recording events.

Race Scoring and Structure

DRL races consist of heats[9] with up to four pilots in each. Each pilot will compete in multiple heats, accumulating points for a race; the winner of the race gets the most points. A crash eliminates a pilot from a particular heat, but that pilot can still earn points by competing in other heats. Points are scored as follows:

> For passing at least two checkpoints and visiting the course in its entirety, pilots are awarded 50 points. For every second underneath the two-minute time cap, pilots are awarded an additional 10 points. Each race features a number of heats. [The final point total is calculated by summing the points across all the heats]. [49]

Race Regulations

Leagues specify their own regulations for competition, like any sport. These cover the following:

[9] A *heat* is a single competitive run through a course.

- **Aircraft specifications** for frame shape and size, propeller shape and size, motors, batteries, and vehicle weight.
- **FPV camera and goggles** may be subject to requirements about what data can be shown.
- **Safety rules** cover how people act within a venue, in particular staff and pilots. They also cover rules about pre-flight inspections, allowed types of flight, first aid, and fire hazards. One DRL safety rule is that the first step in retrieving any crashed drone is to pull the power connector off to ensure its rotors do not accidentally activate.
- **Participant rules and requirements** cover how league personnel and spectators should act.
- **Judgment rules** identify how ambiguous situations in a race will be adjudicated.
- **Frequency management rules** describe requirements for radio transmission within the venue to ensure all pilots maintain a video feed and control without interference.
- **Race levels and classes** identify the number and type of levels in a competition.
- **Scoring structure** specifies how pilots accumulate points and win races.

Tournament Structure

Competition in the DRL starts with the pre-season, then moves through each of the levels, which culminate in Level 5. The competition begins with 16 pilots total, four of whom are eliminated in the pre-season event. The remaining 12 pilots compete to win each of the five levels, based on points accumulated through a number of heats on each of those courses. The heats are organized into races, creating a tournament structure within the level. Points and eliminations do *not* carry forward to the next level.

In general, racing events have qualifying levels that they hold in either a regional or non-regional format. A normal structure is to have a tournament with semifinals, finals, and a championship to eliminate players and declare a champion.

Crash Analysis

A major focus of the present research was to explicate the reasons for drone crashes, and consider their role in the sport. Crashes in the DRL result in pilots being eliminated from the current heat, but not the race, which is a substantial penalty. At the same time, in other competitions, the stakes can be higher (e.g., loss of an expensive drone, complete loss of a competition). We thus expect understanding such incidents to be vital.

An interesting point in the DRL is that all drone hardware is standardized and racers practice with that hardware. This helps to eliminate any problems arising from unfamiliar equipment that could lead to crashes.

From our analysis of crash events, we identified three possible crash types:

- **drone-obstacle collisions** occur when a drone strikes an obstacle, either official or incidental;
- **drone-drone collisions** occur when two racers accidentally collide mid-flight; and
- **stall crashes** occur when a racer places the drone at an attitude such that it has insufficient lift to stay airborne.

In our dataset, we observed 15 drone-obstacle collisions, 1 drone-drone collision, and 2 stall crashes.

Collisions

Understanding the reason for collisions (both drone-obstacle and drone-drone) was a key part of this research. We were able to triangulate crash reasons by looking at multiple linked documents for each crash event. In many cases, racers who crashed were interviewed to understand their reasoning. In addition, since crashes were a focus of the produced race videos, we were often able to observe each crash from the racer's viewpoint, the viewpoint of trailing racers, and the viewpoint of venue cameras.

Regarding the one drone-drone collision, while we take this as its own type, these types of collision are rare. The one instance observed involved two drones taking off simultaneously and out of sight of one another.

Stall Crashes

While the mechanics of collisions are straightforward, stall crashes may be unfamiliar to the reader. Racing drones in the DRL are quadcopter designs with four rotors that provide lift in one direction [33, 42]. If the pilot changes the attitude of the drone and exceeds its critical angle of attack, the drone may slow below its stall speed in level flight, which renders it uncontrollable.

An example of a stall crash was when pilot Hazak crashed in Qualifying Race 2, Heat 1. He was banking over the (empty) stands through a series of gates. After clearing the last gate, he banked especially hard, pushing the drone to be perpendicular to the ground. When that happened, his drone only had thrust to its left and none upward, gravity caused it to drop out of the race and into the stands.

Proper drone piloting techniques prevent stall crashes, as we learned through instructional videos. Avoiding stalls is a key skill that is learned through practice.

Crash Reasons

In interviews, pilots discussed the reasons for crashes in terms of *human* performance. While they mentioned that stress and anxiety are factors for crashes, due to the high stakes of the competition, many pointed to a failure of maneuvering skills as the main reason for crashing. They pointed to two issues: choosing the wrong maneuver at the wrong time and a failure to execute the maneuver correctly.

Our study shows that collisions occurred due to three main reasons: improper maneuvering, errors in perception, and interference from lighting transitions.

Improper Maneuvering. While racing drones are agile, they also move very fast. Many collision crashes were a result of the failure of the pilot to maneuver through a tight space. We identified improper maneuvering as the reason for 7 of the drone-obstacle collisions in different places as well as the two stall crashes.

For example, at one of the sections of Level 1, after drones exit from a tunnel they must turn right to the helix immediately. This transition resulted in many of the drone-obstacle collisions due to the degree of the turn and the speed at which pilots were flying. For instance, pilot M0ke crashed in Final Heat 3 upon his drone exiting from a tunnel and wanting to turn right into the helix. Unfortunately for M0ke, he immediately collided with a column.

Errors in Perception. Errors in visual perception were the second-most prevalent reason for drone racing crashes in our dataset. While racing, pilots must use TTC, depth cues, and other information in their optic flow to choose the lines that they will fly through a course. However, due to the limited field of view of the front-mounted camera, pilots' situation awareness is compromised. Moreover, human perception is imperfect at extreme speeds, thus racers have difficulty judging their potential to avoid obstacles, causing collisions. Errors in perception were the reason for 6 of the observed drone-obstacle collisions.

For instance, when pilot Hazak in the DRL race Semifinal 2 Heat 3 was preparing to enter a tunnel gate, he lined up his drone and flew straight for a full 3 seconds. Believing his drone was aligned with the entrance, he flew directly into the top of the tunnel.

Interference from Lighting Transitions.

Some crashes were caused by drones moving from a dark space into a bright one or vice-versa. This lighting transition, which lasts only a moment, makes it hard for the racer to identify and avoid obstacles, leading to collisions. This was the reason for 2 drone-obstacle collisions.

DISCUSSION

Drone racing user interfaces are simple and direct, modeling the basics of flight. A mental model of quadcopter flying is needed, which is likely readily acquired through practice, in order to manipulate a drone. Further practice helps pilots develop an intuitive sense of the aircraft's aerodynamic capabilities and limitations, especially with regards to stalls. Based on our observed data, an understanding of how the sport is played, an understanding of the practice of spectating, and an understanding of crashes, we expect that there is ample opportunity for new UI designs in drone racing.

Value of Crashes

Watching pilots' performance is a primary motivator for spectators in drone racing and a primary concern in the design of the DRL. The controlled environment of the DRL helps to ensure that pilot skill is the primary point of competition (and the reason for crashes). Careful attention is paid to ensuring that flying drones are consistent, that pilots' capabilities are not technologically hindered, and that everyone has a fair and equivalent experience.

As in car racing, the possibility of crashes increases the drama of races and adds excitement. There is an open question as to whether or not reducing crash rate in professional drone races is desirable, although in other contexts (e.g., non-entertainment flight; drone races with privately owned, expensive drones) it clearly is.

None of the pilot interview data suggested a need for technological intervention; in fact, using a bare-bones design is what enables a DRL drone's speed and agility. The consensus among pilots indicates that they value the opportunity to engage in complex maneuvering and enjoy flying fast. Further, crashes are simply a component of the sport.

Potential for User Interface Improvements

While crashes seem integral to drone racing, we have two perspectives on how more advanced UIs could improve the sport while preserving the value of crashes.

First, DRL pilots represent some of the best drone racing pilots in the world, they are extremely skilled and have practiced their craft extensively. The process of undertaking this practice is time-consuming and expensive, and so augmented drone interfaces could serve to speed up pilot education and better prepare them for DRL-style drone racing.

Second, although skilled, pilots are playing through a technological mediation that does not support human cognition effectively. This failure, especially errors in perception, appears to directly translate into the few crashes that we observed. Further, unlike pilots of manned aircraft, drone pilots lack the physical experience that lends them information about the aerodynamic state of the aircraft. They also fly without basic instruments that are normally needed for flight.

Prior research in the community has focused on how drones might be used as a source of design, but not focused on how to support piloting them. A number of projects have considered using drones for display purposes (e.g., [18, 22, 36]), for playing games (e.g., [22, 28]), or for remote collaboration (e.g., [21]). The UI to control racing drones is, presently, simple, and only a few projects have considered how new technologies might support more interesting control devices and control mappings (e.g., [1, 24]). The projects fall short of addressing the issues we have discovered in drone racing.

Changes to drone UIs could help to develop human skill for more exciting races or could directly improve performance. In the remainder of this section, we look at the ways in which the research community could improve drone UIs for the purposes of racing. Beyond this scope, these improvements could benefit drone pilots, especially training, in general.

While we expect that faster processing, better display technologies, and faster drones will enhance the appeal of the sport, these advancements are straightforward and largely directed at hardware. At the same time, such hardware improvements are likely to exacerbate the existing challenges of flight, pushing it beyond human capabilities. This argues, further, for the need for UI enhancements to the sport.

Supporting Accurate Perception

One part of our results shows that most crashes are due to collisions, and the main reasons for collisions are failures in human perception and performance. This is illustrated by the fact that many crashes happened when racers tried to enter a check point or clear an obstacle but erred in their perception or maneuvering.

UI support could be added to support diagnosis of passability through and around various obstacles. Depending on the stance of drone racers, this could function in a tutorial mode to enable new pilots to understand the inherent difficulties in judging distance through FPV HMD goggles, yet we expect it to be valuable even as a prosthesis to overcome the inherent deficiencies in the setup.

We envision simple augmentations to a pilot's video feed: indicators on the feed of where the drone is projected to be in the near future. More advanced designs could warn of the location of an impending crash.

Technologically, supporting accurate perception can likely be performed through computer vision analysis of live video, to minimize the impact on the lean design of drones. At the same time, augmenting drones with a combination of sensors and / or data on the 3D configuration of their race environment would enable similar capabilities.

Supporting Instrumentation

Stall crashes occur when a drone's angle of attack is such that it loses lift. Stalls are a known issue in flight (both in traditional contexts and drone racing), and we observed a number of training videos and resources aimed at supporting drone racers in avoiding stalls. Drone pilots have to be made aware of the drone aerodynamic states that can lead to stall crashes during maneuvers. Drone racers lack even the most basic instruments and this, combined with being outside the cockpit of their vehicles, increases the likelihood of stall crashes.

We thus suggest that even a basic stall indicator would support drone pilots immensely. Such as system could communicate, through iconography, the lift state of a drone by using small, onboard sensors. Again, even used as a training tool, such an indicator could help drone pilots avoid stall crashes.

Enhancing the Spectator Experience

Drone racing is primarily watched in a technologically mediated way (e.g., professionally produced video from multiple viewpoints, large live screens, HMDs that can tune to multiple drones' frequencies). Spectators are rarely near a race because it is unsafe. Further, the inability to spot speeding drones with the naked eye is challenging even at a close distance.

A straightforward solution for visibility is to add lighting the drones. Some leagues provide or require drones that have bright LEDs on them, as is true of the DRL's Racer drones. Races are held indoors or at night for this reason.

An alternative solution is to have spectators located safely in an area where they can enjoy the race live through HMD goggles. An augmented view of the race could highlight racers and provide insight into their movement vectors. Spectators could select their preferred video feed and engage with the race at a greater depth.

CONCLUSION

In this paper, we have performed a grounded theory analysis of a large corpus of DRL video data to deeply understand the sport of drone racing and develop an understanding of the reasons for crashes. We contribute a first-of-its-kind description of the sport for consumption by the research community. The research has led us to a framework for describing and characterizing crashes. Looking further, we point toward the value of interfaces in this sport and the benefits they could provide.

It is our expectation that the sport of drone racing will continue to advance, pushing the limits of human capability and that, as a sport that is inherently technologically mediated, both for participants and spectators, it stands to benefit from leveraging that mediation. Looking to the future of drone racing, we expect that improving pilots' and spectators' interfaces are the keys to enabling more exciting and entertaining races. Such developments require that drone platforms advance, along with the sophistication of their sensor packages and ability to convey data to the pilot and transmit nuanced control to the drone.

We close with a quote from Stephenson's *Snowcrash*, in which he describes characters engaged in racing in a virtual world (the Metaverse). The description bears a striking resemblance to the experience of drone racing. For us, this quote highlights how drone racing can advance as a sport, but one in which UI advancements are vital in supporting physical advances in racing performance.

> A Metaverse vehicle can be as fast and nimble as a quark. There's no physics to worry about, no constraints on acceleration, no air resistance. Tires never squeal and brakes never lock up. The one thing that can't be helped is the reaction time of the user. So when they were racing their latest motorcycle software through Downtown at Mach 1, they didn't worry about engine capacity. They worried about the user interface, the controls that enabled the driver to steer, accelerate, or brake as quickly as he could think. Because when you're in a pack of bike racers going through a crowded area at that speed, and you run into something and suddenly slow down to a speed of exactly zero, you can forget about catching up. One mistake and you've lost. [40, p. 354]

ACKNOWLEDGEMENTS

This material is based upon work supported by the National Science Foundation under Grant No. IIS-1619273.

REFERENCES

1. Charlie Anderson, Benji Barash, Charlie McNeill, Denis Ogun, Michael Wray, Jarrod Knibbe, Christopher H. Morris, and Sue Ann Seah. 2015. The Cage: Towards a 6-DoF Remote Control with Force Feedback for UAV Interaction. In *Proceedings of the 33rd Annual ACM Conference Extended Abstracts on Human Factors in Computing Systems (CHI EA '15)*. ACM, New York, NY, USA, 1687–1692. DOI: http://dx.doi.org/10.1145/2702613.2732877
2. Ella Atkins, Aníbal Ollero, and Antonios Tsourdos (Eds.). 2016. *Unmanned Aircraft Systems*. John Wiley & Sons Ltd., Chichester, West Sussex, United Kingdom.
3. ATLAS.ti Scientific Software Development GmbH. 2017. ATLAS.ti Windows version 8. Software [Windows]. (2017). http://atlasti.com/product/v8-windows/
4. Reg Austin. 2010. *Unmanned aircraft systems: UAVS design, development and deployment*. John Wiley & Sons Ltd., Chichester, West Sussex, United Kingdom.
5. HaiYang Chao, YongCan Cao, and YangQuan Chen. 2010. Autopilots for small unmanned aerial vehicles: a survey. *International Journal of Control, Automation and Systems* 8, 1 (2010), 36–44.
6. Juliet Corbin and Anselm Strauss. 2008. *Basics of Qualitative Research: Techniques and Procedures for Developing Grounded Theory* (3rd ed.). SAGE Publications, Inc, Thousand Oaks, California, USA.
7. Igor Dolgov. 2016. Moving towards Unmanned Aircraft Systems Integration into the National Airspace System: Evaluating Visual Observers' Imminent Collision Anticipation during Day, Dusk, and Night sUAS Operations. *International Journal of Aviation Sciences* 1, 1 (2016), 41–56.
8. Igor Dolgov and Stephen B. Hottman. 2011. Human Factors in Unmanned Aircraft Systems. In *Introduction to Unmanned Aircraft Systems*, Richard K. Barnhart, Stephen B. Hottman, Douglas M. Marshall, and Eric Shappee (Eds.). CRC Press, 165–180. DOI: http://dx.doi.org/10.1201/b11202-12
9. Igor Dolgov, Elizabeth Kaltenbach, Ahmed S. Khalaf, and Zachary O. Toups. 2017. Measuring human performance in the field: Concepts and applications for unmanned aircraft systems. In *Human Factors in Practice: Concepts and Applications*, H. Cuevas, J. Velasquez, and A. Dattel (Eds.). Taylor & Francis. In press.
10. Mica R. Endsley. 1995. Toward a theory of situation awareness in dynamic systems. *Human Factors* 37, 1 (1995), 32–64.
11. Mica R. Endsley. 2000. Theoretical Underpinnings of Situation Awareness: A Critical Review. In *Situation Awareness Analysis and Measurement*, Mica R. Endsley and D. J. Garland (Eds.). Lawrence Erlbaum Associates, Mahwah, NJ, USA, 3–6.
12. Mattias Esbjörnsson, Barry Brown, Oskar Juhlin, Daniel Normark, Mattias Östergren, and Eric Laurier. 2006. Watching the Cars Go Round and Round: Designing for Active Spectating. In *Proceedings of the SIGCHI Conference on Human Factors in Computing Systems (CHI '06)*. ACM, New York, NY, USA, 1221–1224. DOI: http://dx.doi.org/10.1145/1124772.1124955
13. James J. Gibson. 1950. *The Perception of the Visual World*. The Riverside Press, Cambridge, Massachussets, USA.
14. James J. Gibson. 2014. *The Ecological Approach to Visual Perception* (classic ed.). Psychology Press, New York, New York, USA.
15. Barney G. Glaser. 1978. *Theoretical Sensitivity: Advances in the Methodology of Grounded Theory*. The Sociology Press, Mill Valley, California, USA.
16. Barney G. Glaser. 1998. *Doing Grounded Theory: Issues and Discussions*. The Sociology Press, Mill Valley, California, USA.
17. Barney G. Glaser and Anselm Strauss. 1967. *The Discovery of Grounded Theory: Strategies for Qualitative Research*. Aldine Publishing Company, Chicago, Illinois, USA.
18. Antonio Gomes, Calvin Rubens, Sean Braley, and Roel Vertegaal. 2016. BitDrones: Towards Using 3D Nanocopter Displays As Interactive Self-Levitating Programmable Matter. In *Proceedings of the 2016 CHI Conference on Human Factors in Computing Systems (CHI '16)*. ACM, New York, NY, USA, 770–780. DOI: http://dx.doi.org/10.1145/2858036.2858519
19. Peter A. Hancock and M. P. Manster. 1997. Time-to-Contact: More than Tau Alone. *Ecological Psychology* 9, 4 (1997), 265–297. DOI: http://dx.doi.org/10.1207/s15326969eco0904_2
20. Alan Hobbs. 2010. Unmanned Aircraft Systems. In *Human Factors in Aviation* (2nd ed.), Eduardo Salas and D. Maurino (Eds.). New York: Elsevier, 505–531. DOI: http://dx.doi.org/10.1016/B978-0-12-374518-7.00016-X
21. Brennan Jones, Kody Dillman, Richard Tang, Anthony Tang, Ehud Sharlin, Lora Oehlberg, Carman Neustaedter, and Scott Bateman. 2016. Elevating Communication, Collaboration, and Shared Experiences in Mobile Video Through Drones. In *Proceedings of the 2016 ACM Conference on Designing Interactive Systems (DIS '16)*. ACM, New York, NY, USA, 1123–1135. DOI: http://dx.doi.org/10.1145/2901790.2901847
22. Matjaž Kljun, Klen Čopič Pucihar, Mark Lochrie, and Paul Egglestone. 2015. StreetGamez: A Moving Projector Platform for Projected Street Games. In *Proceedings of the 2015 Annual Symposium on Computer-Human Interaction in Play (CHI PLAY '15)*. ACM, New York, NY, USA, 589–594. DOI: http://dx.doi.org/10.1145/2793107.2810305

23. Jan J. Koenderink. 1986. Optic flow. *Vision Research* 26, 1 (1986), 161–179.

24. Nataliya Kos'myna, Franck Tarpin-Bernard, and Bertrand Rivet. 2014. Bidirectional Feedback in Motor Imagery BCIs: Learn to Control a Drone Within 5 Minutes. In *CHI '14 Extended Abstracts on Human Factors in Computing Systems (CHI EA '14)*. ACM, New York, NY, USA, 479–482. DOI: http://dx.doi.org/10.1145/2559206.2574820

25. David N. Lee. 1976. A theory of visual control of braking based on information about time-to-collision. *Perception* 5, 4 (1976), 437–459.

26. David N. Lee and Paul E. Reddish. 1981. Plummeting gannets: A paradigm of ecological optics. *Nature* 293 (1981), 293–294. DOI: http://dx.doi.org/10.1038/293293a0

27. David N. Lee, Paul E. Reddish, and D. T. Rand. 1991. Aerial docking by hummingbirds. *Naturwissenschaften* 78, 11 (1991), 526–527.

28. Joseph Lindley and Paul Coulton. 2015. Game of Drones. In *Proceedings of the 2015 Annual Symposium on Computer-Human Interaction in Play (CHI PLAY '15)*. ACM, New York, NY, USA, 613–618. DOI: http://dx.doi.org/10.1145/2793107.2810300

29. Jack M. Loomis and Andrew C. Beall. 1998. Visually controlled locomotion: Its dependence on optic flow, three-dimensional space perception, and cognition. *Ecological Psychology* 10, 3-4 (1998), 271–285.

30. Michael K. McBeath, Dennis M. Shaffer, and Mary K. Kaiser. 1995. How baseball outfielders determine where to run to catch fly balls. *Science* 268, 5210 (1995), 569.

31. Don Norman. 2013. *The Design of Everyday Things: Revised and Expanded Edition* (2013 ed.). Basic Books, New York, New York, USA.

32. Carl Pancock, Jr., Ellen J. Bass, and Philip J. Smith. 2016. *UAS human factors and control station design standards: UAS control station literature review*. Technical Report.

33. Quadcopter Flight School. 2014. Vortex Ring State (The Wobble of Death). (2014). http://quadcopter101.blogspot.com/2014/10/vortex-ring-state-wobble-of-death.html.

34. Darren Rovell. 2016. Drone Racing League, ESPN reach broadcasting agreement. (2016). http://www.espn.com/moresports/story/_/id/17544727.

35. G. J. Savelsbergh, H. T. Whiting, and Reinoud J. Bootsma. 1991. Grasping Tau. *Journal of Experimental Psychology: Human Perception and Performance* 17, 2 (1991), 315.

36. Stefan Schneegass, Florian Alt, Jürgen Scheible, Albrecht Schmidt, and Haifeng Su. 2014. Midair Displays: Exploring the Concept of Free-floating Public Displays. In *CHI '14 Extended Abstracts on Human Factors in Computing Systems (CHI EA '14)*. ACM, New York, NY, USA, 2035–2040. DOI: http://dx.doi.org/10.1145/2559206.2581190

37. Dennis M. Shaffer, Igor Dolgov, Andrew Maynor, and Cody Reed. 2013a. Receivers in American football use a constant optical projection plane angle to pursue and catch thrown footballs. *Perception* 42, 8 (2013), 813–827.

38. Dennis M. Shaffer, Igor Dolgov, Eric Mcmanama, Charles Swank, Andrew B. Maynor, Kahlin Kelly, and John G. Neuhoff. 2013b. Blind (fold) ed by science: A constant target-heading angle is used in visual and nonvisual pursuit. *Psychonomic bulletin & review* 20, 5 (2013), 923–934.

39. Dennis M. Shaffer, Richard S. Marken, Igor Dolgov, and Andrew B. Maynor. 2013c. Chasin' choppers: using unpredictable trajectories to test theories of object interception. *Attention, Perception, & Psychophysics* 75, 7 (2013), 1496–1506.

40. Neal Stephenson. 1992. *Snow Crash*. Bantam Books, New York, NY, USA.

41. H-J Sun, DP Carey, and MA Goodale. 1992. A mammalian model of optic-flow utilization in the control of locomotion. *Experimental Brain Research* 91, 1 (1992), 171–175.

42. The Drone Racing League. 2016a. Proximity Stall. (2016). https://thedroneracingleague.com/trick-wiki/proximity-stall/.

43. The Drone Racing League. 2016b. Trick Wiki. (2016). https://thedroneracingleague.com/trick-wiki/.

44. James R. Tresilian. 1999. Visually timed action: Time-out for 'tau'? *Trends in Cognitive Sciences* 3, 8 (1999), 301–310.

45. U.S. Government Publishing Office. 2017. Small Unmanned Aircraft Systems, 14 C.F.R. Part 107. (2017).

46. Kimon P. Valavanis, P. Oh, and Les A. Piegl. 2013. *Unmanned aircraft systems*. Springer.

47. Hermann Wagner. 1982. Flow-field variables trigger landing in flies. *Nature* 297 (1982), 147–148.

48. Adam C. Watts, Vincent G. Ambrosia, and Everett A. Hinkley. 2012. Unmanned aircraft systems in remote sensing and scientific research: Classification and considerations of use. *Remote Sensing* 4, 6 (2012), 1671–1692.

49. Jesse Young. 2017. Everything You Need to Know about Drone Racing. (2017). http://www.droneguru.net/everything-you-need-to-know-about-drone-racing/.

Predictive Physics Simulation in Game Mechanics

Perttu Hämäläinen, Xiaoxiao Ma, Jari Takatalo
Aalto University
firstname.lastname@aalto.fi

Julian Togelius
NYU Tandon School of Engineering
julian@togelius.com

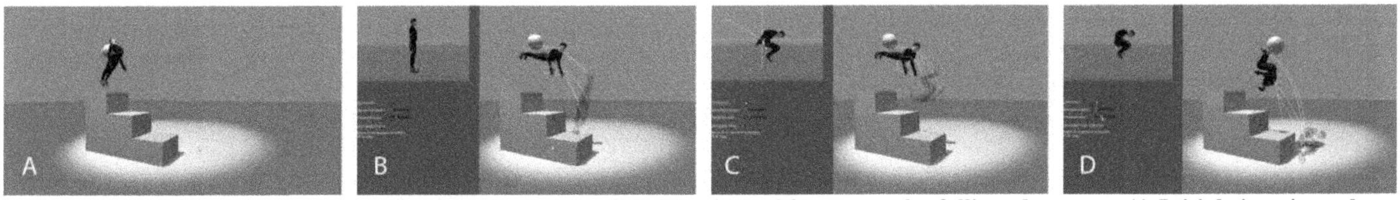

Figure 1. Our "animation as a game" prototype, where the player's goal is to save the falling character. A) Initial situation where the character is hit by a projectile. B) Game interface appears on the left, and the main view shows predictive movement trajectories and future pose; the character will hit its head unless the player acts. C) Using the posing controls (top-left), the player adjusts the future pose. Tucking increases rotation speed, which is predicted and visualized in real-time. D) Once satisfied with the prediction, the player advances the simulation. See the supplemental video at 03:00 for live gameplay.

ABSTRACT

Computers can now simulate simple game physics systems hundreds of times faster than real-time, which enables real-time prediction and visualization of the effects of player actions. Predictive simulation is traditionally used as part of planning and game AI algorithms; we argue that it presents untapped potential for game mechanics and interfaces. We explore this notion through 1) deriving a four-quadrant design space model based on game design and human motor control literature, and 2) developing and evaluating six novel prototypes that demonstrate the potential and challenges of each quadrant. Our work highlights opportunities in enabling direct control of complex simulated characters, and in transforming real-time action into turn-based puzzles. Based on our results, adding predictive simulation to existing game mechanics is less promising, as it may feel alienating or make a game too easy. However, the approach may still be useful for game designers, for example, as it allows one to test designs beyond one's playing skill.

Author Keywords
Game design; visualization; physics simulation;

ACM Classification Keywords
H.5.2. User interfaces: Interaction styles

CHI PLAY '17, October 15–18, 2017, Amsterdam, Netherlands
© 2017 Copyright is held by the owner/author(s).
ACM ISBN 978-1-4503-4898-0/17/10.
DOI: https://doi.org/10.1145/3116595.3116617

INTRODUCTION

Simulation of dynamic physical systems utilizes a set of rules that are unambiguous and mathematically well-defined [5], but can at the same time lead to emergent, rich behavior. This has inspired many types of physically based games and game mechanics, with popular examples such as The Incredible Machine [4], Angry Birds [25], Cut the Rope [36], Where's My Water [3], QWOP [2], and Portal [34]. Gradually, game physics has evolved towards more complex systems, i.e., from 2D to 3D, and from rigid bodies (e.g., stacked objects) to soft bodies (e.g., ropes and cloth) and fluids. During recent years, no fundamentally new physics simulation types have appeared, but on the other hand, personal computing devices can now simulate simple systems hundreds or even thousands times faster than real-time. This paper focuses on capitalizing this excess computing power for novel game mechanics and interfaces.

In this paper, we argue that *real-time predictive physics simulation* provides an underexplored tool for game design. Most games simulate physical systems at a fixed rate such as 60 simulation steps per second, and only use simulations in a *reactive* manner to compute the interactions of objects based on player input. In contrast, we denote by predictive simulation a process of:

1) Saving the current simulation state
2) Simulating the physics forward for multiple steps, up to a prediction horizon,
3) Using the simulation results to preview and evaluate the results of player decisions
4) Restoring simulation state back to the saved state, so that the game may continue without discontinuities.

As a simple example, while the player aims a projectile, one can provide immediate visualization of the predicted trajectories of impacted objects. Figure 1 presents a more complex example of controlling a humanoid model; the same principle of providing immediate feedback through predictive simulation trajectories still applies.

As summarized in Table 1, predictive physics simulation is not a new concept, and it has been increasingly utilized by recent artificial intelligence (AI) and animation research (e.g., [11,32]). However, research has focused on non-player characters or enabling simple high-level control of a simulated avatar, e.g., making a bipedal character walk in a desired direction. This has obvious applications in action games such as God of War [27] or Uncharted [20], which presently need vast quantities of animation data to enable such high-level control. However, there are also various games such as Angry Birds [25] and QWOP [2], where the player directly controls simulations on a low level. In such games, predictive simulation seems less explored. This observation prompts our primary research question: *What novel possibilities and challenges emerge from combining predictive simulation with low-level direct control of simulated characters?*

We contribute to answering the research question through an exploratory research process of 1) defining a four-quadrant design space model based on human motor control theory, and 2) developing and evaluating six novel prototypes that demonstrate the potential and challenges of each quadrant. Thus, using the contribution types of Wobbrock and Kientz [35], we make both a theoretical and an artifact contribution. In the following, we first start with the design space model, and then discuss the relevant background, our prototypes, their evaluation with game designers, and finally, key design insights and lessons learned.

DESIGN SPACE MODEL

In game and animation AI, a primary function of predictive simulation is to help an intelligent controller evaluate different options when making decisions. Such controllers typically use a feedback control model, i.e., decisions are evaluated through comparing simulation results to some goals, and the comparison results then inform further decisions. A key observation behind our design space model is that much of human motor control and decision making can also be modeled using a similar feedback or closed-loop model [29]. Further, control difficulty is heavily affected by the following three factors:

- *Time pressure*, which depends on the control task. Adjusting actions such as steering a car based on sensory feedback from previous actions always takes some time [29].
- *Complexity of actions*, which depends on both the control task and control interface. Complexity also interacts with time pressure, as complex decisions take more time; for example, reaction time grows as a function of the number of stimulus-response mappings [29].
- *Possibility of anticipation*, which depends on information provided by the task and interface. Although our reaction time is limited, we can still execute sequences of quick actions if we can anticipate and plan ahead of time [29]. An example of this is provided by various music games which display timelines of upcoming notes to play, providing more anticipation and reaction time.

	Reactive simulation	Predictive simulation
High-level (abstract) control	Animation-driven action games, e.g., God of War, Uncharted.	Recent AI and animation research.
Low-level (direct) control	Direct physics control games (QWOP, Angry Birds)	***Underexplored.***

Table 1. A categorization of physics simulation uses. Predictive simulation is increasingly used in AI and animation research, which is however focused on high-level control of simulated characters.

	Simple actions	Complex actions
Turn-based control (no time pressure)	2D ball shooting (**Figure 2**)	Character posing, turn-based QWOP, timeline QWOP (**Figures 1,3,4**).
Real-time control (time pressure)	3D car (**Figure 5**)	3D bike (**Figure 6**)

Table 2. A four-quadrant model of the underexplored design space of Table 1, with our prototypes placed in the quadrants.

A key opportunity of predictive simulation is in providing anticipation and enabling rapid evaluation of action results before action is taken, which should help in control tasks with more time pressure and/or increased action complexity. Time pressure and action complexity are up to the game designer to decide, and the decision is crucial since designing appropriately difficult challenges for the player is a central part of game design [26,28]. Hence, we propose the 2D design space model of Table 2, with time pressure and action complexity as the coordinate axes. We have divided the model into four quadrants, and following this division, we have developed and evaluated at least one prototype to explore each quadrant.

To reiterate, the model in Table 2 is based on both game design literature (importance of appropriate difficulty) and human motor control research (factors affecting difficulty). In low-level control of simulated characters, action complexity increases with the number of controlled simulation parameters and the need to plan for multiple actions instead of just a single action. With respect to time pressure, simulations can be controlled in real-time or turn-based fashion. Overall difficulty grows towards the bottom right corner of our model. We do not claim that our model captures all dimensions of the design space; our purpose is to highlight important dimensions that should provide sufficient focus for the rest of this paper. Of the three factors affecting difficulty listed above, anticipation is not explicitly included in the model in Table 2, as improved anticipation is automatically implied by using predictive simulation and visualization. In each quadrant, the degree of anticipation can be fine-tuned by selecting what to visualize and adjusting the prediction horizon.

BACKGROUND AND RELATED WORK

Before describing our prototypes in detail, we now make a brief detour into reviewing related work.

Reactive physics simulation in games

Reactive physics simulation in digital games dates back to at least the gravity simulations of Space War, Lunar Lander and Artillery [18]. Advances in simulation technology and computing power have inspired new game mechanics and types such as the water manipulation in Where's my Water [3]. Initially, simulations were only computed in two dimensions and with rigid bodies, but recently, even 3D large scale water simulation has found use in gameplay [13].

While our work focuses on simple mouse and keyboard interfaces, our Table 1 is inspired by Liu and Zordan [17], who similarly divide game interfaces into literal (low-level) and symbolic (high-level) in the context of gestural interaction. Both interface types have their strengths and weaknesses. Low-level control of simulation parameters such as a bipedal character's joint motor speeds can give rise to emergent and interesting movement, as in the interfaces of Laszlo et al. [15] and later in the games QWOP [2] and Toribash [19]; both games are however extremely difficult. Although the difficulty can give rise to physical comedy [31], many games instead simplify and abstract the interface to a level where the player simply presses a button to trigger complex predefined character animations. Creating and finetuning the animations is however costly, and some degree of movement emergence is lost, although physics simulation can still be used for reactions of the game world.

Predictive physics simulation in animation and AI

Predictive physics simulation is increasingly used in procedural animation and AI research. The basic idea is that since the outcomes of multiple alternative actions can be simulated and evaluated, an optimization algorithm can choose which action to take and which actions to evaluate next. This has a long history in animation synthesis and simulated robot control (e.g., [1,9,16,21]), with recent methods capable of real-time control of 3D humanoid bipeds [11,32]. Predictive physics simulation has also been used, especially together with stochastic search algorithms such as Monte Carlo Tree Search, for controlling non-player characters in video games [7,12], and for providing real-time feedback to level designers regarding the playability and possibilities of level designs [30].

In close relation to our work, Twigg and James [33] investigated predictive trajectory visualizations for adjusting the starting conditions of simulations such as trebuchet shooting; our ball shooting prototype in Figure 2 extends this with the interactive heatmap. We are also inspired by Laszlo et al. [14] who introduced predictive simulation and visualization for animation interfaces close to our prototype in Figure 1. We extend their work with full-body humanoid characters, visualization of trajectories in addition to poses, and the timeline interface of the prototype in Figure 4.

Predictive physics simulation in game interfaces

Although many games such as Angry Birds do visualize predictions of object movement trajectories, it appears that such predictions are mostly computed using more computationally efficient but also more limited methods than predictive simulation. For example, basic ballistic equations allow computing projectile trajectories but not the subsequent complex interactions of impacted objects. Toribash [19] and Peggle [22] provide rare counterexamples. In Toribash, the player controls a 3D simulated humanoid, and the game proceeds in a turn-based fashion. While the player is adjusting simulation controls, the game simulates and renders what will happen in the next few seconds. Interestingly, Toribash frames the complexity of Laszlo et al. [14] style physically based animation as a game challenge. However, predictions are only computed one rendered frame at a time, which adds significant delay in contrast to our immediate visualizations. Peggle employs immediate projectile trajectory visualization akin to Twigg and James [33]. It is noteworthy that although such visualization might make a game too easy, Peggle cleverly uses it as a limited resource, allowing longer predictions as a power-up.

PROTOTYPES

The following lists our prototypes, structured following the four-quadrant model of Table 2, and the monikers used when referring to them in the rest of the paper:

1. *Turn-based control of simple actions*: the "ball shooting" prototype of Figure 2 (supplemental video at 00:20).
2. *Turn-based control of complex actions:* the "character posing" prototype of Figure 1 (video at 03:00), "turn-based QWOP" of Figure 3 (video at 02:02), and "timeline QWOP" of Figure 4 (video at 02:28).
3. *Real-time control of simple actions:* the "car" prototype of Figure 5 (video at 01:05).
4. *Real-time control of complex actions:* the "bike" prototype of Figure 6 (video at 01:28)

We start our discussion from the most straightforward case of simple actions and turn-based control, and then extend the ideas to real-time control and more complex actions.

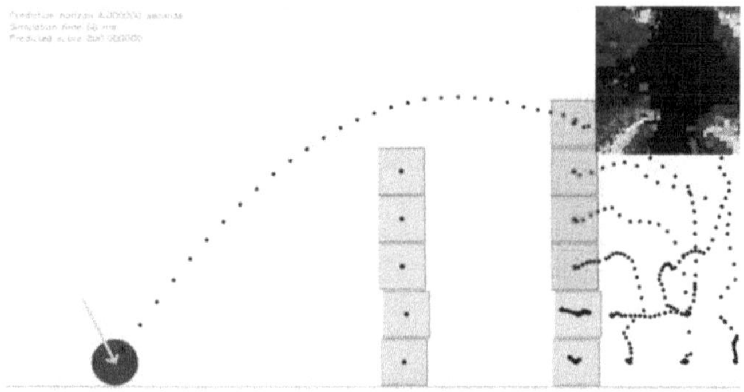

Figure 2. A ball shooting prototype inspired by Angry Birds. The player defines launch speed and angle of the blue ball, with the goal of only moving the green cubes. One can also shoot using a heatmap (top-right), where bright pixels correspond to good speed and angle combinations.

Figure 3. A turn-based version of the game QWOP, where the effect of keypresses is predicted and visualized, and time only advances when the player holds down the spacebar.

Figure 4. Timeline-based version of the game QWOP. In this prototype, the player paints the keystrokes on an animation timeline with tracks for the Q,W,O,P keys. Animation automatically plays in a loop (yellow frame indicator, solid character). The ghost character shows state at mouse position.

A note on the design process: The work towards this paper originates from a serendipitous discovery in context of intelligent animation control research, as the first author developed an initial implementation of the character posing prototype. We considered the prototype interesting, which motivated the construction of the design space model and developing prototypes for the other quadrants. The development of the QWOP versions then followed, as the emergent and rich movements of a simulated humanoid appeared more interesting than the ball, car, or bike.

Turn-based control of simple actions

In turn-based control, feedback is often delayed and the player must try and iterate multiple times to get an action right. Here, the key potential of predictive simulation is in providing feedback already while the player searches for a suitable action. We demonstrate this in the ball shooting prototype of Figure 2. The player controls the launch speed and angle similar to Angry Birds [25], with the goal of only moving the green boxes. We use predictive simulation to provide immediate visualization of the trajectories of objects and a prediction of the score (200 points for every green box that moves more than a threshold, minus 100 points for every gray box that moves).

In the ball shooting case, the action space is only two-dimensional (a shot is fully defined by speed and angle). In such cases, actions can be explored automatically to produce a heat map that gives a visual overview of possible player actions (the top-right grayscale rectangle in Figure 2). Four high-scoring strategies show up as bright clusters, the higher ones corresponding to bouncing the ball off the ground, and rightmost ones corresponding to bouncing the ball off the left wall. The user can interactively browse the heatmap with mouse to view the shot trajectories.

Brute force heatmap computation can be slow; at about 5-10ms per simulation and 256x256 pixel heatmap, the computation takes several minutes. However, as we demonstrate on the supplemental video, a non-negative scoring function can be treated as an unnormalized probability density function, which allows for quick computing of an approximate heatmap using importance-sampling. We use kD-tree Sequential Monte Carlo Sampling [10], which adaptively increases resolution where score is high.

Turn-based control of complex actions

Our prototypes in Figure 1, Figure 3, and Figure 4 extend turn-based control to the more complex case of a simulated humanoid. In our designs, we recombine ideas from three games: QWOP, Toribash, and Backflip Madness [2,8,19]. All three games implement an interface for controlling a physically based simulated humanoid character, but the games differ in how they manage the control complexity. QWOP only uses a 2D character, which prevents falling sideways, and simplifies the controls into discrete keystrokes; Q and W drive the left and right thigh forward, and O and P bend the left and right knee. Toribash uses a full 3D humanoid, but gives the player unlimited time to think – the player can explicitly control when simulation is advanced. Backflip Madness reduces complexity by allowing the player to only control the timing of transitions between predefined poses such as crouching, extended, and tucking.

We consider two main sources of complexity. The character posing prototype of Figure 1 focuses on the high dimensionality of action space, and the QWOP-inspired prototypes of Figure 3 and Figure 4 utilize simplified actions (only a set of 4 actions corresponding to the Q,W,O,P keys) that however require precise timing and coordination.

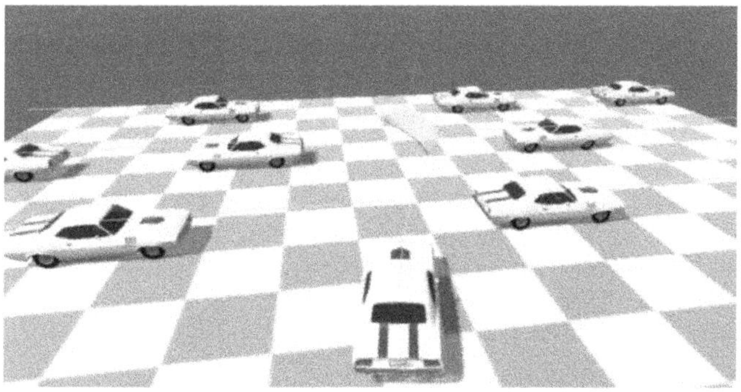

Figure 5. Prototype where the player tries to drive through the traffic at full speed. Holding down ctrl key shows predicted trajectories of all cars. In this image, the end of the player's trajectory is red, which signals predicted future collision.

Figure 6. Prototype where horizontal mouse movement controls the steering of a 3D bike without any artificial balancing. The bike's predicted movement and balance is predicted. Red color signals falling.

In our character posing prototype, the user controls when simulation is advanced; compared to Toribash, we provide faster feedback and more precise control. The game interface features an animation rig that the player can manipulate using a mouse. This defines a target pose that the simulated character is driven towards. The predicted trajectories and the resulting pose at the prediction horizon are also visualized. In Figure 1 the player is making the character tuck to rotate faster and avoid hitting its head. The player can also adjust the prediction horizon with a slider. The supplemental video shows how the character can be landed safely by first tucking, and then extending the body near the ground.

Figure 3 shows a turn-based version of QWOP, where the player is given a fifth key – simulation time advances only when the player holds down spacebar. The effects of other keys are predicted and visualized, allowing the player to explore the best combination of keys.

In initial testing, the turn-based QWOP was found quite difficult despite the unlimited time for deciding on the keypresses. This is why we developed the concept further, resulting in the prototype in Figure 4. Instead of pressing the keys, the player paints the keypresses on a timeline with a track for each key. The painted keypresses can also be freely erased, in essence transforming an originally real-time action game into a puzzle. The interface provides immediate visualization of character state at the mouse position (the semitransparent character) and the character's movement trajectory over the whole timeline.

Real-time control of simple actions

Our car and bike prototypes in Figure 5 and Figure 6 examine how the ideas presented above can be extended to real-time control. The car driving represents the case of simple actions. Horizontal mouse movement is mapped to steering, and the player has also keys for accelerating, braking, and turning on the predictive simulation and visualization. The player's goal is to drive through the traffic at full speed without hitting other cars. The predictive trajectory's color indicates whether the car will collide with others using the present steering direction.

Real-time control of complex actions

As the more complex real-time case we use the 3D bike steering and balancing prototype of Figure 6. We are inspired by the bikes of Trials HD [23], which however are only simulated in 2D. A 3D bike is more complex to control than a 2D bike or a car, as balance is coupled to steering through centripetal force; when steering right, one has to actually first countersteer left to make the bike start falling right. To prevent the bike from falling all the way, one must then steer right. Complexity arises from the needed precise temporal coordination of steering movements. As shown on the supplemental video, balancing is highly difficult because it is nearly impossible to estimate the correct steering magnitude, and both over- and understeering quickly lead to lost balance.

Similar to the car prototype, horizontal movement of the mouse is directly mapped to bike steering. Left mouse button controls throttle.

Technology: simulation cost and determinism

In modern game development, physics simulation is rarely implemented from scratch. Instead, games often use established libraries and toolkits such as the Open Dynamics Engine (ODE), Bullet, or Box2D. Our ball shooting prototype uses Box2D v2.3.0 for simulation and OpenCV for visualization. The other prototypes use Open Dynamics Engine (ODE) integrated with Unity 3D game engine as a native plugin. The predictive simulations take around 5-40ms on a 2.6GHz Intel i7-6700HQ processor, depending on simulation complexity and prediction horizon. The car prototype is the most computationally heavy due to multiple simulated cars and 3D simulation being slower than 2D.

In the implementation, we had to solve the problem of neither ODE or Box2D simulations being *fully deterministic and reproducible*. The simulators do not by default provide functionality for simulating forward from a given state and then restoring the starting state in a way that would ensure exactly same results in further simulations. This was also the reason for us not being able to use Unity3D's built-in physics, which has the additional complication that simulation time cannot be advanced independent of graphics rendering time.

In principle, saving and restoring movement state (position, rotation, velocity, and angular velocity) of all objects should be enough, but subsequent simulations can still diverge, due to the following main reasons:

- Simulators use random numbers, e.g., to process solver constraints in random order for better simulation stability.
- Simulators use additional internal state for speeding up the simulation. For example, ODE caches some variables inside the joint classes, and Box2D builds a dynamic spatial subdivision data structure for faster collision handling.

For deterministic simulation, all internal state, including random number generator state, must be saved and loaded together with movement state. We have implemented this in both ODE and Box2D and the source code is available at *https://bitbucket.org/perttuhamalainen/predictivesimulation*

EVALUATION DESIGN

Participants

We evaluated the prototypes qualitatively with 6 game design M.A. students and one game designer/design teacher (all male, age m=30, sd=5). All participants had experience from designing several games (m=9, sd=4).

Procedure

Each participant played all prototypes for 5-10 minutes while thinking aloud, and then answered a set of final questions. The order of prototypes used Latin Square counterbalancing. The total experiment duration was about 1 hour per participant.

For the prototypes that could also be played "regularly" without the predictive simulation (ball shooting, car, bike), the participant first played without prediction and then again with prediction turned on. We then asked which game version was better and why. The QWOP game versions were played with order altered between participants, and we again asked which version was better and why.

After all prototypes had been tested, we asked the following questions, and also probed further with why-questions:

1. Which of the prototypes were the most interesting?
2. Which of the prototypes were the least interesting?
3. What benefits and challenges does predictive physics simulation present from a game design perspective?
4. Which quadrant of Table 2 would the participant be interested in exploring further or utilizing in a game?

Data analysis

A thematic analysis of participant answers and comments was performed, with the goal of informing future design and research, and to identify the primary benefits and challenges of predictive physics simulation.

EVALUATION RESULTS

In the following, the participants are referred to as P1...P7 and their quotes are in italics.

Most interesting prototypes

The prototypes that were found most interesting were the character posing prototype of Figure 1 (all participants), the QWOP versions (5 participants mentioned one or both of the two, and there was no clear consensus of which version was better), and the bike (two participants). All of these except the bike also frequently resulted in comical blunders that made the participants laugh.

A central theme was that participants found it intriguing to understand and learn about the dynamics of movement. "*You never really pay attention to what parts of the body need to move to execute some actions. You have to think about individual actions that we otherwise are not aware of. Also the motorbike one was interesting because the countersteering is so counterintuitive – learned about how movement and physics work.*" (P2), *"I felt like having a superpower, that I understood better how people and the world work, and I got the character to make an insane acrobatic move"* (P6 on the character posing), *"Something like Quicksilver in X-Men movies"* (P4 on the character posing), *"Somehow makes me want to try again and again"* (P1 on the bike), *"Prediction is better. It seems to teach me how the bike works. I cannot otherwise understand why I fail."* (P6 on the bike), "*A fun variation of the original, which I have tried to learn for a long time. I now succeeded on first try*" (P6 on the turn-based QWOP).

One participant also selected the ball shooting prototype as the most interesting when considering the heatmap as a tool for level design. As a player, he too preferred the character posing prototype.

Least interesting prototypes

The prototypes that were found least interesting were the car (3 participants), the ball shooting (3 participants), the bike (2 participants), and the QWOP versions (1 mention for each).

Most of the mentioned prototypes are games that one could also play without predictive simulation. Although some participants preferred the versions with prediction because they were easier, a recurring concern was that prediction make the gameplay different and even alienating, as one's focus shifts from the controlled character to the trajectory visualizations. *"Prediction system was confusing, I was looking at the line, not the guy."* (P4 on the bike), *"Prediction makes it different, and removes the core game"* (P5 on the car), *"Prediction requires re-learning with the bike and car, because you pay attention to completely different things. I was not looking at the car at all."* (P7), *"It feels like it removes something"* (P6 on driving games), *"No feeling of being an awesome motorcyclist. Hard to be excited when the game's challenge is not to do cool tricks but instead just to follow a line and try to keep it white instead of red"*

(P3), *"I seem to stop using my intuition, I just think of the trajectories"* (P6 on the ball shooting).

An additional reason for mentioning the bike was too hard difficulty. None of the participants could keep the bike balanced without the predictive visualization. Four participants could keep the bike balanced with the predictive visualization, but balancing required so much effort and concentration that they could not steer the bike where they wanted.

Too hard difficulty was also the reason for mentioning the QWOP versions.

Benefits and challenges of predictive simulation

To summarize the pros and cons discussed during testing and in response to our questions 3 and 4, we identified the following main themes:

1. Positive: predictive simulation allows players to tackle new challenges and discover novel solutions and movements. *"An interesting puzzle. I've sometimes tried to play Toribash, but I got nowhere."* (P6 on the prototype of Figure 1), *"Discovery was the most interesting thing about the prediction"* (P2), *"Enables completely new levels and impossible scenarios that have a solution that the player otherwise wouldn't find except through insane trial and error"* (P7), *"Novel game mechanics in the style of the posing prototype."* (P6), *"It was interesting to see that there are four solutions when I assumed there's only one"* (P6)
2. Negative: predictive simulation can make a game too easy. *"Prediction clearly helped, but made the game less interesting due to reduced challenge"* (P7 on the car), *"Prediction is too easy."* (P6 on the car), *"It's hard to balance the challenge – easily either too hard or too easy and feels like cheating"* (P5), *"It would maybe be more fun to use the prediction for searching for a strategy if the puzzle was more difficult"* (P5), *"Prediction makes me lose interest in prototypes that otherwise feel challenging"* (P7 on the car and bike)
3. Mixed: even if always-on predictive simulation can be detrimental in some games, it may be useful in level design and testing or as a limited resource or power-up. *"Prediction is more useful for level designer, if you want to design and test a really hard level"* (P1 on the car prototype), *"Would be useful as a limited resource or power-up. As a player I would not use all the time, if it is not necessary for the game mechanics"* (P1), *"Seeing the prediction ruins the game, but would work for a tutorial"* (P2), *"Useful as a design tool in a car game if I want to test whether something is possible* <for a highly skilled player>*"* (P7), *"The heatmap is useful as it shows distinct solutions and rules out things you might otherwise try in testing"* (P2), *"Prediction would work well for game design and testing"* (P4)

Most interesting quadrants

All participants found turn-based control of complex actions as the most interesting quadrant, although P2 commented: *"As a game designer, turn-based control of complex actions, because I can learn and analyze. As a player, real-time control of complex actions, as I don't want to analyze so much during gameplay"*.

DISCUSSION

In this section, we present some additional observations and revisit our design space dimensions in light of the results.

Turn-based vs. real-time control

Considering all the prototypes and the evaluation results, turn-based control based on predictive simulations seems more promising than real-time control.

In our interpretation, the key difference between turn-based and real-time control is that optimizing the level of challenge is much more difficult in the latter. In real-time gameplay, it can be difficult to process visual information fast enough; predictive simulation can require the player's full attention as in our bike prototype, while still not making the control task easy enough to be enjoyable.

In real-time gameplay, predictive visualization also easily moves the focus of attention away from the controlled object or character, which many participants considered distracting. In our turn-based prototypes that were found most interesting (character posing and QWOP versions), one's focus of attention is not completely on the control interface or predictive visualization; instead, focus shifts back to the character when one advances the simulation or evaluates the animation resulting from keypresses painted on the timeline. Turn-based control also has less restrictions on how much visual information can be processed and utilized.

Simple vs. complex actions

Our prototypes with complex simulations appear more successful, in particular the ones with humanoid characters. In such simulations, predictive visualization can enable novel control interfaces and discovery of interesting emergent movement.

For simple actions, it appears that predictive simulation is not as useful as it can make a game too easy. The movement discovery capabilities provided by predictive simulation might be more useful as a game design and testing tool.

Designing novel mechanics and interfaces

We agree with P4 and P5 who commented that rather than adding predictive simulation to existing games and interfaces, one should probably design novel game mechanics and interfaces around the predictive simulation. Our best performing prototypes (the posed character and QWOP versions) were of the latter type. Although our QWOP versions are based on an existing game, they do not simply reduce the level of challenge; they play completely differently than the original. A key lesson learned is that *predictive simulation and visualization allows transforming real-time action games into turn-based puzzles*. Our prototypes demonstrate that achieving the intended movement is still challenging and can provide surprising outcomes, as slight differences in input can result in large deviations of realized movement. This is characteristic to all physics simulations with contacts; shooting a ball at slightly different angles can result in completely different trajectories depending on whether or not the ball hits an obstacle.

Interestingly, P5 explained that the original QWOP feels more comical because of the faster try and fail cycle, but P6 on the other hand commented that the turn-based QWOP is better because *"I see the possible futures and they are comical in the same way as in the original, but I don't have to fail for real."*

LIMITATIONS AND FUTURE WORK

Due to our qualitative and exploratory research approach, our evaluation data does not provide quantitative evidence in favor or against hypotheses such as "visualization A is better than B in task C". Readers should also use their own judgement in assigning weight to the user comments – they represent the views and experiences of individual players rather than the collective experience of a larger player population.

We opted for this approach as we wanted to gain a broad understanding of the design space and generate a wide variety of examples that could provide ideas for future games and ideas or hypotheses for future research. As an example of such a hypothesis, our results suggest that predictive visualization helps in the complex case of steering and balancing a 3D bike; this could be validated in a quantitative follow-up study, possibly comparing different visualizations in terms of task performance and player enjoyment.

Based on our ball shooting prototype (Figure 2), we also see future potential in characterizing level designs based on multiple simulations – for example, we hypothesize that good levels have multiple bright heatmap areas (i.e., multiple alternative strategies), and each area is large enough (no need for pixel-perfect control). Naturally, with more complex actions, such heatmaps and summary visualizations are likely to need advanced multidimensional data visualization techniques.

Although we have limited ourselves to low-level simulation control as opposed to utilizing predictive simulation for high-level AI-based control, we intend to investigate hybrids of the two approaches in future work; this might provide better tools for adjusting control difficulty and control abstraction/indirection. For example, extrapolating the concept of Draw Race [24] and Flight Control [6] (draw the desired path of a car or a plane to control it), a humanoid parkour character could be controlled indirectly by indicating the desired sequence of foot placements in advance, while getting predictive feedback of how the AI will succeed in obeying the instructions.

CONCLUSION

In this paper, we have proposed a four-quadrant model of the design space of low-level game or simulation control with predictive physics simulation and visualization, based on the key design dimensions of action complexity and time pressure (Table 2). Furthermore, we have presented the design and evaluation of six prototypes that demonstrate novel possibilities and challenges of each quadrant. Drawing on our experiences, observations, and the user comments, we now conclude with a summary of design insights and lessons learned:

1. Predictive physics simulation appears a promising tool for designing novel game mechanics and interfaces, in particular considering turn-based control of complex actions, such as our character posing prototype (Figure 1). Previewing results of player actions before the actions are executed is a useful design pattern, provided that it does not make a game too easy.
2. As demonstrated by our QWOP variations, predictive physics simulation allows creating novel games through transforming a real-time action game into a turn-based puzzle.
3. One must be cautious in simply adding predictive simulation and visualization to existing games and mechanics. For example, it was found detrimental to our car prototype, as it made the game too easy and shifted the player's focus from the car to the trajectory visualizations.
4. Even if predictive simulation does not improve the player's experience, it may still be useful as a limited power-up, in tutorial use, or for the game designer. For example, it can be used to explore strategies that the designer might not otherwise think of, or to test difficult levels beyond the designer's playing ability.
5. Considering technological aspects, it appears that most physics simulators are not designed for predictive simulations. We hope our work informs future game and physics engine development of the need to provide full simulation determinism, reproducibility, and an interface for loading and saving both movement state and all internal state.

ACKNOWLEDGEMENTS

We thank our participants and the anonymous reviewers for their insightful comments. Takatalo is supported by Academy of Finland grant 299358.

REFERENCES

1. Christopher G Atkeson. 2007. Randomly sampling actions in dynamic programming. In *2007 IEEE International Symposium on Approximate Dynamic Programming and Reinforcement Learning*, 185–192.
2. Bennet Foddy. 2008. *QWOP*. http://foddy.net, Game [browser].
3. Creature Feep. 2011. *Where's my Water*. Game [iOS].
4. Dynamix. 1993. *The Incredible Machine*. Game [PC].

5. David H Eberly. 2010. *Game physics*. CRC Press.
6. Firemint. 2009. *Flight Control*. Game [iOS].
7. Jacob Fischer, Nikolaj Falsted, Mathias Vielwerth, Julian Togelius, and Sebastian Risi. 2015. Monte Carlo Tree Search for Simulated Car Racing. In *Proc. FDG'15*.
8. Gamesoul Studio. 2013. *Backflip Madness*. Game [iOS].
9. T. Geijtenbeek and N. Pronost. 2012. Interactive Character Animation Using Simulated Physics: A State-of-the-Art Review. *Computer Graphics Forum* 31, 8: 2492–2515. https://doi.org/10.1111/j.1467-8659.2012.03189.x
10. Perttu Hämäläinen, Sebastian Eriksson, Esa Tanskanen, Ville Kyrki, and Jaakko Lehtinen. 2014. Online Motion Synthesis Using Sequential Monte Carlo. *ACM Trans. Graph.* 33, 4: 51:1–51:12. https://doi.org/10.1145/2601097.2601218
11. Perttu Hämäläinen, Joose Rajamäki, and C. Karen Liu. 2015. Online Control of Simulated Humanoids Using Particle Belief Propagation. *ACM Trans. Graph.* 34, 4: 81:1–81:13. https://doi.org/10.1145/2767002
12. Emil Juul Jacobsen, Rasmus Greve, and Julian Togelius. 2014. Monte Mario: Platforming with MCTS. In *Proceedings of the 2014 Annual Conference on Genetic and Evolutionary Computation* (GECCO '14), 293–300. https://doi.org/10.1145/2576768.2598392
13. Timo Kellomäki. 2015. *Large-Scale Water Simulation in Games*. Tampere University of Technology.
14. Joe Laszlo, Michael Neff, and Karan Singh. 2005. Predictive Feedback for Interactive Control of Physics-based Characters. *Computer Graphics Forum* 24, 3: 257–265. https://doi.org/10.1111/j.1467-8659.2005.00850.x
15. Joseph Laszlo, Michiel van de Panne, and Eugene Fiume. 2000. Interactive Control for Physically-based Animation. In *Proceedings of the 27th Annual Conference on Computer Graphics and Interactive Techniques* (SIGGRAPH '00), 201–208. https://doi.org/10.1145/344779.344876
16. Stephen R. Lindemann and Steven M. LaValle. 2005. Current Issues in Sampling-Based Motion Planning. In *Robotics Research. The Eleventh International Symposium*, Paolo Dario and Raja Chatila (eds.). Springer Berlin Heidelberg, 36–54. https://doi.org/10.1007/11008941_5
17. C Karen Liu and Victor B Zordan. 2011. Natural user interface for physics-based character animation. In *Proc. International Conference on Motion in Games*, 1–14.
18. Henry Lowood and Raiford Guins. 2016. *Debugging Game History: A Critical Lexicon*. MIT Press.
19. Nabi Studios. 2006. *Toribash*. Game [PC].
20. Naughty Dog. 2007. *Uncharted: Drake's Fortune*. Game [PlayStation 3].
21. J. Thomas Ngo and Joe Marks. 1993. Spacetime Constraints Revisited. In *Proceedings of the 20th Annual Conference on Computer Graphics and Interactive Techniques* (SIGGRAPH '93), 343–350. https://doi.org/10.1145/166117.166160
22. PopCap Games. 2007. *Peggle*. Game [PC].
23. RedLynx. 2009. *Trials HD*. Game [Xbox 360].
24. RedLynx. 2009. *Draw Race*. Game [iOS].
25. Rovio Entertainment. 2009. *Angry Birds*. Game [iOS].
26. Katie Salen and Eric Zimmerman. 2003. *Rules of Play: Game Design Fundamentals*. The MIT Press.
27. SCE Santa Monica Studio. 2005. *God of War*. Game [PlayStation 2].
28. Jesse Schell. 2008. *The art of game design a book of lenses*. Elsevier/Morgan Kaufmann, Amsterdam; Boston.
29. R. A. Schmidt and C. A. Wrisberg. 2008. *Motor Learning and Performance*. Human Kinetics.
30. Noor Shaker, Mohammad Shaker, and Julian Togelius. 2013. Ropossum: An Authoring Tool for Designing, Optimizing and Solving Cut the Rope Levels. In *Proc. AIIDE 2013*.
31. Jaroslav Švelch. 2014. Comedy of Contingency: Making Physical Humor in Video Game Spaces. *International Journal of Communication* 8, 0: 23.
32. Yuval Tassa, Nicholas Mansard, and Emo Todorov. 2014. Control-Limited Differential Dynamic Programming. In *Proc. IEEE International Conference on Robotics and Automation* (ICRA'14).
33. Christopher D. Twigg and Doug L. James. 2007. Many-worlds Browsing for Control of Multibody Dynamics. In *ACM SIGGRAPH 2007 Papers* (SIGGRAPH '07). https://doi.org/10.1145/1275808.1276395
34. Valve Corporation. 2007. *Portal*. Game [PC].
35. Jacob O Wobbrock and Julie A Kientz. 2016. Research contributions in human-computer interaction. *interactions* 23, 3: 38–44.
36. ZeptoLab. 2010. *Cut the Rope*. Game [iOS].

"Where's Pinky?": The Effects of a Reduced Number of Fingers in Virtual Reality

Valentin Schwind[a], Pascal Knierim[a], Lewis Chuang[b], Niels Henze[a]
[a]VIS, University of Stuttgart
Stuttgart, Germany
{firstname.lastname}@vis.uni-stuttgart.de
[b]Max Planck Institute for Biological Cybernetics
Tuebingen, Germany
{firstname.lastname}@tuebingen.mpg.de

ABSTRACT
The hands of one's avatar are possibly the most visible aspect when interacting in virtual reality (VR). As video games in VR proliferate, it is important to understand how the appearance of avatar hands influence the user experience. Designers of video games often stylize hands and reduce the number of fingers of game characters. Previous work shows that the appearance of avatar hands has significant effects on the user's presence—the feeling of 'being' and 'acting' in VR. However, little is known about the effects of missing fingers of an avatar in VR. In this paper, we present a study ($N = 24$) that investigated the effect of hand representations by parametrically varying the number of fingers of abstract and realistically rendered hands. We show that decreasing the number of fingers of realistic hands leads to significantly lower levels of presence, which is not the case for abstract hands. Qualitative feedback collected through think-aloud and video revealed potential reasons for the different assessment of realistic and abstract hands with fewer fingers in VR. We contribute design implications and recommend considering the human-likeness when a reduction of the number of fingers of avatar hands is desired.

ACM Classification Keywords
H.1.2 User/Machine Systems: Human factors; I.3.7 Three-Dimensional Graphics and Realism: Virtual reality

Author Keywords
Virtual reality; presence; lacking fingers; immersion; avatars.

INTRODUCTION
With the rise of virtual reality (VR) and head-mounted displays (HMDs), the need for understanding how and why the human brain perceives and accepts the virtual world is becoming more and more important. This is particularly relevant for researchers and designers of immersive VR games and applications. A key feature of upcoming VR technologies and games is rendering the user's body in the virtual world using *avatars*. Avatars in VR significantly increase the user's immersion and the feeling of *presence* [11]—one of the key concepts of 'being' or 'acting' in a virtual environment while physically situated in another place. Avatars in VR also provide a natural and intuitive interface for the user to interact with the surrounding virtual world. The most important body parts for interaction through avatars in VR are one's hands and fingers. Using current game controllers, virtual hands can be displayed in VR. Today's technologies even allow motion tracking of hands and fingers without wearing additional motion controllers or markers. Thus, arms, hands, and fingers can be rendered in VR according to their real pose and location.

For video games, however, it is not only important to provide hands for interaction but also to understand how their appearance influences the experience of the user. Designers of video games have unlimited freedom to vary the appearance of an avatar. Cartoonists, for example, simplify their drawings due to the thickness of black outlines. Thus, to avoid too big hands or overlapping of the black outlines, they reduce the number of fingers of their characters. This kind of stylization was adopted and preserved by many video games such as in *Earthworm Jim*, the *Rayman* series, *The Smurfs*, or *Simpsons – The Game*.

Designers can also reduce the number of fingers in realistic ways. In 2009, the cover art of the game *Left4Dead 2* showed a hand with a severed little finger, ring finger, and thumb. To appease the Entertainment Software Rating Board (ESRB) game developer Valve changed the cover in a way that the index and middle fingers remained [19]. In video games, designers reduce the number of fingers in a realistic way as for the aliens in *Avatar – The Game* or Elizabeth's character in *BioShock Infinite*. Thus, the body structure of game avatars in VR does not necessarily match the structure of the user's body. However, little is known about the effects of a reduced number of fingers on the user experience and perception of presence in VR.

To investigate the effect of varying an avatar's number of fingers we conducted a study in VR. We tested five-, four-, three-, and two-fingered hands rendered with a realistic and an abstract style. We collected quantitative and qualitative data. We not only show that reducing the number of fingers significantly affect the perceived presence but also show that this effect depends on the realism of the avatar. This has consequences for VR users and, thus, is relevant for researchers and designers of immersive VR games and applications. We discuss further effects and potential factors that influence the user experience of being in VR with fewer fingers. We contribute implications for game and VR designers.

CHI PLAY '17, October 15-18, 2017, Amsterdam, Netherlands

DOI: https://doi.org/10.1145/3116595.3116596

RELATED WORK

In the following, we provide an overview of the previous work that is related to the perception of the virtual self and hands in VR. This includes research on the rubber hand illusion, which has contributed to our understanding of own body perception as well as the condition of phantom pain, which is experienced by some amputees in their removed limbs. Both phenomena, established in the real world, pose implications for how one's body avatar ought to be represented in VR. Finally, we discuss how the appearance of virtual avatars affects the illusion of body ownership and the feeling of presence in VR.

The rubber hand illusion experiment by Botvinick and Cohen [4] demonstrated that humans can incorporate prosthetic limbs into their body representation when congruent visual and tactile feedback is provided. Further research of the rubber hand illusion (originally not situated in VR) showed how our body registers the interaction space using self-location [7], self-agency [3], and body ownership [13]. VR allows to further explore the rubber hand illusion from a first person view and for animated false limbs as well as full bodies [23]. The acceptance of structural changes of hands in VR was investigated by Hoyet et al. [10]. The authors examined the rubber hand illusion by using a six-fingered hand in VR. They found that participants experienced relatively high levels of body ownership using an additional finger when compared to using five-fingered hands. Consequently, the authors recommend investigating hands with fewer fingers.

Our work differs conceptually from adding existing body parts in the rubber hand illusion. The removal of limbs is particularly related to work that investigates phantom pain and its treatment in VR. However, it has not yet been investigated how fewer limbs affect acceptance in VR. Murray et al. [16] showed that VR can be used to treat the phantom pain of amputees. Not situated in VR, but also related to our work is the research by Giummarra et al. [9] which compared sensations of amputees and non-amputees. Their findings indicate that both phantom pain and an illusory embodiment, do not necessarily require amputation.

Previous work also shows that the appearance of an avatar affects the VR experience. Lin and Jörg [12] found that more human-like hand models increased the illusion of body ownership. Using a first-person computer-game Christou and Michael [5] found that visual characteristics of the avatar influences the players' behavior. This was confirmed by Argelaguet et al. [1] who found that the appearance of an avatar in VR influences the user's behavior as well. Their results indicate that the sense of agency is stronger for less realistic virtual hands, however, the illusion of body ownership increases for virtual human hands. Peck et al. [17] showed that the manipulation of skin tones caused changes in interpersonal attitudes and decreased participants' implicit racial bias. Not only skin color but also the virtual body size lead to biases in estimating the own weight, which was shown by Piryankova et al. [18].

Research in *presence* is vital, especially as games and virtual environments strive towards becoming more and more immersive. Presence is defined as the "sense of being in another environment" [2] or as "the outcome or a direct function of immersion" [20]. Vinayagamoorthy et al. [25] and Lugrin et al. [14] found that higher degrees of presence were caused by less realistic VR game characters. In both works, the authors assume that their results are influenced by the *Uncanny Valley* phenomenon by Mori [15], who first hypothesized that imperfections of very human-like characters cause uncomfortable sensations. Furthermore, Schwind et al. found gender-related differences when using different virtual hands in VR [21]. Their results indicate that women dislike male hands and men perceive lower levels of presence using non-human avatar hands. The authors suggest avoiding gender swapping in VR by using non-realistic bodies or – if necessary – by using androgyny avatars.

Investigations of the rubber hand illusion [4, 23, 10] and illusion of body ownership [12, 1, 24] are related, but different from the kind of body changes investigated in this paper. They highlight the importance of visual and haptic cues for registering the interaction space of the own body using additional limbs. How the reduction of body parts affects the user experience in VR is currently unknown. For this reason, and especially in context of games, which reduce the number of fingers (*e.g.* for stylized hands), we decided to explore the effects on presence (*cf.* [25, 14, 21]) using avatar hands in VR.

METHOD

Fingers are an integral part of daily interaction and are often removed, for example, for stylization reasons in today's video games. However, previous work did not investigate the effects of removing limbs of VR avatars, however, shows that the degree of realism of the own body has an impact on how users perceive presence. Therefore, we decided to test the effect of fewer fingers with realistic as well as abstract avatar hands in a user study in VR. We used a within-subject study design with the two independent variables REALISM (*abstract* and *realistic*) and FINGERS PER HAND (*two, three, four, five*) resulting in eight conditions. Data was collected quantitatively through questionnaires in VR and qualitatively through the think-aloud method and video observations.

Stimuli

We compared *five*-fingered hands with hands where we successively removed little finger, ring finger, and the middle finger of each hand (see Figure 1). We used a pinch gesture to trigger events in our apparatus and kept both thumbs as well as index fingers. Previous work found that men and women show different levels of presence while using male and female hands. As suggested [21], we used a human androgynous hand model consisting of a mesh blending between male and female hand models provided by the Leap Motion SDK. To remove an effect of the finger movement on the animated skin at adjacent parts of the palm, we removed the stumps of the fingers. Thus, the hands look more natural and not as being cut off or torn, which was achieved by smooth transitions towards the palm of the hand. A professional 3D artist removed the fingers and the influence of their virtual bones on the hand skin using Autodesk 3ds Max. The abstract hand models are based on the white abstract hands used by Argelaguet et al. [1]. They consist of rigid oval shapes for the fingers and arms as well as a circle-shaped palm.

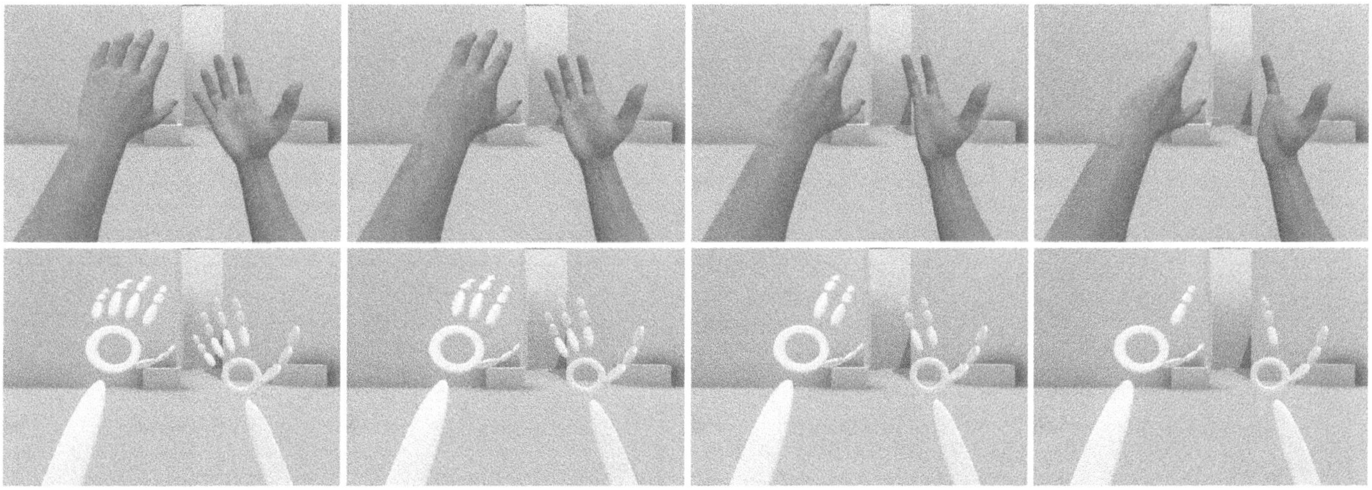

Figure 1. Screenshots of the avatar hand models of the four realistic (1st row) and four abstract (2nd row) hands with five, four, three, and two fingers.

Apparatus

Our system consisted of an HTC Vive HMD and a Leap Motion sensor mounted onto the front of the display using a 3D printed frame. We used a PC with Windows 10, an Intel i7-6700, 16GB RAM, and a Nvidia GTX980 graphics card. Our Unity3D application used hand tracking provided by the Orion SDK of Leap Motion optimized for hand tracking on HMDs. The target frame rate of the application was 60 frames per second. To ensure that the frame rate and the tracking quality was the same for all hands, we used the same tracking system provided by Leap and the same configuration of bones. The surrounding scene was the same for all condition and designed with a neutral white style and a standard sun- and skylight. Real-time global illumination, anti-aliasing, and ambient occlusion were enabled for rendering.

Tasks

Three immersive tasks were used to ensure that the virtual hands are in the field of view of each user. Furthermore, they enabled a versatile and immersive VR experience. We used the tasks purposed and provided by the software by Schwind et al. [21][1]. In the *typing task*, participants operated with a virtual keyboard to enter "I love VR" into a text display. The *draw task* enabled users to perform free hand painting in the surrounding virtual space using the pinch gesture. The *pyramid task* is a physical simulation where participants were advised to staple at least six blocks on a table to build a small pyramid. Black fading was used for transitions between all tasks as well as between the tasks and the final questionnaire.

Measures

We used questionnaires in VR to facilitate a continuously user experience (*cf.* integrated questionnaires in gaming environments by Frommel et al. [8]) as suggested by Schwind et al. [21]. Thus, every participant filled in the questionnaire using the virtual hands whose effect we actually measured. We decided to use the presence questionnaire (PQ) by Witmer and Singer [26]. The questionnaire has been used in a large number of studies, includes items that address related factors such as naturalness or involvement, and all questions can be meaningfully answered in VR. As suggested by previous work [21, 22], we additionally asked for likability, human-likeness, attractiveness, and eeriness on 7-point Likert scales. Participants' feedback and their actions were recorded through think-aloud protocols and video cameras.

Procedure

After signing the consent form, every participant was asked to take a seat in the middle of our VR laboratory. We explained the experimental procedure and introduced the functionality of the HMD as well as the hand tracking sensor. Furthermore, all participants were instructed to "think aloud", which means to verbally articulate all their concerns and thoughts especially considering their virtual embodiments. We pointed out that participants could pause or abort the experiment at any time. The order of the eight virtual hands was given by a balanced Latin square design. The order of tasks was randomized by software. Every task could either be finished by pressing a button or showing a thumbs-up gesture. After completing all tasks a panel with the questionnaire appeared in front of the participant's view. Since all questions could not be displayed at once, panels containing four questions were presented. The participant navigated through these panels of the questionnaire by pressing two buttons labeled "back" and "next". After leaving the VR we handed out a questionnaire where we asked for feedback, general concerns, suggestions. Finally, we also asked for both the hand they prefer and definitely not prefer.

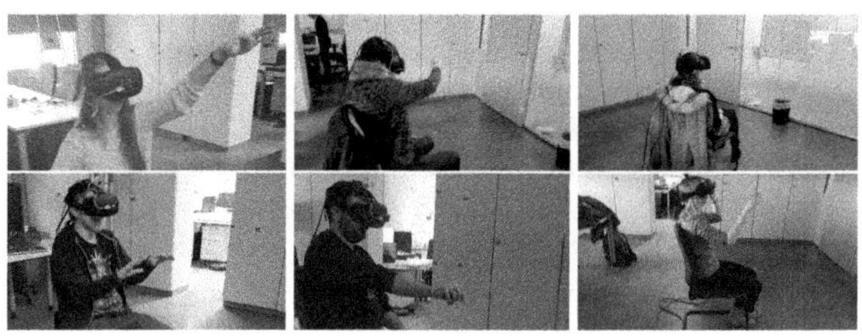

Figure 2. Images of the participants situated and observed in our VR laboratory.

[1] `https://github.com/valentin-schwind/selfpresence`

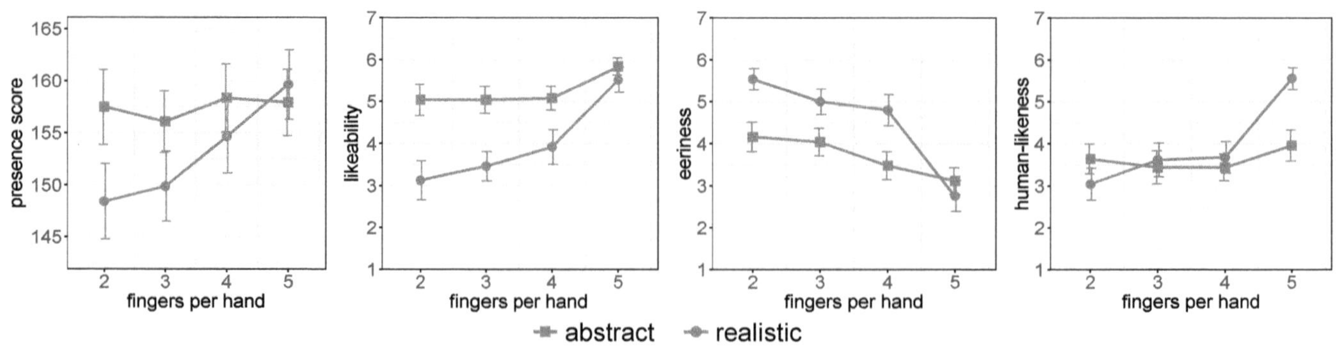

Figure 3. Average presence scores, perceived likeability, eeriness, and human-likeness of abstract and realistic virtual hands with number of fingers per hand. All error bars show standard error of the mean (SE).

Participants

We recruited 24 participants (11 males, 13 females) from our campus via mailing lists and social networks. All participants had light skin tones matching the visual appearance of the realistic virtual hand. None of the volunteers was excluded from participation in the study. The average age of the participants was 21.8 years ($SD = 6.41$). Only four participants mentioned having previous VR experience, 20 of our participants stated that they had no VR experience at all.

RESULTS

On average the study lasted for 75 minutes per participant ($SD = 8.34$). The average task completion time was 3.0 minutes ($SD = 1.8$). Two participants took a 5-minute break.

Quantitative Results

We analyzed the effects of the within-subject factors REALISM and FINGERS PER HAND on our five dependent variables with analyses of variance (ANOVA) using linear mixed-effects models. All effects were taken as random at the participant level. Since we had non-parametric data, we used aligned rank transformations[2] by Wobbrock et al. [27]. All significance levels are at $\alpha = .05$. The results of presence, likeability, eeriness, and human-likeness are depicted in Figure 3. All means (M) and standard deviations (SD) are listed in Table 1.

Presence

A two-way ANOVA showed significant effects of REALISM, $F(1,168.00) = 13.990, p < .001$, and FINGERS PER HAND, $F(3,168.01) = 8.890, p < .001$, on perceived presence. We also found a significant interaction effect between both factors, $F(3,168.01) = 5.890, p < .001$. Pairwise post-hoc comparisons using Tukey's method for p-value adjustment within the levels of the main factors revealed no significant differences of the presence scores between the levels of FINGERS PER HAND using the *abstract hands* (all with $p > .05$). However, the analysis of the *realistic hands* showed significant differences between the levels of FINGERS PER HAND (all with $p < .03$), expect between the *two-* and *three*-fingered ($p = .866$) as well as the *three-* and *four*-fingered hand ($p = 0.066$). Bonferroni-corrected pairwise cross-factor comparisons of REALISM and FINGERS PER HAND revealed significant differences between the *two* and *five*-fingered hand ($p < .001$) and the *three-* and *five*-fingered hand ($p = .021$).

Previous work found an effect of gender using male and female hands [21]. Therefore, we conducted a three-factorial ANOVA including the participant's GENDER as between-subject factor on presence to assess the perception of the used hands. We found no effect of GENDER and no interaction effects of GENDER on REALISM, FINGERS PER HAND, or both (all with $p > .05$). An additional analysis was conducted to determine if participants with previous experiences in VR have potentially influenced the results. We found no effects of PRIOR VR EXPERIENCE as between-subject factor and no interaction effects (all with $p > .05$). The analysis of the quantitative results did not change substantially when persons with previous experience in VR were excluded from the analysis. Therefore, the data of all participants were considered in the analysis.

Likeability

For likeability, we found a significant effect of REALISM, $F(1,168.00) = 33.089, p < .001$, FINGERS PER HAND, $F(3,168.13) = 11.815, p < .001$, and an interaction effect of REALISM × FINGERS PER HAND, $F(3,168.12) = 3.603, p < .015$. Pairwise comparisons showed no significant differences between the abstract hands (all with $p > .05$), but between the *two-* and *five*-fingered, *three-* and *five*-fingered, and *four-* and *five*-fingered realistic hands (all with $p < .001$). Pairwise cross-factor comparisons showed significant differences between the *two-* and *five*-fingered hand ($p = .015$).

Human-Likeness

The measures of human-likeness showed significant effects of REALISM, $F(1,168.00) = 3.956, p = .048$, and on FINGERS PER HAND, $F(3,168.11) = 9.437, p < .001$, and an interaction effect of REALISM × FINGERS PER HAND, $F(3,168.11) = 4.992, p = .002$. Pairwise comparisons showed no significant differences between the abstract hands (all with $p > .05$), but between all realistic hands (with $p < .001$) except for the *two-* and *three*-fingered, *two-* and *four*-fingered, *three-* and *four*-fingered hand. Pairwise cross-factor comparisons showed significance differences between the *two-* and *five*-fingered hand ($p = .001$), the *three-* and *five*-fingered hand ($p = .05$), as well as the *four-* and *five*-fingered hand ($p = .05$).

[2] http://depts.washington.edu/madlab/proj/art/

Realism	Fingers	PQ score		Likeability		Eeriness		Human-like		Attractiveness		Prefer	Not Prefer
		M	SD	M	SD	M	SD	M	SD	M	SD	N	N
Abstract	2	157.480	17.702	5.040	1.843	4.160	1.713	3.640	1.741	4.200	1.876	2	
	3	156.080	14.475	1.843	1.587	4.040	1.612	3.440	1.920	4.520	1.676	2	1
	4	158.360	16.030	4.200	1.412	3.480	1.628	3.440	1.551	4.440	1.675		1
	5	157.920	15.620	1.876	1.007	3.120	1.532	3.960	1.822	5.480	1.473	13	
Realistic	2	148.417	17.364	3.640	2.225	5.542	1.225	3.042	1.815	2.625	1.998		16
	3	149.885	16.714	1.741	1.758	5.000	1.518	3.615	2.000	2.962	1.763		2
	4	154.640	17.085	4.160	2.018	4.800	1.811	3.680	1.827	3.080	1.853		3
	5	159.640	16.473	1.713	1.473	2.760	1.795	5.560	1.267	5.200	1.697	7	1

Table 1. Means (M) and standard deviations (SD) of the quantitative measures (presence score, likeability, eeriness, human-likeness, attractiveness) as well as the number of participants (N) who stated at the end of the experiment to prefer or not prefer an avatar hand.

Eeriness

For eeriness we found significant effects of REALISM, $F(1,168.00) = 11.020, p < .001]$, FINGERS PER HAND, $F(3,168.14) = 17.088, p < .001$, and an interaction effect of REALISM × FINGER PER HAND $[F(3,168.14) = 4.923, p < .001)$. Pairwise comparisons showed significant differences between the abstract hands with *two-* and *five*-fingered hands, *three-* and *five*-fingered hands, as well as between *four-* and *five*-fingered hands (all with $p < .05$). We found significant differences between all realistic hands (with p < .001) except for the *two-* and *three*-fingered, *two-* and *four*-fingered, as well as the *three-* and *four*-fingered hand. Pairwise cross-factor comparisons showed significant differences between the *two-* and *five*-fingered hand ($p = .004$) and the *four-* and *five*-fingered hand ($p = .007$).

Attractiveness

We found significant effects of REALISM, $F(1,168.0) = 29.535, p < .001$, and FINGER PER HAND, $F(3,168.1) = 19.2063, p < .001$, on the perceived attractiveness. There was no significant interaction effect between both factors, $F(3,168.1) = 19.206, p = .09$. Pairwise comparisons showed significant differences between the abstract hands with *two-* and *five*-fingered hands, *three-* and *five*-fingered hands, as well as between *four-* and *five*-fingered hands (both with $p < .05$). Differences were significant between all realistic hands (with p < .05) except for the *two-* and *three*-fingered, *two-* and *four*-fingered, *three-* and *four*-fingered hand. Due to the missing interaction effect, pairwise cross-factor comparisons showed no significant differences (all with $p > .05$).

Final Assessments

After having left the VR, a final questionnaire on a sheet of paper were handed out to the participants in which they were asked, which virtual hand they most prefer and not prefer: 13 participants (52%) prefer the abstract hand with five fingers, 7 participants (28%) the realistic hand with five fingers, 2 participants (8%) the abstract hand with two fingers and 2 participants (8%) the abstract hand with three fingers. 16 participants (64%) would definitely not use the realistic hand with two fingers again, 3 participants (12%) the realistic hand with four fingers, 2 participants (8%) the realistic hand with four fingers, and 1 participant (4%) in each case the realistic hand with five fingers, the abstract hand with three, and the abstract hand with four fingers. The numbers of participants which prefer or not prefer the eight avatar hand pairs are summarized in Table 1.

Qualitative Results

We collected qualitative feedback using the think-aloud method and video to gain further insights into the perception of our participants. Based on the records, protocols of verbal utterances and observed actions were transcribed. The transcribed protocols were annotated and scrutinized through axial coding in two iterations: In the first iteration, two researchers went through all comments to identify further individual *factors* and *effects*, which had not been quantified through our questionnaires. One of the authors scrutinized and annotated effects, the other one factors. Both went through the results of the other and refined or complement their results. Discrepancies between the two sets of annotations were resolved through discussion. There was a total of five factors and two effects which were finally identified.

Additional Factors

In the qualitative analysis, we identified *association, habituation, aesthetics, sensitivity to display/tracking errors,* and *task performance* as non-quantified factors which influence the individual experience of the participants in VR. FINGERS PER HAND and REALISM were previously quantified and are not listed as individual factors in the sections below (P# = participant ID; A/R# = abstract/realistic hand and number of fingers per hand).

(1) **Associations:** We found that having fewer fingers were associated with very different prior mental concepts mainly based on the individual experience. Realistic hands with fewer fingers were associated with "claws" (P5, R2), hands of a "T-Rex" (P6, R3) "aliens" (P12, R3), "mutations" (P12, R2), or with the shape of "pistols" (P12, R2). The abstract hands reminded participants on characters from movie or series such as *Wall-E* (P7, A3), *I, Robot* (P7, A2), *The Simpsons* (P23, A4), or on "crabs" (P14, A5), "skeletons" (P1, A2), and "robot" (P13, A5) hand. Associations were influenced by familiarity and previous knowledge: "Abstract hands are much better than realistic hands because it can be that such robots have fewer fingers." (P22, R2). Associations were also connected with the own emotional state and personal feelings: "I feel crippled. I feel sad. When I could see my body, I would be a little crippled sad robot." (P4, A2). Hands with fewer fingers, mainly while using abstract hands, were often considered as practical or functional tools for completing the tasks: "These hands are more practical because I only need two fingers to complete the tasks." (P11, A3).

(2) **Habituation:** For most of the participants the study was the first VR experience. Entering VR and the impression of being in another body was first exciting and overwhelming for them: "Oh my god, this is so cool". (P4, A4). The enthusiasm to be in another body outweighed a potentially strange feeling at the beginning: "Only four fingers? Oh no! But I am so impressed. I could just look at my hands all day. That's so cool." (P12, A4). We further observed that participants accustomed to all virtual hands as well as to a reduced number of fingers: "You get used to dealing with every hand very quickly." (P22, R4).

(3) **Aesthetics:** Participants were influenced by several aesthetic preferences, e.g. design aspects, in particular, while using abstract hands: "Nicely designed." (P16, A4). We assume that design preferences are potentially connected to personal experiences and familiarity: "To see the fingers in such a design is somehow unfamiliar. You should have put a little more effort into it." (P7, A3) We also found that aesthetic aspects depend on the perceived style of the virtual environment: "Everything looks so sterile. You get used to it, however, the robot [abstract] hand fit very well into it." (P4, A5). Aesthetic aspects were also mentioned when using realistic hands: "The place where the finger is missing looks disgusting." (P14, R4)".

(4) **Sensitivity to display/tracking errors:** Hands of all participants were tracked in the same way. However, some participants responded more sensitively to potential errors during hand tracking or rendering using certain hands. Then, even small errors in hand tracking were perceived unpleasant by some participants: "The tracking is really good unless you turn the hand around quickly." (P12, A4). Not only tracking errors, but the overall loss of control of one's own body evoked negative feelings: "I feel to have no control over my middle finger anymore. This is weird." (P12, R3). Some participants had problems with hand tracking that only allowed inputs when visible in the field of view of the HMD.

(5) **Task performance:** We observed that participants became involved into VR when they tried to solve a task, especially the typing task. Completing a task satisfactorily sometimes lead to positive feedback related to the used hands: "I think two fingers are even better to type or paint'." (P4, A2). To complete a task successfully may be influenced by the association (see beforehand) that participants consider hands with fewer fingers as useful tools: "With those, I can type better since I'm not distracted by the other fingers." (P15, A2). Individual performances may be (reversely) related to other behavioral changes which are considered in the following section about individual effects.

Additonal Effects

Furthermore, we identified *emotional reactions* and changes of *hand interaction* as main categories of additional or individual effects, which have not been explicitly quantified through concepts in our questionnaire. We define emotional reactions as initial and prominent short-term responses. Changes of hand interaction are defined as medium-term tendencies for acting and solving problems with hands differently.

(1) **Emotional Reactions:** We observed strong verbal and physical emotional reactions when participants were confronted with *realistic* virtual hands and less than five fingers. They felt "disgusting", "strange", "creepy", "unfamiliar", or "uncomfortable". Partly the participants were incensed. "What the hell is that?" (P6, R3). This was not the case with fewer fingers on the abstract hands: "It doesn't disturb me that I only have three fingers because the hand is not realistic anyway." (P3, A3). However, we recognized satisfaction of participants getting back virtual hands with five fingers after having a hand with a reduced number of fingers. "I have my pinky again!" (P7, A5). Some participants did not initially noticed that there was a missing finger in the *four*-fingered hand condition. They were scared when they finally realized that they are having a *four*-fingered hand.

(2) **Hand interaction:** We observed that participants changed their way of hand interaction when using a reduced number of fingers. Participants only used the fingers they saw. "It is so crazy. I don't move it [the little finger] automatically." (P4, R4). Some participants recognized by themselves changes of their hand interaction which potentially lead to a reverse effect on their feelings and behavior: "It is a totally strange feeling to grab something. You don't expect to be able to hold things." (P12, R4). They also reflect their behavioral changes after getting a *five*-fingered hand: "Now, I move all the fingers instead of just a few, and that is more natural and immersive." (P12, A5). Participants also tried to use haptic feedback of their real fingers to confirm that they are still there: "Yes, I have five fingers. I see four, however, I can still feel my little finger." (P2, R4).

Discussing Potential Cognitive Mechanisms

In a second feedback analysis, two of the authors repeated the analysis of the protocols provided by think-aloud and video. In this iteration, we used axial coding based on the identified factors and effects (see beforehand) to understand why an individual factor has an effect on the user experience. In the following, we establish five potential *cognitive mechanisms*, which may influence an individual's concept of having an avatar with a reduced number of fingers in VR. The themes were discussed and established when they were supported by the feedback from the participants.

(1) **Visually induced phantom pain** caused by the fear of amputation and limb loss lead to strong emotional and behavioral reactions. We observed participants who painted replacements for their fingers at the stumps of their hands during the draw task. "As if you had phantom pain. You feel it, but don't see it." (P5, R4). We also observed that the level of associated phantom pain increased with the number of missing fingers: "So, I can get over one finger. But not two." (P4, A3).

(2) **Familiarity** emerges through individual prior experiences caused by associations. Associations influence personal preferences through knowledge e.g. about threats. Such preferences can then either be positive or negative: "What? Please no! Reminds me somehow of claws of an animal." (P5, R2). Familiarity influences the individual long-term habituation of using hands with fewer fingers, "I have often seen people with

a missing finger, no problem."(P3, R4). And short-term habituation such as with one participant after getting an abstract hand with five fingers: "[...] and now it's freaky to have all fingers again." (P12, A5).

(3) The **Uncanny Valley** by Mori [15] describes a non-linear relationship of familiarity and human-likeness. It predicts a sudden dip of familiarity in relation to the human-likeness (or realism) of a robot or virtual avatar. Since we have only used two different styles (*abstract* and *realism*), our quantitative data does not allow to infer the shape of a potential Uncanny Valley with virtual avatars and reduced number of fingers. However, qualitative data provided while participants used *five*-fingered hands indicate that there is a potential relation to this phenomenon: "Looks strange. I don't know. I liked the other one [hand, A5] more because of the design. Perhaps it's because these hands look more human than the others." (P2, R5), "I don't know, it's confusing because the hand is too real!" (P14, R5).

(4) A **visually induced identity dysphoria** potentially causes discomfort through lacking coherence between the known appearance of one's own body and the virtually projected self. "I feel it's supposed to be my hand. But I know it's not my hand, so I think it is creepy." (P6, R5), The incongruence of the real and virtual body was recognized and lead to a negative sensation, "Hand is too orange." (P22, R5), and using structural changes such as missing fingers in particular: "What is this? I'm not a Simpson!" (P6, R4). "It's completely unfamiliar because you assume that you have five fingers and then you're thinking: Where's pinky?" (P17, R4).

(5) A **mismatch of visual and haptic cues** lead to decreased proprioception and to a feeling of loosing body control. Getting feedback from fingers that were not displayed was considered as a strange and peculiar feeling. "It is totally creepy when I touch my fingers which are not displayed." (P12, R2). The concept is related to the rubber hand illusion [4] when visual cues are in conflict with tactile sensations. This is also related to findings by Costantini and Haggard [6] who interpret that sensory evidence about "me" is related to a prior mental representation of one's own body.

DISCUSSION AND CONCLUSION

In this paper, we investigate how reducing the number of fingers affects the perception of virtual hands in VR. We decreased the number of fingers from little to the middle finger and tested the hands at two different levels of realism (*abstract* and *realistic*).

We collected quantitative data using questionnaires integrated in VR. Our quantitative results indicate that the number of fingers significantly affects presence and shows interaction effects with the level of realism. The reduction of fingers does not significantly influence presence using abstract hands. However, when using realistic hands, the feeling of presence significantly decreased with the number of fingers. The diverging effect of reducing fingers for abstract and realistic hands is confirmed by significant interaction effects for all questionnaire measures except for attractiveness. Furthermore, through reducing the number of fingers, we found significant effects on likeability, eeriness, human-likeness, and attractiveness. Except for the perceived human-likeness, all measures show that the reduction of fingers lead to stronger effects while participants interacted with realistic hands. Ratings of human-likeness were constantly low for all hands, except for the five-fingered human hand, which indicates that the participants had a clear concept of how human avatar hands should look like.

Through the qualitative analysis of think-aloud protocols and videos, we identified factors and effects that were not captured by the quantitative measures. We derived associations, habituation, aesthetic aspects, sensitivity to display/tracking errors, and the individual performance (e.g. while completing the tasks) as additional factors that influence the experience while using avatar hands with fewer fingers. We also found additional effects including emotional reactions and changes of hand interaction. In the second iteration of the qualitative analysis, we discussed five potential underlying cognitive mechanisms: visually induced phantom pains, familiarity based on prior experiences, the Uncanny Valley, a visually induced identity dysphoria, and the mismatch of visual and haptic feedback.

In context of previous research, our paper presents the first investigation of a VR experience with a reduced number of fingers. We examined the effect on presence, thus, our work contributes to a better understanding of the perception of user's self-embodiment and avatars in VR games and applications. Our findings of the mismatch of visual and haptic cues are related to findings of investigations about the rubber hand illusion, however, adding limbs conceptually differs from removing them [4]. The illusion we created is the opposite of experiences with the rubber hand illusion and lead to mainly negative feedback in VR. This is supported by findings of Hoyet et al. [10] who observed relatively high levels of the illusion of body ownership after adding a sixth finger. We assume that self-perception in VR using structural changes that do not match the structure of the user's body depends on whether limbs are added or removed.

Our observations indicate that the reduction of fingers induced phantom pains. The phantom pain of non-amputees could include pain due to the fear of amputation or "real" phantom pains as observed with people with missing limbs, which are also treated in VR [16]. Interestingly our participants responded emotionally, which indicated that they were highly immersed with their appearance in VR and not with the outer world anymore. Nevertheless, the feeling of presence was negatively influenced by reducing realistic fingers. Some shock moments, however, indicate that the participants still had an immersive VR experience. Source code and assets of our project are available on github[3].

Limitations and Future Work

To keep the length of our study reasonable, we only used two different hand styles (realistic and abstract). Cartoon or comic styles, which often make use of four finger hands for stylized characters, should be considered in further studies to examine

[3] `https://github.com/valentin-schwind/lessfingers`

e.g. also a hypothetical effect of the Uncanny Valley of the own avatar. We symmetrically reduced the number of fingers on both hands. Thus, we could not analyze potential effects of hand or finger asymmetries. Furthermore, we removed little fingers, ring fingers, and middle fingers. Future studies could additionally take thumb and index finger into account. Further research could also investigate the effects of other combinations of removed fingers. For example, it is possible, that the loss of the little finger is easier to handle than the loss of the index finger.

With emotional reactions and effects on the hands interaction, we identified two factors in our qualitative analysis that could be quantified by future research. Furthermore, we derived five potential cognitive mechanisms that influence self-perception in VR with a reduced amount of fingers. To develop a robust and reliable model of virtual self-perception, which also illustrates interrelations and influences the themes, more empirical research is needed. We, therefore, suggest quantifying data of the derived themes to predict potential dependencies and correlations. In line with Schwind et al. [21], we assume that deviations from the own self (e.g. by using altered body scans) should be considered by future research.

VR Game Design Implications

For designers of immersive VR games and applications, we recommend considering the level of realism of an avatar when a reduction of fingers is desired. Using an *abstract* hand style, our VR users felt high levels of presence even with only two fingers left. This was not the case for *realistic* avatar hands. The level of presence decreased according to the number of fingers when using *realistic* avatar hands. Thus, when designers of games create an avatar with less fingers in an abstract way, they profit not only from higher acceptance as opposed to real avatars, but also from less effort they have to spend on implementing highly realistic avatar representations. Emotional reactions of our participants indicate, that a reduction of fingers of realistic hands should only be considered for shocking and horror experiences in VR. We observed habituation effects which potentially indicated that users get used to or even accept hands with a reduced number of *abstract* and *realistic* fingers. However, our participants responded sensitively to any structural changes of the avatar hands. Therefore, we recommend that the number of fingers should be kept consistent during the VR experience or gameplay.

ACKNOWLEDGMENTS

We thank the reviewers for their constructive criticisms and valuable comments, which were of great help in revising the paper. We also thank Thomas Kosch and Cagri Tasci for their organizational and technical support. This work was supported by the German Research Foundation (DFG) through projects C03 and C04 of the SFB/Transregio 161 and by the German Federal Ministry of Education and Research as part of the project Be-greifen (Grant No. 16SV7527).

REFERENCES

1. Ferran Argelaguet, Ludovic Hoyet, Michaël Trico, and Anatole Lécuyer. 2016. The role of interaction in virtual embodiment: Effects of the virtual hand representation. In *2016 IEEE Virtual Reality (VR)*. 3–10. DOI: http://dx.doi.org/10.1109/VR.2016.7504682
2. Frank Biocca and Mark R. Levy. 2013. *Communication in the Age of Virtual Reality*. L. Erlbaum Associates Inc., Hillsdale, NJ, USA. 416 pages.
3. Olaf Blanke and Thomas Metzinger. 2009. Full-body illusions and minimal phenomenal selfhood. *Trends in Cognitive Sciences* 13, 1 (2009), 7–13. DOI: http://dx.doi.org/10.1016/j.tics.2008.10.003
4. Matthew Botvinick and Jonathan Cohen. 1998. Rubber hands' feel'touch that eyes see. *Nature* 391, 6669 (1998), 756. DOI: http://dx.doi.org/10.1016/j.concog.2007.01.001
5. Chris Christou and Despina Michael. 2014. Aliens versus Humans: Do Avatars Make a Difference in How We Play the Game?. In *2014 6th International Conference on Games and Virtual Worlds for Serious Applications (VS-GAMES)*. 1–7. DOI: http://dx.doi.org/10.1109/VS-Games.2014.7012029
6. Marcello Costantini and Patrick Haggard. 2007. The rubber hand illusion: Sensitivity and reference frame for body ownership. *Consciousness and Cognition* 16, 2 (2007), 229 – 240. DOI: http://dx.doi.org/10.1016/j.concog.2007.01.001
7. Frédérique de Vignemont. 2011. Embodiment, ownership and disownership. *Consciousness and Cognition* 20, 1 (2011), 82–93. DOI: http://dx.doi.org/10.1016/j.concog.2010.09.004
8. Julian Frommel, Katja Rogers, Julia Brich, Daniel Besserer, Leonard Bradatsch, Isabel Ortinau, Ramona Schabenberger, Valentin Riemer, Claudia Schrader, and Michael Weber. 2015. Integrated Questionnaires: Maintaining Presence in Game Environments for Self-Reported Data Acquisition. In *Proceedings of the 2015 Annual Symposium on Computer-Human Interaction in Play (CHI PLAY '15)*. ACM, New York, NY, USA, 359–368. DOI: http://dx.doi.org/10.1145/2793107.2793130
9. Melita J. Giummarra, Nellie Georgiou-Karistianis, Mike E. R. Nicholls, Stephen J. Gibson, and John L. Bradshaw. 2010. The Phantom in the Mirror: A Modified Rubber-Hand Illusion in Amputees and Normals. *Perception* 39, 1 (2010), 103–118. DOI: http://dx.doi.org/10.1068/p6519 PMID: 20301851.
10. Ludovic Hoyet, Ferran Argelaguet, and Anatole Lécuyer. 2016. "Wow! I Have Six Fingers!": Would You Accept Structural Changes of Your Hand in VR? *Frontiers in Robotics and AI* 3 (2016), 27. DOI: http://dx.doi.org/10.3389/frobt.2016.00027
11. Konstantina Kilteni, Raphaela Groten, and Mel Slater. 2012. The sense of embodiment in virtual reality. *Presence: Teleoperators and Virtual Environments* 21, 4 (2012), 373–387.

12. Lorraine Lin and Sophie Jörg. 2016. Need a Hand?: How Appearance Affects the Virtual Hand Illusion. In *Proceedings of the ACM Symposium on Applied Perception (SAP '16)*. ACM, New York, NY, USA, 69–76. DOI:http://dx.doi.org/10.1145/2931002.2931006

13. Matthew R. Longo, Friederike Schüür, Marjolein P.M. Kammers, Manos Tsakiris, and Patrick Haggard. 2008. What is embodiment? A psychometric approach. *Cognition* 107, 3 (2008), 978–998. DOI: http://dx.doi.org/10.1016/j.cognition.2007.12.004

14. Jean-Luc Lugrin, Johanna Latt, and Marc Erich Latoschik. 2015. Anthropomorphism and Illusion of Virtual Body Ownership. In *Proceedings of the 25th International Conference on Artificial Reality and Telexistence and 20th Eurographics Symposium on Virtual Environments (ICAT - EGVE '15)*. Eurographics Association, 1–8. DOI: http://dx.doi.org/10.2312/egve.20151303

15. Masahiro Mori, Karl F. MacDorman, and Norri Kageki. 1970/2012. The Uncanny Valley [From the Field]. *Robotics & Automation Magazine, IEEE* 19, 2 (1970/2012), 98–100. DOI: http://dx.doi.org/10.1109/MRA.2012.2192811

16. Craig D. Murray, Stephen Pettifer, Toby Howard, Emma L. Patchick, Fabrice Caillette, Jai Kulkarni, and Candy Bamford. 2007. The treatment of phantom limb pain using immersive virtual reality: Three case studies. *Disability and Rehabilitation* 29, 18 (2007), 1465–1469. DOI:http://dx.doi.org/10.1080/09638280601107385 PMID: 17729094.

17. Tabitha C. Peck, Sofia Seinfeld, Salvatore M. Aglioti, and Mel Slater. 2013. Putting yourself in the skin of a black avatar reduces implicit racial bias. *Consciousness and Cognition* 22, 3 (2013), 779–787. DOI: http://dx.doi.org/10.1016/j.concog.2013.04.016

18. Ivelina V. Piryankova, Hong Yu Wong, Sally A. Linkenauger, Catherine Stinson, Matthew R. Longo, Heinrich H. Bülthoff, and Betty J. Mohler. 2014. Owning an Overweight or Underweight Body: Distinguishing the Physical, Experienced and Virtual Body. *PLOS ONE* 9, 8 (2014), 1–13. DOI: http://dx.doi.org/10.1371/journal.pone.0103428

19. Jim Reilly. 2009. ESRB Made Valve Change Left 4 Dead 2 Cover. (2009). http://www.ign.com/articles/2009/06/17/esrb-made-valve-change-left-4-dead-2-cover

20. Thomas Schubert, Frank Friedmann, and Holger Regenbrecht. 2001. The Experience of Presence: Factor Analytic Insights. *Presence: Teleoperators and Virtual Environments* 10, 3 (2001), 266–281. DOI: http://dx.doi.org/10.1162/105474601300343603

21. Valentin Schwind, Pascal Knierim, Cagri Tasci, Patrick Franczak, Nico Haas, and Niels Henze. 2017. "These are not my hands!": Effect of Gender on the Perception of Avatar Hands in Virtual Reality. In *Proceedings of the 2017 Annual Symposium on Computer-Human Interaction (CHI'17)*. ACM Press, New York, New York, USA. DOI:http://dx.doi.org/10.1145/3025453.3025602

22. Valentin Schwind, Katrin Wolf, Niels Henze, and Oliver Korn. 2015. Determining the Characteristics of Preferred Virtual Faces Using an Avatar Generator. In *Proceedings of the 2015 Annual Symposium on Computer-Human Interaction in Play (CHI PLAY '15)*. ACM Press, 221–230. DOI: http://dx.doi.org/10.1145/2793107.2793116

23. Mel Slater, Bernhard Spanlang, Maria V. Sanchez-Vives, and Olaf Blanke. 2010. First Person Experience of Body Transfer in Virtual Reality. *PLOS ONE* 5, 5 (2010), 1–9. DOI:http://dx.doi.org/10.1371/journal.pone.0010564

24. William Steptoe, Anthony Steed, and Mel Slater. 2013. Human Tails: Ownership and Control of Extended Humanoid Avatars. *IEEE Transactions on Visualization and Computer Graphics* 19, 4 (2013), 583–590. DOI: http://dx.doi.org/10.1109/TVCG.2013.32

25. Vinoba Vinayagamoorthy, Andrea Brogni, Marco Gillies, Mel Slater, and Anthony Steed. 2004. An investigation of presence response across variations in visual realism. In *The 7th Annual International Presence Workshop*. 148–155.

26. Bob G. Witmer and Michael J. Singer. 1998. Measuring Presence in Virtual Environments: A Presence Questionnaire. *Presence: Teleoperators and Virtual Environments* 7, 3 (1998), 225–240. DOI: http://dx.doi.org/10.1162/105474698565686

27. Jacob O. Wobbrock, Leah Findlater, Darren Gergle, and James J. Higgins. 2011. The Aligned Rank Transform for Nonparametric Factorial Analyses Using Only Anova Procedures. In *Proceedings of the SIGCHI Conference on Human Factors in Computing Systems (CHI '11)*. ACM Press, 143–146. DOI: http://dx.doi.org/10.1145/1978942.1978963

Self-Transforming Controllers for Virtual Reality First Person Shooters

Andrey Krekhov
High Performance Computing Group
University of Duisburg-Essen
andrey.krekhov@uni-due.de

Katharina Emmerich
Entertainment Computing Group
University of Duisburg-Essen
katharina.emmerich@uni-due.de

Philipp Bergmann
High Performance Computing Group
University of Duisburg-Essen
philipp.bergmann@stud.uni-due.de

Sebastian Cmentowski
High Performance Computing Group
University of Duisburg-Essen
sebastian.cmentowski@stud.uni-due.de

Jens Krüger
High Performance Computing Group
University of Duisburg-Essen
jens.krueger@uni-due.de

ABSTRACT
Immersive technologies push the boundaries of virtual reality games. In particular, input controllers play an important role for such a player experience. With regard to first-person shooters, a well-crafted controller that resembles its virtual counterpart can increase the feeling of presence. Though controllers often resemble gun handles or even two-handed rifles, the in-game weapon switching is not reflected in the physical controller. That is, swapping a tiny blaster for a big laser rifle does not alter the haptics and the behavior of the device, restricting the feeling of presence.

Our contribution closes that gap and enhances the player experience by introducing the concept of a self-transforming controller. The controller adapts to the current virtual weapon by transforming between a pistol-like controller and a two-handed rifle-like device. We evaluated the concept by comparing the self-transforming controller to a state-of-the-art device. The results show a significant improvement in the player experience in terms of appearance, authenticity, efficiency, experienced realism, and flow.

ACM Classification Keywords
H.5.2. Information Interfaces and Presentation (e.g. HCI): User Interfaces

Author Keywords
Virtual reality controller; shape-changing interfaces; authentic input device; first-person shooter.

CHI PLAY '17, October 15–18, 2017, Amsterdam, Netherlands
Copyright © 2017ACM ISBN 978-1-4503-4898-0/17/10...$15.00
DOI: http://dx.doi.org/10.1145/3116595.3116615

INTRODUCTION
Being there—the feeling of presence in a virtual world—is what excites players about virtual reality (VR). The feeling of being a part of that world can be increased by various immersive devices. In particular, head-mounted displays (HMDs) such as Oculus Rift and HTC Vive are already establishing the VR gaming experience for the broad masses.

With regard to user input, these devices come with handy controllers. For instance, the Vive controller resembles a gun handle with a trigger. That shape promotes first-person shooter interactions and is designed to further increase immersion. Other input controllers mimic the shape of two-handed guns to provide players a more realistic haptics for games with such weapon types.

Relying on a one-handed, pistol-like controller for a game where the weapon should be a two-handed rifle is clearly less realistic than a two-handed input device, and vice versa. Hence, the input controller should be as close as possible to its virtual counterpart. Our contribution aims to close that gap and to provide an optimal controller concept for VR games with in-game weapon switching. The core idea is to create a shape-changing, self-transforming controller. The controller should adjust its shape and handling according to its game representation. In particular, the controller should feel and behave similarly to a pistol-like device in its first state, and similarly to a rifle-like device in its second state.

We propose a shape-changing controller concept covering these requirements and evaluate the results in terms of the impact on the player experience. Additionally, we provide insights into our iterative design thinking approach to building the device. We start off with low-fidelity prototypes to determine optimal weight distribution for both states. We then iteratively improve our concepts by relying on player feedback and finally create a fully functioning and VR-compatible game controller that mechanically transforms its shape based on a telescopic bar approach.

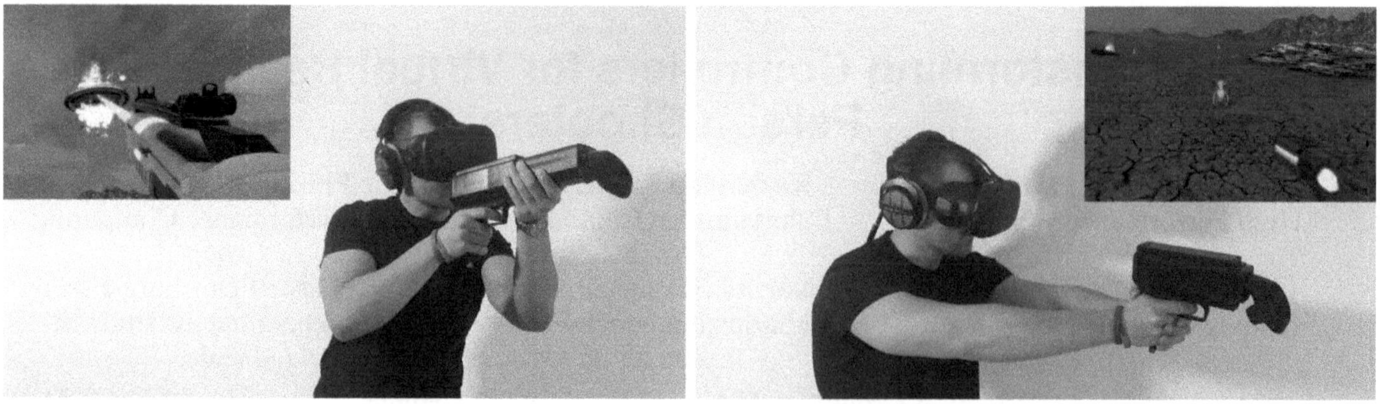

Figure 1. Our final self-transforming controller simulating a two-handed laser rifle (left) and a one-handed blaster (right). The transformation is triggered by a button at the bottom of the handle and works based on a motor and two telescopic tubes. A built-in Vive controller is used for tracking.

To validate our assumptions, we evaluate the impact on the player experience by comparing our device to the state-of-the-art HTC Vive controller. Our context is a futuristic first-person shooter involving a one-handed blaster and a two-handed laser rifle as the two virtual archetypes.

Although our research focuses on first-person shooters and goes into depth with a two-state controller model, the overall results provide significant and novel insights into the general approach of self-transforming controllers. We encourage further research such as developing prototypes for other kinds of games or VR applications, as the shape-changing concept can potentially have an important influence on the feeling of being there.

RELATED WORK

Our contribution is based on insights from a number of research areas discussed in the following. We start off the section by briefly addressing player experience and its manifestation in virtual reality. The main part focuses on game controllers and shape-changing interfaces in general.

Improving the player experience plays a central role in the development of our controller. Player experience is a multi-faceted construct and is usually regarded as a combination of a number of components, such as flow, competence, challenge, and immersion. The work by Bernhaupt [2] provides a set of evaluation approaches with regard to these criteria in order to achieve a positive user experience. IJsselsteijn et al. [13, 14] formalized these elements by proposing the Game Experience Questionnaire (GEQ). The study of Takatalo et al. [41] illustrates how these aspects of player experience might vary when a first-person shooter is played at home or in the lab.

Studying player experience in the context of virtual reality often puts the emphasis on the aspect of immersion. A comprehensive summary can be found in the work by Cairns et al. [6]. As proposed by Slater [37], we will refer to *immersion* mostly when talking about the technical quality of a virtual reality installation [3, 35]. To describe the impact of such immersive technologies on the human perception, we will use the term *presence*. In this area, Poels et al. [30] summarize the overall feelings and experiences of players. Presence, also referred to as the feeling of being there [12], is described by Lombard et al. [22] and IJsselsteijn et al. [15].

The work of Simeone et al. [36] on *Substitutional Reality* shows how users perceive the counterparts of real objects in virtual reality. The authors pair every object in a room with a virtual counterpart to investigate the engagement of the users. Their results form a solid base for the design of such substitutional experiences. For instance, the participants reported a significant mismatch when the paired objects varied in terms of tactile feedback, temperature, and weight. Especially the latter aspect plays an important role with regard to our transformable controller.

The remainder of this section examines existing research on input controllers. A good starting point is the case study of Young et al. [44] on usability testing of video game controllers. The work focuses on two-dimensional pointing tasks but also provides a high-level overview of current work done with regard to controllers and player experience.

With respect to the influence of game controllers on the player experience, Jennet et al. [18] investigated whether immersion can be described in a quantitative way. They also presented a correlation between the mapping of controls to the corresponding in-game action and the overall perceived immersion. Klimmt et al. [21] described the correlation of interactivity and game enjoyment. Their work states that the fun declines if the experiences of effectance are limited. The impact of controller-related issues on user experience was also described by Brown et al. [5]. Their work underlines the importance of a natural controller mapping with regard to experienced fun and immersion.

Birk et al. [4] further examined the impact of controllers on the player experience. They applied self-determination theory to understand the player experience and shared several effects of controllers with respect to the in-game player personality. In terms of player performance, Zaranek et al. [45] evaluated the targeting performance in first-person shooters. The authors compared a mouse, a game controller, the PlayStation Move, and the Kinect, stating that the mouse and controller offered much better performance.

As we propose a novel interaction device, the fact that users have to potentially transition into another controller type is also important. In this area, Gerling et al. [11] compared different interaction paradigms for console and PC by means of two first-person shooter games. Although the players switching to a new platform are more challenged, the overall player experience is not affected by the transitioning aspect.

Another consideration is the age of the players. Pham et al. [29] evaluated how older adults experience button controllers, gesture controllers, and mixed button and gesture controllers. The latter controller type, represented by the Nintendo Wii, performed best. As our controller falls into the same caterogy, these results might also be true for our use case.

Our input device is heavier than the default VR controllers. However, the physical exertion is often preceived positively by players as shown by Zhang et al. [47]. The authors constructed an input device based on multiple sensors that induced more movement compared to default controllers.

Prototyping and building game controllers is a complex and often multidisciplinary task. In many cases researchers apply the ISO 9241-9 standard mentioned in the work of Douglas et al. [8]. The standard describes an evaluation pipeline for pointing devices in terms of performance and comfort. In addition, the work of McNamara et al. [24] equips researchers with the Consumer Products Questionnaire (CPQ), a tool to measure the user satisfaction of their outcomes. Another work by McNamara et al. [23] also encourages us to validate the functionality, usability, and user experience of our prototype.

The research in the area of shape-changing interfaces has led to several novel input devices. Michelitsch et al. [25] presented a shape-changing user interface with force feedback, combining the advantages of tangible and haptic user interfaces. Considering games, Steins et al. [38] researched the concept of *Imaginary Devices* that allow users to freely choose their gesture-based input modality for the current game. Hereby, the transformation is also triggered by the users, however, it does not involve any haptic devices. The *SHAPEIO* controller by Kajiyama et al. [19] adapts to the current item in the game. The controller consists of triangular prisms, which allow the device to mimic several shapes. Iwafune et al. [17] leveraged the shape-changing approach by introducing physically programmable materials suitable for various interface applications. Instead of ridid materials, Nakagaki et al. [27] presented a shape-changing interaction system based on water membranes. Niiyama et al. [28] also avoided rigid materials by relying on liquid metal to achieve programmable mass and volume objects. These approaches have the potential to further extend our transformation procedure by removing rigid weights and replacing them with liquids.

To further explore the advantages of shape-changing in interface design, Suh et al. [40] created a shape-changing pushbutton, the *Button+*, and classified such interfaces based on the context and identity of the users. Similarly, Rasmussen et al. [31] introduced a system for articulating the level of control provided to users via a shape-changing interface. Roudaut et al. [32] focus on the designer's point of view on shape-changing interfaces (or "Changibles") and help to create accurate assemblies out of interactive wireless units.

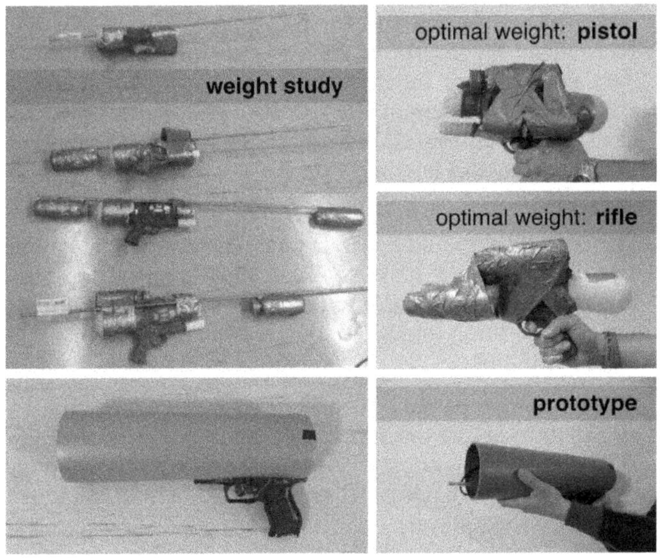

Figure 2. Our first goal was to find out how to balance the controller to evoke the feeling of holding an authentic weapon. Surprisingly, only a small change of the weight distribution is required to differentiate between a pistol and a two-handed rifle. The bottom images depict our first prototype. Inside the grey tube, a motor moves an internal weight to switch between the two weapon kinds.

A recent and related example of utilizing weight shifting for enhancing object perception in VR is *Shifty* by Zenner et al. [46]. The authors present a plexiglass pipe with an internal belt system that transports an object filled with lead. This kind of weight shifting inside the tube allows so modify the rotational resistance, resulting in the virtual object appearing lighter, shorter, or thinner (or vice versa). The presented results show an increase in fun and realism compared with passive haptic feedback objects. Our work shares the idea of shifting weights inside such objects. However, our focus lies more on the iterative design approach, the perceived transformation aspects, and the context of FPS games.

Experimenting with novel VR controllers is not limited to the research area, as various devices are already available to the broad masses. Well-known virtual reality systems such as Oculus Rift [43], PlayStation VR [10], and HTC Vive [7] come with included controllers. Other noteable end products are *StrikerVR* [39] and *The Delta Six Avenger Controller* [9]. These devices offer different haptics, however, none of these supports the self-transformation concept.

CRAFTING THE CONTROLLER

Our research starts at nearly ground zero as, to our knowledge, there is no other self-transforming VR controller fulfilling the requirements stated below. Hence, we rely on an iterative trial-and-error method. Our design thinking process is centered around multiple small-scale evaluations and subsequent adjustments of the prototypes to a point when enough knowledge has been gathered to construct the final version of the controller.

Requirement Analysis
To evaluate the impact of the self-transforming feature, we have construct an input controller and integrate it into an appropriate first-person VR shooter. The controller should have two states: one state representing a one-handed, pistol-like weapon, and another state for a two-handed, rifle-like weapon.

The controller should be able to switch between these states. The player will not have any other input possibilities in our scenario. For that reason, commands such as changing the weapon and firing it must be captured and transmitted via our input controller.

Players cannot see the controller. This is a crucial point, as it allows us to ignore the appearance and focus only on haptics and behavior. In particular, the transformation process should be performed as quickly and smoothly as possible and impose no harm on the player.

Design Thinking Stage
Our first goal was to gather insights into the overall weight distribution and related inertness aspects of weapon-like controllers. We started off by taking water pistols and mounting differently positioned water flasks. We also varied the distance of the weights from the handle in both directions to cover a broad design space. An excerpt of the evaluated mockups is shown in Figure 2.

To find the sweet spot in terms of weight distribution, we conducted an explorative survey ($n = 20$, 11 males, 9 females). In a think-aloud protocol, our goal was to get as much player feedback as possible to narrow down the design space. After a short introduction, participants were blindfolded to imitate the VR scenario. We then handed over our water pistol experiments one by one in a randomized order. The participants were asked to estimate the perceived length of each device and comment in detail on the device haptics. These comments were recorded by the examiner.

The survey provided two important insights. Firstly, the controller does not need to be as long as a real rifle. A total length of 400 mm already suffices to mimic a two-handed gun. Secondly, already a subtle shift of the weights toward the front of the device suffices to represent the transformation from a one-handed pistol to a two-handed rifle. Figure 2 demonstrates the two final water pistol versions, both of approximately the same weight but a slighly shifted balance point.

Based on these observations, we concluded that the self-transformation should rely on shifting the balance point by changing the overall weight distribution. The length of the device does not require significant transformations per se but still plays a certain role when it comes to perceived inertness when players move the device.

To gather further knowledge, we crafted a first mechanical prototype, depicted in Figure 2. With a length of 410 mm and a total weight of 1200 g, the controller relies on a motor and a rack transporting 200 g of lead inside its static tube. The resulting device appeared to be too heavy and slow in terms of its inertness. Therefore, we drew two final conclusions at this stage. Firstly, a static tube must be replaced by a dynamic solution to reduce laggardness. Secondly, the overall weight must be further reduced to improve the controller usability.

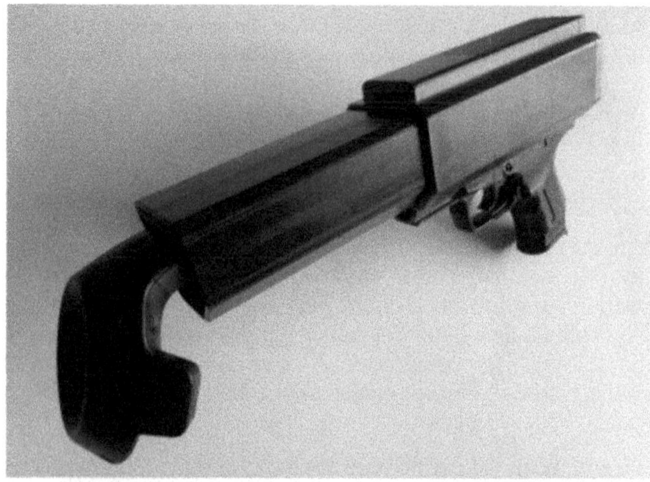

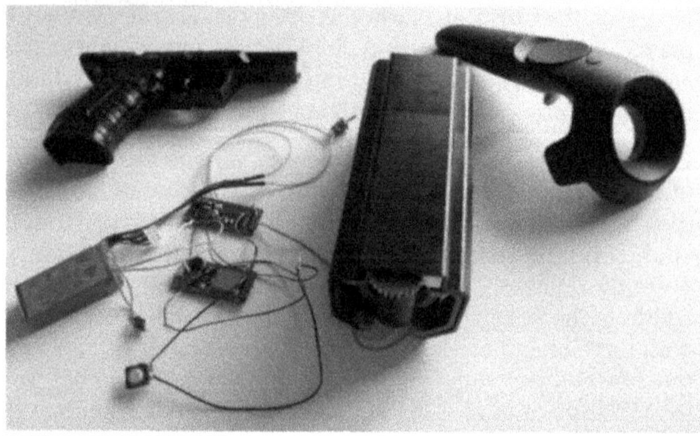

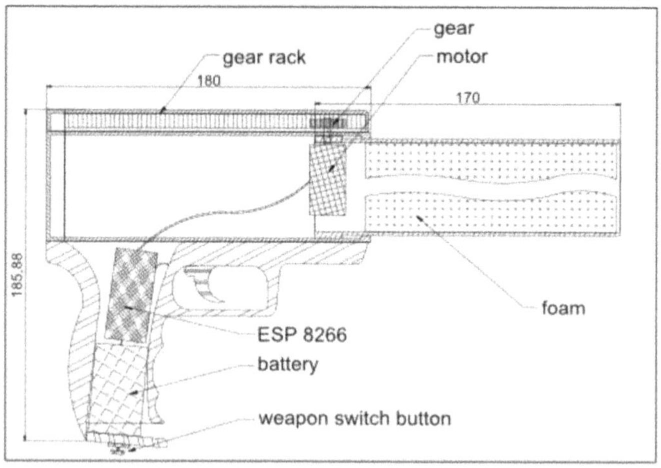

Figure 3. The final controller. The blueprint highlights the important components of our device. The telescoping tubes are moved by a rack and a motor, which is driven by a microcontroller. The HTC Vive controller is plugged into the soft foam.

Device Construction
Our final controller and its components are depicted in Figure 3. To see the device in action, please refer to Figure 1 and the supplementary video. The core functionality is based on

the previous prototype: to achieve the transformation effect, a shift of the balance point is performed by mechanically changing the weight distribution. The total weight of our controller is 710 g, the length in the pistol mode is 230 mm, and the length of the two-handed rifle state is 390 mm.

The handle of the controller is a cropped handle of a toy weapon including the trigger part. A telescopic mechanism is located on top. It consists of two 3D-printed tubes, each one with an approximate weight of 140 g. The inner tube is moved out by a motor-powered rack mechanism.

Instead of adding artificial weights to the device, we have the HTC Vive controller inside the inner tube, such that the tracking circle barely looks out. The Vive controller weighs approximately 200 g and is already included in the 710 g total device weight. Apart from its function as moving weight, the Vive controller is also used to perform spatial tracking of our input device, i.e., no additional tracking is required.

The motor needs around 700 ms to move the telescopic tube in or out. An Arduino-like board [1], the ESP8266, is responsible for the device logic. The board controls the motor and is also wired with the trigger and the weapon transformation buttons. The latter is placed at the bottom of the handle to be easy to hit even when being in VR. Figure 3 depicts the controller components. The ESP8266 has Wi-Fi onboard and is responsible for communicating firing and weapon switching events to our VR game.

Deploying to a Virtual Environment

We created a futuristic first-person shooter to evaluate our device. To focus on the transformation aspects, the game mechanics are mostly limited to shooting and weapon switching. The game is realized with the Unity 3D Engine [42] and takes place on a foreign planet. A human outpost is being attacked by aliens. The player is located on a small platform and has to defend the outpost by warding off the approaching waves as shown in Figure 4.

The enemies are walking aliens and flying spaceships. The former explode when they reach the player platform, whereas the latter start shooting when they come into close range. Although the platform starts to emit smoke after a certain amount of damage is inflicted, the game cannot be lost. The game always finishes after 4 minutes, reporting that the player was able to hold off the enemies.

A detailed in-game tutorial explains the weapon specifics. The player can switch between two types: a one-handed blaster and a two-handed laser rifle. Figure 4 shows the two weapon models. The tutorial also explains that the blaster is more effective versus the ground troops, whereas the laser rifle is best used for spaceships. The player needs about three shots to destroy an enemy with the appropriate weapon. To motivate weapon switching, shooting with the inappropriate weapon requires three times more hits. In addition, the player can move on the tiny platform to get a better aiming angle. Although the our controller needs 700 ms to perform the transformation, we decided not to include a transformation animation, as our pre-test participants did not report any negative impact of that mismatch.

The game is executed on a HTC Vive and supports both the default HTC Vive controller and our self-transforming device. For the default controller, the trigger is used for firing, and the big round thumb button is used for weapon switching. The self-transforming device also fires with a trigger, and the switching is initiated by a button press at the bottom of the handle. Our controller sends the user input to the Unity game via Wi-Fi over the MQTT [26] protocol. The tracking of the weapon position and orientation is done with the built-in HTC Vive controller in the front tube. This combination of standard components and the widespread MQTT protocol also guarantees a wide interoperability with other HTC Vive applications and games to facilitate further research.

EVALUATION

We conducted a study to evaluate our self-transforming controller. We were particularly interested in players' perception and acceptance of the controller, its usability as well as its influence on the player experience compared to a common VR game controller. Hence, we applied a within-subject design with the type of weapon as the independent variable comparing our self-transforming controller to the HTC Vive game controller. Participants played the testbed game with both controllers, and the order of the controllers was randomized as a between-subject factor, thereby controlling for possible sequence and learning effects.

Focus of the Study and Hypotheses

One goal of the study was to gather explorative qualitative and quantitative data about the usability and acceptance of our controller in general to determine the quality of our product. Furthermore, we tested three main hypotheses regarding the comparison of our controller and the standard HTC Vive controller. We assumed that the design and functionality of the self-transforming controller enhances the feeling of actually handling the weapon that is displayed in the virtual world and thus the perceived realism of the interaction. This, in turn, is hypothesized to affect the player experience, particularly in terms of immersion, presence, and flow. Hence, our first hypotheses are:

- H1: Perceived realism is significantly higher for the self-transforming controller than for the HTC Vive controller.
- H2: The use of the self-transforming controller leads to higher
  (a) immersion and feelings of presence
  (b) flow
  (c) positive affect

  than the use of the HTC Vive controller.

Furthermore, we assume that the analogy between our controller and a real gun leads to intuitive and easy handling. Hence, we hypothesize:

- H3(a): The use of the self-transforming controller is perceived as more intuitive than the use of the HTC Vive controller.
- H3(b): Players experience a higher feeling of competence using the self-transforming controller compared to the HTC Vive controller.

Figure 4. Our first-person shooter used for the evaluation of the self-transforming controller. The two weapon kinds, a blaster and a laser rifle, are depicted in the center. The right image shows an attaking spaceship. The ground troops do not shoot and instead explode upon reaching the platform.

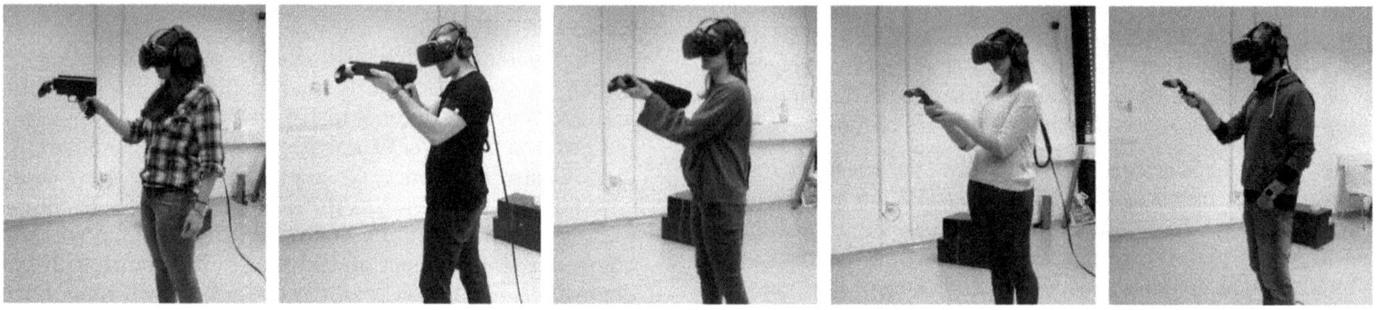

Figure 5. The participants playing our first-person shooter with the default HTC Vive device and our self-transforming controller.

Beside these hypotheses, our self-transforming controller will also be compared to the HTC Vive controller in terms of usability as well as players' in-game behavior and performance.

Procedure and Applied Measures

The study took place in our virtual reality lab at the university. After informing participants about the study's procedure, we administered a first questionnaire to assess age, gender, and their prior experiences with digital games, first-person shooters, real-life guns, and VR gaming systems. We also asked the participants if they had used the common Vive controller before. Subsequently, participants were introduced to the Vive HMD, the game rules, and the first controller. Half of the participants played with the standard Vive controller first, and the other half started with our self-transforming device.

After playing the game for 4 minutes, we asked the participants to fill in questionnaires regarding their player experience and their evaluation of the game controller used. To assess player experience, the Game Experience Questionnaire (GEQ) [14] and the Player Experience of Need Satisfaction (PENS) [33] questionnaire were administered. The GEQ subdivides player experience into the seven subdimensions *positive affect*, *negative affect*, *immersion*, *flow*, *challenge*, *tension/annoyance*, and *competence*. The PENS measures the degree of need satisfaction regarding the needs for *autonomy* and *competence* and also contains the subscale *intuitive controls* referring to the ease of use of the game controls. As feelings of presence and immersion are supposed to be a particularly important part of the experience in VR games, we additionally used the Igroup Presence Questionnaire (IPQ) [34], which assesses the perceived presence in general, as well as the subdimensions *spatial presence*, *involvement*, and *experienced realism*.

Furthermore, participants' evaluation of the game controller was addressed by parts of the the Consumer Products Questionnaire (CPQ) [24] and the Device Assessment Questionnaire (DAQ) [8], which is based on the ISO 9241-9 standard [16]. The CPQ measures user-satisfaction with electronic consumer products. We used the subscales *appearance* and *efficiency* to investigate how participants liked the look and feel of the controller as well as their interaction with it. We added one item referring to the weight of the controller to the appearance scale, because this was an important aspect of the appeal of the controller discussed by participants in the pre-study. In addition, we generated three additional items addressing the perceived authenticity of the controller: '*I felt like actually holding the weapon displayed in the VR world*', '*I felt a shifting of weight when changing the weapon*', and '*Both weapons in the game (pistol and rifle) felt different in my hands*'. The DAQ consists of 13 items referring to the overall usability as well as issues of physical operation (effort, smoothness), accuracy, speed, general comfort, and fatigue (of fingers, wrist, arm, shoulder, and neck).

After filling in the questionnaires, the game was played a second time for another 4 minutes, this time with the other controller. Again, we administered GEQ, PENS, IPQ, CPQ, and DAQ afterwards to assess player experience and controller evaluation for the second controller. At the end, we presented a final questionnaire including questions about participants' physical well-being to control for simulator sickness [20].

Finally, we asked the participants to rate some details of our self-transforming controller to gain comprehensive insights into the evaluation of our specific creation, e.g., the time and process of the weapon transformation, and the look and feel.

Table 1. Mean values and standard deviations regarding dependent variables related to player experience in both controller conditions and results of the repeated measures ANOVA comparing those values.

Dependent Variable	Self-Transforming Controller M (SD)	HTC Vive Controller M (SD)	F (1, 27)	Significance p	
GEQ (scale: 0 - 4)					
Positive Affect	2.77 (0.56)	2.73 (0.65)	0.15	.701	
Negative Affect	0.44 (0.41)	0.47 (0.44)	0.13	.717	
Flow	2.45 (0.85)	2.12 (0.75)	9.46	.005	**
Immersion	1.88 (0.67)	1.78 (0.62)	2.02	.166	
Competence	2.57 (0.66)	2.55 (0.81)	0.06	.817	
Annoyance	0.31 (0.46)	0.32 (0.44)	0.03	.866	
Challenge	1.18 (0.54)	1.05 (0.72)	2.41	.133	
PENS (scale: 1 -7)					
Autonomy	3.60 (1.42)	3.49 (1.44)	0.25	.619	
Competence	5.45 (1.04)	5.07 (1.25)	5.71	.024	*
Intuitive Control	6.49 (0.68)	6.47 (0.70)	0.01	.941	
IPQ (scale: 0 - 6)					
General	4.48 (1.02)	4.31 (1.20)	0.94	.342	
Spatial Presence	4.12 (0.67)	4.20 (0.68)	0.40	.532	
Involvement	4.18 (1.22)	3.75 (1.44)	2.18	.152	
Experienced Realism	2.67 (1.01)	2.27 (0.94)	4.83	.037	*
CPQ (scale: 0 - 4)					
Appearance	3.13 (0.62)	2.47 (0.94)	8.21	.008	**
Efficiency	3.56 (0.44)	3.21 (0.49)	12.07	.002	**
Controller Authenticity	3.01 (0.72)	0.89 (0.84)	85.42	< .001	**

*p <.05, ** p <.01

During the two gaming sessions, we additionally logged relevant gameplay data to record players' performance and in-game behavior. These gameplay metrics include the hit ratio of both weapons, the total number of shots fired, the amount of weapon switches, and the damage taken by the platform.

Results

29 persons (7 females, 22 males), aged 19 to 64 ($M = 26.14$, $SD = 8.56$), participated in the study. Most of them were students ($N = 21$) or employees ($N = 6$). The majority reported to have some experience with playing first-person shooter games ($N = 24$), whereas fewer participants had some prior experiences with VR gaming systems ($N = 13$), the HTC Vive controller ($N = 7$), and real firing arms ($N = 12$). Thus, our sample included mostly players interested in first-person shooter games, and both experienced and inexperienced persons regarding VR gaming, the HTC Vive, and the use of firing arms. No participants reported problems with simulator sickness ($M = 0.21$, $SD = 0.49$).

Evaluation of the Self-Transforming Controller

We asked four questions addressing the design and functionality of our controller. Participants rated their liking of different aspects of the controller on a scale from 0 (*'I did not like it at all'*) to 4 (*'I liked it a lot'*). Results show high mean scores for all items: *'the transformation (shape and weight distribution modification) when switching the weapon'* ($M = 3.59$, $SD = 0.57$), *'the feeling of how the controller fits in the hand'* ($M = 3.31$, $SD = 0.76$), *'the similarity of the controller to the weapon displayed in the VR world'* ($M = 3.07$, $SD = 0.75$), and *'the feeling of holding an authentic weapon'* ($M = 2.86$, $SD = 1.22$).

Participants should also rate their agreement with statements regarding the duration of the transformation on a scale from 0 (*'I don't agree'*) to 4 (*'I totally agree'*). On average, they disagreed that *'the transformation of the controller took too long'* ($M = 0.66$, $SD = 0.86$), or that *'the fact that the transformation is not instant was disturbing'* ($M = 0.55$, $SD = 0.78$). In contrast, they agreed that *'the transformation duration appeared authentic'* ($M = 2.90$, $SD = 0.98$). A summary is depicted in Figure 7.

Scores of the CPQ and the ISO DAQ also provided valuable insight into how participants perceived our controller and its usability. Values on the CPQ subscales are all above 3 on a scale from 0 to 4, indicating very positive evaluations of the look and feel, efficiency, and authenticity of the controller. We tested ther internal consistency of the subscale *controller authenticity*, which we added to the original questionnaire, by calculating Cronbach's alpha. The calculation indicates a sufficient level of consistency for the three items ($\alpha = 0.76$).

Mean scores for all DAQ items are plotted in Figure 6. On a scale ranging from 0 to 4, our controller scored high on the overall ease of use ($M = 3.38$, $SD = 0.73$), smoothness ($M = 2.72$, $SD = 1.07$), and general comfort ($M = 3.07$, $SD = 0.84$). Ratings for all kinds of physical fatigue are very low (all $M < 1.31$). Mean values regarding the required force to operate an action ($M = 1.86$, $SD = 0.58$), the mental effort ($M = 1.62$, $SD = 0.49$), the physical effort ($M = 2.07$, $SD =$

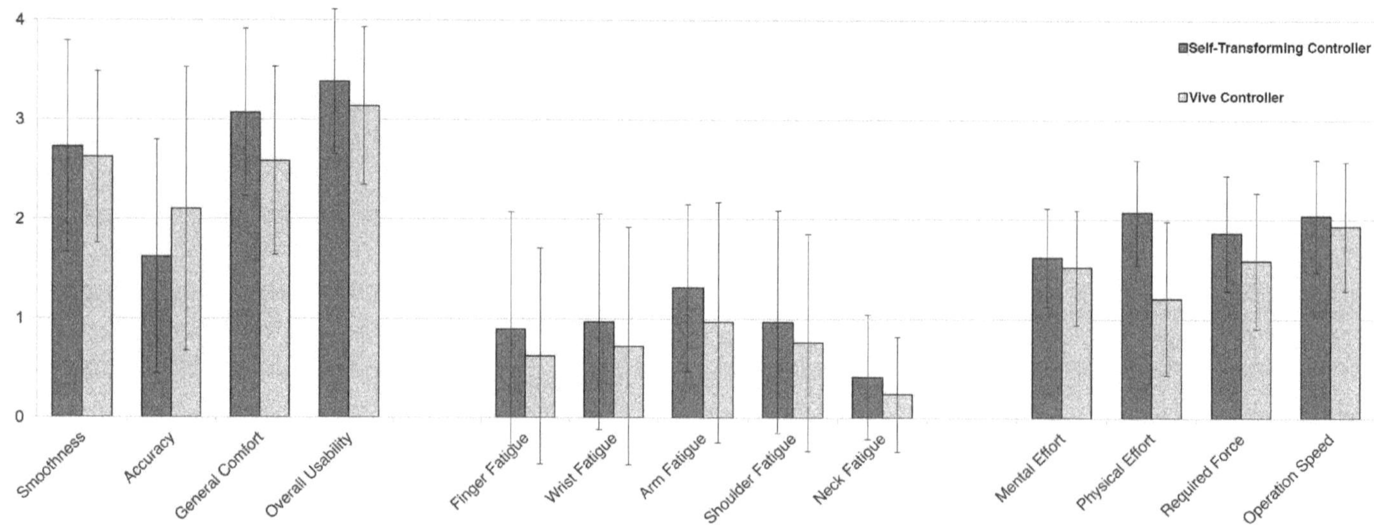

Figure 6. Mean scores and standard deviations for the Device Assessment Questionnaire (DAQ) items with regard to our device and the HTC Vive controller. Note that for the left group, higher values are better. The center group contains items for which lower values are best, and the items of the right group have their optimum in the middle (2.0), i.e., neither too low nor too high.

0.53), and operation speed ($M = 2.03$, $SD = 0.57$) are near the optimum medium rating (with 2.0 indicating that the aspect is neither *too low* nor *too high*).

Comparing the Two Game Controllers

All investigated parameters are approximately normally distributed according to Kolmogorov-Smirnov tests. Hence, we use one-way repeated measures ANOVA to compare measurements for our self-transforming controller and the HTC Vive controller while accounting for the sequence of controller types as a between-subjects factor. Mean values and results of the ANOVA for all variables related to player experience are presented in Table 1.

The GEQ subscales show significantly higher flow values for the self-transforming controller. Mean values of all other GEQ subscales do not differ significantly. However, for the GEQ subdimension *competence*, a significant sequence effect was found: Although, on average, values on the competence scale are quite equal for both controller conditions, the ANOVA indicates that competence is rated significantly higher for the second round of play, independent of controller type, $F(1,27) = 6.78$, $p = .015$.

The analysis of the PENS subscales reveals a higher feeling of competence when playing with the self-transforming controller. No sequence effects or other significant differences were found for the PENS measures. The IPQ addresses feelings of presence on four dimensions. Values for general presence, involvement, and experienced realism are higher for the self-transforming controller, but only the difference for experienced realism is significant. No sequence effects were found.

Results of the ANOVA comparing the CPQ subscales indicate that the self-transforming controller scored significantly higher on appearance, efficiency, and authenticity. In the case of the appearance subscale, the ANOVA also reveals a significant sequence effect: The HTC Vive controller has lower scores for appearance in both sequence conditions, but the difference is particularly high if participants played with the self-transforming controller first and then had to evaluate the Vive controller afterwards. In this case, the appearance rating for the HTC Vive controller is much lower ($M = 2.11$, $SD = 0.99$) than in the reverse playing order ($M = 2.86$, $SD = 0.73$). DAQ scores for the self-transforming controller also indicate high usability, as depicted in Figure 6.

According to the ANOVA, there is only one highly significant difference in terms of physical effort, which is higher for the self-transforming controller ($M = 2.07, SD = 0.53$) than for the HTC Vive controller ($M = 1.21, SD = 0.77$), $F(1,27) = 25.14$, $p < .000$. Differences for difficulties in accurate pointing ($F(1,27) = 3.62$, $p = .068$) and comfort ($F(1,27) = 3.31$, $p = .080$) are not significant and show marginally better scores for our self-transforming controller. Ratings of general comfort also showed a significant sequence effect ($F(1,27) = 4.41$, $p = .045$): The comfort of the self-transforming controller was rated significantly higher than the comfort of the HTC Vive, if participants played with the self-transforming controller first. In contrast, in the other sequence, comfort ratings for both controllers are almost equal.

The analysis of the gameplay data, which was automatically logged during play, results in few significant differences between the two controller types. Regarding the hit ratio with both game weapons, the final damage to the platform, and the total number of shots fired, both controllers show comparable values. In contrast, participants performed significantly fewer weapon changes with the self-transforming controller ($M = 19.07$, $SD = 5.09$) than with the HTC Vive controller ($M = 27.17$, $SD = 8.99$), $F(1,27) = 30.54$, $p < .001$. Furthermore, a sequence effect was detected for the damage taken, which was significantly lower in the second play round independent of controller type, $F(1,27) = 13.34$, $p = .001$, indicating a better player performance.

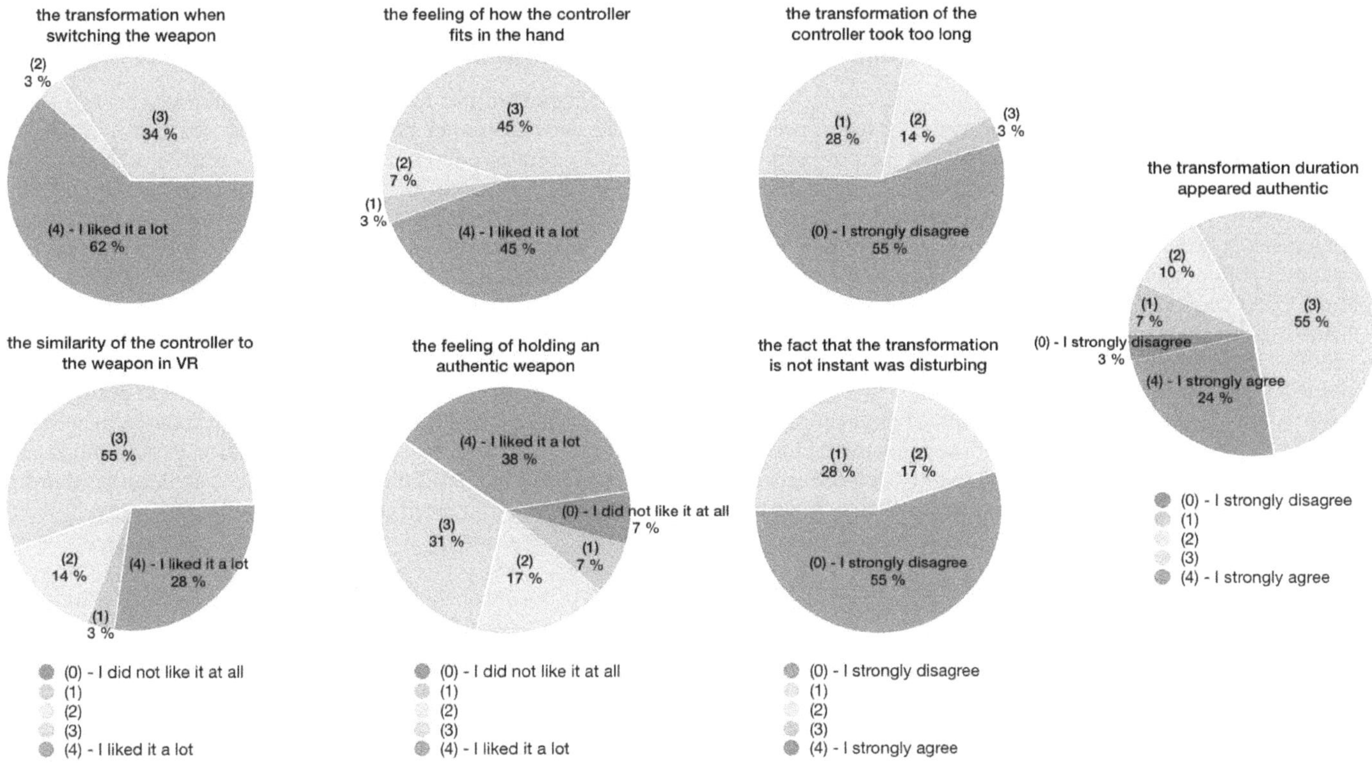

Figure 7. We asked the subjects several questions about the design and functionality of our self-transforming controller. The pie charts illustrate the respective questions and the overall answer distribution of the 29 participants.

DISCUSSION

The scores of the CPQ and the ISO DAQ confirm the outstanding usability of our device. Players reported to enjoy the overall haptics and the transformation concept, as can be seen in the high values of the CPQ subscales. Yet not being an industry product, our device performed significantly better than the Vive controller with regard to appearance, efficiency, and controller authenticity. The ISO DAQ further supports this statement as shown in Figure 6. Our controller achieves high scores in terms of the overall ease of use, smoothness, and general comfort. Futhermore, the mental and physical efforts to operate the device are close to the optimum as is the operation speed.

The favorable feedback on our novel transformation approach is most visible in the rating presented in Figure 7. Nearly 83% of the participants disagreed (1) or strongly disagreed that the transformation (700 ms) took too long. The same percentage is also observable with regard to the question whether the transformation time was disturbing. Although the transformation process happens instantly in the VR game, one might have expected issues related to that kind of delay. However, as the transformation produces a decent noise and also a slight tactile feedback, the 700 ms needed for the physical transformation do not affect players in a negative way. On the contrary, 79% agreed (3) or strongly agreed (4) that the duration appeared authentic. The concept of transformation, being our primary contribution, was liked (3) or liked a lot (4) by **96% of the participants.**

Our device weighs 3.5 times more than the HTC Vive controller (710 g and 200 g, respectively). Nevertheless, the current prototype was not perceived as too heavy by the players. This is underlined by our question referring to the weight that we added to the CPQ on the appearance scale. The result shows an average of 2.97 on a scale ranging from 0 to 4, i.e., players reported that the overall weight is adequate.

The same is true for the experienced fatigue. According to the DAQ results, the overall fatigue is fairly low. The worst rated item is the arm fatigue ($M = 1.31$, $SD = 1.28$). In contrast, the lighter Vive controller is slightly better in all fatigue scales, yet not reaching a level of significance. However, the game was played for only 4 minutes, and longer game sessions might have a more significant impact in terms of fatigue. Tightly coupled to weight and fatigue aspects, the physical effort for our device was significantly higher compared to the Vive controller. However, this is a rather positive outcome as our controller gets significantly closer to the optimum.

We summarize that our controller provided very high comfort and usability overall (DAQ) and shows noticeable trends to outperform the default HTC Vive device. The transformation concept was highly appreciated by the players and resulted in very high acceptance throughout the related scales, such as transformation time.

Our proposed hypotheses are based on the comparison between our device and the default HTC Vive controller. H1 stated that the perceived realism is significantly higher for the self-transforming controller. Both the CPQ authenticity scale

($p < .001$) and the IPQ experienced realism scale ($p = .037$) show significant improvements, and, thus, confirm this hypothesis.

For H2, we assumed that immersion and feelings of presence, flow, and positive affects would be higher for our controller. Firstly, the GEQ and the IPQ confirmed the experienced realism. In terms of presence, as the HMD already offers a highly immersive experience, the resultung values were very high for both controllers according to the IPQ. The immersion scale of the GEQ shows only marginal improvements. We attribute this to the fact that the GEQ questions about immersion mostly relate to the game design and not to the overall experience, including peripherals such as the controller. In a similar way, the positive affects were not significantly better according to the GEQ. Even better, despite the high dependence of the GEQ on the game design, our device significantly outperformed the Vive controller on the flow scale which confirms that part of H2.

H3(a) stated that use of our controller is perceived as more intuitive. The intuitive controls scale of the PENS questionnaire does not show any significant difference: $M = 6.49$ for our controller and $M = 6.47$ for the HTC Vive device on a scale from 1 to 7. Note that both controllers perform extremely well, hence, we argue this is the reason that no significant difference can be established.

In H3(b), we assumed that the feeling of competence would be higher when played with our controller. At a first glance, we have two contradicting results from the PENS and the GEQ here. The PENS questionnaire shows a significant difference ($p = .024$) on the competence scale in favor to our device. That scale mostly assesses competence in terms of the balance between the game's challenge and the player's skills. Such a balance rather resembles the flow scale of the GEQ, which was also significant. The competence scale of the GEQ, in contrast, does not provide significant differences. However, the GEQ shows that the feeling of competence significantly increases in the second game round, no matter which controller was used in the first round. Hence, the competence feeling of the GEQ was mostly influenced by sequence effects and not by the controller type.

We evaluated the order of execution for all measurements and determined three significant sequence effects, apart from the GEQ competence scale. A similar learning effect was observed with respect to the damage taken, which is significantly lower in the second game round. Furthermore, the CPQ appearance score reports that the HTC Vive controller was rated notably worse if players used our self-transforming device in the first round. That is to say, players that were already exposed to the transformation concept clearly less liked the appearance of the Vive controller. The third item with a significant sequence effect is the DAQ comfort rating. Although our controller is not significantly better overall, the difference becomes significant when the subjects played with the self-transforming controller in the first round. In that case, similar to CPQ appearance, our controller was rated significantly better than the Vive controller. The fact further fortifies our statement on the overall very high comfort compared to the HTC state of the art device. All other reported controller differences are not affected by sequence effects.

With regard to the logged gameplay metrics, no significant difference in player performance was observed. Thus, the novel concept does not impose any negative effects on the player performance, as the players were able to aim and shoot reliably. The total amount of performed weapon switching is significantly lower for our controller. We motivate that result by the fact that the transformation process is more complex for our controller. Players have to move their non-leading hand to a button on the bottom of the handle and deal with the transformation time. In contrast, weapon switching with the Vive controller was done by the big thumb button that is always in reach. This is also reflected in the overall physical effort scores. Overall, the transformation process leads to a more conscious, and thus, less frequent switching, and does not affect the player performance in a negative way.

CONCLUSION AND FUTURE WORK

Our contribution is a self-transforming controller concept and its evaluation in a VR first-person shooter game. Based on a telescopic, motor-driven mechanism, the device transforms between a pistol-like and a rifle-like shape. The presented design thinking approach included a think-aloud protocol and gave us insights into the influence of weight distribution on controller perception.

We evaluated our final controller via a user study. Hereby, we compared our device to the HTC Vive controller based on the GEQ, CPQ, IPQ, and PENS questionnaires. The results show that our shape-changing device significantly outperforms the default controller with regard to scales such as appearance, efficiency, authenticity, experienced realism, and flow. Most importantly, 96% of the participants reported to like the overall concept of a self-transforming controller.

In order to further investigate the users' perception of our self-transforming controller, additional studies are of high interest. In particular, we suggest to add non-transforming pistols and rifles to the comparison, as the HTC Vive controller is designed with universality in mind and, thus, possibly does not provide sufficient similarity to its virtual counterpart with respect to haptics. Additionally, this would also further isolate the advantages of the transformation itself. Another subject to investigate is a further reduction in the weight of the controller and a determination of the sweet spot for the total weight.

Although we focused on the transformation between a pistol and a rifle, the same design approach can also be applied to other weapons or virtual objects. Including a second rack that transports an equal weight toward the player would allow to simulate shoulder-fired missile weapons (e.g., bazooka). This would already cover most of the weapon classes for firearm-based FPS games. Making the handle retractable would further increase the design space and allow to simulate sword-shaped virtual objects. In that case, the weight based transformation could simulate the switch between, e.g., a short knife and a two-handed sword.

REFERENCES

1. Arduino. 2017. Arduino Electronics Platform. Website. (2017). Retrieved April 10, 2017 from https://www.arduino.cc.
2. Regina Bernhaupt. 2010. *User Experience Evaluation in Entertainment*. Springer London, London, 3–7. DOI: http://dx.doi.org/10.1007/978-1-84882-963-3_1
3. Frank Biocca and Ben Delaney. 1995. Communication in the Age of Virtual Reality. L. Erlbaum Associates Inc., Hillsdale, NJ, USA, Chapter Immersive Virtual Reality Technology, 57–124. http://dl.acm.org/citation.cfm?id=207922.207926
4. Max Birk and Regan L. Mandryk. 2013. Control Your Game-self: Effects of Controller Type on Enjoyment, Motivation, and Personality in Game. In *Proceedings of the SIGCHI Conference on Human Factors in Computing Systems (CHI '13)*. ACM, New York, NY, USA, 685–694. DOI:http://dx.doi.org/10.1145/2470654.2470752
5. Michael Brown, Aidan Kehoe, Jurek Kirakowski, and Ian Pitt. 2015. Beyond the gamepad: HCI and game controller design and evaluation. In *Game User Experience Evaluation*. Springer, 263–285.
6. Paul Cairns, Anna Cox, and A Imran Nordin. 2014. Immersion in digital games: review of gaming experience research. *Handbook of digital games* (2014), 337–361.
7. HTC Corporation. 2017. HTC Vive. Website. (2017). Retrieved April 10, 2017 from https://www.vive.com/.
8. Sarah A. Douglas, Arthur E. Kirkpatrick, and I. Scott MacKenzie. 1999. Testing Pointing Device Performance and User Assessment with the ISO 9241, Part 9 Standard. In *Proceedings of the SIGCHI Conference on Human Factors in Computing Systems (CHI '99)*. ACM, New York, NY, USA, 215–222. DOI: http://dx.doi.org/10.1145/302979.303042
9. Kotkin Enterprises. 2017. The Delta Six VR Gun. Website. (2017). Retrieved April 10, 2017 from https://www.avengercontroller.com/vr-gun-controller/.
10. Sony Interactive Entertainment. 2017. PlayStation VR. Website. (2017). Retrieved April 10, 2017 from https://www.playstation.com/en-us/explore/playstation-vr/.
11. Kathrin M Gerling, Matthias Klauser, and Joerg Niesenhaus. 2011. Measuring the impact of game controllers on player experience in FPS games. In *Proceedings of the 15th International Academic MindTrek Conference: Envisioning Future Media Environments*. ACM, 83–86.
12. Carrie Heeter. 1992. Being there: The subjective experience of presence. *Presence: Teleoperators & Virtual Environments* 1, 2 (1992), 262–271.
13. Wijnand IJsselsteijn, Yvonne De Kort, Karolien Poels, Audrius Jurgelionis, and Francesco Bellotti. 2007. Characterising and measuring user experiences in digital games. In *International conference on advances in computer entertainment technology*, Vol. 2. 27.
14. Wijnand IJsselsteijn, Wouter Van Den Hoogen, Christoph Klimmt, Yvonne De Kort, Craig Lindley, Klaus Mathiak, Karolien Poels, Niklas Ravaja, Marko Turpeinen, and Peter Vorderer. 2008. Measuring the experience of digital game enjoyment. In *Proceedings of Measuring Behavior*. Noldus Information Tecnology Wageningen, Netherlands, 88–89.
15. Wijnand A. IJsselsteijn, Huib de Ridder, Jonathan Freeman, and Steve E. Avons. 2000. Presence: concept, determinants, and measurement. (2000). DOI: http://dx.doi.org/10.1117/12.387188
16. ISO. 2000. ISO/DIS 9241-9 Ergonomic Requirements for Office Work with Visual Display Terminals, Non-keyboard Input Device Requirements. (2000).
17. Miyu Iwafune, Taisuke Ohshima, and Yoichi Ochiai. 2016. Coded Skeleton: Programmable Deformation Behaviour for Shape Changing Interfaces. In *SIGGRAPH ASIA 2016 Emerging Technologies (SA '16)*. ACM, New York, NY, USA, Article 1, 2 pages. DOI: http://dx.doi.org/10.1145/2988240.2988252
18. Charlene Jennett, Anna L Cox, Paul Cairns, Samira Dhoparee, Andrew Epps, Tim Tijs, and Alison Walton. 2008. Measuring and defining the experience of immersion in games. *International journal of human-computer studies* 66, 9 (2008), 641–661.
19. Hayato Kajiyama, Akifumi Inoue, and Tohru Hoshi. 2015. SHAPIO: Shape I/O Controller for Video Games. In *Proceedings of the 2015 Annual Symposium on Computer-Human Interaction in Play*. ACM, 565–570.
20. Robert S. Kennedy, Norman E. Lane, Kevin S. Berbaum, and Michael G. Lilienthal. 1993. Simulator Sickness Questionnaire: An Enhanced Method for Quantifying Simulator Sickness. *The International Journal of Aviation Psychology* 3, 3 (1993), 203–220. DOI: http://dx.doi.org/10.1207/s15327108ijap0303{_}3
21. Christoph Klimmt, Tilo Hartmann, and Andreas Frey. 2007. Effectance and control as determinants of video game enjoyment. *Cyberpsychology & behavior* 10, 6 (2007), 845–848.
22. Matthew Lombard and Theresa Ditton. 1997. At the heart of it all: The concept of presence. *Journal of Computer-Mediated Communication* 3, 2 (1997), 0–0.
23. Niamh McNamara and Jurek Kirakowski. 2006. Functionality, usability, and user experience: three areas of concern, interactions, v. 13 n. 6. *November+ December* (2006).
24. Niamh McNamara and Jurek Kirakowski. 2011. Measuring user-satisfaction with electronic consumer products: The Consumer Products Questionnaire. *International Journal of Human-Computer Studies* 69, 6 (2011), 375 – 386. DOI: http://dx.doi.org/10.1016/j.ijhcs.2011.01.005

25. G. Michelitsch, J. Williams, M. Osen, B. Jimenez, and S. Rapp. 2004. Haptic Chameleon: A New Concept of Shape-changing User Interface Controls with Force Feedback. In *CHI '04 Extended Abstracts on Human Factors in Computing Systems (CHI EA '04)*. ACM, New York, NY, USA, 1305–1308. DOI: http://dx.doi.org/10.1145/985921.986050

26. mqtt.org. 2017. MQTT. Website. (2017). Retrieved April 10, 2017 from http://mqtt.org.

27. Ken Nakagaki, Pasquale Totaro, Jim Peraino, Thariq Shihipar, Chantine Akiyama, Yin Shuang, and Hiroshi Ishii. 2016. HydroMorph: Shape Changing Water Membrane for Display and Interaction. In *Proceedings of the TEI '16: Tenth International Conference on Tangible, Embedded, and Embodied Interaction (TEI '16)*. ACM, New York, NY, USA, 512–517. DOI: http://dx.doi.org/10.1145/2839462.2856517

28. Ryuma Niiyama, Lining Yao, and Hiroshi Ishii. 2013. Weight and Volume Changing Device with Liquid Metal Transfer. In *Proceedings of the 8th International Conference on Tangible, Embedded and Embodied Interaction (TEI '14)*. ACM, New York, NY, USA, 49–52. DOI:http://dx.doi.org/10.1145/2540930.2540953

29. Tan Phat Pham and Yin-Leng Theng. 2012. Game Controllers for Older Adults: Experimental Study on Gameplay Experiences and Preferences. In *Proceedings of the International Conference on the Foundations of Digital Games (FDG '12)*. ACM, New York, NY, USA, 284–285. DOI: http://dx.doi.org/10.1145/2282338.2282401

30. Karolien Poels, Yvonne de Kort, and Wijnand IJsselsteijn. 2007. "It is Always a Lot of Fun!": Exploring Dimensions of Digital Game Experience Using Focus Group Methodology. In *Proceedings of the 2007 Conference on Future Play (Future Play '07)*. ACM, New York, NY, USA, 83–89. DOI: http://dx.doi.org/10.1145/1328202.1328218

31. Majken Kirkegård Rasmussen, Timothy Merritt, Miguel Bruns Alonso, and Marianne Graves Petersen. 2016. Balancing User and System Control in Shape-Changing Interfaces: A Designerly Exploration. In *Proceedings of the TEI '16: Tenth International Conference on Tangible, Embedded, and Embodied Interaction (TEI '16)*. ACM, New York, NY, USA, 202–210. DOI: http://dx.doi.org/10.1145/2839462.2839499

32. Anne Roudaut, Rebecca Reed, Tianbo Hao, and Sriram Subramanian. 2014. Changibles: Analyzing and Designing Shape Changing Constructive Assembly. In *Proceedings of the 32Nd Annual ACM Conference on Human Factors in Computing Systems (CHI '14)*. ACM, New York, NY, USA, 2593–2596. DOI: http://dx.doi.org/10.1145/2556288.2557006

33. Richard M. Ryan, C. Scott Rigby, and Andrew Przybylski. 2006. The Motivational Pull of Video Games: A Self-Determination Theory Approach. *Motivation and Emotion* 30, 4 (2006), 344–360. DOI: http://dx.doi.org/10.1007/s11031-006-9051-8

34. T. W. Schubert, Frank Friedmann, and H. T. Regenbrecht. 1999. Decomposing the sense of presence: Factor analytic insights. In *2nd international workshop on presence*, Vol. 1999.

35. William R Sherman and Alan B Craig. 2002. *Understanding virtual reality: Interface, application, and design*. Elsevier.

36. Adalberto L. Simeone, Eduardo Velloso, and Hans Gellersen. 2015. Substitutional Reality: Using the Physical Environment to Design Virtual Reality Experiences. In *Proceedings of the 33rd Annual ACM Conference on Human Factors in Computing Systems (CHI '15)*. ACM, New York, NY, USA, 3307–3316. DOI: http://dx.doi.org/10.1145/2702123.2702389

37. Mel Slater. 2003. A note on presence terminology. *Presence connect* 3, 3 (2003), 1–5.

38. Christian Steins, Sean Gustafson, Christian Holz, and Patrick Baudisch. 2013. Imaginary Devices: Gesture-based Interaction Mimicking Traditional Input Devices. In *Proceedings of the 15th International Conference on Human-computer Interaction with Mobile Devices and Services (MobileHCI '13)*. ACM, New York, NY, USA, 123–126. DOI: http://dx.doi.org/10.1145/2493190.2493208

39. Striker VR . 2017. Striker VR. Website. (2017). Retrieved April 10, 2017 from https://www.strikervr.com/.

40. Jihoon Suh, Wooshik Kim, and Andrea Bianchi. 2017. Button+: Supporting User and Context Aware Interaction Through Shape-Changing Interfaces. In *Proceedings of the Eleventh International Conference on Tangible, Embedded, and Embodied Interaction (TEI '17)*. ACM, New York, NY, USA, 261–268. DOI: http://dx.doi.org/10.1145/3024969.3024980

41. Jari Takatalo, Jukka Häkkinen, Jyrki Kaistinen, and Göte Nyman. 2011. User Experience in Digital Games. *Simulation & Gaming* 42, 5 (2011), 656–673. DOI: http://dx.doi.org/10.1177/1046878110378353

42. Unity Technologies. 2017. Unity. Website. (2017). Retrieved April 10, 2017 from https://unity3d.com/.

43. Oculus VR. 2017. Oculus Rift+Touch. Website. (2017). Retrieved April 10, 2017 from https://www.oculus.com/rift/.

44. Gareth W Young, Aidan Kehoe, and David Murphy. 2016. Usability Testing of Video Game Controllers. *Games User Research: A Case Study Approach* (2016), 145.

45. Alexander Zaranek, Bryan Ramoul, Hua Fei Yu, Yiyu Yao, and Robert J Teather. 2014. Performance of modern gaming input devices in first-person shooter target acquisition. In *Proceedings of the extended abstracts of the 32nd annual ACM conference on Human factors in computing systems*. ACM, 1495–1500.

46. A. Zenner and A. Krüger. 2017. Shifty: A Weight-Shifting Dynamic Passive Haptic Proxy to Enhance Object Perception in Virtual Reality. *IEEE Transactions on Visualization and Computer Graphics* 23, 4 (April 2017), 1285–1294. DOI: http://dx.doi.org/10.1109/TVCG.2017.2656978

47. Dapeng Zhang, Zhongjie Cai, Kefei Chen, and Bernhard Nebel. 2009. A game controller based on multiple sensors. In *Proceedings of the International Conference on Advances in Computer Enterntainment Technology*. ACM, 375–378.

Here's Looking At You Anyway! How Important is Realistic Gaze Behavior in Co-located Social Virtual Reality Games?

Sven Seele
Bonn-Rhein-Sieg
University of Applied Sciences
Sankt Augustin, Germany
sven.seele@h-brs.de

Sebastian Misztal
Hochschule Hannover –
University of Applied Sciences
and Arts Hannover, Germany
sebastian.misztal@hs-hannover.de

Helmut Buhler
Bonn-Rhein-Sieg
University of Applied Sciences
Sankt Augustin, Germany
helmut.buhler@inf.h-brs.de

Rainer Herpers[*†]
Bonn-Rhein-Sieg
University of Applied Sciences
Sankt Augustin, Germany
rainer.herpers@h-brs.de

Jonas Schild[‡]
Hochschule Hannover –
University of Applied Sciences
and Arts Hannover, Germany
jonas.schild@hs-hannover.de

ABSTRACT
Simulating eye movements for virtual humans or avatars can improve social experiences in virtual reality (VR) games, especially when wearing head mounted displays. While other researchers have already demonstrated the importance of simulating meaningful eye movements, we compare three gaze models with different levels of fidelity regarding realism: (1) a base model with static fixation and saccadic movements, (2) a proposed simulation model that extends the saccadic model with gaze shifts based on a neural network, and (3) a user's real eye movements recorded by a proprietary eye tracker. Our between-groups design study with 42 subjects evaluates impact of eye movements on social VR user experience regarding perceived quality of communication and presence. The tasks include free conversation and two guessing games in a co-located setting. Results indicate that a high quality of communication in co-located VR can be achieved without using extended gaze behavior models besides saccadic simulation. Users might have to gain more experience with VR technology before being able to notice subtle details in gaze animation. In the future, remote VR collaboration involving different tasks requires further investigation.

*University of New Brunswick, Fredericton, E3B 5A3, Canada
†York University, Toronto, M3J 1P3, Canada
‡Bonn-Rhein-Sieg University of Applied Sciences, Sankt Augustin, Germany

CHI '17, October 15–18, 2017, Amsterdam, Netherlands
ACM 978-1-4503-4898-0/17/10...$15.00
DOI: http://dx.doi.org/10.1145/3116595.3116619

ACM Classification Keywords
H.5.1. Multimedia Information Systems: Artificial, augmented, and virtual realities; I.3.7 Three-Dimensional Graphics and Realism: Animation

Author Keywords
Gaze Behavior; Social Virtual Reality; Eye Tracking; Head-mounted Display

INTRODUCTION
As head-mounted displays (HMDs) become readily available to the mass market, one of the biggest challenges for current virtual reality (VR) developers and experience designers is the lack of industry standards for topics such as navigation, interaction and communication. Academics have investigated these issues in depth (e.g, [6]), but most of the documented findings and suggestions are based on outdated technology. As developers are looking to create ever more immersive experiences, while trying to minimize strain on consumers, one of their biggest hopes lies in social VR. In order to facilitate a believable social experience, users need to feel that they are interacting with another person in a co-located virtual space.

There are many factors, which potentially influence this sense of presence and co-presence. One of the most important factors is gaze behavior. For example, Thomas & Johnson [25] noted that "the audiences watches the eyes, and this is where the time and money must be spent if the character is to act convincingly" (cf. [23]). We believe that this observation can be transferred to user interaction with either conversational agents or other human users within a shared virtual environment. Other researches already showed the importance of being able to portray natural looking eye movements for virtual humans (e.g., [3, 10, 15]). Additionally, eye tracking has been a part of games research for a while and is going to become a commercial success in games according to Velloso et al. [27]. In their survey they were able to identify over 100 sources related to eye tracking in games, extracting more than

100 individual game mechanics that can only be realized with eye tracking. One of the most interesting mechanics is social gaze, which is particularly relevant for designing interactions between players and NPCs (see, e.g., [30]). Besides these social interactions, eye tracking data can additionally be used in game development and research to facilitate alternative input modalities (e.g., gaze gestures, dwell time selection, aiming) or, on a more abstract level, to improve level design, anticipate player actions, or infer player intent and behavior (cf. [1, 27]).

To investigate how closely an avatar's eye movements need to match those of the player, we compared generated gaze behavior, with and without adjusting fixation points, to mapping live eye tracker data to a user's virtual eyes. The setting involved two users situated in the same real and virtual space, who had to engage in a verbal interaction task including two guessing games. We hypothesized that simulating gaze shifts on top of an existing saccadic eye movement model will improve perceived realism and the overall social VR game experience. Simultaneously, we expected the simulated gaze shift model to be indistinguishable from real eye tracking data with regard to the impact on the quality of the social VR interaction.

Since collected questionnaire responses could not reveal significant differences between the three conditions, we discuss likely reasons and possible improvements of the study design. However, the data did show that gaze quality is correlated to the perception of communication and presence. Additionally, the data suggests that high quality social VR experiences are possible even without sophisticated gaze animation; at least for early social VR games. This conclusion may have to be re-investigated as players become more familiar with VR.

RELATED WORK

Long before the current interest in VR, modeling gaze shifts and saccades in combination with eyelid and head movements were topics of interest to researchers from various fields. The social significance of these movements in human communication for expressing emotions, directing attention, or initiating conversations were specific objects of research. With the aim of designing interaction in virtual environments as realistic and natural as possible, it makes sense to adapt these results and to apply them to VR. There are various developments addressing human–avatar communication and a few approaches in the field of verbal and non-verbal human–human communication aided by eye gaze of virtual representations.

Gaze in Communication

The social significance of eye gaze behavior in human communication is shown in the work of Beebe [5] and Burgoon et al. [7]. Comprehension, credibility, likeability, persuasiveness, and attraction are some of many relevant aspects with positive and negative impact on human communication. The effects on these aspects depend on whether or not the eye movement matches the content and the vocal inflection of the conversation. Additionally, Li [16] has shown that cultural differences between communication partners can lead to disrespect, inattentiveness, insincerity and thus to intercultural misunderstanding when eye gaze behavior does not meet expectations and habits. Besides cultural differences he also showed that role disparity can lead to miscommunication. In a doctor–patient relationship, medical doctors suppose that patients looking away do not report all of their symptoms according to Li. At the same time, Heath [12] showed that patients need to receive the doctor's gaze before they reveal their symptoms. These misunderstandings may appear within a virtual environment with embodied conversational agents if eye gaze is not implemented suitably.

Users tend to show more, partly exaggerated emotions as well as facial gestures and movements if their opposite virtual avatar does not express its emotions adequately [3]. This can be explained by the urge of humans to trigger a reaction the more intense they try, like pressing a mouse button harder to get a faster response. Therefore, visualizing as many human gestures and movements as possible, especially eye gaze, is relevant to prevent a distortion of natural communication.

Focusing on conversational attention, Vertegaal et al. [29] found that looking at somebody's face in a four-person setup is a strong indication of who is talking to whom, which is a decisive factor in speech recognition and production systems to decide when the system is the addresser or the addressee. Considering their results, subjects look seven times more at the individual they are listening to than to others. Furthermore, subjects look three times more at individuals they are speaking to. In a subsequent study, Vertegaal et al. [28] compared two three-person setups where gaze behavior of computer controlled characters is synchronized with conversational attention or random. They observed that people are more likely to speak when the conversational counterpart gazes at them more often. However, they found no evidence that people are more likely to speak if gaze behavior is synchronized with conversational attention. In contrast to their procedure, we apply a two-person setup with the main focus on the perceived naturalness of the virtual avatar with regard to eye gaze. We do not specifically consider who is looking at whom.

Garau et al. [9] have shown that using avatars with random eye gaze in a communication does not provide any advantage over a pure audio communication without virtual avatars. However, avatars with inferred eye gaze significantly improve communication. We follow a similar approach and compare eye movements during a conversation in VR. The movements are based on either static fixations, fixations determined by a neural network trained with human eye movements, or fixations recorded by an eye tracker.

Related Experimental Setups

In a study with 13 participants (7 female and 6 male), Fukayama et al. [8] examined their gaze movement model where interface agents, embodied only with bare eyes in front of a black background, showed different impressions. Nine gaze patterns were generated by altering the following parameters: amount of gaze, mean duration of gaze and gaze points while averted. Participants were listening to a recorded conversation (simple question-and-answer format) of an agent and another human and had to report their impression. In comparison to our setting this study has no human–human interaction and the abstract avatar is shown on a 2D screen.

Apart from eye gaze, Peters et al. [21] evaluated if participants could differentiate between horizontal and vertical gaze shifts. Furthermore, the participants had to assess the naturalness of blinking as they were shown animations of a virtual character making a series of eye and head movements. Steptoe et al. [24] had participants compare motion captured eye movements with linearly interpolated eyelid saccades. The animations were ranked in terms of perceived realism (most human-like) and similarity to the source. Trutoiu et al. [26], who examined eye blinking, as well as both Peters et al. and Steptoe et al. showed videos of pre-recorded animations to participants on a 2D screen without human–human interaction.

Bee et al. [4] used verbal interaction in addition to nonverbal interaction in communication. Their goal was to evaluate social dominance of intelligent virtual agents in order to show that gaze behaviors affect dominance perceptions. The study included 19 participants (10 female and 9 male) who were guided through a website after reading an instruction page describing the task.

A framework generating eye gaze based on live or recorded speech input was introduces by Le et al. [14]. In three comparative user studies participants estimated facial gesture as well as head and eye motion. In a forced choice task, participants were shown sequential video clips of the same avatar on a 2D display and had to select the eye gaze animation appearing to be more natural and more perceptually realistic. Andrist et al. [2] used a similar setting, enabling virtual agents to use gaze aversions towards 24 participants (12 female and 12 male) to achieve conversational functions. After giving consent, participants were seated in front of a large 2D display having to talk to life-sized virtual agents in four different tasks. Andrist et al., Bee et al., and Le et al. all did not considered human-human interaction nor did they put users in a 3D virtual environment.

To analyze gaze shifts towards different objects, Pejsa et al. [20] used a split-plot design with two dependent variables: communicative accuracy and perceived naturalness, two aspects which are also considered in our study. 50 males and 46 females watched 32 videos with either an animated virtual character or a human, looking at one of 16 objects. Each participant had to guess at which object the virtual character or human was looking, followed by filling out a questionnaire for subjective evaluation.

Gaze behavior by analyzing convergence (monocular vs. binocular eye-tracker) and the avatar's gaze in mono vs. stereo was addressed by Murray et al. [19]. Using three experiments, they studied how 7 to 12 participants assessed the efficacy of eye gaze and the impact of integrating it into collaborative and immersive virtual environments. The participants watched a virtual scene on a large screen with the eye gaze behavior of the previous participant, recorded with an eye tracker on a head-mounted display and mapped to the virtual character. Similar to [20], participants had to guess at which object the avatar was looking. After each half of the experiment participants were given a questionnaire. Here again, participants performed a human–agent interaction without communication, even if the tracking is close to a human–human interaction.

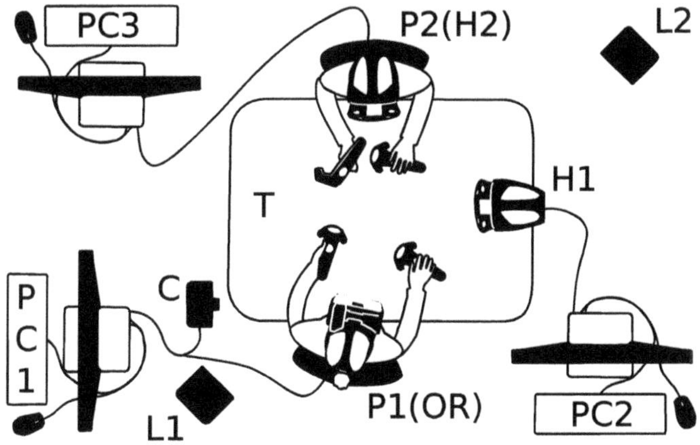

Figure 1: Experimental setup: Two participants (P1 and P2) are seated across a table (T). P1 wears an Oculus Rift DK2 HMD (OR) with an integrated eye tracker attached to PC1. PC2 provides the reference coordinate system for PC1 and PC3 and provides access to the controllers of the HTC Vive (H1). P2 wears the second HTC Vive HMD (H2) and uses the associated set of controllers. The lighthouse base stations (L1, L2) define the tracking volume for both Vive Systems. The tracking camera C tracks the position of the Oculus Rift.

Moubayed et al. [18] tried to avoid the *Mona Lisa Gaze Effect* by augmenting a physical head with eye gaze (i.e. projecting an animated talking head onto it). Participants were asked to look at the head from different angles and perceive gaze targets. The authors mention a possible application where the talking head and especially the eye gaze was captured by a human in real-time and projected to the model of the physical head. But in the study they did not test this scenario and again, there was no direct human–human interaction.

A 3D environment was used by Garau et al. [10] as the setting for a communicational human–human interaction, testing the impact of visual and behavioral realism. 48 participants, not knowing their conversational partner, were either put into a $CAVE^{TM}$-like system or wearing an HMD before they answered a questionnaire. The eye gaze behavior was derived from voice or was random. In both settings all participants were represented by a humanoid avatar. In contrast to our study, participants were not in the same room, but communicated across separate rooms using microphones.

Yu et al. [33] also investigated human–human and human–agent interaction as they analyzed gaze patterns and behavior in an attention task. 48 Participants with head-mounted eye-trackers were sitting towards a table in front of an agent or a human. The results indicated that participants were sensitive to the behavior of their partners (human and agent) and adapted gaze behavior, like in Howard Giles' Communication Accomodation Theory [11]. Unlike in our study, their head-mounted device did not include a display. Participants were looking at a non-virtual scene.

USER STUDY, DESIGN AND SETUP

As has been indicated in the previous section, the simulation of virtual gaze models has been addressed in research before.

Consequently, there are solutions that are readily available for use in modern real-time virtual environments. Two examples for gaze models, well known in the virtual humans community, are Lee et al. [15] and Itti et al. [13]. "Realistic eye movements"* is an implementation based on both approaches. It is available for use within the Unity game engine. Our main goal was to compare such *off-the-shelf* solutions to an extended version with a gaze behavior model and to a gaze behavior that uses an eye tracker for the user's actual eye movements. Our first gaze model represents the reference implementation and has no dynamic fixations, but uses the Realistic Eye Movements asset to handle eye blinks and saccades based on provided parameters. Our underlying assumption is that saccadic eye movements alone are not sufficient to capture realistic human gaze behavior as humans will focus their attention on different salient objects in a scene. Therefore, the first hypothesis is that adding a user's actual eye movements recorded using eye tracking hardware (tracked gaze model) will improve the perceived quality of communication or verbal interaction. At the same time, it will increase the sense of social co-presence within a virtual world shared between two users. Since it is unclear when eye trackers will be a standard component of VR HMDs, the second hypothesis is that a comparable effect can be achieved by simulating gaze behavior using an algorithm (simulated gaze model). The experimental design is mainly based on Garau et al. [9, 10].

Hardware Setup and Virtual Test Environment

The setup involved two participants seated across a real table. The scene was recreated in the Unity game engine such that perception of the real table (using sense of touch) and the virtual representation of the table (using vision) was nearly identical. One participant was wearing an HTC Vive HMD and used the accompanying controllers to control the hands of the virtual avatar. The other participant was wearing an Oculus Rift DK2 with an eye tracker retrofitted by SensoMotoric Instruments (SMI). To provide the same hand controls, the subject wearing the Oculus HMD used the controllers of another HTC Vive HMD, which were connected to the subject's virtual avatar via network. Thus, three PCs were necessary to set up the experiment: the Oculus Rift was attached to one PC, a second PC provided the reference for aligning the virtual worlds of each PC and the controllers for the Oculus avatar's hands via the first HTC Vive, and the second HTC Vive HMD including controllers was attached to the third PC. An appropriate arrangement of two lighthouse base stations provided the tracking volume for both Vive systems. An overview of the setup can be found in Figure 1, and images of the real and virtual scene used in the experiment are shown in Figure 2.

The study followed a between-groups design with three factors, which are the states of the gaze behavior. Observing the avatar of their counterpart, participants could either observe no gaze behavior (i.e. only saccades and blinks were generated by the Realistic Eye Movements asset), simulated gaze behavior (s. Section 3.2), or the actual unfiltered eye movements and blinks of the other participant as recorded by the eye tracker. We decided against a within-subject design to avoid adding a bias to the results by drawing exaggerated attention to the test conditions. We tested 21 pairs of participants; 42 individual subjects divided into the three groups with regard to the tested conditions. Gender balance was maintained between groups and within groups. The distribution of test subjects to groups was as follows: 14 saw only saccades (8 male, 6 female), 14 saw simulated gaze (8 male, 6 female), and 14 saw eye-tracked gaze (8 male, 5 female, 1 other). Participants were assigned an avatar with matching gender. We provided two male and two female avatars such that paired subjects could always be assigned different avatars. Participants were recruited from the university's student body and staff. Participants were paid 10 Euro for the experiment lasting approximately 45 minutes.

Simulated Gaze Algorithm

Most available algorithms that determine a current fixation point are based on multiple maps encoding various features, such as color, motion, or orientation (see, e.g, [13]). In contrast, our approach utilizes only depth information that is readily available in any physics engine, e.g., using raycasts†. Rays are cast from a user's point of view on a 20×20 grid (see Figure 3). Each raycast on the grid determines the distance to the closest object and whether that object represents a face. A neural network processes these 400 data points and produces a probability distribution (saliency) map, which is sampled each time the simulated eye fixates a new target, i.e. the map represents how likely it is that a real human would look towards a specific grid cell. Note that the saccade and blinking simulation is the same as in the reference implementation and independent of the fixation algorithm.

The neural network architecture (see Figure 4) is straightforward; it consists of four input neurons, ten hidden neurons and one output neuron. Each input neuron corresponds to one of the following:

- a normalized distance to the object hit by casting a ray through a specific grid cell (0 for closest object, 1 for the object farthest away),
- the information whether the raycast hit a face (1 for face, 0 for anything else),
- the location on the x-axis of the grid, and
- the location on the y-axis of the grid.

The training data for the neural network was obtained using an HMD with an integrated eye tracker. The data was recorded from a scene that includes several moving images, objects, and characters to provide a multitude of visual stimuli. Training was performed using stochastic gradient descent and back propagation. Nonlinearity was applied in both the hidden layer and output layer using the sigmoid activation function. The mean squared error was used as the cost function. The parameters that control the neural network and the training algorithm (see Table 1) were manually adjusted to minimize the final cost and to prevent overfitting. It took less than one minute to train the network. The final neural network is then used to determine the next simulated eye fixation at a rate

*Tom Knabe, Unity Asset Store, 2016

†Depth information could also be provided by the z-buffer or from software rendering used for occlusion culling.

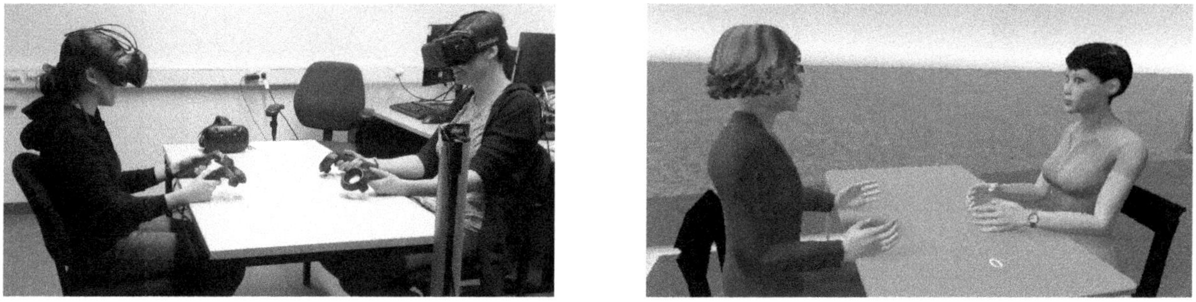

(a) (b)

Figure 2: The experimental scene shown in reality (a) and in the virtual world (b).

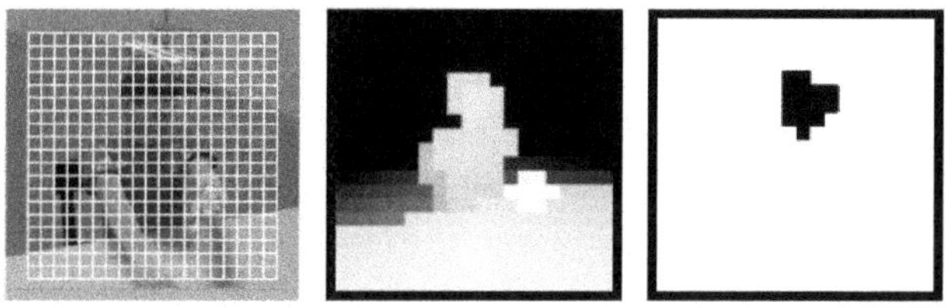

Figure 3: The left most image shows the scene from a participant's point of view. Rays are cast on a 20×20 grid. The center image visualizes the resulting depth map. On the far right a black grid cell indicates where a raycast hit a face.

that is sampled from a distribution corresponding to typical fixation times of humans [31].

Table 1: Hyper parameters

Parameter	Value
Grid Dimensions	20×20
Hidden Neurons	10
Minibatch Size	10
Epochs	15
Learning Rate	0.03

Social VR Gaming Task

With the experiment we wanted to assess whether the type of gaze behavior influenced the perceived quality of the interaction with the virtual representation of another human in a game-like scenario. Therefore, a task was required that encourages participants to look at the conversational partner. At the same time, the task should not reveal the intention of the study to avoid influencing the results. Garau et al. [10] suggest a role playing task to facilitate such an assessment. We specifically excluded tasks based on role playing to eliminate additional preparation time for participants and to avoid the chance of having participants feel uncomfortable playing an assigned role. We assumed that the latter would have a significant influence on the outcome of the experiment. Additionally, allowing participants to have an unconstrained conversation held too much risk of people not engaging in conversation without external encouragement. To gain insights about the applicability of the results to social VR games, the task was supposed to include a simple game-like interaction. As a result, we chose the combination of a free conversation and a game-like interaction. First, participants were asked to introduce themselves and talk about arbitrary topics for a short amount of time (2 minutes) to get accustomed to the situation and to their conversational partner. Afterwards, both participants played a game in which one of the two had to explain a word that only he or she could see. It was not allowed to mention the word itself or parts of it. If the other participant guessed the word both would get one point as a team and the participants would switch roles. If the word was not guessed after one minute, they would switch roles without getting a point. After five minutes the participants would move on to a slightly different game, which is similar to the game "Who am I?" Now the participant that did not see the name had to ask yes-or-no questions to guess who he or she was. The partner was only allowed to answer the questions with "yes", "no", or "I do not know". If the name was guessed within three minutes, the pair received one point. After guessing the name or after the time limit, the participants switched roles. The second game ended after 9 minutes. In both games, the words or names were displayed in front of the partner's forehead to encourage participants to look at each other's faces. To raise motivation for the pseudo tasks (the games), a highscore list was maintained for the duration of the entire experiment. The group that correctly guessed most words and names would receive additional payment in form of a voucher. In case more than one group ended up at the top of the list, the winning group would be chosen by lots.

Participants were assigned to time slots and to another volunteer. The pairs were assigned such that participants within one pair were not familiar with each other. Before starting each experiment, participants signed a consent form acknowledging that they were informed about the general background of the experiment, the procedure, and possible risks of using a VR HMD. Then subjects put on the HMDs, but were not able to see the virtual representation of their partner, because a virtual wall was placed between them. Once the experiment started, the wall was removed. Now participants were asked to have an unconstrained conversation for two minutes, then they would play the word guessing game for five minutes, and finally they

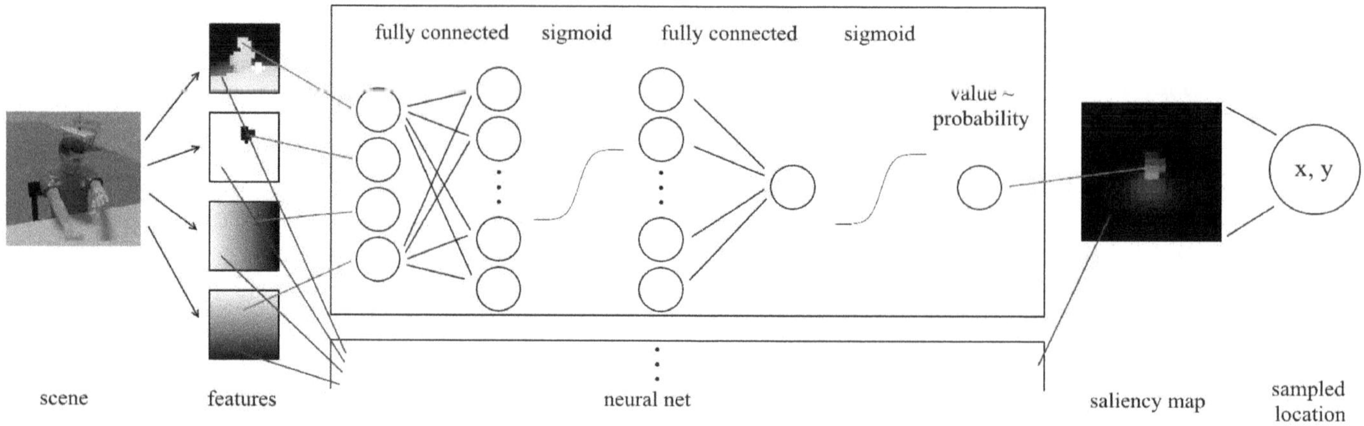

Figure 4: In order to determine the next fixation of the simulated eye movement, depth information for the current view is obtained using raycasts. For every raycast, depth, face information, and location on the grid (x, y) are fed into a neural network. The four input neurons are fully connected to 10 hidden neurons. The hidden layer is fully connected with the single output neuron, which represents the probability of looking at that specific grid location in the view. The saliency map is generated by normalizing the output of each network and represents the probability distribution of the current view. It is sampled to obtain the next fixation target.

would play "Who am I?" for nine minutes. Following the second game they filled out a questionnaire without an HMD.

Participant Responses

The questionnaire consisted of the IPQ to report presence [22], questions to survey explanatory variables (e.g., age), and questions to assess the quality of the conversation or interaction as well as the perception of the eye movements.

Like the experimental design, the main response variable of interest – perceived quality of communication – is based on the study by Gaurau et al. [10]. According to their design, the response is measured based on the following 4 indicators:

- How much does the experience represent a real face-to-face conversation? (Based on 6 items.)
- How much were participants involved in the interaction? (Based on 2 items.)
- How much did participants feel like interacting with another real person? (Based on 2 items.)
- How did participants evaluate their partner? (Based on 5 items.)

The exact wording of the questions can be found in [9] and question responses were rated on a 7-point Likert scale. We agree with Velloso et al. [27] that objective measures, such as task performance, do not adequately capture, e.g., social or emotional states of a user. Therefore, as we were mainly interested in finding out how users perceived interaction quality, we did not consider objective measures in this study.

Explanatory values included age, gender, status, educational level, and technical expertise (cf. [10]). For the latter we added affinity with digital games, interactive VR applications, programming, 3D animation, and general computer usage.

Additionally, to receive specific responses about the perceived realism and appearance of the virtual eye movements (gaze quality) and the avatar realism, the following items were added to the questionnaire (all rated on a 7-point Likert scale):

1. The behavior of the avatar's eyes appeared natural.
2. The general appearance of the avatar was realistic.
3. The eye movements of the avatar were appealing.
4. The eye movements of the avatar were familiar.

Items 1 and 2 are from [24]; items 3 and 4 are based on [17].

RESULTS AND DISCUSSION

The study involved experiments with 42 participants, 14 for each gaze behavior model (i.e. saccades-only, simulated, eye-tracked). All subjects were included in the data.

The three gaze groups were analyzed for dissimilarities in demographic data (age, gender, education, occupation, playing frequency, prior computer/VR/3D asset expertise) using a Kruskal-Wallis-test for k independent samples where the data was not distributed normally, as indicated by results of a Shapiro-Wilk-Test. For frequency of play, an ANOVA was applied. The analysis showed that the three groups were similar regarding all demographic factors.

Our group of participants consisted mainly of students (30) and employees of the university (10). 30 were undergraduates, 11 had a university degree. The mean age was 27.5 years, ranging from 18 years to 53 years. Half of the group was 23 years or younger (median = 23.5). The participants described themselves as 24 males, 17 females and one other gender type. Technical expertise (1 to 7 scale, 7 = highest) was high with computers in general (Median=5.5), medium with programming (Md=3.0), low with 3D assets (Md=2.0) and very low with VR (Md=1.0). All but 5 participants regularly play games, with half of them playing multiple times a week or more frequently (4=daily, 6=multiple times a day). Of the other half, 5 play multiple times a month, 11 play multiple times throughout the year.

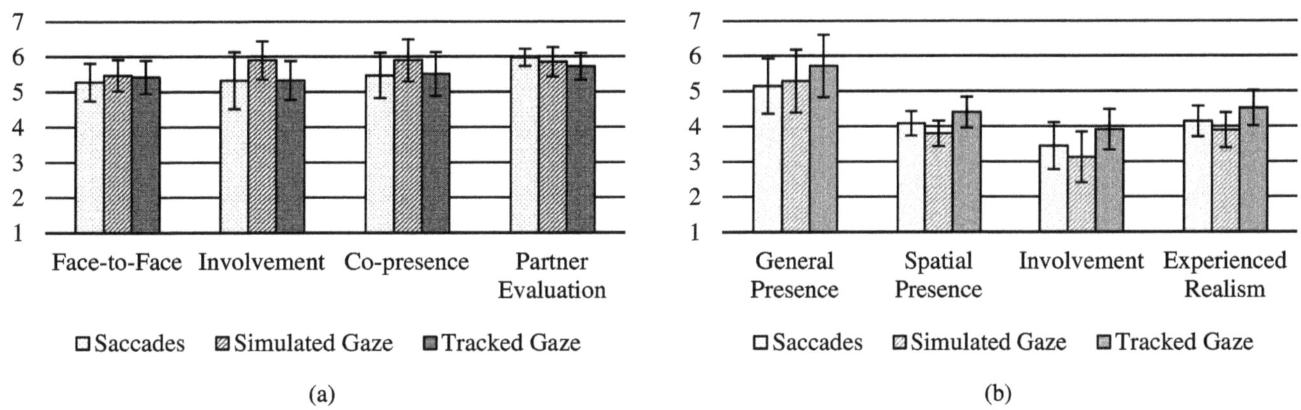

Figure 5: Mean scores of (a) Quality of Communication and (b) iGroup Spatial Presence Questionnaire across the three participant groups. Error bars depict 95% confidence interval.

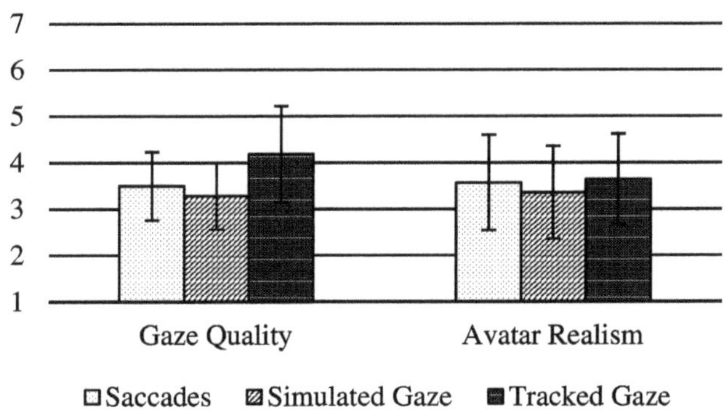

Figure 6: Mean scores of custom metrics for gaze quality and avatar realism. Error bars depict 95% confidence interval.

Quality of Communication

Figure 5 (a) shows mean scores for the four dimensions of quality of communication (QoC): face-to-face, involvement, co-presence, and partner evaluation. Overall, the mean scores all range from 5.27 to 5.97 on a high level. The differences between the three gaze groups were of minor effect and not statistically significant.

Presence

Figure 5 (b) shows mean scores for the four dimensions of the iGroup Presence Questionnaire: general presence, spatial presence, involvement, experienced realism.

The mean scores show highest values for the tracked gaze group, where the reported participant's partners showed eye movements according to tracked data. However, none of these differences are statistically significant.

While the general presence scores are high ($5 < x < 6$), the mean scores for the other three dimensions are at a medium level ($3 < x < 5$).

Gaze Quality and Avatar Realism

We calculated gaze quality by averaging the means of the three related items (items 1., 3., and 4. in Sec. "Participant Responses"). This score and the avatar realism score were distributed normally among subjects. Figure 6 shows medium scores for both metrics. While mean scores of both metrics were highest for the tracked gaze group, an ANOVA revealed no signifant differences between our independent groups.

Correlations

An analysis using Spearman's correlation test (two-sided) revealed correlations between several dimensions of QoC with those of presence (IPQ): IPQ-general presence correlates with IPQ-co-presence ($\rho = .34, p < .05$). IPQ-involvement correlates with QoC-face-to-face ($\rho = .64, p < .001$), QoC-involvement ($\rho = .38, p < .02$), QoC-Co-presence ($\rho = .56, p < .001$), and with QoC-partner evaluation ($\rho = .44, p < .01$). IPQ-experienced realism correlates with QoC-face-to-face ($\rho = .40, p < .01$) and with QoC-co-presence ($\rho = .36, p < .02$).

There was hardly any statistical relation between demographic background and user experience data (IPQ, QoC): We found no correlations between gender, education or player type with UX data; IPQ-involvement negatively correlates with Age ($\rho = -.37, p < .02$) and employment ($\rho = -.33, p < .05$). Frequency of playing negatively correlates with QoC-partner evaluation ($\rho = -.37, p < .02$). Regarding technical expertise, the data only shows a positive correlation between VR expertise and IPQ-involvement. No correlations were found with computer versatility, programming or 3D modelling expertise.

We looked separately into the three gaze behavior groups. Only in the eye tracked gaze group, we again found positive correlations of VR expertise with IPQ-involvement ($\rho = .56, p < .05$) and further with QoC-partner evaluation ($\rho = .78, p = .001$). The data of the group who only saw saccade-based gaze behavior shows a negative correlation between computer versatility and IPQ-experienced realism ($\rho = -.55, p < .05$).

Concerning gaze quality, the data correlates positively with QoC-face-to-face (*Pearson's* $r = .41, p < .01$), QoC-involvement ($r = .47, p < .01$), QoC-co-presence ($r = .34, p < .05$) and IPQ-involvement ($r = .43, p < .001$). Perceived visual realism of the avatar correlates with QoC-face-to-face ($r = .43, p < .01$), QoC-co-presence ($r = .4, p < .01$), and IPQ-involvement ($r = .49, p = .001$). The two metrics directly relate to each other ($r = .64, p < .001$)

Discussion

In conclusion, participants of all three groups rated the quality of the communication in the situation rather high. Similarly, participants of all three groups felt present in the virtual world, but presence concerning the spatial environment, involvement in a virtual situation, and realistic experience can potentially be deepened further. Similarly, the perceived quality of gaze animation and avatar realism scores medium values and leaves room for improvement. With our groups, the tracked gaze condition scored higher means than saccades and our simulation, but these effects are not likely to repeat with other groups.

The technical differences in gaze animation input most likely have no impact on experiencing the proposed task in the depicted scenario. A probable explanation is that most of the participants were overall inexperienced in VR applications, with the majority having no previous experience with VR technology. We assume that the novelty factor of using VR technology dominated any other effect. At the same time the overall experience was too short for the media novelty effect to diminish. Therefore, we hypothesize that participants were unable to notice subtleties, like specific eye movements, within the given setting. Presumably, such details will become more important to more experienced VR users. At the same time, the overall setup or the co-located situation may have influenced the results. It is also possible that the chosen pseudo task does not rely enough on gaze behavior or that the cohort of test subjects may have been too small to reveal any significant differences. Therefore, both our hypotheses of a positive impact of tracked or simulated gaze animation on perceived quality of communication and presence could not be verified, but further studies are necessary before they can be rejected. Subsequent studies should investigate the influence of the mentioned factors. Especially the choice of the pseudo task will have to be re-considered carefully.

Additionally, participants perceived avatar realism as only medium high. Garau et al. [10] argued that the level of avatar realism determines the expectations towards behavioral realism, e.g., eye movements. According to this result, participants may not have observed the avatar's eye movements, because due to their perceived level of realism, they may not have expected gaze behavior to be highly realistic. An insufficient amount of observation could be another explanation for finding only insignificant differences between the three groups.

Interestingly, while involvement ratings regarding the conversation were high for all gaze types, IPQ-involvement was rated lower on medium level. We suspect that because participants shared the same physical space, they may have been overly aware of the real social situation. Furthermore, the means for questionnaire responses regarding QoC-involvement, which were reported in our study, were similar to the values reported by Garau et al. [10]. They argued that involvement was not affected by any of their tested factors, because participants were focused mainly on the other participants voice during their task, because they would not get sufficient feedback through non-verbal channels (e.g., facial expression and lip movements). Consequently, the type of gaze animation and avatar realism do not impact involvement ratings. The same can be argued about our experiment, i.e. the quality of the VR environment did not have much impact on the experience. The amount of positive correlations between experienced quality of communication and presence further undermine this argumentation. To further investigate this assumption, we should compare user experience regarding communicational quality and presence with participants in different physical locations in comparison to co-located subjects.

Overall, we were able to measure questionnaire responses that are very similar to those reported by Garau et al. [10] concerning their inferred gaze group for all QoC dimensions. Compared to the results of their high-realism avatar group, our study showed higher ratings in co-presence and partner evaluation. Both can be explained by the physical setup. In Garau et al.'s design, participants were situated at different physical locations. In our case, we chose a co-located setting, which could explain higher response values as participants could have been overly aware of the real situation and thus may have felt more involved. Also, participants briefly met before the experiment. Having seen the real person behind the avatar might have improved the involvement in the conversation as well as the evaluation of the partner.

Generally, we could have included a comparison to a group without any eye movements in the experiment, as was also the case in the study by Garau et al. [10]. Such a setup would more likely have resulted in significant differences between the group without eye movements and the groups with different gaze models. However, these comparisons have been done in the past and saccadic models of eye movements are readily available. Therefore, assuming that some degree of eye movement will always be available, we think a comparison of different gaze models is more valid to identify promising research directions or to veritably counter intuitive promises by high fidelity technology.

As a last aspect, the applied quiz gaming task in the experiment may not depend critically on realistic gaze behavior. The participants were free to look at each other during conversation or anywhere else, but the success of the task does not directly rely on noticing whether the partner focuses on a specific object or not. Other tasks that involve participants' awareness of each others' focus points concerning different objects or even objectives within a cooperative virtual environment might gain more impact. However, defining such a task without making the purpose of the experiment obvious remains a difficult problem.

Finally, it is important to note that – as our study reveals – while both perceived gaze quality and avatar realism correlate with communication and presence perception, high quality communication in co-located VR is possible without the use of sophisticated gaze animation technology.

CONCLUSIONS

To investigate the impact of avatar eye movement techniques on the perceived quality of a social VR game, on presence, and co-presence, we compared three gaze behavior techniques in a multi-user setting. The simulation of saccades based on existing work was used as a reference technique. The saccadic model was compared to an algorithm that added the ability to choose the current fixation point in the virtual scene based on a neural network and to movements directly recorded from a user using a proprietary eye tracking solution. By testing 42 participants, divided into three groups, we evaluated the impact of eye movements in a between-group design study. Subject pairs were co-located in the same physical and virtual space and engaged in two types of interactions: free conversation and two simple guessing games.

Against our initial assumptions, our results show that participants generally perceived a high quality of communication, but no significant differences between the three gaze behavior models was found for any of the tested responses. A likely explanation is given by the novelty factor of VR technology that could have outweighed any other effect. As a consequence, the perception of details such as specific eye movement techniques may have been prevented. Also, having test subjects share the same physical space might have influenced the results regarding presence and involvement. Further studies with altered conditions, such as a more gaze-reliant task or a larger sample size, are required to evaluate our interpretations and to verify whether our hypotheses indeed need to be rejected. Future experiments could also include two eye tracked HMDs and record how often participants look at each other.

Besides the experimental considerations, our gaze model could be improved by having the neural network learn how to model the parameters of the distribution (e.g., mean and deviation for each dimension) [32]. Bayesian networks, especially with a Hidden Markov model, could also be applied to model probability distributions for time series data. Furthermore, it is to be determined whether a similar approach would also work for simulating head movements. The correlation between head movement and eye movement is currently considered only implicitly by sampling the scene in the user's viewing direction. Because of this correlation, including input neurons based on measured head rotation might produce better predictions of the saliency maps and thus improve the simulated eye movement.

In conclusion, to provide high quality communication within a co-located multi-user virtual environment, details, such as intricate eye movement models, may not have to be considered in early social VR games. One possible reason is that consumers are still too inexperienced to notice such details. Instead, it is important to include any meaningful eye movement algorithm to improve social interactions in VR games and to re-investigate this topic as soon as users become more familiar with the medium. Second, we need to validate these findings for different tasks and in remote collaborative VR environments, where the social impact of being co-located relies more directly on the simulated world.

ACKNOWLEDGMENTS

This work was carried out within the project EPICSAVE (FKZ 01PD15004A), which is being funded as part of the program Digitale Medien in der Beruflichen Bildung 2 by the German Federal Ministry of Education and Research (BMBF) and by the European Social Fonds (ESF).

REFERENCES

1. Samuel Almeida, Ana Veloso, Licínio Roque, and Óscar Mealha. 2011. The Eyes and Games: A Survey of Visual Attention and Eye Tracking Input in Video Games. In *Proceedings of the Tenth Brazilian Symposium on Games and Digital Entertainment. SBGames 11*. IEEE, 1–10.

2. Sean Andrist, Bilge Mutlu, and Michael Gleicher. 2013. Conversational Gaze Aversion for Virtual Agents. In *Intelligent Virtual Agents. IVA 2013 (Lecture Notes in Computer Science, vol 8108)*, Aylett R., Krenn B., Pelachaud C., and Shimodaira H. (Eds.). Springer, Berlin, Heidelberg, 249–262.

3. Jeremy N Bailenson, Nick Yee, Dan Merget, and Ralph Schroeder. 2006. The Effect of Behavioral Realism and Form Realism of Real-Time Avatar Faces on Verbal Disclosure, Nonverbal Disclosure, Emotion Recognition, and Copresence in Dyadic Interaction. *Presence: Teleoperators and Virtual Environments* 15, 4 (2006), 359–372.

4. Nikolaus Bee, Colin Pollock, Elisabeth André, and Marilyn Walker. 2010. Bossy or Wimpy: Expressing Social Dominance by Combining Gaze and Linguistic Behaviors. In *Intelligent Virtual Agents. IVA 2010 (Lecture Notes in Computer Science, vol 6356)*, Allbeck J., Badler N., Bickmore T., Pelachaud C., and Safonova A. (Eds.). Springer, Berlin, Heidelberg, 265–271.

5. Steven A Beebe. 1976. *Effects of Eye Contact, Posture and Vocal Inflection upon Credibility and Comprehension.* Ph.D. Dissertation. University of Missouri–Columbia.

6. Doug Bowman, Ernst Kruiff, Joseph LaViola Jr., and Ivan Poupyrev. 2004. *3D User Interfaces: Theory and Practice*. Pearson Addison Wesley.

7. Judee K. Burgoon, Deborah A. Coker, and Ray A. Coker. 1986. Communicative Effects of Gaze Behavior. *Human Communication Research* 12, 4 (1986), 495–524.

8. Atsushi Fukayama, Takehiko Ohno, Naoki Mukawa, Minako Sawaki, and Norihiro Hagita. 2002. Messages Embedded in Gaze of Interface Agents—Impression Management with agent's gaze. In *Proceedings of the SIGCHI Conference on Human Factors in Computing Systems. CHI 02*. ACM New York, 41–48.

9. Maia Garau, Mel Slater, Simon Bee, and Martina Angela Sasse. 2001. The Impact of Eye Gaze on Communication Using Humanoid Avatars. In *Proceedings of the SIGCHI Conference on Human Factors in Computing Systems. CHI 01*. ACM New York, 309–316.

10. Maia Garau, Mel Slater, Vinoba Vinayagamoorthy, Andrea Brogni, Anthony Steed, and M. Sasse, Angela.

2003. The Impact of Avatar Realism and Eye Gaze Control on Perceived Quality of Communication in a Shared Immersive Virtual Environment. In *Proceedings of the SIGCHI Conference on Human Factors in Computing Systems. CHI 03*. 529–536.

11. Howard Giles. 2016. *The International Encyclopedia of Communication Theory and Philosophy*. John Wiley & Sons, Inc., Chapter Communication Accommodation Theory, 1–7.

12. Christian Heath. 1984. Participation in the Medical Consultation: The Co-ordination of Verbal and Nonverbal Behaviour Between the Doctor and Patient. *Sociology of Health & Illness* 6, 3 (1984), 311–388.

13. Laurant Itti, Nitin Dhavale, and Frédéric Pighin. 2003. Realistic Avatar Eye and Head Animation Using a Neurobiological Model of Visual Attention. In *Prococeedings of the SPIE 48th Annual International Symposium on Optical Science and Technology*, B. Bosacchi, D. B. Fogel, and J. C. Bezdek (Eds.), Vol. 5200. SPIE Press, 64–78.

14. Binh H Le, Xiaohan Ma, and Zhigang Deng. 2012. Live Speech Driven Head-and-Eye Motion Generators. *IEEE Transactions on Visualization and Computer Graphics* 18, 11 (2012), 1902–1914.

15. Sooha Park Lee, Jeremy B. Badler, and Norman I. Badler. 2002. Eyes alive. *ACM Transactions on Graphics* 21, 3 (2002), 637–644.

16. Han Z Li. 2004. Culture and Gaze Direction in Conversation. *RASK* 20 (2004), 3–26.

17. Rachel McDonnell and Martin Breidt. 2010. Face Reality: Investigating the Uncanny Valley for Virtual Faces. In *ACM SIGGRAPH ASIA 2010 Sketches (SA '10)*. ACM New York, Article 41, 2 pages.

18. Samer Al Moubayed, Jens Edlund, and Jonas Beskow. 2012. Taming Mona Lisa: Communicating Gaze Faithfully in 2D and 3D Facial Projections. *ACM Transactions on Interactive Intelligent Systems. TiiS 12* 1, 2, Article 11 (2012), 11:1–11:25 pages.

19. Norman Murray, Dave Roberts, Anthony Steed, Paul Sharkey, Paul Dickerson, and John Rae. 2007. An Assessment of Eye-Gaze Potential Within Immersive Virtual Environments. *ACM Transactions on Multimedia Computing, Communications, and Applications. TOMM 07* 3, 4, Article 8 (2007), 8:1–8:17 pages.

20. Tomislav Pejsa, Sean Andrist, Michael Gleicher, and Bilge Mutlu. 2015. Gaze and Attention Management for Embodied Conversational Agents. *ACM Transactions on Interactive Intelligent Systems. TiiS 15* 5, 1, Article 3 (2015), 3:1–3:34 pages.

21. Christopher Peters and Adam Qureshi. 2010. A Head Movement Propensity Model for Animating Gaze Shifts and Blinks of Virtual Characters. *Computers & Graphics* 34, 6 (2010), 677–687.

22. Holger Regenbrecht and Thomas Schubert. 2002. Real and Illusory Interactions Enhance Presence in Virtual Environments. *Presence: Teleoperators and Virtual Environments* 11, 4 (Aug. 2002), 425–434.

23. K. Ruhland, C. E. Peters, S. Andrist, J. B. Badler, N. I. Badler, M. Gleicher, B. Mutlu, and R. McDonnell. 2015. A Review of Eye Gaze in Virtual Agents, Social Robotics and HCI: Behaviour Generation, User Interaction and Perception. *Computer Graphics Forum* 34, 6 (2015), 299–326.

24. William Steptoe, Oyewole Oyekoya, and Anthony Steed. 2010. Eyelid Kinematics for Virtual Characters. *Computer Animation and Virtual Worlds* 21, 3-4 (2010), 161–171.

25. Frank Thomas and Ollie Jonston. 1995. *The Illusion of Life: Disney Animation*. Disney Editions.

26. Laura C Trutoiu, Elizabeth J Carter, Iain Matthews, and Jessica K Hodgins. 2011. Modeling and Animating Eye Blinks. *ACM Transactions on Applied Perception. TAP 11* 8, 3, Article 17 (2011), 17:1–17:17 pages.

27. Eduardo Velloso and Marcus Carter. 2016. The Emergence of EyePlay: A Survey of Eye Interaction in Games. In *Proceedings of the 2016 Annual Symposium on Computer-Human Interaction in Play. CHI PLAY 16*. ACM New York, 171–185.

28. Roel Vertegaal and Yaping Ding. 2002. Explaining Effects of Eye Gaze on Mediated Group Conversations: Amount or Synchronization?. In *Proceedings of the 2002 ACM Conference on Computer Supported Cooperative Work. CSCW 02*. ACM New York, 41–48.

29. Roel Vertegaal, Robert Slagter, Gerrit Van der Veer, and Anton Nijholt. 2001. Eye gaze patterns in conversations: there is more to conversational agents than meets the eyes. In *Proceedings of the SIGCHI Conference on Human Factors in Computing Systems. CHI 01*. ACM New York, 301–308.

30. Melodie Vidal, Remi Bismuth, Andreas Bulling, and Hans Gellersen. 2015. The Royal Corgi: Exploring Social Gaze Interaction for Immersive Gameplay. In *Proceedings of the 33rd Annual ACM Conference on Human Factors in Computing Systems. CHI 15*. ACM New York, 115–124.

31. V. Vinayagamoorthy, M. Garau, A. Steed, and M. Slater. 2004. An Eye Gaze Model for Dyadic Interaction in an Immersive Virtual Environment: Practice and Experience. *Computer Graphics Forum* 23, 1 (2004), 1–11.

32. Christopher KI Williams and Carl Edward Rasmussen. 1996. Gaussian Processes for Regression. *Advances in neural information processing systems* (1996), 514–520.

33. Chen Yu, Paul Schermerhorn, and Matthias Scheutz. 2012. Adaptive Eye Gaze Patterns in Interactions with Human and Artificial Agents. *ACM Transactions on Interactive Intelligent Systems. TiiS 12* 1, 2, Article 13 (2012), 13:1–13:25 pages.

Evaluating Real-Time Gaze Representations to Infer Intentions in Competitive Turn-Based Strategy Games

Joshua Newn[1], Eduardo Velloso[1], Fraser Allison[1], Yomna Abdelrahman[2], Frank Vetere[1]
[1]Microsoft Research Centre for Social NUI, University of Melbourne, Australia
[2]Institute for Visualization and Interactive Systems, University of Stuttgart, Germany
[1]{newnj,evelloso,fallison,f.vetere}@unimelb.edu.au, [2]yomna.abdelrahman@vis.uni-stuttgart.de

ABSTRACT
In this paper, we investigate nine different visual representations of gaze in a competitive digital game setting. We evaluate the ability of spectators to infer a player's intentions in the game for each visual representation. Our results show that spectators have a remarkable ability to infer intent accurately using all nine visualizations, but that visualizations with certain characteristics were more comprehensible and more readily revealed the player's intent. The real-time *Heatmap* visualization was the most highly preferred by participants and the most effective in revealing intent, due to its ability to balance real-time gaze information with a persistent summary of recent gaze behaviour. Our findings show that eye-tracking visualization can enable playful interactions in competitive games based on players' ability to interpret opponents' attention and intention through gaze information.

ACM Classification Keywords
H.5.2. Information Interfaces and Presentation: User Interfaces: Input devices and strategies

Author Keywords
Eye tracking; Gaze; Nonverbal leakage; Shared gaze; Gaze awareness; Competitive Gaming; Intent Prediction

INTRODUCTION
Players' nonverbal signals are an important element in many competitive board and card games. By monitoring an opponent's body language, facial expressions and gaze direction, a player can infer their next moves or call their bluffs. Gaze is a strong signal of a person's area of attention and interest [9], and can give away unintended information—what psychology researchers call 'nonverbal leakage' [8]. Gaze is equally important in collaborative settings, as a cue for collaborators to monitor each other's attention and coordinate their actions [14]. Despite its importance in co-located settings, shared gaze awareness is typically absent in remote multiplayer games. In this paper, we demonstrate an opportunity to bring shared gaze awareness into this setting by comparing nine different ways of visualising gaze within a digital multiplayer version of a popular board game—*Ticket to Ride*[1].

CHI PLAY '17, October 15-18, 2017, Amsterdam, Netherlands

ISBN 978-1-4503-4898-0/17/10...$15.00
DOI: https://doi.org/10.1145/3116595.3116624

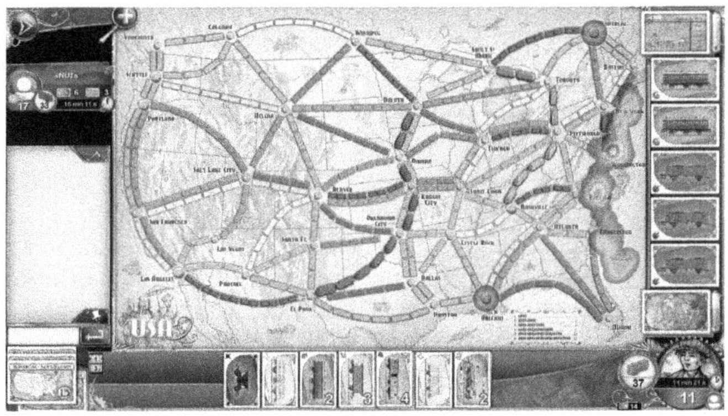

Figure 1: An opponent's gaze presented as a real-time Heatmap over *Ticket to Ride game* showing interest in the east coast of the North America. This is an animated figure and it is best viewed in Adobe Reader.

The advantages in observing a partner's gaze in a *collaborative* task are clear, leading researchers to build multiple systems where users' gaze points are streamed over a network to improve coordination [3]. However, the opportunities for gaze in *competitive* settings are more nuanced. Recent studies have explored these possibilities by using visualizations of players' gaze to open up novel gameplay experiences and increase social presence [16, 20]. Normally in remote multiplayer games, a player's only clues for predicting their opponents' current and future plans are the in-game actions they have previously taken; players do not have access to the bodily cues (such as gaze) that enrich the experience of games played around a table or in a shared space. When given information about an opponent's gaze in a networked game, a player can build hypotheses about what their opponent is thinking through observation of the areas or game elements that receive the most visual attention. This creates further opportunities for a player to deliberately manipulate their own gaze behaviour to deceive an opponent about their plans and goals. This contrast between the tendency for observed gaze to reveal intent and the ability of a player to use their eye movements deceptively makes shared gaze awareness a rich resource for game design.

[1]https://www.daysofwonder.com/online/en/t2r/

However, studies on shared gaze visualizations for various applications have found that the introduction of shared gaze awareness can be *disruptive*, often being referred to as 'distracting' and 'confusing' [6, 16]. We hypothesise that this is caused by two primary problems with gaze visualization for digital interfaces. First, the way in which gaze has been visually represented in past works may be inadequate or ill-suited for the task and setting. This is expected, as the design of visual representations in graphical user interfaces is highly dependent on their context of use. This problem is exacerbated by an inherent problem with gaze: gaze is 'always on', which makes designing gaze representations difficult as the technology cannot distinguish between focused scrutiny and more absent-minded looking.

Second, humans are not accustomed to interpreting visual representations of gaze, as the focal point of gaze is 'invisible' in normal interpersonal interaction. Gaze information can be 'noisy' due to the jittery movements and the way the eyes work (fixation-saccade-fixation cycle), and this is reflected in the representations. Gaze data is difficult to interpret and often misunderstood [6], as even trained professionals in eye-tracking evaluations make use of a range of gaze visualizations to make sense of the same collected data. Further, as gaze is fast-moving and never entirely still, any real-time visualization overlaid on a user interface adds a highly distracting element that may interfere with the viewer's own thought process.

To effectively use gaze awareness in a game, the designer must understand how the choice of gaze visualization will affect players' understanding and enjoyment. Inspired by how players observe the gaze of one another in tabletop boardgames, we selected a popular board game—*Ticket to Ride*—for the purposes of our research. Using recorded clips from eye-tracked gameplay, we assessed nine gaze representations in three different stages of the game (early, mid, late). This paper serves as an initial novel groundwork for determining the characteristics of gaze representations that allow human players to make inferences about other players' intentions and into derivation of potential insights into their strategies (goals and plans).

RELATED WORK

In this section, we summarise related works that require a user to interpret gaze representations of another, which falls into two key areas: research on *shared gaze*, and works that compare and interpret the use of gaze representations. We have chosen to exclude works related to eye-tracking evaluations in which gaze data is interpreted by trained professionals, as our interest is specifically on the ability of non-specialist users to interpret visual gaze representations.

Shared Gaze

Shared gaze systems are those that give users the ability to see the gaze of a partner, typically to improve communication and coordination between pairs in collaborative problem-solving tasks. Here, the eyes are typically not directly visible, and the addition of a gaze visualization provides a complementary layer of nonverbal communication. Knowing where someone is looking can provide rich information, from inference about their intentions to clues about their current cognitive activity (based on behaviours such as scanning, focused interest in an object, and repeated comparison of different objects) [24]. With this knowledge, much research in HCI (Human-Computer Interaction) has used gaze in collaborative settings to foster coordination. For instance, Stein and Brennan [24] found an improvement in problem-solving task performance when another person's gaze was used as a cue. Gaze has been shown to be effective in co-located settings, e.g. when multiple users perform a visual search task on a large display [29]. A common approach is to present a user's gaze as a cursor overlaid on the shared visual display space, to create an awareness of that user's focus area [5, 24].

Gaze has shown promise when used implicitly with other modalities in remote communication. Qvarfordt and Zhai applied gaze in a dialogue system, where a remote assistant is able to detect the interest of a remote user through their gaze patterns while conversing with them (remote user is unaware that their gaze is being tracked) [22]. Tracking gaze behaviour can serve as a natural deictic pointer and thus reveal interest in a natural way. Brennan et al. have demonstrated that shared gaze can be more efficient than speech for the rapid communication of spatial information (spatial referencing) [3].

Despite the numerous benefits mentioned, gaze as an input suffers from inherent problems is that gaze is 'always on', related to the 'Midas Touch' problem that leads to accidental triggering of gaze-enabled interface widgets [12]. To combat this, gaze is often paired with another modality, such as voice interaction; however, this can also lead to confusion when there is a mismatch between gaze and voice inputs [6]. However, in competitive settings, this ambiguity can work as a resource for game design, revealing a glimpse into players' intentions without giving it away entirely.

Gaze Representation

How gaze information is represented strongly influences gaze interaction [4]. We reviewed two recent works in HCI that compare and contrast gaze representations to gather design implications for our study. Zhang et al. evaluate gaze representations for use in co-located collaboration, where two users share a screen and two gaze points are represented [29]. From a review of prior works, the authors selected four different gaze visualization formats for testing—*Cursor*, *Trajectory*, *Highlight* and *Spotlight*—of which participants preferred highlight and spotlight. The authors determined that attaining a balance between *visibility* and *distraction* was one of the biggest challenges when designing and selecting gaze visualizations.

In another work, Li et al. designed and evaluated two gaze representations aimed at improving the coordination between pairs of users [17]: *zoom focus* and *gaze trail*. Both representations used fixations processed from the gaze stream; the former aimed to show the precise location of a fixation, while the latter aimed to show the most recent gaze locations. *Zoom focus* was found to be cognitively demanding and *gaze trail* was found to have excessive information. The authors conclude that when designing gaze representation, one should consider *distraction* and *visual information*.

Games Context and Summary

Gaze is an emerging input in computer games, with a focus on using a player's own gaze as a direct control mechanism to en-

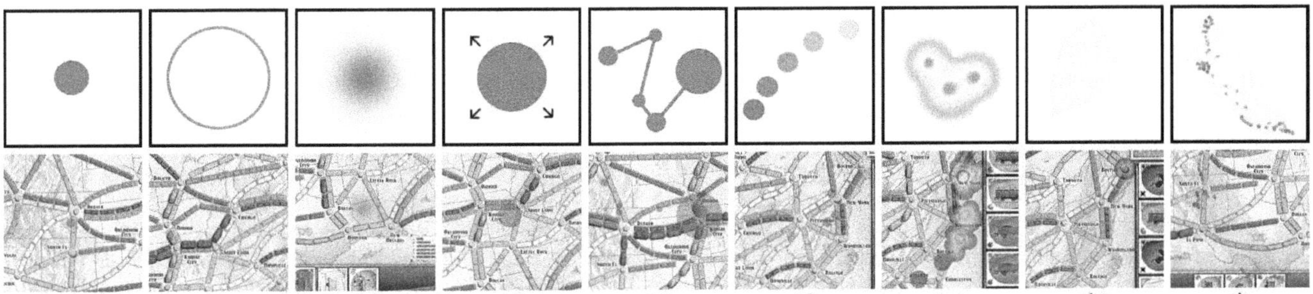

Figure 2: Top: The nine real-time gaze representations selected. Bottom: How each representation appears over the game *Ticket to Ride*. L-R: (a) Dot, (b) Cursor, (c) Spotlight, (d) Fixation, (e) Scanpath, (f) Fixation Trail, (g) Heatmap, (h) Convex Hull and (i) Bee Swarm.

able novel playful experiences [25, 26]. There is growing interest in implementing gaze as a mechanic for multiplayer games, in both cooperative [19, 21] and competitive [16, 20] settings. While the use of gaze in cooperative gameplay can directly leverage the findings of 'shared gaze' literature (e.g. [21]), competitive gameplay presents a different design challenge, as players have opposing objectives and are more likely to see different information on screen. We seek to find a gaze representation for use in competitive games that maintains the game balance, giving neither player a disproportionate edge over their opponent while not being disruptive to gameplay.

The existing literature makes clear that there is a need to balance *visibility*, *distraction* and *visual information*. Furthermore, we note that the problem with a majority of gaze representations is that they are designed to be used in post-processing of gaze data. Therefore, there is a need to design and evaluate novel gaze representations, such as that presented by Li et al. [17], to cater for settings where gaze input is not commonly used. Before we can design novel gaze representations, we need to understand the intrinsic characteristics of existing representations in relation to the context of use. In the next section, we present a variety of visual gaze representations that we have selected for use in our study.

REAL-TIME GAZE REPRESENTATIONS

Figure 2 shows the nine visual gaze representations which were evaluated in this study. For each representation, we provide an account of its current applications, its characteristics and the parameters for our use in the study. Most of the representations are common in existing in eye-tracking software, such as Tobii Pro Studio[2]. These representations are primarily used for gaze data analysis and to replay collected gaze data. We also considered a wide selection of representations from works that: (1) survey gaze representations (e.g. [2, 18]), (2) evaluate gaze representations (e.g. [29]) and (3) use gaze for interaction (e.g. [21]). In making our selection, we required the representations to be clearly distinguishable from one another. The selection was based on the characteristics *conspicuousness* and *visual information* (see Table 1). We chose the term *conspicuousness* (rather than 'visibility') to highlight the degree to which the representations can be used to display and draw attention, beyond just how well the viewer is able to see the representation. *Visual information* refers to the amount of information the representation provides. This is measured by the amount of aggregated gaze data used to generate the representation in addition to its overall size. We further sub-categorised the selected representations by their characteristics into three equally-sized subgroups: (1) Point-based, (2) Trajectory-based and (3) Area of Interest (AOI)-based.

[2]http://www.tobiipro.com

Representation	*Conspicuousness*	*Visual Information*	*Category*
Dot	Low	High	Point
Cursor	Low	Low	Point
Spotlight	Low	Moderate	Point
Fixation	High	Low	Trajectory
Scanpath	High	Moderate	Trajectory
Fixation Trail	Moderate	Moderate	Trajectory
Heatmap	Moderate	High	AOI
Convex Hull	Moderate	Low	AOI
Bee Swarm	High	High	AOI

Table 1: Real-time gaze representations in relation to conspicuousness and visual information.

Point-Based Representations

For this category, we first selected two types of gaze representations previously examined by Zhang et al. [29]: *cursor* and *spotlight*. We then added the commonly-used *dot* representation as a contrast to the first two in terms of precision and visual information. The point-based representations are mapped directly to the real-time gaze coordinates from the eye tracker. To reduce the jittery motions that naturally arise from eye movements, we applied a weighted moving average filter [27] on top of the eye tracker's already lightly filtered data to smooth out the motion. This gave all three representations a hovering effect when a user's eyes moved across the screen and reduced distracting jitter during gaze fixations.

Dot: This representation appears as a translucent red dot, akin to a laser pointer beam or, at larger sizes, a torch beam (Fig. 2a). It has commonly been adopted for use in gaze-based interaction as a deictic pointer and has been demonstrated to be an effective referential pointer to facilitate coordination in remote collaboration [1]. This representation allows a viewer to see gaze with high precision but can be potentially distracting. Our implementation used a 0.5 opacity with a radius of 30-px.

Cursor: This representation is a large ring with a transparent centre (Figure 2b). Its use has been demonstrated by Zhang et al. [29] and in GazeArchers [21], a game in which two players use gaze and touch simultaneously on a shared surface. Further, Tobii divisions has implemented a similar representation in many of their recent products (Tobii Gaming[3] *Gaze Trace*, Tobii Pro *Gaze Share*[4]). Tobii Pro also uses this representation for their wearable eye tracker controller to view the gaze of a user in the real world in real-time. This representation is equivalent to the size of the foveal vision which is about the size of a thumb at arm's length, making explicit the confidence range of the gaze estimation. We matched the size of this representation to default size of Tobii's *Gaze Trace* (150-pixel radius) and coloured the outline in grey to give this a low visibility. This representation provides more visual information than the previous representation (*Dot*) as it allows users to see what is enclosed in the ring as opposed to a specific point.

Spotlight: Figure 2c depicts this representation where the gaze point is shown as a red circle with high opacity in the centre and decreasing opacity towards the edges. This was the most widely preferred representation in Zhang et al.'s evaluation [29]. It was noted to be more subtle and less distracting due to the reduced overall visibility and conspicuousness. We modified the parameters to suit our study, reducing its overall size to a radius of 90 pixels (30 pixels at the highest opacity) and changing the colour to red, as white blended into the light background of the map area of the *Ticket to Ride* game board.

Trajectory-Based Representations

The representations in this category use the sensitive fixation stream provided by the eye tracker's SDK to reveal the sequence of points at which the player has recently looked, leaving behind a short history of the player's gaze. We initially drew from professional eye tracking usability studies that use animated representations to replay gaze data. In our review, we found similar representations being used in eye tracking research. For example, Qvarfordt and Zhai use a scanpath representation to infer dynamic eye movements in their study [22]. We also found proposed representations aimed to enhance remote collaboration, demonstrating the importance of assessing representations that fall into this category [17]. A red fill is used for representations in this category, with each fixation presented as a translucent ellipse.

Fixation: This representation aims to illustrate points of focus by displaying a single, unmoving fixation point as a red dot (Figure 2d). When a player maintains their fixation, the dot remains small in size. If the distance to the next fixation is within a threshold, the dot becomes larger. In real-time, this representation gives the appearance of small eruptions occurring on the interface that indicates whether a player is sustaining attention in an area (large dots) or flicking around between multiple areas (small dots). This representation was inspired by the 'Live Viewer' feature in the Tobii software, which Higuch et al. implemented for use in a remote collaborative scenario [11]. Our adaptation removes the elements of direction (tail, fade) used in other implementations to potentially reduce the mental load. Therefore, participants see a single point that appears then disappears instead of following a point.

Scanpath: The scanpath representation shows the length, duration and direction of gaze by using a sequence of fixations connected by a line (Fig. 2e). Variation of this representation has long been used to visualise gaze patterns in both psychology, eye tracking usability studies and in HCI. This representation has been used unidirectionally such as in Qvarfordt and Zhai's study to show the interest of a remote unaware user, or bi-directionally such as in Jermann and Nussli to improve communication in a remote pair-programming scenario [13, 22]. We implemented this representation based on Goldberg and Helfman [10]. Many approaches have been presented to overcome the problem of visual clutter such as by bundling close fixations into a single point. Another approach is to use time duration such as in previous works (e.g. 5 seconds [28]. Instead, we opted to limit the number of fixation bundles displayed to 5, reduce the visibility of the lines connected the fixation bundle and removed other elements such the numbering of each fixation bundle to reduce visual information.

Fixation Trail: This representation was originally proposed by Li et al. to illustrate gaze paths as opposed to a single fixation point [17]. In our study, we renamed this representation to *Fixation Trail* (originally *Gaze Trail*) as it uses fixation data and leaves a trail of fixations (see Figure 2f). Li et al. believe that the availability of prolonged gaze information allowed participants to make references to multiple locations (e.g. contrasting two different fixation clusters). This representation is different to *Scanpath* in that we fixed the size of the fixation to a 30-px radius. Only 5 fixation points remain fully visible while the remainder fades over time.

AOI-Based Representations

In this category, we selected gaze representations that allow an observer to view the Areas of Interest (AOI) at which the user has looked as a whole rather than a specific point. Representations in this category use fixations aggregated over time. We can control how much visual information is displayed by adjusting its time window. Our implementation uses 120 fixation points ($\tilde{2}$ seconds) so as not occlude the screen (increase visibility, reduce visual information). We selected three representations with varying levels of visual information based on their popularity in eye tracking research.

Heatmap: Heatmaps represent the distribution of gaze points by a colour gradient (Figure 2g). We included this representation as it has commonly been used to visualise data in many domains and is not limited to eye tracking. In eye tracking usability studies it is also used for aggregating the gaze data from multiple participants. While the representation requires the aggregate participant data, it is possible to display a dynamic heatmap of a single tracked user [7]. Our implementation calculates the density of fixations within a 2-second window and displays the heatmap accordingly. The window size in our implementation attempts to balance visual information, allowing several 'hot spots' to be shown but do not remain for too long that it starts to occlude the interface.

Convex Hull: This representation is also known as *Cluster* (Tobii Pro) which display areas with a high concentration of gaze points as polygons to shows areas of interest (Figure 2h). Our implementation uses the fixation data stream in which we use to render a convex hull polygon in real-time using a clustering algorithm. As the stream continuously updates the convex hull, this creates a shifting polygon that shows the

[3]https://www.tobiigaming.com
[4]https://tobiicloud.com/share/

area in which the area is interested in. When the player looks rapidly between two points, the polygon stretches towards the points, but when the focus on a small area is high, the representation becomes small. This representation aims to provide minimal visual information of the area in which the participant has shown interest in.

Bee Swarm: Bee Swarm has been typically used to replay gaze points of several subjects against dynamic content such as videos, allowing efficient comparison of recordings from several subjects. Our variation aims to emulate this representation for use with a single user by displaying all fixation points in the last 2 seconds in which we enclose in a convex hull (Figure 2i). Each point was 5 pixels in radius with a red translucent fill. This visualization allows the player not only to see where the area in which the opponent was looking but the also points within that area. When the user focuses in a particular area, the points will become denser in the area, revealing an interest in the area. This representation has the highest amount of visual information as it combines characteristics from both AOI- and point-based representations.

RESEARCH DESIGN

In this study, we aim to understand the following research questions derived from our review of the literature:

[RQ1] How well are human subjects able to infer intent from a range of gaze representations?

[RQ2] What characteristics of gaze representations enable humans to perform better in predicting intentions?

[RQ3] Do gaze representations have an influence on predicting intent in a competitive gameplay setting?

To answer these questions, we adopted a spectator ('third person') approach. This means that participants other than the players watched clips of gameplay sessions after the fact, with different clips featuring different gaze representations. We chose to make our participants spectators rather than active players in order to simplify the task they were asked to perform, as they could focus on interpreting the gaze data without worrying about managing their own strategy. This decision was informed by the common finding in prior works that live gaze data can be highly distracting from a task at hand [17, 20, 29]. As this was the first study to assess people's ability to infer intent from gaze data of a remote opponent in a game setting, we decided to begin with a more concentrated test of interpretive ability, before introducing the distractions of live gameplay in a future study.

We recorded our data in two stages. In the first, we recruited 8 players to record 4 games of our selected game—*Ticket to Ride* (described below) in which one player's gaze was shared. In the second, a separate group of 27 participants watched short selected clips (< 1 minute) of the recorded gameplay from the perspective of the player who could see the real-time gaze representations. These participants provided an assessment of each clip, which we used in our analysis. A secondary benefit of this two-stage approach was that we were able to conduct a larger number of gaze visualization assessments in a shorter period of time than would have been possible if all participants had had to actively complete multiple games. This enabled a

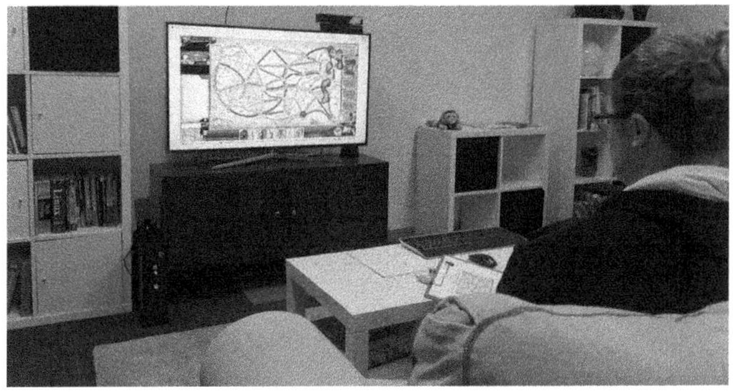

Figure 3: Participant assessing a clip in a lounge room setting.

larger sample size for this foundational work, which we will build on in future studies involving active players.

Application

We developed a custom networked system that overlays real-time gaze visualizations over any application (see through, click through). We used this application to stream gaze data between two laptops, each equipped with a Tobii EyeX eye tracker, in different rooms. We streamed two types of gaze data concurrently from the SDK: the lightly filtered gaze data and the sensitive fixation data. Our application is capable of displaying the gaze of one or both users simultaneously, meaning that we have the ability to switch on the gaze of one user to be visualised by themselves or by another user. Moreover, we can easily switch the gaze between representations through a control window on an extended screen.

Game and Stages

In *Ticket to Ride*, each player competes to claim train routes between cities across a map of North America, seeking to connect certain pairs of cities ('tickets') in a continuous path of linked routes. Only one player can claim each route, and players do not know which cities their opponent is seeking to connect. Therefore, players must place their routes carefully, staying alert to the risk that their opponent will claim a route before them and block the most convenient path between their goal cities. Keeping information hidden plays a large role in *Ticket to Ride*, as a player can gain significant advantages over their opponents by correctly guessing which routes they are planning to take. Hence, *Ticket to Ride* works as an excellent use case for our study for several reasons. First, it is a widely-played board game, already familiar to many, with a digital game version that is almost identical to the board game; and because it has relatively simple rules involving clear goals and actions, which can be learned in under 15 minutes by interested players who have not played it previously. Second, as a tabletop game, it demands constant attention, requiring regular thought processing and frequent changes to short- and long-term strategies. This affords us to obtain a range of behaviours to display. Third, Lankes et al. have determined that turn-based games are better-suited to gaze transfer applications (as opposed to real-time first person shooters) [16]. This is because such games give players the opportunity to alternate between playing their own moves and watching their opponents' behaviour as they take their turn. Fourth, it is a map-based game, in which the players' focus and strategic calculations are closely concentrated on the geography of the

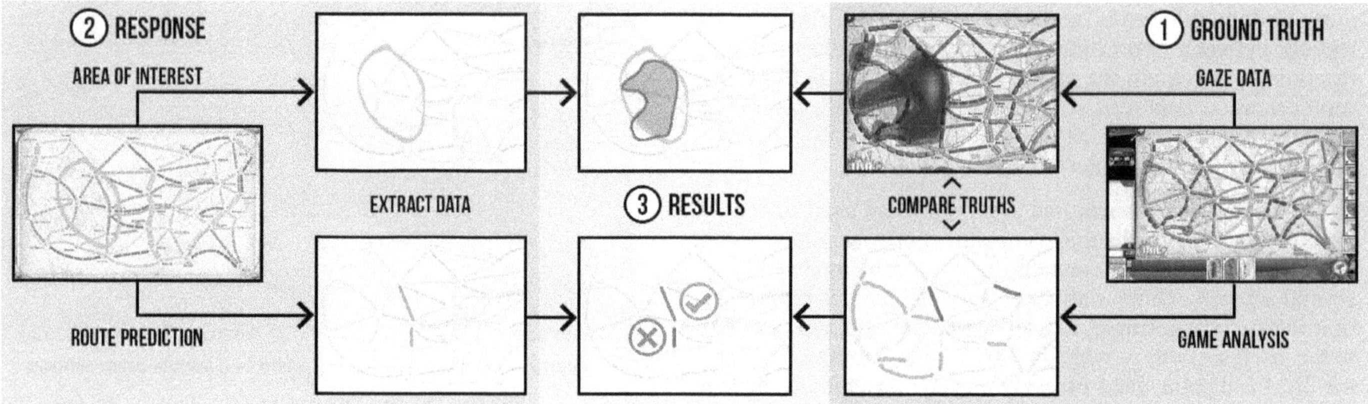

Figure 4: Method for analysis for Area of Interest (AOI) Estimation and Route Prediction.

map; gaze awareness and eye movement studies with map-based applications have been shown to be highly successful, as the static map gives users a point of reference [15, 22, 29].

As a playthrough of *Ticket to Ride* progresses, the map becomes increasingly populated with trains, and the strategic information available to the players becomes consequently richer while their choices of unclaimed routes become more constrained. Each player starts with a stock of 45 trains, and the game ends when any player's stock of unplaced trains falls below three. We use this train stock as a metric for game progression to divide the recorded games into three stages: early (45-31 trains), middle (31-16 trains), late (15-0 trains). The early stage is typically given over to planning, and placing trains are minimised as players try not to give away their goals. The middle stage sees greater competition for routes, and is where players often find themselves clashing over the most efficient paths between their respective goal cities. The late stage involves players either slotting in the last remaining routes that they need, seeking to block their opponent, or looking for other routes they can pick up extra points. We include an even selection of representations of each stage in our study, as we hypothesised that the usefulness and relevance of gaze visualizations might change as the game progresses.

Gaze Visualization Recording

We recruited 8 players (4 pairs) to record the necessary gameplay clips between a *naive player* (whose gaze was being recorded) and an *aware player* (for whom their opponent's gaze was visualised). Both players were placed in separate rooms with an experimenter and given the opportunity to play the in-game tutorial for up to 10 minutes to understand the rules and mechanics of the game. Once the *naive player* was confident with the game, they were asked to perform the default calibration provided by the eye tracker. The *naive player* does not know that they are being watched to record and observe 'natural gaze'. Meanwhile, the *aware player* was briefed that different gaze visualizations would be shown to them and that their opponent was not aware that their gaze was being shown. Each pair played three games, and the gaze representation was changed at every stage of the game. We recorded the displays using *Open Broadcaster Software (OBS) Studio*[5] and logged the gaze data with our custom application.

[5]https://obsproject.com/download

Following the recordings, we reviewed the videos and noted instances in which the naive player exhibited various behaviours, such as planning, checking game counters or tickets, and looking for routes to claim on the map. From the videos, we selected three short clips for each of the nine gaze visualization formats: one in early game, one in middle game and one in late game. This gave us a total of 27 clips, exhibiting a variety of behaviours, and balanced between stages to control for the influence of game stage. Moreover, as different visualizations were used in different stages of different games, we are able to randomise the clips further. The length of the clips ranged between 20 and 60 seconds. All clips were saved without audio, to remove any potential sound clues such as the recorded player speaking aloud about their opponents' plans. As expected, the *aware players* experienced a level of distraction causing them to be drawn away from their own strategy and that some visualizations were preferred over others. However, we disregarded the feedback to avoid any early speculations.

STUDY

For the second stage of our study, we recruited 27 participants from the University of Melbourne. There were 11 male and 16 female participants, aged 18 to 44 years (mean=25.6), and included undergraduate students, graduate students and non-faculty staff. Only two had previously played the board game version of *Ticket to Ride*, but 17 indicated they had played a game of the same type in the past week. Participants were compensated with a $5 coffee voucher for their time. We encouraged participants to watch a short video[6] that describes the rules and objectives as part of the recruitment process.

Procedure

Upon arrival, participants were greeted and seated comfortably in a lounge room setting, facing a 48-inch (1080p) television display connected to a PC as depicted in Figure 3. They completed a consent form and a simple demographic questionnaire and were briefed on the rules of *Ticket to Ride*. The facilitator showed them an example clip of gameplay footage and with it, explained how they should assess each clip on a paper survey, with the measures outlined under 'Measures and Analysis'. Here, the facilitator ensured that the participants understood the rules of the game and what was required of them before starting the study. Each session ran between 30 to 60 minutes.

[6]https://www.youtube.com/watch?v=uDODCHcj6Sg

Representation	*Early*	*Mid*	*Late*	*Overall*
Heatmap	.44(.78)	.68(.63)	.73 (.75)	.62(.72)
Fixation Trail	.48(.41)	.66(.72)	.48 (.75)	.54(.62)
Dot	.59(.49)	.37(.55)	.67(.36)	.54(.47)
Cursor	.46(.73)	.68(.68)	.44(.28)	.53(.56)
Fixation	.63(.72)	51(.87)	.41(.80)	.52(.80)
Scanpath	.40(.65)	.50(.79)	.65(.70)	.52(.71)
Bee Swarm	.59(.58)	.36(.63)	.43(.72)	.46(.64)
Convex Hull	.40(.62)	.17(.44)	.23 (.44)	.27(.50)
Spotlight	.24(.37)	.25(.43)	.28 (.65)	.26(.48)

Table 2: AOI Estimation Results. Precision(Recall).

Representation	*Early*	*Mid*	*Late*	*Overall*
Bee Swarm	.70(.37)	.67(.43)	.43 (.28)	.60(.36)
Cursor	.69(.85)	.54(.37)	.53 (.19)	.59(.47)
Heatmap	.57(.31)	.63(.29)	.50(.63)	.57(.41)
Scanpath	.40(.46)	.45(.26)	.63(.25)	.50(.32)
Spotlight	.50(.22)	49(.26)	.25(.14)	.41(.20)
Fixation Trail	.44(.14)	.50(.17)	.26(.26)	.40(.19)
Dot	.59(.37)	.37(.14)	.10(.04)	.35(.18)
Fixation	.37(.44)	.26(.14)	.27(.21)	.30(.26)
Convex Hull	.25(.11)	.27(.10)	.74(.02)	.20(.08)

Table 3: Route Prediction Results. Precision(Recall).

We employed a repeated-measures design: each participant was shown all 27 (3 stages $\times$ 9 visualizations) clips, each of which was considered one study 'condition', representing one gaze visualization format and one game stage. Participants were divided into three sets (A, B and C), and the order of the clips was randomised for each set.

Participants were given a maximum of 10 seconds to analyse the game and board state before the clip was played. In almost all cases, participants indicated that this was enough time for them to understand the game state, either with a verbal acknowledgement or a non-verbal indication such as a nod of the head. This time limit was imposed to prevent the participant from basing their inferences too heavily on reasoning about the layout of the game board, rather than the visualizations of the gaze data, and in order to more closely approximate a live gameplay setting in which the gaze information would be processed and responded to quickly. The facilitator encouraged participants to *think aloud* about what they were seeing, and to ask for any clarifications about the game if required. After the participant had viewed and assessed all 27 clips, they were finally asked to rank the nine gaze visualization formats from most preferred to least preferred. In summary, we collected a total of 27 participants $\times$ 9 visualizations $\times$ 3 stages $=$ 729 responses for each of our dependent measures.

Measures and Analysis

In response to each clip, participants were asked to record the following five pieces of information: (1) *Area of Interest Estimation*, using a map of the game board they circled the area (or multiple areas) in which they believed the gaze-tracked player had been interested. (2) *Route Prediction*, on the same map they highlighted any specific routes that they thought the gaze-tracked player was planning to build upon. They were also encouraged to write a short interpretation of what the gaze-tracked player was thinking during the clip or to explain their interpretation of the gaze behaviour out. (3) They rated how informative they found the gaze visualization in the clip on a 7-point scale ranging from *Not informative at all* to *Extremely informative*. (4) They rated how well they felt they could predict the gaze-tracked player's intentions in the clip on a 10-point rating scale. Participants were permitted to skip any of these questions when they felt unable to give a response, for example, if they could not predict any routes upon which the gaze-tracked player was considering to build. Finally, we collected (5) *Qualitative Responses* at the end of the session, participants were asked to rank the representations in order of preference and explain the reasoning behind their choices.

Area of Interest Estimation and Route Prediction

To determine how closely each participant guessed the area of interest of the naive player, we compared the intersection of each response against the ground truth for the respective condition. Participants recorded their responses by circling the corresponding area in the map. To be able to analyse this data digitally, we scanned the highlighted pages and extracted the contours of the highlights using a custom-built OpenCV computer vision application. To establish a ground truth, we generated 2D density maps from the gaze data in each clip using the R statistical package. We then refined the AOIs against the manual analysis of the clips, discarding outliers that did not correspond to the routes the player eventually built. We then compared the intersection of the two regions, computing the precision (area of intersection divided by the total area circled by the participant) and the recall (area of the intersection divided by the area of the ground truth contour) of the participant's estimate (see Figure 4, top path).

Similarly to the analysis of the AOI Estimation, we scanned the highlighted maps and extracted the highlighted routes using our OpenCV application (see Figure 4, bottom path). We established the ground truth by recording the routes that the player eventually built after the clip. We also recorded routes that the player was considering to build but never did. We inferred such routes based on evidence from their hidden goal cards, subsequent game actions, and in-game comments. As with the AOI Estimation, we operationalise their performance primarily based on precision and recall, but also considered their harmonic mean i.e. *F-Score* ($F = 2 \times (precision \times recall)/(precision + recall)$). The details of these performance metrics are explained by Rijsbergen [23].

Quantitative and Qualitative Responses

For our third and fourth measure, we will use descriptive statistics to analyse how informative as well as the predictability of the gaze representation. To gain richer insights beyond the quantitative performance data, we collected subjective perceptions in three ways. First, we transcribed all verbal comments as they thought out loud when watching the clips. Second, in the questionnaires for the clips, participants answered an open-ended question that asked them to predict what the player was thinking. Third, we transcribed the interview about their order of preference at the end of the study. We were particularly interested in comments beyond the areas of interest and routes, including potential strategies, such as building a route to block the opponent, planning a route, verifying whether they have enough resources to build a certain route.

Representation	*Early*	*Mid*	*Late*	*Overall*
Spotlight	5.1 (1.0)	5.1 (1.1)	4.8 (1.0)	5.0 (1.0)
Heatmap	4.8 (1.0)	5.0 (0.8)	4.9 (1.0)	4.9 (0.9)
Cursor	4.9 (1.3)	4.8 (1.4)	4.6 (1.3)	4.8 (1.3)
Dot	5.1 (1.6)	4.8 (1.1)	4.1 (1.7)	4.7 (1.5)
Fixation	4.7 (1.0)	4.5 (1.2)	4.6 (1.1)	4.6 (1.1)
Scanpath	4.7 (1.0)	4.5 (1.2)	4.8 (1.0)	4.6 (1.1)
Bee Swarm	4.6 (1.1)	4.6 (1.3)	4.4 (1.4)	4.5 (1.3)
Fixation Trail	4.4 (1.2)	4.7 (1.0)	4.3 (1.0)	4.5 (1.1)
Convex Hull	3.2 (1.2)	3.6 (1.4)	3.0 (1.5)	3.3 (1.4)

Table 4: Ratings of Informativeness Results 1 Not Informative at all - 7 Extremely Informative). Score (Standard Deviation)

RESULTS

We report the results of the nine visualizations at each of the three game stages and their overalls. Five primary metrics are reported: the percentage overlap of the AOI indicated by the participant against the AOI detected by the software; the performance between routes predicted by the participant and routes plausibly considered by the naive player; participant ratings of the visualizations' informativeness; participant self-assessments of how well they can predict what the naive player is planning to do; and participant rankings of gaze visualization preference. Lastly, we compared the scores from their performance in our first two metrics against the last three.

Area of Interest Estimation

Table 2 shows the precision and recall for each representation, ordered by precision. The order of the performance of the visualizations in terms of precision were the *Heatmap* (.62), followed by the *Fixation Trail* (.54), and finally the *Dot* (.54). This means that these are the best representations for selecting areas of interest within the ground truth. In terms of recall, the *Fixation* (.80) was the best performing, followed by the *Heatmap* (.72) and the *Scanpath* (.71). This indicates that these were the representations in which the selected area captured a larger area within the area of interest. If we combine both metrics using the *F-Score*, we find that the overall best representation was the *Heatmap* (.66), followed by the *Fixation* (.63) and the *Scanpath* (.63). To test whether the stage of the game had an effect on the precision and recall, we conducted a repeated-measures ANOVA for each representation. Except for *Spotlight*, we found that the stage had a significant effect on the stage on the precision and recall. Precision significantly increased in the *Heatmap* and *Fixation Trail* as the game progressed, and decreased in the remaining conditions.

Route Prediction

Table 3 shows the computed precision and recall results for each visualization ordered by precision. The best performing visualizations when it comes to route prediction in terms of *F-Score* are *Cursor* (.52), *Heatmap* (.48), and *Bee Swarm* (.45). *Convex Hull* was ranked significantly lower in both precision and recall (.20 and .08 respectively) and this was primarily from the late stage precision score (.02). The other low score noted, also in the late stage, is the *Dot* representation recall score (.04). We tested the effects of the gameplay stage on both precision and recall for each representation using repeated-measures ANOVA. For precision, only the *Scanpath* representation showed significance ($p = 0.014$) in which a

Representation	*Early*	*Mid*	*Late*	*Overall*
Heatmap	6.3 (2.0)	6.7 (1.9)	7.1 (1.7)	6.7 (1.9)
Cursor	7.0 (1.7)	6.1 (2.0)	6.6 (2.0)	6.6 (1.9)
Scanpath	6.0 (1.5)	6.0 (2.2)	6.6 (1.6)	6.2 (1.8)
Fixation	6.9 (1.7)	5.4 (2.1)	6.3 (1.5)	6.2 (1.9)
Spotlight	6.2 (1.7)	6.5 (1.5)	5.6 (1.9)	6.1 (1.8)
Bee Swarm	5.9 (2.1)	6.2 (2.0)	5.8 (2.3)	6.0 (2.1)
Fixation Trail	6.1 (1.7)	6.2 (1.5)	5.6 (2.2)	6.0 (2.0)
Dot	6.9 (2.3)	5.7 (1.8)	3.8 (2.0)	5.5 (2.4)
Convex Hull	4.0 (1.8)	4.7 (2.0)	3.9 (2.1)	4.2 (2.0)

Table 5: Predictive Ability Results. Score (Standard Deviation)

Bonferroni post hoc test showed a significant difference between the mid and late stage ($p = 0.0069$). Here, we note that the *Scanpath* representation is the only representation to have increase in precision from the mid stage ($M = 45.5$) to the late stage ($M = 63.4$). A majority of representations, 6 out of 9 (*Bee Swarm, Heatmap, Spotlight, Fixation Trail, Scanpath and Convex Hull*), remained precise for the early and mid stages but significantly becomes less precise in the late stage. Both *Fixation* and *Cursor* precision dropped significantly from early ($M = 37.3$, $M = 69.1$) to mid game ($M = 27.2$, $M = 54.0$) but remained consistent in the late game. The precision of the *Dot* representation dropped linearly from early to late stage. There was no significant effect on recall on the gameplay stages.

Ratings of Informativeness

The responses follows a normal distribution (*Pearson chi-square normality test*, $p < 0.05$), in which calculated the mean scores and standard deviation for each visualization for each stage, and overalls (see Table 4). We test the effects of stage on their rating on informativeness using repeated-measures ANOVA and found a significance in the mid and late stage ($p = 0.0247$). We tabulated the results and ranked them by overall rating accordingly. We found that *Spotlight* (5.0), *Heatmap* (4.9) and *Cursor* (4.8) received the highest rating while *Convex Hull* was rated significantly lower (3.3). *Heatmap* had the lowest deviation (0.9) among the visualizations showing an agreement among participants on its informativeness.

Self-Assessment of Predictive Ability

We ran the same statistical tests used in the previous measure and found that the responses also follows a normal distribution. We calculated the mean scores and standard deviation of each visualization for each stage and overalls, and ranked them by overall rating (see Table 5). We proceeded to test the effects of stage on the responses using repeated-measures ANOVA and found significance in the early and late stage ($p = 0.331$). The results shows that *Heatmap* (6.7), *Cursor* (6.6) and *Scanpath* (6.2) received the highest rating while *Dot* (5.5) and *Convex Hull* (4.2) was rated significantly lower than the others.

Preference Rankings

Figure 5 shows the ranking data for each representation by all participants, showing that the *Convex Hull* was ranked the lowest ($M = 2.0$) while *Heatmap* was the highest ranked ($M = 6.7$). *Cursor* and *Scanpath* also was ranked highly. We further analysed the ranked data using the Friedman test in which we found a significance ($p < 0.05$). The post hoc test showed that *Convex Hull* representation was ranked significantly lower than

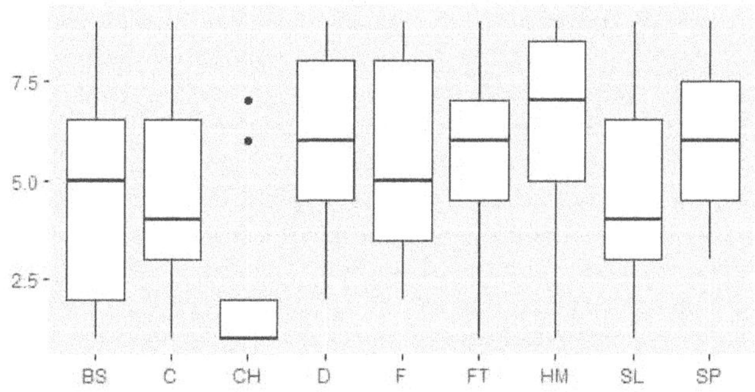

Figure 5: Boxplot of Preference Ratings given for each visualization. (BS) Bee Swarm, (C) Circle, (CH) Convex Hull, (D) Dot, (F) Fixation, (FT) Fixation Trail, (HM) Heatmap, (SL) Spotlight and (SP) Scanpath.

all other representations. We ran the Friedman test once again but this time removing the *Convex Hull* representation from the test. We found that there were no significance differences between the other rest ($p = 0.07547$). We proceeded to analyse the interviews to gain further insights into these preferences.

We received many positive insights into why *Heatmap* was ranked the highest and preferred by a majority of participants. Participants that gave the *Heatmap* a high score mentioned its 'persistence' i.e. the visualization gave them a moment to make an inference before it fades away (e.g. *"I like that it stayed on the screen for awhile" [P3]*). A small number of participants (e.g. P7) noted that they were familiar with the visualization having seen or used them in other domains, noting its inherent usefulness. When participants were asked why they preferred *Heatmap* over the others, a majority they mentioned that they had difficulty following them. Two contributing factors for this were (1) speed (*"too quick" [P16], "moved too much and too quickly"* [P11]) and (2) lack of conspicuousness (e.g. *"more subtle ones are harder to keep track of" [P19], "it was hard to see" [P25]*). Some participants mentioned that the *Scanpath* visualization blended into the game making it hard to differentiate (e.g. P20) while others found it useful (e.g. *"I like it because it gives you a track." [P11]*). Conversely, some participants did rate visualization that falls under point-based category highly. Participant 22 provided his explanation, stating that he preferred the point-based representations as he was able to process the visual information quickly and described trajectory- or AOI-based representations as "a lot going on". Participants often compared *Convex Hull* and *Bee Swarm* and found that the 'red dots' made it better (e.g. P17). *Bee Swarm*'s ability to have persistence yet show movement at the same time it is probably a reason why it scored well in the route prediction measure. Overall, participants provided rich feedback, noting that AOI-based representations were good for predicting overall strategy while point-based representations appear to be better moment-to-moment attention.

DISCUSSION

Our study explored the characteristics of nine visual representations of gaze to determine which was most effective at conveying intent to an observer by exploring relationship between the characteristics of representations and human ability to infer intent from them. This section discusses the results from the five metrics as well as the post study interviews.

Representation Performance and Preference

Once again *Convex Hull* was largely indecipherable to participants, with the lowest scores for route prediction and close to the lowest scores for AOI estimation. However, the other AOI-based visualizations, *Bee Swarm* and *Heatmap*, had among the best results for route prediction. Unlike *Convex Hull*, these visualizations can clearly display both the broad area of sustained interest and the focal point of the player's moment-to-moment attention. The *Heatmap* shows multiple hot spots and recent zones in which the player has looked. Interestingly, *Bee Swarm* performed well for route prediction but relatively poorly in AOI estimation measure. Our version of the *Bee Swarm* is encompassed by a convex hull display, which allows viewers to see at a glance the general region of the player's gaze while their more exact moment-to-moment attention is captured by a large number of rapidly-propagating red dots. We believe that participants used the convex hull to narrow their focus, enabling them to see the routes more clearly; avoiding a visual search for the next sequence.

Conversely, *Fixation Trail* and *Dot* performed strongly for AOI estimation, but relatively poor for route prediction, suggesting that these visualizations were effective at conveying general information but were not fine-grained enough for inferring specific intent. We believe that trajectory-based representations caused participants to divide their attention between two areas of interest and this was specifically mentioned by Participant 22. None of the point-based representations performed particularly well. We believe by the time participants start to make a connection between objects, the visual has moved somewhere else, causing them to start making a new inference elsewhere.

The *Heatmap* gaze representation overall scored highly in all five measures, and this is primarily attributed to its ability to provide a high level of visual information by using averaged information. Moreover, *Heatmap* takes a small amount of time to 'heat up' and cool down, allowing the player to know areas which are gaining interest and losing interest. We earlier noted that *Scanpath* performance increased from the early-mid to late stage of the game which may be reflective of the nature of the game. Towards the late stage players tend to track the missing paths which reduces the search space and enhances the performance of the *Scanpath* gaze representation. Further, with the increased availability of other cues to select from as the game progresses, a sustained gaze (presenting sustained interest) at a location is likely to signal with greater confidence the likelihood of an intention to action. To some degree, we expected the *Heatmap* to have performed the best being a well-used representation. On the other hand, the *Convex Hull* was notably disliked, being given the lowest or second-lowest ranking by all but four participants.

Preferences were mixed for the rest, with a wide variation in scores indicating that different participants valued different characteristics. The trajectory-based representations were all ranked relatively highly; we hypothesise that this is because trajectory-based representations naturally calls attention to the connections between different points of interest as the player moves their gaze between them without overloading the user and therefore remained neutral in our results.

Interplay Between Game Cues and Overall Scores

As expected, we found that participants make use of in-game and behavioural cues to predict routes such as by observing what cards the naive player looked at or picked. From the game analysis, there was 17 showed cards being picked and many participants drew conclusions by matching the route seen and card colour which is a probable cause of differences in scores between the clips. Across all visualizations, prediction accuracy was lower in the late game than in the early and mid game. We consider several factors that may account for this trend, with different implications for the use of gaze visualizations in other contexts. First, the visual clutter on the screen increases as the game progresses, so that in the late game there are substantially more train routes that may potentially distract the viewer from the gaze representation. Second, the number of available routes is lower in the late game, which tends to require players to draw more convoluted routes; the combination of zigzagging existing routes and fewer possibilities may increase the difficulty of recognising an obvious path that the player is aiming for. Third, the behaviour of the player is likely to be different, as they transition from long-term planning in the earlier stages to opportunistic route-grabbing and path-blocking in the late stage; this behaviour may be more difficult for a viewer to interpret. We believe that it is plausible that all three of these factors play a role, but based on our own observation of the game recordings, we expect that the third factor to be the most significant as gaze behaviour clearly shows a different pattern late in the game. This is exhibited in our results such as in the case of the *Dot* representation where the naive player was looking for was considering a route to build between a few potential routes.

Humans naturally rely on explicit actions as they confirm their thoughts, such as in real life. Regardless of representation shown, we are impressed at the ability of participants to put themselves into the mind of the player with the introduction of displayed gaze. In the same way, spectators rely on these actions, and therefore participants employ a variety of cues in making inferences. However, we observed in our study that some participants better than other in keeping track of the elements in the game, allowing them to make better inferences.

Design Implications

Our results present various implications towards the digital games community. First and foremost, we demonstrated the possibilities of using different types of representations to display mental processes (e.g. intention) of players in real-time, which has direct implications towards *game developers*. When using gaze explicitly for use in games, game developers must be wary of how it is actually used in its execution. For example, when we the tested the *Convex Hull* representation, it worked well allowing two developers to reveal what the other was looking at. However, during our evaluation, *Convex Hull* obtained consistently low scores revealing a flaw in our implementation when converting a static visualisation to real-time. Then again, this consistently low score gave us a reference point and confidence in the validity of our data. The design of gaze representations should further consider the amount it reveals without giving it away as it would give a player a disadvantaged. Imagine playing a game and your opponent is constantly one step ahead of you. For the evaluation of games in real-time with gaze visualisation (implicit use), representations such as the *Heatmap* can be used to reveal intentions of players from natural gaze behaviour, and therefore provide insights into whether players understand the task in hand or is making correct strategic decisions. Second, a range of selectable gaze visualizations can implemented in live game streaming platforms such as Twitch, where *audiences* to create sensory excitement and anticipation. For example, audiences can anticipate intentions of live players before the actual move, providing a new experience. Lastly, *players* themselves can benefit from visualisations the gaze of their opponent in the form of an in-game 'power up' to create new gameplay experiences, especially in similar competitive contexts.

CONTRIBUTIONS, LIMITATIONS AND FUTURE WORK

This work presents three main contributions. First, we provide an understanding of the role of gaze and its importance to game designers in choosing and designing the right visualisation. Second, an assessment of how people interpret visual gaze visualisations, which has not been done before in this context. The findings also highlight the effect of the different techniques on the inferring ability. Third, we contribute the assessment of AOI-based representations in the context of gameplay. Limitations wise, we used clips in our study from the entire game session which might not be comprehensive to show the goals of the whole game but enough to determine short term intention. Moreover, as each visualization was tested in only three different clips, it is possible that one outlier clip could affect the overall result for that visualization; nevertheless, we have taken this into account in our reporting of the findings. We also acknowledged that we only used an example of a strategic game to demonstrate gaze. However, we believe our findings apply to similar games.

Our future work focuses on *players*, where we give one player the ability to predict intentions using a real-time *Heatmap*, and with room for deceptive or misinterpreted behaviours to happen. We have also considered testing the viability of our findings with a different game (e.g. on with a less cluttered board) to provide further insights into the generalisation of our results. Furthermore, our work has further implications in gaze-aware artificial intelligence, and we have begun putting together a planning-based AI that predicts players potential intentions based on the recorded games from this study.

CONCLUSION

This paper contributes the groundwork for determining the characteristics of gaze representations that allow human players to make inferences about other players' intentions and to derive insights into potential strategies. This has been achieved by measuring the performance of human in their ability to predict intentions using a range of visual gaze representations. Our results showed us that human subjects have a remarkable ability to infer intent with the introduction of gaze. We conclude that representations that show both characteristics of point- and AOI- based representations would work well in our setting. Our work ultimately contributes gaze input as a viable implicit modality in multiplayer competitive computer games and with broader implications towards the games community.

ACKNOWLEDGEMENTS

We acknowledge the Australian Commonwealth Government and the Microsoft Research Centre for Social NUI for their support on this project. We further acknowledge Zaher Joukhadar for major improvements made on the custom built software.

REFERENCES

1. Deepak Akkil, Jobin Mathew James, Poika Isokoski, and Jari Kangas. 2016. GazeTorch: Enabling Gaze Awareness in Collaborative Physical Tasks. In *Proceedings of the 2016 CHI Conference Extended Abstracts on Human Factors in Computing Systems (CHI EA '16)*. ACM, New York, NY, USA, 1151–1158. DOI: http://dx.doi.org/10.1145/2851581.2892459
2. T. Blascheck, K. Kurzhals, M. Raschke, M. Burch, D. Weiskopf, and T. Ertl. 2014. State-of-the-Art of Visualization for Eye Tracking Data. In *EuroVis - STARs*, R. Borgo, R. Maciejewski, and I. Viola (Eds.). The Eurographics Association. DOI: http://dx.doi.org/10.2312/eurovisstar.20141173
3. Susan E. Brennan, Xin Chen, Christopher A. Dickinson, Mark B. Neider, and Gregory J. Zelinsky. 2008. Coordinating cognition: The costs and benefits of shared gaze during collaborative search. *Cognition* 106, 3 (2008), 1465 – 1477. DOI: http://dx.doi.org/10.1016/j.cognition.2007.05.012
4. Marcus Carter, Joshua Newn, Eduardo Velloso, and Frank Vetere. 2015. Remote Gaze and Gesture Tracking on the Microsoft Kinect: Investigating the Role of Feedback. In *Proceedings of the Annual Meeting of the Australian Special Interest Group for Computer Human Interaction (OzCHI '15)*. ACM, New York, NY, USA, 167–176. DOI: http://dx.doi.org/10.1145/2838739.2838778
5. Mauro Cherubini, Marc-Antoine Nüssli, and Pierre Dillenbourg. 2008. Deixis and Gaze in Collaborative Work at a Distance (over a Shared Map): A Computational Model to Detect Misunderstandings. In *Proceedings of the 2008 Symposium on Eye Tracking Research & Applications (ETRA '08)*. ACM, New York, NY, USA, 173–180. DOI: http://dx.doi.org/10.1145/1344471.1344515
6. Sarah D'Angelo and Darren Gergle. 2016. Gazed and Confused: Understanding and Designing Shared Gaze for Remote Collaboration. In *Proceedings of the 2016 CHI Conference on Human Factors in Computing Systems (CHI '16)*. ACM, New York, NY, USA, 2492–2496. DOI: http://dx.doi.org/10.1145/2858036.2858499
7. Andrew T. Duchowski, Margaux M. Price, Miriah Meyer, and Pilar Orero. 2012. Aggregate Gaze Visualization with Real-time Heatmaps. In *Proceedings of the Symposium on Eye Tracking Research and Applications (ETRA '12)*. ACM, New York, NY, USA, 13–20. DOI: http://dx.doi.org/10.1145/2168556.2168558
8. Paul Ekman and Wallace V. Friesen. 1969. Nonverbal Leakage and Clues to Deception. *Psychiatry* 32, 1 (1969), 88–106. DOI: http://dx.doi.org/10.1080/00332747.1969.11023575
9. Alexandra Frischen, Andrew P Bayliss, and Steven P Tipper. 2007. Gaze cueing of attention: visual attention, social cognition, and individual differences. *Psychological Bulletin* 133, 4 (2007), 694.
10. Joseph H. Goldberg and Jonathan I. Helfman. 2010. Visual Scanpath Representation. In *Proceedings of the 2010 Symposium on Eye-Tracking Research & Applications (ETRA '10)*. ACM, New York, NY, USA, 203–210. DOI: http://dx.doi.org/10.1145/1743666.1743717
11. Keita Higuch, Ryo Yonetani, and Yoichi Sato. 2016. Can Eye Help You?: Effects of Visualizing Eye Fixations on Remote Collaboration Scenarios for Physical Tasks. In *Proceedings of the 2016 CHI Conference on Human Factors in Computing Systems (CHI '16)*. ACM, New York, NY, USA, 5180–5190. DOI: http://dx.doi.org/10.1145/2858036.2858438
12. Robert J. K. Jacob. 1991. The Use of Eye Movements in Human-computer Interaction Techniques: What You Look at is What You Get. *ACM Trans. Inf. Syst.* 9, 2 (April 1991), 152–169. DOI: http://dx.doi.org/10.1145/123078.128728
13. Patrick Jermann and Marc-Antoine Nüssli. 2012. Effects of Sharing Text Selections on Gaze Cross-recurrence and Interaction Quality in a Pair Programming Task. In *Proceedings of the ACM 2012 Conference on Computer Supported Cooperative Work (CSCW '12)*. ACM, New York, NY, USA, 1125–1134. DOI: http://dx.doi.org/10.1145/2145204.2145371
14. Adam Kendon. 1967. Some functions of gaze-direction in social interaction. *Acta Psychologica* 26 (1967), 22 – 63. DOI:http://dx.doi.org/10.1016/0001-6918(67)90005-4
15. Peter Kiefer, Ioannis Giannopoulos, and Martin Raubal. 2013. Using Eye Movements to Recognize Activities on Cartographic Maps. In *Proceedings of the 21st ACM SIGSPATIAL International Conference on Advances in Geographic Information Systems (SIGSPATIAL'13)*. ACM, New York, NY, USA, 488–491. DOI: http://dx.doi.org/10.1145/2525314.2525467
16. Michael Lankes, Bernhard Maurer, and Barbara Stiglbauer. 2016. An Eye for an Eye: Gaze Input in Competitive Online Games and Its Effects on Social Presence. In *Proceedings of the 13th International Conference on Advances in Computer Entertainment Technology (ACE2016)*. ACM, New York, NY, USA, Article 17, 9 pages. DOI: http://dx.doi.org/10.1145/3001773.3001774
17. Jerry Li, Mia Manavalan, Sarah D'Angelo, and Darren Gergle. 2016. Designing Shared Gaze Awareness for Remote Collaboration. In *Proceedings of the 19th ACM Conference on Computer Supported Cooperative Work and Social Computing Companion (CSCW '16 Companion)*. ACM, New York, NY, USA, 325–328. DOI: http://dx.doi.org/10.1145/2818052.2869097

18. Paivi Majaranta, Hirotaka Aoki, Mick Donegan, Dan Witzner Hansen, and John Paulin Hansen. 2011. *Gaze Interaction and Applications of Eye Tracking: Advances in Assistive Technologies* (1st ed.). Information Science Reference - Imprint of: IGI Publishing, Hershey, PA.

19. Bernhard Maurer, Michael Lankes, Barbara Stiglbauer, and Manfred Tscheligi. 2016. *EyeCo: Effects of Shared Gaze on Social Presence in an Online Cooperative Game*. Springer International Publishing, Cham, 102–114. DOI: http://dx.doi.org/10.1007/978-3-319-46100-7_9

20. Joshua Newn, Eduardo Velloso, Marcus Carter, and Frank Vetere. 2016. Exploring the Effects of Gaze Awareness on Multiplayer Gameplay. In *Proceedings of the 2016 Annual Symposium on Computer-Human Interaction in Play Companion Extended Abstracts (CHI PLAY Companion '16)*. ACM, New York, NY, USA, 239–244. DOI:http://dx.doi.org/10.1145/2968120.2987740

21. Ken Pfeuffer, Jason Alexander, and Hans Gellersen. 2016. GazeArchers: Playing with Individual and Shared Attention in a Two-player Look&Shoot Tabletop Game. In *Proceedings of the 15th International Conference on Mobile and Ubiquitous Multimedia (MUM '16)*. ACM, New York, NY, USA, 213–216. DOI: http://dx.doi.org/10.1145/3012709.3012717

22. Pernilla Qvarfordt and Shumin Zhai. 2005. Conversing with the User Based on Eye-gaze Patterns. In *Proceedings of the SIGCHI Conference on Human Factors in Computing Systems (CHI '05)*. ACM, New York, NY, USA, 221–230. DOI: http://dx.doi.org/10.1145/1054972.1055004

23. C. J. Van Rijsbergen. 1979. *Information Retrieval* (2nd ed.). Butterworth-Heinemann, Newton, MA, USA.

24. Randy Stein and Susan E. Brennan. 2004. Another Person's Eye Gaze As a Cue in Solving Programming Problems. In *Proceedings of the 6th International Conference on Multimodal Interfaces (ICMI '04)*. ACM, New York, NY, USA, 9–15. DOI: http://dx.doi.org/10.1145/1027933.1027936

25. Jayson Turner, Eduardo Velloso, Hans Gellersen, and Veronica Sundstedt. 2014. EyePlay: Applications for Gaze in Games. In *Proceedings of the First ACM SIGCHI Annual Symposium on Computer-human Interaction in Play (CHI PLAY '14)*. ACM, New York, NY, USA, 465–468. DOI: http://dx.doi.org/10.1145/2658537.2659016

26. Eduardo Velloso and Marcus Carter. 2016. The Emergence of EyePlay: A Survey of Eye Interaction in Games. In *Proceedings of the 2016 Annual Symposium on Computer-Human Interaction in Play (CHI PLAY '16)*. ACM, New York, NY, USA, 171–185. DOI: http://dx.doi.org/10.1145/2967934.2968084

27. Oleg Špakov. 2012. Comparison of Eye Movement Filters Used in HCI. In *Proceedings of the Symposium on Eye Tracking Research and Applications (ETRA '12)*. ACM, New York, NY, USA, 281–284. DOI: http://dx.doi.org/10.1145/2168556.2168616

28. Nadir Weibel, Adam Fouse, Colleen Emmenegger, Sara Kimmich, and Edwin Hutchins. 2012. Let's Look at the Cockpit: Exploring Mobile Eye-tracking for Observational Research on the Flight Deck. In *Proceedings of the Symposium on Eye Tracking Research and Applications (ETRA '12)*. ACM, New York, NY, USA, 107–114. DOI: http://dx.doi.org/10.1145/2168556.2168573

29. Yanxia Zhang, Ken Pfeuffer, Ming Ki Chong, Jason Alexander, Andreas Bulling, and Hans Gellersen. 2017. Look Together: Using Gaze for Assisting Co-located Collaborative Search. *Personal Ubiquitous Comput.* 21, 1 (Feb. 2017), 173–186. DOI: http://dx.doi.org/10.1007/s00779-016-0969-x

Invisible Walls: Co-Presence in a Co-located Augmented Virtuality Installation

Michael Lankes
Department of Digital Media
UAS Upper Austria
Hagenberg, Austria
michael.lankes@fh-ooe.at

Jürgen Hagler
Department of Digital Media
UAS Upper Austria
Hagenberg, Austria
juergen.hagler@fh-ooe.at

Georgi Kostov
Department of Digital Media
UAS Upper Austria
Hagenberg, Austria
georgi.kostov@fh-ooe.at

Jeremiah Diephuis
Department of Digital Media
UAS Upper Austria
Hagenberg, Austria
jeremiah.diephuis@fh-ooe.at

ABSTRACT

This paper investigates the effects of the virtual players' (VR) representation and verbal communication regarding co-presence in a co-located and playful augmented virtuality (AV) installation for multiple participants. We examine if the incorporation/exclusion of the visualization of the VR players' hands and the absence/presence of verbal communication influences the perceived co-presence. To find answers to our research question, we created an experimental setting called Invisible Walls. Within the installation, players and spectators have various means of interaction at their disposal. Our study findings show a positive impact of the VR player's representation on the perceived co-presence. However, due to the experimental setup, verbal communication did not have the anticipated effect. With these findings we endeavor to reduce the gap between the VR player and the spectators and provide insights for game designers and researchers regarding the inclusion of nonverbal and verbal communication in co-located AV settings.

ACM Classification Keywords

H.5.m. Information Interfaces and Presentation (e.g. HCI): Miscellaneous; K.8.0. General: Games

Author Keywords

Augmented Virtuality; Co-Presence; Co-located Play

CHI '17, October 15–18, 2017, Amsterdam, Netherlands
ACM ISBN 978-1-4503-4898-0/17/10... $15.00
DOI: http://dx.doi.org/10.1145/3116595.3116609

INTRODUCTION

Virtual Reality (VR) devices, such as the HTC Vive[1], have become quite popular during the last year. These technological developments have led not only to a tremendous amount of design and research opportunities—such as offering great potential to incorporate the human body as an interaction design resource—but also to design-related risks [14]. Although there are some exceptions[2], the majority of VR game titles offer a single-player game experience. In public contexts, such as game festivals, demo sessions at conferences, and art exhibitions, typically VR players are being watched by spectators that can see the current game status via a monitor or a projection screen. However, VR technology cannot only be used to grant a unique and engaging experience for one or more VR players, but can also can be harnessed to establish a gateway between virtual and real space (VR players and spectators). One interesting field of research in this context concerns Augmented Virtuality (AV) in co-located settings for multiple participants. AV settings have the potential to create a connection between the VR player and the spectators as they merge real world objects into virtual worlds [9].

Various questions arise, such as how to reduce the gap between the real and the virtual world, or how VR players in such heterogeneous scenarios should come into contact and interact with the spectators [8]. Research efforts within the field are still at an early stage, and fairly little is known about which factors contribute to an engaging co-experience among VR players and spectators.

Thus, this submission proposes an approach via an AV installation that does not just take one VR player into account, but also the spectators of an installation (see Figure 1). Furthermore, it shall be investigated which factors influence the social aspect (co-presence) in an AV context: in detail we are interested in determining whether the virtual representation of the VR

[1] www.vive.com
[2] www.playstation.com/en-us/games/the-playroom-vr-ps4/

Figure 1. The playful experimental co-located AV installation "Invisible Walls" featuring different player roles. The VR player (using a VR device with hand gesture recognition) interacts with a spectator whose position is tracked and visualized as a stylized representation in the VR world, projected at the back of the installation.

player (in our case: hands) and the verbal communication (speech) influence the relationship between him/her and the spectators.

To find answers to our research questions, we created a playful experimental setting called "Invisible Walls". The installation offers different interaction techniques (physical movement and hand gestures) for VR player and the spectator. On the one hand, the VR player is able to come into contact with the spectators by using his/her hands, while, on the other hand, the spectators assume a more passive role by moving through the real/virtual environment (a more detailed description can be found in the section "The installation: Invisible Walls").

Due to the co-located setting, we focused on one specific aspect in a multiplayer setting: co-presence. This phenomenon forms one of the sub-dimensions of social presence, in which players automatically detect and classify a form as another (i.e., possessing agency) [2]. The level of co-presence is influenced by the degree to which players appear to share an environment together, i.e. the degree of mutual salience of the player and the perceived other.

Our submission should shed some light regarding co-presence and its contributing factors in an AV installation, whereas the scope can be framed by the following questions: Does the player's representation in VR (here: hands) foster the mutual salience and sensomotoric accessibility (i.e. co-presence)—and if so, in which way does it affect the experience of co-presence, and how do other channels moderate the effect of co-presence in that regard (in our case: verbal communication)?

Generally, we argue that by providing means for nonverbal communication (i.e., representation of the VR player's hands) and verbal communication during co-located gameplay in AV settings, a new interaction layer for the VR players and the spectators can emerge, leading to a smaller gap between them. Our findings should inform game designers and researchers if the inclusion of a virtual representation in a co-located AV setting changes the perceived co-presence, and how it potentially changes co-located gameplay.

RELATED WORK

For the past few decades, multiplayer VR and AV installations were basically confined to research labs or festival contexts, representing experiments in display technologies, computer graphics and network performance. Although graphics-driven multiplayer online games such as first-person shooters have definitely provided concepts for a shared awareness and an interaction between players, the actual physical, real-world position of players has not been utilized.

However, co-location has been both a key feature and shortcoming of VR and AV installations since the initial CAVE systems [6]. Whereas only one VR user can interact in the CAVE, other users are simply spectators and are provided with the same perspective rendered for the guide. Even if two or more CAVE systems are connected, the co-located users are only offered a passive experience. A quite elaborate approach for a co-located playful experience, however, is proposed in the artistic CAVE installation World Skin[3]. In this interactive artwork, up to three spectators could interact with real photo cameras in a co-located virtual environment (VE). Since real world objects are merged into the VE, this artwork can be classified as one of the first co-located AV installations. Current state-of-the-art approaches, such as proposed by Chague et al. [5] are capable of providing a multi-user AV experience including the sense of touch by connecting the real world with the virtual world. Zhu et al. [17] propose a Shared Augmented Virtual Environment (SAVE), a mixed reality (MR) system that overlays the virtual world with real world objects captured by a Kinect depth camera. In their approach, the synthetic MR world contains both real and virtual objects that are rendered in real time with a correct representation of depth from both worlds. Nevertheless, although advances are being made to create a shared AV experience, many questions remain regarding the inclusion of spectators in such multi-user installations.

One relevant aspect of co-location in VR and AV settings is the phenomenon called "presence", which has received an increased interest by the art and scientific community. Several articles[4] stress the significance and the novelty aspect of the term presence. However, the concept is not new: it is derived from "tele-presence" introduced by Marvin Minsky [10] in the 1980s and has undergone several developmental processes with a variety of definition attempts [4].

Lee [7], for instance, stated that, in general, presence can be understood as a psychological state in which the artificiality of an experience is not noticed by the subjects. In computer-mediated environments, several authors claim that presence refers to the sense of existing or of "being there" in a virtual space (e.g. [1, 13]). Numerous authors support the idea that it is composed of three dimensions: spatial presence, self presence, and social presence [15].

The last sub-dimension and most relevant for our submission, social presence, is experienced when subjects "successfully simulate other humans or non-human intelligences" [7]. In such a scenario, users do not notice the artificiality of the

[3] http://benayoun.com/moben/1997/02/12/world-skin-a-photo-safari-in-the-land-of-war/
[4] https://www.sundance.org/projects/100humans

experienced social actors. Participants within a technologically mediated environment communicate as in a real human-to-human communication [1]. This can be observed as users frequently interact in artificial spaces by applying social rules that they also utilize in the real world.

According to Biocca and Harms [3], social presence can be further sub-divided into the following dimensions: co-presence, attentional allocation, perceived message understanding, perceived affective understanding, perceived affective interdependence, and perceived behavioral interdependence. Our project specifically deals with co-presence, which is the degree to which the recipients believe that they are not alone, their level of awareness of the other, and their sense of the degree to which the other is aware of them. Frank Biocca and Chad Harms [2] give the following definition for co-presence: "Users experience the phenomenal state of co-presence when they automatically detect and classify a form as another (i.e., possessing agency). The level of co-presence is influenced by the degree to which the user and the agent appear to share an environment together, that is the degree of mutual salience and sensorimotor accessibility of the user and perceived other."

Research dealing with co-presence in the context of AV and VR offers diverse opportunities for investigation. Roth et al. [11], for instance, propose an experimental method to investigate the effects of reduced social information and behavioral channels with full-body avatar embodiment on presence. The researchers compared physical-based and verbal-based social interactions in the real world and in VR. Study participants were represented by abstract avatars with a limited set of social cues. The experiment showed that subjects are capable of compensating for missing social cues by shifting to other communication channels.

Many research projects deal with aspects of cooperation. Salimian et al. [12] describe a mixed reality environment in which they employ virtual arm embodiments to visualize the remote collaborator's arms on the physical tabletop. Tang et al. [16] examine the role of the user's body in a collaborative work setting and how it affects presence disparity. They articulate four design implications to mitigate the effects of presence disparity: embodiments should provide local feedback; they should visually portray people's interaction; they should display fine-grain movement and postures of hand gestures; and, last but not least, they should be positioned within the interaction space.

As discussed in this section, the VR-spectator relationship and co-presence are particularly relevant issues in AV and VR approaches. However, research efforts within the field are still at an early stage, and fairly little is known about which factors contribute to co-presence among VR players and spectators.

OUR APPROACH

Based on state-of-the-art approaches, "Invisible Walls" is characterized by a large number of unique features: it is an experimental AV installation [9] that merges a virtual and a real space (approximately 40 square meters) and provides asymmetrical forms of interaction between one VR player and up to ten spectators (see Figure 2). With this playful co-located AV setting, we conducted a controlled experiment that investigates the impact of factors that contribute to the experience of co-presence. These factors are the presence/absence of the visual representation of the VR player and the verbal communication between the VR player and the spectators. Four different conditions (condition 1 (Hands & No Sound), condition 2 (No Hands & No Sound), condition 3 (Hands & Sound), condition 4 (No Hands & Sound)) were defined to investigate whether VR players experience a higher degree of co-presence when they are visually represented within the game; this is based on the assumption that the virtual representation of the hands could foster the conceptual bond between VR players and the spectators. Furthermore, due to the co-located setting, we were also interested in examining the effects of voice communication on co-presence. Thus, the research questions can be formulated as follows :

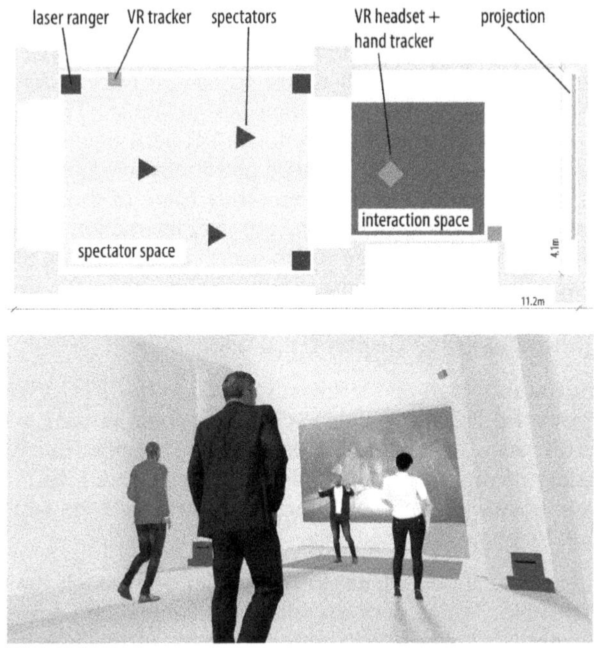

Figure 2. Setup at the Vienna Design Week in 2016: Top: layout of the installation. Bottom: Rendering showing the VR player, spectators, VR headset and trackers, laser rangers and projection.

Research question: Will VR players experience a higher degree of co-presence if their body (in our case: hands) is visually represented in the virtual environment? Does the inclusion/exclusion of exterior audio sources (verbal communication) influence the perceived co-presence?

Generally, we aim to evaluate nonverbal and verbal communication within a co-located and playful AV installation through a controlled experimental setting. The results of our study should contribute to reducing the gap between VR players and spectators. The following sections provide some information on the installation Invisible Walls, a description of the four conditions, the hypotheses, the participants, the procedure, and the results.

The installation: Invisible Walls

Invisible Walls is an experimental AV interaction space that was developed exclusively for the 10th anniversary of Austria's largest design festival, the Vienna Design Week[5]. The concept consists of a large-scale projection, a VR headset that supports hand and finger motions as input, and a sensitive laser position tracking system from the technology forge of the Ars Electronica Futurelab in Linz[6]. The physical interaction space was a 40 square meter garage which had to accommodate the VR player, the spectators and a large wall projection. We decided to design the experience for a single VR user with a high-end VR head-mounted Display (HMD).

The use of a high-end VR headset such as the HTC Vive and a powerful PC allowed us to create complex visuals, a high-performance VR experience and opened the possibility for a variety of input devices. It also provided us with full room-scale positional and head tracking, allowing users to freely walk in a pre-calibrated area.

In terms of input, we explored interaction through the Vive controllers, which perform reliably in games[7] and design applications[8], but require a certain time for users to learn how to use them, which was contrary to the design goals of our installation. We quickly realized that hand-tracked interaction would potentially feel more natural for first-time VR users and also allow us to explore hand presence in VR. The Leap Motion[9] provided us with a sensor, a mount that is attached in front of the VR device and an implementation of their tracking engine for Unity[10].

Another challenge for the installation was properly dividing the interaction spaces and providing both the spectators and the VR player with enough space, while simultaneously avoiding collisions and having enough space for the projection. A couple of possibilities such as a rear projection and merging VR and co-located spaces were discussed, but eventually a decision was made to divide the room into a spectator space and a room-scale VR space for one user.

As shown in Figure 2, the VR player faces the spectators, while the projection behind him/her presents a view of the VE. Participants are represented as 3D sculptures (see Figure 2), moving in sync with the real location of the players in the physical space. The spectator and VR space are physically separated by LED lights, while the VR space warns the player if he/she gets too close to the border, in order to avoid physical collisions. The VE is mapped to the physical location, but removes the walls and presents spectators with an open environment, consisting of gigantic floating objects, morphing sculptures for the spectators and a day-night cycle, which periodically changes the visuals of the environment. The hands of the VR player are visually represented (see Figure 3) and a multitude of gestures such as pointing, waving and clapping can be used to manipulate the environment.

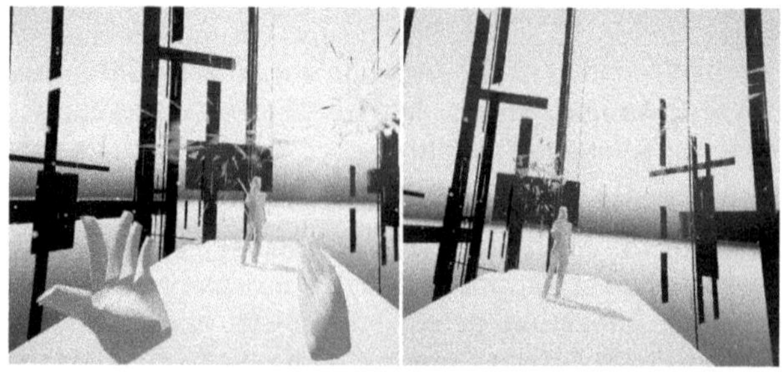

Figure 3. Left: The VR player's viewing area with a virtual representation of his/her hands. Right: The VR player's viewing area without a virtual representation of his/her hands.

In order to identify factors for co-presence, four conditions were defined that support the study scenarios and provide a ground for the hypotheses.

Condition 1 (Hands & Audience Sound) the player's hands are shown in an abstract form that matches the visual style of the virtual space. The hand can be seen by the VR player and the spectators as the VR view is shown on the projection. The VR player and spectators may come into contact via the interaction possibilities granted by the installation and also through voice.

Condition 2 (No Hands & Audience Sound) the player's hands are not represented. Only the results of the player's actions (touching the virtual representations of the spectators, creating fireworks and copies of the sculptures by clapping) are shown to the participants of the installation.

Condition 3 (Hands & No Audience Sound) is similar to condition 1. However, in this condition the VR player has to wear headphones (audio: ambient sounds, sound effects from the installation) to increase the gap between the spectators and the VR player by removing voice communication. VR players should be more immersed in the game world via sound (and the importance of the other installation participants is reduced).

Condition 4 (No Hands & No Audience Sound) is similar to condition 2 and also includes sound to increase the gap between the spectator and the VR player.

Invisible Walls utilizes hand input in a couple of novel ways. The VR player's left hand is used to remotely activate a deform animation in the sculpture of a spectator, while the right hand is used to swap its color. In the real world, people are not accustomed to selecting and manipulating objects at a distance, which is why it is particularly challenging to come up with an intuitive way to do this in a virtual scenario. The implementation uses a raycast from the hand in a forward direction, which returns data about the first object hit. Precision however degrades over distance and is influenced by unsteady motion and the pose of the hand in 3D space. To improve the results, the raycast oscillates between predefined angles, which means

[5] http://www.viennadesignweek.at/
[6] https://www.aec.at/futurelab/
[7] http://www.spacepiratetrainer.com/
[8] https://www.tiltbrush.com/
[9] https://www.leapmotion.com/
[10] https://www.unity3d.com/

that if the user holds his/her hand facing up or straight, the ray will always hit the object directly in front of it.

Another problem is how to visually inform the player about what his/her hand is pointing at. An approach that generates a line or a particle system from the hand was tested, but felt unnatural since it needed a way to be turned on and off by using a specific gesture—otherwise it would always be displayed no matter what the user points at. This approach could be investigated further by snapping the line/particles to the specific object, visualizing it with a curved rather than a straight line. However, we decided to use a more subtle approach, which prompted the user to discover how the system works by waving at the sculptures and observing the effects of his/her actions. The hands of the VR player are colored in red and blue, and a corresponding particle system is created above the currently selected object to signify which hand is currently manipulating it. This is further enhanced by the deform animation and the random color swapping, which are triggered as soon as one of the rays from the hands reaches the object. The proximity between a VR player and spectators also plays an important role. The closer a sculpture is, the higher its transparency becomes. Once this distance is under approximately one meter, the sculpture dissolves into multiple polygons and the hand of the VR player can act as an anti-magnet, pushing the polygons away.

The final interaction capability is clapping, which releases a visual explosion and duplicates the current scene somewhere in the space above the player. The gesture does not involve direct interaction with the spectators, but rather provides the VR player with haptic and auditory feedback to his/her action.

Hypotheses

H1: The VR player will experience a higher degree of co-presence if his/her body (here: hands) is visually represented in the virtual environment.

H1 addresses the question of whether VR players experience a higher degree of co-presence if they are visually represented within the game. It is anticipated that the virtual representation of the hands will strengthen the conceptual bond between the VR player and the spectators of the installation. Without this element, only the outcome of the VR player's interactions (coloring and animating the avatars of the other participants) and not the origin of manipulation (the embodiment that is strongly connected to the VR player) can be perceived. Through the inclusion of the VR player's embodiment, a bridge is being built that connects the VR player with the spectators of the Invisible Wall installation. The feeling should be supported by the natural mapping of hand gestures granted by the Leap Motion device.

H2: The inclusion of other communication channels (here: verbal communication) will have a moderating effect on impact of the VR player's embodiment regarding the perceived co-presence.

Via voice communication, the experienced co-presence should be amplified, while a diminished inclusion of the verbal communication channel (sounds of the game environment through headphones) should tone down the anticipated effect. These considerations lead us to the following assumptions: In condition 1 (Hands & No Sound), the perceived co-presence should be fairly high as the embodiment of VR players builds a link between them and the spectators. Furthermore, the inclusion of verbal communication among participants should foster the feeling of co-presence. The positive impact of embodiment should also be seen in condition 3 (Hands & Sound), but with lower ratings as the verbal communication is toned down via the headsets. Condition 2 (No Hands& No Sound) will have the second lowest ratings in comparison to condition 1 and 3, as no visual representation of the VR player is displayed, but verbal communication is possible. Condition 4 (No Hands & Sound) should lead to the lowest degree of co-presence, because this version does not offer direct communication among participants.

Participants and procedure

The sample consisted of 256 participants, ages 8 to 69 years (123 female, mean age= 34.34, SD= 14.23). 153 participants (59.78%) are employed, 95 subjects are either pupils or students (37.11%), and 5 retired (1.94%). When asked about their frequency of playing games, subjects gave the following answers: daily: 15 subjects (5.86%), several times a week: 24 subjects (9.38%), sometimes: 89 subjects (34.77%), never: 128 subjects (50%). Furthermore participants were asked if they have any experience with VR applications: 7 subjects (2.73%) indicated that they use VR applications several times a week, 71 subjects (27.73%) replied that they sometimes are engaged in VR applications, while 178 participants (69.53%) do not have any experience with VR technology. Furthermore, 4 participants (1.56%) own a VR device. In regards to the procedure, subjects played only one of the four conditions (between subject design). Potential evaluators observing the exhibition space were asked by the experimenter to take part in the study. If the subjects agreed to evaluate the installation, the experimenter would provide a short introduction that gave an overview of the overall procedure. After the VR technology was properly set up, subjects were instructed about the possibilities to interact with the other participants of the installation. When the people confirmed that every aspect was clear to them, the experiment began (see Figure 4). The time to interact with the installation was set to 3 to 5 minutes, which is very well suited to measure the co-presence dimension due to its immediate effects on subjects. When the interaction was completed, the experimenter instructed the participants to fill out the questionnaire (see section measures). Furthermore, the VR players and spectators had the possibility to give comments regarding the perceived game experience via short informal interviews.

Measures

All dependent measures were collected by using validated scales. To measure the co-presence dimension, the Networked Minds Social Presence Inventory by [3] was employed, which is designed to measure social presence and consists of three scales (co-presence, psycho-behavioral interaction, and subjective and intersubjective symmetry). Due to the short interaction time (3 to 5 minutes), we only employed the first scale, co-presence, which forms a core component of social presence

Figure 4. Invisible Walls: a VR player is interacting with the spectators at the Vienna Design Week 2016.

and measures the degree to which the players feel as if they are together in the same space. It emerges when players have the impression that they automatically detect and classify a form as another, which is moderated by the degree to which the user and the agent appear to share an environment together (mutual salience and sensorimotor accessibility of the user and perceived other). For instance, "I think the other participants often felt as if we were in the same virtual space together." is one of the four items that can be rated using a seven-point Likert scale (ranging from "strongly disagree" to "strongly agree"). Apart from the Networked Minds Social Presence Inventory, the evaluation also included an open interview at the end of the test session in order to gain a deeper understanding of the experience. Two open-ended qualitative questions regarding the experience of co-presence were asked by the experimenter ("What did you like most about the installation?" and "What did you dislike most about the installation?"). Furthermore, data on demographics (age, gender, occupation) as well as pre-experience with VR devices and games was gathered.

RESULTS

Table 1 reports the descriptive statistics and table 2 shows the tests of the between-subjects effects. The data (CRF-22 design) was analyzed by means of a univariate analysis of variance (ANOVA) with hands (with hands versus without hands) and headphones (with headphones versus without headphones) as the between-subject factors and co-presence as the dependent variable. The results revealed a marginally significant main effect of hands, $F(1, 252) = 2.99$, $p = .085$. In line with H1, experienced co-presence tended to be higher in the condition in which hands were shown, $M = 4.64$, $SD = 1.09$, as compared with the condition in which no hands were not rendered, $M = 4.44$, $SD = 0.85$. The main effect of headphones was not significant, $F(1, 252) = 0.01$, $p = .946$, and neither was the interaction between hands and headphones, $F(1, 252) = 0.85$, $p = .357$. Thus, H2 was not supported. Furthermore, gender, age, playing games and a prior knowledge in the field of VR as well as occupation were not significantly related to presence ratings.

DISCUSSION

In general, our study showed the positive effects of the VR player's representation towards an increased feeling of co-presence among participants. The approach presented a new

Hands	Headphones	Mean	SD	N
No hands	No headphones	4.49	.87	69
	Headphones	4.39	.82	68
	Total	4.44	.85	137
Hands	No headphones	4.59	1.15	65
	Headphones	4.71	1.03	54
	Total	4.65	1.09	119
Total	No headphones	4.54	1.01	134
	Headphones	4.53	.93	122
	Total	4.54	.97	256

Table 1. Descriptive statistics dependent variable: co-presence.

layer of nonverbal interaction for the players, which in turn, resulted in a range of co-presence qualities emerging from this interaction channel. In the comments, participants emphasized the immersive experience, the idea of merging the real and virtual space, the interaction with real people, and the control via gestures. There were several remarks such as "I like the possibility to change the color and shape of the figures with my hands" or "I felt totally merged with the virtual space". The visual design, especially the abstract representation, lighting, colors and visual effects (particle effects, night/day simulation) were predominantly positively evaluated, although some of the users would have liked a more detailed figure design and reported that the figures were not animated. The response to the interaction design and the feedback to the implementation of the interaction was generally positive.

Most users positively underscored the combination of VR and gesture control, as well as the interaction with real people in virtual space. Only few players perceived the possibilities of interaction as being complicated and awkward. Reasons for this were too little feedback for the interaction, experienced delay and the representation of the other participants. Users with hands (condition 1 and 3) also criticized the offset of the representation of the hands. Furthermore, some users asserted that the possibilities for interaction were not sufficient, the interaction space was too small, and the cables of the VR device were considered as distracting. It has to be noted that only users with headphones (condition 3 and 4) mentioned the sound design. Two users rated the sound positively, two others criticized the sound through headphones because they felt isolated from the others and reported that they could not communicate with the other participants. A significant point in the comments was that users without hands reported that they missed a visual representation of their own hands and even their body.

Virtual representation and co-presence

Study results revealed that the visualization of the VR players' hands does effect the perceived co-presence, which is also indicated by some statements that were given by subjects. In condition 1, and particularly in condition 3, the interaction with hands was assessed more positively to come into contact with the spectators compared to participants with no representation of their hands. In conditions 2 and 4, some remarks about missing the representation of the hands and the body can be found. These impressions include statements such as: "No representation of the hand movements, I cannot come into

Source	Type III Squares	df	Mean Squares	F	Sig.	Partial Eta Squared
Corrected Model	3.47	3	1.16	1.23	.300	.014
Intercept	5242.92	1	5242.92	5563.81	.000	.957
Hands	2.82	1	2.82	2.99	.085	.012
Headphones	.01	1	.01	.01	.946	.000
*Hands * Headphones*	.80	1	.80	.85	.357	.003
Error	237.47	252	.94			
Total	5511.55	256				
Corrected Total	240.94	255				

Table 2. Tests of between-subjects effects.

contact with the others", or "I don't like the fact that I don't see my hands and thereby I do not see a connection to the real world.". Thus, we determined that the visual representation of the VR player is one of the key factors for the perceived co-presence. However, the effect was not as strong as anticipated, which can be explained by some technical issues (in a few cases the tracking of the hands did not function properly, or there was an offset between the player's virtual hands and the effect they had on the spectators). In one situation, for instance, the VR player pointed at a spectator's avatar without any effect, or in another situation, the VR player did not point at an avatar, but the avatar was colorized and animated.

Spectator participation in VR

Comments of spectators show that our AV installation Invisible Walls granted an engaging experience also for spectators. Thus, the installation addresses one of the problems of VR games in public settings (such as: game festivals, demo sessions at conferences, etc.): typically, VR installations feature a single VR player experience in which the player is being watched by an audience that can see the current game status via a monitor or projection screen without any possibility of interacting with the VR player. With Invisible Walls we created not only a unique and engaging experience for one VR player, but also established a connection between the real and the virtual via an AV approach. Spectators were represented within the VE in the form of abstract humans that could be altered by the VR player. Some spectators noted that they liked the idea of being part of the game without the necessity of wearing a VR device. Furthermore, the visual connection (hands) between the spectators and the VR players was received positively by the spectators. Another interesting finding was that some of spectators mentioned they simply were not interested in VR technology, but enjoyed the more passive spectator role. Other spectators noted that they were not keen in trying out the VR technology, because they did not want to be in the center of attention (being watched by others during playing the game), but liked to influence the game state through their actions.

Verbal communication in augmented virtuality

The inclusion of verbal communication did not have a significant impact on the perceived co-presence. This can be explained by the fact that, for safety reasons, it was not possible to completely exclude the verbal communication channel. To guarantee a safe experience for both spectators and VR players, verbal communication was toned down by adjusting the volume level of the headphones. Subjects were able to hear installation-related instructions from the experiment supervisors, such as maintaining awareness of the VR device's cables, instructions to avoid collisions with physical objects, support if something was not clear to the VR players or the spectators, or help when subjects encountered technical issues. Another factor that had an effect on the results was the novelty of the experience (69.53% had never used a VR device before). Players were fascinated by the experience and focused heavily on the visual experience, which, in turn, might have led to lower verbal communication activity. In conclusion, we argue that our approach revealed several interesting findings in the context of VR player representation in an AV setting during co-located gameplay. Via our experimental design, aspects of player representation and nonverbal communication in AV are addressed that should contribute to a smaller gap between the VR player and the spectators. The representation of the VR players created an interpersonal link between them and the spectators, which was fostered by showing VR player's view to the spectators via a projection screen. Our installation proved to be an effective tool to explore the fringes of VR and AV in the context of interactive installations.

CONCLUSION

This paper investigated the effects of the VR players' representation and verbal communication regarding co-presence in a co-located and playful AV installation for multiple players. The submission proposes an approach that does not just take one VR player into account, but also spectators, to investigate which factors influence the co-presence in an AV context. Concretely, with our experimental setting Invisible Walls, we examined whether the incorporation/exclusion of the visualization of the VR players' hands and the presence/absence of verbal communication would influence the perceived co-presence. Results showed the positive influence of the VR player's representation on the perceived co-presence. The inclusion of verbal communication, however, did not reveal any significant results, as for safety reasons, it was not possible to completely exclude the verbal communication channel. Based on our findings, game designers and researchers should have gained some insights regarding the inclusion of nonverbal and verbal communication channels in co-located AV settings to foster the social interaction between VR players and spectators. For future work, we plan to further investigate other settings (different kinds of public spaces) and other interaction channels (for instance: body postures) as well as explore our approach in situations with more than one VR player.

ACKNOWLEDGMENTS

We would like to thank all of our survey participants for their time and for the data they generously provided. Furthermore we thank the organizers of the Vienna Design Week for providing the experiment location.

REFERENCES

1. Elizabeth Behm-Morawitz. 2013. Mirrored selves: The influence of self-presence in a virtual world on health, appearance, and well-being. *Computers in Human Behavior* 29, 1 (2013), 119–128.
2. Frank Biocca and Chad Harms. 2003a. Guide to the Networked Minds Social Presence Inventory v. 1.2. (2003). http://cogprints.org/6743/
3. Frank Biocca and Chad Harms. 2003b. Networked Minds Social Presence Inventory: Measures of co-presence, social presence, subjective symmetry, and intersubjective symmetry. (2003). http://cogprints.org/6742/
4. Gordon Calleja. 2011. *In-Game: From Immersion to Incorporation*. The MIT Press, Cambridge, Massachusetts.
5. Sylvain Chagué and Caecilia Charbonnier. 2016. Real Virtuality: A Multi-user Immersive Platform Connecting Real and Virtual Worlds. In *Proceedings of the 2016 Virtual Reality International Conference (VRIC '16)*. ACM, New York, NY, USA, Article 4, 3 pages. DOI: http://dx.doi.org/10.1145/2927929.2927945
6. Carolina Cruz-Neira, Daniel J. Sandin, Thomas A. DeFanti, Robert V. Kenyon, and John C. Hart. 1992. The CAVE: Audio Visual Experience Automatic Virtual Environment. *Commun. ACM* 35, 6 (June 1992), 64–72. DOI:http://dx.doi.org/10.1145/129888.129892
7. K.M. Lee. 2004. Presence, explicated. *Communication Theory* 14, 1 (2004), 27–50.
8. Stefan Liszio and Maic Masuch. 2016. *Designing Shared Virtual Reality Gaming Experiences in Local Multi-platform Games*. Springer International Publishing, Cham, 235–240. DOI: http://dx.doi.org/10.1007/978-3-319-46100-7_23
9. P. Milgram and F. Kishino. 1994. A Taxonomy of Mixed Reality Visual Displays. *IEICE Trans. Information Systems* E77-D, 12 (Dec. 1994), 1321–1329.
10. Marvin Minsky. 1980. Telepresence. *OMNI magazine* (June 1980).
11. D. Roth, J. L. Lugrin, D. Galakhov, A. Hofmann, G. Bente, M. E. Latoschik, and A. Fuhrmann. 2016. Avatar realism and social interaction quality in virtual reality. In *2016 IEEE Virtual Reality (VR)*. 277–278. DOI: http://dx.doi.org/10.1109/VR.2016.7504761
12. Mohamad H. Salimian. 2015. Exploring Group Awareness in a Mixed Reality Collaborative Environment. In *Adjunct Proceedings of the 2015 ACM International Joint Conference on Pervasive and Ubiquitous Computing and Proceedings of the 2015 ACM International Symposium on Wearable Computers (UbiComp/ISWC'15 Adjunct)*. ACM, New York, NY, USA, 495–501. DOI: http://dx.doi.org/10.1145/2800835.2801654
13. Ulrike Schultze. 2010. Embodiment and presence in virtual worlds: a review. *JIT* 25, 4 (2010), 434–449.
14. Anthony Steed, Sebastian Friston, Maria Murcia Lopez, Jason Drummond, Ye Pan, and David Swapp. 2016. An 'In the Wild' Experiment on Presence and Embodiment using Consumer Virtual Reality Equipment. *IEEE Trans. Vis. Comput. Graph.* 22, 4 (2016), 1406–1414.
15. R. Tamborini and N. Bowman. 2010. Presence in video games. In *Immersed in Media: Telepresence in Everyday Life*, C. Bracken and P. Skalski (Eds.). Routledge, New York, NY, USA, 87–109.
16. Anthony Tang, Carman Neustaedter, and Saul Greenberg. 2007. *VideoArms: Embodiments for Mixed Presence Groupware*. Springer London, London, 85–102. DOI: http://dx.doi.org/10.1007/978-1-84628-664-3_8
17. Yu Zhu, Kang Zhu, Qiang Fu, Xilin Chen, Huixing Gong, and Jingyi Yu. 2016. SAVE: Shared Augmented Virtual Environment for Real-time Mixed Reality Applications. In *Proceedings of the 15th ACM SIGGRAPH Conference on Virtual-Reality Continuum and Its Applications in Industry - Volume 1 (VRCAI '16)*. ACM, New York, NY, USA, 13–21. DOI: http://dx.doi.org/10.1145/3013971.3013979

Drunk Virtual Reality Gaming: Exploring the Influence of Alcohol on Cybersickness

Aliya Iskenderova
Ilmenau University of Technology
Ilmenau, Germany
aliya.iskenderova@tu-ilmenau.de

Florian Weidner
Ilmenau University of Technology
Ilmenau, Germany
florian.weidner@tu-ilmenau.de

Wolfgang Broll
Ilmenau University of Technology
Ilmenau, Germany
wolfgang.broll@tu-ilmenau.de

ABSTRACT
Recently released consumer head-mounted displays (HMD), such as the Oculus Rift, the HTC Vive, or the Sony PlayStation VR, hyped up the market of virtual reality, particularly affecting the gaming industry. Although the technology is now publicly accessible, it is not yet mature enough to guarantee its users an absolutely pleasant experience. Side effects of virtual environments, i.e. cybersickness, pose a threat to the safe use of the devices. Symptoms of cybersickness may worsen if safety instructions are neglected. It is not unlikely that home use of the headsets will entice consumers to combine virtual reality experiences with alcohol consumption.

This paper attempts to discover how alcohol intoxication affects the symptoms of cybersickness caused by immersion in virtual environment. Thirty-one participants were asked to play a video game using the Oculus Rift DK2 headset two times, before and after consuming either alcohol or a placebo.

The study revealed unexpected results: alcohol intoxication at a blood alcohol level of approximately 0.07% significantly reduced symptoms of cybersickness among individuals in the experimental treatment group and did not worsen symptoms among all participants.

ACM Classification Keywords
H.5.1 Information Interfaces and Presentation (e.g. HCI): Artificial, augmented, and virtual realities; H.1.2 User/Machine Systems: Human factors; K.8 Personal Computing: Games

Author Keywords
Virtual reality; cybersickness; alcohol intoxication; games

INTRODUCTION
In recent times, virtual reality (VR) technology has developed to a considerable extent. The progress is driven especially by the video game industry where intensive competition requires constant innovation in terms of realistic design, natural interaction, and improved usability. Substantial increase in the quality and capabilities of the modern virtual reality devices has led to a price decline for the technology, making it available to a wide range of customers.

The *Oculus Rift CV1*, currently among the most advanced VR headsets available to mass consumers, was released in the first quarter of 2016 for the US market and immediately followed by competitors such as the HTC Vive and Sony PlayStation VR. Today, developers offer hundreds of virtual reality games for home entertainment. Promising and captivating, however, the new technology is not yet mature enough to offer its users an entirely pleasant experience.

Interaction within a virtual environment (VE) may cause adverse effects influencing the level of comfort, safety, and health. Depending on the particular factor, side effects can be divided into direct and indirect ones [49]. Direct effects include traumatizing consequences of virtual reality systems on visual (e.g. photic seizures) and auditory systems (e.g. can cause hearing damages) as well as skin and tissue (e.g. bacteria). Indirect effects are presented by psychological effects (e.g. phobias, anxiety), neurological effects on the visual system (e.g. eyestrain), impairments caused in the vestibular system, and motion-sickness symptoms [49]. The latter is often described as the polysymptomatic maladaptation syndrome that may occur during exposure to real or apparent motion or result from synthetic experiences, such as, for instance, simulators, virtual environments, or augmented reality [34]. The dedicated syndrome caused by immersion in a computer generated virtual environment is called cybersickness [35].

Cybersickness is one of the main adverse effects of virtual environments. It is characterized by a number of symptoms including nausea, eye strain, sweating, disorientation, fatigue, headache, and vomiting [9]. There are several theories trying to explain causes of cybersickness occurrence, such as a sensory conflict theory, poison theory, and postural instability theory. However, research is struggling to provide a reasonable explanation of the side effects [33].

Cybersickness may significantly impede commercial success of virtual reality head-mounted displays. More importantly, it constitutes a potential threat to its users. Symptoms of

CHI PLAY'17, October 15 – 18, 2017, Amsterdam, Netherlands

ACM ISBN 978-1-4503-4898-0/17/10... $15.00
https://doi.org/10.1145/3116595.3116618

cybersickness may be exacerbated if consumers neglect manufacturer warnings during at-home application of the HMDs. For instance, according to the Oculus Rift's Health and Safety Instructions[1], the headset is not recommended for use under the influence of alcohol. The warning is vitally important, however, there is little to no research on the impact of alcohol on cybersickness. It has not been yet determined whether alcohol worsens the side effects caused by virtual environments and poses a serious health threat. This paper attempts to study how alcohol intoxication affects cybersickness caused by immersion in VR in order to lower this uncertainty. Therefore, the research question is defined as follows:

How does alcohol intoxication influence cybersickness symptoms of gamers immersed in virtual reality?

Further, we discuss the above-mentioned considerations and the current state of research. Specifically, cybersickness and its underlying causes are described. A brief introduction of the influence of alcohol on a human body is presented. Also, the research approach and study design are explained. Additional variables which might be important for replication comparability are introduced. Finally, results and discussions conclude the study and outline future work.

BACKGROUND AND RELATED WORK

Cybersickness

Although cybersickness is inseparably associated with motion and simulator sickness, these terms are not entirely synonymous. Motion sickness develops from the exposure to real or apparent movement, whereas cybersickness refers to visually induced motion sickness following from immersion in a virtual environment [24, 34]. Simulator sickness is caused by imperfections of the simulation rather than the actual simulated situation [24].

It was suggested that different symptom profiles might be used to distinguish between motion sickness-related ailments [26]. Symptoms, generally assessed by means of the Simulator Sickness Questionnaire (SSQ, [27]), are categorized into nausea (e.g., stomach awareness), oculomotor (e.g., eyestrain), and disorientation (e.g., vertigo). According to Kennedy et al. [26], cybersickness had frequently higher disorientation scores followed by nausea and oculomotor ratings, whereas military simulators had oculomotor symptoms dominating over nausea and disorientation, and sea sickness often had higher nausea and lower oculomotor and disorientation ratings.

Factors increasing likelihood of cybersickness

There are several theories that strive to explain why and how the symptoms of cybersickness occur. In this study, the sensory conflict, poison, and postural instability theories are briefly reviewed. Additionally, factors contributing to the severity of cybersickness are presented (for more detailed information a reader is encouraged to refer to [24]).

Sensory Conflict Theory.

According to the sensory conflict theory, sickness occurs due to inconsistency between the sensory system components that are responsible for providing information regarding the orientation and motion of human body [39, 45]. A person immersed in virtual reality continuously receives visual and auditory stimuli from the simulation, while vestibular and proprioceptive cues are obtained from body motion in the real world. The discrepancy between the senses results in the onset of symptoms. Although the theory is widely practiced, it is considered as insufficient, because firstly, it fails to explain why some people get sick and others do not; secondly, the theory does not have any predictive power. Finally, it does not elaborate on why sensory conflicts induce sickness [33].

Postural Instability Theory.

The theory suggests that postural imbalance may induce sickness as humans always try to minimize instability [42]. For instance, a user is likely to lean forward if the visual environment is moving forward [3]. However, changes in a posture in order to compensate mismatch between visual and vestibular cues destabilize the user and result in the onset of symptoms [24].

Poison Theory.

The poison, or evolutionary, theory argues that the sickening response to virtual environments is a natural reaction of a human body unadjusted to relatively new conditions. The theory claims that, due to the extrinsic sensory input provided by a VE, the human body responds as if it was poisoned. The reaction is similar to intoxication where the ingestion of certain poisonous substances leads to typical symptoms like nausea and vomiting. However, the theory does not have predictive power and does not account for incidents without sickness [33, 42].

Factors increasing susceptibility to cybersickness

The factors which can increase susceptibility to cybersickness can be divided into three groups: individual factors, device factors, and task factors [14].

Individual factors.

Research in the area of motion sickness, simulator sickness and cybersickness emphasized influence of factors like gender, age, and experience on the onset and severity of symptoms. For instance, in a simulated driving experiment conducted by Park et al. [40], female participants had higher drop-out rates and higher symptom incidence than male participants. Although early research suggested that children are more susceptible to motion and simulator sickness [30], more recent data showed that individuals under the age of 15 experienced less cybersickness than adults [2]. Decline of susceptibility with age was proven by early as well as more recent studies [40, 55]. Correlation was found between susceptibility to cybersickness and prior exposures to VEs [18, 25] as well as previous gaming experience [41]. Further, history of motion sickness can predict predisposition to the syndrome [18, 41].

Device factors.

In recent years, more attention was focused on technology issues, such as field of view, navigation, display types, as factors potentially influencing the level of discomfort in a virtual environment. For example, individuals had higher SSQ ratings while watching a 3D movie compared to a monoscopic

[1] https://static.oculus.com/documents/health-and-safety-warnings.pdf, date retrieved: 2017-01-05

condition in the experiment of Naqvi et al. [38]. Stereoscopic displays were found to increase eye strain and, therefore, influence the evolution of the simulator sickness symptoms [50]. It also appears that the sickness symptoms increase with screen size [20]. In the experiment of Bos et al. [5] on the internal and external fields of view, symptoms became less prominent when the ratio between the real and virtual field of view was incremented. Increased navigation speed in a virtual environment was found to contribute to sickness severity [47]. Although stable refresh rates of at least 60 Hz are recommended for a virtual environment [15], increasing the refresh rate was found to decrease simulator sickness symptoms [11]. Current devices allow refresh rates of 90Hz[2]. End-to-end latency in HMDs, defined as the period of time between a user's physical motion and the following update of the frame displayed due to this motion [56], higher than 60 ms can induce simulator sickness [1, 32].

Task factors.
A user behavior in a virtual environment can impact his susceptibility to cybersickness. It was assumed that high level of concentration during immersion reduced the severity of cybersickness [30]. Anxiety caused by the immersion in a virtual environment was named as one of the substantial factors contributing to sickness [7, 8]. Duration of the immersion was described earlier as one of the factors largely contributing to the development of the symptoms. It was shown that the onset and severity of the symptoms increased over time [6, 25]. Quick head movements were found to produce a greater chance of cybersickness [30]. Walker et al. [51] discovered that individuals with high sickness ratings were limiting their head movements supposedly to avoid acerbation.

Miscellaneous.
Some health conditions may affect the onset and severity of symptoms. For example, individuals with an absent or atrophied vestibular system can be unable to experience cybersickness. Further, hangover as well as certain drugs and medications were found to increase individuals vulnerability [18].

Habituation of cybersickness
Symptoms of cybersickness can be reduced by repeated exposures to virtual environments. Hill and Howarth [21] asked their participants to use a game with a non-tracked head-mounted display for 20 minutes on five consecutive days. They found that individuals experienced notably less nausea and aftereffects in comparison with the initial results. Howarth and Hodder [23] suggested that the number of exposures is a key factor in order for habituation to take place.

Alcohol and cybersickness
As mentioned before, the connection between cybersickness and alcohol intoxication is not clearly understood. However, some studies suggested that alcohol might elevate the susceptibility to motion or simulator sickness [4, 31, 55].

[2] https://www3.oculus.com/en-us/rift/, date retrieved: 2017-01-01

BAC (g/dl)	Ranking by lowest BAC level at which significant Impariment was reported for a specific test	Ranking by BAC level above which 50% of studies reported impairment for a specific test
0.100	Critical Flicker Fusion	Simple reaction time, critical flicker fusion
0.090 - 0.099		
0.080 - 0.089		
0.070 - 0.079		
0.060 - 0.069		Cognitive tasks (e.g. digital symbol substitution), psychomotor skills (e.g. balance, finger tapping, manual assembly), choice reaction time
0.050 - 0.059		Adaptation, pursuit, compensatory tracking
0.040 - 0.049	Simple reaction time	Perception (e.g. visual search), visual functions (e.g. visual acuity)
0.030 - 0.039	Vigilance, perception	Vigilance
0.020 - 0.029	Choice reaction time, visual functions	
0.010 - 0.019	Drowsiness, psychomotor skills, cognitive tasks, tracking	Drowsiness (e.g. multiple sleep latency test)
0.001 - 0.009	Driving, flying, divided attention	Driving, flying, divided attention)

Table 1. Alcohol Impairment for Specific Human Performance Tests

Alcohol and human body
Alcohol directly influences the human sensory system. For instance, the *spinning room phenomenon* appearing after alcohol intoxication illustrates the impact of alcohol on the vestibular system [18]. Depending on the level of *blood alcohol concentration* (BAC), effects of alcohol on performance can vary largely (see Table 1, adopted from [36]). Note that the following applies for the table and the remainder of this paper:

$$1g/dl = 1g/100ml = 1\%BAC = 10‰BAC \qquad (1)$$

At the lower BAC ($0.001\% - 0.019\%$) problems with divided attention are registered. At this level, individuals are also prone to drowsiness. Higher levels of BAC ($0.02\% - 0.07\%$) may impair human postural control, adaptation, and perception. In the current user study, the target BAC of 0.07% was selected so that most of these impairments appear. A target BAC higher than 0.07% was not justifiable in order to avoid any negative consequences of possible acute poisoning.

The influence of alcohol on the human body depends on a number of factors, such as age, gender, genetics, body weight, type of beverage, drinking experience, health condition, drug consume [22, 43]. For instance, women were found to be more easily affected by alcohol than men after consuming the same dose of alcohol (e.g. [37]).

USER STUDY

Study Design
In order to answer the research question, the current study employs a quantitative research design. A quasi-experimental design was chosen to collected variables during an experiment to determine if a specific treatment influences an outcome [12]. A between-subject design was used in combination with a within-subject experimental design [19].

System Overview
The presented audiovisual stimulus was the game *MiMiCCs*, developed at Ilmenau University of Technology. It consisted of a virtual hangar, airplanes, boxes, and barrels, as shown in Figure 1. In the game, a player was required to find three cards hidden in the hangar (see Fig. 2). The VR game featured a first-person perspective. Using an XBox 360 controller, an individual controlled a character using the left-thumb stick to run, the right-thumb stick to look left and right, and the A-button to collect the cards. Further, a player could look around using the head tracking capabilities of the HMD. The

interaction design might induce cybersickness due to the possibility of controlling the virtual camera by both, head tracking and controller. For example, a person could turn the virtual camera to the right by twisting his head to the right side At the same time, she could use the right-thumb stick to turn the camera to the left. In addition to that, player movements were executed fast and without any smoothing. Further, the game had some image quality issues, i.e. z-fighting, a visual artifact appearing when two surfaces in a scene are parallel and have the same depth value [54].

We performed the experiment in one of the laboratory rooms of the university. The virtual reality headset Oculus Rift DK2 HMD[3] was used in combination with the original optical-inertial tracking system. The HMD has a resolution of 960×1080 pixels per eye, a 100° field of view. Participants were provided with an XBox 360 controller as input device and headphones, as seen in Figure 3.

Application was installed on a high performance workstation equipped with two Intel Xeon E5-2687W v2 @3.4GHz, 64GB RAM, and two NVIDIA Quadro K6000 graphics cards. Operating system was Windows 10, *MiMiCCs* was compiled with Unity3D version 5.0.3. The game was executed applying a fixed frame rate of 60 frames per second.

Task

The task was to find three cards hidden in an airplane hangar. However, there was only one card, not three, in the hangar that appeared after first five minutes of immersion (see Fig. 2). This deception was necessary to keep participants in the virtual environment for 15 minutes, otherwise the game could be finished earlier. The location of the card remained the same for both trials (before and after treatment). Subjects were encouraged to keep looking for the cards regardless of their level of frustration. They could opt out if they felt uncomfortable in the virtual environment.

The duration of 15 minutes was chosen due to the fact that a longer VR experience might result in higher attrition rates. According to Wilson [53], symptoms of cybersickness usually occurr within the first 15 minutes of the immersion. It was also pointed out by Kennedy et al. [28] that longer playtime induced more side effects.

Sample

A total of $N = 31$ individuals (81% male, 19% female) ranging from $18 - 32$ years of age ($M = 25.42, SD = 3.314$) participated in the experiment. All participants were university students. Participation was voluntary and anonymous. A call for participation was circulated through the university mailing list for active students. Participants were required to be of minimum legal drinking age (18 years old) according to the German "Protection of Young Persons Act" (§9 Jugendschutzgesetz).

Participants were selected on the basis of the criteria that were included in the *General Questionnaire*: no illnesses and physical impairments, no medical or psychiatric conditions, not currently pregnant or lactating, not taking any medications

[3]https://www3.oculus.com/en-us/dk2/, date retrieved: 2017-01-02

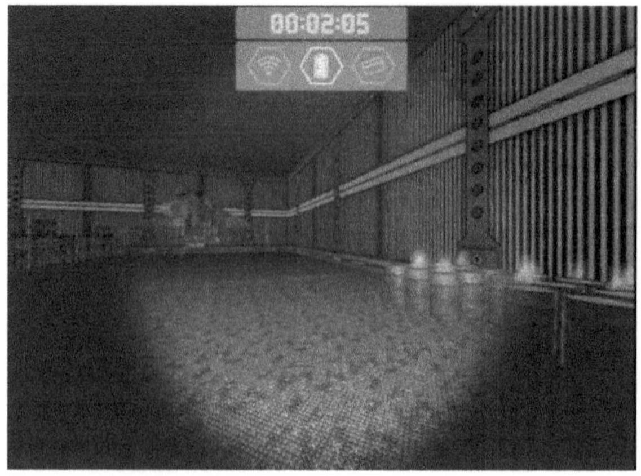

Figure 1. An airplane hangar where players had to search for the card.

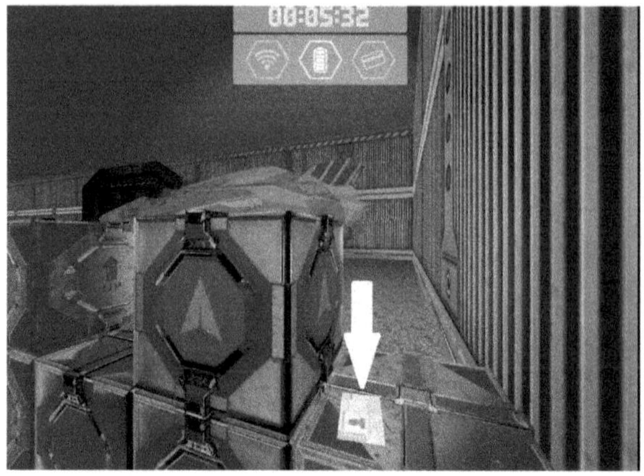

Figure 2. Participants were given a task to to find a key card. White arrow indicates the location of the card. The arrow is edited here for visual demonstration.

or drugs. Normal or corrected to normal vision was required. Individuals were also screened using the *CAGE Substance Abuse Screening Tool* [17]. By that, individuals with potential alcohol problems (alcoholism) were excluded from taking part in the study. However, recent experience with moderate doses of alcohol was a necessary requirement for participation. This way we ensured that no non-alcoholic individuals were introduced to drinking alcohol by the experiment.

Prior to the experiment students interested in the research received a notification. They were asked not to eat anything two hours before the experiment, abstain from alcohol or any drugs for at least a day prior to the experiment and on the day of their participation.

Measures

Measures used in the current study can be divided into two main categories. The first category includes measures directly related to alcohol consumption and cybersickness (*SSQ*, BAC level). The second group are measures related to cybersickness in general (Video Game Usage, Previous Exposure, *MSSQ*, gender, time in VR). We included the additional measures in order to perform a holistic analysis of cybersickness. We aimed to investigate whether they affect the symptoms, as well

Figure 3. Set-up of the experiment with the Oculus Rift DK2, headphones, and an XBox 360 Controller. The movements of the character, could be controlled using the controller and the headset itself due to its tracking camera.

as to provide additional information on the sample for future research with respect to reproducibility and comparability.

General questionnaire.
The questionnaire consisted of 16 items on the participants' background. The items referred to personal information, such as age, gender, weight, height, and educational level. Questions on health condition, e.g. visual and physical impairments, and use of drugs and alcohol, were incorporated in order to exclude unfit individuals from participation.

CAGE questionnaire.
The questionnaire for detection of alcoholism has been developed by Ewing [17]. It was introduced in order to prevent participation of individuals with drinking problems. The clinical interview consists of four closed-ended dichotomous questions that focus on cutting down drinking, annoyance experienced by criticism of drinking habits, guilty feelings and eye-opener. Subjects that scored 2 or above were excluded from further participation in the study.

Video Game Usage Questionnaire.
The questionnaire was adopted from Tolchinsky [48] in order to collect information regarding the participants experience with video games: the average number of hours played per week, average duration of each playing session and what time of day a user typically plays.

Previous Exposure to virtual environments.
Participants were asked if they have experienced virtual reality and 3D computer simulation in the past.

Motion Sickness Susceptibility Questionnaire (MSSQ).
The *MSSQ* [18] was employed to predict individual differences in motion sickness. The questionnaire included a variety of stimuli influencing motion sickness susceptibility. Different types of motion, such as cars, coaches, boats, planes, trains, funfair rides, and swings, were listed. The objective was to evaluate the frequency of usage of the above-mentioned types of stimuli, and severity of sickness experienced by the respondent in his childhood in comparison to adulthood. Participants were supposed to rate each type of motion with the extent to which they experience sickness using a 5-point scale: 0 - *Never*; 1 - *Rarely*; 2 - *Sometimes*; 3 - *Frequently*; 4 - *Always* ($MSSQ_{min} = 0$, $MSSQ_{max} = 380.16$).

Simulator Sickness Questionnaire (SSQ).
The standard instrument in cybersickness research is the *SSQ* developed by Kennedy et al. [27]. It consists of 16 items representing side effects emerging from interaction with virtual environments. The questionnaire offers a 4-point scale from *None*, *Slight*, *Moderate* to *Severe* that are scored respectively as 0, 1, 2 and 3. In the evaluation, scores are combined and weighted with a weight w according to the scoring instructions from the authors into three factors:

- *Nausea* ($Min = 0$, $Max = 200.34$, $w = 9.54$),
- *Oculomotor* ($Min = 0$, $Max = 159.18$, $w = 7.58$)
- *Disorientation* ($Min = 0$, $Max = 292.32$, $w = 3.74$)

The total SSQ score can be calculated by summing up the unweighted scores of each scale and weighting them ($SSQ_{total:min} = 0$, $SSQ_{total:max} = 235.62$, $w = 3.74$).

Blood alcohol concentration (BAC).
The breath alcohol tester *ACE AF-33*[4] was used to estimate blood alcohol level during all tests performed in this study. The analyzer is labeled "Accuracy Class 1" with a precision of $\pm 0.005\%$.

Other measures.
Using a stopwatch, time of immersion in VR was measured. The measurement was started when a participant put on a headset and the game was launched. It was stopped after the game was finished. Further, participants were video recorded during the game. After each immersion individuals were asked to provide subjective evaluation of their current state.

Experiment Protocol

At the beginning of the experiment, participants were informed about the purpose of the study, the individual parts of the experiment, and its approximate length. For ethical reasons all individuals were informed that the study would involve consumption of alcohol. Written informed consent was obtained from all participants. The participants' right to discontinue the experiment at any time was explained.

The procedure was divided into six major parts (see Fig. 4):

1. Screening: selection of healthy participants prior to the experiment.
2. Introduction: randomization, collecting information on the selected participants, and giving instructions on the experiment.
3. First Trial: the first virtual reality exposure.
4. Beverage Manipulation: consumption of experimental or placebo treatment.
5. Second Trial: the second virtual reality exposure.
6. Debriefing

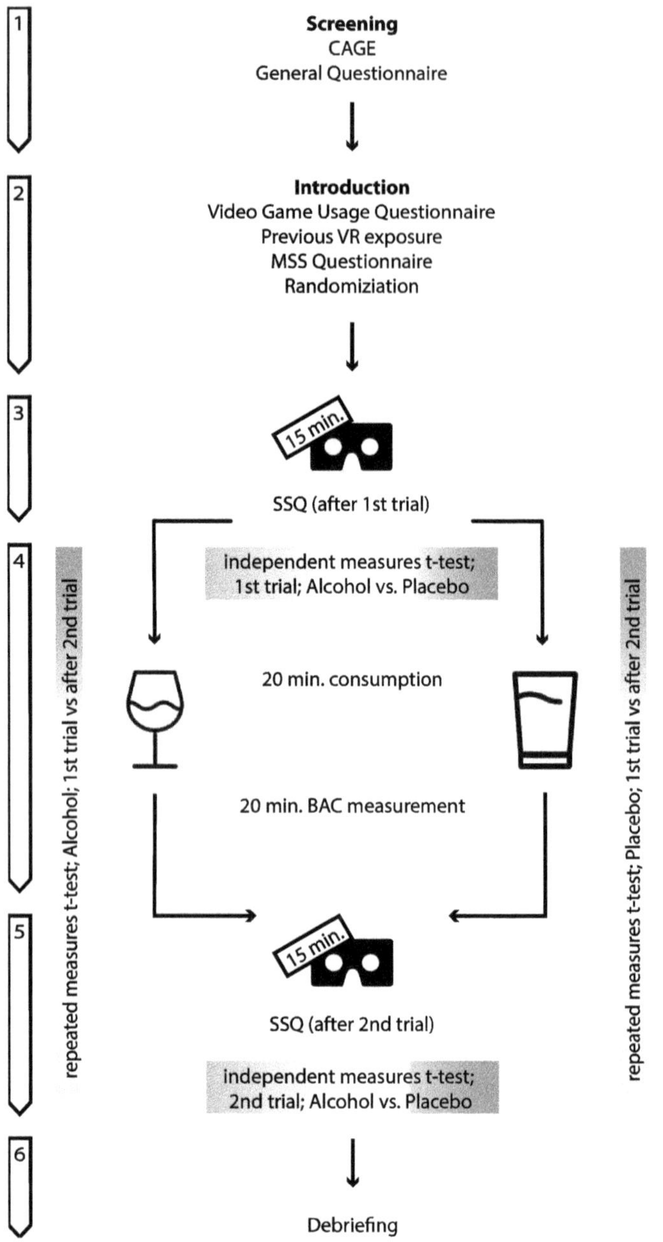

Figure 4. Experimental design including the questionnaires and statistical tests used on different stages of the study. Please note that the colors marking the tests correspond to the ones in Fig. 5 and Fig. 6.

All tests were performed between 13:00 and 17:00 in order to avoid the effects of circadian rhythm [13].

1. Screening.

Prior to the experiment, individuals intending to participate were required to provide personal information and information on their health condition. The selection procedure was based on the responses to the *General Questionnaire* and *CAGE Questionnaire*. As mentioned above, people with alcoholism history, drug abusers, individuals abstaining from alcohol, pregnant and lactating women, people with health conditions, individuals taking medications, and underage were excluded from participation.

2. Introduction.

Individuals who met all criteria were randomly assigned to either alcohol or placebo groups. Participants were not matched, as this would lead to an unequal distribution if participants decided to leave the experiment [44].

In the beginning of the experiment, breath analysis was administered in order to confirm that the participants abstained from alcohol. In this phase, the individuals were introduced to the experiment and its timeline. They were asked about their previous exposure to virtual reality to understand the level of familiarity with virtual environments. Participants were also asked to fill in the *Video Game Usage Questionnaire* and the *Motion Sickness Susceptibility Questionnaire*.

3. First trial.

Both experimental (alcohol) and alternative (placebo) treatment groups were invited to play the video game. Participants received the Oculus Rift DK2, headphones, and the XBox wireless controller with the usage instructions and were asked to play the game for 15 minutes.

After the first virtual reality exposure, individuals were asked to report symptoms experienced during the immersion with the aid of the *SSQ*. The questionnaire was followed by a short interview session, where participants were asked to elaborate on their experience, their condition, and the game.

4. Beverage manipulation.

In the fourth phase, depending on the assigned group, participants were exposed to the experimental or alternative treatment.

As noted before, all participants, regardless of the group they were assigned to, were told that they would receive an alcoholic beverage. All individuals were informed that the BAC would not exceed 0.1%, however they did not receive any information on the amount of alcohol consumed.

The alcohol dose was calculated for each subject individually, taking into consideration participant's weight, gender, height, and anticipated concentration of BAC. First, using Equation 2 or 3, the total body water of the participant was calculated (TBW in [milliliters]).

$$TBW_{male} = 2.447 - (0.09516 \times p_a) + (0.1074 \times p_h) + (0.1074 \times p_h) \quad (2)$$

$$TBW_{female} = -2.097 + (0.1069 \times p_h) + (0.2466 \times p_w) \quad (3)$$

whereas p_h is the participants height in [cm], p_w is the participants weight in [kg], and p_a is the participants age in [years] [52]. The required amount of alcohol in [grams] was then estimated using equation 4.

$$m_{alcohol} = BAC_{target} \times \frac{TBW}{0.8} \quad (4)$$

[4]https://www.alkomat.net/artikeldetails.php?p=ACE1&aid=2848063, date retrieved: 2017-01-04

whereas $m_{alcohol}$ is the amount of alcohol in [grams], $BAC_{target} = 0.07\%$ is the target BAC, and 0.8 is the specific weight of alcohol [29].

Individuals were seated in a comfortable environment and given 20 minutes to finish their drink. It was either orange juice with the calculated amount of alcohol using 40% vodka mixed with orange juice in a 4 : 1 ratio or only orange juice (0% alcohol). To avoid participants noticing the absence of alcohol due to the lack of alcohol-specific smell, the rims of a glass given to individuals from the placebo group were moistened with a cotton ball damped upfront in 40% vodka.

After consumption, breath analysis of the blood alcohol level was performed every three minutes until the plateau was observed. Here, plateau means that two consecutive measurements show decreasing values. This point was indicated as the peak of the BAC and was supposed to range between 0.06% and 0.08%. Participants who did not reach the minimum required BAC were excluded from the second trial. Blood alcohol concentration of the placebo group was also continuously measured in order to avoid the participants from discovering the absence of the experimental treatment.

5. Second Trial.

In the final phase, each participant was required to play the same game for the period of 15 minutes with the same task as in the first trial. Then, blood alcohol concentration was measured again with the help of the breath analyzer. The *SSQ* was distributed to participants in order to collect information on the occurrence and severity of symptoms. Finally, a short interview was conducted to focus on the individual experience of each subject.

6. Debriefing.

Upon completion of the experiment, participants were given safety instructions regarding the consequences of alcohol intoxication and were told not to drive motorized vehicles or operate heavy machinery.

RESULTS

If participants experienced severe discomfort, they could a) terminate the first trial early but still continue with the experiment, b) terminate the second trial early and complete the experiment or c) quit the experiment completely. Dropouts were not included in the following calculations, except where mentioned.

Alcohol Impact on Cybersickness.

Table 2 shows mean *SSQ* scores (total and subscales) for the alcohol and placebo group after the first and after the second trial.

For the alcohol group, mean differences between the two conditions (before and after treatment) were evaluated using a repeated-measures t-test. Figure 5, prefix *A:* illustrates the results. There was a statistically significant difference between total SSQ scores before and after consuming alcohol ($M = 85.44$ ($SD = 44.67$) before alcohol consumption; $M = 50.63$ ($SD = 42.33$) after alcohol consumption; $t(12) = 5.37, p < 0.01$).

	SSQ Scale	SSQ 1st trial Mean	SSQ 1st trial SD	SSQ 2nd trial Mean	SSQ 2nd trial SD
Placebo	Nausea	86.65	25.55	81.88	42.94
	Oculomotor	37.26	20.3	46.11	26.54
	Disorientation	77.72	42.16	96.28	67.79
	Total	73.24	27.59	80.72	45.23
Alcohol	Nausea	82.92	40.73	40.36	35.93
	Oculomotor	54.22	33.87	35.56	28.08
	Disorientation	97.44	68.66	64.24	61.34
	Total	85.44	44.67	50.63	42.33

Table 2. Data table showing mean SSQ scores with standard deviations for alcohol and placebo group after the first and after the second trial.

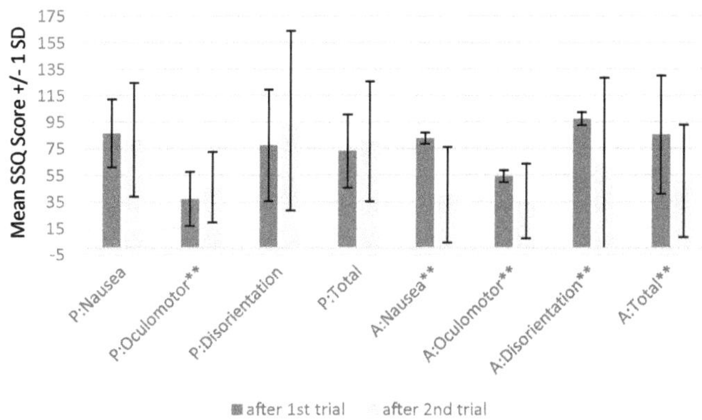

Figure 5. Results of the within-subject design showing the differences between the first and second trials for the placebo (*P:*) and alcohol (*A:*) groups (* indicates p < 0.05, ** indicates p < 0.01).

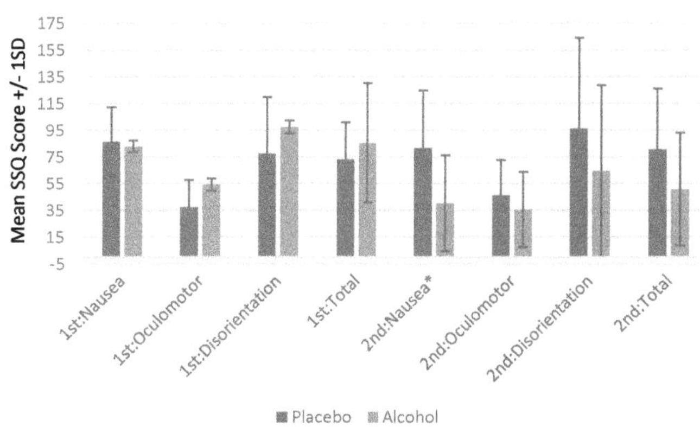

Figure 6. Results of the between-subject design showing the differences between the placebo and alcohol groups for the first (*1st:*) and second trials (*2nd:*) (* indicates p < 0.05.)

Looking at the individual subscales of the *SSQ*, nausea symptoms in the alcohol group decreased by an average of $M = 42.56$ ($SD = 30.81$). Oculomotor symptoms decreased by an average of $M = 18.66$ ($SD = 22.02$). Similarly, disorientation symptoms decreased by an average of $M = 33.19$ ($SD = 28.15$). All differences were found significant ($p < 0.01$, see Fig. 5, prefix *A:*).

For the placebo group, total SSQ scores did not differ significantly between first and second trial as illustrated in Figure 5, prefix *P:*. The *SSQ* subscales nausea and disorientation showed no significant differences between trials. Oculomo-

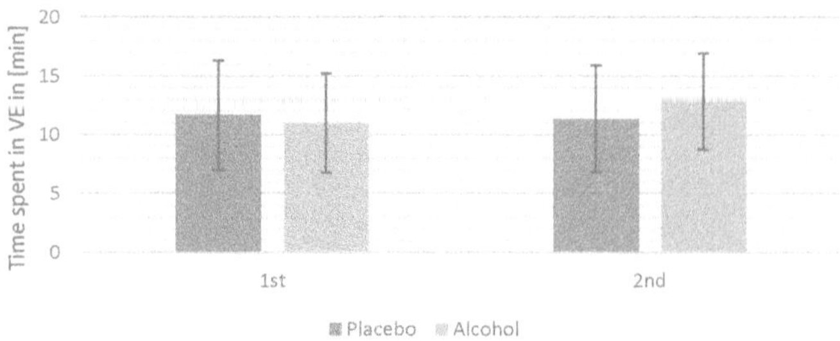

Figure 7. Time spent in VE for the first and second trials. No significant differences were observed.

tor symptoms increased significantly in the placebo group (first trial: $M = 37.26$ ($SD = 20.30$); second trial: $M = 46.11$ ($SD = 26.54$), $p < 0.01$; see Fig. 5, *P:Oculomotor*).

Between-subjects design was implemented to compare mean differences of two independent samples (alcohol and placebo group) across trials. There was no statistically significant difference between the total SSQ scores of individuals who consumed alcohol and individuals who did not consume alcohol (see Fig. 6). Looking at the individual subscales after the second trial (alcohol vs. placebo), no statistically significant differences of oculomotor and disorientation symptoms were found. Individuals who consumed alcohol reported significantly less nausea symptoms than subjects in the control group (alcohol $M = 40.36$ ($SD = 35.93$), placebo $M = 81.88$ ($SD = 42.94$), $p < 0.05$).

Average time of immersion.

For each group, the average time in minutes spent in the virtual environment was analyzed (see Fig. 7). There was no significant difference found for average play time between alcohol and placebo groups for the first and second trials (independent t-test; first trial: placebo $M = 11.67$, $SD = 4.6$, alcohol $M = 11.35$, $SD = 4.56$, $p = 0.86$; second trial: placebo $M = 11.00$, $SD = 4.24$, alcohol $M = 12.84$, $SD = 4.10$, $p = 0.28$).

Subjective Evaluation of VE Experience.

After each trial, participants were asked to evaluate their experience with the virtual environment in order to understand which factors, from their perspective, caused the side effects. After the first trail, fast movements and increased head rotations were mentioned by more than 70% of individuals. Other issues of the game were noted to a lesser extent, i.e. 50% mentioned z-fighting, 30% high end-to-end latency. Individuals from the experimental group reported a more relaxed feeling after the second trial.

Additional Information

In order to support interpretation of the results and reproducibility and comparability, additional data on the participants was collected.

Group Characteristics and Dropouts

Two subjects from the experimental treatment group (2 male) and four subjects (3 male, 1 female) from the control group (19.4% of all the participants) dropped out after the first trial due to severe symptoms of cybersickness. Mean blood alcohol level was between the anticipated range of 0.06% and 0.08% ($M = 0.75, SD = 0.12$). The characteristics of the groups in the beginning of the experiment were similar in terms of age, gender distribution, playing experience, VE experience, but differed in the *MSSQ* mean scores. This situation continued to apply even after drop-outs (see Table 3 and Figure 8).

	Age [a]		Video Game Playing Experience [a]		VE expierence (yes/no) [%]	MSSQ Score		Gender	
	Mean	SD	Mean	SD		Mean	SD	Male	Female
1st:Placebo	25.38	3.89	12.73	4.93	56.3	29.01	26.37	13	3
2nd:Placebo	25.17	3.13	13.09	3.99	58.3	26.92	25.28	10	2
1st:Alcohol	25.47	2.69	13.47	6.1	53.3	47.85	37.61	12	3
2nd:Alcohol	25.77	2.71	13.31	6.55	53.8	43.97	38.99	10	3

Table 3. Data table of group comparison for the first and second trials of the placebo and alcohol groups.

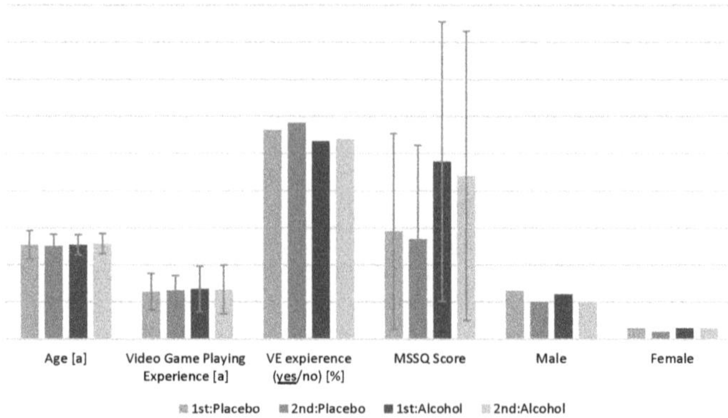

Figure 8. Comparison of the first and second trials for the placebo and alcohol group. There are no significant differences before and after dropouts.

Gender.

In the study, female participants experienced more simulation sickness than male participants. Although the difference was noticeable, no statistical test was applied due to the small number of female participants.

SSQ and previous exposure to virtual reality.

A majority of the participants (54.8%) were not new to virtual reality. Individuals who had been previously exposed to VE actually reported significantly more simulator sickness symptoms than individuals without VR experience (see Table 4; independent t-test between alcohol and placebo group, $t(29) = 1.99, p = 0.049$).

Experience with gaming and cybersickness.

The Pearson correlation was calculated to investigate the relationship between the intensity of playing video games during a typical week and symptoms experienced after the first trial of the experiment. Analysis of the data revealed a significant

	SSQ	
	Mean	SD
Expierience with VR	101.86	3.13
No experience with VR	71.06	47.97

Table 4. SSQ score by previous exposure to virtual reality. The results of the independent-measures t-test were significant (p=0.049).

relationship between the two variables (Pearson correlation, two-tails, $r = -0.38, n = 31, p = 0.04$).

Motion sickness susceptibility.

For all participants, the results of *MSSQ* were correlated with the total *SSQ* scores after the first trial. The variables are positively related with a Pearson correlation of $r = 0.43, p = 0.02$. The mean *MSSQ* score of the alcohol group was twice as high as the mean *MSSQ* of the placebo group. Hence, we calculated the Pearson correlation between the difference of *SSQ* score between trials ($SSQ_{diff} = SSQ_{after1st} - SSQ_{after2nd}$) and the *MSSQ* score. For all participants, there was no relation between the difference in mean *SSQ* scores and motion sickness susceptibility ($r = 0.01, p = 0.95, n = 31$). Looking only at the alcohol group, there was no relation found between the difference in mean simulator sickness scores and motion sickness susceptibility ($r = -0.32, p = 0.28$).

DISCUSSION

One of the main objectives of the current study was to discover the influence of alcohol on the symptoms of cybersickness. An independent measures t-test revealed no significant difference between the total mean simulator sickness scores of the alcohol and placebo groups. However, analyzing only the second trial, individuals that received the experimental treatment experienced less nausea symptoms than the placebo condition. In addition to that, a repeated measures t-test revealed that, individuals of the experimental treatment group reported significantly less symptoms of cybersickness after the ingestion of alcohol compared to the trial before alcohol consumption. This unforeseen result implies that alcohol may reduce symptoms of cybersickness but it is by no means recommended as a general preventive measure. It is noteworthy that the BAC of around 0.07% did not worsen cybersickness on any of the *SSQ* subscales.

It is likely that symptoms of cybersickness were less distinct among the individuals in the experimental treatment group due to the relaxing effect of alcohol. Participants from the alcohol group reported that, during the second trial, they experienced less strain and anxiety.

It is interesting to note that, while the onset and severity of sickness decreased among the participants of the alcohol group after the second trial, average time spent in the VR was not significantly different between the two samples. In fact, individuals who played the game for 15 minutes in the first trial, were also able to last the required time in the second trial.

The *MSSQ* scores of the alcohol group were twice as high as the placebo group ratings, meaning that subjects from the former group were more susceptible to motion sickness-related ailments. Analysis revealed that there was also a significant decrease in simulator sickness symptoms within the alcohol group. However, there was no relation between the difference in mean *SSQ* scores between trials and motion sickness susceptibility scores among all subjects. In other words, individuals who scored high on *MSSQ* did not have a higher probability of experiencing sickness after playing the VR game under influence of alcohol.

According to observations and interview results, the game was found to be highly sickness provoking. Increased head movements along with fast movements of the character in the game were mentioned as one of the main causes for sickness. On one hand, actions caused by head rotations and game scene movements may result in a loss of control over a posture. As mentioned in the literature review, failure to maintain postural stability can be one of the factors causing cybersickness. On the other hand, quick head movements could lead to sickness due to the delay in the display update. This can be explained by the performance issues of the chosen game, for example, low refresh rate (60 Hz), possible issues with latency in tracking, and rendering. However, the performance and graphic issues were rarely mentioned by the participants supposedly because they might not consciously perceive the actual delay.

The sickness-provoking ability of the game resulted in a relatively high attrition rate. About 20% of the individuals dropped out solely due to the severity of the experienced symptoms. Since the attritions were anticipated, time of immersion in the virtual environment was limited to 15 minutes.

We also tested additional variables mentioned in the literature review of the current study. The effect of gender on *SSQ* score is visible but the small sample size does not allow any interpretations regarding the effect of alcohol. Interestingly, the subjects who previously experienced a virtual environment, were actually more prone to cybersickness. We suppose that previous experiences did not lead to a habituation effect because their experiences with virtual environments were of occasional nature. [23]. However, the current study did not focus on habituation, therefore, there was no additional information on the previous exposure to a VE included.

We found a correlation between cybersickness and participants' gaming experience. Individuals with higher gaming experience reported less cybersickness symptoms. This can be a result of habituation of the side effects, since in-game motion sickness can also appear due to excessive playing on non-VR displays [10].

CONCLUSION

The results of this study indicate that a blood alcohol concentration of approximately 0.07% may reduce the symptoms of cybersickness. In other words, this blood alcohol level did not worsen cybersickness symptoms measured by the *SSQ*. This indicates that intoxication equivalent to around 0.07% of BAC while playing a virtual reality game does not pose a serious health threat with respect to cybersickness. We consider this finding important, because it can be anticipated that virtual reality headsets will be used at home, at venues, or at VR arcades by people drinking alcohol. However, results cannot be generalized without further research. Although the findings indicate that the 0.07% BAC does not aggravate sickness, we do not recommend alcohol as a preventive measure for cybersickness.

One of the limitations of the current study is the relatively young age of the participants. It is unclear how alcohol impacts the onset and severity of symptoms in older or younger populations. Further, a rather small sample size prohibits generalization of the results. In addition to that, the game *MiMiCCs* was a first-person game with elements provoking cybersickness and only one specific task. Other types of games and tasks, for example, various levels of mental workload or different virtual cameras, might reveal different relationships between alcohol and cybersickness. In this study, the placebo effect has not been taken into account. Participants from the control group might have reported higher cybersickness because they perceived alcohol as a factor worsening the symptoms. A double-blinded study could shed light on this issue. In the future, we plan to add a baseline group that will receive neither of the treatments to measure the placebo effect directly.

It would also be interesting to observe the impact of various blood alcohol levels. For example, it can be hypothesized that a BAC at 0.03% may not have any influence, whereas 0.1% or higher may have a negative effect and worsen the actual symptoms. Findings of this study could help companies in specifying their safety and health warnings. More importantly, they can enhance the safety and well-being of consumers.

Due to the fact that the current study focused on the influence of alcohol intoxication on cybersickness, as well as the fact that the game task was intentionally designed insolvable, there is no task performance data available. However, how player's frustration caused by the inability to complete a given task impacts cybersickness symptoms should be taken into account in the future VR game research. This could be done either by measuring player movement and grip force (e.g. [16]) or with a questionnaire [46].

Finally, the *Simulator Sickness Questionnaire* is a self-report measure, therefore, it lacks objectivity. The current study would profit from psycho-physiological data, for example, electrogastogram, electrooculogram, galvanic skin response, or respiration, as these measurements reflect biological changes in a human body that are of a great importance when foreign substances such as alcohol are involved. Moreover, it would be beneficial for future studies in this area to incorporate eye tracking due to the fact that pupil dilation, nystagmus, and abnormal smooth pursuit are advantageous in monitoring various levels of alcohol intoxication.

REFERENCES

1. Robert S. Allison, L. R. Harris, M. Jenkin, U. Jasiobedzka, and J. E. Zacher. 2001. Tolerance of temporal delay in virtual environments. In *Proceedings IEEE Virtual Reality 2001*. 247–254. DOI: http://dx.doi.org/10.1109/VR.2001.913793
2. Laura L. Arns and M.M. Cerney. 2005. The relationship between age and incidence of cybersickness among immersive environment users. In *IEEE Proceedings. VR 2005. Virtual Reality, 2005*. IEEE, Bonn, Germany, 267–268. DOI: http://dx.doi.org/10.1109/VR.2005.1492788
3. David R. Badcock, Stephen Palmisano, and James G. May. 2014. *Vision and Virtual Environments*. CRC Press, Chapter Vision and, 39–85. DOI: http://dx.doi.org/10.1201/b17360-6
4. Frank Biocca. 1992. Will Simulation Sickness Slow Down the Diffusion of Virtual Environment Technology? *Presence: Teleoperators and Virtual Environments* 1, 3 (jan 1992), 334–343. DOI: http://dx.doi.org/10.1162/pres.1992.1.3.334
5. Jelte E. Bos, Sjoerd C. de Vries, Martijn L. van Emmerik, and Eric L. Groen. 2010. The effect of internal and external fields of view on visually induced motion sickness. *Applied Ergonomics* 41, 4 (2010), 516–521. DOI:http://dx.doi.org/10.1016/j.apergo.2009.11.007
6. Stéphane Bouchard, Geneviève Robillard, and Patrice Renaud. 2007. Revising the factor structure of the Simulator Sickness Questionnaire. *Annual review of cybertherapy and telemedicine* 5 (2007), 128–137.
7. Susan Bruck and Paul Watters. 2009a. Cybersickness and anxiety during simulated motion: Implications for VRET. *Annual Review of CyberTherapy and Telemedicine* 7 (2009), 169–173.
8. Susan Bruck and Paul A. Watters. 2009b. Autonomic Nervous System Factors Underlying Anxiety in Virtual Environments: A Regression Model for Cybersickness. In *2009 15th International Conference on Virtual Systems and Multimedia (VSMM '09)*. IEEE, Washington, DC, USA, 67–72. DOI: http://dx.doi.org/10.1109/VSMM.2009.16
9. Grigore C. Burdea and Philippe Coiffet. 2003. *Virtual reality technology*. Vol. 1. John Wiley & Sons, New York, NY, USA.
10. Chih-Hui Chang, Wu-Wen Pan, Li-Ya Tseng, and Thomas A. Stoffregen. 2012. Postural activity and motion sickness during video game play in children and adults. *Experimental brain research* 217, 2 (2012), 299–309.
11. Sherrilene Classen, Megan Bewernitz, and Orit Shechtman. 2011. Driving Simulator Sickness: An Evidence-Based Review of the Literature. *American Journal of Occupational Therapy* 65, 2 (2011), 179–188. DOI:http://dx.doi.org/10.5014/ajot.2011.000802
12. John W. Creswell. 2013. *Research design: Qualitative, quantitative, and mixed methods approaches*. SAGE Publications, Inc., Thousand Oaks, California. 25 pages.
13. John C. Dalrymple-Alford, P. Anne Kerr, and Richard D. Jones. 2003. The effects of alcohol on driving-related sensorimotor performance across four times of day. *Journal of studies on alcohol* 64, 1 (jan 2003), 93–7. http://www.ncbi.nlm.nih.gov/pubmed/12608488
14. Simon Davis, Keith Nesbitt, and Eugene Nalivaiko. 2014. A Systematic Review of Cybersickness. In *Proceedings of the 2014 Conference on Interactive Entertainment (IE2014)*. ACM, New York, NY, USA, 8:1—-8:9. DOI: http://dx.doi.org/10.1145/2677758.2677780
15. Michael F. Deering. 1993. Data complexity for virtual reality: where do all the triangles go?. In *Proceedings of IEEE Virtual Reality Annual International Symposium*. IEEE, Seattle, WA, USA, USA, 357–363. DOI: http://dx.doi.org/10.1109/VRAIS.1993.380758

16. Virginia I. Douglas and Penny A. Parry. 1994. Effects of reward and nonreward on frustration and attention in attention deficit disorder. *Journal of Abnormal Child Psychology* 22, 3 (1994), 281–302. DOI: http://dx.doi.org/10.1007/BF02168075

17. John A. Ewing. 1984. Detecting alcoholism. The CAGE questionnaire. *JAMA* 252, 14 (oct 1984), 1905–7. http://www.ncbi.nlm.nih.gov/pubmed/6471323

18. John F. Golding. 2006. Predicting individual differences in motion sickness susceptibility by questionnaire. *Personality and Individual Differences* 41, 2 (jul 2006), 237–248. DOI: http://dx.doi.org/10.1016/j.paid.2006.01.012

19. Frederick J. Gravetter and Larry B. Wallnau. 2016. *Statistics for the behavioral sciences*. Cengage Learning, Boston, MA, USA.

20. Catherine Harvey and Peter A. Howarth. 2007. The effect of display size on visually-induced motion sickness (VIMS) and skin temperature. In *Proceedings of the 1st international symposium on visually induced motion sickness, fatigue, and photosensitive epileptic seizures, Hong Kong*. Hong Kong, 96–103.

21. K. J. Hill and Peter A. Howarth. 2000. Habituation to the side effects of immersion in a virtual environment. *Displays* 21, 1 (2000), 25–30.

22. Louis Holdstock, Andrea C. King, and Harriet de Wit. 2000. Subjective and objective responses to ethanol in moderate/heavy and light social drinkers. *Alcoholism, clinical and experimental research* 24, 6 (jun 2000), 789–94. http://www.ncbi.nlm.nih.gov/pubmed/10888066

23. Peter A. Howarth and Simon G. Hodder. 2008. Characteristics of habituation to motion in a virtual environment. *Displays* 29, 2 (2008), 117–123.

24. Jason Jerald. 2016. *The VR Book* (1st ed.). Morgan & Claypool Publishers All. 637 pages.

25. David M. Johnson. 2005. *Introduction to and review of simulator sickness research*. Technical Report. DTIC Document.

26. Robert S. Kennedy, Julie Drexler, and Robert C. Kennedy. 2010. Research in visually induced motion sickness. *Applied Ergonomics* 41, 4 (2010), 494–503. DOI:http://dx.doi.org/10.1016/j.apergo.2009.11.006

27. Robert S. Kennedy, Norman E. Lane, Kevin S. Berbaum, and Michael G. Lilienthal. 1993. Simulator Sickness Questionnaire: An Enhanced Method for Quantifying Simulator Sickness. *The International Journal of Aviation Psychology* 3, 3 (jul 1993), 203–220. DOI: http://dx.doi.org/10.1207/s15327108ijap0303_3

28. Robert S. Kennedy, Kay M. Stanney, and William P. Dunlap. 2000. Duration and Exposure to Virtual Environments: Sickness Curves During and Across Sessions. *Presence: Teleoperators and Virtual Environments* 9, 5 (oct 2000), 367–368. DOI: http://dx.doi.org/10.1162/105474600566952

29. Ramona Kenntner-Mabiala, Yvonne Kaussner, Monika Jagiellowicz-Kaufmann, Sonja Hoffmann, and Hans-Peter Krüger. 2015. Driving Performance Under Alcohol in Simulated Representative Driving Tasks. *Journal of Clinical Psychopharmacology* 35, 2 (apr 2015), 134–142. DOI: http://dx.doi.org/10.1097/JCP.0000000000000285

30. Eugenia M. Kolasinski. 1995. *Simulator Sickness in Virtual Environments*. Technical Report. DTIC Document.

31. R. V. Kruk. 1992. Simulator sickness experience in simulators equipped with fiber optic helmet mounted display systems. In *Flight Simulation Technologies Conference*. 4135.

32. Steven M. LaValle, Anna Yershova, Max Katsev, and Michael Antonov. 2014. Head tracking for the Oculus Rift. In *2014 IEEE International Conference on Robotics and Automation (ICRA)*. 187–194. DOI: http://dx.doi.org/10.1109/ICRA.2014.6906608

33. Joseph J. LaViola. 2000. A discussion of cybersickness in virtual environments. *ACM SIGCHI Bulletin* 32, 1 (jan 2000), 47–56. DOI: http://dx.doi.org/10.1145/333329.333344

34. Ben Lawson. 2014. Motion Sickness Symptomatology and Origins. In *Handbook of Virtual Environments*. CRC Press, 531–600. DOI: http://dx.doi.org/10.1201/b17360-29

35. Michael E. McCauley and Thomas J. Sharkey. 1992. Cybersickness: Perception of Self-Motion in Virtual Environments. *Presence: Teleoperators and Virtual Environments* 1, 3 (jan 1992), 311–318. DOI: http://dx.doi.org/10.1162/pres.1992.1.3.311

36. Herbert Moskowitz and Dary Fiorentino. 2000. *A review of the literature on the effects of low doses of alcohol on driving-related skills*. Technical Report. NHTSA. https://one.nhtsa.gov/people/injury/research/pub/HS809028/index

37. Martin S. Mumenthaler, Joy L. Taylor, Ruth O'Hara, and Jerome A. Yesavage. 1999. Gender differences in moderate drinking effects. *Alcohol research & health : the journal of the National Institute on Alcohol Abuse and Alcoholism* 23, 1 (1999), 55–64. http://www.ncbi.nlm.nih.gov/pubmed/10890798

38. Syed Ali Arsalan Naqvi, Nasreen Badruddin, Aamir Saeed Malik, Wan Hazabbah, and Baharudin Abdullah. 2013. Does 3D produce more symptoms of visually induced motion sickness?. In *2013 35th Annual International Conference of the IEEE Engineering in Medicine and Biology Society (EMBC)*. IEEE, 6405–6408. DOI: http://dx.doi.org/10.1109/EMBC.2013.6611020

39. Charles M. Oman and Kathleen E. Cullen. 2014. Brainstem processing of vestibular sensory exafference: implications for motion sickness etiology. *Exp Brain Res* 232, 8 (aug 2014), 2483–2492. DOI: http://dx.doi.org/10.1007/s00221-014-3973-2

40. George D Park, R Wade Allen, Dary Fiorentino, Theodore J Rosenthal, and Marcia L Cook. 2006. Simulator Sickness Scores According to Symptom Susceptibility, Age, and Gender for an Older Driver Assessment Study. *Proceedings of the Human Factors and Ergonomics Society Annual Meeting* 50, 26 (2006), 2702–2706. DOI: http://dx.doi.org/10.1177/154193120605002607

41. Lisa Rebenitsch and Charles Owen. 2014. Individual variation in susceptibility to cybersickness. In *Proceedings of the 27th annual ACM symposium on User interface software and technology - UIST '14 (UIST '14)*. ACM Press, New York, New York, USA, 309–317. DOI: http://dx.doi.org/10.1145/2642918.2647394

42. Lisa Rebenitsch and Charles Owen. 2016. Review on cybersickness in applications and visual displays. *Virtual Reality* 20, 2 (2016), 101–125. DOI: http://dx.doi.org/10.1007/s10055-016-0285-9

43. Timothy Roehrs, David Beare, Frank Zorick, and Thomas Roth. 1994. Sleepiness and ethanol effects on simulated driving. *Alcoholism, clinical and experimental research* 18, 1 (feb 1994), 154–158.

44. Robert Rosenthal and Ralph L. Rosnow. 1991. *Essentials of behavioral research: Methods and data analysis*. McGraw-Hill Humanities Social.

45. Frank Schmäl. 2013. Neuronal Mechanisms and the Treatment of Motion Sickness. *Pharmacology* 91, 3-4 (2013), 229–241. http://www.karger.com/DOI/10.1159/000350185

46. Melinda Scime and Jill M. Norvilitis. 2006. Task performance and response to frustration in children with attention deficit hyperactivity disorder. *Psychology in the Schools* 43, 3 (2006), 377–386. DOI: http://dx.doi.org/10.1002/pits.20151

47. Richard H. Y. So, W. T. Lo, and Andy T. K. Ho. 2001. Effects of Navigation Speed on Motion Sickness Caused by an Immersive Virtual Environment. *Human Factors* 43, 3 (2001), 452–461. DOI: http://dx.doi.org/10.1518/001872001775898223

48. Anatol Tolchinsky. 2013. The development of a self-report questionnaire to measure problematic video game play and its relationship to other psychological phenomena. (2013). http://commons.emich.edu/cgi/viewcontent.cgi?article=1928

49. Erik Viirre, B. J. Price, and Bradley Chase. 2014. Direct Effects of Virtual Environments on Users. In *Handbook of Virtual Environments*. CRC Press, 521–529. DOI: http://dx.doi.org/10.1201/b17360-28

50. Raluca Vlad, Olha Nahorna, Patricia Ladret, and Anne Guerin. 2013. The influence of the visualization task on the simulator sickness symptoms - A comparative SSQ study on 3DTV and 3D immersive glasses. In *2013 3DTV Vision Beyond Depth (3DTV-CON)*. IEEE, 1–4. DOI: http://dx.doi.org/10.1109/3DTV.2013.6676647

51. Alexander D. Walker, Erik R. Muth, Fred A. Switzer, and Adam Hoover. 2010. Head movements and simulator sickness generated by a virtual environment. *Aviation, space, and environmental medicine* 81, 10 (2010), 929–934.

52. Patricia E. Watson, Ian D. Watson, and Richard D. Batt. 1980. Total body water volumes for adult males and females estimated from simple anthropometric measurements. *The American journal of clinical nutrition* 33, 1 (jan 1980), 27–39.

53. John R. Wilson. 1997. Virtual environments and ergonomics: needs and opportunities. *Ergonomics* 40, 10 (oct 1997), 1057–1077. DOI: http://dx.doi.org/10.1080/001401397187603

54. Richard S. Wright, Nicholas Haemel, Graham Sellers, and Benjamin Lipchak. 2011. *OpenGL SuperBible* (5 ed.). Pearson Education, Boston. 986 pages.

55. Laurence R. Young. 2003. Spatial Orientation. In *Principles And Practice Of Aviation Psychology*. Lawrence Erlbaum, Mahwah, NJ, 69–113.

56. Jingbo Zhao, Robert S. Allison, Margarita Vinnikov, and Sion Jennings. 2017. Estimating the motion-to-photon latency in head mounted displays. In *2017 IEEE Virtual Reality (VR)*. 313–314. DOI: http://dx.doi.org/10.1109/VR.2017.7892302

Author Index

www.ingramcontent.com/pod-product-compliance
Ingram Content Group UK Ltd.
Pitfield, Milton Keynes, MK11 3LW, UK
UKHW051417290926
15471UKWH00009B/1644

9 781450 356756